European Union Health Law

A contextual analysis of the internal logics of EU health law through four themes: consumerism; (human) rights; interactions between equality, solidarity and competition; and risk. Leading authors in the emergent field explain the interactions and implications of EU health law through thematic reinterpretation of the law in context in key substantive areas, such as the regulation of health research, access of patients to high-quality care, health care professional regulation, organization and funding of health care services and public health. This book offers a fresh perspective and thorough understanding of EU health law through individual and collective or systemic perspectives, and covers health law both within the EU and globally. Essential reading for anyone interested in health law in any EU Member State, or in global health law.

Tamara K. Hervey is Jean Monnet Professor of EU Law and Head of School, School of Law, University of Sheffield.

Jean V. McHale is Professor of Health Care Law and Director of the Centre for Health Law, Science and Policy, University of Birmingham.

The Law in Context Series

Editors: William Twining (University College London),
Christopher McCrudden (Queen's University Belfast) and
Bronwen Morgan (University of Bristol).

Since 1970 the Law in Context series has been at the forefront of the movement to broaden the study of law. It has been a vehicle for the publication of innovative scholarly books that treat law and legal phenomena critically in their social, political and economic contexts from a variety of perspectives. The series particularly aims to publish scholarly legal writing that brings fresh perspectives to bear on new and existing areas of law taught in universities. A contextual approach involves treating legal subjects broadly, using materials from other social sciences, and from any other discipline that helps to explain the operation in practice of the subject under discussion. It is hoped that this orientation is at once more stimulating and more realistic than the bare exposition of legal rules. The series includes original books that have a different emphasis from traditional legal textbooks, while maintaining the same high standards of scholarship. They are written primarily for undergraduate and graduate students of law and of other disciplines, but will also appeal to a wider readership. In the past, most books in the series have focused on English law, but recent publications include books on European law, globalization, transnational legal processes and comparative law.

Books in the Series
Anderson, Schum & Twining: *Analysis of Evidence*
Ashworth: *Sentencing and Criminal Justice*
Barton & Douglas: *Law and Parenthood*
Beecher-Monas: *Evaluating Scientific Evidence: An Interdisciplinary Framework for Intellectual Due Process*
Bell: *French Legal Cultures*
Bercusson: *European Labour Law*
Birkinshaw: *European Public Law*
Birkinshaw: *Freedom of Information: The Law, the Practice and the Ideal*
Brownsword & Goodwin: *Law and the Technologies of the Twenty-First Century*
Cane: *Atiyah's Accidents, Compensation and the Law*
Clarke & Kohler: *Property Law: Commentary and Materials*
Collins: *The Law of Contract*
Collins, Ewing & McColgan: *Labour Law*
Cowan: *Housing Law and Policy*
Cranston: *Legal Foundations of the Welfare State*
Darian-Smith: *Laws and Societies in Global Contexts: Contemporary Approaches*
Dauvergne *Making People Illegal: What Globalisation Means for Immigration and Law*
Davies: *Perspectives on Labour Law*
Dembour: *Who Believes in Human Rights?: The European Convention in Question*
de Sousa Santos: *Toward a New Legal Common Sense*
Diduck: *Law's Families*
Fortin: *Children's Rights and the Developing Law*

European Union Health Law

Themes and Implications

TAMARA K. HERVEY AND JEAN V. McHALE

CAMBRIDGE
UNIVERSITY PRESS

CAMBRIDGE
UNIVERSITY PRESS

University Printing House, Cambridge CB2 8BS, United Kingdom

Cambridge University Press is part of the University of Cambridge.

It furthers the University's mission by disseminating knowledge in the pursuit of education, learning and research at the highest international levels of excellence.

www.cambridge.org
Information on this title: www.cambridge.org/9781107010499

First published 2015

A catalogue record for this publication is available from the British Library

Library of Congress Cataloguing in Publication data
Hervey, Tamara K., author.
European Union health law : themes and implications / Tamara Hervey, Jean McHale.
    pages   cm. – (Law in context)
Includes bibliographical references and index.
ISBN 978-1-107-01049-9 (hardback)
1. Public health laws – European Union countries.   2. Medical care – Law and legislation – European Union countries.   3. Medical laws and legislation – European Union countries.
I. McHale, Jean V. (Jean Vanessa), 1965– author.   II. Title.
KJE6172.H45   2015
344.2404 – dc23   2015002845

ISBN 978-1-107-01049-9 Hardback

To Rosalind, Geneviève and James: ten years older but still a delightful distraction

Contents

Acknowledgements

We gratefully acknowledge support from the following organizations:

The Economic and Social Research Council, Award RES-451-26-0764 (Principal Investigator, Dr Mark Flear)

The University Association for Contemporary European Studies

The School of Law, University of Sheffield

The Sheffield Undergraduate Research Experience (SURE) scheme, University of Sheffield

Birmingham Law School, University of Birmingham

We are also indebted to the following individuals: Rita Baeten, Gordon Bache, Mark Bell, Margot Brazier, Robert Burrell, Paul James Cardwell, Victoria Chico, Glenn Cohen, Marise Cremona, Anniek de Ruijter, André den Exter, Anne-Maree Farrell, Mark Flear, Marie Fox, Larry Gostin, Scott Greer, Leigh Hancher, Vassilis Hatzopoulos, Graeme Laurie, Sheelagh McGuinness, Martin McKee, Thérèse Murphy, Steve Peers, Philip Rostant, Jo Shaw, Morgan Shimwell, Dorte Sindbjerg Martinsen, Lindsay Stirton, Ruth Stirton, Oisin Suttle, Mark Taylor, David Townend, Louise Trubek, Bart Vanhercke, Peter Vincent-Jones, Amanda Warren-Jones; as well as the many students with whom we have shared the ideas in this book.

For excellent and tenacious research assistance: James Harrison.

We have endeavoured to state the law as at 31 December 2014.

Table of cases

Court of Justice of the European Union (alphabetical order)

Court of Justice of the European Union (Opinions)

European Court of Human Rights

EFTA Court

United States of America

Table of instruments and legislation

European Union instruments and legislation

Primary law

Secondary law

EU directives (numerical order)

European Parliament resolutions (chronological order)

International instruments and legislation

Conventions and agreements (alphabetical order)

National legislation (alphabetical order)

Belgium

Part I
Introduction

1

Introduction

In December 2013, the *tribunal correctionnel* in Marseille delivered its verdict in a fraud case affecting an estimated 300,000 women across the globe, around 5 per cent of whom are breast cancer patients, and many of whom suffer mental ill health. The case concerns Jean-Claude Mas, whose business, Poly Implant Prothèse, manufactured breast implants sold either directly or re-branded by intermediaries such as Dutch Rofil Medical to clinics in some sixty-five countries. The *tribunal* found that Mas fraudulently substituted industrial grade silicone for medical silicone in the implants.[1] The production process (although not the industrial grade silicone) for the implants had been approved by a private German certification body, TÜV-Rheinland. The products duly carried a CE marking, to warranty their safety for the European market.

After the matter came to light, the Czech, French, German and Swedish pharmaceuticals and medical devices regulatory authorities advised precautionary removal of the implants. In England, NHS Medical Director Sir Bruce Keogh's 2012 report concluded that there was no need for such removal if the implants had not ruptured, although where a doctor certifies 'medical need' the NHS will pay for removal. The high media profile of the case, and the availability of social media, have given an outlet to women affected by Poly Implant Prothèse to describe their suffering and their sense of injustice, including at the failings of the law. Dominque Terrier[2] speaks for many:

> The pain we went through was psychological and physical . . . we were mutilated, re-operated on. It's not easy to survive that after cancer.

With its very human, but also legal and European, dimensions, the Poly Implant Prothèse story illustrates many of the questions that piqued our curiosity and which we explore in this book. Does European Union law on health products (like the implants in the Poly Implant Prothèse case) treat those products as essentially the same as any consumer product available in the European market?

---

[1] Mas was fined €75 000 and sentenced to 4 years in prison. His appeal is pending. The German certification body was ordered to pay compensation to victims by the civil *tribunal de commerce* on 14 November 2013. It has also appealed.

[2] Speaking to public TV channel *France 3*, reported in A Chrisafis, 'PIP breast implant bosses' trial for aggravated fraud begins in France', *The Guardian*, 16 April 2013.

Is the same true of European Union law on health services? To the extent that it is, what does that mean for how patients are conceptualized by European Union health law? Are patients essentially consumers, subject to rules such as *caveat emptor*, even if they are protected by law from at least some products and services that would harm their health? If that is so, which products or services does European Union health law decide are harmful to health, and through what processes are those decisions made? What about treatments that are ethically controversial, such as beginning or end-of-life health care? What are the implications for health care professionals? What happens to notions of a professional ethic of care, or provision of public service, if European Union health law understands the relationships between doctors and their patients through the lens of **consumerism**?

The women affected by Poly Implant Prothèse spoke of infringements of their dignity and bodily integrity, which have been associated with the human right to privacy. More generally, both nationally and internationally, health rights are often thought of as human rights. Is this the case in European Union health law? What about the **rights** of patients? Are patients' rights seen as *human* rights in European Union health law, or are they more like *consumer* rights? Which, if any, of such health rights are recognized and upheld by European Union health law? If European Union health law involves consumerization of health care, what does that mean for patient autonomy and patient choice, which are both related to human rights? What are the implications of the 'right to health care' in the EU's own Charter of Fundamental Rights, for substantive European Union health law? Is its significance more symbolic than practical? How does European Union health law deal with conflicting rights in health contexts? Might European Union health law strengthen, or weaken, claims to health care resources as claims of right? What might this mean for health care systems?

We tend to think of European Union law as reducing differences between national legal systems. Yet the health authorities in different countries came to very different conclusions about the Poly Implant Prothèse case. Under European Union health law, how much control do national authorities have over determining questions of quality, safety and efficacy of health care products, services and procedures? What is the extent of national autonomy: if the Swedes decide that alcohol is so harmful to health that it should only be sold through one state-controlled monopoly provider, or the Scots decide to change alcohol pricing rules, or the Greeks decide that infant formula milk should only be sold through pharmacies, is that allowed? Can such national decisions, made with a view to promoting good health of the population, be challenged if they disrupt patterns of trade in products or services across European Union borders? If the European Union is supposed to secure safe medical devices, why did Poly Implant Prothèse patients in different European Union Member States have such different experiences? Why doesn't European Union health law offer equivalent protection to all patients? If patients in different countries end up with very different entitlements to treatment, what are the implications of European Union health law for equality of access to medical care?

National arrangements for health care provision in EU Member States allow monopoly, or near monopoly, providers of health care services. What if those providers abuse that position? Does European Union health law scrutinize such behaviour, or the concentration of market power through mergers of health care providers? If so, does this mean that European Union health law is moving health care systems towards market-based models of regulation? To the extent that it does, what are the implications for the organization and underlying ethos of national health systems? Or does European Union health law recognize health care as a 'special case', a type of service that is not subject to the ordinary rules that apply to anti-competitive behaviour of companies?

To the extent that European Union health law involves more patient choice, how does that increased choice affect the delivery of health care through health care systems that are predominantly funded either by taxation or through social insurance, rather than through private mechanisms? The fundamental basis of health care in European contexts is solidarity. Does European Union health law challenge, disrupt, or even destroy, those fundamentals? How does European Union health law balance **equality** and **solidarity** with fair and effective **competition**?

The Poly Implant Prothèse story suggests a very light touch approach to regulation of risk in health contexts – the medical device involved was allowed onto the European market following essentially the same marketing authorization procedure that applies to, say, toys. To what extent is that true of European Union law on other health products or services involving assessment of **risk**? What does European Union health law require in terms of pre- and post-market controls of health care products such as pharmaceuticals, bio- or nano-technology products, and medical devices? What does European Union health law require of other products that are or may be harmful to health, such as tobacco, food, alcohol? Where European Union law must balance risks to patients with freedom to run a business, how is such law made? Given that health industries make a major contribution to the European economy, what are the implications for the European economy, which so desperately needs to grow to escape from recession?

Poly Implant Prothèse operated in a global market for health products. In that case, the European Union legal standards were insufficiently stringent to prevent harm to thousands of women. What should we make of the oft-repeated claim that the European Union is *too strict* in its regulatory approach to risk, is significantly more risk-averse than, say, the USA? Are firms operating in the EU therefore saddled with competitive disadvantage when seeking to compete globally? Does this hamper innovation in European health industries? What does this mean for economic growth? What does it mean for patients who are waiting for a treatment for their currently incurable conditions? What does it mean for patients across the world, who are dying because the health industry invests in novel products for the rich global North, not in products that are needed by patients in the poor global South? What, if anything, does EU law do to make health products affordable to the poorest in the world? To what extent does European Union health law affect such questions of global health ethics?

And, of course, it isn't only health products that move across borders globally. What, if anything, are the implications of European Union health law for global 'medical tourism'? And what about global movement of public health threats, both from products that have important health implications (food, alcohol, tobacco) and from communicable diseases? How does European Union health law interact with global health law?

These questions illustrate our research agenda. One colleague, to whom we presented our work before publication, suggested that an introduction with over forty questions might be somewhat overwhelming for our readers, and wondered whether we were really going to answer all the questions we ask here. For those who would like a brief answer to each question, we have provided that summary, with references to the relevant chapters, in an Appendix. The detailed legal analysis supporting those brief answers is found in the body of the book.

Our inquiry into European Union health law is organized thematically. The questions arising from the Poly Implant Prothèse story can be arranged into four key themes: consumerism; protection of (human) rights; interactions between equality, solidarity and competition; and risk regulation. Our premise, which we support through the substantive chapters in Parts II, III and IV of the book, is that these are the themes of European Union health law. Our research agenda is to illuminate the significance of each theme, and its implications, for European Union health law.

We organize our analysis of those themes as follows. In Parts II and III of the book, we focus on the EU's *internal* health law, that is, how EU health law applies within the European Union and its Member States. In Part IV, our focus is on EU *external* health law, that is, how EU health law applies outside of the EU, in relations between the EU and states which are not EU members, and other international organizations. As far as we are aware, coverage of both internal and external EU health law in a single analytical framework is unique in the literature to date.

In our approach to the themes, we distinguish between two broad perspectives: an *individual perspective* and a *systemic or collective perspective*. The themes of consumerism and rights apply predominantly to ways that *individuals* experience EU health law. Part II of the book therefore places the individual patient and health care professional in the centre of its analytical perspective. The themes of solidarity, equality, competition and risk engage predominantly with the *systemic* effects of EU health law, and on *collective* experience. Therefore, the analysis in Part III of the book is based upon a collective or systemic analytical perspective. Likewise, the discussion of the EU's *external* health law, in Part IV of the book, considers each perspective in turn.

Of course, there are limitations to this broad division of focus, perspectives and themes. The EU's internal health law can have important implications for its external health law, and vice versa. An example is the ways in which EU health law embodies and reinterprets the Council of Europe's law on human tissue or organs. Associating each theme with one of two perspectives may obfuscate aspects of that theme which are associated with the other perspective. For instance, equality, which we consider mainly within the collective perspective, can be individual focused, such as in the context of non-discrimination litigation. And of course the four themes are far from distinct; they overlap and cut across one another. For instance, a consumer also enjoys (human) rights, and must be protected from unacceptable risk of harm. By being attentive to the potential drawbacks of our thematic approach, we are able at least in part to mitigate them. Particularly in the Conclusions, but also in the substantive chapters of the book, part of our contribution is to draw out exceptions and overlaps between our focuses, perspectives and themes.

The research agenda we set for ourselves essentially requires us to use the methods of standard legal scholarship, to understand the meanings of legal texts and the modes of legal reasoning and conceptualizations that underpin them. We are interested in how EU health law has shaped or may shape the behaviour of relevant actors, such as patients, national governments, health care professionals, the pharmaceutical or medical devices industry, health researchers, those bodies which finance or otherwise regulate the provision of health care, or protection of human health, and so on. But in seeking to draw out the significance of EU health law, and to understand its themes and their implications, we also need to draw on at least some literature in cognate fields, such as health policy and EU studies. In terms of the way in which we understand the EU and its legal system (our 'methodology'[3]), without going into too much detail here,[4] we see the EU as a constitutionalized, pluralist legal order, within which EU, international and national legal rules, as well as processes of regulation or governance that are formally non-binding, but nonetheless have normative effects, interact with one another. Thus, our methodological approach means that we have included within the scope of our analysis some of the more important sources of soft law, and governance processes, which apply to the substantive topics under discussion. Nevertheless, this book is essentially a piece of *legal* scholarship. Our central focus is on the EU's *law*, in the sense of its formally binding legal rules, as found in its foundational Treaties (the Treaty on European Union and Treaty on the Functioning of the European Union), the legislation adopted by its institutions (the European Commission, Council and European Parliament) and the jurisprudence of its court (the Court of Justice of the

---

[3] On the distinction between 'method' and 'methodology' in (EU) legal research, see Cryer et al., *Research Methodologies in EU and International Law* (Hart 2011).

[4] There is a vast literature on the EU's legal order, and on the interfaces between law, regulation, governance and policy in EU contexts.

European Union (CJEU)). We recognize that legal rules emanating from national, EU or international institutions are not in hierarchical relationships within one another. However, we do concentrate on the ways in which EU legal rules, which bind the governments of Member States and are applicable to individuals within and beyond the EU, change or may change situations or relationships. This focus might be read as implying a hierarchy, but is unavoidable as our central concern in this book is EU law.

In this book, we do not try to defend the concept of 'EU health law'. We recognize that the book begins from an implicit position that 'EU health law' exists as an entity with respect to which one can discern themes, and that not everyone will agree with this assertion.[5] Neither do we try to determine whether there should be 'EU health law', or whether the EU should be involved in health law: our approach implies that, even if we could demonstrate definitively, from some kind of standpoint of external critique, that it should not be, it is too late for that kind of observation to make much difference to law or policy. Moreover, we are not offering an evaluative assessment of EU health law – for instance, determining whether it is an 'achievement, failure or missed opportunity', or what the 'added value' of EU law is to health policy. Others have already offered such evaluations.[6]

In approaching EU health law through four themes and two broad perspectives, we are contributing a new analytical framework to the existing literature in the field. The four themes enable us to draw together disparate areas of EU health law and to understand them as a meaningful whole. They liberate us from the cognitive constraints of the existing organizing structures deployed to set out and interpret health law and EU law. This book is organized neither along the lines of a book on health law nor along the lines of a book on EU law. Adopting a new organizing structure, or taxonomy, is a crucial move in developing a new field of study: EU health law. It has the added benefit of allowing us to consider each particular substantive topic in a holistic or relatively holistic way.

Organizing the themes into two broad perspectives (individual and collective) sharpens our analysis, by assisting us to draw out the implications and potential implications of each theme with more precision than we would otherwise be able to achieve. Focusing on the internal separately from the external provides added clarity. Furthermore, we are able to rely on our organization of the material to draw out tensions and contradictions in EU health law. These are

---

[5] This position is a departure from Hervey and McHale, *Health Law and the European Union* (CUP 2004), see p 4. We will develop the analysis supporting the assertion that 'EU health law' is a meaningful analytical category in a companion piece, probably a journal article.

[6] See, for instance, Rosenkötter, Clemens, Sørensen, 'Twentieth anniversary of the European Union health mandate: taking stock of perceived achievements, failures and missed opportunities: a qualitative study' (2013) 13 *BMC Public Health* 1074; Clemens, Michelsen and Brand, 'Supporting health systems in Europe: added value of EU actions' (2013) 9(1) *Health Economics Policy and Law* 49.

illuminated in several ways: by comparing and contrasting how the themes play out in the EU's internal health law and its external health law; by contrasting the different perspectives across the themes; and by considering the individual and the collective perspective within each theme.

Using our analytical framework, we are able to reinterpret the academic and policy-focused literature on a range of topics, which share a concern with how EU law affects, or has the potential to affect, human health. Essentially, and to oversimplify our overall findings, each theme is associated with one or more claims in the existing literature about its significance and implications for health. Some of these claims are stated or implied by the questions that we outlined above. For instance, it is claimed that EU law undermines national health systems based on solidarity, that EU law pushes competitive market models into health, that EU law supports the choices of (wealthy and relatively healthy) patients, that EU law stifles health innovations, that EU law makes it difficult for national authorities to protect the health of their populations, and so on. Our overall findings are that, while the strong version of each claim is not borne out, once we immerse ourselves in the details of law in its policy contexts, a weaker version may well be defensible.

But we are getting ahead of ourselves. Before we explore the first of our themes, the following two chapters provide an explanation of the scope of the enquiry. To that end, we consider first how we are defining 'health law' (chapter 2), and, second, how we are defining 'European Union health law' (chapter 3).

2

What is health law?

Introduction

The development of health law as a discipline has been gradual and incremental. One of the complexities in ascertaining the nature and scope of health law is that, across the EU as a whole, health law is at different stages of development. As we shall see, the origins of health law stretch back for many centuries, but its evolution has been more rapid and concentrated over the last half-century. Secondly, even the words that describe the discipline are not consistently utilized across or within EU Member States, or indeed in the rest of the world. In some jurisdictions, the term used is 'medical law', whereas elsewhere it is 'health care law' or simply 'health law.' Understanding the evolutionary development of the discipline is critical to effective engagement with the discipline. Derek Morgan writing in 2001 suggested that

> Medical law is indeed not *just* a subject; it is also a responsibility. Whether medical law is a legal category in itself is beside the point. The framing of responses properly lying within medical law is part of an intellectual responsibility that lies at the heart of the academic obligation which, as John Fleming has otherwise observed, is to be 'sensitive to movement and direction . . . [being] concerned with whence, whither and most important, with why'.[1]

The fact that not many textbook writers, or indeed many academic commentators, across the EU have engaged explicitly with such development is a source of regret. It is also, more importantly, problematic for others attempting to understand the nature and scope of the discipline. Hence we begin our book by briefly examining what is understood by 'health'. In the second section of the chapter, we consider the disciplinary derivations of health law, and its legal evolution. This leads directly to a third section, in which we analyse the extent to which the evolution of health law is integrally connected to the development of biomedical ethics. There, we explore the relationship between biomedical ethics and professional ethics and the impact of both discourses upon health law itself. We conclude the chapter with a discussion of what we mean by 'health law' in the context of our research agenda in this monograph.

---

[1] Morgan, *Issues in Medical Law and Ethics* (Cavendish 2001) 3

What is health?

In common with many who write on health law,[2] we take as our starting point the WHO and UNICEF Declaration of Alma Ata, 1978. This provides that:

> health, which is a state of complete physical, mental and social well-being and not merely the absence of disease and infirmity, is a fundamental human right and that the attainment of the highest possible level of health is a most important worldwide social goal whose realisation requires the action of many other social and economic sectors in addition to the health sector.[3]

Such an expansive definition can, however, be seen as laudably aspirational but lacking in practical focus. 'Well-being' goes far beyond the scope of modern medicine. The relations between the physical and the psychological mean that 'well-being' extends into the promotion of good mental health, but also into the provision of social care.[4] Expressing health in terms of well-being, as in this definition and the UN Covenant[5], involves reference to a philosophical concept. In large parts of the world, because living standards are so low, and indeed life itself is so regularly threatened by conditions of extreme poverty, the practical realization of the concept is limited to attempting to reduce disease.[6] Hence, a broad definition of 'health' may, in practice, lead to considerable problems in both the definition and the conceptualization of the discipline of 'health law'. If 'health' is 'a state of complete physical, mental and social well-being', how can we determine the practical content of any 'right to health'? What legal obligations does it entail – on health care professionals, on governments?

An alternative, if we cannot conclusively define 'health', is to attempt to define what constitutes 'illness'. At first this might seem a more straightforward approach, but on reflection this too may be seen as fundamentally problematic. Ian Kennedy, referring to Oliver Wendell Holmes's remark that medicine is as highly sensitive to context (political, religious, philosophical, imaginative) as any other socially constructed concept, points out, correctly, that illness, 'a central concept of medicine, is not a matter of objective scientific fact. Instead it is a term used to describe deviation from a notional norm'.[7] This means that whether someone is deemed 'ill' depends upon the choice of comparative

---

[2] Such as: e.g. Herring, *Medical Law and Ethics* (5th edn, OUP 2014) 6; Brazier and Cave, *Medicine, Patients and the Law* (5th edn, Penguin 2011) paragraph 2.18; Murphy, *Health and Human Rights* (Hart 2013).

[3] WHO, 'Declaration of Alma-Ata 1978' (WHO 1978).

[4] The boundaries between health and social care have become blurred in some contexts, notably long term care for physical illness and disability, and care of persons with mental disabilities. Indeed in the UK over a decade ago, Brazier and Glover suggested that health care law might eventually collapse into social care law: Brazier and Glover, 'Does Medical Law have a Future?' in Hayton (ed), *Law's Futures* (Hart 2000).

[5] UN International Covenant on Economic Social and Cultural Rights 1996, Article 12.

[6] Fluss, 'The Development of National Health Legislation in Europe: The Contribution of International Organisations' (1995) 2 *European Journal of Health Law* 193.

[7] Kennedy, *The Unmasking of Medicine* (Allen and Unwin 1981) 7–8.

norm, and this of course is a matter of judgement. The judgement of what constitutes illness, while inherently subjective, is something which, in the past, has been largely entrusted to the medical profession. But such determination of what constitutes ill health may not always be effective, conclusive, nor indeed necessarily appropriate.[8]

For the purposes of this book, we regard 'health' as centrally focused upon the individual, and consequently upon what has been termed an 'engineering model'. Such a model, as Jonathan Montgomery suggests, is concerned with repairing the defective human machine.[9] In the context of twenty-first-century Europe, the central focus here is on ill health as defined mainly (though not solely) by health care professionals, in the context of the global North, where poverty-related ill health of course remains an issue for some, but is not experienced on the same scale or to the same degree as in less developed countries.[10] In that context, and for these purposes, 'health' includes both physical and mental health.[11]

Charles Foster and Jonathan Herring have highlighted the social and relational aspects of individual health.[12] They argue that it is wrong to regard individuals simply as 'atomistic, static entities'.[13] Drawing upon the work of some commentators writing from a disability perspective, Herring and Foster suggest that health can be seen as a 'social notion'.[14] We recognize that 'health' may be affected by a range of other considerations, beyond the immediate focus of an individual. Nonetheless, we propose that there may be dangers in straying too far from that focus. An individual may be, or feel, separated from potentially relevant communities. Conceptualization of relations between individuals, and between an individual and various communities, may be exceedingly fluid. The fact that individuals may not always operate in an isolated fashion does not necessarily require us to depart entirely from a conception of 'health' that is based on individuals. We recognize the force of Foster and Herring's argument, which draws on the work of Martha Fineman, to the effect that '[a]utonomy is used not only to disguise our own vulnerability but also to justify inequalities

---

[8] See further: Kennedy (Allen and Unwin 1981), above n 7, 10–11, 16.

[9] Montgomery, 'Recognising a Right to Health' in Beddard and Hill (eds), *Economic, Social and Cultural Rights: Progress and Achievement* (Macmillan 1992); and see the further discussion in: Montgomery, *Health Care Law* (OUP 2002) 2–4.

[10] We recognise that some EU Member States, in particular Romania and Bulgaria, are not 'very high human development countries' as the other EU Member States are, in UN terms. This has implications for EU health law, which has been largely developed in the context of those Member States that are in the category of most developed countries.

[11] Of course, particularly in mental health contexts, questions of social care may also be important. For instance, legal entitlements, constraints or obligations following a patient's discharge from hospital under mental health legislation are part of the experience of that patient, and differ significantly across the EU. Nonetheless, we exclude social care from the scope of our inquiry here, as to include it would involve a differently focused research agenda.

[12] Foster and Herring, 'What is Health?' in Freeman, Hawkes and Bennett (eds), *Law and Global Health: Current Legal Issues Volume 16* (OUP 2014).

[13] Foster and Herring, above n 12, 24.   [14] Foster and Herring, above n 12, 25.

in society'.[15] Foster and Herring point out that people themselves do not want a medical model of health[16] and moreover that dependency 'should not be something to be afraid of or ashamed of'.[17] But while some individuals may not seek such an individually focused model, others may very well do, perhaps for some of the reasons outlined above. A medical model has its own limitations, but so does a more relational-based approach with its implications, for example, for individually enforceable human rights.

We do recognize that an individual focus needs to be set in the context of collective needs. When it comes to matters such as population health, we understand 'health' as reaching beyond the individual human being. Moreover, we recognize that the boundaries of individuals', and indeed societal, conceptions of 'health' and 'illness' change over time, and in many instances are highly subjective. In many situations, the individual and the broader community in which he or she finds himself or herself[18] cannot be easily severed. The context-specific nature of 'health' precludes an all-embracing, fixed definition. Our understanding of 'health' for the purposes of this book is thus both geographically and temporally contingent.

The origins of 'health law'

From early times and across jurisdictions, whilst there was no defined body of 'health law' as such, nonetheless law was utilized to regulate personal health choices and behaviours, whether on ethical grounds or on the broader public interest basis of disease prevention, through the use of 'public health' measures. So, for example, references to the isolation of lepers are to be found in the Old Testament.[19] Practices of quarantine can be traced back to 1000, and Venetian legislative statutes concerning plague quarantine date from 1127.[20]

Aspects of health law as we understand them today in the EU have evolved from the 'primary' or core principles of law in the relevant Member States. But those primary elements, and their jurisdictional bases, differ both between states and over time. Brazier and Ost point to the Mesopotamian Code of Hammurbai of over 3,000 years ago, which involved a (draconian) criminal penalty for a surgeon who 'caused the death of a lord'.[21] In many European states, from early times it was the criminal law which formed the basis for the legal regulation of

---

[15] Foster and Herring, above n 12, 29.   [16] *Ibid.*   [17] Foster and Herring, above n 12, 30.

[18] In this book, we use 'he' to refer to a patient or consumer, and 'she' to refer to a health professional. Legal entities are referred to as 'it'.

[19] See, for example: Leviticus 13: 45–46; Numbers 5: 1–3. See further discussion in: Gostin, *Public Health Law: Power, Duties and Restraints* (University of California Press 2000) 204.

[20] Gostin (2000) above n 19, 205.

[21] In such a case, the surgeon's hand was to be cut off; on the other hand, if he saved the lord's life, he was granted a pecuniary reward. See: Brazier and Ost, *Medicine and Bioethics in the Theatre of the Criminal Process* (CUP 2013) 16; see also: Montgomery, 'Medicalizing Crime – Criminalizing Health? The Role of Law' in Erin and Ost (eds), *The Criminal Justice System and Health Care Law* (OUP 2007).

health behaviours. In recent years, there has been much greater emphasis upon the use of civil liability or of other regulatory structures and processes.

In the UK, which is one EU Member State where there is considerable academic literature concerning health law and medical law, the discipline has evolved gradually from the interface between case law and statute law. The law concerning abortion finds its roots in ecclesiastical Canon Law. The recent statutory regulation began in the early 1800s and the current law criminalizing 'procuring a miscarriage' dates from 1861.[22] Moreover, health care practitioner regulation was initially bolstered by the operation of the criminal law. For example, in the UK, the London College of Physicians was granted a charter by King Henry VIII, which was followed by a statute in 1522, permitting the College to license physicians practising either in London or within seven miles of the city.[23] Practising without a licence was punishable by the criminal law. In Germany, Medicinal Orders were enacted in the fourteenth and fifteenth centuries, and until the eighteenth century medical law defined itself largely by reference to the criminal law.[24]

While the broad parameters of health law began to emerge in Member States by the turn of the nineteenth century, it has taken much longer for health law to cohere as a discipline. The disciplinary evolution of health law from its location within different primary legal principles has taken different forms. A notable illustration is the introduction of specific legislation addressing health, either health systems legislation, or sector-specific regulation of particular aspects of health care. So, for example, in Italy, the Crispies law of 1890 required that organizations which provided free health care through charity would be subject to legal regulation.[25] In the UK, the introduction of the National Health Service (NHS) was effected by legislation in the 1940s. Later specific statutory regulation covers evolving health technologies, for example, relating to human reproduction.[26]

Such an evolutionary trajectory was not, however, immediately characterized as 'health law'. In many instances, the discipline evolved as 'medical law'.[27]

---

[22] UK Offences Against the Person Act 1861, section 58.

[23] See further Brazier and Ost, above n 21, 17.

[24] Spranger, *Medical Law in Germany* (2nd edn, Kluwer Law International 2012) 21.

[25] Bassetti, Gulino et al., 'The Old Roots of the Italian Health Legislation' (2011) 2(2) *Mediterranean Journal of Social Science* 9.

[26] Belgium: Law on Research into Embryos In Vitro 2002 and the Law on Medically Assisted Reproduction and the Disposition of Supernumerary Embryos and Gametes 2007; France: Law on the Donation and Use of Elements and Products of the Human Body, Medically Assisted Procreation, and Prenatal Diagnosis, No. 94-654 (1994); Italy: Medically Assisted Procreation Law (2004); Spain: Law 35/88 on assisted reproduction, 1988, now Law 14/2006 on Assisted Human Reproduction Techniques, 2006; UK: Human Fertilisation and Embryology Act 1990 (as amended).

[27] See the project of the various Medical Law Books published by Kluwer: Nys (ed), *International Encyclopedia of Laws: Medical Law* (Kluwer Law International 1994); Den Exter and Hermans, *The Right to Health Care in Several European Countries* (Kluwer Law International 1995); WHO, *Promotion of the Rights of Patients in Europe* (Kluwer Law International 1995).

John Coggon has drawn attention to both the critical self-reflection of medical lawyers, and to the views of some scholars in other disciplines, who see medical law as a 'dubious or incoherent area of inquiry.'[28] We agree that the question of coherence of any area of legal study is open to question. For instance, Peter Cane has described tort law as 'conceptually disorganized and ramshackle', noting that the boundaries of a legal subject are created through custom and practice, in particular the analytical systematization by academic lawyers, and are thus much more contingent than we might imagine.[29]

The evolution of 'health law' as 'medical law' in the EU[30] is perhaps on reflection unsurprising, given the focus in European societies over the last century upon care being provided by doctors responsible for the primary diagnosis and treatment of patients. Moreover, the doctor has traditionally been the director of health care delivery. This remains the case, although in many Member States a greater role in making autonomous clinical judgements is now being given to other health professionals, such as nurses and pharmacists.[31] Law's engagement with health was predominantly cast in terms of the primary actors in the litigation process, and focusing on doctors and their legal obligations. The seminal comparative law text in this area, Dieter Giesen's *International Medical Malpractice Law*, reflects the dominance of the doctor in health professional negligence litigation.[32] Herman Nys's *International Encyclopaedia for Medical Law*,[33] which covers many EU Member States,[34] has a similar focus. In the UK, in *Medical Law: Text and Materials*, first published in 1991, Ian Kennedy and Andrew Grubb defined the discipline as 'medical law', and outlined its parameters in terms of the interrelationship between the patient and her doctor, the primary actors in the courtroom at that time.[35] This focus was repeated across Europe. So Nys' text *La Médicine et Le Droit*, published in 1995,[36] is primarily physician focused. While it discusses many of the doctor–patient issues to be

---

[28] Coggon, 'Would responsible Medical Lawyers lose their patients?' (2012) 20(1) *Medical Law Review* 130.

[29] Cane, *Atiyah's Accidents, Compensation and the Law* (6th edn, CUP 2004) 25, cited in Coggon, above n 28; Grey, 'Accidental Torts' (2001) 54 *Vanderbilt Law Review* 1225, cited in Ruger, 'Health Law's Coherence Anxiety' (2008) 96 *Georgetown Law Review* 625.

[30] This also appears to be the case in other highly developed countries, such as Canada, the USA, Australia and New Zealand, although exploration of this question is outwith the scope of this book.

[31] This is illustrated, for example, through the extension of powers to independently prescribe given to nurse practitioners and to pharmacists, see, for instance, UK Independent Prescribing Guidance and related regulations. See: National Prescribing Centre, 'Non-Medical Prescribing Competency Frameworks' (*NPC*, 20 May 2011).

[32] Giesen, *International Medical Malpractice Law* (JCB Mohr (Paul Siebeck) Martinus Nijhoff 1988).

[33] Nys (ed), above n 27.

[34] Austria, Belgium, Bulgaria, Czech Republic, France, Germany, Greece, Hungary, Ireland, the Netherlands, Poland, Portugal, Slovakia, Slovenia, Spain, Sweden, and the UK.

[35] Kennedy and Grubb, *Medical Law: Text with Materials* (Butterworths 2000).

[36] Nys, *La Médicine et Le Droit* (Kluwer Edit Juridiques 1995), which was the first such book in two decades to be published in the French-speaking part of Belgium.

found in standard UK texts, only title XII discusses relationships of the physician with other health professionals and institutions. *La Médicine et Le Droit* was followed by *Medical Law in Belgium*, with a similar focus.[37] In Ireland, Deidre Madden has published two recent texts, *Medicine, Ethics and the Law in Ireland*[38] and *Medical Law in Ireland*,[39] part of the same series of books in which Nys' 2012 book was published. In Sweden, Lotte Westerhäll's book *Medical Law* again focuses on the physician–patient relationship, with only five pages being devoted to consideration of other professional relationships.[40] The approach is similar in Germany, in Adolf Laufs and Wilhelm Uhlenbruck's *Handbuch des Artzrechts*[41] and Tade Spranger's *Medical Law in Germany*.[42] The University of Zagreb, in the EU's newest Member State, offers a module in 'Medicine and Law' using a text entitled *Health Law*,[43] which deploys a similar approach.

Over time, however, this approach was criticized for failing to engage with the changing dynamics of clinical practice (health care being delivered by interdisciplinary 'teams' of health care practitioners) and to take account of the trend towards other professionals being given greater degrees of responsibility.[44] Montgomery, for example, suggested that these developments mean that 'medical law' should be defined in terms of 'health care law'. For Montgomery, 'health care law' stretches beyond the practice of medicine to the non-medical health care professions, but also the organization and administration of health services (which falls largely within public law, rather than torts), as well as law's involvement in public health. Montgomery also takes the view that a narrow concept of law would not capture all that is important in 'health care law', noting that legislation and judicial decisions 'are not the only type of binding norm that is relevant to health care law'.[45]

But 'health care law' has not superseded 'medical law'. Indeed, the nature of medical law and its boundaries remain the subject of lively debate.[46] In over two decades since Montgomery's observations, there has been a plethora of new 'medical law' textbooks in the UK[47] and, as noted above, numerous medical law textbooks exist in other EU Member States. The UK academic commentators, Kennedy and Grubb, sought to respond to criticism about the

---

[37] Nys, *Medical Law in Belgium* (Kluwer Law International 2012).
[38] Madden, *Medicine, Ethics and the Law in Ireland* (Bloomsbury Professional 2011).
[39] Madden, *Medical Law in Ireland* (Kluwer Law International 2014)
[40] Westerhäll, *Medical Law: An Introduction* (Fritzes 1994).
[41] Láufs, Uhlenbruch and Genzel, *Handbuch des Artzrechts* (CH Beck 2002).
[42] Spranger, above n 24.
[43] Babić and Roksandić, Uvod u zdravstveno pravo (Introduction to Health Law) (Tipex 2006).
[44] Montgomery (OUP 2002) above n 9; Montgomery, 'Time for a Paradigm Shift? Medical Law in Transition' (2000) 53 *Current Legal Problems* 363; Brazier and Glover, above n 4; Sheldon and Thompson (eds), *Feminist Perspectives on Health Care Law* (Cavendish 1998) Introduction
[45] Montgomery, above n 9, 4.
[46] See: e.g. Veitch, *The Jurisdiction of Medical Law* (Ashgate 2013).
[47] See for example, three notable new books published in that period: Jackson, *Medical Law: Text, Cases, and Materials* (OUP 2014); Herring, above n 2; Pattinson, *Medical Law and Ethics* (Sweet and Maxwell 2014).

scope of their textbook in their third edition: 'We see it ['medical law'] as essentially concerned with the relationship between health care professionals (particularly doctors and to a lesser extent hospitals or other institutions) and patients'.[48] They go on to emphasize the ethical dimension of the discipline – respect for autonomy, consent, truth telling, confidentiality, respect for persons, respect for dignity and respect for justice. Moreover, Kennedy and Grubb believe that medical law today has one unifying theme, namely that of human rights.[49] This perspective is reflected in scholarship from other EU Member States, such as Elisabeth Rynning and Mette Hartlev's *Nordic Health Law in a European Context*,[50] although there the discipline is termed 'health law'.

For the purposes of this book, our view is that, while respect for fundamental human rights is undeniably an important theme in either medical or health law, it is by no means the single unifying characteristic. As we shall see below, the picture is considerably more complex. Across Europe, including in general in the UK, there is an observable trend towards the terminology of 'health law' rather than 'medical law' or 'health care law'. The first national society of health law in Europe was founded in 1967.[51] A programme of health law has been developed since 1977 by the Regional Office of the World Health Organization. In 1994, the *European Journal of Health Law* was established. This replaced an earlier journal entitled *Medicine and Law* and its change in title reflected a perceived shift away from a focus on malpractice litigation.[52]

A matter of ethics?

We noted above that Kennedy and Grubb defended the discipline (for them, 'medical law') as centrally focused around ethics. Is it ethics which is crucial in understanding what health law is and how it operates? The interface between law and biomedical ethics has been prevalent from the earliest times. Codes of ethical conduct of health care professionals date back at least as far as the Hippocratic Oath in the days of Ancient Greece around 420 BCE.[53] For centuries, law has engaged with some of the great ethical dilemmas of clinical practice, such as

---

[48] Kennedy and Grubb, above n 35, 3.   [49] *Ibid.*

[50] Rynning and Hartlev (eds), *Nordic Health Law in a European Context: Welfare State Perspectives on Patients' Rights and Biomedicine* (Martinus Nijhoff 2011); see also: Hartlev, 'Diversity and Harmonization. Trends and Challenges in European Health Law' (2010) 17(1) *European Journal of Health Law* 37.

[51] Leenen, 'The European Journal of Health Law: A New Publication' (1994) 1 *European Journal of Health Law* 1.

[52] Carmi, 'Health Law towards the 21st Century' (1994) 1 *European Journal of Health Law* 225.

[53] This reliance has, however, been the subject of some critical discussion. Thompson suggests that the Hippocratic Oath was not universally supported and only re-emerged in the nineteenth century as a means of medical practice enveloping itself in respectability; see further: Thompson, 'Fundamental ethical principles in health care' (1987) 295 *British Medical Journal* 1461. For a discussion of the development of the discipline in the light of Hippocrates see: Montgomery, 'Medical Law in the Shadow of Hippocrates' (1989) 52 *Modern Law Review* 566.

abortion and decisions at the end of life. As clinical practice developed rapidly over the last half century, accompanied by new technological developments, so the ethical controversies have multiplied, to include, for instance, sex-selection, cloning, face transplants and genetic screening. Consequently, the engagement of bioethicists and indeed theologians[54] with lawyers and the law has increased. The implications for health law as a discipline are drawn out by Montgomery, who observes that, traditionally, medical lawyers conceptualized ethics, law and medicine as in a hierarchical relationship. Ethics is at the apex, and its substance should be reflected in the law, which should then exert its coercive power over medicine. 'Medical law is thus a species of applied medical ethics.'[55]

This is a strong statement. Whether it is now or has ever been the case remains questionable. There is a danger in assuming that medical or health law is predicated upon ethics, as this may be true in some areas but is not the case across the board. Whether ethics is at the apex of the hierarchy, or whether ethics is a subset of the discipline of philosophy remains a matter of dispute,[56] but such questions go beyond our agenda, and we do not need to resolve them here. Moreover, Montgomery's account suggests that there are universally agreed 'medical ethical' principles, whereas such principles differ both across and within jurisdictions, and also evolve over time.[57] Religious and cultural perspectives have important practical effects on biomedical principles. So, for example, a concept such as the sanctity of life is commonly respected by different faith groups, and is inherent in legal frameworks across jurisdictions. But 'sanctity of life' can mean very different things when applied in practice.[58] Its application is predicated upon agreement as to what 'life' means and when

---

[54] For a few notable illustrations of this point, representing merely the tip of a vast iceberg: see, for example: Beauchamp and Childress, *Principles of Biomedical Ethics* (OUP 2001); Harris, *The Value of Life* (Routledge 1985); Gillon, *Philosophical Medical Ethics* (John Wiley and Sons 1986); Ashcroft, 'The Troubled Relationship between Bioethics and Human Rights' (2008) 11(22) *Law and Bioethics* 31; Ashcroft, 'Could human rights supersede bioethics?' (2010) 10 *Human Rights Law Review* 639.

[55] Montgomery, 'Time for a Paradigm Shift? Medical Law in Transition' (2000) 53 *Current Legal Problems* 363. It is interesting to note here that one of the leading exponents of health law is here himself characterizing the discipline as medical law.

[56] See for example: Koch, 'Bioethics? A grand idea' (2008) 178(1) *Canadian Medical Association Journal* 116.

[57] Abel and Terribas, 'The Dynamics of the Bioethical Dialogue in Spain' in Pessini, de Paul de Barchifontaine and Lolas Stepke (eds), *Ibero-American Bioethics* (Springer 2011) 245-260.

[58] See: e.g. Perrett, 'Buddhism, euthanasia and the sanctity of life' (1996) 22 *Journal of Medical Ethics* 309; Clarfield, Gordon, Markwell, Shabbir and Alibhai, 'Ethical Issues in End-of-Life Geriatric Care: The Approach of Three Monotheistic Religions—Judaism, Catholicism, and Islam' (2003) 51(8) *Journal of the American Geriatrics Society* 1149. See also, generally: Widdows, 'Christian Approaches to Bioethics'; Rosner, 'Judaism and Medicine: Jewish Medical Ethics'; Sachedina, 'The Search for Islamic Bioethics Principles'; Hughes, 'Buddhist Bioethics'; Coward, 'South Asian Approaches to Health Care Ethics'; Jing-Bao, 'The Specious Idea of an Asian Bioethics: Beyond Dichotomizing East and West' all in Ashcroft, Draper, Dawson and Macmillan (eds), *Principles of Health Care Ethics* (Wiley-Blackwell 2007).

it begins and ends. In addition, while the principle may be agreed in general, the extent to which it is amenable to exceptions may vary considerably.

The rise of 'ethics consciousness' in turn has been driven at least initially by engagement of health care professionals with biomedical ethical concepts, and less by the law. Certainly professional ethical tenets existed centuries before the recent development of biomedical ethics. One of the earliest statements of such a professional code was that of the Hippocratic Oath in Ancient Greece, one provision of which, exhorting health professionals to keep their patients' secrets, resonates throughout health care professional codes in the Western world today.

This is an interesting development as such engagement has undoubtedly helped to frame the manner in which health professionals self-regulate through the evolution of professional ethical codes. Thus biomedical ethics translates into professional ethics. Such professional ethical standards can ultimately affect health care law, in the evolution of legal standards.[59] Biomedical ethicists today sit on ethics committees of medical professional regulatory bodies, assisting in the development of those professional guidelines.

There is undoubtedly an interface between professional biomedical ethics and health law. José Miola talks of a 'symbiotic relationship'.[60] Coggon argues that there is also an interface between academic medical law and academic medical ethics. Although their approaches and analytical concerns differ, both have developed in response to particular questions such as how, and why, should medical practices be governed. Each informs the other. The conclusions they reach are often strikingly similar and are reflected in laws, regulations, guidance, and even dominant professional norms and mores.[61] Equally, rather than 'academic medical ethics', others take the view that the better terminology should be 'health care ethics' or 'health ethics'.[62]

What do we mean by 'health law'?

Having given a brief overview of the evolution of health law and its relationships with medical law and ethics, in this section, rather than attempting a definitive contemporary definition, we outline our understanding of the scope of health law for the purposes of this book. In so doing, we recognize that delineating health law should always be a provisional exercise, because health law develops in tandem with medicine, and indeed science and technology more generally.

---

[59] See for example the evolution of the UK law concerning informed consent and the role played by professional practice guidelines here, General Medical Council (GMC), 'Consent guidance: patients and doctors making decision together' (GMC 2008); Jones, 'Informed Consent and other fairy stories' (1999) 7(2) *Medical Law Review* 104; McLean, "From *Sidaway* to *Pearce* and Beyond: Is the legal regulation of consent any better following a quarter of a century of judicial scrutiny?' (2012) 20(1) *Medical Law Review* 108.

[60] Miola, *Medical Law and Medical Ethics: A Symbiotic Relationship* (Hart 2007).

[61] Coggon, above n 28.

[62] Note that the one of the leading compendiums in the area of biomedical ethics is Ashcroft, Draper, Dawson and Macmillan (eds), above n 58.

Moreover, we agree with Coggon, that 'although we might imagine a narrow area characterised as medical law within larger fields labelled health care law, health law, and public health law, it is not entirely clear in practice how neatly the categories can be divided'.[63] Nonetheless, we do need to give readers some indication of the substantive scope of our research agenda in this book.

We have suggested that health law should be conceived as extending beyond the professional–patient relationship. This was true a decade ago, but it is much more so today. Patients as consumers increasingly access particular health care services without professional involvement. Far greater information about treatments and procedures is available directly to patients. Nonetheless the professional nexus has not yet dissolved totally. Professionals remain the gatekeepers for access to service in many instances, and certainly across the EU, for the vast majority of forms of hospital care. Where procedures are wholly private, admittedly a different dynamic does operate. Cosmetic surgery provides one such example, but even in such areas there is a degree of retrenchment to public provision, not least, as we saw in the case of Poly Implant Prothèse, because of the fear of what can happen when private medical procedures go wrong.[64]

In this book, our focus is 'health law'. We recognize that medical law and health care law do exist as disciplinary constructs. It is undoubtedly the case that the precise content of health law varies between jurisdictions, partly due to differences in levels of sophistication of engagement with the discipline; partly due to differences in medical practice, the organization of health care systems, and the parameters of public health law. Nonetheless, there are certain 'core' identifiable elements of health law at national level, discernible across the Member States of the EU.[65] We identify six such core elements, which of course overlap to some extent: a concern with individual human rights; professional liability; access to and practising of health care professions and regulating health care institutions; funding and organization of health systems; public health; and regulation of human material in health contexts.

First, health law is about a concern with individual human rights, specifically, as these apply in health care settings. Human rights are central to the scope of health law in several respects. Perhaps most notably, human rights are inherent in health law in principles of bodily integrity. Health law covers legal rules on consent to treatment, and the human right to individual decision-making autonomy. The specifics of recognition of principles of consent do vary between Member States, but nonetheless the concept of consent is recognized across EU jurisdictions. This concept has been bolstered, as we shall see in chapters 7 and 12, by engagement with human rights at national levels. It is particularly

---

[63] Coggon, above n 28.
[64] Keogh, 'Review of the Regulation of Cosmetic Interventions' (DoH 2013).
[65] See further: Mason and Laurie, *Law and Medical Ethics* (2013); Madden, above n 39.

the case in the very notion of decision-making autonomy being derived from a right to privacy.[66]

Individual human rights also frame health law where questions arise concerning who has decision-making capacity in a specific situation, and which rules apply, to adults, to children and to those who may lack mental capacity. Human reproductive choices (such as abortion or access to reproductive technologies) can be seen as human rights, or as ethical questions. While these fall within health law, in many jurisdictions they are also part of family law, and an uneasy degree of overlap remains. Moreover, human rights inform health law in the specifics of information provision to patients, for instance, rights to access medical records, and rights to know, and not know, genetic information.[67] This is an area of health law that is becoming increasingly aligned in many respects across the EU.

The question of a 'right to health care', while a concern of health law, is far less engaged as a concept at national level, although, as we shall see, the right to health care is incorporated into the EU Charter of Fundamental Human Rights in Article 35. One of the challenges is that of asserting such a right, given that an individual claim to health care might conflict with the competing right of another person to health care resources.

To say that health law is concerned with human rights does not necessarily mean that this is a single defining feature, not least because of the lack of consensus as to what fundamental rights mean, how they operate in practice, and how they should be interpreted in a particular context. Health lawyers are also concerned with engaging with the limitations of fundamental rights, when, for example, principles such as liberty may be legitimately curtailed to further therapeutic ends such as in treatment for mental illness.[68] Human rights analysis

---

[66] This arises in various areas see eg on privacy and autonomy and the use of personal information and genetic material: Laurie, *Genetic Privacy: A Challenge to Medico-Legal Norms* (CUP 2007); Taylor, *Genetic Information and the Law: A Critical Perspective on Privacy Protection* (CUP 2012); on consent to treatment including the debates concerning reproductive choices see: e.g. Jackson, *Regulating Reproduction: Regulating Reproduction: Law, Technology and Autonomy* (Hart 2001); Marshall, 'A right to personal autonomy at the European Court of Human Rights' (2008) 13(3) *European Human Rights Law Review* 337; Valongo, 'Human Rights and Reproductive Choices in the Case law of the Italian and European Courts' (2014) 24(2) *European Journal of Health Law* 123.

[67] Chadwick, Levitt, Shickle (eds), *The Right to Know and the Right Not to Know: Genetic Privacy and Responsibility* (CUP 2007); Ost, 'The 'right' not to know' (1984) 9(3) *The Journal of Medicine and Philosophy* 301; Harris and Keywood, 'Ignorance, information and autonomy' (2001) 22(5) *Theoretical Medicine and Bioethics* 415; Laurie, 'In defence of ignorance: genetic information and the right not to know' (1999) 6(2) *European Journal of Health Law* 119; Laurie, 'Protecting and promoting privacy in an uncertain world: further defences of ignorance and the right not to know' (2000) 7(2) *European Journal of Health Law* 185; Laurie, above n 66; UK Human Genetics Commission, *Inside information—balancing interests in the use of personal genetic data* (UK HGC 2002); Taylor, above n 66; Chico, 'Known unknowns and unknown unknowns: the potential and the limits of autonomy in non-disclosure of genetic risk' (2012) 28(3) *Journal of Professional Negligence* 162.

[68] *X v UK* (1981) Series A no 46; *Winterwerp v the Netherlands* (1979) Series A no 33; *Rakevich v Russia* App no 58973/00 (ECtHR, 28 November 2003);.*Ashingdane* v *UK* (1985) Series A no 93;

may also be problematic where specific claimed rights clash. Classic examples include the rights of a woman to an abortion, in contest with the right of a foetus to life; or the reproductive rights of a couple where one wishes to use a stored frozen embryo created using the couples' gametes and the other opposes it – that is, a right to reproduce against a right not to reproduce.[69]

Secondly, health law is concerned with liability of health care professionals, and also of health care institutions. A major feature of health law across the last half century has been the evolution of the law on compensation for harms caused by medical procedures or treatments.[70] The gradual change in litigation culture in certain European countries fuelled discussion of a 'malpractice crisis' akin to that in the USA.[71] This change was assisted by increased awareness of legal processes and easier access to litigation across many Member States. Furthermore, over time there was simply less deference to professional expertise and less acceptance of professional 'mistakes' when things went wrong.[72] While in the latter part of the twentieth century, the concern with professional responsibility manifested itself predominantly in civil litigation, there has been an increasing willingness to engage with criminal liability of health professions. So, for example, in the case of *Vo* v. *France*, the issue of criminal liability arose where there was a negligent performance of a clinical procedure due to a mistake over the identity of the patient which resulted in a miscarriage.[73] Contamination of blood has led to criminal litigation in France.[74] End-of-life decision-making raises difficult questions of professional ethics, legal liability and patient choice or rights.[75] In the UK, there is a debate about the potential

---

DN v Switzerland, no. 27154/95, ECHR 2001-III; *HL v UK*, no. 45508/99, ECHR 2004-IX;.*Herczegfalvy v Austria* (1992) Series A no 244; *Witold Litwa v Poland*, no. 26629/95, ECHR 2000-III; *Keenan v UK*, no. 27229/95, ECHR 2001-III .

[69] *Evans v UK*, no. 6339/05, ECHR 2007-I. See also chapters 4 and 7.

[70] In his introduction to Giesen's treatise on *International Medical Malpractice Law* in 1988, Lord Kilbrandon quoted from the judgment given in a Scottish case, *Farquhar v Murray* (1901) 3 F. 859, 862: "This action is certainly one of a particularly unusual character. It is an action of damages by a patient against a medical man. In my somewhat long experience I cannot remember having seen a similar case before." See: Giesen, above n 32.

[71] See: Dute, 'Medical Malpractice Liability. No easy solutions' (2003) 10(2) *European Journal of Health Law* 85.

[72] See further: Miola, 'The Impact of Less Deference to the Medical Profession' in Algrahni, Bennett and Ost (eds), *The Criminal Law and Bioethical Conflict: Walking the Tightrope* (CUP 2012).

[73] *Vo v France*, no. 53924/00, ECHR 2004-VIII.

[74] Farrell and Kazarian, 'The role of the criminal law in healthcare malpractice in France: examining the HIV Blood Contamination Scandal' in Sanders and Griffiths (eds), *Medicine, Crime and Society* (CUP 2013).

[75] *Pretty v UK*, no. 2346/02, ECHR 2002-III; Griffiths, Weyers and Adams, *Euthanasia and the Law in Europe* (Hart 2008); *R (Purdy) v DPP* [2009] UKHL 45; Hirst, 'Assisted Suicide after Purdy: the unresolved issue' (2009) 12 *Criminal Law Review* 870; Lewis, *Assisted Dying and Legal Change* (OUP 2007). Lewis and Black, 'Reporting and Scrutiny of reported cases in four jurisdictions where assisted dying is lawful. A review of the cases in Belgium, Oregon, the Netherlands and Switzerland' (2013) 13(4) *Medical Law International* 221.

relevance of the crimes of corporate and gross negligence manslaughter to deaths resulting from extreme negligence in health settings.[76]

Thirdly, related to questions of professional liability, although in jurisdictional basis frequently distinct, health law is also concerned with the structure of the regulation of health care. This comprises both the regulation of practitioners and the regulation of premises on which health care procedures are conducted, especially hospitals and clinics. Access to medical professions, including entitlement to use certain professional titles, is subject to legal restrictions. Health care practice is subject to licensing or other legal authorization in many instances. Authority to operate as various types of health care institution is also normally subject to some sort of authorization, often prescribed in detailed legislation. This is true, for instance, of blood banks, clinical laboratories and pharmacies. In this book, all of these matters form an important part of health law.

Both people and premises are regulated primarily to ensure patient and population safety, but also to promote quality of health care. The approach taken to different professions varies across EU Member States. Even the question of who is a 'practitioner' and what constitutes a 'profession' may differ significantly across jurisdictions. In many respects, the very fact that a profession is regarded as 'legitimate' relates to whether it is formally regulated. A nascent profession may be regulated to some extent, albeit less formally. A good illustration here is the position of complementary and alternative medicine.[77]

A common pattern appears to be the evolution of self-regulatory structures into more formal state-led regulation, often precipitated by politically critical events. However, the detailed practical operation of regulatory controls may well remain in the hands of health care professionals, especially doctors, rather than being replaced by independent regulation. So, for example, in the UK, major inquiries into clinical practice at the children's cardiac paediatric unit at Bristol Royal Infirmary and following the prosecution of the multiple murderer Dr Harold Shipman,[78] led to regulatory restructuring and increased oversight by the medical professional regulatory body, the General Medical Council, although this was also accompanied by the development of independent bodies overseeing both professional regulation and standards of safety and quality.

EU Member States also have different forms and types of regulation of health professionals. We have noted different balances between state and self-regulation. The balance between formal and informal rules also varies. Legislative or administrative rules are often supplemented by detailed 'soft law' guidance and 'good practice' statements, which have significant effects on

---

[76] Wells, 'Medical Manslaughter: Organisational Liability' in Sanders and Griffiths above n 74.

[77] See further: Stone and Matthews, *Complementary Medicine and the Law* (OUP 1996); Saks, 'Professionalization, Regulation and Alternative Medicine' in Saks and Allsop (eds), *Regulating the Health Professions* (Sage 2002).

[78] See further: Kennedy, 'The report of the public inquiry into children's heart surgery at the Bristol Royal Infirmary 1984-1995: learning from Bristol' (Bristol Royal Infirmary Inquiry 2001); Smith, 'Sixth Report – Shipman: The Final Report' (The Shipman Inquiry 2005).

professional practice, even if they are not technically legally binding. The regulatory structures for health professionals also encompass engagement with professional ethics.

The regulation of health care premises reflects a fundamental concern with quality and safety, by requiring basic standards of hygiene in the performance of clinical procedures and in offering patient care. The addressees of these regulatory rules may be heath care professionals, but they may equally be other service providers, such as porters, cleaners or caterers, or those responsible for their actions. The question of basic hygiene is, perhaps surprisingly in the twenty-first century,[79] an increasingly important regulatory concern, with the rise of Methicillin-resistant *Staphylococcus aureus* (MRSA) and other potentially lethal hazards in hospitals and other health care premises. It is also a source of debate when non-surgical procedures, such as cosmetic enhancements, are undertaken for allegedly therapeutic purpose in non-health care premises, such as hair salons and beauty parlours.[80]

Fourthly, for us, as for others,[81] health law is concerned with the funding of health care services. The ways in which health care services are funded vary across the EU. There is, however, consistency in that there is always some state-centred control over the allocation of resources for such services. We say more about the different ways in which health care services are funded in the introduction to Part III of the book. For now, it is sufficient to note that, across the EU, both national health social insurance schemes, based on the compulsory insurance of categories of persons, and national health systems funded by general taxation, are found. Health care schemes may be integrated into the general social security system, or the administration of health insurance may be entrusted to public or semi-public bodies, such as sickness funds. In addition, the growing evolution of private health care has meant that increasingly the relationship between patients, health insurance funds and private providers may become important. Health law is concerned with all the legal structures that surround these relationships.

Also central to the discipline of health law, in addition to funding structures, is the related question of who has access to health care resources within the national social insurance or national health system. Put simply, patients' entitlements and expectations can relate closely to the funding structures which are

---

[79]   Given the work of Florence Nightingale and others nearly 160 years ago.

[80]   Keogh, 'Review of the Regulation of Cosmetic Interventions' (Department of Health 2013). See also: Latham, '"If it aint broke don't fix it": Scandals, "Risk" and Cosmetic Surgery Regulation in the UK and France' (2014) 22(3) *Medical Law Review* 384.

[81]   Buijsen, 'The Concept of Health Law' (14th World Health Law Congress, Maastricht, 2002) 1, on file with the authors. Jost also regards health care organisation and finance as a major area of health law: see: Jost, *Readings in Comparative Health Law and Bioethics* (Carolina Academic Press 2007); as does Montgomery, above n 9. See also: Greer, 'The Three Faces of European Union health policy: Policy, markets, austerity' (2014) 33(1) *Policy and Society* 13.

employed. Inevitably, the more directly the patient funds the care in question, the greater their own personal expectations are likely to be of the standards of care delivered. Funding structures and entitlements thus interact with the regulatory questions of quality and safety outlined above. Equally, if patients are denied funding, this may give rise to legal challenges to the allocation of resources, whether this arises through a national health service[82] or through prioritization processes which operate in the context of socially funded insurance. Such legal challenges may be formulated in terms of patients' human rights to demand health care services.[83]

Our fifth area of concern is the public dimension of health. A classic definition of 'public health' dates from 1920:

> Public Health is the science and art of preventing disease, prolonging life and promoting physical health and efficiency through organised community efforts for the sanitation of the environment, the control of community infections, the education of the individual in principles of personal hygiene, the organisation of medical and nursing service for the early diagnosis and preventative treatment of disease, and the development of social machinery which will ensure to every individual in the community a standard of living adequate for the maintenance of health.[84]

Public health law has its roots in concern for preventing the spread of communicable diseases, and considered the legitimacy of detention for such purposes. These questions remain much disputed among public health lawyers, as illustrated notably by the continuing national[85] and international[86] controversy in the context of HIV and AIDS. SARS, H1N1 and H5N1 prompted similar concerns in the 2000s. The lawfulness, or otherwise, of such deprivation of liberty, to protect public health, is a fundamental part of health law.

But the ambit of public health law goes well beyond this relatively narrow focus. Public health law is centrally concerned with constraining both the rights of individuals and those of commercial entities in the name of collective or community health protection, and the promotion of good community health. The range of factors that contribute to health protection and promotion is vast. Many are encapsulated in the UK's Nuffield Council on Bioethics 2007 Report, 'Public Health: The Ethical Issues'. The report notes that, in addition

---

[82] Syrett, *Law, Legitimacy and the Rationing of Health Care* (CUP 2007).

[83] O'Sullivan, 'The allocation of scarce resources and the right to life under the European Convention on Human Rights' [1998] *Public Law* 389.

[84] Winslow, 'The Untilled Fields of Public Health' (1920) 51 *Science* 23, 23.

[85] For instance, in 1985, in the UK, a man suffering from AIDS was controversially detained in hospital. See: Editorial, 'Detaining Patients with AIDS' (1985) 291 *British Medical Journal* 1002.

[86] See, for example, Erin and Bennett (eds), *HIV and AIDS: Testing screening and confidentiality* (OUP 1999); Gostin and Lazzarini, *Human Rights and Public Health in the AIDS Pandemic* (OUP 1997); Haigh and Harris, *AIDS and the Law* (Routledge 1995).

to lifestyle choices, other factors determining collective good health are 'genetic background, social and economic living standards, the built environment, the availability of and access to preventative and curative health services and the influence of commercial organisations such as the food and drink industries'.[87] In addition, over time, the approaches taken to what constitutes public health have also evolved in the light of developments in medical science. Here the public interest in safe and effective medical innovations forms an interface with individual interests in privacy, bodily integrity and other human rights protection (such as consent), as well as ethical safeguards.

Thus, health law also covers the regulation of experimental health procedures and indeed of clinical research. The proper regulation of clinical research has become of international concern following the 1945–46 Nuremberg Trials and the production of the Declaration of Helsinki in 1964.[88] For health law, the challenge of regulating health research engages with the law on consent to participation and specific rules concerning children and adults lacking mental capacity. In addition, an important part of research is public health research, and thus the question arises of regulating the relationships between state interests, public interests and commercial interests.[89] Research is also concerned with professional responsibility, and with questions of public safety. This aspect of health law determines the responsibilities of researchers, of the relevant industries, and of the state. In the context of an increasingly globalized medical research industry, health lawyers are also concerned with ethical questions, for instance, about the involvement of patients in developing countries in trials for medicines that their countries will never be able to afford.[90]

It follows that public health law might, for instance, permit, or even require, disease surveillance and the reporting of health information (including, for example, making large health datasets available for research) in ways that affect individual privacy or confidentiality. Public health law might impose mandatory prophylactic treatment (in particular, immunization), testing or screening that affects bodily integrity or property rights. Public health law also includes mandatory rules that apply to certain industries, such as the pharmaceutical and medical devices industries, tobacco industry, alcohol industry or food industry, in ways that affect their freedom to trade.[91] Many such specific elements of

---

[87] Nuffield Council on Bioethics, *Public Health: Ethical Issues* (Cambridge Publishers 2007), paragraph 1.4. For a discussion, see: Baldwin, Brownsword and Schmidt, 'Stewardship, Paternalism and Public Health: Further Thoughts' (2009) 2(1) *Public Health Ethics* 113.

[88] See also discussion of regulation of research below at chapter 12.

[89] McHale, 'Law, Regulation and Public Health Research: A Case for Fundamental Reform?' (2010) 63(1) *Current Legal Problems* 475.

[90] See further: chapter 17; Jackson, *Law and the Regulation of Medicines* (Hart 2012); Goldacre, *Bad Pharma: How Medicine is Broken, and How We Can Fix It* (Fourth Estate 2013); Altavilla, 'Ethical Standards for Clinical Trials Conducted in Third Countries: The New Strategy of the European Medicines Agency' (2011) 18(1) *European Journal of Health Law* 65.

[91] See further: chapters 12–15 and 18. Gostin, *Public Health Law: Power, Duty and Restraint* (University of California Press 2008) 20.

public health law have been discussed by legal and bioethics commentators. For example, the coercion entailed in fluoridation of water has prompted debate.[92] Health lawyers are also concerned with questions such as the interface between lifestyle choices and access to treatment in national health or social insurance systems.[93]

Other non-coercive methods of public health policy have grown in their use over the last two decades, accompanied by the evolution of 'nudging', regulation by design and other mechanisms of persuasion as a regulatory concept.[94] Health lawyers are interested in the relationships between coercive and non-coercive aspects of health law, particularly in contexts of technological development.[95]

Extrapolating from these definitions of public health, public health *law* is potentially an almost impossibly wide concept, encompassing communications law (transport, telecommunications, infrastructure), environmental law (air and water quality, built environments, waste management), welfare law (social security, social care, housing, education), consumer protection law; and the list goes on. There are challenges in adopting a very broad definition here. As Gostin notes, if a definition is too broad, it may be problematic if it encompasses issues such as redistribution of wealth and social restructuring, which fundamentally enter the general *political* arena[96] rather than constituting part of *health law*. Perhaps this goes some way to explaining why public health law, while crucially important in practice, still is not a matter of major concern in many health law textbooks.[97] In this book, partly for practical reasons, we exclude some

---

[92] See for example: Nuffield Council on Bioethics, above n 87, ch 7.

[93] See, for instance: Pallot, 'Sympathy wanes for sufferers of the 'self-inflicted illnesses' *The Telegraph* (London, 24 January 2006); Editorial, '"Get tough" on unhealthy – survey' (*BBC News*, 22 November 2005); Runner's World, 'Should the NHS treat 'self inflicted' illness?? – Clubhouse – Runner's World' (*Runners World*, 11 February 2014). See: Newdick, *Who Should We Treat? – Rights, Rationing and Resources in the NHS* (OUP 2005); Syrett, above n 82.

[94] Thaler and Sunstein, *Nudge: Improving Decisions about Health, Wealth, and Happiness* (Yale University Press 2008); Brownsword, 'Code, Control , and Choice: Why East is East and West is West' (2005) 21 *Legal Studies* 1; Marteau, Oliver and Ashcroft, 'Changing behaviour through state intervention: When does an acceptable nudge become an unacceptable shove?' (2009) 338(7687) *British Medical Journal* 121; House of Lords Science and Technology Select Committee, *Behaviour Change (second report)* (HL 2010-12, 179-I).

[95] Nuffield Council on Bioethics, above n 87, paragraph 1.4; Baldwin, Brownsword and Schmidt, 'Stewardship, Paternalism and Public Health: Further Thoughts' (2009) 2(1) *Public Health Ethics* 113; Murphy, *New Technologies and Human Rights* (OUP 2009); Flear, Farrell, Hervey and Murphy (eds), *European Law and New Health Technologies* (OUP 2013).

[96] Gostin, 'Public Health, Ethics and Human Rights: A Tribute to the Late Jonathan Mann' (2001) 29 *Journal of Law, Medicine and Ethics* 121. See also further: Rothstein, 'Rethinking the Meaning of Public Health' (2002) 30 *Journal of Law, Medicine and Health* 144.

[97] Some indeed emphasised its separateness as a discipline. Tobey, writing in 1926: it "should not be confused with medical jurisprudence which is concerned only in the legal aspects of the application of medical and surgical knowledge to individuals . . . Public health is not a branch of medicine but a science in itself, to which, however, preventative medicine is an important contributor. Public health law is that branch of jurisprudence which treats . . . the application of common law and statutory law to the principles of hygiene and sanitation", see: Tobey, *Public Health Law: A Manual of Law for Sanitarians* (Williams and Wilkins Co 1926) 6–7, cited in Areen et al., *Law, Science and Medicine* (Foundation Press 1996) 485.

aspects of the list above, notably communications, environmental and welfare law. But we do include communicable disease law, regulation of medical and other health-related research,[98] and the law on certain consumer products with clear implications for public health promotion and protection. These, at least for us, are areas where the law can be understood through the primary analytical lens of health.

Finally, in the context of both research and of health care and treatment, health law also covers the regulation of human material. Human material is a huge category, extending from solid organs for transplantation, to blood, plasma and serum, and to small slivers of tissues or cells, for instance, used in biotechnological or nanotechnological contexts. It is therefore not surprising that the broad heading 'human material regulation' encapsulates a range of diverse forms of regulation. Historically, the law was concerned with the use of material for anatomical examinations.[99] As clinical science has developed, for example to permit organ transplantation, the law has reached further. Today health law can be seen as covering those categories, but also extending to the use of human material for research purposes. As well as seeking to safeguard quality and safety, the reasons for regulation here concern respect for individual human rights, notably respect for individual decision-making autonomy and bodily integrity, although property rights have also been implicated.[100] Several EU Member States have experienced significant controversies in the unauthorized use of human materials within health care contexts:[101] health law is concerned with determining responsibility for the consequences and seeking to prevent undesirable future events.

Conclusions

The main aim of this chapter was to begin to delineate some substantive boundaries of our inquiry in this book. We have set out some of the broader disciplinary and historical contexts for that inquiry. We have also explained the substantive scope of health law for our purposes, as focused around six overlapping core elements. These are a concern with individual human rights; professional liability; access to and practising of health care professions and regulating health

---

[98] Although not the regulation of science more generally, as to do so would involve a different research agenda.

[99] E.g. Richardson, *Death, Dissection and the Destitute* (Phoenix Press 2001).

[100] See: *Moore v University of California* (1990) 793 P 2d 479; and see further: Hardcastle, *Law and the Human Body: Property Rights, Ownership and Control* (Hart 2009); Andrews and Nelkin, 'Whose Body is it Anyway? Disputes Over Body Tissue in a Biotechnology Age' (1998) 351(9095) *The Lancet* 53; Herring, Gould, Greasley and Stene (eds), *Persons, Parts and Property: How Should We Regulate Human Tissue in the 21st Century?* (Hart 2014).

[101] Redfearn, 'The Royal Liverpool Children's Inquiry Report' (HC12-II, The Stationary Office 2001); Bristol Inquiry Interim Report, 'Removal and Retention of Human Material' (2000); and see also: Metx and Hoppe, 'Organ Transplantation in Germany: Regulating Scandals and Scandalous Regulation' (2013) 20(2) *European Journal of Health Law* 113; Colgan, *Trust Betrayed: How the Organ Retention Scandal Devastated Irish Families* (Poolbeg Press 2009).

care institutions; funding and organization of health care systems; public health; and regulation of human material in health contexts.

We recognize that, in seeking to explain how we are conceptualizing health law for our purposes here, we have drawn distinctions that may seem rather fine. Perhaps these simply highlight the fluid nature of disciplinary boundaries. In other work, we might therefore choose to adopt different terminology, or different definitions of the nature of our subject of inquiry. But in this book our agenda concerns health law as we have set it out above – in particular, the health law of the European Union. We turn to the scope of European Union health law in the next chapter.

3

What is European Union health law?

Introduction

Chapter 2 indicated the reach of our inquiry in terms of how we are defining health law for the purposes of this book. In this chapter, we further specify the scope of our research agenda, by explaining what we mean by 'European Union health law'. We first give some historical context. The EU's legal order is relatively unstable, certainly when compared to the constitutional settlements of its Member States, in the sense of being subject to significant constitutional changes over short periods of time. It is therefore rather pointless to describe the state of EU law only at a particular moment. Rather, what is needed is an understanding of EU law as a process: a video rather than a snapshot.[1] Second, we outline the key sources of EU health law: treaties and legislation, case law, and soft law. These will be explained in much greater detail in the chapters that follow. We also explain the 'transversal' nature of the scope of EU health law, using the concept of 'mainstreaming'. Finally, as we hope that among our readership will be those who are unfamiliar with EU law, we explain some of the key actors and processes involved in making EU health law.

This chapter covers only the EU's internal health law – that is, the law emanating from the EU's constitutional, legislative and judicial sources that applies to countries within the EU. The scope of the EU's external health law – that is EU law that applies outside of the EU – is considered in Part IV of the book, where we turn to our global focus.

History of EU health law

Early years

Where should we start with a history of EU health law? There is a strong argument that, although health was not an explicit EU competence[2] at the time,

---

[1] Pierson, 'The Path to European Integration: a Historical Institutionalist Analysis' (1996) 29 *Comparative Political Studies* 123. On the EU's changing constitution see, inter alia: Weiler and Wind, *European Constitutionalism Beyond the State* (CUP 2003); Craig and de Búrca (eds), *The Evolution of EU Law* (2nd edn, OUP 2011); Walker, Shaw and Tierney (eds), *Europe's Constitutional Mosaic* (Hart 2011); de Búrca and Weiler, *The Worlds of European Constitutionalism* (CUP 2011).

[2] See further below.

the place to begin is the very foundation of the 'European Economic Community' (EEC), which has now become the European Union (EU).[3] The EEC was established by international treaty between six states in Western Europe in 1957.[4] Its aims were to promote peace and stability in Europe, through collaborative economic growth and development.[5] The centrepiece of its activities was the creation of the 'common market'.[6] This is an area without internal frontiers within which the free movement of the factors of production (products (goods); services; workers, professionals and companies; capital) is to be legally secured.[7] The EEC also developed common policies in several areas, most important of which was the Common Agriculture Policy (CAP). The CAP responded to the pressing need for Western Europe to become more self-sufficient in food, and to alleviate the extreme poverty and starvation that followed the Second World War.[8]

From the point of view of those who include public health law within their conception of the scope of EU health law,[9] the earliest pieces of EU health law are found in the law of the Common Agricultural Policy and that of the 'common market' (now known as the 'internal market'). For instance, legislation from the 1960s was concerned with the safety of food intended for human consumption,[10] food being an important disease vector. The EU continues to protect human health by regulating food safety.[11] However, today's EU

---

[3] The Treaty of Lisbon 2007, which entered into force on 1 December 2009, provides that the European Union 'shall replace and succeed the European Community', Article 1 TEU. The 'European Community' was the successor to the 'European Economic Community', according to the Treaty of Maastricht, 1992.

[4] The European Union now has 28 Member States: Austria, Belgium, Bulgaria, Croatia, Cyprus, Czech Republic, Denmark, Estonia, Finland, France, Germany, Greece, Hungary, Ireland, Italy, Latvia, Lithuania, Luxembourg, Malta, Netherlands, Poland, Portugal, Romania, Slovakia, Slovenia, Spain, Sweden, United Kingdom.

[5] Article 2 EEC Treaty.

[6] On the history of the EU, see further: Bache, George and Bulmer, *Politics in the European Union* (OUP 2011) 79-222; Urwin, *The Community of Europe: A History of European Integration since 1945* (Longman 1995); Milward, *The European Rescue of the Nation State* (Routledge 2000); Weiler, *The Constitution of Europe* (CUP 1999).

[7] Article 26 (2) TFEU.

[8] For more on these aspects of European history, see: Judt, *Postwar: A History of Europe since 1945* (Vintage 2010).

[9] There is some variation in approaches here. For instance: Den Exter and Hervey, *European Union Health Law: Treaties and Legislation* (Maklu 2012) includes very little public health legislation; Mossialos, Permanand, Baeten and Hervey's (eds), *Health Systems Governance in Europe: The Role of European Union Law and Policy* (CUP 2010) has only one chapter on public health; whereas Hervey and McHale, *Health Law and the European Union* (CUP 2004), included a great deal. Some of the very earliest texts are only on public health, e.g. McCarthy and Rees, *Health Systems and Public Health Medicine in the EC* (Royal College of Physicians 1992). For a more recent text on this area, see: Greer and Kurzer (eds), *European Union Public Health Policy: Regional Global Trends* (Routledge 2013).

[10] The very first EU food Directive, concerning colours in foodstuffs, was adopted in 1962. This provision has no number, as no formal system for numbering of EEC laws was in operation at the relevant time. See: O'Rourke, *European Food Law* (Palladian Law Publishing 1999).

[11] See: Grant, 'Agricultural Policy, Food Policy and Communicable Disease Policy' (2012) 37 *Journal of Health Politics, Policy and Law* 1029.

agriculture law has a more significant *indirect* effect on health. Whereas in the 1950s and 60s, the food-related health concerns of Europe were of *insufficient* nutrition, in the 2010s, the concerns are of *over-consumption* and of consumption of unhealthy foods.[12] In terms of internal market law, legislation also dating from the 1960s concerned the need to protect patients as consumers of pharmaceuticals, products that circulate freely within the internal market.[13] This legislation provided that all pharmaceuticals marketed in the EU are required to have a marketing authorization from a national regulatory authority. The procedures established under the legislation provide an institutional forum for the mandatory coordination of national pharmaceutical marketing authorization systems.

Others conceptualize EU health law more narrowly, focusing more closely on patients, professionals and health care systems,[14] and excluding public health and pharmaceuticals regulation from its substantive scope. But even with a narrower focus, EU health law begins at this foundational period. Although the main aims of the EEC were related to trade and agriculture, some of its early legislation concerned the social security position of workers (one of the factors of production) moving between the original six Member States.[15] This legislation included entitlements to access health care systems in host Member States for migrant workers and members of their families, and hence falls within the aspects of EU health law concerning patients' entitlements and heath care systems.

By the 1970s, the EEC legislature had also turned its attention to the free movement of professionals and professional services. Specific EU legislation facilitating professional mobility covered doctors, nurses responsible for general

---

[12] For discussion of how the EU's Common Agricultural Policy has affected nutrition and health, see: Kurzer, 'Non-communicable diseases: The EU Declares War on Fat' in Greer and Kurzer (eds), above n 9.

[13] Pharmaceuticals regulation is covered in Hermans, Casparie and Paelinck (eds), *Health Care in Europe after 1992* (Dartmouth 1992); Normand and Vaughan (eds), *Europe without Frontiers: The Implications for Health* (Wiley 1993); Randall, *The European Union and Health Policy* (Palgrave 2001); Busse, Wismar, Berman (eds), *The European Union and Health Services* (IOS Press 2002); Hervey, 'Mapping the Contours of EU Health Law and Policy' (2002) 8 *European Public Law* 69; Mossialos and McKee (eds), *EU Law and the Social Character of Health Care* (PIE Peter Lang 2004); McKee, Mossialos and Baeten (eds), *The Impact of EU Law on Health Care Systems* (PIE Peter Lang 2003); Hervey and McHale, above n 9; Mossialos et al., above n 9; Hancher and Sauter, *EU Competition and Internal Market Law in the Health Care Sector* (OUP 2012); Greer and Kurzer, above n 9.

[14] These areas are covered in all the literature in ns 9 and 13 above, and also in Mossialos, Dixon, Figueras and Kutzin (eds), *Funding Health Care: Options for Europe* (Open University Press 2002); Nihoul and Simon (eds), *L'Europe et les soins de santé: Marché intérieur, sécurité sociale, concurrence* (Larcier 2005); Thomson, Foubister and Mossialos, 'Financing health care in the European Union: Challenges and policy responses' (WHO 2009) <http://www.euro.who.int/—data/assets/pdf_file/0009/98307/E92469.pdf>; Van de Gronden, Szyszczak, Neergaard and Krajewski (eds), *Health Care and EU Law* (Springer 2011).

[15] Regulation 1612/68/EEC [1968] OJ L257/2, Article 7 (2); Regulation 1408/71/EEC [1971] OJ L149/2, Article 22.

care, dentists, midwives and pharmacists.[16] The relevant legislation followed a
fixed pattern, based on the mutual recognition of specified courses of medical
training, explicitly listed in the annexes to the legislation. Agreeing these lists of
recognized diplomas was possible only where the professions were sufficiently
common to all Member States, and so this 'sectoral' approach does not apply
to other health care professionals. In practice, the numbers of healthcare professionals moving within (as opposed to into) the EU was highly limited until
after the 2004 EU enlargement to include many Central and Eastern European
Member States,[17] and still involves relatively small numbers.[18]

As we will see below, the sources of EU health law include both legislation and
case law. The EU judiciary comprises both courts in the Member States, which
are obliged to apply EU law where relevant, and the EU's own Court of Justice
(CJEU).[19] During this foundational phase of the EU, the CJEU established
several key constitutional principles of EU law, which formed the basis for future
development of aspects of EU health law. The CJEU held that certain provisions
of EU law are 'directly effective', that is, they are enforceable by individuals,
in national courts.[20] Over time, the CJEU established that all the key Treaty
provisions setting up the internal market and rules of competition law have the
quality of direct effect.[21] Moreover, lawfully adopted measures of EU law enjoy
'primacy' or 'supremacy' over conflicting measures of national law.[22] The EU's
legal order also recognizes fundamental human rights, particularly those found
in the European Convention on Human Rights, as 'general principles' of EU
law.[23]

---

[16] Directive 75/362/EEC [1975] OJ L167/1; Directive 75/363/EEC [1975] OJ L167/14; Directive
77/452/EEC [1977] OJ L176/1; Directive 77/453/EEC [1977] OJ L176/8; Directive 78/686/EEC
[1978] OJ L233/1; Directive 78/687/EEC [1978] OJ L233/10; Directive 80/154/EEC [1980] OJ
L33/1; Directive 80/155/EEC [1980] OJ L33/8; Directive 85/432/EEC [1985] OJ L253/34;
Directive 85/433/EEC [1985] OJ L253/37.

[17] Commission, 'Work of the High Level Group on Health Services and Medical Care in 2006'
(HLG/2006/8, 10 October 2006) Zajac, 'EU Accession: Implications for Poland's Healthcare
Personnel' (2002) 8 *Eurohealth* 13.

[18] Peeters, McKee and Merkur, 'EU Law and Health Professionals' in Mossialos et al., above n 9;
Howat, Ulicna and Harris, 'Study Evaluating the Professional Qualifications Directive against
recent educational reforms in EU Member States' (Danish Technological Institute 2011) 78-85
<http://ec.europa.eu/internal_market/qualifications/docs/policy_developments/final_report_
en.pdf>.

[19] Although the Court of Justice of the EEC did not technically become the CJEU until 2009, the
abbreviation CJEU is used throughout the book, for clarity.

[20] *Van Gend en Loos* C-26/62, EU:C:1962:42; *Defrenne v SABENA (No 2)*, C-43/75, EU:C:1976:56;
Commission v Italy, C-39/72, EU:C:1973:13; *Grad v Finanzamt Traunstein*, C-9/70,
EU:C:1970:78; *Van Duyn*, C-41/74, EU:C:1974:133.

[21] *Iannelli and Volpi*, C-74/76, EU:C:1977:51; *Pigs Marketing Board*, C-83/78, EU:C:1978:214
(goods); *Van Binsbergen*, C-33/74, EU:C:1974:131 (services); *Van Duyn* EU:C:1974:133
(workers); *BRT v SABAM*, C-127/73, EU:C:1974:25; *Courage and Crehan*, C-453/99,
EU:C:2001:465; *Manfredi and Others*, C-295/04, C-296/04, C-297/04 and C-298/04,
EU:C:2006:67 (competition law).

[22] *Costa v ENEL*, C-6/64, EU:C:1964:66.

[23] *Internationale Handelsgesellschaft*, C-11/70, EU:C:1970:114; *Nold v Commission*, C-4/73,
EU:C:1977:1; *Rutili*, C-36/75, EU:C:1975:137.

1980s and 1990s: health in the (internal) market

The mid-1980s saw the introduction of a new regulatory strategy for the internal market – the 'new approach' – brought in by the European Commission,[24] underpinned by the reasoning of the European Court of Justice in *Cassis de Dijon*,[25] and formally backed by the governments of the Member States in 1986.[26] Principally applied to the free movement of goods, the significance of this approach for EU health law, at least as defined by those who include pharmaceuticals regulation within its scope, became apparent in the context of free movement of pharmaceuticals. Underlying the 'new approach' was the principle of 'mutual recognition', according to which products lawfully produced and marketed in one Member State must be accepted in all other Member States, unless the latter can justify more restrictive production or marketing rules for its home producers by reference to a relevant legitimate public interest. The 'direct effect' and 'supremacy' of relevant provisions of EU law meant that individual traders could bring litigation in their national courts to challenge national rules, which, while protecting such public interests, also made free trade more difficult. In the case of pharmaceuticals, several such possible public interests might apply, such as protecting patients from harm arising from consumption of pharmaceuticals; or securing national health care systems' budgets from opportunistic 'parallel imports' of pharmaceuticals taking advantage of different pricing mechanisms in different Member States; or protecting intellectual property rights in pharmaceuticals or their packaging. The CJEU considered whether such public interests might justify rules such as those prohibiting private or trade[27] import of prescription-only medicines; or (although rather later in time) restricting the sale of pharmaceuticals to physical (as opposed to mail order, or online) sales.[28] The CJEU's approach in these cases is to reason that because the marketing of pharmaceuticals is regulated in every Member State, and pharmacists' qualifications have been the subject of EU-level legislation, therefore Member States must in principle recognize each other's regulatory strategies as providing sufficient protection for the relevant public interests. Yet, generally speaking, where Member States justified restrictions on

---

[24] Under the dynamic leadership of Commission President Jacques Delors. See: Commission, 'Completing the Internal Market: White Paper from the Commission to the European Council' (White Paper) COM (85) 0310 final.

[25] *Cassis de Dijon*, C-120/78, EU:C:1979:42; Commission Practice Note on Import Prohibitions, 'Communication from the Commission concerning the consequences of the judgment given by the Court of Justice on 20 February 1979 in Case 120/78 ('*Cassis de Dijon*')' [1980] OJ C256/2.

[26] The Single European Act [1986] OJ L169/29, which amended the original EEC Treaty in several significant respects, in particular by removing the national veto on EU internal market legislation by introducing qualified majority voting in Council, entered into force on 1 July 1987.

[27] *Schumacher*, C-215/87, EU:C:1989:111; *Eurim-Pharm*, C-347/89, EU:C:1991:148.

[28] *DocMorris*, C-322/01, EU:C:2003:664; *Neumann-Seiwert (DocMorris)* C-171/07 and C-172/07, EU:C:2009:316.

free movement of pharmaceuticals on public health grounds, this was usually respected by the CJEU.[29] At this stage, the CJEU paid little attention to the broader contexts in which such litigation was brought, in particular the very different prices of pharmaceuticals in different Member States.

The EU legislature did attempt to tackle the lack of any meaningful internal market in pharmaceuticals, due to the various measures used by governments of Member States (as the main purchasers) to control pharmaceuticals prices,[30] through its Directive 89/105/EEC on the transparency of measures regulating the pricing of medicinal products for human use and their inclusion in the scope of national health insurance schemes. However, this legislation does little more than require Member States to communicate their policies to the European Commission, and in the absence of its robust enforcement through litigation it has proved rather toothless.[31]

The 'new approach' to internal market law distinguishes between 'what is essential to harmonise, and what may be left to mutual recognition of national regulations and standards'.[32] The former is established through EU legislation, based on the Treaty provision giving the EU competence to adopt such legislation necessary to create and sustain the internal market.[33] It is possible for Member States to secure permission to adopt higher standards, on the basis of 'major needs referred to in Article 36', which include the protection of human health, but only through a special procedure set out in the Treaty.[34] Otherwise, compliance with the EU-level standard[35] secures access to the whole of

---

[29]   See, for example: *De Peijper,* C-104/75, EU:C:1976:67; *Kortmann,* C-32/80, EU:C:1981:20; *Royal Pharmaceutical Society,* C-266/87 and 267/87, EU:C:1989:205; *Delattre,* C-369/88, EU:C:1991:137; *Monteil and Samanni,* C-60/89, EU:C:1991:138; *Medical Reagents,* C-55/99, EU:C:2000:693.

[30]   For discussion of the main types of such measures, see: Hervey and McHale, above n 9, 321; Mossialos and Abel-Smith, 'The Regulation of the European Pharmaceutical Industry' in Stavridis, Mossialos, Morgan and Machlin (eds), *New Challenges to the EU: Policies and Policy-Making* (Dartmouth 1997).

[31]   The European Commission has proposed a revision to the Directive, to take account of significant changes in the pharmaceuticals market since the 1980s, especially the increased availability of generic medicines, as well as to tackle the slowness with which Member States make decisions on the pricing and availability of pharmaceuticals within their national health systems, see: Commission, 'Proposal for a Directive relating to the transparency of measures regulating the prices of medicinal products for human use and their inclusion in the scope of public health insurance systems' COM (2012) 84 final.

[32]   COM (85) 0310 final, paragraph 65.

[33]   Now Article 114 TFEU. The EU's pharmaceuticals legislation is a key example of such legislation.

[34]   Article 114 (4) – (10) TFEU. This has been used rarely. For instance, it was used in 2003 by Denmark to maintain national measures governing food additives that were more restrictive than those set by the relevant EU-level Directive.

[35]   These 'European industry standards', such as the 'CE mark', are elaborated by specialist non-state corporate actors in the relevant fields, thus allowing for the development of consensus on essential safety in rapidly developing fields. The application of this system to medical devices has become increasingly uncomfortable as bio- and nano-technology has developed in ways that mean that pharmaceuticals and medical devices are much more similar than they were in the 1980s, see further below.

the internal market for a product. This was very much the EU's approach to medical devices regulation. The medical devices Directives adopted in the early 1990s set essential manufacture and design criteria, and established procedures for ensuring conformity with those criteria, evidenced by a CE mark. 'Notified bodies' provide oversight of the conformity assessment procedure. They are private companies, authorized by national authorities and officially notified to the European Commission and listed on its database.[36] By the 2010s, the short-comings of this system with respect to medical devices, especially given scientific developments through new technologies,[37] had become apparent. In particular, it came to light that a French manufacturer of breast implants (Poly Implant Prothèse) had used an inappropriate silicone, causing harm to thousands of women. The European Commission called for urgent reform to bring EU med-ical devices regulation more into line with pharmaceuticals regulation.[38]

Where the health of consumers might be harmed by products circulating in the internal market, the EU's product liability legislation, adopted in the mid-1980s, is supposed to provide protection through a strict tortious liability system. However, Member States may exclude strict liability for 'development risks', if at the time of manufacture, the state of scientific knowledge was such that the risk of harm was not foreseeable. Almost all Member States have done so. Although some Member States exclude pharmaceuticals[39] and products derived from the human body and human body parts[40] from the development risk exclusion, in other Member States, the shortcomings of this aspect of EU law for protecting patients became apparent in cases such as those involving blood from Hepatitis C-infected donors.[41]

Further EU-level patient protection legislation adopted during this time con-cerns the labelling and packaging of pharmaceuticals;[42] and direct-to-consumer prescription-only pharmaceuticals advertising, which is currently forbidden in the EU.[43] Special legislation aimed at encouraging the development of 'orphan

---

[36] Commission, 'NANDO (New Approach Notified and Designated Organizations) Information System' (*Commission*, 25 August 2014) <http://ec.europa.eu/enterprise/newapproach/nando/>.

[37] For instance, products manufactured using non-viable human tissues or cells, or using nanotechnologies. See: Hoppe, 'Innovative Tissue Engineering and its Regulation: The Search for Flexible Rules for Emerging Health Technologies' and Dorbeck-Jung, 'The Governance of Therapeutic Nanoproducts in the EU: A Model for New Health Technology Regulation?' both in Flear, Farrell, Hervey and Murphy (eds), *European Law and New Health Technologies* (OUP 2013).

[38] Commission, 'Proposal for a Regulation of the European Parliament and of the Council on medical devices, and amending Directive 2001/83/EC, Regulation (EC) No 178/2002 and Regulation (EC) No 1223/2009' COM (2012) 0542 final.

[39] Such as Germany and Spain.   [40] Such as France.

[41] *A* [2001] 3 All ER 289. See: Jackson, *Law and the Regulation of Medicines* (Hart 2012) 116-119; Navarro-Michel, 'New Health Technologies and their Impact on EU Product Liability Regulations' in Flear et al., above n 37.

[42] Originally covered by Directive 92/27/EEC [1992] OJ L113/8, which aimed to harmonise these consumer protection rules within the internal market. Now covered by Directive 2001/83/EC [2001] OJ L311/67.

[43] Directive 2001/83/EC [2001] OJ 311/67, Article 88.

medicines', used to treat rare diseases, was adopted in 2000. This legislation gives protocol assistance for marketing authorizations, possible fee waivers, and a ten-year exclusive marketing right.[44] The EU also adopted various measures of soft law concerning blood safety, responding to the global AIDS epidemic, and the fact that the EU was reliant on blood from developing and transitional economies, especially in the global South. These soft law measures set out non-binding principles for blood donation in the EU, and recommended that the Member States should 'encourage the voluntary and unpaid donation of blood or plasma',[45] on the basis that this is the safest source of human blood.[46]

During this time, the CJEU was also developing its case law on free movement of services, in ways which would eventually lead to EU-level legislation on the rights of patients seeking cross-border health care. In a suite of cases concerning private medical treatment,[47] medical treatment in the context of 'social insurance' health care systems,[48] and in other contexts altogether,[49] the CJEU established that health services are to be treated as 'services' in internal market law. Much of the literature on EU health law takes this case law, in particular the *Kohll* case, as its starting point.[50] The CJEU has been roundly criticized by the health law and policy community,[51] although from the point of EU law the *Kohll* ruling is doctrinally uncontroversial.[52] The numbers of migrant patients

---

[44] Regulation 141/2000/EC [2000] OJ L18/1, especially Article 8. Syrett, 'Looking After the Orphans? Treatments for Rare Diseases, EU Law, and the Ethics of Costly Health Care' in Flear et al., above n 37.

[45] Council Recommendation 98/463/EC [1998] OJ L203/14, paragraph 14.

[46] See further: Farrell, *The Politics of Blood: Ethics, Innovation and the Regulation of Risk* (CUP 2012).

[47] *Luisi and Carbone,* C-286/82 and C-26/83, EU:C:1984:35; *SPUC* v *Grogan,* C-159/90, EU:C:1991:378. There are also relevant decisions of national courts, for instance the English Court of Appeal in *R v Human Fertilisation and Embyology Authority, ex parte Blood* [1997] 2 All ER 687.

[48] *Kohll,* C-158/96, EU:C:1998:171.

[49] E.g., establishing that remuneration for a service need not come directly from the recipient of a service, see: *Bond van Adverteerders,* C-352/85, EU:C:1998:196; and that the Treaty provision covers the right to receive, as well as provide, cross-border services, see: *Cowan,* C-186/87, EU:C:1989:47.

[50] See: e.g. Nihoul and Simon, above n 14 Van de Gronden et al., above n 14 Hancher and Sauter, above n 13.

[51] See literature cited in: Hervey and McHale, above n 9, 138-144, for instance: Editorial, 'Public Health Insurance and Freedom of Movement within the European Union' (1999) 6 *European Journal of Health Law* 1; Cabral, 'Cross-border medical care in the European Union—bringing down a first wall' (1999) 24 *European Law Review* 387; Nickless, 'Were the ECJ decisions in *Kohll* and *Decker* right?' 7 (1) *Eurohealth* (2001) 16; Nickless, 'The internal market and the social nature of health care' in McKee, Mossialos, Baeten (eds), (PIE Peter Lang 2003) above n 13; Baeten, 'European Integration and National Healthcare Systems: a challenge for social policy' (2001) 8 *Infose* 1; Baeten, McKee, Mossialos, above n 9 and Gekiere, Baeten, and Palm, 'Free Movement of Health Services in the EU and Health Care' in Mossialos et al., above n 9.

[52] See: Greer, 'Power struggle: the politics and policy consequences of patient mobility in Europe' (Policy Paper No.2, Observatoire social européen 2008) <http://www.ose.be/files/publication/policy_papers/OSEPolicypaper2_Greer_EN.pdf;> Greer, 'Choosing paths in European Union health services policy: a political analysis of a critical juncture' (2008) 18 *Journal of European*

are also relatively low,[53] suggesting that the judgment is of more symbolic than practical significance.

From the point of view of health care systems, the CJEU's case law on free movement of services and freedom of establishment as applied to health care institutions and professionals is more significant. Again, this period saw the beginnings of case law that would become more widely applied in such contexts in the decades to come. The CJEU held that the Treaty rules on freedom of establishment apply in principle to providers of health care services within a national health system, such as clinical biological laboratories,[54] or nursing homes.[55] Restricting access to the health care profession on grounds that *de facto* discriminated on the basis of nationality was also held to be contrary to EU law.[56] In the meantime, the EU legislature was also affecting professional practice by adopting its first legislation on working time;[57] its first legislation on the practice of 'posting' workers;[58] and new legislation on the mutual recognition of the qualifications of health care professionals other than those covered in the original 'sectoral' Directives.[59]

For those who include the regulation of health research within the scope of EU health law, another significant development during the 1980s and 90s was EU regulation of,[60] and support for, health and health-related research. The former includes incipient EU law on the ethics of (bio)medical research,[61] a foundation which was built upon in the 2000s and beyond. In terms of the latter, two strands of EU policy are important: the general 'Framework Programmes'

Social Policy 219, describing the cases as a 'critical juncture', which is a break with the past practice; Hervey, 'If only it were so simple: Public Health Services and EU Law' in Cremona (ed), *Market Integration and Public Services in the EU* (OUP 2011).

[53] For details on different types of cross-border patient activity, see: Rosenmöller, McKee, and Baeten, (eds), *Patient Mobility in the European Union: Learning from Experience* (European Observatory on Health Systems and Policies 2006); Glinos and Baeten, *A Literature Review of Cross-Border Patient Mobility in the European Union* (Observatoire social européen 2006) <http://www.ose.be/files/publication/health/WP12_lit_review_final.pdf>.

[54] *Clinical Biological Laboratories,* C-221/85, EU:C:1987:81 .

[55] *Sodemare,* C-70/95, EU:C:1997:301.

[56] The rules in this instance prohibited doctors and dentists from practising in France while remaining registered to practice in another Member State, see *Doctors and Dentists,* C-96/85, EU:C:1986:189.

[57] Directive 93/104/EC [1993] OJ L307/18.

[58] Directive 96/71/EC [1997] OJ L018/1, covers the question of which legal system covers workers employed in one Member State, but deployed by their employer to work in another Member State.

[59] Directive 89/48/EEC [1989] OJ L019/16; Directive 92/51/EEC [1992] OJ L209/25.

[60] Directive 87/18/EC [1987] OJ L15/29; Directive 88/320/EEC [1988] OJ L145/35. This legislation draws from the OECD's work and on International Standards for audit, accreditation and technical competence. See further: Bache et al., 'The Defining Features of the European Union's Approach to Regulating New Health Technologies' in Flear et al., above n 37.

[61] The EU's 'Group of Advisors on the Ethical Implications of Biotechnology' was established in 1991. This was replaced by the European Group on Ethics in Science and New Technologies in 1997. See: Hervey, Busby and Mohr, 'Ethical EU Law: The influence of the European Group on Ethics in Science and New Technologies' (2008) 33 *European Law Review* 803.

for research,[62] which supported health projects among other areas; and the more specific public health programmes. The latter began informally, with 'Europe against Cancer' in 1986,[63] and 'Europe against AIDS' in 1991.[64] In 1993,[65] the EU was formally empowered to support and promote public health, and from 1996 onwards it adopted public health programmes in specific areas.[66] Projects funded under these small scale programmes covered exchange of information and personnel, training, pilot projects, information campaigns, and networking of organizations and experts. The explicit EU public health competence only formalized what was already happening, and was severely constrained, in that it by and large excluded harmonization,[67] and contained only very weak provision for health to be considered in the context of other EU policies.[68] Nevertheless, from the point of view of EU health lawyers, this Treaty recognition set health law on the road to becoming a recognized aspect of EU law.

The EU's pharmaceuticals regulation continued to evolve during this period. A new EU body, the European Medicines Evaluation Agency (now the European Medicines Agency), began operation in 1995.[69] This body grants marketing authorizations for certain pharmaceuticals under a new 'centralized procedure', which complements the 'decentralized procedure' already in place since the 1960s.[70] The European Medicines Agency operates through its scientific committees, comprised of national experts. It proposes marketing authorizations based on the criteria of quality, safety and efficiency, having assessed dossiers of clinical trials evidence.[71] The EU also introduced legislation to enhance

---

62 The first Framework Programme 1984-87 (Council Resolution [1983] OJ C208/1) included 'improving safety and protecting health' under its objective 6; the second and third Framework Programmes covered biotechnology and biomedical and health research, under their objective 4, 'Life sciences and technologies'; the fourth Framework Programme also covered research into evaluating new pharmaceuticals, biomedical engineering, including medical devices, orphan diseases, health systems research and bio-medical ethics. Hervey and McHale, above n 9, 240-241. See also: Commission, 'Framework Programme for Research 1984-87' COM (83) 260 final. These research programmes became increasingly strongly linked to the EU's economic growth agenda, see: e.g., Commission, 'White Paper - Growth, Competitiveness, Employment' (White Paper) COM (93) 700 final.

63 See: Hervey and McHale, above n 9, 369-374; Trubek, Nance and Hervey, 'The Construction of a Healthier Europe: Lessons from the Fight Against Cancer' (2008) 26 *Wisconsin International Law Journal* 804.

64 Decision 91/317/EEC [1991] OJ L175/26; see: Hervey and McHale, above n 9, 336-340.

65 The Treaty of Maastricht 1992 (Treaty on European Union [1992] OJ C191/01), which entered into force in 1993, introduced Article 152 EC into the EC Treaty. See: Hervey and McHale, above n 9, 72-84; Van der Mei and Waddington, 'Public Health and the Treaty of Amsterdam' (1998) 5 *European Journal of Health Law* 129.

66 AIDS, cancer, drug dependence, health promotion, health monitoring, injury prevention, rare diseases, pollution-related diseases.

67 Save in the areas of human organ, tissue and blood safety, and agricultural policy measures that have the direct objective of protecting public health, (ex) Article 152 (4) (a), (b) and (c) EC.

68 Article 168 TFEU.   69 Regulation 2309/93/EC [1993] OJ L214/1.

70 Described in Hervey and McHale, above n 9, 290-319.

71 For critique of the system see: Jackson, above n 41; Abraham and Lewis, *Regulating Medicines in Europe: Competition, expertise and public health* (Routledge 2000).

intellectual property rights in novel pharmaceuticals, to compensate for the longer time between patent filing and putting the new pharmaceutical on the market, given the time it takes for the pre-clinical and clinical trial evidence to be gathered, in order to satisfy the EU's marketing authorization regulation.[72]

The final aspect of EU health law to note during this period is that relating to fundamental human rights.[73] The EU built on its early recognition of fundamental human rights in the case law of the CJEU, through specific pieces of legislation, as well as adopting the Community Charter on Fundamental Social Rights for Workers 1989, which eventually fed into the EU's much broader Charter of Fundamental Rights, adopted in 2000.[74] Examples of relevant specific legislation include the EU's data protection legislation, which concerns the right to privacy,[75] and makes special provision for health contexts. The EU's Directive on the Legal Protection of Biotechnological Inventions[76] excludes from patentability the use of human embryos for industrial or commercial purposes, in line with the Council of Europe's Convention on Human Rights and Biomedicine, which, in accordance with the principle of human dignity, prohibits the creation of human embryos for research purposes.

2000s and 2010s: greater coherence

The governments of the Member States and the EU institutions have imposed (or at least sought to impose) greater coherence on EU health law from the 2000s onwards. For example, the human rights aspects of EU health law continued to develop into the 2000s and 2010s, bringing a rights-based focus around which EU health law could potentially be said to cohere.[77] The EU's Charter of Fundamental Rights (EU CFR) was given 'the same legal value as the Treaties'[78] in 2009. The EU CFR protects[79] a range of civil and political rights which

---

[72] Regulation 1768/92/EEC [1992] OJ L182/1.

[73] See: Toebes, Hartlev, Hendriks and Hermann (eds), *Health and Human Rights in Europe* (Intersentia 2012), especially ch 2 on the EU.

[74] The EU CFR is now part of the EU Treaties (Charter of Fundamental Rights of the European Union [2012] OJ C326/391).

[75] Directive 95/46/EC [1995] OJ L281/31.   [76] Directive 98/44/EC [1998] OJ L213/13.

[77] We will explore the extent to which this is the case in chapters 7 and 8. The literature to date tends to focus on the 'patchwork' nature of EU health law and human rights, see: Herrmann and Toebes, 'The EU and Human Rights' in Toebes et al., above n 73; McHale, 'Fundamental Rights and Health Care' in Mossialos et al., above n 9; Hervey, 'The right to health in EU law' in Hervey and Kenner (eds), *Economic and Social Rights under the EU Charter of Fundamental Rights* (Hart 2003).

[78] Article 6 (1) TEU.

[79] The EU CFR contains 'rights, freedoms and principles'. The difference, and the significance of differences, between the three is contested. See: e.g. Goldsmith, 'A charter of rights, freedoms and principles' (2001) 38 *Common Market Law Review* 1201; Lenaerts and Foubert, 'Social Rights in the Case-Law of the European Court of Justice' (2001) 28 *Legal Issues of Economic Integration* 267; Gijzen, 'The Charter: a milestone for social protection in Europe?' (2001) 8

have significance for EU health law.[80] In addition, the EU CFR provides special protection for members of vulnerable groups whose vulnerabilities mean that their rights need special attention in health law contexts.[81] The EU CFR also prohibits non-discrimination on any forbidden ground, and articulates the principle of equality.[82] Finally, the EU CFR states that 'everyone has the right of access to preventive health care and the right to benefit from medical treatment' in accordance with national conditions.[83]

Human rights – or at least the *language* of human rights[84] – permeate various aspects of EU health legislation adopted during this period. For instance, EU legislation on the entitlements of free moving patients seeking health care services in Member States other than their 'home' Member State is termed the 'patients' rights Directive'. Legislation on paediatric clinical research and medicinal products for paediatric use, and on 'orphan' medicines, is framed in terms of the rights of children and sufferers of rare diseases to equal access to health care and medical treatment. EU legislation on clinical trials stresses consent, a concept central to the human rights to autonomy and dignity. Human rights and ethical concerns are often combined in EU health law, and this is certainly true during this period. For instance, the EU's clinical trials Directive requires Member States to establish research ethics committees, and sets out their broad duties and parameters of operation, which include protection of human rights of trial participants. In the context of EU research funding, only proposals that meet ethical and human rights standards may be funded.[85] The EGE provides oversight, and has adopted what has been said to be 'a human rights approach'.[86] The CJEU, and especially its Advocates General (AGs), have relied increasingly on human rights and ethical reasoning in health law cases, for instance, concerning the 'right to health' itself,[87] medical

---

Maastricht Journal of European and Comparative Law 33; Peers, Hervey, Kenner and Ward (eds), *The EU Charter of Fundamental Rights: A Commentary* (Hart 2014).

[80] Human dignity, Article 1 EU CFR; the right to life, Article 2 EU CFR; integrity of the person, Article 3 EU CFR; private life, Article 7 EU CFR; protection of personal data, Article 8 EU CFR; right to marry and found a family, Article 9 EU CFR; freedom of thought, conscience and religion, Article 10 EU CFR. See McHale, 'Fundamental Rights and Health Care' in Mossialos et al., above n 9.

[81] Children, the elderly and persons with disabilities, Articles 24-26 EU CFR.

[82] Article 21 EU CFR; Article 20 EU CFR.

[83] Article 35 EU CFR. See: Hervey and McHale, 'Article 35' in Peers et al., above n 79.

[84] For more on the 'framings' of rights (and other frames), in the context of EU law on new health technologies, see: Bache et al., 'The Defining Features of the European Union's Approach to Regulating New Health Technologies' in Flear et al., above n 37.

[85] Regulation 1906/2006/EC [2006] OJ L391/1, Article 15 (2).

[86] Herméren (the former Chair of the EGE), 'Accountability, Democracy and Ethics Committees' (2009) 2 *Law, Innovation and Technology* 153.

[87] *Deutsches Weintor*, C-544/10, EU:C:2012:526; *Susisalo*, C-84/11, EU:C:2012:374; *Pérez and Gómez*, C-570/07 and C-571/07, EU:C:2010:300, *Rossius and Collard*, C-267/10 and 268/10, EU:C:2011:332, was found inadmissible for lack of jurisdiction. See also Opinions of the

research and research involving human tissue,[88] data protection,[89] or even food regulation.[90]

A second salient example of the emerging greater coherence for EU health law during this period is the evolution of the Treaty provisions giving the EU competence in (public) health. The competence provisions in Part I of the TFEU affirm that public health is a shared competence between the EU and its Member States,[91] and that the EU has power to support, coordinate or supplement national policy in the protection and improvement of human health.[92] The 'mainstreaming' provision of Article 168 TFEU has been strengthened, and is now also reflected in Part I of the TFEU, which affirms that the EU must take into account 'protection of human health' in all its policies and activities.[93] The main provision, now Article 168 TFEU, introduced into EU law at the Treaty of Maastricht, was strengthened by the Treaty of Amsterdam, and again by the Treaty of Lisbon. At least four key inter-connected changes are important: a refocusing of substantive scope; a gathering of competences leading to institutional adjustments; a strengthening of the democratic legitimacy of EU health law; and a reaffirmation and elaboration of the respective powers of the EU and the Member States.

The substantive scope of EU competence has been increasingly focused away from disease prevention and towards health promotion and the broader determinants of good health. Both physical and mental health are now covered. This prevention aspect of EU competence means that the EU has been increasingly empowered to adopt law focused more on individuals, in addition to law that adopts a collective or 'public health' approach. The 'patients' rights Directive' is one example of such legislation.

The symbolic and institutional importance of bringing together pre-existing EU competences under one textual umbrella should not be understated. At Lisbon, power to adopt EU legislation on the quality and safety of pharmaceuticals and medical devices; to undertake global disease surveillance; to encourage health services in cross-border regions to complement one another; and an explicit endorsement of EU (non-harmonizing) measures about tobacco and alcohol from a public health perspective were all added to the EU's explicit health competences under what is now Article 168 TFEU. The gathering of EU health competence in a much more coherent and logical form than the pre-Amsterdam treaty provisions, and addition of new health competences,

---

Advocates General in *Stamatelaki*, C-444/05, EU:C:2007:24; and *Josemans*, C-137/09, EU:C:2010:433.

[88] See, most saliently: Opinion of the Advocate General in *Brüstle*, C-34/10 EU:C:2011:138; contrast Opinion of the Advocate General in *International Stem Cell* C-364/13 EU:C:2014:2104.

[89] *Lindqvist*, C-101/01, EU:C:2003:596.   [90] *Deutsches Weintor* EU:C:2012:526.

[91] Article 4 (2) (k) TFEU.   [92] Article 6 (a) TFEU.

[93] Article 9 TFEU, although human health protection does not (yet) merit a 'mainstreaming provision' all of its own, in the way that non-discrimination (Article 10 TFEU), environmental protection (Article 11 TFEU) consumer protection (Article 12 TFEU) and animal welfare (Article 13 TFEU) do.

paved the way for institutional developments. The key institutional change was the moving of more health law and policy operations into DG SANCO, the Directorate General of the European Commission responsible for health and consumer protection. DG SANCO had worked hard since the early 2000s to enhance its legitimacy by building links with health policy communities.[94] In 2010, SANCO was given responsibility for oversight of pharmaceuticals regulation, an area which had previously been part of the DG responsible for the internal market. This meant a change of policy focus for EU pharmaceuticals regulation, to being conceptualized as more about health, and not just thought of as essentially similar to any other potentially hazardous product circulating in the internal market.[95] However, DG SANCO's legitimacy was seriously shaken in 2012, when Commissioner Dalli resigned in the wake of allegations of links with the tobacco industry.[96]

The importance of the EU's health law and policy to the European public was underlined by the obligation on the European Commission to 'fully inform' the European Parliament (as the democratic representative of the European electorate) of its health initiatives. The European Parliament has been gradually developing its capacity to respond from the point of view of health to various legislative and other proposals, particularly through its Committee for the Environment, Public Health and Food Safety, but also through other Parliamentary Committees.[97] Also pertaining to democratic legitimacy of EU health law, at the same time as developing EU public health competence, the Treaty explicitly states that Member States are responsible for their health policies, the organization, management and delivery of health services, and resource allocation. This more precise elaboration of national and EU spheres of competence is consistent with the more general move by the Treaty of Lisbon to attempt to clarify and contain EU competences.[98]

---

[94] For instance, it established the EU Health Policy Forum in early 2001, bringing together some fifty umbrella organisations in the health sector; it began sending its officials to the 'Gastein' annual European Health Forum; it established a 'High Level Group on Health Services and Medical Care' in 2004, (Commission, 'Follow-up to the high level reflection process on patient mobility and healthcare developments in the European Union' (Communication) COM (2004) 301 final), to respond to the work of the EU health ministers who had been meeting as the 'High Level Process of Reflection on Patient Mobility and Healthcare Developments in the EU' since 2003, (European Commission, HLPR/2003/16, 9 December 2003).

[95] Vestlund, 'Changing Policy Focus through Organisational Reform? The case of the pharmaceutical unit in the European Commission' (2006) Arena Working Paper 6/2012.

[96] See: Hildebrand, 'Open Government in the EU: Dalligate tests the European Parliament's oversight over the European Commission' (*ACELG*, 20 November 2012).

[97] For instance, the EP Legal Affairs Committee and Committee on Industry, Research and Energy have considered the health aspects of the proposed revisions to EU data protection law. For discussion of the roles of the EU institutions in EU health law and policy, see Greer, The Politics of European Union Health Policies (Open University Press 2009).

[98] See: e.g. Craig, *The Lisbon Treaty: Law, Politics and Treaty Reform* (OUP 2010); Griller and Ziller (eds), *The Lisbon Treaty: EU Constitutionalism without a Constitutional Treaty* (Springer 2008). On the law of EU competence, see: Weatherill, 'Competence creep and competence

The new competence provisions gave the EU the legal power to adopt a suite of measures regulating quality and safety of human blood, tissues and cells, and organs. These follow a standard risk regulation model, requiring Member States to establish institutions (called 'competent authorities') to ensure quality assurance procedures are followed, in the collection, testing, processing, storage and distribution of human materials, with the aim of securing minimum safety standards. The EU's blood safety laws have been criticized for failing to acknowledge sufficiently the reality of the EU market for human blood and plasma products.[99] The underlying approach, which is replicated in the other legislation, does stress voluntary donation and an ethic of altruism, although there is some scope for out-of-pocket payments[100] and the organs Directive does recognize that living organ donors might need to be compensated for loss of income.[101] In 2010, the CJEU ruled that Austrian legislation prohibiting importation of blood products where payment had been made for the donation of the blood breached EU law on free movement of goods, and was not justified by the need to protect public health.[102] In its reasoning, the CJEU relied in part on the fact that the blood safety Directive permits reimbursement of donors' expenses and other small tokens of payment. Implicitly, therefore, the CJEU accepted that EU law does not require that the donation of human material in health contexts be completely separated from market concepts, such as free movement of goods, or, by implication, payment for services.

The EU's human blood, organs and tissue regulation is an example of a third way in which EU health law has become more coherent during the 2000s and 10s. At least until this period, EU health law occupied at best a tenuous and uncertain position vis-à-vis EU internal market law. The root of the uncertainty is often termed EU law's 'constitutional asymmetry'.[103] Put simply, this is the (contested) idea that social or welfare policies are rendered constitutionally subservient to the economic laws of the internal market. As we have seen, in the context of EU health law, the idea means that national laws or policies that aim to protect or promote human health must be *justified* if they impinge upon market liberalization or upon competition. Freedom of movement and competition are the rule; health protection or health promotion are exceptions. At the same time, the EU's powers to adopt its own laws or policies protecting or promoting human health are severely constrained. Hence the notion of asymmetry. As we

control' (2004) 23 *Yearbook of European Law* 1; Weatherill, 'Competence and Legitimacy' in Barnard and Odudu (eds), *The Outer Limits of EU Law* (Hart 2009).
[99] See: Farrell (2012) above n 46.
[100] Directive 2002/98/EC [2003] OJ L33/30, Article 20; Directive 2004/23/EC [2004] OJ L102/48, Article 12; Directive 2010/53/EU [2010] OJ L207/14, Article 13 (2) (This is the correct number – see: Corrigendum to Directive 2010/45/EU [2010] OJ L243/68); see *Humanplasma*, C-421/09, EU:C:2010:760, paragraph 44.
[101] Directive 2010/53/EU [2010] OJ L207/14.   [102] *Humanplasma* EU:C:2010:760.
[103] See, seminally: Scharpf, 'A new social contract? Negative and positive integration on the political economy of European welfare states' (1996) European University Institute Working Paper RSC 94/44. See also the references in chapter 9, n 2-10.

entered the 2000s, the extent to which this idea of constitutional asymmetry applied to health law, or whether relationships between EU health law and EU internal market law were differently configured, was unclear.[104] During this period, however, the relationships between internal market law and health law have been significantly (although not entirely) clarified, in ways which enhance the coherence of EU health law.

The broader contexts for changes to EU internal market law include the EU's 'Lisbon agenda' for growth and development. In 2000, the EU set itself the target of being the world's most dynamic and competitive knowledge-based economy by 2010.[105] The reasons for its failure to achieve this goal were multiple,[106] and obviously among them were the global economic crisis, the Eurozone crisis, and subsequent economic downturn. The EU has now launched a new growth strategy, 'Europe 2020', which sets targets on employment, innovation, education, social inclusion and climate/energy.[107] The social inclusion target includes aspects of health care systems, and the innovation target includes the development of new medical technologies.[108] The original Lisbon agenda was associated with a turn to 'new modes of governance', that is, the use of non-binding processes of target setting, data gathering, peer review and mutual learning to align Member States with good practice, rather than the adoption of binding legal rules harmonizing national laws.[109] During the 2000s, as part of its governance of social policy, the EU developed an 'open method of coordination'[110]

---

[104] For early literature explicitly considering these questions *in the context of health law*, see: Hervey, 'Social solidarity: a buttress against internal market law' in Shaw (ed), *Social Law and Policy in an Evolving European Union* (Hart 2000); Hervey, 'Buy Baby: the European Union and regulation of human reproduction' (1998) 18 *Oxford Journal of Legal Studies* 207.

[105] European Council, 'Presidency Conclusions 23 and 24 March 2000' (European Parliament 2000).

[106] See: Commission, 'Lisbon Strategy Evaluation Document' SEC (2010) 114 final.

[107] European Council, 'Presidency Conclusions June 2010' (European Council, EUCO 13/10, 17 June 2010).

[108] See: Commission Staff Working Document, 'Investing in Health - Accompanying the document Commission Communication, Towards Social Investment for Growth and Cohesion including implementing the European Social Fund 2014-2020' SWD (2013) 43 final; Greer, 'The Three Faces of European Union Health Policy: Policy, markets, austerity' (2014) 33(1) *Policy and Society* 13; Figueras and McKee (eds), *Health Systems, Health, Wealth and Societal Well-being: Assessing the case for investing in health systems* (Open University Press 2011).

[109] The literature on 'new modes of governance', and how they relate to law, is considerable. For an overview, see: Dawson, *New Governance and the Transformation of European Law* (CUP 2011); De Búrca and Scott (eds), *Law and New Governance in the EU and the US* (Hart 2006).

[110] The 'open method of coordination' (OMC) is a 'new mode of governance', inspired by the work of the OECD and first used by the EU in the 1990s to coordinate the Member States' economic and fiscal policies. It was subsequently applied to the European Union's employment strategy. OMC uses mutual learning, benchmarking, best practice and peer pressure to steer national policies towards objectives, expressed in 'guidelines' agreed at EU level. The EU guidelines are translated into 'national action plans', with the support of various actors (including non-governmental actors) at national and sub-national level. Each Member State's performance is then evaluated against the EU objectives, using quantitative (or qualitative) indicators, and examples of best practice are identified, to serve as benchmarks as

in health, which sought to gather and compare data on health systems indicators, such as life expectancy.[111] Although these new modes of governance continue to be used by the EU, to some extent there has been a return to 'old law' in the European Commission's revised approach to the internal market from 2011, and in 'Europe 2020',[112] as well as continued use of hybrid blends of the 'old' and the 'new'.[113] The early 2000s also saw the development of a concern with 'good governance' in the internal market, recognizing that the internal market is not just concerned with liberalization of markets, but must also be legitimated in terms of the values expressed through its regulatory output.[114] At the same time, from the mid-2000s, the European Commission moved towards greater harmonization at EU level of rules that protect consumers within the internal market.[115] These ideas are now being reformulated as part of the Commission's 'smart regulation' agenda.[116] Many of these changes are reflected in the Lisbon Treaty, most prominently in the statement that the EU's internal market is based on a 'social market economy'.[117]

the process of guideline-setting begins anew. On the relationships between OMC and law, see, seminally: Scott and Trubek, 'Mind the Gap: law and new approaches to governance in the European Union' (2002) 8 *European Law Journal* 1.

[111] For further information, see: Hervey and De Ruijter, 'Healthcare and the Lisbon Agenda' in Copeland and Papadimitriou (eds), *The EU's Lisbon Strategy: Evaluating Success, Understanding Failure* (Palgrave 2012).

[112] See: Commission, 'Single Market Act: Twelve levers to boost growth and strengthen confidence 'Working together to create new growth' COM (2011) 206 final; and, Commission, 'Europe 2020: A Strategy for Smart, Sustainable and Inclusive Growth' (Communication) COM (2010) 2020 final, which include enforcement of existing laws, as well as proposals for new legislation.

[113] For discussion of such hybrids in EU health law and policy, see Hervey and Vanhercke, 'Health care and the EU: The law and policy patchwork' in Mossialos et al., above n 9.

[114] Literature on legitimacy in the EU's internal market law includes Barnard and Scott (eds), *The Law of the Single European Market: Unpacking the Premises* (Hart 2002); Moravcsik, 'In defence of the democratic deficit: reassessing legitimacy in the EU' (2002) 40(4) *Journal of Common Market Studies* 603; Scharpf, 'Economic Integration, Democracy and the Welfare State' (1997) 4(1) *Journal of European Public Policy* 18; Scharpf, 'The Joint-Decision Trap: Lessons from German Federalism and European Integration' (1988) 66(3) *Public Administration* 239; Scharpf, 'The Joint-Decision Trap Revisited' (2006) 44(4) *Journal of Common Market Studies* 845; Lord and Magnette, 'E Pluribus Unum? Creative Disagreement about Legitimacy in the European Union' (2004) 42(1) *Journal of Common Market Studies* 183; Schmidt, 'Democracy and Legitimacy in the European Union Revisited: Input, Output *and* "Throughput"' (2013) 61(1) *Political Studies* 2. For an overview, see: Bache, George and Bulmer, above n 6, 66-76.

[115] Commission, 'Green Paper on the Review of the Consumer Acquis' (Green Paper) COM (2006) 744 final. *Antroposana*, C-84/06, EU:C:2007:535 and *Gintec*, C-374/05, EU:C:2007:654 confirm that the EU's legislation on pharmaceuticals marketing authorisation establish an exhaustive level of consumer protection, and Member States may not therefore impose higher consumer protection standards, even on their home producers.

[116] Commission, 'Smart Regulation in the EU' (Communication) COM (2010) 543 final.

[117] Article 3 (3) TEU. This provision was widely perceived to be a response to the French referendum rejecting the Treaty establishing a Constitution for Europe, see: Maher, 'Introduction: Regulating Markets and Social Europe: New Governance in the EU' (2009) 15 *European Law Journal* 155, 156.

Some, in particular those writing towards the beginning of the 2000s, take the view that the EU's internal market law still enjoys a hegemonic and ultimately disruptive position vis-à-vis EU health law.[118] But for others,[119] the clarification that EU health law enjoys a relationship with internal market law that is more complex than the 'rule-exception' formulation of the 'constitutional asymmetry' position, has helped to create a sense of distance from internal market law, and hence a greater coherence for EU health law during this period. Rather than being comprised of a series of unrelated exceptions to free trade rules, the underlying principles of EU health law, particularly in the context of 'good governance' or 'smart regulation', have begun to emerge. We say more about these principles below. Their emergence can be seen in both the activities of the CJEU and in those of the EU legislature. In both instances, the emergent EU health law is based on a respect for national competences for national health systems, on a set of values said to be common to all EU health systems, and on human rights protection. At the same time, it is increasingly recognized that health is not only a matter of rights or social welfare, but also a factor in a productive economy.

For example, the CJEU has recognized a series of related 'objective public interests' that are relevant for the ways in which EU health law understands the roles of national health care systems within the EU. Rather than allowing the liberalizing effects of the free movement rules to present fundamental, and perhaps insurmountable, challenges to the structures of national health systems, the CJEU has increasingly recognized the need to protect the coherence of those systems. Thus CJEU case law during this period recognized the objective public interest in the financial viability of social security systems.[120] This more recent case law builds on earlier CJEU rulings which recognized, for instance, the

---

[118] Hatzopoulos, 'Killing national health and insurance systems but healing patients?' (2002) 39 *Common Market Law Review* 683; Hatzopoulos, 'Health Law and Policy: The Impact of the EU' in De Búrca (ed), *EU Law and the Welfare State: In Search of Solidarity* (OUP 2005); Montgomery, 'The impact of EU Law on English health care law' in Dougan and Spaventa (eds), *Social Welfare and EU Law* (Hart 2005); Newdick, 'Citizenship, free movement and health care: Cementing individual rights by corroding social solidarity' (2006) 43(6) *Common Market Law Review* 1645; Gekiere, Baeten and Palm, 'Free movement of services in the EU and health care' in Mossialos et al., above n 9; Davies, 'Legislating for Patients' Rights' and Newdick, 'Disrupting the Community – Saving Public Health Ethics from the EU Internal Market', both in Van de Gronden et al., above n 14.

[119] Hervey and Vanhercke, 'Health care and the EU: the law and policy patchwork' in Mossialos et al., above n 9; Hervey, (OUP 2011) above n 52; Hervey, 'The European Union's Governance of Health Care and the Welfare Modernization Agenda' (2008) 2 *Regulation and Governance* 103. Hancher and Sauter, above n 13, see both dynamics of greater coherence *and* dynamics of disruption.

[120] *Vanbraekel*, C-368/98, EU:C:2001:400; *Geraets-Smits*, C–157/99, EU:C:2001:404; *Leichtle*, C-8/02, EU:C:2004:161; *Watts*, C-372/04, EU:C:2006:325; *Stamatelaki*, C-444/05, EU:C:2007:231; *Hartlauer*, C-169/07, EU:C:2009:141; *Major Medical Equipment*, C-512/08, EU:C:2010:579; *Laboratory Analyses*, C-490/09, EU:C:2011:34. See: Hatzopoulos and Hervey, 'Coming into line: The EU's Court Softens on Cross Border Healthcare' (2013) 8 *Health Economics Policy and Law* 1.

social protection provided by national social security systems;[121] rules about the organization of health care professions, qualifications and professional ethics;[122] or consumer protection.[123] Similarly, in the context of EU competition law, the CJEU[124] and also national courts[125] and competition authorities,[126] have extended the application *in principle* of EU competition law and state aids law to health contexts during this period. Nonetheless, at the same time, they have recognized that health as a 'service of general economic interest' occupies a special place in EU competition law.[127] And in public procurement law, both the CJEU and the EU legislature have explicitly recognized health systems as operating not entirely within ordinary markets.[128]

Of course, internal market legislation that itself protects 'non-market' interests already existed long before this period, particularly regulating pharmaceuticals, medical devices, and products that are harmful to health (in particular tobacco, but also food and alcohol). The place of this legislation within the scheme of EU law has changed over time. For instance, in 2001, the European Commission launched a major review of its pharmaceuticals regulation. This review was steered by a High Level Group on Innovation and Provision of Medicines in the EU. It embodies the multi-faceted and more holistic approach to EU health law that characterizes its relationships with internal market law during this period. Set up by the Commissioner for DG Enterprise *and* the Commissioner for DG SANCO, the group represents health and industry ministers, different industry sectors, as well as patients' representatives. Its work led eventually to a significant amendment of the EU pharmaceuticals legislation in 2004. The ongoing evolution of that legislation[129] now takes place through this new frame for pharmaceuticals within EU health law. Likewise, proposed amendments to EU medical devices legislation are taking account of the various

---

[121] *Guiot v Climatec*, C-272/94, EU:C:1996:147.

[122] *Van Binsbergen* EU:C:1974:131; *Gulling*, C-292/86, EU:C:1988:15; *Ramrath*, C-106/91, EU:C:1992:230.

[123] *Commission v Germany*, C-205/84, EU:C:1986:463; *Gouda*, C-288/89, EU:C:1991:323; *Sager*, C-76/90, EU:C:1991:331; *Schindler*, C-275/92, EU:C:1994:119.

[124] *Ambulanz Glöckner*, C-475/99, EU:C:2001:577; *FENIN*, T-319/99, EU:T:2003:50; *FENIN*, C-205/03, EU:C:2006:453; *Medipac-Kazantzidis*, C-6/05, EU:C:2007:337; *BUPA Ireland*, T-289/03, EU:T:2008:29; *AG2R*, C-437/09, EU:C:2011:112.

[125] See, for example: the UK Competition Appeal Tribunal's decisions in *BetterCare Ltd* [2002] CAT 7, *Napp Pharmaceutical Holdings* [2002] CAT 1, and *Genzyme Ltd* [2004] CAT 4; the Austrian Federal Supreme Court's decision in Case 16 Ok 14/97 *Apotheker*; the Belgian Supreme Court's decision cited in *e-Competitions Law Bulletin* No 15370 (2006).

[126] See the many examples cited in: Lear, Mossialos and Karl, 'EU Competition Law and Health Policy' in Mossialos, et al., above n 9; see also chapters 9, 10 and 11.

[127] For a detailed discussion, see Hervey, (2011) above n 52. See further, in general: Prosser, 'EU Competition Law and Public Services' in Mossialos et al., above n 9; Prosser, *The Limits of Competition Law: Markets and Public Services* (OUP 2005).

[128] See: the '*Altmark* package': *Altmark*; C-280/00, EU:C:2003:415; Decision 2005/842/EC [2005] OJ L312/67.

[129] In 2007 for high/new technology pharmaceuticals: Regulation 1394/2007/EC [2007] OJ L324/1; in 2010 and 2012 on 'pharmacovigilance' (post-marketing surveillance of adverse reactions): Directive 2010/84/EU [2010] OJ L348/74; and in 2011 on counterfeits: Directive 2011/62/EU [2011] OJ L174/74.

different interests concerned, and do not simply regard the relevant law as solely part of internal market legislation.[130] On the other hand, ongoing proposals to loosen the current EU-wide prohibition on direct-to-consumer advertising of prescription-only pharmaceuticals do place pharmaceuticals more firmly within a consumerist frame.[131] Similarly, EU tobacco regulation, originally very much associated with the EU's internal market powers (which proved problematic from a health promotion point of view[132]) has now become much more associated with the EU's health law and policy agendas. Although the tobacco industry still dominates policy processes, other players are also present, and debates are increasingly framed in terms of health. For instance, pressure to lift the EU's ban on smokeless tobacco has so far failed,[133] and part of the reason is that the EU legislature paid attention to DG SANCO's report on the health risks of smokeless tobacco.[134] Opponents of the ban refer to the EU's drive for 'smarter regulation' in the internal market, but also cite health data.[135]

The idea of health as a factor in a productive economy,[136] related to internal market law, the Lisbon Agenda and now 'Europe 2020', is reflected in aspects of EU pharmaceuticals law that seek to support the European pharmaceuticals industry, and in particular innovation within that industry, such as enhanced intellectual property rights.[137] It is also reflected in the EU's support for health-related research, particularly through its Framework programmes, and now

---

[130] Commission, 'Proposal for a Regulation of the European Parliament and Council on medical devices, and amending Directive 2001/83/EC, Regulation (EC) No 178/2002 and Regulation (EC) No 1223/2009' COM (2012) 542 final.

[131] Commission, 'Amended proposal for a Directive of the European Parliament and of Council amending Directive 2001/83/EC as regards information to the general public on medicinal products subject to medical prescription amending, as regards information to the general public on medicinal products subject to medical prescription, Directive 2001/83/EC on the Community code relating to medicinal products for human use' COM (2012) 48 final.

[132] The CJEU held that the original Tobacco Advertising Directive (Directive 98/43/EC [1998] OJ L213/9), based on the EU's internal market competences, was invalid: see *TAD*, C-376/98, EU:C:2000:544. However, subsequent case law revealed this case to be more of an exception than the rule, see, e.g., *TAD2*, C-380/03, EU:C:2006:772; *Swedish Match*, C-210/03, EU:C:2004:802; *BAT and Imperial Tobacco*, C-491/01, EU:C:2002:741.

[133] The CJEU upheld the ban in 2004, see: *Arnold André*, C-434/02, EU:C:2004:800; and Directive 2014/40/EU [2014] OJ L127/1 retains the ban.

[134] Commission, 'Scientific Committee on Emerging and Newly Identified Health Risks (SCENIHR) Opinion on: Health Effects of Smokeless Tobacco Products, February 2008' (Health and Consumer Protection Directorate-General 2008). See further: McKee, Hervey and Gilmore, 'Public health policies' in Mossialos et al., above n 9.

[135] See, for instance: *Stotesbury (Head of Regulatory Science at Imperial Tobacco), 'Smokeless Tobacco: EU Dogma or Dialogue' (*EurActiv, 16 October 2012); Ross, 'Smoking Kills, so why ban smokeless tobacco' (*European Voice*, 9 January 2013).

[136] Greer, above n 108.

[137] On the ways in which EU intellectual property law seeks to influence industry behaviour, see: Jackson, above n 41; Hervey and Black, 'The European Union and the governance of stem cell research' (2005) 12 *Maastricht Journal of European and Comparative Law* 3. For examples of relevant EU legislation during this period see: Regulation 1901/2006/EC, Directive 2001/20/EC, Directive 2001/83/EC and Regulation (EC) No 726/2004 [2006] OJ L378/1, Article 36; Regulation 141/2000/EC [2000] OJ L18/1, Articles 8 and 9.

their successor 'Horizon 2020', which aims to create the 'European Research Area'.[138] The relevant strand of 'Horizon 2020' is entitled 'Health for Growth', and it was proposed to succeed the EU's second public health programme which ran from 2008 to 2013.[139] In addition to investing in research into novel health products or processes, the EU has also invested in research into health system reform.[140] The Commission and the Council's Economic Policy Committee have identified areas where, in their view, structural reforms and efficiency gains could improve the future sustainability of health systems.[141] The EU's 'cohesion funds', similarly tied into the EU's growth agenda, which provide co-financing to projects supporting the EU's poorest regions and groups, are also being used to invest in health infrastructure.[142] The extent to which the rationale for EU health law as part of the EU's competitive advantage is consistent with, or runs counter to, other rationales, such as EU health law as supporting equity or promoting equality is discussed in chapters 9, 10, 11 and 18. Be that as it may, the underlying idea of health as a productive factor has the effect of enhancing the cohesiveness of EU health law.

A fourth and final example of greater coherence for EU health law is found in the 'Conclusions on Common Values and Principles in European Union Health Systems' adopted by the EU's Council in 2006.[143] The 'common values and principles' were endorsed by the European Commission in its 2007 White Paper,

---

[138] Supposed to be a border-free zone for research, in which resources are efficiently deployed in order to enhance both employment and competitiveness in the EU, see: Commission, 'Towards a European Research Area' COM (2000) 6 final.

[139] Commission, 'Proposal for a Regulation of the European Parliament and of the Council on establishing a Health for Growth Programme, the third multi-annual programme of EU action in the field of health for the period 2014-2020' COM (2011) 709 final. The proposal, now adopted as Regulation 282/2014/EU [2014] OJ L86/1, repeals Decision 1350/2007/EC [2007] OJ L301/3. See also: Commission Staff Working Document, 'Investing in Health - Accompanying the document Commission Communication, Towards Social Investment for Growth and Cohesion including implementing the European Social Fund 2014-2020' SWD (2013) 43 final; European Court of Auditors, *The European Union's Public Health Programme 2003-2007: An Effective Way to Improve Health?* (Court of Auditors 2009).

[140] Decision 1350/2007/EC [2007] OJ L301/3; Decision [2012] OJ C198/7; Commission, 'Towards Social Investment for Growth and Cohesion including implementing the European Social Fund 2014-2020' COM (2013) 83 final.

[141] Commission and the Economic Policy Committee, 'Joint Report on Health Systems' (European Economy Occasional Papers 74, December 2010) <http://ec.europa.eu/economy_finance/publications/occasional_paper/2010/pdf/ocp74_en.pdf;> and, Council of the European Union, '3054th Council meeting Economic and Financial Affairs' (7 December 2010).

[142] See: Commission Staff Working Document, 'Social investment through the European Social Fund' SWD (2013) 44 final; Commission, 'Proposal for a Regulation of the European Parliament and Council establishing Horizon 2020 the Framework Programme for Research and Innovation (2014–20)' COM (2011) 809 final; Commission, 'Towards Social Investment for Growth and Cohesion including implementing the European Social Fund 2014-2020' (Communication) COM (2013) 83 final; Commission, 'Solidarity in health: reducing health inequalities in the EU' (Communication) COM (2009) 567 final.

[143] Council Conclusions on Common values and principles in European Union Health Systems [2006] OJ C146/1.

'Together for Health',[144] and subsequently, although not always explicitly.[145] They have also been supported by the European Parliament.[146] The history of the 'common values and principles' lies in the debate over whether health care services should be included in the Directive on services in the internal market.[147] The case law of the CJEU on freedom to receive health services across borders in the EU from the end of the 1990s onwards[148] increased uncertainty for the authorities of national health care systems. By the early to mid-2000s, the case law had built up a sufficient head of steam that governments of the Member States were keen to resolve that uncertainty through EU-level legislation. However, the difficulty was that the obvious route, via internal market law, was not politically acceptable. This is because health care is not seen as an economic 'service' in European societies, and to attach health care to a general Directive on services in the internal market was politically impossible. Significant opposition to the proposed EU legislation liberalizing services provision, in part prompted by the (failed) Treaty establishing a Constitution for Europe, heightened its salience.[149] In the revised services Directive, health care was explicitly excluded,[150] and eventually the EU adopted a separate Directive on 'patients' rights in cross border health care'.[151] But, in the meantime, the governments of the Member States, acting within the EU Council, had taken the opportunity to articulate some values and principles that are supposed to be held sufficiently common to apply to all EU health care systems. This was no mean feat. During the period since 2000, the EU has nearly doubled in terms of numbers of Member States, with the significant enlargements to the east and south.[152] The EU now includes more than twenty-eight different health care systems, which vary in terms of their institutional and funding arrangements, as well as their histories.[153]

---

[144]   Commission, 'White Paper: Together for Health: A Strategic Approach for the EU 2008-2013' (White Paper) COM (2007) 630 final.

[145]   See, for instance: Commission, COM (2013) 83 final; Commission Staff Working Document, SWD (2013) 44 final; Commission Staff Working Document, 'Investing in Health - Accompanying the document Commission Communication, Towards Social Investment for Growth and Cohesion including implementing the European Social Fund 2014-2020' SWD (2013) 43 final; Commission, 'Annual Growth Survey 2013' (Communication) COM (2012) 750 final; Commission COM (2009) 567 final; Commission, COM (2011) 709 final.

[146]   For instance, European Parliament Resolution of 9 October 2008 on 'Together for Health: A Strategic Approach for the EU 2008-2013' [2010] OJ CE 9/56.

[147]   The so-called 'Bolkestein Directive': Directive 2006/123/EC [2006] OJ L376/36.

[148]   See above, ns 40 and 120.

[149]   Barnard, 'Unravelling the Services Directive' (2008) 45(2) *Common Market Law Review* 323; De Witte, 'Setting the Scene: How Did Services get to Bolkestein and Why?' (2007) Edinburgh Europa Institute Mitchell Working Paper Series 3/2007 O'Leary, 'Free Movement of Persons and Services' in Craig and de Búrca (2011) above n 1.

[150]   Directive 2006/123/EC, Article 2 (2) (f).   [151]   Directive 2011/24/EU [2011] OJ L88/45.

[152]   In 2000, the EU had 15 Member States: the original 6, Ireland, Denmark and the UK joining in 1973, Greece in 1981, Spain and Portugal in 1986, and Austria, Finland and Sweden in 1995. A further 10 joined in 2004: the Czech Republic, Cyprus, Estonia, Hungary, Latvia, Lithuania, Malta, Poland, Slovakia and Slovenia. Bulgaria and Romania joined in 2007, Croatia in 2013.

[153]   For an overview, see Introduction to Part III.

Not surprisingly, the 'common values and principles' are expressed in very general terms. The 'values' are 'universality, access to good quality care, equity, and solidarity'. The principles, 'which all EU citizens would expect to find in any health care system across the EU', are quality, safety, evidence-based ethical care, patient involvement, redress, privacy and confidentiality. This articulation of the values and principles of EU health law thus overlaps with the human rights focus noted above. Although they have not yet been explicitly endorsed by the CJEU, the 'common values and principles' are beginning to find expression in some EU legislation,[154] and proposed legislation,[155] as well as in the EU's public health programmes. Some commentators, including ourselves, have expressed significant reservations as to the practical fulfilment of these principles, particularly those of solidarity and equity, but also those of human rights protection, within EU health law. In particular, as we have just seen, there is concern about the extent to which EU health law, as it relates to EU internal market law, can ever support such principles.[156] There is also concern over whether the quality principle is sufficiently fulfilled where EU health law seeks to support technological innovation.[157] Some of these concerns reflect the EU's constrained competences in health. However, for our purposes, what is more important is not whether these 'common values and principles', and the human rights expressed in the EU CFR, are honoured in every specific instance. Rather, their very generality, as well as their expression as *principles*, lends support to the greater coherence of EU health law.

More recently, Council has reiterated the 'common values and principles', in the context of 'Europe 2020'.[158] This reiteration adds the new aspect of

[154] Notably, Directive 2011/24/EU above n 151.

[155] For instance, the European Commission launched a consultation on the mutual recognition of qualifications directives in 2010: Commission, 'Green Paper on modernising the Professional Qualifications Directive' (Green Paper) COM (2011) 367 final; and a proposal for a new Directive: Commission, 'Proposal for a Directive of the European Parliament and of the Council amending Directive 2005/36/EC on the recognition of professional qualifications and Regulation on administrative cooperation through the Internal Market Information System' COM (2011) 883 final, followed part of the revised approach to the internal market, the 'Single Market Act', see above n 112, these consider concerns about the quality of care provided by health care professionals, particularly those who have been debarred from professional practice in one Member State. Proposed new legislation will extend the 'alert mechanism' already in place for health care professionals covered by the services Directive, to health professionals covered by the 'sectoral' rules on mutual recognition of qualifications. This is explicitly framed as being about providing 'guarantees to patients' concerning quality of care. See: Commission, 'Proposal for a Directive of the European Parliament and of the Council amending Directive 2005/36/EC on the recognition of professional qualifications and Regulation on administrative cooperation through the Internal Market Information System' COM (2011) 883 final, proposed new Article 56a.

[156] See, for instance: Hervey, (2003) above n 77; McHale, 'Fundamental Rights and Health Care' in Mossialos et al., above n 9.

[157] Bache et al., 'The Defining Features of the European Union's Approach to Regulating New Health Technologies'; Abraham and Davis, 'Science, Law, and the Medical-Industrial Complex in EU Pharmaceutical Regulation: The Deferiprone Controversy' both in Flear et al., above n 37.

[158] Commission, 'Solidarity in health: reducing health inequalities in the EU' (Communication) COM (2009) 567 final.

health as a productive factor. The context is the Eurozone crisis, and the EU's continued inability to develop economic policies that will bring the EU back into a period of strong economic growth. The austerity policies that are being imposed on various Member States by the EU and the International Monetary Fund are already having implications for national health care systems, and will continue to do so. For instance, reports from Greece suggested that fiscal austerity measures led the Ministry of Health to call for a 40 per cent cut to hospital budgets in 2011.[159] Similar concerns have been raised about the Spanish health system.[160] It was reported in 2013 that hospitals in such Member States were reluctant to treat chronically ill patients from other Member States.[161] In its 2011 'Conclusions: Towards Modern, Responsible and Sustainable Health Systems',[162] the Council calls on Member States and the European Commission to focus on the idea of health as a *contributor* to economic growth rather than solely an expenditure. We can expect to see that aspect of EU health law emerge more strongly during the years ahead. Scott Greer reads these developments as a third strand of EU health policy, distinct from its support for data, networks, agencies and research; and the application of internal market law.[163]

Sources of EU health law

EU legislation and treaty provisions

The legislative content of EU health law is based in part on the explicit health competences given to the EU legislature in the TFEU,[164] and in part on other competences.[165] Deciding what legislation should be included involves determining the extent or scope of health law in general. We have discussed that question in the previous chapter, and explained our position that, for the purposes of this book, we understand health law to be concerned with six key dimensions: individual human rights; professional liability; access to and practising of health care professions and regulating health care institutions; funding

---

[159] Kentikelenis and Papanicolas, 'Economic crisis, austerity and the Greek public health system' (2012) 22 *European Journal of Public Health* 4. Human rights scholars, such as Keith Ewing, have argued that the Greek austerity measures are contrary to European human rights law, and have suggested that the European Court of Human Rights would have jurisdiction to hear such a claim, see: Sweet, 'Greek austerity illegal says UK professor' (*Neoskosmos*, 30 April 2013). The CJEU held in *Pringle*, C-370/12, EU:C:2012:756, that Article 51 (1) and (2) EU CFR mean that the European Stability Mechanism is not subject to scrutiny under the EU CFR, because the Member States are not implementing Union law when they establish such a mechanism.

[160] Legido-Quigley et al., 'Will austerity cuts dismantle the Spanish health care system?' [2013] *British Medical Journal* 346:f2363.

[161] Sindbjerg Martinsen and Vollaard, 'Implementing Social Europe in Times of Crises: Re-established Boundaries of Welfare' (2014) 37(4) *West European Politics* 677.

[162] Council of the European Union, 'Council conclusions: towards modern, responsive and sustainable health systems' [2011] OJ C202/10.

[163] Greer, above n 108.

[164] Article 168 TFEU.   [165] Principally, though not exclusively, Article 114 TFEU.

and organization of health care systems; public health; and regulation of human material in health contexts.

In the literature on EU health law, we see several different approaches to the question of legislative scope. There is an emerging division between those who focus on EU law (or policy) *and* health;[166] and those who seek to analyse EU health law *per se*. The former approach, and group of scholars, tends to have a wider substantive focus than the latter. Both include EU legislation on patient mobility; on mobility of health care services;[167] on patient/consumer safety legislation; and on entry into the medical profession and entitlement to practise. These areas, at least, form the core substance of EU health legislation.

Secondly, from the point of view of the rights and responsibilities of individual patients or health professionals, many scholars include EU legislation on data protection and privacy; and on employment conditions. In terms of legislation pertaining to health-related institutions, as opposed to individuals, some scholars cover EU law concerning the organization of health care systems,[168] such as EU legislation on pharmaceuticals pricing; on fair competition, state aids and public procurement in the context of 'services of general interest'; and on health insurance. Some include legislation governing the EU's health-related institutions.

A third significant area of relevant substantive EU legislation concerns pharmaceuticals and medical devices. Much of the literature includes legislation on clinical trials; on manufacture, marketing, labelling and advertising; 'pharmacovigilance'; and liability for pharmaceuticals. Similarly, EU legislation on medical devices falls within this area. Several scholars include the EU's intellectual property legislation, as it is particularly important in practice for the development of new health technologies.

The literature is divided on the question of whether public health law (that is, the law surrounding the conditions of good health) is included within EU health law.[169] EU legislation covers communicable diseases, for instance, through blood safety, human tissues, cells and organs, and food safety. It also covers

---

[166] Sometimes known as 'the law of the horse', taken from Easterbrook's discussion of cyberlaw in: Easterbrook, 'Cyberspace and the Law of the Horse' [1996] *University of Chicago Legal Forum* 207, or as the notion of 'law and a banana', see: Annas, 'Health Law at the Turn of the Century: from White Dwarf to Red Giant' (1989) 21 *Connecticut Law Review* 551, cited in Hall, 'The Legal and Historical Foundations of Patients as Medical Consumers' (2008) 96 *Georgetown Law Journal* 583.

[167] The relevant legislation, Directive 2006/123/EC, above n 147, explicitly excludes all 'healthcare services', Article 2 (2) (f). But free movement of such services is guaranteed under Article 56 TFEU.

[168] As the title suggests, the primary focus of Mossialos et al., above n 14, is systemic. See also: Mossialos, Dixon, Figueras and Kutzin, above n 9; Thomson, Foubister and Mossialos, *Financing health care in the European Union: Challenges and policy responses* (WHO 2009).

[169] For instance, Den Exter and Hervey, above n 9, include very little public health legislation; whereas Hervey and McHale, above n 9, included a great deal. Some of the very earliest texts are only on public health, e.g. McCarthy and Rees above n 9. For a more recent text on this area, see: Greer and Kurzer, above n 9.

the promotion of good health, for instance through cancer and tobacco regulation, or law relating to alcohol. A few scholars have included EU road safety legislation in this category.[170] Arguably, EU environmental legislation ought to be included, as air and water quality play a significant role in promoting good health.[171] There is also the question of whether general EU 'social law' on poverty, or on economic growth is part of EU health law, as there is evidence that good health is linked to economic prosperity.[172] As we said in chapter 2, these areas fall outside the scope of our inquiry.

Finally, few scholars include the small amount of relevant legislation concerning the EU's external health law, that is to say concerning EU law governing relations with the rest of the world, in the area of health. We are unaware of any holistic scholarly treatment of EU external health law. We consider this legislation in Part IV of the book, which includes our attempt to provide a first mapping of that field.

Case law of the CJEU

As we have already seen, much of the EU's health law has been developed by the CJEU, although there are aspects of EU health law where other sources dominate. Of the various heads of the CJEU's jurisdiction, three are important in this respect: applications for judicial review of acts of the EU institutions,[173] Commission allegations of non-compliance with EU law on the part of Member States[174] and preliminary references from national courts.[175] Within EU health law, examples of the first include rulings that the tobacco advertising Directive 98/43/EC was invalid,[176] and, conversely, upholding Directive 98/44/EC on the legal protection of biotechnological inventions.[177] Exercising the second, its compliance jurisdiction, the CJEU has, for instance, repeatedly found aspects of national law regulating health care professionals to be in breach of EU law.[178]

---

[170]   Greer, Hervey, McKee and Mackenbach, 'Health Law and Policy of the European Union' (2013) 381(9872) *The Lancet* 1135.

[171]   We are not aware of any source dealing with EU environmental legislation as part of EU health law.

[172]   The correlation between poverty and health is not a perfect or direct one, but many studies show that poverty is a key indicator for poor health. For some global research see: Dood and Munck, 'Dying For Change: Poor people's experience of health and ill-health' (WHO and World Bank 2000); for European examples see: Koller, 'Poverty, Social Exclusion and Health Systems in the WHO European Region' (WHO Regional Office for Europe 2010); and Koller (ed), 'Poverty and Social Exclusion in the WHO European Region: health systems respond' (WHO Regional Office for Europe 2010) and for recent examples from the USA, see research cited here: Multiple Authors (Spotlight on Poverty and Opportunity, continuous).

[173]   Article 263 TFEU.   [174]   Article 258 TFEU.   [175]   Article 267 TFEU.

[176]   *TAD* EU:C:2000:544.   [177]   *Biotechnology,* C-377/98, EU:C:2001:523.

[178]   *Clinical Laboratories* EU:C:1987:81; *Opticians,* C-140/03, EU:C:2005:242; *Psychotherapists,* C-456/05, EU:C:2007:755; *Pharmacies,* C-141/07, EU:C:2008:492; *Pharmacies,* C-531/06, EU:C:2009:315; *Bio-Medical Analysis Laboratories II,* C-89/09, EU:C:2010:772; *Laboratory analysis* EU:C:2011:34.

The third is, however, by far the most significant.[179] The CJEU is empowered to give authoritative rulings on the validity and interpretation of EU law, where such questions are raised before any national court or tribunal in the Member States. Because of the supremacy of EU law, these authoritative interpretations have the effect of rendering inapplicable any national rules that are inconsistent with that of the CJEU.[180] The preliminary reference procedure is not an appeal: the national court refers questions to the CJEU and must ultimately decide the case in the light of the CJEU's answers. As a matter of practical judicial politics, in virtually every situation, the national courts have respected the authority of the CJEU to give definitive interpretations of EU law, and thus have lent their authority to its decisions. This is so even where the rulings of the CJEU have been surprising, particularly where the CJEU adopts methods of interpretation beyond the literal approach, a practice which has been common for the CJEU since the 1960s. Consequently, the reach of EU law into national legal orders is significantly enhanced, compared to that of other international organizations.[181]

However, at the same time, the preliminary reference procedure supports the heterarchical relationships between the EU legal order and national legal orders that make EU law so significant in terms of its reach and effects.[182] The structure of the preliminary reference procedure is such that national courts are ultimately gatekeepers to court-based development of EU law. Not only may they, for the most part,[183] choose whether or not to make a reference, but they also make the final decision in the instant case, translating the practical meaning of the CJEU's articulation of the principles of EU law into national contexts. So, for instance, when the Irish courts were faced with various challenges to Irish abortion law

---

[179] See: e.g. de la Mare and Donnelly, 'Preliminary Rulings and EU Legal Integration: Evolution and Stats' in Craig and de Búrca, above n 1; de Burca and Weiler (eds), *The European Court of Justice* (OUP 2001); Arnull, *The European Union and its Court of Justice* (OUP 2006).

[180] *Costa v ENEL* EU:C:1964:66; *Factortame2* [1991] 1 AC 603.

[181] Alter, 'The European Court's Political Power' (1996) 19 *West European Politics* 458.

[182] A selection of the more recent literature on this topic includes: Walker, Shaw and Tierney, above n 1; Maduro and Azoulai (eds), *The Past and Future of EU Law: The Classics of EU Law Revisited on the 50th Anniversary of the Rome Treaty* (Hart 2010), chs on *Van Gend en Loos* and *Costa v ENEL*; Beck, 'The Lisbon Judgment of the German Constitutional Court, the Primacy of EU Law and the Problem of *Kompetenz-Kompetenz*: A Conflict between Right and Right in Which There is No *Praetor*' (2011) 17 *European Law Journal* 470; De Witte, 'Direct Effect, Primacy and the Nature of the Legal Order' in Craig and de Búrca (2011) above n 1; Wendell, 'Lisbon Before the Courts: Comparative Perspectives' (2011) 7 *European Constitutional Law Review* 96; Walker, 'Beyond boundary disputes and basic grids: Mapping the global disorder of normative orders' (2008) 6(3) & (4) *International Journal of Constitutional Law* 373; Von Bogdandy, 'Pluralism, Direct Effect, and the Ultimate Say' (2008) 6 *International Journal of Constitutional Law* 397.

[183] See: Article 267 TFEU; *CILFIT*, C-283/81, EU:C:1982:335. On the possibility of damages under infringement proceedings against Member States for judicial failure to make a reference to the CJEU, see: *Köbler*, C-224/01, EU:C:2003:513; *Commission v Italy*, C-129/00, EU:C:2003:656.

during the 1980s and 90s,[184] they could have referred questions to the CJEU on the proper interpretation of EU law on freedom to receive services within the internal market, and hence on whether the Irish provisions were consistent with the relevant EU law. But they chose not to do so, rather deciding the points of EU law raised themselves. Without referring to the CJEU, the English Court of Appeal decided that the EU law on transparency of pricing of pharmaceuticals had not been breached when the Secretary of State for Health restricted the circumstances under which Viagra could be funded by the NHS.[185] Equally, when the CJEU decided the *Kohll* case on free movement of patients in 1998, many Member States took the view that the principles established therein did not apply to the vast majority of health care provided within their national health systems, on the basis that the term 'services' in EU law did not cover such health care, and so chose not to adjust their national policies[186] (a position that the CJEU later ruled was incorrect). In the English *Watts* case, widely regarded as highly problematic from the point of view of national health systems based on taxation, the question of whether there had, in fact, been 'undue delay', entitling Mrs Watts to reimbursement for her hip operation carried out in France, was a matter for the national court, not the CJEU. As it happened, the case settled, and the national rules were changed so that the NHS in effect used spare capacity in the private sector to treat patients who had been waiting for a long time for operations. The feared mass exodus of patients to other EU Member States did not take place.

The health policy community in particular has been very critical of the phenomenon of the CJEU developing EU health law.[187] They point to the unpredictability of law that is made through litigation, the difficulty of determining the precise implications or scope of individual rulings without legislative guidance, and the fact that not all relevant interests are taken into account where law is developed in this way. In addition, it has often been pointed out that not all patients are willing or able to litigate and that it may actually be the patients with

---

[184] See, for instance: *AG (SPUC) v. Open Door Counselling* [1988] 2 CMLR 443; *AG v X* [1992] 2 CMLR 277.

[185] *R (on the application of Pfizer)* [2002] EWCA Civ 1566.

[186] See, for instance, regarding Sweden and Denmark: Martinsen and Blomqvist, 'The European Union: single market pressures' in Magnusson, Vanbræk and Saltman (eds), *Nordic Healthcare Systems: Recent Reforms and Current Policy Challenges* (Open University Press 2009), regarding Denmark: Sindbjerg Martinsen and Vrangbæk, 'The Europeanisation of Healthcare Governance: Implementing the market imperatives of Europe' (2008) 86 *Public Administration* 169 (and no Danish court or tribunal has referred a question on the issue to the CJEU); Germany did not introduce reforms until 2004; France and the Netherlands in 2005, see: Palm and Glinos, 'Enabling Patient Mobility in the EU' in Mossialos et al., above n 9; Martinsen, *EU for the Patients: Developments, Impacts, Challenges* (Report No. 6, Swedish Institute for European Policy Studies 2007).

[187] See literature cited in Hervey and McHale, above n 9, 138-144, for instance: Baeten, 'European Integration and National Healthcare Systems: a challenge for social policy' (2001) 8 *Infose* 1, 1; Baeten, McKee, Mossialos, above n 9; Nickless, 'Were the ECJ decisions in *Kohll* and *Decker* right?' (2001) 7(1) *Eurohealth* 16.

lesser clinical needs who do so. Hence, the implications of making EU health law in this way may be that resource decisions are skewed inappropriately.[188] The view that EU health law should not be made primarily through the CJEU's case law is a specific variant of a more general strand of literature on EU law. This literature concerns the benefits and drawbacks of pursuing economic integration through litigation, and is long-standing,[189] but remains of current concern.[190] And, of course, that literature itself fits within the general literature on whether courts make, or merely interpret, law.[191]

There is no doubt that court-made law is an important source of EU health law. But the particular criticisms noted above essentially concern only one aspect thereof, that on free movement of patients. In other contexts, the criticism has been of *insufficient* activity by the CJEU in the development of EU health law. For instance, the CJEU has refused to involve itself where challenges have been made to the granting of pharmaceuticals marketing authorizations, holding that it did not have jurisdiction to hear a judicial review claim brought by a scientist whose study was relied upon in a marketing authorization granted by the EMA.[192] It is, therefore, also important not to overstate the significance of this particular source of EU health law. There are aspects of EU health law where the CJEU's contribution is minimal, and the key relevant sources are legislation, perhaps supplemented by soft law.[193] There are also areas – for instance, EU

---

[188] Newdick, 'Citizenship, free movement and health care: Cementing individual rights by corroding social solidarity' (2006) 43(6) *Common Market Law Review* 1645; Newdick, *Who Should We Treat? - Rights, Rationing and Resources in the NHS* (OUP 2005).

[189] Among the earliest scholars to write on this topic are: Stein, 'Lawyers, Judges and the making of a Transnational Constitution' (1971) 75 *American Journal of International Law* 1; Cappelletti, Seccombe and Weiler (eds), *International Through Law: Europe and the American Federal Experience* (3 Vols, de Gruyter 1985); Weiler, 'The Transformation of Europe' (1991) 100(8) *Yale Law Journal* 2403.

[190] See, for instance, Kelemen, *Eurolegalism: The Transformation of Law and Regulation in the Euroepan Union* (Harvard University Press 2011); Augenstein (ed), *Integration Through Law Revisited* (Ashgate 2012).

[191] Ross, *On Law and Justice* (University of California Press 1959). For an overview of Scandinavian Legal Realism, and comparison and contrast with American Legal Realism, see, e.g. Zamboni, 'Legal Realisms and the Dilemma of the Relationship of Contemporary Law and Politics' (Stockholm Institute for Scandinavian Law 2010).

[192] In *Olivieri*, T-326/99, EU:T:2003:351, Dr Olivieri, the original scientific lead researcher on a research project involving deferiprone, a thalassaemia drug, sought judicial review of a marketing authorisation for the drug. She was acting following adverse findings, having lost confidence in the promise of the drug, whereas the sponsoring company, Apotex, had continued with the trials and applied for marketing authorisations to various authorities across the world, including the EMA. The CJEU held she had no *locus standi* to bring 9 judicial review claim to protect public health and the application was dismissed. See further: Abraham and Davis, 'Science, Law, and the Medico-Industrial Complex in EU Pharmaceutical Regulation: The Deferiprone Controversy' in Flear et al., above n 37.

[193] For instance, in practice the EU's good laboratory practice and good clinical trials legislation is interpreted through the issuing of guidance notes, which, though non-binding, have a binding effect in practice, because compliance with the guidance, though formally not mandatory, is normally required for studies used to support applications for clinical trial or market authorization.

communicable diseases law – where the CJEU is neither the most important driver of legal developments nor completely irrelevant.[194]

'Softer' types of law

'Soft law' and 'governance' are concepts that have come under greater scrutiny within legal scholarship, including scholarship on EU law, since the 1990s.[195] At risk of greatly oversimplifying a rich and complex literature, the ambiguity of relationships between formal legal rules and other, less formal, but nonetheless normative measures, and how each relates to social practices, has intrigued legal scholars both in the EU and elsewhere.[196] For our purposes, it is sufficient to note that the literature on EU *health* law considers that at least some types of 'soft law', in particular those associated with 'governance', are included within its scope. Only Hervey and den Exter, which is a collection of EU health law *legislation*, excludes all soft law measures from its scope.

The roles of soft law and governance within EU health law include preparatory and informative instruments, such as green papers, which fulfil a 'pre-law' function. Soft law also performs a 'post-law' function, by providing greater specificity of more general rules;[197] or providing guidance that is *de facto* followed, even though it is technically not mandatory.[198] Sometimes described as fulfilling a 'para-law' function,[199] a third category of soft law or governance instruments steer behaviour in ways other than through legislation. For instance, the EU provides formal mechanisms for comparison of national

---

[194] See: Hervey, 'The Role of the European Court of Justice in the Europeanization of Communicable Disease Control: Driver or Irrelevance?' 37 (2012) *Journal of Health Politics, Policy and Law* 975.

[195] See: e.g. Senden, *Soft Law in European Community Law* (Hart 2004); Senden, 'Soft law, self-regulation and co-regulation in European Law: where do they meet?' (2005) 9 *Electronic Journal of Comparative Law* 1, 18. For earlier examples, see Wellens and Borchardt, 'Soft Law in European Community Law' 14 (1989) *European Law Review* 267; Kenner, 'The EU Employment Title and the "Third Way": Making Soft Law Work?' (1999) 15 *International Journal of Comparative Labour Law and Industrial Relations* 33.

[196] See, non-exhaustively, Scott and Trubek, 'Mind the Gap: Law and New Approaches to Governance in the European Union (2002) 8 *European Law Journal* 1; Loebel, 'The Renew Deal: The Fall of Regulation and the Rise of Governance in Contemporary Legal Thought'(2004) 89 *Minnesota Law Review* 262; De Búrca and Scott (2006), above n 109; Trubek and Trubek, 'New Governance and Legal Regulation: Complementarity, Rivalry and Transformation' (2007) 13 *Columbia Journal of European Law* 539; Gunningham, 'The New Collaborative Environmental Governance: The Localization of Regulation' (2009) 36 *Journal of Law and Society* 145; NeJaime, 'When New Governance Fails' (2009) 70 *Ohio State Law Journal* 323; De Schutter and Lenoble, *Reflexive Governance: Redefining Public Interest in a Pluralistic World* (Hart 2010); Sabel and Zeitlin (eds), *Experimentalist Governance in the European Union* (OUP 2010); Dawson, above n 109.

[197] See, for example, the '*Altmark* package' above n 128.   [198] Such as clinical trials standards.

[199] Senden (2004) above n 195, 182-3, 458; Senden, 'Soft law, self-regulation and co-regulation in European Law: where do they meet?' (2005) 9 *Electronic Journal of Comparative Law* 1, 23-25.

systems against benchmarks and thus disseminating good practice;[200] or provides resources to support certain (desired) types of behaviour;[201] or makes recommendations or adopts codes of conduct.[202] There is some evidence that such 'steering' may affect national health systems, for instance, the English responses to poor cancer statistics in the late 1990s, comparatively high rates of perinatal mortality provoking changes in Dutch health policy, and the French reaction to high rates of HIV infection among the homeless.[203]

Mainstreaming: 'health in all policies'

Interpreting the scope of EU health law involves engaging with its 'transversal' nature. Unless one takes the view that EU health law is *only* legislation adopted on the basis of the EU's public health competence provision, and case law interpreting and applying those measures,[204] EU health law cuts across the taxonomy accepted by EU lawyers[205] as establishing the categories of EU law.[206] For instance, and non-exhaustively, provisions on the recognition of health care professionals' qualifications, and their ability to practise across borders within the EU; on access to health care of mobile workers and their families in another EU Member State; on patients accessing health care services across borders; and on restrictions on health care providers setting up and offering their services in another Member State, fall within various areas of EU free movement law. Measures on the marketing and advertising of pharmaceuticals and medical devices fall within EU free movement and consumer protection law. Perhaps counter-intuitively, legislation on data protection also falls within EU free movement law. Special arrangements for the provision of health care services paid for by the

---

[200] For instance, the 'Europe 2020' comparative indicators on health and health systems include comparative data on health expenditure and projected expenditure, reported unmet medical needs, and healthy life years at birth, see: Commission, 'Health and Health Systems' (Commission 2014); and those for poverty include 'access to healthcare', see: Commission, 'Europe 2020 Targets: Poverty and Social Exclusion Active Inclusion Strategies' (Commission 2014).

[201] Such as dissemination, investigation and implementation of the European Cancer Code being supported by the EU public health programmes.

[202] For example, Council Recommendation 98/463/EC [1998] OJ L203/14; Council of the European Union, 'Council conclusions: towards modern, responsive and sustainable health systems' [2011] OJ C202/10.

[203] See: Greer et al., above n 170.

[204] Article 168 TFEU. None of the published literature on the topic takes this approach to the scope of EU health law. Hancher and Sauter, above n 13, 161, distinguish between legislation 'which directly concerns healthcare' and legislation which can be applied across sectors.

[205] Represented, for instance, in the main chapter headings in textbooks on EU law, in the way in which the TEU and TFEU are organised into different parts and chapters, each covering different legal topics, and in the taxonomy according to which the EU institutions, particularly the European Commission organise EU law.

[206] Part of what we achieved in our 2004 book was a 're-reading' of these places where EU law and health law interact, through the categories of health law, rather than those of EU law.

public purse, through, for instance, granting exclusive licences, authorizations or other restrictive measures, at least potentially fall within EU competition law. Legislation on working conditions and working time in health care institutions, such as hospitals, which goes to enhancing patient safety and quality of care, falls within EU labour law. Provisions on development, authorization and marketing of novel health technologies fall within EU research and development law as well as free movement law. International treaty provisions and EU legislation on access to essential medicines across the globe fall within EU external relations law.[207] Measures ensuring safety of food, as a major disease vector, or the regulation of sale, labelling and advertising of food, tobacco and alcohol, major contributors to 'life-style' diseases, fall within EU agricultural law, free movement law and consumer protection law. In addition, provisions of EU Treaty law, which have a constitutional quality, on allocation of competences,[208] 'mainstreaming' duties[209] and the place of human rights in EU law,[210] also form part of EU health law. These provisions have important implications for how the more detailed legislative provisions are both adopted and interpreted.

The 'transversal' nature of EU health law is now expressed in the TFEU. Article 9 TFEU requires the EU to 'take into account' 'requirements linked to ... the protection of human health' when it defines and implements its policies. This 'mainstreaming' provision is repeated more or less verbatim in the first sentence of Article 168 (1) TFEU. The TFEU's health mainstreaming provisions are consistent with the EU's aim of promoting 'the well-being of its peoples' (Article 2 TEU). The 'mainstreaming' of health across all EU laws and policies is said to have been originally added to the Treaty in 1996, in response to the arguments of the UK government in *UK* v. *Commission (BSE)*,[211] concerning the emergency measures adopted by the EU in response to the bovine spongiform encephalopathy crisis of the mid-1990s.[212] However, traces of the

---

[207] These are discussed further in chapters 16 and 17.

[208] Article 5 TEU; Articles 4 and 6 TFEU; Article 46, 48, 50 TFEU (free movement); Article 114 TFEU (internal market); Article 153 TFEU (social policy); Article 168 TFEU (public health); Article 169 (consumer protection); Article 352 TFEU (implied powers).

[209] Article 9 TFEU: 'In defining and implementing its policies and activities, the Union shall take into account requirements linked to ... a high level of ... protection of human health'; Article 10 TFEU: 'In defining and implementing its policy and activities, the Union shall aim to combat discrimination based on sex, racial or ethnic origin, religion or belief, disability, age or sexual orientation'. For a discussion, see: Geyer and Lightfoot, 'The Strengths and Limits of New Forms of EU Governance: The Cases of Mainstreaming and Impact Assessment in EU Public Health and Sustainable Development Policy' (2010) 32(4) *European Integration* 339.

[210] Article 6 TEU; Article 16 TFEU.   [211] Order in *BSE*, C-180/96-R, EU:C:1996:308.

[212] See: Geyer, *Exploring European Social Policy* (Polity 2000) 175. The UK argued that the measures (banning the export of bovines, meat from bovines and products obtained from bovines liable to enter the animal feed or human food chain, or materials destined for use in pharmaceuticals or cosmetics) were adopted on the basis of economic measures and the need to reassure consumers and protect the beef market. The UK sought an interim suspension of the ban with respect to various products for which the risk of BSE was not established or had been eliminated by national measures. Essentially, the UK argued that the ban was not justified for such products. The CJEU disagreed (at the time the link between BSE and nvCJD

mainstreaming of health were already in the Treaty as early as the mid-1980s. According to Article 114 TFEU, which was originally added to the Treaty by the Single European Act, internal market legislation must provide 'a high level of protection' in matters concerning 'health, safety, environmental protection and consumer protection'. The mainstreaming provisions could be used by the EU institutions to justify giving greater weight to health protection, or could even potentially ground an argument that EU legislation is invalid,[213] although they have not been successfully relied upon in this respect to date. The health mainstreaming provisions of the TEU and TFEU could be interpreted as confirming quite the reverse of our view that EU health law is now more coherent than during earlier phases of its development. After all, if EU health law is already a coherent aspect of the EU's legal system, then there is no need for a legal expression of the need to ensure that it is secured through all policies. Worse, if the primary means of securing health protection and promotion is through the law in *other* areas, it is difficult to argue that EU health law is a coherent entity. However, we suggest that the mainstreaming provisions are further evidence of the greater coherence of EU health law. Many other areas of EU law, several of which have long been accepted as core parts of EU law, are also 'mainstreamed' in EU law. These include equality between men and women (Article 8 TFEU), employment, social protection and education (Article 9 TFEU), non-discrimination on forbidden grounds (Article 10 TFEU), protecting the environment, consumers and animal welfare (Articles 11–13 TFEU).

Each of the different areas of EU law, through which EU health law has been developed and conceptually situated, has its own history, its own rationales and formal legal basis, and its own communities of expertise, with shared understandings of problems and their (legal) solutions. These differences go a long way to explaining what is distinctive about EU health law, as opposed to health law in any of the EU's Member States. Indeed, the history, rationale and shared understandings inform the themes of EU health law that are the main subject of this book. Thus, for instance, the *Luisi and Carbone* decision,[214] to the effect that restrictions on currency movement, where the currency was to be used to pay for medical treatment, are *prima facie* contrary to EU law; or the *Grogan* ruling,[215] to the effect that restrictions on abortion advertising are *prima facie* contrary to EU law, though can be justified,[216] can now be understood as embodying the EU's approach to its health law, through the EU's 'common principles' of EU health law: human rights protection, quality of care,

---

was unclear). The CJEU reasoned implicitly that the protection of human health was a duty of the EU institutions (*BSE* EU:C:1996:308) paragraph 63). The 'mainstreaming' provision of Article 168 TFEU made this assumption explicit.

[213]   Van der Mei and Waddington, 'Public Health and the Treaty of Amsterdam' (1998) 5 *European Journal of Health Law* 129, 134.

[214]   *Luisi and Carbone* EU:C:1984:35.   [215]   *SPUC v Grogan* EU:C:1991:378.

[216]   See also: *AG v X* [1992] 2 CMLR 277.

patient safety, evidence-based and ethically robust care, patient involvement, redress, and privacy and confidentiality, all within the context of constrained EU competences.

How is EU health law made?

The European Union's founding treaties establish its legislative and judicial institutions, and determine the processes by which EU law is made, interpreted and applied. The basic position is that the EU only has the legislative competences given to it in the Treaties; that the European Commission proposes legislation and the Council and European Parliament decide; and that the CJEU adjudicates. We have already outlined the key jurisdictional competences of the CJEU, and explained their significance for EU health law, so these are not repeated here. But in order to provide context for the rest of the book for those unfamiliar with the EU's institutions and legal system, the remainder of this section considers how the EU institutions operate to create EU health law.

The treaties (Treaty on European Union and Treaty on the Functioning of the European Union) are like a constitution for the European Union. Treaties are agreed by the governments of the Member States, and must be ratified by each Member State according to its constitutional requirements. For EU health law, the key Treaty provisions are the competence provisions (which set out the powers of the EU institutions to make law) and the directly effective provisions on free movement of the factors of production and fair competition. These have already been outlined above and are discussed in much greater detail later in the book.

EU health legislation is adopted in accordance with the legislative procedures set out in the TFEU. The ordinary legislative procedure is the relevant procedure for virtually all the EU health legislation that we discuss in this book. EU legislation offers several advantages over the rather general Treaty rules.[217] Legislation offers greater structure for relationships between relevant actors; it provides valuable detail and certainty; it consolidates and codifies the CJEU's case law, making it generally applicable and giving it greater democratic legitimacy; and it allows for special arrangements to be made for particular sectors. The latter has been especially valuable in the context of EU health law, for instance, in the special internal market legislation governing the marketing of pharmaceuticals, and tortious liability for defective products in health care settings. It is also the driver behind the proposed changes to EU medical devices legislation. Sometimes EU health legislation is adopted as a *reaction against* the CJEU's case law, for instance, in the case of patients' rights legislation or in the proposed changes to direct-to-consumer advertising of pharmaceuticals. Three

---

[217] See: Kilpatrick, 'Internal Market Architecture and the Accommodation of Labour Rights: As good as it gets?' in Syrpis (ed), *The Judiciary, the Legislature and the Internal Market* (CUP 2012).

main EU institutions are involved in the adoption of legislation: the European Commission, Council and Parliament.

The European Commission is made up of a President, a college of Commissioners, and a permanent staff, divided into Directorates General (DGs), each responsible for a particular policy area. The Commission plays both administrative and legislative roles in the EU. It enjoys a significant agenda-setting power in the legislative process, in that, in general,[218] it alone may initiate legislative proposals. In practice, before proposing legislation, the European Commission undertakes formal and less formal consultations with relevant stakeholders. At least five different policy domains, associated with different DGs of the Commission, are relevant in the development of EU health law: the internal market, social affairs, public health, enterprise and economic policy.[219] As might be expected, different Commission DGs have relationships with different groups of stakeholders. For instance, DG SANCO uses the EU Health Policy Forum to interact with almost fifty umbrella organizations in the health sector. DG Enterprise consults with both global firms and SMEs working on novel health technologies. The existence of these different policy domains has allowed the Commission to advance its health law proposals even in the face of political opposition, by shifting the proposal to a different policy domain. For instance, in the early 2000s, the Commission secured Council agreement on an OMC in health, by linking health with the 'elderly', which was much less contested than health per se.[220] The Commission is increasingly using the economic policy domain to progress its health proposals.[221] However, strongly divergent views from different DGs can also constrain the development of EU health law. For instance, the 'turf war' between DG EMPL and DG SANCO over responsibility for EU legislation on migrant patients contributed to delays in proposing the patients' rights Directive.

---

[218] There are some exceptions, see Article 289 TFEU; none has yet been applied in EU health law. The 'European citizens' initiative' whereby one million EU citizens representing at least one quarter of Member States, has been invoked in several public health-related petitions, mainly concerning the environment; none has yet reached the stage of a European Commission proposal. Article 11 TEU; Article 24 TFEU; Regulation 211/2011/EU [2011] OJ L65/1. The Commission has responded to a citizens' initiative proposal on access to water (Commission, 'Communication on the European Citizens' Initiative "Water and sanitation are a human right! Water is a public good, not a commodity!"' (Communication) COM (2014) 177 final); and one on stem cell research/abortions in EU development funding (Commission, 'A decent Life for all: from vision to collective action' (Communication) COM (2014) 355 final), but did not propose EU legislation in either case.

[219] Hervey and Vanhercke, 'Health care and the EU: the law and policy patchwork' in Mossialos et al., above n 9.

[220] See: European Council, 'Presidency Conclusions: Barcelona European Council 15-16 March 2002' (European Council 2002)

[221] See: De Ruijter and Hervey, above n 111. For an example of how national actions are 're-framing' health in similar ways, see: Vincent-Jones and Mullen, 'From Collaborative to Genetic Governance: The Example of Healthcare Services in England' in De Schutter and Lenoble, above n 196.

The Council is composed of the relevant ministers of the Member States, depending upon the subject matter under discussion. Although in general the voting in Council is by qualified majority, Member States still threaten to veto EU legislation as a diplomatic manoeuvre, as was the case, for instance, in UK Prime Minister John Major's use of the veto in response to perceived non-cooperation of other Member States in resolving the BSE crisis of the 1990s.[222] The different domains of EU health law also imply different Council config-urations. Although the ministers of health of the Member States have been meeting since at least the mid-1980s, the main relevant Council configura-tion for EU health legislation is the Employment, Social Policy, Health and Consumer Affairs Council. However, EU health legislation also often goes to the Competitiveness Council (which covers the internal market, research and industry), and indeed increasingly to the powerful ECOFIN Council of Eco-nomic and Finance Ministers. Thus, the relevant ministers voting in Council are usually not health ministers, nor even those with any particular expertise in health. This aspect of EU health law making has been criticized vociferously by health policy communities. In addition, the position of governments of Member States in Council may be strongly divergent on proposed EU health law, depending upon how they understand national interests on a particular issue. For instance, in pharmaceuticals regulation, and intellectual property and similar rights, there are important differences between the preferences of those Member States who seek to rely on generic medicines in their national health systems, and have no industry developing novel, on-patent medicines, and those Member States where such industry actors are located.

In the past, the European Parliament has had a much weaker role in adopting EU legislation, but changes introduced gradually, and most recently by the Lis-bon Treaty, mean that the European Parliament has strengthened its role to one of co-legislature with Council. EU health legislation must be agreed by both the European Parliament and the Council, and both institutions have opportu-nities to propose amendments to the Commission's text during the legislative process. European Parliament scrutiny of Commission proposals takes place through parliamentary committees, and here again there have been questions of where EU health law 'belongs' within the structures of EU law. There is no 'health' parliamentary committee *per se*, but the idea of health as a special case has helped the European Parliament's 'ENVI' committee (Environmental Pub-lic Health and Food Safety) wrest control of at least some health proposals away from its IMCO committee (Internal Market and Consumer Protection). Like the European Commission, the European Parliament has developed capacity in health fields over time, through interaction with various stakeholders. A good example is tobacco regulation, where both the industry and anti-smoking

---

[222] See: Salmon, 'The Structures, Institutions and Powers of the EU' in Gower (ed), *The European Union Handbook* (Fitzroy Dearborn 2002).

pressure groups, as well as health professionals and policymakers, seek to inform and persuade influential MEPs.

Alongside the EU's legislative institutions, an array of EU regulatory and executive agencies operates in the practical determination, administration and application of EU health law. As the EU's competences expanded, so did its need to take executive decisions in various policy areas,[223] including health. The practice of pursuing European integration through decisions of technical experts, often in committees made up of representatives of the European Commission, national civil servants and private or quasi-private bodies, has been termed 'infranationalism'.[224] The legal structures for EU administrative law (known as 'comitology') developed incrementally and originally outside of the formal Treaty provisions, lending them an 'extra-legal' feel that contributed to the EU's legitimacy deficit, especially during the 1980s and 1990s. Far from being merely 'technical' or 'implementing', EU executive decision-making can have profound implications for those affected, and may also reach into the realms of 'political' decision-making. A well-known example, with public health ramifications, is the 2004 decision to allow genetically modified maize to be grown in the EU, in spite of opposition from a majority of EU Member States. The 'comitology' system was eventually rationalized in legislation,[225] and the Treaty of Lisbon made further changes to the legal arrangements for delegated EU legislation.[226] Many of the EU's agencies are based on previous comitology structures, and were most recently rationalized in a review in 2012.[227]

More than forty different agencies and other bodies, of various types,[228] contribute to EU executive rule-making, or other governance activities, such as 'steering' of behaviour through soft law or through financial incentives. The EU's regulatory agencies are bodies with legal personality, governed by EU law, set up by EU legislation, with financial and administrative autonomy, and independence in carrying out their assigned tasks. Most are funded from the EU's budget, and they are physically located across the Member States. Some have the power to take legally binding decisions. In the area of EU health law, key regulatory agencies are the European Medicines Agency (EMA), the European Food Safety Agency (EFSA) and the European Centre for Communicable Disease Control (ECDC). The EMA advises the Commission as to whether to

---

[223] Some 2500 'technical' measures are adopted every year, many of which are truly technical, but some of which are not, see: Guéguen, 'Comitology: hijacking European power?' (European Training Institute 2010) 47.

[224] Weiler (1999) above n 6.

[225] Originally: Decision 1999/468/EC [1999] OJ L184/23; amended by: Decision 2006/512/EC [2006] OJ L200/11. See now: Regulation 182/2011/EU [2011] OJ L55/13.

[226] Articles 290 and 291 TFEU.

[227] See: European Parliament, Council and Commission, 'Joint Statement of the European Parliament, the Council of the EU and the European Commission on decentralised agencies' (19 July 2012)

[228] Different typologies of EU agencies have been developed, see: e.g. Geradin and Petit, 'The development of agencies at EU and national levels: conceptual analysis and proposals for reform' (2004) Jean Monnet Working Paper No 01/04.

grant marketing authorizations for pharmaceuticals. All applications under the 'centralized procedure' (which essentially covers most categories of novel pharmaceuticals) are processed by the EMA. Although the Commission formally takes the final and binding decision on marketing authorizations, the EMA takes some binding decisions that affect third parties, for instance, waivers from the obligation to produce certain information for paediatric medicines.[229] The EFSA supports the European Commission in its food regulation role. The EFSA provides technical scientific advice to the Commission, directly assisting it in internal market decision-making, by carrying out risk and safety assessments. Even more so than EMA, the EFSA works with national food safety agencies, coordinating their efforts and communicating to consumers across the EU.[230] Through their interactions with internal market law, and in determining what products are deemed sufficiently safe to reach the EU market, these agencies have considerable *indirect* effects on national health systems.[231] The decisions of the EMA cannot, however, affect the core powers of national authorities, for instance, to set prices of pharmaceuticals within their national health systems, or to determine which therapeutic indications or pack sizes are covered by those systems.[232] And even the EU food market is not a true single market, with EU-wide health-based determinations of food marketing regulations.[233] The effects on national health law of the ECDC, which gathers, analyses and forwards information on communicable diseases to relevant EU and national institutions, have been even more muted.[234]

Rather different from these regulatory agencies, the Executive Agency for Health and Consumers manages the EU's multi-annual public health programmes; and the European Research Council and the Research Executive Agency manage the EU's 'Framework Programmes', which, as we have seen, support health research. These agencies are covered by a legal framework[235] which is different from that which applies to regulatory agencies. They are charged with implementing and managing any EU activity, set of activities or other initiative, where the Commission is required to benefit one or more categories of specific persons, by committing expenditure.[236]

Finally, we should mention some of the other bodies which may influence the ways in which EU health law is made.[237] These include the Experts Group

---

[229] See: Regulation 726/2004/EC [2004] OJ L136/1, Article 57 (1) (t); Regulation 1901/2006/EC [2006] OJ L378/1, Article 7.
[230] See further: Vos and Wendler, *Food Safety Regulation in Europe* (Intersentia 2006).
[231] For further discussion, see Permanand and Vos, 'EU regulatory agencies and health protection' in Mossialos et al., above n 9.
[232] Regulation 726/2004/EC [2004] OJ L136/1, Article 1.
[233] See: Permanand and Vos, in Mossialos et al., above n 9, 163.
[234] Greer, 'Catch Me If You Can: Communicable Disease Control' in Greer and Kurzer (eds), above n 9.
[235] Regulation 58/2003/EC [2003] OJ L11/1.
[236] Regulation 58/2003/EC [2003] OJ L11/1, Article 2 (b).
[237] See further: Greer and Vanhercke, 'The hard politics of soft law: the case of health' in Mossialos et al., above n 9; Greer (2009), above n 97.

on Health Information, successor to the High Level Group on Health Services and Medical Care, which brings health expertise from the Member States into the cooperation between DG SANCO and the Council on health matters. The Social Protection Committee was the hub for the health Open Method of Coordination, which brought together the work of various EU working groups, as well as work done by the OECD and WHO, on comparative health indicators. Now, under 'Europe 2020', healthcare is subsumed within the 'European Platform Against Poverty',[238] which is thus far untested in terms of its ability to make concrete changes. Similar scepticism surrounds the 'Platform on Diet, Nutrition, and Physical Activity', a forum that brings together governments, firms and NGOs to discuss food policy objectives, but that does not result in any enforceable commitments being made, although may feed into the legislative process.[239] Finally, the European Group on Ethics in Science and New Technologies (EGE) is mandated to provide multidisciplinary advice to EU decision-makers on the ethical dimensions of new technologies, many of which have health implications.[240]

We conclude with three further observations which enhance our understanding of how EU health law works in practice. First, of course, the formal legal procedures outlined above should be understood within their political contexts. Many of the interactions in practice between the EU institutions take place on the basis of inter-institutional agreements.[241] Consensus is the preferred mode of operation for the EU institutions, and they rarely operate through oppositional modes of interaction. So, for instance, formally speaking, the 'constitutional' Treaty provisions are primary EU law, and therefore the CJEU has the power to strike down any EU legislation that is inconsistent with the Treaty. It has done so in some health contexts, most notably in striking down the first Tobacco Advertising Directive.[242] However, in practice, the CJEU tends to avoid interpreting EU law in such a way as to create a conflict between Treaties and EU legislation. This was the case, for instance, in *Inizan*,[243] concerning a French patient who sought multidisciplinary pain treatment at a German clinic. A question arose as to whether the system of national authorization for cross-border health care, set up by EU legislation dating from the 1970s, was a 'restriction' on free movement of services and thus contrary to the Treaty

---

[238] See: Marlier and Natali (eds) with van Dam, *Europe 2020: Towards a More Social EU?* (PIE Peter Lang 2010).

[239] The ill-fated proposal for a 'traffic light' system in EU food labelling law is an example, see further chapter 15.

[240] For further discussion, see: Busby, et al., 'Ethical EU law?: The influence of the European Group on Ethics in Science and New Technologies' (2008) 33 *European Law Review* 803; Plomer, 'The European Group on Ethics: Law, Politics and the Limits of Moral Integration in Europe' (2008) 14 *European Law Journal* 839.

[241] The EU budget, for instance, is the subject of an inter-institutional agreement, see further: Commission, 'Financial Programming and Budget: Interinstitutional agreements' (*Commission*, 14 November 2013).

[242] *TAD* EU:C:2000:544; *Arnold André* EU:C:2004:800.   [243] *Inizan*, C-56/01, EU:C:2003:578.

rules. The CJEU held that both the legislation *and* the Treaty provisions were vectors of integration and thus should be interpreted as compatible with one another. This particular line of argument in the judgment originated from the Commission's DG Employment and Social Affairs.

Second, in understanding how EU health law works, it is helpful to consider how the EU institutions interface and interact with national institutions. The European Parliament and Commission have developed relationships with national and regional health administrations in the Member States. There is also clear evidence of interactions with industry actors, such as those in the tobacco, food and alcohol industries. The notion of the EU as a 'multilevel' legal system has been used to describe this feature of EU law.

Third, most of the literature agrees that interactions between 'hard' and 'softer' law, and 'hybrid' arrangements where law and governance are intertwined, are the most appropriate way of understanding EU (health) law. While some see litigation as essentially driving the process of EU law making,[244] in general legal scholars who study EU law in context agree that *interactions* between litigation, legislation and softer modes of governance are the key to understanding how EU law is made.[245] Softer modes of governance include steering by providing incentives for certain activities or behaviours: the measures by which such incentives may be lawfully provided by the EU are themselves legally determined, and thus form part of EU health law. Studies of EU health law that consider these interactions and hybrids have been published since at least the mid-2000s.[246]

Conclusions

Writing in 2010, Hervey and Vanhercke conceptualized the EU's effects on healthcare using the metaphor of a 'patchwork'.[247] The EU has had, and still largely has, a limited formal competence in the field of health. Because its explicit competences are still largely based on public health, the EU's formal legal powers are especially limited in the field of health care. Yet, since the very beginnings of what is now the EU, other areas of EU law have had unintended

---

[244] Keleman, above n 190.

[245] Kilpatrick, 'Internal market architecture and the accommodation of labour rights' in Syrpis (ed), above n 217.

[246] Hervey and McHale, above n 9; Hervey, 'The European Union and the governance of health care' in de Búrca and Scott, (2006) above n 109; Hervey and Trubek, 'Freedom to provide health care services within the EU: An opportunity for Hybrid Governance' (2007) 13(3) *Columbia Journal of European Law* 623; Trubek, Nance and Hervey, 'The Construction of a Healthier Europe: Lessons from the Fight Against Cancer' (2008) 26 *Wisconsin International Journal* 804; Greer and Vanhercke, 'The hard politics of soft law: the case of health' in Mossialos et al., above n 9; Mossialos et al., 'Health Systems Governance in Europe: the role of EU law and policy' in Mossialos et al., above n 9; De Ruijter and Hervey 'Healthcare and the Lisbon Agenda' in Copeland and Papadimitriou, above n 111.

[247] Hervey and Vanhercke, above n 113.

effects in health care contexts. These effects were characterized by their lack of connection or legal coherence.

Our argument in this chapter has been that, since at least the early 1990s, the EU has responded to these unintended consequences in ways that conceptualize health, and health care, as central, rather than incidental or peripheral. It is true that, because the EU has no explicit formal powers to develop its own health care law, these provisions constitutionally 'belong' to different legal or policy domains: the internal market, public health, social affairs, enterprise and economic policy, external trade, and so on. But for the purposes of this book we take the position that these aspects of EU law (those based on its public health competence and those based on other competences, but with health as their central concern) have, over time, sufficiently coalesced to become a sufficiently coherent entity for study: EU health law. The remainder of the book is concerned with EU health law: its themes and its implications.

Part II
EU internal health law: the individual focus

Introduction

In chapter 2, we saw how health law has evolved from the criminal law and civil law, which determine individual legal responsibility in health settings. One of the key tasks of health law is to determine the liabilities of individual health care professionals, where medical treatment goes wrong. Initially, health care professionals were regulated through the criminal law, but the rise of civil malpractice litigation led to the emergence of 'medical law', as being centrally concerned with the relationship between an individual doctor and her patient. More recently, criminal law liability is making something of a comeback in health contexts. The Poly Implant Prothèse case, with which we began the book, is one example.

In addition, we saw that health law is also focused on certain individual human rights. These are usually said to include respect for human dignity, respect for autonomy, respect for bodily integrity, consent, confidentiality and privacy. How health law promotes respect for autonomy, and rules on consent to treatment in particular, resonates strongly with notions of patient choice. Health law is thus concerned with guaranteeing individual choice in health care settings. Health lawyers are also interested in the limitations of individual human rights in health contexts: in practice, in situations where two people have competing human rights claims in a health context, where does one person's right begin and another's end?

The institutional aspects of relationships between health care professionals and their patients, and the legal duties and powers of health care institutions, are also part of the discipline. Alongside the emergence of public health law, which has a longer pedigree, they claimed the attention of health lawyers in European Union Member States from the late 1990s onwards. But, in general, for health law, the individual (patient, health care professional) came first.

We therefore begin our substantive analysis looking at the EU's internal health law (that is, the ways in which EU health law applies within the EU and its Member States) from an individual perspective. Here, our central focus is on two of our main themes: consumerism and (human) rights. As we said in the introduction, we are interested in the extent to which EU law treats health products and services as essentially the same as other consumer products or services available on the EU market. To the extent that this is the case, we wish to explore the implications: for patients and for health care professionals. We are also interested in the question of how EU health law treats human rights. To the extent that health rights are human rights, how, if at all, does EU health law reflect that, and what are the implications?

Of course, implications for patients and health care professionals cannot really be separated from implications for health care institutions and health care systems. And, equally, internal EU health law cannot really be separated from external EU health law (how EU health law applies outside the EU's borders). Their separation here is purely for practical purposes, to sharpen the analytical focus. We explore the systemic implications of EU health law (including its focus on consumerism and (human) rights), and both individual and systemic implications of external EU health law, in Parts III and IV.

4

Consumerism: the moving patient

Introduction

To what extent does EU health law understand patients, and their relationships with health care professionals, through the lens of consumerism? Of course, exploring the idea that the EU might be a driver in a process of 'consumerization' of health care relationships does not preclude the idea that any such move to consumerism may also emanate from other processes. These might include, for instance, the increased availability of medicines over the counter, or via the internet; the rise of 'complementary and alternative' medicines and therapies; or the increased blurring of boundaries between 'therapeutic' health care (associated with national (social insurance) health systems), and 'non-therapeutic' (private) health care.[1]

However, our focus here is on the themes of EU health law, and their implications. The claim that, in holding that EU law applies to health care products and services, the Court of Justice of the European Union (and perhaps also other EU institutions) conceptualizes health care as a consumer service, has been made both by the health policy community and in academic contexts,[2] including by us in 2004.[3] Given the historical context of health care provision within the EU's Member States, which is based on solidarity and social citizenship, this claim is controversial. The idea that EU law moves European societies away

---

[1] See: e.g. Brazier and Cave, *Medicine, Patients and the Law* (Penguin 2011) 277-279; Montgomery, *Health Care Law* (OUP, 2002), ch 9; Jackson, *Law and the Regulation of Medicines* (Hart 2012).

[2] See: e.g. Hancher and Sauter, *EU Competition and Internal Market Law in the Healthcare Sector* (OUP 2012) 53-83, but see 133-137; Gekiere, Baeten and Palm, 'Free movement of services in the EU and health care' in Mossialos et al. (eds), *Health Systems Governance in Europe: The Role of European Union Law and Policy* (CUP 2010); Hartlev, 'Diversity and Harmonisation. Trends and Challenges in European Health Law' (2010) 17(1) *European Journal of Health Law* 37; Newdick, 'The European Court of Justice, Transnational Health Care, and Social Citizenship – Accidental Death of a Concept?' (2009) 26 Wisconsin International Law Journal 845; Newdick, 'Preserving Social Citizenship in Health Care Markets – There May be Trouble Ahead', (2008) 2 McGill Journal of Law and Health 93; Newdick, 'Citizenship, Free Movement and Health Care: Cementing Individual Rights by Corroding Social Solidarity' (2006) 43 Common Market Law Review 1645; Davies, 'The process and side-effects of harmonisation of European welfare states', (2006) Jean Monnet Working Paper 2/06.

[3] Hervey and McHale, *Health Law and the European Union* (CUP 2004) 393-4.

from solidarity and social citizenship, towards markets, is a variant of a more general strand of EU legal scholarship, which draws inter alia on Polanyi.[4] Its underlying basis is the view that EU law inverts the relationships between market and society. EU law sees social relations as embedded within the economic system, rather than vice versa, and consequently sees relationships in society as essentially based on contract.[5] To return to our context, in so doing, the CJEU has reframed[6] patients as consumers of health care within a market or markets.

What do we mean by 'consumerism' in this context? As we noted above, others in the EU health law field have also considered this question. Like them, by consumerism, we mean conceptualizing and organizing health systems and health care settings through a lens of a relationship between a consumer of a service (e.g., health care, medical treatment, medical advice) or a product (e.g., pharmaceuticals, medical devices) and the provider of that service or product. The focus in this chapter is principally the connections between patients and health care professionals. Our broader enquiry also includes the nexus between patients, health care professionals and health care systems more generally.[7] Consumerism assumes that relationships are defined essentially through contract.[8] This idea resonates well with the underlying ideas of EU internal market law concerning the benefits of free trade within the EU's single internal market.[9] The assumption is that the products and services of health care are essentially to be treated the same way as any other commodity that is being lawfully sold to consumers within the EU.

The consumerist frame is not, however, based on unrestricted freedom to trade or freedom of contract, as it also includes the idea that one party to the contract (the consumer) is in a position of lesser power (perhaps through having less complete information, for instance, with respect to risks and benefits arising from a product or service) than the other party.[10] Nevertheless, although regulatory interventions are considered necessary within a consumerist frame, they are justified by the need to correct the market externalities that arise from the imbalance of power between the parties in contracting for sale of a commodity or service. They are not justified by models of solidarity,[11] according to which some

---

[4] Polanyi, *The Great Transformation: The Political and Economic Origins of our Time* (republished, 2nd edn, Beacon Press 2002).

[5] See: Chalmers et al., *European Union Law* (CUP 2014) 832-33.

[6] The idea that the way in which the law 'frames' or 'conceptualises' something is crucial to the way in which it operates is familiar in legal sociology and policy studies. See: e.g. Hajer and Laws 'Ordering Through Discourse' in Moran et al. (eds), *Oxford Handbook of Public Policy* (OUP 2006).

[7] See chapters 9, 10 and 11, where we look at those relationships through the lens of solidarity, equality and competition.

[8] See: e.g. Howells and Weatherill, *Consumer Protection Law* (2nd edn, Ashgate 2005), ch 1.

[9] See: e.g. Barnard, *The Substantive Law of the European Union: The Four Freedoms* (OUP 2010) 3-8; Barnard and Scott, *The Law of the Single European Market: Unpacking the Premises* (Hart 2002).

[10] See: e.g. Howells and Weatherill, above n 8, ch 1, and 108-118.

[11] See: Baldwin, *The Politics of Social Solidarity: Class Bases of the European Welfare State 1875-1975* (CUP 1992); Stjernø, *Solidarity in Europe: The History of an Idea* (CUP 2009). On

public goods (such as health care) are subject to and organized through redistribution of resources (between generations, between classes, between regions), and access to the resource is determined by some criterion (for instance, medical need) other than ability and willingness to enter into a contractual relationship for the commodity or service. Thus, a consumerist frame, although to some extent relied upon within the health care system of every Member State of the EU, stands in stark opposition to the predominant frame of all European health care systems, which are organized on the basis of solidarity, in terms of resourcing; and equality of access according to medical need, in terms of distribution.[12]

To explore this question, this chapter considers the first of two examples, both from the perspective of the patient. This first example concerns situations where patients use EU free movement law as recipients of services, where the patient himself[13] moves to another Member State to receive a medical treatment or other health care service and seeks reimbursement from the national health (insurance) system of his own Member State. The following chapter turns to a second example, with a longer history, but lower profile, where patients use EU free movement law as recipients of goods and services, by the good or service itself moving between Member States. The implications of this body of law are changing, as the use of electronic communications in health care delivery is increasing.

Moving patients as recipients of services in EU law

Quite possibly the best-known part of EU health law is that on free movement of patients, beginning with the *Kohll/Decker* litigation,[14] and, in the *Watts* case,[15] applied to national health systems funded largely by taxation (rather than social insurance) with most health care treatment free at the point of receipt. The

---

the roles of 'solidarity' in EU law, see: Ross, 'The Value of Solidarity in European Public Services Law' in Krajewski, Neergaard and Van de Gronden (eds), *The Changing Legal Framework for Services of General Interest in Europe* (TMC Asser Press 2009); Ross, 'Promoting Solidarity: From Public Services to a European Model of Competition' (2007) 44 *Common Market Law Review* 1057; Boeger, 'Solidarity and EC competition law' (2007) *32 European Law Review* 319. For further discussion of solidarity, see chapters 9, 10 and 11.

[12] Of course, there are significant differences in the detail in terms of how health care systems are organised in the EU Member States. For an overview, see the introduction to Part III; Hervey, 'If only it were so simple: Public Health Services and EU Law' in Cremona (ed), *Market Integration and Public Services in the EU* (OUP 2011). Although now somewhat dated, information on the Member States' health care systems is available in the documentation for the health care Open Method of Coordination (OMC), and in the healthcare strands of the OMC on social protection and social inclusion. The relevant National Preliminary Reports, National Action Plans and National Strategy Reports can be found via the document database here: There is also rich data in the European Observatory on Health Care Systems, 'Health Care Systems in Transition Studies' (*WHO*, various dates).

[13] In this book, we use 'he' to refer to a patient or consumer, and 'she' to refer to a health professional.

[14] *Decker*, C-120/95, EU:C:1998:167; *Kohll*, C-158/96, EU:C:1998:171.

[15] *Watts*, C-372/04, EU:C:2006:325.

application of this body of EU law to patients is based on a consumerist frame – in order successfully to rely on the law, the patient must cast his relationship with the health care system(s) at issue as that of recipient of a service from a provider, for remuneration. The fact that the Court of Justice of the EU has been willing to support such an approach in its case law in itself suggests that consumerism is one of the themes of European health law. But how significant is the role of consumerism in this context? And what are the implications for patients? We explore those questions through a close analysis of relevant EU law. We begin with the general EU Treaty law on restrictions on freedom to receive services within the internal market and its interfaces with EU legislation on coordination of national social security schemes. We then examine decisions of the CJEU on free movement of patients since 2010; the 2011 Patients' Rights Directive;[16] the law on 'objective public interest justifications', which are an exception to free movement law; and the application of EU free movement law to matters of ethical sensitivity.

Restrictions on freedom to receive services and the interface with social security coordination

The underlying legal principles of the CJEU's case law on free movement of patients were established in mostly relatively uncontroversial cases, many not involving health services at all, and some involving privately remunerated health care, taking place outside of national health care (insurance) systems. The legal starting point is Article 56 TFEU, which provides, pithily, that 'restrictions on freedom to provide services within the Union shall be prohibited'. The CJEU has interpreted this provision to establish a consumer-based right for individuals to travel to another Member State to *receive* services.[17] A 'service' must be provided for remuneration, and privately remunerated health services fall within the Treaty provisions on freedom to provide services.[18] However, remuneration need not come directly from the recipient of the services.[19] Article 56 TFEU

---

[16]   Directive 2011/24/EU [2011] OJ L88/45. On the implementation of the Directive, see special edition of the European Journal of Health Law , volume 21(1) 2014; Sindbjerg Martinsen and Vollaard, 'Bounded Rationality in Transition Processes: The Case of the European Patients' Rights Directive' (2014) 37(4) *West European Politics* 711; Zanon, 'Healthcare across borders: Implications of the Directive on crossborder health care for the English NHS' (2011) 17(2-3) *Eurohealth* 34.

[17]   *Cowan*, C-186/87, EU:C:1989:47, paragraph 16; *Eurowings*, C-294/97, EU:C:1999:524, paragraphs 33 and 34; *Gambelli*, C-243/01, EU:C:2003:597, paragraph 55; *Commission v Spain*, C-211/08, EU:C:2010:340, paragraph 49.

[18]   See: *Luisi and Carbone*, C-286/82 and 26/83, EU:C:1984:35, paragraph 16; *SPUC* v *Grogan*, C-159/90, EU:C:1991:378, paragraph 18. On the growing market for cross border private health services, especially in areas of fertility treatment, as well as experimental treatments of various sorts, both within the EU and globally, see: Cortez, 'Patients Without Borders: The Emerging Global Market for Patients and the Evolution of Modern Health Care' (2008) 83 *Indiana Law Journal* 71.

[19]   *Bond van Adverteerders*, C-352/85, EU:C:1988:196.

applies to publicly funded health care services if there is an element of choice, either for the service recipient, or for the body paying for the service, or for both.[20] Later cases established that the way in which the relevant health care system is organized (even where it involves a monopoly state provider of free-to-recipients health care, either funded as a national health service through taxation or through social insurance) is not relevant: what matters is whether the transaction in the Member State where the patient receives the treatment is based on remuneration.[21] But the CJEU's pre-*Kohll* jurisprudence already established that there is no *general* exclusion for health care (or other welfare) services from Article 56 TFEU.[22] Furthermore, the CJEU determined that the term 'restriction' in Article 56 TFEU includes any measure that actually or even potentially inhibits provision of services between Member States,[23] a wide definition that could potentially catch many arrangements of national health care systems.[24]

As we have already noted, this pre-existing case law meant that the ruling in *Kohll*[25] to the effect that health care paid for by a national sickness insurance fund could fall within the Treaty concept of services was totally uncontroversial from the point of view of EU law. From the point of view of the health care community, however, it was highly controversial.[26] The *Kohll* case applied Article 56

---

[20] Contrast the Court's ruling in the field of education in: *Belgian State* v *Humbel*, C-263/86, EU:C:1988:451; see also the Opinion of the Advocate General in *Gravier*, C-293/83, EU:C:1985:15.

[21] *Watts* EU:C:2006:325, paragraph 90. See: Sokol, 'Rindal and Elchinov: A(n) (Impending) Revolution in EU Law on Patient Mobility' (2010) 6(6) *Croatian Yearbook for European Law and Policy* 167; Van de Gronden, 'Cross-Border Health Care in the EU and the Organization of the National Health Care Systems of the Member States: The Dynamics Resulting from the European Court of Justice's Decisions on Free Movement and Competition Law' (2009) 26 *Wisconsin International Law Journal* 705.

[22] See: e.g. *Sodemare*, C-70/95, EU:C:1997:301 applying both Article 56 and Article 49 TFEU in the context of a care home for the elderly.

[23] *Cowan* EU:C:1989:47, paragraphs 15–17; *Säger*, C-76/90, EU:C:1991:331, paragraph 12; *Vander Elst*, C-43/93, EU:C:1994:310, paragraph 14; *Guiot and Climatec*, C-272/94, EU:C:1996:147, paragraph 10.

[24] See: Gekiere, Baeten and Palm, 'Free Movement of Health Services in the EU and Health Care' in Mossialos et al., above n 2; Hancher and Sauter, above n 2, 82–83.

[25] *Kohll* EU:C:1998:171.

[26] For discussion see: e.g. Van der Mei, 'Cross-Border Access to Medical Care within the European Union – Some Reflections on the Judgments in *Decker* and *Kohll*' (1998) 5 *Maastricht Journal of European and Comparative Law* 277; Bayens, 'Free movement of goods and services in health care: a comment on the Court cases *Decker* and *Kohll* from a Belgian point of view' (1999) 6 *European Journal of Health Law* 373; Editorial, 'Public Health Insurance and Freedom of Movement within the European Union' (1999) 6 *European Journal of Health Law* 1; Cabral, 'Cross-border medical care in the European Union – bringing down a first wall' (1999) 24 *European Law Review* 387; Nickless, 'The internal market and the social nature of health care' in McKee, Mossialos and Baeten (eds.), *The Impact of EU law on Health Care Systems* (PIE-Peter Lang 2003); Glinos and Baeten, 'A Literature Review of Cross-Border Patient Mobility in the European Union' (Observatoire social européen 2006); Sieveking, 'ECJ rulings on health care services and their effects on the freedom of crossborder patient mobility in the EU' (2007) 9(1) *European Journal of Migration and Law* 25; Obermeier, *The End of*

TFEU to a Member State where health care is financed largely through a social insurance model, operating on the basis of cash benefits in the form of refunds for medical treatment received. This principle was extended in *Vanbraekel*[27] and *Geraets-Smits*[28] to Member States that operate a benefits-in-kind social insurance system and extended further in *Watts*[29] and *Stametelaki*[30] to national health systems financed largely by public taxation, where, after paying the foreign health care provider for treatment, the patient subsequently seeks reimbursement from the home system.[31] The application of the principle in the context of a home (paying) Member State which, given the relative levels of development of the two Member States, is able to invest significantly less in its national health care system than the Member State where the treatment takes place was confirmed in *Elchinov*.[32] The principle was extended from care provided outside a hospital situation (*Kohll*) to hospital care in *Geraets-Smits/Peerbooms*,[33] although the Member State may more easily justify restrictions on free movement of services in such a case (see below).

In this case law, the CJEU has had to grapple with the relationship between the rights to free movement in Article 56 TFEU and the EU's long-standing legislative arrangements for coordination of social security systems between the Member States. This legislation includes entitlements to 'sickness insurance'

Territoriality? The Impact of ECJ rulings on British, German and French social policy (Ashgate 2009); Greer, 'Ever Closer Union: Devolution, the EU and Social Citizenship Rights' in Greer (ed), *Devolution and Social Citizenship in the United Kingdom* (Policy Press 2009); Newdick, 'The European Court of Justice, Transnational Health Care, and Social Citizenship – Accidental Death of a Concept?' (2009) 26 *Wisconsin International Law Journal* 845; Gekiere, Baeten, Palm, 'Free Movement of Health Services in the EU and Health Care' in Mossialos et al. (eds), (CUP 2010) above n 2; Zanon, above n 16; Cruz, 'The Case Law of the ECJ on the Mobility of Patients: An Assessment' Pennings, 'The Draft Patient Mobility Directive and the Coordination Regulations of Social Security' both in Van de Gronden, Szyszczak, Neergaard and Krajewski (eds), *Healthcare and EU Law* (Springer 2011); Hancher and Sauter, *EU Competition and Internal Market Law in the Healthcare Sector* (OUP 2012) 60-83; Greer and Sokol, 'Rules for Rights: European Law, Health Care and Social Citizenship' (2014) 20(1) *European Law Journal* 66; Sindbjerg Martinsen and Vollaard, 'Implementing Social Europe in Times of Crises: Re-established Boundaries of Welfare' (2014) 37(4) *West European Politics* 677; Sindbjerg Martinsen and Vollaard, 'Bounded Rationality in Transition Processes: The Case of the European Patients' Rights Directive' (2014) 37(4) *West European Politics* 711.

[27] *Vanbraekel*, C-368/98, EU:C:2001:400.

[28] *Geraets-Smits/Peerbooms*, C-157/99, EU:C:2001:404.

[29] *Watts* EU:C:2006:325.   [30] *Stamatelaki*, C-444/05, EU:C:2007:231.

[31] Note, however, that in those cases, the Court was not required to answer the specific question whether hospital treatment provided by a national health system funded largely by taxation constitutes a service in the sense of Article 56 TFEU, because, in those cases, the patients themselves had directly remunerated a hospital in another Member State which provided the health service at issue.

[32] Involving a Bulgarian national having received advanced treatment in a specialist German clinic; *Elchinov*, C-173/09, EU:C:2010:581.

[33] *Geraets-Smits/Peerbooms* EU:C:2001:404; confirmed in *Müller-Fauré/Van Riet*, C–385/99, EU:C:2003:270. For discussion see: Flear, 'Annotation of Case C–385/99 *Müller-Fauré*' (2004) 41 *Common Market Law Review* 209; Davies, 'Health and Efficiency: Community Law and National Health Systems in the Light of *Müller-Fauré*' (2004) 67 *Modern Law Review* 94.

for people moving between Member States in the EU, now found in Regulation 883/2004/EC.[34] Because of the constitutional position of Article 56 TFEU in EU law, the CJEU has, at least in the past, effectively bypassed, and thus rendered increasingly unsatisfactory, this legislative settlement,[35] although on its face the CJEU's jurisprudence finds no clash or contradiction between the two legal provisions.[36] With the exception of emergency medical treatment,[37] Regulation 883/2004/EC, and its predecessor, Regulation 1408/71/EEC,[38] envisage Member States *authorizing* the patients for whom they are responsible to receive health care or medical treatment in another Member State, in advance of the medical treatment taking place.[39] The legislation envisages the only exception to this 'home Member State control' as the situation where the treatment (a) is covered by the health (insurance) system in the home Member State; and (b) cannot be given to the patient within a 'treatment time limit which is medically justifiable' in the home Member State – taking into account the patient's 'current state of health and the probable course of his/her illness'.[40]

However, because of the very wide definition of 'restriction' in Article 56 TFEU as essentially precluding 'the application of any national rules which have the effect of making the provision of services between Member States more difficult than the provision of services purely within a Member State',[41] prior authorization rules under Regulation 883/2004/EC may *themselves* constitute 'restrictions' on free movement of services, wherever such a system of prior authorization 'prevents or deters' patients from seeking health care from

---

[34] Regulation 883/2004/EC [2004] OJ L166/1. For a corrected version of the text, see: Corrigendum to Regulation 883/2004/EC [2004] OJ L200/1. This Regulation replaced Regulation 1408/71/EEC [1971] OJ L149/2, and entered into force on 1 May 2010.

[35] The EU legislation has responded with Directive 2011/24/EU [2011] OJ L88/45, discussed below.

[36] *Inizan,* C-56/01, EU:C:2003:578, paragraphs 21, 22 and 25; *von Chamier-Glisczinski,* C-208/07, EU:C:2009:455, paragraphs 64, 66 and 85; *Commission v Spain* EU:C:2010:340, paragraph 45; *Social Care Equipment,* C-562/10, EU:C:2012:442. See: Hervey, (2011) above n 12.

[37] Regulation 883/2004/EC [2004] OJ L166/1, Article 19. In determining whether the healthcare or medical treatment has become necessary on medical grounds during a stay in another Member State, account must be taken of the nature of the health care or medical treatment and the expected length of the stay.

[38] Regulation 1408/71/EEC, above n 34.

[39] Regulation 883/2004/EC, above n 34, Article 20. Some Member States, such as Luxembourg and Malta, use the ability to authorize treatment in other Member States relatively often; others, such as the UK, hardly at all. See: Palm and Glinos, 'Enabling patient mobility in the European Union: between free movement and coordination' in Mossialos et al., above n 2; Muscat, Grech, Cachia, and Xuereb, 'Sharing capacities— Malta and the United Kingdom' in Rosenmöller, McKee, and Baeten (eds), *Patient Mobility In The European Union—Learning From Experience* (European Observatory on Health Systems and Policies 2006) 119–136.

[40] Regulation 883/2004/EC, above n 34, Article 20(2). The 'home' Member State retains control over further referral to a third state, see: *Keller,* C-145/03, EU:C:2005:211.

[41] *Stamatelaki* EU:C:2007:231, paragraph 25. See also: *Commission* v *France,* C-381/93, EU:C:1994:370, paragraph 17; *Kohll* EU:C:1998:171, paragraph 33; *Vanbraekel* EU:C:2001:400, paragraph 45; *Geraets-Smits/Peerbooms* EU:C:2001:404, paragraph 61; *Watts* EU:C:2006:325, paragraph 94.

providers in other Member States.[42] If authorization is granted only where the treatment is 'normal within the professional circles concerned' in the home Member State, and the treatment is a 'medical necessity',[43] this constitutes a 'restriction' in the sense of Article 56 TFEU.[44] The proper interpretation of Regulation 883/2004/EC, Article 22 (2) requires national authorities to consider whether a treatment method available in another Member State 'corresponds to benefits provided for' by the legislation of the home Member State.[45] If it does, then prior authorization rules that refuse to reimburse a treatment carried out in another Member State, on the grounds that that treatment is not available in the home Member State, breach EU law. Where a patient would receive a lower level of cover under the prior authorization rules where scheduled treatment[46] is received in another Member State from the 'home' Member State,[47] this also constitutes a 'restriction' under Article 56 TFEU,[48] although a patient may not make a profit from the application of this rule.[49]

Other 'restrictions' include a rule, applicable only where the health care is sought abroad, making reimbursement for travel, board and lodging[50] conditional on a health care professional finding that the treatment is 'absolutely necessary owing to the greatly increased prospects of success outside the

---

[42] *Leichtle,* C-8/02, EU:C:2004:161, paragraph 30; *Watts* EU:C:2006:325, paragraphs 95-98; *Elchinov* EU:C:2010:581, paragraph 49; *Major Medical Equipment,* C-512/08, EU:C:2010:579 *Petru* C-268/13 EU:C:2014:2271. Greer and Sokol have described the set of legal principles by which the CJEU – and implicitly national courts applying EU law – judge national administrative decisions in health care settings as 'rules for rights'; see Greer and Sokol, 'Rules for Rights: European Law, Health Care and Social Citizenship' (2014) 20(1) *European Law Journal* 66.

[43] Meaning that adequate treatment cannot be obtained without undue delay in hospitals in the home Member State that have a contractual relationship with the sickness fund.

[44] *Geraets-Smits/Peerbooms* EU:C:2001:404, paragraphs 60-69; *Müller-Fauré/Van Riet* EU:C:2003:270, paragraphs 37-44. For discussion, see: Flear, above n 33; Davies, 'Health and Efficiency: Community Law and National Health Systems in the Light of *Müller-Fauré*' (2004) 67 *Modern Law Review* 94.

[45] *Elchinov* EU:C:2010:581, paragraph 62 *Petru* EU:C:2014:2271, paragraph 30.

[46] Where the treatment sought is provided for under the patient's home legislation and the treatment is not available for that patient—in terms of their current state of health—within the time regarded as medically justifiable for obtaining that treatment in their home Member State, Regulation 883/2004/EC, above n 34, Article 20 (2).

[47] Usually, the Member State in which the patient is socially insured, see Regulation 883/2004/EC, above n 34, Article 1 (s) and (q).

[48] *Vanbraekel* EU:C:2001:400, paragraphs 38-53; *Commission v Spain* EU:C:2010:340, paragraphs 56-57; *Elchinov* EU:C:2010:581, paragraph 78.

[49] Where cross-border health care is received under Article 56 TFEU, and the patient seeks cross-border health care without seeking prior authorisation, the reference point for determining the amount to be reimbursed is that of the home Member State: *Müller-Fauré/Van Riet* EU:C:2003:270. But the patient is entitled only to the amount which would have been reimbursed had the treatment been provided in the home Member State and within the limits of the actual costs incurred in the Member State where the treatment is given; see: *Watts* EU:C:2006:325, paragraphs 131 and 143; and Opinion of Advocate General in *Watts,* C-372/04, EU:C:2005:784, paragraphs 106 to 119.

[50] Board and lodging constituting part of the healthcare itself, see: *Leichtle* EU:C:2004:161, paragraph 43. See also: *Herrera,* C-466/04, EU:C:2006:405.

home State'.[51] If there is no need to seek prior authorization to have medical treatment in national health service hospitals, free of charge, in the home Member State, but prior authorization is needed to receive treatment from a hospital in another Member State, at the expense of the national health service, that is also a 'restriction'.[52] Similarly, an entitlement to receive emergency medical treatment in a public hospital or a private hospital located in the home Member State (whether or not that hospital has an agreement with the national health system) without paying at the time; whereas emergency treatment in a private hospital in another Member State must be paid for by the patient himself at the point of receipt, is also a 'restriction'.[53] The CJEU has yet to rule on whether a rule prohibiting reimbursement of treatment in a private healthcare provider in another Member State is a 'restriction'.[54] Also, a national rule preventing reimbursement of costs of medical laboratory analyses and tests where these are carried out in another Member State, by operating a system only of direct billing of costs to sickness insurance funds, rather than reimbursement of patients, constitutes a 'restriction'.[55]

All of these rulings, through their very generous interpretation of the rights of service recipients in EU internal market law, to include patients crossing EU borders to consume health care services, have the potential to force the replacement of the solidarity-based provision of health care with a consumer-based provision. This potential effect has implications for the question of which patients are more able to access health care, and exercise choice and autonomy in that context. The ability to choose to travel to another Member State for health care privileges those patients who are able to behave as consumers of health care. Such patients are those who are able and willing to travel; those who are wealthy enough to pay for treatment in advance and to weather the time-consuming litigation that might follow if reimbursement is not granted; and those who are able to discover where more advanced treatments, or more timely treatments, are available to treat their conditions. The reason that a patient chooses to move may well be because of a dispute with the health care professionals with whom he is relating in his national (social insurance) health system, perhaps about which treatment should be made available to him, or the time frame within which it should be made available. The patient himself therefore is reframing the relationship he may have with such health care professionals, away from a more paternalistic 'doctor knows best' type of relationship, towards a position in which the patient himself becomes the expert in his own health requirements. He may also be changing his relationship with the health care system itself, be that the social insurance fund or the taxation-based NHS. In essence, he is claiming that his assessment of his medical need, coupled with his choice and

---

[51] *Leichtle* EU:C:2004:161, paragraph 41.
[52] *Watts* EU:C:2006:325, paragraphs 95–96.   [53] *Stamatelaki* EU:C:2007:231, paragraph 27.
[54] The CJEU was asked this question in *Reinke* but found there was no need to answer the question referred, see: Order in *Reinke*, C-336/08, EU:C:2010:604.
[55] *Medical Laboratory Tests*, C-490/09, EU:C:2011:34.

autonomy and ability to receive health care across borders within the EU, is of greater importance than national systemic rules which are designed to restrict such patient autonomy on the basis of the collective need to allocate scarce public resources by reference to a different value, such as medical need, as assessed by health care professionals, or systemic rules about which treatments are available, under what circumstances, and within what time frames. Patients who have these characteristics are likely to be among the better educated, more wealthy and relatively healthier patients within the EU. They are not necessarily the patients most in need of health care. They are unlikely to include among them those patients who are the most vulnerable, who are unable to travel, have no disposable income from which to pay for cross-border health care even if it were to be later reimbursed, and who have no knowledge or experience of other EU Member States. The implications of EU health law in this context are enhanced patient choice and autonomy, and a move away from notions of equal access based on (professionally determined) medical need.

In response to this CJEU case law, Member States may seek to regain control over cross-border patient movement relying on rights in EU law. As the case law has developed, Member States may do this by determining which medical treatments are covered by their national health (insurance) system. Member States may be led to define entitlements under their national systems with ever greater precision.[56] A striking example is the *Elchinov* case. If the Bulgarian state had specified the precise medical treatments to which its patients were entitled, rather than specifying only types of benefits available for the treatment of certain conditions, Mr Elchinov would not have had a basis for his claim in EU law. But the very specification of individual entitlements to particular medical treatments in itself moves national health care systems away from a model based on care determined by medical need, based on professional decisions with respect to such medical need, and towards an individual consumer model, based on ability to consume, as determined by a patient's personal desires and available resources.

But before we reach too hasty a conclusion, we must take into account four interlocking and countervailing elements of this area of EU law. These are: first, the softening of the CJEU's interpretation of 'restriction' in this context; second, the adoption of the Directive on Patients' Rights in Cross-border Health Care; third, the CJEU's jurisprudence on justifications for restrictions on free movement of services; and fourth, the extent to which the reach of the

---

[56] Greer and Sokol, above n 42. See, for instance, Spain's Royal Decree-Law 16/2012 of 20 April 2012 which provides a catalogue of basic, supplementary and accessory health services within the national health system, see: Requejo, 'Cross-border Healthcare in Spain and the Implementation of Directive 2011/24/EU on the Application of Patients' Rights in Cross-border Healthcare' (2014) 21(1) *European Journal of Health Law* 79; Finland's amended Healthcare Act (No. 1326/2010, section 7 (a)), see: Kattelus, 'Implementation of the Directive on the Application of Patients' Rights in Cross-border Healthcare (2011/24 EU) in Finland' (2014) 21(1) *European Journal of Health Law* 23.

consumerizing effects of EU law in this area extends to matters of national ethical sensitivity.

Countervailing elements of EU law

Recent cases

The CJEU's very wide interpretation of 'restriction' in its case law on free movement of patients has been tempered in cases since around 2010. A good example is Case C-211/08 *Commission* v. *Spain (Emergency Hospital Care)*.[57] There the CJEU held that, where the patient has travelled to the host Member State as a tourist or student or for some reason other than to receive health care services, reimbursement rules concerning 'unscheduled' treatment, that is, emergency care,[58] that do not guarantee that the patient receives at least the same level of reimbursement as he would have if he had received the treatment in the home Member State, do not constitute a 'restriction'.[59] This decision confines the rulings in *Vanbraekel* and *Müller-Fauré* to the application of Article 56 TFEU to reimbursement of 'scheduled' treatment in the sense of Article 20 (2) of Regulation 883/2004/EC. In other circumstances, 'the rules of the Treaty on freedom of movement offer no guarantee that all hospital treatment services which may have to be provided ... unexpectedly in the Member State of stay will be neutral in terms of cost'.[60] Here, the 'consumption' by the patient of the health care service in the host Member State is not being interpreted solely within the consumerist frame of internal market law. Rather, the CJEU is also taking into account the coordinated arrangements of national health care systems treating patients as *patients*, in need of emergency care, under Regulation 883/2004/EC. The CJEU explicitly notes that to find that the home Member State must pay for emergency care at the rate of the home Member State would 'undermine the very fabric of the system which Regulation [883/2004] sought to establish'.[61]

The decisions in *Elchinov* and *Petru* also mark the CJEU taking a different approach with respect to the relationship between Article 56 TFEU and Regulation 883/2004/EC. In both *Elchinov*[62] and *Petru*[63] the CJEU reconfirmed, that nothing in EU law requires Member States to extend the list of medical benefits that are reimbursed by their own social security system. This new approach tempers the consumerist push of Article 56 TFEU, by respecting the arrangements in Regulation 883/2004/EC which conceive of the patient as a person insured (against sickness) within their home Member State, rather than contracting

---

[57] *Commission v Spain* EU:C:2010:340.

[58] Under Regulation 883/2004/EC above n 34, Article 19

[59] *Commission v Spain* EU:C:2010:340, paragraph 72.

[60] *Commission v Spain* EU:C:2010:340, paragraph 61. See also: *Bosch*, C-193/03, EU:C:2004:630.

[61] *Commission v Spain* EU:C:2010:340, paragraph 79.   [62] *Elchinov* EU:C:2010:581.

[63] *Petru* EU:C:2014:2271 following *Geraets-Smits/Peerbooms* EU:C:2001:404, paragraph 87.

for (health care) services within any Member State. The Regulation's arrangements do not expect a single market in (health care) services, but require only the coordination of separate, nationally-based (health care) welfare systems, to the extent that this is possible, given their fundamentally territorial basis. The approach has also been echoed by the EFTA Court. In *Rindal*,[64] the EFTA Court held that, where treatment available abroad is no more medically advanced than treatment available in the home state, and the patient's medical condition does not necessitate treatment more quickly than the home state can provide, there is no entitlement in EEA law to such treatment. This approach suggests that the desires of the patient as consumer to have treatment quickly cannot be supported by EEA law, where to do so would be to undermine the home state's rationally planned health care system.[65]

However, it should be noted that, in *Rindal*, *Elchinov* and *Petru*, the courts took a different approach with respect to the situation where treatment abroad is more medically advanced than in the home Member State. In that context, if the treatment available in the other Member State is more advanced, according to the internationally accepted views of the medical profession, then 'the state may no longer justify prioritizing its own offer of treatment'[66] but must interpret its list of types of treatment appropriately, taking into account 'the available scientific data' and not simply refuse to authorize treatment on the basis that that particular treatment is not available in the home Member State.[67] Moreover, lack of medical infrastructure, medication and basic medical supplies can be a reason that authorization must be given because 'the same or equally effective treatment cannot be given in good time' in the home Member State.

Nevertheless, in *Petru*, the CJEU left the factual question of whether there was a lack of medical infrastructure to the national court, pointing out that Petru could have approached other hospitals in Romania which did have the requisite means necessary to carry out her treatment. Hence the CJEU gave a strong steer to the national court – essentially, to be successful, Petru would have to show that *no* Romanian hospital had the means necessary to carry out her treatment – a requirement that poses significant practical barriers to successful litigation. It would take a courageous national court to make such a decision in these circumstances, given the threat to the national health system that would ensue were thousands of Romanian patients in similar situations to seek expensive treatment in German and other Western European hospitals, on the basis that their local hospitals lacked appropriate infrastructure,

[64] *Rindal v Norway (E-11/07)/Slinning v Norway (E-1/08)* [2009] 3 CMLR 32 (Judgment of the EFTA Court, 19 December 2008).
[65] The CJEU rejected the Commission's claim against Germany in a case involving charging for the hire of care equipment outside of Germany, on the basis that Germany had complied with Regulation 1408/71/EEC above n 34, see: *Care Equipment* EU:C:2012:442.
[66] *Rindal v Norway*, above n 64, at [83].   [67] *Elchinov* EU:C:2010:581, paragraph 62.

pharmaceuticals and medical staff. On the other hand, the ruling does leave open the possibility that national health systems in developing, or fiscally constrained, Member States would have to either reduce the 'benefits normally provided for' under their health systems, or re-invest resources in high cost medical care, to secure against the threat of such successful litigation based on individual patient choice.

Also, in *Commission* v. *Portugal (Non-hospital Medical Care)*,[68] the CJEU considered the very restrictive conditions on which prior authorization for non-hospital health care was granted by the Portuguese health service. The Commission withdrew its claim concerning health care using specialist equipment.[69] Under the Portuguese rules, authorization was available only with a request from a hospital belonging to the national health system and a detailed medical report, approved by both the health service manager and a specialist health care professional, responsible for the final decision. This requirement was stated to be as 'an instrument for hospital management'.[70] In its defence, Portugal argued that either Regulation 1408 (the precursor to Regulation 883/2004) meant that prior authorization for cross-border health care was lawful in EU law, or in the alternative that an objective public interest was present. The former argument had already been excluded in the CJEU's earlier case law, and the CJEU was not impressed with Portugal's argument that that case law involved a different aspect of the CJEU's jurisdiction (Article 267 TFEU, rather than Article 258 TFEU). None of the possible justifications advanced by Portugal was accepted by the CJEU. Granted, Portugal failed to adduce any evidence of sufficient numbers of migrant patients to jeopardize the financial stability of its health care system, and nor was the CJEU convinced that the special nature of the Portuguese health system was a sufficient justification. Neither is surprising – they are both consistent with the earlier case law on objective public interest justifications. From these rulings, we conclude that the post-2010 rethinking of the consumerist tendencies of the CJEU's case law on free movement of patients is only partial and does not represent a complete retreat from the implications of the earlier case law.

The patients' rights directive

Second, some of the effects of EU internal market law with respect to the 'consumerization' of relationships between patients and health care systems have been tempered by the latest EU legislative intervention in the field: Directive

---

[68] *Non-hospital Medical Care*, C-255/09, EU:C:2011:695.

[69] Such as a scintillation camera, a positron emission coincidence detector, emission tomography, nuclear magnetic resonance imaging, a hyperbaric chamber, or a cyclotron, see: *Non-hospital Medical Care* EU:C:2011:695, paragraph 20.

[70] *Non-hospital Medical Care*, paragraph 28.

2011/24/EU on Patients' Rights in Cross-border Health Care.[71] The very title of this Directive (explicitly *not* a directive on freedom to provide or receive health care services in the internal market), as well as its legal basis (the dual legal basis of Articles 114 TFEU (internal market) and 168 TFEU (public health)), suggest a conceptualization that is about patients and health care rather than recipients of a service no different in any important respect to any other. The exclusion of health care services from the general Directive 2006/123/EC on services in the internal market is also consistent with this pattern.[72]

Although the 'general principle' of Directive 2011/24/EU is that the Member State of affiliation (the home Member State, in which the patient is insured/covered for national health care provision) must reimburse the costs of patients receiving cross-border health care,[73] this apparently consumerist frame, in line with the CJEU's jurisprudence discussed above, is qualified by three significant exceptions. First, the rule applies only if the treatment concerned is among the benefits to which that patient is entitled in the home Member State.[74] Thus the home Member State controls the 'basket' of health care entitlements, and the *desire* of a patient to consume health care services available in another Member State, but not the home Member State, has not been translated into a *right* embodied in EU legislation to do so. Second, the rule is subject to Regulation 883/2004/EC. Taking into account the CJEU's post-2010 case law on Regulation 883/2004/EC, such as *Elchinov*, the proper interpretation of Regulation 883/2004/EC, Article 22 (2) requires national authorities to consider whether a treatment method available in another Member State 'corresponds to benefits provided for' by the legislation of the home Member State. If it does, then prior authorization rules that refuse to reimburse a treatment carried out in another Member State, on the grounds that that treatment is not available in the home Member State, breach EU law.[75] Reasoning *a contrario*, if it does not, then there is no obligation to authorize treatment in another Member State and there will be no obligation to pay for such treatment under the Patients' Rights Directive either. Third, the rule is subject to Articles 8 and 9 of the Patients' Rights Directive.

Article 8 provides that Member States may provide for a system of prior authorization for reimbursement of the costs of cross-border health care. The provision lists the types of health care that may be subject to prior authorization.

---

[71] Directive 2011/24/EU [2011] OJ L88/45. For a general discussion of the Directive, see: Quinn and De Hert, 'The European Patients' Rights Directive: A clarification and codification of individual rights relating to cross border healthcare and novel initiatives aimed at improving pan-European healthcare cooperation' (2012) 12(1) *Medical Law International* 28; Di Federico, 'Access to Healthcare in the Post-Lisbon Era and the Genuine Enjoyment of EU Citizens' Rights' in Rossi and Casolari (eds), *The EU After Lisbon: Amending or Coping with the Existing Treaties* (Springer 2014).
[72] Directive 2006/123/EC [2006] OJ L376/36, Article 2 (2) (f).
[73] Directive 2011/24/EU, above n 71, Article 7 (1).
[74] *Ibid.*   [75] *Elchinov* EU:C:2010:581, paragraph 62 *Petru* EU:C:2014:2271, paragraph 30.

The list is inspired by the CJEU's jurisprudence,[76] but goes much further. The following types of health care may be subject to prior authorization:

(a) Health care that is 'made subject to planning requirements relating to the object of ensuring sufficient and permanent access to a balanced range of high-quality treatment in the Member State concerned or to the wish to control costs and avoid, as far as possible, any waste of financial, technical and human resources and:
   (i) involves overnight hospital accommodation of the patient in question for at least one night; or
   (ii) requires use of highly specialised and cost-intensive medical infrastructure or medical equipment;'[77]
(b) Health care that 'involves treatments presenting a particular risk for the patient or the population', or
(c) Health care that is 'provided by a healthcare provider that, on a case-by-case basis, could give rise to serious and specific concerns relating to the quality or safety of the care, with the exception of healthcare which is subject to Union legislation ensuring a minimum level of safety and quality throughout the Union'.

Member States may therefore refuse to authorize reimbursement of cross-border health care under the terms of the Directive. Again, this tempers the effect of EU law of bringing health care entitlements within a consumerist frame, as the preferences of the patient as consumer are not guaranteed to be met under the entitlements that the patients enjoys in EU law. Nevertheless, there are circumstances in which Member States must authorize cross-border treatment. These are outlined in Article 8 (5):

> when the patient is entitled to the healthcare in question in accordance with Article 7, and when this healthcare cannot be provided on its territory within a time limit which is medically justifiable, based on an objective medical assessment of the patient's medical condition, the history and probable course of the patient's illness, the degree of the patient's pain and/or the nature of the patient's disability at the time when the request for authorisation was made or renewed.

As noted above, the provision is consistent with the system under Regulation 883/2004/EC, in that it leaves the control over the 'basket' of health care entitlements with the home Member State. Moreover, the Patients' Rights Directive contains a further protection for the national health systems of home Member States. According to Article 8 (6), authorization need not be granted where:

(a) 'the patient will, according to a clinical evaluation, be exposed with reasonable certainty to a patient-safety risk that cannot be regarded as acceptable,

---

[76] See: e.g. *Geraets-Smits/Peerbooms* EU:C:2001:404; *Müller-Fauré/Van Riet* EU:C:2003:270.
[77] See also: *Major Medical Equipment* EU:C:2010:579.

taking into account the potential benefit for the patient of the sought cross-border healthcare;

(b) the general public will be exposed with reasonable certainty to a substantial safety hazard as a result of the cross-border healthcare in question;

(c) this healthcare is to be provided by a healthcare provider that raises serious and specific concerns relating to the respect of standards and guidelines on quality of care and patient safety, including provisions on supervision, whether these standards and guidelines are laid down by laws and regulations or through accreditation systems established by the Member State of treatment;

(d) this healthcare can be provided on its territory within a time limit which is medically justifiable, taking into account the current state of health and the probable course of the illness of each patient concerned'.

Again, the arrangements under the Patients' Rights Directive not only give significant control to the national health authorities in the home (paying) Member State, but they also involve a stronger degree of professional determination of what the patient's health care needs are. If health care can be given anywhere in the home Member State, within a time limit 'medically justifiable', which presumably in practice means 'justifiable by a health care professional', then again the patient's desire to receive the service more quickly, by consuming it in another Member State, is not promoted by EU law. The claim that EU law enhances patient choice, at the expense of the determinations of national health (social insurance) systems, or health care professionals, cannot be supported in its most extreme form.

Objective public interest justifications

The third major feature of this body of EU health law that tempers its consumerist tendencies is the CJEU's jurisprudence on the justification of restrictions to free movement of services within the internal market.[78] Article 56 TFEU is not and has never been a right without exceptions. Throughout the history of its case law on the internal market's 'four freedoms', the CJEU has recognized not only the explicit exemptions to those freedoms as set out in the Treaties,[79]

---

[78] For similar exemptions from or exceptions to the other free movement rules, see: Articles 36, 45 (3) and (4), 52 (1), 62 and 65 TFEU; and the jurisprudence of the CJEU on 'mandatory requirements' (see: e.g. *Cassis de Dijon*, C-120/78, EU:C:1979:42) or 'objective public interests' (see: e.g. *Van Binsbergen*, C-33/74, EU:C:1974:131; *Thieffry*, C-71/76, EU:C:1977:65; *Alpine Investments*, C-384/93, EU:C:1995:126; *Gebhard*, C-55/94, EU:C:1995:411). For further discussion, see: Scott, 'Mandatory or Imperative Requirements in the EU and the WTO' in Barnard and Scott (eds), *The Law of the Single European Market: Unpacking the Premises* (Hart 2002).

[79] Articles 36, 45 (3) and (4), 52 (1), 62 and 65 TFEU.

but also the ability of Member States to offer 'objective public interest justifications' for restrictions on free movement.[80] Such justifications must be applied in an objective, non-discriminatory manner,[81] and based on judicially reviewable criteria known in advance.[82] There must be imperative reasons relating to the public interest (mandatory requirements). The public interest must not be already protected by the state of establishment (equivalence).[83] The restriction must not be disproportionate to its ends (proportionality).[84]

The CJEU has long recognized that the social protection provided by national social security systems can be an 'objective public interest' justifying restrictions on the free movement of services.[85] In the context of cases involving patients moving to receive healthcare services, the CJEU had until 2010 in practice distinguished between 'extra-mural' and 'hospital' care. In the *Kohll* case, the CJEU found that 'reimbursement of the costs of dental treatment provided in other Member States, in accordance with the tariff of the state of insurance, has no significant effect on the financing of the social security system'.[86] The restriction on free movement of services at issue was not justified. However, in later cases involving hospital care,[87] the CJEU refers to the distinct characteristics of the hospital sector, in particular, the planning of the number of hospitals, their geographical distribution, the way in which they are organized, the equipment with which they are provided, and the nature of the health services they are able to offer. The planning of hospital provision aims to ensure sufficient and permanent access to a balanced range of high-quality medical services, to protect public health and even the survival of a population in the relevant Member State. Hospital planning promotes efficiency in the deployment of financial, technical and human resources. It assists with cost control, in the context of increasing demand with limited financial resources. Hence the CJEU has held that rules requiring prior authorization for hospital treatment may be justified, although they must be appropriate and necessary to meet their aims.[88]

---

[80]　For the earliest case in the context of services see: *Van Binsbergen* EU:C:1974:131, paragraph 12, in which the Court held, '[T]aking into account the particular nature of the services to be provided, specific requirements imposed on the person providing the service cannot be considered incompatible with the Treaty where they have as their purpose the application of... rules justified by the general good... which are binding upon any person established in the State in which the service is provided.'

[81]　If distinctions are made on the basis of nationality, then the measure can be justified only under the grounds set out in Articles 45(3) and 52 TFEU.

[82]　*Geraets-Smits/Peerbooms* EU:C:2001:404, paragraph 90; *Müller-Fauré* EU:C:2003:270, paragraph 85; *Watts* EU:C:2006:325, paragraphs 116-120.

[83]　See: e.g. *Guiot and Climatec* EU:C:1996:147.

[84]　See: e.g. *Lawyers Services*, C-427/85, EU:C:1988:98, paragraph 26.

[85]　*Guiot and Climatec* EU:C:1996:147.　　[86]　*Kohll* EU:C:1998:171, paragraph 42.

[87]　*Geraets-Smits/Peerbooms* EU:C:2001:404, paragraphs 76-82; *Müller-Fauré/Van Riet* EU:C:2003:270, paragraphs 67-71 and 76-83; *Inizan* EU:C:2003:578, paragraph 56; *Watts* EU:C:2006:325, paragraphs 102-110; *Stamatelaki* EU:C:2007:231, paragraphs 31-32; *Major Medical Equipment* EU:C:2010:579.

[88]　*Geraets-Smits/Peerbooms* EU:C:2001:404, paragraph 82; *Watts* EU:C:2006:325, paragraphs 106 and 114, *Stamatelaki* EU:C:2007:231, paragraph 34.

Although the *fact patterns* of the pre-2010 cases involve a distinction between hospital and non-hospital care, the CJEU's *reasoning* in these decisions does not limit the possibility of justifying restrictions to access to cross-border receipt of health care services, for instance, through requiring prior authorization, to hospital care. On the contrary, the *rationes* of the decisions imply that objective public interest justifications are available, where they are made out and are non-discriminatory and proportionate, in accordance with the CJEU's general case law on the internal market. This interpretation of the pre-2010 cases was confirmed in the CJEU's decision in Case C-512/08 *Commission v. France (Major Medical Equipment)*. In that case, the CJEU held that a prior authorization rule applicable to treatment involving the use of major medical equipment, such as PET (positron emission tomography) scanners, MRI (magnetic resonance imaging) scanners, hyperbaric chambers and cyclotrons, outside hospital infrastructures, could be justified on the basis of the planning necessary to ensure a balanced range of high-quality treatment, and at the same time control costs by avoiding wastage of resources.[89] It can also be inferred from the Commission's withdrawal of its claim about the Portuguese prior authorization rules for major medical equipment in Case C-255/09 *Commission v. Portugal (Non-hospital Medical Care)*.

The possibility of justifying restrictions on cross-border receipt of services by patients receiving healthcare in non-hospital settings has also been signalled strongly by the EU legislature, in the Directive on Patients' Rights in Cross-border Health Care. As noted above, the Directive considers that 'hospital care' in this context means either where the patient stays overnight in hospital for at least one night or where the treatment involves using 'highly specialised and cost-intensive medical infrastructure or medical equipment', even if not within a hospital.[90] Furthermore, the Directive also envisages that prior authorization be required for particularly risky health care treatments, either from the point of view of the patient or of the population, for example, the *Bexero* vaccine for Meningitis B immunization of children.[91] In addition, excepting health care that complies with EU legislation on safety and quality,[92] Member States may require prior authorization if they have a serious and specific concern about the quality and safety of the care provided by the healthcare provider in the host Member State. This provision of the Directive has yet to be tested but could perhaps be used where a patient seeks care in a Member State where quality and safety assurance procedures are less developed than in the home Member State. The Directive thus envisages that the Member State may take a view of the best

---

[89] *Major Medical Equipment* EU:C:2010:579, paragraph 33.
[90] Directive 2011/24/EU, above n 71, Article 8 (1).
[91] See: UK Joint Committee on Immunistaion and Vaccination, 'Interim Position Statement on use of Bexsero meningococcal B vaccine in the UK' (*DoH*, 24 July 2013).
[92] See for example: EU legislation on pharmaceuticals and medical devices, discussed in chapters 13 and 14.

interests of the patient with respect to risk assessment and patient safety, and in this respect EU health law does not simply promote the consumption of health care services based on the preferences of the patient as consumer.

The CJEU is not, of course, obliged to follow the legislature where it interprets Treaty provisions such as Article 56 TFEU, but in practice it usually does so.[93] The *Major Medical Equipment* case suggests that the CJEU is likely to do so on the question of justification. Moreover, given that the Directive does not 'occupy the field', that is, completely displace all national regulation of the matter, but is a 'minimum harmonization' measure, it would still be open to a Member State or public health authority within a Member State to claim, under Article 56 TFEU, that restrictions on access to cross-border non-hospital care, or other restrictions based on an 'objective public interest', were justified, provided that the strict proportionality test of the case law had been met.[94]

Matters of national ethical sensitivity

Finally, in reaching a balanced conclusion on the 'consumerizing' effects of EU health law in situations where the patient moves, we consider the application of the relevant EU health law in matters of national ethical sensitivity. A range of areas of health law, particularly those pertaining to human reproduction and end-of-life decision-making, are characterized by significant divergences in approach between the EU's Member States. Access to abortion services, to assisted reproduction, or to certain end-of-life decisions, differs widely across Europe.[95] If EU health law had a strong 'consumerizing' effect, we might expect these ethically based differences to be subject to significant challenges, based on individual choice and autonomy, and relying on rights of patients to provision of medical services in EU law. We might even expect a convergence towards an EU standard along those lines.

In practice, however, any such 'consumerizing' tendencies to ethical varia-tion *that may flow from EU health law* are distinctly muted. Looking at the example of abortion, national abortion laws differ significantly across the EU. In Malta, abortion is illegal on any grounds.[96] In Ireland, it is severely restricted

---

[93] See, for instance: the CJEU's case law on citizenship of the EU, which follows in many respects the provisions of Directive 2004/38/EC [2004] OJ L158/77. Another example is the CJEU following Council's amendment to Regulation 1408/71/EEC, above n 34, Regulation 1247/92/EEC [1992] OJ L136/1; see: Sindbjerg Martinsen, 'Social Security Regulation in the EU: The De-Territorialisation of Welfare' in De Búrca (ed), *EU Law and the Welfare State: In Search of Solidarity* (OUP 2005) 100-101.

[94] See: Hervey, (2011) above n 12; Di Federico, above n 71.

[95] The World Health Organisation, Europe region, has compiled rich comparative data on law and policy on human reproductive and sexual health, and on dignity at the end of life, in European countries, see: generally (WHO 2014) and, on 'Healthy Ageing' (WHO 2014).

[96] See: Criminal Code, section 241. See also: United Nations, 'World Abortion Policies 2013' (Department of Economic and Social Affairs, United Nations 2013).

to instances where it is necessary to save a mother's life.[97] On the other hand, in the majority of EU Member States[98], abortion is available on a wide range of grounds, including on request, and medical terminations of pregnancy are covered under the national health (insurance) system.[99] Depending in part on contraceptive use, abortion rates in some of those countries are significantly higher than the EU average.[100] We have already noted the *Grogan* case,[101] involving the distribution of information by a students' union in an Irish University, about abortion services in Member States where termination of pregnancy is lawful on a range of grounds, in contrast to the position in Ireland. The CJEU held that abortion is a 'service' in the sense of Article 56 TFEU. But the CJEU went on to decide that the link between the actions of the Irish students' union and medical terminations of pregnancies in clinics in other Member States was 'too tenuous' for the prohibition of distributing information to constitute a 'restriction' on free movement of services.[102] Restricting advertising by a body unconnected with the abortion services was thus not covered by EU law.

The *Grogan* ruling prompted speculation as to the extent to which the principles of EU free movement law undermine ethical principles, especially those enshrined in national constitutional law, and the extent to which this is desirable.[103] The Member States have since enshrined the continued diversity of national abortion rules within the EU's 'constitutional' texts.[104] The debate about how far EU and national law are in a hierarchical relationship, with the former displacing the latter, goes to the heart of the EU's constitutional law. In its broader manifestation, it has been the subject of a great deal of literature, much of which now understands relationships between the EU's constitutional rules and those of Member States as non-hierarchical.[105] Such an understanding is

---

[97] Irish Constitution, Article 40.3.3.

[98] Austria, Belgium, Bulgaria, Czech Republic, Croatia, Denmark, Estonia, France, Germany, Hungary, Latvia, Lithuania, Netherlands, Portugal, Romania, Slovakia, Spain and Sweden: WHO, 'Facts and figures about abortion in the European Region' (WHO 2014).

[99] See: United Nations, 'World Abortion Policies 2013' (Department of Economic and Social Affairs, United Nations 2013) .

[100] WHO, 'Facts and figures about abortion in the European Region' (WHO 2014).

[101] *SPUC v Grogan* EU:C:1991:378.   [102] *SPUC v Grogan* EU:C:1991:378, paragraph 24.

[103] See: e.g. Phelan, 'The Right to Life of the Unborn v Promotion of Trade in Services: The European Court of Justice and the Normative Shaping of the European Union' (1992) 55 *Modern Law Review* 670;

[104] Protocol No 35, annexed to the TEU and TFEU (formerly, Protocol No 17, Annexed to the Treaty on European Union 1992); Protocol No 7, annexed to the Accession Treaty 2003. Protocols are "an integral part" of the EU's Treaties, Article 51 TEU.

[105] See, for instance: De Búrca and Weiler, *The Worlds of European Constitutionalism* (CUP 2011); Walker, Shaw and Tierney (eds), *Europe's Constitutional Mosaic* (Hart 2011); Maduro, 'How Constitutional can the European Union be? The Tension between Intergovernmentalism and Constitutionalism in the European Union'. (2004) Jean Monnet Working Paper 5/04; Itzcovich, 'Legal Order, Legal Pluralism, Fundamental Principles: European and its Law in Three Concepts' (2012) 18(3) *European Law Journal* 358; Walker, 'The Idea of Constitutional Pluralism'. *Modern Law Review* (2002) 65(3) 317; MacCormick, *Questioning Sovereignty: Law,*

certainly consistent with our view here that the *Grogan* case has not in practice had the effect of replacing national ethics-based positions about the availability of certain medical treatments with decisions based on consumer choice.

Moreover, *Grogan* is very much the exception. No other litigation involving abortion has so far reached the CJEU.[106] And this is also true for other ethically controversial health care services. Consider, for instance, the tragic story of Alan and Louise Masterton, from Scotland. The couple, who already had several sons, sought access to pre-implantation gender selection to enable them to have another daughter, after their only daughter was killed in a bonfire accident. They considered a challenge under the UK Human Rights Act 1998, and were eventually given an apology from the UK's Human Fertilisation and Embryology Authority, following an Ombudsman investigation.[107] But as far as we are aware no consideration was given to a possible EU law claim, to the effect that UK law prohibiting pre-implantation gender selection is an unjustified restriction on free movement of services. Certainly no such litigation reached the courts. In fact, the couple sought treatment in Italy, although sadly they were unsuccessful.[108] At the start of the 2000s, Robert Lee and Derek Morgan[109] noted that significant numbers of patients from France and elsewhere were seeking fertility treatment in Belgium, where the regulatory structures are significantly less restrictive, and this pattern appears to be continuing.[110] Although fertility treatment in France is publicly funded, it is available only where a *projet parental* is involved, that is, a heterosexual couple, married or cohabiting for at least two years, and of 'reproductive age'.[111] Other Member States restrict egg or embryo donation, or surrogate motherhood, or restrict the age at which fertility treatments are available.[112] In addition, differences in national rules on gamete donor payments, in donor anonymity, in waiting times and in the costs of

---

State, and Nation in the European Commonwealth* (OUP 1999). Contrast, for instance, Schütze's *European Constitutional Law* (CUP 2012), and see the discussion in Chalmers et al., *European Union Law* (CUP 2014) 219-225.

[106] Other relevant cases have been considered by national courts alone, see, for instance: *AG v Open Door Counselling Ltd* [1988] 2 CMLR 443; *AG v X* [1992] 2 CMLR 277.

[107] UK Science and Technology Committee, *Report: Human Reproduction and the Law* (HC 2004-05, HC 7-II [Incorporating HC 559 i-ix of session 2003-04]), Appendix 49.

[108] Editorial, 'Rise of the Fertility Tourist' (*BBC News*, 06 March 2001) Editorial, 'Couple abandon battle for baby of their choice' (*The Sunday Times (Scotland)* 23 January 2005).

[109] Lee and Morgan, *Human Fertilisation and Embryology: Regulating the Reproductive Revolution* (Blackstones Press 2001) 278-80.

[110] See: Pennings et al., 'Cross Border Reproductive Care in Belgium' (2009) 24(12) *Human Reproduction* 3108.

[111] Latham, *Regulating Reproduction: A Century of Conflict in Britain and France* (Manchester University Press 2002).

[112] See discussion in: Berg Brigham, Cadier and Chevreul, 'The Diversity of regulation of and public financing of IVF in Europe and its impact on utilization' (2013) 28(3) *Human Reproduction* 666. Italy introduced a very restrictive law in 2004 replacing a regime providing straightforward access to treatment. This has been subsequently the subject of numerous legal challenges, see further: Hanafin, 'Law Biopolitical and Reproductive Citizenship: The Case of Assisted Reproduction in Italy' (2013) 4(1) *Italian Journal of Science and Technology Studies* 45.

treatment, all play a part in encouraging would-be parents to seek fertility treatment outside of their home state, particularly in Belgium, Spain, and Central and Eastern European states.[113] Again, although such cross-border fertility tourism[114] is on the increase, we are not aware of any EU health law litigation having been involved. Likewise, cases involving patients seeking to cross EU borders to receive end-of-life treatment not available at home[115] have not involved arguments from EU law.

In some cases, litigation has involved arguments in EU law but the CJEU has not been involved. This was the case for some decisions of the Irish courts during the 1980s and 90s concerning abortion.[116] The 'gate-keeping' role of national courts, especially their control over the preliminary reference procedure,[117] is thus an important factor here. So, for example, although EU law was raised in the *Diane Blood* case,[118] it was considered only by the national court, as the case was not referred to the CJEU. Diane Blood had planned to have a family with her husband Stephen. Stephen subsequently contracted meningitis, and, while he was in a coma on a life support machine, sperm was taken from him with a view to subsequent IVF treatment for Diane. As Stephen had not given explicit consent to the taking of his sperm, the UK Human Fertilisation and Embryology Authority[119] decided that its removal, and subsequent use by Diane, was illegal.[120] Diane sought to have the sperm exported, in order to allow her to receive treatment in Belgium, where the national rules would permit this. The Human Fertilisation and Embryology Authority refused to authorize the

---

[113] Culley, Hudson, Rapport, Blyth, Norton, and Pacey, '*Crossing borders for fertility treatment: motivations, destinations and outcomes of UK fertility travellers*' (2011) 26 (9) *Human Reproduction*, 2373; Editorial, 'The cost of fertility treatment tourism' (*BBC News*, 24 April 2011); Campbell, 'Destination Spain: the rise and rise of fertility tourism' *The Guardian* (London, 22 August 2010) Devlin, 'Hundreds of women risk health by fertility tourism' *The Telegraph* (London, 29 June 2009).

[114] Others refer to this as "cross border reproductive care" see: Pennings et al., 'ESHRE Task Force on Ethics and Law 15: Cross-border reproductive care' (2008) 23(10) *Human Reproduction* 2182. Van Hoof and Pennings, 'Cross-Border Reproductive Care Around the World: Recent Controversies' in Botterill, Pennings and Mainil (eds), *Medical Tourism and Transnational Health Care* (Palgrave Macmillan 2013), though note also criticism of this term: Dickenson, *Bioethics: All that Matters* (Hodder and Staughton 2013) 28.

[115] *Pretty* [2001] UKHL 61; *Purdy* [2009] UKHL 45.

[116] See, for instance: *AG v Open Door Counselling* [1988] 2 CMLR 443; *AG v X* [1992] 2 CMLR 277.

[117] Article 267 TFEU.

[118] *Blood* [1997] 2 All ER 687. See the discussion in Morgan and Lee, 'In the Name of the Father? Ex parte Blood: Dealing with Novelty and Anomaly' (1997) 60 *Modern Law Review* 840; Hervey, 'Buy Baby? The European Union and Regulation of Human Reproduction' (1998) 18 *Oxford Journal of Legal Studies* 207.

[119] The body charged with the regulation of infertility treatment under the UK Human Fertilisation and Embryology Act 1990 (as amended).

[120] This decision was supported by Schedule 3 of the UK Human Fertilisation and Embryology Act 1990 (as amended), and also by a decision of the UK House of Lords in *Re F* [1990] 2 AC 1, concerning non-therapeutic medical procedures (such as the removal of sperm) and adults lacking mental capacity.

export. It was argued that this refusal breached Article 56 TFEU as it restricted the free movement of services. The English Court of Appeal agreed, holding that the Treaty provisions were applicable, and that the HFEA should have taken this into account in reaching their decision. Following this ruling, the HFEA reconsidered their decision, authorized the export of the sperm, and Diane subsequently gave birth to two sons: Liam in 1998 and Joel in 2001.

Again, the *Blood* case is very much the exception. A crucial part of the national court's reasoning was that its decision would not create an unwelcome precedent, as the relevant national legislation and guidelines had already been clarified so as to prevent such a situation arising in the future. Neither the question of the legality of the removal of the sperm, nor of its storage, were covered by the national court's ruling, which focused only on the export of the sperm.[121] Had the question of the legality of the national rules on removal or storage been the subject of a challenge for consistency with EU law, the national court could have relied on an objective public interest justification, for instance, respect for human dignity.[122]

So, although there has been increasing discussion of the possible impact of EU free movement law on the ethical dimensions of health care provision, there is still considerable limitation on its scope, both in terms of which cases reach the CJEU at all, and in terms of how national ethical values assert themselves in such cases. The most we might expect is a change to the way courts *express* the discussion in such cases – a certain suppression of explicit consideration of ethical questions, replaced by a discussion of trade in goods or services.[123] But, overall, in this context, there is scant evidence of even that sort of 'consumerizing' effect from EU law in this context. It is true that Member States can no longer retain control over the types of treatments that 'their' patients may access, even on the most deeply held ethical grounds. The 'Easy Jet/Motorbahn' factor of increased ability (if one has the financial resources) to leap onto a plane or into a car and receive medical services anywhere in Europe, and indeed the world,[124] has put paid to such draconian controls. But this factor, which is supported by EU free movement law, has not undermined the internal application of national ethical laws or policies on medical treatment. If anything, the ability of (sufficiently wealthy) patients to seek ethically restricted treatments in other countries operates as a safety valve. Increasing global movement of such wealthy patients is probably more significant than movement within the EU.[125]

---

[121] See: Hervey and McHale, above n 3, 151; Kennedy and Grubb *Medical Law* (Butterworths 2000), 1304.

[122] Human dignity has been recognised by the CJEU as a permissible objective public interest justification in *Omega*, C-36/02, EU:C:2004:614.

[123] See: Hervey, above n 118.

[124] See: Cohen, *Patients with Passports: Medical Tourism, Law and Ethics* (OUP 2015), and see further the discussion in the introduction to Part IV and chapter 17.

[125] See, for instance: Cohen (2015) above n 124; Cohen, 'Transplant Tourism: The Ethics and Regulation of International Markets for Organs' (2013) 41(1) *Journal of Law, Medicine and Ethics* 269; Chen and Flood, 'Medical Tourism's Impact on Health Care Equity and Access in

The easy bypassing of national restrictions by those who oppose them means that there is little incentive or pressure for change to existing national rules. The overall effect of EU law here, far from moving towards an increasingly homogenized, consumer-based EU norm,[126] is in fact to promote and protect diversity across different EU Member States.

Conclusions

Overall, then, what does the CJEU's jurisprudence concerning movement of patients across an EU border to receive health care services[127] imply for consumerism as a theme of EU health law? This area of EU health law has the potential to undermine health care system models that eschew consumerist concepts, in particular through the stronger articulation of patient choice than is usually found in national health systems funded predominantly from general taxation or social insurance. The entitlements of patients under these aspects of EU health law to receive health care that they would not have received, or would not have received in the same terms, at home, are based on the choices made by those individual patients to exercise their rights as consumers of services within EU law. The very application of internal market law to health care in itself thus involves a *de facto* reconceptualization of the relationships between patients and the health care systems through which health care is provided. Because it is founded within the law of the internal market, the body of EU health law discussed in this chapter therefore exemplifies consumerism as a key theme of EU health law. It also supports the argument that EU health law at least complements moves to the 'consumerization' of relationships between

Low-and Middle-Income Countries: Making the Case for Regulation' (2013) 41(1) *Journal of Law, Medicine and Ethics* 286; Mutcherson, 'Open Fertility Borders: Defending Access To Cross Border Fertility Care In The United States' in Cohen (ed), *The Globalization of Health Care: Legal and Ethical Issues* (OUP 2013); Biggs and Jones, 'Tourism: A Matter Of Life And Death In The United Kingdom' in Cohen (ed), OUP 2013) above; Levine and Wolf, 'The Roles And Responsibilities Of Physicians In Patients' Decisions About Unproven Stem Cell Therapies' in Cohen (ed), above, Master, Zarzeczny, Rachul and Caulfield, 'What's Missing? Discussing Stem Cell Translational Research in Educational Information on Stem Cell "Tourism"' (2013) 41(1) *Journal of Law Medicine and Ethics* 254; Cortez, 'Patients Without Borders: The Emerging Global Market for Patients and the Evolution of Modern Health Care' (2008) 83(1) *Indiana Law Journal* 71; Horowitz, Rosensweig and Jones, 'Medical Tourism: Globalization of the Healthcare Marketplace' (2007) 9(4) *Medscape General Medicine* 33 and see further the discussion in the introduction to Part IV and chapter 17.

[126] Although there were reports of a 'citizens initiative' (see Article 11 (4) TEU) on abortion rights in the EU (see: Camilleri, 'EU citizens initiative to force abortion' *Times of Malta* (19 July 2009) a search of the official Commission website reveals no trace of such an initiative being registered. The European Commission's communication following the 'citizens initiative' on stem cell research stresses that the question of whether or not stem cell research is permitted is a matter of national competence, see: Commission, 'A decent Life for all: from vision to collective action' (Communication) COM (2014) 355 final.

[127] Framed within the Treaty rules on free movement of services, and concerning the interface with Regulation 883/2004/EC, which has the very different frame of coordination of national social security systems.

patients and health care professionals, as well as health care systems, even if EU health law does not drive such changes. This reconfiguring of health care relationships has positive implications for patient autonomy and patient choice (at least of some patients), but negative implications for equity and principles such as access according to professionally assessed medical need.

However, the discussion above has shown that it is necessary to add nuance to this account. There are elements of EU health law here that shift the focus away from the consumer of services in the internal market. These include many post-2010 decisions of the CJEU, as well as the dual legal basis and the terms of the Patients' Rights Directive – which, after all, is *not* entitled the 'Directive on Free Movement of Health Care Services.'[128] The nuance is also found in the CJEU's case law on justification through objective public interests. EU law is also constitutionally organized[129] so as to protect and even promote diverse national laws on ethically controversial health care. The exercise of patient choice need not be seen as a consumer activity, but rather through a lens of human rights.[130]

Nevertheless, the main implication of this aspect of EU health law is that the *very structure* of EU law sets up a tension between the preferences of an individual consumer of services and the priorities of a national health (insurance) system, and frames those preferences and priorities as oppositional. The question of whether a national policy or practice is justified does have to be carried out within that frame. Member States are required to evidence a specific policy that is appropriate and necessary to meet an objective public interest justification. In both the case law and under the Patients' Rights Directive Member States are effectively obliged to do so on an individual (rather than strategic or systemic) basis. We therefore conclude that, although the strongest version of these claims cannot be sustained in light of detailed analysis, overall and on balance, the principal implication of EU health law on free movement of patients is to increase patient choice and autonomy, and to change relationships between at least some patients and health care professionals.

[128] And could never have been so, as there was strong political opposition to the notion of health care services as "ordinary" services in the internal market.

[129] Greer and Jarman show how the Member States have used legislation and 'bureaucratic resistance' to mitigate the effects of CJEU rulings, see: Greer and Jarman, 'Managing Risks in EU health services policy: Spot markets, legal certainty and bureaucratic resistance' (2012) 22(3) *Journal of European Social Policy* 259.

[130] We discuss the human rights dimensions of patient rights in chapters 7 and 8.

5

Consumerism: the moving health care product or service

Introduction

In the previous chapter, we considered the implications of the ways in which EU health law conceptualizes health care as a consumer service, focusing on the law applicable when a patient crosses borders within the EU. Continuing this theme, our focus in this chapter is where patients and others rely on or benefit from EU free movement law as recipients or providers of products ('goods' in EU law) and services, in circumstances where the product or service itself moves between Member States. As in the previous chapter, we are primarily interested in relationships between patients and health care professionals, although we also consider relationships between patients, health care professionals and health care systems more generally.[1] In the following chapter, we consider the theme of consumerism in the context of EU health law covering health care professionals.

The area of EU health law covered in this chapter has a significantly longer history than that considered in the previous chapter. The notion of free moving *patients* only really became a topic for EU health law from the 1990s. The movement across borders within the EU of health care *products* (pharmaceuticals, vaccines, medical devices, equipment, other health care products) has been supported by EU law from the 1950s onwards, and the earliest relevant litigation dates from the 1970s. In the 1950s and 60s, health care products and services effectively enjoyed a territorial protection within each EU Member State. Patients, even those accessing private health care, sought out health care products and services locally. The relevant industries also treated each Member State as a distinct market, often having different versions of the same product for different states. This is particularly true of the pharmaceutical industry, and largely remains the case today.

However, patients, especially those bearing the cost (or some of the cost) of their health care individually, are increasingly seeking medical services or purchasing pharmaceuticals or medical devices across borders, including via mail order and the internet. Where national rules inhibit such consumer choice, individual patients can rely upon directly effective provisions of EU law

---

[1] See further chapters 9, 10 and 11.

(on the free movement of products and services) in litigation challenging those national rules. The very application of EU law to such relationships is based on a consumerist frame. In order successfully to rely on EU law, patients must cast their relationship with the health care system(s) at issue as that of a consumer purchasing goods or services across a border within the EU's internal market. Perhaps this is achieved by taking the relationship outside the national health (insurance) system altogether, by constructing it as a purely private contractual relationship. Perhaps there is involvement of a national health insurance system in the payment: some Member States give patients an element of choice over the source of the provider of their health care products, and all national health systems in the EU involve some elements of co-payment.[2]

But not all of the relevant litigation is brought by patients as consumers. In fact, patient-led litigation of this type is relatively unusual. What is much more common is that producers or distributors of health care products rely on EU law to open up new markets in EU Member States. Pharmaceutical companies often bring such litigation, challenging marketing environments that are territorially closed. But also producers of a wide range of medical devices that can be marketed directly to patients, such as contact lenses, as well as other products that are used in health care settings, such as infant formula milk, have used EU free movement law. Where national health care policies and practices have the effect of partitioning the EU market along national lines, they are particularly susceptible to such challenges before the national courts, and, by reference,[3] to the CJEU. The underlying idea of EU free movement law is that, ultimately, consumers should benefit from the greater economies of scale inherent in creating a single European market. Where commercial actors (such as the pharmaceutical industry) have brought claims based on EU law, those claims have thus been underpinned by the interests of an ultimate consumer of those products, whose interests EU law at least notionally serves. Such litigation brought on the basis of EU law must in effect be constructed in terms of consumer relationships within the market. As a consequence, at worst, the systemic aims or effects of the national regulatory arrangements under review are rendered irrelevant; at best, they are interpreted as an exception to the rule of free movement, or are sidelined. The consumerist frame is central.

Significant movements of health care *services* across borders are a more recent phenomenon. But, as health services are increasingly supported by electronic communications, this area of EU health law is also developing, and has the potential to develop further. In the context of increased direct access of patients to their preferred health services, the points made above apply equally to health services.[4] In order to fall within EU law, any litigation must be constructed in

---

[2] See further the introduction to Part III, which outlines the different types of health care system within the EU.

[3] Under Article 267 TFEU.

[4] Hancher and Sauter also discern a trend in the jurisprudence on freedom of establishment, and in free movement of capital, in which the CJEU has 'gradually departed' from the caution

terms of a service recipient receiving a service from a provider, for remuneration. Although such litigation may well involve private health care services, recall that, in EU law on free movement of services, the service recipient need not be the person who pays for the service, so long as there is remuneration.[5] Therefore the provisions of EU law discussed in the previous chapter, in which EU law on free movement of services applies even where the patient is reimbursed by a national health (insurance) system, apply equally in this context.

Cross-border health care products or services: applicable law

EU law seeks to secure free movement of goods[6] and services[7] within the internal market. These rules, found in the EU's Treaties, grant directly effective[8] rights to individuals facing unjustified 'restrictions' on free movement of those factors of production. That is the starting point, or the 'constitutional' basis for the applicable EU law. It is the basis on which much of the relevant litigation has been brought.

There is also a significant body of EU legislation (Directives, Regulations) that seeks to protect consumers of products and services within the internal market. In every Member State of the EU, the products and services associated with health care are highly regulated with respect to their quality, safety and efficacy. In terms of health products, much of this regulation is mandated by EU-level legislation, both general in its terms and specific to health products or services. Specific EU legislation governs the development, production, licensing, importation, distribution, marketing and retail of pharmaceuticals[9] and medical devices.[10] These provisions must also be considered in the context of increasingly streamlined and homogenous rules developed at international level, in particular through the International Conference on Harmonisation of Technical Requirements of Pharmaceuticals for Human Use (ICH).[11]

The key piece of general EU consumer protection legislation covering products is the Product Liability Directive.[12] As the CJEU has confirmed, in the context of case law concerning liability for harm caused by medical devices and

---

exercised in *Sodemare*, C-70/95, EU:C:1997:301, see: Hancher and Sauter, *EU Competition and Internal Market Law in the Healthcare Sector* (OUP 2012) 105, 118-120, and *Minister voor Wonen, Wijken en Integratie v Woningstichting Sint Servatius*, C-567/07, EU:C:2009:593, concerning housing cooperatives investing across borders.

[5] *Bond van Adverteerders*, C-352/85, EU:C:1988:196; *Kohll*, C-158/96, EU:C:1998:171; *Watts*, C-372/04, EU:C:2006:325.

[6] Article 28 TFEU.   [7] Article 56 TFEU.

[8] *Van Gend en Loos*, C-26/62, EU:C:1963:1; *Van Duyn*, C-41/74, EU:C:1974:133; *Defrenne v SABENA*, C-43/75, EU:C:1976:5; *Reyners*, C-2/74, EU:C:1974:68.

[9] Directive 2001/83/EC [2004] OJ L311/67.

[10] Directive 90/385/EEC [1990] OJ L189/17; Directive 93/42/EEC [1993] OJ L169/1; Directive 98/79/EC [1998] OJ L331/1.

[11] See further chapters 16–18.   [12] Directive 85/374/EEC [1985] OJ L210/29.

medical equipment,[13] this Directive aims to promote free movement within the EU of such products that comply with its terms. The Directive replaces various different national liability laws, which might impede free movement, with an EU-level consumer protection standard. That EU standard is a no-fault liability for damage caused to consumers[14] by defective products. However, the Product Liability Directive gives Member States the option to derogate from its terms where the state of scientific and technical knowledge at the time when the product was put into circulation was insufficient to identify the defect (the 'development risks defence'). The reason for the defence is to provide a balance between consumer protection and industry innovation – a particularly tricky balance in the context of health products and services, as numerous examples, such as thalidomide, or contaminated blood scandals, have shown. Most Member States have implemented the development risks defence,[15] although some exclude relevant products, such as pharmaceuticals,[16] or products derived from the human body.[17] The Product Liability Directive has been the subject of litigation,[18] in particular because Member States are not permitted explicitly by the Directive to adopt provisions that secure a higher level of consumer protection, such as in the case of Spanish law pre-dating the Directive as applicable to defective blood used in blood transfusions.[19] The CJEU's rulings in these cases mean that the Directive is 'frozen in time': a position which is problematic in the context of health products where there is significant innovation as well as changes in political preference for consumer protection levels.[20] Other consumer protection legislation has not yet been relied upon in litigation involving health products, although the potential is there.[21]

In terms of health services, as noted in the previous chapter, the EU's general Services Directive 2006/123/EC does not apply to health care services.[22] Likewise, the EU's legislation on non-life insurance, which, inter alia, seeks to protect consumers by ensuring that insurance providers are sufficiently financially sound, and by setting out risk management principles, explicitly exempts

---

[13] *Medipac-Kazantzidis*, C 6/05, EU:C:2007:336, paragraph 51; *Nordiska Dental*, C-288/08, EU:C:2009:718, paragraph 20. However, a hospital using defective medical equipment of which it is not the producer is not liable under the Directive, see: *Dutrueux*, C-495/10, EU:C:2011:869.

[14] In *Moteurs Leroy Somer*, C-285/08, EU:C:2009:351 the CJEU confirmed that the Directive does not cover damage to property used in a professional capacity, e.g. by health professionals in a hospital.

[15] Except Finland and Luxembourg.   [16] Germany and Spain.   [17] France.

[18] *Aventis Pasteur*, C-358/08, EU:C:2009:744; *Commission v France*, C-52/00, EU:C:2002:252; *Commission v Greece*, C-154/00, EU:C:2002:254; *Medicina Asturiana*, C-183/00, EU:C:2002:255.

[19] *Medicina Asturiana* EU:C:2002:255.

[20] See: Navarro-Michel, 'New Health Technologies and their Impact on EU Product Liability Regulations' in Flear, Farrell, Hervey and Murphy (eds), *European Law and New Health Technologies* (OUP 2013).

[21] See, for instance, the 'doorstep selling' Directive 85/577/EEC [1985] OJ L372/31; Directive 93/13/EEC [1993] OJ L095/29; Directive 97/7/EC [1997] OJ L144/19. The majority of litigation relying on this legislation concerns financial services.

[22] Directive 2006/123/EC [2006] OJ L376/36.

health insurance schemes that 'may serve as a partial or complete alternative to health cover provided by the statutory social security scheme'.[23] This provision, aimed at those Member States who operated private health insurance systems as part of their overall national health systems,[24] has been the subject of discussion in terms of its relationship to EU law on 'services of general economic interest'. It will be discussed further in chapter 9, along with the EU legislation on 'public procurement', concerning the ways that EU law constrains public entities, including those that are part of national health systems, in entering into contracts for services and goods.

However, other specific EU legislation concerning services could apply in health care settings. The consumer protection legislation cited above applies also to services contracts.[25] Another example is the 'E-Commerce Directive' 2000/31/EC, which applies to certain 'information society services', that is, services provided by electronic means.[26] This Directive has been relied upon in *KerOptika*, a case concerning the provision of contact lenses via the internet.[27] Note that, in *KerOptika* it was held that, although the *sale* of contact lenses by internet was covered by the Directive,[28] the subsequent *supply* of contact lenses was not.[29] Rather, the national rules on supply were subject to Articles 34 and 36 TFEU, on the free movement of goods.[30] The *KerOptika* case demonstrates the interactions between Treaty rules and EU legislation, a theme to which we shall return later in the chapter.

---

[23] Council Directive 92/49/EEC [1992] OJ L228/1, Article 54; now see Directive 2009/138/EC [2009] OJ L335/1, Article 206.

[24] Ireland, the Netherlands, Germany. For further discussion, see: Hancher and Sauter, above n 4, 129-132; Thomson and Mossialos, 'Private health insurance and the internal market' in Mossialos, Permanand, Baeten and Hervey (eds), *Health Systems Governance in Europe: The Role of European Union Law and Policy* (CUP 2010).

[25] The 'doorstep selling' Directive 85/577/EEC above n 21; Directive 93/13/EEC above n 21; Directive 97/7/EC, above n 21.

[26] Directive 2000/31/EC [2000] OJ L178/1, Article 2 (a) defines 'information society services' as: 'services within the meaning of Article 1(2) of Directive 98/34/EC as amended by Directive 98/48/EC'. This technical specifications Directive, as amended, defines 'information society services' as 'any service normally provided for remuneration, at a distance, by electronic means and at the individual request of a recipient of services'. It explicitly excludes 'services provided in the physical presence of the provider and the recipient, even if they involve the use of electronic devices', such as '(a) medical examinations or treatment at a doctor's surgery using electronic equipment where the patient is physically present'; and 'services which are not provided via electronic processing/inventory systems', such as '(a) voice telephony services; (b) telefax/telex services; (c) services provided via voice telephony or fax; (d) telephone/telefax consultation of a doctor'; (Annex V). Recital 18 of Directive 2000/31/EC [2000] OJ L178/1 states that 'information society services' include 'selling goods online', although the delivery of goods or the provision of services off-line are not covered, and that 'activities which by their very nature cannot be carried out at a distance and by electronic means such as . . . medical advice requiring the physical examination of a patient' are not 'information society services'.

[27] See: *Ker-Optika*, C-108/09, EU:C:2010:725.

[28] *Ker-Optika*, paragraphs 28, 40; being separable from the examination by an ophthalmologist, paragraphs 33-40.

[29] *Ker-Optika*, paragraph 31.   [30] *Ker-Optika*, paragraphs 41-78.

Important EU internal market law concerns the protection of individuals in the context of free movement of data within the internal market. The Data Protection Directive[31] provides that the 'processing' of personal data must not jeopardize the rights of individuals to privacy.[32] Where 'special' personal data (a category which includes data concerning health[33]) is processed, this is lawful only where one of a series of criteria is met. The criteria include where explicit consent has been given, and where processing is necessary to meet the vital interests of the data subject or a third party and the data subject is incapable of consenting.[34] The Directive could have important ramifications in health care contexts,[35] for instance where patients seek information-based services, such as genetic profiling for disease susceptibility, across EU borders. The CJEU has adopted a wide definition of 'data concerning health', encompassing 'information concerning all aspects, both physical and mental, of the health of an individual'.[36]

All of this EU internal market legislation is conceived within a consumerist frame. Its main *raison d'être* is the protection of consumers within the internal market. Even those pieces of EU legislation (such as EU data protection legislation) that have other equally important aims (in that instance, protection of civil liberties, the right to privacy) are nonetheless framed in terms of consumer protection in the internal market in terms of their legal basis, as the EU does not have competence to adopt human rights measures per se.[37] Although few cases relying on the legislation so far involve health products or services, potential is there. Moreover, when the CJEU interprets the free movement Treaty provisions, it does so in the context of this internal market legislation.

In theory, therefore, there is a 'single market' within the EU for pharmaceuticals and other health products, and for health services where 'remuneration' is present. In that single market, consumers are protected, in part through EU legislation, in terms of safety, quality and the inequality of power that characterizes consumer contracts. However, in practice, this single market has not been fully realized.

---

[31] Directive 95/46/EC [1995] OJ L281/31. Repeal proposed by the European Commission: Commission, 'Proposal for a Regulation of the European Parliament and of the Council on the protection of individuals with regard to the processing of personal data and on the free movement of such data (General Data Protection Regulation)' COM (2012) 11 final.

[32] Directive 95/46/EC, above n 31, Article 1 (1).

[33] Directive 95/46/EC above n 31, Article 8 (1).

[34] Directive 95/46/EC above n 31, Article 8 (2).

[35] Taylor, *Genetic Data and the Law* (CUP 2012); Taylor and Grace, 'Disclosure of Confidential Patient Information and the Duty to Consult: The Role of the Health and Social Care Information Centre' (2013) 21(3) *Medical Law Review* 415; Taylor, 'Health research, data protection, and the public interest in notification' (2011) 19(2) *Medical Law Review* 267.

[36] *Lindqvist*, C-101/01, EU:C:2003:596.

[37] Article 5 TEU, Article 6 TEU: 'the provisions of the Charter [of Fundamental Rights of the EU, 2000] shall not extend in any way the competences of the Union as defined in the Treaties'; Articles 2-6 TFEU.

The Member States of the EU have used various regulatory strategies to keep their national markets in health care products and services territorially closed. This is usually, at least notionally, because of a commitment to equitable access to health care products and services on the basis of professionally assessed medical need. Having open markets for the supply of medical products and services is unattractive to governments for several reasons. First, in such open markets, some providers will enter only the more lucrative parts of the market, leaving those which are less lucrative uncovered. The health care needs of those in the less lucrative parts are thus left unmet. Member States therefore often use obligations of universal supply, or redistributive measures,[38] to prevent this kind of 'cream-skimming', and hence to secure equal access based on medical need. Second, in an 'ordinary' market, supply increases only in so far as consumer demand – and ability to pay – dictates. Where a market involves expensive new products or services, these are sought after only in so far as they are affordable to those who consume them. These 'ordinary' market conditions do not apply to health care products or services.[39] The vast majority of health care across the EU is paid for by the public purse (either through social insurance or taxation), rather by individual patients. As all Member States are under pressure to avoid excessive government deficits,[40] having a consumer-demand-led market in health care products and services would lead to an undesirable ever-increasing burden on the public purse. Therefore, Member States have adopted various regulatory arrangements that aim to control costs to the national health care system. All Member States use mechanisms such as closed lists for services and products available through the national health (insurance) system, or pricing arrangements,[41] such as fixed prices or profitability agreements with the pharmaceutical industry. Intellectual property rights (held in national law) may be used to reinforce such pricing arrangements. National prior authorization rules, discussed at length in chapter 4, are another example.

Third, in the context of the EU, if privately contracted health care 'goes wrong', the national health (insurance) system often has to 'pick up the tab', because the public national health system then treats the patient. Member States have therefore sought to protect their own patients, even those who are able to pay

---

[38] Such as at issue in *BUPA*, T-289/03, EU:T:2008:29, concerning Irish law providing that private health insurers who have lower risks than the average should pay into a central fund, while those insurers who have higher risks than average should receive monies from that central fund.

[39] See: e.g. Arrow, 'Uncertainty and the Welfare Economics of Medical Care' (1963) 53(5) *The American Economic Review* 941.

[40] Article 126 TFEU; Article 136 TFEU; Protocol No. 12 on the Excessive Deficit Procedure annexed to the TEU and TFEU [2008] OJ C155/279; Treaty on Stability, Coordination and Governance in the EMU, 2012; Treaty establishing the European Stability Mechanism, 2012; Regulation 1173/2011/EU [2011] OJ L306/1; Regulation 472/2013/EU [2013] OJ L140/1.

[41] The CJEU has held the rules which control prices may breach free movement law, see: e.g. *Cipolla*, C-94/04 and C-202/04, EU:C:2006:758 (price of legal fees fixed); *Cullet*, C-231/83, EU:C:1985:29 (minimum fuel price); *Van Tiggele*, C-82/77, EU:C:1978:10 (minimum price of gin); although such rules may be justified by objective public interests, such as consumer protection or the safeguarding of the proper administration of justice (*Cipolla*, paragraph 64).

for health care themselves, from risky treatments or products, particularly those which are relatively new and untested, for instance, by restricting the supply of such services or products, through licensing laws. National rules designed to protect patients from being provided, supplied or sold inappropriate treatments for their medical conditions, include a variety of protective measures. Probably the best-known of these is the distinction between over-the-counter and prescription-only pharmaceuticals and other medical products. Other provisions, such as rules on importation and distribution of pharmaceuticals or other medical products, rules on where pharmaceuticals or medical devices may be sold, and rules on establishment of pharmacies, play a similar role. Rules that regulate the supply of medical services, such as professional qualifications rules, also fall into this category – they are discussed in more detail in the next chapter. All of these protective rules are based on the relationships between health care professionals and patients, and are framed in terms of the responsibilities of doctors and other medical specialists, and pharmacists, to their patients. They may be similar to general consumer protection laws, but they have an additional rationale beyond general consumer protection.

EU free movement law runs in opposition to the underlying rationales of all these national territorially based regulatory arrangements. And EU free movement law is enforceable by individuals. EU law litigation challenging such national provisions has been deployed since the 1970s,[42] often by repeat litigants, such as the pharmaceutical company Centrafarm[43] and the internet and mail order pharmacy DocMorris.[44]

Litigation brought by private individuals

A relatively small body of litigation brought by private individuals has sought to challenge national regulation of health care products or services, on the basis that the rules restrict cross-border trade in the EU. An example from the 1980s is *Schumacher*.[45] Heinz Schumacher, a German resident, ordered a medicinal product (Chophytol), used to treat dyspepsia and as a diuretic, from a French pharmacy. The order was for his personal use, not for subsequent resale. Chophytol was licensed for over-the-counter marketing in both Germany and France. However, it was considerably cheaper in France. Schumacher

---

[42] The litigation essentially involves cases brought against companies, supplying medicinal or medical products, for breaching national rules of various types, which the companies in turn, in their defence, alleged breached EU law. For discussion of EU law being used as a cause of action or a defence in health settings, see: Hervey and McHale, *Health Law and the European Union* (CUP 2004) 44-47.

[43] E.g. *Centrafarm* v *Sterling Drug*, C-15/74, EU:C:1974:114; and *Centrafarm* v *Winthrop*, C-16/74, EU:C:1974:115; *De Peijper*, C-104/75, EU:C:1976:67.

[44] *DocMorris*, C-322/01, EU:C:2003:664; *Neumann-Siewert*, C-171/07 and C-172/07, EU:C:2009:316; Order in *Apotheke DocMorris*, T-173/10, EU:T:2011:381; Order in *Apotheke DocMorris*, T-196/10, EU:T:2011:382.

[45] *Schumacher*, C-215/87, EU:C:1989:111.

successfully challenged German law prohibiting private importation of pharmaceuticals, as contrary to EU law on free movement of goods. The relevant national law[46] provided that medicinal products subject to marketing authorization rules could be imported only if the consignee was a pharmaceutical undertaking, a wholesaler, a veterinary surgeon, or operated a pharmacy. Germany argued that its national law was justified on the basis of consumer protection: to give consumers proper information, advice and guarantees of quality, safety and efficacy.

The CJEU was not impressed. It pointed out that, where a pharmaceutical is authorized for over-the-counter sale in both Member States, the consumer is protected by purchasing the product from a pharmacy in the Member State in which it is purchased.[47] This protection is all the more guaranteed, given EU legislation that restricts access to the profession of pharmacist to suitably trained and qualified professionals.[48] The CJEU relied on the equivalence of such professional qualifications regulation to justify its conclusion that the restriction to free movement of goods was not justified in this instance.

The CJEU's reasoning is similar in later cases. Nor does it make a difference whether the medical product or health care service itself is paid for by the patient, or ultimately paid for through the national health (insurance) system. We have already noted the *Kohll* case on health care services.[49] Its partner case, *Decker*,[50] decided by the CJEU on the same day, concerned cross-border purchase of vision-correcting spectacles. Nicolas Decker, a Luxembourg national, purchased a pair of spectacles from an optician in Arlon, Belgium. He had supplied the Belgian optician with a prescription from an ophthalmologist in Luxembourg. He then sought reimbursement from the Luxembourg social health insurance fund. The relevant national legislation allowed medical treatment and services to be given by non-Luxembourg providers, but only where authorization has been granted in advance. The fund therefore refused Decker's request, on the basis that he had failed to seek prior authorization.

Decker challenged this refusal, arguing that the national rules breached directly effective EU law on free movement of goods.[51] The CJEU dealt first with the question of the scope of EU free movement law, finding that, although EU law 'does not detract from the powers of the Member States to organise their social security systems',[52] national law which 'may affect the marketing of medical products, and indirectly influence the possibilities of importing those

---

[46] Paragraph 73(1) of the Gesetz zur Neuordnung des Arzneimittelsrechts of 24 August 1976.

[47] *Schumacher* EU:C:1989:111, paragraphs 18-20.

[48] Then Directive 85/432/EEC [1985] OJ L253/34; and Directive 85/433/EEC [1985] OJ L253/37; now Directive 2005/36/EC [2005] OJ L255/22.

[49] *Kohll* EU:C:1998:171. See chapter 4.

[50] *Decker*, C-120/95, EU:C:1998:167.   [51] Article 34 TFEU.

[52] *Decker* EU:C:1998:167, paragraph 21, citing *Duphar*, C-238/82, EU:C:1984:45 and *Sodemare*, C-70/95, EU:C:1997:301.

products' falls within EU law on free movement of goods.[53] The CJEU then applied its long-established legal test for breach of Article 34 TFEU: is the rule capable of hindering, directly or indirectly, actually or potentially, intra-EU trade?[54] The very generous nature of this test, which encompasses *potential* and *indirect* disruptions to cross-border trade in goods, meant that the CJEU found easily that the Luxembourg rules were inconsistent with Article 34. The CJEU therefore turned to the question of justification. The Luxembourg government had argued that its rules were justified by the need to control health expenditure. However, the facts of this case were such that this justification was not established. Costs were fixed according to a flat rate, irrespective of where the spectacles were purchased, and so any effect on Luxembourg's health expenditure was, according to the CJEU, neutral.[55]

The Belgian, German and Netherlands governments, intervening in *Decker*, argued that the Luxembourg rules were justified by the need to protect public health, by ensuring access of patients to high-quality health care. Vision-correcting spectacles must be supplied by qualified ophthalmologists or opticians. If such spectacles are provided in another Member State, it is impossible for the home Member State to exercise sufficient control to protect patients and ensure high quality and appropriate standards.[56] The CJEU was absolutely scathing in its analysis of this supposed justification. In its view, the regulation of the relevant professions is covered by EU legislation,[57] and therefore 'the purchase of a pair of spectacles from an optician established in another Member State provides guarantees equivalent to those afforded on the sale of a pair of spectacles by an optician established in the national territory'.[58] This may, or may not, be true. It is certainly hotly contested by the health care profession[59] – a fact which was blithely ignored by the CJEU in its judgment. For our purposes, this is not the point. The point is, that although the litigation was brought within the context of EU free movement of goods law, hence on the basis of consumerism, the CJEU did not conceptualize the relationships concerned entirely on that basis. Rather, the professional–patient relationship was seen by the CJEU within the framework of regulation of professional practice,

---

[53] *Decker* EU:C:1998:167, paragraph 24.   [54] *Dassonville*, C-8/74, EU:C:1974:82, paragraph 5.

[55] *Decker* EU:C:1998:167, paragraph 40. In subsequent cases, as we have seen, the CJEU has been prepared to accept the financial stability of health care systems as a justification for national rules that inhibit free movement of products or services, where the national rules actually have the effect of protecting such financial stability. See chapter 4.

[56] *Decker* EU:C:1998:167, paragraph 41.

[57] Directive 92/51/EEC [1995] OJ L209/25; Directive 95/43/EC [1995] OJ L184/21.

[58] *Decker* EU:C:1998:167, paragraph 43.

[59] See: e.g., the discussion in Peeters, McKee and Merkur, 'EU Law and Health Professionals' in Mossialos et al., above n 24; Glinos and Baeten, *A Literature Review of Cross Border Patient Mobility* (Observatoire Social Européen 2006); Cabral, 'Cross-border medical care in the European Union – bringing down a first wall' (1999) 24 *European Law Review* 387; Nickless, 'The internal market and the social nature of health care' in McKee, Mossialos and Baeten (eds.), *The Impact of EU law on Health Care Systems* (PIE-Peter Lang 2003).

which was regarded by the CJEU as guaranteeing the protection of public and individual health.[60]

The effect of the application of EU law in the types of situation represented by *Schumacher* and *Decker* is to require mutual recognition of and trust in the patient protection arrangements made in the other Member State. The way that the litigation is framed involves conceptualizing the relationship between a patient and a provider of health care goods and services through a consumerist lens, as a relationship between a producer and consumer in a market. In that sense, the relationship is not primarily seen as based on professional trust and protection of a patient. Nonetheless, the patient protection arrangements which the CJEU requires Member States to recognize are not based on consumerism. They rely strongly on a patient–professional relationship that goes beyond seeing patients as mere consumers of health care products or services. Therefore, in so far as the CJEU relies on the professional qualifications of relevant providers of health care products and services in its reasoning on justification, the litigation cannot be seen as a strong example where consumerism undermines other values of health care. A more nuanced conclusion on the implications of consumerism as a theme of EU health law is necessary.

Litigation brought by the European Commission and by legal persons

The same is true when we look in detail at litigation brought by the European Commission and by firms offering health care products or services within the EU, rather than litigation brought by individual patients. All this litigation falls within EU internal market law, and hence a consumerist frame. But can the claim that EU health law changes legal understandings of relationships between patients and health care professionals be supported in its strong form? Does EU health law see these relationships as based in contract, rather than solidarity; on exchange, rather than trust; on choice and autonomy, rather than equity? We explore those questions through close analysis of the relevant EU law, concerning (i) intellectual property law; (ii) national rules on patient protection; (iii) price and profit regulation, and restrictions on reimbursement. We also consider (iv) the case of regulation of pharmacies, as an area that exemplifies the approach of EU health law particularly well.

Intellectual property rules

Traders, particularly the pharmaceutical industry, have used EU law to challenge national intellectual property rules as applied to health products, particularly pharmaceuticals. These litigants, though not consumers themselves, rely on the

---

[60] *Decker* EU:C:1998:167, paragraph 44: 'Furthermore, in the present case, the spectacles were purchased on a prescription from an ophthalmologist, which guarantees the protection of public health'.

consumerist frame of EU law to bring litigation that challenges the ways in which intellectual property law interacts with market-dividing national regulations that are based, at least in part, on national health (social insurance) systems.

Intellectual property law, especially trade-mark law, partitions markets in health care products along national lines. Significant differences in prices of pharmaceuticals in different Member States (arising largely from differences in arrangements for the purchase of pharmaceuticals by national authorities) are supported, inter alia, by intellectual property rights, in particular, trade-marks, held in national law. The price differences are sufficiently great to encourage 'parallel importers', who buy pharmaceuticals in a Member State where they are relatively cheap, and sell them in a Member State where they attract a higher price. Differences in national rules and consumer preferences with respect to packaging pharmaceuticals mean that parallel importers frequently have to repackage pharmaceuticals in order to sell them. To show the propriety of the product, the parallel importers re-affix the trade-mark or allow it to remain visible through the new packaging. The original manufacturers seek to rely on their intellectual property rights to prevent the parallel import of the pharmaceuticals from a Member State in which they are cheaper, into a Member State in which they are more expensive. The parallel importers rely on EU law to challenge the exercise of intellectual property rights in such circumstances. The question then arises, do these intellectual property rights prevail over EU law on the free movement of goods?[61]

The TFEU provides that 'The Treaties shall in no way prejudice the rules in the Member States governing the system of property ownership'.[62] Restrictions on the free movement of goods can be justified by the protection of industrial and commercial property.[63] But, nevertheless, the CJEU held in the 1970s that, once the intellectual property rights have been 'exhausted' by the product being placed on the market in one Member State, restrictions on parallel imports of goods are in principle an unjustified breach of what is now Article 30 TFEU on the free movement of goods.[64] Further cases followed.[65]

The EU legislature has intervened, in an attempt to clarify the place of trade-marks in internal market law. The first Trade-Mark Directive 89/104/EEC[66] provided for exhaustion of trade-mark rights within the internal market,[67] unless there are legitimate reasons to oppose further commercialization of the

---

[61] See: Opinion in *Bristol-Myers Squibb*, C-427/93, C-429/93 and C-436/93, EU:C:1995:440, paragraphs 2-4.

[62] Article 345 TFEU.   [63] Article 36 TFEU.

[64] *Centrafarm v Sterling Drug* EU:C:1974:114; and *Centrafarm v Winthrop* EU:C:1974:115.

[65] *Pharmon BV v Hoechst AG*, C-19/84, EU:C:1985:304; *Merck v Stephar*, C-187/80, EU:C:1981:180; *Hoffman La-Roche v Centrafarm*, C-107/76, EU:C:1977:89; *De Peijper* EU:C:1976:67.

[66] Directive 89/104/EEC [1988] OJ L40/1, repealed by Directive 2008/95/EC [2008] OJ L299/25, Article 7 of which is identical to that of Directive 89/104/EEC.

[67] Directive 89/104/EEC above n 66, Article 7 (1).

product.[68] The CJEU interpreted this provision, which remains identical in the current Trade-Mark Directive 2008/95/EC,[69] in *Bristol-Myers Squibb*,[70] a case involving repackaging and parallel import of pharmaceuticals. The CJEU held that a trade-mark may be upheld to prevent further marketing of a repackaged medicinal product, unless five conditions are met: the trade-mark would artificially partition markets along national lines; the repackaging would not affect the original product; the new packaging clearly identifies both the repackager and the manufacturer of the original product; the packaging does not damage the reputation of the trade-mark holder; and the importer notifies the trade-mark owner in advance of marketing. In other words, so long as the parallel importer complies with the notification requirement, identifies the original manufacturer and packages appropriately, once a trade-marked pharmaceutical is placed on the market in one Member State, those trade-mark rights are exhausted. In 2006, AG Sharpston observed (quoting the English Court of Appeal) that the law here was a 'pickle',[71] and that it was high time that the principles of the case law were applied by national courts without regular recourse to the CJEU. Her argument was that the *Bristol-Myers Squibb* test was a sufficiently clear interpretation of Article 7 (2) of the Trade-marks Directive. Trade-mark rights will not be exhausted if there are legitimate reasons for the holder of the trade-mark to oppose further marketing of the product, and repackaging will constitute a 'legitimate reason' unless the *Bristol-Myers Squibb* test is satisfied.[72] The CJEU agreed.[73]

Thus, trade-marks may not be used to protect high prices within a particular Member State – the application of internal market law makes lawful cross-border trade in trade-marked pharmaceuticals. In this respect, EU health law influences what Hancher has called the 'market pathway' for regulating pharmaceutical products: the prices and conditions under which pharmaceuticals are purchased, primarily by national health care bodies (authorities, insurance bodies), but also ultimately by patients themselves.[74] Here, then, EU health law reframes those purchases as fundamentally based in consumerism, that is, they are seen as based upon exchange in a market.

However, EU health law has not gone so far as redressing the underlying barrier to cross-border trade – the very existence of price differentials for pharmaceuticals and other medical products across the Member States. The only piece of EU-level legislation here is the Transparency Directive 89/105/EEC,[75] which

---

[68]   Directive 89/104/EEC above n 66, Article 7 (2).
[69]   Directive 2008/95/EC [2008] OJ L299/25.
[70]   *Bristol-Myers Squibb*, C-427/93, C-429/93 and C-436/93, EU:C:1996:282.
[71]   Opinion in *Boehringer Ingelheim 2*, C-348/04, EU:C:2006:235, paragraph 2.
[72]   Opinion in *Boehringer Ingelheim 2* EU:C:2006:235, paragraph 16-20.
[73]   *Boehringer Ingelheim 2*, C-348/04, EU:C:2007:249, paragraph 31.
[74]   Hancher, 'The EU Pharmaceuticals Market: parameters and pathways' in Mossialos et al., above n 24, 635-682.
[75]   Directive 89/105/EEC [1989] OJ L40/8. For discussion, see: Hancher and Sauter, above n 4, 168-173.

imposes what are basically procedural requirements on the Member States, to provide annual information on pharmaceutical prices that have been fixed during that year,[76] or information on the criteria for determining profitability,[77] where that is the mechanism chosen for price control. In 2011, the Commission was reported to have abandoned legislative attempts to strengthen the Transparency Directive for procedures that support developing a wider policy consensus on pharmaceutical pricing within the EU.[78] However, it proposed a new Directive, which clarifies the case law and tightens time limits and enforcement, in 2012.[79] Legislative attempts to create the single market here have failed, and thus it is not a surprise that litigation continues to be used to tackle barriers to cross-border trade, both by private litigants and by the Commission itself.[80]

What is important for the analysis here is that the way that these cases are framed and reasoned, and the rationales of the EU legislation where it applies. How does EU health law consider the position of intellectual property holders, parallel importers and consumers in the internal market? Bringing these matters within the purview of EU law necessarily frames disputes in those terms, and removes from the debate the wider questions of the need to 'close' national health (insurance) systems from extra-territorial competition. Such measures operate to protect negotiated prices for pharmaceuticals or medical services, within a health care system seeking to provide access to health care on the basis of medical need, in the context of a need to control prices because of national budget constraints. Those questions are certainly invisible in terms of the text of the Transparency Directive, suggesting that consumerism is strongly present here. On the other hand, the Directive is not, on its face, concerned with consumers. So, it is also difficult to sustain the argument that the EU legislation represents a strong example of EU health law as promoting consumerization. On balance, however, the silence of the Directive on the subject of the broader contexts of health systems is probably enough to support such an argument.

It is also difficult to assess the extent to which litigation involving parallel imports of pharmaceuticals exemplifies the consumerization tendency of EU health law. The reasoning in the CJEU's case law makes very little reference at all to the wider context in which this litigation takes place. The only place where it does so is where the CJEU assesses whether the trade-mark will 'artificially

---

[76] Directive 89/105/EEC, Article 2 (3) and 3 (3).   [77] Directive 89/105/EEC, Article 5 (a)-(d).

[78] See: Hancher, above n 74 637-8; 661; 672-77.

[79] Commission, 'Proposal for a Directive relating to the transparency of measures regulating the prices of medicinal products for human use and their inclusion in the scope of public health insurance systems' COM (2012) 84 final. See: Hancher and Sauter, above n 4, 173.

[80] See: e.g. *Boehringer Ingelheim* EU:C:2007:249; *Pharmacia & Upjohn v Paranova*, C-379/97, EU:C:1999:494; *Phytheron*, C-352/95, EU:C:1997:170; *Loendersloot*, C-349/95, EU:C:1997:530; *Merck Sharp & Dohme*, C-267/95 and C-268/95, EU:C:1996:468; *Biogen*, C-181/95, EU:C:1997:32; *Pharmon* EU:C:1985:304; *Merck v Stephar* EU:C:1981:180; *Hoffman La-Roche v Centrafarm* EU:C:1977:89; *De Peijper* EU:C:1976:67. See also the judgment of the EFTA Court in *Paranova v Merck (E-3/02)* [2003] 3 CMLR 7.

partition markets'. In so doing, the CJEU does pay attention to effects of the trade-mark upon the underlying rules, such as those authorizing packaging only of a certain size, or making reimbursement under a national health insurance scheme conditional on the size of the packaging, or medical prescription practices that are based on standard sizes recommended by health care professionals, or by national health insurance bodies.[81] To that extent, therefore, the CJEU does look beyond the individual trading relationships, based on an underlying notion of contract or exchange, to the wider context of the national health system. But the very invisibility of these debates in the litigation in general suggests that this area could be a strong example of consumerization: EU law simply does not construct the relationships involved in such a way as to reflect solidarity, trust or equity: it constructs them as relationships of trade and consumption.

Patient or consumer protection rules

In addition to using EU law to bring litigation challenging intellectual property rules, companies operating within the EU's health systems have used EU law to challenge national patient or consumer protection rules. The US cosmetics firm Estée Lauder brought some of the earliest litigation using EU free movement law to tackle national rules which sought to protect patients from misleading product descriptions or misleading advertising.[82] Estée Lauder marketed cosmetics under the name 'Clinique' in several EU Member States. But German law prohibited marketing of cosmetics using names liable to mislead consumers by attributing to those products attributes that they do not possess. Germany claimed that the name 'Clinique' could mislead consumers into thinking that the cosmetics had medicinal properties. Estée Lauder therefore sold the same products under a different name – 'Linique' – in the German market. Seeking to save on reduced packaging and advertising costs, by selling their products with the same packaging and advertising across the EU, Estée Lauder challenged the German law.

As the relevant EU legislation in force at the time[83] did not fully harmonize national laws on prohibition of misleading advertising, Member States were permitted to maintain their own national laws on the subject, provided these were consistent with the Treaty rules on free movement of goods.[84] Applicable EU legislation was to be interpreted consistently with those Treaty rules. But the extra expense of different packaging and advertising costs constituted a *prima facie* breach of those rules, which had to be justified. The CJEU found no justification whatsoever. There was no evidence that consumers in other

---

[81] *Bristol-Myers Squibb* EU:C:1996:282, paragraph 53.
[82] *Wettbewerb*, C-315/92, EU:C:1994:34.
[83] Directive 84/450/EEC [1984] OJ L250/17; Directive 76/768/EEC [1976] OJ L262/169.
[84] *Wettbewerb*, paragraphs 9-17.

Member States were fooled by the name 'Clinique'. The products were sold in perfumeries and department stores, not pharmacies. Hence the German law was not justified by the need to protect human health.[85]

On the other hand, in *Ortscheit*, a pharmaceuticals importer, Eurim-Pharm GmbH, was unsuccessful in challenging national law. Eurim-Pharm relied on EU law as a defence in a claim brought by a competitor, Lucien Ortscheit GmbH. Ortscheit sought an order against Eurim-Pharm on the basis that it was breaching German law prohibiting the advertisement of pharmaceuticals (Heilmittelwerbegesetz, para. 8) which were not authorized for marketing in Germany. The relevant pharmaceuticals had marketing authorizations in other Member States. German law (Arzneimittelgesetz (Law on Medicinal Products), para. 73 (3)) allowed their import, but only where, in each individual case, there was a medical prescription and an order from a pharmacist. The national rule obviously treated foreign pharmaceuticals differently from domestically produced pharmaceuticals, and thus *prima facie* fell foul of EU law on free movement of goods. Was it justified on the grounds of protection of human health? Yes. Applying a test of proportionality, the CJEU pointed out that, at the time, no EU-level legislation was yet in force harmonizing patient-protection rules on pharmaceuticals marketing and advertising. A Directive was in the pipeline, but had not yet entered into effect. So Member States were entitled to prohibit entirely the marketing on their territory of pharmaceuticals that were not authorized for consumption there. Otherwise, if pharmaceuticals that were not authorized in Germany could be advertised there, then the German authorization rules – which form an important element of patient protection – could be bypassed altogether. Pharmaceuticals manufacturers could simply gain authorization in another Member State, where authorization was easier to achieve, and then import them into Germany, having encouraged individual orders through effective advertising campaigns. Heilmittelwerbegesetz, Para 8 was held to be consistent with EU law.

What matters for our purposes is how the CJEU interpreted the relationships between patients and pharmacists. The idea that, were the CJEU not to uphold the Heilmittelwerbegesetz, para. 8, pharmaceuticals importers could access patients through advertising, suggests that the CJEU understands patients as autonomous actors, able to be targeted directly by producers. The idea is of a consumer, exercising choice, rather than a patient, being cared for by a health care professional, or treated within the context of equal access to care through a national health (insurance) system. For sure, patients need to be protected. But as *consumers*, not in any other way.

The German Heilmittelwerbegesetz, para. 8 was challenged again some twelve years later,[86] this time with a different outcome. Pharmaceuticals trader Juers Pharma Import–Export GmbH specialized in the trade of products which fell within that provision of national law. Its marketing model was to send to

---

[85] *Wettbewerb*, paragraphs 21-22.   [86] *Juers Pharma*, C-143/06, EU:C:2007:656.

pharmacists lists of medicinal products, not authorized for marketing in Germany, identified by trade name, and noting information about packaging size, dosage (where different dosages are offered in a particular product), country where the product is authorized or country of origin and price. The German pharmacists would then order the products they required. A pharmacy, Ludwigs-Apotheke München Internationale, whose business was threatened by other pharmacies taking advantage of the services of Juers Pharma, sought an injunction to stop Juers Pharma from sending the lists.

By this time, EU legislation covered pharmaceuticals advertising. As we have already noted, what is now Directive 2001/83/EC,[87] as amended, prohibits the marketing of pharmaceuticals in the EU without a prior marketing authorization.[88] There is an exception in Article 5 (1) allowing Member States to exclude from the Directive, 'medicinal products supplied in response to a bona fide unsolicited order, formulated in accordance with the specifications of an authorised health-care professional and for use by an individual patient under his direct personal responsibility' in order to 'fulfil special needs':[89] in other words, pharmacists and medical professionals may supply pharmaceuticals tailor-made for a specific individual patient, without having the normal marketing authorization. In 2001, specific provisions covering advertising were added to the pre-existing EU legislation on pharmaceuticals. The Directive defines advertising as 'any form of... information... or inducement designed to promote the prescription, supply or consumption of medicinal products', aimed either at the general public or at pharmacists or medical professionals with the authority to prescribe medicines.[90] The definition excluded 'factual, informative announcements and reference material, relating, for example, to pack changes... trade catalogues and price lists, provided they include no product claims'.[91] At first instance, the German court held that the lists supplied by Juers Pharma fell within this concept, and were not advertising. On appeal, the national court referred to the CJEU, asking whether the first instance court was correct in its interpretation of the definition of advertising of pharmaceuticals, and what was the relationship between the EU legislation and national legislation that governs pharmaceuticals advertising?

EU legislation such as Directive 2001/83/EC seeks to create the internal market (here in medicinal products) by 'harmonizing' the trading conditions for those products. The EU legislature has adopted various approaches to 'harmonization', which range from a 'maximum harmonization' approach, in which the EU legislation exhaustively regulates a particular field, leaving no discretion

[87] As amended by Directive 2004/27/EC [2004] OJ L136/34.
[88] Directive 2001/83/EC [2001] OJ L311/67, Article 6 (1): 'No medicinal product may be placed on the market of a Member State unless a marketing authorisation has been issued by the competent authorities of that Member State in accordance with this Directive or an authorisation has been granted in accordance with Regulation 2309/93/EEC OJ 1993 L214/1'.
[89] Directive 2001/83/EC, Article 5 (1).   [90] Directive 2001/83/EC, Article 86.
[91] Directive 2001/83/EC, Article 86 (2).

to Member States to have different national rules; to a 'minimum harmonization' approach, in which Member States are required to comply with an EU minimum level of consumer protection, but are free to impose higher standards, so long as those higher standards do not breach the Treaty rules on free movement of goods.[92] The question in *Juers Pharma* was, essentially, which of those was the case for the EU rules on pharmaceuticals advertising?

The CJEU held that the Artzneimittelgesetz, para. 73 (1), gave effect in Germany to the general prohibition on marketing of unauthorized pharmaceuticals. But para. 73 (3) permits pharmacists, in order to meet an order from an individual, to obtain limited quantities of pharmaceuticals that are not authorized in Germany, but are authorized for marketing in another Member State.[93] Thus, reasoned the CJEU, this provision of German law gives effect to Directive 2001/83/EC, Article 5 (1). Accordingly, the advertising provisions of the Directive are not applicable to pharmaceuticals supplied under para. 73(3).[94] The CJEU went on to decide whether, in the absence of applicable EU *legislation*, the German rules were inconsistent with the *Treaty rules* on free movement of goods. Applying *Ortscheit*, the CJEU held that the German advertising law constitutes a *prima facie* breach of the Treaty. But, on the justification question, the CJEU held this time that the proportionality principle was *not* satisfied. Even though the EU legislation did not apply, the specific provisions on advertising in the EU legislation 'strengthened the exceptional nature'[95] of the rule in Article 5 (1). The derogation was understood by the CJEU as casting pharmacists in the 'passive role of intermediaries', responding only to individual patient requests. Where the information being supplied by Juers Pharma was in the form of lists of products, with no substantive information about therapeutic effects, the claim that the German law on the advertising of medicines (Heilmittelwerbegesetz, para. 8), which prohibits advertising of pharmaceuticals that could be acquired under Artzneimittelgesetz, para. 73 (3), was necessary to protect patients by limiting the volume of imports from other Member States of pharmaceuticals that were not authorized to be marketed in Germany, was 'not very plausible'.[96] Such information could not be regarded as encouraging, or even permitting, pharmacists to recommend the importation of such pharmaceuticals.[97]

We might well quibble with CJEU's reasoning here. If the role of pharmacists were really so passive, why would Juers Pharma expend resource in supplying the lists to its clients? That would make little business sense. The pharmaceuticals industry is a complex web of market actors, each seeking to maximize its profits, as a private enterprise, responsible ultimately to its shareholders. In reasoning that the German law was not justified, the CJEU plays down the

---

[92] The CJEU held that Directive 2001/83/EC brings about 'complete harmonisation' in *Gintec*, C-374/05, EU:C:2007:654, paragraph 39.

[93] *Juers Pharma* EU:C:2007:656, paragraph 20.   [94] *Juers Pharma*, paragraph 23.

[95] *Juers Pharma*, paragraph 35.   [96] *Juers Pharma*, paragraph 39.   [97] *Ibid.*

role of the national legislation in protecting patients *qua* patients. It bases its reasoning on the notion of a reasonably informed consumer (patient), who is an active participant in his own health care, exercising choices, and articulating those to the (implicitly passive) supplying pharmacy. The EU legislation restricting direct-to-consumer pharmaceuticals advertising is there to protect such consumers, within this consumerist frame. But outside of the scope of that legislation, there is no longer any need (the EU legislature having provided sufficient consumer protection) for national patient protection laws. Consumer choice is paramount.

A similar approach is seen in *Humanplasma*,[98] involving another piece of 'minimum harmonization' EU legislation, Directive 2002/98/EC on human blood safety.[99] Austrian legislation (Blutsicherheitsgesetz 1999, para. 8(4)) prohibited paid blood donation. Imports of blood products into Austria were prohibited unless the blood was donated without any payment whatsoever being made (Arzneiwareneinfuhrgesetz 2002, para. 7(1a)).[100] The relevant EU legislation encourages,[101] but does not require, unpaid donation. Moreover, it explicitly permits Member States to have more stringent rules, in particular 'requirements for voluntary and unpaid donations', provided these are consistent with the EU Treaty.[102] A hospital association in Vienna had issued an invitation to tender for a contract for supply of blood products. HumanPlasma GmbH tendered for the contract, and its tender was cheaper than that of the only competitor, the Austrian Red Cross (a charity). But the Austrian legislation was amended, inserting para. 7(1a), during the time between HumanPlasma making its tender, and the hospital association deciding which of the two tenderers to choose. The hospital association deemed HumanPlasma's tender rejected, on the grounds that it could not guarantee compliance with the new Austrian law on blood donation. HumanPlasma sought review of this decision before a national public procurement review tribunal. The question was whether the Austrian law was consistent with the EU Treaty on free movement of goods.

Again the CJEU found that the measure was *prima facie* in breach of the Treaty. The CJEU held that the aim of ensuring blood safety, and of pursuing the objective of unpaid blood donations, as enshrined in EU legislation, could in principle justify such a restriction on free movement of goods.[103] But the Austrian legislation was deemed to be too restrictive of free movement of goods. In banning even reimbursement of travel expenses associated with blood donation, the Austrian legislation had gone further than was necessary to pursue those aims. Blood safety was ensured by compliance with the minimum requirements in the EU legislation.[104] In its assessment, the CJEU also adopted a comparative approach, noting that many Member States do allow payment

---

[98] *Humanplasma* C-421/08, EU:C:2010:760.   [99] Directive 2002/98/EC [2003] OJ L33/30.

[100] The national law included exceptions for the case of urgent need in an acute emergency, allowing blood donors' expenses to be covered in such cases.

[101] Directive 2002/98/EC [2003] OJ L33/30, Recital 23; Article 20 (1).

[102] Directive 2002/98/EC, Article 4 (2).   [103] *Humanplasma* EU:C:2010:760, paragraph 33.

[104] *Humanplasma*, paragraph 42, 44.

of expenses, small tokens, and refreshments.[105] As in *Juers Pharma*, the CJEU here essentially adopts an interpretation of the Treaty that is consistent with the notion that the EU legislation itself is sufficient to guarantee consumer protection.

One difference between *Clinique*, on the one hand, and *Ortscheit*, *Juers Pharma* and *HumanPlasma*, on the other, is that *Clinique* concerns a product that is not a health product – and indeed it concerns a product that is neutral in terms of its health effects. In that context, any restrictions based on protecting human health are not easily justified. In the context of the CJEU's jurisprudence on pharmaceuticals (*Ortschiet*, *Juers Pharma*), on products deriving from human blood (*HumanPlasma*) and on medical devices (see *Ker-Optika*,[106] discussed above), the CJEU distinguishes between instances where there is EU legislation and those where there is not. Before the EU has adopted relevant legislation, the CJEU respects the patient protection measures put in place by the relevant Member State. Thereafter, the CJEU regards the EU legislation as securing sufficient patient protection. The latter is the case even where the legislation secures only minimum harmonization. The reliance on EU legislation as the source of patient protection perforce constructs the question of application of EU law as one essentially of consumer protection law, because that is the basis of the EU legislation itself. The interactions between the EU Treaty and EU legislation are such that the EU's consumer protection legislation is effectively seen as making it almost impossible to justify more trade-restrictive patient protection rules imposed at national level. But, irrespective of whether there is EU legislation or national legislation, the point is that the frame – that of consumer protection – remains constant.

But this consumer protection frame is incomplete – or at least its strongest version is not always present in the CJEU's more recent case law. In the past, where the product itself is potentially *harmful* to health, such as is the case with alcohol, the CJEU has traditionally adopted a trade-favourable approach, holding, applying the proportionality test, that effective labelling is sufficient to protect consumers. The classic example of this approach is the 1979 *Cassis de Dijon* ruling[107] in which the CJEU held that rules fixing alcohol content of certain drinks contravened EU free movement law, and were not justified on grounds of health protection.[108] Similarly, some years later, in *German Beer Purity Law*,[109] the CJEU noted that consumers could be protected from unwitting consumption of harmful products through the information given in product labels, rather than more trade-restrictive rules, such as those banning additives in alcohol products.[110] In *Rosengren*, the CJEU found the Swedish alcohol monopoly rules contrary to free movement law and not justified by public health protection.[111]

---

[105] *Humanplasma*, paragraph 41.   [106] *Ker-Optika* EU:C:2010:725.

[107] *Cassis de Dijon*, C-120/78, EU:C:1979:42.   [108] *Cassis de Dijon*, paragraphs 10-11.

[109] *Beer Purity*, C-178/84, EU:C:1987:126.   [110] *Beer Purity*, paragraphs 35-36.

[111] *Rosengren*, C-170/04, EU:C:2007:313.

Yet this approach has come increasingly under scrutiny over the last decade.[112] In 2004, the French *Loi Evin*,[113] which prohibits direct or indirect TV advertising of alcohol, was held to be a proportionate public health protection measure, even though it impedes free movement of advertising services. Two years later, the CJEU upheld the Finnish *Alkoholilaki*[114] 'Law on Alcohol', which, inter alia, prohibits the unlicensed importation of products with an alcohol content of over 80 per cent alcohol by volume.[115] The Scottish Court of Session, applying EU law, held in 2013 that the Alcohol (Minimum Pricing) (Scotland) Act 2012 was lawful,[116] although subsequently at least five EU Member States have approached the Commission[117] with a view to further litigation.[118] In the courts' reasoning in all of these cases, the collective public health imperatives are much more prominent than the individual consumer protection frame. And in a case in which a claim that an alcoholic beverage was *beneficial* to human health came under scrutiny[119] the CJEU adopted a different approach altogether, by focusing on human rights. The CJEU reasoned that national rules prohibiting the labelling of wine with health claims ('easily digestible') were necessary to ensure compliance with the right to health in Article 35 of the EU's Charter of Fundamental Rights. Again, it is difficult to defend the strongest form of the claim that EU health law alters legal understandings of relationships between patients and health care professionals, or national health care systems. EU health law does not construct those relationships as solely based on individual consumption, where choice and autonomy are protected through contract (albeit regulated contracting). EU health law also sees the bigger picture of group solidarity, the need to protect scarce public resource, and the protection of public health through a range of regulatory measures, including through collective, even paternalistic, values.[120]

[112] On the ways in which the CJEU has developed the idea that public health protection is a matter for EU law, not a matter to be left to Member States, and thus vulnerable to challenge for being restrictive of trade, see Hervey, 'The Role of the European Court of Justice in the Europeanization of Communicable Disease Control: Driver or Irrelevance?' (2012) 37 *Journal of Health Politics, Policy and Law* 975. See also the approach in *Josemans*, C-137/09, EU:C:2010:433 as applied to the smoking of marihuana in 'coffee shops' in Maastricht, near the Netherlands/German border.

[113] Law No 91-32 of 10 January 1991 on the campaign against smoking and alcoholism ('Loi Evin') (JORF of 12 January 1991) 6615.

[114] Alkoholilaki (The Alcohol Act) No. 1143/1994 (8 December 1994).

[115] *Ahokainen and Leppik*, C-434/04, EU:C:2006:609.

[116] *The Scotch Whisky Association v Lord Advocate* [2013] CSOH 70.

[117] See: Cook, 'Minimum alcohol pricing: Five countries oppose Scottish drink plan' (*BBC News*, 25 July 2013).

[118] Under Article 258 TFEU. By contrast, the CJEU held in 2014 that Italian legislation seeking to impose minimum prices for cigarettes, to combat the activities of cigarette manufacturers on price, is contrary to EU law, see: *Yesmoke Tobacco* C-428/13 EU:C:2014:2263.

[119] *Deutsches Weintor*, C-544/10, EU:C:2012:526.

[120] For a discussion of the expression of such values of paternalism in health contexts by institutions 'beyond the state', see: Flear (ed), 'Special Issue: "A symposium with Professor Roger Brownsword:super-stewardship in the context of public health"' (2011) 62(5) *Northern Ireland Legal Quarterly* 569, especially Hervey, 'The European Union, Its Court of Justice, and

Price and profit regulation and restrictions on reimbursement

A similar conclusion is supported if we consider the example of national measures designed to support national health (insurance) systems through price and profit regulation, or through national restrictions on reimbursement for pharmaceuticals, and other health care products or services. In the 1980s, in general, the CJEU adopted a 'strict scrutiny' of such measures. For instance, *Roussel*[121] concerned the Dutch system of fixing pharmaceutical prices, so as to make the sale of imported pharmaceuticals more difficult than the sale of domestic pharmaceuticals. The CJEU held this was contrary to Article 34 TFEU, without even discussing possible justifications, such as the need to protect the Dutch health care system from the exploitative efforts of parallel pharmaceuticals importers. Fixing of pharmaceuticals prices by Italian national authorities was found contrary to Article 34 TFEU, also without explicit discussion of justification, although 'developing the national pharmaceutical and research industries' was mentioned in the judgment.[122]

Nonetheless, even during this time period, the CJEU was not adopting reasoning based entirely on a notion of a consumer-based market in pharmaceuticals. The *Duphar* case[123] is an important example. Several pharmaceuticals companies sought to challenge the Dutch *Besluit farmaceutische hulp ziekenfondsverzekering* (Sickness Insurance Fund (Provision of Medicinal Preparations) Order) 1982.[124] The Order provided that a range of listed pharmaceuticals would not normally be provided to patients under the national health insurance scheme, unless, exceptionally, such a refusal to authorize payment would have an unacceptable harmful effect on an individual patient. The context of the litigation was the beginning of the reform of the Dutch health care system, which continued throughout the 1980s and 1990s. The purpose of the Order was specifically to reduce the burden on the Dutch health care scheme and to eliminate its considerable deficit. While the CJEU held that mere economic considerations, such as matters that were primarily budgetary, could not justify a restriction on free movement of goods,[125] it also observed, canonically, that

> [EU] law does not detract from the powers of Member States to organize their social security systems and to adopt, in particular, provisions intended to govern the consumption of pharmaceutical preparations in order to promote the financial stability of their health-care insurance schemes.[126]

By the 1990s, such reasoning was firmly embedded in the CJEU's approach. In 2012, the European Federation of Pharmaceutical Industries and Associations

---

"Super-Stewardship" in Public Health' in Flear (ed), (2011) 62(5) *Northern Ireland Legal Quarterly* 633.

[121] *Roussel*, C-181/82, EU:C:1983:352.   [122] *Pharmaceuticals Pricing*, C-56/87, EU:C:1988:295.

[123] *Duphar* EU:C:1984:45.   [124] Staatscourant No 139 of 23 July 1982.

[125] *Duphar* EU:C:1984:45, paragraph 23.

[126] *Duphar* EU:C:1984:45, paragraph 16. This principle has been repeated by the CJEU in numerous cases, see further chapter 4.

relied on it (unsuccessfully) in asking the European Commission to restrict parallel imports by a temporary ban, following a report that price cuts for pharmaceuticals, in Greece and other countries badly affected by the Eurozone crisis, to help people afford their medicines, had resulted in wholesalers buying up pharmaceuticals in those Member States and reselling them elsewhere.[127] A Commission challenge to Belgian pharmaceuticals price fixing was unsuccessful.[128] In the same case, the Commission sought to challenge the Belgian rules as to which pharmaceutical products would be authorized for reimbursement under the national health insurance system. These rules, in the Commission's view, operated to confer an advantage on national producers, and thus divided up the internal market. The CJEU disagreed. In its reasoning, the CJEU recognized the special nature of trade in pharmaceuticals, noting that this is not trade in a 'normal' market, because the vast majority of the trade consists in sales to national health (insurance) systems. Hence, held the CJEU, Member States must be permitted to regulate the consumption of pharmaceuticals, for instance, by deciding which pharmaceuticals were reimbursable under national health system arrangements. In particular, this is necessary to secure the financial sustainability of national health (insurance) systems. Of course, this reasoning was mirrored in the litigation brought by individuals, such as the *Decker* and *Kohll* cases, discussed above and in chapter 4. It illustrates, as we have already seen, that the strong form of the claim that EU health law reconfigures relationships within a consumerist frame, cannot be supported once we enter into detailed analysis of the relevant case law.

Services and products provided by pharmacies

Probably the best illustration of this conclusion is EU health law governing services or products provided by pharmacies. In a series of cases involving rules relating to the arrangements for sale and supply of products related to health care, the CJEU has confirmed that, in principle, national rules relating to selling arrangements that affect differently the selling of the relevant products by traders within the relevant state, to selling by traders from other Member States,[129] breach Article 34 TFEU. Many such rules relate to the role of pharmacists, and pharmacies, within national health care systems.

In the mid-1990s, the European Commission sought to challenge Greek rules to the effect that infant formula milk could be sold only in pharmacists shops.[130]

---

[127] Fox, 'Drugs supplies to Euro crisis countries at risk, warn health analysts' (*EUObserver*, 23 August 2012).

[128] *Pharmaceuticals Pricing*, C-249/88, EU:C:1991:121. Although the system of 'programme contracts', whereby pharmaceuticals producers entered into contracts with the state authorities, entailing commitments to research, investment and employment, in exchange for authorized prices and reimbursement, was found to breach Article 30 TFEU. This was because the system was such that only national companies could enter into the programme contracts. See also: *AGIM*, C-471/07 and C-472/07, EU:C:2010:9, paragraph 16.

[129] See, classically: *Keck*, C-267/91 and C-268/91, EU:C:1993:905, paragraph 16.

[130] *Infant Milk*, C-391/92, EU:C:1995:199.

Although, in fact, there were no domestic producers of infant formula milk, the CJEU held that the rules affected domestic traders and cross-border traders alike, and found that the rules fell outside the scope of EU law. Likewise, professional conduct rules of a pharmacists' professional association prohibiting pharmacists from advertising 'quasi-pharmaceutical products'[131] outside of the pharmacy itself fall outside the scope of EU law.[132] In those cases, therefore, the consumerist frame of EU law did not apply to the national rules aimed at protecting public health, by promoting breast feeding, or by ensuring professionalism among pharmacists. Although not expressly reasoned on this basis, the rationale of the CJEU implicitly reflects the professional activity and role of pharmacists, as well as the need to secure an adequate supply of medicinal products, using pharmacists as part of the national health system.[133]

Even in cases where the CJEU finds that national rules regulating pharmacies or pharmacists fall within the scope of EU law, analysis of the judgments reveals that the consumerist frame of internal market law is only weakly articulated in these cases. This jurisprudence dates back to the 1980s. In *R. v. Royal Pharmaceutical Society of Great Britain*,[134] the CJEU considered the Royal Pharmaceutical Society's Code of Ethics, which, *inter alia*, prohibited a pharmacist from substituting a therapeutically equivalent product for the product prescribed by a doctor. Doctors are free to prescribe pharmaceuticals by their generic name, or, in the case of proprietary medicinal products, by a specific brand name. The case concerned an attempt to prohibit certain pharmacists from dispensing parallel imports of products that were either generics, or were branded differently from the specification in the prescription, but contained the same active ingredients and preparation. Obviously, the parallel imports were cheaper, so the broader context of the case was also about protecting those parts of the pharmaceutical industry which create and market new products protected by intellectual property rights, in particular trade-marks, rather than the producers of generic medicines. The CJEU found that the rules at issue fell within the scope of Article 34 TFEU. But, on the question of justification, the CJEU did not refer at all to the question of consumer choice, or even the question of access to cheaper products. Rather, the CJEU found that the relevant rules 'are part of the national public health system'.[135] So long as no EU legislation covered the matter, under Article 36 TFEU, Member States have a significant margin of discretion within which to protect public health within their territories.[136]

---

[131] Without wanting to go into too much detail, 'quasi-pharmaceuticals' or 'quasi-drugs' are defined or categorised differently in different legal systems. They may be defined as 'over the counter pharmaceuticals', or as cosmetics, or as quasi-drugs. They include products such as mouthwashes or deodorants, for treating bad breath or body odour; bathing products designed to prevent inflammation or prickly heat; hair removal cream; hair re-growth cream; anti-acne soap or shower gel; or tooth whitening preparations.

[132] *Hünermund*, C-292/92, EU:C:1993:932.

[133] Contrast, for instance: Opinion in *Hünermund*, C-292/92, EU:C:1993:863, paragraph 30.

[134] *Royal Pharmaceutical Society of Great Britain*, C-266/87 and 267/87, EU:C:1989:205.

[135] *Royal Pharmaceutical Society of Great Britain*, paragraph 21   [136] *Ibid.*

The margin of discretion applies also to national rules that seek to inhibit cross-border trade in pharmaceuticals though the internet. Here the pharmacy DocMorris has been a repeat litigant. DocMorris, established in the Netherlands, operates directly, through subsidiaries, or by franchise arrangements, in various Member States, including Ireland, Sweden, Italy, and Germany, as well as offering direct-to-patient products by mail order through its website. DocMorris' principal market is Germany. German law (Arzneimittelgesetz (Law on Medicinal Products), para. 43(1))[137] prohibited sale by mail order of pharmaceuticals that may only be sold in pharmacies. The establishment of DocMorris's original centre of operation in the Netherlands, around 10 km from the German border, was a deliberate move to circumvent this restriction, as mail order supply of pharmaceuticals is permitted in the Netherlands. A German association of pharmacists brought a claim before the German courts to the effect that DocMorris's activities were unlawful.[138] DocMorris relied on EU law in its defence.

The CJEU began its analysis by distinguishing pharmaceuticals which were authorized for sale in Germany and those which were not. With respect to the latter, German law implemented EU legislation intended to protect patients, and was not unlawful under the Treaty rules.[139] With respect to the former, the CJEU considered first whether the matter was covered by EU legislation on distance sales and electronic commerce.[140] This legislation is very much cast in terms of consumer protection. It sets a minimum level required to protect consumers, and permits Member States to adopt more stringent rules, including a ban on marketing pharmaceuticals by means of distance contracts.[141] These more stringent consumer protection rules are, however, subject to the TFEU rules on free movement.[142] Applying the standard *Dassonville* test, the CJEU found that the rules fell within the scope of EU law. The German prohibition affected the sale of domestic pharmaceuticals differently to the way in which it affected the sale of pharmaceuticals being imported from other Member States: there was therefore a 'direct or indirect, actual or potential' effect on cross-border trade.[143]

So far, the CJEU's analysis is standard free movement analysis, very much based in an underlying consumerist frame. But, when it turned to the question of justification, the CJEU conceptualized the purchasers and suppliers of *prescription-only* pharmaceuticals differently. For *over-the-counter* pharmaceuticals, the likely dangers posed by their purchase through the internet are such that, so long as the pharmacist is lawfully established within one Member State, it must be permitted to trade with consumers in all Member States, on the basis of what are essentially consumer transactions, albeit transactions

---

[137] Artzneimittelgesetz (Law on Medicinal Products) BGBl, 1998 I, p 2649.
[138] *DocMorris* EU:C:2003:664.   [139] *DocMorris*, paragraphs 52-54.
[140] Directive 97/7/EC [1997] OJ L144/19.   [141] Directive 97/7/EC, Article 14.
[142] *DocMorris*, paragraphs 63-65.   [143] *DocMorris*, paragraphs 66-76.

that are regulated through professional conduct rules. But for *prescription-only* pharmaceuticals, the reasoning is reversed. Where a pharmaceutical has been designated prescription-only, the greater risk involved should that product be consumed by the wrong consumer, or inappropriately, justifies the requirement for the pharmacist physically to check the prescription and ensure that the pharmaceutical reaches the correct patient, and appropriate advice is provided. Two reasons are given for this in the CJEU's judgment: the greater risk to patients presented by prescription-only pharmaceuticals and the need to protect the arrangements for pharmaceuticals pricing within national health systems.[144] In the CJEU's reasoning, therefore, patients are not simple consumers, and the broader context of the role of pharmacists within the national health system is taken into account.

Similar rationales are expressed by the CJEU in cases concerning national rules on pharmacies contracted to supply public hospitals;[145] rules restricting who may operate a pharmacy;[146] rules which restrict, on a geographical basis, the opening of new pharmacies;[147] rules on the licensing of pharmacies;[148] and rules on opening times, duty rotas and holidays for pharmacies.[149] In all of these cases, the CJEU respects the margin of discretion of the Member States to protect patients, and public health, through the regulation of pharmacies and pharmacists. The relationships between patients, prescribing doctors, pharmacists and national health systems, are conceptualized in ways that go beyond standard consumer relations of choice and autonomy. Rather, the solidarity-based aspects of national health care systems, and the professional–patient relationships embedded in the way in which they are organized, are respected by the CJEU.

This approach to the place of pharmacists and pharmacies in EU law is also reflected in the Patients' Rights Directive.[150] Although the Directive provides that, 'in principle', prescriptions should be recognized across borders,[151] the detail of the Directive's Article 11 recognizes the role of prescriptions within national health systems. Cross-border recognition of prescriptions may be limited to protect public health, to protect rules on reimbursement of pharmaceuticals or medical devices within national health care systems, or where restrictions are 'based on legitimate and justified doubts about the authenticity, content or

---

[144] *DocMorris*, paragraph 117, although the latter ground was not, in fact, supported by sufficient evidence in that particular instance.
[145] *Hospital Pharmacies*, C-141/07, EU:C:2008:492.
[146] *Pharmacists*, C-531/06, EU:C:2009:315; *Apothekerkammer des Saarlandes*, C-171/07 and C-172/07, EU:C:2009:316.
[147] *Pérez and Gómez*, C-570/07 and C-571/07, EU:C:2010:300; Order in *Grisoli*, C-315/08, EU:C:2011:618.
[148] *Susisalo*, C-84/11, EU:C:2012:374.
[149] *Sbarigia*, C-393/08, EU:C:2010:388. In this instance, the CJEU held that no EU law was applicable to the circumstances of the case.
[150] Directive 2011/24/EU [2011] OJ L88/45.   [151] Directive 2011/24/EU, Recital 53.

comprehensibility of an individual prescription'. Special recognition of the ethical basis of professional conduct is expressly included:

> In particular, the recognition of prescriptions shall not affect a pharmacist's right, by virtue of national rules, to refuse, for ethical reasons, to dispense a product that was prescribed in another Member State, where the pharmacist would have the right to refuse to dispense, had the prescription been issued in the Member State of affiliation.

Thus the ethical and professional basis of the relationships between prescribing doctors, pharmacists and patients are protected and reflected in the EU's legislature as well as its case law. This is not simply a relationship of consumer interactions. Pharmacists are recognized as playing an important role in securing patient safety, efficacy of treatment and in controlling costs to the national health (insurance) system in all Member States.[152] Nor does it seem that pharmacists are a 'special case' in this respect. We have already seen similar reasoning applied in the case of other health care professionals, such as opticians.[153]

Summary

Considering litigation brought by the European Commission and legal persons in the round, and in the context of relevant EU legislation, a mixed picture emerges as to whether EU health law changes legal understandings of relationships between health care professionals and their patients, and moves them towards a consumerist frame. In some contexts, in particular where intellectual property rights are concerned, we do see a strong articulation of consumerism, at least implicitly, through EU health law. But in other areas the consumerist frame is at best incomplete. In general, and on balance, therefore, the strong claim to the effect that EU health law 'consumerizes' patient–professional relationships cannot be supported on the evidence, once examined in detail.

Conclusions

To what extent does EU health law treat health products and services as essentially the same as other consumer products or services available within its internal market? We began these chapters with the observation that the strong version of the claim that EU health law does so is highly controversial. Health law in the EU is traditionally based on relationships of solidarity, of ethics and

---

[152] Appleby and Wingfield, *Dale and Appleby Pharmacy and Medicines Law* (10th edn, Pharmaceutical Press 2013); Weedle and Clarke, *Pharmacy and Medicines Law in Ireland* (Pharmaceutical Press 2011); German Pharmacy Act Geset uber das Apothekenwesen, last amended by the Act for the Structural development of Nursing Care Institutions of May 28th 2008 (Fed Law Gazette 1, page 876).

[153] *Ker-Optika* EU:C:2010:725; *Ottica New Line*, C-539/11, EU:C:2013:591, paragraph 45, explicitly drawing out the similarity with the pharmacy case law.

professional trust, and of dignity. It is not based on relationships of commodification, which is precisely what a strong version of consumerism would imply.
We are now in a position to reach a more balanced conclusion on this question,
with respect to EU health law concerning patients, health care products, or
services.

As was the case with EU health law examined in the previous chapter, when
we consider EU health law involving a health product or service that moves
across borders, our analysis must begin with the observation that the *very
application* of EU law to such products or services requires conceptualizing
relationships within a consumerist frame. Relevant EU legislation is based on
the EU's competence to protect consumers of products or services within its
internal market. Litigation reaches the CJEU because there is a question of free
movement of one of the factors of products at issue: by definition, that means
that there must be some kind of exchange of a commodity for consideration. At
the moment at which the CJEU decided that health was not somehow 'special'
and therefore beyond the reach or scope of EU law, EU health law was cast
within a consumerist frame. There is no doubt, therefore, that consumerism is
a theme of EU health law.

But we have also seen that the strong version of the claim that EU health
law replaces relationships of trust, solidarity or professional ethics with those
of consumer relations cannot be supported once a detailed analysis of the
relevant legislation and litigation is carried out. In some contexts, in particular
the ways in which EU law has dealt with the interplay between intellectual
property rights, parallel imports of pharmaceuticals and cost control measures
for national health (insurance) systems, on balance, consumerism holds sway.
This is so not least because other considerations are rendered invisible in the
legal texts (both legislation and case law). Another such context is where EU
consumer protection law in effect 'occupies the field' driving out national
discretionary space for patient protection rules.

But the same is not true in other contexts. More recent case law concerning protection of consumers from products harmful to health shows increased
respect for collective (national) public health imperatives, such as to reduce
costs to health care systems, and suffering of patients, resulting from alcohol abuse. The same may be said for more recent case law on national price
and profit regulation of pharmaceuticals and the pharmaceutical industry. The
need to secure financial sustainability of national health (insurance) systems
is increasingly recognized by both the CJEU and the EU legislature. This is
all the more critical in the context of fiscal austerity and the Eurozone crisis.
Individual consumer choice does not outweigh the collective needs or entitlements expressed through such arguments. Above all, in its recognition of
the place of health professionals, as *professionals*, not 'service providers', within
national health systems; in its respect for the place of professional judgment
within national health care systems; and in its attention to the broader context
beyond the particular individual claim to a product or service across a border

in the EU, EU health law is not solely based on consumerism. EU health law implies a movement towards a consumerist frame, but the consequences are less significant or wide-ranging than the 'standard narrative' asserts.

To the extent that EU health law does have a weak consumerizing effect, what are the implications for patients? As we already noted in the previous chapter, moves towards 'consumerizing' health care relationships have positive implications for patient autonomy and choice – although those are limited to certain patients (in particular, those most able to exercise autonomy and choice). But, as we have seen in this chapter, it is rarely patients who have taken advantage of EU law in this context. The vast majority of litigants are market actors – companies and professionals seeking to challenge national rules which divide markets and restrict their abilities to capitalize on free movement through economies of scale. And the European Commission has taken the opportunity to pursue its notion of a liberalized market in health products and services too – although not always successfully. There may be benefits to patients *qua* consumers of increased efficiencies through such economies of scale. But there may also be risks – for instance, those inherent in the scaling up of provision of personal services within specific local contexts, such as provided by neighbourhood pharmacies. The implications for patients of the weak consumerizing effect of EU health law are thus that any benefits arising from economies of scale or increased choice are significantly mitigated by the restrictions imposed by the EU legislature and CJEU. Conversely, looking at patients as a whole, in terms of fulfilling their needs to adequate health care, on the basis of medical need, through a solidarity-based national health (insurance) system, EU health law protects those needs. Through recognizing that individual patient desires should not always trump collectively determined allocations of public resource, EU health law may facilitate the protection of those patients who are least able to exercise choice and autonomy: the elderly, the immobile and the impoverished or otherwise excluded. On balance, therefore, EU health law looks a great deal more like the health law of any of its Member States than the strong claim about consumerism as a theme of EU health law implies.

So much for the implications of consumerism as a theme of EU health law for patients. We turn now to the third and final chapter considering the question of the claims made about the consumerizing tendencies of EU health law. In that chapter, EU health law on health professionals is centre stage.

6

Consumerism: the moving health care professional

Introduction

The category of 'health professional' encapsulates an extremely diverse range of professional roles and activities. Any nuanced analysis needs to disaggregate that category, along at least six continua. First, health professionals range from the highly specialized, technologically expert provider of cutting-edge complex health care services (open heart surgery; application of cultured cells to promote healing, such as for burns) through to the provider of health services that border on social care services (community nurse, low grade nurse on geriatric hospital ward). Second, they range from professionals operating within a complex team (which could include laboratory technicians, pharmacists, surgeons, anaesthetists, physiotherapists, psychotherapists or psychiatrists, nurses and so on) through to sole practitioners. Third, a health professional may have been practising for many years, and may have accumulated significant experience (along with practices that may or may not need to be refreshed in the light of new evidence on best practice), or may be newly qualified, or even a student or prospective student. Fourth, in the context of EU health law, we also need to take account of the important legal and contextual differences between a health professional who provides occasional services in a Member State other than that in which she is qualified, and one who is permanently practising in a Member State other than that in which she originally qualified (either because she is employed in that 'host state', or because she is permanently established there as a self-employed professional).[1] Fifth, there are important distinctions in EU law between health professions which are recognized as equivalent in all Member States (general practitioner is an example) and those which are recognized (and hence regulated) in few Member States, or even only one Member State (the German 'Heilpraktiker' is an example). And, sixth, as a broad generalization, the position of health professionals in the EU's northern/western Member States differs from that in its eastern/southern Member States. Levels

---

[1] Irene Glinos distinguishes six types of mobile health professionals: the 'livelihood migrant', 'the career oriented', 'the backpacker', 'the commuter', 'the undocumented' and 'the returner', see: Glinos, 'Going beyond numbers: A typology of professional mobility inside and outside the European Union' (2014) 33(1) *Policy and Society* 25.

of economic development across the EU have significant consequences for their health care systems, including the position of health professionals within them. Large numbers of health professionals are migrating from lower income to higher income countries.[2]

All Member States of the EU regulate health professionals operating within their territories. The rationales for such regulation include the need to correct an imbalance of power between a health professional and her patients, who are in a vulnerable position, with incomplete expertise or information to make informed choices about the health services they receive, and to guard against possible abuses of that imbalance of power. They include the desire to protect the dignity and autonomy of patients, in the context of provision of services which may be extremely personal and intrusive of privacy and bodily integrity. Thus, a strong ethical strand underpins regulation of health professionals. There are also important systemic and public health reasons for regulating health professionals in the context of health care systems where a significant funding burden lies with the public purse (either through taxation or through social insurance),[3] and where the health of the population is an important contributor to national security (for instance, in the context of infectious disease control), equality of all citizens, protection of the most vulnerable in society (such as children and the elderly) and to economic growth.

National regulation of health professions covers educational requirements for access to the profession, use of professional titles, specific skills and attributes demonstrating fitness to practise, continuous professional development, conduct while practising, and ethical behaviour or even attitudes. A wide range of regulatory approaches is found across the EU's Member States, including everything from the force of criminal law to 'soft', non-binding guidance;[4] from state-based regulation to professional association-based regulation to self-regulation; and from models based on detailed behavioural control to those based on trust and professionalism.[5]

Despite all of these significant differences, the aim of this chapter is to draw out some general conclusions on the consequences of EU health law for health professionals, with a focus on individuals and on the consumerist theme. These

---

[2] See: Dayrit et al., 'WHO code of practice on the international recruitment of health personnel' (2008) 86(10) *Bulletin of the World Health Organization* 737, although as Glinos points out, it is extremely difficult to determine accurate numbers of migrating health professionals globally or within the EU: Glinos, above n 1.

[3] For instance, several Member States restrict the numbers of health professionals operating on their territory in various ways; for instance, Germany and Spain limit the number of pharmacists. See: Hervey and McHale, *Health Law and the European Union* (CUP 2004) 192-3.

[4] Some Member States, such as Finland, place a heavier reliance on prevention of poor practice, allowing for a greater range of possibilities for patient redress, such as statements, instructions and guidelines, which do not involved disciplinary measures against a particular health professional. See: Hervey and McHale, above n 3, 192.

[5] For instance, in Belgium, doctors are regulated through the Order of Physicians, initially established by the Law of 25 June 1938. In the UK, doctors are regulated through the General Medical Council, under the Medical Act 1983. See: Hervey and McHale, above n 3, 191.

general conclusions should be understood in the context of the significant differences outlined above. Where possible, the different contexts will be elaborated in the analysis. As with the two preceding chapters, the general points we make here emerge from detailed analysis of relevant legal provisions in their specific contexts. And again, as with the two preceding chapters, of course it is not really possible to separate the individual from the collective frame, or the EU's internal health law from its external health law, but we do so here to sharpen the analytical focus. We return to the systemic implications of EU health law for health professionals in Part III, and some aspects of the international context of health professional practice in Part IV.

As with EU health law as applied to moving patients, or to moving health care products or services, the claims made about consumerism as a theme of EU health law in the context of health professionals focus around the commodification of health care. The strongest version of the claim is that the effect of EU health law is a tendency for relationships between professionals and patients to be understood through consumerism, rather than solidarity. EU health law treats health professionals as first and foremost market actors, as 'service providers', subject to consumer law; not as professionals, subject to the legal and ethical frameworks of professional regulation. Service providers are understood as operating in a market; professionals as operating in the context of national health (insurance) systems.

Some claim that benefits arise from the consumerist frame. They focus on the promise of economies of scale inherent in the creation of a single European market in services and labour. For instance, the larger market of the EU, rather than the atomised markets of its twenty-eight Member States, creates benefits in highly specialized care, where the very best treatments can be made available at EU level in contexts where the scale of required investment per patient would not be viable within a particular Member State, especially those with less developed economies. Miek Peeters, Martin McKee and Sherry Merkur[6] begin their analysis of EU law on health professionals with a story of the world's first ever face transplant operation taking place in France, with the involvement of health professionals from more than one Member State. The idea of 'European reference networks' linking health professionals within 'centres of expertise' for highly specialized, or technologically innovative, health care is a legal and policy reflection of the promise of this type of benefit from economies of scale.[7] The larger EU market is also said to manage more effectively the surpluses and shortages of health professionals across the EU's territory, as qualified health

---

[6] Peeters, McKee and Merkur, 'EU Law and Health Professionals' in Mossialos et al. (eds), *Health Systems Governance in Europe: the role of European Union Law and Policy* (CUP 2010).

[7] Directive 2011/24/EU [2011] OJ L88/45, Article 12; Regulation 141/2000/EC [2000] OJ L18/1; The European Union Committee of Experts on Rare Diseases (EUCERD), formally established via Decision 2009/872/EC [2009] OJ L315/18, advises the European Commission on European reference networks, see: Aymé and Rodwell (eds), '2013 Report on the State of the Art of Rare Disease Activities in Europe' (EUCERD, European Union 2013).

professionals can move to where the 'market' needs them.[8] In border areas, particularly of geographical remoteness, enabling health professionals to work across borders makes good sense for reasons of practical economy.[9] In short, the claim is that a single market in EU health professionals is necessary to make the best use of professional resources.

But of course this notion has a darker side. The significant economic disparities between EU Member States mean a de facto brain drain from east and south to north and west in the EU. This movement of health professionals threatens the viability of Central and Eastern European health care systems which are based on a plentiful supply of cheap labour, in the absence of more expensive health technologies.[10] Moreover, cross-border movement of health professionals to provide a service on a temporary basis (rather than to become established) threatens quality of care from a patient perspective. Lack of effective information exchange, for instance, about differences in professional practice between different Member States, may have unfortunate consequences, and may even threaten very basic patient safety. Where national rules on privacy differ, information about fitness to practise may not be shared across borders, and, consequently, unjustified assumptions about fitness to practise of such migrant health professionals may be made by patients, health authorities or employers.[11]

More fundamentally, in the context of EU health law, regulation of health professionals, rather than being seen as a protection for patients, or inherent in the proper functioning of national health care systems, is conceptualized as an obstacle to the operation of the market. To that extent, a health professional is treated in EU law as equivalent to any other professional who provides services, takes up employment or establishes herself in a Member State other than the state in which she became professionally qualified. The way in which health professionals are regulated in EU law takes little or no account of the special nature of health services. There are fundamentally divergent views across the EU

---

[8] Buchan et al. (eds), 'Health professional mobility in a changing Europe: New dynamics, mobile individuals and diverse responses' (WHO 2014); Glinos, above n 1; Wismar et al. (eds), 'Health Professional Mobility and Health Systems: Evidence from 17 European countries' (WHO 2011); Peeters, McKee and Merkur, above n 6.

[9] Legido-Quigley et al., 'Patient Mobility in the European Union' (2007) 334 *British Medical Journal* 188.

[10] Dussault and Buchan, 'The economic crisis in the EU: Impact on health workforce mobility' in Buchan et al. (eds), 'Health professional mobility in a changing Europe: New dynamics, mobile individuals and diverse responses' (WHO 2014); Galan et al., 'Emergent challenge of health professional emigration: Romania's accession to the EU' in Wismar et al., above n 8; but see also: Kautsch and Czabanowsk, 'When the grass gets greener at home: Poland's changing incentives for health professional mobility' in Wismar et al., above n 8; Peeters, McKee and Merkur, above n 6, 589-90.

[11] For instance, different Member States interpret the requirements of Directive 95/46/EC [1995] OJ L281/31 differently in circumstances where a health professional has been suspended from practice pending investigation, or barred from some activities but not others.

about relationships between the state and health professionals, and consequently the relationships between health professionals and their patients.[12] For instance, some Member States base their regulation of at least some health professionals on strong traditions of liberal professionalism, with consequent reliance on self-regulation and trust.[13] At the other end of the spectrum are those Member States which regulate at least some health professionals through detailed state or even quasi-private control, including through structures of new managerialism.[14] These structures control professional behaviour through offering incentives to certain practices or activities, such as payment schedules for family general practitioners, codes of conduct or highly specified protocols (e.g., for hand washing or waste disposal). These incentives or protocols are often coupled with management control of professional practices, particularly in large institutions such as hospitals, where risk management and reporting are used as part of the landscape of regulation of health professionals.

These regulatory approaches, and their rationales, stand in stark contrast to the rationales underlying EU health law. The homogenizing effects of EU free movement law *in and of themselves* challenge national values, where those values conflict with the creation of a single European market. Relevant values include patient safety, protection of dignity, and compensating for information deficits and imbalance of power between patient and health professional. Where Member States express such values through regulation, in EU law, these are regulatory 'measures' which impede free movement. Thus, in EU law, regulatory controls are conceptualized as (potentially justifiable) market inhibitors. EU law achieves this doctrinally by placing free movement, a tool of integration and creation of a single European market, in conflict with other values embedded in national regulation, including regulation of professionals. The 'public good' emanating from free movement is conceptualized in EU law as legally superior to other 'public goods': free movement is the rule; 'public goods' are the exception. It follows that national regulation of health care professionals may be permitted, or even encouraged, in EU health law, *but* it always has to be *justified* as an *exception* to the rule of free movement. At root then, EU health law sees professional regulation as about a 'market' of mobile professionals, rather than seeing it as fundamentally about quality of care. The very act of bringing regulation of health professionals within EU health law is thus *per se* in tension with other regulatory goals.

---

[12] Klein, *The New Politics of the NHS: From Creation to Reinvention* (Radcliffe 2010); Freeman, *The Politics of Health in Europe* (Manchester University Press 2000), especially ch 6; Tuohy, *Accidental Logics: The Dynamics of Change in the Health Care Arena in the United States, Britain and Canada* (OUP 1999); Johnson, Larkin and Sachs (eds), *Health Professions and the State in Europe* (Routledge 1995); Moran and Wood, *States, Regulation and the Medical Profession* (Open University Press 1993).

[13] See: e.g. Jacobs, *Doctors and Rules: A Sociology of Professional Values* (Transaction Publishing 1999).

[14] See: e.g. Friedson, *Profession of Medicine: Study of the Sociology of Applied Knowledge* (University of Chicago Press 1988).

These are strong, and potentially mutually inconsistent, claims. Does EU health law on health professionals bring benefits for patients as consumers, or indeed governments or national health care system institutions as 'consumers' of professional services? Or does the consumerist basis on which EU health law operates threaten the very foundations of health professional relationships, both with patients and with the state? In order to reach a conclusion on the extent to which either of these claims can be supported, the chapter considers each claim in turn, disaggregating the different contexts as outlined above. Before that, we set out the relevant EU legal framework.

Health professionals: applicable law

EU health law seeks to secure free movement of health professionals, either as self-employed persons establishing themselves in a Member State other than that in which they qualified, or as workers employed by a health institution within another Member State. Where health professionals are workers, as opposed to self-employed persons, EU employment law also applies. The key area of contention here has been EU rules on working time, where special arrangements and opt-outs have been applied to the health professional sector.[15] EU health law also covers health professionals who move across borders in the EU as providers of health services. In general, the free movement rules operate through prohibiting barriers ('restrictions') to access of economic actors (here, health professionals) to markets in other Member States than their 'home' Member State (here, the one in which they originally qualified). In addition, the CJEU and the EU legislature have relied upon the legal principle of mutual recognition of professional qualifications.

Self-employed and employed health professionals

Where a (health) professional[16] seeks to practise in a Member State other than that of which she is a national, or other than that in which she is entitled to practise, the Treaty provisions on freedom of establishment, or free movement of workers, may apply. Article 49 TFEU prohibits 'restrictions on the freedom of establishment of nationals of a Member State in the territory of another Member State'. It does so by prohibiting both directly and indirectly discriminatory barriers to cross-border establishment;[17] and also by prohibiting non-discriminatory

---

[15] See below. Hervey and McHale, above n 3, 194-7; Peeters, McKee and Merkur, above n 6, 623-32.

[16] Who is a "citizen of the European Union" or of an EEA state – the position is more complex for the position of "third country" nationals, see: Hervey and McHale, above n 3, 230-233; *Hocsmann*, C-238/98, EU:C:200:440.

[17] The right to take up and pursue activities as a self-employed person is to be under the conditions laid down for the pursuit of such activities applicable to nationals by the host Member State, Article 49 TFEU. This is a specific example of the general principle of non-discrimination on grounds of nationality, see: Article 18 TFEU. Indirect discrimination is

'hindrances', 'obstacles' or 'impediments' to market access.[18] Article 45 TFEU provides that 'free movement for workers shall be secured within the Union'. It also prohibits national rules that discriminate on the basis of nationality; and rules that do not do so directly, but have the effect of impeding market access.[19] An important type of national rule that impedes professionals from accessing the market in another Member State is the failure to recognize professional qualifications from the home state. Other barriers include requirements about the status of the directors or operators of a company providing health services,[20] or about the legal form of such a company,[21] or prohibiting a professional from having more than one place of operation,[22] or reserving certain kinds of health services for professionals with particular qualifications,[23] or reserving offering of private health services to those who have been authorized to provide services within the national health insurance system,[24] or requiring a health professional to have a bank account with a bank in a particular Member State,[25] or rules on territorial distribution of health establishments.[26] National rules on access to university courses of medical training have also been held to infringe EU law entitling EU citizens to move across the EU as students.[27] Articles 45 and 49 TFEU are directly effective, and thus may be relied upon by an individual in proceedings before national courts in order to tackle national regulatory measures that impede freedom of establishment, irrespective of whether EU-level harmonizing or coordinating legislation has been adopted.[28]

The CJEU defines 'establishment' as 'the actual pursuit of an economic activity through a fixed establishment in another Member State for an indefinite period',[29] where presence in another Member State is 'stable and continuous'.[30] Permanence is thus a key feature of establishment, as distinct from the provision of services, which implies a temporary basis.[31] Establishment also denotes

---

where national rules *de facto* place nationals of another Member State at a disadvantage, for instance, by imposing upon them a "double burden" of regulatory requirements with which to comply, see: *Vlassopoulou*, C-340/89, EU:C:1991:193.

[18] *Haim 2*, C-424/97, EU:C:2000:357; *Payroll Data Services*, C-79/01, EU:C:2002:592; *Wouters*, C-309/99, EU:C:2002:98; *Computer Games*, C-65/05, EU:C:2006:673; *Apothekerkammer des Saarlandes* C-171/07 and 172/07, EU:C:2009:316; *Biomedical analysis laboratories 2*, C-89/09, EU:C:2010:772.

[19] *Bosman*, C-415/93, EU:C:1995:463.

[20] *Clinical Laboratories*, C-221/85, EU:C:1987:81; *Pharmacists*, C-531/06, EU:C:2009:315.

[21] *Sodemare*, C-70/95, EU:C:1997:301.   [22] *Opticians*, C-140/03, EU:C:2005:242.

[23] *MacQuen*, C-108/96, EU:C:2001:67.   [24] *Psychotherapists*, C-456/05, EU:C:2007:755.

[25] *Commission v Austria*, C-356-08, EU:C:2009:401.

[26] *Pérez and Gómez*, C-570/07 and C-571/07, EU:C:2010:300.

[27] *University Education*, C-147/03, EU:C:2005:427; *Morgan and Bucher*, C-11/06 and C-12/06, EU:C:2007:626; *Bressol*, C-73/08, EU:C:2010:181; *Commission v Netherlands*, C-542/09, EU:C:2012:346.

[28] *Walrave and Koch*, C-36/74, EU:C:1974:140; *Boukhalfa*, C-214/94, EU:C:1996:174; *Angonese*, C-281/98, EU:C:2000:296; *Reyners*, C-2/74, EU:C:1974:68; *Thieffry*, C-71/76, EU:C:1977:65; *Patrick*, C-11/77, EU:C:1977:113.

[29] *Factortame 3*, C-221/89, EU:C:1991:320.   [30] *Sodemare* EU:C:1997:301.

[31] *Gebhard*, C-55/94, EU:C:1995:411. See discussion below on cross border service provision.

independence of activity. Where work is carried out 'for and under the direction of another person',[32] the free movement of workers regime applies.

As is the case with freedom to provide and receive services,[33] restrictions on the freedom of establishment and free movement of workers in EU law may be justified. The Treaty itself provides for two types of exemption from the general free movement rules. One (exercise of official authority[34]) does not apply to the health profession.[35] The other, permitting restrictions on grounds of 'public policy, public security and public health',[36] is also reflected in the Treaty provision on free movement of workers, Article 45 (3) TFEU,[37] and the CJEU's jurisprudence may probably be read across both provisions. The CJEU has developed a third type of exemption, applicable where restrictions on the freedom of movement are not measures directly discriminating on grounds of nationality, but are equally applicable to nationals and non-nationals. This line of CJEU jurisprudence recognizes that the TFEU does not envisage a completely deregulated single European market,[38] but rather recognizes that there are differences between national regulatory regimes, and that some national regulation is justified in the public interest. Therefore, freedom of establishment must be reconciled with legitimate national regulatory measures. The legal means by which this balance is reached is the rule that indirectly discriminatory and non-discriminatory restrictions on free movement of persons, including health professionals, are permitted if they are justified in pursuance of a public interest. Such public interest must be objectively defined, and the restrictive national measure must be suitable and proportionate to the aim of protecting the public interest.[39]

So, for instance, in *Commission* v. *France (Establishment of Doctors and Dentists)*,[40] the CJEU considered as possible justification the 'concern that individuals enjoy the most effective and complete health protection possible'; 'the need to ensure continuity of medical treatment'; and considerations of 'medical ethics'.[41] Although, in this particular instance, the CJEU found that such concerns did not, in fact, justify the particular restrictions at issue, the principle is that such aims constitute potential objective public interests. In *Gullung*,[42] the CJEU held that the requirement that lawyers must be registered at a bar must be regarded as lawful in EU law, provided that such

---

[32] *Lawrie-Blum*, C-66/85, EU:C:1986:284.   [33] As we saw in chapters 4 and 5.

[34] Article 51 TFEU.

[35] It applies only to professions concerned with the exercise of the prerogative powers of the state, such as the judiciary: *Reyners* EU:C:1974:68.

[36] Article 52 (1) TFEU.

[37] The grounds are also found in the 'Citizenship Directive', Directive 2004/38/EC [2004] OJ L158/77, Article 27 (1).

[38] See, with respect to freedom of establishment in particular: Edward, 'Freedom of Movement for the Regulated Professions' in White and Smythe (eds), *Current Issues in European and International Law: Essays in Memory of Franck Dowrick* (Sweet and Maxwell 1990) 40.

[39] *Gebhard* EU:C:1995:411.   [40] *Doctors and Dentists*, C-351/90, EU:C:1992:266.

[41] *Doctors and Dentists*, paragraphs 10 and 14.   [42] *Gullung*, C-292/86, EU:C:1988:15.

registration is open to all EU citizens without discrimination. The CJEU observed that such a requirement 'seeks to ensure the observance of moral and ethical principles and the disciplinary control of the activity of lawyers, and thus constitutes an objective worthy of protection'.[43] Such objective public interests presumably also apply in the case of registration requirements for health professionals.

The exact contours of the concept of objective public interest are difficult to discern with precision.[44] This is also true of the public health exemption. Nonetheless, some general observations can be made. The EU legislature has given some guidance on the public health ground. Directive 2004/38/EC[45] lists those diseases that justify a refusal of entry on the grounds of public health.[46] Thus, 'public health' is understood in a narrow, technical and disease-based sense, not a broader meaning, such as protecting the ways in which health professionals interact with a national health (insurance) system, or protecting national ethical rules concerning health care in non-private contexts. In *Commission* v. *France (Establishment of Doctors and Dentists)*,[47] the CJEU held that national rules prohibiting doctors and dentists from practising in France where they were already established in another Member State, unless they relinquished that registration in the Member State of origin, were not justified on public health grounds. On the other hand, in *Bressol*, the CJEU accepted that, at least in principle, a difference in treatment based indirectly on nationality (here, restriction to 30 per cent of the number of non-Belgians enrolled on some medical courses) may be justified by the objective of maintaining, into the future, a 'balanced high-quality medical service open to all, in so far as it contributes to achieving a high level of protection of health'.[48] Here, 'public health' is being interpreted more broadly.

The main thrust of the CJEU's jurisprudence on both the public health exemption and on objective public interest justifications is to limit the restrictions on the freedom of movement as much as possible. The grounds of exemption do not provide a wide discretion to Member States to preserve national policies. Rather, Member States must show a clear, objective and proportionate imperative of public policy, public security or public health. More importantly, the interpretation of the exemption provisions is a matter of EU, not national, law to be determined by the CJEU.[49] Any suggestion that the exemption is being relied on to protect national interests from competition from other Member

---

[43] *Gullung,* paragraph 29.

[44] Scott, 'Mandatory or Imperative Requirements in the EU and the WTO' in Barnard and Scott (eds), *The Law of the Single European Market: Unpacking the Premises* (Hart 2002) 269-294.

[45] Directive 2004/38/EC [2004] OJ L158/77, Article 29.

[46] It does so by reference to the relevant instruments of the World Health Organisation on diseases with epidemic potential, Directive 2004/38/EC, Article 29 (1).

[47] *Doctor or Dentist,* C-96/85, EU:C:1986:189.   [48] *Bressol* EU:C:2010:181, paragraph 62.

[49] *Rutili,* C-36/75, EU:C:1975:137. However, the application of the exemption in a particular case would be a matter for the tribunal of fact, at national level, albeit operating under a duty to apply EU law (Article 267 TFEU; Article 4(3) TEU).

States is generally regarded by the CJEU as being evidence that the exemption is not justified.[50]

Much of the CJEU jurisprudence on the Treaty is now also reflected in EU legislation on free movement of professionals. In particular, the legislation elaborates the principle of mutual recognition of professional qualifications. Originally, EU legislation on mutual recognition of professional qualifications took two broad approaches: a 'sectoral' approach that covers specific professions (such as dentist or midwife); and a 'general' approach that applies to other professional qualifications. The two approaches were brought together into one legislative instrument in 2005,[51] which has been revised several times, most recently in 2013.[52] The operation of the legislation is subject to a Code of Conduct,[53] which sets out the national administrative practices which fall under the relevant legislation.

Some of the first professions to be subject to EU legislation, using the 'sectoral' approach' to mutual recognition of qualification were the medical and nursing professions: doctors, dentists, pharmacists, midwives, general care nurses. The essential aim of this approach is to enable the automatic recognition in all Member States of a licence to practise a profession in one Member State. Each sector was originally covered by two directives. One defined at EU level the minimum educational requirements for access to the profession. Member States were required, where necessary, to adjust their national degree programmes in order to meet these requirements. The other directive simply listed, by official title, all diplomas which satisfy the requirements. These Directives had important effects on Central and Eastern European Member States when they joined the EU in 2004 and 2007. Nursing, in particular, underwent significant reforms.[54] Host Member States are allowed to ensure that health professionals covered by this system have sufficient language skills to communicate with their patients.[55] But otherwise, at least in theory, the beauty of the sectoral system is its simplicity: it allows for recognition of qualifications without the need for assessing the qualifications of each migrant professional on an individual basis.

---

[50] See also: Directive 64/221/EEC [1964] OJ L056/850, Article 2 (1), which provides that the grounds of exemption may not be used to serve economic ends.

[51] Directive 2005/36/EC [2005] OJ L255/22.

[52] See: Directive 2013/55/EU [2013] OJ L354/132. In general, the amendments sought to further liberalize services markets across the EU, promote growth through exploiting economies of scale, and make it easier for professionals to relocate and set up in another Member State, hence creating more jobs and tackling workforce skills shortages in some Member States. See: Commission, 'Proposal for a Directive of the European Parliament and of the Council amending Directive 2005/36/EC on the recognition of professional qualifications and Regulation on administrative cooperation through the Internal Market Information System COM (2011) 883 final.

[53] Code of Conduct approved by the Group of Coordinators for Directive 2005/36/EC on the recognition of professional qualifications [2005] OJ L255.

[54] See: Keighley, 'Nursing and the EU Accession Process' (2006) 53(2) *International Council of Nurses* 81.

[55] Confirmed in *Haim 2* EU:C:2000:357.

In the late 1980s, the EU adopted 'general' directives on mutual recognition of qualifications, covering all other professions. The two systems (general and sectoral) were consolidated in Directive 2005/36/EC,[56] which is the current applicable legislation. As noted above, many of its key principles were established through the CJEU's case law. Under the general system, the basic logic is the idea of mutual recognition of equivalence. Member States are required to consider, on a case-by-case basis, whether a qualification from another Member State is equivalent to its own qualification. Host Member States must take into account professional qualifications, and experience of practice in another Member State, and compare the knowledge and abilities certified by the professional qualification, and experience, with those required by national rules.[57] If the qualification is not equivalent, then the Member State must decide what 'compensating measures' must be taken by a health professional seeking to establish herself or to work in the host Member State. 'Compensating measures' can take the form of an aptitude test, or a period of adaptation. Health professions differ quite significantly across the EU, so Member States consider compensating measures to be justified in the vast majority of health professions covered by the 'general' system.

An assessment of the implications of EU health law on freedom of establishment of health professionals and free movement of health professionals as employees must take into account both the possibility that national professional regulatory arrangements, even if they impede free movement, could be justified, and the fact that, in practice, justification is difficult to show. It must also take into account the ability of Member States to require compensating measures to mobile health professionals in the vast majority of instances. We turn to that assessment below. First, however, we set out the key provisions of EU health law on free movement of services as applicable to health professionals. The important difference here is that, while a health professional permanently establishing herself or working in another Member State from that in which she qualified will essentially be subject to the professional regulatory rules of the state in which she practises, that is not necessarily the case for health professionals providing temporary services.

Service providers and posted workers

Where a (health) professional[58] seeks to offer a service in a Member State other than that in which she normally works or is established, the Treaty provisions on free movement of services may apply. Article 56 TFEU prohibits 'restrictions on the freedom to provide services within the EU'. It does so by prohibiting both

[56] Directive 2005/36/EC [2005] OJ L255/22.   [57] Directive 2005/36/EC, Article 14.
[58] Who is a "citizen of the European Union" or of an EEA state – see below for the position of "third country" nationals.

directly and indirectly discriminatory barriers to cross-border movement of services;[59] and also by prohibiting non-discriminatory 'hindrances', 'obstacles' or 'impediments' to market access.[60] As with freedom of establishment and free movement of workers, national rules that impede professionals from accessing the market in another Member State by not recognizing their professional qualifications could be such an impediment. Another type of impediment is the operation of national health insurance rules, which recognize only providers of health services that are established in the home Member State.[61] Article 56 TFEU is directly effective.[62]

As noted above, the free movement of services rules apply only to the temporary offering of services. Although the *proposal* for the current relevant legislation suggested that permanence should be defined as providing the service for more than sixteen weeks per year,[63] the Directive as adopted is less specific. It provides only that a service must be pursued on a 'temporary and occasional basis', to be assessed individually in the context of each case.[64]

We have already noted that restrictions on the freedom to provide and receive services may be justified. The principles applicable to freedom of establishment, free movement of workers, and in the context of free movement of patients apply equally in this context. For instance, in 2009, the Commission brought a claim against Luxembourg, seeking to open up the market in laboratory analyses and tests for patients covered by the Luxembourg national health insurance system. The Luxembourg rules meant, in practice, that providers established outside Luxembourg could not be reimbursed by the national health insurance system for such services.[65] The CJEU accepted that 'the objective of maintaining a balanced medical and hospital system applicable to all' and 'the risk of seriously undermining the financial balance of the social security system' could justify such a restriction. In this particular instance, Luxembourg had failed to show why this was the case. But in principle such justification is available.

Particularly in an internal market of twenty-eight Member States, with very different living standards, employment law traditions, and wage levels across different Member States, free supply of labour services across borders poses particular challenges for the EU. Both the EU legislature and the CJEU have responded to these challenges. In terms of applicable legislation, the general

---

[59]   *Van Binsbergen*, C-33/74, EU:C:1974:131.
[60]   *Geraets-Smits/Peerbooms*, C-157/99, EU:C:2001:404; *Bond van Adverteerders*, C-352/85, EU:C:1988:196.
[61]   See: e.g. *Laboratory analyses*, C-490/09, EU:C:2011:34.
[62]   *Van Binsbergen* EU:C:1974:131.
[63]   Commission, Proposal for a Directive of the European Parliament and Council on the recognition of professional qualifications' COM (2002) 119 final, amended by: Commission, 'Amended proposal for a Directive of the European Parliament and of the Council on the recognition of professional qualifications (presented by the Commission pursuant to Article 250 (2) of the EC Treaty)' COM (2004) 317 final, Article 5.
[64]   Directive 2005/36/EC [2005] OJ L255/22, Article 5 (2).
[65]   *Laboratory analyses* EU:C:2011:34, paragraphs 40-41.

'Services Directive' 2006/123/EC explicitly excludes health services from its scope,[66] so we do not discuss it further here. However, health professionals are covered by what is known as the 'Posted Workers' Directive 96/71/EC.[67] A 'posted worker' is an employee who is sent by her employer on a temporary basis to carry out work in another Member State, for instance, because the employer has won a contract in that Member State.[68] The posted workers legislation aims to protect labour standards, in particular minimum wage levels, in circumstances where cheaper labour is used to provide a service in another Member State, thus potentially undermining the arrangements for employment rights and other elements of social protection, such as collective bargaining arrangements, in that host Member State. The legislation has been significantly challenged by the CJEU's reinterpretation of its provisions, alongside Articles 49 and 56 TFEU.[69] This means in practice that the circumstances in which the labour standards of the host Member State can be imposed on posted workers have been restricted.[70] Member States retain discretion to determine employment conditions, such as the minimum wage, but this must not impede free movement of services.[71]

In addition, Title II of Directive 2005/36/EC applies to free movement of services. This provides that, *in general*, host Member States may not restrict provision of *services* for any reason relating to professional qualifications. If the service provider is lawfully established in one Member State, they must be allowed to provide services in any other.[72] The general rule is that 'compensating measures' apply only to the exercise of freedom of *establishment*.[73] However, what is important here is that this general rule does *not* apply to health services. Directive 2005/36/EC explicitly allows Member States to check

---

[66] Directive 2006/123/EC [2006] OJ L376/36, Article 2 (2) (f).

[67] Directive 96/71/EC [1997] OJ L18/1.

[68] The application of public procurement legislation to posted workers is unclear. There is no explicit obligation in the relevant legislation to comply with local labour standards, though some have claimed that this is because compliance is assumed. See: McCrudden *Buying Social Justice: Equality, Government Procurement and Social Change* (OUP 2007), cited in: Kilpatrick, 'Internal Market Architecture and the Accommodation of Labour Rights' in Syrpis (ed), *The Judiciary, The Legislature and the EU Internal Market* (CUP 2012), 214. The CJEU has had some sympathy for the use of labour market criteria in decisions by public authorities to accept or award tenders for services, see e.g. *Beentjes*, C-31/87, EU:C:1988:422; *Nord-Pas-de-Calais*, C-225/98, EU:C:2000:494. See further: Kilpatrick, above.

[69] *Viking*, C-438/05, EU:C:2007:772; *Laval*, C-341/05, EU:C:2007:809; *Rüffert*, C-346/06, EU:C:2008:189; *Commission v Luxembourg*, C-319/06, EU:C:2008:350; *Isbir*, C-522/12, EU:C:2013:711.

[70] See: Kilpatrick, above n 68.

[71] *Isbir* EU:C:2013:711, paragraph 37. The European Commission proposes a clarification of these rules; see: Commission, 'Proposal for a Directive of the European Parliament and of the Council on the enforcement of Directive 96/71/EC concerning the posting of workers in the framework of the provision of services' COM (2012) 131 final.

[72] Directive 2005/36/EC [2005] OJ L255/22, Article 5 (1). This rule is also reflected implicitly in Directive 2006/123/EC [2006] OJ L376/36, Article 16.

[73] The distinction between establishment and services here is about permanence or temporary activity. Directive 2005/36/EC, Article 5 (2); *Gebhard* EU:C:1995:411.

the professional qualifications of the health service provider prior to the first provision of services.[74] This exception to the general rules on service providers forms an important part of the context for an assessment of the implications of these rules. Before turning to that, however, we set out the final element of applicable law: EU employment law.

Employment law

Health professionals employed within the EU enjoy rights under EU employment law. This legislation sets minimum requirements in various employment-related fields, especially working conditions, and health and safety at work. Its objectives are to protect employees, and to enhance their working conditions. It is part of the EU's social policy, rather than the measures discussed so far in this chapter, which, at least in theory, seek to create the EU's internal market. The relevant EU employment legislation was not drafted with the health sector in mind. But its impacts in that sector can be significant, and are often unintended. The most important aspect of this EU law is the EU's working time legislation, as interpreted by the CJEU.[75]

The currently applicable Directive 2003/88/EC,[76] represents a consolidation of previous legislation. Various aspects of this Directive are regarded as unsatisfactory, and the European Commission sought to bring in new legislation, also to clarify CJEU rulings, shortly after it was adopted.[77] Nearly five years of negotiations from 2004 to 2009, resulted in a stalemate.[78] A further review was launched in late 2009, involving negotiations between the 'social partners' (management and the trades unions, at EU level), but these negotiations broke down in late 2012.[79] In particular, it has proved impossible to reach agreement on three crucial points: the opt-outs, on-call time and multiple contracts. The former two of these are important in the context of health professionals.

---

[74] Directive 2005/36/EC, Article 7 (4).
[75] For general discussion of the application of EU working time law to the health sector, see: Hancher and Sauter, *EU Competition and Internal Market Law in the Health Care Sector* (OUP 2012) 153-159.
[76] Directive 2003/88/EC [2003] OJ L299/9.
[77] Commission, 'Proposal for a Directive of the European Parliament and of the Council amending Directive 2003/88/EC concerning certain aspects of the organisation of working time' COM (2004) 607 final; Commission, 'Amended proposal for a Directive of the European Parliament and of the Council amending Directive 2003/88/EC concerning certain aspects of the organisation of working time' COM (2005) 246 final.
[78] The Commission may, if it so chooses, draft a new proposal from scratch. It should be noted that this was the first time that no agreement had been reached at the stage of 'conciliation' between the European Parliament and Council since the entry into force of the Amsterdam Treaty, which significantly extended the scope of the procedure according to which European Parliament and Council are 'co-legislators'.
[79] See: NHS Employers, 'Working Time Directive' (NHS Employers 2014). The European Commission informed the Employment, Social policy, Health and Consumer Affairs Council on 28 February 2013 that the European social partners had failed to come to an agreement on the review of the Working Time Directive.

The Working Time Directive sets minimum requirements to protect health and safety of workers. Member States may go further than these minimums if they wish. The Directive specifies a maximum working week of forty-eight hours[80] (averaged over a four-month reference period);[81] provisions on rest periods and breaks;[82] special provisions for night and shift workers;[83] and measures on annual leave.[84] CJEU case law involving health professionals clarified the meaning of 'working time' in the context of on-call work. The assumption had been that time spent ready to respond to health emergencies, but not actually working, was not included within 'working time'. Many health sector employers across the EU organized their professionals' shifts on this basis, and there is evidence that some still do so.[85] But the CJEU has held[86] that time spent on-call where the health professional is required to be at the place of employment (even if resting or asleep) counts as 'working time', as does time actually working, in circumstances where the professional is 'on-call' in the sense of being contactable, but not actually present at the place of employment.

The other important feature of the Working Time Directive is its significant provision for derogations, exemptions and 'opt-outs'. Under Article 22, Member States may decide to allow individual workers to opt out of the forty-eight-hour working week by agreement. According to a Commission report of 2010,[87] some sixteen Member States use the opt-out.[88] Of these, five[89] allow its use in any sector, while eleven only allow its use in connection with on-call time (in some cases, only within public health services).[90] Article 18 allows derogation from aspects of the Directive by collective agreement. Article 17 allows derogations for shift work, which, given the nature of health care, applies to many health professionals; and for specific activities, including 'activities involving the need for continuity of service or production, particularly services relating

---

[80] Directive 2003/88/EC [2003] OJ L299/9, Article 6.   [81] Directive 2003/88/EC, Article 16.

[82] Directive 2003/88/EC, Articles 3 and 4.   [83] Directive 2003/88/EC, Articles 8-13.

[84] Directive 2003/88/EC, Article 7.

[85] For instance in France, Greece, Hungary, see: Commission Staff Working Paper, 'Detailed report on the implementation by Member States of Directive 2003/88/EC concerning certain aspects of the organisation of working time ('The Working Time Directive')' SEC (2010) 1611 final, especially 156-7.

[86] *SIMAP*, C-303/98, EU:C:2000:528; *Jaeger*, C-151/02, EU:C:2003:437; *Pfeiffer*, C-397/01, C-398/01, C-399/01, C-400/01, C-401/01, C-402/01 and C-403/01, EU:C:2004:584; *Dellas*, C-14/04, EU:C:2005:728.

[87] Commission Staff Working Paper, 'Detailed report on the implementation by Member States of Directive 2003/88/EC concerning certain aspects of the organisation of working time ('The Working Time Directive')' SEC (2010) 1611 final.

[88] This is a significant increase on the one Member State relying upon it in 2000 (the UK). The report also notes "It is important to emphasise that due to the rapid and widespread introduction of opt-out clauses in different Member States, the Commission services do not have full information on their application in practice in different Member States": Commission SEC (2010) 1611 final, 88.

[89] Bulgaria, Cyprus, Estonia, Malta, and the United Kingdom.

[90] Belgium, Czech Republic, France, Germany, Hungary, Latvia, the Netherlands, Poland, Slovakia, Slovenia, and Spain.

to the reception, treatment and/or care provided by hospitals or similar establishments, including the activities of doctors in training'. The fact that Member
States have made widespread use of the derogations[91] forms part of the context
in assessing the implications of EU health law for health professionals, and their
relationships with patients.

Assessment of EU health law on health professionals

By and large, EU health law on health professionals falls squarely within the
theme of consumerism that is the subject of this group of chapters. The rules on
free movement (of workers, self-employed professionals and service providers)
certainly rely on a notion of a 'market' in health professionals. The claim is that
efficient deployment of resource in that 'market' will lead to greater benefits to
consumers of health professional services, whether we see the 'consumers' of
those services as governments, health care systems or as patients themselves. The
claim relies on a notion of economies of scale in the single European market. It is
consistent with the European Commission's general focus on the liberalization
of services, as part of its drive to improve the European economy, and to create
more jobs, within its 'Europe 2020' programme.[92] Even the EU employment
law on working time is justified in part by a concern for the safety of consumers
of health services. Patients receive a better quality of care if professionals are
sufficiently rested and have not worked unacceptably long hours in a particular
shift.

In assessing the implications of this consumerist theme in the context of this
aspect of EU health law, we separate out the rules on entry into a health profession, from those on the practice of a health profession. All the Member States
deploy rules on professional training and licensing/authorization of health professional practice, including the use of particular professional titles. Those rules
on initiation into the profession have a territorial and national basis – there are
no EU-level health qualifications. We consider the implications of EU health
law for those national rules first.

Entry into health professions

For health professionals covered by the 'sectoral approach', the main benefit
claimed of the system is the automatic recognition of a formal qualification, as
listed in Directive 2005/36/EC, Annex V. In theory, health professionals falling
within the principle of 'automatic recognition'[93] (doctor, specialized doctor,

---

[91]   Commission SEC (2010) 1611 final, 108.
[92]   See: Recommendation 2010/410/EU [2010] OJ L191/28; Decision 2010/707/EU [2010] OJ
       L308/46; Commission, 'Europe 2020: A strategy for smart, sustainable and inclusive growth'
       (Communication) COM (2010) 2020 final.
[93]   Directive 2005/36/EC, Article 21.

nurse responsible for general care, dental practitioner, specialized dental practitioner, pharmacist, midwife) may work or establish themselves in another
Member State without the need for further formalities concerning qualifications, save for ensuring that the professional has the necessary linguistic
knowledge.[94] The host Member State must recognize their qualification and
may not require any further proof of fitness to enter into the profession in the
host Member State. The benefit to patients (or to the institutions of national
health systems) as 'consumers' of professional services is that health professionals are able to move to the parts of the EU where demand for their services is
greatest. Hence it is claimed that efficient allocation of the 'resource' of health
professionals is achieved.

However, in practice, benefits from that freedom of movement are distinctly
muted. Even setting aside the objection that the assumed benefits from the
sectoral approach rely on the assumption that health services are a service like
any other being offered in a market, which is refuted by many, given the special nature of health services,[95] there are several problems with the notion that
the sectoral system entails benefits for patients. The sectoral approach of EU
health law on entry into health professions does not in itself create mutual
trust in qualifications. In practice, lack of trust means that in many Member States non-national health professionals are not universally automatically
accepted.[96] The official minimum training requirements are seen as inadequate, as they do not cover specific content of training, or dictate the level of
competence that a professional must reach. For instance, comparisons between
the number of patients that trainee doctors are required to treat before qualifying reveal significant differences in approach. One study from the 1990s
showed that UK trainee doctors had to see around 210 patients with trauma
before qualifying, whereas the equivalent figure in Sweden, Finland, the Netherlands and France was around thirty patients.[97] A Commission evaluation in
2011 found that the minimum training requirements need to be updated, as
some are over forty years old, in order better to reflect current professional
practice.[98]

---

[94] Directive 2005/36/EC, Article 53. This aspect of control by the receiving state was bolstered
by the 2013 reform of the legislation, see: Commission, COM (2011) 883 final. Directive
2005/36/EC, Article 53 (3) makes explicit that Member States may check linguistic ability
for professions with 'patient safety implications'.

[95] Arrow, 'Uncertainty and the Welfare Economics of Medical Care' (1963) 53(5) *The American
Economic Review* 941.

[96] The European Commission receives regular complaints in this regard, see: e.g. *Commission
v Spain*, C-232/99, EU:C:2002:291; Klemperer, 'Working abroad as a doctor' in Eysenbach
(ed), *Medicine and Medical Education in Europe: The Eurodoctor* (Thieme 1998).

[97] See: Eldridge, 'Junior Doctors' Hours' (1993) 308 *British Medical Journal* 417, cited in Finch,
'Professional Recognition and Training of Doctors – The 1993 EC Directive' (1995) 2(2)
European Journal of Health Law 163, 171.

[98] Commission, 'Evaluation of the Professional Qualifications Directive' (Commission 2011) 6.

Worse, the need for full EU legislative agreement means it is difficult to change educational requirements to reflect changes in scientific understanding or good practice in medical education. The qualifications recognized under the sectoral approach may therefore be detrimentally ossified. In the past, the EU's Advisory Committee on Medical Training kept under review the need for medical training to adapt to developments in both medical science and pedagogy. But this Committee was disbanded in 1999.[99] A recent attempt to alter merely the basic period of medical training, which is set at five years minimum, was unsuccessful.[100] This example shows how difficult it would be for the EU to alter the content or approach to health professional training, where covered by the sectoral approach. The EU's role in determining medical professional training, and maintaining high standards of professional practice through limiting access to the profession in that way, is distinctly constrained.

Moreover, the sectoral system works only for professions where there is a general consensus across the Member States about the scope and meaning of a particular professional title. This is not the case for many health professions, such as psychologists, chiropractors, osteopaths or opticians. For those, the general system applies. Although in theory the general system works on the assumption of mutual recognition of equivalence, in practice Member States regularly use 'compensating measures', such as an aptitude test or adaptation period, which *de facto* exclude health professionals with qualifications from another Member State. Moreover, administrative practices often exclude migrant health professionals from host Member States. The UK's Department for Business Innovation and Skills cites a UK-qualified physiotherapist who waited for four months for the relevant authorities in a host Member State to reply to his application for his qualifications to be recognized. He was then told he needed to submit further information. He did so, and seven months later was asked to supply the same information again, in a different format, which he did. A further six months later, he had still received no decision from the authorities in the host Member State.[101] Thus, the reality of the general approach is that compensating measures impede free movement because they are administratively burdensome. The ability of host Member States to control access of health professionals from other Member States to their patients by applying such compensating measures does belie the concern that mutual recognition of qualifications is detrimental for patients, for instance, because it allows health professionals with less

[99]   Hervey and McHale, above n 3, 209.

[100] See: Commission, COM (2011) 883 final. This was in part due to opposition from health professionals in the UK, where the 5 year 'fast track' basic medical training is seen as a valuable training route. See: Royal College of Physicians, 'European Parliament votes on doctors' qualifications' (*Royal College of Physicians*, 31 January 2013) British Medical Council, 'EU maintains minimum length of medical training' (*British Medical Association*, 21 November 2013).

[101] See: Department for Business Innovation & Skills, 'UK Government Response: European Commission Public Consultation on the Mutual Recognition of Professional Qualifications Directive' (Department for Business Innovation & Skills 2011) .

stringent qualifications to enter into professional practice or be employed in a host Member State. The evidence suggests that although this may be the case in theory, it is not so in practice, save perhaps in exceptional circumstances.

A related claim that EU health law on health professionals' entry into professional practice is detrimental for patients concerns national provisions that impede access of students to educational courses for various medical professions. These provisions are intended to secure sufficient numbers of qualified professionals to ensure patients are properly cared for into the future. They are necessary in the context of countries where language barriers do not impede students from other, invariably larger, countries, coming to study in the host Member State, with the intention of returning home after their studies are complete. The small Member States of Belgium (with the larger France) and Austria (with the larger Germany) both have such measures in place, to secure future provision of health services for their patients.

In the mid-2000s, the European Commission brought both Belgium and Austria before the CJEU, which found that national rules restricting the numbers of students accessing training for paramedics and other health professionals impeded EU internal market law, and were not justified.[102] In 2006, both countries adopted new legislation, seeking to achieve the same ends, and attempts by the European Commission to sanction this were derailed by the political process of adopting the Lisbon Treaty.[103] However, a further case reached the CJEU by the preliminary reference procedure, brought by private litigants – in this case French students who were unable to study physiotherapy, podiatry and midwifery in French-speaking Belgian universities.[104] As we saw above, the CJEU accepted that the protection of 'public health' could include the need to 'maintain a balanced high-quality medical service open to all'. In assessing whether the justification was proportionate, the national court could take into account the possible future deterioration of the health services provided to patients within the particular Member State. But the CJEU was insistent that the assessment must be based on concrete data, and could not rely on assumptions, such as, for instance, an assumption that all non-Belgians, or non-resident students, would return home, or that all Belgian, or resident, students would remain. The need to justify such rules places the home Member States on the back foot in terms of evidentiary burden. Although the link between health professionals trained within a particular Member State, and an assumption of a future service to patients within that state, is not entirely broken, it is certainly significantly challenged by this jurisprudence. The education and training of health professionals is thus no longer conceptualized as falling within an ethic of service to particular community of patients (territorially defined). Rather, it

[102] *Commission v Belgium*, C-65/03, EU:C:2004:402; *University Education* EU:C:2005:427.
[103] For discussion, see: Garben, 'Case Note on *Bressol*' (2010) *47 Common Market Law Review* 1493.
[104] *Bressol* EU:C:2010:181.

is conceptualized as the equipping of an economic actor to offer professional services within a wider European market.

Finally, even if we were to accept the benefits of free movement of health professionals through economies of scale and market creation, there would still be negative consequences for patients in some parts of the EU. Although data is incomplete, the trend of movement of health professionals is East-to-West and North-to-South in the EU, with significant flows into the EU from elsewhere in the world.[105] There is emergent information to the effect that health professionals are migrating from the EU Member States worst hit by the Eurozone crisis, and certainly health systems are affected in those countries.[106] The EU law on freedom of establishment, and the posted workers law, can be relied upon to support such professional migration. Free movement of health professionals in this context is likely to have negative effects for individual patients, as better-qualified or more experienced professionals leave their home health care system. It also poses significant systemic challenges, because the national health systems in the EU's former communist Member States were based on a plentiful supply of cheap labour, which compensated for the lack of investment in technology.

The ethics of free movement of health professionals in the context of health care systems in countries with very different levels of economic development have been considered by the EU since at least the 2000s.[107] Policy initiatives include professional migration within the EU, as well as involving countries outside of its borders.[108] The EU has used its development policies, including with accession and candidate countries, to build health professional capacity in many countries. But no hard law has been adopted to restrict the movement of health professionals from wealthier to less wealthy countries.

Health professional practice: workers and self-employed professionals

One of the most important criticisms of EU health law on health professionals is that its underlying focus on free movement, and on entry into the profession,

---

[105] Glinos, above n 1, 28.

[106] Glinos, above n 1, 28; Ognyanova and Busse, 'A destination and a source: Germany manages regional health workforce disparities with foreign medical doctors' in Wismar et al. (eds), above n 8; Fahy, 'Who is shaping the future of European health systems?' (2012) 334 *British Medical Journal* (2012) e1712; Greer, 'The Three Faces of European Union Health Policy: Policy, markets, austerity' (2014) 33(1) *Policy and Society* 13.

[107] Peeters, McKee and Merkur, above n 6, 622-623.

[108] See, for instance: the Code of Conduct on Ethical Cross-border Recruitment and Retention in the Hospital Sector, signed by the European Federation of Public Service Unions and the European Hospital and Healthcare Employers Association, April 2008: HOSPEEM and EPSU, 'EPSU- HOSPEEM code of conduct and follow up on Ethical Cross-Border Recruitment and Retention in the Hospital Sector' (HOSPEEM and EPSU 2008); Commission, 'Ethical cross-border Recruitment and Retention: European social partners in the hospital sector signed a code of conduct' (*Commission*, 7 April 2008).

detracts from the importance of regulation of health professional practice. In all the Member States, professional practice in health care settings is concerned first and foremost with ethical concerns, and with quality of care. In the most extreme cases, it is concerned with very basic patient safety and with the management of risk – with minimizing the chance that those skilled health professionals, who exercise a great deal of control over the patient experience, do not injure, or even kill, the patients within their care. EU health law does not start from ethics, or quality of care, or even basic safety: it begins from the idea of a market of free moving professionals.

Thus the EU's legal framework has been heavily criticized for its lack of engagement with the need for continuing professional development and accreditation and lack of coordination of disciplinary measures. Due to the nature of the professional services being provided, where patients' health, or even lives, are at risk, there is a strong public interest in retaining home state control by keeping health professionals 'home grown'. Health professionals not only have obligations to the patients whom they treat. They also at least arguably have obligations to the broader community in which they work, and to the public in general, within the state in which they practice. The interests of the state in protecting patients and the population more generally through having an effective health system, including one with effective professional regulation, are supported inter alia through obligations of whistleblowing, where unsafe practices come to light. The roles and obligations of health professionals are very different to those in ordinary employment or service provision relationships. But the very way that EU health law is structured gives insufficient attention to those interests.

It is not simply a question of regulating quality of care in a technical, medical sense. As our understandings of the holistic nature of human health have developed, so too have our understandings of the ways in which professional communications with patients, and ethical questions of respect for dignity, also have a bearing on health outcomes. Inadequate levels of service in health care cannot simply be compensated financially. Where (public or private) health care 'goes wrong', in all the EU's Member States, it is the national health (insurance) system which will be responsible for seeking to improve the health and extend the life of the patient concerned. Hence there is an added incentive for Member States to keep controls on the health professionals practising within their territories. Such controls include which health professionals are recognized within national health (insurance) systems. All of this goes a long way to explaining the lack of trust that contributes to the failure in practice of the mutual recognition of qualifications. But the inability for the EU to intervene to set professional standards of practice is not simply because of lack of legal competence to do so, or even because of lack of political will to agree legislation based on the internal market. It relates more fundamentally to the mismatch between the rationale for such regulation in the context of EU health law, and the rationales in national contexts.

Where disciplinary measures are concerned, the existing law applies as follows. It is inconceivable that an individual finding of unfitness to practise would not justify the exclusion of a particular health professional from establishing herself, or providing services, within the health system of a host Member State. There is an obligation on Member States to exchange 'information regarding disciplinary action or criminal sanctions taken or any other serious, specific circumstances which are likely to have consequences for the pursuit of'[109] freedom of establishment, free movement of workers, or provision of services. Since 2013, there is an obligation on the host Member State exchange information with other Member States on 'disciplinary action or criminal sanctions or other serious specific circumstances' which are likely to have consequences for professional practice.[110] But what is the situation where a health professional is banned from practice in one Member State because of practices which are perfectly legal in another Member State?[111] Nor is there a single understanding of what 'disciplinary action' means in this context, and, as we have seen, Member States have very different approaches in this respect.[112] If, for instance, a health professional is suspended from practising without pay, pending investigation of the alleged misconduct, there is nothing to prevent that professional from seeking employment, or to establish herself, in another Member State. If the host Member State does not recognize such a status as attracting the penalty of being barred from practice, perhaps because until there is a finding of fact from an investigation, the professional is to be presumed innocent, then to refuse a professional from another Member State access to the profession would be directly discriminatory on grounds of nationality, and thus would, *prima facie* at least, apparently breach EU Treaty law. But this is inconsistent with the ability of Member States to justify *indirectly* discriminatory restrictions on free movement on objective public interest grounds.

These sorts of differences, and the lack of legal clarity, are compounded by the application of EU privacy and data protection law. The reporting obligation in Directive 2005/36/EC is explicitly[113] subject to EU data protection law,[114] and

---

[109]   Directive 2005/36/EC, Article 56 (1).

[110]   Directive 2005/36/EC, Article 56 (2).

[111]   The examples of abortion and euthanasia seem obvious ones. Others such as certain types of *in utero* genetic testing might be others.

[112]   See: e.g. Peeters, McKee and Merkur, above n 6, for examples.

[113]   Directive 2005/36/EC, Article 56 (1). Article 56 (2) states that Member States must respect the rules in Directive 95/46/EC [1995] OJ L281/31, but these are interpreted differently in different Member States.

[114]   Directive 95/46/EC [1995] OJ L281/31; Directive 2002/58/EC [2002] OJ L201/37. This aspect of EU law is under revision, see: Commission, 'Safeguarding Privacy in a Connected World A European Data Protection Framework for the 21st Century' COM (2012) 09 final; Commission, 'Proposal for a Directive of the European Parliament and of the Council on the protection of individuals with regard to the processing of personal data by competent authorities for the purposes of prevention, investigation, detection or prosecution of criminal offences or the execution of criminal penalties, and the free movement of such data' COM (2012) 10 final; Commission, 'Proposal for a Regulation of the European Parliament and of

also implicitly subject to EU law on protection of human rights.[115] But Member States differ in their interpretations of these privacy rules. Application of data protection law is sometimes used as a reason to withhold information.[116] Thus the legal position is such that assumptions may be made about fitness to practise of a mobile health professional, which may be based on local understandings, but which turn out to be inaccurate. The consequence could be that a mobile health professional could be allowed to practise in a host Member State where there has been a question over her fitness to do so in the home Member State.

These fears were covered in the 2013 amendments to the Directive, but have not been completely addressed. Article 56a contains a new proactive 'alert mechanism', covering health professionals falling within the 'sectoral' approach of automatic recognition of qualifications (general practitioner, specialist doctor of medicine, general care nurse, dentist and specialized dentist, midwife, pharmacist), as well as 'other professionals exercising activities that have patient safety implications, where the professional is pursuing a profession regulated in that Member State'.[117] National authorities are obliged to inform all other Member States and the European Commission 'about the identity of a professional who has been prohibited by national authorities or courts from pursuing, even temporarily' their professional activities in the home Member State.[118] The extent of the concept of a professional 'exercising activities that have patient safety implications' is unclear. Arguably, it could extend to a massive range of professionals within the health sector, given the integrated nature of 'patient safety', which extends well beyond clinical practice, to include, for instance, technicians, porters, dieticians, cleaning managers, and so on, although not all of these activities would count as 'professions regulated in that Member State'. For health professionals not within these categories, the obligation is to inform not all Member States, but only 'the Member States concerned', as under the pre-2013 legal position.[119] Article 56a is also subject to privacy and data protection law, which differs in its interpretation between Member States.

Unfitness to practise is one thing. But what about the question of whether a host Member State could impede a mobile health professional not because

the Council on the protection of individuals with regard to the processing of personal data and on the free movement of such data (General Data Protection Regulation)' COM (2012) 11 final.

[115] For discussion of the ways in which EU law respects human rights, see chapters 7 and 8.

[116] Peeters, McKee and Merkur, above n 6, 620.

[117] Directive 2013/55/EU, Article 56a (1) (k).   [118] Directive 2013/55/EU, Article 56a (1).

[119] For further discussion of the alert mechanism, see responses of the Royal College of Nurses, UK, and the UK government, to the consultation on the reform of mutual recognition qualifications: Royal College of Nurses, 'Royal College of Nursing Briefing: Free Movement of Health Professionals in Europe – Proposed Changes to EU Legislation in 2012' (Royal College of Nurses 2012); Department for Business Innovation & Skills, 'UK Government Response: European Commission Public Consultation on the Mutual Recognition of Professional Qualifications Directive' (Department for Business Innovation & Skills 2011)

she has been formally banned from practice, but because her continuing professional education is insufficiently developed? Merely having a formal qualification is increasingly being seen as insufficient evidence of fitness to (continue to) practise. Indeed there is at least some evidence that certain health professional skills actually decline over time.[120] Different Member States have adopted different policy responses, ranging from basic continuing knowledge-based medical education focused on state of the art of particular health specialisms, through to practice-based systematic peer review, inspection and external evaluation and reaccreditation.[121] There is little agreement over what types of regulatory interventions are most effective.[122] Some attempts have been made to coordinate these kinds of discussions, and to share 'good practice', for instance through the European Accreditation Council for Continuing Medical Education, established in 2000.[123] But in terms of the formal legal position, EU health law on mobility of health professionals focuses almost exclusively on initial entry to the profession. One of the key criticisms raised of EU law here is that EU law does not concern itself sufficiently with continuing professional education, and, on balance, this is a fair criticism.

In terms of ability of mobile health professionals to exercise 'softer' professional skills, including those of effective and appropriate communication with their patients, the existing law does allow Member States to require appropriate language skills.[124] But there are gaps in the existing legal provision.[125] The sectoral directives were silent on the question of linguistic ability. Nonetheless, the ability of a health professional to communicate with patients justifies subjecting an individual mobile health professional to linguistic tests, provided these meet the proportionality test.[126] But systematic language tests, across all categories of health professionals, would not be justified, not least because different language skills are necessary for different health professionals. For instance, a psychiatrist would require exceptionally advanced linguistic skills; a laboratory technician would need less advanced language capability. Subjecting the ability of Member States to control for linguistic abilities to a proportionality test has been criticised. The lack of ability of a host Member State to impose systematic language checks at the point of registration is seen as a practical impediment to patient

---

[120] See: Choudry, Fletcher and Soumerai, 'Systematic Review: The Relationship Between Clinical Experience and Quality of Health Care' (2005) 142 *Annals of Internal Medicine* 260.

[121] Merkur et al., 'Physician Revalidation in Europe' (2008) 8 *Clinical Medicine* 371; Peeters, McKee and Merkur, above n 6, 615-8.

[122] Peeters, McKee and Merkur, above n 6, point out that some have argued that over-regulation could itself be harmful, see: O'Neill, *A Question of Trust* (CUP 2002).

[123] See: European Accreditation Council for Continuing Medical Education <http://www.uems.eu>

[124] Directive 2005/36/EC, Article 53 (1): 'Professionals benefiting from the recognition of professional qualifications shall have a knowledge of languages necessary for practising the profession in the host Member State'. Confirmed/elaborated in *Haim 2* EU:C:2000:357.

[125] Commission, 'Evaluation of the Professional Qualifications Directive' (Commission 2011) 6.

[126] *Haim 2* EU:C:2000:357.

safety. Employers are able to impose these checks, but of course many health professionals operate in a self-employed capacity.[127]

The 2013 amendments to Directive 2005/36/EC somewhat tighten the ability of Member States to impose language controls on those operating in the health sector. The original proposal would have imposed an obligation on Member States to check linguistic ability, after deciding on the mutual recognition of a professional qualification, 'if there is a serious and concrete doubt about the professional's sufficient language knowledge in respect of the professional activities this person intends to pursue'.[128] Imposing a standard obligation on Member States to this effect would have enhanced patient protection, not least because it would have been enforceable by patients who subsequently suffered harm caused by a Member State's failure to comply.[129] The legislative text imposes no obligations, although it does give Member States discretion to adopt such controls.[130] Moreover, for 'professions with patient safety implications', under the proposal, this obligation to make an individual assessment of linguistic ability was to have been supplemented by a provision empowering Member States to make blanket assessments of linguistic abilities, through procedures of language checking of all professionals concerned. This provision, if adopted, would have given Member States significant control over the influx of health professionals. It would have been limited only by the following requirements: (i) there must be an express request for systematic checking, either from the national health system, or representative national patient organizations; (ii) it must be free of charge to the health professionals affected; (iii) it must be proportionate; and (iv) there must be a right of appeal of the decision to national courts. The legislative text does not adopt this approach. It allows Member States to impose language controls on professionals where the profession to be practised has 'patient safety implications', and in other instances, where there is a 'serious and concrete doubt' about a professional's language competencies in terms of what is sufficient for the specific professional activity.[131] Such controls are subject to the proportionality test, and the professional concerned must have a right of appeal in national law.[132]

Health professional practice: working time

The implications of EU law on working time for health professional practice are equally difficult to disentangle. Although the underlying aim of the relevant law

---

[127] See: Department for Business Innovation & Skills, 'UK Government Response: European Commission Public Consultation on the Mutual Recognition of Professional Qualifications Directive' (Department for Business Innovation & Skills 2011).

[128] Commission, COM (2011) 883 final, Article 53 (2).

[129] Directives are directly effective against 'emanations of the state', see: *Marshall*, C-152/84, EU:C:1986:84.

[130] Directive 2005/36/EC, Article 53.   [131] Directive 2005/36/EC, Article 53 (3).

[132] Directive 2005/36/EC, Article 53 (4).

is the protection of *workers*, particularly in health contexts, this rationale is also supplemented by a focus on patient safety. There is no doubt that 'posting' of workers does take place in some health contexts. In the early 2000s, controversy arose when certain British hospitals contracted nurses from Spain to cope with problems of British under-capacity.[133] The legal position of those nurses, in particular which systems' working hours applied to them, was unclear. EU law did not assist in the resolution of the dispute.

In terms of the application of EU working time law in the health sector, major criticisms of its application to health professionals were raised on the grounds that it was insufficiently attentive to national contexts. Particularly in the UK and Ireland, the concerns were that EU law would severely disrupt established provisions of health professional training (particularly the long working hours of junior doctors) and would lead to severe capacity problems, jeopardizing patient safety and quality of care.[134] Several Member States changed their national laws, or their practices, in order to comply with the CJEU's interpretation of the 'on-call' provisions. The European Commission[135] cites Czech Republic, France, Germany, Hungary, the Netherlands, Poland, Slovakia and the UK as having done so. Presumably these changes have resulted in increased patient safety, as they have the effect of reducing the number of 'on-call' hours a health professional can be expected to work per week. But this assessment must be tempered by the fact that several Member States (Czech Republic, France, Germany, Hungary, the Netherlands, Poland, Slovakia, Slovenia, Spain) relied on the Directive's 'opt out' provisions,[136] as part of these changes. Some Member States also continued to rely on the derogation for doctors in training,[137] right up until July 2011.[138] In 2013 and 2014, the European Commission initiated litigation against three Member States for failing to comply with EU law on health professional working hours, and a fourth Member State is at the 'reasoned opinion' state of the litigation process.[139]

---

[133] See discussion in Hervey and McHale, above n 3, 197-9.

[134] See Hervey and McHale, above n 3, 196.

[135] Commission, 'Report from the Commission to the European Parliament, the Council, the European Economic and Social Committee and the Committee of the regions on implementation by Member States of Directive 2003/88/EC ('The Working Time Directive')' COM (2010) 802 final; Commission Staff Working Paper, 'Detailed report on the implementation by Member States of Directive 2003/88/EC concerning certain aspects of the organisation of working time ('The Working Time Directive')' SEC (2010) 1611 final, 56.

[136] Directive 2003/88/EC [2003] OJ L299/9, Article 22.   [137] Directive 2003/88/EC, Article 6.

[138] Commission, COM (2010) 802 final; Commission SEC (2010) 1611 final, 60.

[139] Italy, see: Commission, 'Working time: Commission refers Italy to Court for not respecting EU rules in public health services' (*Commission*, 20 February 2014); Ireland, see: Commission, 'Working time: Commission refers Ireland to Court for not respecting EU rules in public health services' (*Commission*, 20 November 2013) Greece, see: Commission, 'Working time: Commission refers Greece to Court for not respecting EU rules in public health services' (*Commission*, 20 November 2013); Spain, see: Commission, 'MEMO: Working Time: Commission requests spain to respect forensic doctors' rights to maximum working hours and minimum rest periods' (*Commission*, 20 February 2014).

As for the failed proposed reform of EU working time law, the main stumbling block was the opt-out clause. The European Parliament and Council were in stark opposition. Parliament sought to make opt-outs both exceptional and temporary; Council was adamant that they were necessary as a permanent part of the regulatory landscape. The proposal sought to constrain the CJEU's interpretation of the 'on-call' provisions, which Parliament felt was a retrograde step. Also, the institutions were unable to agree on how to approach the situation where workers are covered by more than one employment contract. Should the relevant calculations be made by reference to the individual human being or by reference to each contract?[140] As patterns of work change, in particular in the context of a recovering European economy, including in the health sector, this is an important question to resolve. EU law has done little towards that resolution.

Health professional practice: service providers

We saw above that the general rule that service providers are subject only to regulatory measures in the Member State in which they are established is explicitly excluded for health professionals.[141] Any criticism of EU health law on the basis that it fails to protect patients in cross-border service contexts for failure to check professional qualifications is thus unfounded. Host Member States may lawfully check the professional credentials of health service providers within their territories.

Nevertheless, this ability to check qualifications of health professionals who provide cross-border services has not always been effectively used. Moreover, in itself, it is insufficient to secure patient safety. Various Member States have used the EU service mobility rules to bring in locums (temporary staff) from other Member States so as to fill gaps in national capacity and provide continuity of care, particularly at unpopular times, such as weekends. Another model is where health professionals are contracted to provide services for a few weeks or months each year.[142] The tragic case of David Gray provides a high-profile example of the problems that may arise from this phenomenon. David Gray was killed by a German locum, Daniel Ubani, on his first UK shift. Ubani had administered a lethal dose of diamorphine, and later admitted that he was not familiar with

---

[140] See: European Parliament, 'Final decision by Conciliation Committee' (2004/0209 (COD), 29 April 2009).

[141] Directive 2005/36/EC, Article 5 (1), which prohibits 'compensating measures' for service providers, hence if a service provider is lawfully established in one Member State, another Member State may not lawfully restrict free provision of services for any reason relating to professional qualifications. However, there is an explicit exemption for health professions in Article 7 (4).

[142] See: Glinos, above n 1; Kautsch and Czabanowsk, 'When the grass gets greener at home: Poland's changing incentives for health professional mobility'; Saar and Habicht, 'Migration and attrition: Estonia's health care sector and cross-border mobility to its northern neighbour' both in Wismar et al., above n 8.

the drug as used in British contexts. He was convicted of manslaughter and gross negligence, and struck off the UK register of GPs, although apparently was able to continue to practise in his home Member State. The case of Gray is an illustration of how differences in professional practice between different Member States can have devastating consequences for an individual patient.

Conclusions

Overall, and on balance, the principal implication of EU health law for health care professionals is to recast their relationships with the states in which they operate. EU health law understands health professionals through a model of a (fictitious) pan-EU market for health services, with its concerns for economies of scale and efficiency. It stands in contrast to models built from an ethic of professional service, based on territorial solidarity.

The consequences for relationships between health professionals and patients are difficult to determine. They vary depending upon the legal and geographical context, and the type of health professional. At an EU level, there may be benefits to patients with rare medical conditions. The bringing together of health professional expertise in a 'European centre of excellence' represents an opportunity for enhanced care for those patients. But people with rare diseases would, however, only enjoy such enhanced care if the home Member State authorizes them to access the care available, or they could otherwise access sufficient means to pay for it. Thus, patients may benefit from legally supported professional mobility which improves the ability of Member States to secure the services of a health professional to fill gaps in national capacity. Patients in northern/western Member States may benefit significantly from migration of health professionals, at all levels. Given capacity gaps at the less well remunerated ends of health professional practice, the benefits may be significant where lower-paid health professionals are concerned. A corresponding detriment may apply to patients in southern/eastern Europe.

On the other hand, EU law on health professionals represents at best a lost opportunity to benefit from economies of scale where matters such as continuing professional education are concerned. The EU has legal competence to harmonize national regulatory measures which impede the free movement of services, or freedom of establishment or workers, within the EU. However, structures regulating health professionals vary significantly across the EU in their overall approach,[143] as well as in the specifics of how they engage with codes of professional ethics, questions of medical negligence, and biomedical ethics more generally. Given the very diverse cultures of health professional

---

[143] Rosso-Gill, Legido-Quigley, Panteli and McKee, 'Assessing the Role of Regulatory Bodies in Managing Health Professional Issues and Errors in Europe' (2014) 26(4) *International Journal for Quality in Health Care* 348.

regulation across the EU, agreement on a 'European' model of regulation of health professionals is a practical impossibility.

Most fundamentally, the problem with EU law in this context is that it is not the aim of the EU provisions to protect patients or to ensure high-quality, cost-effective care. Rather, EU law seeks to promote the free movement of service providers and freedom of establishment of professionals and employees. The relevant EU Directives do not grant individual rights to patients, and thus cannot be enforced by patients receiving substandard care from a professional moving between Member States in reliance upon the Directive.

In the final analysis, probably the most important implication of EU health law on mobile professionals, as seen through the consumerist lens, is that health services are more like any other service than national legal provisions suggest. EU health law does not go so far as to treat health services as essentially identical to all other consumer services. The exemptions for free movement of services, and in the working time context, are good examples of instances where health services are seen as special, and their different legal treatment is justified. As we concluded in the previous chapter, the strongest version of the claim that EU health law replaces relationships of trust, solidarity or professional ethics with those of consumer relations is not supported in this context by a detailed analysis of the relevant legislation and litigation. But, in many respects, EU health law does proceed on the assumption that this is not the case, and that any special treatment of health services must be specifically justified. This has implications for the nature of the role of health professionals within the EU. At the very least, it complicates and disrupts the traditional understanding of a professional role founded on an ethic of public service, which includes a duty of care to individual patient/consumers, as well as a solidarity-based connection with the national health system in which it applies.

7

Rights: health rights as human rights

Introduction

Health rights are often seen as human rights – in international law, in (European) regional human rights law, and in national constitutions, including those of the EU's Member States. Rights are a potent theme in health law and biomedical ethics.[1] Recognition for fundamental human rights and the notion of respect for individual decision-making autonomy, privacy and human dignity have played an important part in the evolution of health law internationally and across individual Member States of the EU.[2] One important catalyst for the development of health rights as human rights in European contexts was, of course, the events of the middle of the twentieth century.[3] In particular, the atrocities perpetuated in Nazi Germany, and the response of the international community, led to the United Nations' Universal Declaration of Human Rights 1948,[4] the Council of Europe's European Convention of Human Rights and Fundamental Freedoms 1950 (ECHR)[5] and the later European Social Charter 1961.[6]

---

[1] See, for example: Mann, Gruskin, Grodin and Annas (eds), *Health and Human Rights: A Reader* (Routledge 1999); Mann, Gostin, Gruskin, Brennan, Lazzarini and Fineberg, 'Health and Human Rights' (1994) 1(1) *Health and Human Rights* 6; Wicks, *Human Rights and Health Care* (Hart 2007); Hendriks, 'The Right to Health' (1998) 5 *European Journal of Health Law* 389; McHale, 'Enforcing Health Care Rights in the English Courts' in Burchill, Harris and Owers (eds), *Economic, Social and Cultural Rights: Their Implementation in UK Law* (University of Nottingham Human Rights Centre 1999); Toebes, 'Right to Health and Health Care', *Encyclopaedia for Human Rights* (2009) vol 1, 365; Toebes, *The Right to Health as a Human Right in International Law* (Intersentia 1999).

[2] Beyleveld and Brownsword, *Human Dignity in Bioethics and Biolaw* (OUP 2001).

[3] Fundamental rights in European countries of course went back much further as demonstrated, for example, by the age of the Enlightenment and post Revolutionary France.

[4] Universal Declaration of Human Rights 1948.

[5] European Convention of Human Rights and Fundamental Freedoms 1950.

[6] European Social Charter 1961. The European Social Charter was opened for signature originally in 1961, with a revised Charter being opened for signature in 1996. States must provide which provisions of the Charter that they accept (in contrast to Treaties which require them to enter a reservation). Article 20 of the ESC and Article A of the Revised ESC provide that states must accept a minimum of the provisions. States are also required to report upon their progress in implementation on a biannual basis in relation to the so-called "core provisions" and on a four

The EU is not, or not predominantly, a human rights organization.[7] But of course no international organization, least of all the EU, with its roots in post-conflict peacekeeping and economic development, could ever actively reject human rights.[8] According to its constitutive Treaties, the EU is founded upon 'respect for dignity . . . and human rights'.[9] Acts of its institutions, bodies, offices and agencies, which have legal effect, are invalid if they breach human rights.[10] Indeed, should a Member State engage 'in a serious and persistent breach' of those values, there is (at least theoretical) provision for sanctions.[11] The principles of equality and non-discrimination are to be protected and respected.[12]

Standard accounts of the EU's engagement with human rights over time tell a story of a gradual unfolding or recognition of human rights, initially led by the CJEU[13] and culminating in the incorporation of the EU's Charter of Fundamental Rights (EU CFR) within its 'constitutional' texts at the Treaty of Lisbon[14] and the (eventual) accession of the EU to the ECHR.[15] Whether we agree with this story, and whether we judge it a 'human rights success' is not our central concern in this chapter. For our purposes, the focus is on the place of health rights as human rights in the EU's contemporary legal order. The EU has recognized health as a human right in its policy documents, such as the European Commission's White Paper, 'Together for Health'.[16] But to what extent is this reflected in EU health law? This is not an easy question to answer because, as we shall see, EU human rights law both draws inspiration

---

year basis in relation to the rest. In addition to the traditional international law mechanisms of reporting, the ESC provides a complaints mechanism, whereby specific organisations, such as the European Trade Union Confederation may file a complaint which is heard by the European Committee of Social Rights. For more information, see: Council of Europe, 'The European Social Charter' (*Council of Europe*, 2014) See generally: Cullen, 'The Collective Complaints System of the European Social Charter: Interpretative Methods of the European Committee of Social Rights' (2009) 9(1) *Human Rights Law Review* (2009) 61.

[7]   De Búrca, 'The Road Not Taken: The EU as a Global Human Rights Actor' (2011) 105(4) *American Journal of International Law* 649; Besson, 'The EU and Human Rights: Towards a Post-National Human Rights Institution' (2006) 6 *Human Rights Law Review* 323; Von Bogdandy, 'The EU as a Human Rights Organisation: Human Rights and the Core of the EU' (2000) 37 *Common Market Law Review* 1307; Alston (ed), *The EU and Human Rights* (OUP 1999).

[8]   Douglas-Scott, 'The European Union and Human Rights after the Treaty of Lisbon' (2011) 11(4) *Human Rights Law Review* 645.

[9]   Article 2 TEU.   [10]   Article 263 TFEU; Article 51 (1) EU CFR.

[11]   Including suspension of voting rights in Council, see: Article 7 TEU.

[12]   Article 2 TEU, Articles 8, 10, 18 TFEU, Chapter III, especially Articles 20, 21, 23, EU CFR.

[13]   Contrast, e.g. *Stork*, C-1/58, EU:C:1959:4; with *Stauder*, C-29/69, EU:C:1969:57.

[14]   See, for instance: Clapham, *Human Rights and the European Community, A Critical Overview* (Nomos 1991); Alston, above n 7; Lenaerts and Gutiérrez-Fons, 'The Place of the Charter in the EU Constitutional Edifice' in Peers, Hervey, Kenner and Ward (eds), *The EU Charter of Fundamental Rights: A Commentary* (Hart 2014).

[15]   Article 6 (2) TEU. Opinion 2/13 on the Accession of the EU to the European Convention for the Protection of Human Rights and Fundamental Freedoms EU:C:2014:2454.

[16]   Commission, 'Together for Health: A Strategic Approach for the EU 2008-13' (White Paper) COM (2007) 630 final.

from and interlocks with other human rights orders, and is in non-hierarchical relationships with those other legal systems.[17]

A brief note before we begin our analysis. Sometimes discussions of health and human rights draw on a distinction between 'civil and political rights' and 'economic and social rights'. The former are seen as of higher legal value, and enforceable as a 'freedom from' state interference. The latter are regarded as aspirational 'claims on' the state for protection and assistance, involving expenditure of resources, and are characteristic of more affluent societies. Fundamental civil and political rights, such as the right to life, the right to privacy and bodily integrity, freedom of religion and the right to family life, are often brought to bear in litigation and legislation in health contexts. Relevant economic and social rights include the 'right to health' as well as associated rights, such as protection from poverty or access to essential medicines. A right to health was first explicitly stated in the Preamble of the Constitution of the World Health Organization in 1946.[18] Some international human rights provisions, such as the right to a standard of living adequate for health and well-being,[19] the need for recognition of the highest ascertainable standard of physical and mental health[20] and protection of health in the workplace,[21] directly address health rights. Certain other provisions contained in international statements of human rights, while they may not make a direct reference to health, may be seen as relevant in claims for rights to particular medical treatments, particularly at the beginning and end of life.[22]

---

[17]   There is a significant literature on this question. See: e.g. Gragl, 'Agreement on the Accession of the European Union to the European Convention on Human Rights' in Peers et al., above n 14; Sarmiento, 'Who's Afraid of the Charter? The Court of Justice, National Courts and the New Framework of Fundamental Rights Protection in Europe' (2013) 50 *Common Market Law Review* 1267; Canor, 'My Brother's Keeper? Horizontal *Solange*: An Ever Closer *Distrust* Among the Peoples of Europe' (2013) 50 *Common Market Law Review* 38; Rosas, 'The Charter and Universal Human Rights Instruments' in Peers et al., above n 14; Itzcovich, 'Legal Order, Legal Pluralism, Fundamental Principles: European and its Law in Three Concepts' (2012) 18(3) *European Law Journal* 358; Klabbers, 'Völkerrechtsfreundlich? International Law and the Union Legal Order' in Koutrakos, (ed) *European Foreign Policy: Legal and Political Perspectives* (Edward Elgar 2011); Walker, 'Beyond boundary disputes and basic grids: Mapping the global disorder of normative orders' (2008) 6(3) & (4) *International Journal of Constitutional Law* 373; Krisch, 'The open architecture of European human rights law' (2008) 71(2) *Modern Law Review* 183; Eckes, 'Does the European Court of Human Rights provide protection from the European Community? The Case of Bosphorus Airways' (2007) 13(1) *European Public Law* 47; Douglas-Scott, 'A Tale of Two Courts: Luxembourg, Strasbourg and the Growing European Human Rights *Acquis*' (2006) 43 *Common Market Law Review* 629; Canor, '*Primus Inter Pares*: Who is the Ultimate Guardian of Fundamental Rights in Europe?' (2000) 25 *European Law Review* 3.

[18]   For an accessible overview of different approaches to the 'right to health', and an articulation of the author's own 'domain-based' approach, see: e.g. Eleftheriadis, 'A Right to Health Care' (2012) 40 *Journal of Law, Medicine & Ethics* 268.

[19]   Universal Declaration of Human Rights 1948, Article 25.

[20]   International Covenant on Economic, Social and Cultural Rights, Article 12 (1).

[21]   Universal Declaration of Human Rights 1948, Article 6.

[22]   See: Universal Declaration of Human Rights 1948, Article 3; and International Covenant on Civil and Political Rights, Article 6. See, in the Council of Europe context: e.g. *Pretty*, no.

Many contemporary human rights scholars, including those working on health and human rights, reject the dichotomy between civil/political and economic/social rights.[23] They point out that civil and political rights have no practical force without the ability to enjoy them, and that rights have value in terms other than judicial enforcement. We are broadly sympathetic to this position, and so, in this chapter, we discuss health rights as encapsulating a cluster of rights, falling in both categories. What is of interest to us here is not whether health rights as human rights in the EU's legal order are a particular type of human right. Our agenda for this chapter, and the next, is to discover the extent to which, and the circumstances in which, EU health law recognizes health rights as human rights, and to draw out the implications.

One claim which has been made in this respect relates to the standard accounts of human rights in EU law. This is the idea that fundamental health rights have become increasingly significant in the EU's legal order. The chapter investigates the extent to which this is true for health rights by tracking the place of health rights as human rights in EU health law across time. To do so, we consider the position before and after the year 2000, the date on which the EU CFR was promulgated.[24] The chapter then considers some of the implications of this story. The focus here is on whether, and if so, the extent to which, and in what contexts, fundamental human rights provide a basis for effectively changing and reforming health law or policy within the EU and its Member States. The question of whether human rights provide a platform for reforming *external* EU health law is considered in Part IV.

An important aspect of health rights as human rights is the question of human rights claims to health resources. In the EU context, typically such rights approaches have arisen in connection with the movement of patients across internal EU borders. We have already seen the ways in which free movement rights encapsulated in Treaty provisions have provided a platform for patients to seek treatment in other jurisdictions, and to claim reimbursement of the cost of such treatment from the social insurance/national health system of their home Member State.[25] Such claims themselves have led to the new 'Patients' Rights Directive', a document somewhat confusingly labelled, given that, in contrast to the domestic legislation of certain EU Member States, it does not provide a 'patients' rights manifesto', still less a Patients' Rights Act.[26] Instead,

---

2346/02, ECHR 2002-III. See: Clarke, 'Abortion: A Rights Issue?' in Lee and Morgan (eds), *Birthrights* (Routledge 1989); Harris, *The Value of Life: An Introduction to Medical Ethics* (Routledge 1985) ch 8; Lewis, *Assisted Dying and Legal Change* (OUP 2007); Huxtable, *Euthanasia, Ethics and Law from Conflict to Compromise* (Routledge 2007); Keown, *Euthanasia, Ethics and Public Policy: An Argument Against Legalisation* (CUP 2002); Mason and Laurie, *Mason & McCall Smith's Law and Medical Ethics* (9th edn, OUP 2013) chapters 16 and 17.

[23] Murphy, *Health and Human Rights* (Hart 2013); See also, by implication: Toebes, Hartlev, Hendriks and Hermann (eds), *Health and Human Rights in Europe* (Intersentia 2012); Selgelid and Pogge (eds), *Health Rights* (Ashgate 2010).

[24] [2000] OJ C83/2.   [25] See further the cases discussed in chapter 4.

[26] Directive 2011/24/EU [2011] OJ L88/45. See further chapter 8.

the Directive clarifies the free movement case law, builds in further controls upon free movement from Member States, and seeks to perpetuate a health care standards agenda. Scott Greer and Tomislav Sokol read this law as an emergent model of social citizenship expressed as 'rules for rights' rather than a social rights model per se.[27] The question of whether EU health law protects mobile patients' rights, in the sense of claims to resources, *as human rights*, is the subject of the following chapter.

The development of health rights as human rights in EU law

Judicial development: human rights as 'general principles' of EU health law

The CJEU recognized human rights as 'general principles' of EU law in the 1960s.[28] One of the most important sources of such general principles of EU law is the ECHR.[29] Its position in EU law was recognized in the EU's founding Treaties in the early 1990s, and it is now found in Article 6 (3) TEU, which asserts that the ECHR's fundamental rights are general principles of EU law.

The ECHR is a traditional civil and political statement of human rights.[30] It was drafted in the aftermath of the Second World War, and came into force in 1953. All the EU's Member States are signatories to the ECHR and thus individual citizens of all EU Member States may enforce their rights before the European Court of Human Rights.[31] A considerable number of actions brought before the European Court of Human Rights relate to health. For instance, Article 1 ECHR, which safeguards the right to life, has been used in claims concerning the status of the foetus and abortion,[32] resource allocation[33] and the right to die.[34] Article 5 ECHR, which safeguards the position of liberty and security of the person, has been used extensively in mental health claims.[35] Article 8 ECHR, the right to privacy of home and family life, has been used in the context of health privacy and confidentiality of patient information, autonomy of treatment decisions, and reproductive rights.[36] Article 12 ECHR, the right

---

[27] See: Greer and Sokol, 'Rules for Rights: European Law, Health Care and Social Citizenship' (2014) 20(1) *European Law Journal* 66.

[28] *Stauder* EU:C:1969:57.

[29] *Nold*, C-4/73, EU:C:1974:51; *Rutili*, C-36/75, EU:C:1975:137; *Johnson v RUC*, C-222/84, EU:C:1986:206.

[30] See further: White and Overy, *The European Convention on Human Rights* (OUP 2010).

[31] There are important limitations on this entitlement, in particular the doctrine of exhaustion of domestic remedies.

[32] *H v Norway* App no 17004/90 (ECtHR, 19 May 1992); *Open Door and Dublin Well Woman v Ireland* (1992) Series A no 246; *Paton v UK* App no 8416/78 (ECtHR 13 May 1980); *A, B, C v Ireland*, no. 25579/05, ECHR 2010-I.

[33] *Osman v UK*, no. 23452/94, ECHR 1998-VIII. *Scialaqua v Italy* App no. 34151/96 (ECtHR, 1 July 1998).

[34] *Pretty v UK*, no. 2346/02, ECHR 2002-III.

[35] See: e.g. *Winterwerp v The Netherlands* (1992) Series A no 33; *Aerts v Belgium*, no. 25357/94, ECHR 1998-V.

[36] *Evans v UK*, no. 6339/05, ECHR 2007-I.

to marry and found a family, has featured in claims concerning reproductive rights.[37]

The various ECHR rights relevant to health contexts, as general principles of EU law, did not feature directly in a claim before the CJEU in a health context during this phase of the EU's human rights law development. The *SPUC* v. *Grogan* case[38] from the 1980s concerned abortion, but this was discussed in terms of free movement of services, and the CJEU was reluctant to engage with the human rights aspects of the litigation. Similarly, national courts applying EU law in circumstances concerning reproductive medical treatments, such as the UK's Court of Appeal in *R.* v. *Human Fertilisation and Embryology Authority ex parte Blood,*[39] did not refer directly to ECHR rights to life, privacy or family life.

In its general jurisprudence, the CJEU has also recognized some other regional and international human rights instruments.[40] Those which are of particular relevance in the health field include the Council of Europe's Convention for the Protection of Human Rights and Dignity of the Human Being with regard to the Application of Biology and Medicine,[41] 1997, a statement which, as its title suggests, is specifically targeted at biomedicine.[42] Article 1 of the Biomedicine Convention states that its purpose and object is safeguarding the dignity and identity of all human beings, and respecting their integrity and other fundamental rights and freedoms. The Convention refers to rights to consent,[43] private life and the right to information,[44] controls on genetics and prohibition on discrimination,[45] research[46] and removal of organs and tissue from living donors for transplantation purposes.[47] The Council of Europe has also

[37] *Dickson v UK,* no 44362/04, ECHR 2007-V.

[38] *Grogan,* C-159/90, EU:C:1991:378. See: De Búrca, 'Fundamental Human Rights and the Reach of EC Law' (1993) 13 *Oxford Journal of Legal Studies* 283; Rossa Phelan, 'Right to Life of the Unborn v Promotion of Trade in Services: the ECJ and the normative shaping of the EU' (1992) 55 *Modern Law Review* 670.

[39] [1997] 2 All ER 687. See: Hervey, 'Buy Baby: the European Union and the Regulation of Human Reproduction' (1998) 18 *Oxford Journal of Legal Studies* 207; Morgan and Lee, 'In the Name of the Father? *Ex parte Blood*: Dealing with Novelty and Anomaly' (1997) 60 *Modern Law Review* 840.

[40] *Defrenne v SABENA,* C-149/77, EU:C:1978:130, paragraph 26, in which the CJEU drew on the European Social Charter.

[41] Recognised by the CJEU in: Opinion in *Biotechnology Directive,* C-377/98, EU:C:2001:329, paragraph 210; although in *De Fruytier,* C-237/09, EU:C:2010:316, paragraph 27, the CJEU noted that the Convention on Human Rights and Biomedicine has been ratified by only a small number of Member States and not by the EU itself. As at January 2014, 17 Member States have ratified the Convention, 5 have signed but not ratified, and 6 have not even signed.

[42] Convention for the Protection of Human Rights and Dignity of the Human Being with Regard to Biology and Medicine: Convention on Human Rights and Biomedicine 1997; and see also: Zilgavis, 'The European Convention on Biomedicine: Its Past, Present and Future' in Garwood-Gowers, Tingle and Lewis (eds), *Healthcare Law: The Impact of the Human Rights Act 1998,* (Routledge-Cavendish 2001).

[43] Biomedicine Convention, Articles 5-9.   [44] Biomedicine Convention, Article 12.

[45] Biomedicine Convention, Articles 11-13.   [46] Biomedicine Convention, Articles 15-18.

[47] Biomedicine, Articles 21-22.

produced additional protocols on cloning,[48] transplantation[49] and biomedical research.[50]

Again, the CJEU did not rely on these provisions in health litigation during this period of time. *Netherlands* v. *European Parliament and Council (Biotechnology Directive)*,[51] concerning the validity of Directive 98/44/EC on the legal protection of biotechnological inventions,[52] was one possible opportunity in which to do so. However, the CJEU's judgment considered only 'the fundamental right to human dignity and integrity'.[53] The Advocate General referred to the ECHR, and to the Biomedicine Convention once,[54] but did not rely significantly on this human rights instrument in his reasoning.

The Council of Europe's European Social Charter (ESC),[55] Article 11, covers the 'right to the protection of health', obliging states to 'take appropriate measures' to 'remove as far as possible the causes of ill-health', 'to provide advisory and educational facilities for the promotion of health and the encouragement of individual responsibility in matters of health', and 'to prevent as far as possible epidemic, endemic and other diseases as well as accidents'. The work of the European Committee of Social Rights, including under the complaints mechanism, has elaborated a 'jurisprudence' of social rights, in particular articulating the values (autonomy, dignity, equality and solidarity) which underpin the ESC. As Cullen has noted, the ways the Committee understands these values supports a generous interpretation of ESC rights, for instance, solidarity is seen as 'a value supporting inclusion and protection against vulnerability'.[56] Although, again, the ESC and the European Committee's work could form a resource for the

---

[48] Additional Protocol to the Convention for the Protection of Human Rights and Dignity of the Human Being with Regard to Biology and Medicine on the Prohibition of Cloning Human Beings 1998.

[49] Additional Protocol to the Convention on Human Rights and Biomedicine, on Transplantation of Organs and Tissues of Human Origin 2002. The Council of Europe has adopted a Convention against Trafficking in Human Organs, 9 July 2014; see: Council of Europe, 'Towards a Council of Europe convention to combat trafficking in organs, tissues and cells of human origin' (*Committee on Social Affairs, health and Sustainable Development*, Council of Europe, 20 December 2012); Council of Europe, 'Committee of Experts on Trafficking in Human Organs, Tissues and Cells (PC-TO)' (*European Committee on Crime Problems (CDPC)*, Council of Europe).

[50] Additional Protocol to the Convention on Human Rights and Biomedicine, on Biomedical Research 2005.

[51] *Biotechnology Directive*, C-377/98 EU:C:2001:523.

[52] Directive 98/44/EC [1998] OJ L213/13.

[53] *Biotechnology Directive* EU:C:2001:523, paragraphs 6 and 70.

[54] Opinion in *Biotechnology Directive* EU:C:2001:329, paragraph 210, referring to the principle of free and informed consent.

[55] First recognised by the CJEU in: *Defrenne* EU:C:1978:130.

[56] Cullen, 'The Collective Complaints System of the European Social Charter: Interpretative Methods of the European Committee of Social Rights' (2009) 9(1) *Human Rights Law Review* 61, 92.

CJEU, in practice connections between EU law and the ESC are notable in their absence during this period.[57]

Another important source of human rights as 'general principles' of EU law is the constitutional traditions of the Member States.[58] The Member States protect ECHR rights, including those relied upon in health contexts, in their constitutions. The concept of human dignity from the German constitution has been particularly influential on the CJEU.[59] Although the CJEU has stated that the concept of human dignity has an independent meaning in EU law,[60] the ways in which national and EU human rights orders interlock[61] is underlined by Article 52 (4) EU CFR, which provides that rights from the common constitutional traditions of the Member States are to be interpreted 'in harmony with those traditions'.[62] A majority (18/28) of Member States' constitutions explicitly recognize a 'right to health'.[63]

Although the Member States share health rights as human rights at the level of general legal or constitutional provisions, when it comes to the specifics of how these rights are understood and implemented, there are significant differences. Abortion, and the status of the human embryo, is the canonical example;[64] but others include details on free and informed consent to medical treatment,

---

[57] Hervey, 'We Don't See a Connection: The 'Right to Health' in the EU Charter and European Social Charter' in De Búrca and De Witte (eds), *Social Rights in Europe* (OUP 2005) 305.

[58] Article 6 (3) TEU.   [59] See: Dupré, 'Article 1 – Human Dignity' in Peers et al., above n 14.

[60] *Omega*, C-36/02, EU:C:2004:614.

[61] See, for instance: Lenaerts, 'Interlocking Legal Orders in the EU and Comparative Law' (2003) 52 *International and Comparative Law Quarterly* 873.

[62] For further discussion, see Peers and Prechal, 'Article 52 – Scope and Interpretation of Rights and Principles' in Peers et al., above n 14.

[63] Article 23 of the Belgian Constitution; Chapter 2, Article 52 of the Bulgarian Constitution; Article 59 of the Croatian Constitution; Article 4 Czech Charter of Fundamental Rights and Freedoms; Article 28 of the Estonian Constitution; section 19 (3) of the Finnish Constitution; Article 70 D of the Hungarian Constitution; Article 32 of the Italian Constitution; Article 111 of the Latvian Constitution; Article 53 of the Lithuanian Constitution, Article 11(5) of the Luxembourg Constitution; Article 22 (1) of the Netherlands Constitution; Article 68 of the Polish Constitution; Article 64 (1) of the Portuguese Constitution; Article 34 of the Romanian Constitution; Article 40 of the Spanish Constitution; Article 51 of the Slovenian Constitution; Article 43 of the Spanish Constitution. According to the former UN Special Rapporteur on the Right to Health, Paul Hunt, over 100 national constitutional provisions now include the right to health, the right to health care, or health-related rights such as a right to a healthy environment. Hunt, 'The human right to the highest attainable standard of health: new opportunities and challenges' (2006) 100(7) *Transactions of the Royal Society of Tropical Medicine and Hygiene* 603, 603 cited Toebes et al., above n 23, 91.

[64] Ireland, Malta, and Poland are outliers in this respect, and their position is enshrined in the Protocol No. 35 on Article 40.3.3 of the Constitution of Ireland annexed to the TFEU and the Protocol No. 7 on Abortion in Malta, annexed to the Treaty of Accession of the Czech Republic, Estonia, Cyprus, Latvia, Lithuania, Hungary, Malta, Poland, Slovenia and Slovakia [2003] OJ L236/17 . Other Member States, including Lithuania and Spain, have recently considered or implemented more restrictive abortion laws. As the CJEU observed in *Brüstle*, C-34/10, EU:C:2011:669, paragraph 30, the definition of embryo is 'marked by [the Member States'] multiple traditions and value systems'.

or participation in clinical trials; details on the arrangements for donation of blood, organs and other human tissue; how human rights apply in the context of biotechnological and nanotechnological research; and on how privacy rights are reconciled with other interests in the context of the handling of health data. As we will see, EU law allows for reasonably significant variations in this regard.[65]

Treaty amendments: health rights in the EU Charter of Fundamental Rights

The formal place of human rights in the EU's legal order changed with the incorporation of the EU's Charter of Fundamental Rights and Freedoms 2000 (EU CFR) into the Treaties in December 2009.[66] Assessments of the significance of the EU CFR vary. Certainly the promulgation of the instrument in 2000, as a measure of soft law, was a low-key affair. The CJEU did not cite the EU CFR until 2006, but continued its practice of referring to the ECHR.[67] Since then, however, references to the EU CFR have increased, and, since the Treaty of Lisbon, its provisions now have the 'same legal value' as Treaty provisions.[68]

The EU CFR brings together a long list of human rights, drawing inspiration from international and regional human rights instruments, EU legislation and the jurisprudence of the CJEU. Its provisions are organized into six substantive 'Chapters', of which those on dignity, freedoms, equality, and solidarity are of most relevance to health rights. The EU CFR distinguishes between 'rights',

---

[65] Although, where the internal market and free movement law are engaged, not as much discretion to the Member States as the ECtHR's 'margin of appreciation'. The margin of appreciation doctrine allows discretion to individual States Parties to interpret Convention provisions taking into account their particular national circumstances and traditions, such as cultural practices or religious or historic traditions. See generally: Arai-Takahashi, *The Margin of Appreciation Doctrine and the Principle of Proportionality* (Intersentia 2002). The ECtHR has been prepared to afford a wide margin of appreciation to States Parties where the issues which come before it are acutely ethically controversial in nature. Examples include abortion (see: *Paton v UK* App no 8416/78 (ECtHR 13 May 1980); *Vo v France* ECHR [2004] 2 FCR 577; *A,B,C v Ireland,* no. 25579/05, ECHR 2010-I; end of life decision-making (see: *Pretty v UK*, no. 2346/02, ECHR 2002-III) and reproductive rights (see: *Evans v UK*, no. 6339/05, ECHR 2007-I. See: O'Donovan, 'Taking a Neutral Stance on the Legal Protection of the Fetus' (2006) 14 *Medical Law Review* 115; Hewson, 'Dancing on the Head of a Pin: Foetal Life and the European Convention' (2005) 13 *Feminist Legal Studies* 363; Mason, 'What's in a Name? The Vagaries of *Vo v France* (2005) 17(5) *Child and Family Law Quarterly* 97; Plomer, 'A Foetal Right to Life? The Case of *Vo v France*' (2005) 5(2) *Human Rights Law Review* 311; Krishnan, 'What's the consensus: The Grand Chamber's decision on abortion in *A, B and C v Ireland*' (2011) 2 *European Human Rights Review* 200; McGuinness, '*A, B and C* leads to D for delegation!' (2011) 19(3) *Medical Law Review* 476; Freeman, 'Denying Death its Dominion: thoughts on the Dianne Pretty case' (2002) 10 *Medical Law Review* 245; Tur, 'Legislative Techniques and human rights; the sad case of assisted suicide' (2003) *Criminal Law Review* 3.

[66] Commission, 'Declaration concerning the Charter of Fundamental Rights of the EU' (European Union 2010) 337.

[67] Douglas-Scott, 'The European Union and Human Rights after Lisbon' (2011) 11(4) *Human Rights Law Review* 645.

[68] Article 6 (1) TEU.

'freedoms' and 'principles', although does not explicitly identify which provisions fall in which category.[69] While 'rights' and 'freedoms' are (potentially) individually enforceable, 'principles' are 'judicially cognisable only in the interpretation of' legislative and executive acts of the EU, and national acts which implement EU law.[70]

Since 2009, health rights (whether 'rights' or 'principles') have been expressed in the EU's 'constitutional' legal texts. However, as we have seen, this development may not be as significant in practice as it appears, given that most relevant rights had already been recognized as general principles of EU law, as noted above. In some ways, the EU CFR could be read as seeking to *restrict*, rather than encourage, the CJEU-led development of human rights in EU law. For instance, the Treaties explicitly state that the EU CFR 'does not extend the field of application of Union law beyond the powers of the Union, or establish and new power or task for the Union, or modify powers or tasks as defined by the Treaties'.[71] The CJEU's case law establishes that human rights as general principles of EU law apply where Member States derogate from EU law; the Charter provides explicitly that it applies to the Member States 'only when they are implementing Union law'.[72] However, the CJEU has stated more recently that the EU CFR applies 'in all situations governed by EU law'.[73]

On the other hand, it is at least arguable that the incorporation of the EU CFR in the EU's Treaties has enhanced the role and significance of human rights in EU law.[74] In the context of health rights, looking at the jurisprudence of the CJEU, for instance, we see an increased willingness to consider human rights implications in EU litigation. For instance, the EU CFR's 'right to health care'[75] was cited by the CJEU only once before 2009 (and that only in an AG Opinion),[76] but has been cited five times since then.[77]

---

[69] According to the EU CFR's 'Explanations' (non-binding explanatory text adopted at the same time as the EU CFR itself), an Article of the EU CFR may contain elements of a right and a principle, see: Explanations to Article 52(2) EU CFR.

[70] Article 52 (5) EU CFR. On the difference, see: Peers and Prechal, 'Article 52 – Scope and Interpretation of Rights and Principles' in Peers et al., above n 14, and the literature cited therein.

[71] Article 52 (2) EU CFR; and Commission, 'Declaration concerning the Charter of Fundamental Rights of the EU' (European Union 2010) 337.

[72] Article 51 (1) EU CFR.

[73] *Fransson*, C-617/10, EU:C:2013:280, paragraph 19. See also: Opinion in *Ruiz Zambrano*, C-34/09, EU:C:2010:560. See discussion in Ward, 'Article 51 – Field of Application' in Peers et al., above n 14.

[74] Peers et al., 'Editors' Preface' in Peers et al., above n 14; Cartabia, 'Europe and Rights: Taking Dialogue Seriously' (2009) 5(1) *European Constitutional Review* 5; Peers and Ward (eds), *The EU Charter of Fundamental Rights: Politics, Law and Policy* (Hart 2004); Hervey and Kenner (eds), *Economic and Social Rights under the EU Charter of Fundamental Rights* (Hart 2003).

[75] Article 35 EU CFR.

[76] Opinion in *Stamatelaki*, C-444/05, EU:C:2007:24.

[77] *Deutsches Weintor*, C-544/10, EU:C:2012:526; *Susisalo*, C-84/11, EU:C:2012:374; *Pérez and Gómez*, C-570/07 and C-571/07, EU:C:2010:300; Opinion in *Josemans*, C-137/09,

Furthermore, it is also at least arguable that, with the incorporation of the EU CFR into EU Treaty law, the *possibilities* for health claims being articulated as human rights claims in EU law have increased. Articulating a claim within a human rights frame may have implications for both legal reasoning and for legal outcomes, such as determining the standard of proof required to interfere with free movement rules. The CJEU has long recognized that the protection of human rights objectively justifies restrictions on free movement.[78] For instance, what if a cross-border patient in a situation such as that in the *Peerbooms* case were in a *life-threatening* coma?[79] Would the burden of proof on a Member State refusing to authorize cross-border treatment be greater in such a circumstance than if the right to life were not engaged? Equally, could a Member State more easily justify refusal to authorize cross-border treatment that could be interpreted as infringing the right to life, such as euthanasia[80] or abortion?[81] Only future litigation would determine the answers to these questions, but the power of human rights-based reasoning in European legal traditions suggests that it is at least conceivable that human rights reasoning could make a difference.

Moreover, some relevant rights were given increased prominence in the EU CFR. The best example is Article 1 EU CFR, on human dignity. Although this human right was recognized in pre-2009 litigation,[82] as well as legislation,[83] its explicit articulation, and its place (the first provision of the EU CFR), suggest an increased importance. That said, the CJEU has delivered rulings referring to or explicitly relying upon Article 1 EU CFR only a few times, in cases involving asylum.[84] However, particularly in combination with other provisions, such as the right to life,[85] human dignity has significant potential in the EU's regulation of novel health technologies in particular.[86]

Institutional developments: the European Fundamental Rights Agency

The argument that health rights as human rights have become increasingly significant in EU law is lent strength by considering institutional developments

---

EU:C:2010:433. Another case, Order in *Rossius and Collard*, C-267/10 and C-268/10, EU:C:2011:332, was found inadmissible for lack of jurisdiction.

[78] *ERT*, C-260/89, EU:C:1991:254; *Schmidberger*, C-112/00, EU:C:2003:333.

[79] See Wicks, 'Article 2 – Right to Life' in Peers et al., above n 14, 26.

[80] See: Michalowski, 'Health Care Law' in Peers and Ward, above n 74, 295-6.

[81] See: Wicks, above n 79, 27.

[82] *P v S and Cornwall CC*, C-13/94, EU:C:1996:170; *Biotechnology Directive* EU:C:2001:523.

[83] For discussion of examples, which range from children's audiovisual service to reception conditions for asylum seekers, see: Dupré, above n 59.

[84] Judgment in *NS v Secretary of State for the Home Department*, C-411/10, EU:C:2011:865.

[85] Wicks, above n 79.

[86] See: Millns, 'Reproducing inequalities: assisted conception and the challenge of legal pluralism' (2002) 24 *Journal of Social Welfare and Family Law* 19; Flear et al., 'A European Law of New Health Technologies' in Flear et al. (eds), *European Law and New Health Technologies* (OUP 2013).

beyond the role of the CJEU. In 2007, the EU established a Fundamental Rights Agency (FRA),[87] replacing an earlier institution, with a narrower remit.[88] The EU's FRA has an advisory role, gathering and disseminating information and good human rights practice to the EU institutions and the Member States and (through its Fundamental Rights Platform) promoting dialogue within civil society to raise human rights awareness.

The FRA works through a 'Multiannual Framework', which is agreed by the EU legislature. The first such Framework ran from 2007 to 2012.[89] Its basic focus, at first glance, is on traditional 'civil and political rights', particularly in areas such as access to justice and exercise of democratic rights. Much of the FRA's early work, therefore, cannot be said to be increasing the ways in which EU law or policy treats health rights as human rights. However, several of the Framework's thematic priorities were relevant to health rights, in particular when combined with principles of non-discrimination. The relevant thematic priorities are tackling racism and xenophobia, discrimination based on a range of forbidden grounds, rights of the child and protection of children, asylum and respect for private life and personal data protection. A good illustrative example is its first Annual Report published after the EU CFR was incorporated into the Treaties.[90] Health does not feature generally, but it is mentioned in the context of an examination of discrimination safeguards, particularly in terms of the social and economic position of members of the Roma community in the EU[91] and tensions between religious belief and health provision.[92]

The current Multiannual Framework runs from 2013 to 2017.[93] Its thematic priorities are very similar to those of the previous Framework, although 'Roma integration' features as a specific priority in this Framework. In 2011, the FRA reported a serious data deficiency in terms of the human rights position of the Roma, including in terms of social and economic rights such as health.[94] The FRA set about rectifying that information gap, commissioning research and making recommendations of good practice. Research from surveys, reviews of official information and qualitative data through participatory action research reveals that Roma are systematically worse off than other Europeans, in a range of areas including health and life expectancy.[95] The headline figures of its key

---

[87] Regulation 168/2007/EC [2007] OJ L53/1.

[88] The European Monitoring Centre on Racism and Xenophobia.

[89] Decision 2008/203/EC [2007] OJ L63/14.

[90] European Union Agency for Fundamental Rights (FRA), 'Annual Report. Fundamental Rights: challenges and achievements in 2010' (FRA 2011).

[91] FRA, 'Annual Report. Fundamental Rights: challenges and achievements in 2010' (FRA 2011) 15, 21–22.

[92] FRA, above n 90.   [93] Decision 252/2013/EU [2013] OJ L79/1.

[94] The FRA began its work on Roma as the European Monitoring Centre on Racism and Xenophobia (EUMC). Its first report concerned health. EUMC, 'Breaking the Barriers – Romani Women and Access to Public Health Care' (EUMC 2003).

[95] FRA, 'Multi-Annual Programme' (*FRA*, 2013) and Commission, 'National Roma Integration Strategies: a first step in the implementation of the EU Framework' (Communication) COM

report are shocking: one out of three Roma respondents aged 35 to 54 report health problems limiting their daily activities; on average, about 20 per cent of Roma respondents are not covered by medical insurance or do not know if they are covered.[96] Drawing on the work of the FRA, the European Commission called upon Member States to improve integration of Roma in four areas, one of which is health.[97] A working group is developing indicators and measuring progress towards these goals.[98]

The FRA also uses a more legal approach in instances where its reports highlight deficiencies in implementing relevant EU law, or untapped potential legal avenues for enforcing human rights, often coupled with the principle of non-discrimination.[99] Directive 2000/43 on race equality, for instance, applies to 'social protection, including . . . healthcare'.[100] A report on the Directive highlights the judicial, administrative and alternative dispute mechanisms available to enforce it.[101] The FRA has also worked on the health rights of people with disabilities.[102] In addition, a major FRA report in 2013 considered questions of 'intersectionality' in health inequalities.[103] It found that unequal and unfair treatment in access to health and quality of health care persists across the EU, with particularly ill-served groups being those who experience discrimination on more than one 'forbidden ground' (for instance, a Muslim, older, woman with a disability). The report cites examples of discrimination at the intersection of sex, ethnicity and disability in violations of human rights provisions on informed consent to treatment, coupled with rights to human reproduction, such as sterilization of Roma women and women with disabilities.

The FRA has highlighted the limitations of the law and legal processes in remedying such human rights infringements in health contexts. Barriers include tolerance of or failure to recognize unlawful discrimination,[104] difficulties in

---

(2012) 226 final; FRA, 'Collecting secondary data and mapping official data sources' (*FRA*, ongoing) FRA, 'Multi-Annual Programme' (*FRA*, 2013).

[96] FRA, 'The Situation of Roma in 11 Member States' (FRA 2012) 12 and 21.

[97] Commission, 'An EU Framework for National Roma Integration Strategies up to 2020' (Communication) COM (2011) 173 final.

[98] FRA, 'Assisting Member States to measure the progress of Roma integration' (*FRA*, ongoing).

[99] Article 21 EU CFR.

[100] Directive 2000/43/EC [2000] OJ L180/22. The CJEU has not heard a claim involving a health context based on the Directive. In *Kamberaj*, C-571/10, EU:C:2012:233, involving housing benefit rules, the CJEU found that the Directive does not cover nationality discrimination. But there is no reason why it should not cover race discrimination in health contexts.

[101] FRA, 'The Race Equality Directive: application and challenges' (FRA 2011).

[102] FRA, 'Involuntary placement and involuntary treatment of persons with mental health problems' (FRA 2012); FRA, 'Choice and control: the right to independent living' (FRA 2012); FRA, 'Legal capacity of persons with intellectual disabilities and persons with mental health problems' (FRA 2013).

[103] FRA, 'Inequalities in multiple discrimination in access to and quality of healthcare' (FRA 2013) For more information about 'intersectionality' in EU law, see: Schiek and Lawson (eds), *European Union Non-Discrimination Law and Intersectionality: Investigating the Triangle of Racial, Gender and Disability Discrimination* (Ashgate 2011).

[104] FRA, 'The Race Equality Directive', above n 101.

evidencing discrimination, and in choice of comparator, and lack of under-standing of intersectionality by lawyers and judges alike. The consequence is that disputes are often pursued through non-human rights legal frame-works, such as medical negligence, or alternative dispute mechanisms such as Ombudsmen.[105] So, on balance, although the FRA's work on the Roma com-munities of Europe is probably its most significant practical contribution to health and human rights,[106] the mechanisms used here are not the traditional mechanisms of human rights law.[107] Again, therefore, the conclusion is that the claim that health rights as human rights are increasingly significant in EU law may have some merit, but needs some nuance.

The implications of increased significance of health rights as human rights in EU law

To the extent that fundamental health rights, as human rights, have become more significant in the EU's legal order, what are the implications? Have health rights made a difference – to national or EU level health policies? In what contexts? What opportunities arise from the recognition by EU law of health rights as human rights? In 2004, we concluded that many health rights were already protected within EU law, as general principles of law, and so little change was expected, even if the EU CFR were to become binding EU law,[108] as has now taken place. Writing in 2003, of the 'right to health', Hervey concluded that, were the right to health to become articulated more strongly in EU law, *in some contexts* change could be anticipated. In the context of internal market litigation, there might be changes in terms of how claims were articulated and decisions made, but the *outcomes* of any relevant decisions would remain unaltered. The area of most promise, in terms of promoting the health status of some of the most vulnerable human beings within the EU, was that of human migration.[109]

The remainder of this chapter considers the current position, some ten years later. We consider first the scope for health rights as human rights to affect the

---

[105] FRA, 'Inequalities in multiple discrimination in access to and quality of healthcare' (FRA 2013).

[106] Although it is too soon to assess its effects.

[107] For a discussion of the FRA's potential, and its contribution to 'an administrative law of fundamental rights protection and promotion', see: Von Bogdandy and Von Bernstoff, 'The EU Fundamental Rights Agency within the European and International Human Rights Architecture: The Legal Framework and Some Unsettled Issues in a new field of Administrative Law' (2009) 46 *Common Market Law Review* 1035; Toggenburg, 'The role of the new EU Fundamental Rights Agency: debating the "sex of angels" or improving Europe's human rights performance? (2008) 33 *European Law Review* 385. For a critique of the FRA's use of comparative statistics as a technique of government, see: Sokhi-Bulley, 'Governing (Through) Rights: Statistics as Technologies of Governmentality' (2011) 20 *Social and Legal Studies* 139.

[108] Hervey and McHale, *Health Law and the European Union* (CUP 2004) 406-7.

[109] Hervey, 'The right to health in EU law' in Hervey and Kenner (eds), above n 74.

validity of EU legislation and administrative acts, and how EU law is interpreted. Either or both of these processes can have the effect of making a difference to EU health law or policy. We also consider the national context, examining ways in which health rights as human rights affect the interpretation of national implementing legislation. Coupled with the doctrine of supremacy of EU law, such interpretations often, *de facto*, amount to testing the consistency of national legislation with EU law. Second, we consider an important example of how health rights as human rights may extend individual entitlements, particularly in claims against state bodies. This is the possibility of health rights being coupled with equality and non-discrimination, in interpreting EU law, national implementing law or both. Third, we consider the relevance of human rights in the context of internal market law, where Member States seek to justify restrictions on free movement on the basis that they breach a health right of some sort. Finally, we consider some more nebulous or indirect effects of health rights as human rights in EU health law.

The validity and interpretation of EU legislation or administrative decisions and national implementing acts

Acts of the EU institutions which breach fundamental human rights are invalid. The CJEU has jurisdiction to hear judicial review claims on this (and other) ground(s),[110] brought by the 'privileged' applicants of the EU institutions and Member State governments, and by individuals in certain restricted circumstances.[111] In principle, therefore, health rights could act as a constraint on the EU's law and policymaking powers. In practice, however, such constraining effects have been very limited.

As noted above, the CJEU mentioned human dignity[112] in its judicial review of Directive 98/44/EC on the legal protection of biotechnological inventions.[113] But none of the EU's other legislation concerning development of new health technologies, or involving the use of human material in clinical research, has been challenged on grounds of breaching fundamental rights. The Advanced Therapy Medicinal Products Regulation,[114] for instance, establishes a special

---

[110] Article 263 TFEU.

[111] The main context in which an individual may bring a claim is where an act of an EU institution is addressed to that individual. The restricted *locus standi* of individuals in EU law has been controversial in some health contexts, such as the CJEU's ruling in *Olivieri v Commission*, T-326/99, EU:T:2003:351, that Dr Nancy Olivieri did not have *locus* to review the decision of the European Medicines Agency to authorise deferiprone, a drug whose clinical trials she originally directed. Dr Olivieri left the deferiprone trials when she became concerned about the safety of the drug. See further: Abraham and Davis, 'Science, Law and the Medical-Industrial Complex in EU Pharmaceutical Regulation: The Deferiprone Controversy' in Flear et al., above n 86.

[112] *Biotechnology Directive* EU:C:2001:523, paragraphs 70–77.

[113] Directive 98/44/EC [1998] OJ L213/13.

[114] Regulation 1394/2007/EC [2007] OJ L324/121.

marketing authorization system for novel products based on genes, cells and tissues, at the boundaries between pharmaceuticals and medical devices, and using human material. Although the Regulation itself declares compliance with human rights instruments,[115] it is at least arguable that even developing these products at all, let alone authorizing their marketing, breaches fundamental human rights such as dignity or the right to life, as expressed through the idea that the human body is not a commodity. But no litigation was brought challenging the validity of the provisions of the Regulation. Nor has there been litigation challenging EU administrative acts, for instance, the decision to fund, or not to fund, certain types of research – even though such a decision might be claimed to breach human dignity, the right to life, or, conversely, freedom of scientific research.[116]

On reflection, however, this is not such a surprise. The European Court of Human Rights is ambivalent about the application of the 'right to life' in the context of novel health technologies,[117] and there is every reason to expect similar caution from the CJEU. Perhaps this is in part because of the presence of competing rights (to life, to dignity) of those patients who might benefit from future therapies, and because a public interest justification applies in the context of developing novel health technologies. The EU CFR explicitly prohibits 'the reproductive cloning of human beings',[118] but is silent on the question of so-called 'therapeutic cloning',[119] perhaps implying that such uses of human material do not infringe human rights according to EU law.

---

[115] Regulation 1394/2007/EC, Recital 8: 'This Regulation respects the fundamental rights and observes the principles reflected in the Charter of Fundamental Rights of the European Union and also takes into account the Council of Europe Convention for the Protection of Human Rights and Dignity of the Human Being with regard to the Application of Biology and Medicine: Convention on Human Rights and Biomedicine.'

[116] Article 13, EU CFR. See: Sayers, 'Article 13 – Freedom of the Arts and Sciences' in Peers et al., above n 14, 394.

[117] Gevers and O'Connell, 'Fixed Points in a Changing Age? The Council of Europe, Human Rights and the Regulation of New Health Technologies' in Flear et al., above n 86; Hervey and McHale, above n 108, 400-402; Nys, 'Comparative health law and the harmonisation of patients' rights in Europe' (2001) 8(4) *European Journal of Health Law* 317; Millns, 'Consolidating Bio-rights in Europe' in Francioni (ed), *Biotechnologies and International Human Rights* (Hart 2007); Brownsword, 'Human Dignity, Ethical Pluralism and the Regulation of Modern Biotechnologies' in Murphy (ed), *New Technologies and Human Rights* (OUP 2009); Mason and Laurie, above n 22.

[118] Article 3 (2) (d) EU CFR.

[119] Defined by the UK Human Genetics Advisory Commission (HGAC) as: "medical and scientific applications of cloning technology which do not result in the production of genetically identical foetuses or babies. These techniques may be undertaken to advance fundamental research and therefore not all such applications will lead to immediate therapeutic utility", UK HGAC, 'Cloning Issues in Reproduction Science and Medicine (Consultation Document)' (HGAC 1998) Annex B. See further: Hervey and McHale, above n 108, 271-273; UK HGAC and UK Human Fertilisation and Embryology Authority (HFEA), 'Cloning Issues in Reproduction, Science and Medicine' (HGAC and HFEA 1998) 19-23.

Health rights as human rights have, however, played a stronger role in the *interpretation* of EU law. The CJEU was asked to interpret the Biotechnology Directive in the 2011 *Brüstle* case,[120] in the context of German patents for 'neural crest cells' (a type of cell that can develop into many types of cells and tissues), derived from a blastocyst (the entity which has developed around five days after fertilization of an ovum), and the process of deriving these cells. These cells offer the promise of treatment of diseases such as Parkinson's disease. The national referring court asked whether the patent was excluded from patentability, in so far as it concerns cells obtained from embryonic stem cells. To answer that question, the CJEU was required to interpret Article 6 (2) (c) of the Biotechnology Directive, which provides that 'uses of human embryos for industrial or commercial purposes' shall be unpatentable. In essence, this involved an interpretation of the term 'human embryo', in this context.

The CJEU's judgment, and in particular the Opinion of its Advocate General, AG Bot, strongly articulate human rights as the rationale underpinning the decision. AG Bot goes so far as to say that the EU is 'not only a market to be regulated', but also 'has values [in particular that of human dignity] to be expressed'.[121] The CJEU's interpretation of the Directive begins from 'fundamental rights and the dignity of the person',[122] and it is on this basis that the CJEU concludes that

> The context and aim of the Directive . . . show that the European Union legislature intended to exclude any possibility of patentability where respect for human dignity could thereby be affected. It follows that the concept of 'human embryo' within the meaning of Article 6(2) (c) of the Directive must be understood in a wide sense.[123]

Hence, according to the CJEU in *Brüstle*, 'human embryo' includes any fertilized human ovum; a non-fertilized human ovum into which a mature human cell nucleus has been transplanted ('therapeutic cloning'); and a non-fertilized human ovum whose division and further development has been stimulated by parthenogenesis (a form of reproduction where embryos grow without fertilization, which has been achieved in human embryos since around 2004). The ruling means that these entities, and processes, are not patentable in the EU – although the CJEU left to the national court the final determination of whether the specific products and processes at issue in the *Brüstle* case fell within this definition.[124] In this context, therefore, the human rights engaged meant that the concept of 'human embryo' was given a wide interpretation, hence

---

[120] *Brüstle*, C-34/10, EU:C:2011:669.   [121] Opinion in *Brüstle*, paragraph 46.
[122] *Brüstle*, paragraph 32.   [123] *Brüstle*, paragraph 34.
[124] *Brüstle*, paragraph 38. See: Harmon, Laurie and Courtney, 'Dignity, plurality and patentability: the unfinished story of *Brüstle v Greenpeace*' (2013) 38(1) *European Law Review* 92; Varju and Sandor, 'Patenting Stem Cells in Europe: The Challenge of Multiplicity in EU Law' (2012) 49(3) *Common Market Law Review* 1007; Bonadio, 'Biotech Patents and Morality after *Brüstle*' (2012) 34(7) *European Intellectual Property Review* 433.

excluding patentability of a range of possible novel health technologies on the basis of the imperative of protecting human dignity.

By contrast, however, in *International Stem Cell*,[125] the wide definition of *Brüstle* was not embraced. *International Stem Cell* concerned the patentability of a 'parthenote' – an oocyte which can, once activated chemically and/or electrically, develop into a blastocyst (over about 5 days) but can never develop to term, because it lacks paternal DNA. Admittedly, the CJEU in *International Stem Cell* restates the *Brüstle* principle that 'human embryo' in Article 6 (2) (c) of the Directive must be interpreted broadly.[126] But, following its Advocate General, the CJEU reasoned that 'human embryo' in that context 'must... have the inherent capacity of developing into a human being'.[127] In *Brüstle*, that was the case. Here, it is not, and hence the cases must be distinguished. The question of capability of the particular invention concerned to develop into a human being was left ultimately for the national court.

It has been claimed that the ruling in *Brüstle* will encourage certain types of research or certain types of industry behaviour. The *International Stem Cell* case certainly suggests that the patent concerned was for a process deliberately designed to avoid the creation of an entity that could, in theory, develop into a human being. The EU CFR's protection of 'freedom of the arts and sciences'[128] is unlikely to change future CJEU rulings on the subject, as it must be exercised consistently with Article 1 EU CFR on human dignity. It has been suggested that *Brüstle* is likely to encourage research using adult, rather than embryonic, stem cells. Greater investment in non-European companies developing these new technologies, and greater use of trade secrecy, are both expected,[129] although little concrete evidence of widespread changes of behaviour has yet been reported.

The CJEU adopts a similar wide interpretation of provisions, where human rights are engaged, in the context of the EU's Data Protection Directive.[130] In *Lindqvist*,[131] the CJEU was asked to interpret the term 'personal data... concerning health'.[132] This category of data is given special treatment within

---

[125] *International Stem Cell* C-364/13 EU:C:2014:2451.

[126] *International Stem Cell* EU:C:2014:2451, paragraph 24.

[127] *International Stem Cell* EU:C:2014:2451, paragraph 27.

[128] Article 13, EU CFR; and see: Sayers, above n 116, 380, 393-4.

[129] See: Bache et al., 'The Defining Features of the European Union's Approach to Regulating New Health Technologies' in Flear et al., above n 86, 14, and the sources cited therein.

[130] Directive 95/46/EC [1995] OJ L281/31. This Directive is currently being revised, see: Commission, 'Safeguarding Privacy in a Connected World A European Data Protection Framework for the 21st Century' COM (2012) 09 final; Commission, 'Proposal for a Directive of the European Parliament and of the Council on the protection of individuals with regard to the processing of personal data by competent authorities for the purposes of prevention, investigation, detection or prosecution of criminal offences or the execution of criminal penalties, and the free movement of such data' COM (2012) 10 final; Commission, 'Proposal for a Regulation of the European Parliament and of the Council on the protection of individuals with regard to the processing of personal data and on the free movement of such data (General Data Protection Regulation)' COM (2012) 11 final.

[131] *Lindqvist*, C-101/01, EU:C:2003:596.   [132] Directive 95/46/EC, Article 8 (1).

the Directive. The rationale for the Directive is to enable the transmission of data between Member States. Hence, the general approach of the Directive is harmonize information privacy. Without such harmonization, Member States with higher levels of privacy protection could prevent data sharing across borders within the EU, and thus impede the creation of the internal market in data, and data-based services. So the main thrust of the Directive is to allow legitimate and lawful processing of data, including personal data. The Directive covers two types of personal data. Ordinary personal data may be legitimately processed only if the person concerned has unambiguously given consent.[133] But for special categories of data the presumption is reversed. The processing of this type of data (which includes data concerning health),[134] is prohibited under the Directive, unless one of a list of exceptions applies.[135] A broad interpretation of 'data concerning health' thus extends the scope of the exceptional category within the Directive. This is the approach taken by the CJEU in *Lindqvist*. Although the underlying rationale of the Directive is market creation, the CJEU expresses its purposes as multiple, and states that a key purpose of the Directive is human rights protection. Hence, 'in light of the purpose of the Directive', the term 'data concerning health' must be interpreted widely – it includes 'information concerning all aspects, both physical and mental, of the health of an individual'.[136]

A third illustration of the way in which the CJEU interprets health rights is found in cases which also demonstrate an important feature of human rights litigation – how to reconcile competing rights. In *Deutches Weintor*,[137] the CJEU considered the interpretation of a Regulation on nutritional claims on food labelling.[138] The Regulation provides that 'beverages containing more than 1.2 per cent by volume of alcohol shall not bear health claims'.[139] The CJEU held that the phrase 'easily digestible' constitutes such a claim. The CJEU then turned to the question of whether the prohibition of such a product description nonetheless breaches Articles 15 (1) and 16 EU CFR, on freedom to

---

[133] Directive 95/46/EC, Article 7 (a). For a discussion of 'unambiguous consent' in this context, see: Kranenborg, 'Article 8 – Protection of Personal Data' in Peers et al., above n 14, 250-251. Consent may be implied in other circumstances, such as where it is necessary to protect the vital interests of the individual concerned, or on public interest grounds, see: Directive 95/46/EC, Articles 7 (b) (c) (d) (e). The proposed new Regulation strengthens the conditions for consent.

[134] The ECtHR has confirmed that health data have a special relationship with the right to privacy and family life, see: *I v Finland* App no 20511/03 (ECtHR, 17 July 2008), paragraph 38. For discussion of the Data Protection Directive in health research, see: Beyleveld, Townend, Rouillé-Mirza and Wright, *Implementation of the Data Protection Directive in Relation to Medical Research in Europe* (Ashgate 2004).

[135] These include where explicit consent has been given, where necessary to meet the vital interests of the individual or a third party and the individual is incapable of consenting, see: Directive 95/46/EC, Article 8 (2) (a)-(e). A specific exemption applies where data processing is required in a health care context: Directive 95/46/EC, Article 8 (3).

[136] *Lindqvist* EU:C:2003:596, paragraph 50.　　[137] *Deutsches Weintor* EU:C:2012:526.

[138] Regulation 1924/2006/EC [2007] OJ L12/3.　　[139] Regulation 1924/2006/EC, Article 4 (3).

pursue an occupation and to conduct a business. It found that 'the prohibition does not in any way affect the actual substance' of those freedoms.[140] In its reasoning, the CJEU balanced the freedom to conduct a business with Article 35 EU CFR, second sentence, which provides that 'a high level of human health protection shall be ensured in the definition and implementation of all the Union's policies and activities.'[141] The CJEU's rationale in so doing was that health protection is among the principal aims of the Regulation.[142] Assessment of the validity of the Regulation must reconcile such competing fundamental rights, striking a 'fair balance' between them.[143] The EU's legislature was entitled to prohibit such health claims, in order to ensure a high level of health protection for consumers.[144] A similar balancing approach between freedom of thought, conscience and religion, and health rights, is found in the ECtHR's ruling in *Pichon and Sajous* v. *France*,[145] upholding national policy requiring pharmacists to supply contraceptives, because of the need to protect health policy, as well as the rights and freedoms of others.

The effect of human rights law, as a tool for interpretation of these areas of EU health law, is to articulate a particular version of the EU's internal market. The underlying context and aims of the relevant legislation is to create and sustain the market for health products, data or services, or products that might have an effect on health. But this market is heavily regulated, and not only for reasons of patient safety. It is also regulated in order to protect an ethic of human dignity, expressed through human rights. Human rights claims must be balanced with market objectives, as well as with other human rights claims. The significance of human rights as health rights in this context is an underlying process of legitimization – the EU's claim to rule over human health is bolstered by its protection of human rights.[146]

However, the effects of human rights in this respect are limited. For instance, it is highly unlikely that the CJEU would interpret the Patients' Rights Directive by reference to the right to life and the right to health care so as to find an individual entitlement to access life-saving treatment for a particular patient.[147] Another example of the limitation of health rights as human rights in EU law is that the CJEU's case law has done little, if anything, to disrupt the Data Protection Directive's position over one of the major concerns of the health policy community: the use of 'big data' in health contexts, particularly clinical and epidemiological research and public health monitoring. This is an

---

[140] *Deutsches Weintor*, paragraph 58.   [141] *Deutsches Weintor*, paragraph 45.

[142] *Deutsches Weintor*, paragraph 45, referring to Regulation 1924/2006/EC [2007] OJ L12/3, Recitals 1 and 18.

[143] *Deutsches Weintor*, paragraphs 44-47.   [144] *Deutsches Weintor*, paragraph 52.

[145] *Pichon and Sajous v France*, no. 49853/99, ECHR 2001-X.

[146] See: further, Bache et al., above n 129, 30-41.

[147] See: Wicks, above n 79, 28, Di Federico, 'Access to Healthcare in the Post-Lisbon Era and the Genuine Enjoyment of EU Citizens' Rights' in Rossi and Casolari (eds), *The EU After Lisbon: Amending or Coping with the Existing Treaties* (Springer 2014); and see further chapter 8.

area where there are significant differences between national approaches, and moves to a greater use of electronic record keeping in health contexts mean that the traditional protections for human rights through health data management between patient and health care provider are under challenge.[148] The consent provisions of the Directive have come under particular criticism from the research community. If taken literally, they would seem to impede research using health data collected from young children, or adults who are mentally incompetent to give consent. Moreover, much of the data held in banks of health information, such as cancer registries, could contravene the Directive, as it was information that had been transferred and used without explicit consent being given, and where none of the exceptions in the Directive appeared to apply.[149] It may be that making such health data anonymous, as the Directive implies is to be effected wherever possible, is sufficient to protect privacy and data protection rights, although it is not clear how anonymization or 'depersonalization' is defined in the Directive.[150]

The CJEU is yet to rule on this question, but some national courts have done so, interpreting their implementing legislation. In the *Source Informatics* case,[151] the English Court of Appeal held that collection by a private company of data about the prescribing habits of general practitioners collected from pharmacists did not contravene the Directive. Indeed, the Court held that the fact that the data was anonymized *protected* the patients' privacy, rather than undermining it.[152] In the context of that ruling, then, health rights as human rights have made little difference in terms of disrupting the legislative settlement, either through challenge to the validity of legislation, or its interpretation. We might therefore expect a similar approach by national courts to the interpretation of implementing legislation in a range of areas where human rights might be engaged. These include implementation of the Patients' Rights Directive where the right to found a family might be impeded; of the Clinical Trial Directive, regarding consent of mentally incapacitated adults; or of freedom of expression where EU law places restrictions on advertising, for instance, of alcohol or tobacco.[153]

Health rights plus non-discrimination/equality

Where health rights have the potential to make the most difference to interpretation of EU legislation is where they are combined with the principles

---

[148] See: Kranenborg, above n 133, 254.   [149] See: Hervey and McHale, above n 108, 179-80.

[150] Directive 95/46/EC, Article 6 (1) (e). See: Hervey and McHale, above n 108, 172–4.

[151] *Source Informatics* [2001] QB 424 (CA).

[152] For critical discussion, see: e.g. Beyleveld and Histed, 'Anonymisation is not Exoneration' (1999) 4 *Medical Law International* 69.

[153] Neither the CJEU nor the ECtHR have yet decided a case concerning access to reproductive technologies, see: e.g. Choudry, 'Article 9 – Right to Marry and Right to Found a Family' in Peers et al., above n 14, 271-2, 284. On freedom of expression and tobacco advertising, see: Opinion in *Tobacco Advertising*, C-376/98, EU:C:2000:324. See also: Hervey and McHale, above n 108, 408-9.

of non-discrimination[154] or equality.[155] These principles are a potent 'bridge' between the social and the civil rights components of the EU CFR.[156] For instance, as Claire Kilpatrick suggests, were access to cross-border health care to be denied because of morbid obesity, Article 21 EU CFR on non-discrimination on grounds of disability would be engaged.[157] Equally, as EU law plays an increasingly important role in health, as well as social, care, the rights of the elderly in the EU CFR apply.[158]

The link between social rights and enforceable entitlements is particularly important where some of the most vulnerable people in the EU are concerned: asylum seekers, unaccompanied migrant children, members of the Roma community, people with physical or mental disabilities, elderly people.[159] While there is yet to be a decision of the CJEU involving the 'right to health care' in this regard, the *Kamberaj* case,[160] concerning housing benefit, applies by analogy.

Servet Kamberaj, an Albanian national, was a lawful long-term resident in Italy. He was refused housing benefit, because the fund for 'third country' (non-EU) nationals ran out of resources. A separate fund covered housing benefit for EU nationals. Kamberaj claimed that this breached the 'Long-term residents Directive',[161] Article 11 of which provides that long-term residents are to be treated equally with nationals, as regards social assistance and social protection (as defined nationally). Member States may, however, limit equal treatment in social assistance and social protection to 'core benefits'.[162] The CJEU was asked to interpret the Directive, in particular whether housing benefit was 'social assistance or social protection', and whether it was a 'core benefit'.

Referring explicitly to Articles 12 and 34 EU CFR, the CJEU held that

> when determining the social security, social assistance and social protection measures defined by their national law and subject to the principle of equal treatment enshrined in Article 11(1)(d) of Directive 2003/109, the Member States must comply with the rights and observe the principles provided for under the Charter, including those laid down in Article 34 thereof. Under Article 34(3) of the Charter, in order to combat social exclusion and poverty, the Union (and thus the Member States when they are implementing European Union law) 'recognises and respects the right to social and housing assistance so as to ensure a decent existence for all those who lack sufficient resources, in accordance with the rules laid down by European Union law and national laws and practices'.[163]

---

154 EU CFR, Article 21.
155 EU CFR, Article 20. The legal distinction between the two provisions appears to be that Article 21 enumerates several 'suspect grounds', whereas Article 20 is a residual provision, covering other types of distinction, see: Bell, 'Article 20 – Equality before the Law' in Peers et al., above n 14.
156 See: Kilpatrick, 'Article 21 – Non-Discrimination' in Peers et al., above n 14, 586.
157 See: Kilpatrick, above n 156, 581.
158 See: O'Cinneide, 'Article 25 – The Rights of the Elderly' in Peers et al., above n 14, 694.
159 See: Hervey, 'The Right to Health in EU Law', in Hervey and Kenner, above n 74, 217-222.
160 *Kamberaj* EU:C:2012:233.   161 Directive 2003/109/EC [2003] OJ L16/44.
162 Directive 2003/109/EC, Article 11 (4).   163 *Kamberaj* EU:C:2012:233, paragraph 80.

Technically, the question of application of the Directive to housing benefit is a matter for the national court. But the CJEU gives a 'very strong steer'[164] to the national court, stressing the basic nature of housing benefit, as well as the 'right to ensure a decent existence for all those who lack sufficient resources'.[165]

Although yet to be tested, the reasoning in *Kamberaj* should apply also to core health care benefits, especially as the Long-term Residents Directive itself refers to 'assistance in case of illness, pregnancy' in recital 13. By extension, and more significantly, it applies also in the context of EU asylum law. The qualification Directive 2011/95/EU[166] requires Member States to grant access to health care to refugees or those with 'subsidiary protection', on the same basis as nationals.[167] The reception conditions Directive 2013/33/EU[168] provides that applicants for asylum must be given 'an adequate standard of living for applicants, which guarantees their subsistence and protects their physical and mental health', although this may be means tested.[169] When implementing the Directive, Member States must take into account the needs of vulnerable applicants, including 'persons with serious illnesses', 'persons with mental disorders', disabled people, elderly people and pregnant women. And Directive 2008/115/EC on common standards and procedures for returning illegally staying third-country nationals (the returns Directive)[170] gives safeguards pending return of third country nationals, including 'emergency health care and essential treatment of illness'.[171] These provisions apply even to some of the categories of third country nationals which Member States may exclude from the Directive,[172] such as those who have been apprehended by the border authorities because of an irregular crossing of an external EU border, and who do not subsequently obtain an authorization to stay in that Member State.[173]

The potential for health rights as human rights to make a difference in this context is significant. The ECtHR has stressed that the particularly vulnerable position of asylum seekers requires special attention to their material needs, including health protection.[174] The public health conditions in detention

---

[164] White, 'Article 34 – Social Security and Social Assistance' in Peers et al., above n 14, 940. The CJEU states that housing benefit 'cannot be considered . . . as not being part of core benefits': *Kamberaj* EU:C:2012:233, paragraph 92.

[165] *Kamberaj*, paragraph 92.   [166] Directive 2011/95/EU [2011] L337/9.

[167] Directive 2011/95/EU, Article 30 (1). Article 30 (2) makes special mention of 'beneficiaries of international protection who have special needs, such as pregnant women, disabled people, persons who have undergone torture, rape or other serious forms of psychological, physical or sexual violence or minors who have been victims of any form of abuse, neglect, exploitation, torture, cruel, inhuman and degrading treatment or who have suffered from armed conflict', who are entitled to adequate healthcare, including treatment of mental disorders when needed.

[168] Directive 2013/33/EU [2013] OJ L180/96.   [169] Directive 2013/33/EU, Article 17 (2).

[170] Directive 2008/115/EC [2008] OJ L348/98.   [171] Directive 2008/115/EC, Article 14 (1) (b).

[172] Directive 2008/115/EC, Articles 4 (4) and 2 (2) (a).

[173] Directive 2008/115/EC, Article 2 (2) (a).

[174] *MSS v Belgium and Greece* App no 30696/09 (ECtHR, 2011), paragraphs 250-251, 263. See: Den Heijer, 'Article 18 – Right to Asylum' in Peers et al., above n 14, 522-3.

centres are a matter of concern for human rights groups.[175] They highlight, in particular, the position of children,[176] with significant breaches of their right to health, in contravention of the UN Convention on the Rights of the Child. The FRA has also identified uneven protection for the right to health care for irregular migrants in the EU, both 'undetected' and 'non-removed' people. In its view, 'EU Member States should disconnect healthcare from immigration control policies'.[177] As noted above, the FRA's work concerning inequalities and multiple discrimination in health care[178] is based on Articles 21 and 35 EU CFR.[179]

Justifying restrictions on free movement

According to Article 51 (1) EU CFR, the provisions of the EU CFR apply to Member States 'only when they are implementing EU law'. However, as noted above, the CJEU has held that human rights (as general principles of EU law) apply where Member States act 'within the scope of application of EU law'.[180] The case law on this topic is complex, and demonstrates the ways in which EU law, ECHR law and national constitutional law interact in non-hierarchical relationships.[181] Whether the EU CFR applies when Member States derogate from free movement rules (by justifying restrictions on freedom of movement within the internal market, on the basis of an objective public interest which is the protection of a human right) is not yet definitively settled by the CJEU.[182] For our purposes, however, the focus is on the implications of health rights as human rights in the context of internal market law. Two important questions arise. The first is the implication of interpreting an objective public interest (an *exception* to internal market law) as a human right. The second is the

---

[175] Médicins Sans Frontières, 'Not Criminals' (Médicins Sans Frontières 2009); FRA, 'Coping with a fundamental rights emergency: the situation of persons crossing the Greek land border in an irregular manner' (FRA 2011).

[176] Human Rights Watch, 'Left to Survive: Systematic Failure to Protect Unaccompanied Migrant Children in Greece' (Human Rights Watch 2008); Hammarberg (Commissioner for Human Rights of the Council of Europe), 'Human Rights of Asylum Seekers and Refugees' (CommDH(2009)31, Council of Europe 2009) ; FRA, 'Separated asylum-seeking children in EU Member States: a comparative report' (FRA 2011). See: Lamont, 'Article 24 – The Rights of the Child' in Peers et al., above n 14.

[177] FRA, 'Migrants in an irregular situation: access to health care in 10 EU Member States' (FRA 2011) 10.

[178] FRA, 'Inequalities and multiple discrimination in healthcare' (FRA 2012).

[179] For further discussion, see: Hervey and McHale, 'Article 35 – The Right to Health Care' in Peers et al., above n 14, 958-9, 961-4.

[180] See: *ERT* EU:C:1991:254; *Familiapress*, C-368/95, EU:C:1997:325; *Schmidberger* EU:C:2003:333. Moreover, the CJEU has stated more recently that the EU CFR applies 'in all situations governed by EU law', see: *Fransson* EU:C:2013:280, paragraph 19.

[181] *Melloni*, C-399/11, EU:C:2013:107; *Fransson* EU:C:2013:280 and see above n 17.

[182] Ward, 'Article 51 – Field of Application' in Peers et al., above n 14, 1427. Advocate General Sharpston takes the view that it does, see: Opinion in *Pfleger*, C-390/12, EU:C:2013:747, paragraphs 45-46.

question of who gets to decide on the detailed contours of the interpretation of a particular human rights measure. Whether this is a matter for ECHR law, national constitutional law, or EU law, is essentially unresolved, although (put simplistically) from the point of view of the CJEU, it is the latter.[183]

The CJEU has been consistently criticized by the human rights community for placing human rights as technically subordinate to market freedoms in EU law (free movement is the rule; human rights protection is the exception).[184] However, the practical implications are probably less significant than would appear. Although the ways in which litigation may be carried out, and the reasoning of national courts, may be affected, the *outcomes* of relevant rulings are rarely, if ever, affected by human rights reasoning. For instance, in cases involving human reproduction, although free movement of services was engaged, national constitutional protections of human rights were ultimately safeguarded.[185] Human rights may provide analytical tools, but much more rarely will provide clear cut solutions.

The latter question (who gets to decide, and according to what standard) is potentially more significant. This question is illustrated by a case concerning human dignity, although not in a health context. It concerns the banning of laser 'killing games' by a German public authority. The provider of the games, Omega Spielhallen, challenged this decision as breaching EU law on free movement of services. In holding that the prohibition was justified on public policy grounds, and was a proportionate response, the CJEU referred to the concept of human dignity *as corresponding with the level of protection of human dignity found in the German constitution.*[186] The CJEU therefore implied that, although it retained the authority to decide on a question of interpretation of EU law, the standard according to which it would decide is the national standard. This approach is also reflected in Article 52 (4) EU CFR, which provides that where fundamental rights in the EU CFR come from constitutional traditions common to the

---

[183] Contrast, for example, the positions of the German, Polish, Czech national constitutional courts. The position of the ECtHR in *Bosphorus Airways v Ireland*, no. 45036/98, ECHR 2005-VI suggests that the ECtHR will review the CJEU's interpretation of human rights provisions only if there is a manifest breach of the ECHR. See further: Peers and Prechal, 'Article 52 – Scope and Interpretation of Rights and Principles' in Peers et al., above n 14, 1469; Canor, (2013) above n 17; Krisch, above n 17; Eckes, above n 17; Douglas-Scott, above n 8; Canor, (2000) above n 17. See also Opinion on the Accession of the EU to the European Convention for the Protection of Human Rights and Fundamental Freedoms EU:C:2014:2454.

[184] See, seminally: Coppell and O'Neill, 'The European Court of Justice: Taking Rights Seriously?' (1992) 29 *Common Market Law Review* 669, and the robust two-part rebuttal in Weiler and Lockhart, '"Taking Rights Seriously" Seriously: The European Court and its Fundamental Rights Jurisprudence Part I' (1995) 32(1) *Common Market Law Review* 51, and Weiler and Lockhart, '"Taking Rights Seriously" Seriously: The European Court and its Fundamental Rights Jurisprudence Part II' (1995) 32(2) *Common Market Law Review* 579.

[185] See: e.g. *Grogan*, EU:C:1991:378; *Blood* [1997] 2 All ER 687; *AG v X* [1992] CMLR 227; and see: Hervey and McHale, above n 108, 144-55.

[186] *Omega* EU:C:2004:614, paragraph 30.

Member States, these rights 'should be interpreted in harmony with those traditions'.[187]

If adopted more broadly, the approach of the CJEU in *Omega* would have significant consequences. Any restriction on free movement could be readily justified by reference to a national constitutional tradition, encapsulated in a human rights provision (and reflected in the EU CFR). Multiple examples in the health field spring to mind. As noted above, health rights can be derived from traditional civil and political rights, such as rights to life, to family life, and to privacy. However, the precise contours of entitlements, and general approaches to these human rights, differ considerably between the Member States, because of the potential fluidity of interpretation of human rights provisions. So, for example, the right to life, recognized universally, is subject to significant disparity in interpretation across EU Member States. Notable here is the scope for disagreement as to when life itself actually begins.[188] Equally, the right to found a family is interpreted very differently in different national contexts. So is the right to health care. The implication would be that health rights as human rights in EU law would prevent the application of internal market law from disrupting national interpretations of health entitlements.[189]

However, there are reasons to suggest that *Omega* may be an exceptional case. The German Constitution is undoubtedly the source of inspiration for Article 1 EU CFR, and has been highly influential in the Opinions of several Advocates General, when developing the concept of human dignity as a 'general principle' of EU law, as well as when interpreting Article 1.[190] By contrast, other provisions of the EU CFR, where a variety of different national understandings of the meaning of the human rights provision exist, may be interpreted by the CJEU by reference to an EU law, rather than national, standard. For instance, the CJEU has adopted an EU approach to interpretation of Article 35 EU CFR, in determining whether national laws regulating pharmacies are consistent with internal market law on freedom of establishment.[191]

---

[187] The EU CFR Explanations note that this should not be a 'lowest common denominator approach'.

[188] So for example, in the Republic of Ireland where constitutional protection is given to the position of the foetus, Article 40.3.3 of the Constitution provides that "The State acknowledges the right to life of the unborn, and with due regard to the equal right to life of the mother, guarantees in its laws to respect, and as far as practicable by its laws to defend and vindicate that right". Similar constitutional protections for the position of the foetus apply in Poland and Malta. The ECtHR has recognized an emerging European consensus on the provision of lawful abortion in *A, B, C v Ireland* App no 255579/05 (ECtHR, 16 December 2010), but it gave Ireland a very wide margin of discretion. See: Wicks, '*A, B, C v Ireland*: Abortion Law under the European Convention on Human Rights' (2011) 11 *Human Rights Law Review* 556. Similarly, the CJEU in *Brüstle* EU:C:2011:669, paragraph 30, acknowledged that 'the definition of a human embryo is a very sensitive issues in many Member States, marked by their multiple traditions and value systems'.

[189] For further discussion, see chapter 8.

[190] Dupré, above n 59, 11-12; Jones, 'Common Constitutional Traditions': Can the Meaning of Dignity under German Law Guide the European Court of Justice?' [2004] *Public Law* 167.

[191] *Susisalo* EU:C:2012:374; *Pérez and Gómez* EU:C:2010:300.

More nebulous or indirect effects

Finally, we consider some of the more indirect effects of health rights as human rights in EU law.

As we have seen in the above, human rights considerations have affected the terms of EU legislation in several areas relevant to human health. In particular, the non-commodification of the human body, as a specific expression of Articles 1 and 3 EU CFR features in a range of EU legislation on human blood, organs, tissues and cells. Similarly, Article 2 EU CFR has influenced EU administrative decisions concerning the funding of different types of health research. Shazia Choudry suggests that the right to marry and found a family may have effects on EU law and policy in health contexts, as the EU's competence in this field expands.[192]

However, although there may be agreement at the level of a general statement of a human right among the EU's Member States, there is often little agreement about its practical meaning in concrete circumstances. One of the most practical challenges arises where human rights conflict. One individual's human right may come in conflict with that of another individual. Or individual rights may come into conflict with rights of a broader group of persons. The ways in which these conflicts are managed differ significantly between EU Member States. The ECHR system manages these differences through the doctrine of margin of appreciation. And, in practice, EU law does little to change this. Now that EU law increasingly recognizes health rights as human rights, we might expect an increased reference to the *rhetoric* of rights, in both legislation and litigation, but no difference in terms of substantive outcomes of litigation, or the content of legislation.

Conclusions

While the rhetoric or language of health rights as human rights has increased significantly since the foundation of the EU, and exponentially since 2000, the strong version of the claim that the EU now protects health rights as human rights cannot be supported. On the other hand, neither can it be claimed that the EU ignores or is blind to the idea of health rights as human rights. It remains true to say that the EU's legal order *recognizes* health rights as human rights in ways that it did not do before. Health rights as rhetoric underpin Europeanization processes, such as those pursued by the FRA, but it is rare that this happens through legal processes such as litigation.

It may well be that the *potential* for legal entitlements to health protection, or even particular types of medical treatment, being articulated as human rights within the EU has increased. But the practical implications, in terms of the legal position of patients, health professionals and the obligations owed to them by

---

[192] Choudry, 'Article 9 – Right to Marry and Right to Found a Family' in Peers et al., above n 153, 271-3.

Member States, are negligible, if not non-existent – at least in litigation and in the context of the EU's 'internal' health law.[193] In the final analysis, the EU's increasing recognition of health rights as human rights has not made much of a difference. No EU legislation, or administrative acts, in the health context have been set aside by the CJEU for breaching human rights. The specificities of human rights protection in health contexts remain determined at national level, in accordance with the ECHR's margin of appreciation. EU law does not disrupt this position. In this respect, our overall conclusions in this chapter support those of human rights scholars or activists who are sceptical about the EU's tangible commitment to human rights.[194]

Nonetheless, health rights as human rights have played an important role in the context of interpretation of EU law, and national law implementing EU obligations. Here, the CJEU has articulated a particular version of the EU's internal market law – one in which human rights are protected. While this articulation may lend legitimacy to the EU's regulation of health contexts through its internal market law, again, in practice, it does little to alter the entitlements of individuals, or the significant variations between national approaches in many key areas of health law. Rather, the CJEU's position effectively leaves EU or national legislation unchallenged. The one possible exception to this general conclusion concerns an area of potential development, rather than representing the current legal position. This is where health rights as human rights apply alongside the principle of non-discrimination/equality. Here, especially as applied to people such as asylum seekers, or migrant children, health rights as human rights in EU law may require Member States to extend the entitlements of their health care systems to some of the most vulnerable individuals within the EU.

---

[193] The EU's 'external' health law is discussed in Part IV of the book.

[194] See: e.g. Williams, *The Irony of Human Rights in the European Union* (OUP 2004). Human Rights organisations such as Amnesty International regularly call upon the EU to do more to protect, respect and fulfil human rights, see the reports available here: Multiple Authors (*Amnesty International*, 2009).

8

Rights: mobile patients' rights as human rights

Introduction

We saw in the previous chapter that the idea of health rights as human rights has become part at least of the rhetoric of EU health law. A discourse of rights (including 'fundamental' or 'human' rights) has also imbued the part of EU health law that has come to be known as concerning 'patients' rights'. Patients' rights in EU law have now been embodied in the Directive on the application of Patients' Rights in Cross-border Health Care 2011/24/EU (the Patients' Rights Directive).[1] This piece of EU legislation is our central focus in this chapter, although of course the law in this area has not ceased to develop with the adoption of the Directive. Indeed, as the Directive is transposed, interpreted and applied in the future, we will enhance our understanding of patients' rights in EU law.

At least four strands of EU health law have come together in the Patients' Rights Directive. These strands are as follows: first, patients' rights legislation in some Member States, and the concept of 'patients' rights' as developed by international organizations, especially WHO Europe; second, coordination of social security entitlements of mobile workers and their families; third, CJEU jurisprudence on rights to receive services for mobile service recipients/consumers; and fourth, human rights discourse on access to health care, and the notion of European citizenship. A fifth possible emergent strand is the idea of rights to health related to economies of scale in the single EU market.

This chapter tracks the evolution of those strands, and explains how they fed into the eventual legislative text. The aim is to understand the overlapping meanings of patients' rights in EU health law, and, consequently, the extent to which patients' rights are understood as human rights in EU health law. The implications of the relative importance of the different strands are then drawn out. Finally, we draw some more general conclusions about the theme of 'rights' in EU health law. Are patients' rights seen as *human* rights in European Union health law, or are they more like *consumer* rights?

---

[1] Directive 2011/24/EU [2011] OJ L88/45.

Each of the strands of EU health law discussed here has been developed and continues to be developed through different legal mechanisms. The EU has engaged in some comparative law and policy discourse by reference to those Member States which have enacted national patients' rights legislation, or soft law, such as charters or bills of patients' rights. In so doing, the EU has referred to various international and national statements of patients' rights, in particular the work of WHO (Europe). Social security coordination is mainly found in EU level legislation,[2] as interpreted and applied by national courts and the CJEU. The right to receive services,[3] as part of EU free movement law, has been developed mainly by the CJEU. Some legislation has been developed on service movement, but the general legislation[4] expressly excludes health care services. Possibilities for benefiting from economies of scale from cross-border economic activity, which go to the heart of internal market law, are thus curtailed in this context. The Patients' Rights Directive fits partly within the category of movement of services within the internal market, but, as we shall see, also goes further. The human right to health, which includes the right of patients to access timely health care, is also part of the legal discourse here. As we have seen in the previous chapter, this right is found in the EU CFR, which has 'constitutional' status in EU law.

Patients' rights in international and comparative contexts

The EU legislature adopted the Patients' Rights Directive 2011/24/EU in response to the uncertainty engendered by decisions of the CJEU concerning the rights of patients to receive cross-border health care services, under EU law on free movement of services. The Commission's initial response to this problem was to include health care in its proposal for a Directive on Services in the Internal Market.[5] However, because health is not seen solely as a 'service' in European societies, including healthcare within the general services Directive proved politically impossible. The Directive was watered down: Directive 2006/123/EC[6] does not apply to '(f) healthcare services whether or not they are provided via healthcare facilities, and regardless of the ways in which they are organised and financed at national level or whether they are public or private'.[7]

---

[2] Regulation 883/2004/EC [2004] OJ L166/1. For a corrected version of the text, see: Corrigendum to Regulation 883/2004/EC [2004] OJ L200/1. This Regulation replaced Council Regulation 1408/71/EEC [1971] OJ L149/2, and entered into force on 1 May 2010.

[3] Article 56 TFEU.   [4] Directive 2006/123/EC [2006] OJ L376/36.

[5] For discussion of the health services proposals in the original proposal, see: Palm and Glinos, 'Enabling patient mobility in the EU: between free movement and coordination' in Mossialos, Permanand, Baeten and Hervey (eds), *Health Systems Governance in Europe: The role of EU law and policy* (CUP 2010).

[6] Directive 2006/123/EC [2006] OJ L376/36.

[7] Directive 2006/123/EC, Article 2 (2) (f). For discussion of the Services Directive, see: Barnard, 'Unravelling the Services Directive' (2008) 45(2) *Common Market Law Review* 323.

The European Parliament and Council then called for a specific legal instrument on health services in the internal market.

But how to frame such a Directive on healthcare services, without running into the same political opposition? It seems that during DG SANCO's public consultation in 2006–07 to inform its proposal, the idea of patients' rights as a politically acceptable framing idea for the proposal emerged. An unofficial document circulating in late 2007 was entitled 'A Community Framework for the Application of Cross-border Healthcare Patients' Rights'. The formal Commission proposal, entitled 'A Proposal for a Directive on the Application of Patients' Rights in Cross-border Healthcare', appeared in July 2008.[8]

The notion of patients' rights had already appeared in some EU policy documentation before 2008. For instance, the important 2006 Council Conclusions on Common values and principles in European Union Health Systems[9] noted that some Member States had expressed the value of equity (equal access to healthcare according to need, regardless of ethnicity, gender, age, social status or ability to pay) in terms of patients' rights. The Council Conclusions note that rights to redress if things go wrong and rights to privacy and confidentiality are important 'operating principles', shared across the EU's Member States. In 2008, the European Economic and Social Committee (an EU institution that advises the EU legislature) adopted its opinion on patients' rights.[10] This opinion refers to the work of the umbrella NGO, the 'Active Citizenship Network', which brings together national citizens' NGOs, which had adopted a 'European Charter of Patients' Rights' in 2002.[11] In turn, this document refers to the work of the Council of Europe and the WHO on patients' rights, undertaken during the 1990s.

Following a quite extensive consultation and data gathering exercise,[12] WHO (Europe) adopted a Declaration on the Promotion of Patients' Rights in Europe in 1994. The Declaration was supposed to inspire national patients' rights policies, in the context of emergent healthcare system reforms. The Declaration

---

[8] Commission, 'Proposal for a Directive of the European Parliament and of the Council on the application of patients' rights in cross-border healthcare' COM (2008) 414 final.

[9] Council Conclusions on Common values and principles in European Union Health Systems [2006] OJ C146/1. These Conclusions draw on the Open Method of Coordination in social and health fields (see: Hervey and De Ruijter, 'Healthcare and the Lisbon Agenda' in Copeland and Papadimitriou (eds), *The EU's Lisbon Strategy: Evaluating Success, Understanding Failure* (Palgrave 2012); and the High Level Process of Reflection on Patient Mobility; see: Hervey and Vanhercke, 'Health care and the EU: the law and policy and Greer and Vanhercke, 'The hard politics of soft law: the case of health' both in Mossialos et al., above n 5.

[10] Economic and Social Committee, 'Opinion of the European Economic and Social Committee on Patients' rights' [2008] OJ C10/67.

[11] Active Citizenship Network, 'European Charter of Patients' Rights' (*Active Citizenship Network*, 2002).

[12] Reported in: WHO, 'The Rights of Patients in Europe' (WHO 1993). See also: Leenen, 'The rights of patients in Europe' (1994) 1 *European Journal of Health Law* 5; Abbing, 'Twenty Year WHO Principles of Patients' Rights in Europe, a Common Framework: Looking Back to the Future' (2014) 21(4) *European Journal of Health Law* 323.

explicitly calls for cooperation between WHO (Europe), the Council of Europe and the EU, in the area of patients' rights. The Council of Europe's Convention on Human Rights and Biomedicine of 1997 echoes many of the patients' rights found in WHO (Europe)'s Declaration.

Feeding into and flowing from the work of the WHO and Council of Europe, several Member States of the EU have developed patients' rights instruments.[13] Finland adopted a Patient's Rights Law in 1992,[14] the Netherlands in 1995,[15] Lithuania in 1996,[16] Denmark in 1998,[17] Belgium in 2002,[18] France in 2002,[19] Bulgaria in 2004,[20] Cyprus in 2005,[21] and Slovenia in 2008.[22] Hungary's Law on Rights and Obligations of Healthcare Workers,[23] Estonia's Law of Obligations Act 2001[24] and the Scottish Government's consultation on patients' rights and responsibilities[25] mainly express patients' rights in terms of duties of healthcare professionals, but contain many of the same ideas. Many of the relevant national instruments, such as the Netherlands Medical Checks Law 1997,[26] the Danish Order no. 665 of 14 September 1998 on Information and Consent and the Communication of Information Relating to Health,[27] Finland's Personal Data Law 1999,[28] Italy's 1999 Decree-Law on Health-related Personal Data,[29] and

---

[13] See: Fallberg, '"Patients" Rights in Europe: Where do we stand and where do we go?' (2000) 7 *European Journal of Health Law* (2000) 1; Leenen, 'Development of Patients' Rights and Instruments for the Promotion of Patients' Rights' (1996) 3 *European Journal of Health Law* 105.

[14] Act on the Status and Rights of Patients 1992. For further discussion, see: Fallberg, 'Patients' Rights in the Nordic Countries' (2000) 7 *European Journal of Health Law* 123-143; Kattelus, 'Implementation of the Directive on the Application of Patients' Rights in Cross-border Healthcare (2011/24 EU) in Finland' (2014) 21(1) *European Journal of Health Law* 23.

[15] Act on the Medical Treatment Contract 1995.

[16] Now found in the General Health Law of June 2005, Division III.

[17] Now consolidated in the Health Act 2005.

[18] Law on the Rights of Patients, 2002, WHO International Digest of Health Legislation; Katholieke Universiteit Leuven, 'National Patient Rights Legislation: Belgium' (*Euro Patient Rights,* 2008).

[19] Law on Patients' Rights and the Quality of the Health System, 2002 WHO International Digest of Health Legislation.

[20] Health Act 2004, section 2, patients' rights and obligations: see Katholieke Universiteit Leuven, 'National Patient Rights Legislation: Bulgaria' (*Euro Patient Rights,* 2008)

[21] Law on the Protection of the Rights of Patients and related issues 2005, WHO International Digest of Health Legislation; Katholieke Universiteit Leuven, 'National Patient Rights Legislation: Cyprus' (*Euro Patient Rights,* 2008).

[22] Act on Patients' Rights 2008: see Katholieke Universiteit Leuven, 'National Patient Rights Legislation: Slovenia' (*Euro Patient Rights,* 2008).

[23] Rights and Obligations of Healthcare Workers according to Act CLIV of 1997, on Health.

[24] Katholieke Universiteit Leuven, 'National Patient Rights Legislation: Estonia' (*Euro Patient Rights,* 2008).

[25] NHS Scotland, 'Patient Rights and Responsibilities: A draft for consultation' (The Scottish Executive 2003).

[26] <http://waml.haifa.ac.il/index/reference/legislation/netherlands/denmark1.htm>.

[27] <http://waml.haifa.ac.il/index/reference/legislation/denmark/denmark2.htm>.

[28] WHO International Digest of Health Legislation   [29] *Ibid*

Spain's Patients' Autonomy and Rights Law 2002,[30] implement the EU's Data Protection Directive,[31] and focus primarily on rights to health information privacy.

All of these international and national policy strands converge around a consensus of three basic types of patients' rights: to privacy and confidentiality; to dignity, especially to consent to or refuse treatment; and to be informed (or choose not to be informed) about risk. Notably, none of these types of patients' rights reflects the collectively enjoyed social right to health care; on the contrary, all are expressions of individual rights, to be enjoyed and enforced by individual patients. This aspect of patients' rights is reflected in the Patients' Rights Directive. The Directive sets out responsibilities of the Member States with regard to cross-border health care, distinguishing between the obligations of the Member State of treatment (where the cross-border healthcare takes place) and those of the Member State of affiliation (where the patient is 'insured' or part of a national health system). Member States of affiliation must reimburse the cost of cross-border healthcare,[32] giving individual patients a (limited) right to such healthcare, in accordance with the provisions of the Directive (discussed below). Patients' rights to information feature strongly. Member States of affiliation must provide information about rights and entitlements to reimbursement for cross-border healthcare, and mechanisms for enforcement of those rights.[33] Member States of treatment must set up 'national contact points' to provide information on patients' rights, treatment options, quality and safety standards in healthcare, prices, authorization systems, and system of professional liability.[34] This information is supposed to 'help individual patients make an informed choice'.[35] The right to privacy also features strongly, with multiple references to the protection of personal data, as found in the EU Charter of Fundamental Rights, Article 8, and Directive 95/46/EC.[36] Patients have the right to access their medical records (an obligation of the Member State of affiliation);[37] and to access the record of their cross-border treatment (an obligation of the Member State of treatment).[38] To stress the individual nature of these rights, the Directive requires that patients be given information on enforcement of rights, dispute settlement procedures, complaints procedures and remedies.[39]

---

[30] Laying down basic rules concerning the autonomy of patients and their rights and duties with regard to clinical information and documentation, WHO International Digest of Health Legislation; Katholieke Universiteit Leuven, 'National Patient Rights Legislation: Spain' (*Euro Patient Rights,* 2008). Some of the Spanish nationalities and regions have adopted their own patients' rights laws.

[31] Directive 95/46/EC [1995] OJ L281/31.

[32] Directive 2011/24/EU [2011] OJ L88/45, Article 5 (a); Articles 7-9.

[33] Directive 2011/24/EU, Article 5 (b). See: Delnoij and Sauter, 'Patient Information under the EU patients' rights Directive' (2011) 21(3) *European Journal of Public Health* 271.

[34] Directive 2011/24/EU, Article 4 (2) (a) and (b); Article 6 (3).

[35] Directive 2011/24/EU, Article 4 (2) (b).

[36] Directive 2011/24/EU, Recital 25 and Article 4 (2) (e) and (f).

[37] Directive 2011/24/EU, Article 5 (d).   [38] Directive 2011/24/EU, Article 4 (2) (f).

[39] Directive 2011/24/EU, Article 4 (2) (c); Article 6 (3).

The version of patients' rights reflected in this strand of EU law and policy is thus strongly individuated, focused on the central value of patient choice (instrumentalized through the requirement to give patients information) and concerned with enforcement of individual rights. Rights in the sense of human rights are present as individual civil and political rights, in particular the right to privacy and to human dignity (consent). There is very little attention to patients' rights as a collective phenomenon, as part of national health systems, which are themselves part of national welfare or social security systems. This latter aspect of patients' rights is, however, reflected in the second strand that feeds into EU law and policy on patients' rights, that of coordination of social security entitlements.

Coordination of social security entitlements

Historically speaking, the coordination of social security entitlements is the oldest of the strands that builds towards patients' rights in EU health law and policy. These social security entitlements are based on the provisions of the TFEU which require that 'freedom of movement for workers shall be secured' within the EU,[40] and that restrictions on the freedom of establishment shall be prohibited.[41] No discrimination on the grounds of nationality is permitted, in terms of employment or establishment rights, and secondary legislation extends this principle to discrimination with respect to 'social advantages'.[42] The term 'social advantages' has been broadly defined.[43] It thus includes access to national health systems in the host Member State to which the worker or self-employed person has migrated. These prohibitions are extended to family members of workers[44] and, in some circumstances, to citizens of the EU,[45] by secondary legislation, in particular the 'Citizens Directive' 2004/38/EC.

But free movement of natural persons could not be achieved in practice simply by these Treaty provisions, and this was recognized by the EU legislature as long ago as the early 1970s.[46] To make free movement for workers and self-employed people a practical reality, without those migrants losing their social security entitlements earned in the home state, EU secondary legislation (the latest version of which is Regulation 883/2004/EC) coordinates the social security entitlements (including access to health insurance – or rather 'sickness insurance' – or the taxation-based national health system, or the combination

---

[40] Article 45 TFEU.   [41] Article 49 TFEU.
[42] Regulation 1612/68/EEC [1968] OJ L257/2, Article 7(2).
[43] *Christini*, C-32/75, EU:C:1975:120.
[44] Directive 2004/38/EC [2004] OJ L158/77, Article 2 (2).
[45] Directive 2004/38/EC, Article 3(1); Chapter II (right of exit and entry); Chapter III (right of residence); Chapter IV (right of permanent residence); Article 24 (right of equal treatment, with exceptions as provided elsewhere in EU law, and a derogation for social assistance and student benefits).
[46] Regulation 1408/71/EEC [1971] OJ L149/2 has now been replaced by Regulation 883/2004/EC [2004] OJ L166/1.

of the two) of those who work in different Member States during their active lives.[47]

The technical operation of this system of coordination of national social security systems is the subject of many detailed rules and numerous interpretative rulings of the CJEU.[48] The personal scope of the Regulation covers EU citizens,[49] stateless persons and refugees residing in a Member State, who are or have been subject to the social security legislation of one or more Member States; members of their families and their survivors;[50] and survivors of non-EU citizens who have been subject to the social security legislation of one or more Member States, where the survivors are EU citizens, or stateless persons or refuges residing in one of the Member States.[51] The scope is thus broad, and catches almost everyone who is 'insured' within a social security system in the EU.[52] The material scope of the Regulation covers all social *security* provision, including (of relevance to patients' rights) 'sickness benefits', 'maternity benefits', 'invalidity benefits', 'benefits in respect of accidents at work and occupational diseases', whether part of a general or special social security scheme, contributory or non-contributory.[53] It does not, however, cover social and medical *assistance*.[54] If a benefit accrues as of right, following a period of employment or affiliation under a social security scheme, then it is social security; if it involves an element of individual means-testing, it is social assistance.[55] The general system established by Regulation 883/2004 is based on the principles of non-discrimination on grounds of nationality;[56] aggregation or apportionment of benefit rights;[57] exportability of benefits between Member States;[58] and the 'single state' rule for affiliation, contribution and benefit entitlement.[59] In general, each migrant worker or self-employed person is the responsibility of a

---

[47] Regulation 883/2004/EC [2004] OJ L166/1.

[48] See, for instance: Luckhaus, 'EU Social Security Law' in Ogus and Wikeley (eds), *The Law of Social Security* (OUP 2002); Barnard, *EU Employment Law* (OUP 2012) 254-282; and the regular reviews of case law on Regulation 1408/71/EEC in the *Common Market Law Review*.

[49] 'nationals of a Member State'.   [50] Regulation 883/2004/EC, Article 2 (1).

[51] Regulation 883/2004/EC, Article 2 (2).

[52] Directive 2009/103/EC [2009] OJ L16/44, Article 11 (1) (d) grants third country nationals who are lawfully resident in the EU rights of equal treatment to social security, social assistance and social protection.

[53] Regulation 883/2004/EC, Article 3 (1) and (2).   [54] Regulation 883/2004/EC, Article 3 (5).

[55] See, for instance: *Piscitello v INPS*, C-139/82, EU:C:1983:126; *Hosse*, C-286/03, EU:C:2006:125, paragraph 37; *Habelt and Others*, C-396/05, C-419/05 and C-450/05, EU:C:2007:810, paragraph 63; *Petersen*, C-228/07, EU:C:2008:494, paragraph 19; *Stewart*, C-503/09, EU:C:2011:500, paragraph 32.

[56] Migrant workers and their families must be entitled to equal treatment with nationals in terms of access to and benefits provided under national health (insurance) systems, where these fall within the scope of Regulation 883/2004/EC, Recitals 33-35, Article 1 (i), Article 17.

[57] Where a Member State makes the acquisition of sickness benefits conditional upon completion of periods of employment, insurance or residence, such periods in another Member State must be aggregated to periods completed in the host Member State, and treated as though they were periods in that Member State. Regulation 883/2004/EC, Article 6.

[58] Regulation 883/2004/EC, Recitals 33, 37 and 42.

[59] Each migrant worker (and his or her family) is the responsibility of a "competent Member State", in which the worker is insured at the time of the application for benefit, or would be

'competent state', usually the state in which the migrant person is or has been employed or self-employed.[60]

For our purposes, the detailed provisions of the Regulation on sickness insurance are of most interest. In general, under the coordination of social security schemes, the person receiving health care in another Member State is not moving qua *patient*, but as a worker, self-employed person or family member of such. Title III, Chapter I of the Regulation covers sickness benefits. Where someone falls within the scope of the Regulation, and resides in a Member State other than the competent Member State, they are entitled to receive benefits in kind in the Member State of residence, on behalf of the competent Member State, as if they were insured in the place of residence.[61] There are special rules for 'frontier workers'.[62] As one of the typical migration patterns in this area is for retired persons to move from northern to southern 'sunshine' Member States,[63] a special section of the relevant Chapter of the Regulation covers sickness benefits and benefits in kind entitlements of migrant pensioners.[64]

Under the Regulation, people within its scope also have rights to *emergency* health care which becomes necessary during a stay (for vacation, temporary work, or other reason) in another Member State. Again, the person concerned is not moving *qua* patient, but is entitled to health care as a patient under EU law on an emergency basis. These health care benefits are provided on behalf of the competent institution (that of the home Member State) by the institution of the place of stay, in accordance with the provisions of the legislation it applies, as though the persons concerned were insured under the said legislation.[65] The 'European Health Insurance Card', introduced by the European Commission

---

entitled to health care benefits (sickness or maternity benefits, in the terms of the Regulation) if resident in the Member State concerned: Regulation 883/2004/EC, Articles 11, 13 and 40 (2).

[60] Regulation 883/2004/EC, Article 65.   [61] Regulation 883/2004/EC, Article 17.

[62] Regulation 883/2004/EC, Article 18.

[63] Havighurst discusses the effects of this migration pattern in the United States, observing that the "sunshine states" of California and Florida reduced welfare benefits in an attempt to avoid an influx of poor people, see: Havighurst, 'American Federalism and American Health Care: Lessons for the European Community' in Hermans, Casparie and Paelinck, *Health Care in Europe after 1992* (Dartmouth 1992) 42. In the EU context, see: Sieveking, 'The Significance of the Transborder Utilisation of Health Care Benefits for Migrants' (2000) 2 *European Journal of Migration and Law* 143. In fact, many such migrants, while resident in host Member States, also returned regularly for short visits to their home Member States to access public health care benefits and services, such as prescription medicines, there. See: Dwyer, 'Retired EU Migrants, healthcare rights and European social citizenship' (2001) 23 *Journal of Social Welfare and Family Law* 311. Cohen, *Patients with Passports: Medical Tourism, Law and Ethics* (OUP 2015) discusses the relevance of the migration of patients to and from southern 'retirement' Member States, in particular Spain, to the adoption of the Patients Rights Directive.

[64] Regulation 883/2004/EC, Articles 23-30. The interactions between the version of these provisions in Regulation 1408/71/EEC and the general provision were discussed in *IKA*, C-326/00, EU:C:2003:101; and *ANOZ*, C-156/01, EU:C:2003:389; and the Regulation was amended to bring the entitlements of the rights of other patients more closely into line with the rights of these pensioner patients. See also: *Care Equipment*, C-562/10, EU:C:2012:442 in which the CJEU applies Regulation 883/2004/EC rather than Article 56 TFEU.

[65] Regulation 883/2004/EC, Article 19.

from 2004, evidences entitlement to such health care, and covers all the Member States of the EU, plus Iceland, Lichtenstein, Norway and Switzerland.[66]

Finally, patients also have rights under the Regulation where they travel to another Member State *for the purpose of* receiving health care or medical treatment. Here the patient *is* moving as a patient. The origins of this entitlement lie in the authorization system set up by Regulation 1408/71/EEC (the precursor to Regulation 883/2004/EC). A Member State may authorize a patient to go to another Member State, with the purpose of receiving medical treatment for his or her illness or condition.[67] That patient receives benefits in kind from the health care system of the host Member State, as if they were a patient within that system, provided on behalf of the competent Member State which has authorized the treatment. The original Regulation provided that authorization 'may not be refused where the treatment in question cannot be provided for the person concerned within the territory of the Member State in which he resides'.[68] Interpretation by the CJEU of this provision in *Pierik (No. 1)*[69] suggested that that an individual seeking medical treatment according to a procedure which is not available in his or her own Member State could rely on the coordination of social security Regulation to *require* his or her Member State's national health insurance to meet the cost. Whether or not this broad interpretation of the

---

[66] Decision 2003/751/EC [2003] OJ L276/1.

[67] Regulation 883/2004/EC, Article 20. Some Member States, such as Sweden, France and the UK traditionally granted authorisation only very rarely, for instance, where waiting lists were deemed "too long". At the other end of the spectrum, Luxembourg and Belgium grant authorisation relatively often. Some Member States, such as Denmark, Germany, Greece, Ireland, Netherlands and Portugal, grant authorisation for types of treatment (often new treatments) which are not available in their own country, see: Palm, Nickless, Lewalle and Coheur, *Implications of Recent Jurisprudence on the Coordination of Health Care Protection Systems: Summary Report produced for DG Employment and Social Affairs* (AIM 2000); Van der Mei, *Free Movement of Persons within the European Community: Cross-Border Access to Public Benefits* (Hart 2003) 256; Mossialos and McKee, *EU Law and the Social Character of Health Care* (PIE Peter Lang 2004) 84–85; Jorens, 'The Right to Health Care Across Borders' in McKee, Mossialos and Baeten (eds), *The Impact of EU Law on Health Care Systems* (PIE Peter Lang 2003) 91; Busse, 'Border-crossing patients in the EU' (2002) 8(4) *eurohealth* 19; and Busse, 'Consumer choice of healthcare services across borders' in Busse, Wismar and Berman (eds), *The European Union and Health Services: The Impact of the Single European Market on Member States* (IOS Press 2002). At least some Member States, for example, Denmark, changed their practice, in the light of the CJEU's jurisprudence discussed below, see: Sindbjerg Martinsen, 'The Europeanisation of Welfare: The Domestic Impact of Intra European Social Security' (2005) 43 *Journal of Common Market Studies* 1027; Sindbjerg Martinsen, 'Social Security Regulation in the EU: The De-Territorialisation of Welfare' in de Búrca, ed, *EU Law and the Welfare State: In Search of Solidarity* (OUP 2005); Sindbjerg Martinsen, 'Conflict and Conflict Management in the cross-border provision of healthcare services' (2009) 32 *West European Politics* 792.

[68] Regulation 1408/71/EEC [1971] OJ L149/2, Article 22 (2).

[69] *Pierik 1*, C-117/77, EU:C:1978:72. The case involved physiotherapeutic treatment for a rheumatic ailment, where the individual concerned had already received treatment in Germany, and a medical expert in the Netherlands was of the opinion that no treatment available in the Netherlands would be as effective as the treatment sought in Germany.

Regulation would have been upheld by the CJEU was unclear,[70] but the legislature intervened, to make clear that patients do not have the *right* under the Regulation to claim financial support from their home Member State for treatments received in another Member State which are not available, or not publicly funded, in the home Member State. The legislative amendment also aimed to prevent patients from circumventing waiting lists in the home Member State by claiming an EU law 'right to be treated' in another Member State.[71] The legislature reasserted the general rule that control over the authorization procedure remains firmly at the discretion of the Member States,[72] and is not the subject of individually enforceable *rights* in EU law, either to obtain authorization for types of treatment not included in the competent Member State's insurance package, nor to circumvent waiting lists in that state. However, that general rule is subject to an exception. The Regulation provides that authorization must be given – in other words a patient has a right to cross-border health care – only where (a) the treatment in question is covered by the home Member State's health care system and (b) where the patient cannot be given such treatment within a medically justifiable time limit, taking into account his or her current state of health and the probable course of his illness.[73]

Under EU law on coordination of social security systems, patients enjoy rights to cross-border health care in three main situations. First, when they have moved to another Member State to work or conduct their own business (or are the family member of such a person), they have the right to access the health system of the host Member State as if they were part of that health system, and their home system will pay for the treatment. Second, people who fall within the scope of the Regulation have an entitlement to health care on an emergency basis in another Member State. Third, as an exceptional case, patients moving to receive health care have the right to treatment in another Member State where their home Member State must authorize the treatment because it is covered within the system of their home State, and they cannot be given the treatment at home within a medically justifiable time limit, based on an individual assessment of their health and illness. These rights are, by and large, uncontroversial, because the person who receives the health care has

---

[70] A subsequent ruling on the same issue as *Pierik 1* EU:C:1978:72 suggests that the CJEU would perhaps have been unlikely to interpret Regulation 1408/71/EEC to this very broad effect. In *Pierik 2*, C-182/78, EU:C:1979:142, the CJEU was asked whether Regulation 1408/71/EEC applied where the home Member State *deliberately* excluded a medical treatment from its national health service, on cost containment or "medical-ethical" grounds. Although the facts of Pierik's case did not require the CJEU to consider this issue (see: *Pierik 2* EU:C:1979:142, paragraph 10; see also: Opinion in *Pierik 2*, C-182/78, EU:C:1979:120, paragraph 2), the submissions of the Commission suggest that Member States are permitted to refuse authorisation, for instance, for treatments "seriously contrary to the ethical rules prevailing" in its jurisdiction, on the grounds that Member States retain competence to regulate public morality, see: Watson, *Social Security Law of the European Communities* (Mansell 1980) 258.

[71] Van der Mei (2003) above n 67, 256.

[72] Jorens, (2003) above n 67, 92–93.   [73] Regulation 883/2004/EC, Article 20 (2).

contributed to the relevant health care system, through their social security or social insurance payments. The version of patients' rights here is concerned primarily with the social right to health care, access to which is mediated through the particular state to which the patient is affiliated, and is determined by the resources available to that state. However, this strand of EU law on patients' rights is not the whole story: to it, we must add EU law on free movement of services.

Free movement of services

The TFEU prohibits 'restrictions' on the freedom to provide services within the EU.[74] This directly effective (individually enforceable) provision of the Treaty includes freedom to receive services.[75] As we have already seen in chapter 4, the legal test for 'restriction' in this context is a very generous one, in line with the underlying rationale of the provision, which is to create the internal market (an area in which the factors of production move freely) through removing all national regulations that impede its creation. The essence of the CJEU's approach is to consider the *potential* for the restriction to inhibit inter-Member State provision of services.[76] Prohibited restrictions include physical restrictions, measures which made it impossible or excessively difficult in practice for the person to receive the service sought,[77] and also any other measures which have the effect of making the provision of services between the Member States more difficult than the provision of services purely within one Member State.[78]

The right to rely on this provision of EU law to seek private health care abroad is (largely[79]) non-contentious, and has been a well-established feature of EU law since at least the mid-1980s.[80] However, in a series of cases beginning in the 1990s,[81] the CJEU has interpreted this very general provision to give patients in the EU the right to receive health care in another Member State, *and to have the cost of that health care reimbursed by their home national health*

---

[74] Article 56 TFEU.

[75] See: *Van Gend en Loos*, C-26/62, EU:C:1962:42; *Laval*, C-341/05, EU:C:2007:809.

[76] See: *Cowan*, C-186/87, EU:C:1989:47, paragraphs 15-17; *Säger* v *Dennemeyer*, C-76/90, EU:C:1991:331, paragraph 12; *Vander Elst*, C-43/93, EU:C:1994:310, paragraph 14; *Guiot and Climatec*, C-272/94, EU:C:1996:147, paragraph 10.

[77] For instance, in *Luisi and Carbone*, C-286/82 and C-26/83, EU:C:1984:35 a prohibition on export of foreign currency above a certain amount was held to restrict the freedom to receive services, as it prevented the transfer of currency necessary to pay for services received (including medical treatment) in another Member State.

[78] *Commission* v *France*, C-381/93, EU:C:1994:370, paragraph 17; *Kohll*, C-158/96, EU:C:1998:171, paragraph 33; *Vanbraekel*, C-368/98, EU:C:2001:400, paragraph 45; *Geraets-Smits/Peerbooms*, C-157/99, EU:C:2001:404, paragraph 61; *Watts*, C-372/04, EU:C:2006:325, paragraph 94. Greer and Sokol have characterized this as a 'rules for rights' approach, see: Greer and Sokol, 'Rules for Rights: European Law, Health Care and Social Citizenship' (2014) 20(1) *European Law Journal* 66.

[79] But see: *SPUC* v *Grogan*, C-159/90, EU:C:1991:378.   [80] *Luisi and Carbone* EU:C:1984:35.

[81] *Kohll* EU:C:1998:171; *Decker*, C-120/95, EU:C:1998:167.

system. This was a surprise to those familiar with health policy, as, in order to fall within the Treaty, a service must be provided for remuneration – the essential characteristic of remuneration being that it constitutes consideration for the service in question.[82] National health care systems within the EU are organized on the basis of solidarity, rather than contractual arrangements,[83] and so it was assumed that, as payments within national health systems do not appear to be 'remuneration', health care under a national health system would not count as a 'service' within EU law. Notwithstanding, the CJEU, relying on an earlier ruling to the effect that remuneration need not come directly from the recipient of the services,[84] held in the *Kohll* case[85] that medical treatment paid for by a sickness insurance fund, or a charitable organization, could fall within the Treaty concept of services, in other words, that 'remuneration' is present in the provision of some forms of publicly funded medical services. In certain circumstances, medical treatment or health care reimbursed under a national social security scheme may fall within Article 56 TFEU.[86] For instance, this is so where treatment is paid for by the patient, but reimbursed by a public sickness insurance fund, and provided extramurally 'outside any hospital [i.e., public] infrastructure'.[87]

As we have seen in chapter 4, the CJEU then extended this principle in subsequent case law.[88] It applies to all Member States, irrespective of the organization of their health system. This must be correct, as patients' right to cross-border health care cannot differ across the EU depending on the type of national health system at issue – not least because the different health systems within the EU share many features with one another as hybrid arrangements, drawing on different types, become more common.[89] Rights to free movement in EU law apply to all EU citizens and others falling within its scope. We have also seen that the broad interpretation of the concept of a 'restriction' on free movement of services means that application of the prior authorization rules under Regulation 883/2004/EC may in itself be a 'restriction' in the sense of Article 56 TFEU, wherever such a system of prior authorization 'prevents or deters' patients from seeking health care from providers in other Member States.[90]

---

[82] *Humbel*, C-263/86, EU:C:1998:451, paragraph 17. For discussion of the application of this aspect of EU law to health services, see the literature cited in chapter 4.

[83] See further the Introduction to Part III.

[84] *Bond van Adverteerders*, C-352/85, EU:C:1988:196.   [85] *Kohll* EU:C:1998:171.

[86] *Ibid.*   [87] *Kohll* EU:C:1998:171, paragraph 29.

[88] *Geraets-Smits/Peerbooms* EU:C:2001:404, paragraphs 55-58; see also: *Vanbraekel* EU:C:2001:400, paragraph 42; *Müller-Fauré/Van Riet*, C-385/99, EU:C:2003:270; *Inizan*, C-56/01, EU:C:2003:578; *Leichtle*, C-8/02, EU:C:2004:161, paragraph 30; *Keller*, C-145/03, EU:C:2005:211; *Watts* EU:C:2006:325, paragraphs 95-98; *Herrera*, C-466/04, EU:C:2006:405; *Stamatelaki*, C-444/05, EU:C:2007:231; *von Chamier-Glisczinski*, C-208/07, EU:C:2009:455; *Elchinov*, C-173/09, EU:C:2010:581; *Major Medical Equipment*, C-512/08, EU:C:2010:579; *Commission v Spain*, C-211/08, EU:C:2010:340; *Medical Laboratory Tests*, C-490/09, EU:C:2011:34; *Non-hospital Medical Care*, C-255/09, EU:C:2011:69; *Social Care Equipment*, C-562/10, EU:C:2012:442.

[89] See Introduction to Part III.   [90] See further chapter 4, and the literature cited therein.

Of course, freedom to receive services in EU law is not a right without exceptions. Restrictions on the freedom to provide and receive services may be justified in various circumstances. In interpreting the Treaties, the CJEU has recognized that some differences between national regulatory arrangements are justified in the public interest, even though they restrict free movement.[91] The CJEU has recognized various interests, for instance, the application of professional rules, including those relating to the organization of professions, qualifications or professional ethics, for the public good,[92] the social protection provided by national social security systems,[93] the financial viability of such social security systems[94] and consumer protection.[95]

This case law based on Article 56 TFEU has profoundly affected the position of patients under the Regulation on coordination of social security systems discussed above, because the provision of EU law that is involved here is a piece of 'primary' and 'directly effective' Treaty law, and thus gives rights to individuals, enforceable in the national courts, that cannot be removed by legislation. However, again as we saw in chapter 4, in more recent case law, following the proposal and eventual adoption of the Patients' Rights Directive, even though the CJEU is not applying the Directive, but the Treaty provisions, the CJEU has softened its 'revolutionary' position, and essentially interprets Article 56 TFEU in line with the Directive.[96] In view of this case law, the content of patients' rights in the sense of this strand of EU law going forward is likely to be significantly influenced by the entitlements set out in the Patients' Rights Directive.

The Patients' Rights Directive consolidates the case law on patients' rights to cross-border health care, and also extends it.[97] It also seeks to clarify the

---

[91] See: Articles 28 TFEU; Article 45 (3) and (4) TFEU; Article 52 TFEU; Article 62 TFEU; Article 65 TFEU; and the jurisprudence of the European Court of Justice on "mandatory requirements" (see: e.g. *Cassis de Dijon*, C-120/78, EU:C:1979:42) or "objective public interests" (see: e.g. *Van Binsbergen*, C-33/74, EU:C:1974:131; *Thieffry*, C-71/76, EU:C:1977:65; *Alpine Investments*, C-384/93, EU:C:1995:126; *Gebhard*, C-55/94, EU:C:1995:411). For further discussion, see: Scott, 'Mandatory or Imperative Requirements in the EU and the WTO' in Barnard and Scott (eds) *The Law of the Single European Market: Unpacking the Premises* (Hart 2002).

[92] *Van Binsbergen* EU:C:1974:131, paragraph 14; *Gulling*, C-292/86, EU:C:1988:15, paragraph 29; *Ramrath*, C-106/91, EU:C:1992:230.

[93] *Guiot and Climatec* EU:C:1996:147.

[94] *Decker* EU:C:1998:167; *Kohll* EU:C:1998:171; *Geraets-Smits/Peerbooms* EU:C:2001:404; *Vanbraekel* EU:C:2001:400; *Müller-Fauré/Van Riet* EU:C:2003:270; *Leichtle* EU:C:2004:161; *Watts* EU:C:2006:325, paragraph 145.

[95] *Commission* v *Germany*, C-205/84, EU:C:1986:463, paragraph 30; *Gouda*, C-288/89, EU:C:1991:323, paragraph 27; *Säger* EU:C:1991:331, paragraph 15; *Schindler*, C-275/92, EU:C:1994:119, paragraph 58.

[96] See: *Emergency hospital care* EU:C:2010:340; *Major Medical Equipment* EU:C:2010:579; Hatzopoulos and Hervey, 'Coming into Line: The EU's Court Softens on Cross-Border Healthcare' (2013) 8(1) *Health Economics, Policy and Law* 1.

[97] On the implications of the Directive, see the literature cited in chapter 4.

relationship between that case law and Regulation 883/2004/EC. Although the Directive is couched in the language of entitlements of patients, its substantive content is largely concerned with the position of national health systems. So, although the relevant part of the Directive[98] begins with patients' rights to cross-border health care, much of its detail is taken up with exceptions to those rights. The Patients' Rights Directive covers almost all[99] cross-border healthcare provided as part of national health systems[100] within the Member States of the EU, irrespective of the way in which a particular system is organized, provided or financed.[101] The 'general principle' established by the Directive is that cross-border health care must be reimbursed by the Member State to which the patient is affiliated,[102] without the need for prior authorization.[103] The principle applies only to healthcare that is 'among the benefits to which the insured person is entitled' in that Member State.[104] Entitlement to cross-border healthcare must be assessed on the same basis (conditions, criteria of eligibility, regulatory and administrative formalities) as entitlement to healthcare within the Member State. Assessing individual entitlement to cross-border healthcare may be carried out by a health professional or health administrator. If such assessments constitute obstacles to the free movement of patients, they must be objectively justified, by 'planning requirements relating to the object of ensuring sufficient and permanent access to a balanced range of high-quality treatment in the Member State concerned or to the wish to control costs and avoid, as far as possible, any waste of financial, technical and human resources'.[105] The right to reimbursement applies only up to the level of costs that would have been paid for the healthcare in that Member State,[106] and only to the actual healthcare, not to associated costs such as travel or accommodation costs.[107]

However, the 'general principle' is subject to significant exceptions. These allow Member States to subject cross-border healthcare to prior authorization – in other words patients do not have a *right* to cross-border healthcare – in the following circumstances. Six categories of healthcare fall within the exception:[108]

---

[98] Directive 2011/24/EU [2011] OJ L88/45, Chapter III.

[99] Allocation of and access to organs for transplantation and public vaccination programmes are excluded; long term care in terms of support for people who need assistance carrying out routine everyday tasks is also excluded: Directive 2011/24/EU, Article 1 (3).

[100] The Directive does not affect situations un-related to cross-border healthcare. 'In particular, nothing in this Directive obliges a Member State to reimburse costs of healthcare provided by healthcare providers established on its own territory if those providers are not part of the social security system or public health system of that Member State.' Directive 2011/24/EU, Article 1 (4).

[101] Directive 2011/24/EU, Article 1 (2).   [102] Directive 2011/24/EU, Article 5 (a); Article 7 (1).

[103] Directive 2011/24/EU, Article 7 (8).   [104] Directive 2011/24/EU, Article 7 (1).

[105] Directive 2011/24/EU, Article 7 (7); also Article 7 (9); Article 8 (2).

[106] Directive 2011/24/EU, Article 7 (4).   [107] Directive 2011/24/EU, Article 7 (4).

[108] Directive 2011/24/EU, Article 8 (2).

(a) Healthcare which is subject to planning requirements relating to the object of ensuring sufficient and permanent access to a balanced range of high-quality treatment in the Member State concerned or to the wish to control costs and avoid, as far as possible, any waste of financial, technical and human resources' and involves overnight hospital accommodation for at least one night;[109]

(b) Healthcare which is subject to planning requirements relating to the object of ensuring sufficient and permanent access to a balanced range of high-quality treatment in the Member State concerned or to the wish to control costs and avoid, as far as possible, any waste of financial, technical and human resources' and requires use of highly specialized medical infrastructure or equipment;[110]

(c) Healthcare involving treatments presenting an unacceptable risk to the patient, taking account of a clinical evaluation of risks and benefits to that patient;[111]

(d) Healthcare involving treatments presenting a particular risk ('substantial safety hazard') to the population;[112]

(e) Healthcare provided by a provider that, on a case-by-case basis, could give rise to serious and specific concerns relating to the quality or safety of the care;[113]

(f) Healthcare which can be provided in the Member State of affiliation within a time limit which is medically justifiable, taking into account an objective medical assessment of the patient's current state of health and probable course of the illness, the degree of the patient's pain and/or the nature of their disability.[114]

Thus patients' rights to cross-border healthcare under the Directive, although apparently important, are in practice significantly constrained. In this strand, the interests of national health systems, their viability, their planning and coverage, their procedures concerning quality and safety and so on are much more dominant than the title of the Directive suggests. Individual patients' rights to medical treatment are present in the text, for sure, but the actual legal content is more concerned with collective provision of healthcare within the different national health systems and with protecting those systems from unpredictable consequences of individual patient movement.

---

[109] Directive 2011/24/EU, Article 8 (2) (a) (i).   [110] Directive 2011/24/EU, Article 8 (2) (a) (ii).
[111] Directive 2011/24/EU, Article 8 (2) (b); Article 8 (6) (a).
[112] Directive 2011/24/EU, Article 8 (2) (b); Article 8 (6) (b).
[113] Directive 2011/24/EU, Article 8 (2) (c); Article 8 (6) (c).
[114] Directive 2011/24/EU, Article 8 (6) (d); Article 8 (5).

Coordination of social security entitlements combined with free movement of services

Even though they are actually based on very different rationales,[115] the CJEU has (cleverly) stressed the interconnected nature of these two strands of EU law on patients' rights in its jurisprudence. This connection is also stressed in the Patients' Rights Directive, the aim of which is to 'clarify the relationship' between 'access to safe and high-quality cross-border healthcare' and coordination of social security under Regulation 883/2004/EC.[116] The CJEU has held that Regulation 1408/71/EEC, Article 22 (now Regulation 883/2004/EC, Article 20) relates to Article 56 TFEU in that the Regulation 'helps to facilitate the free movement of persons';[117] and 'to the same extent, the cross-border provision of medical services between Member States'.[118] Thus, the Treaty does not invalidate the provisions of the Regulation.[119] Rather, the Regulation must be interpreted consistently with the Treaty provisions. At least four elements of the relationship have been considered by the CJEU: the question of when an authorization system is justified, which we covered in chapter 4; the question of what counts as 'undue delay' so as to require an authorization to receive cross-border care; the amount of reimbursement to which a patient is entitled; and the 'basket of care' that is covered by a health system.

On the question of 'undue delay', in *Inizan*,[120] the CJEU interpreted the term 'within the time normally necessary for obtaining the treatment in question' of Regulation 1708/71/EEC (the precursor to Regulation 883/2004/EC), adopting the interpretation it had given for the term 'without undue delay' in cases involving the free movement provisions (now Article 56 TFEU) *Geraets-Smits and Peerbooms*[121] and *Müller-Fauré and Van Riet*.[122] In *Watts*, the CJEU explicitly considered the relationship between the concepts of 'within the time normally necessary for obtaining the treatment in question' in Regulation 1408/71/EEC and 'without undue delay' in the context of Article 56 TFEU. The CJEU began its analysis[123] with the point noted above, that Article 22 of Regulation 1408/71/EEC 'helps to facilitate the free movement of persons'[124] and 'to the same extent, the cross-border provision of medical services between Member States'.[125] The Regulation and Article 56 TFEU, according to the CJEU, therefore share an internal market aim, and the implication is that the approach

---

[115] De La Rosa, 'The Directive on Cross-Border Healthcare or the Art of Codifying Complex Case Law' (2012) 49 *Common Market Law Review* 15, 22.
[116] Directive 2011/24/EU, Article 1 (1).   [117] *Vanbraekel* EU:C:2001:400, paragraph 32.
[118] *Inizan* EU:C:2003:578, paragraph 21.
[119] *Inizan* EU:C:2003:578; see also *von Chamier-Glisczinski* EU:C:2009:455, paragraphs 62-66.
[120] *Inizan*, paragraphs 45 to 46.
[121] *Geraets-Smits/Peerbooms* EU:C:2001:404, paragraphs 103-104.
[122] *Müller-Fauré/Van Riet* EU:C:2003:270, paragraphs 89-90.
[123] *Watts* EU:C:2006:325, paragraph 54.   [124] *Vanbraekel* EU:C:2001:400, paragraph 32.
[125] *Inizan* EU:C:2003:578, paragraph 21.

to each should be consistent with the other. This, as we have seen above, is not quite accurate: the 'internal market aim' of the free movement provisions involves creating the internal market by harmonization (indeed, through the 'deregulatory' move of rendering unlawful all 'restrictions' on free movement); whereas the 'internal market aim' of the social security legislation involves creating the internal market by coordination of national systems. However, the CJEU ignored this difference and held that there is no reason to have a different approach to interpretation of the two concepts concerned.[126] Given the relationship between the two provisions, the concept of 'undue delay' also requires an individual assessment of the specific medical and other circumstances of the patient concerned, in the context of the health system of the home Member State generally, not the specific hospital or health institution in which the patient finds himself.[127] Mere reliance on the existence of general waiting lists in the home Member State is not a sufficient basis for a decision that there is no 'undue delay'.[128] For good measure, the CJEU also refers[129] to the provision of Regulation 883/2004/EC (Article 20) which replaced Regulation 1408/71/EEC, Article 22. This sets a duty to grant authorization where the medical treatment cannot be given in the home Member State 'within a time limit which is medically justifiable, taking into account his/her current state of health and the probable course of his/her illness'. The legislation and the CJEU thus agree that the two concepts are inter-related and indeed possibly interchangeable. This interpretation is reflected in the Patients' Rights Directive.[130]

The *Vanbraekel* case[131] concerned the question of the amount of reimbursement to which a cross-border patient is entitled. Vanbraekel (a Belgian national) sought orthopaedic surgery for bilateral gonarthrosis (a disease of the knees). The patient was insured under the Belgian social insurance system and sought authorization for the treatment to be carried out in France. Under Belgian law, authorization under Article 22 of Regulation 1408/71/EEC was only to be given in very exceptional cases, where an expert medical specialist certified that the treatment was not available in Belgium. Authorization was therefore refused, on the grounds that the patient did not have a supporting opinion from a doctor practising in a national university institution. In fact, the patient went ahead with the operation in France, and then sought reimbursement. An expert report subsequently sought by the national court determined that the patient's condition necessitated treatment abroad. The court therefore ordered reimbursement of the costs of treatment. However, the costs came to 38,608.99 francs if the reimbursement was calculated according to French legislation; but 49,935.44 francs if calculated according to Belgian legislation. This amounted to a difference of nearly 1,700 euros. The CJEU held that where the application of

---

[126] See: Opinion in *Watts* EU:C:2005:784, paragraph 101.
[127] *Petru* C-268/13, EU:C:2014:2271.
[128] *Watts* EU:C:2006:325, paragraphs 59, 60, 62, 63 and 64.
[129] *Watts*, paragraph 65.   [130] Directive 2011/24/EU, Article 8 (5) and 8 (6) (d).
[131] *Vanbraekel* EU:C:2001:400.

the prior authorization rules under Regulation 1408/71/EEC results in a lower level of cover where treatment is received in another Member State to that in which the patient is insured, this constitutes a restriction in the sense of Article 56 TFEU. This ruling attracted significant criticism, as it implies that patients could actually make a profit from using cross-border healthcare. However, as we predicted in 2004,[132] the ruling in *Vanbraekel* is limited to the application of Article 56 TFEU to reimbursement of 'scheduled' treatment.[133] In its decision in Case C-211/08 *Commission* v. *Spain (Emergency Hospital Care)*, the CJEU explicitly takes into account the coordinated arrangements of national health care systems, under Regulation 883/2004, noting that to find otherwise would 'undermine the very fabric of the system which Regulation [883/2004] sought to establish'.[134] Again, the Patients' Rights Directive reflects this position: reimbursement is up to the level of costs that would have been provided in the home state, without exceeding the actual costs of healthcare received.[135]

On the question of 'basket of care', the decision in *Elchinov*[136] and *Petru*[137] also demonstrate the CJEU's approach to the relationship between Article 56 TFEU and Regulation 883/2004. In *Elchinov* and *Petru*, the CJEU reconfirmed (following *Smits and Peerbooms*) that nothing in EU law requires Member States to extend their own reimbursable 'basket of care'. The approach has also been echoed by the EFTA Court in Cases E-11/07 and 1/08 *Rindal*, (2008). However, in all three cases, the courts took a slightly different approach where treatment available abroad is more medically advanced than in the home Member State. In that context, if the treatment available in the other Member State is more advanced, according to the internationally accepted views of the medical profession, then 'the state may no longer justify prioritizing its own offer of treatment'[138] but must interpret its list of types of treatment appropriately, taking into account 'the available scientific data' and not simply refuse to authorize treatment on the basis that that particular treatment is not available in the home Member State. In this respect, the CJEU's case law continues the line of earlier decisions. The Patients' Rights Directive takes a different approach. The general principle that costs of cross-border health care should be reimbursed by the Member State of affiliation applies only 'if the healthcare in question is among the benefits to which the insured person is entitled' in that Member State.[139]

---

[132] Hervey and McHale, *Health Law and the European Union* (CUP 2004) 143: 'the rulings will be unlikely to apply in the context of emergency treatment'.

[133] See: *Emergency hospital care* EU:C:2010:340.

[134] *Emergency hospital care* EU:C:2010:340, paragraph 79.

[135] Directive 2011/24/EU, Article 7 (4).

[136] *Elchinov*, C-173/09, EU:C:2010:581.   [137] *Petru* EU:C:2014:2271.

[138] *Rindal v Norway (E-11/07)/Slinning v Norway (E-1/08)* [2009] 3 CMLR 32 (Judgment of the EFTA Court, 19 December 2008), paragraph 83.

[139] Directive 2011/24/EU, Article 7 (1); Recital 5: 'In particular, decisions about the basket of healthcare to which citizens are entitled ... must be taken in the national context'; Recital 7: 'This Directive respects and is without prejudice to the freedom of each Member State to decide what type of healthcare it considers appropriate'.

Nevertheless, the decisions in *Elchinov, Petru* and *Rindal* are consistent in the sense that the list of types of treatment is to be determined by the Member State concerned. It is simply that the interpretation of the list is subject to EU law on free movement.

Looking at the second and third strands of law and policy feeding into EU law on patients' rights together, again we see that the focus is not so much on *individual* rights, but rather there is significant attention paid to the *collective* notion of rights to health care, in the context of different systems, with different resources and approaches.

The right to access healthcare and EU citizenship

The fourth strand of EU health law and policy that feeds into EU law on patients' rights and in particular to the Patients' Rights Directive concerns the rights of EU citizens. The Council Conclusions on Common values and principles in EU Health Systems[140] are stated to promote 'clarity for our citizens', and this idea is picked up in the Directive.[141] In some contexts, notably the coordination of social security systems discussed above, the concept of access to health care for citizens in EU health law and policy is limited to those who are covered by the social insurance or national health system. In others, it is limited to 'economic' actors, that is to say recipients of services, relying on internal market law. However, there are places in EU law and policy where the right to access healthcare is conceived as a human right, or at least as a citizens' right, enjoyed by all EU citizens on the basis of their citizenship.

Principal among these is Article 35 of the EU Charter of Fundamental Rights, which now has 'the same legal value as the Treaties'.[142] As we saw in the previous chapter, this provision, entitled 'Health care', states that 'Everyone has the right of access to preventive health care and the right to benefit from medical treatment under the conditions established by national laws and practices.' The EU CFR applies to the EU institutions, and to the Member States only when they are implementing EU law,[143] and does not extend the EU's powers,[144] or

---

[140] Council Conclusions on Common values and principles in European Union Health Systems [2006] OJ C146/1.

[141] Directive 2011/24/EU, Recital 9. See, by contrast: Di Federico, 'Access to Healthcare in the Post-Lisbon Era and the Genuine Enjoyment of EU Citizens' Rights' in Rossi and Casolari (eds), *The EU After Lisbon: Amending or Coping with the Existing Treaties* (Springer 2014) 199, who takes the view that neither Directive nor CJEU case law effectively takes 'the opportunity to link citizenship to healthcare services'.

[142] Article 6 (1) TEU.

[143] EU CFR, Article 51 (1). The EU's Fundamental Rights Agency has investigated inequalities in health care, which could fall within the EU's race discrimination Directive, (Council Directive 2000/43/EC of 29 June 2000 implementing the principle of equal treatment between persons irrespective of racial or ethnic origin [2000] OJ L180/22), see: European Union Agency for Fundamental Rights (FRA), 'Inequalities and multiple discrimination in healthcare' (FRA 2012).

[144] EU CFR, Article 51 (2).

competences,[145] or the scope of the Treaties. An important question about the status of human rights in EU law is thus their scope of application.

In a line of cases dating back to at least the early 1990s, the CJEU has held that fundamental human rights protection (as a 'general principle' of EU law) applies to citizens who move between the Member States. Any national of one Member State who pursues an economic activity in another Member State may, as a matter of EU law, invoke the protection of his or her fundamental human rights. The principle was famously articulated by Advocate General Jacobs in *Konstantinides*:[146]

> In my opinion, a Community national who goes to another Member State as a worker or self-employed person . . . is entitled not just to pursue his trade or profession and to enjoy the same living and working conditions as nationals of the host State; he is in addition entitled to assume that, wherever he goes to earn his living in the European Community, he will be treated in accordance with a common code of fundamental values, in particular those laid down in the European Convention of Human Rights. In other words, he is entitled to say '*civis europeus sum*' and to invoke that status in order to oppose any violation of his fundamental rights.

Although the Advocate General characterizes the position of EU citizens as relying on a 'common code of European values', the CJEU's decision is based on the principle of non-discrimination on grounds of nationality and restrictions on free movement,[147] and thus on the exercise of rights within EU internal market law.

However, since the 1990s, and in particular since the CJEU's expansive interpretation[148] of the provisions (now found in the TFEU) on citizenship of the EU,[149] there is an argument to be made that the CJEU has 'transformed the paradigm of *homo economicus* into that of *homo civitatis.*'[150] The scope of EU

---

[145]   Article 6 (1) TEU.

[146]   *Konstantinides*, C-168/91, EU:C:1992:504, paragraph 46. The idea of a 'common code of fundamental values' applying in the area of EU free movement law has been repeated by Advocate General Gulmann, in *Bostock*, C-2/92, EU:C:1993:141, paragraph 31; *Petersen*, C-228/07, EU:C:2008:281, paragraph 16; Advocate General Maduro in *Centro Europa 7*, C-380/05, EU:C:2007:505, paragraph 16; and Advocate General Sharpston in *Ruiz Zambrano*, C-34/09, EU:C:2010:560, paragraph 83.

[147]   See also: e.g. *Avello*, C-148/02, EU:C:2003:539; *Grunkin and Paul*, C-353/06 EU:C:2008:559; *Sayn-Wittgenstein*, C-208/09, EU:C:2010:806.

[148]   Perhaps most famously, the CJEU found that citizenship of the EU is 'destined to be the fundamental status of nationals of the Member States': *Grzelczyk*, C-184/99, EU:C:2001:458, paragraph 31; see also: *Martínez Sala*, C-85/96, EU:C:1998:217.

[149]   Articles 20-24 TFEU.

[150]   Opinion in *Petersen* EU:C:2008:281, paragraph 15, citing: Editorial, 'Two-Speed European Citizenship? Can the Lisbon Treaty help close the gap?' (2008) 45(1) *Common Market Law Review* 1, 2-3. Even the *homo economicus* approach was used to support extension of rights to EU citizens, see, eg *Cowan* EU:C:1989:47 in which tourists were given equal access to a compensation scheme; and *Wood*, C-164/07, EU:C:2008:321 in which a non-national father was given compensation for an act that took place outside of the EU, on the same basis as nationals.

law has been extended to people who did not traditionally fall within its scope: students;[151] those claiming benefits;[152] and nationals of third countries who are related to a citizen of the EU.[153] Most recently, the scope of EU citizenship law has been extended to situations where there is no obvious cross-border element.[154] The concept of citizenship, and the human rights that inhere in citizens, rather than barriers to entry into another Member State, or non-discrimination, have gradually emerged as a new force behind European integration.[155] In *Ruiz Zambrano*,[156] Advocate General Sharpston suggests that fundamental rights should extend to all areas of EU competence. In her view, *Konstantinidis* 'ceased to be merely a case about discrimination on grounds of nationality and became a case about the fundamental right to personal identity'.[157] One possible interpretation of these developments is that simply being deprived of your human rights as an EU citizen is in itself sufficient to bring a situation within the scope of EU law. If this is right, then Member States are required to 'respect the rights, observe the principles and promote the application thereof' within the EUCFR (including Article 35 EUCFR[158]) in such situations. But the decisions in *Rottmann*,[159] *Zambrano* and subsequently,[160] suggest that the CJEU has not quite gone this far: EU law precludes national measures which have the effect of depriving citizens of the EU of the genuine enjoyment of *the substance of the rights conferred by virtue of their status as citizens of the EU* – in the case of *Rottmann*, the status of EU citizen (as Mr Rottman would have de

---

[151] E.g. *Bidar*, C-209/03, EU:C:2005:169; and *Morgan and Bucher*, C-11/06 and C-12/06, EU:C:2007:626.

[152] *Grzelczyk* EU:C:2001:458; and *Tas-Hagen*, C-192/05, EU:C:2006:676.

[153] *Carpenter*, C-60/00, EU:C:2002:434; and *Baumbast*, C-413/99, EU:C:2002:493.

[154] *Ruiz Zambrano*, C-34/09, EU:C:2011:124; see also: *Rottmann*, C-135/08, EU:C:2010:104, where although there was a cross-border dimension, the CJEU did not rely on it in its decision.

[155] Opinion in *Petersen* EU:C:2008:281, paragraph 27-28; also Advocate General Colomer's Opinions *Shingara and Radiom*, C-65/95 and C-111/95, EU:C:1996:451, paragraph 34; *Baldinger*, C-386/02, EU:C:2003:671, paragraph 25 *Collins*, C-138/02, EU:C:2003:409, paragraphs 56-74; *Morgan and Bucher*, C-11/06 and 12/06, EU:C:2007:174, paragraphs 37-68.

[156] Opinion in *Ruiz Zambrano* EU:C:2010:560.

[157] Opinion in *Ruiz Zambrano* EU:C:2010:560, paragraph 83. Other Advocates General have made similar points about citizenship and solidarity, see: e.g. Opinion of Advocate Maduro in *Nerkowska*, C-499/06, EU:C:2008:132, paragraph 23: 'Citizenship of the Union must encourage Member States to no longer conceive of the legitimate link of integration only within the narrow bounds of the national community, but also within the wider context of the society of peoples of the Union.'; and Advocate General Trstenjak in: *Habelt, Möser and Wachter*, C-396/05, C-419/05 and C-450/05, EU:C:2007:392, paragraph 83: 'I fail to see why integration into the society of the Federal Republic of Germany should not at the same time always entail integration into the society of peoples within the European Union, particularly as the declared aim of the EC Treaty is, according to the first recital in the preamble, to lay the foundations of an ever closer union among the peoples of Europe.'

[158] Di Federico, above n 141. There is a debate about whether Article 35 (and the other rights in EU CFR, Chapter IV) are 'rights' in the sense of individually enforceable entitlements, or merely 'principles'. See: Jääskinen, 'Fundamental Social Rights in the Charter – Are They Rights? Are They Fundamental?' in Peers et al. (eds), *The EU Charter of Fundamental Rights* (Hart 2014), and the material cited therein.

[159] *Rottmann* EU:C:2010:104.   [160] See, e.g., *Dano* C-333/13 EU:C:2014:2358.

facto lost this status); and in the case of *Zambrano*, the right of residence (as Mr Zambrano's children would in practice have to leave the EU with their parents). To go further and extend this to all human rights found in the EU CFR would be to undermine the statements about scope of EU law and fundamental rights in the TEU and EU CFR.[161]

In the area of patients' rights, citizenship and human rights arguments have been discussed by the CJEU and its Advocates General in a few cases, which reflect this position. In *Stamatelaki*,[162] Advocate General Colomer notes that

> although the case-law [on patients' rights] takes as the main point of reference the fundamental freedoms established in the Treaty, there is another aspect which is becoming more and more important in the Community sphere, namely the right of citizens to health care, proclaimed in Article 35 of the Charter of Fundamental Rights of the European Union.[163]

The notion of patients' rights that the Advocate General has in mind here is not simply the right to healthcare that inheres in those who contribute to social security systems, since

> being a fundamental asset health cannot be considered solely in terms of social expenditure and latent economic difficulties. This right is perceived as a personal entitlement unconnected to a person's relationship with social security and the Court of Justice cannot overlook that aspect.[164]

However, the judgment of the CJEU in *Stamatelaki* focuses only on social security coordination, and on whether the relevant national law on authorization involves a 'restriction' on free movement of services, and does not mention rights, citizenship or Article 35 EU CFR at all. Advocate General Sharpston's Opinion in *O and B* considers 'exceptionally derived rights of residence' which might arise from a situation in which an EU national seeks cross-border care and wishes his non-EU national wife to accompany him, under circumstances where the wife is not authorized to reside in his home Member State.[165] The Advocate General considered that 'that decision belongs to the sphere of his private and family life'. Again, the CJEU ruling does not consider such a question.[166]

Citizenship as a basis for cross-border healthcare rights is considered by the CJEU for the first time in *von Chamier-Glisczinski*.[167] The patient concerned,

---

[161] See chapter 7.

[162] Opinion in *Stamatelaki*, C-444/05, EU:C:2007:24.

[163] Opinion in *Stamatelaki* EU:C:2007:24, paragraph 40. This is the only patients' rights case mentioning EU CFR, Article 35; other cases that mention it involve public health, see: Order in *Rossius and Collard*, C-267/10 and C-268/10, EU:C:2011:332; *Josemans*, C-137/09, EU:C:2010:774; *Pérez and Gómez*, C-570/07 and C-571/07, EU:C:2010:300.

[164] Opinion in *Stamatelaki* EU:C:2007:24, paragraph 40, citing: Economic and Social Committee, 'Opinion of the European Economic and Social Committee on "Healthcare"' [2003] OJ C234/36.

[165] Opinion in *O and B*, C-456/12, EU:C:2013:837, paragraphs 131 and 138.

[166] It did not need to do so, given the facts of the reference: *O and B*, C-456/12, EU:C:2014:135.

[167] *von Chamier-Glisczinski* EU:C:2009:455, paragraphs 78-85.

Ms von Chamier-Gliczinski had moved from Germany to a care home in Austria, because her husband was seeking work or self-employment in Austria. She was thus neither a worker, nor a service recipient. The CJEU therefore considered her entitlements as an EU citizen. The CJEU noted that free movement of citizens in EU law would be ineffective if citizens were deterred from moving between Member States because they would be *de facto* penalized for doing so.[168] It was not disputed that Ms von Chamier-Gliczinski was in a worse position than she would have been if she had not moved to another Member State. But the free movement rights of EU citizens are subject to the limitations and conditions laid down in the Treaty and in the measures adopted to give them effect.[169] These include Regulation 883/2004/EC, which provides for the coordination, not the harmonization, of the legislation of the Member States. Therefore, 'substantive and procedural differences between the social security systems of individual Member States, and hence the rights of person who are insured persons there, are unaffected by that provision'.[170] Citizenship rights cannot guarantee that moving to another Member State will be 'neutral as regards social security',[171] including patients' rights.

This strand of EU law on patients' rights is thus the least well-developed of the four discussed in this chapter. While linking human rights, including the right to access health care in the EU CFR, to citizenship of the EU remains a possible way of understanding patients' rights in EU law and policy, it seems that this version of patients' rights is unlikely to unfold in the near future. Rather, the status of the right to health as a *citizen's* right in EU law is subject to the pre-existing measures of EU law that instrumentalize free movement of EU citizens, in particular in the context of coordination of social security systems.

Conclusions

This chapter considered the different legal and policy strands that have come together to constitute the legal discourse of patients' rights in EU law. We have seen that the single legal text of the Patients' Rights Directive encompasses at least four different notions of patients' rights: one drawing on international and national patients' rights laws; a second drawing on coordination of social security systems in EU law; a third drawing on free movement of services in the EU's internal market; and a fourth drawing on EU citizenship and access to healthcare as a citizen's right.

Having examined the history of patients' rights in EU health law and policy, we are now in a better position to understand the meaning and significance of 'rights' in this context. There are significant tensions between the conceptions

---

[168] *von Chamier-Glisczinski* EU:C:2009:455, paragraph 82, citing: *Morgan and Bucher* EU:C:2007:626, paragraph 26; and *Zablocka-Weyhermüller*, C-221/07, EU:C:2008:681, paragraph 34 and case law cited in both.

[169] *von Chamier-Glisczinski* EU:C:2009:455, paragraph 81, Article 21 (1) TFEU.

[170] *von Chamier-Glisczinski* EU:C:2009:455, paragraph 84.

[171] *von Chamier-Glisczinski* EU:C:2009:455, paragraph 85.

of patients' rights reflected in the different strands. The first strand strongly suggests that patients' rights are individual rights, and enforceable as such. The third strand appears to echo this individual conception, but actually, following the CJEU's interpretation of Article 56 TFEU in the light of the Patients' Rights Directive, now has become more attentive to collective rights ideas, in particular the need to protect general national health systems from the unbalancing of their collectively determined provisions by individual claims of entitlement. The second strand definitely conceives of patients' rights as collective rights. It is too soon to tell what, if anything, the fourth strand will stand for, although at present it appears to reflect the second strand.

We conclude that at least one strand of patients' rights in the context of EU law and policy (the first strand) is in practice more closely related to consumerism than to human rights. It relies strongly on the idea of patients as consumers, endowed with sufficient information to make informed choices about their health care. But there is more to EU patients' rights law than this narrow vision. The Patients' Rights Directive, and now the jurisprudence of the CJEU, conceives of patients' rights to access healthcare as *social* rights – collectively enjoyed, subject to the differences of resource and approach in different Member States, but not individually enforceable, save in the case of unreasonable or disproportionate administrative arrangements. This conclusion suggests that EU law has moved beyond the narrow market-based consumerist notion of patients' rights, and reflects and respects the European organization of health care, on the basis of solidarity.[172]

To balance the various interests here, EU health law uses various legal mechanisms. The language of 'rights' suggests a 'trumping' of other interests – after all, a right is a right. But rights interfere with the rights of others, and there must then be a balancing exercise. As we have seen, EU law has 'fudged' the different types of rights (collective and individual) here, which also helps to manage such clashes of interests. Also individual rights in EU law interfere with national competences – again requiring a balancing exercise. EU law uses (both in case law and in legislation here) the notion of rule and exception, especially the exception of 'overriding reasons of general interest'. In this context, that concept is used to preserve the specificities of the different national health systems, as a vehicle for delivering collective health care rights, in the face of individual rights claims by mobile patients.[173]

The different legal mechanisms entailed by the four strands themselves have different consequences. Detailed legislation promotes certainty and consistency of application (though not totally so, as Member States transpose EU law differently within their own health systems). Patients can usually enforce such specific legal entitlements relatively easily, and, in order to comply with obligations in EU law, national administrative systems must be adjusted to grant the relevant rights without the need for litigation. Conversely, litigation usually develops the law incrementally, and with a great deal of uncertainty, but occasionally

---

[172] See: Part III.   [173] De La Rosa, above n 115, 24.

involves an unexpected 'step change', which often meets resistance in terms of practical implementation within the national legal orders. A limited number of individual (litigious) patients are well-served, but their hard-won legal victories do not necessarily translate into widespread change in administrative practice. In theory, human rights have an elevated legal status within legal systems, including those of the EU and its Member States. In practice, as we saw in the previous chapter, the general wording of human rights entitlements, and the broad margin of discretion that Member States have when interpreting human rights texts in specific contexts, tend to mean that specific legal entitlements are very difficult to enforce through the human rights route. This is particularly the case for those seeking to access specific medical treatments through social rights, such as the right to health care. In addition, health rights have been linked to EU citizenship, but the implications of this are yet to be fully understood.

Unravelling the meaning and significance of patients' rights in EU health law thus is far from straightforward. We conclude with three observations on the nature of patients' rights in EU law at present.

First, the main contributions that EU law has made to patients' rights are to procedural rights and rights to information. As noted above, rights to information may in practice have the greatest effect on patients' rights within the Member States. In terms of procedural rights, the case law of the CJEU as consolidated in the Patients' Rights Directive entitles patients seeking cross-border healthcare to access to an authorization procedure which must be (a) individualized; (b) timely; (c) transparent in terms of the criteria to be applied; (d) subject to judicial review for arbitrariness.[174] This aspect of EU health law represents a much more 'rights-based' approach to access to healthcare than a 'welfare-based' approach, which might depend more on clinical judgment that lacks transparency, or on arbitrary application of welfare entitlements rules by administrative authorities or indeed social insurance institutions. Stephane De La Rosa argues that the enhanced procedural rights under the Patients' Rights Directive, especially the entitlement to a prior authorization decision that is based *only* on the patient's medical condition, constitute an expression of the values that the Patients' Rights Directive claims to support – namely, 'universality, access to good quality care, equity and solidarity'.[175]

Second, EU law does entitle patients to the substantive right to non-hospital, non-'special in some other way' (not involving expensive medical infrastructure, not involving risk to the patient or population) healthcare in another Member State. But in practice this right applies only to those in emergency situations; those authorized under Regulation 883/2004 (which is arguably not a 'right'); and those who have the money to pay in advance (as the right under the Patients' Rights Directive is only the right to be reimbursed for cross-border healthcare after it has been provided). The classical understanding of the right to access health care is a right to be enjoyed regardless of ability to pay. In EU law, the right to cross-border health care is not really a 'right' in a 'full' or 'human

---

[174] Directive 2011/24/EU, Article 9.   [175] De La Rosa, above n 115, 34-35.

Table 1 World Bank database, *World development indicators,* 2011 and 2012 (latest figures)

	GDP per capita (current US$)	Health expenditure per capita (current US$)	Life expectancy at birth (total years)	Infant mortality rate (per 1,000 live births)
Austria	46,642	5,280	81	3
Belgium	43,372	4,962	80	3
Bulgaria	6,978	522	74	11
Croatia	13,881	1,138	77	4
Cyprus	26,070	2,123	79	3
Czech Republic	18,683	1,507	78	3
Denmark	56,326	6,648	80	3
Estonia	16,717	987	76	3
Finland	45,721	4,325	80	2
France	39,772	4,952	82	3
Germany	41,863	4,875	81	3
Greece	22,083	2864	81	4
Hungary	12,831	3,986	75	5
Ireland	45,932	4,542	80	3
Italy	33,072	3,436	82	3
Latvia	14,008	841	74	8
Lithuania	14,183	875	74	4
Luxembourg	103,828	8,798	81	2
Malta	20,848	1,706	82	6
Netherlands	45,955	5,995	81	3
Poland	12,708	899	77	4
Portugal	20,165	2,311	81	3
Romania	9,036	500	75	11
Slovak Republic	16,847	1,534	76	6
Slovenia	22,000	2,218	80	3
Spain	28,624	3,027	82	4
Sweden	55041	5,331	82	2
United Kingdom	39,093	3,609	81	4

rights' sense. Moreover, in terms of substantive rights, as De La Rosa points out, there is nothing in the Patients' Rights Directive that requires Member States to cooperate to improve quality of care or access to care.[176] Some have suggested that the Directive may contribute *indirectly* to increased awareness of poor quality or unsafe care, for instance, where a Member State articulates a precise national standard or guideline, which is made available under the information provisions of the Directive.[177] Others note that the Directive has had no such discernible effects.[178]

---

[176] De La Rosa, above n 115, 36.
[177] Schwebag, 'Implementation of the Cross-border Care Directive in EU Member States: Luxembourg' (2014) 21(1) *European Journal of Health Law* 56.
[178] Prudil, 'Implementation of the Directive 2011/24/EU in the Czech Republic' (2014) 21(1) *European Journal of Health Law* 15.

Are there any patients' rights in EU law that can be claimed and enforced in wholly internal situations – that is, where neither the patient nor the health care service has moved? In principle, there are no such new rights – existing rights to data protection and privacy in Directive 95/46/EC have merely been spelled out in this specific context. But, in practice, the Patients' Rights Directive, once implemented, may well actually affect patients' rights *within* Member States because of its information and transparency requirements. Member States are now obliged to provide information (ostensibly for cross-border health care recipients) on a range of patients' rights matters, including what health care is provided in the national health system; prices; professional liability schemes; complaints procedures, and so on. It is inconceivable that this information will not be of interest to patients (and in particular patients' rights NGOs) within the relevant Member State, even if they have no intention of moving to another Member State for healthcare. Once such information is in the public domain, comparisons can (and will) be made across and between Member States (and even within Member States, where health care is a devolved responsibility) and pressures to change national policies towards an EU 'benchmark' will no doubt increase. The EU has already been supporting such a process in its health policy, in a very slow and incremental, but nonetheless a discernible, way, through developing various statements of best practice in terms of health care and treatments.

Thirdly, it is very important to note that nothing in the Patients' Rights Directive will address the major discrepancies in access to health care when one compares patients' rights across different Member States. Simply looking at the amounts spent on health care in each Member State gives an idea of just how wide the gaps are here (see Table 1). In terms of per capita expenditure on health, Romania and Bulgaria spend, respectively, US$ 500 and US$ 522, whereas Denmark spends US$ 6,648, the Netherlands US$ 5,995 and Luxembourg a generous US$ 8,798. Within those bare figures, a very different range of entitlements to access different types of care is found across different Member States. True substantive 'patients' rights' in EU law to access health care would smooth out those discrepancies.

Overall, therefore, we conclude as follows. Although the notion 'rights' in this context has a relationship to the 'fundamental human rights' discussed in the previous chapter, in many ways that relationship is symbolic rather than representing legal reality. In the context of EU law, patients' rights are in practice probably more closely related to consumerism than to human dignity.

Part III
EU internal health law: the systemic focus

Introduction

So far in the book, the *individual* – in particular, the individual patient, but also the individual health care professional – has been the dominant perspective. We have seen the ways in which the themes of 'consumerism' and of 'rights' are playing out in EU health law. These themes are deeply embedded in the law, and, although each provides an important counterpoint to the other, both consumerism and rights have a strong significance for the contours and trajectory of EU health law.

We turn now to a different perspective: that of the collective or systemic. As well as being experienced by individuals (patients, health care professionals), health care is provided within the EU Member States through health *systems*. Every Member State offers health care to its citizens (and, indeed, to others resident within its borders) through a systemic arrangement of various public and quasi-market relationships, rather than health services being provided entirely through private contracts. At least, arguably, each Member State is under an obligation in international law to have such a national health (insurance) system in order to protect and secure the 'right to health' within its territory.[1] In this group of chapters, we are concerned with the extent to which the application of EU law in health settings has resulted in challenges or opportunities for health from a systemic perspective. Looking systemically, we add two further themes of EU health law: the interface between competition, solidarity and equality; and the regulation of risk.

Considering the first theme: just as there are those who have claimed that, in holding that EU law applies to the health services that patients receive, the EU institutions have reconceptualized health care to involve a 'consumerist' approach, or to provide an increased stress upon individual (human? consumer?) rights, there are those who argue that the involvement of EU law in health *systems* has resulted or will result in increased attention to competition

---

[1] This obligation arises from Council of Europe Treaties, in particular: the European Social Charter 1961 and Revised European Social Charter 1996, not from membership of the EU. For further discussion, see: Toebes, *The Right to Health as a Human Right in International Law* (Intersentia 1999) and see further: chapter 7.

within such systems. There are corresponding implications for the values of solidarity, and equality, which are in tension with such competition. The argument is that the balance between the three elements, which must be accommodated within any health system, is disrupted as EU health law develops and its reach extends. Further, it is argued that the consequent realignment of the elements is detrimental to the values of solidarity and equality. After an explanation of how EU competition law applies to health systems, chapters 9, 10 and 11 consider the extent to which this view is sustainable, when the detail of relevant EU health law, and how it is applied, are analysed.

Turning to the second theme, chapters 12, 13, 14 and 15 consider the EU's approach to the regulation of risk, which is now implicated in law in many areas of health systems. Legal responses to risk are found in the public health aspects of health systems, but also in law concerning safety of pharmaceuticals, medical devices, blood, human tissue and organs, and the regulation of medical research, especially involving novel technologies, and at the stage of clinical research. Here, the dominant views in the literature contradict one another. Some maintain that the EU is, comparatively speaking, risk averse, to the detriment of market actors and the economy more generally. For instance, David Vogel concludes that in the context of regulating not only health but also safety and the environment since the 1990s, the EU has adopted policies of greater 'regulatory stringency' than the USA.[2] Others imply that the EU under-regulates for risks associated with health.[3] It is said that EU law's focus on the regulation of risk within markets has detrimental implications for bio-ethical values, related to human dignity. The entitlement to equal treatment as a human being, inherent in respect for human dignity, is said to be compromised, for instance, by the ways in which EU law treats aspects of risk regulation in health systems as part of a market in health technologies. But there is also a strand of literature that tracks the *contributions* of EU law to the integration of such ethical standards within health systems.[4] We are interested in the extent to which these strong claims withstand detailed analysis of the legal position.

'Competitiveness' – the idea that health contributes to economic development and hence to the potential to compete in global markets – is related to the themes of equality, solidarity and competition, and risk regulation. Competitiveness is therefore considered in this part of the book and also in the final chapters, where we examine European health industries in their global contexts.[5]

Before we turn to the analysis, however, we describe some of the pertinent aspects of the arrangements of health systems within the EU. Of course, we

---

[2] Vogel, *The Politics of Precaution: Regulating Health, Safety and Environmental Risks in Europe and the United States* (Princeton University Press 2012).

[3] The principal source of this set of claims is those who analyse regulation of the global pharmaceutical industry, see: chapters 12, 13, 14, 17 and 18.

[4] See: chapters 12, 13, 14, 17 and 18.   [5] See: chapters 16, 17 and 18.

cannot enter here into a detailed account of more than twenty-eight health systems.[6] In any event, to do so would not serve our research agenda, which is to consider the themes of EU health law and the significance of each. As Theodore Marmor, Rudolph Klein, Carolyn Tuohy and others within the health policy community have pointed out,[7] although there is something to learn from comparison, it is misguided to assume that health systems are comparable with one another in all (important) respects. Generalizations about the impact of EU health law on a particular system through comparative analysis with another should therefore be treated with caution. However, given a sufficient degree of similarity, such analysis may support conclusions about the application or potential application of EU law. What we do here, therefore, is outline the similarities between health systems within the EU. This is followed by discussion of a series of typologies through which we can understand the differences between them. Finally, we introduce a simple typology to which we refer in the following chapters.

Health systems within the EU in the twenty-first century: key similarities

The health systems of the EU Member States – each of which is part of the national welfare system[8] – share four features: a dignity-based 'right to health care'; reliance on the concept of 'solidarity' in funding arrangements; with consequent respect for equality; and pressure for reform, especially to increase systemic efficiencies.

A 'right to health care'

We have already noted the internationally recognized 'right to health'. The 'right to health care' was discussed, among other (human) rights, from the point of view of *patients*, in chapters 7 and 8. All EU Member States have health systems

---

[6] Some Member States have more than one health system, for instance the UK where, in part due to the devolved legal systems, the health systems in Northern Ireland, Scotland and Wales are subject to a range of different organizational structures than those in England. Information gathered by the EU on the different health systems in the EU is available from the database here: http://cc.europa.eu/social/keyDocuments.jsp?langId=en. There is also rich data in the European Observatory on Health Care Systems, *Health Care Systems in Transition* studies (WHO, various dates).

[7] Marmor and Klein, *Politics, Health and Health Care: Selected Essays* (Yale University Press 2012); Tuohy, *Accidental Logics: The Dynamics of Change in the Health Care Arena in the US, Britain and Canada* (OUP 1999); Klein, 'Learning from Others and Learning from Mistakes: Reflections on health policy making' in Marmor, Freeman and Okma (eds), *Comparative Studies and the Politics of Modern Medical Care* (Yale University Press 2009); Marmor, Freeman and Okma, 'Comparative Perspectives and Policy Learning in the World of Health Care' (2005) 7(4) *Journal of Comparative Policy Analysis* 331.

[8] On the relationships between welfare systems and social policy and healthcare, see: Hatzopoulos, 'Health Law and Policy: The Impact of the EU' in De Búrca (ed), *EU Law and the Welfare State* (OUP 2005).

that operate, at least in principle, on the idea of universal access to necessary health care, irrespective of the ability of the patient to pay. In several Member States, the 'right to health care' is a constitutionally protected entitlement.[9]

Internationally recognized human rights must be provided on the basis of non-discrimination with respect to irrelevant differences. Sex, race, religion, sexuality, age, social class and so on are 'forbidden grounds', according to which health systems may not lawfully differentiate between individuals. Other irrelevant grounds, in particular ability to pay, are also recognized within health systems within the European Union.

Solidarity

To achieve this dignity-based right to health, European health systems operate on the basis of the redistributive principle of social justice known as 'solidarity'. Solidarity is expressed within both social democratic and Christian democratic traditions of European politics, in Roman Catholic social teaching and Protestant ethics, all of which underpin the development of the welfare state in European countries.[10] Recently, discussions of bio-medical ethics have also engaged with solidarity.[11] In probably the best-known contemporary piece of literature on the subject, Stjernø defines solidarity as 'the preparedness to share resources by personal contribution to those in struggle or in need and through taxation and redistribution organised by the state'.[12] Solidarity thus implies three elements: (i) mandatory cross-subsidization of one group within a state by another; (ii) cross-subsidization organized by the state (using either a taxation or a social insurance model); (iii) a bounded community (usually territorially based; here the state), in terms of entitlement and obligation to contribute.

All health systems of the EU Member States embody solidarity. Cross-subsidization takes place through compulsory income- or wealth-related contributions, independent of the extent to which the contributing person uses or will use the system. European health systems consequently imply

---

[9] See for instance: Article 23 of the Belgian Constitution; Chapter 2, section 19 (3) of the Finnish Constitution; Article 70 D of the Hungarian Constitution; Article 32 of the Italian Constitution; Articles 43, 50 and 51 of the Spanish Constitution.

[10] See: Stjernø, *Solidarity in Europe: The History of an Idea* (CUP 2005); Esping-Andersen, *The Three Worlds of Welfare Capitalism* (Princeton University Press 1990); Baldwin, *The Politics of Social Solidarity: Class Bases of the European Welfare State 1875–1975* (CUP 1992).

[11] See: Prainsack and Buys, *Solidarity, Reflections on an Emerging Concept in Bioethics* (Nuffield Council on Bioethics 2012); Dawson and Verweij, 'Solidarity: a moral concept in need of clarification' (2012) 5(1) *Public Health Ethics* 1.

[12] Stjernø, above n 10, 2. On the roles of 'solidarity' in EU law see: Ross, 'The Value of Solidarity in European Public Services Law' in Krajewski, Neergaard, and Van de Gronden (eds), *The Changing Legal Framework for Services of General Interest in Europe* (TMC Asser Press 2009); Ross, 'Promoting Solidarity: From Public Services to a European Model of Competition' (2007) 44 *Common Market Law Review* 1057; Boeger, 'Solidarity and EC competition law' (2007) 32 *European Law Review* 319; Guibboni, 'Free Movement of Persons and European Solidarity' (2007) 13 *European Law Journal* 360.

cross-subsidization between healthy and unhealthy, rich and poor, and also across different age groups.[13] States use taxation and social insurance to organize the redistribution of resources required by their health systems. Every health system within the EU relies to some extent on both taxation and insurance (including private insurance). No European health system is organized entirely on the basis of private activity within (regulated) markets, although private funding, including co-payments for some public healthcare services, also plays a role in all systems.[14] Health care is paid for on the basis of either refund/reimbursement or benefits-in-kind. Under a reimbursement scheme, patients choose their healthcare provider (sometimes from a closed list), and the sickness fund repays the expense.[15] Under a benefits-in-kind scheme, health care and treatment are free for the patient at the point of receipt.[16] Health systems within the EU also involve public institutions, such as public hospitals. Entitlements to health care are limited to those within that state's system, whether that is decided on a contribution-based approach, or residence-based criteria.

European health systems are *national*. Within Europe, health care, in common with other welfare entitlements, is not based on pan-European solidarity.[17] Health care within Europe is systemically organized at national, regional and local levels, based on a bounded notion of shared social responsibility for the well-being of one's co-citizens *within each Member State*.

Equality

Solidarity implies universal (or near universal) health system coverage;[18] mandatory affiliation;[19] and mandatory acceptance of patients.[20] Solidarity also implies that, as coverage is based on the medical needs of the patient, all patients are treated equally, regardless of their contributions to the system.

---

[13] Given that both poverty and old age are significant indicating factors for ill health see: e.g. Daniels, *Just Health: Meeting Health Needs Fairly* (CUP 2008) especially chapter 13; Sachs, *The End of Poverty: How We Can Make It Happen In Our Lifetime* (Penguin 2005), especially chapter 1, 12, 13.

[14] Indeed, solidarity may be seen as rationale or justification for regulation; see: Prosser, 'Regulation and Social Solidarity' (2006) 33 *Journal of Law and Society* 364.

[15] Broadly speaking, this is the case, for instance, in France, Belgium and Luxembourg.

[16] Broadly speaking, this is the case in Beveridgean systems, and in some sickness insurance systems, such as Austria and Germany.

[17] See, for example: Davies, 'The process and side-effects of harmonisation of European welfare states' (2006) Jean Monnet Working Paper, No 02/06, 11–12; Ferrera, *The Boundaries of Welfare: European Integration and the New Social Politics of Social Welfare* (OUP 2005); Guibboni, above n 12 .

[18] Everyone within the state concerned is assumed to be included in the system. The position of those who are unlawfully present within a state has arisen in the context of human rights law; see further: chapters 7 and 8.

[19] No one may opt out of contributing to the system.

[20] Sickness insurance funds or national health systems may not exclude some categories of persons.

Solidarity thus has important links with the theme of equality. At least in principle, all Member States share a commitment to equality in their health systems.

Equality also relates directly to the protection of human rights. As we saw in chapters 2, 7 and 8, the legal principle of non-discrimination on 'forbidden grounds' plays important roles in health law more generally, and EU health law more specifically, from the perspective of individual legal entitlements. Taking a systemic perspective, legal obligations to secure equality for *groups* of people may be pertinent for the development of different policy approaches, and for the disbursement of public resource.

Reform pressures and efficiency

European health systems share a sense of reform pressure. They have been more or less constantly the subject of major restructuring at least since after the Second World War, more intensively since the 1980s, and especially following the 2008 Eurozone crisis. All the EU Member States are currently facing challenging changes[21] to the policy contexts for health.[22] Of course, reform pressures are expressed and experienced differently depending on national context.[23] But common pressures include the following:

changing demographics, in particular older populations;
changing disease patterns, especially multi and chronic disease (for example, cardiovascular disease) outstripping infectious disease;
new health care technologies,[24] especially the products of biotechnology, nanotechnology and information technology;
changing consumer/patient expectations, especially increased expectations of information leading to meaningful choice and corresponding decreased trust in professional advice or opinion;
post-Fordism, in the sense of changing patterns of employment and contribution to welfare institutions;

---

[21] At least, what is true to say is that the relevant policy and academic discourse treats the situation as one of change and challenge. Whether it is actually changing any more than at any other historical period of time is a different question – this book treats the 'change/challenge thesis' as a given.

[22] Szyszczak, 'Modernising Healthcare: The Quest for the Holy Grail' in Krajewski, Neergaard, and Van de Gronden, above n 12; Greer, *The Politics of European Union Health Policies* (Open University Press 2009); Taylor-Gooby (ed), *Ideas and Welfare State reform in Western Europe* (Palgrave Macmillan 2005); Marmor, Freeman and Okma, above 12 332-333; Taylor-Gooby (ed), *New Risks, New Welfare* (OUP 2004).

[23] Dixon and Poteliakhoff, 'Back to the Future: 10 Years of European Health Reforms' (2012) 7 *Health Economics Policy and Law* 1; Marmor, Freeman and Okma, above 12 337.

[24] See, in particular: Flear, Farrell, Hervey and Murphy (eds), *European Law and New Health Technologies* (OUP 2013); Jost (ed), *Health Care Coverage Determinations: An International Comparative Study* (Open University Press 2004).

a situation of 'permanent welfare austerity',[25] in particular, in the Eurozone in response to the need for governments to meet the budgetary commitments required by economic and monetary union, in the context of the global economic downturn; and

increasing recognition that the health of a population is a crucial factor in competitiveness, growth and economic development.

These changes[26] imply that European health systems are under increased financial stress. At the same time, however, the political context requires a continued commitment from national governments to a 'European' model of health care. This model is based on an existing paradigm, involving principles of equality of access and solidarity in funding arrangements.

Facing these challenges, Member States are examining and reforming[27] the design of their health systems, and the balance between the roles of the state, the family and the market, central and local government, and non-governmental bodies, such as the 'third sector'.[28] Such 'modernization' programmes seek to meet the goals of access to high-quality care, on the basis of need, while ensuring financial sustainability. The health systems modernization agenda takes different forms (Paul Pierson[29] notes recommodification, cost containment and recalibration; Anna Dixon and Emmi Poteliakhoff[30] note input-control, budgets and other forms of output-control and competition). At its core lies a shared understanding that these apparently contradictory goals can be achieved by increasing *efficiency* in health care provision. In the health policy community, a key aspect of increasing systemic efficiency is through public health interventions, particularly those which involve the regulation of food, tobacco or alcohol, all known factors in population ill-health across the EU. Another major aspect, in the context of an ageing Europe, is the relation between 'health care' and 'social care'. The question of regulation of the development of novel health technologies (pharmaceuticals, medical devices) also resonates with efficiencies, through debates about whether the current regulatory structures serve the interests of increasing value for money in such health technologies,[31] or

---

[25] Pierson, 'Coping with Permanent Austerity: Welfare State Restructuring in Affluent Democracies' in Pierson (ed), *The New Politics of the Welfare State* (OUP 2001).

[26] Many of which are summarised in: Pestieau, *The Welfare State in the European Union: Economic and Social Perspectives* (OUP 2005), 116-124.

[27] Note that we are not taking a view on whether these reform programmes actually result in any significant changes. The institutional 'stickiness' of health care organisations has been widely noted in the literature, see: e.g. Pierson, 'Increasing Returns, Path Dependence, and the Study of Politics' (2000) 94(2) *American Political Science Review* 251; Saltman, 'The role of comparative health studies for policy learning' (2012) 7 *Health Economics, Policy and Law* 11, citing Hofstede, *Culture's Consequences: International Differences in Work-Related Values* (Sage Publications 1980) 475; Greer, 'Choosing paths in European Union health services policy: a political analysis of a critical juncture' (2008) 18 *Journal of European Social Policy* 219.

[28] Dixon and Poteliakhoff, above n 23, 3; Multiple Authors, 'Special Issue on Legacies and Latitude in European Health Policy' (2005) 30(1-2) *Journal of Health Politics, Policy and Law* 1.

[29] Pierson (2001), above n 25.   [30] Dixon and Poteliakhoff, above n 23.

[31] Syrett, *Law, Legitimacy and the Rationing of Healthcare* (CUP 2007).

those of the capital-led pharmaceuticals and medical devices industries. While there may be some examples of policy transfers across a significant number of Member States,[32] a wide variety of approaches as to how to achieve such efficiency can be discerned.

Health systems within the EU in the twenty-first century: key differences

Notwithstanding the universal access principle, solidarity, equality and human rights, and common reform pressures, the detailed arrangements for health systems differ significantly between (and sometimes within) European countries. Differences concern which treatments are covered (the 'basket of care'[33]); how such decisions are made; and where and by whom treatments are provided (hospital, clinic, or outpatient treatment; by specialist practitioner, general practitioner, nurse, health visitor).[34] Ideally, health care coverage would be described according to a standard taxonomy, with detailed information on eligibility, benefits, reimbursement, financing and delivery systems (as well as data on actual usage). But no such taxonomy is internationally accepted.[35]

To make our subsequent analysis manageable, and to distinguish significant from insignificant differences, we review various typologies of health systems, before setting out our own very simple typology. Of course, as with all typologies, this is a *model*, a heuristic device by which to make sense of the world,

---

[32] For instance, activity-based funding for hospitals, based on the 'Diagnosis-Related Group (DRG) classification spread from the USA since the 1980s and is now the main mechanism for reimbursing hospitals across Europe. See O'Reilly et al., 'Paying for hospital care: the experience with implementing activity-based funding in five European countries' (2012) 7 *Health Economics, Policy and Law* 73. However, as O'Reilly et al. show in a study involving five EU Member States, its implementation and development varies widely across different Member States. Another example is health technology appraisal, which again originated in the USA. As Sorenson and Chalkidou, 'Reflections on the evolution of health technology assessment in Europe' (2012) 7 *Health Economics, Policy and Law* 25 show, over the last 30 years, many EU Member States, including France, Spain, Sweden, England, Germany, Poland and Hungary, have set up new institutions to carry out health technology assessment. Again, there is a wide variety in terms of institutional organisation, operations, and impact on health care policy and clinical practice.

[33] The OECD looks at health care utilization, surgical procedures, pharmaceutical consumption, long term care and so on, (see: OECD, 'List of Variables in OECD Health Data' (OECD 2011)) but this does not reveal which types of health care fall within the 'basket of care' covered within a national system.

[34] For further discussion of the differences between the public healthcare systems of the Member States of the EU, see: McKee, Mossialos and Baeten (eds), *The Impact of EU Law on Health Care Systems* (PIE Peter Lang 2003); Mossialos and McKee, *EU Law and the Social Character of Health Care* (PIE Peter Lang 2002); Hatzopoulos, above n 8; Steffen (ed), *Health Governance in Europe: Issues, Challenges and Theories* (Routledge 2005); Wendt, 'Mapping European Healthcare systems: a comparative analysis of financing, service provision and access to healthcare' (2009) 19(5) *Journal of European Social Policy* 432, and the literature cited therein.

[35] Schieber, Poullier and Greenwald, 'Health care systems in twenty-four countries' (1991) 10(3) *Health Affairs* 22.

rather than an accurate description of social reality. Each national health (insurance) system maps more or less strongly to a particular type, but each system includes elements of all the types.

Administrative/legal typologies

One way of organizing health systems into types[36] is to consider patterns of influence of key actors and institutions. Mark Field's[37] early typology distinguishes between pluralistic health systems (where a variety of coexisting institutions provide health services); health insurance systems (where financial transfers to service providers are made by third parties); health service systems (where most facilities are state owned/nationalized and mostly independent medical professionals are paid from the treasury); and socialized health systems (where all facilities are owned by the state and all health professionals are state employees). More recently, Carolyn Tuohy[38] focuses on the balance between control of health systems by the state (whose basis of power in a health system is authority), the medical profession (whose basis of power in a health system is skill) and private finance (whose basis of power in a health system is wealth); and on the mix of elements of social control, that is hierarchy, market and collegiality. Systems are arranged into types depending on the mix of institutions in three categories: state hierarchy; private market; and professional collegial. For instance, European health systems, in general, involve a strong role of self/peer regulation through the role of professional associations, rather than state control. Colleen Flood's[39] comparative discussion of health system reforms in four countries (including the UK and the Netherlands) focuses on accountability relationships between patients, purchasers, and health professionals, and divides reforms into 'internal market' type (the UK) and 'managed competition' (the Netherlands).

Administrative or legal structures also concern the extent of centralization of health system administration. Some Member States administer their public health system at national level; others at sub-national levels. Over the last ten years or so, there has been a move among some Member States to more centralization or state control of the health system, and a corresponding move away from decentralized administration. Examples include Denmark, Germany, Netherlands, Ireland and Estonia. This trend is seen even where state control is used to impose more 'market-related' structures, for example, in the EEA

---

[36] For a discussion that brings together all these different types into a single typology, see: Wendt, above n 34.

[37] Field, 'The Concept of the "Health System" at a Macrosociological Level' (1973) 7 (10) *Social Science & Medicine* 763.

[38] Tuohy (1999) above n 7; Tuohy, 'Agency, Contract and Governance: Shifting Shapes of Accountability in the Health Care Arena' (2003) 28 *Journal of Health Politics, Policy and Law* 195.

[39] Flood, *International Health Care Reform* (Routledge 2003).

state of Norway. However, there are also counter-examples, such as in England, following the Health and Social Care Act 2012, where the emphasis of some legislative provisions and policy statements has moved in the opposite direction, to more localized control of budgets. Moreover, Member States such as Spain, Sweden and Finland remain firmly committed to decentralization.[40]

A similar categorization of health systems considers the legal/constitutional status of health providers, and legal relationships between health care institutions and the state. Although there is a lively tradition of comparative medical law,[41] this aspect of comparative legal scholarship is less well represented.[42] Relationships between the state, health care institutions (such as hospitals, clinics and sickness funds) and health care providers (including medical professionals across a wide range of disciplines) range from those governed by private law to state ownership or employment by the state.[43]

Funding typologies: Beveridge versus Bismarck

Funding for health services within national health systems was traditionally categorized through a binary model: either a 'social insurance' 'Bismarckian' model or a taxation-based 'Beveridgean' national health system. On a social insurance model, healthcare is paid for by compulsory insurance. In the first instance, people are insured by reference to their membership of a professional group or employment sector, industry, organization or company. Sickness insurance funds[44] hold contributions from the employer and employee. Those who are not employed are covered by schemes that 'fill the gaps'. The sickness insurance funds contract with hospitals, clinics and other health care providers.[45] The Beveridge model starts from citizenship, rather than economic activity. Everyone is covered, because of their citizenship (or presence in the national

---

[40] Saltman, above n 27.

[41] See Grubb, 'Comparative European Health Law' (1999) 2 *European Journal of Health Law* 291; Jost, 'Comparative and International Health Law' (2004) 14 *Health Matrix* 141; Jost, *Readings in Comparative Health Law and Bioethics* (Carolina Academic Press 2007).

[42] So, for instance, Jonathan Montgomery's excellent textbook *Health Care Law* (OUP 2002) considers such legal relationships in the context of England and Wales, but not comparatively (not even with Scotland and Northern Ireland).

[43] For instance, both Diane Longley, *Health Care Constitutions* (Routledge 1996) 187; (the UK, Canada and New Zealand) and Colleen Flood (2003) above n 39 (the USA, Netherlands, New Zealand and the UK) saw health system reforms of the 1980s and 90s within broader moves towards 'New Public Management', where the legal relationship of contract, and the introduction of quasi-markets, defined public service delivery. See also: Walsh, *Public Services and Market Mechanisms: Competition, Contracting and the New Public Management* (Palgrave Macmillan 1995). Flood focuses on legal or administrative relationships within the system. Longley is attentive to differences in the constitutions of the comparator states, so, for instance, the role of the Canadian provinces is an important explanatory factor in differences between Canada's health care system and those of the UK or New Zealand.

[44] With manifestations in law as either public or private bodies.

[45] Which may be public or private bodies.

territory[46]). The system is financed by state taxation. Health care facilities are usually public institutions. Although it is difficult to categorize precisely, just under one half of the current Member States of the EU fall into the latter type, and just over one half into the former.[47]

No individual health system conforms directly to either Bismarck or Beveridge.[48] Moreover, the types refer to the foundation of European social welfare systems,[49] rather than the way that European welfare settlements are developing in the twenty-first century. Some prominent policymakers, such as Josep Figueras,[50] argue that 'Beveridge versus Bismarck' is a 'dead debate' and that boundaries between the two have become irrelevant as meso- and micro-level policy change and analysis ignore them.[51] Member States such as Germany, Belgium, Netherlands and France, traditionally thought of as Bismarck states, are using new blends of social insurance, tax and private insurance.[52] Since the 1990s, private insurance has played a greater role in many Member States,[53] as complementary, substitutive or supplementary insurance, for instance, covering services excluded from the 'basket of care'.[54] Central European Member States have adopted new 'hybrid' models.[55]

---

[46] As in the case of the National Health Service in the England and Wales.

[47] Flear, 'Does the Free Movement of Persons Cause Change in Healthcare Systems?' (Unpublished PhD thesis, University of Nottingham 2006) on file with author; Hatzopoulos, above n 8; Palm, Nickless, Lewalle and Coheur, *Implications of Recent Jurisprudence on the Coordination of Health Care Protection Systems* (AIM 2000); Marreé and Groenewegen, *Back to Bismarck: Eastern European Health Care Systems in Transition* (Ashgate 1997); Ferge, 'Welfare and 'Ill-fare' Systems in Central and Eastern Europe' in Sykes, Palier, and Prior (eds), *Globalization and European Welfare States: Challenges and Change* (Palgrave Macmillan 2001) 127; WHO and Commission, *Health Status Overview for Countries of Central and Eastern Europe that are Candidates for Accession to the European Union* (European Communities and WHO 2002).

[48] Bismarck and Beveridge form ideal types, not representations of reality.

[49] Baldwin, above n 10.

[50] Director of the European Observatory on Health Systems and Policies and head of the WHO European Centre on Health Policy in Brussels.

[51] Dixon and Poteliakhoff, above n 23, 5; Wendt, above n 34.

[52] For instance, in 2006 the Netherlands introduced a scheme of health insurance that is both statutory (compulsory) and private (it is operated by private insurers and governed by private law). See: Thomson and Mossialos, 'Private health insurance and the internal market' in Mossialos, Permanand, Baeten and Hervey (eds), *Health Systems and Governance in Europe: The Role of European Union Law and Policy* (CUP 2010), 420.

[53] Especially Central and Eastern European Member States. See: Thomson, 'What role for voluntary health insurance?' in Kutzin, Cashin and Jakab (eds), *Implementing health financing reform: lessons from countries in transition* (WHO on behalf of the European Observatory on Health Systems and Policies 2010). Ireland is an important example, where private insurance covers about 50% of the population, see: Thomson and Mossialos, above n 52, 423.

[54] Such as occupational therapy or dental care.

[55] Such as Estonia, Hungary (with only one social health insurance fund) and the Czech Republic (with a limited number of social health insurance funds), where the social health insurance fund is a direct arm of the national government, rather than a private not-for-profit organisation (as in the case of Germany or the Netherlands), and where the funds receive a significant proportion of their revenues from national taxation. Note that the Former Yugoslav Republic of Macedonia, a candidate country, is also in this category. See: Saltman, above n 27.

Planned economy　　　constrained competition/modified liberalism　　　neo-liberal

Figure 1 Types of European national health (insurance) systems

Our typology: a simple continuum

In the analysis that follows in chapters 9, 10 and 11, we draw on these existing typologies. Rather than using 'Beveridge versus Bismarck', we consider European health systems within a continuum from a 'planned economy', through 'constrained competition' or 'modified liberalism', towards 'neo-liberalism' (see Figure 1).[56] The latter two categories draw on Peter Hall and David Soskice's 'Varieties of Capitalism'.[57] Hall and Soskice differentiate between liberal and coordinated market economies. Liberal market economies are characterized by fluid labour markets, shorter time horizons for capital and relatively easy entry to (and exit from) markets. Coordinated market economies feature relatively inflexible but consequently highly skilled labour, 'patient' capital investment and embedded enterprises with dense and ongoing relational contracting. Obviously, Hall and Soskice's types do not map directly to health systems. But we were inspired by their expression of the discussion on how best to create an efficient system. In particular, the role of competition within markets and the significance of individual choice differ between the two categories, and for us this is a key distinction between health systems that tend towards the planned end and those that tend towards the neoliberal end of the continuum. Perhaps unsurprisingly, given that no EU Member State has a 'planned economy' or 'neoliberal' health system, we would locate the health systems of the EU Member States near the centre. The ends of the continuum assist in understanding variations between those systems.

The planned economy type involves a highly centralized health system, funded by state budgets. This type of health system was found in variations on the Russian 'Semashko system', operating in Central and Eastern European states[58] before the 'velvet revolution' beginning in the late 1980s. State-owned facilities, operated by district and regional authorities, but under direct central government control, offered free access to health care to all. Industrial workers accessed occupational medical facilities. The system emphasized hospital care; little provision was made for primary care; health care professionals' salaries were low. No current EU Member State fits well within this type, although elements remain in Central and Eastern European Member States, and candidate countries.[59]

---

[56] For a discussion of many other (more complex) typologies, see: Wendt, above n 34. For our purposes, given that we are concerned with mapping the themes of *EU* health law and policy, and their significance for EU and national law and policy, a simpler typology will suffice.

[57] Hall and Soskice, 'An Introduction to Varieties of Capitalism' in Hall and Soskice (eds), *Varieties of Capitalism: The Institutional Foundations of Comparative Advantage* (OUP 2001).

[58] Many of which are now Member States of the EU.

[59] Hervey and McHale, *Health Law and the European Union* (CUP 2004) 416-7; WHO and Commission, 'Health Status Overview for Countries of Central and Eastern Europe that are Candidates for Accession to the European Union' (European Communities and WHO 2002);

At the other end of our continuum is a neoliberal type health system, with a focus upon the market as the means of providing the delivery of health care. Enhanced engagement with market principles in health contexts remains acutely controversial.[60] Under a neoliberal type system, risks of ill health are mitigated by private insurance contracts. Private insurance funds contract with privately owned health providers. Health providers raise capital on the same basis as any other firm, and compete with one another in a market. Consumers choose from the market of health insurance providers, and from the market of health care providers. Perhaps a residual state involvement provides for those too indigent to enter into the market, on the basis of the obligation to protect the human 'right to health care'.

The World Bank's health care policies provide an example of promotion of neoliberal approaches to health system reform. At the same time as linking health to development, during the 1990s the World Bank[61] advocated privatization of some elements of health services in developing states.[62] The World Bank now plays an important role in health policy in those states, which include some Member States of the EU.[63] According to the World Bank, the key elements of a neoliberal approach to health system reform are liberalization in the sense of opening access to national health markets to private suppliers;[64] privatization of entities previously owned by the state;[65] competition between

Ferge, above n 47; Deacon, 'Eastern European welfare states: the impact of the politics of globalization' (2000) 10(2) *Journal of European Social Policy* 146; Marrée and Groenewegen, above n 47.

[60] See: e.g. Satz, *Why Some Things Should not be for Sale: The Moral Limits of Markets* (OUP 2010); Stacey Taylor, *Stakes and Kidneys: Why Markets in Human Body Parts are Morally Imperative* (Ashgate 2005); Price, *Legal and Ethical Aspects of Organ Transplantation* (CUP 2000); Wilkinson, *Bodies for Sale: Ethics and Exploitation in the Human Body Trade* (Routledge 2003); Cohen, 'Transplant Tourism: The Ethics and Regulation of International Markets for Organs' (2013) 41(1) *Journal of Law, Medicine and Ethics* 269; Cohen, *Patients with Passports: Medical Tourism, Law, and Ethics* (OUP 2015); Savulescu, 'Is the sale of body parts wrong? (2002) 29(3) *Journal of Medical Ethics* 138; Duxbury, 'Do Markets Degrade?' (1996) 59(3) *Modern Law Review* 331. See further chapter 17.

[61] World Bank, 'World Development Report 1993: Investing in Health' (World Bank 1993).

[62] Abbasi, 'The World Bank and world health' *British Medical Journal* (1999) 318, 865-9; 933-7; 1003-7; 1206-8; Brunet-Jailly, 'Has the World Bank a strategy on health?' (1999) 51(161) *International Social Science Journal* 347; De Beyer, J., Preker, A and Feacham, R., 'The Role of the World Bank in international health: renewed commitment and partnership' (2000) 50 *Social Science and Medicine* 169; Wagstaff, 'Economics, health and development: some ethical dilemmas facing the World Bank and the international community' (2001) 27 *Journal of Medical Ethics* 262; Lethbridge, 'The Promotion of Investment Alliances by the World Bank: Implications for National Health Policy' (2005) 5 *Global Social Policy* 203; Prah Ruger, 'The Changing Role of the World Bank in Global Health' (2005) 95 *American Journal of Public Health* 60.

[63] For instance, the World Bank's work on health care in Bulgaria during the early 2000s was more significant than that of the EU; see: Kotzeva, *International Influence on Bulgarian Health Law and Policy.* (Unpublished PhD thesis, University of Wisconsin-Madison 2006), on file with author.

[64] For example, suppliers of pharmaceuticals, medical devices and equipment, physical infrastructure, insurance, and health care services.

[65] Such as hospitals, clinics, blood banks, laboratories, insurance providers.

suppliers of goods and services within a health system; and consumer choice.

A few EU Member States have undoubtedly moved further than the majority towards the neoliberal end of the continuum in their health system reforms. We should stress here that none has moved particularly far down the continuum. In research pre-dating the Eurozone crisis, Hervey[66] identified Germany, the Netherlands, the UK[67] and to some extent Hungary as a small group of Member States experimenting the most with health system reforms. Julia Lear, Elias Mossialos and Beatrice Karl, writing in 2010 before the English 2012 health system reform, found that the Netherlands had gone the furthest in incorporating competition policy within its health system.[68] Victoria Chico, Hervey, Ruth Stirton and Amanda Warren-Jones' assessment of the 2012 reforms suggests some further movement in England.[69]

However, these Member States are very much the outliers. For around half the Member States, there is little indication of movement in a neoliberal direction.[70] A further significant minority[71] express greater patient choice in their systems, but little else of the neoliberal model. Karsten Vrangbaek et al.[72] considered the significance of hospital choice policies in England, Sweden, Denmark and the Netherlands, noting a change in emphasis on patient choice from twenty years ago. They found that patient choice was associated with competition only in the Netherlands and England: in Sweden and Denmark, the emphasis was more on patient empowerment. The impression is of constrained patient choice, within the need to make rational provision of health care to the whole population, and within existing social insurance health care systems, which are based on solidarity principles of risk pooling and cross-subsidization, as well as universal, or near universal, population coverage. A similar example is Finland's 'service voucher system', covering both health and long-term care, brought into

[66] Hervey, 'The European Union's governance of health care and the welfare modernization agenda' (2008) 2(1) *Regulation and Governance* 103.

[67] See also: Le Grand, *The Other Invisible Hand: Delivering Public Services through Choice and Competition* (Princeton University Press 2007).

[68] Lear, Mossialos, and Karl, 'EU Competition Law and Health Policy' in Mossialos et al., above n 52, 372.

[69] Chico, Hervey, Stirton and Warren Jones, 'Markets and Vulnerable Patients: Health Law after the 2012 Act' (2014) 22(2) *Medical Law Review* 157. See also: Klein, *The New Politics of the NHS: From Creation to Reinvention* (8th edn, Radcliffe Publishing 2013); Lewis, Harrison and Smith, *From Quasi Markets to Markets in the NHS: What does this mean for the purchasing of health services?* (The Kings Fund 2009).

[70] Belgium, France, Finland, Ireland, Italy, Latvia, Poland, Portugal, Slovakia, Spain, Sweden, Romania had no, or virtually no, mention of any concepts related to neo-liberal models of health care in their 2008 NAPs. Furthermore, a few explicitly rejected some of the relevant concepts; For instance, Austria's National Action Plan states that "the political consensus is to keep the existing statutory compulsory insurance. There is no intention of introducing a free choice of health insurance funds" Austria NAP, p. 33.

[71] For instance, Estonia, the Czech Republic, Lithuania, Luxembourg and Malta.

[72] Vrangbaek, Robertson, Winblad, Van de Bovenkamp and Dixon, 'Choice Policies in Northern European Health Systems' (2012) 7 *Health Economics Policy and Law* 47.

effect in 2009, which is expected to enhance responsiveness of health service providers to patient choice.[73] In these examples, and in the 'outlier' Member States, competition is 'packaged' as patient choice, rather than a market model per se. Furthermore, even in the 'outlier' group, the objectives of not only choice and quality but also equity and solidarity remain important.[74] These systems involve heavily regulated competition.

To summarize, health (insurance) systems across the EU, despite reforms over the last 10–20 years, occupy neither the 'planned economy' nor the 'neoliberal' end of the continuum. Rather, the norm is different mixes of constrained competition or modified liberalism. However, within those different mixes, a few Member States have moved further down the continuum towards neoliberal health systems; other Member States remain more towards the planned economy end.

Risk on the continuum?

At least in theory, our continuum may also be useful for analysis of different approaches to risk. Approaches to risk regulation vary, depending on how risk-averse, stringent, innovative and precautionary they are. In particular, a precautionary approach to risk regulation involves a desire to reduce the risks of 'false negatives'. Here, the default response to novel and uncertain technologies is to ban them, or otherwise confine or constrain the ability of producers to reach potential consumers, until a position of greater certainty about the risks entailed can be reached. Regulation of nano-technologies in health contexts is a good example.

By contrast, risk regulation approaches may prefer to focus on the risk of 'false positives'. The assumption is that risk regulation should be focused on judging whether products or services are safe, and good regulatory systems adopt robust procedures for making those judgements, in accordance with *existing* knowledge and understanding. This approach recognizes that there is a risk – of a different nature – inherent in adopting a precautionary approach. The risk is, broadly speaking, that inherent in impeding the development and marketing of new technologies and thus the development of the economy.

Questions of the balance between the role of the market in protecting health and the need for regulation can thus be expressed as preferences for more, or less, interference in markets. Regulating to reduce risk inevitably involves such an interference with market preferences. It also involves interference with freedom to conduct one's business affairs. Countries with less stringent approaches to regulation of risk thus give greater freedom to market actors, including those operating in health contexts. They may be located more towards the neoliberal

[73] Finnish Competition Authority, 'Competition – Key to Efficiency: Finnish Competition Authority Yearbook 2009' (Finnish Competition Authority 2010).
[74] Hervey, (2008) above n 66.

end of our continuum. By contrast, countries which adopt a more precautionary approach to risk regulation are located towards the centre of our continuum, in adopting a 'constrained liberalism' approach.

As we will see, however, in chapters 12, 13, 14 and 15, the continuum of health systems from planned economy to neoliberal is limited in its utility in analysis of approaches to risk. It is not feasible to map general approaches to risk in health systems to particular Member States. Rather than adopting a single risk approach, Member States adopt different approaches depending upon the specific issue under consideration. So, for instance, the regulation of human materials may be more or less precautionary in different Member States, as may the regulation of alcohol or tobacco consumption. In addition, as the previous paragraphs hint, there are also questions about what constitutes 'risk' in these contexts.[75] Determining a particular approach to risk thus depends also on whether the focus is on risk of death, of physical harm, of danger to public health, of harm to fundamental values such as free trade, or human dignity, or of adverse policy outcomes. A particular policy area may be dealt with more cautiously in terms of the legal requirements to guard against risks, but risk is rarely if ever the sole regulatory driver.

Conclusions

What does EU health law mean for the health systems of its Member States? As health systems are not the same, they experience the effects of EU health law differently. The continuum set out in this chapter will help us to move beyond generalizations, and understand the implications of EU law for different types of health systems. The next three chapters consider those implications for one of our themes of EU health law: the interface between competition; equality; and solidarity. The following four chapters consider the theme of risk. They explore the ways in which various conceptions of risk have influenced EU health law, and the implications for its scope, content and effects.

---

[75] See further: chapter 12.

9

Competition, solidarity, equality: health insurance

Introduction

This chapter and the following two chapters consider the significance of EU law on freedom to trade across borders (free movement law) and on free and fair competition within the EU's market or markets (competition law) for national health systems. We have already considered the implications of EU free movement law for *individual* patients and health care professionals in chapters 4 and 6, in terms of its tendencies towards 'consumerization'. The perspective in these chapters is the *systemic* level, and we explore the systemic tensions between competition, solidarity and equality. After a summary of the claims in the existing literature associated with the application of free movement and competition law to health systems in the EU, the chapter sets out the key provisions of EU competition law. The overall questions with which we are concerned are (a) how does EU law affect systemic matters, such as the organization of health systems and how the bodies within them interact with one another?; and (b) how does EU law seek to reconcile competition-driven efficiencies and solidarity-based equality of access? What are the implications of that resolution?

Some have claimed that EU law, in particular free movement and competition law, implies a threat to European welfare systems (of which health systems form an important part), and will move them towards the neoliberal end of our typology of health systems. As we noted in chapter 4, these accounts draw either explicitly or implicitly on Polanyi's claims about relations between markets and society.[1] Fritz Scharpf[2] has argued that, while 'economic policy' and 'social protection' policy in the Member States enjoy the same constitutional status,

---

[1] Polanyi, *The Great Transformation: The Political and Economic Origins of our Time* (2nd edn, Beacon Press 2002).

[2] Scharpf, 'A new social contract? Negative and positive integration on the political economy of European welfare states' (1996) European University Institute Working Paper RSC 94/44 ; Scharpf, 'The European Social Model: Coping with the Challenges of Diversity' (2002) 40(4) *Journal of Common Market Studies* 645; Scharpf, 'Legitimate Diversity: The New Challenge of European Integration' (n. 1/2002, *Les Cahiers européens de Sciences Po*, n° 01Paris: Centre d'études européennes at Sciences Po 2002) <http://www.cee.sciences-po.fr/erpa/docs/wp_2002_1.pdf>; Scharpf, 'The Joint-Decision Trap Revisited' (2006) 44(4) *Journal of Common*

the direct effect and supremacy of internal market and competition law,[3] in the absence of equivalent EU social law, mean that this is not the case at EU level. Rather, national social protection policies remain vulnerable to challenge through private or Commission-sponsored litigation, on the basis that they infringe internal market or competition law. This has implications for health systems. If EU law on free movement of the factors of production, or the provisions on free and fair competition, applies to health care services,[4] EU law has set in train a process of deregulatory liberalization of those health systems.

Claus Offe[5] contrasts 'Continental European capitalism' (based on a constrained or socially controlled market economy) with 'Anglo Saxon capitalism' (based on market liberalism). He explains that these two welfare paradigms are in a non-equal relationship to one another. Just as it is easier to make fish soup from an aquarium than the other way around (!), so it is much easier to move from a Continental European welfare model to a liberal one. This is because the constrained elements of the Continental European model are more easily dismantled than achieved. The implication for Member States of the EU is that it is possible for a Europeanized welfare policy paradigm to take the EU Member States effectively down a 'one-way street' towards a liberal welfare model. Like Scharpf, Offe[6] also notes the possible trend from negative integration (the single market and economic and monetary union) towards depriving Member States of the powers to keep in place their welfare systems. Offe suggests that the EU may be using policy learning tools, such as the 'Open Method of Coordination', to persuade the political elites in the Member States that they need to recalibrate their welfare systems.[7] The EU's 'hidden curriculum' in this respect is a move toward liberal welfare models.

Luis Moreno and Bruno Palier[8] suggest that convergence in welfare policy paradigms between EU countries and between actors in Member States is towards a 'liberal' social welfare system. As examples, they cite moves towards 'workfare' in France, German labour market policies, and private Spanish providers filling the gaps left by the retreat by women from a family-based welfare system. Above all, they show how the UK, which belongs in the 'liberal'

Market Studies 845; Scharpf, 'The asymmetry of European integration, or why the EU cannot be a "social market economy"' (2010) 8(2) *Socio-Economic Review* 211.

[3] It will be recalled that the 'direct effect' of EU law means that it is enforceable by individuals before their national courts, which, following the doctrine of 'supremacy' must uphold EU law in preference over contradictory national law, see: *Van Gend*, C-26/62, EU:C:1963:1.

[4] Which they do, see: *Kohll*, C-158/96, EU:C:1998:171; and see further the cases discussed in chapters 4-8; *Ambulanz Glöckner*, C-475/99, EU:C:2001:577 and see further the cases discussed below.

[5] Offe, 'The European Model of "Social" Capitalism: Can it survive European integration?' (2003) 11(4) *Journal of Political Philosophy* 437.

[6] Offe, above n 5, 447, 457.   [7] Offe, above n 5, 463.

[8] Moreno and Palier, 'The Europeanisation of Welfare: Paradigm Shifts and Social Policy Reforms' in Taylor-Gooby, *Ideas and Welfare State Reform in Western Europe* (Palgrave Macmillan 2005).

world of welfare capitalism,[9] has led the way with many European welfare reforms, in particular in extending private services, expanding the for-profit sector and constraining state spending. Nevertheless, for Moreno and Palier, this is a modified and constrained liberal model. In their view, the EU's overall influence 'remains qualitatively distinct from purely market-driven liberalism'.[10] The implication of Moreno and Palier's analysis for health services is that EU law is moving health care towards a modified liberal model, and towards the neoliberal end of our spectrum, but not all the way there. In this policy orientation, market drivers are welcomed as mechanisms to increase efficiency, but ultimately are constrained by the social welfare needs to safeguard equality of access to health care, on the basis of solidarity.

These accounts focus on welfare systems more generally, and in particular on the interactions between welfare and employment policies and relationships. Our task in these chapters is to consider the extent to which they are sustainable in the specific context of the effects of EU law on health systems. To this effect, the chapters are structured as follows. First, we outline the principal relevant elements of EU competition law, for readers who may be unfamiliar with those. We then briefly recap the salient features of EU free movement law (already explained in chapter 4). The substantive analysis that follows considers the implications of these aspects of EU health law for health systems. In this chapter, we consider only one – very important – aspect of health systems: health insurance. Given that the majority of EU Member States use social insurance as the principal funding mechanism for their health system, the ways in which EU health law affects health insurance are central in understanding how EU health law manages the interactions between competition, solidarity and equality. The following chapter considers some of the other main health institutions typically found in EU Member States: hospitals, pharmacies, laboratories, blood and tissue banks, dental clinics, opticians. Chapter 11 turns to the systemic effects of EU law on the pharmaceuticals, medical devices and medical equipment industries, and the ways in which they relate to health systems. The conclusion to the three chapters draws these areas together, to determine the significance for EU health law of competition and free trade within the EU's market(s). How are the tensions between themes of competition, solidarity and equality resolved? What are the implications?

EU competition law and freedom to trade

The three main areas of EU competition law are its anti-cartel rules; its monopolies rules; and its rules regulating mergers. In addition, the EU has developed significant procedural norms that accompany these rules. Until 2004,

---

[9] Esping-Andersen, *The Three Worlds of Welfare Capitalism* (Princeton University Press 1990).
[10] Moreno and Palier, above n 8, 168.

enforcement of EU competition law was carried out by the European Commission. Much of the detailed enforcement of EU competition law is now devolved to national competition authorities.[11] This devolved authority means that, particularly in a politically sensitive area such as health systems, there is scope for a variety of approaches between Member States.[12] (The practical consequence is that our investigation of the effects of 'EU competition law' on health systems must consider the work of these national competition authorities,[13] not just decisions of the EU institutions.) Formal legal enforcement powers may also involve courts. Enforcement by individuals is possible,[14] though in practice relatively rare, even in general, but more so in the politically sensitive health sector.[15] However, often the effects of the application of competition law in the health sector come from pressure to comply with competition law, rather than formal legal sanctions. For instance, in October 2011, the Italian Antitrust Authority (*Autorità Garante della Concorrenza e del Mercato*) announced that, in response to its (non-mandatory) investigation, six companies offering parents storage of umbilical cord blood had agreed to change their marketing material better to inform potential consumers about current scientific developments in the field.[16]

---

[11] Though their decisions are subject to scrutiny by the European Commission, see: Regulation 1/2003/EC [2003] OJ L1/1, Article 11 (4)-(6); and the discussion in Monti, *EC Competition Law* (CUP 2007) 414-419.

[12] Lear, Mossialos and Karl, 'EU competition law and health policy' in Mossialos, Permanand, Baeten and Hervey (eds), *Health Systems Governance in Europe: The Role of European Union Law and Policy* (CUP 2010) 369-71 contrast the Italian Antitrust Authority which has been active in opposing anticompetitive behaviour in various parts of the health system since the 1990s, and the Finnish and Hungarian Competition Authorities, which have supported health system reforms aimed at increasing competition within elements of the health system; with the Estonian Competition Board, which though investigating pharmacies, health insurance funds and a pharmaceutical cartel, found no liability, and the UK Office of Fair Trading, now the UK Competition and Markets Authority (CMA), which did not consider activities of the new entities, such as Foundation Trusts, set up following English national health system reforms until May 2014: CMA, 'CMA clears Foundation Trust hospitals merger' (*CMA*, 14 May 2014).

[13] The first to provide an effective analysis of this were Lear, Mossialos and Karl, above n 12.

[14] *Courage*, C-453/99, EU:C:2001:465; Judgment in *Manfredi*, C-295/04, C-296/04, C-297/04 and C-298/04, EU:C:2006:461. Commission, 'White Paper on Damages Actions for breach of the EU Antitrust rules' (White Paper) COM (2008) 165 final.

[15] The decision in *Bettercare* [2002] CAT 7, discussed below, is an exception. Lear, Mossialos and Karl, above n 12, 374 suggest that it could be a pioneer, rather than an anomaly, as companies seek to enter health care markets following modernization of health systems.

[16] Information was to be given about 'the actual therapeutic applications for hematopoietic stem cells from umbilical cords, the number of transplants performed in two different categories (autologous, for services purchased by future parents, and allogeneic - with samples provided by the National Healthcare Service through the blood bank network for solidaristic donations), the guaranteed shelf-life for blood sample preservation (15-16 years) as compared to the even longer 20-25 years for the preservation services being offered, the genetic compatibility of family members and the obstacles to bringing samples home for use in Italy', see: Autorità Garante della Concorrenza e del Mercato (AGCM), 'Umbilical Cord Preservation: Antitrust intervenes to change the advertising messages of six companies' (*AGCM*, 24 October 2011).

In sectors involving services of general interest, with significant state involvement in provision of such services, such as health, the EU competition rules interact with the EU rules prohibiting unlawful granting of aid to national industries ('state aids law'[17]), which seek to prevent inefficient 'propping up' of failing national firms by their governments, and also with the law relating to public procurement of goods and services, which seeks to open up access to markets for public services to competition.[18] As Vassilis Hatzopoulos has pointed out, the two sets of rules are two sides of the same coin: they are designed 'to prevent public authorities from meddling with markets'.[19] Advocate General Fenin put it very neatly:

> The power of the State which is exercised in the political sphere is subject to democratic control. A different type of control is imposed on economic actors operating in a market: their conduct is governed by competition law. But there is no justification when the State is acting as an economic operator, for relieving its actions of all control.[20]

EU competition law applies to 'undertakings', and 'associations of undertakings',[21] and prohibits 'agreements, concerted practices' (essentially cartels) 'which have as their object or effect the prevention, restriction or distortion of competition within the common market'[22] and 'abuse of dominant position within the common market or in a substantial part of it' (essentially monopolies).[23] A special exemption applies to 'public undertakings and undertakings to which Member States grant special or exclusive rights'.[24] If such undertakings are 'entrusted with the operation of services of general economic interest',[25] they are only subject to the Treaty rules, including those on competition, 'insofar as the application of such rules does not obstruct the performance, in law or in fact, of the particular tasks assigned to them'.[26] All these matters have been developed through a significant body of case law of the Court of

---

[17] On the application of state aids law to health care financing, see: Van de Gronden, 'Financing Health Care in EU Law: Do the European State Aids Rules Write Out an Effective Prescription for Integrating Competition Law with Health Care?' (2009) 6(1) *Competition Law Review* 5.

[18] For instance, the German Bundeskartellamt decided in May 2007 that statutory health insurance funds are subject to public procurement law, see: Bundeskartellamt, 'Statutory Health Insurance Funds to be seen as Public Contracting Entities' (*Bundeskartellamt*, 11 May 2007).

[19] Hatzopoulos, 'Public procurement and state aid in national health care systems' in Mossialos et al., above n 12, 381.

[20] Opinion in *FENIN*, C-205/03, EU:C:2005:666, paragraph 26.

[21] For an example of an 'association of undertakings' in the health context, see: *CNOP*, T-23/09, EU:C:2010:452, involving French pharmacies and medical laboratories, and see also the decisions of the French Conseil de la Concurrence on the subject. See further: Lear, Mossialos, Karl, above n 12, 343; Hancher and Sauter, *EU Competition and Internal Market Law in the Healthcare Sector* (OUP 2012) 227.

[22] Article 101 (1) TFEU. An exemption is available under Article 101 (3) TFEU.

[23] Article 102 TFEU.   [24] Article 106 TFEU.

[25] Under Article 106 (2) TFEU.   [26] Article 106 (2) TFEU.

Justice of the European Union, and also Commission Decisions and soft law guidance.[27] A brief illustration is in order here, relying on two high-profile cases concerning health services: *BetterCare Ltd* v. *Director of Fair Trading*[28] and *Ambulanz Glöckner*.[29]

An 'undertaking' is a body engaged in an 'economic activity'.[30] An 'economic activity' is the offering of goods and services in a market.[31] A body may be an undertaking for some activities but not for others.[32] According to the Commission, 'matters ... such as compulsory basic social security schemes' are not carried out by undertakings.[33] Whether an activity is 'economic' for these purposes depends on whether it is organized on the basis of 'social solidarity'[34] and the extent to which it is subject to state control.[35] Health providers are

[27] See, for a detailed discussion: Neergaard, 'Services of General Economic Interest: The Nature of the Beast' in Krajewski et al. (eds), *The Changing Legal Framework for Services of General Interest in Europe: Between Competition and Solidarity* (TMC Asser Press 2009); Goyder and Albors-Llorens, *Goyder's EC Competition Law* (OUP 2009); Whish and Bailey, *Competition Law* (OUP 2012); Jones and Sufrin, *EU Competition Law: Text, Cases, and Materials* (OUP 2014); Monti (CUP 2007) above n 11.

[28] [2002] CAT 7. For other examples of national competition authorities applying the CJEU jurisprudence on this subject see: e.g. Van de Gronden, 'Purchasing Care: Economic Activity or Service of General (Economic) Interest?' (2004) 25(2) *European Competition Law Review* 87, in particular at 90 (Germany); Decision of the Spanish National Anti-Trust Tribunal, 29 January 1997, *Cruz Roja Española* (Expte R 179/96); *Kilpailuvirasto*, 17 March 2000, dnro 343/61/1997 (Finland); Decision No 358 of the competition authority of 12 October 1994 in *FDB v Southern Health Board* (Ireland); and the examples in Lear, Mossialos, and Karl, above n 12.

[29] *Ambulanz Glöckner*, C-475/99, EU:C:2001:577.

[30] Regardless of the legal status of the body or the manner in which its activities are financed, see: *Höfner and Elser*, C–41/90, EU:C:1991:161; *Pavlov*, C–180/98, C-181/98, C-182/98, C-183/98 and C-184/98, EU:C:2000:428, paragraph 75.

[31] *Commission v Italy*, C-118/85, EU:C:1987:238, paragraph 7; *Commission v Italy*, C–35/96, EU:C:1998:303, paragraph 36; *Pavlov* EU:C:2000:428, paragraph 75; *Ambulanz Glöckner* EU:C:2001:577, paragraph 19. See: Odudu, *The Boundaries of EC Competition Law* (OUP 2006) 26–45.

[32] *Commission v Italy* EU:C:1987:238, para 7.

[33] Commission, 'Green Paper on Services of General Interest' (Green Paper) COM (2003) 270 final, paragraph 45; Prosser, 'EU competition law and public services' in Mossialos et al., above n 12. This view is underpinned by the CJEU rulings in *Eurocontrol*, C–364/92, EU:C:1994:7 (air traffic regulation); *Calì*, C–343/95, EU:C:1997:160 (pollution surveillance) and contrast *Ordre National des Pharmaciens* T-90/11 EU: T:2014:1049 (a professional organisation).

[34] *Poucet and Pistre*, C–159/91 and 160/91, EU:C:1993:63 (compulsory social security scheme not an 'undertaking'); *INAIL*, C–218/00, EU:C:2002:36 (compulsory worker compensation scheme not an 'undertaking'); *AOK*, C–264/01, C–306/01, C-354/01 and C–355/01, EU:C:2004:150 (sickness insurance funds not 'undertakings'); contrast *FFSA*, C–244/94, EU:C:1995:392 (voluntary supplementary pension insurance scheme was an 'undertaking'); *Albany*, C–67/96, EU:C:1999:430; *Brentjens*, C–115/97, EU:C:1999:434; *Bokken*, C–219/97, EU:C:1999:437; *Pavlov* EU:C:2000:428 (pension fund with optional membership, capitalization, and benefits in proportion with contributions was an 'undertaking'); *Ambulanz Glöckner* EU:C:2001:577 (medical aid organization providing ambulance services was an 'undertaking').

[35] *Kattner Stahlbau*, C-350/07, EU:C:2009:127 (an employers' liability insurance association is not an undertaking where employers in a particular industry must be affiliated to it, and the insurance fulfils an 'exclusively social function', operating on the principle of solidarity. Solidarity satisfied where contributions to the scheme and benefits paid under the scheme are not proportionate to the risk or the insured person's earnings. (see: *Kattner Stahlbau* EU:C:2009:127, paragraphs 44, 50-55, 61-62, 64-68)); *SELEX*, C-113/07, EU:C:2009:191 (An

'undertakings', and subject to EU competition law, if they are engaged in an 'economic activity'. Self-employed health professionals may be undertakings, whereas those who are subject to employment relationships are not. One element of the legal test is the question of who assumes the risk for the service provided. In *Pavlov*,[36] the CJEU held that medical specialists, who provide health services in a market, and assume the risks associated with their professional activity, are 'undertakings'.

In the *BetterCare* case, a Northern Irish local authority had purchased nursing and social care services, in BetterCare's residential homes, under a standard contract. The local authority itself also provided such residential nursing and social care services, in the same market. In BetterCare's view, the contract for the care services offered unreasonably low prices and unfair contract terms, and was thus abuse of a dominant position. The original complaint was dismissed[37] on the basis that the local authority was not acting as an 'undertaking', because they were purchasing nursing and social care in an 'act of solidarity', for people who lacked the means of their own to pay. That decision was overturned.[38] Although some acts of the local authority (such as for instance refusing to register a home as licensed to contract with the authority to provide residential care) would be an exercise of official authority, acts such as contracting out provision of care to the private sector[39] are 'economic', because, when the local authority acquired places in BetterCare's residential care homes on this basis, it was entering into contracts for services in a market.[40]

The Tribunal went on to hold that the prohibition on 'abuse of a dominant position' applies to unfair purchase prices or unfair trading conditions imposed by a dominant buyer, just as it does to unfair purchase prices imposed by a dominant seller. Likewise, the potential abuse of applying dissimilar conditions to equivalent transactions with other trading parties, is not limited to sellers, but may equally apply to buyers. Moreover, the Tribunal found that the local authority was also active as a seller of services on the relevant market.[41] The transactions on this market were 'economic activities' carried out on a commercial basis.[42]

international organisation such as the European Organisation for the Safety of Air Navigation (Eurocontrol) is not an undertaking for the purposes of EU competition law. Taken as a whole, Eurocontrol's activities, by their nature, their aim and the rules to which they are subject, are connected with the exercise of powers relating to the control and supervision of airspace, which are typically those of a public authority, not of an economic nature. Eurocontrol does not offer goods or services on a market. (see: *Eurocontrol* EU:C:1994:7, paragraphs 70-72, 76-77, 79, 92, 96, 102, 114)).

[36] *Pavlov* EU:C:2000:428.   [37] By the Director General of Fair Trading.

[38] By the Competition Appeal Tribunal.

[39] The CAT distinguished *Calì* EU:C:1997:160 and *Eurocontrol* EU:C:1994:7. In a later case involving Eurocontrol, *SELEX*, T-155/04, EU:T:2006:387, paragraph 7, the Court of First Instance took a different approach, but the CJEU (*SELEX* EU:C:2009:191) has since ruled that the CFI erred in finding that Eurocontrol's activity was an 'economic' activity, see: *SELEX* EU:C:2009:191, paragraph 80.

[40] [2002] CAT 7, paragraphs 168–171.   [41] [2002] CAT 7, paragraphs 200–201.

[42] For further discussion, see: Hervey, 'If only it were so simple: Public Health Services and EU Law' in Cremona (ed), *Market Integration and Public Services in the EU* (OUP 2011).

Ambulanz Glöckner[43] involved emergency and non-emergency ambulance services. The public authorities of a German *Land* had entrusted two medical aid organizations[44] to provide the *Land*'s public ambulance service. This exclusive licence was challenged by a private firm seeking to enter the market, on the basis that the licence was an abuse of a dominant position. The CJEU held that the medical aid organizations were 'undertakings',[45] reasoning that because the activity of providing emergency transport services and patient transport services has not always been, and is not necessarily, carried on by public authorities, this was a service, for remuneration from users, on a market, and hence the activity was an economic activity.[46] There was an abuse of a dominant position, because the *Land* was required to consult with the medical aid organizations before granting any further licences.

On the question of whether the grant of exclusive rights to the medical aid organizations was justified as the operation of a 'service of general economic interest', the CJEU held[47] that, if the exclusive rights were necessary to ensure that those organizations could perform the tasks entrusted to them,[48] it would be permitted. The revenue from non-emergency transport off-set the costs of providing emergency transport, and that was what made the service economically viable. If private operators were to be allowed to enter the market, and take the more profitable elements of it, this would affect how much that cross-subsidization could continue, and ultimately jeopardize the quality and reliability of the public service.[49] Essentially, the CJEU applies a proportionality test in its reasoning here: the objective public interest justifying the monopoly or anti-competitive practice is balanced against the restriction on competition.[50] Member States may create undertakings that operate in ways that breach EU competition law only where this is justified by a legitimate national

---

43 *Ambulanz Glöckner* EU:C:2001:577.   44   The German Red Cross and the Maltese Aid Service.

45 *Ambulanz Glöckner* EU:C:2001:577, paragraph 22. In the subsequent case of *Spezzino* C-113/13 EU:C:2014:2440, involving provision of ambulance services by the Italian Red Cross (Croce Rossa Italiana), the CJEU did not consider the application of competition law, and so did not need to make a finding on this point.

46 *Ambulanz Glöckner* EU:C:2001:577, paragraph 20.

47 *Ambulanz Glöckner* EU:C:2001:577, paragraphs 51–65.

48 *Ambulanz Glöckner* EU:C:2001:577, paragraph 56.

49 *Ambulanz Glöckner* EU:C:2001:577, paragraph 61. This 'no cream-skimming' argument is found in several earlier cases on what is now Article 106(2) TFEU, to the effect that Article 106(2) TFEU protects the 'economic equilibrium' of public service provision, which would be upset if further private operators were permitted to enter the market and take the more profitable elements of it, undermining the solidarity-based cross-subsidization that the grant of special or exclusive rights permits, see: e.g. *Corbeau*, C–320/91, EU:C:1993:198. The 'no cream-skimming' argument would not be available only if it could be shown that the undertakings entrusted with the operation of the public ambulance service were manifestly unable to satisfy demand, *Ambulanz Glöckner* EU:C:2001:577, paragraph 62.

50 *Sacchi*, C-155/73, EU:C:1974:40; *Corbeau* EU:C:1993:198; *Almelo*, C–393/92, EU:C:1994:171; *Corsica Ferries*, C–266/96, EU:C:1998:306; *TNT Traco*, C–340/99, EU:C:2001:281; *Albany* EU:C:1999:430. See also: Opinion in *AOK*, C–264/01, C–306/01, C–354/01, and C–355/01, EU:C:2003:304. See further: Edward and Hoskins, 'Article 90: Deregulation and EC Law. Reflections arising from the XVI FIDE Conference' (1995) 32 *Common Market Law Review* 157.

objective, and where the consequent restriction of competition is limited to what is necessary to achieve this objective.

EU competition law thus applies in principle to 'undertakings' (non-state actors), with modifications in terms of how it applies to states, acting through the various mechanisms of public or quasi-public bodies associated with the exercise of administrative power in the twenty-first century. In that it seeks to create effective conditions for free and fair trade, EU competition law plays an important role in the creation of the EU's internal market. In this respect, it is the legal counterpart to the provisions of EU free trade law, which we considered in earlier chapters. These rules prohibit unjustified restrictions on the free movement of the factors of production.

As Member States of the EU experiment with changes to their health systems that involve the state 'acting as an economic operator', the application of EU competition and state aids law, as well as free trade law, to health system increases. It is not possible to make blanket statements about the applicability of EU competition or free trade law to health systems – every health system is different and thus detailed analysis of particular arrangements is necessary. But what is possible is to draw some general conclusions, based on the different types of health systems outlined in our typology. In order to do this, we consider four different aspects of health systems: health insurance; health institutions; health professionals; and the pharmaceuticals, medical equipment and medical devices industries. Some of these areas have seen the application of EU competition and free trade law for decades. For others, application of EU competition and free trade law is relatively recent.

Health insurance

As we saw in the introduction to this section of the book, many Member States have structured their health systems using social insurance models. Moreover, in all Member States, private health insurance plays at least some part in the system, not least because capacity in the public system is released by those who use the private system. In some Member States, notably the Netherlands, the blend between social and private insurance involves a mandatory social health insurance scheme, implemented by for-profit (private) insurance companies.[51] The systemic place of private health insurance ranges from supplementary social insurance or tax-based systems (where faster access and consumer choice drive the market in supplementary private health insurance), through complementary (where the scope of benefits or the proportion of cost of what is met by the public system drive the private health insurance market), to substitutive (where the lack of inclusiveness of the public system drives the private health insurance market).[52]

---

[51] See: Den Exter and Guy, 'Market Competition in Health Care Markets in the Netherlands: Some Lessons for England?' (2014) 22(2) *Medical Law Review* 255.

[52] See: Thomson and Mossialos, 'Private health insurance and the internal market' in Mossialos et al., above n 12, 422, Table 10.1.

In at least some of these instances, it is possible that EU competition and free movement law applies to health insurance. Insurance, as well as being covered by EU competition law, is also covered by EU free movement law, in particular law on free movement of services and capital, and the EU's Non-Life Insurance Directives.[53] The basic idea behind the EU's free movement law in this area is that of 'home state control'. Home state control means that a single Member State governs the provision of insurance – authorizing providers and regulating the terms under which they provide the financial service of insurance, for instance, ensuring financial probity and sufficient solvency. If a Member State allows for the private insurance of a particular type of risk (in our case, the risk of ill health), then any insurer authorized in its home state to cover that risk must be allowed to access the market in that Member State. In the case of non-life insurance, the EU legislation involves several exceptions which may take the provision of health insurance outside of these general principles.

If EU law applies, the expectation is that it is likely to move the system more towards the neoliberal end in our typology, if we work from the underlying assumption that competition law is about promoting economic welfare through minimizing costs and maximizing benefits to consumers, through enhanced consumer choice. If insurance funds are dominant players, with monopolies on the market, an ability to contract with all doctors or hospitals could lead to abuse of that position, for instance, through unfair contractual terms. Or if there is an over-supply of health care providers, the procedures for selecting those with which the insurance fund contracts could also be anti-competitive, if subjective or arbitrary.[54] The legal debate in this area has focused around two key points: whether there is an 'undertaking', and whether any anti-competitive behaviour is nonetheless justified.

Competition law requires control of monopolies and of collusive behaviour. From the point of view of health systems, however, both monopolistic and collusive practices may seem entirely appropriate. They respond to a need to provide health care on the basis of equal access according to need, under solidaristic funding arrangements such as progressive taxation or social insurance. They do so in the context of constrained resources and the desire for significant efficiencies through state control or at least economies of scale. This is seen as more efficient than the atomization of service provision implied by a standard market with many, smaller private providers competing on the basis of price. For instance, health insurance funds might agree to share markets for particular services, to make gains from specialization. They might also benefit from relational contracting, where ongoing interactions between a few larger actors are seen as preferable to the instability of constant renegotiation of contracts with new providers. All of these matters are highly contested from the point of view of competition law.

[53] Now see: Directive 2009/138/EC [2009] OJ L335/1.
[54] Lear, Mossialos, and Karl, above n 12, 361-2

Where private health insurance of a *supplementary* nature is at issue, there is no question that EU competition (and indeed free movement) law could apply to that part of a health system. So, for instance, in 2011, the UK Office of Fair Trading[55] referred[56] the market for privately funded health care, which is supplementary within UK health systems,[57] to the Competition Commission for investigation.[58] Reporting in 2014, the Competition and Markets Authority (the successor to the Competition Commission) found both structural and transactional aspects of the overall market for private health care to involve 'adverse effects on competition'.[59] However, the Authority found no aspects of the private health insurance market to be anti-competitive.[60] The practice of 'fee capping' (whereby insurers, such as BUPA and Axa PPP, only 'recognize' consultants who agree not to charge patients more than the relevant insurer's maximum reimbursement rate) was not at present distorting competition, but it could do in the future if insufficiently transparent oversight was not in place. The Authority urged insurers to be transparent in their interactions with both policy-holders and consultants.[61] Beyond that, the potential application of EU law had no consequences.

It also seems clear that, conversely, *substitutive* private health insurance ought to fall outside the reach of EU law, because it is essentially performing a social solidarity role, in substituting for the public/social insurance or taxation-based system. In the context of free movement law, 'insurance forming part of a statutory system of social security'[62] falls outside of the EU rules, although the precise scope of that provision remains open to question.[63] Furthermore, insurance that 'may serve as a partial or complete alternative to health cover provided by the statutory social security scheme' is exempt from the principle that Member States may not intervene in the setting of insurance premiums and

---

[55] The UK OFT and the UK Competition Commission ceased to operate on 31 March 2014. Their duties have passed to several other bodies, including the UK Competition and Markets Authority, and Monitor, the competition regulator for the health sector.

[56] OFT, 'OFT provisionally decides to refer private healthcare market to Competition Commission' (*OFT*, 8 December 2011).

[57] There is a small market for complementary health insurance, to meet the costs of co-payment for prescription medicines.

[58] Features of the market suggesting possible breach of competition law include lack of information to patients, GPs or insurers, on quality and costs; insufficient numbers of undertakings on the market (e.g. some local areas where private healthcare providers own the only local hospital); and barriers to new market entrants such as pricing structures and loyalty payments used to keep competitors out of markets.

[59] CMA, 'Private Healthcare Market Investigation Final Report' (CMA 2014).

[60] The market structure is one of concentration (e.g. Bupa alone holds 39.5% of the overall market), but no abuse of that dominant position was found.

[61] CMA, above n 59, 8-9, paragraphs 7-112 and 7-135.

[62] Directive 73/239/EC [1973] OJ L228/3, Article 2 (1) (d).

[63] See: *Accidents at Work*, C-206/98, EU:C:2000:256; Letter from Commissioner Bolkestein to Hans Hoogervorst, Dutch Minister for Health, regarding Dutch health insurance system (25 November 2003); see: further Hancher and Sauter, above n 21, 128-9.

conditions.[64] This provision was adopted to cater for Ireland, the Netherlands and Germany, which at the time all operated private health insurance systems as substitutes or partial substitutes for state (public) schemes. The underlying idea was to secure protection from EU free movement law for provisions which play a solidarity-based role within health systems. The view that this idea applies also in competition law has not yet been fully tested in the case law, but the *AOK* case,[65] in which the CJEU held that German sickness insurance funds are not undertakings,[66] supports this proposition. Leigh Hancher and Wolf Sauter take the view that the CJEU's case law on the competition law concept of 'undertaking' treats what they call 'public law' (in our view, substitutive) providers of health insurance differently from other undertakings operating in health systems.[67] Moreover, we can gain further insights into the position of substitutive private health insurance by considering the case law involving systems with *complementary* private health insurance. In that case, although the systems are subject to scrutiny for compliance with EU competition law, it seems that the control is only 'light touch' proportionality control.

Ireland has a taxation-funded national healthcare system, but around 50 per cent of the population rely instead on private health insurance. This is in part to supplement the public system, but it also plays a complementary rule in terms of the relatively narrow scope of benefits covered by the public system. Private health insurance in Ireland was offered by a body called the Voluntary Health Insurance Board. In 1997, following Irish legislation liberalizing the market, BUPA Ireland entered the Irish market for private health insurance, as a competitor to the Voluntary Health Insurance Board.[68] The relevant national law introduced a 'risk equalization scheme', which essentially provides that private health insurers who have lower risks than the average should pay into a central fund, and those insurers who have higher risks than average should receive monies from that central fund. In practice, this meant transfer of funds from BUPA Ireland to the Voluntary Health Insurance Board. BUPA Ireland

---

[64] Directive 2009/138/EC [2009] OJ L335/1, Recital 84, Article 206 (1).

[65] *AOK* EU:C:2004:150 ; and see further: *Non-Life Insurance*, C-185/11, EU:C:2012:43.

[66] Contrast: *FFSA* EU:C:1995:392 (voluntary supplementary pension insurance scheme was an 'undertaking'); *Albany* EU:C:1999:430; *Brentjens* EU:C:1999:434; *Bokken* EU:C:1999:437; *Pavlov* EU:C:2000:428 (pension fund with optional membership, capitalization, and benefits in proportion with contributions was an 'undertaking'). Whether EU competition law applies depends on how the insurance scheme is organised – factors are 1) standardised contribution and benefit levels; 2) compulsory membership; 3) lack of competitors in the market; 4) delegated state mandate to provide public services. If those are present, then the body concerned is not an undertaking. But if elements of variation in contribution and benefit, depending on individual risk, optional membership, competitors from the private sector in the relevant market, and independent discretion of the body concerned in providing its services, then the body concerned is likely to be an undertaking.

[67] Hancher and Sauter, above n 21, 227.

[68] BUPA Ireland had a market share of around 15 per cent, with the Voluntary Health Insurance Board having the other 85 per cent.

challenged the risk equalization scheme as a 'state aid', contrary to Article 107 TFEU.

The EU law in this area is quite complex, but basically a payment to an undertaking is not an 'aid' in the sense of Article 107 TFEU if it is a reasonable payment for a 'public service obligation', and the recipient has been chosen either through a public procurement process or, if not, where the payment is that which would be made to an efficient undertaking for the service received.[69] Special treatment is given to hospitals[70] and to 'services of general economic interest meeting social needs as regards health and long-term care ... and the care and social inclusion of vulnerable groups'.[71] In the *BUPA Ireland* case,[72] the European Commission thought that the way the scheme was structured did not involve a state aid at all. It was organized on the basis of solidarity, in the context of a public service, rather than being an unwarranted interference in a market. In the alternative, the Commission decided that even if it was a state aid, it was justified as a 'service of general economic interest'. The Court of First Instance focused on the public service obligation of the Voluntary Health Insurance Board. The Court rejected BUPA's argument that the compensation to the Voluntary Health Insurance Board under the risk equalization scheme was not necessary because the Voluntary Health Insurance Board could avoid burdens by partitioning the market in health insurance according to the risk insured, in accordance with a commercial strategy.[73] The aim of the risk equalization scheme was not to compensate costs of specific services, but rather to equalize the additional burdens where one health insurer has a negative risk profile, compared to the average market risk profile.[74] The Commission was correct in finding the scheme necessary and proportionate. This aspect of the Court's ruling in *BUPA Ireland* shows sensitivity to the *systemic* structures of the Irish health system, rather than focusing upon a strict and literal application of EU

---

[69] See: *Altmark*, C–280/00, EU:C:2003:415; Directive 2005/81/EC [2005] OJ L312/47; Decision 2005/842/EC [2005] OJ L312/67; and Commission, 'Community framework for State aid in the form of public service compensation' (Communication) [2005] OJ C297/04. See: Hervey, (2011) above n 42; Hancher and Sauter, above n 21, 268-273. These provisions (known as the 'Altmark package') were replaced in 2011 and 2012 by the 'Alumnia package', comprising: Commission, 'Communication from the Commission on the application of the European Union State aid rules to compensation granted for the provision of services of general economic interest' (Communication) [2012] OJ C8/4; Commission, 'Communication from the Commission — Approval of the content of a draft for a Commission Regulation on de minimis aid for the provision of services of general economic interest' (Communication) [2012] OJ C8/23; Regulation 360/2012/EU [2012] OJ L114/8; Decision 2012/21/EU [2012] OJ L7/3; Commission, 'Communication from the Commission: European Union Framework for State aid in the form of public service compensation' (Communication) [2012] OJ C8/15; Sauter, 'The Altmark Package Mark II: New Rules for State aid and the compensation of services of general economic interest' (2012) 33(7) *European Competition Law Review* 307; Commission, 'EU Competition Policy Newsletter 2012-1' (Various Authors 2012).
[70] Decision 2012/21/EU, Article 2 (1) (b).   [71] Decision 2012/21/EU, Article 2 (1) (c).
[72] *BUPA*, T–289/03, EU:T:2008:29.   [73] *BUPA* EU:T:2008:29, paragraphs 229–232.
[74] *BUPA* EU:T:2008:29, paragraph 235.

state aids law rules.[75] Even though the Court assumed that the Voluntary Health Insurance Board was an undertaking, and thus fell within the scope of EU law, the scrutiny of its activities was subject only to a light touch proportionality control. If the Court had decided otherwise, the Voluntary Health Insurance Board would have had to either adopt the market partitioning approach, or raise premiums overall, to make up the lost income from the risk equalization scheme. Given that BUPA Ireland had 'skimmed' the group with the least risky profiles (that is, those least likely to need to access health care), either of these results would have meant less equality within the system as a whole, in terms of equality of access according to medical need. The market partitioning approach would have had a worse effect on equality, as it would have meant either higher premiums or lower benefits for those individuals with the riskiest profiles. The light touch proportionality control respects the solidarity- and equality-based systemic position of the risk equalization scheme.

Similarly, the European Commission's assessment of the new Netherlands framework for health insurance, brought in in 2005, was assessed in terms of the exception under Article 106 (2) TFEU. The system involved transforming previously public entities into private health insurance bodies, allowing them to keep their reserves; requiring that the whole population be covered, using a risk equalization scheme and open enrolment; and providing half of the financing received by the health insurance bodies from a public fund. The Commission decided that the keeping of the reserves constituted a 'state aid', but that a service of general economic interest under Article 106 (2) TFEU was engaged. The aid was justified, on the basis that it was a proportionate response to the need to develop certain economic areas (here health insurance) and did not adversely affect trade to an extent contrary to the common interest.[76]

Likewise, in *AG2R*,[77] the CJEU (disagreeing with its Advocate General) found that a body responsible for complementary health insurance in France was an 'undertaking'. Under the French health system, employees' health care costs are reimbursed in part by the basic social security scheme. The remainder of the costs may be reimbursed in part by complementary private health insurance, and sectoral collective agreements between employers and employees provide for such complementary schemes. Only certain types of bodies may provide such schemes, and they may not refuse access to the scheme for employees within the sector, even on grounds of failure to pay. Beaudout, a traditional

---

[75] See further: Hervey, (2011) above n 42.

[76] Article 107 (3) (c) TFEU. Decision of the Commission of 3 May 2005 with regard to state aid N 541/2004. See: Hancher and Sauter, above n 21, 274-5.

[77] *AG2R*, C-437/09, EU:C:2011:112. Contrast: *Fontaine*, C-603/11, EU:C:2012:731 in which the CJEU rejected as manifestly inadmissible a claim that French law on the relations between social insurance bodies and the providers with which they contract are contrary to EU competition law, inter alia on the grounds that no evidence had been provided that the relevant body was an 'undertaking'.

bakery firm, refused to join AG2R's scheme, which covers the bakery sector. They challenged the rule to the effect that membership is compulsory for firms in the sector, for breach of EU competition law. The CJEU held[78] that, although there was a high degree of solidarity,[79] there was insufficient state control over the body's activities[80] for AG2R to fall outside the concept of an 'undertaking'. However, the CJEU found that the French legislation at issue, which provided for compulsory membership of the complementary schemes, may have involved an anti-competitive agreement, or placed AG2R in a position where it abused its position of market dominance, but it was *justified* under Article 106 (2) TFEU. Again, the scrutiny of AG2R's position was 'light touch': despite evidence to the effect that allowing exemptions from the compulsory membership rule would not endanger AG2R's financial viability, the CJEU found it would not be possible for AG2R to continue to fulfil its statutory obligations under 'economically acceptable conditions'.[81]

The conclusion that substitutive health insurance falls outside the scope of EU law is also supported by the relevant EU (free movement) law on (non-life) insurance services,[82] the aims of which are to promote cross-border provision of insurance services within the EU and encourage competition among insurance providers. The relevant Directive explicitly exempts social health insurance schemes from its scope.[83] However, if an insurance fund operates a social security scheme at its own risk, then this constitutes an 'economic activity' and falls within the Directive.[84] In general, Member States are prohibited from restricting prices or conditions of insurance services that fall under EU law. Nonetheless, Member States may impose such restrictions on 'insurers providing a partial

---

[78] Applying the case law on an 'undertaking', as summarised by the Advocate General, 'In the context of social security, the Court has established two main criteria for determining whether or not the activity in which the body or bodies responsible for the various schemes concerned is/are engaged is economic in nature. There are two key elements: does the scheme apply the principle of solidarity? To what extent is the scheme subject to state control? [cites *Poucet and Pistre* EU:C:1993:63, paragraphs 8-15; *INAIL* EU:C:2002:36, paragraphs 37-46; *AOK*, EU:C: 2004:150, paragraphs 47-57; and *Kattner Stahlbau*, paragraphs 43 to 68.] If the scheme applies the principle of solidarity and is under State control, the body in charge of managing the scheme will be considered not to be engaged in an economic activity and will therefore fall outside the scope of [EU competition law]' (Opinion in *AG2R*, C-437/09, EU:C:2010:676, paragraph 59).

[79] The scheme involved fixed-rate contributions, so rate of contributions not based on the risk insured (ie the scheme does not take account of age, health etc., when fixing contributions rates); Benefits paid are not necessarily linked to amount of contributions made. Hence there is a 'high degree of solidarity' (*AG2R* EU:C:2011:112, paragraphs 47-52).

[80] Insufficient state control. AG2R enjoys a degree of autonomy – social partners chose to have a sectoral level collective agreement; social partners chose AG2R from among various possible operators on the health insurance market, including private companies (which in fact offered identical services to AG2R's before AG2R was appointed/chosen by the sector).

[81] *AG2R* EU:C:2011 :112, paragraphs 75-77.   [82] Directive 2009/138/EC [2009] OJ L335/1.

[83] Directive 2009/138/EC, Article 3.

[84] *Commission v Belgium* EU:C:2000:256, interpreting the earlier Directive 92/49/EEC [1992] OJ L228/1.

or complete alternative to health cover provided by the statutory social security system' to 'protect the general good'.[85] This category would include open enrolment, community rating, standardized benefits packages and risk equalization schemes. The Directive thus operates on the basis that health insurers who provide insurance that *substitutes* for social health insurance are to be exempt from the constraints of EU free movement (and, at least implicitly, competition) law, whereas *supplementary* health insurance should be subject to the rules of the market.[86]

However, the conclusion that *BUPA Ireland* and *AG2R* are authority for the proposition that anti-competitive behaviour by undertakings providing complementary private health insurance can be readily justified as a 'service of general economic interest' might be less certain, in the light of the CJEU's 2012 ruling that Slovenia's complementary health insurance system is not fully in line with the Third Non-Life Insurance Directive.[87] Admittedly, the basis of the Slovenian case is not competition law, but free movement law. Under the Slovenian Health Care and Health Insurance Act, foreign health insurers were required to appoint a representative in Slovenia (a potential restriction on freedom of establishment), health insurers were restricted from using their profits for distribution to their shareholders (a potential restriction on free movement of capital), and insurers were required to notify the Slovenian supervisory authority of their insurance terms (a breach of the Directive). The Slovenian authorities had argued, relying on the *BUPA Ireland* case, that the complementary insurance market is a part of the broader social security system and is a 'service of general economic interest'. Sarah Thomson and Elias Mossialos take the view that the Slovenian government had a stronger case than the Irish government did in *BUPA Ireland* 'because the complementary market [in Slovenia] makes a more significant contribution to social protection than the predominantly supplementary market in Ireland'.[88] Unfortunately, the CJEU was not required to deal with this question. The points on the applicability of the free movement provisions in the Treaty were held to be inadmissible. On the question of infringement of the Directive, Slovenia did not deny the infringement, and had already initiated a legislative reform to comply with the Directive. It is difficult, therefore, to draw firm conclusions on the legal position from the *Slovenia* case.

Perhaps the explanation for the difference in approach between the *Slovenia* case and the *AG2R* and *BUPA Ireland* cases is that the proportionality test is light touch in the context of EU competition law, but much stricter in the context of

[85] Directive 2009/138/EC, Article 206. See also: Commission, 'Commission Interpretative Communication - Freedom to Provide Services and the General Good in the Insurance Sector' (Communication) [2000] OJ C43/5.

[86] For further analysis, see: Thomson and Mossialos, above n 52.

[87] *Non-Life Insurance* EU:C:2012:43.   [88] Thomson and Mossialos, above n 52, 445-7.

EU free movement law.[89] Nevertheless, we can draw some interim conclusions from the case law discussed so far.

(Interim) conclusions

Perhaps the most important conclusion so far is that nothing about EU competition or free movement law requires Member States to organize the insurance aspects of their health systems in any particular way. The precise blend of private supplementary, complementary or substitutive insurance, with social insurance and taxation, is a matter of national policy. Different Member States have chosen different settlements in this regard, placing themselves at different points on the continuum from 'planned economy' to 'neoliberal' health systems. In terms of the claim that EU law moves health systems (as opposed to welfare systems more generally) towards neoliberalism, the example of health insurance suggests that this cannot be supported in its most general or strongest form. EU law *itself* does not move health systems along the continuum towards neoliberalism.

This conclusion is illustrated, for instance, by the *Bettercare* litigation. It was the *choice* of Northern Ireland to provide nursing care through a (partial) market in which private providers competed with local authority providers. In that context, the local authority providers were defined by competition law as 'undertakings', and thus were required to behave consistently with the requirements of competition law. Had the provision of nursing care remained entirely a matter of local authority provision, the question of the application of EU law would never have arisen.

Furthermore, some caution must be exercised in drawing conclusions about even those systems which most resemble the neoliberal ideal type. The three roles for private health insurance (substitutive, complementary, supplementary) do not map directly to our continuum of health systems typology. For instance, one might find systems towards the neoliberal pole with either substitutive private health insurance (such as Germany), or with supplementary private health insurance (such as the UK).[90] If, as has been suggested above, EU law treats different roles that private health insurance plays in the systems differently, in particular, if it applies competition law to supplementary private health insurance, but not to substitutive private health insurance, then this suggests that the claim that EU law is moving *all* systems towards the neoliberal end of the continuum needs to be modified. It does not explain why substitutive systems, such as that found in Germany, which fall *outside* the scope of EU law, are nevertheless towards the neoliberal end of the spectrum.

---

[89] Sauter, 'Proportionality in EU Law: A Balancing Act?' (2013) 15 *Cambridge Yearbook of European Legal Studies* 439; Sauter, 'The Impact of EU Competition Law on National Healthcare Systems' (2013) 38(4) *European Law Review* 457.

[90] Lear, Mossialos and Karl, above n 12, 422, Table 10.1

A better explanation might be that EU law finds a way to respect the national settlement concerning the systemic place of both substitutive and supplementary private health insurance, either by finding that it falls outside the scope of EU law altogether, or by allowing national anti-competitive policies to be easily justified by the 'light touch' proportionality review. *Ambulanz Glöckner* illustrates this point in the context of ambulance services; *BUPA Ireland* and *AG2R* illustrate it in the context of health insurance. Member States determine what constitutes a 'service of general interest', and that is reviewable only in the case of 'manifest error'.[91] As Thomson and Mossialos point out[92]

> Not only do national governments have considerable discretion in deciding what is in the general interest, but the regulations in place themselves contribute to the definition of a particular service as being in the general interest. In other words, if the Irish Government defines a service as being in the general interest, regulations such as open enrolment and community rating can only strengthen the government's case, although the necessity and proportionality tests would still apply. This apparently circular argument reflects the complexity of determining what is and is not a service of general economic interest in the absence of a central definition, but it reinforces the significant scope for MS autonomy in this area.

The Irish Government claimed that private health insurance in Ireland is an important element of Irish health policy (its 'second pillar'), and that its nature is supplementary rather than substitutive. It relied on the population coverage (about half of the population) as evidence of the substantial contribution that private health insurance makes to the Irish health system. These claims are beyond the scrutiny of the European Commission or the CJEU.

If these arguments were taken to apply to all elements of national health systems, it would be possible for Member States to justify virtually every aspect of their national health system, even if organized according to a market basis, by claiming that it was a key element of their health policy overall. These aspects of the health system would still be subject to scrutiny under EU competition law, but this would be extremely light touch, as the test for a permissible service of general interest involves only light proportionality scrutiny. The margin of discretion permitted in Member States determining what counts as 'within' their national health system would itself not be subject to scrutiny, save in the case of manifest error. If this argument is taken to its logical conclusion, it would presumably be open to a Member State to organize the whole of its national health service using private undertakings and subject to the ordinary rules of the market (free movement and competition law), but to justify special treatment for certain undertakings within that market on the grounds that they were providing a service of general interest. It seems unlikely that the EU institutions would accept such an argument in the extreme case outlined here,

---

[91]   *BUPA* EU:T:2008:29, paragraph 165.   [92]   Thomson and Mossialos, above n 52, 444-5.

but there is every reason to conclude that they *would* accept such an argument in a case with some of these features.

As Leigh Hancher and Wolf Sauter put it, EU law accommodates the role of solidarity in health care not only in those health systems which have consciously moved towards a more neoliberal model (in terms of the blend of market and solidarity-based provision), but also in those 'mixed' systems where solidarity-based systems tolerate the co-existence of private insurance, in order to meet pent-up demand.[93] Only where private health insurance is entirely *supplementary* – in other words where it is a consumer commodity, rather than a part of the provision made to ensure equal access to health care according to medical need – does the full rigour of EU competition law apply. However, the stronger version of proportionality applicable in the context of free movement law may result in a different conclusion with respect to that aspect of EU health law.

At most, the application of EU law could, should a Member State choose to move towards a more neoliberal model, help to protect that choice. EU law undoubtedly requires market-like conditions in sectors in which Member States have introduced market-like mechanisms. So, for instance, should the private health insurance providers operating in England and Wales fail to operate contractual relationships in a sufficiently transparent way, with sufficient benefit for consumers, competition law will apply to those potentially anti-competitive agreements. Once those market-like mechanisms are in place, in practice it may be more difficult to retreat from them than it was to adopt them. In that sense, Offe's idea of a 'one-way street' (the making of fish soup from an aquarium, but not vice versa) applies in the context of health systems. André den Exter and Mary Guy make this point also in their analysis of the Netherlands health insurance system following the reforms adopted in 2006.[94] They show the ways in which competition on price has increased choice and reduced costs. But for some groups in the population there is no real increase in choice, because, given their income and health, any options they have to change insurers are limited to those which conflict with their interests in being able to access high quality health care. These individuals include many elderly people, and members of lower socio-economic groups. Consequently, the principle of equality of treatment under the health insurance system has been negatively affected. Moreover, the government's interventions in terms of regulated competition (for instance, in bundling payments for particular categories of care, particularly long-term care; governmental price setting; cost-containment agreements)[95] meant that there was a *de facto* retreat from equitable access, at the same time as incomplete gains from competition on price through consumer choice. In their words,

---

[93] Hancher and Sauter, above n 21, 88; see also: Van de Gronden and Sauter, 'Taking the temperature: EU Competition Law and Health Care' (2011) 38(3) *Legal Issues of Economic Integration* 213.

[94] Den Exter and Guy, above n 51.

[95] These were tested – unsuccessfully – before the courts – see: District Court Breda 23 November 2010, LNJ BO4755.

'unwillingness to leave matters to the market triggers the question of whether there is a way back'.[96] If it can be shown that markets in aspects of health insurance are detrimental to equality, then in this regard the balance in EU law between solidarity, equality and competition involves a retreat from equality.

But EU law *itself* does not make health systems treat health insurance as a matter that must be considered within competitive frameworks, where values of equality and solidarity have to be managed within an overarching framework of competition law. On the contrary, EU law permits health insurance to be treated as part of an overarching framework of solidarity, in which equal access to health care is achieved in accordance with progressive resourcing models, either through taxation, or through social insurance.

[96] Den Exter and Guy, above n 51, 273.

10

Competition, solidarity, equality: health institutions and professions

Introduction

This chapter continues our discussion of the tensions in EU law between solidarity, equality and competition in health systems. Its focus is on the key institutions that make up a health system: hospitals, pharmacies, laboratories, blood and human tissue centres, dental clinics, opticians. The next chapter considers the key industries with which health systems interact, that is the pharmaceuticals, medical devices and medical equipment industries. As in the previous chapter, we are interested in the implications of EU health law for how these tensions are managed.

Health Institutions and professions

Hospitals

Several Member States, especially those in Central and Eastern Europe, have experimented with reforms that open up previously publicly owned and managed hospitals to the private sector. For instance, Estonia and Lithuania have altered the legal status of many hospitals since the 1990s.[1] Member States such as Germany and Austria have seen an increase in private hospitals, but also new hybrids such as publicly-owned hospitals with independent private status; publicly owned, but privately managed hospitals; out-sourcing of non-clinical services; and various other forms of public–private partnerships.[2] In England and Wales, the 'any qualified provider' concept, whereby those who purchase health services for the national health system may choose with whom to contract (and patients have a choice too), has led to an increase of private hospitals providing services within the national health system framework. All of these

---

[1] Lear, Mossialos and Karl, 'EU competition law and health policy' in Mossialos, Permanand, Baeten and Hervey (eds), *Health Systems Governance in Europe: The Role of European Union Law and Policy* (CUP 2010) 348-9.

[2] Lear, Mossialos and Karl, above n 1, 349 and literature cited therein. Fidler et al., 'Incorporation of public hospitals: a 'silver bullet' against overcapacity, managerial bottlenecks and resource constraints' (2007) 81 *Health Policy* 328.

changes increase the likelihood that EU competition and free movement law will apply to hospitals within the health system.

For instance, the German Competition Authority (*Bundeskartellamt*) has scrutinized the structure of markets for hospital services. A good example is the Tübingen and Zollernalb hospital merger. Until 2003, the hospitals in Albstadt, Balingen and Hechingen belonged to the Zollernalb administrative district. In late 2003, the private company Zollernalb-Klinikum gGmbH was set up as an operating company. The University Hospital of Tübingen and the Zollernalb administrative district were equally represented in the company. The business operations of the hospitals in Balingen, Hechingen und Albstadt were entrusted to Zollernalb Klinikum gGmbH in early 2004. Under threat of proceedings brought by the Competition Authority, the firms concerned chose to reverse the merger. There was no question that the activities of the hospitals, though part of the 'public sector', that is the German health system, were carrying out 'economic activities' and therefore fell within the scope of competition law.[3] Attempts to challenge the German Competition Authority's policy through the courts have been unsuccessful.[4]

The Netherlands Competition Authority has been particularly active in this field. In December 2011, it reported that it had taken more than 150 decisions about mergers and proposed mergers in the health sector since 2004.[5] More recently, it has decided that a proposed merger between two hospitals near the western Dutch city of Haarlem may reduce competition in the market for hospital care, and that therefore a merger licence would be necessary.[6] The Netherlands has also investigated mergers aimed at creating 'integrated care', whereby multidisciplinary 'care groups' come together to offer diagnostic services, primary care, and pharmacy services, along with hospital care, particularly for management of long-term health problems such as diabetes. From the point of view of the health needs of groups of particularly vulnerable patients, such multidisciplinary care packages offer quality of care. Organizing health care on such a basis promotes the value of equality of treatment for those groups of patients. From the point of view of social health insurance provision, they offer value for money, through the ability to negotiate on price, and through efficiencies by offering 'joined up care'. Organizing health care on such a basis thus also promotes the value of solidarity. But from the point of view of market structure, such arrangements can constitute anti-competitive mergers, and the Netherlands is apparently considering reintroducing a ban

---

[3] Bundeskartellamt, 'Bundeskartellamt obtains reversal of merger between the University Hospital of Tübingen and Zollernalb District' (*Bundeskartellamt*, 14 May 2009).

[4] For instance, the German Federal Court of Justice has confirmed the Competition Authority's merger control practice in the hospital sector, see: Bundeskartellamt, 'Federal Court of Justice confirms merger control practice in the hospital sector' (*Bundeskartellamt*, 17 January 2008).

[5] Netherlands Competition Authority (NMa), 'NMa blocks merger of health care providers in central Netherlands' (NMa, 20 December 2011).

[6] Netherlands Competition Authority (NMa), 'NMa says proposed hospital merger in western Netherlands requires a license' (NMa, 14 February 2012).

on 'vertical integration' where a health insurer merges with a hospital.[7] Advice from the King's Fund has suggested that application of merger rules should not undermine the provision of integrated care in the English context,[8] following the introduction of 'Health and Wellbeing Boards' under the Health and Social Care Act 2012.

In addition, the Netherlands Competition Authority has investigated exchange of information between hospitals, for compliance with anti-cartel law. Following tip-offs from patients and an investigative report by local radio, the Competition Authority carried out unannounced dawn raids at two Amsterdam-based hospitals. The allegation that the hospitals were refusing patients access solely based on their postcodes, and thus unlawfully sharing the market through collusive behaviour, was not supported by the evidence, but the Authority found that there had been inappropriate sharing of competition-sensitive information between the hospitals.[9] These kinds of collusive behaviour may become more common now that the Netherlands has lifted its ban on for-profit hospitals,[10] thus potentially opening a route for challenging provisions or arrangements that are aimed at equal access to health care according to need, in the context of needing to contain costs where funding is undertaken through solidarity mechanisms, such as variants of social insurance.

However, the use of EU competition law to challenge arrangements for hospitals is not necessarily straightforward, even in Member States which have gone as far as the Netherlands in terms of liberalization of hospital care. Marco Varkevisser et al. explain how the application of different possible approaches to defining hospital markets to the Netherlands context gave widely differing results as to what the relevant market is and whether a particular hospital might be dominant on the market.[11] In terms of the product market (the least controversial element), although a generally accepted definition is 'a broad group of medical and surgical diagnostic and treatment services for acute medical conditions where the patient must remain in a health care facility for at least 24 hours for recovery or observation',[12] arguments can be made for and against the inclusion of outpatient care within the relevant market. In terms of the geographical market, in an investigation into a merger between two general hospitals, the Netherlands Competition Authority considered patient preferences (both stated and revealed).

---

[7]   Den Exter and Guy, 'Market Competition in Health Care Markets in the Netherlands: Some lessons for England?' (2014) 22(2) *Medical Law Review* 255.

[8]   Ham and Walsh, 'Making Integrated Care Happen at Scale and Pace' (The King's Fund 2013).

[9]   NMa, 'NMa confirms investigation into two Amsterdam-based hospitals' (*NMa*, 11 February 2010); and NMa, 'Amsterdam-based hospitals to adjust their information exchange processes after NMa investigation' (*NMa*, 4 January 2011).

[10] Den Exter and Guy, above n 7.

[11] Varkevisser, Capps and Schut 'Defining hospital markets for antitrust enforcement : new approaches and their applicability to The Netherlands' (2008) 3(1) *Health Economics Policy and Law* 7.

[12] US Department of Justice and US Federal Trade Commission, 'Improving Health Care: A Dose of Competition' (US DoJ and US FTC 2004).

Article 106 (2) TFEU limits the application of competition law in the case of 'undertakings entrusted with the operation of services of general ... interest'. Hospitals – if they are 'undertakings' at all – fall within that category of 'undertakings'. So, for instance, in 2011 the Netherlands Ministry of Health concluded an Agreement with various health stakeholders with the aim of containing costs through 'high volume contracting'. The idea is to allow insurers to limit and concentrate the volume of hospital care, through specific arrangements with a limited number of hospitals. These are intended to increase quality of care, even though there is no clear evidence that high-volume contracting improves health outcomes. The Agreement was challenged by hospitals which were not selected, but the challenge was unsuccessful.[13] Competition law does not apply to 'undertakings entrusted with the operation of services of general ... interest', where, as in this case, the application of competition law obstructs the performance of the tasks assigned to those undertakings.[14]

Similarly, the EU's state aids law is modified when it applies to hospitals. Since the 'Altmark package', hospitals have an explicit exemption from the application of state aids law, and this has been extended by the 'Alumnia package'[15] to health and long-term care more generally. This exemption applies *only* where a hospital is 'entrusted' with providing a service of general interest, and the compensation which it is given for so doing does not exceed what is required by the needs of an efficient undertaking. These requirements mean there is scope for oversight of arrangements through the lens of EU law. In the *IRIS-H* case,[16] payments to certain hospitals in Brussels (known as the IRIS hospitals) under a system, where the metropolitan authorities paid for services to patients who presented themselves, regardless of degree of medical emergency, or the patient's social situation or ability to pay, were regarded as state aid, but the 'Altmark condition' of appropriate compensation was not met. The European Commission nonetheless considered the system to be justified as necessary and proportionate to provide a service of general interest.[17] But the General Court found, on review of the decision, that there were 'serious doubts' as to whether there was a clearly defined hospital services mandate entrusted specifically to the IRIS hospitals, whether the parameters for compensation for services were appropriately defined, and whether sufficiently robust procedures for avoiding over-compensation were in place. The hospital sector is scrutinized for compliance with EU competition and state aids law. However, the scrutiny is relatively light touch. So, for instance, the General Court dismissed an earlier judicial review claim brought by private German hospitals complaining that

---

[13] District Court Breda 23 November 2010, LNJ BO4755, cited in Den Exter and Guy, above n 7, 266.

[14] Article 106 (2) TFEU.   [15] Decision 2012/21/EU [2012] OJ L7/3, Article 2 (1) (b) and (c).

[16] *CBI*, T-137/10, EU:T:2012:584.

[17] Decision C(2009) 8120 of 28 October 2009, concerning State aid NN 54/09 implemented by the Kingdom of Belgium for the financing of the public hospitals of the IRIS network in the Région Bruxelles-Capitale.

the Commission should have taken proceedings against a number of public hospitals said to be in receipt of state aids, in the form of unlimited guarantees.[18] The matter was covered by the provisions in the 'Altmark' package on services of general interest.

In terms of free movement law, and its effects on individual patient choice, we have already noted how both CJEU case law and EU legislation gives a special position to the care provided by hospitals. The CJEU has confirmed that, in principle, free movement law applies to hospital care.[19] If carried to its logical extreme, on a *systemic* level, the reasoning in cases such as *Kohll* and *Watts*[20] would mean that individual patients exercising their 'right' to choose health services in other Member States would cause significant disruption to hospital provision. Such disruption was feared by the early commentators on those cases,[21] who expected cataclysmic impacts on the stability and internal balance of national health systems, and the viability of their goals to provide equal access to health care, according to medical need, on the basis of solidarity. Because Member States calculate their health care needs by reference to their populations, the rulings were expected to have detrimental effects on planning and capacity maintenance, particularly in the hospital sector, as the unpredictability of influxes and effluxes of patients made effective planning impossible. Too much movement of patients, it was feared, would lead to the over-burdening of some hospitals, and the corresponding under-use of others, leading to closures. Use of 'waiting lists' and other cost control measures designed to ensure access to hospital care for those with the greatest medical need, in the context of a system with limited resources, would be undermined. Because the patients who can move tend to be the healthier and wealthier patients, all of these consequences were expected to have a negative effect on equality and solidarity.

But EU free movement law has recognized the special place of hospitals within health systems. While in principle freedom to receive and provide services applies to services provided in hospitals, so long as 'remuneration' is present, the special nature of the hospital sector, the need for planning and the possible significant disruption to the organization and financing of national social security systems mean that Member States may justify measures that are technically restrictive of free movement.[22] The Patients' Rights Directive permits Member States to require prior authorization for cross border healthcare which:

---

[18] *Asklepios Kliniken*, T-167/04, EU:T:2007:215.

[19] *Smits/Peerbooms*, C-157/99, EU:C:2001:404.

[20] *Kohll*, C-158/96, EU:C:1998:171; *Watts*, C-372/04, EU:C:2006:325.

[21] See discussion, and references in: Hervey and McHale, *Health Law and the European Union* (CUP 2004) 138-144.

[22] *Smits/Peerbooms* EU:C:2001:404, paragraphs 76-82; *Müller-Fauré/Van Riet*, C-385/99, EU:C:2003:270, paragraphs 67-71 and 76-83; *Inizan*, C-56/01, EU:C:2003:578, paragraph 56; *Watts* EU:C:2006:325, paragraphs 102-110; *Stamatelaki*, C-444/05, EU:C:2007:231, paragraphs 31-32; *Major Medical Equipment*, C-512/08, EU:C:2010:579. See further: chapter 4.

(a) is made subject to planning requirements relating to the object of ensuring sufficient and permanent access to a balanced range of high-quality treatment in the Member State concerned or to the wish to control costs and avoid, as far as possible, any waste of financial, technical and human resources and: (i) involves overnight accommodation of the patient in question for at least one night.[23]

The CJEU's case law, and now the Directive, distinguish between hospital (and other expensive) care, and outpatient care. The significant negative systemic effects for hospitals predicted from the CJEU's early patient mobility case law have been averted, both by the CJEU itself in its more recent case law, and by the EU legislature. EU health law recognizes the special place of hospitals in health systems, and even where Member States have moved towards the neoliberal end of the spectrum, this special place is still accommodated. The legal concept of 'service of general interest' is the main route through which this protection is achieved.

Pharmacies

Across the EU, there is a range of approaches to the regulation and control of pharmacies as part of the health system. Regulation can be through any or all of the following: control of entry to the profession of pharmacist; control of establishment criteria, including licensing, concessions and geographical restrictions; restrictions on ownership of pharmacies; restrictions on terms of trade, such as opening hours, mandatory product range; risk equalization schemes between pharmacies; and control of pharmacies' profit and retail prices. Some Member States, such as Ireland, the Netherlands, Sweden and the UK, have moved toward less restrictive regulation of pharmacies, drawing on consumer choice justifications and introducing more competition-led models within the market.

In the mid-1990s, there was little attention to the pharmacy sector from EU law.[24] But by the mid-2000s this had changed. One particular area of pharmacy regulation that has been under strong reform pressure, including from EU law, is the restriction on sale of non-prescription-only ('over-the-counter') pharmaceuticals. A 2009 report of the Estonian Competition Authority[25] suggests that over-the-counter pharmaceuticals may lawfully be sold outside pharmacies in Bulgaria, Netherlands, Poland, Sweden, Germany, Finland, Denmark, Czech Republic, Hungary and the UK. The Authority found that, since the only reason given for restricting sale of such products to pharmacies was the need for advice to be given by a pharmacist, but that in practice consumers were purchasing

---

[23] Directive 2011/24/EU [2011] OJ L88/45, Article 8 (2) (a) (i).
[24] See, for a rare example: *Infant Formula*, C-391/92, EU:C:1995:199,where the relevant rules were found to be outside the scope of EU law.
[25] Estonian Competition Authority, 'Annual Report 2009' (Estonian Competition Authority 2009) 19–21.

over-the-counter pharmaceuticals in pharmacies without consulting pharmacists, there was no justification for continuing with the anti-competitive policy. They called for the opening up of pharmaceutical sales to the supermarket sector, expecting significant price decreases for consumers as a consequence. Comparisons with practice in other Member States were used to support this recommendation.

The German Competition Authority has taken action against collusive behaviour of pharmacies, and associations of pharmacists and pharmaceutical manufacturers,[26] seeking to retain the benefits of price controls, removed when that aspect of the sector was liberalized in early 2004. For instance, when a discount pharmacy announced plans to open in the Hildesheim area in late 2006/early 2007, about fifty pharmacies based in that area, through a joint advertising group, advertised joint prices for selected over-the-counter medicines, to seek to make market entry difficult or impossible for the new pharmacy, and prevent price competition within the market. This was found to be an unjustified violation of anti-cartel law.[27] In France, behaviour of the *Ordre national des pharmaciens* in hindering the development of groups of clinical biology laboratories and imposition of minimum prices was the subject of an investigation by the European Commission, which imposed a significant fine.[28] Competition law has been used to attack legislative proposals[29] that would have reversed the liberalization process for the 'parapharmacy' sector in Italy.[30] Parapharmacies offer a range of health care and personal hygiene-associated products, including phytotherapy and dietary supplements, and over-the-counter medicines, with their core business focusing around dermo-cosmetic and nutritional supplement brands. This example shows how competition law can play a 'one-way street' role, once a Member State chooses to liberalize an aspect of its health system.

Scrutiny of arrangements for the sale by pharmacies of *prescription* medicines for compliance with competition law has also taken place. In Ireland, this has focused around the terms on which pharmacies contract with the Health Service

---

[26] See: e.g. Bundeskartellamt, 'Bundeskartellamt imposes fines against pharmacist associations and manufacturers of pharmaceuticals for asking pharmacists to observe non-binding price recommendations of manufacturers' (*Bundeskartellamt*, 8 January 2008) reporting fines totalling 465,000 euros against nine Land pharmacist associations, the Federal Association of Pharmaceutical Manufacturers (BAH) and five pharmaceuticals manufacturers.

[27] Bundeskartellamt, (2008) above n 26.

[28] Commission Decision of 8 December 2010 on a proceeding under Article 101 TFEU (Case COMP/39.510 EU:T:2014:1049. See further below).

[29] Just one example is Proposed amendment no. 1,206 to Decree Law No 225 of 29 December 2010, Gazzetta Ufficiale della Repubblica Italiana, Serie generale No 303, 29.12.2010 (a.k.a. milleproroghe - the annual decree extending the life of various measures), the Antitrust Authority has blown the whistle on proposed amendments that were intended to nullify the effects of liberalization and, in particular, to block the opening of new sales points by making the process more difficult or to create a sort of 'personnel plan' for parapharmacies.

[30] Autorità Garante della Concorrenza e del Mercato (AGCM), 'Milleproroghe Decree: Antitrust Authority – No To Amendments Blocking New Parapharmacies' (*AGCM*, 3 February 2011).

Executive. Until 2007, this had involved negotiation over prices, but in 2007 the Health Service Executive unilaterally altered the arrangements, announcing that to continue to negotiate in this respect would breach competition law. Unsurprisingly, many pharmacies and their professional association (the Irish Pharmacy Union) objected to this, and threatened a collective withdrawal of their services. Although the Competition Authority took the view[31] that the requirement to consult did not in itself constitute an anti-competitive agreement,[32] they also found that an agreement between the pharmacies to withdraw services would be likely to be in breach of competition law.[33]

The CJEU upheld restrictions on sale of prescription-only medicines in pharmacies in Germany in the first *DocMorris* case in 2003.[34] The relevant German law (the Arzneimittelgesetz 1998) prohibited the sale by mail order, and associated advertising, of medicinal products which may be sold only in pharmacies. DocMorris, a company established in the Netherlands, and situated near the German border, operated as a pharmacy in accordance with Netherlands law, and also operated a mail order pharmaceutical business. DocMorris's website was clearly targeted at the German market, as it had a prominent German language version. A German pharmacists association challenged DocMorris's activities for breaching German law. DocMorris's defence was that EU law on free movement of goods (Article 30 TFEU) applied. The CJEU made two key distinctions in its ruling. The first was between medicines authorized for sale in Germany and those not so authorized.[35] With regard to the latter, the Arzneimittelgesetz was ensuring that Germany was compliant with EU law on the authorization of pharmaceuticals marketing. It therefore fell outside the scope of the Treaty rules on free movement of goods. The second distinction made by the CJEU was between over-the-counter and prescription-only pharmaceuticals. The CJEU found that the Arzneimittelgesetz constituted a restriction on free movement of goods, because it was more of an obstacle to pharmacies outside Germany than to those within it.[36] Noting national discretion to ensure protection of public health,[37] the CJEU considered whether

---

[31] Applying the *Italian Lawyers* principle, see: *Arduino*, C-35/99, EU:C:2002:97; *Cipolla*, C-94/04 and C-202/04, EU:C:2006:758, paragraph 46: 'Although Article [101 TFEU] is, in itself, concerned solely with the conduct of undertakings and not with laws or regulations emanating from Member States, that article, read in conjunction with Article [4 (3) TEU], nonetheless requires the Member States not to introduce or maintain in force measures, even of a legislative or regulatory nature, which may render ineffective the competition rules applicable to undertakings.'

[32] Confirmed by the Irish High Court in: *Hickey* [2008] IEHC 373.

[33] The Competition Authority, '*Notice in Respect of Collective Action in the Community Pharmacy Sector*' (*The Competition Authority*, 23 September 2009) >; Decision No. N/09/001, The Competition Authority 2009) 17. N.B. The Competition Authority is not the decision-making body for competition law purposes in Ireland – the courts are. It issues only guidance and its considered opinion on the application of competition law in this context.

[34] *DocMorris*, C-322/01, EU:C:2003:664.

[35] All medicinal products marketed in the EU must have an appropriate marketing authorization, Directive 2001/83/EC [2001] OJ L311/67, Article 6 (1). See further chapter 13.

[36] *DocMorris*, EU:C:2003:664, paragraph 74.   [37] *DocMorris*, EU:C:2003:664, paragraph,103.

this restriction was justified by 'the need to provide individual advice to the customer and to ensure his protection when he is supplied with medicines and . . . the need to check that prescriptions are genuine', given the inherently dangerous nature of pharmaceuticals.[38] For over-the-counter medicines, the prohibition of mail order sales was not justified. But, for prescription-only medicines, the greater risks attaching to their misuse meant that the German rules were permissible.

In terms of pharmacy ownership rules, the European Commission began infringement proceedings in the mid-2000s, against several Member States, for various aspects of their national legislation, including ownership rules and limits on the choice of legal form, but also discriminatory licensing provisions, territorial planning provisions, limits on number of pharmacies in a geographical area and minimum distance between them. But the European Commission was largely unsuccessful. In the case of German rules, the effect of which was to ensure that a hospital was supplied from a locally situated pharmacy, the CJEU held that any restriction on free movement was justified.[39] The CJEU referred to similar reasoning to that noted above about the need to plan the number, geographical distribution and organization of hospitals, both to protect public health and to ensure prudent use of financial, technical and human resources in the hospital sector.[40] In principle,

> although the Community rules on the free movement of goods do not require that it should be possible for all hospitals situated in the Member States to obtain supplies of medicinal products from external pharmacies, when a Member State provides for such a possibility, it opens that activity to the market and is accordingly bound by Community rules.[41]

But, in practice, although the national rules were subject to scrutiny for compliance with EU law, the need to protect public health, and to secure efficient use of public resources in the hospital sector, were respected by EU health law. Similarly, in the case of Italian rules restricting ownership of pharmacies to qualified pharmacists, the CJEU found that any restrictions on free movement (freedom of establishment, Articles 49 and 54 TFEU or free movement of capital, Article 63 TFEU) were justified. Again, the CJEU referred to the national discretion to protect public health, the inherently dangerous nature of pharmaceuticals, and also to the need to secure solidarity-based mechanisms of social insurance. The CJEU drew a direct link between the Member State's financial resources deployed to run its health system and the profits of pharmacies, because in most Member States the cost of prescription-only medicines is borne by the national health system.[42] In 2009, the CJEU considered the compatibility with

---

[38] *DocMorris* EU:C:2003:664, paragraphs 7-8.
[39] *Hospital Pharmacies*, C-141/07, EU:C:2008:492, paragraphs 61-63.
[40] Citing *Smits/Peerbooms* EU:C:2001:404, paragraphs 76-80; *Müller-Fauré/van Riet*, EU:C:2003:270, paragraphs 77-80; *Watts* EU:C:2006:325, paragraphs 108-109.
[41] *Hospital Pharmacies*, EU:C:2008:492, paragraph 41.
[42] *Pharmacies*, C-531/06, EU:C:2009:315, paragraph 57.

EU free movement law of a German rule that pharmacies must not only be run, but also be owned, by an independent and qualified pharmacist.[43] There was no question that the rule constituted a *prima facie* breach of Articles 49 and 54 TFEU on freedom of establishment. Referring to the earlier *DocMorris* case,[44] and the discretion Member States enjoy in terms of public health protection, the CJEU noted that it is permissible to restrict free movement to ensure that 'the provision of medicinal products to the public is reliable and of good quality'.[45] The rule was justified because it was necessary to protect public health, as well as to secure the financial stability of the national health system.

Similarly, the need to ensure reliable provision of good quality pharmaceuticals justified Spanish rules on geographical disbursement of pharmacies which restricted freedom of establishment.[46] The relevant rules provided that pharmacies could be opened only by qualified pharmacists, who were accredited to open a pharmacy. Accreditation was based on system designed to limit the number of pharmacies by reference to population and to make sure that pharmacies were not opened within 250 metres of another pharmacy. A points system operated by which accreditation decisions were made. This gave more points for professional experience in small towns. The rules were challenged by Spanish pharmacists seeking to open new pharmacies as breaching EU law on freedom of establishment (Article 49 TFEU). In principle, in such a 'wholly internal situation', where Spanish pharmacists challenge Spanish law, there is no cross-border element in the case, and so one would expect that EU free movement law is not at issue. However, the Court found that the Spanish legislation was a restriction on the freedom of establishment, by reference to a *hypothetical* pharmacist from another Member State.[47] This raises significantly the opportunity for EU law to be used in what is essentially internal litigation, where individuals (or, more likely, companies) seek to challenge all sorts of national regulatory rules whose rationale is the organization and structuring of a national health system. But the CJEU is sensitive both to the 'wholly internal situation' point,[48] but more especially to the place of pharmacies within national health systems, allowing Member States to justify policies which are restrictive of free trade, but which protect public health and the national health system.

The CJEU has followed its reasoning in several further cases on similar points.[49] As is the case with hospitals, the special place of pharmacies, and the

---

[43] *Neumann-Siewert*, C-171/07 and C-172/07, EU:C:2009:316.
[44] *DocMorris* EU:C:2003:664, paragraph 103.
[45] *Neumann-Siewert*, EU:C:2009:316, paragraph 28.
[46] *Pérez/Gómez*, C-570/07 and C-571/07, EU:C:2010:300.
[47] *Pérez/Gómez* EU:C:2010:300, paragraphs 39-40.
[48] See, e.g: Sbarigia, C-393/08, EU:C:2010:388.
[49] *Venturini*, C-159/12, C-160/12 and C-161/12, EU:C:2013:791; *Susisalo* , C-84/11, EU:C:2012:374.

pharmacists who own, run and operate within them, is recognized by EU health law. This recognition is also found in the CEJU's interpretation of the scope of the obligations on Member States to recognize pharmacists' qualifications.[50] The CJEU constructs pharmacists as not simply economic actors, intent on pursuing profit maximization, but also as public servants, with a duty to their patients flowing from their professional status and expectations of professionally based ethical conduct:

> It is undeniable that an operator having the status of pharmacist pursues, like other persons, the objective of making a profit. However, as a pharmacist by profession, he is presumed to operate the pharmacy not with a purely economic objective, but also from a professional viewpoint. His private interest connected with the making of a profit is thus tempered by his training, by his professional experience and by the responsibility which he owes, given that any breach of the rules of law or professional conduct undermines not only the value of his investment but also his own professional existence.[51]

Another area of pharmacy regulation that has been under some pressure concerns regulation of trading rules, in particular opening hours. For instance, the Belgian Supreme Court has considered a local pharmacists' association rule that fixed mandatory opening hours for pharmacies. A pharmacist breaching the rule by opening on Saturdays was sanctioned by the association, and argued in his defence that the rule breached competition law. The Court held that the association was an undertaking, so was subject to competition law, even though it was also obliged to ensure 'the administration of health care'.[52] However, the CJEU found inadmissible a claim brought before it challenging Italian law concerning opening hours for pharmacies for consistency with EU competition and free movement law.[53]

Arrangements reflecting the public service nature of the pharmacy sector, such as the Danish insolvency scheme (in force from 1998 to 2004), have been respected by competition authorities. The scheme, involving an agreement between the Danish Pharmaceutical Association and the three and only pharmaceutical wholesalers on the Danish market, sought to make sure that insolvent pharmacies could consolidate and settle their debts, while continuing to operate. The wholesalers agreed to supply to insolvent pharmacies on their usual credit terms, and, in return, the pharmacies were not allowed to switch

---

[50] See: e.g. *McCauley Chemists*, C-221/05, EU:C:2006:474 where the CJEU declined to allow the mutual recognition of qualifications legislation to be used to undermine national rules regulating the establishing of new pharmacies. On the mutual recognition of professional qualifications, see chapter 6.

[51] *Neumann-Siewert*, EU:C:2009:316, paragraph 37.

[52] Ballet, 'The Belgian Supreme Court held that obligatory opening and closing hours for pharmacists violate the Competition Act' (2006) *e-Competitions Law Bulletin* No. 15370, cited Lear, Mossialos and Karl, above n 1, 354.

[53] *Sbragia* EU:C:2010:388.

between suppliers during the period in which they were covered by the scheme.[54] The Danish Competition Appeals Tribunal, agreed that such an arrangement involved anti-competitive market sharing, but found that there was insufficient evidence to support the assertion that the market sharing agreement had actually had a negative impact on the market.[55]

Similarly, the Netherlands Competition Authority did not find that a group of pharmacies which had participated in an electronic filing system, including patient information, thus sharing considerable market power, had breached the anti-cartel rules, because efficiency and services to patients were significantly improved through the agreement.[56]

In addition to scrutiny of anti-competitive behaviours, competition authorities in some Member States have also been involved in sectoral enquiries that have supported calls for greater liberalization of the pharmacy sector. The UK Office of Fair Trading[57] reported in March 2010 that reforms in 2005, liberalizing the market, had increased consumer choice, provided pharmacy services for extended periods of time, shortened travel times and waiting times for patients. Access to lower-priced over-the-counter medicines has also improved. The OFT claimed that the changes 'have led to new pharmacies opening and greater competition in the market, stimulating improvement to services and delivering significant benefits. None of the feared ill-effects to consumers have so far materialised.'[58] These reforms followed a 2003 market study carried out by the Office of Fair Trading.

The Danish Competition and Consumer Authority's sectoral enquiry into pharmacies reaches more cautious conclusions, in particular a need for further investigation.[59] The Authority found that pharmacy regulation in Denmark is anti-competitive, in that it restrains entrance to the market, excludes price competition and provides no incentives for pharmacies to compete on

---

[54] If, for instance, a pharmacy had shared its purchases between two wholesalers on a 40/60 % basis, it was not allowed to deviate from this allocation.

[55] Danish Competition and Consumer Authority, 'Decision by the Danish Competition Appeals Tribunal: The insolvency scheme of the pharmaceutical sector' (*Danish Competition and Consumer Authority*, 8 June 2007); Lear, Mossialos and Karl, above n 1, 352; Defossez, 'The Danish Competition Council found an insolvency agreement between three medical wholesale dealers and the Danish Pharmaceutical Association to be incompatible with Art. 81 EC and relevant national competition law provision' (2005) *Bulletin e-Competitions Healthcare* Art. N° 24451.

[56] Lear, Mossialos and Karl, above n 1, 359-60. But it was found that the pharmacies had abused their dominant position because new pharmacies were arbitrarily excluded from the scheme. The case settled when the pharmacies adopted some proper admission rules, with objective and transparent criteria and a procedure for appeal.

[57] The competition functions of the UK OFT were taken over by the UK Competition and Markets Authority in April 2014, see: Competition and Markets Authority (CMA), 'New competition authority comes into existence' (*CMA*, 1 October 2013).

[58] Office of Fair Trading (OFT), 'Consumers benefit from pharmacy liberalisation' (*OFT*, 22 March 2010).

[59] Danish Competition and Consumer Authority, 'Regulation of Pharmacies' (*Danish Competition and Consumer Authority*, 23 February 2010).

service(s). A number of ensuing 'inefficiencies' were highlighted, such as long waiting times (in urban areas) and inefficient operations in terms of profits (in rural areas). However, the report stresses the need for strong public regulation of pharmacies, in order to protect public safety, quality in the distribution of pharmaceuticals, equality of access to medicines for citizens, and control of public health expenditure. Interestingly, the Competition Authority noted (unfavourable) comparisons with other EU countries, in terms of number of inhabitants per pharmacy. The Authority recommended some deregulation, to increase efficiency,[60] but with care not to compromise quality, safety and equal accessibility.

Laboratories

Relationships between biomedical laboratories providing diagnostic and investigative services to other health care institutions, in particular hospitals, within some Member States of the EU, have been subject to challenge recently for breach of EU free movement law. It seems that the market in laboratory services in the health care field is undergoing some significant changes, as larger international companies seek to exploit economies of scale by breaking into previously fragmented small markets, operating on national or local bases. The opportunities for economies of scale if the European market in biomedical analysis were to be realized are significant,[61] and the area of biomedical analysis, particularly in the context of new genetic technologies, is an area of interest to the European Commission in seeking to develop the EU's economy in the context of the Eurozone crisis and global economic recession.

National measures, similar to those which apply to hospitals and pharmacies, which keep biomedical laboratories within the solidarity-based health system, pull against this aim of capturing the benefits of free trade and effective competition. In 2004, the CJEU held that French rules requiring biomedical laboratories to have their 'seat of establishment' in France breached freedom of establishment and free movement of services measure and were not justified.[62] But the CJEU had recognized the need to regulate biomedical laboratories, as part of the health system,[63] and in any event has softened its approach in more recent rulings. As was the case with pharmacies, ownership rules were at issue in a 2010 case in which the European Commission challenged French

---

[60] In particular, the Authority recommends repealing the profit equalization scheme and promoting freer entry to the market, by repealing the ownership restrictions and the requirement that the manager must be a qualified pharmacist.

[61] The European market for clinical laboratory testing services has been estimated at €25 billion, see *Ordre National des Pharmaciens* EU:T:2014:1049.

[62] *Biomedical Laboratories 1*, C-496/01, EU:C:2004:137.

[63] *Clinical Biology Laboratories*, C-221/85, EU:C:1987:81. Belgian law provided that clinical biology services could be reimbursed under the national health system only if the laboratory in question is operated by a qualified doctor or pharmacist, or if a for-profit company, its members, partners or directors are doctors or pharmacists.

rules excluding those who are not professional biologists from owning more than 25 per cent of shares in laboratories undertaking biomedical analysis, and a prohibition on holding shares in more than two companies operating jointly one or more such laboratories.[64] The CJEU found a restriction on freedom of establishment (Article 49 TFEU). The French rules make it difficult, or even impossible, for companies established and operating laboratories in other Member States, which do not meet the share capital criteria required in France, to set up in France.[65] On the question of justification, however, the CJEU found that the sector is 'special' and that a parallel should be drawn between the service of biomedical analysis and that of a pharmacist supplying medicines.[66] The negative consequences from incorrect or inappropriate performance of biomedical analyses, both for health of the patients concerned and for the social welfare system, mean that Member States may lawfully maintain such measures. The European Commission failed to show that other measures, such as quality management, would be a more proportionate response.

EU competition law has also been applied to such relationships. The French *Ordre national des pharmaciens* (pharmacy and biomedical laboratory industry association) was fined for price fixing, contrary to anti-cartel rules,[67] in the same year as the free movement case noted above.[68] The anti-competitive agreements included blocking price discounts of over 10 per cent, and keeping outsiders from acquiring capital in the relevant firms. The result was prices for biomedical laboratory testing services were two or three times higher in France than in other Member States. The General Court upheld the Commission Decision, pointing out that the *Ordre national des pharmaciens* does not have sufficient regulatory powers to fall outside of the concept of an 'undertaking'.[69] The various measures that the *Ordre national des pharmaciens* had used to exclude groups of laboratory companies, operating in France and elsewhere in the EU, from the market, and to impose minimum prices, breached EU anti-cartel rules. Scrutiny of the precise nature of the market was crucial to a merger control decision of the German Competition Authority clearing the acquisition of a company offering clinical laboratory services by the international medical diagnostics company Sonic Healthcare Ltd.[70] The Competition Authority defined the relevant product

---

[64] *Biomedical Laboratories 2*, C-89/09, EU:C:2010:772.

[65] *Biomedical Laboratories 2* EU:C:2010:772, paragraph 47. See also: *Laboratory Analyses and Tests*, C-490/09, EU:C:2011:34 concerning reimbursement for laboratory treatments under a national social security scheme.

[66] *Biomedical Laboratories 2* EU:C:2010:772, paragraph 56.

[67] Commission Decision of 8 December 2010 on a proceeding under Article 101 TFEU (CASE COMP/39.510 – LABCO / ONP) (C(2010)8952.

[68] Hancher and Sauter note that 'the corporatist arrangements involved were not innocuous', Hancher and Sauter, *EU Competition and Internal Market Law in the Healthcare Sector* (OUP 2012) 105.

[69] *Ordre National des Pharmaciens* T-90/11 EU:T:2014:1049.

[70] Bundeskartellamt, 'Clearance of two laboratory acquisitions: Sonic Healthcare/Lademannbogen and BC Partners/ Futurelab' (Bundeskartellamt 2010).

market for outpatient clinical laboratory services as comprising general as well as special laboratory services provided for general practitioners and other senders such as hospitals. This market covers the laboratory services provided to third parties by special laboratory practices, medical centres and hospital laboratories. Other laboratory services, for instance, those provided by the treating general practitioners themselves or within a hospital, on the other hand, are not part of the relevant product market. Where independent laboratories provide services which have been outsourced by hospitals, these also do not belong to the product market for outpatient clinical laboratory services. The Competition Authority thus drew on the distinction between 'inpatient' and 'outpatient' care in reaching its decision, reconfirming the special place of hospitals in EU health law.

That said, activities of hospitals in seeking to dominate markets in laboratory services, by effectively excluding private operators, are potentially subject to competition law. In 2003, the Finnish Competition Authority investigated public hospitals which had expanded into providing private laboratory services, offered at below market rates. This was found to be unlawful abusive behaviour. The Competition Authority pointed out that the 'marketization' (in this context, privatization and liberalization) of a public service requires competition authorities to make sure that private companies are able to compete in the field that used to be supplied only by the public sector.[71] In general, however, in this field as with the others we have discussed so far, the Commission and the CJEU, as well as national competition authorities 'tread carefully' around national institutional arrangements.[72]

Blood and human tissue centres

We have already noted the unilateral decision of six umbilical cord blood storage companies to alter their marketing material in response to an investigation by the Italian Antitrust Authority in 2011.[73] The Maltese National Blood Transfusion Centre was also subject to censure by the competition authority,[74] when it abused its dominant position in the market for blood and blood products.[75] The National Blood Transfusion Centre had indeed been entrusted with a service of general economic interest (that is, the collection and management of blood and blood products). But because the National Blood Transfusion

[71] Finnish Competition Authority, 'Finish Competition Authority Yearbook 2003' (Finish Competition Authority Yearbook 2003). cited in Lear, Mossialos and Karl, above n 1, 47.
[72] Hancher and Sauter, above n 68, 234-5.
[73] See: AGCM, 'Umbilical cord preservation: Antitrust intervenes to change the advertising messages of six companies' (*AGCM*, 24 October 2011).
[74] Then the Office for Competition; since May 2011, the Malta Competition and Consumer Affairs Authority.
[75] Lear, Mossialos and Karl, above n 1, 364-5; Case Comment, 'Malta, Abuse of Dominant Position, Blood' (2007) 28 *European Competition Law Review* 120.

Centre was required by law to commercialize the distribution of its products, it was competing on the market for such products with private enterprises. It is established law that Member States may not lawfully grant an undertaking the power to regulate, or to set standards, in a market in which that undertaking also competes.[76]

Attempts by private actors to use the health/human tissue, organs, blood exemptions in the EU's VAT legislation have failed. In a case concerning the VAT Directive,[77] the CJEU held that a *private* stem cell bank holding umbilical cord blood is not a 'hospital, centre for medical treatment or diagnosis' or similar body. It is thus subject to VAT, like any other private service provider.[78] A self-employed person who transports human organs and samples for hospitals is also subject to VAT.[79] The service concerned is the transportation and the fact that national law prohibits trade in human organs was thus irrelevant.[80]

Dental clinics

Of course, the *Kohll* case[81] on free movement of services involved a dental clinic. The implications of that ruling, to the effect that cross-border patients in a social insurance system should be entitled to access dental clinics in other Member States to receive dental services could, if extended to all contexts, have significant effects for national health systems. However, dental clinics are among the part of the health sector within EU health systems that is often covered by the supplementary private insurance market, as many dental treatments do not fall within the 'basket of care' covered by public health systems. Moreover, several central European Member States, in particular Hungary, have developed reputations for high-quality dental services, and, on joining the European Union, have sought access to consumers of dental care and treatment in Western Member States, in particular targeting Germany, Austria and the UK. Some of these patients are being paid for by the social insurance system; others by private insurance.

An attempt in 2008 to overturn national rules prohibiting the advertising of dental services using EU competition law was unsuccessful.[82] The relevant EU law provides that if a Member State's regulatory arrangements require or even encourage cartel-like behaviour contrary to Article 101 TFEU, these arrangements breach EU law,[83] and private parties are exempt from liability

---

[76]   *RTT*, C-18/88, EU:C:1991:474.

[77]   Directive 77/388/EEC [1977] OJ L145/1, now Directive 2006/112/EC [2006] OJ L347/1.

[78]   *CopyGene*, C-262/08, EU:C:2010:328; *Future Health*, C-86/09, EU:C:2010:334.

[79]   *De Fruytier*, C-237/09, EU:C:2010:316.

[80]   On the shifting notions of blood and human tissue banks in European contexts, see: Busby, 'Trust, Nostalgia and Narrative Accounts of Blood Banking in England in the 21st century' (2010) 14 (4) *Health* 369.

[81]   *Kohll* EU:C:1998:171.   [82]   *Doulamis*, C-446/05, EU:C:2008:157.

[83]   Under the 'duty of sincere cooperation', Article 4 (3) TEU.

under competition law.[84] A Belgian dentist relied on EU law in his defence in criminal proceedings for breaching the national rules prohibiting advertising of dental services. In a short judgment, the CJEU rejected the idea that there was any link between the national rules and anti-competitive behaviour.[85]

We might expect that the parts of the dental sector that are not covered by private insurance would not be subject to scrutiny for compliance with EU competition law. After all, substitutive private insurance does not fall within EU law, and provision of health services without the involvement of any 'undertakings' likewise fall outside its scope. However, the UK's Office of Fair Trading announced in September 2011 that it would begin an investigation of the dental sector – to include *both* private *and* NHS dental care.[86] The terms of reference of this OFT investigation would seem to be a recognition that, *de facto*, dental care is not within the traditional structures of the English NHS, but that it is offered throughout the UK system by 'undertakings' operating on the market. Interestingly, the OFT notes that unfavourable comparison with prices for dental care with the rest of the EU are part of the rationale for the study. The OFT reported in 2012,[87] concluding that a sector investigation was not necessary, given the scale of anti-competitive behaviour, and legal and policy changes to the NHS dental contract already in the pipeline.[88]

Arrangements for dental clinics have also been subjected to scrutiny under EU free movement law. The *Hartlauer* case[89] concerned a challenge to Austrian rules on the authorization of setting up of private dental clinics. Authorizations may only lawfully be given where, taking into account existing provision, there is a 'need'. Hartlauer, a company established in Germany, applied for authorization to set up a private outpatient dental clinic in Vienna. The Wiener Landesregierung refused, relying on a report produced by an official medical expert. According to the report, dental care was adequately ensured in Vienna by public and private non-profit-making health institutions and other contractual practitioners offering comparable services. That assessment had been

---

[84] *Van Eycke*, C-267/86, EU:C:1988:427.

[85] The CJEU did not consider the possible application of free movement law.

[86] Unfortunately the OFT press release is no longer available, but a news report of it is available here: Private HealthCare UK, 'OFT launches dentistry market study' (*Private HealthCare UK*, 16 September 2011).

[87] OFT, 'Dentistry: An OFT market study' (OFT 2012). The report focuses on how dentistry services are sold, whether patients are given appropriate information to help them choose between dental practices, the types of treatments on offer and different payment methods in the context of both NHS and private dentistry. It also looks at how easy it is to change dentists, and whether the system for customer redress was effective. The report also examines whether there are any unnecessary barriers to new practices entering either private or NHS funded markets, and considers the issue of professional restrictions on direct access to specialists or providers of auxiliary services, such as hygienists.

[88] These are ongoing, see: UK Department of Health (DoH), 'Policy Paper: NHS dental contract reform: feedback wanted' (*DoH*, 15 August 2013) with several pilots being extended into 2015, see: DoH, 'NHS dental contract pilots – Learning after two years of piloting' (DoH 2014).

[89] *Hartlauer*, C-169/07, EU:C:2009:141.

carried out on the basis of the ratio of the number of inhabitants to the number of dental practitioners, which was 2,207 inhabitants per practitioner. On the basis of the expert's findings, the Wiener Landesregierung concluded that the health institution whose establishment was sought would not have the effect of substantially accelerating, intensifying or improving the provision of dental medical care for patients resident in Vienna, so that there was no need for the institution.[90] Hartlauer challenged that decision as contrary to EU law on freedom of establishment and freedom to provide services. Referring to the case law on free movement of patients, the CJEU repeated that restrictions such as at issue here can be justified by reference to the need to protect health by maintaining a high quality health service open to all, and to prevent the risk of financial instability in the social security system.[91] In this case, in contrast to the others discussed in this chapter, the CJEU found that the rules were not justified. There was inconsistency in their application – group practices were not subject to the same restrictive conditions as new outpatient clinics, and the question of whether there was a 'need' was approached in different ways in different contexts.[92] This consistency scrutiny has not, however, been applied strictly in the context of other health institutions.

Opticians and ophthalmologists

Like dental services, the services provided by ophthalmologists, opticians and related health professionals are not always covered by the 'basket of care' falling within a national health system. Again, this is a market where there is scope for considerable economies of scale, and where new business models, using non-qualified staff to undertake some aspects of the services formerly undertaken by qualified health professionals, have proliferated. In that context, some national regulatory measures may infringe EU law, as protectionist measures. The CJEU has considered national regulation of opticians and ophthalmologists for consistency with free movement law. The *MacQuen* case[93] involved the practice of the UK-based Vision Express, and its subsidiaries in Belgium. Vision Express offered various eyesight examinations in its shops, including using computers to test for various eye problems. These practices were challenged by the Belgian Association of Ophthalmologists and Eye Surgeons, as inconsistent with Belgian rules that limited eye testing to qualified ophthalmologists. The CJEU held that, as access to the profession had not been harmonized by EU legislation, it was for Member States to secure protection for health, including through professional regulation. This could lawfully differ between Member States, and the fact that the German Constitutional Court had recently found[94] that computer-assisted

---

[90] *Hartlauer* EU:C:2009:141, paragraph 18.   [91] *Hartlauer* EU:C:2009:141, paragraph 47.
[92] *Hartlauer* EU:C:2009:141, paragraphs 63, 66-67.   [93] *MacQuen*, C-108/96, EU:C:2001:67.
[94] Decision of 7 August 2000 (1 BvR 254/99).

optician examinations were not detrimental to public health made no difference to the CJEU's ruling.

But, in 2005, the CJEU held that an ownership rule, to the effect that only authorized opticians could own and operate opticians shops, breached Article 49 TFEU.[95] In this context, in stark contrast to the pharmacies and laboratories case law, the CJEU explicitly considered that public health could be protected by other measures, less restrictive of trade, such as 'requiring the presence of qualified, salaried opticians or associates in each optician's shop, rules concerning civil liability for the actions of others, and rules requiring professional indemnity insurance'.[96]

Similarly, a Hungarian rule prohibiting the sale and supply of contact lenses on the internet was challenged for consistency with EU free movement law – in this case, both the Treaty rules and the 'e-commerce Directive'.[97] The CJEU found that the measures were justified for the first supply of contact lenses, given the risks to health which exist if lenses are worn incorrectly. Member States may require contact lens sales to be carried out by qualified staff, who can alert the potential wearer to any risks, examine them, recommend (or advise against) particular lenses, check the positioning of the lenses on the eyes and provide the wearer with information on the correct use and care of the lenses.[98] On the other hand, subsequent supply of contact lenses, including through the internet, may not be so restricted, as to do so is an unjustified restriction on free trade.

(Interim) conclusions

EU health law on health institutions obviously involves interactions between actors at different levels. These include national public authorities (such as competition authorities), private bodies which play a quasi-regulatory role (such as professional associations), the EU legislature and the CJEU. The CJEU has played a particularly important role in those Member States which have liberalized their health systems to the greatest extent.[99] At least at first glance, the notion of 'one-way street', or Offe's aquarium-to-fish-soup concept, seems to be borne out in the context of the health institutions that we examine in this chapter, as well as health insurance as we concluded in chapter 9. As Hancher and Sauter observe, there is no obligation on Member States to liberalize their health sectors, but 'once these have been liberalized, turning back the clock becomes difficult'.[100] If this is so, the implications of EU health law for systems

---

[95] *Opticians*, C-140/03, EU:C:2005:242. [96] *Opticians* EU:C:2005:242, paragraph 35.
[97] Directive 2000/31/EC [2000] OJ L178/1. [98] *Opticians* EU:C:2005:242, paragraph 63.
[99] Hervey and McHale, above n 21; Mossialos et al., above n 1, Hancher and Sauter, above n 68, 88.
[100] Hancher and Sauter, above n 68, 87.

towards the neoliberal end of the continuum in our typology of health systems are far more significant than for those towards the other end.

The CJEU has been criticized for making decisions about health systems with insufficient attention to their histories of promoting solidarity and securing equal access to health care.[101] Indeed, the involvement of courts in matters of social welfare has been widely discussed, particularly in the context of literature on 'social rights'.[102] Creating EU health law through litigation has the effect of substituting judicial decisions for political decisions. The proper allocation of the resources of a state should be a matter for appropriately legitimated political processes, not the decisions of courts in those (few) cases that are subject to litigation. The criticism of EU health law that we raised in 2004[103] – that it is inappropriate that it is created to such an extent through litigation (before the CJEU or before national courts) – thus still stands to a significant degree. But the EU legislature has contributed more in recent times. Certainly for hospitals, for instance, the Patients' Rights Directive changes matters considerably in terms of providing legal certainty for the exclusion of hospitals from the full rigours of EU free movement law.

Once we bring into our perspective the involvement of institutions other than the CJEU, as we have done in the detailed analysis in this chapter, the 'one-way street' ('liberalization breeds liberalization')[104] conclusion becomes more difficult to support in its simplest form. The EU legislature has accommodated

---

[101] Hatzopoulos, 'Killing National Health and Insurance Systems but Healing Patients?' (2002) 29 *Common Market Law Review* 683; Nickless, 'The Internal Market and the Social Nature of Health Care' in Baeten et al. (eds), *The Impact of EU Law on Health Care Systems* (PIE Peter Lang 2003); Newdick, 'Citizenship, free movement and health care: Cementing individual rights by corroding social solidarity' (2006) 43(6) *Common Market Law Review* 1645; Newdick, 'Preserving Social Citizenship in Health Care Markets - There May be Trouble Ahead' (2008) 2 *McGill Journal of Law and Health* 93; Newdick, 'The European Court of Justice, Transnational Health Care, and Social Citizenship - Accidental Death of a Concept?' (2009) 26 *Wisconsin International Law Journal* 845.

[102] See, for instance: O'Connell, *Vindicating Socio-Economic Rights: International Standards and Comparative Experiences* (OUP 2012); Khosla, 'Making social rights conditional: Lessons from India' (2010) 8 *International Journal of Constitutional Law* 739; Young, 'The Minimum Core of Economic and Social Rights: A Concept in Search of Content' (2008) 33 *Yale Journal of International Law* 1; Tushnet, 'Social Welfare Rights and the Forms of Judicial Review' (2003) 82 *Texas Law Review* 1895; and in the specific context of health rights: King, 'Constitutional Rights and Social Welfare: A Comment on the Canadian *Chaoulli* Health Care Decision' (2006) 69 *Modern Law Review* 631; Yamin and Parra-Vera, 'How do courts set health policy? The case of the Colombian Constitutional Court' (2009) 6(2) *PLOS Medicine* 147; Yamin and Parra-Vera, 'Judicial Protection of the Right to Health in Colombia: From Social Demands to Individual Claims to Public Debates' (2010) 33 *Hastings International & Comparative Law Review* 431; Flood and Xavier, 'Health care rights in Canada: The *Chaoulli* legacy' (2008) 27 *Medicine & Law* 617; Flood, '*Chaoulli*'s legacy for the future of Canadian health care policy' (2006) 44 *Osgoode Hall Law Journal* 273; Marmor, 'Canada's Supreme Court and Its National Health Insurance Program: Evaluating the Landmark *Chaoulli* Decision from a Comparative Perspective' (2006) 44 *Osgoode Hall Law Journal* 311; Cousins, 'Health care and human rights after *Auton* and *Chaoulli*' (2009) 54 *McGill Law Journal* 717.

[103] Hervey and McHale, above n 21, 143.   [104] Hancher and Sauter, above n 68, 87.

the special position of health institutions through, for instance, its 'Alumnia package', which allows for the modification of EU state aids law. National competition authorities do not always pursue a free competition approach where health institutions are concerned. Even when we look at the CJEU's stance, while there are indeed some examples of this effect, such a general conclusion is hard to sustain. For instance, as Hancher and Sauter themselves note, the CJEU has permitted very obvious restrictions on free trade within the EU, even in contexts where a Member State has opened up markets in health provision, on the basis that 'the profit motive is inherently suspect in health markets'.[105] Moreover, they note that the CJEU's logic is sometimes difficult to follow and its application of the proportionality test is inconsistent.[106] For instance, there is no particular reason why pharmacist-owners are inherently more immune from the profit motive than other owners. If a pharmacist-owner does not have the burden of financial responsibility, then, at least arguably, she is in a better position to live up to professional ethical standards, unfettered from the need to keep half an eye on the profit motive when advising patients. Alternatively, a more proportionate response to requiring ownership would be to insist on alternative safeguards for patient safety – there are other ways to secure such safety that do not require a pharmacist-owner to be present on the premises. More generally, across the CJEU's case law, liberalization *per se* does not necessarily mean that the full rigour of competition and free trade applies.

Rather than reading these as 'mixed signals' from the CJEU,[107] we suggest that the CJEU is distinguishing between those health institutions which are most closely integrated with the national health (insurance) system and those where the CJEU perceives that there is a distancing between the institution and the publicly funded system. Obviously the distinction is one of degree, with particular institutions within particular health systems occupying a position on a continuum between the most and the least closely associated institutions. This distinction is also present in the legislation, although less obviously. Those health institutions constructed in EU health law as more 'central' to the 'public' health system are hospitals, laboratories and blood centres. The more peripheral ones are dental clinics and opticians. Pharmacies, because they take many different forms, including 'parapharmacies', fall in a middle ground. Broadly speaking, the more peripheral a health institution to the national health (insurance) system, the stricter the scrutiny in terms of the application of free movement and competition law.

The CJEU is using two legal mechanisms to draw this distinction between the ways in which EU health law applies to different health institutions. These mechanisms are (a) the scope of EU law, and (b) the concept of an exception to

---

[105] See: Hancher and Sauter, above n 66, 88-89, discussing Judgment in *Neumann-Siewert* EU:C:2009:316.
[106] Hancher and Sauter, above n 66, 109.   [107] Hancher and Sauter, above n 66, 89.

a general rule. The scope of EU law is drawn through the concept of an 'undertaking' in competition law, and through the definition of relevant geographical or product markets. In free movement law, the concept of a 'wholly internal situation', and the idea of a rule relating to a selling arrangement that does not discriminate in fact or in law, are both used to exclude national arrangements from scrutiny. The exception to a general rule notion is contained in EU legislation (in particular, the Patients' Rights Directive exclusion of hospitals), as well as in the concept of an 'objective public interest', recognized in the CJEU's case law. Objective public interests include securing access to high quality, safe health care, as well as protecting the financial stability of the national health (insurance) system.

11

Competition, solidarity, equality: the pharmaceuticals, medical devices and medical equipment industries

Introduction

Having considered in the previous two chapters the effects of EU law and policy on the social insurance arrangements by which national health systems are funded, the (public) institutions which make up the health system (such as hospitals, pharmacies and laboratories) and the role and place of health professionals within health systems, this chapter turns to the arrangements for supplying products (pharmaceuticals, medical devices and medical equipment) to health systems. As with the previous chapters, we consider the effects of competition and free movement within a single European market, supported by EU law, on two important features shared by European health systems: equality in access to health and the concept of solidarity on which national health systems within the EU are based.

The implications of EU health law and policy on pharmaceuticals, medical equipment and medical devices *for health systems* essentially concern the arrangements by which national health systems contract with the pharmaceutical, medical devices and medical equipment industries for products to be used within the national health systems. A product may be authorized to be marketed within the EU, and consumers may be able to access such a product over-the-counter, or using distance sales via the internet. But in practice many products will only become available to patients within the EU on a widespread basis if they are covered by a national health system. Each national market has its own regulatory arrangements in this regard. Member States consider cost-effectiveness and relative efficacy in comparison to other treatments in the same therapeutic class, in order to determine price, funding and use in the national health (insurance) system. These national rules must balance the need for national health systems to be financially sustainable, in the context of ever-expanding demand for novel health technologies (pharmaceuticals, devices, equipment) and requirements for cost containment, including those mandated by fiscal prudence within the Eurozone. All Member States therefore limit the products which are eligible for reimbursement under social insurance systems or are available within taxation-based systems. There are significant differences between national approaches.[1] The national 'basket' of eligible products within a national health system also therefore indirectly affects innovation in the relevant industries, which is discussed in chapters 12, 13 and 14. Profit-maximizing firms will seek to influence which products are available in national health systems, and will pursue new technologies that are likely to achieve such recognition.

Markets for pharmaceuticals, devices and equipment

There is no single European market in the pharmaceuticals and other health care products that health systems purchase. As pricing arrangements are different in each market, the relevant markets are *de facto* still national. Wide differences in pharmaceutical pricing in different Member States are underpinned by intellectual property rights, such as patents and trade-marks. Intellectual property rights are also largely based on national territories.[2] These rights are used to prevent the 'parallel import' of pharmaceuticals from a Member State in which they are cheap to a Member State in which they are expensive. Early case law on the free movement of goods attempted to tackle these barriers to trade in the internal market.[3] But the CJEU has consistently held that such measures are *justified* by the need for Member States to secure financial stability of their health systems.[4] At the same time, the CJEU required sufficient transparency in pharmaceuticals pricing so as to enable courts to check that rules were free from unlawful protectionist discrimination based on the origin of products.

In the 1980s, the European Union legislature consolidated this case law, and attempted to tackle the distortions in trade in pharmaceuticals that are implicit in the different national laws controlling public expenditure on pharmaceuticals. It did so through the Transparency of Pharmaceuticals Pricing Directive.[5] This Directive imposes obligations on national authorities to publish annual

---

[1] Syrett, 'Looking after the Orphans? Treatments for Rare Diseases, EU Law, and the Ethics of Costly Healthcare' in Flear, Farrell, Hervey and Murphy (eds), *European Law and New Health Technologies* (OUP 2013) 131, cites a 2011 survey of pricing and access to medicines for rare diseases which showed that of the products that had been granted marketing authorization for the EU, 93% were available to patients in France, but only 25% in Greece. Moreover, as Syrett goes on to explain, different Member States approach the very assessment of the relative value to the national health system of novel health technologies very differently, with different blends of focus including on the actual cost of a novel technology; the absolute or overall cost to society as a whole, taking into account, for example, employability; the opportunity costs of treatments which must be foregone if a particular new treatment is provided; and the ethics and social values that underpin such judgments.

[2] Moves to harmonise European patents are ongoing, under the European Patent Office's "Tegernsee Process", see: European Patent Office, 'Substantive Patient Law Harmonisation: The Tegernsee process' (*European Patent Office*, 14 May 2014).

[3] *Centrafarm v Sterling Drug*, C-15/74, EU:C:1974:114; *Centrafarm v Winthrop*, C-16/74, EU:C:1974:115.

[4] See: e.g. *Roussel Laboratoria*, C-181/82, EU:C:1983:352; *Duphar*, C-238/82, EU:C:1984:45; *Commission v Belgium*, C-249/88, EU:C:1991:121.

[5] Directive 89/105/EEC [1989] OJ L40/8.

lists[6] of pharmaceuticals prices, and to publish the 'objective and verifiable criteria' on which they operate their systems, be they direct or indirect profitability controls,[7] or positive or negative lists.[8] It requires decisions on pricing to be made within a specific timeframe, to be reasoned, and to be subject to judicial review. This legislation applies *only* to pharmaceuticals, not to medical devices or equipment. It is minimal in its approach, as it does not directly affect how national health systems set pharmaceuticals prices, or how those aspects of national health systems are organized. All that the relevant legislation does is seek to ensure *transparency* – its obligations are concerned with procedure rather than substance.

As markets have developed (particularly in generic pharmaceuticals), and pressures on national health spending have increased, the Member States have adopted ever wider measures and procedures for pricing and reimbursement of pharmaceuticals within national health systems. For instance, in England and Wales, the 'therapeutic equivalence' concept has been used to influence doctors' prescribing practices – for example, to increase use of generic medicines or to affect the prescription of certain non-generic pharmaceuticals, in particular, statins[9] – through operation of financial incentives. Notwithstanding the generous approach of the CJEU to interpretation of the Directive,[10] the Transparency Directive does not achieve even its very modest objectives, as its scope does not extend to all such new measures. In addition, Member States regularly exceed the time limits prescribed by the Directive for making decisions on pricing and reimbursement.

In 2012, the European Commission proposed a new Transparency Directive.[11] The aims of the proposal remain the same as those of the original Directive: to secure timely decision-making, prevent barriers to parallel trade and to protect the financial viability of national social security systems, as well as national competence to determine the details of such systems. Its approach remains similar too. Changes reflect the changing nature of national systems, so that the scope of the proposal extends to all national measures,

---

[6] Member States may adopt pricing measures more than once a year *Menarini*, C-352/07 to C-356/07, C-365/07 to C-367/07 and C-400/07, EU:C:2009:217.

[7] Directive 89/105/EEC, Article 5.   [8] Directive 89/105/EEC, Articles 6 and 7.

[9] Substances that reduce cholesterol, used in treating cardiovascular disease, see: NHS, 'Statins' (*NHS Choices*, 25 March 2014).

[10] See: e.g. *Commission v Austria*, C-424/99, EU:C:2001:642; *Commission v Finland*, C-229/00, EU:C:2003:334; Judgment in *Pohl-Boskamp*, C-317/05, EU:C:2006:684; *Menarini*, C-352/07, C-353/07, C-354/07, C-355/07, C-356/07, C-365/07, C-366/07, C-367/07 and C-400/07, EU:C:2009:217; *ABPI*, C-62/09, EU:C:2010:219.

[11] Commission, 'Proposal for a Directive of the European Parliament and of the Council relating to the transparency of measures regulating the prices of medicinal products for human use and their inclusion in the scope of public health insurance systems' COM (2012) 84 final; Amended by: Commission, 'Amended proposal for a Directive of the European Parliament and of the Council on the transparency of measures regulating the prices of medicinal products for human use and their inclusion in the scope of public health insurance systems' COM (2013) 168 final.

defined generically rather than specifically, including 'demand side' measures which are used by some Member States to control or promote the prescription of certain pharmaceuticals. The proposal also reflects the changing nature of the pharmaceuticals market, and novel technological developments.[12] The proposal attempts to reduce overlap between the marketing authorization procedure (at which such equivalence or similarity is already determined) and the procedure for national health (insurance) system pricing and reimbursement rules. In so doing, it seeks to support the global competitiveness of the EU's pharmaceutical industries, by decreasing the regulatory stages that a novel product must go through before it is available within national health systems. In this regard, the proposal might be read as supporting competition. The proposal also seeks to increase equality in that, in theory, patients across the EU should be able to access a new pharmaceutical both more quickly and at the same time as each other, assuming each Member State reaches the same 'evidence-based' conclusion about making that new pharmaceutical available. At the same time, the proposal might be read as problematic for solidarity, because it reduces the ability of Member States to rely on national decisions and mechanisms designed to balance the desire of some patients for (expensive) novel products with the needs of those patients who can be treated with (cheaper) products already available within a national health system. However, the proposal does permit Member States to continue to use data on equivalence or similarity as part of the health technology assessment process. Notwithstanding the provision for cooperation on health technology assessment in the Patients' Rights Directive,[13] the assessment of the medical, social, economic and ethical aspects of new health technologies, in the light of existing treatments, in reaching a decision on value for money from the point of view of health (insurance) systems, remains very much a matter of national competence.

Furthermore, the scope of the Directive extends only to pharmaceuticals.[14] It does not cover medical devices or medical equipment. The purchase of devices and equipment within health systems is potentially subject to general EU internal market law, in particular the law of public procurement.[15] Where a 'body

---

[12] For instance, it covers the biosimilarity of biosimilar products and the bioequivalence of generic pharmaceuticals, with the reference product. A 'biopharmaceutical product' is a pharmaceutical manufactured through biological (rather than chemical) processes. They include old technologies such as vaccines and blood components, but also novel technologies, such as allergenics, somatic cells, gene therapies, tissues, recombinant therapeutic protein and living cells. 'Biosimilars' (sometimes called 'follow-on biologics') are a version of a biopharmaceutical product whose patent protection has expired. See: European Medicines Agency (EMEA), 'Guideline on Similar Biological Medicinal Products' (CHMP/437/04, EMEA 2005). A wide range of technologies are covered by the term, and there is a lack of consistency in the use of terminology. See: Warren-Jones, 'Mapping Science and New Health Technologies: In Search of a Definition' in Flear et al., above n 1.

[13] Directive 2011/24/EU [2011] OJ L88/45, Article 15.

[14] This is also the case for the proposal see: Commission, COM (2013) 168 final, Article 2.

[15] The rules on public procurement are an application of free movement rules and must be interpreted in the light of the Treaty: see: e.g. Opinion in *Commission v France*, C–225/98, EU:C:2000:121, paragraph 76.

governed by public law'[16] enters into a major contract[17] for goods, it is subject to public procurement law. These rules also apply to the public purchase of 'works' or services. Many entities within national health (insurance) systems are thus subject to those rules when they purchase medical devices and medical equipment. If, on the other hand, a genuinely competitive regime (a matter of both law and fact) applies to a public entity, then it is excluded from the operation of the public procurement rules.[18] If an entity is an 'undertaking',[19] then its purchasing activities are instead subject to control under EU competition and state aids law. We have already noted the ways in which the application of competition and state aids law has been developed in the context of national health (insurance) systems, through the operation of the 'Altmark' and 'Alumnia' packages.[20] These rules apply also where 'undertakings' within national health systems purchase pharmaceuticals, medical devices or medical equipment.

[16] The public procurement rules cover central, regional, municipal, and local government departments, bodies covered by public law, and public undertakings, see: Directive 2004/18/EC [2004] OJ L134/114, Article 1 (9). Annex III includes a non-exhaustive list of entities deemed by the Member States to be 'contracting authorities'. Some Member States include very broad categories of healthcare bodies, e.g. établissements publics hospitaliers (public hospitals) (France); others include specific bodies, such as the various Belgian sickness insurance funds. A 'body governed by public law' in this context can take any legal form, (*BFI Holding*, C–360/96, EU:C:1998:525; *Oymanns*, C-300/07, EU:C:2009:358). For instance, it can be a public entity, or a private company in national law. The conditions are that the entity must have legal personality, be owned, controlled or financed for the most part by (an emanation of) the state, and be established to meet 'needs in the general interest, not having an industrial or commercial character'. For a discussion of the definition see: Bovis, 'Recent Case Law Relating to Public Procurement: A Beacon for the Integration of Public Markets' (2002) 39 *Common Market Law Review* 1025, 1037–43.
[17] Defined by reference to certain 'threshold' amounts, see: Directive 2004/18/EC [2004] OJ L134/114, as amended.
[18] See: *BT*, C–392/93, EU:C:1996:131; *BFI Holding* EU:C:1998:525; *Agorà*, C–223/99 and C-260/99, EU:C:2001:259; *Mannesmann*, C–44/96, EU:C:1998:4.
[19] See further chapter 9 for an explanation of this term in EU competition law.
[20] See: *Altmark*, C–280/00, EU:C:2003:415; Directive 2005/81/EC [2005] OJ L312/47; Decision 2005/842/EC [2005] OJ L312/67; and Commission, 'Community framework for State aid in the form of public service compensation' (Communication) [2005] OJ C297/04. See: Hervey, 'If only it were so simple: Public Health Services and EU Law' in Cremona (ed), *Market Integration and Public Services in the EU* (Collected Courses of the Academy of European Law, OUP 2011); Hancher and Sauter, *EU Competition and Internal Market Law in the Healthcare Sector* (OUP 2012), 268-273. These provisions (known as the 'Altmark package') were replaced in 2011 and 2012 by the 'Alumnia package', comprising: Commission, 'Communication from the Commission on the application of the European Union State aid rules to compensation granted for the provision of services of general economic interest' (Communication) [2012] OJ C8/4; Commission, 'Communication from the Commission — Approval of the content of a draft for a Commission Regulation on de minimis aid for the provision of services of general economic interest' (Communication) [2012] OJ C8/23; Regulation 360/2012/EU [2012] OJ L114/8; Decision 2012/21/EU [2012] OJ L7/3; Commission, 'Communication from the Commission: European Union Framework for State aid in the form of public service compensation' (Communication) [2012] OJ C8/15; Sauter, 'The Altmark Package Mark II: New Rules for State aid and the compensation of services of general economic interest' (2012) 33(7) *European Competition Law Review* 307; Commission, 'EU Competition Policy Newsletter 2012-1' (Various Authors 2012) and see: Order in *BUPA*, T–289/03, EU:T:2005:78; and follow up CJEU ruling: *BUPA*, T-289/03, EU:T:2008:78; Van de Gronden, 'Financing Health Care in EU Law: Do the European State Aids Rules Write Out an Effective Prescription

The EU legislation on public procurement[21] is now consolidated in Directive 2014/24/EU,[22] which establishes a system of technical rules[23] about contracts for public goods, works or services, and seeks to secure compliance with these rules. The Directive applies only where the value of the contract is above certain thresholds (just over 200,000 euros for most public contracts). Although the Directive establishes a special regime for contracts for 'social and health services',[24] its general rules apply to sufficiently high value contracts for *products* in health services contexts. Where the contract is worth more than the threshold value, the Directive governs the procedures by which public health sector organizations procure products.

However, EU law also affects public contracts of a value *below* the thresholds. Although the Directive does not apply, the CJEU's general internal market jurisprudence does. It requires 'adequate publicity, extended mutual recognition and, most importantly, does not allow for clauses that would exclude, directly or indirectly, operators from other Member States'.[25] General principles of non-discrimination and equal treatment regardless of nationality, transparency (which essentially means adequate publicity), proportionality and mutual recognition[26] apply to public contracting authorities when public

---

for Integrating Competition Law with Health Care?' (2009) 6(1) *Competition Law Review* 5. See further chapter 9.

[21] See: Arrowsmith (ed), *EU Public Procurement Law: An Introduction* (EU Asia Inter University Network for Teaching and Research in Public Procurement Regulation 2011).

[22] Directive 2014/24/EU [2014] OJ L94/65. The Member States must transpose the new rules in the Directive by April 2016.

[23] Concerning matters such as advertising through standard form notices, negotiations with bidders, selection of tenderers, award procedures, and award criteria (lowest price, or most economically advantageous tender).

[24] Directive 2014/24/EU [2014] OJ L94/65, Articles 74-77. The thresholds for health *services* are €750 000, which is significantly higher than for other public contracts (just over €200 000), see: Directive 2014/24/EU, Article 4. The special regime is because, according to the Directive, 'by their nature', they have a limited cross-border dimension, are unlikely to be of interest to providers in other Member States, and apply 'within a particular context that varies widely amongst Member States, due to different cultural traditions': Directive 2014/24/EU, Recital 114. The spirit of the lighter touch regime of the Directive was upheld in *Spezzino*, C-113/13, EU:C:2014:2440, even though the Directive is not applicable in that case, as the facts took place before the Directive entered into force. While the latter rationale is undoubtedly true, the former is not necessarily the case for all health services. The special regime includes an obligation to issue a notice of intention to contract, Directive 2014/24/EU, Article 75, but excludes many of the other obligations in the Directive. Most of the relevant procedures thus remain governed by national rules.

[25] See further: Commission, 'Commission interpretative communication on the Community law applicable to contract awards not or not fully subject to the provisions of the Public Procurement Directives' [2006] OJ C179/2. Hatzopoulos, 'Public procurement and state aid in national health care systems' in Mossialos, Permanand, Baeten and Hervey (eds), *Health Systems Governance in Europe: The Role of European Union Law and Policy* (CUP 2010).

[26] *Nord Pas de Calais*, C-225/98, EU:C:2000:494; *Telaustria*, C–324/98, EU:C:200:669; *Parking Brixen*, C–458/03, EU:C:2005:605; *Coname*, C–231/03, EU:C:2005:487; *Contse*, C–234/03, EU:C:2005:644. See also: Commission, 'Commission interpretative communication on the Community law applicable to contract awards not or not fully subject to the provisions of the Public Procurement Directives' [2006] OJ C179/2, which interprets this case law.

contracts are awarded, or wherever public money[27] is put onto the market. Equally, although the EU legislation makes special arrangements for emergency and patient transport ambulance services, the principles of non-discrimination, proportionality and mutual recognition also apply to those services.[28]

As we have already seen, in the context of application of EU free movement law to free movement of patients, scrutiny of national measures turns on the application of the proportionality test. EU free movement law does not require free trade in all circumstances, but allows for Member States to protect 'objective public interests', including the protection of human health. The key question is whether the measure (here the purchase of pharmaceuticals, medical devices, or medical equipment) could be adjusted so as to continue to protect the public interest, but be less restrictive of trade. Bodies purchasing such products may not simply limit their contracts to one provider, or a small select group of providers, on the basis that an 'objective public interest' is served in so doing. They must consider whether that approach to protecting the public interest concerned is the least restrictive of trade. The application of EU law therefore has the effect of opening up markets to providers in other Member States. Through the application of competition within the EU internal market, this could have the effect of reducing prices of the relevant products, which could secure greater value for public money, and thus have a positive effect on solidarity-based health systems. Of course, it could have the effect of driving domestic firms out of particular markets, thus increasing concentration of market share in fewer, larger firms operating across borders. In theory, as we have already seen, EU competition law prevents the 'abuse' of such market concentration.

So, for instance, until 1992, the UK banned imports of diamorphine, an opium derivative used as an analgesic. A UK company, Macfarlan Smith, had exclusive rights to manufacture diamorphine for the UK market, and another UK company, Evans Medical, held exclusive rights to process it (by freezing, dehydration and packaging). The rationale for the ban was to ensure a reliable supply of the product to the UK and to avoid the risk of diamorphine being diverted to illicit trade. The ban was lifted in 1992, following the development of EU law to secure the single market in goods, in part because the UK government took the view that the continued operation of the ban would breach EU free movement law. A Dutch company, Generics Ltd, was then able to access the UK market, and supply diamorphine more cheaply. Macfarlan and Evans challenged the lifting of the ban.[29] Their argument was that the UN Convention on Narcotic Drugs 1961, to which the UK is a signatory, applied, and meant that the UK should rely on a public security exemption to leave the ban in place. In terms of security of supply of the product, the CJEU held that maintaining the ban in place merely to safeguard the survival of the UK firms would not be justified, although protecting human health through securing a reliable supply of a

---

[27] Or indeed non-financial limited public resources, such as a fixed number of licences, see: *Placanica*, C–338/04, C–359/04, and C–360/04, EU:C:2007:133.

[28] *Spezzino*, EU:C:2014:2440.   [29] *Evans Medical*, C-324/93, EU:C:1995:84.

particular product could be justified, *so long as it was proportionate.* The CJEU rejected the argument that it was necessary to limit the firms who could tender for the contract so as to make sure that the product was not diverted into illicit trade. It pointed out that the contracting public authority could secure such protection by specifying that the suppliers' ability to implement proper security measures was to form part of the contract. EU free movement law here operated to increase competition among providers of diamorphine to the UK market, resulting in a lowering of the cost to the UK national health system. At the same time, the UK was permitted to keep in place proportionate measures to secure patient safety and to protect public health.

What is a proportionate measure to protect patients is a matter over which there may be legitimate scientific and professional disagreement and dispute. The interactions between EU public procurement law and EU law securing the safety of consumers of products sold in the EU are important here. Medical devices sold in the EU fall under the CE system, which seeks to secure a single European market in products that are safe for consumers. The Medical Devices Directive[30] harmonizes the inspection and certification processes applicable to medical devices to be sold within the EU. It provides that such devices must be

> designed and manufactured in such a way that, when used under the conditions and for the purposes intended, they will not compromise the clinical condition or the safety of patients, or the safety and health of users or, where applicable, other persons, provided that any risks which may be associated with their use constitute acceptable risks when weighed against the benefits to the patient and are compatible with a high level of protection of health and safety.[31]

A product bearing a CE certification must be presumed to meet these requirements.[32] Should a Member State seek to dispute such a certification, because in its view and according to the scientific or professional assessments upon which its view is based, the medical device compromises patient safety, it may do so, and may withdraw the product from its market with immediate effect. But it must also follow a procedure of notification to the European Commission, which then considers whether the EU-wide standards for that particular product need to be adjusted, or whether the Member State must reopen its market to that product.[33]

In *Medipac,*[34] the CJEU applied internal market law to a contract with the general hospital of Heraklion, Greece for surgical sutures with a value below the

30 Directive 93/42/EEC [1993] OJ L169/1 (as amended), in particular by: Directive 98/79/EC [1998] OJ L331/1; Directive 2000/70/EC [2000] OJ L313/22; Directive 2001/104/EC [2002] OJ L6/50; and Regulation 1882/2003/EC [2003] OJ L284/1.
31 Directive 93/42/EEC, Article 3 and Annex I.
32 Directive 93/42/EEC, Article 4 (1), and Article 17.   33 Directive 93/42/EEC, Article 8.
34 *Medipac,* C-6/05, EU:C:2007:337.

thresholds.[35] The tender specification referred to the CE system, and Medipac duly offered its sutures which bore the CE mark. But the hospital's surgeons persuaded the hospital administration to exclude Medipac from the contractors under consideration. Their experience was that the particular sutures on offer from Medipac were an insufficiently high-quality product – knots slipped easily and closed prematurely, needles frequently twisted or broke and the sutures did not retain adequate strength for sufficiently long. The CJEU held that the hospital could not exclude from its tendering process products that met the requisite CE standards, given that the basis of the tender was the CE standards themselves. The Greek government could, however, have challenged the CE marking of those particular sutures, using the procedures in the Medical Devices Directives. As they had not, the exclusion of Medipac from the tendering process was a disproportionate restriction on trade and contrary to EU free movement law. If the hospital genuinely needed sutures of a higher quality, that should have been made clear in the tender specification.

These examples illustrate the conclusion that the requirements of the CJEU's jurisprudence in this context, like those of the Transparency of Pharmaceutical Pricing Directive, are essentially *procedural*. Moreover, litigation relying on EU health law has rarely been used to disrupt existing arrangements. So long as entities within national health (insurance) systems contract with sufficient transparency, their underlying discretion is relatively untouched by EU health law. The principal contribution of EU law is to secure such transparency – EU law operates to ensure that decisions made by national health system bodies (such as hospitals and the like) to purchase pharmaceuticals, medical devices or medical equipment are made on a basis under which it can be checked whether these are trade-protectionist measures. This may have some effects in terms of opening up markets and increasing efficiency of provision, for instance, through lower prices. But, otherwise, different national bodies may take different views on what type, quality and so on of such products are best suited to their national market. EU law does not, therefore, harmonize decisions about what products produce best value for money across the whole of the EU. The calculation of 'best value' takes into account the need to secure products of a sufficiently high quality to be fit for their purpose. In that regard, EU health law could be interpreted as not going as far as it could to secure equal access to patients across the EU to high-quality products used in health care settings. But, given the different national health (insurance) systems, with very different levels of resourcing,[36] it is hard to see how it could conceivably do so.

In general, therefore, it would seem that EU health law is thus limited in terms of its effects on competition, and by extension on solidarity and equality, in

---

[35] Contrast: *Ambulance Services*, C–532/03, EU:C:2007:801, in which the CJEU found that the Commission had not made out its case that internal market law should apply to a contract with the Irish Eastern Regional Health Authority for ambulance services.

[36] See further: Introduction to Part III.

terms of how national health (insurance) systems interact with the pharmaceuticals, medical devices and medical equipment industries. Certainly, nothing in the above supports the thesis that this aspect of EU law moves national health systems closer to the neoliberal end of our typology. Nonetheless, there are some specific instances where EU health law may have had greater effects in this context. These are where EU competition and free movement law have been used to promote generic competition, including by mounting challenges to pricing regimes; and to challenge the structure of the pharmaceuticals, medical devices and medical equipment industries and their relations with health professionals. The remainder of the chapter considers those specific contexts.

Challenging pricing and promoting generic competition

Governments of Member States (or, more accurately, their national competition authorities) may use competition law to tackle anti-competitive arrangements that affect the benefit to their national health systems of contracting with suppliers who have colluded or otherwise acted anti-competitively. EU competition law represents an opportunity for governments to intervene in anti-competitive arrangements, in order to enhance their national health systems.

At the level of particular anti-competitive agreements or other collusive behaviour, many national competition authorities have tackled behaviour that affects pricing of pharmaceuticals, medical equipment and medical devices. As early as 1999, we have an Italian case against two pharmaceutical companies for colluding to fix prices and share the market;[37] more recent examples from Italy include tackling collusive behaviour over a tender for electro-medical equipment used for diagnostic imaging,[38] and a competition-restricting agreement over provision of flu vaccines.[39] A Latvian monopolist in the medical gas market was fined for price discrimination; the Hungarian Competition Council fined a medical equipment distributor for establishing an exclusive distribution scheme.[40] The Danish Competition Council found a supply maintenance agreement between pharmaceutical wholesalers that sought to help insolvent pharmacies to be an anti-competitive cartel agreement. This decision is part of its general project to increase competition in the pharmaceutical sector.[41] In 2007, the German Bundeskartellamt took action against a price-fixing cartel

---

[37] Cited in: Lear, Mossialos and Karl, 'EU competition law and health policy' in Flear et al., above n 1, 350.

[38] Autorità Garante della Concorrenza e del Mercato (AGCM), 'Healthcare: Antitrust, over 5.5 million in fines for competition-distorting agreement among 4 suppliers of magnetic resonance equipment' (*AGCM*, 5 August 2011).

[39] AGCM, 'Flu Vaccines: Antitrust launches investigation into possible competition-restricting agreement between Solvay Pharma and Sanofi Pasteur MSD' (*AGCM*, 22 December 2009).

[40] Both cited in: Lear, Mossialos and Karl, above n 37, 351.

[41] Defossez, 'The Danish Competition Council found an insolvency agreement between three medical wholesale dealers and the Danish Pharmaceutical Association to be incompatible with Art. 81 EC and relevant national competition law provision' (2005) *Bulletin e-Competitions Healthcare* Art. N° 24451.

among four companies in the pharmaceutical distribution sector;[42] the Hungarian Competition Council fined three companies for collusion over tendering processes for information systems management for University hospitals; and the French Competition Council fined two medical devices manufacturers for collusion over market share during a tendering process.[43] The Bundeskartellamt reported proudly in 2008 that it had put a stop to price increase arrangements between two manufacturers of colistin antibiotics, and forced a price reduction, thus making significant savings for the German health insurance funds in the future, as well as securing a reimbursement to those funds of the extra costs that they had already incurred from the unlawful price agreements.[44] More recent examples from Germany include fines on a group of manufacturers of ophthalmic lenses and the association of opticians, for price-fixing agreements and exchange of information on terms and conditions and coordinating price increases;[45] and persuading the major manufacturers of ophthalmic lenses to give up their non-binding price recommendations from until further notice.[46]

A well-known UK example is the 2001 *Napp* case,[47] in which Napp became 'superdominant'[48] in morphine tablets and capsules, and their predatory pricing was held to be abusive. In that case, even though the hospital market (in which Napp held over 90 per cent of the market share) represented only around 10 per cent of the total market, the court agreed with the UK OFT that the hospital market is a crucial market segment, because it is only through hospitals that new patients access morphine.[49] A 2011 follow-up report found 'our action against Napp has already resulted in cost savings for the NHS, and therefore the taxpayer, in excess of £13 million',[50] indicating at least a narrative of the use

---

[42] See: Bundeskartelamt, 'Fines against pharmaceutical wholesalers are final' (*Bundeskartellamt*, 19 April 2007), cited in: Lear, Mossialos and Karl, above n 37, 350–1.

[43] Hungarian Competition Authority, 'Bidders cooperated in university hospitals public procurement, Municipial Court of Budapest upheld' (*Hungarian Competition Authority*, 21 February 2007); Autorité de la Concurrence, 'Medical gases for use in hospitals: the Conseil de la concurrence sanctions practices by two subsidiaries of the Air Liquide Group' (Autorité de la Concurrence, 20 January 2003), both cited in: Lear, Mossialos and Karl, above n 37, 351.

[44] Bundeskartellamt, 'Agreement on price increase for pharmaceuticals retractes after application leniency' (*Bundeskartllamt*, 7 May 2009).

[45] Bundeskartellamt, 'Fine proceedings against manufacturers of ophthalmic lenses' (*Bundeskartellamt* 2010).

[46] Bundeskartellamt, 'Non-binding price recommendations for ophthalmic lenses to be discontinued' (*Bundeskartellamt*, 25 March 2009).

[47] *Napp Pharmaceutical 4* (Competition Commission Appeal Tribunal) [2002] CAT 1.

[48] [2002] CAT 1 at paragraph 214: "very significant market power which their superdominance confers so as to preclude the emergence either of a new or additional competitor. Where an undertaking, or group of undertakings whose conduct must be assessed collectively, enjoys a position of such overwhelming dominance verging on monopoly" (quoting Advocate General Fennelly's Opinion in *Compagnie Maritme Belge*, C-395/96 P and C-396/96 P, EU:C:1998:518, paragraph 137); at paragraph 288: "undertaking pricing selectively and below direct cost in order to protect a market share"; paragraph 463: "with the aim of protecting its monopoly in the community segment."

[49] Lear, Mossialos and Karl, 'above n 37, 361.

[50] UK Office of Fair Trading (OFT), 'OFT evaluation of Napp case finds increased competition in morphine market' (*OFT*, 6 June 2011).

of competition law by national competition authorities to support solidarity within national health systems.

Closely related to tackling abusive pricing arrangements, or collusive pricing-related agreements, is the use of EU competition law to promote generic competition. The French *Autorité de la concurrence* has been quite active here, with cases brought against Glaxo for predatory pricing for its injectable antibiotic (Zinnat) that hindered the entry of generic medicines into hospitals.[51] It was alleged that Glaxo did so by 'sending a signal' to deter generic manufacturers from entering the market in which Glaxo sells its flagship product (Zovirax), an injectable anti-viral.[52] However, the decision was overturned by the Paris Court of Appeals, and this was upheld by the Cour de Cassation (Supreme Court). It was found that there was no particular link between the two markets, and so no link between the predatory pricing on the market in which Glaxo was not dominant and the market on which it was dominant. The *Autorité de la concurrence* also investigated a complaint by Teva Santé to the effect that Sanofi-Aventis France was in effect driving from the market generic versions of one of its flagship products, Plavix.[53]

Another example is the Italian Antitrust Authority's decision[54] in January 2012 to the effect that the Pfizer group, a multinational company in the pharmaceuticals sector, abused its dominant position in the market for commercializing glaucoma medicines based on the active ingredient *latanoprost*. This abuse took the form of complex strategy, based on artificially prolonging patent protection, designed to obstruct the entry of generic drugs into that market. The Antitrust Authority explicitly pointed out that the delayed entry of generic drugs to the Italian market cost its national health system about 14 million euros. When the generics entered the market, prices dropped immediately to *half* their previous level.

Following a pattern of such individual cases, we see pressure building up for reforms to pricing arrangements at a more systemic level. So, for instance, in 2006, the Finnish Competition Authority, finding anti-competitive pricing arrangements between pharmaceutical companies and pharmacies, called for

---

[51] See: Autorité de la Concurrence, 'Conseil de la concurrence imposes €10 millions fine on GlaxoSmithKline for having abusively hindered the entry of certain generic drugs to hospitals' (*Autorité de la Concurrence*, 14 March 2007) Temple-Boyer, 'No abuse of dominant position without a link between the predatory practice and the dominated market' (Soulier Advocats 2009) discussed in: Lear, Mossialos and Karl, above n 37, 360.

[52] The Competition Authority relied on the ruling of the CJEU in *AKZO*, C-62/86, EU:C:1991:286, to the effect that 'if a dominant company can seek to protect its position in applying predatory prices on the dominated market, it can do so on an ancillary market if this practice helps it protect or strengthen its position on the dominated market' (see also: *TetraPak*, C-333/94 P, EU:C:1996:436.

[53] Autorité de la Concurrence, 'The Autorité de la concurrence does not declare emergency measures against Sanofi-Aventis but continues its investigation on the merits regarding the complaint by Teva Santé' (*Autorité de la Concurrence*, 18 May 2010).

[54] AGCM, 'Drugs: Pfizer sanctioned with 10.6 million euro fine for abuse of dominant position' (*AGCM*, 17 January 2012).

a full reform of pharmaceuticals pricing and distribution,[55] and repeated that call in 2009.[56] The Irish Competition Authority issued a Guidance Note in September 2009.[57] The Competition Council of Latvia has carried out such a sectoral inquiry, reporting in February 2011.[58] The report stressed opportunities to reduce prices by increasing competition and adopting appropriate regulation. Its recommendations include requiring medical prescriptions to refer only to active ingredients, so as to promote price competition between producers; removing restrictions on parallel imports and trade in generics; prohibiting volume discounts; and allowing pharmacies to purchase direct from producers, to tackle the market power of distributors. Such changes have quite profound effects at a systemic level on a health system as a whole, as well as on the industry concerned.

Industry challenges to pricing

We have already noted the early free movement litigation seeking to challenge practices that impede free movement of pharmaceuticals, medical equipment or medical devices, through closing down 'parallel' pharmaceutical trade.[59] Here we concentrate on the use by industry actors of EU competition law to challenge pricing practices of the industry that are anti-competitive. EU competition law offers two main possibilities: an opportunity for firms in the sectors to challenge the status quo, where agreements or abusive behaviour impede market access or profitability; and an opportunity for firms to challenge regulatory structures, on the basis that they are abusive of a dominant position.

Considering first the use of competition law by firms in the pharmaceuticals, medical equipment and devices markets as an opportunity to challenge the current market arrangements, where agreements or abusive behaviour make it more difficult for the competitor firm to access the market or gain from it, we find many examples of such behaviour. For instance, in 2009, the Cyprus

---

[55] Finnish Competition Authority, 'Finnish Competition Authority Yearbook 2006' (Finnish Competition Authority 2006).

[56] Finnish Competition Authority, 'Finnish Competition Authority Yearbook 2009' (Finnish Competition Authority 2009).

[57] Irish Competition Authority, 'Notice in Respect of Collective Action in the Community Pharmacy Sector' (Decision No. N/09/001, Irish Competition Authority 2009).

[58] Koncurences Padome (Latvian Competition Council), Existing Regulation impedes Price Competition in Medicine Market' (*Latvian Competition Council*, 13 May 2011), the Competition Council concludes that existing Regulation impedes Price Competition in Medicine Market.

[59] See chapter 5. Competition law can also be used to challenge parallel trade restrictions. For instance, in October 2011, the Romanian Competition Council (Decisions no 51 and 52/28.10.2011) sanctioned two suppliers of prescription-only medicines, Belupo Iijekovi & kozmetica d.d. Croatia and Baxter AG Switzerland and their distributors on the Romanian market, for restricting parallel exports outside the Romanian market. See: Commission, 'Romania: The Competition Council imposes Fines on Pharmaceutical Companies Baxter, Belupo and their distributors' (*Commission*, January 2012); Romanian Competition Council, 'The Competition Council sanctioned the companies Baxter, Belupo and their distributors with fine of RO 7,8 million' (*Romanian Competition Council*, October 2011).

Commission for the Protection of Competition found, in response to a complaint by a firm forced out of the market by the practice, that a system of discounts for the supply of meningococcal vaccine (Meningitec) constituted an abuse of a dominant position.[60] As well as pricing-related abuses, bundling of services and products can also be an abuse, as found by the UK OFT in a case involving the pharmaceutical company Genzyme, which was bundling the price of Cerezyme services[61] to include the cost of home delivery.[62] The application of competition law in these sorts of contexts could be read to be supporting solidarity within national health systems, in that it opens the market to greater efficiencies and challenges practices that translate into pricing regimes that do not offer maximum value for public money. On the other hand, where pricing practices are based on negotiated prices, opening these processes up to competition may have the opposite effect. They may also disrupt best medical practice, of securing patient-focused, integrated health care services across different medical professional specialisms.

The flexibility of competition law and its application by national competition authorities mean that such complaints against dominant providers of pharmaceuticals, medical devices or medical equipment to national health (insurance) systems are not always successful. For instance, in 2012, the Croatian Competition Agency rejected a complaint from a leading pharmaceutical company to the effect that the Croatian Institute for Health Insurance was abusing its dominant position.[63] The Competition Agency took the view that the Institute for Health Insurance was performing activities under the Act on Compulsory Health Insurance, with a high degree of solidarity and on the principle of universal coverage. It was therefore not acting as an undertaking. This approach has been upheld by the CJEU. For instance, in the *AOK* case,[64] where sickness funds set maximum prices for some prescription medicines, and pharmaceuticals companies complained that the sickness funds were acting anti-competitively, using collusive behaviour, the CJEU held that the funds were not undertakings, so fell outside the scope of competition law. Likewise, in the *FENIN* case[65] the bodies running the Spanish national health service, about whose practices a complaint from suppliers of medical devices, equipment and so on alleged abuse of a dominant position, it was held that the relevant bodies were not 'undertakings' so competition law did not apply. So a strong claim to the effect that the application

---

[60] Cyprus Commission for the Protection of Competition Decision number: 14/2009, 29 January 2009; see: Commission for the Protection of Competition (Cyprus), 'Annual Report 2009' (Commission for the Protection of Competition 2009) 22.

[61] Long-term enzyme replacement therapy for paediatric and adult patients with a confirmed diagnosis of Type 1 Gaucher disease that results in one or more of the following conditions: anaemia, thrombocytopenia, bone disease, hepatomegaly or splenomegaly.

[62] Lear, Mossialos and Karl, above n 37, 361; *Genzyme* [2004] CAT 4.

[63] Croatian Competition Agency (AZTN), 'Exclusively Croatian Institute for Health Insurance decides on prescription drug benefit programmes' (*AZTN*, 6 February 2012).

[64] *AOK*, C-264/01, C-306/01, C-354/01 and C-355/01, EU:C:2004:150.

[65] *FENIN*, C-205/03, EU:C:2006:453.

of EU competition law increases competition, to the detriment of solidarity or equality, cannot be sustained in this context.

The second way in which competition law may be used by industry actors in this area is more controversial. It offers national authorities an opportunity to challenge the use by pharmaceutical and other companies of regulatory structures, in particular, intellectual property bodies, to delay entry into the market of generic competitors. As Hancher explains,[66] the 60 million euros fine imposed on AstraZeneca by the Commission in 2005 was surprising in that it was previously assumed that, irrespective of market dominance, such behaviour could not constitute 'abuse', so long as access to the procedures was available to all market competitors. The Commission found that the 'allegedly misleading representations' to patent authorities were part of a strategy on AstraZeneca's part to protect its leading product, Losec, from generic competition, even after the patent on its active ingredient had expired.

AstraZeneca sought judicial review of the Commission's decision before the CFI.[67] The CFI upheld the Commission's approach to assessing dominance, including taking account of AstraZeneca's intellectual property rights. As for AstraZeneca's argument that there was no precedent for applying Article 102 TFEU to applications for acquiring or extending intellectual property rights, the CFI upheld the Commission's decision in all important respects. (The CFI found that the Commission had erred in determining the date on which the abuse began,[68] and that the Commission had not established that the behaviour of AstraZeneca in Denmark and in Norway was capable of restricting parallel imports).[69] AstraZeneca appealed, and the Commission cross-appealed on the points it had lost.[70] The CJEU rejected all the appeals. Citing some relatively early case law,[71] the CJEU confirmed that Article 102 TFEU 'prohibits a dominant undertaking from eliminating a competitor and thereby strengthening its position by using methods other than those which come within the scope of competition on the merits'.[72]

Hancher[73] sees this use of Article 102 TFEU by the Commission as an important part of its strategy to open up market access for generic pharmaceuticals. This in turn is part of a move towards focusing on exclusionary (rather than exploitative) practices, in the enforcement of EU competition law.[74] Indeed, the Commission began a sector-wide inquiry into such practices in the pharmaceutical industry in 2008. Its conclusions included observations on the

---

[66] Hancher, 'The EU pharmaceuticals market: parameters and pathways' in Mossialos et al., above n 25, 655-9.

[67] *AstraZeneca*, T-321/05, EU:C:2010:266.

[68] *AstraZeneca* EU:C:2010:266, paragraphs 374-381, 161.

[69] *AstraZeneca* EU:C:2010:266, paragraph 865.   [70] *AstraZeneca*, C-457/10 P, EU:C:2012:770.

[71] *AKZO* EU:C:1991:286, paragraph 70.   [72] *AKZO* EU:C:1991:286, paragraph 75.

[73] Hancher, above n 66.

[74] Hancher and Sauter, above n 20, 242-3; Commission, 'Guidance on the Commission's enforcement priorities in applying Article 82 of the EC Treaty to abusive exclusionary conduct by dominant undertakings' [2009] OJ C45/7.

significant impediments to access of patients to generics within national health (insurance) systems. The Commission announced that it intends to continue to enforce competition law to improve matters in this regard, and to encourage national competition authorities to do so also.[75] In July 2012, it launched investigations into agreements about Citalopram, an antidepressant;[76] Perindopril, a cardio-vascular medicine;[77] and Fentanyl, a pain killer,[78] which may have hindered the entry of generic products into various EU Member States. The 'pay for delay' arrangements, under which firms agreed to delay market entry of generics, despite the relevant patents having expired, have resulted in fines for some of the companies involved.[79] Lundbeck, which held the basic patent for Citalopram, a 'blockbuster' antidepressant and Lundbeck's best-selling product, was fined 90 million euros for entering agreements with producers and potential producers of generic versions of the pharmaceutical. The agreements were worth tens of millions of euros, and guaranteed Lundbeck that the potential competitors would stay out of the market for the duration of the agreement. No compensating access to the market thereafter was involved (as is the norm in such patent dispute settlements). The European investigations mirror similar claims in the US context.[80] They are controversial, in that they are the first time that the EU authorities have found such settlements of patent disputes to breach competition law, and the circumstances in which they arose may be exceptional.[81]

The Commission also urged Member States to introduce systems which would make generics available within national health systems automatically, where the corresponding original product has such a status. This includes the request that Member States 'disregard' submissions to their authorization and funding processes which raise patent, bioequivalence or safety issues for such generics. But the EU has no power to mandate such behaviour, and the very fact that it is requesting it suggests that the behaviour continues to be widespread.

---

[75] Commission, 'Pharmaceutical Sector Inquiry: Final Report' (Commission 2009); Willis, 'Something "rotten" in EU pharmaceutical sector, says Kroes' (*EU Observer*, 8 July 2009); De Souza, 'Competition in Pharmaceuticals: the challenges ahead post *AstraZeneca*' (Competition Policy Newsletter 2007) 39.

[76] Commission, 'Antitrust: Commission sends Statement of Objections to Lundbeck and others for preventing market entry of generic antidepressant medicine' (*Commission*, 25 July 2012).

[77] Commission, 'Antitrust: Commission sends Statement of Objections on perindopril to Servier and others' (*Commission*, 30 July 2012).

[78] Commission, 'Antitrust: Commission sends Statement of Objections to J&J and Novartis on delayed entry of generic pain-killer' (*Commission*, 31 January 2013).

[79] Commission, 'Antitrust: Commission fines Lundbeck and other pharma companies for delaying market entry of generic medicines' (*Commission*, 19 June 2013). See further: Ancelin et al., 'The pay-for-delay settlements in the pharmaceutical sector' (2014) 2 Art. No. 65478 *Concurrences Journal* 12.

[80] See: US Supreme Court decision: *Federal Trade Commission v Actavis*, 570 US, 12-416 (2013).

[81] See: EU Competition Commissioner Alumni's press release which stresses that the Commission pursues only a few small number of the hundreds of these settlements that have taken place over the last few years: Almunia, 'Commission fines Lundbeck and other pharma companies for delaying market entry of generic medicines: statement by Vice-President Almunia' (*Commission*, 19 June 2013).

As Hancher and Sauter point out, to date, the application of EU competition law on dominance abuse in health contexts has been limited.[82] Even in the pharmaceuticals sector, where competition law has been applied, it is more likely to be through national competition authorities rather than the EU institutions themselves. The contexts in which EU competition law are likely to be applied are those where liberalization of national markets means increased opportunities for cross-border trade. Again, therefore, the liberalization *itself* is not driven by EU law, but by national policies. EU competition law may provide a mechanism to respond to those opportunities for new market entrants, but in itself it does not move national health (insurance) systems towards the neoliberal end of our typology.

Scrutiny of the structure of the industry and relations with health professionals

Finally, EU competition law has been used to scrutinize the way that the industry for pharmaceuticals, medical devices and medical equipment is structured, and its relationships with health care professionals. As the global pharmaceutical industries' major players approach the 'patent cliff' (the expiry of patents on blockbuster pharmaceuticals worth billions of euros), firms are considering mergers and other restructuring arrangements. These may be scrutinized by national competition authorities where national interests are at stake. For instance, the high-profile merger of Canadian firm Valeant Pharmaceuticals with Lithuania's Sanitas was of particular interest to the Polish Office for Competition and Consumer Protection of Poland, as both Valeant and Sanitas already had Polish subsidiaries.[83]

The French competition authority (the *Conseil de la concurrence*), following a complaint by Santéclair, a company providing specialist complementary health insurance cover, fined the National Board of the French Dental Surgeons Association (*Conseil national de l'Ordre des chirurgiens-dentistes*) and several of its regional boards for encouraging dental surgeons to boycott a partnership with the company Santéclair, thus trying to force it out of the market.[84] Santéclair's partnership arrangements aimed to keep down treatment costs, and to promote access to the so-called 'tiers-payant' (or third-party payment) system, where insurance companies settle treatment and pharmaceuticals costs directly

---

[82] Hancher and Sauter, above n 20, 246.
[83] The Polish competition authority authorized the merger. See: Polish Office of Competition and Consumer Protection, 'Consent to concentration: Valeant Pharmaceuticals' (*Polish Office of Competition and Consumer Protection*, 17 August 2011).
[84] Autorité de la Concurrence, 'The Conseil de la concurrence fines the National Board of the French Dental Surgeons Association (Conseil national de l'Ordre des chirurgiens-dentistes) and several of its regional boards for encouraging dental surgeons to rule out a partnership with the company Santéclair' (*Autorité de la Concurrence*, 12 February 2009).

with the dentist. The decision was appealed, but the appeal was unsuccessful.[85] The consequence of finding such agreements to be anti-competitive in principle means that other suppliers can enter the market. But again, in practice, whether this means greater access to cheaper pharmaceuticals within the national health (insurance) system is less difficult to determine. From the point of view of competition law, such partnership arrangements are suspect. But from the point of view of national health law, they are part of the ways in which the Member State contains costs and secures high quality and value for public money.

It is one thing to apply competition law to agreements of health care professional associations on pricing, market sharing or even arrangements for trade. It is more controversial to apply competition law to agreements that impose restrictions on who may prescribe or otherwise provide pharmaceuticals or medical devices to patients within a health care system, or otherwise seek to secure standards of high quality and ethical health care. As many Member States have delegated the task of regulating access to health care professions to professional associations, such rules play an important role within health systems, in terms of protecting public health, and ensuring quality of service provided within the system. This is an emergent area where EU competition law is being applied, and the way in which competition authorities have balanced the aims of preventing or sanctioning anti-competitive behaviour with other public policy goals, in particular, protecting patients from unskilled health professionals and ensuring quality control, will be an important feature of EU health law into the future.

Some competition authorities and courts have permitted such restrictions on competition, on public health grounds. For instance, the French Constitutional Court heard a complaint from a distributor of contact lenses to the effect that the law, enforced by the Optician's Trade Association, requiring suppliers of optical care appliances be qualified opticians, breached competition law. It held that the aim of protecting public health could justify such rules.[86] The Netherlands Competition Authority has said that health care providers could collaborate in the purchasing of medical equipment and medical devices,[87] following the German model where collectives of up to 100 hospitals use professional independent commercial purchasing organizations to do so, to drive down prices and hence costs to the insurance bodies. Obviously, such collusive behaviour would be *prima facie* in breach of anti-cartel law.

---

[85] Appealed to Paris Court of Appeals. Commercial Supreme Court rejected appeal from there: Kovar, 'Jurisdiction of the French NCA: The French Commercial Supreme Court rejects an appeal against a decision of the Court of Appeal of Paris (CNOCD, "Santéclair")' (2011) 3(38200) *Concurrences* 212.

[86] *Laboratoire de Prothèses Oculaire v Union Nationale des Syndicats d'Opticiens de France* [1994] *European Competition Cases* 457, cited in: Lear, Mossialos and Karl, above n 37, 354.

[87] Netherlands Competition Authority (NMa), 'NMa: an efficient purchasing process helps control costs of medical equipment' (*NMa*, 15 February 2012).

Others have adopted a stricter approach. For instance, the Polish Office for Competition and Consumer Protection has required the Polish Chamber of Physicians and Dentists to cease its practice of disciplining members who prescribe homeopathic products.[88] The Office for Competition and Consumer Protection stated that it was not expressing an opinion on the effectiveness of homeopathic products,[89] but of course the authority's decision has the effect of changing the availability to patients of such products. Similarly, the Netherlands Competition Authority fined the Netherlands National Association of General Practitioners for its practice of recommending that new GPs be accepted in a certain area only if the established GPs in that area agree to such an entry into the market.[90] Such a barrier to entry into a market reduces choice for both patients and insurers. Likewise, the Competition Authority in Ireland has censured the arrangements by which general practitioners in Ireland provide services under the national health system: the General Medical Services ('GMS') contract. A GMS contract is very valuable to a GP practice; in practice, very few Irish GP practices operate without one. In a report in December 2009/2010,[91] the Competition Authority found that this system was restricting competition and was detrimental to both public and private patients. The system was changed in September 2011, to increase competition,[92] and a Health (Provision of General Practitioner Services) Act 2012 opens access to all qualified GPs to GMS contracts and removes the power of the Health Services Executive to consider 'economic viability' of existing GP practices when granting GMS contracts,[93] or to make restrictions on geographical location. The Competition Authority reports over 100 new applications for contracts in the first six months of operation, the vast majority of which have been granted.[94] In July 2013, the

---

[88] Polish Office for Competition and Consumer Protection, 'Professional association of medical doctors violated the law' (*Polish Office of Competition and Consumer Protection*, 8 August 2011).

[89] "UOKiK is not the party to discussions on the effectiveness of homeopathic products. This issue was not at all subject of our interest. We found that the practice of the Polish Chamber of Physicians and Dentists is a violation of competition by restricting market access to undertakings selling products approved for legal trade, and thus the availability of these products for consumers" according to the President of UOKiK Małgorzata Krasnodębska-Tomkiel, see: Polish Office for Competition and Consumer Protection, "Professional association of medical doctors violated the law' (*Polish Office of Competition and Consumer Protection*, 8 August 2011).

[90] NMa, 'NMa fines Dutch National Association of General Practitioners for illegal establishment recommendations' (*NMa*, 9 January 2012).

[91] Irish Competition Authority, 'Competition in Professional Services: General Medical Practitioners' (Irish Competition Authority 2010) .

[92] The Competition Authority reported on 15 September 2011 that "The changes to the system for GPs treating medical card holders announced by the Minister for Health Dr James O'Reilly yesterday are good news for patients. These changes will impact on all patients; medical card holders and those who pay the full cost of visiting a GP. Last year the Competition Authority called for exactly these changes to this system", Irish Competition Authority, 'Patients will benefit from changes to GP system' (*Irish Competition Authority*, 15 September 2011).

[93] Irish Health (Provision of General Practitioner Services) Act 2012, section 5.

[94] Irish Competition Authority, 'General Medical Practitioners (GPs)' (*Irish Competition Authority*, June 2013).

Competition Authority began proceedings against the Irish Medical Organisation, representing doctors in Ireland,[95] claiming that its GP Committee decision
to withdraw patient services as a response to proposed reductions in fees paid
under GMS contracts[96] amounted to an unlawful cartel agreement.[97] The case
settled in May 2014.[98] It is too soon to assess whether these types of interventions
have detrimental effects on equality of access for patients or solidarity-based
arrangements for health provision.

Conclusions

This chapter has considered various ways in which EU competition and free
movement law affect, or have the potential to affect, the place of industries
providing pharmaceuticals, medical devices and medical equipment within
health systems. We began with the general EU laws governing the ways in which
such products become available in national health (insurance) systems, noting
that, in general, this is still essentially a matter of national competence. We then
considered three areas in which EU law has had greater effects, or at least it has
been claimed that this is so. These are: challenges to pricing arrangements (which
are crucial given the cost containment pressures on all European health systems);
the related promoting of generic competition (because generics, requiring less in
terms of investment for research and development, can be made more cheaply);
and challenges to the structure of the markets for pharmaceuticals, medical
devices and equipment, including through regulation of health professionals
(who mediate that market access in practice).

   The aims of EU law are in tension here, because we do not have a situation
where competition is being promoted in a relatively simple consumer market
with many suppliers and many consumers. The ultimate 'consumer', the patient,
is not (in most cases) the person who pays for the services or products. In
general, the national health social insurance or taxation-based system pays. The
provider (the health professional or health institution) need not necessarily be
(although may be) the purchaser. In the market for pharmaceuticals, medical
equipment and medical devices, the main purchasing role within the health
system (however that is organized) is not performed directly by individual
patients. This is a highly regulated market, due to the nature of the products at
issue. There are particular concerns about safety of pharmaceuticals, medical
equipment and medical devices, as well as concerns about their quality and

---

[95] Irish Medical Organisation (September 2014).
[96] Introduced in response to the austerity measures required by the Eurozone crisis. See the Irish
      Financial Emergency Measures in the Public Interest Act 2009.
[97] Irish Competition Authority, 'Competition Authority secures High Court undertakings from
      the Irish Medical Organisation' (*Irish Competition Authority*, 28 May 2014); Irish Competition
      Authority, 'What's the story . . . with the IMO representing their members?' (*Irish Competition
      Authority*, 3 July 2014); Commission, 'Ireland: The Competition Authority secures High Court
      Undertakings from Irish Medical Organisation' (Commission 2014).
[98] Irish Competition Authority, 'The Competition Authority and The Irish Medical
      Organisation: Heads of Agreement' (Irish Competition Authority 2014).

efficacy in comparison with alternatives. Regulation is justified by the need to take account of the information deficit of the ultimate consumers (patients). Health systems are under pressure to contain costs, even more so during this period of welfare austerity following the global financial and Eurozone crises, but they are under pressure also to make available novel health technologies within their health systems. EU and national law makers must also promote research and development, and sustain the European pharmaceuticals, medical equipment and medical devices industries.

Our conclusion in this chapter, as in the previous two, is that there is scant evidence for the strong claim that EU health law moves health care systems towards the 'neoliberal' end of the spectrum in our typology of health systems. It may be that once Member States decide to open up that aspect of their health systems to markets, EU law has a 'sticky' quality, which prevents a reversion to a non-market-based system. The opening up of the UK market to suppliers of diamorphine in other Member States is an example. But the foregoing detailed analysis shows that a claim to the effect that EU health law *itself* changes the relationships between equality, solidarity and competition, so that competition has become the dominant force, cannot be sustained in the context of the ways in which EU law regulates the pharmaceuticals, medical devices and medical equipment industries. The role of the Member States remains more significant than the claims about the effects of EU health law imply.

Taking the last three chapters together, what can we conclude about how the themes of competition, solidarity and equality are playing out in EU health law, and what are their implications for its trajectories at the systemic level? It is widely accepted that health systems, though a national responsibility, are affected by EU law. Thus, Member States do not have total control over health law. In the area of health systems, Member States of the EU are now only 'semi-sovereign' in Leibfried and Pierson's[99] sense. Indeed we go further than this, in suggesting that the EU's *own* health law forms part of the overlapping multi-level legal system that exists in the interactions within and between the EU and its Member States. Every health system has to resolve the tension between solidarity (how much cross-subsidy there is between generations, rich and poor, young and old within the system); equality (how far is the system organized to achieve 'equal' health for all – equal in what sense, health inputs, health outcomes?); and competition (how far competitive behaviour with markets is used to promote efficiency in the system). Health law contributes to the resolution of those tensions, and EU health law is no different.

An overarching research question for this group of chapters was to consider how the *European Union's* health law resolves those tensions. Because they retain competence to act in the area of health, the Member States can 'translate' EU law in different ways, to suit local contexts, and perhaps to mitigate its effects. We have seen several examples of this – for instance, in the different approaches

---

[99] Leibfried and Pierson (eds), *European Social Policy: Between Fragmentation and Integration* (The Brookings Institution 1995).

that national competition authorities have to the application of EU competition law in health contexts. However, because of the constitutional status of EU law within national law, the way that EU health law resolves these tensions has important implications for national systems. As the CJEU has often stated, the organization of health systems is a matter for each Member State, but, when exercising that power, the Member States must comply with EU law. In principle, therefore, EU competition law and free movement law apply to health systems within the EU.

The basic aims of EU competition law are to prevent anti-competitive behaviour and to punish it where it occurs.[100] Within that bland statement lie a range of positions as to the reasons for having competition law, and indeed what 'competition' means.[101] In particular, there is no universal agreement about whether competition law is only about promoting economic welfare through minimizing costs and maximizing benefits to consumers, through enhanced consumer choice;[102] or whether competition law can be used to pursue other political, social or ethical goals.[103] A similar debate takes place in the context of free movement law. Whether free movement law can be used to achieve goals other than free trade, such as protection of the environment, security of national welfare systems, or public health, is disputed. Recognizing that the principal tools of EU 'market' law (free movement and competition law) are not necessarily only about creating free markets contributes to a more nuanced understanding of claims that EU law is 'bad' for solidarity and equality at a systemic level. It is not possible to support blanket statements about whether markets per se are a force for good or bad in health contexts.[104]

These uncertainties about the aims and scope of EU competition and free movement law have important implications for its application to health systems, and thus for EU health law. It is not always the case that EU competition or free trade law is applied to health systems in such a way as to achieve the aim of promoting economic efficiency, or free/fair trade, in the narrow sense. This and the previous two chapters have shown how EU competition law has been

---

[100] Monti, *EC Competition Law* (CUP 2007).

[101] Putting it very simply, 'structural' economists seek to ensure that markets are served by many firms, so that the interactions between many buyers and many sellers will optimise efficiency and therefore consumer welfare. The 'Chicago School' argues that the number of firms in a market is not the only determining factor, but that other features of the market need to be considered in order to determine whether competition law needs to interfere in order to promote consumer welfare. See: Monti, above n 100, 2-19.

[102] In this respect we disagree with Tony Prosser, whose view is that 'the underlying purpose' of competition law is to do those things, Prosser, 'EU competition law and public services' in Mossialos et al. (eds), above n 25, 317.

[103] Monti suggests as possible goals: 'to maximise economic freedom, preserve employment, promote national champions, facilitate restructuring, protect small firms, safeguard cultural values, conserve the environment and so on': Monti, above n 100, 4.

[104] Den Exter and Guy, 'Market Competition in Health Care Markets in the Netherlands: Some lessons for England?' (2014) 22(2) *Medical Law Review* 255; and Stirton, 'Back to the Future? Lessons on the Pro-Competitive Regulation of Health Services' (2014) 22(2) *Medical Law Review* 180 both make this point. But see: Sandel, *What Money Can't Buy: The Moral Limits of Markets* (Allen Lane 2012).

or could be used to promote a range of other objectives within the context of health systems. It may well be that there is scope to consolidate these aspects of EU health law, to secure 'health-specific' approaches which would enhance legal certainty.[105] But, at the systemic level, we cannot conclude that EU health law simplistically promotes competition, at the expense of solidarity and equality.

The conclusions to these chapters, with their systemic perspective, differ markedly to those from the earlier chapters, where the individual informed the dominant perspective. Like us, Hancher and Sauter note a difference between the way the EU, and in particular the CJEU, has treated individual patients and the way they treat health care institutions which also seek to rely on freedom to trade across borders. EU health law supports individual patient mobility and the right to individual freedom of choice.[106] Yet, at the systemic level, the CJEU frequently endorses the protection of public health and the discretion Member States have to determine the level of health protection.[107] For Hancher and Sauter, this presents a puzzle. They question whether the national competence to regulate the quality of health care and its delivery should imply that Member States have unfettered discretion to organize the means of its delivery as well.[108] As they succinctly put it,

> Why [has] the CJEU been prepared to support patient mobility and the right to freedom of choice in the health care sector but has been reluctant to embrace the freedom of health care providers to compete across borders to widen that choice?[109]

Our analysis, and our separate treatment of first the individual and subsequently the systemic perspective, casts further light on this puzzle within EU health law. At an *individual* level, freedoms, choice and rights enjoy greater protection from EU health law. National discretion is fettered as a consequence or by-product. But, at the *systemic* level, the balance between competition, equality and solidarity is such that EU health law gives far greater weight to solidarity and equality than in the individual context, with consequent limiting of the application of legal concepts of free trade and fair competition.

---

[105] Hancher and Sauter are critical of the lack of 'health sector specific precedents or guidance' on how EU competition law applies, Hancher and Sauter, above n 20, 258-9. They call for 'a competition law framework that is based on a coherent approach and strikes an adequate balance between competition concerns and health care objectives' (Hancher and Sauter (OUP 2012) above n 20, 259). This point is also developed by Van de Gronden, 'The Treaty Provisions on Competition and Health Care' in Van de Gronden et al. (eds), *Health Care and EU Law* (Springer 2011); and Van de Gronden and Sauter, 'Taking the temperature: EU Competition Law and Health Care' (2011) 38(3) *Legal Issues of European Integration* 213.

[106] Hancher and Sauter, above n 20, 89.

[107] Hancher and Sauter, above n 20, 88.   [108] Hancher and Sauter, above n 20, 89.

[109] *Ibid.*

12

Risk: clinical trials

Introduction

Risk and the need for its regulation have been perceived as posing major legal challenges in recent years. The idea that we live in a 'risk society' in which risk is a constructed concept pervades cultural, political, sociological and legal understandings of risk.[1] From insurance to traffic management systems, there is no doubt that risk calculations form a fundamental part of everyday life in the twenty-first century EU, just as in other parts of the world. But the language of risk has been with us for many centuries. The term 'risk' was developed by explorers in the sixteenth and seventeenth centuries, referring to sailing in unchartered waters. Although the ways in which we understand the concept of risk have evolved, the essence of uncertainty, and equally of promise, remains.[2] Risk can be seen as double-edged. It is both a negative force and yet also encapsulates exciting new possibilities.[3] Risk is associated with, but not coterminous with, the anticipation of danger. Since the 1980s, new technologies in particular have been linked to this aspect of risk: nuclear radiation, chemical and industrial waste, lead poisoning, genetically modified food – all involving danger or potential danger of harm to human health. The 'risk industry' and 'risk governance' are concerned with prevention of harm from such anticipated dangers. Risk is also associated with opportunity. In business contexts, new

---

[1] There is a significant literature here, which we only touch upon. See, for instance: Douglas and Wildavsky, *Risk and Culture: An Essay on the Selection of Technological and Environmental Dangers* (University of California Press 1983); Beck, *Risk Society: Towards a New Modernity* (Sage 1992); Douglas, *Risk and Blame: Collected Works* (Routledge 2002); Franklin (ed), *The Politics of Risk Society* (Polity 1998); Denney, *Risk and Society* (Sage 2005); Mythen and Walklate (eds), *Beyond the Risk Society: Critical Reflections on Risk and Human Security* (Open University Press 2006); Taylor-Gooby and Zinn (eds), *Risk in Social Science* (OUP 2006). Legal scholars have also taken up the notions of risk society, see for example: Sunstein, *Risk and Reason: Safety, Law and the Environment* (CUP 2002); Steele, *Risks and Legal Theory* (Hart 2004); Fisher, *Risk Regulation and Administrative Constitutionalism* (Hart 2007); Woodman and Klippel (eds), *Risk and the Law* (Routledge 2009); Everson and Vos (eds), *Uncertain Risks Regulated* (Routledge-Cavendish 2009); Alemanno et al. (eds), *Better Business Regulation in a Risk Society* (Springer 2013).
[2] See further: Denny (Sage 2005) above n 1.   [3] Denny (Sage 2005) above n 1, 11.

technologies present opportunities for exploitation and commercial gain:[4] a promising new pharmaceutical may reap major rewards for shareholders who are prepared to risk investing in the companies which develop and market it. In both contexts, risk can also mean a device for calculation of probabilities or possibilities, and hence a tool to support decision-making.[5]

The desire to welcome new technological developments, along with their perceived health and also commercial benefits, has been tempered by concerns regarding the risks of harm which novel technologies may pose to patients and consumers, and indeed to society at large. Where risk to patients potentially conflicts with economic development, there are risks inherent in adopting either too stringent or too lax a regulatory approach.[6] At a crude level, the negative effects of conservatism in the light of promising novelty can be blamed as the 'health and safety' culture. But it is undeniable that new health technologies may pose physical risks to individuals. There are notable examples of what can happen if scientific advances are introduced too fast, too soon and without effective scrutiny. If harms associated with such risks eventuate, the implications are devastating, at both an individual human level, and collectively.

EU health law has responded to the opportunities and threats associated with health risks. Pregnant women given the drug Thalidomide in the 1960s led to children subsequently being born with major disabilities.[7] This eventually was one trigger across the EU for what is now a complex regulatory regime for pharmaceuticals. As we will see,[8] this regime attempts to balance the need to protect future patients from harmful products, but at the same time to encourage the development of beneficial ones. Yet the treatment of pharmaceuticals as inherently riskier than other products used within health systems (in particular medical devices) was brought into sharp relief more recently during 2011 and 2012, when it was revealed that certain silicone breast implants implanted into thousands of women contain industrial rather than medical-level silicone. The Poly Implant Prothèse incident[9] has led to the governments of various Member States being drawn into the controversy, and has provided a further platform for the EU to reform the regulation of medical devices.[10] The infection of hundreds

---

[4]   Beck, 'Politics of Risk Society' in Franklin (ed), (Polity 1998) above n 1; Giddens, 'Risk Society: The Context of British Politics' in Franklin (ed), (Polity 1998) above n 1; Franklin, 'Politics and Risk' in Mythen and Walklate (eds), (Open University Press 2006) above n 1.

[5]   Steele (Hart 2004) above n 1, 18–36.

[6]   Brownsword, *Rights, Regulation, and the Technological Revolution* (OUP 2008); Brownsword and Yeung, (eds), *Regulating Technologies: Legal Futures, Regulatory Frames and Technological Fixes* (Hart 2008); Brownsword and Somsen, 'Law, Innovation and Technology: Before We Fast Forward – A Forum for Debate' (2009) 1(1) *Law, Innovation and Technology* 1.

[7]   See generally on the Thalidomide disaster: *Distillers v Thompson* [1971] AC 458; Teff and Munro, *Thalidomide: The Legal Aftermath* (Saxon House 1976); Ferguson, *Drug Injuries and the Pursuit of Compensation* (Sweet and Maxwell 1996).

[8]   In this chapter; and chapters 13 and 18.

[9]   Editorial, 'Implants: France recommends removal but UK does not' (*BBC* News, 23rd December 2011), see chapter 1.

[10]   For discussion of the reform proposals, see chapter 14.

of haemophiliacs with defective blood[11] was instrumental in the development of the EU's blood safety law.[12] Incidents such as the 2006 Northwick Park Hospital, London phase I trial of the monoclonal antibody TGN1412, in which six healthy adults immediately suffered life-threatening multiple organ failure on being administered the drug, provide high-profile examples of the need to regulate risks arising from the processes through which novel health technologies are developed.[13] Risk regulation in clinical procedures has been reflected in EU measures directed explicitly at addressing concerns for patient safety.[14] EU health law seeks to ensure that technological advances adopted within health systems are not only clinically effective, but also clinically safe. At the same time, of course, there is no such thing as a completely safe medical treatment, process or product.

Equally, novel consumer products, or novel methods of producing such consumer products, may pose risks to health. Food is a major example. Concerns about the relationships between genetically modified food and allergies, which form part of a debate between the EU and USA on the environmental risks of genetically modified food, are dwarfed by the threats from food-borne diseases and other risks to health from the food chain. Hormones in beef, dioxins in pork; E coli, salmonella, campylobacter, listeria; norovirus and rotavirus[15] are all examples of health risks to consumers to which the EU has responded – a response which is necessary given the single EU market in food. Novel methods of recovering meat and other parts of bovines, as well as the use of parts of other animals in animal feed, contributed significantly to the EU's BSE/vCJD crisis of the 1990s. This incident led to a major revision of EU food law, designed to reduce risks to both consumers and the EU's agriculture and food industries.[16] The EU's involvement in regulating the risks inherent in alcohol consumption has been more low-key, although observers have noted recent moves towards a more interventionist approach.[17] EU tobacco regulation has

---

[11] See further: Farrell, *The Politics of Blood: Ethics, Innovation and the Regulation of Risk* (CUP 2012).

[12] See chapter 14.

[13] See the report of the expert scientific group established by the Secretary of State in the light of the Northwick Park incident *The Expert Group on Phase One Clinical Trials: Final Report* (2006).

[14] Commission, 'Communication on patient safety, including the prevention and control of healthcare-associated infections' (Communication) COM (2008) 836 final; Council Recommendation of 9 June 2009 on patient safety including prevention and control of healthcare associated infections [2009] OJ C151/1.

[15] See, WHO Europe's data and statistics on the topic: WHO, 'Data and statistics' (*WHO*, various dates) and the European Food Safety Authority's (EFSA) information: EFSA, 'Food-borne zoonotic diseases' (*EFSA* 19 February 2014).

[16] See: Alemanno and Gabbi (eds), *Foundations of EU Food Law and Policy: Ten Years of the European Food Safety Authority* (Ashgate 2014).

[17] Cisneros Örnberg, 'Alcohol policy in the European Union' in Greer and Kurzer (eds), *European Union Public Health Policies: Regional and Global Trends* (Routledge 2013); McKee, Hervey and Gilmore, 'Public health policies' in Mossialos, Permanand, Baeten and Hervey (eds), *Health Systems Governance in Europe: The Role of EU Law and Policy* (CUP 2010).

a long history, dating back to 1989[18] and now encompassing regulation of the composition, marketing, advertising and taxation of traditional tobacco products. The development of a new generation of products – e-cigarettes – has prompted EU regulatory responses as the risks (as well as benefits) of these products are slowly becoming better understood.[19]

The following chapters explore the ways in which EU health law regulates risk arising from products or services which might be harmful to health. As these chapters adopt a systemic perspective, we focus mainly on products or processes made available or applied to patients/consumers within national health systems: pharmaceuticals, medical devices, human blood, tissue and cells,[20] and those novel technologies which involve combinations of two, or more, of the above.[21] We consider how EU health law regulates the development of novel pharmaceuticals and other products through the clinical trials process; through restrictions on the marketing of such risky products; and through compensating for harms that result from their use. We contrast the EU's regulation of medical devices, and show how the trend towards applying more precautionary risk-based approaches to regulation of medical devices has increased in the wake of the Poly Implant Prothèse incident. Finally, we consider what EU health law requires of other products that are or may be harmful to health, such as tobacco, food, alcohol.

EU health law, risk and precaution

Our analysis starts from the proposition that, gradually since the 1950s, the EU has taken on many of the roles in regulating risk that were previously associated with nation states.[22] In health contexts, the aftermath of the blood contamination crises in the 1980s and 1990s led to increased EU involvement in risk regulation in public health domains.[23] The EU's involvement in risk regulation underwent a step change in the 1990s, following the BSE/vCJD crisis.[24] Although the detailed arrangements for risk regulation differ between

---

[18] See chapter 15.

[19] See: Directive 2014/40/EU of the European Parliament and of the Council of 3 April 2014 on the approximation of the laws, regulations and administrative provisions of the Member States concerning the manufacture, presentation and sale of tobacco and related products and repealing Directive 2001/37/EC [2014] OJ L127/1. See further chapter 15. Henley, 'E-cigarettes: miracle or health risk?' *The Guardian* (London, 5 May 2104); Clarke, 'E-cigarettes may not be as safe as you think' *Huffington Post* (Washington, 17 April 2014).

[20] Human organs are considered more fully in chapter 17.

[21] For some examples, see further: Flear, Farrell, Hervey and Murphy (eds), *European Law and New Health Technologies* (OUP 2013).

[22] See: Majone, *Regulating Europe* (Routledge 1996).

[23] Farrell, 'The emergence of EU governance in public health: the case of blood policy and regulation' in Steffen (ed), *Health Governance in Europe: Issues, Challenges and Theories* (Routledge 2005).

[24] Hervey and McHale, *Health Law and the European Union* (CUP 2004) 348–357; Westlake, '"Mad Cows and Englishmen": The Institutional Consequences of the BSE Crisis' in Nugent

EU Member States, as EU law is implemented, interpreted and applied differently in different national contexts, the broad approaches to risk regulation are driven by the EU institutions. The relevant literature makes several overlapping and interlocking claims about the EU's approaches to risk regulation, both in general and in specific health contexts.

In theory, risk regulation can be divided into risk assessment and risk management. Risk assessment is based on a scientific analysis (usually using mathematical modelling) of identification of a hazard; quantification of its potency; assessment of who is exposed to the hazard; and characterization of the risk.[25] So, for instance, risk assessment might consider whether a substance is carcinogenic; how powerful a carcinogen it is; who is exposed to the carcinogen and how (through air, water etc.); and what is the likelihood of someone exposed to the carcinogen developing cancer. Risk management on the other hand takes into account the economic, legal, ethical and above all political dimensions of the risk. In a particular democratically legitimated polity (a state, a regional organization, a global trading system), what is an acceptable and legitimate level of risk? This is not a question susceptible to 'scientific' measurement.

In practice, however, it is rare to find risk assessment and risk management, or the 'scientific' and 'political' elements of legal or policy decisions concerning risky or potentially risky products, processes or services, being treated as distinct. The implicit distinction between science-driven and value-driven decision-making is recognized to be a false distinction. Value-driven or political decision-making itself determines what 'counts' as 'scientific' knowledge, how facts should be interpreted and applied when decisions are made, and vice versa. This is the idea (from sociology) of 'coproduction' of knowledge.[26] Risk is not a rationally measurable absolute, which can be scientifically determined. Rather, it is socially constructed, may appear irrational, and is fundamentally contingent upon geographical or temporal circumstances.[27] It follows that what matters, in terms of understanding the ways that law approaches risk, is the public acceptability of risk,[28] rather than a scientific assessment of risk alone.

Some commentators take the view that the EU's approach to risk regulation involves a greater reliance on the scientific than on the political or democratically

(ed), *European Union 1996: the annual review* (published in association with *Journal of Common Market Studies* 1997); Vos, 'EU food safety legislation in the aftermath of the BSE crisis' (2000) 23(3) *Journal of Consumer Policy* 227; Streinz, 'Risk Decisions in Cases of Persisting Scientific Uncertainty: the precautionary principle in European food law' in Woodman and Klippel (eds), (Routledge 2009) above n 1.

[25] US National Research Council, *Risk Assessment in the Federal Government: Managing the Process* (National Academy Press 1983).

[26] See: Jasanoff, *The Fifth Branch: Science Advisers as Policymakers* (Harvard University Press 1998); Everson and Vos (eds), (Routledge-Cavendish 2009) above n 1, 3; Fisher (Hart 2007) above n 1, 16–18.

[27] Jasanoff, *Designs on Nature: Science and Democracy in Europe and the United States* (Princeton University Press 2007).

[28] See: Lee, 'Beyond Safety: The Broadening Scope of Risk Regulation' (2009) 62(1) *Current Legal Problems* 242.

legitimated than elsewhere. They observe a tendency in the EU to focus on expert calculations of risk.[29] The EU's founding Treaties imply that this is the case. According to Article 114 (3) TFEU, when making proposals for legislation governing health, safety, environmental protection and consumer protection in the internal market, the Commission, 'will take as a base a high level of protection taking into account in particular of any new development based on scientific facts'. The EU's risk regulation thus has a particular form, being concerned with promoting the operation of the EU's single market in goods and services.[30] Flear, Farrell, Hervey and Murphy have argued that 'European law' (which includes, but is not limited to, EU law) of new health technologies mediates risk regulation through a central focus on markets.[31] The risk to markets, particularly the EU's single market, is ever-present in the ways in which the EU's legal order seeks to regulate risk. Others also take the view that this leads the EU, under the oversight of the European Commission, to rely particularly strongly on scientific advice in its risk regulation structures.[32]

A related strand of literature shows how the EU uses risk regulation as a tool to enhance its own legitimacy.[33] Here, the reference to the perceived objectivity of science is used to obfuscate political disagreement, or to present particular legislative (or judicial) settlements as rational and optimal. Risk regulation as a means of legitimation of public authority relies on considerations of the extent to which 'science-driven' risk regulation 'fits' with the concerns of relevant actors; whether risk regulation meets its self-defined aims; and the procedural

---

[29] Stokes, 'Something Old, Something New, Something Borrowed: Emerging Health Technologies and the Continuing Role of Existing Regulations' in Flear et al., above n 21.

[30] Heyvaert, 'Europe in a Climate of Risk: Three Paradigms at Play' (2010) LSE Law, Society and Economy Working Papers 06/2010 Bache et al., 'The Defining Features of the European Union's Approach to Regulating New Health Technologies' and Flear et al., 'A European Law of New Health Technologies' in Flear above n 21.

[31] Flear, Farrell, Hervey, Murphy, 'A European Law of New Health Technologies?', in Flear above n 21, 396–398.

[32] Commission, 'Communication from the Commission on the Precautionary Principle' (Communication) COM (2000) 1 final; Corkin, 'Science, legitimacy and the law: regulating risk regulation judiciously in the European Community' (2008) 33(3) *European Law Review* 359; Kritikos, 'Traditional risk analysis and releases of GMOs into the European Union: space for non-scientific factors?' (2009) 34(3) *European Law Review* 405; Farrell above n.11, 201.

[33] Flear, *Governing Public Health* (Hart 2015); Flear, 'Clinical Trials Abroad: The Marketable Ethics, Weak Protections and Vulnerable Subjects of EU Law' in Albors-Llorens, Armstrong, and Gehring (eds), *Cambridge Yearbook of European Legal Studies, Vol 16 2013–2014* (Hart 2014); Flear and Pfister, 'Contingent participation: imaginaries of sustainable technoscientific innovation in the European Union' in Cloatre and Pickersgill (eds), Knowledge, Technology and Law *(Routledge 2014);* Flear and Pickersgill, 'Regulatory or Regulating Publics? The European Union's Regulation of Emerging Health Technologies and Citizen Participation' (2013) 21(1) *Medical Law Review* 39; Flear and Vakulenko, 'A Human Rights Perspective on Citizen Participation in the EU's Governance of New Technologies' (2010) 10(4) *Human Rights Law Review* 661; Flear, 'The EU's Biopolitical Governance of Advanced Therapy Medicinal Products' (2009) 16(1) *Maastricht Journal of European and Comparative Law* 113; Farrell, above n11, 203; citing Follesdal 'Legitimacy Theories of the European Union' (2004) ARENA Working Papers WP 04/15.

arrangements for securing transparency within the regulatory regime. The European Commission continues to claim that its health law enhances public trust.[34] But it has also been shown how novel health technologies, such as nanotechnology, challenge the use of existing scientific frameworks for assessing risk,[35] as probabilities of certain events are not possible to calculate, given existing knowledge about these technologies. These levels of uncertainty raise questions as to whether self-defined aims are appropriate. In the context of the regulation of pharmaceuticals, it has been argued that the law is used to *impede* transparency, through enforcement of contractual and intellectual property claims which restrict the opportunities for scrutiny of information by courts, or through other mechanisms, such as alternative dispute resolution.[36]

Others, by contrast, see EU risk regulation as essentially driven by the political acceptability (or otherwise) of risk. They show that, far from being the province of science alone, a broad range of stakeholders are involved in law and policymaking, including through 'new governance' mechanisms.[37] The scientific expertise that informs internal market law on risk is balanced by the use of ethical expertise and advice, including through the EU's own institutions such as the European Group on Ethics in Science and New Technologies.[38] A related body of literature is interested in the ways in which EU regulation in

---

[34] See for instance: Commission, 'Synthetic Biology: From Science to Governance' (Commission 2010).

[35] Stokes, 'Nanotechnology and the products of inherited regulation' (2012) 39(1) *Journal of Law and Society* 93; Stokes, 'Demand for command: responding to technological risks and scientific uncertainties' (2013) 21(1) *Medical Law Review* 11; Stokes, 'Something Old, Something New, Something Borrowed: Emerging Health Technologies and the Continuing Role of Existing Regulations' in Flear above n 21.

[36] See: Judgment in *Oliveri*, C-482/01 and C-493/01, EU:C:2004:262; Abraham and Davis, 'Science, Law, and the Medico-Industrial Complex in EU Pharmaceutical Regulation: The Deferiprone Controversy' in Flear above n 21; see also the discussion of the Nordic Cochrane Centres attempts to gain access to clinical trials data in: Goldacre, *Bad Pharma: How Drug Companies Mislead Doctors and Harm Patients* (Fourth Estate 2012); Gøtzsche and Jørgensen, 'Opening Up Data at the European Medicines Agency' (2011) 342 *British Medical Journal* p.d2686, which are ongoing, see: European Ombudsman, 'European Ombudsman reaction to EMA's 12 June 2014 statement issued after its Management Board meeting' (*European Ombudsman*, 13 June 2014); Letter from Emily O'Reilly (European Ombudsman) to José Manuel Barroso (European Commission President) (3 June 2014); European Ombudsman, 'European Ombudsman concerned about change of policy at Medicines Agency as regards clinical trial data transparency' (*European Ombudsman*, 16 May 2014) and documents therein. See also: Farrell above n 11, 171. The European Ombudsman's decisions, although not legally binding, are usually followed in practice by the body to which they are addressed, see: Tsadiras, 'The European Ombudsman's Remedial Powers: An Empirical Analysis in Context' (2013) 38(1) *European Law Review* 52.

[37] De Búrca and Scott, 'Introduction: New Governance, Law and Constitutionalism' in De Búrca and Scott (eds), *Law and New Governance in the EU and the US* (Hart 2006); and see further references in chapter 3, n. 196.

[38] Hervey, Busby and Mohr, 'Ethical EU Law: The influence of the European Group on Ethics in Science and New Technologies' (2008) 33 *European Law Review* 803; Plomer, 'The European Group on Ethics: Law, Politics and the Limits of Moral Integration in Europe' (2008) 14 *European Law Journal* 839.

health fields goes beyond a concern with risk. EU health law is at least as much concerned with rights, or indeed with dignity, as it is with risk.[39]

Equally, commentators are divided on whether the EU is inherently more protectionist than the USA in its approach to risk.[40] It is said that the USA tends to view risk as opportunity, whereas the EU is more cautious. For some commentators, the EU is too strict in its regulatory approach to risk. For others, it is not strict enough. It has also been argued that the EU focuses on risk assessment of processes, whereas the USA's focus is on products. Much of the comparative debate has focused on the 'precautionary principle'. The precautionary principle provides a way in which risk may be assessed and calibrated, based on future events.[41] It allows for proactive public action to be taken in the absence of full scientific certainty about threats to human health or well-being.[42] Originally associated with protection of the environment, the principle began to be used in health contexts in 1990s, beginning with public health protection.[43] In the USA, the precautionary principle is associated with science-based decision-making, particularly in biotechnology.[44] As noted above, such an approach tends to play down or even ignore the social construction of risk, or the ethical dimensions of risk decisions.[45]

The EU tends to be associated with a stronger version of the precautionary principle. In the EU, the principle is legally recognized, widely used in policy and regulatory processes and relied upon in a range of adjudicatory contexts.[46] A Commission Communication from 2000 provides that

[39] See, for instance: Murphy, *Health and Human Rights* (Hart 2013), and Murphy (ed), *New Technologies and Human Rights* (OUP 2009). Also: Brownsword, 'Human Dignity, Ethical Pluralism, and the Regulation of Modern Biotechnologies' in Murphy (ed), (OUP 2009); Brownsword and Yeung (eds), (Hart 2008) above n 6.

[40] See: Jasanoff (Princeton University Press 2009) above n 26; Wiener, Rogers, Hammitt and Sand (eds), *The Reality of Precaution: Comparing Risk Regulation in the US and Europe* (RFF Press 2010); Vogel, *The Politics of Precaution: Regulating Health, Safety and Environmental Risks in Europe and the United States* (Princeton University Press 2012).

[41] Murphy (2009) above n39, 12; Boisson de Chazournes, 'New Technologies, the Precautionary Principle and Public Participation' in Murphy (2009) above n39, 162.

[42] Rio Declaration on Environment and Development 1992, Principle 15; Wingspread Consensus Statement on the Precautionary Principle 1998; Commission, 'Communication from the Commission on the Precautionary Principle' (Communication) COM (2000) 1 final.

[43] See further: Boisson de Chazournes, 'New Technologies, The Precautionary Principle and Public Participation' in Murphy (ed), above n 39.

[44] See: National Research Council, *Risk Assessment in the Federal Government: Managing the Process* (National Academy 1993).

[45] Jasanoff, 'Citizens at Risk: Cultures of Modernity in the US and the EU' (2002) 11(2) *Science As Culture* 363, 374-5; Brownsword, 'Regulating Nanomedicine – The Smallest of Our Concerns' (2008) 2(1) *Nanoethics* 73; Nelkin, *Technological Decisions and Democracy: European Experiments in Public Participation* (Sage 1977); Sclove, *Democracy and Technology* (Guilford Press 1995); Nelkin (ed), *Controversy: Politics of Technical Decisions* (Sage 1992).

[46] See: De Sadeleer, 'The precautionary principle in EC environmental and health law' (2006) 12(2) *European Law Journal* 139; Corkin, 'Science, legitimacy and the law: regulating risk regulation judiciously in the European Community' (2008) 33(3) *European Law Review* 359; Lee, 'The Precautionary Principle in the Court of First Instance' (2003) 14(1) *King's College Law Journal* 86; Fisher (Hart 2007) above n 1, 208–11.

The precautionary principle is not defined in the Treaty, which prescribes it only once – to protect the environment. But in practice, its scope is much wider, and specifically where preliminary objective scientific evaluation indicates that there are reasonable grounds for concern that the potentially dangerous effects on the environment, human, animal or plant health may be inconsistent with the high level of protection chosen for the Community.[47]

For some, the EU's application of the precautionary principle in health contexts constitutes a justified impediment to unproven technological developments, especially in health contexts. For example, xenotransplantation (transplantation into humans of genetically modified animal organs) is a controversial technology whose development has stalled in recent years through concerns about risks of the technology including animal to human transmission of viruses. The EU took the view that precautionary measures were necessary to protect the human rights of xenotransplant patients, given their vulnerabilities in the face of a novel risky health technology.[48]

But, for others, the way the EU applies the precautionary principle in health contexts is simply to mask a trade protectionist agenda. For example, it is claimed that the EU's banning of certain growth hormones in beef, in response to concerns about their effects on the development of pre-pubescent children, was not based on objective scientific evidence of harm, but on consumer pressure.[49] Understanding of the effects of hormones on humans when ingested through the food chain is without doubt incomplete, and the EU bans are based on precaution rather than certainty.

Finally, there are many commentators who observe that the precautionary principle is used differently in different contexts.[50] There is no blanket 'EU' or 'US' approach to precaution in risk regulation. As we will see in the context of the detailed discussions below, this is the position which we find most

---

[47] Commission, 'Communication from the Commission on the Precautionary Principle' (Communication) COM (2000) 1 final. See also: Bureau of European Policy Advisors (BEPA), 'Second Dialogue EU-US on Precaution in Risk Management Science and Society Projects (M. D. Rogers), Project 1: "The Reality of Precaution: Comparing Transatlantic Approaches to Risks and Regulation"' (*BEPA*, 22 February 2010) European Parliament resolution on the communication from the Commission on application of the precautionary principle and multiannual arrangements for setting TACs (COM(2000) 803) [2002] OJ CE 177/139.

[48] Council of Europe, 'Recommendation Rec(2003)10 of the Committee of Ministers to member states on xenotransplantation: (Adopted by the Committee of Ministers on 19 June 2003 at the 844th meeting of the Ministers' Deputies)' (Council of Europe, 2014) discussed in: Guerra, 'European Regulatory Issues in Nanomedicine' (2008) 2(1) *Nanoethics* 87, 94.

[49] See, for instance: Petersmann and Pollack (eds), *Transatlantic Economic Disputes: The EU, the US, and the WTO* (OUP 2003); Skogstad, 'The WTO and Food Safety Regulatory Policy Innovation in the European Union' (2001) 39(3) *Journal of Common Market Studies* 485; Scott, *The WTO Agreement on Sanitary and Phytosanitary Measures: A Commentary* (OUP 2007). For details on the WTO's involvement in the dispute, see: WTO, 'European Communities – Measures Concerning Meat and Meat Products (Hormones)' (*WTO*, 2014).

[50] For instance: Majone, 'What price safety? The precautionary principle and its policy implications (2002) 40(1) *Journal of Common Market Studies* 89; Hammitt, Weiner and Swedlow et al., 'Precautionary regulation in Europe and the US: a quantitative comparison' (2005) 25(5) *Risk Analysis* 1215; Farrell above n 11, 171–3; Fisher (Hart 2007) above n 1, 208.

persuasive. None of the strong claims about the EU's approach to regulation of risk, articulated above, applies to *every* health context. However, the significance of risk does resonate and influence EU health law in various different ways, depending on the specific context.[51] To illustrate this proposition, in the remainder of this chapter and the chapters that follow, we first consider the EU's regulation of some important processes for health systems. The processes by which new health technologies – particularly pharmaceuticals – become available within health systems have already been considered, from the point of view of equality, solidarity and competition, in chapter 11. Here we consider those processes – in particular the clinical trials process – from the point of view of risk. In the next chapter, we turn to the ways in which the EU regulates access of risky health products to the EU market. First, we consider products used within health systems (pharmaceuticals and medical devices), as well as products derived from or involving human blood, tissue and cells. Finally, in chapter 14, we discuss products available to consumers outside of health systems, but which have important effects on human health.

EU health law on clinical trials

Introduction

Research is an inherently risky activity. It involves testing the untested, stepping into the unknown. Health research which is undertaken involves risks of physical or mental harm to the participants in the research (who are often patients), and the patients who may eventually use the product or experience the process being tested. It involves risks to the public more generally, as well as to the national health (insurance) system, should research be insufficiently robustly regulated so as to ensure that unacceptably risky products or processes do not reach national health systems or markets. Should such an event occur, there are also risks to reputation, and possibly legal liability, of the companies associated with the research. There are also risks of lost opportunity, should health research be impeded. These include to patients suffering from currently untreatable diseases or disabilities, or those whose conditions could be better managed with a novel health technology. They also include risks to the opportunities for economic growth from new products, processes and technologies.

In the remainder of this chapter, we explore the ways in which EU health law regulates research processes in health contexts. EU law does not attempt to regulate this area systematically. Rather, there is specific regulation of certain specific research activities. The most notable example of relevant EU legislation is the Clinical Trials Directive,[52] which is to be repealed and replaced by the

[51] Flear et al., above n 21, show a distinctive 'European' way of regulating new health technologies, part of which involves a particular role and place for risk in those regulatory structures.
[52] Directive 2001/20/EC of the European Parliament and of the Council of 4 April 2001 on the approximation of the laws, regulations and administrative provisions of the Member States

Clinical Trials Regulation[53] at some point after 28 May 2016.[54] This legislation regulates the conditions under which certain health-related research, namely, clinical trials of pharmaceutical products, may be conducted within the EU.

Background to and rationales for the Clinical Trials Directive and the Clinical Trials Regulation

The background to the Clinical Trials Directive and the Clinical Trials Regulation can be found in the drive post-Nuremberg to regulate the conduct of clinical research for ethical reasons. A series of international statements[55] were produced, with the aim of facilitating ethical practice in clinical trials worldwide. The ethical aspects of EU clinical trials regulation were its key historical driver, and remain a central focus, both in the Clinical Trials Directive and Regulation, and in other contexts.[56]

But at least three other rationales also apply. These resonate more obviously with risk.[57] Clinical trials regulation is driven by a concern for patient safety. EU law on marketing and licensing of pharmaceutical products requires that researchers in trials of such new products comply with 'good clinical practice'.[58] The idea of such practice is to ensure that harms to research participants (who are often also patients) are minimized. Participant/patient safety is framed to some extent within a human rights idiom, with particular reference to rights to physical and mental integrity, and privacy, found within the legislation. Second, regulation is driven by the public safety aspect of risk. Inspections,

relating to the implementation of good clinical practice in the conduct of clinical trials on medicinal products for human use [2001] OJ L121/34.

[53] Regulation 536/2014/EU of the European Parliament and of the Council of 16 April 2014 on clinical trials on medicinal products for human use, and repealing /EC [2014] OJ L158/1.

[54] Regulation 536/2014/EU, Article 99: 'It shall apply as from six months after the publication of the notice referred to in Article 82(3), but in any event no earlier than 28 May 2016'. The notice in Article 82 (3) is a notice from the European Commission to the effect that the new 'EU portal' and 'EU database' – through which the new procedures for clinical trials will operate – have achieved full functionality.

[55] Such as the Declaration of Helsinki 1964, adopted by the World Medical Assembly; the Council of Europe Convention on Human Rights and Biomedicine 1997; and the UNESCO Universal Declaration on the Human Genome and Human Rights 1997. For discussion of a longer list, see: Sprumont, 'Legal Protection of Human Research Subjects in Europe' (1999) 6(1) *European Journal of Health Law* 25.

[56] See, in particular: the position in EU law of patenting of life forms under Directive 98/44/EC of the European Parliament and of the Council of 6 July 1998 on the Legal Protection of Biotechnological Inventions [1998] OJ L213/13; and Judgment in *Brüstle*, C-34/10, EU:C:2011:669, discussed in chapter 7.

[57] Mark Flear argues that risk supports a neoliberal approach, which supports broader phenomena of pharmaceuticalisation and suppresses certain ethical concerns (such as broader public health equality) while favouring a safety-based market-oriented focus. See: Flear, *Governing Public Health* (Hart 2015); Flear, 'Offshoring Clinical Trials: The Mutable Ethics, Weak Protections and Vulnerable Subjects of EU Law' (2013) Centre for European Legal Studies Seminar Paper.

[58] Directive 2001/83/EC, OJ L311/67 Annex 1, Part 4.

along with reporting, monitoring and surveillance procedures, seek to ensure that health and safety procedures are followed, and members of the general public (in addition to research participants) are not endangered by the conduct of a clinical trial, through its various phases. There is also a concern to ensure that research is carried out in matters of public interest, such as developing treatments for diseases for which there is currently no effective cure.[59] Third, the Directive and Regulation are driven by economic or commercial concerns, notably to ensure that the approval procedures for trials, which are regarded as lengthy by the pharmaceuticals industry, are speeded up to facilitate the progress of scientific research and make it more efficient. The Clinical Trials Directive was supposed to support an EU-wide effective approach to the conduct of clinical trials, as part of the EU's internal market, and the 'European research area'.[60] These three different rationales may be seem to be in tension, but this is not necessarily so. If trials are unsafe and harm results to participants, there is the risk of considerable reputational damage, leading to consequent adverse financial impact upon the research organization, which may be the arm of a pharmaceutical company. It is a question of balance between the different rationales, which may be mutually supportive.

The intention behind the structure of the Clinical Trials Directive was to facilitate the efficient approval of proposals to conduct trials, in addition to addressing questions of patient safety during the trial, as well as drug safety, along with protecting human rights and securing ethical principles. The evidence from the working of the Directive was that the drafters may have erred on the side of risk aversion and procedural safeguards, at the expense of facilitating research. Rather than speeding up trial processes, it could instead slow them down,[61] and in practice lead to a reduction in the number of trials undertaken. European Commission figures indicated a decrease of 25 per cent in the number of applications for clinical trials in the period from 2007 to 2011.[62] Some studies found that trial approval processes were considerably

---

[59] As we saw in chapter 11, the EU's involvement in health technology assessment is at present minimal, and EU law is limited to seeking to secure transparency of national health (insurance) system decisions about which products or treatments are covered. See also: chapter 13 on EU pharmaceuticals law, and chapter 18 on the global dimensions of the question of development of new health technologies.

[60] Introduced by the 'Fifth Framework Programme' for research, see: Commission, 'Towards a European Research Area' COM (2000) 6 final; see further: Hervey and McHale (CUP 2004) above n 24, 239–247. The EU's current research programme is Horizon 2020, see: Regulation 1291/2013/EU of the European Parliament and of the Council of 11 December 2013 establishing Horizon 2020 – the Framework Programme for Research and Innovation (2014–2020) and repealing Decision No 1982/2006/EC [2013] OJ L347/104.

[61] See: Commission, 'Assessment of the functioning of the Clinical Trials Directive 2001/20/EC – Public Consultation Paper' (Commission 2009); Commission, 'Assessment of the functioning of the Clinical Trials Directive, 2001/20/EC: Summary of Responses to the Public Consultation Paper' (Commission 2010).

[62] Commission, 'Proposal for a Regulation of the European Parliament and of the Council on clinical trials on medicinal products for human use and repealing Directive 2001/20/EU' COM

slower than in comparable markets such as the USA,[63] implying a need to read-just the EU approach to be less precautionary. However, other studies reached different conclusions.[64] Perhaps an overall reduction in the number of tri-als is explained by a trend towards 'fewer, larger, higher quality trials, with a reduction in the number of poorly designed and managed trials as well as duplicate trials'.[65] A further problem with the Directive was that the procedural safeguards it introduced increased the cost of clinical trials. In 2007, the run-ning costs of non-commercial cancer trials in the UK were reported to have doubled since the Directive was implemented in 2004.[66] In addition, the delay for beginning a clinical trial after approval had increased by 90 per cent to 152 days.[67] The number of staff needed to operate the process for authorization of such studies had also increased by 107 per cent since implementation of the Directive.[68]

These aspects of the Directive suggest that the EU's approach to risk in the context of clinical trials is indeed highly (or even overly) precautionary, and stricter than that in the USA. However, this conclusion assumes that the Direc-tive effectively harmonized the approach to trials regulation across the EU. While the initial intention was that the Directive would facilitate consistency in pharmaceuticals approval processes, in practice there was considerable diver-gence in approach across Member States in the Directive's implementation.[69] In part this is because, although the inspiration for the ethical underpin-nings of the Directive is international, Member States do not share inter-pretations of or approaches to particular ethical questions. In addition, the structures for approval of clinical trials differ considerably across Member States.[70]

(2012) 369 final. The legal basis for the Regulation is Article 114 TFEU and Article 168 (4) (c), paragraph 1 TFEU.

[63] Lambers Heerspink, Dobre, Hillege, Grobbee and De Zeeuw, 'Does the Clinical Trials Directive really improve clinical trial approval time' (2008) 66(4) *British Journal of Clinical Pharmacology* 546.

[64] See: e.g. Berendt, Håkansson and Bach et al., 'Effect of the European Clinical Trials Directive on academic drug trials in Denmark: retrospective study of applications to the Danish Medicines Agency, 1993–2006' (2008) 336(7634) *British Medical Journal* 33.

[65] Robinson and Andrews, ' "(More) trials and tribulations"; the effect of the EU directive on clinical trials in intensive care and emergency medicine, five years after its implementation' (2010) 36(8) *Journal of Medical Ethics* 322.

[66] See further: Hearn and Sullivan, 'The impact of the Clinical Trials Directive on the cost and conduct of non-commercial cancer trials in the UK', 43 *European Journal of Cancer* (2007) 8–13.

[67] Commission Proposal 2012 above n.62.   [68] Commission Proposal 2012 above n.62.

[69] Hoey, 'The EU Clinical Trials Directive: 3 years on' (2007) 369(9575) *The Lancet* 1777.

[70] See, for example: Megone et al., 'The Structure, Composition and Operation of European Research Ethics Committees' in Mason and Megone (eds), *European Neonatal Research: Consent, Ethics Committees and Law* (Ashgate 2001); Nys, 'Ethical Committees in Belgium' (1995) 2 *European Journal of Health Law* 175; Garanis Papadatos and Dalla Vorgia, 'Ethical Review Procedures for Clinical Trials in Greece' (2000) 7 *European Journal of Health Law* 441; Glass (ed), *Ethics Committees in Central and Eastern Europe* (Institute of Medical Ethics and Bioethics Foundation 2001).

The Clinical Trials Regulation is a response to these concerns,[71] although there is no intention to alter completely the way in which the regulation of risk in this area is undertaken.[72] Using the legal form of a Regulation means assessment of an application for authorization of a clinical trial is now based on identical text, rather than potentially diverging national measures transposing a Directive.[73] The main changes in the Regulation include the streamlining of the trial approval process; a move closer to consistency and central control with the concept of the 'reporting Member State', the dossier, the portal and the power of the EU to investigate Member States' compliance.[74] All imply reduction in national discretion. But, at the same time, the Regulation recognizes the variety of national approaches to trial approval, especially where ethical decision-making is concerned.

Scope, obligations and responsibilities

The EU Clinical Trials Directive is limited in its scope, in that it only regulates the conduct of trials on pharmaceuticals, or 'medicinal products', as the legislation terms them.[75] This covers trials on pharmaceuticals which are in a developmental stage, but also what are termed 'investigational medicinal products'. Such products are not novel per se, but are defined in the Directive as being

> a pharmaceutical form of an active substance or placebo being tested or used as a reference in a clinical trial, including products already with a marketing authorization but used or assembled (formulated or packed) in a way different from the authorized form, or when used for an unauthorized indication or where used to gain further information about the authorized form.[76]

---

[71] Commission, 'Safe, innovative and accessible medicines: a renewed vision for the pharmaceutical sector' (Communication) COM (2008) 666 final; Commission, 'Assessment of the functioning of the Clinical Trials Directive 2001/20/EC/– Public Consultation Paper' (Commission 2009).

[72] Commission, 'Fostering EU's attractiveness in clinical research; Commission proposes to revamp rules on trials with medicines' (Commission, 17 July 2012).

[73] Nys, 'New European Rules Regarding the Approval of Clinical Trials, the Role of Research Ethics Committees and the Protection of Subjects' (2012) 60(6) *Archivum Immunologiae et Therapiae Experimentalis* 405, 413.

[74] See further below.

[75] "Medicinal products" are defined as being "any substance or combination of substances presented for preventing disease in human beings or animals" and "any substance . . . which may be administered to human beings or animals with a view to making a medical diagnosis or to restoring, correcting or modifying physiological functions in human beings or in animals", Council Directive 65/65/EEC of 26 January 1965 on the approximation of provisions laid down by law, regulation or administrative action relating to medicinal products [1965] OJ L22/369, Article 1 (2); now in Directive 2001/83/EC of the European Parliament and of the Council of 6 November 2001 on the Community code relating to medicinal products for human use [2001] OJ L311/67 (as amended), Article 6 (1).

[76] Directive 2001/20 /EC, Article 2 (d).

The new Regulation's definition is broader in scope. It includes the category of a 'clinical study', defined as

> any investigation in relation to humans intended
>
> (a) to discover or verify the clinical, pharmacological or other pharmacodynamics effects of one or more medicinal products or
> (b) to identify any adverse reactions to one or more medicinal products or
> (c) to study the absorption, distribution, metabolism and excretion of one or more medicinal products;
>
> with the objective or ascertaining their safety or efficacy.[77]

On the face of it, this increase in scope might suggest that risk regulation has become more stringent. However, closer examination reveals a more complex picture. It is recognized that clinical risks may differ between trials and as a result it may be better to temper the nature and scope of regulation to the level of risk involved.[78] The Regulation thus is constructed to show recognition that in the case of lower risk trials (called 'low-intervention clinical trials')[79] the regulatory process will be streamlined.

Neither the Directive nor the Regulation applies to non-interventional clinical research, or to other health-related research that does not involve 'medicinal products'.

The Directive applies to trials undertaken in single or in multiple sites, whether in one or more Member State.[80] The Directive does not effectively address the challenge of the regulation of multi-state trials. In practice, it seems that multi-state trials have not been supported by the Directive, as highlighted in recent consultations on its reform.[81] The Regulation sets out procedures to regulate these trials, thus *de facto* extending its scope. In contrast, although the Regulation states that it applies to all clinical trials conducted within the

---

[77] Regulation 536/2014/EU/EU, Article 2 (2).

[78] See, in the UK context, NHS Health Research Authority's work on proportionate consent for simple and efficient trials, following the National Institute for Health Research's call for simple and efficient trials in 2014: NHS Health Research Authority, 'NIHR call for simple and efficient trials (closed)' (*NHS Health Research Authority*, 2014)

[79] Defined in Regulation 536/2014/EU, Article 2 (3), as a clinical trial in which all of the following conditions are met: 'the investigational medicinal products, excluding placebos, are authorized'; according to the trial protocol 'the investigational medicinal products are used in accordance with the terms of the marketing authorization; or the use of the investigational medicinal products is evidence-based and supported by published scientific evidence on the safety and efficacy of those investigational medicinal products in any of the Member States concerned'; and 'the additional diagnostic or monitoring procedures do not pose more than minimal additional risk or burden to the safety of the subjects compared to normal clinical practice in any Member State concerned'.

[80] Directive 2001/20/EC Articles 2 (a) and (b).

[81] See: Commission, 'Assessment of the functioning of the Clinical Trials Directive 2001/20 /EC – Public Consultation Paper' (Commission 2009) Commission, 'Assessment of the functioning of the Clinical Trials Directive, 2001/20/EC: Summary of Responses to the Public Consultation Paper' (Commission 2010).

EU,[82] in fact, it does not make explicit provision for multi-centred trials *within* a Member State. The focus of the Regulation is upon the conduct of multi-centred trials *across* Member States,[83] and how Member States must cooperate for the authorization of such trials. Given that there is no need for such cooperation if the trial is taking place within a Member State, the Regulation does not deal with mono-centric trials or even multi-centred trials in only one Member State.[84] Why this is the case is uncertain. It may be a question of *de minimis*, as on average studies with over forty participants apply across more than one state.[85] It may also be that EU law would not be concerned with matters which took place within only one Member State,[86] or the EU may not have formal legal competence to regulate such matters.[87] But, if patient and public safety and risk minimization are paramount, or even if efficient regulation of the 'European research area' is sought, a better approach would be to regulate the approval of multi-centred trials within Member States, as well as cross-border trials.

Clinical trials in the EU must be subject to scientific and ethical review, and may not take place unless authorized.[88] Rights, safety, dignity and well-being must be protected, and trials must be designed so as to generate reliable and robust data.[89] The Clinical Trials Regulation establishes an authorization process to secure these protections. One response to the perceived procedural inhibitors and administrative inefficiency under the Clinical Trials Directive is that, under the Regulation, the trial authorization process is streamlined. It is seen as critically important that applications are approved rapidly to ensure that the EU is a commercially attractive place where trials can be conducted.[90] The Regulation establishes a single computer system for applications for clinical trials, linked to an EU database, the 'EU portal'.[91] Applicants will have to submit a dossier[92] providing information about the conduct of the trials, the investigators, sites, sponsors, the medicinal products being trialled and the measures which are to be put into place to safeguard the position of trial subjects.[93] It remains to be seen whether the concerns which were expressed about the Directive on the administrative complexity of the process will be satisfactorily addressed through the use of the portal. The European Group on Ethics have questioned whether in fact the documentation under the new

---

[82] Regulation 536/2014/EU, Article 1.
[83] Regulation 536/2014/EU, Articles 5 and 6. See: Nys, 'New European Rules Regarding the Approval of Clinical Trials, the Role of Research Ethics Committees and the Protection of Subjects' (2012) 60(6) *Archivum Immunologiae et Therapiae Experimentalis* 405.
[84] Nys above n. 83, 407.   [85] Nys, above n. 83, 405.   [86] Nys, above n. 83.
[87] Note that Regulation 536/2014/EU is based on both Article 168 TFEU (public health competence) and Article 114 TFEU (internal market competence).
[88] Regulation 536/2014/EU, Article 4.
[89] Regulation 536/2014/EU, Article 3.
[90] Commission, 'Safe, innovative and accessible medicines: a renewed vision for the pharmaceutical sector' (Communication) COM (2008) 666 final, at 16, paragraph 8.
[91] Regulation 536/2014/EU, Article 5 and Article 80.
[92] Regulation 536/2014/EU, Article 5.
[93] Regulation 536/2014/EU, Article 25, and Annex I.

proposed Regulation will be any less onerous.[94] Moreover, it is uncertain as to how the new portal will interact with the current established EU clinical trials database system, the EudraCT system.[95]

To support the authorization process, the Regulation introduces the concept of the 'reporting' Member State.[96] An application on submission will propose a Member State to be the reporting state. The state may accept this or it may ask for the application to be referred to another state.[97] The reporting state completes 'Part I' of the assessment report, dealing only with the matters covered in Article 6, which is focused mainly on the risk assessment aspects of the Regulation, concerning therapeutic and public health benefits, risks and inconveniences for research participants. Part I is circulated to all other Member States concerned. Those Member States assess, each for their own territory, various ethical and human-rights aspects, covered in Article 7, including informed consent, privacy and data protection, recruitment, reward or compensation of participants, and liability for damage. These form 'Part II' of the assessment report. A new Clinical Trials Coordination and Advisory Group, which will address issues which arise in the approval process, is to be established.[98] Nonetheless, the Regulation leaves considerable scope for differences of approach between Member States. In this respect, the hoped-for aim of a harmonized clinical trials law for the EU is yet to be achieved.

The Regulation does seek to harmonize the time frames within which trial authorization decisions must be taken. This is another instance of the tension between commercial efficacy and patient or public safety. The Clinical Trials Directive established explicit time limits as part of the approval process, a standard limit of sixty days.[99] However, in practice, delays still proved problematic. The Regulation also imposes time limits, for both stages of the new assessment process. The period was to have been shorter, but, following criticisms from the European Group on Ethics,[100] in the final Regulation there is little

---

[94] European Group on Ethics in Science and New Technologies, 'Statement of the European Group on Ethics in Science and New Technologies on the Proposal for a Regulation of the European Parliament and the Council on Clinical Trials on Medicinal Products for Human Use and repealing Directive 2001/20/EC (COM 2012), 369 final' (European Group on Ethics in Science and New Technologies 2013) 4, paragraph 10.

[95] See also <https://eudract.ema.europa.eu/index.html>.

[96] Regulation 536/2014/EU, Article 5(1).

[97] Regulation 536/2014/EU, Article 5.

[98] Regulation 536/2014/EU, Article 85.

[99] Directive 2001/20/EC Article 9. In the past this approach was criticized, see: Bayens, 'Implementation of the EU Clinical Trials Directive: Pitfalls and Benefits' 9 *European Journal of Health Law* (2002) 31. There is provision for a further 30-day extension in the case of medicinal products for gene therapy and somatic cell therapy (this includes xenogenic cell therapy).

[100] See: European Group on Ethics in Science and New Technologies above n 94, 409. Heringa and Dute were also critical of these aspects of the proposal, taking the view that rushed approaches processes are unethical, see: Heringa and Dute, 'The Proposed EU Regulation on Clinical Trials on Medicinal Products: An Unethical Proposal?' (2013) 20(4) *European Journal of Health Law* 347.

difference. The reporting Member State has ten days within which to 'validate' the application, and a further forty-five days within which to submit Part I,[101] during which time the other concerned Member States must also complete their assessments.[102] There is scope for extension of time where additional information is needed. In this regard, the Regulation fits within an assessment of the EU as tending towards a precautionary approach to risk.

The Regulation gives more flexibility to sponsors, so that applications may be able to be submitted on the back of documents assessed by Member States as to where the trial may be conducted. To facilitate cross-border trials, the Regulation enables the extension of such trials without needing applications to be reassessed by the Member States involved in initial trial authorization.[103] This is likely to raise problems in terms of tracking approval processes given the greater degrees of discretion now given to Member States in establishing such processes.[104]

According to the Directive and the Regulation, clinical trials falling within their scope must be undertaken in accordance with 'good clinical practice.'[105] Commission Directive 2005/28/EC sets out principles and detailed guidelines for good clinical practice.[106] These refer to the International Conference on Harmonisation of Technical Requirements for Registration of Pharmaceuticals for Human Use (ICH), effectively the 'gold standard'. ICH guidelines should be followed by those conducting trials, unless other specific guidance is given by the Commission. In effect, this aspect of EU clinical trials law is harmonized, in a way which protects trial participants from harm; protects compliant trial sponsors from negligence claims; and protects the EU's economy from an over-strict regulatory approach, given that it is based on global standards.

One important question for any clinical trial is who ultimately carries the responsibility for its oversight and liability if problems occur? In an attempt to address at least some of these issues, the Clinical Trials Directive introduced the concept of the 'sponsor'. The 2001 Directive defines the sponsor as 'an individual, company, institution or organization which takes responsibility for the initiation, management and/or financing of a clinical trial'.[107] While the sponsor can be seen as an effective method of addressing the question of responsibility, it was also suggested this could be problematic for those trials

[101] Regulation 536/2014/EU, Articles 5 (3) and 6 (4).
[102] Regulation 536/2014/EU, Article 7 (2).
[103] Regulation 536/2014/EU, Chapter III.
[104] Commission, 'Safe, innovative and accessible medicines: a renewed vision for the pharmaceutical sector' (Communication) COM (2008) 666 final, at 17, paragraph 16.
[105] Directive 2001/20/EC, Article 1 (4); Regulation 536/2014/EU, Article 47; Commission, 'Safe, innovative and accessible medicines: a renewed vision for the pharmaceutical sector' (Communication) COM (2008) 666 final, at 19, paragraph 29.
[106] Commission Directive 2005/28/EC of 8 April 2005 laying down principles and detailed guidelines for good clinical practice as regards investigational medicinal products for human use, as well as the requirements for authorisation of the manufacturing or importation of such products [2005] OJ L91/13.
[107] Directive 2001/20/EC, Article 2 (e).

which are funded through public and charitable sources, where the funders may not be happy to undertake such a role, with its consequent responsibilities and potential liabilities, and may indeed be unable to take out appropriate indemnity insurance.[108] During the reform process, the introduction of 'consistent risk-based insurance conditions throughout a multinational trial' was suggested.[109] Possible alternative approaches which were mooted included establishing a not-for-profit insurance body for clinical trials, or the examination of whether such studies could be explored through the national health systems of Member States.[110]

The Regulation takes a broader approach to sponsorship than that under the Directive. Under the Regulation, a trial may have one or several sponsors and the task of a sponsor may be delegated to another individual company/institution or organization.[111] In a situation in which there are a number of sponsors, all the sponsors are subject to the obligations of sponsorship unless this is determined otherwise by a contract between the sponsors.[112] The role of the sponsor remains critical for risk minimization. Sponsors must monitor the conduct of the trial with the aim of ensuring reliability of results.[113] Sponsors are required to make the relevant Member State aware of serious breaches in the rules concerning the trials.[114] Suspected unexpected serious adverse reactions to medicines, along with other events, must be reported to the European Medicines Agency.[115] Data must be recorded and stored with the aim of ensuring the safety of trial participants and effective monitoring and reporting.[116] Such steps highlight the focus on scientific risk assessment within the Regulation.

Identifying who is responsible for monitoring and reporting goes some way towards minimizing risks of harm to trial participants. The question of who will be legally accountable and indeed liable should harm result is another matter.

---

[108] See further: Watson, 'EU legislation threatens clinical trials' (2003) 326(7403) *British Medical Journal* 1348; and Editorial, 'Who's afraid of the European Clinical Trials Directive?' (2003) 361(9376) *Lancet* 2167.

[109] See: Federation of the European Academies of Medicine (FEAM), 'Opportunities and Challenges for Reforming the EU Clinical Trials Directive: Statement' (FEAM 2010) 8.

[110] FEAM, 'Opportunities and Challenges for Reforming the EU Clinical Trials Directive: Statement' (FEAM 2010) 8.

[111] Regulation 536/2014/EU, Articles 71 and 72.

[112] Regulation 536/2014/EU, Article 72.

[113] Commission, 'Safe, innovative and accessible medicines: a renewed vision for the pharmaceutical sector' (Communication) COM (2008) 666 final at 19, paragraph 30; Regulation 536/2014/EU, Article 48.

[114] Regulation 536/2014/EU, Article 52.

[115] Regulation 536/2014/EU, Articles 40 and 41. The European Medicines Agency is established by Regulation 726/2004/EC of the European Parliament and of the Council of 31 March 2004 laying down Community procedures for the authorisation and supervision of medicinal products for human and veterinary use and establishing a European Medicines Agency [2004] OJ L136/1. Its principal responsibilities are the authorization of all pharmaceuticals that may be marketed within the EU. It is also responsible for monitoring the safety of authorized pharmaceuticals. It does so through the 'Eudravigilance' database, to which all serious adverse reactions to pharmaceuticals are supposed to be reported. See further: chapter 13.

[116] Regulation 536/2014/EU, Article 56 and 57.

In the discussions leading to reform of the Directive, a backstop in the form of indemnity provision was considered. The Directive provides applicants must demonstrate that there are indemnity provisions in place, to compensate for harm suffered.[117] The Regulation takes a different approach. It provides that, in a situation in which either there is no additional specific risk or where risks are negligible, then there is no requirement to have a specific indemnity in place.[118] It is assumed that this will smooth the passage of 'low intervention clinical trials'[119] through the approval process. Nonetheless, the adjustment towards a more industry-favourable approach to perceived 'low risk' trials could prove exceedingly problematic. If something goes wrong in what was thought to be a 'low risk' trial, this could cause considerable problems for an injured research participant seeking redress, particularly if even successful litigation for harm caused does not lead to actual compensation.[120]

The original proposal for the Regulation was that Member States would set up a national indemnification system, which was to work on a 'not-for-profit' basis.[121] Mandating indemnity in this manner would have involved a greater degree of harmonization than under the Directive. However, this proposal was highly controversial. Major research bodies and pharmaceutical companies would have been required to work with Member States, and indeed to contribute to the financing of this body. Such bodies might have preferred to conduct trials in another jurisdiction, thus harming the 'European research area'. It was unclear how the proposal would operate alongside existing systems for

---

[117] Directive 2001/20/EC, Article 3 (2) (f), Articles 6 (3) (h) and (i).

[118] Regulation 536/2014/EU, Article 76.

[119] Regulation 536/2014/EU, Article 2 (3) defines such trials as those in which (a) the investigational medicinal products, excluding placebos, are authorised; and (b) according to the protocol of the clinical trial, (i) the investigational medicinal products are used in accordance with the terms of the marketing authorisation; or (ii) the use of the investigational medicinal products is evidence-based and supported by published scientific evidence on the safety and efficacy of those investigational medicinal products in any of the Member States concerned; and (c) the additional diagnostic or monitoring procedures do not pose more than minimal additional risk or burden to the safety of the subjects compared to normal clinical practice in any Member State concerned'.

[120] Broader concerns, about the subsequent use of data collected for a different purpose, arise in the context of 'big data' research. These concerns pertain to the undermining of public trust, as well as ethical and human rights questions about consent and privacy. There is significant literature on these questions, which are not able to cover in detail here. See, for instance: Barber, 'Patient data and security: an overview' (1998) 49(1) *International Journal of Medical Informatics* 19; Dickenson, *Property in the Body: Feminist Perspectives* (CUP 2007); Lemmens, 'Pharmaceutical Knowledge Governance: A Human Rights Perspective' (2013) 41(1) *Journal of Law, Medicine and Ethics* 163; Laurie and Postan, 'Rhetoric or reality: What is the legal status of the consent form in health-related research?' (2013) 21(3) *Medical Law Review* 371; Taylor and Grace, 'Disclosure of Confidential Patient Information and the Duty to Consult: The Role of the Health and Social Care Information Centre' (2013) 21(3) *Medical Law Review* 415; Sterckx and Cockbain, 'The UK National Health Service's "Innovation Agenda": Lessons on Commercialisation and Trust' (2014) 22(2) *Medical Law Review* 221. For discussion of Directive 95/46/EC of the European Parliament and of the Council of 24 October 1995 on the protection of individuals with regard to the processing of personal data and on the free movement of such data [1995] OJ L281/31, see: chapter 7.

[121] Commission (2012) above n. 62, Article 73.

compensating negligent harm. In general, compensation systems for personal injury are a matter for national legislation.[122] In the final text, the proposal has been dropped. A single provision, Article 76, requires that a system of damage compensation 'appropriate for the Member State concerned where the clinical trial is conducted' must be in place. There remain genuine concerns about malpractice litigation in the EU in cross-border care situations. Where a patient's care or treatment includes participation in a clinical trial, these questions remain unresolved – the Member State in which the trial takes place is the determining factor, and in instance of cross-border care this may not be clear. Nonetheless, while this was considered during the discussions which led up to the Patients' Rights Directive, here too this question has been left to individual Member States.[123]

In terms of the obligations imposed within the scope of the EU's clinical trials law, there is no standard approach to precaution, or to the way that risks inherent in authorizing – or equally not authorizing – a particular clinical trial are assessed. In some respects, the Clinical Trials Directive and Regulation adopt a harmonized, EU-level approach. But, in many significant respects, differences remain between national approaches. Equally, although many aspects of the Directive and Regulation focus on the scientific approach to risk assessment and risk management, equally, many cover ethical and human rights concerns. A claim that EU health law is too focused on risks to industry, to the detriment of other interests, cannot be supported. Equally, neither can a claim that EU health law focuses entirely on risks to the health or safety of patients or other trial participants. The specific context is what matters. This is all the more obvious when we consider the Directive and Regulation's approach to risk, rights and ethics.

Risk, ethics and human rights: ethics committee review and consent provisions

On the face of it, the EU's Clinical Trials Directive and Regulation can be seen as classic risk avoidance measures. Pharmaceuticals trials involve risky untested products which can cause harm. As a consequence, the EU regulates to ensure that there are appropriate checks and balances in place. While risk assessment is fundamental to clinical trials regulation in the EU, the reality of the processes and criteria involved demonstrates that this is not a crude 'science-based' safety calculation, but rather is much more engaged with the politics and economics of novel health technologies, as well as with ethics and human rights.

---

[122] Commission, 'Safe, innovative and accessible medicines: a renewed vision for the pharmaceutical sector' (Communication) COM (2008) 666 final, at 21, paragraph 45. See further: chapter 13.

[123] Directive 2011/24/EU of the European Parliament and of the Council of 9 March 2011 on the application of patients rights in cross-border healthcare [2011] OJ L88/45. See further: chapters 4, 7 and 8. See also: Peeters, 'Free Movement of Patients: Directive 2011/24 on the Application of Patients' Rights in Cross-Border Healthcare' (2012) 19(1) *European Journal of Health Law* 29.

The ethics and governance structures for approval of clinical trials in general differ considerably across Member States.[124] The Clinical Trials Directive promoted greater consistency, but at the same time recognized the need to respect subsidiarity, both in the operation of ethics and governance processes in general, and in the specific question of consent. We consider each of these in turn.

Under the Directive, clinical trials on medicinal products require authorization by the 'national competent authority', typically a state medicines agency.[125] But in addition they also require ethics committee approval. Research ethics committees have been an important part of research governance in the last fifty years, providing independent system of review and scrutiny of research trials. Whether or not the legislation in individual Member States required reference to a research ethics committee, in practice reference to such a committee has become virtually mandatory. Reputable scientific journals will not generally accept articles for publication unless it can be shown that the research has received approval from a research ethics committee. For many researchers, such publications in refereed journals are critical for their careers. Research ethics committees are multidisciplinary and typically contain members drawn from medical, scientific and social science backgrounds, along with lay members.[126] The Clinical Trials Directive required that the operation of those committees, to the extent to which they concern trials on medicinal products, should be placed upon a formal basis and makes reference to them mandatory.[127] Under the Directive, a trial cannot commence unless a favourable opinion has been given by a research ethics committee.[128]

The Directive provides the ethics committee with a series of criteria which it must take into account.[129] First is the relevance of the trial and its design.[130] Second, the committee is required to weigh up any foreseeable risks and inconveniences against any anticipated benefit which may accrue to the participant in the trial.[131] Benefits to be considered here include those not only to the trial participant, but also to other present and future patients. The Directive thus implicitly recognizes both therapeutic trials (those which may benefit the

---

[124] See, for example: Megone et al., 'The Structure, Composition and Operation of European Research Ethics Committees' in Mason and Megone (eds.), (Ashgate 2001) above n 70; Nys, 'Ethical Committees in Belgium' (1995) 2 *European Journal of Health Law* 175; Garanis-Papadatos and Dalla Vorgia, 'Ethical Review Procedures for Clinical Trials in Greece' (2000) 7 *European Journal of Health Law* 441; Glass (ed), (Institute of Medical Ethics and Bioethics Foundation 2001) above n 70.

[125] E.g. in the UK, the Medicines and Health Care Products Regulatory Agency.

[126] Hernandez et al., 'Harmonisation of ethics committees practice in 10 European countries' (2009) 35(11) *Journal of Medical Ethics* 696.

[127] Directive 2001/20/EC, Article 6.

[128] Directive 2001/20/EC, Article 9.   [129] Directive 2001/20/EC n. 52 Article 6 (3).

[130] Directive 2001/20/EC, Article 6 (3) (a) and see also: Commission, 'Detailed Guidance on the application form and documentation to be submitted in an application for an ethics committee opinion on the clinical trials of medicinal products for human use' (Revised, Commission 2006).

[131] Directive 2001/20/EC, Article 6 (3) (b) and see Article 3 (2) (a).

participant personally) and non-therapeutic trials.[132] Third, the protocol is to be considered,[133] in addition to the suitability of investigator and supporting staff[134] and quality of the facilities.[135]

Although the drafting under the Regulation is different, essentially similar risks and benefits must be assessed.[136] The Regulation provides that there are matters concerning approval on which Member States will be required to cooperate, but also some matters devolved to Member States. Those matters covered in 'Part II' of the assessment report are in the latter category. They include ethical issues, such as informed consent, reward, compensation and recruitment of participants; data protection; suitability of investigators and trial sites; liability, compensation and indemnity.[137] In addition, Member States are under an obligation to ensure that those considering the proposal do not have conflicts of interest, are independent of the sponsor, trial site and investigators and or other undue influence.[138]

The Regulation does, however, move from a requirement of guaranteed compulsory review by a research ethics committee. This aspect of the Regulation has been criticized. The German Medical Association saw it as undermining the safety mechanism which research ethics committees currently provide.[139] The EU Group on Ethics in Science and New Technologies (EGE) expressed 'deep concern' at the proposal to remove a 'globally accepted mechanism' for ethical decision-making and human rights protection.[140] The fact that the Regulation requires that the timelines for ethical review must be 'compatible with the timelines and procedures'[141] for trial authorization also suggests a focus on securing timely authorization, rather than protecting trial participants. The EGE also argued that such a change is problematic not only in terms of risks and of ethics, but also could have an adverse impact upon the authorization of pharmaceuticals, and indeed could make the EU less economically competitive,[142] given that in the USA independent multidisciplinary ethics committee review is a requirement before regulators will approve pharmaceuticals to be placed on the market.[143]

The Regulation requires Member States to ensure that a 'reasonable number' of persons consider the application, and they must 'collectively have the

---

[132] Directive 2001/20/EC, Article 3 (2) (a).
[133] Directive 2001/20/EC, Article 6 (3) (c).
[134] Directive 2001/20/EC, Article 6 (3) (d).
[135] Directive 2001/20/EC, Article 6 (3) (f).
[136] Regulation 536/2014/EU, Article 6.
[137] Regulation 536/2014/EU, Article 7.
[138] Regulation 536/2014/EU, Article 9 (1).
[139] Editorial, 'German Medics Challenge New EU Clinical Drugs Trials' (*BBC News*, 25 September 2012).
[140] European Group on Ethics in Science and New Technologies above n. 94, 4, paragraph 2.
[141] Regulation 536/2014/EU, Article 4.
[142] European Group on Ethics in Science and New Technologies above n. 94 4, paragraph 10.
[143] Ibid.

necessary qualifications and experience.'[144] Moreover, at least one layperson must participate.[145] This is a departure from the Clinical Trials Directive, which provides that the ethics committee must include 'health care professionals and non-medical members'.[146] Lay representation and patient involvement have been increasingly common in clinical trials processes.[147] On the other hand, such involvement may simply be tokenism. Certain trials require specific professional expertise in the decisions concerning the scientific validity and the ethical desirability of involvement of certain population groups. Both the Clinical Trials Directive and the Regulation provide for involvement of those with specific expertise concerning children. The Regulation provides that, in the case of research concerning minors, paediatric expertise or advice on clinical, ethical and psychosocial problems in paediatrics will be required.[148] For adults lacking mental capacity, a similar provision is included in the Regulation as in the Directive, namely, that, in determining the application, expertise on the particular disease and patient population must be considered or advice must be taken on clinical, ethical and psychosocial questions, in the field of this disease and patient population.[149]

Whether Member States depart from the safety of a research ethics committee approval system remains to be seen. In any event, the need for research ethics committee approval for publication in career-enhancing journals is probably enough to secure the continued use of research ethics committees across the EU. But this is shared practice, rather than a legally mandated, harmonized approach to the ethical aspects of clinical trials regulation across the EU.

Similarly, the ethical and human rights question of consent to clinical trial participation is a matter that is only harmonized at the most general level within EU law. Consent is a fundamental part of respect for the human rights and dignity of research participants. The importance of consent is recognized in Article 3(2) of the EU Charter of Fundamental Rights.[150] Given this, it was thus unsurprising that the Clinical Trials Directive and Regulation provide for informed consent, and moreover for consent procedures for persons lacking

---

[144] Regulation 536/2014/EU, Article 9 (2).

[145] Regulation 536/2014/EU, Article 9 (3). The original proposal was that the view of at least one person whose "primary area of interest is non-scientific" must be taken into account, and the view of at least one patient: Commission, 'Proposal for a Regulation of the European Parliament and of the Council on clinical trials on medicinal products for human use and repealing Directive 2001/20/EC' COM (2012) 369 final, Article 9 (3).

[146] Directive 2001/20/EC, Article 2 (k).

[147] See generally regarding the role of the lay member: Green, 'Further thoughts on the Recruitment of REC Lay Members' (2007) 3(1) *Research Ethics Review* 8.

[148] Regulation 536/2014/EU, Article 10 (1).

[149] Regulation 536/2014/EU, Article 10 (2).

[150] See: e.g. Convention on Human Rights and Biomedicine 1997, Article 16. For discussion of Article 3 EU CFR, see: Michalowski, 'Article 3 – Right to the Integrity of the Person' in Peers, Hervey, Kenner and Ward (eds), *The EU Charter of Fundamental Rights: A Commentary* (Hart 2014).

decision-making capacity.[151] This approach is continued under the Regulation. In both Directive and Regulation, informed consent in writing is required.[152] A competent individual has the right both to consent and to withdraw consent.[153]

The Clinical Trials Directive and Regulation include detailed provision for consent in trials concerning minors[154] and adults lacking mental capacity.[155] The Directive provides that ethics committees must examine the justification for undertaking research on those persons who are incapable of providing informed consent.[156] The Regulation does not fundamentally change these provisions, save for the removal of the requirement of reference to a research ethics committee.[157] In both Directive and Regulation, persons who lack capacity may only be included in clinical trials, where this would have a direct benefit to them, that is, in a therapeutic trial. Thus, non-therapeutic trials on persons who lack capacity remain unlawful.[158] Under both Directive and Regulation, in the case of the minor, consent should be obtained from the parents or legal representative; in the case of the adult, consent should be obtained from the 'legal representative'.[159] While it is commonly the case, at individual Member State level, that consent will be routinely sought from the person with parental responsibility on behalf of their children, the use of a legal representative, in the case of the adult is somewhat different. Both the Directive and Regulation are silent on procedures to be used to ascertain who is the 'legal representative', leaving it to Member States to formulate policy. While the Directive affords discretion to Member States here, in fact it has actually driven change in the law concerning consent in at least one Member State. The requirement for a

---

[151] Directive 2001/20/EC, Article 3; Regulation 536/2014/EU, Articles 28–31.
[152] Directive 2001/20/EC, Article 3 (2) (d); Regulation 536/2014/EU, Article 2 (2), 28 (1), 29–35.
[153] Regulation 536/2014/EU, Article 28 (3). The fact that such withdrawal is not retrospective is something which should be included from the outset in the consent process, in order that the research participant is aware of the limitations of personal autonomy in this context.
[154] Directive 2001/20/EC, Article 4; Regulation 536/2014/EU above n.53, Article 32.
[155] Directive 2001/20/EC, Article 5; Regulation 536/2014/EU above n.53, Article 31.
[156] Directive 2001/20/EC, Article 6 (3) (g).
[157] Regulation 536/2014/EU above n.53, Articles 31 and 32.
[158] See: Nys, 'New European Rules Regarding the Approval of Clinical Trials, the Role of Research Ethics Committees and the Protection of Subjects' 60(6) *Archivum Immunologiae et Therapiae Experimentalis* (2012) 405, 411; see also: Hervey and McHale (CUP 2004) above n 24.
[159] Directive 2001/20/EC, Articles 4 (a) and 5 (a); Regulation 536/2014/EU, Chapter V; see further in relation to the Clinical Trials Directive and children: Gevers, 'Medical Research Involving Children' (2008) 15(2) *European Journal of Health Law* 103; Altavilla, 'Clinical Research with Children. The European Legal Framework and its implementation in French and Italian Law' (2008) 15(2) *European Journal of Health Law* 109; Pixton, Direick and Nys, 'The Implementation of Directive 2001/20/EC1 EC into Belgian Law and Specific Provisions on Paediatric Practice' (2008) 15 *European Journal of Health Law* 153; Abbing, 'Patients' Rights in a Technology and Market Driven-Europe' (2010) 17 *European Journal of Health Law* 11, 16–18.

legal representative led the UK to enact a specific new provision, giving a legal representative consent power.[160]

Which risks to trial participants are regarded as legitimate may be highly subjective, and can be influenced by inducements.[161] The Directive and Regulation prohibit incentives or financial inducements (except compensation for lost earnings or expenses) to minors and incapacitated adults.[162] In contrast, there is, however, no provision in the Directive prohibiting such incentives or inducements for competent adults, although the Regulation prohibits such incentives for pregnant or breastfeeding women.[163] This perhaps is unsurprising given that some suggest that few competent adults would volunteer without such an inducement. Nonetheless, the very fact of inducement may serve to compromise the quality of consent.

One concern raised under the Directive was its application in emergency situations, such as where a patient suffers a sudden heart attack.[164] In some emergency situations, valid advance consent may be possible because a sudden adverse event is anticipated, perhaps because the patient is already in hospital and a relapse is considered likely. But in many such situations this is impossible because the event could not have been predicted. Moreover, the circumstances may be such that it is simply not practicable to obtain consent from a legal representative.[165] In the years which followed the Directive's implementation, some Member States enacted law to address this question and to enable a waiver of consent, although this was not uniform across the EU. The Commission highlighted concerns about emergency medicine in their review of the Directive. It suggested that it should be possible to include such individuals in trials in some situations. However, there is recognition that this may be ethically controversial

---

[160] See generally as to the implications of the Directive in the context of persons lacking mental capacity: Liddell et al., 'Medical Research involving incapacitated adults, implications of the EU Clinical Trials Directive' (2006) 14 *Medical Law Review* 367; De Klerk, 'Protection of Incapacitated Elderly in Medical Research' (2012) 19(4) *European Journal of Health Law* 367.

[161] See generally: McNeill, 'Paying People to Participate in Research: Why Not?' (1997) 11(5) *Bioethics* 390; Wilkinson and Moore, 'Inducements in Research' (1997) 11(5) *Bioethics* 373; Wilkinson and Moore, 'Inducements Revisited' (1999) 13(2) *Bioethics* 114; Bentley and Thacker, 'The Influence of Risk and Monetary Payment on the Research Decision Making Process' (2004) 30(3) *Journal of Medical Ethics* 293.

[162] Directive 2001/20/EC, Articles 4 (d) and 5(d); Regulation 536/2014/EU, Articles 31 and 32.

[163] The notion that a woman, when pregnant or breastfeeding, is somehow less competent than a man has been roundly rejected by feminist critiques, and its inclusion in the Regulation is thus controversial. It is probably explicable by the desire to protect particularly 'vulnerable' groups of trial participants, including the foetus, or baby/ies being breastfed, or to discourage clinical trials on those groups.

[164] See further: Nys, 'New European Rules Regarding the Approval of Clinical Trials, the Role of Research Ethics Committees and the Protection of Subjects' (2012) 60(6) *Archivum Immunologiae et Therapiae Experimentalis* 405, 412.

[165] See further: Singer and Mullner, 'Implications of the EU Directive on clinical trials for emergency medicine: Many trials in emergency medicine will not be possible' (2002) 324(7347) *British Medical Journal* 1169.

and that safeguards will be necessary. Very clear rules are needed to determine where patients should be included. This is a provision which will need to be interpreted carefully as it represents a difficult balancing test between the interests of the individual patient and those of the broader community. Article 35 of the Regulation now makes specific provision for the emergency situation. It provides that research may be authorized first where, due to the sudden urgency which results from a 'sudden life threatening or other sudden serious medical condition', prior informed consent is impossible. In addition, the person may be included only if no legal representative is available and if there are no previous known objections which have been expressed. Finally, Article 35 applies only in a situation in which research concerns a medical condition which means prior informed consent is impossible, the trial is of minimal risk and imposes a minimal burden. In any event, under Article 35(2), informed consent must be subsequently obtained as soon as possible from the legal representative of the child or the adult lacking mental capacity. This provision seeks to provide a balanced response to a difficult issue.

The Regulation seeks to redress concerns that overly complex or individualized consent procedures are inappropriate in the context of low-risk[166] 'cluster trials', where groups of participants are randomly allocated to receive different pharmaceutical products under investigation. Such trials seek to improve understanding of the comparative benefits of different treatments that are already authorized, through analysis of 'big data' (large datasets which can now be 'mined' using information technology).[167] Article 30 of the Regulation allows for simplified consent procedures to be used in such trials. Simplified consent amounts to an 'opt out' – participants must be given certain key information about the trial, and may opt out, but otherwise are deemed to have consented. Details on the implementation of this provision[168] are likely to vary between Member States.[169]

Beyond these provisions, the specifics of informed consent are left to the individual Member States to determine, by reference to existing provisions of domestic law. There is no EU law informed consent doctrine. This is

---

[166] Defined as 'low intervention clinical trial', see: Regulation 536/2014/EU, Article 2.

[167] See, for discussion of the US context: Faden, Beauchamp and Kass, 'Informed Consent, Comparative Effectiveness and Learning Health Care' (2014) 370(8) *New England Journal of Medicine* 766; Sox and Greenfield, 'Comparative Effectiveness Research: A Report from the Institute of Medicine' (2009) 151(3) *Annals of Internal Medicine* 203; Luce et al., 'Rethinking Randomized Clinical Trials for Comparative Effectiveness Research: The Need for Transformational Change' (2009) 151(3) *Annals of Internal Medicine* 206. And see: Naci, Spackman, and Fleurence, 'National approaches to comparative effectiveness research' in Sobolev (ed), *Handbook of Health Services Research* (forthcoming, Springer 2017) for a discussion of the approach in various European countries.

[168] Such as, for instance, whether the information may be displayed on a poster.

[169] For discussion of the data protection/human rights aspects of such research, see: Kranenborg, 'Article 8 – Protection of Personal Data' in Peers et al. (eds), (Hart 2014) above n 150, 254; and chapter 7.

unsurprising, given the different approaches across the EU.[170] Nonetheless, there is the prospect that practice may become aligned through exchange of information by regulatory agencies and between researchers themselves. Overall, the conclusion is that EU risk regulation in the context of ethics and consent procedures in clinical trials is highly context specific.

Risk monitoring and transparency

Various measures in the Regulation concern the monitoring of risk. A Member State is permitted to revoke, suspend or require modification of a clinical trial which it considers is no longer compliant with the Regulation.[171] The Commission may conduct controls to check whether Member States have correctly supervised compliance with the Regulation and whether the regulatory system applicable to trials outside the EU also complies.[172] In addition, the Commission is to be empowered to undertake inspections where necessary.[173] A Member State must establish national contact points, through which information is shared.[174] Obligations are placed upon the Commission to support the Member States in the authorization procedures.[175] All of these provisions imply significant control for national authorities in terms of the practicalities of implementation of the Directive, as well as scope for different approaches, even within the framework of the Regulation.

One of the more controversial aspects of regulation of clinical trials concerns the lack of transparency of trial data. Several commentators take the view that both the EU and the USA are insufficiently attentive to risks arising from the inability to undertake independent assessment of clinical trial data.[176] This lack of transparency arises because of the *de facto* control that the pharmaceutical industry has over clinical trials. It is claimed that the industry manages information flow in ways that enhance the likelihood of authorization of their novel products, and, ideally, the taking up of those new products by national health (insurance) systems.[177] Nothing in the Clinical Trials Directive changes this position. However, the Regulation takes a modest step towards transparency. The sponsor is required to report to the Member States the start and end of a

---

[170] See further Nys, 'Comparative Health Law and the Harmonisation of Patients' Rights in Europe' (2001) 8(4) *European Journal of Health Law* 317, 324.

[171] Regulation 536/2014/EU, Article 77.

[172] Regulation 536/2014/EU, Article 77 (1) and 79.

[173] Regulation 536/2014/EU, Article 78.

[174] Regulation 536/2014/EU, Article 83.

[175] Regulation 536/2014/EU, Article 84.

[176] See, for instance: Goldacre (Fourth Estate 2012) above n 36; Fisher, *Medical Research for Hire: The Political Economy of Pharmaceutical Clinical Trials* (Rutgers University Press 2008); Figert and Bell, 'Big Pharma and Big Medicine in the Global Environment' in Kleinman and Moore (eds), *Routledge Handbook of Science, Technology and Society* (Routledge 2014); Dukes, Braithwaite, Moloney, *Pharmaceuticals, Corporate Crime and Public Health* (Edward Elgar 2014), and see further: chapters 13 and 18.

[177] See further the discussion in chapter 13.

clinical trial, and this modest transparency requirement could assist in scrutiny of clinical trials. Clinical trials reports are no longer to be assumed to be commercially confidential. Where the clinical trial is to be used to support a future marketing authorization, the 'clinical study report' (a report on the clinical trial presented in an easily searchable format, prepared in accordance with requirements for an application for marketing authorization),[178] must be submitted to the EU database. However, otherwise, for instance, if the trial is unsuccessful, the sponsor is required only to submit a summary of the results of the trial after one year. Beyond these obligations, full data-sharing, for instance, of the mandatory 'clinical trial master file',[179] is on a voluntary basis only.[180] EU health law does not oblige the publication of unsuccessful clinical trial data. Moreover, the Regulation applies only to new pharmaceuticals – it does not rectify the lack of transparency of data on existing pharmaceuticals and other products or procedures regularly used within national health systems. The question of transparency of data supporting marketing authorizations for pharmaceuticals within the EU is considered further in the next chapter.

Conclusions

The EU does not systematically or exhaustively regulate medical or health research across the EU. As we have seen, the scope of the provisions discussed in this chapter is limited. Only clinical trials of pharmaceuticals are covered by the Directive and Regulation. This leaves some matters of risk assessment and management of the research associated with novel health products or procedures for the Member States. In some respects, the new Regulation extends the scope of EU law, but in others it consolidates the approach of respecting different national preferences. Even within the ambit of EU clinical trials law, divergent national approaches, protecting national preferences, are in tension with a desire for harmonization, in order to capitalize on economies of scale.

The observation that the EU tends to use 'scientific' justifications for risk regulation is evidenced by some aspects of EU clinical trials law. 'Science-based' assessment is used to justify a consistent EU-wide approach, underpinned by the idea of a single 'European research area' and the single EU market. The concern to support innovation as a driver of economic development within the EU runs through both the Directive, and, more strongly, the Regulation. Some aspects of the Regulation (such as the different approach to 'low-risk' trials) represent a shift in the EU towards a less stringent approach to risk, but equally others (such as the continued lengthy time periods given for assessment) leave the legal position as under the Directive.

---

[178] Regulation 536/2014/EU, Article 2 (2) and (35).
[179] Regulation 536/2014/EU, Article 57.
[180] Regulation 536/2014/EU, Article 36.

EU clinical trials law is not only focused on risk, or on the idea that risks within the EU's market should be minimized. Equally, the provisions of EU clinical trials law are not only about the safety of individuals – they also seek to secure public health and to protect other public interests, including in access to data. The Directive and Regulation are replete with provisions that seek to protect human rights, and secure ethical decision-making. These provisions, along with the 'science-base' of the assessment of clinical trials in the EU, are used to enhance the legitimacy of EU decision-making in this context. However, the considerable scope for differences in approach between Member States that remains, along with the lack of transparency in available clinical trials data, undermines those regulatory objectives.

13

Risk: health system products – pharmaceuticals

Introduction

The previous chapter considered the ways in which the EU regulates the risks associated with the development of new products which are eventually to be used in health systems. This is far from systematic. The EU has a relatively dense regulatory regime for clinical trials of pharmaceuticals; other aspects of technological innovation in health fields are less closely regulated by the EU.[1] This chapter and the next continue the discussion of EU regulation of risks inherent in the products that are used within health systems – pharmaceuticals, products derived from human blood and tissue, medical devices. The focus here is on what happens after the research phase. Supposing trials show that a novel health system product is a promising new technology, how does EU law affect its access to the market for health products – the main 'market' of course being national health (insurance) systems themselves?[2] And what is the significance of the theme of risk for EU health law in these areas?

By and large,[3] EU law regulates pharmaceuticals, products derived from human blood and tissue, and medical devices separately. It does not define 'health system products', or 'health technologies', as a single regulatory category. EU legislation concerned with the safety of products circulating on

---

[1] See, for instance: Directive 2010/63/EU of the European Parliament and of the Council of 22 September 2010 on the protection of animals used for scientific purposes [2010] OJ L276/33 which seeks to harmonise the wide variety of practice across the EU on welfare standards for animals used in experiments. See: Wells, 'Animal Welfare and the 3Rs in European biomedical research' (2011) 12451(1) *Annals of the New York Academy of Sciences* 14.

[2] Chapter 11 has already covered the question of EU law's (relatively minimal) contribution to determining whether such products are available to patients within the 'basket of care' covered by national health systems (the health technology assessment phase).

[3] There are some important exceptions – in particular the EU's data protection laws apply to all three categories. The EU's Data Protection Directive (Directive 95/46/EC of the European Parliament and of the Council of 24 October 1995 on the protection of individuals with regard to the processing of personal data and on the free movement of such data [1995] OJ L281/31) is referred to in an array of relevant EU legislation. See further: Bache et al., 'The Defining Features of the European Union's Approach to Regulating New Health Technologies' in Flear, Farrell, Hervey and Murphy (eds), *European Law and New Health Technologies* (OUP 2013) 16-17; Chowdhury, *European Regulation of Medical Devices and Pharmaceuticals* (Springer 2014).

the EU's single market distinguishes pharmaceuticals ('medicinal products')[4] from 'medical devices'.[5] In terms of the distinction between pharmaceuticals or devices and human blood, tissues and cells, whole human blood is subject to a separate regulatory regime. Human tissue and cells other than blood cells are also treated separately. This chapter, and the next, explore the significance of risk as a theme of EU health law, through examining the contours and trajectory of the EU law applicable to each of these categories of products.

EU law may see pharmaceuticals, medical devices and human tissue as distinct. But many novel products which use human tissue or cells (such as 'biotechnology medicine' or 'biotechnology-derived pharmaceuticals';[6] 'advanced therapy medicinal products' (ATMPs);[7] and 'nanomedicine'[8]) potentially fall within at least two of the categories of pharmaceuticals, medical devices and human tissue. Examples include human artificial chromosomes (used as a vector for gene delivery); adult stem cells within a 'scaffold' (for instance, used for regenerating spinal cord); monoclonal antibodies (for instance, used to carry cancer drugs or

---

[4] Directive 2001/83/EC of the European Parliament and of the Council of 6 November 2001 on the Community code relating to medicinal products for human use [2001] OJ L311/67 (as amended).

[5] Council Directive 93/42/EEC of 14 June 1993 concerning medical devices [1993] OJ L169/1 (as amended).

[6] The terms 'biotechnology medicine' or 'biotechnology-derived pharmaceutical' are generally used (European Medicines Agency (EMA), 'ICH Guideline S6 (R1) – Preclinical Safety Evaluation of Biotechnology-Derived Pharmaceuticals' (CHMP/ICH/302/95, EMA 2009) to cover the medicines derived from the processes listed in section 1 of the Annex (recombinant DNA technology, controlled expression of genes coding for biologically active proteins in prokaryotes and eukaryotes including transformed mammalian cells, hybridoma and monoclonal antibody methods) to Regulation 726/2004/EC of the European Parliament and of the Council of 31 March 2004 laying down Community procedures for the authorisation and supervision of medicinal products for human and veterinary use and establishing a European Medicines Agency [2004] OJ L136/1.

[7] Advanced therapy medicinal products (ATMPs) are still classed as medicinal products and are included in section 1a of the Annex to Regulation 726/2004/EC of the European Parliament and of the Council of 31 March 2004 laying down Community procedures for the authorisation and supervision of medicinal products for human and veterinary use and establishing a European Medicines Agency [2004] OJ L136/1. Under the definition of ATMPs, Regulation 1394/2007/EC of the European Parliament and of the Council of 13 November 2007 on advanced therapy medicinal products and amending Directive 2001/83/EC and Regulation (EC) No 726/2004 [2007] OJ L324/121, includes gene therapy medicinal products, somatic cell therapy medicinal products, tissue engineered products and combined ATMPs. See: Mahalatchimy, 'Access to Advanced Therapy Medicinal Products in the EU: Where do we stand?' (2011) 18(3) *European Journal of Health Law* 305.

[8] The EMA's, 'Reflection Paper on Nanotechnology-Based Medicinal Products for Human Use' (EMEA/CHMP/79769/2006, EMA 2006), uses the term 'nanomedicinal product'; Commission, 'Amended proposal for a Council Decision concerning the 7th framework programme of the European Atomic Energy Community (Euratom) for nuclear research and training activities (2007-2011) (presented by the Commission pursuant to Article 250 (2) of the EC Treaty)' COM (2006) 364 final, highlights the importance of 'nano-medicine' under the theme of 'Nanosciences, Nanotechnologies, Materials and new Production Technologies'. Moreover, see: Dorbeck-Jung, Bowman and Van Calster (eds), 'Governing Nanomedicine: Lessons from within, and for, the EU Medical Technology Regulatory Framework' (2011) 33(2) *Law & Policy* 215.

radiation to cancer cells); nanotechnological[9] products such as liposomes used to deliver drugs or cells at the nano level; and biodegradable synthetic polymers used in tissue engineering.[10] In EU law, because of the way in which the pharmaceuticals regime has developed,[11] many of these products are subsumed within the category of pharmaceuticals.[12] We therefore begin our discussion with EU pharmaceuticals law. EU law on human blood, tissue and cells; and on medical devices, is considered in the next chapter.

EU pharmaceuticals law

Introduction and scope

Pharmaceutical regulation has been an important part of EU law since the 1960s.[13] The relevant EU law now operates within the context of the International Conference on Harmonisation of Technical Requirements of Pharmaceuticals for Human Use (ICH). The ICH draws together standards and approaches of regulatory authorities in the EU, Japan and the USA,[14] and experts from the pharmaceutical industry in those regions. Its focus is scientific and technical aspects of the regulation of pharmaceuticals. It also has the task of providing recommendations for greater harmonization of such technical requirements, with a view to promoting greater efficiency through avoiding duplication in the testing needed for new pharmaceuticals, and the consequent delay in bringing new products to the various markets.[15] The ICH very much operates within a

---

[9] Defined as materials whose structure is on the scale of nanometers, i.e. billionths of a metre. See further: McHale, 'Nanomedicine and the EU: Some Legal, Ethical and Regulatory Challenges' (2009) 16(1) *Maastricht Journal of European and Comparative Law* 65; Dorbeck-Jung, Bowman and Van Calster (eds), 'Governing Nanomedicine: Lessons from within, and for, the EU Medical Technology Regulatory Framework' (2011) 33(2) *Law & Policy* 215; Dorbeck-Jung, 'The Governance of Therapeutic Nanoproducts in the European Union: A Model for New Health Technology Regulation?' in Flear et al., above n 3; Dorbeck-Jung and Chowdhury, 'Is the European Medical Products Authorisation Regulation Equipped to Cope with the Challenges of Nanomedicines?' (2011) 33(2) *Law & Policy* 276.

[10] For further examples, see: Warren-Jones, 'Mapping Science and New Health Technologies: In search of a definition' in Flear et al. (eds), above n 3.

[11] See, in particular: Regulation 1394/2007/EC of the European Parliament and of the Council of 13 November 2007 on advanced therapy medicinal products and amending Directive 2001/83/EC and Regulation (EC) No 726/2004 [2007] OJ L324/121, which extends the marketing authorization rules applicable to pharmaceuticals to various categories of these novel products.

[12] See further: Bache et al., above n 3.

[13] Council Directive 65/65/EEC of 26 January 1965 on the approximation of provisions laid down by Law, Regulation or Administrative Action relating to proprietary medicinal products.[1965] OJ L22/369; Hervey and McHale, *Health Law and the European Union* (CUP 2004) 288-290.

[14] The WHO, the European Free Trade Area, represented by Switzerland, and Canada have observer status in the ICH.

[15] For further information see: <http://www.ich.org/>. In 2000, ICH adopted a "Common Technical Document" providing a harmonised format for new product applications. In the EU, this was implemented by the CPMP, as a new Notice to Applicants, issued in June and September 2001: EMA, 'Common Technical Document for the Registration of Pharmaceuticals for Human Use' (CPMP/ICH/2887/99, EMA 2004).

safety framework, and its work is imbued with the notions of risk assessment and risk management.

In EU Law, pharmaceuticals ('medicinal products') are defined by the (regularly amended)[16] 2001 'Community Code Relating to Medicinal Products for Human Use'.[17] The definition has two limbs: by 'presentation' ('any substance or combination of substances presented for treating or preventing disease in human beings') or by 'function' ('any substance or combination of substances which may be used in or administered to human beings either with a view to restoring, correcting or modifying physiological functions by exerting a pharmacological, immunological or metabolic action, or to making a medical diagnosis').[18] The definitions are broadly construed.[19] For instance, in the interface between pharmaceuticals and foodstuffs (such as vitamins C and E; bacterial cultures used to assist in gastroenterological problems; bioflavonoids; herbs or herb extracts), where one Member State regulates such products as foodstuffs, but another as pharmaceuticals, the Community code applies.[20] Equally, a product classified as a medical device in one Member State may be classified as a pharmaceutical in another Member State, if it has the characteristics of a pharmaceutical.[21] And industrially processed plasma, intended for transfusions, if it falls within the definition of the Community code, is covered by that code for the purposes of processing, storage and distribution.[22]

---

[16] Most recently in 2012, see: Directive 2012/26/EU of the European Parliament and of the Council of 25 October 2012 amending Directive 2001/83/EC as regards pharmacovigilance [2012] OJ L299/1; and also in 2011, see: Directive 2011/62/EU of the European Parliament and of the Council of 8 June 2011 amending Directive 2001/83/EC on the Community code relating to medicinal products for human use, as regards the prevention of the entry into the legal supply chain of falsified medicinal products [2011] OJ L174/74.

[17] Directive 2001/83/EC of the European Parliament and of the Council of 6 November 2001 on the Community code relating to medicinal products for human use [2001] OJ L311/67 (as amended).

[18] Directive 2001/83/EC, Article 1 (2). A product is a medicinal product if it falls within either of those definitions, see: *Monteil and Samanni*, C-60/89, EU:C:1991:138, paragraphs 10 and 11. On presentation by function, see: *Hecht-Pharma GmbH v Staatliches Gewerbeaufsichtsamt Lüneburg*, C-140/07, EU:C:2009:5; *BIOS Naturprodukte GmbH v Saarland*, C-27/08, EU:C:2009:278.

[19] *Tissier*, C-35/85, EU:C:1986:143, paragraph 26; *Monteil and Samanni* EU:C:1991:138, and *Upjohn*, C-112/89, EU:C:1991:147, paragraph 16; *Staat der Nederlanden v Antroposana, Patiëntenvereniging voor Antroposofische Gezondheidszorg and Others*, C-84/06, EU:C:2007:535, paragraph 31; *Chemische Fabrik Kreussler v Sunstar Deutschland*, C-308/11, EU:C:2012:548.

[20] A product which constitutes a 'medicinal product' within the meaning of Directive 2001/83/EC may be imported into another Member State only with a marketing authorisation issued in accordance with the provisions of that Directive, even where it is lawfully marketed as a foodstuff in another Member State, see: *HLH Warenvertriebs GmbH and Orthica BV v Bundesrepublik Deutschland*, C-211/03, C-299/03 and C-316/03 to C-318/03, EU:C:2005:370, paragraph 60; *Hechtpharma* EU:C:2009:5. On the other hand, a Member State may classify a product as a 'medicinal product' only if it meets the definitions in Directive 2001/83/EC. See: *Commission of the European Communities v Kingdom of Spain*, C-88/07, EU:C:2009:123.

[21] See: *Laboratoires Lyocentre*, C-109/12, EU:C:2013:626, paragraph 48; *Commission v Austria*, C-150/00, EU:C:2004:237, paragraph 60; *HLH Warenvertriebs GmbH and Orthica BV v Bundesrepublik Deutschland* EU:C:2005:370, paragraph 56.

[22] *Octapharma France*, C-512/12, EU:C:2014:149.

EU pharmaceutical law includes measures aimed (broadly) at protection of patients as the consumers of pharmaceuticals. For instance, no new medicinal product may be marketed within the EU without a prior marketing authorization; EU law requires surveillance of safety of pharmaceuticals during their life on the market ('pharmacovigilance'); there are restrictions on labelling and packaging of pharmaceuticals; and on advertising of pharmaceuticals. The requirement for a marketing authorization aims to ensure quality controls in the development of new pharmaceutical products. It fits squarely within a standard risk regulation model. Equally, it is not concerned with relative therapeutic benefit, or whether a new pharmaceutical meets a real health need.[23] There is evidence that the number of truly new pharmaceuticals being authorized in the EU is falling.[24] The model of risk here does not take into account the risk to health systems of 'me-too' pharmaceuticals – versions of patented pharmaceuticals that differ in some small way from a product under patent, and benefit from their own patent protection. One of the key risks here is that of 'evergreening' of patents – the practice of the pharmaceutical industry of gaining significant contracts with national health systems for newly patented pharmaceuticals which are only slightly different from existing pharmaceuticals, generic versions of which would be much cheaper.[25] That risk is not explicitly accounted for in EU pharmaceuticals law. Moreover, provisions such as labelling rules may operate more within a consumer choice framework, by enabling consumers to make their own judgements of risk.

The Community Code relating to medicinal products for human use is a provision of 'exhaustive harmonization'. It is applicable to the vast majority of pharmaceuticals marketed within the EU. However, its scope does not extend to products prepared in a pharmacy for an individual patient, or to advanced therapy medicinal products prepared on a non-routine basis according to specific quality standards and to be used under the direction of a specific practitioner for a specific patient.[26] The risks associated with such use of pharmaceuticals are governed by national laws, leaving discretion to health professionals within that context. We note, therefore, that any claims about *EU law*'s approach to risk do not apply to *all* uses of pharmaceuticals within health systems. Within its

---

[23] The EU's network for health technology assessment, EUnetHTA, published its project work in a special issue of (2009) 25 *International Journal of Technology Assessment in Health Care* 1. As we have already seen in chapter 11, virtually no EU law regulates processes by which novel medical products are produced, authorized, or included within national health systems on the basis of their overall relative therapeutic benefit, to individuals and systemically. For discussion of the role of litigation in health technology assessment in the UK, Australia and New Zealand, see: Syrett, 'Health technology appraisal and the courts: accountability for reasonableness and the judicial model of procedural justice' (2001) 6(4) *Health Economics, Policy and Law* 469.

[24] Jackson, *Law and the Regulation of Medicines* (Hart 2012) 77–81.

[25] Jackson above n24, 81–82. See further below.

[26] Directive 2001/83/EC, Article 3. For a case study in the power of the global pharmaceutical industry to use such 'off label' rules, see: Applbaum, 'Shadow science: Zyproxa, Eli Lilly and the globalization of pharmaceutical damage control' (2010) 5 *Biosocieties* 236.

scope, however, national authorities may not adopt different provisions, even if these seek to grant greater protection to patients.[27] In this context, therefore, the effects of EU law on risk regulation are to secure a unified approach to risks that may arise from the marketing of pharmaceuticals and their use within national health systems. The Community code may therefore have the effect of reducing the levels of protection to consumers in some contexts and in some Member States; but equally of increasing them in others. So, for instance, France is permitted to have a more stringent regime than other Member States for plasma which is prepared by a method involving an industrial process (a 'medicinal product') *only* for its collection and testing.[28] But France is not permitted to have its own standards for processing, storage and distribution, because those fall within the Community code, which sets a single regulatory standard for the whole EU.[29] The Community code therefore implies a particular risk regulation/consumer safety model for areas for which some Member States, for instance, France, may have otherwise chosen a more precautionary approach, or indeed an approach based more on ethics or human dignity.[30]

Marketing authorization, centralized and decentralized procedures

Pharmaceuticals falling within the scope of the Community code may not be made available within the EU without a marketing authorization.[31] This rule includes generic versions of proprietary medicines which have a marketing authorization, although special arrangements apply for securing marketing authorizations for such generics. The marketing authorization rules interact with EU law on research processes, because marketing authorizations cannot be given without compliance with principles of good laboratory/clinical practice.[32]

---

[27] *Deutscher Apothekerverband eV v 0800 DocMorris NV and Jacques Waterval*, C-322/01, EU:C:2003:664; *Staat der Nederlanden v Antroposana, Patiëntenvereniging voor Antroposofische Gezondheidszorg and Others* EU:C:2007:535; *Gintec*, C-374/05, EU:C:2007:654; *HLH Warenvertriebs GmbH and Orthica BV v Bundesrepublik Deutschland* EU:C:2005:370.

[28] Under Directive 2002/98/EC of the European Parliament of the Council of 27 January 2003 setting standards of quality and safety for the collection, testing, processing, storage and distribution of human blood and blood components and amending Directive 2001/83/EC [2003] OJ L33/30, Article 4 (2).

[29] *Octapharma France* EU:C:2014:149.

[30] For discussion of the cultural and legal place of human blood and other tissues and cells in France, see: Farrell, *The Politics of Blood: Ethics, Innovation and the Regulation of Risk* (CUP 2012); Hervey and McHale, above n 13, 343. France was particularly badly affected by the contamination of blood by HIV during the 1990s.

[31] Directive 2001/83/EC, Article 6 (1).

[32] E.g., Directive 2004/10/EC of the European Parliament and of the Council of 11 February 2004 on the harmonisation of laws, regulations and administrative provisions relating to the application of the principles of good laboratory practice and the verification of their applications for tests on chemical substances [2004] OJ L50/44, Recital 4, provides that the EU's marketing legislation lays down 'that non-clinical tests on pharmaceutical products are to be carried out in accordance with the principles of . . . [good laboratory practice] in force in the Community for chemical substances, compliance with which is also required by other

EU law provides two procedures by which a marketing authorization may be secured: the 'centralized' and 'decentralized' procedures. The centralized procedure is compulsory for new biotechnological products and innovative 'high technology' products.[33] Most truly novel pharmaceuticals fall into these categories. The centralized procedure may also be selected for other pharmaceuticals involving a 'new active substance', or 'a significant therapeutic, scientific or technical innovation', or if the centralized procedure is 'in the interests of patients or animal health at EU level'.[34] Under the centralized procedure, applications are submitted to the European Medicines Agency, which grants and subsequently supervises marketing authorizations.[35]

The European Medicines Agency (EMA), based in London, began operation as the European Medicines Evaluation Agency in February 1995.[36] As an EU agency, the EMA assists the EU institutions with the scientific and technical side of their activities.[37] The EMA operates through its scientific committees.[38] Under the centralized procedure, it is the Committee for Medicinal Products for Human Use, a 'scientific committee' of the European Medicines Agency, which prepares opinions on pharmaceuticals intended for humans. Its

Community legislation.'; see also: Commission Directive 2005/28/EC of 8 April 2005 laying down principles and detailed guidelines for good clinical practice as regards investigational medicinal products for human use, as well as the requirements for authorisation of the manufacturing or importation of such products [2005] OJ L91/13, Recital 3. See: Bache et al., above n 3.

33 Regulation 726/2004/EC of the European Parliament and of the Council of 31 March 2004 laying down Community procedures for the authorisation and supervision of medicinal products for human and veterinary use and establishing a European Medicines Agency [2004] OJ L136/1, Article 3 (1) and Annex. These refer to medicinal products developed through recombinant DNA technology, controlled expression of gene coding for biologically active proteins in prokaryotes and eukaryotes; those which contain a new active substance which when the Regulation came into force was not authorized in the EU and is intended for treatment of AIDS, cancer, neurogenerative disorders, diabetes, auto-immune diseases and other immune dysfunctions, viral diseases and designated 'orphan medicinal products' (those for treating rare diseases, see further below).

34 Regulation 726/2004/EC, Article 3 (2).

35 Regulation 726/2004/EC, Article 4.

36 It was established by Council Regulation 2309/93/EEC of 22 July 1993 laying down Community procedures for the authorization and supervision of medicinal products for human and veterinary use and establishing a European Agency for the Evaluation of Medicinal Products [1993] OJ L214/1, see now: Regulation 726/2004/EC.

37 The current EMA structure was established in September 2013. It is headed by an Executive Director, supported by a Deputy Executive Director. There are also eight specific divisions, the Human Medicines Research and Development Support Division, the Human Medicines Evaluation division, the Procedure Management and Business Support Division, The Inspections and Human Medicine Pharmacovigilance Division, Veterinary Medical Products Division, Stakeholders and Communications Division, Information Technology Division and the Administration Division.

38 These are: the Committee for Medicinal Products for Human Use, the Pharmacovigiliance Risk Assessment Committee, the Committee for Medicinal Products for Veterinary Use, the Committee for Orphan Medical Products and the Committee on Herbal Medicinal Products, the Committee for Advanced Therapies and the Pediatric Committee.

opinions are based on scientific assessments of efficacy, quality and safety. In addition, it is involved in post-authorization activities (such as modifications or variations to authorizations), arbitration between national authorities and decisions where 'urgent action is necessary to protect human health or the environment'.[39]

The development of the centralized procedure, and the establishment of EMA, were welcomed by the EU's proprietary pharmaceutical industry, which operates within global markets. The opportunity to secure an EU-wide marketing authorization provides a significant efficiency, and quicker returns on investment in developing novel products. However, especially given understandings that 'scientific' decision-making cannot be divorced from 'political' decision-making, the very notion of a nationally determined risk assessment is a casualty of the centralized procedure. The EMA's role may leave the outcome of risk assessments vulnerable to regulatory capture or corporate bias. The interactions between the EMA and the pharmaceutical industry, with individuals moving between the industry and regulatory bodies such the EMA, during the course of their careers, have been highlighted as a matter of concern.[40] The strong criticism that the institutional structure of the system itself, 'emanating from DG Enterprise and centrally concerned with the single market in pharmaceuticals',[41] is only peripherally concerned with health protection no longer stands, as pharmaceuticals regulation moved to DG SANCO in 2010. But the idea that the system as a whole tends to favour industry interests, at the expense of patient safety, still holds validity. The risk focus is about risk to industry of inefficient authorization processes. Those risks could take the form of a system which is too precautionary. Equally, though, they could take the form of the reputational risk that is associated with allowing to market a product that harms significant numbers of patients, or causes significant harm to a small number of patients. A conclusion that the risk agenda is insufficiently precautionary, because it is 'too focused on industry interests', lacks sufficient nuance.

Applications to the EMA are made on the basis of a standardized dossier of information. It must include details such as the name of the product, its constituent parts, description of manufacturing methods, test results and compliance with good clinical practice.[42] This includes certification that, where clinical trials have been undertaken outside the EU, they comply with the

---

[39] Regulation 726/2004/EC, Article 20 (4).
[40] See: e.g. Dukes, Braithwaite, Moloney, *Pharmaceuticals, Corporate Crime and Public Health* (Edward Elgar 2014); Braithwaite, *Corporate Crime in the Pharmaceutical Industry* (Routledge 1984); Abraham and Lewis, *Regulating Medicines in Europe: Competition, Expertise and Public Health* (Routledge 2000); Mossialos and Abel Smith, 'The Regulation of the European Pharmaceutical Industry' in Stavridis, Mossialos, Morgan and Machlin (eds), *New Challenges to the EU: Policies and Policy-Making* (Dartmouth 1997); Jackson (Hart 2012) above n 24, 91.
[41] Hervey and McHale above n 13, 296.
[42] Directive 2001/83/EC, Article 8 (3) and Annex I.

requirements of the Clinical Trials Directive or Regulation.[43] The Committee for Medicinal Products for Human Use must scrutinize the application and give its opinion within 210 days of a valid application being received.[44] The European Commission must prepare a draft decision within fifteen days of receipt of the Opinion,[45] and final decision after a further fifteen days.[46] The fixed timelines are seen as being beneficial to both the industry and to patients, as they speed up the authorization process. However, they have been criticized as promoting time-to-market for new pharmaceuticals, at the expense of public health.[47]

The decentralized procedure applies to all other pharmaceuticals.[48] The decentralized procedure has been compulsory for all medicinal products to be marketed in a Member State, other than that in which they were first authorized, since 1 January 1998.[49] Under the decentralized procedure, the application for marketing authorization is made to the competent body of the Member State concerned.[50] Where authorization is sought for more than one Member State, the application is made to a 'reference Member State'. In general, the decision of the competent authority of the reference Member State must be recognized by the other Member States.[51] This has raised concerns that the least demanding

---

[43] Directive 2001/83/EC, Article 8 (3) (i), Annex I, and Article 6. For discussion of the Clinical Trials Directive 2001/20/EC of the European Parliament and of the Council of 4 April 2001 on the approximation of the laws, regulations and administrative provisions of the Member States relating to the implementation of good clinical practice in the conduct of clinical trials on medicinal products for human use [2001] OJ L121/34, and Regulation 536/2014/EU of the European Parliament and of the Council of 16 April 2014 on clinical trials on medicinal products for human use, and repealing Directive 2001/20/EC [2014] OJ L158/1, see chapter 12.

[44] Directive 2001/83/EC, Article 17 (1).

[45] Directive 2001/83/EC, Article 33.   [46] Directive 2001/83/EC, Article 34.

[47] Mossialos and McKee, *EU Law and the Social Character of Health Care* (PIE Peter Lang 2004) 113-4.

[48] Directive 2001/83/EC, Article 6 (1).

[49] The decentralized procedure is the successor to the "multi-state procedure", see: Hervey and McHale above n 13, 291-292, 296-298; Sauer, 'The European Community's Pharmaceutical Policy' in Casparie, Hermans and Paelinck, (eds), *Health Care In Europe After 1992* (Dartmouth 1992) 135; Gardner, 'The European Agency for the Evaluation of Medicines and European Regulation of Pharmaceuticals' (1996) 2 *European Law Journal* 48, 53–54 according to which a producer of a medicinal product authorized in one Member State could request extension of this authorization to two or more (originally five or more – see: Directive 75/319/EEC of 20 May 1975 on the approximation of provisions laid down by law, regulation or administrative action relating to medicinal products [1975] OJ L147/13, now repealed and replaced by Directive 2001/83/EC) other Member States. A formal opinion on authorization was to be provided by the CPMP. However, under the multi-state procedure, the CPMP could not impose its view on Member States. In the final analysis, Member States remained free to make their own independent decisions on marketing authorizations.

[50] Directive 2001/83/EC, Article 8.

[51] Directive 2001/83/EC, Article 28. Exceptions include the power of Member States to exclude certain 'advanced therapy' products from their markets, which allows Member States to protect national ethical settlements for instance concerning embryonic stem cells, see: Flear, 'The EU's Biopolitical Governance of Advanced Therapy Medicinal Products' (2009) 16(1)

Member State (chosen by manufacturers seeking authorization) will in effect set the standard, a 'race to the bottom' not appropriate in the context of pharmaceuticals.[52]

Applications under the decentralized procedure require the same information as in the standard dossier for the centralized procedure, including clinical trials results,[53] along with copies of marketing authorization given in another Member State or another country outside of the EU. Details of any decisions refusing marketing authorization must also be included.[54] This latter provision, introduced in 2010, tightens up the EU's procedures in response to the criticism that the pharmaceutical industry was not required to be transparent about such previous refusals.[55] It seeks to respond to concerns that 'pharmacovigilance' information does not effectively reach the bodies making marketing authorization decisions. It is particularly applicable to pharmaceuticals with a new active substance and biological medicinal products, including biosimilars, where a competent authority has granted conditional marketing authorization, for instance, requiring additional monitoring through a post-authorization safety study. It seeks to ensure that such post-authorization information is available to competent authorities making further marketing authorizations in other Member States. Although the post-2010 provisions are undoubtedly an improvement in terms of transparency, in view of the broader criticisms of lack of transparency in the pharmaceuticals authorization process (see further below), they still embody an approach to risk regulation which limits the effects of access to information on regulatory, health professional and patient/consumer decisions.

Where a pharmaceutical is a generic version of an already-authorized pharmaceutical (the 'reference product'[56]), EU law does not require submission of trial data in the authorization process.[57] Reference products are given a

---

Maastricht Journal of European and Comparative Law 113; Roche, 'Advanced Technologies and the Outer Limits of DNA Legislation: New Horizons for Patients or a Scaffold Too Far?' (2008) 3(4) *Journal of Intellectual Property Law and Practice* 210. On the scope of national discretion under Article 28, see *R (on the application of Synthon BV) v Licensing Authority of the Department of Health*, C-452 /06, EU:C:2008:565.

[52] Hervey and McHale above n 13, 297.

[53] In *Commission v Lithuania*, C-350/08, EU:C:2010:642, and *Commission v Poland*, C-385/08, EU:C:2010:801, Lithuania and Poland were found in breach of EU law for maintaining a marketing authorization for pharmaceuticals, which had been granted by Lithuania and Poland (i.e. before their accession to the EU), on the basis of information that did not include trial data.

[54] Directive 2001/83/EC, Article 8 (3) (l).

[55] See, for instance: Abraham and Lewis (Routledge 2000) above n 40, 89–92; Gibson and Lemmens, 'Niche Markets and Evidence Assessment in Transition' (2014) 22(2) *Medical Law Review* 200.

[56] See: *R (on the application of Generics (UK) Ltd) v Licensing Authority*, C-527/07, EU:C:2009:379.

[57] Directive 2001/83/EC, Article 10. The procedure under Article 10 applies also where marketing authorization is sought for a third product, essentially similar to a second product, which is a new pharmaceutical form of the original reference product, which has been authorized for

ten-year protection period under Directive 2001/83/EC. The definition of generic product is based on its composition in active substances, as well as its 'pharmaceutical form' (where various immediate-release oral forms, such as tablets or capsules, are considered the same). For biosimilar products,[58] the bioequivalence with the reference product must be demonstrated by bioavailability studies. However, 'the different salts, esters, ethers, isomers, mixtures of isomers, complexes or derivatives of an active substance shall be considered to be the same active substance, unless they differ significantly in properties with regard to safety and/or efficacy'.[59] If there are differences in raw materials or manufacturing processes of the biosimilar product, then trial data must be provided.[60]

The obligation to recognize marketing authorizations granted under the decentralized procedure applies also to authorizations for generics.[61] National authorities may not unilaterally apply their own versions of the equivalence test. If they are concerned about the public health implications of a marketing authorization for a generic product, they are required to use the procedure set out in Directive 2001/83/EC, Article 29, involving the giving of detailed reasons, an attempt to reach agreement among the relevant Member States, and the eventual involvement of the European Medicines Agency. A Member State may not circumvent the marketing authorization rules for generics on the grounds that a generic obtained from outside the EU is cheaper than an authorized generic.[62] The provisions for individual prescription by health professionals,[63] which delineate the scope of the Directive, are not to be interpreted in such a way as to undermine its overall objective, of protecting public health. These interpretations by the CJEU of the marketing authorization rules support a legislative settlement which has been widely criticized as being too generous to the (non-generic) pharmaceutical industry.[64]

marketing within the EU for at least a 10 year period, see: *R (on the application of Approved Prescription Services Ltd) v Licensing Authority*, C-36/03, EU:C:2004:781.

[58] Products where the active ingredient is either made by or derived from a living organism, using recombinant DNA or controlled gene expression methods. Biosimilars are made by a different company to that holding the intellectual property rights on the original innovative product. Biosimilars are a controversial form of generics, because the generic manufacturer does not have access to the original cell bank, or the precise methods for its preparation.

[59] Directive 2001/83/EC, Article 10 (2) (b).   [60] Directive 2001/83/EC, Article 10 (4).

[61] *R (on the application of Synthon BV) v Licensing Authority of the Department of Health* EU:C:2008:565.

[62] *European Commission v Republic of Poland*, C-185/10, EU:C:2012:181.

[63] Directive 2001/83/EC, Article 5, refers to an individual pharmaceutical order to fulfil special needs, formulated in accordance with the specifications of an authorised health professional and for use by an individual patient under the direct personal responsibility of the health professional, see: *European Commission v Republic of Poland* EU:C:2012:181, paragraph 29.

[64] Marqusee, *The Price of Experience: Writings on Living with Cancer* (OR Books 2014); advance extract available in <https://www.opendemocracy.net/ournhs/mike-marqusee/held-hostage-by-big-pharma>; Figert and Bell, 'Big Pharma and Big Medicine in the Global Environment' in Kleinman and Moore (eds), *Routledge Handbook of Science, Technology and Society* (Routledge 2014); Dukes, Braithwaite, Moloney (Edward Elgar 2014) above n 40;

Homeopathic medicine has been explicitly included in Directive 2001/83/EC since 2004.[65] Article 13 provides that homeopathic medicines must be authorized under the Directive, unless they were already authorized before 31 December 1993. Certain homeopathic products are subject to a special simplified registration process.[66] These provisions highlight the increased recognition of homeopathy in some jurisdictions,[67] and also some of the concerns regarding the safety of such products. Again, Member States may not substitute their own procedures for those required by EU law, even if their procedures are driven by increased patient safety concerns.[68] A special simplified registration process also applies to traditional herbal medicinal products.[69] These are particularly challenging for the EU to regulate, as they have significant cultural resonances, and are regulated as medicines, food, or entirely unregulated, in different EU Member States.[70] The EU became concerned after an incident in the 1990s in which *Aristolochia* (birthwort[71]) had been prescribed to Belgian patients as part of a slimming programme and some 135 suffered kidney damage.[72] Annabelle Littoz-Monnet shows how cooperation between the UK Medicines Control Agency and the EMA was effectively able to legitimate EU involvement in the field, and defeat the 'natural health lobby', which saw the matter as consumer-choice, rather than risk-regulation based. The particular challenges of herbal medicine have been recognized by the EMA, which now includes a specific Committee for Herbal Medicinal Products, established in 2004 and replacing an earlier Working Party on Herbal Medicinal Products.[73] The

---

Badcott and Sahm, 'The dominance of Big Pharma: unhealthy relationships?' (2013) 16(2) *Medicine, Health Care and Philosophy* 245; Goldacre, *Bad Pharma: How Drug Companies Mislead Doctors and Harm Patients* (Fourth Estate 2012), and see further: chapter 18.

[65] Directive 2004/24/EC of the European Parliament and of the Council of 31 March 2004 amending, amending, as regards traditional herbal medicinal products, Directive 2001/83/EC on the Community code relating to medicinal products for human use [2004] OJ L136/85.

[66] Directive 2001/83/EC, Article 14.

[67] Also its championing by high profile figures such as Prince Charles, the Prince of Wales in the UK.

[68] See: *Meta Fackler KG v Bundesrepublik Deutschland*, C-444/03, EU:C:2005:288, a national law precluding the use of Directive 2001/83/EC, Articles 14 and 15, for a pharmaceutical composed of several known homeopathic substances, where its use as a homeopathic product is not generally known, is prohibited.

[69] Directive 2001/83/EC, Article 16 (a). Herbal medicine is a "medicinal product whose only active ingredients are herbal substances or herbal preparations" or both. Herbal preparation concerns "preparation obtained by subjecting herbal substances to processes such as extraction, distillation, expression, fractionation, purification, concentration". Herbal substances refers to "a plant or part of a plant, alga, fungus or lichen". It also includes unprocessed exudate of plants defined by the plant part used. See: Directive 2004/24/EC; Directive 2001/83/EC, Article 1 (1).

[70] Littoz-Monnet, 'The role of independent regulators in policy making: Venue shopping and framing strategies in the EU regulation of old wives cures' (2014) 53(1) *European Journal of Political Research* (2014) 1.

[71] One of the most poisonous plants in the world, see: The Poison Garden, 'Aristolochia clematitis, birthwort' (*The Poison Garden*, 2014).

[72] Littoz-Monnet, above n 70.

[73] Established by Directive 2001/83/EC, Article 16 (h).

Committee's assessments are based on both long-standing use and lack of specific harm.[74]

Some commentators have been critical of the kind of approach adopted by the EU to risks to patients associated with such 'complementary and alternative' medicines. For instance, Emily Jackson (in an analysis of UK law which applies equally to the EU law we outline here) points out that authorizing such products within the same processes as other pharmaceuticals may lend a spurious 'official stamp of legitimacy'. At the same time, lighter touch regulation is justified by the assumption that 'natural' remedies are essentially harmless (though perhaps not very effective), and that such remedies are used mainly by the 'worried well', for whom lower level consumer protection approaches to safety are appropriate, rather than the approach adopted to protect patients with serious illnesses or disabilities. Both these assumptions are inaccurate.[75]

Paediatric medicine and 'orphan drugs'

A special set of provisions of EU law, which operate within the general EU and ICH framework,[76] apply to pharmaceuticals for paediatric use. Many pharmaceuticals currently used to treat children have not in fact been subject to clinical trials involving children. Regulation 1901/2006/EC[77] responds to concerns about risks arising from the appropriateness of medication, dosage and inadequacy of information to the relevant health professionals.[78] The Regulation itself explicitly recognizes that market forces by themselves are insufficient to address the significant challenges arising.[79] The Regulation provides for EU-wide data

---

[74] The criteria which will be considered as to whether the product is authorized are its traditional history and pharmacological properties. The licensing authorities may authorize if it has been in continuous medicinal use for 30 years and has been in continuous medicinal use in the EU for 15 years, see: Directive 2001/83/EC, Article 1 (2) inserting a new Article 16 (a) (1) (e) and a new Article 16 (c) (1) (c) into the Directive. Moreover there must be sufficient information such that it has been established that the traditional use is not harmful and the product's pharmacological effects/efficacy are plausible in the light of the longstanding experience of the products.

[75] Jackson above n 24, 12–13.

[76] Directive 2001/20/EC of the European Parliament and of the Council of 4 April 2001 on the approximation of the laws, regulations and administrative provisions of the Member States relating to the implementation of good clinical practice in the conduct of clinical trials on medicinal products for human use [2001] OJ L121/34; and EMA, 'ICH Guideline E11: Note for Guidance on Clinical Investigation of Medicinal Products in the Paediatric Population' (CPMP/ICH/2711/99, EMA 2001), are noted as important reference points for the Committee's work; See: Regulation 1901/2006/EC of the European Parliament and of the Council of 12 December 2006 on medicinal products for paediatric use and amending Regulation (EEC) No 1768/92, Directive 2001/20/EC, Directive 2001/83/EC and Regulation (EC) No 726/2004 [2006] OJ L378/1, Recital 8.

[77] Regulation 1901/2006/EC.   [78] See: Bache et al., above n 3, 37.

[79] Regulation 1901/2006/EC, Recital 2.

collection of paediatric studies;[80] a special regulatory committee, the Paediatric Committee; and an EU 'network of excellence'.[81] EU funds[82] support the network, as well as other incentives, such as assessment by the EMA of paediatric investigation plans, fee waivers for scientific advice, information and transparency measures, and research.[83] The general EU marketing authorization system makes available a special paediatric use marketing authorization.[84] An applicant for such a marketing authorization is able to refer to data contained in the dossier of a medicinal product which is or has been authorized in the EU, in order to provide an 'incentive to encourage small and medium-sized enterprises to develop off-patent medicinal products for the paediatric population'.[85]

These provisions seek to steer a course between encouraging the development of pharmaceuticals for use with children; ensuring that they are safe and effective, by subjecting them to research that complies with ethical standards (where consent is more challenging than in adult trials); and improving information to health professionals. They also seek to avoid introducing delays to the authorization of pharmaceuticals for adult patients.[86] The Regulation provides a mechanism – the 'paediatric investigation plan'[87] – which compels pharmaceutical companies to envisage the possibility of use of their novel products by children. At the same time, the Regulation provides for various waivers from the obligation to do so,[88] for instance, if there is evidence showing that the disease or condition for which the product is intended occurs only in adult populations.[89] CJEU interprets these waivers narrowly,[90] essentially encouraging the development of paediatric medicine. Bache, Flear and Hervey argue that this area of EU pharmaceutical law is more focused on ethics and human

---

[80] The database on clinical trials established by Directive 2001/20/EC clinical trials on medicinal products for human use [2001] OJ L121/34, 'should include a European register of clinical trials of medicinal products for paediatric use comprising all ongoing, prematurely terminated, and completed paediatric studies conducted both in the Community and in third countries', see: Regulation 1901/2006/EC, Recital 31 and Article 41.

[81] Which 'should contribute to the work of strengthening the foundations of the European Research Area in the context of Community Framework Programmes for Research, Technological Development and Demonstration Activities, benefit the paediatric population and provide a source of information and expertise for industry' see: Regulation 1901/2006/EC, Recital 33 and Article 44.

[82] Regulation 1901/2006/EC, Recital 35.

[83] Regulation 1901/2006/EC, Recital 30 and Article 40.

[84] Regulation 1901/2006/EC, Recital 19.   [85] Regulation 1901/2006/EC, Recital 20.

[86] Regulation 1901/2006/EC, Recital 4.

[87] Regulation 1901/2006/EC, Article 2 (2). An applicant who intends to make an application for marketing authorisation of a medicinal product is under an obligation to draw up a paediatric investigation plan and submit it to the EMA for approval, in accordance with Regulation 1901/2006/EC, Article 15 (1).

[88] Regulation 1901/2006/EC, Article 11.   [89] Regulation 1901/2006/EC, Article 7 (1) (a).

[90] *Nycomed Danmark ApS v European Medicines Agency (EMA)*, T-52/09, EU:C:2011:738.

rights than on a straightforward risk-based analysis within the framework of the market for pharmaceuticals.[91]

Innovations in pharmaceutical medicine have enabled the development of treatments for very rare conditions which affect only small numbers of patients.[92] Regulation 141/2000/EC[93] makes provision for such 'orphan drugs'. This Regulation is aimed at facilitating a harmonized approach and effective regulatory environment which enables the EU to compete internationally.[94] An 'orphan medicinal product' is one intended for diagnosis, prevention or treatment of conditions which vary between 'serious and chronic' to 'life threatening'.[95] It must be shown that there is no alternative, authorized and satisfactory method for the diagnosis, prevention and the treatment of the particular condition or, in the alternative, where such a method does exist, that such a new medicine would 'be of significant benefit to those affected by the condition'.[96] In addition, the product must be targeted at a disease which concerns a maximum of five in 10,000 persons in the EU or 'that without incentives it is unlikely that the marketing of the medicinal product in the [EU] would generate sufficient return to justify the necessary investment'.[97]

Pharmaceuticals are designated orphan drugs following an opinion from the EMA's Committee for Orphan Medicinal Products, although the assessment of their marketing authorization is undertaken by the Committee for Medicinal Products for Human Use.[98] Designation as an 'orphan drug' attracts significant benefits, such as prior assistance/advice in protocol development, access to the centralized procedure,[99] fee reductions or waivers,[100] and, crucially, a ten-year agreement by the EMA not to accept applications for similar medicinal products indicated for the same condition.[101] The Regulation does seem to have

---

[91] Bache et al., above n 3, 37-38, 41.
[92] The precise definition of such drugs varies across jurisdictions see: e.g. Syrett, 'Looking After the Orphans Treatments for Rare Diseases, EU Law and the Ethics of Costly Health Care' in Flear et al., above n 3, 125.
[93] Regulation 141/2000/EC/EC of the European Parliament and of the Council of 16 December 1999 on orphan medicinal products [2000] OJ L18/1.
[94] Bache et al., above n 3, 39.
[95] Regulation 141/2000/EC, Article 3.
[96] Regulation 141/2000/EC, Article 3.
[97] Regulation 141/2000/EC, Article 3.
[98] Regulation 141/2000/EC, Article 4.
[99] Directive 2004/27/EC of the European Parliament and of the Council of the 31st March 2004 amending Directive 2001/83/EC on the Community Code relating to medicinal products for human use [2004] OJ L136/34.
[100] See: Syrett, 'Looking After the Orphans Treatments for Rare Diseases, EU Law and the Ethics of Costly Health Care' in Flear et al. (eds), (OUP 2013) above n 3, 129.
[101] Regulation 141/2000/EC, Article 8. This may be reduced to 6 years if the product is deemed to be sufficiently profitable without market exclusivity. Also see: Commission 'Guideline on aspects of the application of Article 8(1) and (3) of Regulation 141/2000/EC: Assessing similarity of medicinal products versus authorised orphan medicinal products benefiting from market exclusivity and applying derogations from that market exclusivity (Communication) COM (2008) 4077 final.

resulted in an increase in approvals for orphan drugs, without reducing the quality of approval processes.[102] But the availability of the special designation to pharmaceuticals 'that without incentives it is unlikely that the marketing of the medicinal product in the [EU] would generate sufficient return to justify the necessary investment' is controversial. Some 'orphan drugs', such as Cerezyme (a recombinant enzyme), sell as 'blockbusters', that is, generating sales of more than $1 billion per annum, showing that the orphan drug business is hardly a charitable activity.[103] The CJEU has held that 'orphan drug' designation is available only if an application for such designation is made *before* marketing authorization is granted.[104] The CJEU's approach supports a broad array of industry interests, patient interests and significant state and EU interests, at the expense of the interests of manufacturers, such as CSL Behring, whose pharmaceuticals are already on the market.[105]

Packaging, labelling and advertising

EU law has long required detailed, harmonized provisions on the packaging and labelling of pharmaceuticals. The Community code now addresses labelling of pharmaceuticals, their packaging, and the leaflets inserted in such packaging. Compulsory packaging information includes matters such as active ingredients, method and route of administration.[106] Warnings must be included to keep medicinal products away from children, expiry dates and storage requirements where appropriate. The name of the holder of and number of the marketing authorization are also to be included.[107] Particulars are to be given in the official language or languages of the Member State where the product is placed on the market.[108] This is, of course, a serious impediment to a true single market in pharmaceuticals. Nothing prevents the indication of the particulars in several languages, but physical space on the packaging would preclude more than one or two languages being used. As Thompson points out, in terms of finished pharmaceutical products, only blister packs placed within outer packaging

---

[102] See further: Aymé and Rodwell (eds), '2011 Report on the State of the Act of Rare Disease Activities in Europe of the European Union Committee of Experts on Rare Diseases-Part 1' (European Union Committee of Experts on Rare Diseases 2011); but see: Kreeftmeijer-Vegter et al., 'The Influence of the European Paediatric Regulation on marketing authorization of orphan drugs for children' (2014) 9 *Orphanet Journal of Rare Diseases* 120, who find only a minor impact from the Regulation.

[103] Bache et al., above n 3, 38; Faeh, 'A Just Distribution of Health Care in the Case of Orphan Medicinal Products: Aligning the Interests of European Economic Integration and National Welfare Policy' (2012) 14(1) *European Journal of Social Security* 21.

[104] *CSL Behring GmbH v European Commission and European Medicines Agency*, T-264/07, EU:T:2010:371.

[105] Bache and Hervey, 'Incentivising Innovation or Supporting Other Interests? European Regulation of Orphan Medicinal Products: *CSL Behring GmbH v European Commission and another* (2011) 19(1) *Medical Law Review* 123.

[106] Directive 2001/83/EC, Articles 54-57.   [107] Directive 2001/83/EC, Article 54.

[108] Directive 2001/83/EC, Article 63 (1).

could, therefore, be marketable in each Member State. Even in that case, the blister packs would have to be placed within outer packaging with information in the official language of each Member State.[109] Given the consumer safety precautions that must be taken with this information, it is difficult to envisage any other solution.

The Community code also regulates the use of package leaflets.[110] These must be drawn up to reflect the summary of product characteristics, which is part of the marketing authorization application. Required information includes contraindications, precautions for use and interactions with other pharmaceuticals, alcohol, tobacco and foodstuffs. In addition, side-effects (defined as 'undesirable effects which can occur under normal use of the medicinal product'[111]) must be stated. Leaflets do not carry the same constraints of space that apply to packaging itself. It would be significantly cheaper for the pharmaceutical industry to exploit the economies of scale implied by a single European market by inserting different language version leaflets into identically labelled finished packages. This would suggest that the best regulatory approach would be to provide for a bare minimum of information on the package label itself, but to require a leaflet in the appropriate language or languages before marketing in a particular area of the EU. However, the institutions of the EU have not so far adopted that approach. This is presumably because of concerns that leaflets, unlike the immediate packaging of the product, are not physically attached to the product and therefore there is scope for producer or consumer error. Further, consumers may pay significantly less attention to the information on a leaflet than that displayed on the packaging itself. Also, even if the leaflet approach were to be adopted, no single national authority would be able to approve a leaflet in all the languages of the EU. It is not simply a question of translation, since national authorities retain discretion as to the summary of product characteristics and the information to be included in a leaflet.[112]

The approach to risk here, therefore, is a blend between a standard risk-regulation and a consumer protection approach. At a general level, risks from pharmaceuticals are regulated through the marketing authorization provisions and so on, which determine what is 'acceptable' risk, in the sense of a pharmaceutical product being generally available in the EU. But, at an individual level, a more subjective approach applies, leaving the appropriately informed patient to determine whether that particular risk is acceptable to him. This distinction in the EU's approach to risk matters more in an age of widening access to over-the-counter pharmaceuticals and the increasing accessibility of pharmaceuticals via the internet. EU packaging and labelling rules can be seen as supporting patients, as they make informed personal decisions. They resonate

[109] Thompson, *The Single Market for Pharmaceuticals* (Butterworths 1994) 217.
[110] Directive 2001/83/EC, Articles 58–60.
[111] Directive 2001/83/EC, Article 59 (1) (e).
[112] Thompson (Butterworths 1994) above n 109, 223.

with patient choice, human rights to autonomy, as found in the Council of Europe's Convention of Human Rights and Biomedicine and the EU's Charter of Fundamental Rights and Freedoms.[113] But such rules also imply an approach to risk that leaves significant responsibilities with the consumer.[114]

When it comes to advertising of pharmaceuticals, however, the EU's approach is significantly less consumer-focused than the approach in the USA.[115] Advertising, defined as 'any form of door-to-door information, canvassing activity or inducement designed to promote the prescription, supply, sale or consumption of medicinal products',[116] is closely regulated by the Community code. Products without a marketing authorization may not be advertised at all.[117] Advertising must comply with the summary of product characteristics, must 'encourage the rational use of the medicinal product, by presenting it objectively and without exaggerating its properties', and must not be misleading.[118] The CJEU has adopted a wide approach to interpretation of 'advertising' in this context. Advertising includes third-party activity, such as journalism or the use of the internet intended to promote products classed as pharmaceuticals.[119] This is the case even where the product is regarded as a 'health food' by some, or where the third party receives no remuneration for the activity. Equally, quotations taken from medical journals or other scientific works which are included in advertisements for medicinal products directed at persons qualified to prescribe or supply medicines are covered by the Directive's advertising rules.[120] Quotations, tables and other illustrative matter taken from medical journals or other scientific works must be clearly identified by a precise indication of the source, so that health professionals are informed of them and can verify them.[121]

The Community code prohibits all direct-to-consumer advertising of prescription-only pharmaceuticals.[122] The most recent attempt to revise the ban, by including a new provision on information to the general public on prescription-only pharmaceuticals,[123] was eventually withdrawn by the

---

[113] See further: chapters 7 and 8.

[114] Such as checking that the pharmaceutical will not cause allergies.

[115] Only the USA and New Zealand permit direct-to-consumer pharmaceuticals advertising that makes product claims, see: Ventola, 'Direct-to-Consumer Pharmaceutical Advertising: Therapeutic or Toxic?' (2011) 36(10) *Pharmacy and Therapeutics* 669.

[116] Directive 2001/83/EC, Article 86.

[117] Directive 2001/83/EC, Article 87.

[118] Directive 2001/83/EC, Article 87 (3).

[119] *Criminal proceedings against Frede Damgaard*, C-421/07, EU:C:2009:222.

[120] *Novo Nordisk AS v Ravimiamet*, C-249/09, EU:C:2011:272.

[121] *Novo Nordisk AS v Ravimiamet* EU:C:2011:272.

[122] Directive 2001/83/EC, Article 88 (1). Officially supported vaccination campaigns are exempted, see: Directive 2001/83/EC above n 17, Article 88 (4).

[123] Commission, 'Amended proposal for a Directive of the European Parliament and of the Council amending Directive 2001/83/EC as regards information to the general public on medicinal products subject to medical prescription amending, as regards information to the general public on medicinal products subject to medical prescription, Directive 2001/83/EC

European Commission in May 2014.[124] EU law also permits Member States to ban advertising to the general public of pharmaceuticals which may be reimbursed within a national health insurance system, or are available within a 'free at the point of receipt' national health system.[125] At the same time, national incentive schemes, for instance, aimed to encourage health professionals to prescribe cheaper generics, are permitted, because they are not commercial promotion.[126] Directive 2001/83/EC, Article 88 is a measure of exhaustive harmonization, so Member States may not adopt more restrictive measures, such as prohibiting distribution to pharmacists of lists of non-approved pharmaceuticals products, containing only trade name, packaging size, dose and price,[127] or using a third-party survey or prize draw.[128] On the other hand, dissemination on a website of information relating to a pharmaceutical which goes beyond simply faithfully reproducing the packaging and leaflet information ('the literal and complete reproduction of the package leaflet or the summary of the product's characteristics') counts as advertising. Selectively reproducing or rewriting information, which can be explained only by an advertising purpose, is prohibited.[129]

In view of the literature on the ways in which the pharmaceutical industry uses both its relationships with health professionals and the power of consumer-led campaigns, these provisions of EU law provide an important check on a consumer-choice approach to risk arising from pharmaceuticals consumption. However, the prohibition of direct-to-consumer advertising of prescription-only pharmaceuticals may be of decreasing significance.[130] Many pharmaceuticals have been reclassified as 'over-the-counter', and these may be advertised to health professionals and consumers alike. Advertising may encourage patients to prefer branded, rather than cheaper generic, versions of pharmaceuticals, and changing relationships with health professionals may encourage patients to persuade health professionals to prescribe branded versions. The power of patient groups over professional practice should not be underestimated,

---

on the Community code relating to medicinal products for human use' COM (2012) 48 final; see: Hancher and Sauter, *EU Competition and Internal Market Law in the Healthcare Sector* (OUP 2012) 215-7.

[124] Commission, 'Withdrawal of obsolete Commission proposals' [2014] OJ C153/3.

[125] Directive 2001/83/EC, Article 88 (3).

[126] *R (on the application of Association of the British Pharmaceutical Industry) v Medicines and Healthcare Products Regulatory Agency*, C-62/09, EU:C:2010:219.

[127] *Ludwigs-Apotheke München Internationale Apotheke v Juers Pharma*, C-143/06, EU:C:2007:656.

[128] *Gintec* EU:C:2007:654.

[129] *MSD Sharp & Dohme GmbH v Merckle GmbH*, C-316/09, EU:C:2011:275.

[130] Jackson above n 24, 127-158; Badcott and Sahm, 'The dominance of Big Pharma: unhealthy relationships?' (2013) 16(2) *Medicine, Health Care and Philosophy* 245; Womack, 'Ethical and Epistemic Issues in direct-to-consumer drug advertising: where is patient agency?' (2013) 16(2) *Medicine, Health Care and Philosophy* 275; Law, *Big Pharma: How the World's Biggest Drug Companies Control Illness* (Constable 2006); Angell, '*The Truth about Drug Companies: How They Deceive Us and What to Do About It* (Random House 2005).

and those groups are regularly supported by the pharmaceutical industry. Furthermore, advertising to health professionals *is* permitted – along with many other industry practices including gift-giving, sponsorship and involvement in continuing medical education, which have been shown to influence professional practice.[131]

More significantly, industry practices such as 'disease mongering'[132] or selling future risk of disease,[133] part of a general trend to medicalization,[134] show that advertising of pharmaceuticals in the sense covered by Directive 2001/83/EC is but the tip of the iceberg. Jackson's analysis is supported by the work of those such as David Healy[135] and Gilbert Welch, Lisa Schwartz and Steven Woloshin.[136] The argument is that the power of the pharmaceutical industry has shifted dramatically relative to that of both regulatory authorities and health professionals since the 1970s. New pharmaceuticals, and new means of testing for future and chronic diseases, have led to a changed focus on promoted pharmaceuticals, such as statins, which 'modify risk and lifestyle factors, rather than save lives'.[137] As Trudo Lemmens reminds us, 'almost all major pharmaceutical companies have been associated with problematic promotional practices of blockbuster drugs that may have caused significant injuries and death'.[138] In this context, the EU's attempts to regulate the use of a narrow range of advertising practices seems a woefully inadequate response to the risks implied by this literature as inherent in a pharmaceuticals industry whose activities are so embedded in 'normal practice' that we cease to see them as 'advertising' at all.

Intellectual property and the 'market pathway'

Leigh Hancher distinguishes between the EU's 'regulatory pathway', which has been the subject of this chapter so far, and its 'market pathway'. The EU's 'market pathway' is 'the prices and conditions under which products are purchased by national health care providers and insurance companies, and,

---

[131] Sahm, 'Of Mugs, Meals and More: The Intricate Relations Between Physicians and the Medical Industry' (2013) 16(2) *Medicine, Health Care and Philosophy* 265.

[132] Payer, *Disease-mongers: How Doctors, Drug Companies, and Insurers are Making You Feel Sick* (Wiley 1992).

[133] Moynihan and Cassels, *Selling Sickness: How the World's Biggest Pharmaceutical Companies are Turning Us All into Patients* (Nation Books 2006).

[134] 'Treating ordinary feelings, or the normal consequences of ageing, as medial problems', see: Jackson n 24, 132. On 'pharmaceuticalisation', see, for example: Fox and Ward, 'Pharma in the Bedroom . . . and the Kitchen . . . The Pharmaceuticalisation of Daily Life' (2008) 30(6) *Sociology of Health and Illness* 856; Bell and Figert, 'Medicalisation and Pharmaceuticalisation at the Intersections: Looking Backward, Sideways and Forward' (2012) 75(5) *Social Science and Medicine* 775.

[135] Healy, *Pharmageddon* (University of California Press 2012).

[136] Gilbert Welch, *Overdiagnosed: Making People Sick in Pursuit of Health* (Beacon Press 2011).

[137] Healy, above n 135, 5.

[138] Lemmens, 'Pharmaceutical Knowledge Governance: A Human Rights Perspective' (2013) 41(1) *Journal of Law, Medicine and Ethics* 163, 165.

indeed, patients'.[139] It is subject to significant national control, but also EU level legislation and CJEU jurisprudence. One crucial aspect of the 'market pathway' is the ways in which intellectual property rights, in particular trade-marks and patents, interact with free trade rules. Without seeking to delve too deeply into this complex area of European law (where national, EU and European Patent Organization rules interact), we briefly consider the implications of this aspect of EU pharmaceuticals law.

As noted in chapter 5, different arrangements according to which institutions within national health systems purchase pharmaceuticals lead to significant differences in the prices of pharmaceuticals across the EU. In practice, therefore, pharmaceuticals markets in the EU are divided along national lines. 'Parallel importers' exploit the opportunities this brings by purchasing pharmaceuticals in a relatively low-cost Member State and selling them in a higher-price Member State. To do this effectively, parallel importers often repackage the pharmaceuticals as part of the process, in order to meet national regulatory requirements and consumer preferences. The division of pharmaceuticals markets within the EU is maintained, *inter alia,* by trade-marks, which are held in the law of each relevant Member State. So the repackaging usually either involves re-affixing the trade-mark to the pharmaceuticals packaging or deploying packaging which allows the original trade mark to remain visible even after the repackaging. This practice is necessary to demonstrate the propriety of the product and thus secure the confidence of health professionals and consumers alike. But leaving the trade-mark intact means that the original manufacturers, whose interests in maintaining a divided market across the EU are not well served by parallel importing, may seek to rely on their intellectual property rights to prevent parallel imports. In response, parallel importers seek to enforce the relevant EU law. Which is applicable – intellectual property rights or EU law on the free movement of goods?[140]

The TFEU provides explicitly that restrictions on the free movement of goods can be justified by the protection of industrial and commercial property.[141] Nonetheless, the notion of 'exhaustion of intellectual property rights' in this context is a long-standing principle of EU law, deriving from decisions of the CJEU from the 1970s.[142] If a product is placed on the market in one Member State, that act 'exhausts' any rights based on trade-marks. Parallel importers may rely on the free movement of goods rules, as, in principle, the restrictions inherent in exercise of intellectual property rights are not justified.[143]

---

[139] Hancher, 'The EU pharmaceuticals market: parameters and pathways' in Mossialos, Permanand, Baeten and Hervey (eds), *Health Systems Governance in Europe: The Role of European Union Law and Policy* (CUP 2010) 635.

[140] See: Opinion of the Advocate General in *Bristol-Myers Squibb,* C-427/93, C-429/93 and C-436/93, EU:C:1995:440, paragraphs 2–4.

[141] Article 345 TFEU.   [142] Article 36 TFEU.

[143] *Centrafarm v Sterling Drug,* C-15/74, EU:C:1974:114; *Centrafarm v Winthrop,* C-16/74, EU:C:1974:115. The principle has been confirmed many times, see: e.g. *Pharmon BV v*

Following this judge-made law, the EU legislature attempted to promote certainty as to how trade-marks apply in internal market law. In the late 1980s, a Trade-Mark Directive 89/104/EEC[144] consolidated the case law. Trade-mark rights are exhausted within the internal market,[145] unless legitimate reasons ground opposition to further commercialization of the product.[146] This provision remains identical in the current Trade-Mark Directive 2008/95/EC.[147] The leading case on interpretation of the relevant provisions is *Bristol-Myers Squibb*,[148] from the mid-1990s, which involves repackaging and parallel import of pharmaceuticals. The CJEU established the basis on which trade-marks may, and may not, be relied upon in parallel import situations. If five conditions are met, the CJEU held that a trade-mark may not be relied upon to prevent further marketing of a repackaged medicinal product. To be able effectively to rely on EU free movement law, a parallel importer needs only to notify the holder of the trade-mark, and identify the original manufacturer and packages appropriately. The scope for litigation as to whether the conditions had been met, in particular circumstances, however, meant continuing uncertainty as to the legal position in particular cases, and this has been criticized by national courts and at least one Advocate General of the CJEU.[149] In 2007, the CJEU clarified matters, holding explicitly that:[150]

> Article 7(2) of Directive 89/104 must be construed as meaning that the proprietor may legitimately oppose further commercialisation of a pharmaceutical product imported from another Member State in its original internal and external packaging with an additional external label applied by the importer, unless
>
> – it is established that reliance on trade mark rights by the proprietor in order to oppose the marketing of the overstickered product under that trade mark would contribute to the artificial partitioning of the markets between Member States;

Hoechst AG, C-19/84, EU:C:1985:304; *Merck v Stephar*, C-187/80, EU:C:1981:180; *Hoffman La-Roche v Centrafarm*, C-107/76, EU:C:1977:89; *De Peijper (Managing Director of Centrafarm)*, C-104/75, EU:C:1976:67.

[144] Council Directive 89/104/EEC of 21 December 1988 to approximate the laws of the Member States relating to trade-marks [1988] OJ 40/1, repealed by Directive 2008/95/EC of the European Parliament and of the Council of 22 October 2008 to approximate the laws of the Member States relating to trade-marks [2008] OJ L299/25, Article 7 of which is identical to that of Council Directive 89/104/EEC of 21 December 1988 to approximate the laws of the Member States relating to trade-marks [1988] OJ 40/1.

[145] Council Directive 89/104, Article 7 (1).

[146] Council Directive 89/104, Article 7 (2).

[147] Directive 2008/95/EC of the European Parliament and of the Council of 22 October 2008 to approximate the laws of the Member States relating to trade-marks [2008] OJ L299/25.

[148] *Bristol-Myers Squibb*, C-427/93, C-429/93 and C-436/93, EU:C:1996:282.

[149] Opinion of the Advocate General in *Boehringer Ingelheim No 2*, C-348/04, EU:C:2006:235, paragraph 2.

[150] Opinion of the Advocate General in *Boehringer Ingelheim No 2* EU:C:2006:235, paragraphs 16–20.

- it is shown that the new label cannot affect the original condition of the product inside the packaging;
- the packaging clearly states who overstickered the product and the name of the manufacturer;
- the presentation of the overstickered product is not such as to be liable to damage the reputation of the trade mark and of its proprietor; thus, the label must not be defective, of poor quality, or untidy; and
- the importer gives notice to the trade mark proprietor before the overstickered product is put on sale, and, on demand, supplies him with a specimen of that product.[151]

Thus, cross-border trade in trade-marked pharmaceuticals (provided the conditions are met) is protected by internal market law, price differentials stemming from different arrangements within national health systems notwithstanding. Of course, as this statement implies, EU law has failed to redress the underlying barrier to cross-border trade. Significant price differentials for pharmaceuticals and other medical products continue across the Member States. As we saw in chapter 5, EU legislation explicitly tackling this lack of a single EU-wide market imposes only procedural and transparency obligations on the Member States. The Transparency Directive 89/105/EEC[152] requires Member States to provide annual information on pharmaceutical prices that have been fixed during that year,[153] or information on the criteria for determining profitability,[154] where that is the mechanism chosen for price control. The Commission is seeking to strengthen the Transparency Directive,[155] as well as relying upon non-binding procedures that support developing a wider policy consensus on pharmaceutical pricing within the EU.[156] But, so far, the Commission has been unable to create a single pharmaceuticals market through legislation. So litigation, brought both by private litigants and by the Commission itself,[157] continues to be used to challenge barriers to cross-border trade.

---

[151] *Boehringer Ingelheim No 2*, C-348/04, EU:C:2007:249, paragraph 31.

[152] Council Directive 89/105/EEC of 21 December 1988 relating to the transparency of measures regulating the prices of medicinal products for human use and their inclusion in the scope of national health insurance systems [1989] OJ L40/8. See further: chapter 11.

[153] Council Directive 89/105, Articles 2 (3) and 3 (3).

[154] Council Directive 89/105, Article 5 (a)–(d).

[155] Commission, 'Proposal for a Directive relating to the transparency of measures regulating the prices of medicinal products for human use and their inclusion in the scope of public health insurance systems' COM (2012) 84 final. See: Hancher and Sauter, above, n 123, p. 173.

[156] See: Hancher, above n 139, 637-8, 661, 672-77.

[157] See the discussion chapter 11 and see: e.g. *Commission v Austria*, C-424/99, EU:C:2001:642; *Commission v Finland*, C-229/00, EU:C:2003:334; *Pohl-Boskamp*, C-317/05, EU:C:2006:684; *Menarini Industrie Farmaceutiche Riunite and Others*, C-352/07, C-353/07, C-354/07, C-355/07, C-356/07, C-365/07, C-366/07, C-367/07 and C-400/07, EU:C:2009:217; *R (on the application of Association of the British Pharmaceutical Industry) v Medicines and Healthcare Products Regulatory Agency* EU:C:2010:219; *Boehringer Ingelheim and Others*, C-143/00, EU:C:2002:246; *Pharmacia & Upjohn v Paranova*, C-379/97, EU:C:1999:494; *Phytheron*, C-352/95, EU:C:1997:170; *Loendersloot*, C-349/95, EU:C:1997:530; *Merck Sharp & Dohme Ltd*

What is important for the analysis here is the implications of this aspect of EU pharmaceuticals law for risk. In short, the only risks that are even remotely explicit in the relevant EU law are those to the continued competitiveness of the EU's pharmaceuticals industry. The law is framed and reasoned from the position of intellectual property holders, parallel importers and consumers in the internal market. Bringing these matters within the purview of EU law necessarily frames disputes in those terms, and removes from the debate the wider questions of the risks to closed national health (insurance) systems from extra-territorial competition, where negotiated prices for pharmaceuticals apply, in the context of a need to control prices because of national budget constraints. EU law simply does not consider matters in that way: it constructs them as relationships of trade and consumption.[158]

What about the risks to patients and health care systems from patent protection? EU law does consider risks to patients and health systems from application of patents to prevent generic companies from producing cheaper pharmaceuticals. Where a non-patented version of a widely used product reaches the market, there may be price falls of up to 80 per cent.[159] This is obviously beneficial to health systems and patients alike. For this reason, some Member States do not offer full patent protection to pharmaceuticals. This lack of full patent protection was not regarded by the CJEU as a reason to exclude the doctrine of exhaustion – once a pharmaceutical product was on the market in the EU, parallel imports could not be impeded by reference to lack of protection in the importing Member State.[160]

In general, patents prevent generics manufacturers from commencing the process leading to marketing authorization until the patent has expired. However, since 2004, the EU's 'Bolar exemption' has allowed for generic research and development before that date.[161] Member States have implemented the exemption in different ways, leading to fears of 'forum shopping', both within the EU and between the EU and the USA, which interprets the exemption

---

v *Primecrown*, C-267/95 and C-268/95, EU:C:1996:468; *Biogen Inc. v Smithkline Beecham Biologicals*, C-181/95, EU:C:1997:32; *Pharmon BV v Hoechst AG* EU:C:1985:304; *Merck v Stephar* EU:C:1981:180; *Hoffman La-Roche v Centrafarm* EU:C:1977:89; *De Peijper (Managing Director of Centrafarm)* EU:C:1976:67. See also: the judgment of the EFTA Court in *Paranova v Merck* (E-3/02) [2003] 3 C.M.L.R 7.

[158] See: chapters 4-6.

[159] Hancher, 'The EU pharmaceuticals market: parameters and pathways' in Mossialos et al. (eds), (CUP 2010) above n 139, 641.

[160] *Merck v Primecrown* EU:C:1996:468; Hancher, 'EC Competition Law, Drugs and Intellectual Property: Recent Developments' in Goldberg and Lonbay (eds), *Pharmaceutical Medicine, Biotechnology and European Law* (CUP 2001).

[161] Directive 2004/27/EC of the European Parliament and of the Council of the 31st March 2004 amending Directive 2001/83/EC on the Community Code relating to medicinal products for human use [2004] OJ L136/34; Regulation 726/2004 abov n.34004] OJ L136/1. The exemption is based on the US Hatch-Waxman Act 21 USC 355(j), s. 505(j), and followed the USA Supreme Court *Roche Products Inc v Bolar Pharmaceuticals Col Inc* 733 F 2d 858 (Fed Cir 1984).

differently from the EU.[162] A recent reference to the CJEU from a German court[163] seeks to challenge the view that the exemption does not apply to third parties supplying ingredients to a generics company seeking to conduct bioequivalency studies.[164] Given the structure of the industry, and the increasing presence of specialized small and medium-sized enterprises supplying active pharmaceutical ingredients to even relatively large generics companies, this could change the balance between generic producers and patent holders quite significantly. But, in general, as Hancher shows, although the EU law on generics and biosimilars involves a recognition that risks to health systems arise from overprotection of the research-based pharmaceuticals industry, nonetheless, risks to the global competitiveness of that industry remain paramount in the overall legislative settlement.[165]

EU law also protects the research-based industry, by providing a 'supplementary patent certificate', allowing an extension of patent protection for either up to five years, or fifteen years from the first EU marketing authorization.[166] This recognizes that the time from filing for a pharmaceutical patent, through pre-clinical and clinical trials, to its eventual marketing authorization, may last between six and twelve years, so the EU's twenty-year patent protection would otherwise rarely be enjoyed in practice.

Finally, we note that the European Commission, as well as the industry itself, has been increasingly willing to supplement the regulatory and market pathways with use of competition law. Unlike the pre-market controls discussed so far, competition law is an ex-post control, with the limitations that implies. Nonetheless, Hancher argues, it is becoming increasingly important in the overall balance of the objectives of encouraging pharmaceuticals innovation while at the same time encouraging a European market in generics. The 2005 fine of AstraZeneca, and subsequent sector investigation, discussed in chapter 11, are important examples. The European Commission's investigation highlighted 'patent settlements', in which generic manufacturers agreed to limit their freedom to market products in return for significant fees, as another anticompetitive feature of the market.[167] Another example is Novartis' challenge of

---

[162] Kretzschmar, 'Drug safe harbour provisions in the USA and Europe: implications for the emerging biosimilars industry' (2014) 9(4) *Journal of Intellectual Property Law & Practice* 298; Cohen and Peirson, 'The UK Research and "Bolar" Exemptions: Broadening the Scope for Innovation?' (2013) 8(11) *Journal of Intellectual Property Law & Practice* 837.

[163] *Polpharma S.A. Pharmaceutical Works v Astellas Pharma Inc,* 5 December 2013, Court of Appeals in Düsseldorf, Docket no. I-2 U 68/12.

[164] Morée et al., 'It might take three to Bolar' (*Lexology,* 10 February 2014) Allekotte, 'The Bolar exemption: the question of third parties', (*Life Sciences Intellectual Property Review,* 28 February 2014).

[165] Hancher, above n 139, 649–655.

[166] Regulation 469/2009/EC of the European Parliament and of the Council of 6 May 2009 concerning the supplementary protection certificate for medicinal products [2009] OJ L152/1. Introduced in 1992 by Council Regulation (EEC) No 1768/92 of 18 June 1992 concerning the creation of a supplementary protection certificate for medicinal products [1992] OJ L182/1.

[167] Jackson above n 24, 90.

the production, by Apozyt, of single doses of products developed using recombinant DNA technology, hybridoma and monoclonal antibody methods[168] from vials originally authorized for marketing as a one-use vial, with any residual product to be discarded (the result being that the contents of the vials are used for several injections, hence the final price of an injection is significantly decreased). Novartis claimed, unsuccessfully,[169] that this constituted 'unfair competition', and that a separate marketing authorization should be required. The CJEU also rejected various safety-based arguments, such as the risk of infiltration of bacteria when the product is transferred to a different container, and the problems that might arise from the shelf-life of the product.

Conclusions

The examples discussed in detail in this chapter point to one obvious conclusion: any generalized statements about the EU's approach to risk in its pharmaceuticals law should be treated with caution, if not suspicion. The ways in which risk is understood, and its significance and implications, depend upon the particular context, and the particular risk or risks at issue. While risk is undoubtedly an important theme in EU pharmaceuticals law, other themes, such as consumerism, but also ethical or human rights considerations, are also in play. We continue our analysis of the EU's regulation of risks arising from products available in health systems – pharmaceuticals, products derived from human blood and tissue, medical devices – in the next chapter.

---

[168] Lucentis® and Avastin®.   [169] *Novartis v Apozyt*, C-535/11, EU:C:2013:226.

14

Risk: health system products (human blood, tissue and cells, organs) and medical devices

Introduction

The US President's Council on Bioethics has called this the 'golden age' for biology, medicine and biotechnology.[1] Sequencing the human genome, genetic testing, research at cellular (particular stem cell) and nano levels, and advances in tissue engineering techniques suggest huge promise for understanding and treating human illness, disease and disability.[2] Yet such power to 'intervene into the workings of our bodies and minds and to alter them by rational design'[3] also holds significant risks. Moreover, using human cells, blood or tissue in non-autologous settings raises the dimension of ethics and human rights. In European cultural contexts, commercial dealing in 'human material' is regarded as highly controversial,[4] and Member States have sought to regulate on the basis that the human body may not be the subject of commercial gain, even though markets in parts of the human body exist. A straightforward risk-regulation approach is therefore not regarded as appropriate.

This chapter continues our analysis of how risk – conceptualized in various ways – has permeated EU health law in the context of various aspects of health systems. In this chapter our focus is products involving human tissue, cells or blood, and medical devices. As we saw in the previous chapter, these

---

[1] President's Council on Bioethics, 'Beyond Therapy' (President's Council on Bioethics 2003) 6. See also: Murphy, 'Repetition, Revolution, and Resonance' in Murphy (ed), *New Technologies and Human Rights* (OUP 2009) 2-3; Brownsword, 'Human Dignity, Ethical Pluralism, and the Regulation of Modern Biotechnologies' in Murphy (ed), *New Technologies and Human Rights* (OUP 2009); Brownsword and Somsen, 'Law, Innovation and Technology: Before We Fast Forward – A Forum for Debate' (2009) 1(1) *Law, Innovation and Technology* 1; Flear, 'Introduction to 'New Technologies, European Law and Citizens' Symposium: New Technologies, European Law and Citizens - Editorial' (2009) 16(1) *Maastricht Journal of European and Comparative Law* 3.

[2] European Ethics Group on Science and New Technologies Opinion No 21, *Ethical Aspects of Nanomedicine* (EGE 2007) and Opinion No 25, *The Ethics of Synthetic Biology* (EGE 2009); Genetics White Paper 'Our Inheritance, Our Future: Realising the Potential of Genetics in the NHS' (June 2003); McHale, 'Nanomedicine and the EU: Some Legal Ethical and Regulatory Challenges' (2009) 16(1) *Maastricht Journal of European and Comparative Law* 65.

[3] President's Council on Bioethics, 'Beyond Therapy' (President's Council on Bioethics 2003) 6.

[4] Titmuss, *The Gift Relationship: From Human Blood to Social Policy*, Oakley and Ashton (eds), (LSE Books 1997); Duxbury, 'Do Markets Degrade?' (1996) 59(3) *Modern Law Review* 331.

regulatory categories overlap, in important respects, with each other, and with pharmaceuticals. Again, we are interested in investigating the various statements, observations or claims made about EU health law, how it conceptualizes or understands risk, and the implications. Bache, Flear and Hervey, for instance, found that EU law sees risks inherent in novel health technologies through a dominant frame of markets.[5] It has been suggested that EU law's focus on the regulation of risk within markets implies a corresponding devaluation of ethics and human rights.[6] Some take the view that the EU over-regulates, intervening in industry competitiveness; many claim that the EU does not regulate the risks associated with these aspects of health systems tightly enough.[7]

EU law on human materials

Blood

International blood donation has a long and chequered history.[8] The very real risks that unsafe human materials present within health systems were graphically highlighted in the 1980s and 90s, with major incidents of HIV-infected blood transfusions, in particular to haemophiliacs.[9] During the mid-1980s, some 4,000 people in France were given transfusions of HIV-infected blood and many died. It was reported in 1993 that over 350 haemophiliacs in Germany had been infected with the HIV virus from blood products, as a result of the testing of the blood products by using pooled plasma from three donors, instead of testing each donation separately.[10]

The European Commission first proposed a programme of action in the area of blood safety in the early 1990s, and the 2002 Blood Safety Directive[11] followed

---

[5] Bache et al., 'The Defining Features of the European Union's Approach to Regulating New Health Technologies' in Flear, Farrell, Hervey and Murphy (eds), *European Law and New Health Technologies* (OUP 2013).

[6] See: e.g. Mahalatchimy, 'Access to Advanced Therapy Medicinal Products in the EU: Where do we Stand?' (2001) 18(3) *European Journal of Health Law* 305; Lee, 'Risk and Beyond: EU Regulation of Nanotechnology' (2010) 35(6) *European Law Review* 799; Roscam, 'Patients' Rights in a Technology and Market Driven-Europe' (2010) 17(1) *European Journal of Health Law* 11; Farrell, 'Risk, Legitimacy, and EU Regulation of Health Technologies' in Flear et al., above n 5; Farrell, *The Politics of Blood: Ethics, Innovation and the Regulation of Risk* (CUP 2012) and see further below.

[7] See further below.

[8] See further: e.g. Starr, *Blood: An Epic Story of Medicine and Commerce* (Alfred A. Knopf 1998).

[9] See: Editorial, 'Aids Scandals around the world' (*BBC News*, 9 August 2001); and Giesen, 'Liability for Transfer of HIV Infected Blood in Comparative Perspective' (1994) 10 *Professional Negligence* 2.

[10] Abraham and Lewis, *Regulating Medicines in Europe: Competition, Expertise and Public Health* (Routledge 2000) 73.

[11] Directive 2002/98/EC of the European Parliament and of the Council of 27 January 2003 setting standards of quality and safety for the collection, testing, processing, storage and distribution of human blood and blood componentsand amending Directive 2001/83/EC [2003] OJ L33/30

in the wake of these tragic incidents.[12] Anne Maree Farrell has argued that its creation can thus be seen in terms of 'the politics of precaution'.[13] The main legacies of the HIV-infected blood incidents are 'the increased use of the precautionary principle to manage risk, as well as a much stronger patient-centred approach to promoting safety and achieving good clinical outcomes'.[14] Although Farrell draws on rich data from the USA, France and the UK, in the final analysis she shows that all three countries have adopted a precautionary risk approach to blood safety, in the context of the political fallout from the HIV-infected blood episodes, fuelled by the use of (national) legal mechanisms for redress by blood safety campaigners. Variations between the countries are about where to draw the line in a precautionary approach, rather than whether to have one at all.[15] Thus, in the context of blood safety, our view is that the overall conclusion that the EU is more precautionary than the USA is not supported.

Although the precautionary principle itself has not been used explicitly within the Blood Safety Directive,[16] or the successor Directives on human tissue, cells and organs, the principle made an important contribution to the debate. This debate places the EU's law on the use of human materials in health settings very much within a risk regulation framework, with notions of patient safety and public health security as central to the regulatory arrangements. As we write, human blood, tissue and organs are listed under the Europa Public Health Website under the subheading of 'Ensuring Health Security'.[17]

The Blood Safety Directive applies to collection and testing of human blood and blood components, irrespective of intended purpose, and to their processing, storage and distribution when intended for transfusion.[18] In principle, the Directive covers whole human blood, and red cells, white cells, platelets and plasma. But its scope does not extend to 'medicinal products' involving plasma – they are covered by the pharmaceuticals regime. The normal *lex specialis* rule is thus inverted – the pharmaceuticals regime has priority wherever a product falls within its scope.[19] The consequence here is that 'medicinal products' involving

---

[12] See further: Farrell, 'The emergence of EU governance in public health: the case of blood, politics and regulation' in Steffen (ed), *Health Governance in Europe* (Routledge 2005).

[13] See further: Farrell above n 6, ch 7; Farrell, 'The Politics of Risk and EU Governance of Human Material' (2009) 16(1) *Maastricht Journal of European and Comparative Law* 41; Farrell, 'Is the Gift Still Good? Examining the Politics and Regulation of Blood Safety in the EU' (2006) 14(2) *Medical Law Review* 155. See also: Farrell, 'Adding Value? EU Governance of Organ Donation and Transplantation' (2010) 17(1) *European Journal of Health Law* 51; and Robinson and Hampson, 'The EU Blood Safety Directive and its implications for blood services' (2007) 93(2) *Vox Sanguinis* 122.

[14] Farrell above n 6, 4.   [15] Farrell n 6, 194.

[16] Directive 2002/98/EC [2003] OJ L33/30, Recital 2 says that: 'precautionary measures' need to be taken 'making appropriate use of scientific progress in the detection and inactivation and elimination of transfusion transmissible pathogenic agents'.

[17] Commission, 'Public Health: Health' (*Commission*, 1 August 2014).

[18] Directive 2002/98/EC, Article 2 (1).

[19] Implied by: *Octapharma France*, C-512/12, EU:C:2014:149. See further: chapter 13.

blood or plasma may not be used within the EU without a marketing authorization. Blood stem cells are explicitly excluded from the Directive.[20] Moreover, the Directive does not cover all national blood safety matters. Only some aspects of the Directive apply to hospital blood banks.[21]

The Directive provides that only duly accredited, authorized or licensed national blood establishments may collect and test human blood.[22] A 'responsible person', qualified in medical or biological sciences to at least university degree level, must be in charge, and their identity must be notified to national authorities.[23] The Directive sets various inspection requirements and quality control systems with respect to blood establishments.[24] Quality control systems must include particular elements of record keeping, and must respect the principle of traceability, meaning that 'blood and blood components collected, tested, processed, stored, released and/or distributed ... can be traced from donor to recipient and vice versa'.[25] The Directive obliges Member States (using a process laid down in the Directive)[26] to establish common criteria for the testing of donations to ensure quality and safety.[27] These are now found in a series of Commission Directives.[28] All future blood donors in the EU will have to provide at least a form of identification, health history and a signature.[29] Potential donors must be interviewed and examined by a qualified health professional before giving blood.[30] The implication is that, had such measures been in place in the 1980s and 90s, the various blood contamination incidents noted above could probably have been avoided.

With its accreditation and authorization measures, and provisions on record-keeping and traceability, Directive 2002/98/EC is very much focused on facilitating safety. The technical safety requirements were further elaborated in 2004.[31]

---

[20] Directive 2002/98/EC, Article 2 (4).   [21] Directive 2002/98/EC, Article 6.

[22] Directive 2002/98/EC, Articles 4 and 5.   [23] Directive 2002/98/EC, Article 9.

[24] Directive 2002/98/EC, Articles 5–8; 11–13.

[25] Directive 2002/98/EC, Article 14 (1). Data must be kept for at least 30 years: Article 14 (3).

[26] Directive 2002/98/EC, Articles 18 and 29. The Directive refers to the European Commission's powers to adopt implementing decisions through arrangements known as 'comitology', involving committees of national representatives who work with the Commission. The procedures are now found in Regulation 182/2011/EU of the European Parliament and of the Council of 16 February 2011 laying down the rules and general principles concerning mechanisms for control by Member States of the Commission's exercise of implementing powers [2011] OJ L55/13.

[27] Directive 2002/98/EC, Articles 21, 23, 29.

[28] Commission Directive 2005/61/EC of 30 September 2005 implementing Directive 2002/98/EC of the European Parliament and of the Council as regards traceability requirements and notification of serious adverse reactions and events [2005] OJ L256/32; Commission Directive 2005/62/EC of 30 September 2005 implementing Directive 2002/98/EC of the European Parliament and of the Council as regards Community standards and specifications relating to a quality system for blood establishments [2005] OJ L256/41; Commission Directive 2004/33/EC of 22 March 2004 implementing Directive 2002/98/EC of the European Parliament and of the Council as regards certain technical requirements for blood and blood components [2004] OJ L91/25.

[29] Directive 2002/98/EC, Article 17.   [30] Directive 2002/98/EC, Article 19.

[31] Commission Directive 2004/33/EC.

The 2004 Directive sets out detailed information requirements, donor eligibility requirements, storage transport and distribution conditions, and quality control measures.[32] But EU law does not exhaustively harmonize blood safety standards. Member States are not precluded from adopting more-stringent national protective measures.[33] All Member States apply additional testing requirements to take into account their specific national epidemiological situation.[34] The Directive does not require that hospital blood services are subject to licensing and accreditation procedures. Farrell has argued that this is problematic in ensuring that quality and safety standards are achieved.[35] It certainly makes it difficult to argue that the EU has replaced national judgments on safety standards with its own judgments. This is all the more so when we consider how the EU has regulated the ethical and human rights aspects of human blood donation, which we do below.

Human tissue and cells

The Human Tissue and Cells Directive 2004/23/EC[36] applies to a broad range of materials – reflecting the complexity of the human body and the multiple contemporary uses of human material by scientists.[37] The Directive's scope extends to 'human tissues and cells intended for human applications.'[38] Again, the overlaps with other areas of EU regulation are notable. The Directive applies to 'donation, procurement, testing, processing, preservation, storage and distribution of human tissues and cells intended for human applications'. It also applies

---

[32] See: Commission Directive 2004/33, Annexes II-V.

[33] Directive 2002/98/EC, Article 4 (2). Such measures must be compliant with internal market law, see: *Humanplasma*, C-421/09, EU:C:2010:760 and Opinion of Advocate General Mengozzi in *Léger*, C-528/11, EU:C:2014:2112; and see further below.

[34] Virtually all Member States apply tests in addition to those established as minimum requirements in the Directive. See: Commission, 'Communication from the Commission to the Council, the European Parliament, the European Economic and Social Committee and the Committee of the Regions on the application of Directive 2002/98/EC setting standards of quality and safety for the collection, testing, processing, storage and distribution of human blood and blood components and amending Directive 2001/83/EC' (Communication) COM (2010) 0003 final.

[35] Farrell, above n 6, 208.

[36] Directive 2004/23/EC of the European Parliament and of the Council of 31 March 2004 on setting standards of quality and safety for the donation, procurement, testing, processing, preservation, storage and distribution of human tissues and cells [2004] OJ L102/48.

[37] Directive 2004/23/EC, Article 3 provides that:
   (a) 'cells' means individual human cells or a collection of human cells when not bound by any form of connective tissue;
   (b) 'tissue' means all constituent parts of the human body formed by cells;
   (c) 'donor' means every human source, whether living or deceased, of human cells or tissues;
   (d) 'donation' means donating human tissues or cells intended for human applications;
   (e) 'organ' means a differentiated and vital part of the human body, formed by different tissues, that maintains its structure, vascularisation and capacity to develop physiological functions with an important level of autonomy.

[38] Directive 2004/23/EC, Article 1.

to 'manufactured products derived from human tissues and cells intended for human applications'. But where such products are covered by other Directives – in particular, of course, Directive 2001/83/EC, as amended by the Advanced Therapy Medicinal Products Regulation 1394/2007/EC[39] – the Tissue and Cells Directive applies only to donation, procurement and testing,[40] and not to the marketing (including to the national health system) of the relevant products. Blood and blood components explicitly remain covered by the Blood Safety Directive.[41] Organs or parts of organs being used for the same purpose as the entire organ in the human body; and tissues and cells used 'as an autologous graft within the same surgical procedure' are all excluded.[42]

Some have claimed that the effects of the application of the EU's pharmaceuticals regulatory regime to products involving human tissue and cells are the over-regulation of such products.[43] Others go further, and note that the concepts underlying the EU's blood, tissue and cells law – such as safety and quality *in the context of transferring materials from one human to another* – make little sense in the context of novel technologies involving human tissues and cells. For instance, Nils Hoppe[44] explains EU law's application to the decellularized homograft heart valve,[45] which is increasingly becoming the 'gold standard'[46] for the treatment of young adults and children with dysfunctional pulmonary heart valves. As he points out, the Human Tissue and Cells Directive treats 'connective tissue' (in particular, the extracellular matrix component, which is the part that provides structure and is made up largely of collagen, which is protein) as if it were a 'vital donor cell'. Such connective tissue is derived from the human body. But the process of decellularization, used to create the homograft

---

[39] Regulation 1394/2007/EC of the European Parliament and of the Council of 13 November 2007 on advanced therapy medicinal products and amending Directive 2001/83/EC and Regulation 726/2004/EC [2007] OJ L324/121.

[40] Regulation 1394/2007/EC.

[41] Directive 2004/23/EC, Article 2 (2).   [42] Directive 2004/23/EC, Article 2 (2).

[43] E.g. Hoppe, 'Innovative Tissue Engineering and Its Regulation: The Search for Flexible Rules for Emerging Health Technologies' in Flear et al., above n 5, 122, argues that the 'decellularized homograft heart valve' is 'overregulated' because it is treated as analogous to a 'medicinal product' – a classification apparently aimed 'to establish the highest possible level of safety and protection' for a novel process. This makes no sense because 'a heart valve functions solely on mechanical principles and exhibits no pharmacological, immunological or metabolic function.' Yet it is clearly not a medical device in the sense of Council Directive 93/42/EEC of 14 June 1993 concerning medical devices [1993] OJ L169/1.

[44] Hoppe, above n 43; see also: Favale and Plomer, 'Fundamental Disjunctures in the EU Legal Order on Human Tissue, Cells and Advanced Regenerative Therapies (2009) 16(1) *Maastricht Journal of European and Comparative Law* 89, 111, who highlight the 'open-ended and indeterminate character' (111) of the relevant EU law and 'areas of overlap and disjunction'.

[45] A technique of tissue engineering which 'removes vital cells and leaves only a collagen scaffold behind', thereby increasing the transplant's lifetime and recipient tolerance. The process has significant advantages over conventional methods, e.g., the speed of manufacture and operation, increased recipient tolerance due to the lack of vital donor cells, evidence suggesting the scaffold is homogenously populated by autologous cells and a reduction in infection and calcification of the transplant: Hoppe, above n 43.

[46] Hoppe, above n 43, 110.

valve, 'entails the complete removal of all vital donor cells from the collagen matrix'. Indeed, this is a crucial part of the technology, because this removal of all vital donor cells means that recipient cells can subsequently repopulate the valve once it is in place. The consequence of the EU's inappropriately conceptualized regulatory approach is that valuable new technologies are impeded from reaching the market – and hence the patients whom they would help.

Like the Blood Safety Directive, the Tissue and Cells Directive is based on the idea of a 'competent authority' – a body which must be established by each Member State to implement the Directive.[47] These 'competent authorities' must be 'accredited, designated, authorised or licensed'.[48] A register of accredited or licensed tissue establishments must be in place.[49] The individuals involved in using such human materials must be trained and accredited.[50] Member States must establish inspection and control mechanisms.[51] There is a requirement to retain data for thirty years. Member States must ensure that such standards also apply to imports and exports.[52] They must set up procedures for notification of serious adverse incidents.[53] Quality measures are to be put in place as to the management and storage of tissue and cells.[54] Systems for identification of tissue and cells[55] are to be established as traceability, as in the case of human blood, is seen as key to safety and protection of public health as well as the health of individuals. The European Commission works with Member States to establish codification systems. The Directive was followed by Commission Decision 2010/453/EU,[56] which established more specific guidelines concerning inspections and quality standards.

Again, like the Blood Safety Directive, this aspect of EU health law is very much based on a standard risk regulation model. Yet, as is the case with the Blood Safety Directive, questions of ethics are also implicated in the Human Tissue and Cells Directive.[57] We consider this further below. Before we do so, however, we briefly consider a different mechanism that the EU has used to regulate the use of human tissues and cells in health research contexts – that of intellectual property law.[58] Intellectual property rights, in particular patents, are used to encourage or discourage certain types of uses of human tissue and cells. In reality, the inventor of a new medical treatment will require a reasonable prospect for commercial exploitation of its invention, otherwise the research

---

[47] Directive 2004/23/EC, Article 4.   [48] Directive 2004/23/EC, Article 6 (1).
[49] Directive 2004/23/EC, Article 10.   [50] Directive 2004/23/EC, Article 5.
[51] Directive 2004/23/EC, Article 7.   [52] Directive 2004/23/EC, Article 9.
[53] Directive 2004/23/EC, Article 11.   [54] Directive 2004/23/EC/EC, Articles 16-18.
[55] Directive 2004/23/EC, Article 8.
[56] Commission Decision 2010/453/EU of 3 August 2010 establishing guidelines concerning the conditions of inspections and control measures, and on the training and qualification of officials, in the field of human tissues and cells provided for in Directive 2004/23/EC of the European Parliament and of the Council (notified under document C(2010) 5278) [2010] OJ L213/48.
[57] See further below.
[58] For a discussion of intellectual property law as an indirect mode of regulation in this area see: Hervey and Black, 'The European Union and the Governance of Stem Cell Research' (2005) 12(1) *Maastricht Journal of European and Comparative Law* 11.

investment necessary will not be commercially viable. By granting the inventor a protected period of time, within which the patent holder has a monopoly over the invention, a patent is a mechanism for encouraging such research investment.[59] Thus, by making patents available for certain types of invention involving human materials, regulatory authorities are able to provide a strong steer in terms of what research actually takes place, even if other research is permitted in theory.

The relevant EU legislation is Directive 98/44/EC on the Legal Protection of Biotechnological Inventions.[60] The background to this Directive is the global development of gene technology, the perceived need to protect the European Union's biotechnology sector, and the application of the European Patent Convention to the sector.[61] The Directive confirms that the general rules of patent law (that inventions must be new, non-obvious, and have an industrial application) apply to human materials.[62] However, 'the human body . . . and the simple discovery of one of its elements including the sequence or partial sequence of a gene, cannot constitute patentable inventions'. Nonetheless, 'an element isolated from the human body or otherwise produced by means of a technical process including the sequence or partial sequence of a gene, may constitute a patentable invention'.[63] Article 6 of the Directive contains a 'morality' clause to the effect that inventions are unpatentable 'where their commercial exploitation would be contrary to *ordre public* or morality'. For example,

---

[59] Patents are only for "inventions" and not mere "discoveries" of what already exists in nature. However, the *process* of discovering something occurring in nature may be patentable. See further: European Patent Office, 'Guidelines for Examination of Patent Applications: Part G: Patentability' (European Patent Office 2013); and see also Directive 98/44/EC of the European Parliament and of the Council of 6 July 1998 on the legal protection of biotechnological inventions [1998] OJ L213/13, Article 3 (2): "Biological material which is isolated from its natural environment or produced by means of a technical process may be the subject of an invention even if it previously occurred in nature."

[60] Directive 98/44/EC.

[61] The European Patent Convention, administered by the European Patent Office, is not part of the EU's legal order and does not aim to harmonise national patent laws. The EPO grants centralized 'European patents' which give the same rights as national patent laws in the contracting states designated on the application. See further: Hervey and McHale, *Health Law and the European Union* (CUP 2004) 260-4. In 2012, the EU adopted Regulation 1257/2012/EU of the European Parliament and of the Council of 17 December 2012 implementing enhanced cooperation in the area of the creation of unitary patent protection [2012] OJ L361/1; and an Agreement on a Unified Patent Court (Agreement on a Unified Patent Court [2013] OJ C175/1) followed in 2013. The former will enter into force once the latter has been ratified by 13 of its 25 member countries, including Germany, the United Kingdom and France (the three Contracting Member States in which the highest number of European patents had effect in 2012). So far, as at September 2014, 5 states had ratified, see: Council of the European Union, 'Agreement and Ratification Database' (*Council of Europe*, 2014).

[62] Directive 98/44/EC Article 2 and Recital 22. The recitals of a measure of EU Law do not have any binding impact, and only represent a form of soft law (see, for example: Snyder, 'The Effectiveness of European Community Law: Institutions, Processes, Tools and Techniques' (1993) 56(1) *Modern Law Review* 19). However, this does not necessarily mean that recitals do not have any effect. In particular, when the content of a recital is reflected in a binding provision, the recital can be used as the basis for interpretation of the binding provision.

[63] Directive 98/44/EC, Article 5 (1) and (2).

production of chimeras from germ cells, reproductive cloning of human beings and 'uses of human embryos for industrial and commercial purposes' are not patentable.[64]

Adopting a purposive approach, the CJEU has interpreted the term 'human embryo' in Article 6 (2) (c) of the Directive in two cases to date: *Brüstle*[65] and *International Stem Cell*.[66] *Brüstle* concerned a patent for 'isolated and purified neural precursor cells, processes for their production from embryonic stem cells, and the use of neural precursor cells for the treatment of neural defects'.[67] The patents at issue in *International Stem Cell* were for 'methods of producing pluripotent human stem cell lines from parthenogenetically-activated oocytes and stem cell lines produced according to the claimed methods' and 'methods of producing synthetic cornea or corneal tissue, which involve the isolation of pluripotent stem cells from parthenogenetically-activated oocytes, and product-by-process claims to synthetic cornea or corneal tissue produced by these methods'.[68] The product and the process of transplanting the neural precursor cells at issue in *Brüstle* into the nervous system are used in the treatment of neural disorders, such as Parkinson's Disease, for which there is currently no cure. Similarly, it is hoped that the inventions at issue in *International Stem Cell* will help develop more effective treatments for retinal degenerative diseases, which affect millions of people worldwide.

The CJEU considers that the Directive aims both to 'promote investment in the field of biotechnology' and to protect human dignity.[69] Its purpose is not 'to regulate the use of human embryos in the context of scientific research'.[70]

---

[64] Directive 98/44/EC, Article 6 and Recitals 36-42.

[65] *Brüstle v Greenpeace*, C-34/10, EU:C:2011:669.

[66] *International Stem Cell*, C-364/13 EU:C:2014:2451.

[67] *Brüstle v Greenpeace*, paragraph 15. The science is complex here, and consequently so are its legal and ethical implications. Neural precursor cells are specialised, immature cells, which have the capacity to develop into various parts of the mature human body, in particular to do with the nervous system. In the very early stages of fertilisation, they are found in the blastocyst, the pre-embryonic entity that has developed 5-6 days after the ovum (egg) is fertilised. Brüstle's neural cell product and process involve obtaining these neural precursor cells from human embryonic stem cells. The process of doing so involves destroying the blastocyst. But what does 'the human embryo' mean, in Directive 98/44/EC, Article 6? Does it mean all stages of human life, from the moment of fertilisation of the ovum? Does it include the blastocyst? Does it include ova fertilised by transplantation of a nucleus from a mature human cell (sometimes called 'therapeutic cloning'), or by stimulating an unfertilised ovum to grow through cell division by parthenogenesis (a form of asexual reproduction where growth occurs without fertilisation)?

[68] *International Stem Cell*, paragraph 10. The referring national court explained the science here as follows, 'parthenogenesis consists in the activation of an oocyte, in the absence of sperm, by a variety of chemical and electrical techniques. That oocyte, referred to as a 'parthenote', is capable of dividing and further developing. However, according to current scientific knowledge, mammalian parthenotes can never develop to term because, in contrast to a fertilized ovum, they do not contain any paternal DNA, which is required for the development of extra-embryonic tissue. Human parthenotes have been shown to develop only to the blastocyst stage, over about five days', *International Stem Cell*, paragraph 17.

[69] *Brüstle v Greenpeace*, paragraph 32.   [70] *International Stem Cell*, paragraph 22.

Hence 'the human embryo' must be interpreted widely, to include any fertilized human ovum, including ova fertilized through 'therapeutic cloning' and non-fertilized ova where growth and development have been stimulated through parthenogenesis.[71] By the same token, a product whose creation involves the destruction of a human embryo by removing the stem cell from the embryo at the blastocyst stage is also unpatentable.[72] On the other hand, a non-fertilized human ovum is only a 'human embryo' if it is 'capable of commencing the process of development of a human being'.[73] Following its Advocate General in *International Stem Cell*, the CJEU held that to be a 'human embryo' in this context the non-fertilized human ovum 'must necessarily have the inherent capacity of developing into a human being'.[74] This was not the case, because, at the current stage of international medical science, although the ovum can develop into the blastocyst phase it cannot develop further because it does not have the necessary paternal DNA. In both *Brüstle* and *International Stem Cell*, the questions of whether embryonic stem cells derived from a blastocyst are capable of commencing the process of development into a human being, in the light of scientific developments,[75] and whether the parthenotes have the inherent capacity of developing into a human being,[76] was a matter for the national court.

Again, therefore, we see that this aspect of EU health law does not focus solely on risk – even on the risks to competitiveness of the European biotechnology industry of too stringent an approach to the unpatentability of products or processes involving human material.[77] Where matters of national sensitivity are concerned, the CJEU[78] does not set up an opposition between 'market' and ethics or human rights. Rather, the CJEU articulates a strong ethic of human dignity, drawing on Europe's human rights tradition, but ultimately leaves the

---

[71] The CJEU's reasoning is that such ova are 'capable of commencing the process of development of a human being': *Brüstle v Greenpeace*, paragraph 36.

[72] *Brüstle v Greenpeace* paragraphs 47-52.   [73] *International Stem Cell*, paragraph 27.

[74] *International Stem Cell*, paragraph 28, following the Opinion of the Advocate General, paragraph 73.

[75] *Brüstle v Greenpeace*, paragraph 37. The German Federal Court held that they were not, reasoning that *in vitro* stem cells could not develop without significant intervention. Thus stem cells derived from a blastocyst are patentable in the EU (or at least in Germany). The German Federal Court accepted that, although this was not the case when Brüstle filed for the patent, scientific techniques do now exist whereby human embryonic stem cells can be obtained without destroying a human embryo. Therefore, products deriving from a line of stem cells that did not involve the destruction of a blastocyst are also patentable. See further: Hervey, 'EU Health Law' in Barnard and Peers, *EU Law* (OUP 2014); Bache et al., above n 5, 32-34.

[76] *International Stem Cell*, paragraph 36.

[77] Some of the commentary on the *Brüstle v Greenpeace* EU:C:2011:669 suggested that its consequence would be the exit of the biotechnology industry from Europe – see, eg, Bache et al., above n 5, 14, and the literature therein. Probably the most important consequence is that science has moved on and different, less controversial techniques are now being deployed, see: Harmon, Laurie and Courtney, 'Dignity, plurality and patentability: the unfinished story of *Brüstle v Greenpeace*' (2013) 38(1) *European Law Review* 92.

[78] Unlike its Advocate General.

practical application to a national actor (the national court), which is able to be sensitive to local understandings of ethics or interpretations of human rights.

Human organs

Organ transplantation was one of the great clinical advances of the twentieth century. Initially beginning with kidney transplantation, and moving to liver and heart transplantation, the technology has broadened, enabling a wide range of human material to be used for transplantation purposes. Contemporary transplants of human material include limbs, wombs and faces.[79] The EU Member States differ considerably in their approaches to human organs regulation.[80] National organ donation systems are usually understood as either 'informed consent' or 'presumed consent', but within those types significant differences exist. For instance, Germany[81] and the UK operate an informed consent system, with an organ donor register.[82] Austria has been a presumed consent country, with an 'opt out' system,[83] since 1982;[84] likewise Portugal.[85] Belgium has also a presumed consent system, but with absolute priority given to the will of the deceased.[86] Spain operates under a presumed consent law, introduced in 1979.[87] However, the Spanish system is unusual, in that, unlike many other presumed consent countries, it does not have a formal opt-out procedure. Organ donation rates also differ considerably.[88] Spain has the highest number of successful donations per million population in the world.[89] Bulgaria also has a presumed consent system, yet its per million population value is significantly lower.[90] This suggests that legislation is not always the strongest determinant of successful donation rates, and, furthermore, that variable procedures in the

---

[79] Briggs, 'Full face transplant a success' (*BBC* News, 23rd April 2010).

[80] See: e.g. Price, *Legal and Ethical Issues of Organ Transplantation* (CUP 2000); Fabre, Murphy and Matesanz, 'Presumed consent: a distraction in the quest for increasing rates of organ donation' (2012) 341 *British Medical Journal* 4973. Thanks to the medical students on the 'Student Selected Component' at the University of Sheffield who studied organ donation with the School of Law in 2012 and 2013 (Joseph Abrams, Abigail Aitken, Joanne Bowers, Alys Cawson, Claire Cooke, Mairead Denney, Christopher Field, Simeon Holland, Charlotte Loftus, Thomas Pinnock, Oshini Siriwardena), and to Lindsay Stirton who supervised this work.

[81] Germany's system was introduced in November 1997, by the Act on the Donation, Removal and Transplantation of Organs 1997.

[82] British Medical Association Ethics Committee, 'Building on progress: Where next for organ donation policy in UK?' (British Medical Association 2012).

[83] Objections are evidenced by carrying a 'non-donor' card or signing the opt-out register.

[84] Blaicher, Pokorny, Rockenschaub, Puhalla and Mühlbacher, 'Organ transplantation in Austria' (1996) 1(3) *Annals of Transplantation* 41.

[85] Pereira, 'Transplantation of Organs and Tissues and Some Reflections on the "Solidarity" of the Human Cadaver in Portugal' 18(1) *European Journal of Health Law* 55.

[86] Michielsen, 'Presumed consent to organ donation: 10 years' experience in Belgium' (1996) 89(12) *Jounal of the Royal Society of Medicine* 663.

[87] Fabre, Murphy, Matesanz, above n 80.

[88] Rithalia, McDaid, Suekarran, Myers and Sowden, 'Impact of presumed consent for organ donation on donation rates: a systematic review' (2009) 338 *British Medicial Journal* 3162.

[89] 34.0/1 million population in 2008.   [90] 0.8/1 million population in 2008.

laws of consent, and in particular in the practice of consulting family members, can cause these differences.[91] Moreover, the religious or cultural dimensions of organ donation may affect attempts to increase donation in unpredictable ways.

At EU level, organ transplant policy developed in the late 2000s.[92] A major EU focus is the concern to facilitate the supply of donor organs for transplantation. Nonetheless, there are significant concerns as to the safe supply of organs, and the need to put in place effective measures to address these. As this involves global trade, we discuss it in more detail in chapter 17, but here we touch briefly on the aspects of EU organ transplant law that mirror those of the Blood and Tissue and Cells Directives. The Organ Transplant Directive 2010/53/EU[93] does so in many respects. Its very title – 'on standards of quality and safety of human organs intended for transplantation' – highlights its aim to address questions of quality and safety. Like the other Directives discussed in this chapter, it requires Member States to establish authorized 'competent authorities',[94] responsible for the quality and safety framework required by the Directive. An implementing Directive 2012/25/EU[95] sets out information procedures which

[91] Mossialos, Costa-Font and Rudisill, 'Does organ donation legislation affect individuals' willingness to donate their own or their relative's organs? Evidence from European Union survey data' (BMC Health Services Research 2008). Jurgen De Wispelaere and Lindsay Stirton have therefore argued that systemic changes would reduce the number of family refusals, and increase donation rates, see: De Wispelaere and Stirton, 'Advance commitment: an alternative approach to the family veto problem in organ procurement' (2010) 36(3) *Journal of Medical Ethics* 180. See further New, Solomon, Dingwall, McHale *King's Fund Research Report No 18 A Question of Give and Take* (King's Fund 1994); Department of Health *Organs for Transplant* (Organ Donation Task Force 2008).

[92] Commission, 'Action plan on Organ Donation and Transplantation (2009-2015): Strengthened Cooperation between Member States' (Communication) COM (2008) 819 final; Directorate-General for Health and Consumer, 'Organ Donation and Transplantation: Policy Actions at EU level: Consultation Document' (Commission 2006) ; Commission, 'Report on the Open Consultation Policy Options for Organ Donation and Transplantation at EU level' (Commission 2006); Commission, 'Organ Donation and Transplantation: policy action at EU level' (Communication) COM (2007) 275 final; European Parliament resolution of 22 April 2008 on organ donation and transplantation: Policy actions at EU level (2007/2210 (INI)) [2009] OJ CE 259/1. See also: Farrell, 'Addressing organ shortage in the European Union: getting the balance right' in Farrell, Price and Quigley (eds), *Organ Shortage: Ethics and Pragmatism* (CUP 2011); Farrell, 'Adding Value? EU Governance of Organ Donation and Transplantation' (2010) 17(1) *European Journal of Health Law* 51.

[93] Directive 2010/53/EU of the European Parliament and of the Council of 7 July 2010 on standards of quality and safety of human organs intended for transplantation [2010] OJ L207/14. This is the correct number – see: Corrigendum to Directive 2010/45/EU of the European Parliament and of the Council of 7 July 2010 on standards of quality and safety of human organs intended for transplantation [2010] OJ L243/68. Organ transplants are explicitly excluded from the Patients' Rights Directive, Directive 2011/24/EU of the European Parliament and of the Council on the application of patients' rights in cross-border healthcare [2011] OJ L88/45, Article 1 (3) (b), see: Nys, 'Organ Transplantation and the Proposed Directive on Cross-Border Care' (2010) 17(5) *European Journal o f Health Law* 427.

[94] Directive 2010/53/EU, Article 17.

[95] Commission Implementing Directive 2012/25/EU of 9 October 2012 laying down information procedures for the exchange, between Member States, of human organs intended for transplantation [2012] OJ L275/27.

will help to facilitate traceability of information concerning donation[96] and also information concerning adverse events.[97] The Directives do not attempt to harmonize donation systems, or diagnosis of death and use of brain stem death criteria, providing only that organ procurement must be consistent with national consent rules.[98]

On their face, the Blood, Tissue and Cells and Organs Directives are fundamentally concerned with clinical risk, reduction of risk of infection of an individual patient, or public health risks, as well as risk to the EU's internal market if the regulatory environment is not conducive to the development of novel products or processes involving human materials. However, as we have already noted, and as discussed in the following section, although risk concerns may be a basis for EU law in these areas, they are by no means the whole picture.

Biomedical ethics and human rights

EU health law on human materials is expressed in terms of risk. Some have suggested that this means that EU law on human materials does not adequately address ethical or human rights questions.[99] Others, such as Elen Stokes, have argued that EU health law is deficient in this regard, because it tends to lock itself into established analytical frameworks (a standard risk regulation model) rather than being open to evolution over time and in different contexts.[100] Maria Lee has argued that, for all its apparent concern with ethics, relevant EU regulation of nanotechnology (which of course includes both human and non-human materials) is essentially only concerned with risk, in the sense of safety.[101] Anne-Maree Farrell takes the view that EU health law on human materials would be more effective if it moved beyond a narrow 'risk as safety' focus, and considered the ways in which risk is socially and culturally constructed, and therefore fundamentally linked to questions of ethics.[102] Human rights scholars have deplored the lack of embedding of Europe's common human rights framework (meaning that of the European Convention on Human Rights) in these aspects of EU health law.[103] For instance, Directive 98/44/EC on the Legal Protection

---

[96] Directive 2012/25/EU, Article 5 requires information to be transferred in relation to donor characteristic.

[97] Directive 2012/25/EU, Article 7 sets out procedures for notification of information concerning suspected serious adverse events concerning organ transplantation.

[98] Directive 2010/53/EU, Article 14.   [99] See: e.g. Mahalatchimy, above n 6.

[100] Stokes, 'Something Old, Something New, Something Borrowed: Emerging Health Technologies and the Continuing Role of Existing Regulations' in Flear et al., above n 5, 233.

[101] Lee, 'Risk and Beyond: EU Regulation of Nanotechnology' (2010) 35(6) *European Law Review* 799. See also: Altenstetter, 'Medical Device Regulation and Nanotechnologies: Determining the role of Patient Safety Concerns in Policymaking' (2011) 33(2) *Law and Policy* 227.

[102] Farrell, 'Risk, Legitimacy, and EU Regulation of Health Technologies ' in Flear et al., above n 5; Farrell, above n 6.

[103] See: e.g. Abbing, 'Patients' Rights in a Technology and Market Driven-Europe' (2010) 17(1) *European Journal of Health Law* 11, who argues that the 'common European human rights

of Biotechnological Inventions and Directive 2004/23 on Tissues and Cells are regarded as a lost opportunity to protect human rights, in that they failed to restrict the use of human cloning technologies across the EU.[104]

Yet examination of the detail of the legislation considered in this section of the chapter shows that it does include human rights and principles of biomedical ethics. This is also reflected in the literature – for instance, the Biotechnology Directive has been said to be 'an instance of direct incorporation of ethics within EU law'.[105] We illustrate this point through two examples: the consent provisions; and the provisions on non-commodification of the human body. Both examples reflect human rights, in particular to human dignity, integrity of the person and private life; as well as ethical principles including altruism, and autonomy/non-paternalism. The Directives on Tissue and Cells, and Organ Safety have several explicit references to human rights,[106] and the Blood Safety Directive covers data protection rights[107] explicitly, and includes provisions on confidentiality and information provision to donors, which implicitly protect rights to privacy and autonomy.

Although the Blood Safety Directive does not explicitly cover consent, the implementing Directive 2005/62/EC[108] does refer to procedures for donor 'suitability interview'. The requirements here are set out in Directive 2004/33/EC.[109] They focus on the information that must be given to blood donors, which includes 'the significance of "informed consent"'. Donors must sign a questionnaire, to confirm their informed consent. The Tissue and Cells Directive 2004/23/EC[110] and the Organ Safety Directive 2010/53/EU[111] both contain explicit provisions on consent, emphasizing the need to obtain such consent

framework' ought to be embedded into EU law where patients cross borders to receive health care, where health care crosses borders (e.g. direct-to-consumer screening technology), or in the context of cross-border medical research.

[104] Of course, it can equally be argued the developing cloning technologies would *protect* human rights.

[105] Hennette-Vauchez, 'Biomedicine and EU Law: Unlikely Encounters?' (2011) 38(1) *Legal Issues of Economic Integration* 5, 9; see also: Favale and Plomer, 'Fundamental Disjunctions in the EU Legal Order on Human Tissue, Cells and Advanced Regenerative Therapies' (2009) 16(1) *Maastricht Journal of European and Comparative Law* 89; Farrell, 'Governing the Body: Examining EU Regulatory Developments in Relation to Substances of Human Origin' (2005) 27(3) *Journal of Social Welfare and Family Law* 427.

[106] Directive 2010/53/EU, Recitals 7, 19 and 23, Article 16.

[107] Directive 2002/98/EC, Article 24.

[108] Commission Directive 2005/62/EC of 30 September 2005 implementing Directive 2002/98/EC of the European Parliament and of the Council as regards Community standards and specifications relating to a quality system for blood establishments [2005] OJ L256/41.

[109] Commission Directive 2004/33/EC of 22 March 2004 implementing Directive 2002/98/EC of the European Parliament and of the Council as regards certain technical requirements for blood and blood components [2004] OJ L91/25, Annex II.

[110] Directive 2004/23/EC, Article 13.

[111] Directive 2010/53/EU, Articles 4 and 14. see: Corrigendum to Directive 2010/45/EU of the European Parliament and of the Council of 7 July 2010 on standards of quality and safety of human organs intended for transplantation [2010] OJ L243/68.

before human materials are donated. Either the donor, or the next of kin or others who can grant authorization (or at least absence of objection) on the donor's behalf, in accordance with national law, must be given sufficient information to secure consent that is properly informed.

The CJEU has confirmed that EU's consent rules fall within the human right to integrity of the person, found in Article 3 EUCFR.[112] This provision states explicitly that in medicine and biology 'free and informed consent of the person concerned' must be respected. Article 3 EUCFR is linked to Article 8 (1) of the European Convention on Human Rights, the right to privacy, and is closely linked to the medical law/medical ethics concept of autonomy.[113]

Article 3 EUCFR also expresses the idea of non-commodification of the human body. It states that the 'prohibition on making the human body and its parts as such a source of financial gain' must be respected. The source of that prohibition is, *inter alia*, the Council of Europe's Oviedo Convention, Article 21.[114] Non-commodification of human material is also related to the right to human dignity, found in Article 1 EUCFR. In Case C-377/98 *Netherlands v. Parliament and Council (Biotechnology Directive)*,[115] it was argued that 'the patentability of isolated parts of the human body reduces human living matter to a means to an end and undermines human dignity'.[116] The CJEU did not refer to the EUCFR, or human dignity, in the judgment, but, as Catherine Dupré points out, in stating that 'human living matter could not be reduced to a means to an end', the CJEU in effect adopted that reasoning.[117]

The idea that the human body should not be commodified is expressed in the ethic of altruism, and more specifically in the idea of voluntary and unpaid donations,[118] which is found in all the legislation discussed in this section of the chapter.[119] A good example is the Blood Directive, Article 20, which

---

[112] *Netherlands v Parliament and Council (Biotechnology Directive)*, C-377/98, EU:C:2001:523. The judgment also includes confirms that Article 3 EU CFR encompasses the free and informed consent of donor and recipient, paragraph 69, and see Text of Explanatory Note to EU CFR, Article 3.

[113] Michalowski, 'Article 3 – Right to the Integrity of the Person' in Peers, Hervey, Kenner and Ward (eds), *The EU Charter of Fundamental Rights: A Commentary* (Hart 2014) 47.

[114] Council of Europe Convention on Human Rights and Biomedicine 1997, Article 21 – 'the human body and its parts shall [not] as such give rise to financial gain'.

[115] *Netherlands v Parliament and Council (Biotechnology Directive)* EU:C:2001:523.

[116] Ibid.

[117] See: Dupré, 'Article 1 – Human Dignity' in Peers et al., above n 113, 14. There is no consensus on the exact meaning and scope of human dignity, see: e.g. McCrudden, 'Human Dignity and Judicial Interpretation of Human Rights' (2008) 19(4) *European Journal of International Law* 655, and it is 'often deployed to resolve very sensitive issues which lack a clear political and social consensus' – uses of human embryonic cells being such an issue, see: Dupré, in Peers et al., above n 113, 15.

[118] These principles are reflected in the work of Titmuss (LSE Books 1997) above n 4, concerning both the inefficiency of commercialization of human material and also its fundamentally problematic nature of such issues.

[119] Directive 2004/23/EC, Article 12; Directive 2002/98/EC of the European Parliament and of the Council of 27 January 2003 setting standards of quality and safety for the collection, testing,

provides that 'Member States shall take the necessary measures to encourage voluntary and unpaid blood donations with a view to ensuring that blood and blood components are in so far as possible provided from such donations.' The prohibitions on non-commodification reflect the idea that commercial dealing in human material breaches fundamental human rights, such as integrity and human dignity. They also reflect broader policy concerns within a global market in human material, which is characterized by deep inequalities between jurisdictions and between citizens within jurisdictions, and the consequent potential for unsafe practices and exploitation.[120]

However, EU health law also respects national divergences in interpretation and approach to ethics and human rights in this context. Many questions remain a matter for national resolution – for instance, what counts as 'human' material for the purposes of the Directives, and how does that definition interface with 'human' rights, such as 'human dignity', which is a right that does not apply to non-human entities?[121] The European Court of Human Rights has respected significant differences between Member States in this regard,[122] and there is no reason to expect the CJEU to behave differently.[123]

Furthermore none of the Directives defines 'voluntary and unpaid donations'.[124] For instance, the Tissue and Cells Directive provides that Member States are to encourage voluntary donations, but permits expenses to be provided.[125] This approach respects national ethical diversity. As Farrell notes, it can be seen as a compromise, given the diverging approaches across

---

processing, storage and distribution of human blood and blood components and amending Directive 2001/83/EC [2003] OJ L33/30, Article 20; Directive 2010/53/EU. Corrigendum to Directive 2010/45/EU of the European Parliament and of the Council of 7 July 2010 on standards of quality and safety of human organs intended for transplantation [2010] OJ L243/68), Article 13; Directive 98/44/EC of the European Parliament and of the Council of 6 July 1998 on the legal protection of biotechnological inventions [1998] OJ L213/13, Recital 16. The idea of non-commodification is also found in Regulation 1394/2007/EC of the European Parliament and of the Council of 13 November 2007 on advanced therapy medicinal products and amending Directive 2001/83/EC and Regulation (EC) No 726/2004 [2007] OJ L324/121, Recital 15; and in the Clinical Trials Directive 2001/20/EC of the European Parliament and of the Council of 4 April 2001 on the approximation of the laws, regulations and administrative provisions of the Member States relating to the implementation of good clinical practice in the conduct of clinical trials on medicinal products for human use [2001] OJ L121/34, Articles 4 (d) and 5 (d); and Regulation 536/2014/EU of the European Parliament and of the Council of 16 April 2014 on clinical trials on medicinal products for human use, and repealing Directive 2001/20/EC [2014] OJ L158/1, Articles 31-33, which prohibit financial incentives other than compensation for vulnerable trial participants.

[120] This is particularly highlighted by the global debate concerning trafficking organs from "donors" in less economically developed nations to recipients in more economically developed nations, see further: chapter 17.

[121] See: Dupré, 'Article 1 – Human Dignity' in Peers et al., above n 113, 16.

[122] For instance, recognising the constitutional protection for life before birth (eg Ireland) (or even life since conception e.g. Hungary since 2012, Dupré, 'Article 1 – Human Dignity' in Peers et al., n 113, 17), or constitutional protection for dignity only after birth.

[123] See e.g. *Grogan*, C-159/90, EU:C:1991:378.

[124] Farrell above n 6, 207.   [125] Directive 2004/23/EC, Article 12.

Member States to how blood is sourced, ranging from totally not-for-profit in the Netherlands and Finland, through to the UK practice of importing of blood provided by commercial donors.[126] In *Humanplasma*,[127] the Austrian ban on the importation of blood products for use in direct transfusion where they had been obtained with 'any payment whatsoever having been made', was challenged for consistency with EU law on free movement of goods. The Austrian Government accepted that this constituted an infringement of free movement, but argued that the legislation was justified on public health grounds and fell within the discretion given to Member States to adopt certain measures to encourage voluntary donation. The CJEU rejected this argument. It held that payment by itself did not necessarily adversely impact upon the safety and quality of the donation. The restriction imposed was not necessary or proportionate.

Farrell is critical of the ruling, arguing for greater consistency as to what constitutes voluntary donation and 'expenses' across Member States.[128] Reliance on voluntariness may not by itself promote safety in blood donation, so EU law should place more emphasis on blood being sourced from low-risk populations.[129] The EU's ideological commitment to self-sufficiency in blood through voluntary unpaid donation led to 'a form of institutional and political "blindness"' to the realities of global blood markets'.[130] But it could equally be argued that the approach of the EU legislation both respects national diversity and recognizes the reality of the 'market' or quasi market in blood, and, by extension, in human tissue/cells and organs. But the key point here is that, whichever approach is taken, the position that the relevant EU law concerns itself with risk alone is unsustainable.

At the very least, EU legislation reflects the need for some kind of ethical consensus in order to protect the internal market.[131] The *Humanplasma* ruling of the CJEU shows the extent of national discretion does not extend to disproportionate measures, given the approach taken in the Blood Safety Directive to reimbursement of donors' expenses. Many Member States do permit such 'payments' for blood, and that is recognized in the Directive itself.[132] Austria was an 'ethical outlier', and that position is not protected in internal market law – free movement of goods, *within the biomedical ethical consensus*, prevails. This position may be strengthened if the CJEU follows the Opinion of its Advocate General in Case C-528/13 *Léger* to the effect that French law prohibiting a gay man from giving blood does not fall within the term 'Persons whose behaviour or activity places them at risk of acquiring infectious diseases that may be

---

[126] Farrell above n 6, 209.   [127] *Humanplasma* EU:C:2010:760.
[128] Farrell above n 6, 213.   [129] Farrell n 6, chapter 3.
[130] Farrell, 'Is The Gift Still Good? Examining the Politics and Regulation of Blood Safety in the European Union' (2006) 14(2) *Medical Law Review* (2006) 155, 163.
[131] See: Hervey and Black, above n 58, 47–48.
[132] *Humanplasma* EU:C:2010:760, paragraph 41.

transmitted by blood' in Annex III of Directive 2004/33/EC,[133] and that Member States, when applying their discretion under the Directive, must respect human rights, including the principle of non-discrimination on grounds of sexual orientation. Even Bache et al., who find that ethics and human rights 'seem to operate less as a stand-alone frame, and more as a link, inflection, and support, or even as a "false front" for markets and risk',[134] do nonetheless concede that ethics and rights pervade Directive 98/44/EC on Legal Protection of Biotechnological Inventions[135] and the 'product safety' Directives on blood, human tissue and cells and human organs.[136]

Finally, in contrast to those who criticize the EU for being insufficiently concerned with human rights and ethical questions in its law on human materials, others have argued that the EU *should not* be concerned with the ethical or human rights questions that arise from the use of the human body in medical contexts. As we have seen, there is certainly a great deal of diversity of approach over the regulation of human material across the EU Member States. Much of the diversity concerns differences in ethical approach. It is argued that the EU is not the appropriate body to regulate such questions of ethics or to provide the detailed interpretation and implementation of general human rights provisions. Rather, these should be resolved at national level, not harmonized by EU legislation.

It is the case that, where the EU does concern itself with ethics or human rights, specific ethical and human rights content is often determined by committees (in which national interests are represented), national governments or national courts.[137] The *Brüstle*[138] case is a good example. Equally, the relevant EU legislation is mainly found in Directives, and there is therefore scope for strong variations in national implementation.[139] But, as Flear et al., and others,[140] have shown, EU law may be 'pluralist' in this regard, but it is not 'infinitely malleable'. There is a discernible 'minimum core' of non-negotiable human rights content, focused on autonomy and privacy. In terms of substantive rights, it requires the giving of adequate information (including about benefits and risks) to inform consent.[141] Equally, procedurally or institutionally speaking, EU law imposes on the Member States a non-negotiable institutional obligation, to have a 'competent authority', with obligations to report to the EU's institutions, even if the details of operation of national 'competent

---

[133] Commission Directive 2004/33/EC.   [134] Bache et al., above n 5, 30.
[135] See Bache et al., above n 5, 31-35.   [136] Bache et al., above n 5, 35.
[137] Bache et al., above n 5, 39; Tallacchini, 'Governing by Values. EU Ethics: Soft Tool, Hard Effects' (2009) 47(3) *Minerva* 281, 293-95.
[138] *Brüstle v Greenpeace* EU:C:2011:669.   [139] See further Flear et al., above n.5.
[140] Michalowski, 'Article 3 – Right to the Integrity of the Person' in Peers et al., above n 113, 47-48.
[141] Flear et al., 'Conclusion: A European Law of New Health Technologies?' in Flear et al., above n 5, 401-2.

authorities' vary significantly.[142] Overall, therefore, the strong claims to the effect that EU health law does not, or should not, cover the ethical or human rights aspects of uses of human materials in health contexts cannot be sustained.

EU Law on medical devices

Medical devices are health technologies which can transform a patient's life, for good or for ill. Of course, there is a huge variety of such devices. They include something as simple as a tongue depressor; through to hearing aids, contact lenses; prosthetic limbs; artificial cardiac pacemakers; hip replacements; breast implants. Developing medical device technologies include cell-based vectors for nerves and high-confidence medical devices – tiny implants which it is intended will be ultimately developed utilizing human cells and which will have the ability to feed back information about the patient, thus potentially anticipating health problems. Such technology necessarily carries considerable risks through introducing foreign matter into the human body. Here we explore the drivers for EU law on medical devices, and the extent to which these accord with the strong argument that the theme of risk is the fundamental frame for law in this area.

History

There was relatively little attempt globally to regulate medical devices prior to the 1940s, and regulation as we know it can be traced to the USA Medical Devices Amendments in the 1970s.[143] In Europe, some medical device regulation began prior to EU involvement.[144] Italy was the first European country to regulate medical devices separately to pharmaceuticals.[145] Serious implementation of these provisions began in the late 1970s. In the 1980s, the UK produced guides to Good Manufacturing Practice and some devices such as collagen and inter-uterine devices were included under the UK Medicines Act 1968.[146] Within the UK National Health Service, notification procedures have been around for more than forty years.[147] These have enabled faults and dangers in medical devices to be identified and collated, and this information subsequently utilized. In other Member States, such as France, the picture was more complex, with medical devices being partly regulated under consumer protection laws; partly

[142] See: Flear et al., 'Conclusion: A European Law of New Health Technologies?' in Flear et al., above n 5, 403; For examples of variation in the operation of 'competent authorities' see: e.g. Farrell, 'Risk, Legitimacy, and EU Regulation of Health Technologies' and, Stokes, 'Something Old, Something New, Something Borrowed: Emerging Health Technologies and the Continuing Role of Existing Regulations' both in Flear et al., above n 5.
[143] See further: Higson, *Medical Device Safety: The Regulation of Medical Devices for Public Health* (Institute of Physics Publishing 2002).
[144] Higson above n 143, 9.
[145] See: Law on Public Health, 23 June 1927, cited in Higson above n 143, 14.
[146] As amended.   [147] Higson above n 143.

by specific legal provisions on devices;[148] and partly by a general law on medical research.[149] In Germany, medical devices also fell under a range of different sources of law, such as the Artzneimittelgesetz or German Medical Preparations Act. Regulations on the Safety of Medical Technical Equipment were introduced in 1985, following controversy over failure of medical equipment.

Three EU Directives (Directive 90/385/EEC on active implantable medical devices[150] Directive 93/42/EEC on medical devices,[151] Directive 98/79/EC on *in vitro* diagnostic devices[152]) currently regulate medical devices in the EU, although a proposal to replace these with two Regulations is currently with the EU legislature.[153] The Directives are based on the need to create a safe EU market in medical devices, to ensure that trade within the EU is not impeded by tariff barriers and to respond to developing global medical devices markets.[154] The commercial sector initially opposed the Directives, because of the move away from self-regulation they implied. The gap in time (of eight years) between the adoption of these Directives is because of the enhanced involvement of the European Parliament[155] in the adoption of the *in vitro* diagnostic device Directive.[156] There was disquiet from various quarters about devices including human tissue and animal products and their derivatives.[157] As Christa Altenstetter notes, it was only by 'divorcing' animal and human derivatives that the legislative process was able to move forward. This highlights how the Directives, while concerned with risk, safety and engineering, are also integrally related to broader debates concerning ethics and fundamental rights, which increasingly have underpinned EU health law. Safety is not the sole (or perhaps even the predominant) driver for EU medical devices law.

---

148 Law of 23rd July 1983 concerning the safety of consumers: Code de le Sante Publique, *General Guide for the Homologation of Medical Products* 1983.
149 Law of December 1988 concerning the protection of patients undergoing biomedical research.
150 Council Directive 90/385/EEC of 20th June 1990 on the approximation of the laws of the Member States in relation to active implantable medical devices [1990] OJ L189/17 (as amended).
151 Council Directive 93/42/EEC of 14th June 1993 concerning medical devices [1993] OJ L169/1 (as amended).
152 Directive 98/79/EC of the European Parliament and of the Council of 27 October 1998 on in vitro diagnostic medical devices [1998] OJ L331/1.
153 The European Commission proposed a package of provisions on medical devices in September 2012, see: Commission, 'Safe, effective and innovative medical devices and in vitro diagnostic medical devices for the benefit of patients, consumers and healthcare professionals' (Communication) COM (2012) 540 final; Commission Proposal COM (2012) 542 final; Commission, 'Proposal for a Regulation of the European Parliament and of the Council on *in vitro* diagnostic medical devices' COM (2012) 541 final. See further below.
154 See further: Altenstetter, *Medical Devices, European Union Policy Making and the Implementation of Health and Safety in France* (Transaction Publishers 2008).
155 Under the then new 'co-decision' legislative procedure, which requires agreement of both the European Parliament and Council.
156 Altenstetter above n 154, 233. A proposal had been issued by the Commission in 1991, see: Commission, 'Proposal for a Council Directive concerning medical devices' COM (1991) 287 final.
157 Altenstetter above n 154.

Scope and regulatory approach

A 'medical device' is defined by Directive 93/42/EEC, as amended, as:

> any instrument, apparatus, appliance, software, material or other article, whether used alone or in combination, including the software intended by its manufacturer to be used specifically for diagnostic and/or therapeutic purposes and necessary for its proper application, intended by the manufacturer to be used for human beings

for one or more of several purposes. These purposes are:

> diagnosis, prevention, monitoring, treatment or alleviation of disease; diagnosis, monitoring, treatment, alleviation of or compensation for an injury or handicap; investigation, replacement or modification of the anatomy or of a physiological process; [or] control of conception.[158]

To fall within this definition, the device must 'not achieve its principal intended action in or on the human body by pharmacological, immunological or metabolic means',[159] but it 'may be assisted in its function by such means'.[160]

In vitro devices are defined as:

> any medical device which is a reagent, reagent product, calibrator, control material, kit, instrument, apparatus, equipment, or system, whether used alone or in combination, intended by the manufacturer to be used *in vitro* for the examination of specimens, including blood and tissue donations, derived from the human body

where the purpose of the device is 'solely or principally' for providing information about one of the following:

> a physiological or pathological state, or; a congenital abnormality, or; to determine the safety and compatibility with potential recipients, or to monitor therapeutic measures.[161]

---

[158] Council Directive 93/42/EC of 14 June 1993 concerning medicial devices [1993] OJ L169/1, Article 1 (2).

[159] If it does, it falls within the EU's pharmaceuticals law, see: Directive 2001/83/EC of the European Parliament and of the Council of 6 November 2001 on the Community code relating to medicial products for human use [2001] OJ L311/67 (as amended), Article 1 (2); and chapter 13, n 18.

[160] Council Directive 93/42/EC of 14 June 1993 concerning medicial devices [1993] OJ L169/1, Article 1 (2).

[161] Specimen receptacles are also considered to be *in vitro* diagnostic medical devices. 'Specimen receptacles' are those devices, whether vacuum-type or not, specifically intended by their manufacturers for the primary containment and preservation of specimens derived from the human body for the purpose of *in vitro* diagnostic examination. Directive 98/79/EC of the European Parliament and of the Council of 27 October 1998 on in vitro diagnostic medical devices [1998] OJ L331/1, Article 1.

As Altenstetter notes, this definition considerably widens the scope of the Directives as it may encompass a reagent, a kit or indeed a whole laboratory device.[162] Under the Directives, medical devices are classified in accordance with the risk they pose, and a procedure is specified for classification. Greater scrutiny is required for higher risk devices.[163]

The overall approach of the Directives is to create a special, sector-specific, version of the general system of 'CE' product safety certification, a process governed in general in the EU by the 'General Product Safety Directive'.[164] The focus in the Medical Devices Directives is upon the need for conformity with EU standards, as evidenced by the 'CE' mark, placed upon the device. This is a legal requirement which demonstrates the claim of the manufacturer that this product complies with minimum product safety and performance requirements, as set out in the Directives. The 'CE mark' acts as a 'passport' for the product, allowing it to be placed on the EU market and to circulate freely within in it.[165] For the majority of medical devices,[166] CE marking is carried out by a 'notified body'.

In undertaking this task, a notified body determines whether the medical device meets certain 'essential requirements', as specified in the Directives. The manufacturer or their authorized representative draws up a 'declaration of conformity' of the device to the requirements.[167] Medical devices also undergo a pre-market clinical evaluation. This is defined under Commission Guidelines as being the assessment of clinical data pertaining to a medical device to verify the clinical safety and performance of the device.[168] What amounts to 'clinical safety' is defined as being the absence of clinical risks in a situation in which a device is used in accordance with the instructions of the manufacturer.

Notified bodies are nationally based, are under the oversight of a national 'competent authority',[169] and are certified by Member States. Crucially, notified bodies are for-profit organizations. They vary in their approach and capacity.

---

[162] Altenstetter above n 154, 234.

[163] There are four categories of such devices listed under in Directive 93/42/EC: Class I, Class II a, Class II b and Class III. The classification criteria are complex, and are expressed as a set of rules found in Annex IX. The rules are based on the concepts 'non-invasive device', 'surgically invasive device', 'implantable device', 'reusable surgical instrument', 'active medical device', 'active therapeutic device', 'active device for diagnosis'. For instance, 'All devices incorporating, as an integral part, a human blood derivative are in Class III' (Rule 13).

[164] Directive 2001/95/EC of the European Parliament and of the Council of 3 December 2001 on general product safety [2002] OJ L11/4.

[165] Hodges, 'The Regulation of Medicinal Products and Devices' in Grubb, Laing and McHale (eds), *Principles of Medical Law* (3rd edn, OUP 2010) paragraph 17.124.

[166] 'Class I' medical devices can be self-certified by the manufacturer self-executing a declaration of conformity and placing the device on the market.

[167] If the manufacturer follows a national standard which is a European harmonized standard to some aspect of the product, there is a *prima facie* presumption of conformity for this standard. See: Hodges, 'The Regulation of Medicinal Products and Devices' in Grubb, Laing and McHale (eds), (3rd edn, OUP 2010) above n 165, paragraph 17.124.

[168] See: Commission, 'Guidance MEDDEVs' (*Commission*, 18 September 2014).

[169] Which reports to the Minister of Health.

Moreover, their efficiency has been somewhat shrouded in secrecy. The numbers of these bodies vary from state to state, as does information concerning their effectiveness.[170] Daniel Kramer et al. note a 'near total lack of empirical evidence as to the performance of [the EU] system', as well as 'the lack of public access to either pre-market or post market data'.[171] As Imgard Vinck et al. have commented, although the system may be focused on risk of harm to patients, it does not guarantee equality in patient safety. A medical device manufacturer may 'forum shop' by choosing a notified body which is less stringent in its approach.[172]

Specific provisions of the Directives target post-market surveillance, with a technical mechanism and a vigilance clause for incident reporting. Since 1988, each competent authority has access to a European database on medical devices, EUDAMED.[173] This provides information about manufacturer approval, but in practice the use of such information has been variable. Generally, the coordination of adverse incident reporting varies across Member States.

Gordon Higson suggests that the Medical Devices Directives 'broke new ground'[174] and constituted an 'engineering response'[175] to the regulation of medical devices. The Directives not only restricted marketing of devices which compromised safety of patients, users and other persons, but went further in containing a list of 'essential requirements' as to what is deemed to constitute a safe product. The approach of the Directives is more of an industry-based or standards-based regulatory system than that pertaining to pharmaceuticals.[176] The difference can be explained by the view that the impact of medical devices on the body was usually, though not exclusively, external, and when removed their impact ceased. Fewer tests were required on living persons to ascertain the efficacy of the device.[177] Others have suggested that the approaches used in pharmaceuticals regulation, such as placebos and evidenced based trials, do not successfully translate to medical device regulation.[178]

Nonetheless the differences between the EU's regulatory structures for medical devices in comparison to pharmaceutical products are notable. Essentially, pharmaceuticals operate under centralized systems. There is a centralized

---

[170] Altensteller n. 154, 240.

[171] Kramer et al., 'Regulation of Medical Devices in the USA and the EU' (2012) 366(9) *New England Journal of Medicine* 848.

[172] Vinck et al., 'Market Introduction of Innovative High Risk Medical Devices: Towards a recast of the Directive concerning medical devices' (2011) 18(5) *European Journal of Health Law* 477, 481.

[173] See generally: Kramer et al., above n 171.

[174] Higson above n. 143, 2.   [175] Higson above n. 143, 3.

[176] Dorbeck-Jung and Chowdhury, 'Is the European Medical Products Authorisation Regulation Equipped to Cope with the Challenges of Nanomedicines?' (2011) 33(2) *Law and Policy* 276, 282.

[177] Higson above n 143, 4.

[178] See discussion in: Altenstetter, 'EU and Member states Medical Devices Regulation' (2003) 19(1) *International Journal of Technology Assessment in Health Care* 228.

single market authorization from the Commission, following a recommendation from the European Medicines Agency. Marketing authorizations given by individual Member States must be mutually recognized, and taken into account in other Member States. The regulation of medical devices is characterized by far more diversity. Although the thrust of the Directive is towards addressing risk and safety questions, the discretion allowed within different national contexts and indeed even between different notified bodies may *de facto* operate against this. The piecemeal pre- and post-market vigilance structures raise fundamental questions if the true aim of the Directive is addressing patient safety.[179] Furthermore, as Christopher Hodges suggests, if we consider the legal bases of the Directives, although a high level of health and safety must be secured in the EU's internal market, their main aim is facilitating trade, rather than patient safety per se.[180] Like the legislation considered earlier in this chapter, the EU's medical devices law also concerns risk to the internal market should unsafe products circulate therein – a different notion of risk from that focused on patient safety.

Reform

The EU system for approval of medical devices has come under criticism. The existing fragmented and complex structures, and the absence of centralization and harmonization, inhibit effective regulatory oversight of medical devices. The procedures depend upon the manufacturer rather than a separate regulatory body. While a single market in medical devices was achieved, Altenstetter suggests that EU law fell short in enforcement, implementation and accountability.[181] At the same time, reform proposals were concerned with other questions, in particular, as with pharmaceutical regulation, the tension between scientific development, economic innovation and safety. Calls to review the Directives were initially supported by the UK and France, although resisted for some time by Germany.

The European Commission held public reform consultations in 2008.[182] At the time, many respondents thought that further action would be

---

[179] See discussion in: Altenstetter above n 154, 243; see also Chowdhury, *European Regulation of Medical Devices and Pharmaceuticals* (Springer 2014).

[180] Hodges, 'Do we need a European Medical Devices Agency?' (2004) 12(3) *Medical Law Review* 268, 269.

[181] Altenstetter above n 154, 243.

[182] Commission, 'Recast of the Medical Devices Directives Summary of Responses to the Public Consultation' (ENTR/F/3/D(2008) 39582, Commission 2008). See further: Commission, 'Revision of Directive 98/79/EC of the European Parliament and of the Council of 27th October 1998 on In Vitro Diagnostic Medical Devices: Summary of Responses to Public Consultation' (Commission 2011). The European Commission initially committed itself to the re-evaluation of the Directives in 2005, see: Commission, 'Implementing the Community Lisbon programme: A strategy for the simplification of the regulatory environment' (Communication) COM (2005) 535 final.

premature,[183] and favoured the existing approach.[184] The Commission issued a separate public consultation in June 2010 on the specific area of *in vitro* diagnostic medical devices.[185] Following these consultations, and the Poly Implant Prothèse breast implant incident,[186] in September 2012, the Commission published a proposal for two new Regulations, repealing the Directives and reforming EU law on medical devices.[187] The proposals embrace many of the ideas in the consultation documents. The objective of the proposed new Regulations is 'to provide a simple and easily understandable regulatory environment for all medical devices that is supportive of innovation and the competitiveness of the European medical devices industry',[188] addressing gaps in EU law. As with the Clinical Trials Directive reform,[189] the proposal moves away from Directives, thus constraining the discretion of Member States in implementation.

One of the new Regulations (the Medical Devices Regulation) will replace both Directives 90/385 EEC and 93/42/EEC, extending to all medical devices, other than *in vitro* diagnostic devices.[190] The other (the *in vitro* Medical Devices Regulation) will replace the *in vitro* Directive.[191]

The scope of the Medical Devices Regulation will extend to products currently not within the scope of the Directives.[192] As we saw above, some devices

---

[183] Commission 2008 above n 182. This was because of other on-going developments, in particular revisions of Council Directive 90/385/EEC of 20th June 1990 on the approximation of the laws of the Member States in relation to active implantable medical devices [1990] OJ L189/17 and Directive 93/42/EC to be implemented in March 2010 and also the adoption of the new legal framework in January 2010.

[184] To include 'accreditation; designation and monitoring of notified bodies; post market surveillance; obligations for importers and distributors': Commission 2008 above n 182.

[185] Commission, 2011, above n 182.

[186] The European Parliament asked the Commission to establish a legal framework with the aim of guaranteeing the safety of the technology, see: European Parliament, 'Resolution of 14th June 2012 on defective silicone gel breast implants made by French company PIP (2012/2621(RSP)' (European Parliament 2012). Council also requested the Commission to take action see: Conclusions of the Council of the European Union on innovation in the medical device sector' [2011] OJ C202/7.

[187] Commission, 'Safe, effective and innovative medical devices and in vitro diagnostic medical devices for the benefit of patients, consumers and healthcare professionals' (Communication) COM (2012) 540 final; Commission Proposal COM (2012) 542 final; Commission, 'Proposal for a Regulation of the European Parliament and of the Council on *in vitro* diagnostic medical devices' COM (2012) 541 final. There was no consensus on consolidating the Directives.

[188] "In an internal market with 32 participating countries and subject to constant technological and scientific progress, substantial divergences in the interpretation and application of the rules have emerged thus undermining the main objectives of the Directives i.e. the safety of medical devices and their free movement within the internal market": Commission Proposal COM (2012) 542 final, page 2. See also: Commission, 'Safe, effective and innovative medical devices and in vitro diagnostic medical devices for the benefit of patients, consumers and healthcare professionals' (Communication) COM (2012) 540 final.

[189] See: chapter 12.   [190] Commission Proposal COM (2012) above n. 190.

[191] Commission, Proposal COM (2012) above n 187.

[192] The consultation revealed concerns about classification of medical devices, as well as questions about the boundaries between pharmaceuticals, medical devices, human tissue and cells, biocides, cosmetics and food. A wide range of products were seen as not included in the

which consisted entirely of non-viable human cells and/or derivatives are not effectively regulated at EU level.[193] The Regulation will cover products which have been manufactured using non-viable tissues or cells or their derivatives, 'which have undergone substantial modification'.[194] However, products within this category will be excluded from the Regulation if they are advanced therapy medicinal products, covered by Regulation 1394/2007/EC. Human tissues and cells, and products derived from them, which have not been 'substantially modified', will remain within the scope of the Tissues and Cells Directive 2004/23/EC.[195] The Regulation will not apply to some 'implantable or other invasive products without a medical purpose that are similar to medical devices in terms of characteristics and risk profile',[196] such as aesthetic implants and non-corrective contact lenses.[197] The scope of the *in vitro* Medical Devices Regulation clarifies the current position. Current interpretations suggest that 'only genetic tests that have a medical purpose are covered by [the] Directive'.[198] The question of what is a 'medical purpose' may be differently understood in different Member States, for instance, for certain predictive and lifestyle tests.[199] The Regulation will include genetic tests for predisposition to medical conditions and tests to predict treatment response. A high majority (86 per cent) of consultation respondents suggested increased oversight, or even

Directives or not sufficiently regulated. These included assisted reproduction/fertilisation technologies, diagnosis services, predictive testing, and invasive and non-invasive custom-made medical devices., 'Recast of the Medical Devices Directives Summary of Responses to the Public Consultation' (ENTR/F/3/D(2008) 39582, Commission 2008) 3. Commission Proposal COM (2012) 542 final above n 187, recital 43.

[193] Commission, 2008, above n 182.

[194] The example given is that of syringes prefilled with human collagen.

[195] The consultation included suggestions that the EU's medical devices law should also include devices where: 'human tissues are "utilised" during manufacture': Commission 2008 n 182. Such proposals, if adopted, would have ramifications across other areas of EU health law. For example, tissue banks were concerned about links to Directive 2004/23/EC.

[196] Commission Proposal COM (2012) 542 final above n 187, page 4.

[197] Consultation opinions diverged on implantable or aesthetic devices used for medical purposes, such as wrinkle fillers or contact lenses. Industry responses were in general opposed to such devices being covered by the EU medical devices law; others suggested that products with a medical purpose should be included: Commission, 2008, above n 182.

[198] Commission, 'Revision of Directive 98/79/EC of the European Parliament and of the Council of 27th October 1998 on In Vitro Diagnostic Medical Devices: Summary of Responses to Public Consultation' (Commission 2011) 13. The consultation document for *in vitro* devices reveals that the current EU medical devices law may be inappropriately configured for new and emerging technological developments in genetic testing.

[199] The consultation asked whether all genetic tests should be explicitly included by the use of the words 'results obtained by analysis of the genome', and if so whether, for instance, DNA tests for paternity should be explicitly excluded at the same time. A clear majority (83%) of respondents suggested that such wording would simply not be broad enough to cover all tests, such as analysis of RNA or protein biomarkers. Alternatively, the consultation asked whether 'tests, including genetic tests with a direct or indirect medical purpose' should be included within the scope of the Regulation: Commission, 2011 above n 198. An inconclusive 54% were opposed, however, some felt that a clear definition would be beneficial.

prohibition, of direct-to-consumer genetic tests.[200] In addition, some wanted advertising of direct-to-consumer testing to be regulated by the EU.[201] These suggestions were not taken up in the proposal. In recognition of the uncertainty surrounding the scope of the proposed Regulations, definitions are to be aligned with existing international and European definitions and guidance. In addition, the Commission may also establish a group of experts from sectors such as medical devices, products and human tissue and cells to support it in this task.[202]

Virtually all respondents agreed that the scheme of classification for medical devices should be changed to a 'rules-based risk classification' based on Global Harmonization Task Force (GHTF) guidance.[203] This has been done in both proposals. While it might lead to significant rises in costs, the consultation suggested that GHTF alignment would also improve public health, give greater flexibility and improve European exports.[204] Some reclassification, or clarification of classification, is proposed. For instance, products which are 'composed of substances or combinations of substances that are intended to be ingested, inhaled or administered rectally or vaginally and that are absorbed by or dispersed in the human body'[205] are classified in the highest category of risk. They must also comply with Annex I of Directive 2001/83/EC.[206] The current special arrangements for custom-made devices continue.[207] Some concerns were raised as to whether a risk-based approach would be appropriate for genetic testing.[208] It was suggested that a range of other factors should be taken into

---

[200] Commission, (2011) above n 198.
[201] See also discussion of this issue in UK Human Genetics Commission, *Common framework of principles of direct to consumer genetic testing services* (UK HGC 2009).
[202] See generally: Commission, 'Communication from the President to the Commission: Framework for Commission Expert Groups: Horizontal Rules and Public Registers (C(2010) 7649 final, Commission 2010).
[203] Commission, 2008 above n 182; Commission, 'Revision of Directive 98/79/EC of the European Parliament and of the Council of 27th October 1998 on In Vitro Diagnostic Medical Devices: Summary of Responses to Public Consultation' (Commission 2011) 5.
[204] Commission, (2008) above n 182, at 3; Commission, 'Revision of Directive 98/79/EC of the European Parliament and of the Council of 27th October 1998 on In Vitro Diagnostic Medical Devices: Summary of Responses to Public Consultation' (Commission 2011) 3, 4.
[205] Commission Proposal COM (2012) above n 187, page 5.
[206] Directive 2001/83/EC of the European Parliament and of the Council of 6 November 2001 on the Community code relating to medicial products for human use [2001] OJ L311/67 (as amended), Annex I.
[207] Commission, Proposal (2012) above n.186 l, Articles 8 (3) (5) (6), 18, 19, 23, 24, 25, 26, 42, 61. The consultation also suggested that existing exemptions should be retained for in-house tests for rare diseases or population-specific tests: Commission (2008) above n 182, 10. This is needed to enable rapid response, not least because testing for global health threats from infectious diseases would otherwise be slowed down if all new assays were subject to the CE process.
[208] Commission, 'Revision of Directive 98/79/EC of the European Parliament and of the Council of 27th October 1998 on In Vitro Diagnostic Medical Devices: Summary of Responses to Public Consultation' (Commission 2011) 4.

account, such as the impact of genetic testing and its results on patients and on their families.[209]

The underlying idea of the proposal is that legal obligations on manufacturers should be proportionate to the risk of the device.[210] The proposed Medical Devices Regulation adopts the concept of 'common technical specifications' (already found in the *in vitro* devices Directive). This will allow future inclusion of further safety and technical requirements, and clinical evaluation and post-market clinical follow up.[211] The practice of reprocessing medical devices is permitted to continue, but is to be subject to stringent new safeguards.[212] In particular, reprocessing of single-use devices for surgical purposes should be prohibited.[213]

In terms of the overall approach, many aspects of the Regulation remain the same. Neither the consultation's suggestion of a centralized pre-market authorization procedure, such as applies to pharmaceuticals,[214] nor the idea of extending the European Medicines Agency (EMA) role to cover oversight of medical devices approval across the EU,[215] are found in the proposed Regulations. Although health professionals, the academic community and patient community were supportive of involving the EMA,[216] for this to be properly taken forward, any new medical devices division of the EMA needed to be properly funded, and as a consequence the existing structure and budget of the EMA would need to be revised. Given the timing, with the Eurozone crisis and global economic downturn, this was potentially problematic, and the Member States diverged in their views on possible expansion of the EMA.[217]

---

[209] Commission, 'Revision of Directive 98/79/EC of the European Parliament and of the Council of 27th October 1998 on In Vitro Diagnostic Medical Devices: Summary of Responses to Public Consultation' (Commission 2011) 10. However, the exemption could be more carefully defined, and limited to those situations in which either there were no suitable in vitro devices available or where those devices which were commercially available did not address users' needs.

[210] Commission Proposal COM (2012) above n 187, page 6.

[211] Commission Proposal COM (2012) n 187, page 6 and proposed regulations, Annex I and Annex XIII.

[212] Commission Proposal COM (2012) n 187, page 6.

[213] Commission Proposal COM (2012) n 187, page 7.

[214] Most consultation responses were opposed to this idea.

[215] However this option was also rejected by the majority of respondents: Commission (2008) above n 182; in particular both industry and the notified bodies. It was suggested that the EMA did not have appropriate expertise, and that its involvement would lead to delays in approval processes, which would impede sufficiently rapid access to innovative medical devices.

[216] Commission, (2008) above n 182, 9.

[217] An alternative suggestion from the Commission was that the EMA could be concerned with only with 'highest risk' devices. This attracted little support, perhaps unsurprisingly given the opposition by certain interest groups to the expansion of the EMA role. The majority of respondents also rejected the EMA as the body to deal with borderline cases in classification of products, in terms of whether they fell within the pharmaceuticals, human materials, or medical devices regime in EU law. However the need for effective procedures to address such borderline cases, was recognized: Commission, above n 182, 12. The consultation document

However, one view supported by many Member States was the need for a body such as a Medical Devices Agency/Health Products Agency or Management Committee.[218] Hodges had examined the case for such a new medical devices oversight body in 2004.[219] He suggested that, as the justification for any agency can be seen as expertise, a permanent agency could facilitate consistency in decision-making over time.[220] Furthermore, if the remit was wide enough, it could also lead to a proactive stance on patient safety. Nonetheless, he also noted the possibility that establishing a specialist agency could lead to regulatory capture, where the regulatory agenda becomes dislocated from the general public.[221] The proposal envisages an expert committee (the Medical Devices Coordination Group) to facilitate harmonization.[222]

The existing structure, with national notified bodies, remains.[223] Stricter and more detailed criteria for the designation and monitoring of notified bodies by Member States are proposed, although implementation is left to the Member States.[224] The idea is to reduce the risk of manufacturers 'forum shopping'.[225] Both new designations and ongoing monitoring of notified bodies will operate through 'joint assessments' by experts from other Member States and from the Commission.[226] Conformity and assessment procedures have been tightened.[227] National competent authorities remain responsible for designation and monitoring of notified bodies, for conformity with criteria set out in the proposed

responses suggested, in effect, a 'kind of supra-Directives Committee on Borderlines'. This is now found in the proposed 'expert group' which the Commission may establish.

[218] Commission (2008), above n 182, 9. This was seen as advantageous, because it could bring together the views of public bodies and provide oversight.

[219] Hodges, 'Do we need a European Medical Devices Agency?' (2004) 12(3) *Medical Law Review* 268.

[220] Hodges above n 219.   [221] Ibid.

[222] Commission Proposal COM (2012) 542 final above n 187 Chapter VIII, Article 78. The proposal stops short of situating this work within the EMA: "taking into account the clear preference expressed by stakeholders, including many Member States, the proposal mandates the Commission to provide technical, scientific and logistic support to the Medical Devices Coordination Group. Commission, (2008) above n 182.

[223] Consultation respondents thought that designation and monitoring should remain with the Member States, rather than being transferred to the Commission or to another centralised body.

[224] Commission, (2008) above n 182, 7-8. See also Commission Proposal COM (2012) above n 187, paragraph 3.4, and Annex VI. The responses to the consultation clearly indicated that the role of notified bodies and the manner in which they operated should be improved, through harmonisation and possibly centralisation of the oversight of notified bodies. In particular, the consultation responses indicated that existing regulators should be subject to greater standardisation. There should initially be more rigorous designation and monitoring of such bodies, to ensure that they would operate at 'a uniform(ly) high level of competence': Commission (2008) above n 182. The consultation suggested that enhanced scrutiny of notified bodies could be achieved by public authorities having access to the evaluation reports for all devices: Commission (2008) above n 182 at 10. rather than this being the included as part of an expanded role of the European Medicines Agency.

[225] Commission, (2008) above n 182, 8.

[226] Commission (2012) above n 187, page 8 and Annex VI.

[227] Commission (2012) above n 187, page 8 and Annexes VIII-X.

Regulation.[228] It is proposed that the Commission will have power to 'suspend, restrict or withdraw' a notification, following a procedure of investigation and collaboration with national competent authorities.[229] A system of peer review of national competent authorities is proposed, to facilitate a uniform level of competency.[230]

In some respects, the proposed Regulations are being aligned with EU law on pharmaceuticals, on human tissue, and on clinical trials. For example, the manufacturers' organization will require a 'qualified person' who is responsible for regulatory compliance.[231] In the light of the concerns regarding the safety of breast implants, the proposal provides for enhanced patient information, vigilance[232] and traceability.[233] Those patients who have been implanted with a device will be entitled to 'essential information', regarding the device, so that it can be identified.[234] There is to be a new central registration database.[235] The concept of a 'sponsor' (which can be the manufacturer, its authorized representative or another organization, and in practice is often a 'contract research organization' conducting clinical research for the manufacturers), as found in the proposed reform to the Clinical Trials Directive, is to be introduced.[236] Clinical investigations of medical devices 'must be registered in a publicly accessible electronic system',[237] which is to be 'interoperable' with the proposed new database concerning trials on pharmaceuticals discussed in chapter 13. The proposal envisages an EU portal where manufacturers must report serious incidents and corrective actions to reduce the prospect that these would reoccur.[238]

The proposals represent a movement towards facilitating greater harmonization as a response to the concerns regarding fragmented regulation, highlighted in the Poly Implant Prothèse breast implant incident. The proposals reveal the definitional challenges of regulation across health technologies, noting the complexity of the area and the fact that new and emerging technologies lead

---

[228] Commission Proposal COM (2012) above n 187, Article 33, and Annex VI.
[229] Commission Proposal COM (2012) above n 187, Article 36. The consultation suggested that notified bodies should be subject to sanctions, such as withdrawal of their designation, see Commission (2008) n 182, 8.
[230] Commission Proposal COM above n 187, Article 26 (8). The consultation suggested oversight of competent authorities by the European Commission: Commission (2008) above n 182, 8.
[231] Commission Proposal COM (2012) above n 187, page 6.
[232] The consultation revealed support for strengthening of the vigilance system. Health professional and patient groups suggested closer links between vigilance systems for devices and pharmaceuticals. Mandatory reporting of problems by health professionals and patients was suggested, given the current different jurisdictional approaches. 'Over-reporting' could be addressed through reporting being undertaken through the filter of the health professional: Commission, (2008) n 182, 11.
[233] The consultation called for improved traceability and identification of devices, for example, through the use of a 'unique device identifier' Commission (2008) above n 182, 6.
[234] Commission Proposal COM (2012) above n 187, page 6.
[235] Commission Proposal COM (2012) above n 187, page 7.
[236] Commission Proposal COM (2012) above n 187, page 9.
[237] Commission Proposal COM (2012) above n 187, page 9.
[238] Commission Proposal COM (2012) above n 187, page 10.

to uncertainties as to the applicability of the frameworks provided by EU law. Considerable national variations in classification and borderline cases need clarification. The proposals represent increasing alignment of this area with that of the regulation of pharmaceuticals, but they stop short of bringing the whole field within the oversight of the European Medicines Agency. The proposals are an example of a regulatory response triggered by a breach of patient safety (the Poly Implant Prothèse case), which to a significant extent explains their greater emphasis placed upon risk to patients rather than to creating the internal market, which was the original impetus behind EU medical devices law. But the EU's approach is not simply focused on risk to patients and a precautionary approach. Risks to the internal market and the global competitiveness of European industry are also factored into the approach. As we have seen, of course, the therapeutic and commercial agendas can be seen as aligned. Patients seek new treatments, manufacturers seek to bring new products to market. The speed of technological advances provides real practical challenges, and not all stakeholders will take the view that the balance is right. The centralization of and enhanced clarity in risk regulation of medical devices has come under heavy criticism from trade organizations. The EUComed trade organization has gone so far as to say it would create an 'FDA like organisation that will kill patients and kill innovative companies'.[239]

Medical devices conclusions

In EU health law, pharmaceuticals are seen as inherently dangerous. Human material is seen as inherently in need of special regulation, both because of significant safety concerns and because of its ethical and human rights resonances. By contrast, at least originally, the assumption of EU law on medical devices has been that they are essentially like other consumer products. Medical devices need to be regulated to secure consumer safety, and to create and protect the internal market, but not beyond that. Adjustments to the *caveat emptor* principle are necessary to take into account information asymmetries. But, unlike pharmaceuticals, or human materials, it has been assumed that there is no need for EU law to provide special regulation of the processes, entities which produce, or sites of production of medical devices. The proposed reform of EU medical devices law moves it towards the approach taken for pharmaceuticals and human materials. Risks to patient safety play a stronger role than hitherto, although they remain balanced with risks to competitiveness and of technological stagnation.

---

[239] Cohen, 'Devices and Desires; Industry Fights Toughening of Medical Device Regulation in Europe' (2013) 347 *British Medical Journal* 1.

Compensation for harm

While individuals who claim that they have suffered harm from a pharma-ceutical or other product used in the course of their treatment (device, organ, tissue-based product) are able to bring actions in their national courts, under the applicable laws on civil liability, establishing such liability frequently presents major difficulties to the litigant, not least due to the problems in establishing causation.[240] Given the public interests in securing safe health systems, and securing protection of patients who are harmed, it is often argued that a dif-ferent approach to liability is appropriate. Essentially, under such a different approach, the cost of liability for harm is met by the insurers of those producing the pharmaceutical or other health product. Liability in itself becomes a man-ufacturing 'cost', as the assumption of risk is built into the equation from the outset.[241] A risk reduction approach and indeed a potentially powerful deterrent to the production of harmful products is the introduction of strict liability.

In general, EU health law does not extend to compensation for harms result-ing from health care *procedures*, as these have been seen as beyond the scope of EU competence.[242] But the EU's Product Liability Directive 85/374/EEC[243]

---

[240] See, for example, the notable UK case of *Loveday v Renton* [1989] 1 Med LR 117 and for a controversial series of litigation concerning MMR, see the discussion in: Goldberg, *Medicinal Product Liability and Regulation* (Hart 2013) chapter 6, and the contributions to the special edition (2003) 10 (2) *European Journal of Health Law*: and for further extensive consideration of the scope of liability in medical negligence in the UK context, see: Jones, *Medical Negligence* (4th edn, Sweet & Maxwell 2008).

[241] The rationale for special protection in the context of vaccine damage in the UK, as stated by the Pearson Commission, was that of public policy to compensate for injury in a situation in which the state itself supported vaccination, see: Pearson Commission, *Report of the Royal Commission on the Civil Liability and Compensation for Personal Injury* (Cmnd 7054-1, 1978), chapter 25. Thus Pearson, whilst rejecting a general no-fault scheme for medical compensation, was of the view that this was necessary in relation to vaccine damage, leading to the introduction of the Vaccine Damage Payments Act 1979. A further review of this issue undertaken by the UK Chief Medical Officer, Liam Donaldson in: Chief Medical Officer, 'Making Amends: a consultation paper setting out the proposals for reforming the approach to clinical negligence in the NHS' (Department of Health 2003), led to the introduction of the NHS Redress Act 2006 which would lead to a new redress scheme for low value claims. To date this legislation has not been implemented. See: Devaney and Farrell 'Making Amends or Making Things Worse: Clinical Negligence Reform and Patient Redress in England' 27 *Legal Studies* (2007) 360 and generally: McLean, 'Can No-Fault Analysis Ease the Problems of Medical Injury Litigation?' and Brazier, 'The Case for a No-Fault Scheme for Medical Accidents' both in McLean (ed), *Compensation for Damage: An International Perspective* (Ashgate 1993).

[242] Liability for harm from the treatment within hospitals is outside the scope of the Directive, see: *Dutrueux*, C-495/10, EU:C:2011:869, concerning whether a hospital was liable under the Directive for harms caused during surgery from a defective heated mattress. That is not to say that the prospect of harm resulting from negligence liability is something which is avoided in EU policy discussions, as illustrated by the debates concerning the Patients Rights Directive and also the reform of the Clinical Trials Directive. See further: chapters 4–8 and 12.

[243] Council Directive 85/374/EEC of 25 July 1985 on the approximation of the laws, regulations and administrative provisions of the Member States concerning liability for defective products [1985] OJ L210/29.

gives consumers the right to compensation for defective *products* on a strict liability basis.[244] The Directive was introduced following the major scandals over pharmaceutical and blood product safety in the EU. But it is not simply a measure focused on reduction of risk of harm to patients, or patient safety approach. The Product Liability Directive is an internal market measure. Its aim is to harmonize national laws on the liability of producers for damage caused by the defectiveness of their products. Its rationale is that otherwise divergences in national laws will distort competition and affect the free movement of goods within the EU.[245] Institutionally, the Directive is not within the purview of DG-SANCO, which of course covers other EU consumer protection and health law. The Directive was controversial from the outset, as it reduced the discretion of some Member States to offer greater protection to consumers of certain products,[246] including defective pharmaceuticals and other products used in health settings.[247] This interpretation was confirmed by the CJEU:[248] 'The margin of discretion available to the Member State in order to make provision for product liability is entirely determined by the Directive itself.'[249] However, the CJEU has been relatively generous in granting Member States *procedural* discretion.[250] Thus, in terms of its legal basis, the Directive does not represent an unmitigated patient safety approach to the compensation for harm in health settings.

The position in some Member States, in particular Germany, may not be entirely consistent with the Directive, following these cases. Germany had been heavily involved in the Thalidomide scandal.[251] It had subsequently introduced strict liability under the Medicines Act (Arzneimittelgesetz) 1976 (AMG).

---

[244] Directive 85/374, Article 1. For discussion of the history of the Directive, see: Hervey and McHale (CUP 2004) above n 61, 307–312.

[245] Directive 85/374, Preamble and Recital 5. There is some doubt as to whether such differences in national laws do in fact distort competition in this way, suggesting that the consumer protection motivations form a more realistic rationale for the measure. See: Howells and Wilhelmsson, *EC Consumer Law* (Ashgate 1997) 34.

[246] If the main rationale was simply that of the reduction of risk then in those situations in which a Member State already had an operational system of tort liability providing rigorous accountability and effective compensation this would suggest that the Directive should provide a base-line of liability but nothing more. Rather the 'tougher' Member States should be able to maintain their 'tougher' stance.

[247] For instance, the German Arzneimittelgesetz of 1961 was amended following the Thalidomide tragedy to include strict liability for harm from defective pharmaceuticals, even when the adverse effects of the product became discernible after it reached the market. The Spanish General Law 26/1984 for the Protection of Consumers and Users provides a strict liability regime for various products, including pharmaceuticals. The French law has been interpreted by the *Cour de Cassation* to requires that blood suppliers were not able to rely on the undiscoverability of HIV at the time when contaminated blood products were circulating during the 1980s. See: Navarro-Michel, 'New Health Technologies and Their Impact on EU Product Liability Regulation' in Flear et al., above n 5, 174–7.

[248] *Commission v France*, C-52/00, EU:C:2002:252; *Commission v Greece*, C-154/00, EU:C:2002:254; *Gonzalez Sanchez v Medicina Asturiana SA*, C-183/00, EU:C:2002:255.

[249] *Gonzalez Sanchez v Medicina Asturiana SA* EU:C:2002:255, paragraph 25.

[250] *O'Byrne*, C-127/04, EU:C:2006:93; and *Aventis Pasteur*, C-358/08, EU:C:2009:744.

[251] Howells, *Comparative Product Liability* (Dartmouth Publishing 1993) 136, 138-41.

Initially, the AMG imposed liability on manufacturers where injurious effects were produced by a pharmaceutical product as unjustifiable in the light of medical knowledge and its source was found in the development or in the manufacture of the drug, or if physical damage flowed from labelling, instructions from use or where instructions were provided to professionals but which did not correspond with medical knowledge.[252] It has also reversed the burden of proof of causation through amendments to the primary legislation. The burden is now on the manufacturer to demonstrate that the source of the harmful effect did not originate from the development or the manufacture of the drug.[253] A State Compensation Act covers Hepatitis C virus patients infected in the old German Democratic Republic in the period 1978–79 through the compulsory post-partum administration of anti D-immunoglobins.[254] The German Product Liability Act enacted following the Directive does not cover pharmaceutical products. Since the Directive seems to suggest maximum harmonization, the amendment to the AMG may not fall within the exception contained in Article 13.[255]

In terms of its wording, the Product Liability Directive 85/374/EEC also does not fit readily within a standard patient safety approach to risk. Two aspects of the Directive are evidence here: the definition of 'product' and the concept of the 'development risks defence'. The term 'product' in the Directive includes pharmaceuticals, products made from or using human tissue and materials, including blood products, and medical devices.[256] Under the Directive, producers are liable for damage caused by defects in their product, irrespective of negligence or culpability.[257] This approach was chosen on the grounds that it is the fairest apportionment of risks between consumers and producers (and, presumably, their insurers) in an age of increasing technological change.[258] A product is defined as defective when it does not provide the safety which 'the public is entitled to expect', taking into account the presentation of the product, its reasonable uses and the time it was put into circulation.[259] There is no distinction drawn between manufacturing or production defects and those

---

[252] See: Goldberg (Hart 2013) above n 240.

[253] Drucksache 14/8780, Deutscher Bundestag-14-Wahlperiode, 16th April 2002. AMG, in Clause 84.

[254] Act on assistance for patients affected with the hepatitis V virus by anti D immunoglobulins, Gesetz uber die Hilfe dur durch Anti D Immunprophylaxe mit dem Hepatitis C-Virus Infizierte Personen (Anti-D-Hilfegesetz. Anti-DHG), BGBl I 2000.

[255] See discussion in: Goldberg (Hart 2013) above n 240, 13.

[256] Directive 85/374 Article 2, Article 1: "'Product' means all movables even if incorporated into another movable or into an immovable. 'Product' includes electricity."

[257] The term "producer" is broadly defined, to include the manufacturer of a finished product, the producer of any raw material or the manufacturer of a component part and any person who, by putting his name, trademark, or other distinguishing feature on the product, presents himself as the producer. Persons who import products into the Community for sale, hire, leasing or distribution are also deemed to be "producers" for the purposes of the Directive: Directive 85/374, Articles 3 (1) and (2). On the application of the Directive in the context of an organ transplant in a public hospital, see: *Henning Veedfald v Århus Amtskommune*, C-203/99, EU:C:2001:258.

[258] Council Directive 85/374 Preamble, Recital 6.   [259] Directive 85/374, Article 6.

defects which may arise from design or from failure to warn.[260] For this purpose, 'the public' refers to the general public rather than a specialist group,[261]
or has been suggested rather to 'consumer expectations'.[262] Expectations may
be pitched at a higher than baseline standard, in the sense that there may be a
risk-benefit-utility calculation here.[263]

The scope of the strict liability of producers for defects in their products is reduced, potentially significantly, by an optional measure in Directive
85/374/EEC, known as the 'development risks defence'.[264] The Directive provides that, should a Member State opt in to the defence, if, at the time of
manufacture of the product, the state of scientific and technical knowledge was
such that the risk of harm was not foreseeable, the producer will not be liable
under the Directive.[265] Most Member States have a developmental risks defence,
with the exception of Luxembourg and Finland, but the approach of Member
States to products used within health care settings is far from harmonized. In
some instances, the defence applies only in specific contexts. Germany adopted
the defence except for pharmaceuticals.[266] In Spain, the defence does not apply
to food or pharmaceuticals.[267] In France, it does not apply to products derived
from the human body.[268]

---

[260] These are recognized in the USA and it has been suggested that such an approach into
"manufacturing defects", "design defects" and " warning defects" may prove a more
efficacious approach and one best suited to medicinal products. See: Goldberg (Hart 2013)
above n 240, 32–37 and chapters 3 and 4.

[261] See criticism of this by Navarro-Michel, 'New Health Technologies and Their Impact on EU
Product Liability Regulation' in Flear et al., above n 5, 187. In the English courts in *A v
National Blood Authority*, Burton J held that Hepatitis C infected products were defective
because "the public at large was entitled to expect that the blood transferred to them would be
free from infection": *A v National Blood Authority* [2001] 3 All ER 289.

[262] An approach drawn from the Article 402 A US Restatement, Second Torts (1965). See:
Goldberg (Hart 2013) above n 240, 20–22.

[263] See: Goldberg (Hart 2013) above n 240, 21.

[264] In the evolution of the Directive, this was very controversial. The European Commission was
opposed to such a defence while the Parliament were in favour. The defence was eventually
included after pressure from the UK Conservative government, led by Margaret Thatcher, to
safeguard the interests of producers, and it was only when this was included that the UK was
prepared to agree to the Directive in Council, See the discussion in: Goldberg, 'The
development risk defence and the European Court of Justice; increased injury costs and the
Supplementary Protection Certificate' in Goldberg and Lonbay (eds), *Pharmaceutical
Medicine, Biotechnology and European Law* (CUP 2001) 186.

[265] Council Directive 85/374/EC Article 7 (e).   [266] ProdHasft G 1989, Article 15.

[267] Goldberg has speculated that the Spanish approach can be related to a toxic syndrome
involving cooking oil and to a number of defective drug incidents including MER 29 (a
cholesterol reducing drug) which led to blindness, a child vaccine, "quadrigen", leading to
brain inflammation and Thalidomide: Goldberg, 'The development risk defence and the
European Court of Justice; increased injury costs and the Supplementary Protection
Certificate' in Goldberg and Lonbay above n 264, 194; Goldberg (Hart 2013) above n 240,
175. See also Navarro-Michel, 'New Health Technologies and Their Impact on EU Product
Liability Regulation' in Flear et al., above n 5.

[268] Following the controversy on contaminated blood, Commission, 'Liability for Defective
Products' (Green Paper) COM (1999) 396 final, pages 34–35.

The European Commission's view that the development risks defence should be defined narrowly was not upheld by the CJEU.[269] The UK's implementing legislation, which includes discoverability of the risk within the defence, was not contrary to the requirements of the Directive.[270] The decision has been subject to considerable critical comment and discussion.[271] Despite casting the defence in terms of objectivity, in fact there is still a subjective element, in that the national court is left to ascertain, on a case-by-case basis, whether a reasonable producer might have been expected to have discovered the defect.[272] Further, it has been suggested that the ambiguity of the relevant section of the UK Act[273] protected the UK against claims that it has not implemented the Directive correctly because such a 'covert, paraphrased reasonableness standard is potentially misleading in its impact'.[274] In practice, the availability of the development risks defence in most Member States of the EU has significantly reduced the relevance of the Product Liability Directive in the field of pharmaceuticals, and other products used in health settings. In the case of such products, risks either manifest themselves during the preclinical or clinical trial stage, before marketing authorization is granted, or not until some years after, as in the case of side-effects with a long latency period. Indeed, it has been suggested that the standard required under the Directive is so high that it may arguably never succeed.[275] Again, this leads to the conclusion that EU product liability law is not as patient-safety focused as it may at first appear.

While there have been periods where reform of the Directive seemed likely, for instance, following the rulings of the CJEU in actions involving France, Greece and Spain, this has not happened to date.[276] The effectiveness of the Directive as a measure for compensation and indeed deterrence remains questionable. As the Fourth Report of the Commission on the Directive noted, it has not

---

[269] See: *Commission v UK (Product Liability Directive)*, C-300/95, EU:C:1997:255.

[270] For further comment, see Howells and Wilhelmsson (Ashgate 1997) above n 245, 42–3; McHale and Fox, *Health Care Law: Text and Materials* (2nd edn, Sweet and Maxwell 2007) 192–193; Newdick, 'The Development Risk Defence of the Consumer Protection Act 1987' 47 *Cambridge Law Journal* (1988) 455; Goldberg, 'The development risk defence and the ECJ' Goldberg and Lonbay (eds), (CUP 2001) above n 264.

[271] Goldberg and Lonbay, above n.258; Newdick, above n 269.

[272] Goldberg, 'The development risk defence and the European Court of Justice; increased injury costs and the Supplementary Protection Certificate' in Goldberg and Lonbay above n. 258; see: Goldberg (Hart 2013) above n 240, 180; and also: Stapelton, 'Products Liability in the UK: The Myths of Reform' (1999) 34(1) *Texas International Law Journal* 45, 59–60.

[273] UK Consumer Protection Act 1987, section 4.

[274] Goldberg, 'The development risk defence' above n 272, 193.

[275] See discussion in Goldberg, 'The development risk defence' above n 272 and also Hodges, 'Developmental Risks: Unanswered Questions' (1998) 61(4) *Modern Law Review* 560.

[276] See: Council Resolution of 19 December 2002 on amendment of the liability for defective products Directive' [2003] OJ C26/2. In *Commission v France* EU:C:2002:252; *Commission v Greece* EU:C:2002:254; *Gonzalez Sanchez v Medicina Asturinana SA* EU:C:2002:255, the Court took the approach that individual Member States who imposed provisions on supplier liability, which went beyond the scope of the Directive, and were unduly onerous, could be found in breach of their obligations under the Directive.

in itself had a significant impact upon the type and success of such claims.[277] A Commission-sponsored study on the economic implications for consumers, industry, insurance and society of the development of risks defence[278] concluded that the defence constituted 'a significant factor in achieving the Directive's balance between the need to preserve incentives to innovation and consumers interests'.[279] The Directive's contribution to relative stability of insurance costs in Europe and keeping litigation levels 'reasonable' were also valued.[280] The history of the Directive, as a relatively early engagement with product liability, may explain why, despite consideration of reform, it has not taken place, whereas in other jurisdictions, notably the USA, the law has evolved. The very existence of the Directive could be seen in terms of being a risk reduction measure. But the continuation of the consensus to permit significant national discretion in the balance of patient safety, innovation and industry competitiveness must be read more broadly – this is not an area of EU law that can be understood entirely through the lens of risk of harm to patients.

Conclusions

As this chapter and the two preceding it have shown, EU health law deals separately with pharmaceuticals, human material (blood, tissue, cells, organs) and medical devices. This fractured approach is becoming less and less convincing, logical or defensible. It is fundamentally challenged by the emergence of novel technologies that are not easily categorized as device, pharmaceutical or human tissue/cell-based.[281] Technologies already exist that combine the categories, and this is set to continue in unforeseen ways. There is a growing awareness that the dangers inherent in each category are similar, so different approaches to the regulation of the risks are increasingly difficult to justify. In that sense, the theme of risk reveals an important insight into EU health law, which might also indicate its direction of travel. As we have seen in this chapter, although the different substantive areas of this aspect of EU health law remain distinct, they may be slowly converging around common ideas or approaches: regulation through institutional and procedural obligations,[282] an approach to risk

---

[277] Commission, 'Fourth report on the application of Council Directive 85/374/EEC of 25 July 1985 on the approximation of the laws, regulations and administrative provisions of the Member States concerning liability for defective products amended by Directive 1999/34/EC of the European Parliament and of the Council of 10 May 1999' COM (2011) 547 final.

[278] Alaimo et al., 'An Analysis of the Economic Impact of the Development Risk Clause as provided by Directive 85/374/EEC on Liability for Defective Products: Final Report' (Foundazione Rosselli 2004).

[279] Alaimo et al., above n 278, 135.　　[280] Alaimo et al., above n 278, 135.

[281] Dorbeck-Jung, Bowman and Van Calster, (eds), 'Governing Nanomedicine: Lessons from within, and for, the EU Medical Technology Regulatory Framework' (2011) 33(2) *Law & Policy* 215.

[282] For instance, the obligation to have a 'competent authority' at national level, with particular duties and responsibilities.

regulation that considers risk to markets and also bioethical and human rights dimensions.

In general, however, it is difficult to sustain overarching conclusions about this aspect of EU health law. There are important distinctions between areas where there is increasing EU regulatory oversight over time, areas where there is some EU law but significant national discretion and areas where EU law does not apply at all. Examples of increasing EU law involvement include traceability of products, vigilance systems and possibly medical devices regulation, if the reform proposals are adopted. Areas of significant national discretion include blood safety standards, and human rights and ethical interpretations across the board. Areas where there is little or no EU law include processes or techniques, such as novel surgical techniques.[283]

That said, national discretion in regulating risk from health-related products reaching the market has become increasingly constrained. It is significantly more constrained than national discretion over health services or procedures or health research. The idea of the single market in products, and regulating risk within (and to) that single European market, is strong in the context of authorization of pharmaceuticals. The near exhaustive harmonization of this area means that thinking about Member States along a continuum from more to less stringent in terms of risk regulation (as we considered in the introduction to these chapters) is not very helpful. By contrast, (most) medical devices were originally assumed to be 'low risk' and therefore regulated as 'ordinary' consumer products. This means that Member States had significant control over national producers, although they were required to permit marketing of devices which could be sold in other Member States. It is possible that Member States could be mapped to such a continuum, but the paucity of information about the operation of national 'notified bodies' makes this difficult in practice. Over time, this position has changed, most recently by responses to the Poly Implant Prothèse affair.

Uses of human blood, tissues or cells in health contexts were originally not conceptualized as belonging to this category of risk regulation at all. In European traditions, parts of the human body are not 'products', and their regulation cannot therefore be undertaken in terms of market- or trade-based risk to consumers. Rather, ethical or human rights frameworks are applied. In EU health law, this is reflected by the different legal bases for the provisions on human materials, in comparison with those for pharmaceuticals or medical devices. The former are based on the EU's public health competence, the latter on its internal market competence. However, more recent legislation has a dual basis. In part, this reflects technological developments, and the development of EU health law has followed those. Again in this context we have seen that there is significant discretion for Member States, especially in terms of the practical

---

[283] Bache et al., 'The Defining Features of the European Union's Approach to Regulating New Health Technologies' in Flear et al., above n 5, 13.

and detailed interpretation of ethical and human rights provisions. While it would be difficult to map Member States on a continuum of more to less risk averse, it would be feasible to distinguish Member States which are more open to exploration of novel technologies involving the human body (for instance, the UK) from those which are less so.[284]

Whatever the area of EU law on human blood, tissues, cells, organs or medical devices (or indeed clinical trials or pharmaceuticals), it is not comprehensible solely through the theme of risk of harm to patients. Other risks, principally to the EU market (such as trade barriers), or the EU's industry (such as impediments to innovation) also inform the shape and direction of EU health law. Moreover, other concerns are not susceptible to risk regulation approaches at all. Ethics and human rights play a significant role in determining the contours of EU health law in this area, particularly pertaining to human materials. Nonetheless, risk does play a significant role in providing the principal underpinning justification, and in that sense it is an important theme of EU health law.

The question of over- or under-regulation, which we raised at the beginning of this chapter, is taken up in the conclusion to the next chapter, the last in this section of the book. In that chapter, we consider risk to 'patient' safety not from products which are used within national health systems but from products which are in common consumer use within the EU, but which pose significant threats to population health: tobacco, food and alcohol.

[284] For discussion of this ethical continuum, see: Hervey and McHale (CUP 2004) above n 61, 400–404.

15

Risk: tobacco, food, alcohol

Introduction

Abuse of tobacco, food and alcohol accounts for a great deal of ill health. Smoking is the most significant cause of premature death in the EU, responsible for nearly 700,000 deaths each year.[1] WHO figures show that smoking causes around 16 per cent of all deaths in the WHO Europe region,[2] which includes all the EU Member States. Around half of all smokers die prematurely. Smokers also suffer poor health, because many forms of cancer, cardiovascular and respiratory diseases are linked to smoking. Obesity is fast becoming Europe's most significant health problem, accounting for six of the seven leading risk factors for ill health in Europe.[3] Poor diet and inadequate exercise is linked to a range of illnesses, particularly heart disease, diabetes, breast and colon cancer, stroke, hypertension, and depression. The latest WHO Europe figures indicate that one in three European eleven-year-olds is overweight or obese.[4] After tobacco and hypertension, alcohol is the factor responsible for the third most deaths in the EU.[5] Globally, in high income countries, it is the second on the list, after tobacco.[6] Alcohol misuse causes around 195,000 premature deaths in the EU each year.[7] It is difficult to estimate the costs to health systems of tobacco, food or alcohol misuse, but cardiovascular and respiratory disease are the two highest costing diseases in Europe.[8] Headline figures such as these mask important differences between different

---

[1] Commission, 'Public Health: Tobacco Policy' (*Commission*, 6 August 2014)

[2] WHO, 'WHO Global Report: Mortality Attributable to Tobacco' (WHO 2012).

[3] European Union Platform on Diet, Physical Activity and Health, '2010 Annual Report' (European Union Platform on Diet, Physical Activity and Health 2010).

[4] WHO, 'Obesity: Data and Statistics' (*WHO Europe*, 2014).

[5] Commission, 'Factsheet: Alcohol-related harm in Europe – Key Data' (Commission 2006). Top 9 risk factors for ill-health in the EU, Adapted from: WHO, 'Global Burden of Disease study' (WHO 2004); Anderson and Baumberg, 'Alcohol in Europe: A Public Health Perspective' (Institute of Alcohol Studies 2006).

[6] Epianalysis, 'Alcohol use around the globe: new data trends' (*EpiAnalysis*, 28 February 2012).

[7] Commission, 'Factsheet: Alcohol-related harm in Europe – Key Data' (Commission 2006).

[8] Mladovsky et al., 'Health in the European Union: Trends and Analysis' (European Observatory on Health Systems and Policies 2009) 28, 40. Tobacco use has been estimated to cost €98–130 billion annually, or 1.04–1.39% of GDP for the year 2000: ASPECT Consortium, 'Tobacco or Health in the European Union: Past, Present and Future (Commission 2004). See also: Merkur,

socio-economic groups. Ill-health caused by tobacco, food and alcohol misuse is worse for those in lower socio-economic groups, exacerbating inequalities in health.[9] What, if anything, has EU health law done to address these problems?[10]

As we explained in chapter 3, for our purposes, EU health law includes EU public health law. What constitutes 'public health', and 'public health law' remain the subject of debate. C. E. A. Winslow's 1920 definition has become the classic point of reference:

> Public health is the science and art of preventing disease, prolonging life and promoting physical health and efficiency through organised community efforts for the sanitation of the environment, the control of community infections, the education of the individual in principles of personal hygiene, the organisation of medical and nursing services for the early diagnosis and preventative treatment of disease, and the development of social machinery which will ensure to every individual in the community a standard of living adequate for the maintenance of health.[11]

Awareness of public health factors has increased since 1920. The Nuffield Council on Bioethics' 2007 Report includes lifestyle choices, 'genetic background, social and economic living standards, the built environment, the availability of and access to preventative and curative health services, and the influence of commercial organizations such as the food and drink industries'.[12] As is the case with 'health',[13] if the definition of 'public health' is too broad, as a diffuse collection of ideas, it may be limited or even useless in effect.[14] Such a definition, encompassing wealth redistribution and social restructuring, moves beyond the legal arena.[15] But perhaps 'public health' will always generate questions of the political and the 'public interest'.[16]

Sassi and McDaid, 'Promoting health, preventing disease: Is there an economic case?' (European Observatory on Health Systems and Policies, WHO Europe, 2013).

[9] Mladovsky et al., 'Health in the European Union: Trends and Analysis' (European Observatory on Health Systems and Policies 2009) 28, 40; Kulik et al., 'Educational Inequalities in Three Smoking-Related Causes of Death in 18 European Populations' (2014) 16(5) *Nicotine and Tobacco Research* 507; WHO, 'Inequalities in Young People's health: Health Behaviour in School-Aged Children. HBSC International Report from the 2005/2006 Survey' (WHO 2008).

[10] For further discussion of what the EU might do about inequality in health see: Hervey, 'Health Equality, Solidarity and Human Rights in European Union Law' in Silveira et al. (eds), *Citizenship and Solidarity in the EU: From the Charter of Fundamental Rights to the Crisis, The State of the Art* (Peter Lang 2013) 341–66.

[11] Winslow, 'The Untilled Fields of Public Health' (1920) 51 *Science* 23, 23.

[12] Nuffield Council on Bioethics, *Public Health: Ethical Issues* (Cambridge Publishers 2007) paragraph 1.4.

[13] See: chapter 2.

[14] Griffiths and Hunter, 'Introduction' in Griffiths and Hunter (eds), *New Perspectives in Public Health* (2nd edn, Radcliffe 2006).

[15] See: Gostin, 'Public Health, Ethics and Human Rights: A Tribute to the Late Jonathan Mann' (2001) 29 *Journal of Law, Medicine and Ethics* 121.

[16] Rothstein, 'Rethinking the Meaning of Public Health' (2002) 30 *Journal of Law, Medicine and Health* 144; but see: Goldberg, 'In Support of a Broad Model of Public Health: Disparities, Social Epidemiology and Public Health Causation' (2009) 2(1) *Public Health Ethics* 70; and

Public health debates may be inspired by libertarianism;[17] or by collectivism, utilitarianism or social contract theory.[18] A central issue in public health is 'the extent to which it acceptable for the state to establish policies that will influence population health'.[19] This may involve constraining the rights of individuals, particularly commercial entities, in order to protect or promote collective good health.

In the context of the EU, public health law is a classic example of the 'transversal' nature of EU health law.[20] The EU has had formal competence in public health since the early 1990s, but it is significantly constrained.[21] What is more important, therefore, is how public health is promoted through other areas of EU law, principally the law of the internal market.

In the preceding chapter, we considered one area of EU public health law, that pertaining to human blood, tissue, cells and organs. There are many determinants of population health, ranging from those over which EU law has little direct influence (such as poverty; access to clean water and shelter, adequate means; relative equality[22]) to those over which EU law has some influence (such as road traffic safety; air and water pollution control, where the EU has played a part in lowering health hazards).[23] In this chapter, we focus on three related aspects of public health where EU health law has had, or at least has the potential to have, quite some influence – the regulation of the marketing and consumption of tobacco, food and alcohol. These examples are chosen because they highlight the ways in which the 'transversal' nature of EU health

---

response by Rothstein, 'The Limits of Public Health: A Response' (2009) 2(1) *Public Health Ethics* 84.

[17] Derived from John Stuart Mill's, *On Liberty* (reprint, Penguin 1985), to the effect that 'the only purpose for which power can be rightfully exercised over another member of a civilised community against his well is to prevent harm to others'.

[18] Nuffield Council on Bioethics above n 12, paragraphs 2.5–7.

[19] Nuffield Council on Bioethics above n 12, Executive Summary, and paragraphs 2.27–38.

[20] See: Article 9 TFEU, Article 114 TFEU, Article 168 (1) TFEU. See chapter 3, pp 60–63.

[21] Most of the EU's explicit public health competence does not allow the EU to adopt harmonizing legislation; rather it must 'respect the responsibilities of the Member States for the definition of their health policy', Article 168 (7) TFEU.

[22] The correlation between poverty and health is not a perfect or direct one, but many studies show that poverty is a key indicator for poor health. Poverty both causes and is a result of poor health. For some global research see: World Bank, 'Dying For Change: Poor People's Experience of Health and Ill-Health' (World Bank 2005); for European examples see: WHO, Poverty, Social Exclusion and Health Systems in the WHO European Region' (WHO Europe 2010) WHO, 'Poverty and Social Exclusion in the WHO European Region: Health Systems Respond' (WHO Europe 2010) and for recent examples from the USA, see research cited here: Multiple Authors, 'Spotlight on Poverty and Opportunity' (*Spotlight on Poverty and Opportunity*, continuous).

[23] Road traffic deaths have declined by 43% in the EU27 over the years 2001–2010, European Traffic Safety Council (ETSC), '2010 Road Safety Target Outcome: 100,000 fewer deaths since 2001' (5th Road Safety PIN Report, ETSC 2011). EU air emission policies are estimated to have reduced the negative health impact of the road transport sector in Europe as a whole: European Environment Agency (EEA), 'Impact of selected policy measures on Europe's air quality' (EEA Technical Report No. 8/2010, EEA 2010). See: Greer, Hervey, McKee and Mackenbach, 'Health Law and Policy of the European Union' (2013) 381(9872) *The Lancet* 1135. Of course, the EU now has 28 Member States.

law operates, given that tobacco, food and alcohol are products that circulate freely in the single market. The choice also allows for comparisons between the three examples, as all concern consumer products which have ramifications for population health. All three examples could be understood through a standard risk regulation model, directed at protecting consumers from harm. One of the questions for this chapter is the extent to which risk is the guiding theme for this aspect of EU health law.

We are also interested in the ways in which EU health law balances risks to consumers with freedom to make lifestyle choices, to run a business, or the free pursuit of profit maximizing by capital investors. Here we immediately see how EU public health law could be constructed not as concerned with questions of protection of consumers from harm but as unjustified paternalism or restriction of individual autonomy, or even human dignity in the sense of choice over one's own affairs, including bodily integrity. To what extent does EU tobacco, food or alcohol law explicitly present itself as considering these sorts of ethical questions? What are the consequences?

Of equal interest is the extent to which EU law constrains *national* autonomy. Can the intention to protect (national) population health justify different approaches to regulation of tobacco, food or alcohol, in the different Member States? After all, population health differs quite considerably across the EU, not only between Member States, but also within them. The logic of the internal market, and its mandating of free trade in goods throughout the EU, pulls against finely grained laws that seek to tackle specific public health problems, which may be geographically or culturally limited to certain parts of the EU. Does EU health law support population health in those circumstances?

Tobacco

EU tobacco law has been hailed as the EU's public health success story, and perhaps with some justification. Starting from a very low base (the EU's first tobacco law was subsidizing tobacco farmers, under its Common Agricultural Policy), the EU is now considered to be an important global actor in the regulation of tobacco.[24] The EU first placed tobacco control on its policy agenda in its 'Europe against Cancer' programme,[25] and legislative proposals, drawing on the comparative data made available through the programme,[26] were developed

---

[24] We take up the global context further in the final section of the book, see: chapter 18.
[25] Resolution of the Council and the Representatives of the Governments of the Member States, meeting within the Council, of 7 July 1986, on a programme of action of the European Communities against cancer [1986] OJ C184/19.
[26] See: Trubek, Nance and Hervey, 'The Construction of Healthier Europe: Lessons from the Fight against Cance' (2009) 26(3) *Wisconsin International Law Journal* 804; Trubek et al., 'Improving Cancer Outcomes through Strong Networks and Regulatory Frameworks: Lessons from the US and EU' (2011) 14(1) *Journal of Health Care Law and Policy* 119.

from the late 1980s. By the early 1990s, some seven Directives[27] (and a non-binding Resolution) on tobacco product regulation and labelling/packaging, and on taxation, had been adopted. These were gradually developed so that today, for instance, the minimum tax is nearly 60 per cent of product price, warning labels must take up a high proportion of the packaging, and some forms of tobacco are banned altogether.[28] Given that in some Member States there was virtually no tobacco control legislation prior to EU involvement, and in others measures were purely voluntary, this constitutes a significant encroachment on national autonomy.

After the early 1990s, however, EU lawmaking proceeded at a much slower pace. As Martin McKee, Anna Gilmore and others have shown,[29] this is almost certainly attributable to the change in focus of the global tobacco industry, which until then had effectively discounted the EU as a relevant site for lobbying. Nonetheless, and despite industry opposition,[30] including from the industry that produces equipment for tobacco manufacture,[31] Directive 98/43/EC

[27] Directive 89/552 Audiovisual Media Services Directive) [1989] OJ L298/23; Council Directive 89/622/EEC of 13 November 1989 on the approximation of the laws, regulations and administrative provisions of the Member States concerning the labelling of tobacco products [1989] OJ L359/1; Council Directive 90/239/EEC of 17 May 1990 on the approximation of the laws, regulations and administrative provisions of the Member States concerning the maximum tar yield of cigarettes [1990] OJ L137/36; Council Directive 92/41/EEC of 15 May 1992 amending Directive 89/622/EEC on the approximation of the laws, regulations and administrative provisions of the Member States concerning the labelling of tobacco products [1992] OJ L158/30; Council Directive 92/78/EEC of 19 October 1992 amending Directives 72/464/EEC and 79/32/EEC on taxes other than turnover taxes which are levied on the consumption of manufactured tobacco [1992] OJ L316/5; Council Directive 92/79/EEC of 19 October 1992 on the approximation of taxes on cigarettes [1992] OJ L316/8; Council Directive 92/80/ EEC of 19 October 1992 on the approximation of taxes on manufactured tobacco other than cigarettes [1992] OJ L316/10. For discussion, see McKee, Hervey and Gilmore, 'Public health policies' in Mossialos, Permanand, Baeten and Hervey (eds), *Health Systems Governance in Europe: The Role of European Union Law and Policy* (CUP 2010) 257–261.

[28] In particular, snus, a form of smokeless tobacco, although this ban does not apply in Sweden, see: Directive 2014/40/EU of the European Parliament and of the Council of 3 April 2014 on the approximation of the laws, regulations and administrative provisions of the Member States concerning the manufacture, presentation and sale of tobacco and related pr Article 1 and Article 17.

[29] Gilmore and McKee, 'Tobacco policy in the European Union' in Feldman and Bayer (eds), *Unfiltered: Conflicts Over Tobacco Policy and Public Health* (Harvard University Press 2004); Gilmore and McKee, 'Tobacco control policy: the European dimension' (2002) 2(4) *Clinical Medicine* 335; McKee, Hervey and Gilmore, 'Public health policies' in Mossialos et al., above n 27, 260–262; Studlar, 'Tobacco Control: The End of Europe's Love Affair with Smoking?' in Greer and Kurzer (eds), *European Union Public Health Policies: Regional and Global Trends* (Routledge 2013); Mandal, Gilmore et al., 'Block, amend, delay: Tobacco industry efforts to influence the EU's Tobacco Products Directive (2001/37/EC)' (SmokeFree Partnership 2009); Weishaar, Collin and Amos, 'Tobacco Control and Health Advocacy in the European Union: Understanding effective coalition-building *Nicotine and Tobacco Research* 2015 forthcoming.

[30] Adamini et al., 'European policy making on the tobacco advertising ban: the imbalance of escape routes' (2011) 6(1) *Health Economics Policy and Law* 65, 79 describe the Directive as 'a pure conflict between health and industrial interests'.

[31] Much of which is located in Germany.

on Tobacco Advertising and Sponsorship[32] was adopted in the late 1990s. This Directive extended the pre-existing ban on TV advertising of tobacco products,[33] to a near-comprehensive ban on tobacco advertising and sponsorship. The Tobacco Advertising Directive was successfully challenged by Germany through judicial review before the CJEU;[34] but a revised Directive[35] covering cross-border advertising in print media, on the radio and on the internet, withstood a further attempted judicial review claim.[36] Revisions to the tobacco products and labelling legislation were adopted in Directive 2001/37/EC, after difficult negotiations. They represent a product of compromise, and were challenged (again largely unsuccessfully) before the CJEU and national courts.[37]

More recently, however, the EU's anti-tobacco credentials have been rocked by further controversy. Italian legislation imposing a minimum price on cigarettes, in order to combat the harmful effects of cheap cigarettes on the health of the Italian population, was successfully challenged as breaching Directive 2011/64/EU on tobacco excise duty.[38] The litigation was brought by Yesmoke, an Italian-based cigarette manufacturer whose market strategy is to produce and sell cheaper cigarettes than produced by the four biggest global tobacco manufacturers: Philip Morris International, British American Tobacco,[39] Japan Tobacco and Imperial Tobacco. Yesmoke's claim was that Italian law seeks to prevent it from competing on price in the Italian market with those firms. That is indeed the effect of the relevant legislation, which sets, for cigarettes with a lower selling price than the most popular price category, excise duty at 115 per cent of the excise duty applicable to cigarettes with the most popular

---

[32] Directive 98/43/EC of the European Parliament and of the Council of 6 July 1998 on the approximation of the laws, regulations and administrative provisions of the Member States relating to the advertising and sponsorship of tobacco products [1998] OJ L213/9.

[33] Directive 89/55/EC Audiovisual Media Services Directive) [1989] OJ L298/23; as amended by: Directive 97/36/EC of the European Parliament and of the Council of 30 June 1997 amending Council Directive 89/552/EEC on the coordination of certain provisions laid down by law, regulation or administrative action in Member States concerning the pursuit of television broadcasting activities [1997] OJ L202/60; and Directive 2007/65/EC of the European Parliament and of the Council of 11 December 2007 amending Council Directive 89/552/EEC on the coordination of certain provisions laid down by law, regulation or administrative action in Member States concerning the pursuit of television broadcasting activities [2007] OJ L332/27, in response to new digital media technologies.

[34] *Germany* v *Parliament and Council,* C-376/98, EU:C:2000:544.

[35] Directive 2003/33/EC of the European Parliament and of the Council of 26 May 2003 on the approximation of the laws, regulations and administrative provisions of the Member States relating to the advertising and sponsorship of tobacco products [2003] OJ L152/16.

[36] *Germany* v *Parliament and Council,* C-380/03, EU:C:2006:772.

[37] *BAT v Commission,* T-311/00, EU:T:2002:167; *R v Secretary of State for Health ex parte BAT and Imperial Tobacco,* C-491/01, EU:C:2002:741; *Swedish Match,* C-210/03, EU:C:2004:802; *Arnold André,* C-434/02, EU:C:2004:800. There was also litigation before national courts, see: McKee, Hervey and Gilmore, 'Public health policies' in Mossialos et al. (eds), (CUP 2010) above n 29, 267–8.

[38] OJ 2011 L 176/24.   [39] *Yesmoke Tobacco,* C-428/13, EU:C:2014:2263.

selling price.[40] The Directive allows Member States to impose a minimum excise duty on tobacco, subject to certain requirements, including that 'proportional excise duty' and 'specific excise duty' must be the same for all cigarettes. The Preamble to the Directive states that EU 'fiscal legislation on tobacco products needs to ensure the proper functioning of the internal market and at the same time a high level of health protection'.[41] To do so, the Directive provides a single overall excise duty for all cigarettes. Although it distinguishes other tobacco products, cigarettes are a single category of product for its purposes.[42] Therefore, according to the CJEU, Member States may not have different excise duties for cigarettes based on differences in characteristics, or price.[43] The effect of the CJEU's ruling is to deprive national governments of one of the most effective mechanism of anti-tobacco legislation – the setting of minimum prices.[44]

The latest EU tobacco legislation, Directive 2014/40/EU, which amends, updates and consolidates Directive 2001/37/EC, was adopted against the odds. It was claimed that just one of the three major global tobacco firms operating in the EU, Philip Morris International, had spent up to 1.5 million euros in lunches and dinners to lobby MEPs about the proposal. [45] Roberto Bertollino, the WHO representative at the EU, noted that while there were some twenty people advocating the health policy side of the Directive, the tobacco companies had more than 160 lobbyists involved.[46] In October 2012, the then EU Health Commissioner John Dalli resigned, following a meeting with the European Commission President, José Manuel Barroso. This was amid allegations by the EU's anti-fraud office, that a Maltese entrepreneur, who had organized meetings between Dalli and the industry, had sought bribes from Swedish Match, a firm that manufactures oral tobacco.[47] In June 2014, the European Ombudsman began an investigation following a complaint made to him by the Corporate European Observatory into claims that the European Commission has not disclosed some 114 meetings with lobbyists from the tobacco industry, in contravention of UN rules.[48] These allegations are disputed by the

---

[40] *Yesmoke Tobacco*, paragraph 32.   [41] Directive 2011/64/EU, Recital 2.

[42] *Yesmoke Tobacco*, paragraphs 28–29.   [43] *Yesmoke Tobacco*, paragraph 30.

[44] The legality of Scottish minimum price legislation is currently before the CJEU, see: *The Scotch Whisky Association*, C-333/14 (case in progress).

[45] Nielson, 'Tobacco Giant spent up to €1.25 mn on EU lobbying in 2012' (*EU* Observer, 3 October 2013).

[46] Maurice, 'The European Union adds teeth to its anti-tobacco legislation' (2014) 383(9920) *The Lancet* 857.

[47] European Anti-Fraud Office, 'OLAF press statement (*Commission*, 19 October 2012). The matter is under investigation by the Maltese criminal authorities: European Anti-Fraud Office, 'OLAF statement in light of recent comments made by the Maltese Police Commissioner' (*Commission*, 2 June 2014): "The OLAF Report clearly stated that there is no conclusive evidence that Commissioner Dalli was either a mastermind or an accomplice to this criminal activity." The European Ombudsman investigation concluded in September 2014 that the documents need not be disclosed while the matter was before the CJEU (see: *Dalli* v *Commission*, T-562/12 (case in progress), but recommended that they should be disclosed thereafter.

[48] Nielson, 'Judges to cross-examine Barroso in tobacco lobby case' (*EU Observer*, 3rd July 2014).

Commission. Dalli is bringing legal proceedings seeking annulment of the request for his resignation, compensation for loss of earnings as an EU Commissioner, and non-financial damages suffered.[49] In July 2014, Barroso answered questions at the CJEU, concerning the meeting between Dalli and Barroso.[50] At the time of writing, the matter remains unresolved.

The Tobacco Products Directive 2014/40/EU entered into force in May 2014. Member States have until 20 May 2016 to bring their national law into line with the new Directive, at which point the existing Directive 2001/37/EC will be repealed.[51] The Directive was hailed by the EU Health Commissioner Tonio Berg as:

> a great day for EU health policy. The new rules will help to reduce the number of people who start smoking in the EU. These measures put an end to products which entice children and teenagers into starting to smoke in the EU.[52]

Several of the Directive's provisions do focus on young people. These include packaging measures on the size and content of health warnings; on information about nicotine and tar content; on package sizing and design; and product measures on flavoured cigarettes; e-cigarettes and herbal cigarettes. The Directive also includes other measures, including anti-smuggling provisions, and measures on emissions. We consider each of these in turn.

Packaging

Some of the most important changes to EU law made by the Directive concern packaging. Very detailed provisions on health warnings are specified.[53] Some of these were in the original legislation, but some are new. Changes to labelling and packaging rules have been driven by scientific evidence suggesting that, for example, statements of emission levels on packets have led consumers to think that some cigarettes are not as harmful as others.[54] The Directive now

---

[49] *Dalli v Commission*, T-562/12 (case in progress). Nielson, 'Judges to cross-examine Barroso in tobacco lobby case' (*EU Observer*, 3rd July 2014); Nielson, 'Barrosso faces Dalli at EU Court in Tobacco Lobby case' (*EU Observer*, 8 July 2014) Editorial, 'EU's top court hears dispute over EU Commissioner Dalli' (*BBC News*, 8 July 2014).

[50] This is the first time the European Commission President has appeared before the CJEU in this manner.

[51] Directive 2014/40/EU of the European Parliament and of the Council of 3 April 2014 on the approximation of the laws, regulations and administrative provisions of the Member States concerning the manufacture, presentation and sale of tobacco and related pr Articles 30 and 31. Transitional arrangements, until 20 May 2017, apply to products manufactured or released for free circulation, and labelled in compliance with Directive 2001/37/EC of the European Parliament and of the Council of 5 June 2001 on the approximation of the laws, regulations and administrative provisions of the Member States concerning the manufacture, presentation and sale of tobacco products [2001] OJ L194/26 (as amended), before 16 May 2016; electronic cigarettes before 20 November 2016; herbal products before 20 May 2016.

[52] Gallagher, 'Tough EU Smoking rules approved' (*BBC News*, 24th February 2014).

[53] Directive 2014/40/EU Articles 8–14.   [54] Directive 2014/40/EU Recital 25.

states that packaging and labelling shall not encourage consumption by creating the wrong impression in relation to emission levels, health risks and other characteristics.[55] Labels may no longer include any information about the nicotine, tar or carbon monoxide content of the product.[56] In another measure aimed at discouraging tobacco consumption, the Directive provides that incentives such as discounts, vouchers and other offers are expressly prohibited.[57]

Manufacturers continue to be required to place graphic and clearly prescribed warnings on packets.[58] The Directive continues the policy of the earlier Directive, but with stronger warnings. Member States are explicitly obliged to ensure that such labelling is clear and visible.[59] The warnings must be a combination of warning of the dangers of smoking and also information as to support services available to help those who wish to stop smoking.[60] The Directive requires only 65 per cent of the cigarette packaging to contain a warning – a compromise agreed during the passage of the proposal. On smokeless products, warnings must also be placed on both sides of packaging and also cover 30 per cent of the packaging.[61] The proposal was that cigars and pipe tobacco would have warnings similar to those required for cigarettes under the 2001 Directive.[62] Again as a compromise, Member States may depart from the packaging rules on health warnings for products other than cigarettes, roll-your-own tobacco and water pipe tobacco, although a general warning[63] must still be included.[64] The Directive also sets out provisions for appearance and content of packets of cigarettes and roll-your-own tobacco, notably aiming to ban 'lipstick' style packs targeting women with the requirement that packs should contain at least twenty cigarettes.[65] Again, this will impede young peoples' access to cigarettes, as smaller packs, which are more affordable, will no longer be available.

Many of those in the health community commentators view the new packaging rules favourably.[66] However, the EU has not gone as far as Australia, which has adopted plain packaging laws.[67] Plain packaging is controversial

---

[55] Directive 2014/40/EU Article 13 (1).   [56] Directive 2014/40/EU Article 13 (1).

[57] Directive 2014/40/EU Article 13 (2).

[58] Directive 2014/40/EU Article 9.   [59] Directive 2014/40/EU Recital 3.

[60] Directive 2014/40/EU Articles 9 and 10.   [61] Directive 2014/40/EU Article 12.

[62] Commission, 'Proposal for a Directive of the European Parliament and of the Council on the approximation of the laws, regulations and administrative provisions of the Member States concerning the manufacture, presentation and sale of tobacco and related products' COM (2012) 788 final, at paragraph 3.2.

[63] As per Directive 2014/40/EU Article 9 (1), as well as one of the text warnings listed in Annex I, and a reference to services to help consumers to stop using the product.

[64] Directive 2014/40/EU Article 11.

[65] Directive 2014/40/EU Article 14.

[66] See, for instance: UK Royal College of Nurses, 'Policy Briefing 9/14: Tobacco Products Directive' (Royal College of Nursing 2014); the British Medical Association (BMA), 'Standardised Packaging' (*BMA*, 2014).

[67] One of the potential barriers to such laws, which has also dominated the EU discussions on the topic, is intellectual property law. See: Frankel and Gervais, 'Plain Packaging and the Interpretation of the TRIPS Agreement' (2013) 46(5) *Vanderbilt Journal of Transnational Law* 1149.

and is likely to be the subject of legal challenges. In August 2014, Philip Morris International indicated that it would be prepared to seek compensation from the UK government, should it introduce plain packaging, as is currently under consideration.[68] The Directive does, however, allow Member States to introduce their own packaging standardization measures, on grounds of public health, which are proportionate and do not create unjustified barriers to trade within the EU. In June 2014, the UK began a consultation on such standardized packaging, following the Chantler Report[69] which concluded that standardized packaging would have a positive impact on children's health in the UK.[70]

Product regulation

The Directive prohibits cigarettes and roll-your-own tobacco 'with a characterizing flavour'.[71] These products, such as chocolate-, vanilla- or menthol-flavoured cigarettes, have been used by the industry to target younger consumers. In addition, some additives have been represented as having health benefits and having properties which enable them to increase physical performance or mental alertness.[72] Again, these may be designed to appeal to younger consumers, for instance, students. Additives had not been included under the 2001 Directive and in subsequent years Member States had taken measures to address this.[73] While the 2014 Directive does not totally stop the use of additives, it obliges manufacturers to reduce additives, so that they no longer result in a characterizing flavour.[74]

The Directive also prohibits a list of additives, as follows:

(a) vitamins or other additives that create the impression that a tobacco product has a health benefit or presents reduced health risks;
(b) caffeine or taurine or other additives and stimulant compounds that are associated with energy and vitality;
(c) additives having colouring properties for emissions;
(d) for tobacco products for smoking, additives that facilitate inhalation or nicotine uptake; and

---

[68] See: Savage, 'Tobacco Giant Could Sue for £11bn over plain pack "injustice"' *The Times* (London, 12 August 2014).

[69] Chantler, 'Standardised Packaging of Tobacco: Report of the independent review undertaken by Sir Cyril Chantler' (Williams Lea 2014).

[70] Across the UK, over 200 000 children aged 11–15 start smoking every year. See: UK Parliament, 'Statement on standardised packaging of tobacco products: 3 April 2014' (*UK* Parliament, 3 April 2014) UK regulations could be introduced without the need for primary legislation, following the provision in the Children and Families Act 2014, section 94.

[71] Directive 2014/40/EU Article 7 (1). The prohibition does not cover additives which are 'essential for manufacture', such as sugar used to replace sugar lost during production.

[72] Directive 2014/40/EU Recital 18.

[73] Commission, 'Proposal for a Directive of the European Parliament and of the Council on the approximation of the laws, regulations and administrative provisions of the Member States concerning the manufacture, presentation and sale of tobacco and related products' COM (2012) 788 final, at paragraph 3.1.

[74] Directive 2014/40/EU, Recital 17.

(e) additives that have carcinogenic, mutagenic or reprotoxic properties in unburnt form.[75]

Flavourings in other components such as filters or packages are also prohibited.[76] Where an additive has been demonstrated to increase toxic or addictive effects of tobacco, and where it is prohibited in at least three Member States, the Commission is to have the power via delegated acts to impose maximum levels of content of these additives.[77]

The new prohibitions are a crucial element of the EU tightening up its restrictions on the activities of the industry, in order to decrease smoking levels within the EU. This has been partially successful, although lobbying during the passage of the Directive means that menthol flavoured cigarettes (the most commonly found flavour in the EU) will not be covered until 2020.[78]

E-cigarettes were not previously subject to comprehensive EU regulation.[79] The Directive requires Member States to take steps such that e-cigarettes[80] and their refill containers may only be marketed in accordance with the Directive,[81] save where they come within either EU pharmaceuticals or medical devices law.[82] The Directive thus allows e-cigarettes to be classed as consumer goods. This is reported to be due to industry pressure.[83] Notification of intention to place on the market[84] and disclosure of a range of product data[85] are required. The Directive specifies the size of containers[86] and nicotine levels,[87] and restricts additives.[88] But the Directive does not harmonize all aspects of e-cigarettes or refill containers. For example, the responsibility for adopting rules on flavours remains with the Member States. Member States must ensure that e-cigarette instruction leaflets state that the product is not recommended for young people

---

[75] Directive 2014/40/EU, Article 7 (6).

[76] Directive 2014/40/EU, Article 6 (7).   [77] Directive 2014/40/EU, Article 7 (11).

[78] Directive 2014/40/EU, Article 7 (14). See further: Maurice, 'The European Union adds teeth to its anti-tobacco legislation' (2014) 383(9920) *The Lancet* 857.

[79] Syx, 'The Case of the Electronic Cigarette in the EU' (2014) 21(2) *European Journal of Health Law* 161.

[80] Defined in Directive 2014/40/EU, Article 2 (16) as "electronic cigarette' means a product that can be used for consumption of nicotine-containing vapour via a mouth piece, or any component of that product, including a cartridge, a tank and the device without cartridge or tank. Electronic cigarettes can be disposable or refillable by means of a refill container and a tank, or rechargeable with single use cartridges". The health risks associated with e-cigarettes are as yet unknown though 'likely to be less harmful than cigarettes' (Anna Gilmore), cited in Henley, 'What's the new buzz?' *The Guardian, G2* (London, 6 May 2014).

[81] Directive 2014/40/EU, Article 20 (1).

[82] Council Directive 93/42/EEC of 14th June 1993 concerning medical devices [1993] OJ L169/1 (as amended).

[83] Maurice, above n 78.   [84] Directive 2014/40/EU, Article 20 (2) (a).

[85] Details of ingredients, emissions, toxicology data, information on anticipated nicotine doses, description of the product and its parts, an explanation of production processes and statement from manufacturer and importer that they have full responsibility for its quality and safety: Directive 2014/40/EU, Article 20 (2) (b)-(g).

[86] Directive 2014/40/EU, Article 20 (3) (a).   [87] Directive 2014/40/EU, Article 20 (3) (b).

[88] The e-cigarrette may not contain additives as listed in Article 7 (6): Directive 2014/40/EU, Article 20 (3) (c).

or non-smokers.[89] Ingredients must be listed, there must be recommendations to keep out of the reach of children and e-cigarettes must carry set health warnings.[90] Advertising is severely restricted.[91] Scrutiny of the operation of e-cigarette manufacturers by Member States will be facilitated through a requirement to submit data concerning sales, consumer preferences, modes of sale and summaries of any market surveys which manufacturers have conducted.[92] In addition, Member States are to require manufacturers and importers to develop and operate systems for collecting information concerning the adverse effects of these products on human health.[93] There is a notification procedure for adverse events.[94] It appears that provisions in the Directive concerning e-cigarettes will soon be challenged by a UK e-cigarette manufacturer 'Totally Wicked', which is arguing that e-cigarettes will be subject to greater regulation than some other forms of tobacco and that Article 20 of the Directive is disproportionate.[95] Leave has been given for judicial review and a hearing in the English courts.

The Directive also extends the scope of EU law to herbal products which are smoked. These must carry a warning that 'smoking this product damages your health'.[96] Health warnings are required to be printed on front and back and must comply with the general health warning provisions.[97] Manufacturers and importers of herbal products must submit lists of the ingredients and quantities used in each brand, and also inform the competent authorities of any variations in this information.[98] As with other tobacco products,[99] such information must be made publicly available, while aligning this with the need to safeguard trade secrets.[100]

One concern is the extent to which industry may be able to circumvent existing EU prohibitions by producing new products which would not fall within current regulatory structures. These novel products are often aimed at emerging markets, in particular young people. The Directive addresses this by requiring manufacturers and importers of 'novel tobacco products' to notify Member States' competent authorities some six months prior to the product

---

[89] Directive 2014/40/EU, Article 20 (4) (a). Other information such as contra-indications, impacts on certain groups at risk, adverse effects, and also how toxic and/or addictive they are in addition to the details concerning manufacturer/ importer, is also required.

[90] Directive 2014/40/EU, Article 20 (4) (b).

[91] Publications promoting e-cigarettes are expressly prohibited save in relation to the professional e-cigarette business market or those which have been printed/published in "third countries where those publications are not principally intended for the Union market." Directive 2014/40/EU, Article 20 (5). Radio and television adverts and direct/indirect contributions to programmes are prohibited: Directive 2014/40/EU, Article 20 (5) (b), (c) and (e).

[92] Directive 2014/40/EU, Article 20 (7).

[93] Directive 2014/40/EU, Article 20 (9).   [94] Directive 2014/40/EU, Article 20 (9).

[95] ITV News, 'Lancashire Firms Legal Challenge over e-cigarettes' 20 August 2014 and see also Nicotine Science & Policy 'Legal Challenge Against EU Tobacco Directive' 20 August 2014.

[96] Directive 2014/40/EU, Article 21 (1).

[97] Directive 2014/40/EU, Article 21 (3). Herbal cigarettes must comply with the requirements generally set out for products under Directive 2014/40/EU, Article 9 (4).

[98] Directive 2014/40/EU, Article 22 (1).

[99] See Directive 2014/40/EU, Article 5 (4).   [100] Directive 2014/40/EU, Article 22 (2).

being placed upon the market.[101] The notification must contain information including a detailed description of the product and applicable scientific studies concerning its addictiveness; the market research on preferences of various consumer groups such as young people and existing smokers; and other available information concerning, for example, risk benefit calculations.[102] These provisions are designed to improve regulatory information deficits, so that national 'competent authorities' have access to the marketing information that is being relied upon by the tobacco industry in developing novel products. Whether they are effective will depend upon take-up by the Member States. The Directive goes as far as to permit a system of pre-authorization of novel tobacco products, should Member States wish to implement it.[103] Member States may, for instance, deem certain e-cigarettes to be medical devices, and thus subject to marketing authorization procedures under medical devices law. The UK has indicated that e-cigarettes that contain nicotine will be regulated as pharmaceuticals from 2016, so in the UK they will require prior marketing authorization.[104] The European Parliament sought to make this marketing authorization obligation extend to all novel tobacco products, but this proposal was not reflected in the final text.[105] It does not go so far as implementing such a system at EU level.

The Directive also provides that the ban on oral use of tobacco should continue.[106] This is in line with the judgment of the CJEU in *Arnold André GmbH & Co. KG* v. *Landrat des Kreises Herford*.[107] Sweden's exemption for *snus*, negotiated under its Accession Treaty, continues, provided that *snus* is not sold outside of Sweden.

Other provisions

Rules on maximum yields of tar, nicotine and carbon monoxide remain unchanged.[108] But independent verification of emissions levels (tar, nicotine

---

[101] Directive 2014/40/EU, Article 19.

[102] Directive 2014/40/EU, Article 19 (1).   [103] Directive 2014/40/EU, Article 19 (3).

[104] MHRA, 'UK moves towards safe and effective electronic cigarettes and other nicotine-containing products' (*MHRA*, 12 June 2013).

[105] European Parliament Committee on Environment, Public Health and Food Safety, 'Draft Report on the proposal for a directive of the European Parliament and of the Council on the approximation of the laws, regulations and administrative provisions of the Member States concerning the manufacture, presentation and sale of tobacco and related products (COM(2012)0788 – 2012/0366(COD)) (European Parliament 2013) Amendments 10, 16, 48, 51–53.

[106] Commission, 'Proposal for a Directive of the European Parliament and of the Council on the approximation of the laws, regulations and administrative provisions of the Member States concerning the manufacture, presentation and sale of tobacco and related products' COM (2012) 788 final, at paragraph 3.4 and Directive 2014/40/EU, Article 17.

[107] *Arnold André* EU:C:2004:800.

[108] Commission, 'Proposal for a Directive of the European Parliament and of the Council on the approximation of the laws, regulations and administrative provisions of the Member States

and carbon monoxide levels) is to be effected by reference to internationally recognized 'ISO' standards.[109] Verification of such standards should be undertaken using laboratories independent from the tobacco industry and Member States should be able to use laboratories of other Member States.[110] To ensure that regulation is undertaken effectively, manufacturers and importers must make information concerning ingredients and emissions from tobacco products publicly available.[111]

The 2001 Directive contained powers on traceability and identification of products, but these had not been implemented by the Commission.[112] The Commission proposal envisaged an EU tracking and tracing system taking place across the supply chain of products.[113] This is now found in the Directive. Packets must have a 'unique identifier' (a hologram) which will be 'irremovably printed or affixed'.[114] The aim of the identifier is to track to where the product was made, when, how, where it was intended to be marketed and through what routes.[115] This will help to address illicit trading. One argument advanced by tobacco companies is that this kind of regulation will drive the trade itself underground, but there does not appear to be evidence that this has in fact been the case, and illicit trade has not increased in those EU countries where there is already strong regulation. Evidence to the EU Parliament by Anna Gilmore suggested that there was active involvement by the tobacco industry in illicit trafficking.[116]

Some aspects of selling arrangements[117] are now covered by the Directive. The Directive allows Member States to ban cross-border distance sales of tobacco products.[118] To try to control such sales, the Directive also provides that Member States should require those retail outlets who intend to undertake cross-border retail sales to register with the competent authority both of the Member State where the outlet itself is located, and where they intend to trade.[119] Outlets will also be required to provide information about their retail service, dates of provision of service and websites used.[120] They may only market products once this registration has been confirmed. In addition, Member States must retain a list of those products which are available.[121] A further restriction is that the Directive gives Member States discretion to nominate a person to confirm that

---

concerning the manufacture, presentation and sale of tobacco and related products' COM (2012) 788 final, at paragraph 3.1, Directive 2014/40/EU, Article 3.

[109] Directive 2014/40/EU, Article 4.   [110] Directive 2014/40/EU, Recital 11 and Article 4 (2).

[111] Directive 2014/40/EU, Recital 13 and Article 5 (4), although manufacturers may take into account the need to protect trade secrets when doing so, which in practice will reduce the information flow from this obligation.

[112] *Ibid* at para 3.3.   [113] *Ibid* at para 3.3.

[114] Directive 2014/40/EU, Article 15 (1).   [115] Directive 2014/40/EU, Article 15 (2).

[116] Maurice, above n 78.

[117] Though not all, for instance, regulation of tobacco vending machines is still a national matter.

[118] Directive 2014/40/EU, Recital 33 and Article 18 (1).

[119] Directive 2014/40/EU, Article 18 (1).   [120] Directive 2014/40/EU, Article 18 (1) (a) (b) (c).

[121] Directive 2014/40/EU, Article 18 (2).

the tobacco products do fall within the Directive.[122] In line with the Directive's concern to target tobacco consumption amongst the young, the Directive also provides that such outlets shall operate an 'age verification system' so that at point of sale individuals meet minimal national requirements in the Member State concerned.

The formal legal basis of the 2014 Tobacco Products Directive[123] is such that it is presented as a measure of internal market law. The Directive is not an exhaustive measure of harmonization. Outside of the scope of the Directive, Member States retain discretion to adopt their own rules, to protect public health. These national measures must be non-protectionist and proportionate. However, the latter category, in particular, could be difficult to meet, given the very narrow definition of proportionality in free movement law.[124]

The Directive is not based on the EU's public health powers, nor is it presented as a public health measure per se. Rather, it is justified by divergent national rules, and the desire of Member States to adapt legislation to new developments, such as the new understandings that for instance emissions information can mislead consumers.[125] This represents masterful drafting on the part of the EU legislature – it is difficult to see how this Directive could be successfully challenged through judicial review processes, as was the fate of the original Tobacco Advertising Directive.

The idea that tobacco is inherently a harmful product is very much muted in terms of how the 2014 Directive is cast.[126] But the harmful nature of tobacco *de facto* informs much of EU tobacco law. It simply does not make regulatory sense otherwise. In the 2014 Directive, the obligation to 'take as a base a high level of health protection', when adopting internal market law, is associated with the special need to protect children and young people.[127] This comes across more strongly than in earlier EU tobacco legislation. It represents the direction of travel of EU tobacco law. Tobacco products used by older people[128] are less heavily regulated by the EU.

Donley Studlar has characterized the EU as adopting a 'harm reduction' approach, rather than 'neo-prohibitionist' approach (such as that adopted by Australia on packaging).[129] Others have called it a 'nudging strategy'.[130] This

---

[122] Directive 2014/40/EU, Article 18 (3).   [123] Articles 53 (1), 62 and 114 TFEU.

[124] See chapter 5.   [125] Directive 2014/40/EU, Recitals 1–12, 15–18, 36, 43, 49 and 60.

[126] It is not until one reaches Directive 2014/40/EU, Recital 34 of the preamble that the fact that 'all tobacco products have the potential to cause mortality, morbidity and disability' is mentioned.

[127] Directive 2014/40/EU, Recital 21, see also Recital 19, 26, 33.

[128] Cigars, cigarellos (Article 1 of Directive 2014/40/EU states that 'cigarillo' means a small type of cigar and is further defined in Article 8 (1) of Council Directive 2007/74/EC of 20 December 2007 on the exemption from value added tax and excise duty of goods imported by persons travelling from third countries [2007] OJ L346/6 and pipes.

[129] Studlar, 'Tobacco Control: The End of Europe's Love Affair with Smoking?' in Greer and Kurzer (eds), (Routledge 2013) above n 29.

[130] Nudging is a tool which has become fashionable by governments and policy makers in the 2010s. See: Alemanno, 'The revised EU's Tobacco Products Directive seeks to "nudge" citizens

approach is easier to square with the underlying internal market focus of the legislation, and its inherent focus on freedom to trade. The 2014 Directive itself expresses the 'squaring of the circle' between individual liberties, health protection and free trade in a way which obfuscates the real trade-offs between these three regulatory desiderata. It recognizes that 'several fundamental rights are affected by this Directive', and notes that obligations imposed on manufacturers and importers of tobacco and tobacco products must therefore 'not only guarantee a high level of health and consumer protection, but also protect all other fundamental rights and [be] proportionate with respect to the smooth functioning of the internal market'.[131] Relevant fundamental rights include individual decision-making autonomy and the right to a private life in particular.[132] EU tobacco law's increasing focus on young people is consistent with a 'harm reduction'/ or 'nudging' approach. The inherent paternalism in such restriction of freedom to trade is justified by the vulnerability of the consumers in focus, the fact that they are not adults, may not be fully competent to take their own decisions, and hence that they are subject to a different duty of care on the part of states[133] and regulatory entities such as the EU. Given that 70 per cent of smokers in the EU start before the age of eighteen and 94 per cent before the age of twenty-five,[134] it is difficult for the health profession to object to the EU's approach. Equally, it is an approach that is more difficult for the industry to tackle.[135] It makes sense, therefore, for the EU institutions to adopt that approach.

But the 'harm reduction' or 'nudging' approach implies that competent adults should not be further constrained in their autonomous choices, rather should be able to take decisions about risks of damage to their own health. This position ignores risks to family members who may become passive smokers with consequent risks to their own health, as well as to health care systems for the costs of tobacco-related disease. Moreover, given the ways in which industry is able to influence consumer behaviour in ways that are barely perceptible to consumers themselves,[136] there is a further question as to what extent the

whilst preserving individual choice about smoking' (*LSE*, 27 March 2012) Allemanno, 'Out of Sight, Out of Mind: Towards a New EU Tobacco Products Directive' (2012) 18(2) *Columbia Journal of European Law* 197; Elsmore and Obolevich, 'Thank you for not smoking: The Commission's proposal for a new Tobacco Products Directive – legally sound but does it hit the spot?' (2013) 38(4) *European Law Review* 552; and see: Thaler and Sunstein, *Nudge: Improving Decisions About Health, Wealth and Happiness* (Yale University Press 2009).

[131] Directive 2014/40/EU, Recital 59.

[132] On the "right to smoke" at domestic level see: *R (N) v Secretary of State for Health* [2009] EWCA Civ 795.

[133] As noted above, for instance, in the UK a source of relevant regulatory powers is the Children and Families Act 2014.

[134] Commission, 'Special Eurobarometer 385: Attitudes of Europeans Towards Tobacco: Report' (Commission 2012).

[135] The tobacco industry has used civil liberties and human rights as a plank of its campaigning in various ways, focussing on freedom to smoke, see further: McKee, Hervey and Gilmore, 'Public health policies' in Mossialos et al. (eds), (CUP 2010) above n 27.

[136] The politically sophisticated tobacco industry seeks to use all kinds of mechanisms to undermine anti-tobacco policy at national, EU, and international levels, see: Smith et al.,

individual choosing to smoke is making an autonomous decision or individual choice, free of outside influence.

Concerns from the health community focus around the extent to which the EU can continue to effectively follow an approach which recognizes the inherently harmful nature of tobacco, and hence seeks to reduce the risk of harm to the health of European populations. The content of the 2014 Directive is concerned with serious public health considerations, and seeks to facilitate a high level of health protection in the internal market. But the interests of the global tobacco industry, which is dominant on that market, are diametrically opposed to the goal of reduction in tobacco consumption.[137] The sophistication of the industry's engagement with EU policy and legal developments[138] may mean that EU tobacco law has now more or less reached its limits as public health law, focused on risk of harm to populations.

Food

All European States regulate the production, processing, distribution and retail of food. Food is a very densely regulated sector in EU law, with over 100 pieces of EU-level legislation on the subject. One key rationale for food law is public health protection, even if health professionals have sometimes found it difficult to see the link.[139] Food is a significant disease vector; additives in food can cause harm to health, particularly to vulnerable people such as children; and over-consumption of food (coupled with lack of exercise) leads to being overweight or obese, which are major causes of disease and disability.

The food and drink sector is extremely important for the EU's economy, as its largest manufacturing section in terms of turnover and

'Working the system' British American tobacco's influence on the European union treaty and its implications for policy: an analysis of internal tobacco industry documents' (2010) 7(1) *PLoS Medicine* e1000202.

[137] Maier-Rigaud, 'The Commission proposal for a European Tobacco Products Directive- A critical evaluation of the Roland Berger studies' (2013) IESEG Working Paper Series No.2013-ECO-06.

[138] For instance, the formal consultation that preceded Directive 2014/40/EU elicited some 85 000 responses. Many of these presented as 'citizen' responses, but were actually the product of concerted efforts to solicit responses (for example in Italy where a campaign was undertaken by an organization comprised of some 75% of tobacconists in that state leading to some 30,000 responses of which 95% were duplicate). The responses following this consultation came out against changes to the existing Directive. In contrast the Eurobarometer survey, a random survey published in May 2012, found that EU citizens were generally supportive of tobacco control measures: Commission, 'Proposal for a Directive of the European Parliament and of the Council on the approximation of the laws, regulations and administrative provisions of the Member States concerning the manufacture, presentation and sale of tobacco and related products' COM (2012) 788 final, pages 3–4.

[139] See: Hervey and McHale, *Health Law and the European Union* (CUP 2004) 348–9. Other reasons include the desire to protect certain agricultural lifestyles or land use; to guard against unemployment; to promote animal welfare, protection of natural areas or biodiversity, see: Rippe, 'Novel Foods and Consumer Rights: Concerning food policy in a liberal state' (2000) 12(1) *Journal of Agricultural and Environmental Ethics* 71.

employment.[140] Food also has important social and cultural resonances, including, for instance, the French/southern European idea of *terroir*, which is associated with identity.[141] Since the 1950s, the global food industry[142] has undergone significant changes, and notions of food as associated with the land or an agrarian economy now appear more than a little romantic. Food is now a technologically enhanced product. The food European consumers eat is increasingly processed and convenience food. It is the result of technological developments (or manipulations, depending upon one's view), for instance, through use of genetically modified organisms in foodstuffs, or changes to the palatability or desirability of food, in particular, its sugar, salt and fat content. Many ingredients common in today's food were simply not around in the 1950s. Food retailing is increasingly dominated by supermarkets, in out-of-town sites. Small and medium-sized actors in the industry often have little choice but to supply these dominant retailers, which enjoy huge *de facto* market power. Niche marketing of high-quality (and high-price) foods, and movements such as the 'slow food movement',[143] or farmers markets, affect only a small fraction of overall food consumption in the EU.

Development of EU food law

Seen through a lens of public health law,[144] broadly speaking, EU food law has moved through four main phases. Each of these can be understood through a

---

[140] The EU food industry is made up of about 310 000 companies, with an annual turnover in excess of €900 billion. It provides jobs for more than 4 million people. See: Commission, 'Enterprise and Industry: Food Industry' (*Commission,* 5 February 2013); and O'Rourke, *European Food Law* (Sweet and Maxwell 2005).

[141] Roth-Behrendt, 'A View of EFSA from the European Parliament' in Alemanno and Gabbi (eds), *The Foundations of EU Food Law and Policy: Ten Years of the European Food Safety Authority* (Ashgate 2014). For a non-European exploration of *terrior*, see: Trubek, *The Taste of Place: A Cultural Journey into Terrior* (University of California Press 2009).

[142] We discuss the global context further in chapter 18. This chapter focuses on the EU's internal food law.

[143] For an accessible historical and cultural critical overview of slow food, terroir, and gastronomy, see: Laudan, 'Slow Food: The French Terroir Strategy, and Culinary Modernism. An Essay Review of Carlos Petrini, trans. William McCuaig. *Slow Food: The Case for Taste* (New York: Columbia University Press, 2011)' (2004) 7(2) *Food Culture and Society: An International Journal of Multidisciplinary Research* 133.

[144] Not all of EU food law is concerned with health. For instance, claims of origin, or nomenclature rules for food have consumed a great deal of EU legislative attention. Protected geographical food names (such as Greek feta, Parma ham, Cheddar cheese) were introduced in 1992, revised in 2006, 2011 and 2012. Current definitions are found in Regulation 1151/2012/EU of the European Parliament and of the Council of 21 November 2012 on quality schemes for agricultural products and foodstuffs [2012] OJ L343/1, and distinguish 'destination of origin' (e.g. Single Gloucester cheese); 'geographical indication' (e.g. Czech beer); and 'traditional speciality guaranteed' (e.g. Mozzarella). Thanks to the students in Hervey's LLM Internal Market Law seminar groups in 2009–14, for research assistance. There are parallels here with tobacco – just as not all EU law on tobacco is anti-cancer/cardiovascular disease, not all EU food law is anti-obesity.

risk frame, though the risk in each is different. EU food law began as the law of the Common Agricultural Policy. It was shaped by the need for security of food supplies in a literally starving post-war Europe,[145] and the powerful farmers' lobbies. From the 1970s, through the CJEU's case law and followed by legislation, EU food law focused on tackling the risks to the internal market from protectionist behaviour of Member States. The 1990s brought a concern with risks from food as a disease vector, particularly from animal-to-human zoonoses, but also from toxic chemical elements introduced via the food chain. Most recently, EU food law at least has the potential to be concerned with risk from obesity. This includes a human rights strand, based on non-discrimination. We now see all of these public health elements in EU food law.

As EU food law has expanded, the discretion of the Member States to regulate risk to food consumers has correspondingly decreased. Increasingly, national decisions, made with a view to promoting good health of the population, can be challenged for inconsistency with EU internal market law, if they disrupt patterns of trade in products or services across European Union borders. We track those developments here, beginning in the 1970s.

The EEC Treaty itself did not make it clear how human health should be protected in the internal market. Indeed, its provisions could be interpreted to mean that health protection is a matter for Member States. But the CJEU took the contrary view – that human health is protected *by EU law*.[146] It did so first in a rhetorical move in a 1976 case concerning not food, but pharmaceuticals.[147] The CJEU then re-asserted the principle in several subsequent cases,[148] embedding it in its jurisprudence.

Over time, the idea that *the EU* (and not only its Member States) is responsible for health protection allowed the CJEU to change its understanding of which restrictions on free trade (including in food) are justified by the need to protect public health. As we have already seen,[149] the legal mechanism used to judge consistency with free movement law of national rules, which restrict trade but for which there is an 'objective public interest', is proportionality. Proportionality is a highly malleable legal concept.[150] In assessing human health protection claims

---

[145] See the discussion in: Judt, *Postwar: A History of Europe Since 1945* (Vintage 2010).

[146] For further discussion, see: Hervey, 'The Role of the European Court of Justice in the Europeanization of Communicable Disease Control: Driver or Irrelevance?' (2012) 37(6) *Journal of Health Politics, Policy and Law* 977.

[147] 'Health and life of humans rank first among the property or interests protected by [the Treaty] . . .': *De Peijper*, C-104/75, EU:C:1976:67, paragraph 15. Having made this move as a matter of rhetoric, the CJEU then went on to find, in that particular case, that the national rules at issue were not 'necessary' to protect that interest.

[148] Explicitly in *Schumacher*, C-215/87, EU:C:1989:111; *Freistaat Bayern v Eurim-Pharm GmbH*, C-347/89, EU:C:1991:148; *Commission of the European Communities v Federal Republic of Germany*, C-62/90, EU:C:1992:169; *Ortscheit*, C-320/93, EU:C:1994:379, paragraph 16.

[149] See chapter 5.

[150] Sauter, 'Proportionality in EU Law: A Balancing Act?' (2013) 15 *Cambridge Yearbook of European Legal Studies* 439.

in food law cases (for instance, on national laws on pesticides),[151] the CJEU applied a weaker version of the proportionality test from the beginning of the 1970s, into the mid-1980s. Its reasoning stresses that EU law does not cover the clearly established risks to human health from pesticides. Member States may therefore adopt different approaches. The CJEU applied a similar approach in cases where the science was less clear. Member States were not required to prove conclusively the risk of harm to human health; it was enough to show a reasonable belief in the harmful nature of the product.[152] This approach was applied to cases concerning food additives,[153] where the scientific uncertainty itself formed part of the rationale for granting significant national discretion. The CJEU continued to take this view into the mid-1980s.[154] The weaker version of proportionality supports the position that, although the EU and its Member States share competence for protection of public health, essentially the Member States hold primary responsibility. Given that, the implication is that there is no particular need to develop a dense system of EU level public health institutional mechanisms or capacities.

But, piece by piece, from the mid-1960s onwards, the EU *did* develop its administrative capacity to regulate some sources of risk to human health within the food chain. Originally part of the Common Agricultural Policy, these activities fed into the strand of internal market law that is EU food law today. The 'panel of veterinary experts' and the Standing Committee on Foodstuffs, both established in the 1960s,[155] now form part of the Standing Committee on the Food Chain and Animal Health[156] that operates within the European Food Safety Authority.[157] Originally deciding on matters that seem only

---

[151] *Heijn BV*, C-94/83, EU:C:1984:285; and *Mirepoix*, C-54/85, EU:C:1986:123. In *Mirepoix* EU:C:1986:123, paragraph 15, the CJEU explained: 'In so far as the relevant Community rules do not cover certain pesticides, the Member States may regulate the presence of residues of those pesticides on foodstuffs in a way which varies from one country to another according to the climatic conditions, the normal diet of the population and their state of health'. Likewise, in *Melkunie*, C-97/83, EU:C:1984:212, involving the prohibition of certain levels of active coliform bacteria and active micro-organisms in milk products, the CJEU readily accepted that a real danger to public health was present and that therefore a Member State could lawfully inhibit free trade.

[152] See: *Rewe-Zentralefinanz Gmbh* v *Landwirtschaftskammer*, C-4/75, EU:C:1975:98, paragraph 8.

[153] *Sandoz*, C-174/82, EU:C:1983:213, paragraphs 10–11: *Eyssen*, C-53/80, EU:C:1981:35, paragraph 13.

[154] See: *Motte*, C-247/84, EU:C:1985:492; and *Muller*, C-304/84, EU:C:1986:194.

[155] To recommend whether infected bovines or swine could lawfully be prohibited entry into a Member State, Council Directive 64/432/EEC of 26 June 1964 on animal health problems affecting intra-Community trade in bovine animals and swine [1964] OJ L121/1977, Article 10; Council Decision 69/414/EEC of 13 November 1969 setting up a Standing Committee for Foodstuffs [1969] OJ L291/9.

[156] Regulation 178/2002/EC of the European Parliament and of the Council of 28 January 2002 laying down the general principles and requirements of food law, establishing the European Food Safety Authority and laying down procedures in matters of food safety [2002] OJ L31/1 (as amended).

[157] See further below.

technical,[158] over time these comitology procedures built up a body of EU-level decisions about the risk to human health of various food additives and hazards in food (including toxins and biological hazards such as bacterial pathogens/zoonotic agents).[159] An example is the Commission's administrative decision that the additive Konjac (E425), used in jelly mini-cups, marketed at children, was no longer authorized within products marketed in the EU.[160] Rather than simply allowing Member States to make their own decisions, the EU began to develop its own idea of tolerable (and intolerable) levels of hazard to human health within the food chain.

Perhaps responding to these developments, but certainly supporting their continued proliferation, by the early 1990s, the CJEU began to modify its jurisprudence in this field, by adding a procedural dimension to its application of proportionality. In a series of cases involving the addition of sorbic acid;[161] the nutrient L-Carnitine and taurine;[162] and the nutrient Co-enzyme Q10,[163] the CJEU was asked to assess whether a procedure requiring a national marketing authorization was permissible in EU law. Although the rhetoric of the CJEU's judgments defers to national discretion where there is scientific uncertainty,[164] the rulings moved towards a stricter version of proportionality, by scrutinizing the transparency, speed and accessibility of the national marketing authorization procedures at issue. As Hervey has shown,[165] this process set up a 'virtuous circle of mutual reinforcement' between CJEU reasoning and EU administrative capacity building in food law. Through the proliferation and deepening of the remit of EU scientific committees and agencies, the EU administrative authorities developed their scientific knowledge. The CJEU developed an increasingly suspect position towards nationally determined versions of hazard. Given the

---

[158] e.g., whether a particular additive counts as a 'colour' for the purposes of EU legislation (Directive 94/36/EC of the European Parliament and of the Council of 30 June 1994 on colours for use in foodstuffs [1994] OJ L237/13); whether additives are being used in accordance with EU legislation (Directive 95/2/EC of the European Parliament and of the Council of 20 February 1995 on food additives other than colours and sweeteners [1995] OJ 61/1 (as amended)).

[159] Any bacterium, virus or parasite which is likely to cause a zoonosis (i.e. a disease and or infection transmitted from animals to humans). Includes brucellosis, salmonellas, listeria, rabies, tuberculosis.

[160] Commission, 'Food Safety Member States support emergency suspension of the sale of jelly mini-cups containing "konjac" (E425) food additive' (*Commission*, 19 March 2002). Holland and Pope, *EU Food Law and Policy* (Kluwer 2004) 55–56; Van der Meulen and Vaskoka, 'Rule of Science: A Food Law Professor's Perspective' in Alemanno and Gabbi (eds), above n 134.

[161] *Bellon*, C-42/90, EU:C:1990:475.

[162] *Commission* v *France (Red Bull)*, C-24/00, EU:C:2004:70; *Max Rombi and Arkopharma*, C-107/97, EU:C:2000:53. France lifted the ban on Red Bull in 2008, see: Kogustowska, 'France allows taurine in Red Bull' (*FoodBev*, 2 June 2008).

[163] *Greenham and Abel*, C-95/01, EU:C:2004:71.

[164] '[I]t is of course left to Member States to decide the level of protection to life and health of humans they wish to provide, in the absence of harmonisation and where there is scientific uncertainty': *Greenham and Abel* EU:C:2004:71, paragraph 37.

[165] Hervey, above n 146.

social and political construction of 'scientific knowledge',[166] this unfolding process represents a significant *de facto* reduction of national discretion in food law.

Alongside the administrative and judicial actors, the EU legislature has also played a significant role in protecting human health through EU food law, although opinions differ as to whether it has been sufficiently effective, or sufficiently distant from the global food industry to be so. Starting in the 1970s, the EU has adopted a significant body of food legislation. The framework for this legislation encompasses the common agricultural policy; the internal market; and EU consumer protection policy. We consider the two key areas: general food safety and food labelling.

General food safety law

EU food law took a major change of direction – and, indeed, for some,[167] came into being – at the time of the BSE/vCJD crisis. This was a moment of high political salience in the development of EU food law, and public health law more generally.[168] The approach to food regulation[169] that had been adopted up to that point was insufficiently robust to cope with a new and fatal food and feed-borne human disease, present within the EU, the spread of which had not been contained, and about which consumers had been misinformed.[170] The EU's general Food Safety Regulation 178/2002/EC,[171] adopted in the aftermath of the BSE/vCJD affair, arises from dissatisfaction with the previous approach, brought sharply into relief by BSE/vCJD. It involves a significant restructuring of administrative responsibilities for food in the EU, including the establishment of a new agency, the European Food Safety Authority.

---

[166] Jasanoff, *Designs on Nature: Science and Democracy in the US and Europe* (Princeton University Press 2007); Jasanoff, 'Citizens at Risk: Cultures of Modernity in the US and the EU' (2002) 11(2) *Science As Culture* 363, 374–5; Brownsword, 'Regulating Nanomedicine – The Smallest of Our Concerns' (2008) 2(1) *Nanoethics* 73; Nelkin, *Technological Decisions and Democracy: European Experiments in Public Participation* (Sage 1977); Sclove, *Democracy and Technology* (Guilford Press 1995); Nelkin (ed), *Controversy: Politics of Technical Decisions* (Sage 1992).

[167] Alemanno and Gabbi (eds), above n 141.

[168] Vos, 'EU Food Safety Regulation in the aftermath of the BSE Crisis' (2000) 23(3) *Journal of Consumer Policy* 227; Westlake, ' "Mad Cows and Englishmen": The Institutional Consequences of the BSE Crisis' in Nugent (ed), *European Union 1996: the annual review* (published in association with the *Journal of Common Market Studies* 1997); Krapohl, 'Risk Regulation in the EU between Interests and Expertise: The Case of BSE' (2003) 10(2) *Journal of European Public Policy* 189.

[169] The so-called 'new approach', which involved mutual recognition of national standards, see further: Hervey and McHale above n 139, 53–59.

[170] For further details, see: Hervey and McHale above n 139, 351–7.

[171] Regulation 178/2002/EC [2002] OJ L31/1. Amended in 2003 by Regulation 1642/2003/EC [2003] OJ L245/4; in 2006 by Regulation 575/2006/EC [2006] OJ L100/3; in 2008 by Regulation 202/2008/EC [2008] OJ L60/17; in 2009 by Regulation 596/2009/EC [2009] OJ L188/14; and in 2014 by Regulation 652/2014/EU [2014] OJ L189/1.

The scope of the Food Safety Regulation extends to 'any substance or product, whether processed, partially processed, or unprocessed, intended to be, or reasonably expected to be ingested by humans'.[172] Food thus includes drink, water and any substance incorporated into food during its manufacture.[173] The Regulation sets requirements for food and feed safety, relying on the principle of traceability of food and feed.[174] The effectiveness of these provisions has been repeatedly brought into question, for instance, during the horsemeat in supermarket burgers incident in 2013.[175] Sanctions for non-compliance with the Food Safety Regulation are set at national level. The CJEU has confirmed that Member States must set rules which are 'effective, proportionate and dissuasive'. So, for instance, a strict liability fine, imposed on a supermarket manager where the levels of salmonella present in fresh poultry meat on sale in the supermarket, is not necessarily disproportionate.[176] The main focus of the Regulation is with hazards within the food chain, and these are numerous. Focusing on the years 2005–11, Raymond O'Rourke discusses semicarbazide (from packaging) in baby foods, GM foods, trans fatty acids, aspartame, pork contamination with dioxins and e-coli.[177] Focusing only on 2007–11, James Lawless mentions melamine in food, pork contamination with dioxins, mineral oil in sunflower oil, 4-methylbenzophenone in breakfast cereals, nicotine in mushrooms, chlormequat in table grapes, volcanic ash, e-coli and Schmallenburg virus.[178]

The Regulation's underlying basic principle is the separation of risk assessment, risk management and risk communication. The institutional structures set up by the Regulation support this. A new entity within the European Commission, DG-SANCO, was established in 2000, to tackle the long-standing problem of division of responsibilities for food across various of the Directorates General. DG-SANCO is responsible for the risk management aspects of the system.[179]

Risk assessment is the responsibility of separate, 'scientific' bodies.[180] The pre-existing system had numerous problems, such as lack of scientific support for the system of scientific advice, inadequacies in monitoring and surveillance on food safety issues, gaps in the rapid alert system, and lack of coordination of scientific cooperation and analytical support. The previously good reputation of

---

[172] Regulation 178/2002/EC, Article 1.
[173] It does not include pharmaceuticals, cosmetics or tobacco.
[174] Regulation 178/2002/EC (as amended), Articles 14, 15, 17, 18 and 20.
[175] Lawrence, 'Horsemeat scandal: Where did the 29% horsemeat in your Tesco burger come from?' *The Guardian* (London, 22 October 2013).
[176] *Reindl*, C-443/13, EU:C:2014:2370.
[177] O'Rourke, 'EFSA's Communication Strategy: A Critical Appraisal' in Alemanno and Gabbi (eds), above n 134.
[178] See: Lawless, 'EFSA Under Pressure: Emerging Risks, Emergencies and Crises' in Alemanno and Gabbi (eds), (Ashgate 2014) above n 141.
[179] Regulation 178/20022002] OJ L31/1 (as amended), Article 6 (2).
[180] In this respect, the EU's food law differs from the US FDA approach, see: Hervey and McHale above n 132, 361.

the Standing Committee on Foodstuffs was shattered by the BSE/vCJD affair.[181] These problems were all to be tackled by establishing a new agency – the European Food Safety Authority (EFSA). The main role of EFSA is to provide 'scientific advice and scientific and technical support for the [EU's] legislation and policies in all fields which have a direct or indirect impact on food and feed safety'.[182] Its role is to assess risk and provide independent information and scientific advice, through its Scientific Committee and ten Scientific Panels,[183] to support the European Commission in its administrative and legislative duties.

Risk communication is undertaken by the EFSA, in collaboration with the European Commission and the Member States. This is supposed to secure coherence, essential for restoring consumer confidence over food safety following an incident of harm or potential harm. But there is no obligation on national food authorities to coordinate with EFSA, leaving the risk communication aspect of EU food law vulnerable to lack of credibility in situations where national authorities act independently of EFSA's advice.[184]

Food labelling law

The earliest significant[185] piece of EU food legislation is Directive 79/112/EC[186] on food labelling. This Directive prohibited labelling likely to mislead consumers, and set eight compulsory items to be included on all food labels.[187]

---

[181] Vos, above n 168. See also: Gray, 'The Scientific Committee for Food' in Van Schendelen (ed), *EU Committees as Influential Policy Makers* (Dartmouth 1998).

[182] Regulation 178/2002/EC, Article 22 (2). The EFSA has published around 3000 scientific outputs 2003–2013, see: Silano, 'EFSA's Science Strategy: Taking Stock and Looking Ahead' in Alemanno and Gabbi (eds), (Ashgate 2014) above n 141.

[183] The Panel members are voluntary experts who are not employed by the EFSA. They are appointed in their personal capacity by the EFSA Management Board, through a procedure designed to secure balanced representation of nationalities and geographic spread. The Panels are supported by Working Groups, which are 'hyper-specialized scientific fora aimed at eviscerating a very specific matter', i.e. the experts who serve on them are selected for expertise alone. On the strengths and weaknesses of this system, see: Gabbi, 'The Scientific Governance of the European Food Safety Authority' in Alemanno and Gabbi (eds), (Ashgate 2014) above n 141.

[184] O'Rourke, 'EFSA's Communication Strategy: A Critical Appraisal' in Alemanno and Gabbi (eds), (Ashgate 2014) above n 141.

[185] The first EU food Directive, concerning colours in foodstuffs, was adopted in 1962. This provision has no number, as no formal system for numbering EEC laws was in operation at the time, see: O'Rourke, *European Food Law* (Sweet and Maxwell 2005). A series of detailed legislation was adopted setting compositional standards for various foods, such as honey, jam, and chocolate. See: Hervey and McHale, above n 139, 351–4.

[186] Council Directive 79/112/EEC of 18 December 1978 on the approximation of the laws of the Member States relating to the labelling, presentation and advertising of foodstuffs for sale to the ultimate consumer [1979] OJ L33/1.

[187] Namely: name, ingredients, net quantity, 'use by date', any special storage or use conditions, name and address of manufacturer, packager or seller established in the EU, and place of origin where required, instructions for use where necessary: Council Directive 79/112, Article 3. For general discussion of EU food labelling law see: Von Heydebrand u.d. Lasa, 'Free Movement of Foodstuffs, Consumer Protection and Food Standards in the EU: Has the Court

The EU's general food labelling legislation is now found in Regulation 1169/2011/EU.[188] Its general objectives are expressed as supporting 'informed consumer choice',[189] by providing consumers information to use food safely, and hence protect their health. The Regulation thus is expressed in terms not only of risk of harm to consumers, but also individual autonomy. It represents a compromise between a risk-regulation approach based on consumer safety, under which public bodies take on the responsibility for making expert assessments of risk, and an 'autonomy-centred' approach, in which consumer sovereignty is guaranteed by requiring consumer information.[190]

The Regulation's key changes from the pre-existing EU law are to add to the food labelling requirements[191] new mandatory nutrition labelling on processed foods; and to require better legibility of information. The Regulation also requires mandatory origin labelling for meat; and highlighting common allergens on the list of ingredients. In theory, the Regulation applies in full from 13 December 2014, although the new nutrition information obligations apply only from 13 December 2016, and work on meat origin labelling is ongoing at the time of writing.

Regulation 1169/2011/EU defines food by reference to the EU's general Food Safety Regulation.[192] The Regulation applies to the whole food industry, where its activities concern consumer information.[193] Regulation 1169/2011/EU applies without prejudice to Directive 2009/39/EC on food for particular nutritional uses, a *lex specialis*.[194] The new nutrition labelling rules also do not apply to food supplements or mineral waters,[195] nor to unprocessed products, products that have only matured, rather than been artificially processed, food supplied directly to the final consumer in small quantities, and comprising only

of Justice got it wrong?' (1991) 16(5) *European Law* Review 391; MacMaoláin, 'Free Movement of Foodstuffs, Quality Requirements and Consumer Protection: Have the Court and the Commission Both Got It Wrong?' (2001) 26(5) *European Law Review* 413; MacMaoláin, 'Waiter! There's a Beetle in my Soup. Yes Sir, That's E120: Disparities Between Actual Individual Behaviour and Regulating Food Labelling for the Average Consumer in EU Law' (2008) 45(4) *Common Market Law Review* 1147.

[188] Regulation 1169/2011/EU of the European Parliament and of the Council of 25 October 2011 on the provision of food information to consumers, amending Regulations (EC) No 1924/2006 and (EC) No 1925/2006 of the European Parliament and of the Council, and repealing Commission Directive 87/250/EEC, Council Directive 90/496/EEC, Commission Directive 1999/10/EC, Directive 2000/13/EC of the European Parliament and of the Council, Commission Directives 2002/67/EC and 2008/5/EC and Commission Regulation (EC) No 608/2004 [2011] OJ L304/18.

[189] Regulation 1169/2011/EU, Article 3 (1).

[190] See further: Hervey and McHale above n 139, 349–51.

[191] Detailed in Regulation 1169/2011/EU, Articles 17–28.

[192] Boundary issues, e.g. with pharmaceuticals provide that Directive 2001/83/EC of the European Parliament and of the Council of 6 November 2001 on the Community code relating to medicinal products for human use [2001] OJ L311/67 applies in priority toRegulation 1169/2011, see: e.g. *Orthica,* C-211/03, C-299/03, C-316/03, C-317/03 and C-318/03, EU:C:2005:370, paragraph 45.

[193] Regulation 1169/2011/EU, Article 1 (3).   [194] Regulation 1169/2011/EU, Article 29.

[195] Regulation 1169/2011/EU, Article 29.

a single ingredient, and a small range of other products such as herbal infusions, chewing gum, and food in packaged in very small quantities.[196]

The nutrition labelling provisions are the most controversial aspects of the Regulation. The original proposal[197] was to require a wide range of information (calories, total fat, saturated fat, salt, carbohydrates), in a specific place on the packing, with a minimum font and contrasting background, to make the information easy to find and read. The idea of 'traffic light' labels – red, yellow or green to indicate whether high medium or low fat or sugar – supported by all medical, public health and consumer advocacy NGOs,[198] did not feature in the original Commission proposal.[199] The Regulation's basic obligation is that of 'fair information' – the idea that food information should not be misleading.[200] This provision had been elaborated in the equally controversial Regulation 1924/2006/EC on nutrition and health claims made on foods.[201]

Regulation 1924/2006/EC was supposed to tighten up on unfounded claims on food packages such as 'rich in vitamin C' or health claims such as 'good for your heart'. It was also supposed to deal with accurate but misleading health claims, such as 'low in fat' when a product is high in sugar or salt.[202] Some Member States prohibited these claims altogether, but the CJEU found such national measures a disproportionate restriction on free movement.[203]

---

[196]   Regulation 1169/2011/EU, Annex V.
[197]   Commission, 'Proposal for a Regulation of the European Parliament and of the Council on the provision of food information to consumers' COM (2008) 40 final.
[198]   The NGOs relied on research findings that colour coding was 'the easiest format for consumers to understand, especially when shopping in a hurry, see: Kurzer, 'Non-communicable Diseases: The EU Declares War on 'Fat'' in Greer and Kurzer (eds), (Routledge 2013) above n 29, citing Borgmeier and Westenhoefer, 'Impact of Different Food Label Formats on Healthiness Evaluation and Food Choice of Consumers: A Randomised-Controlled Study' (2009) 9(1) *BMC Public Health* 184.
[199]   Attempts to persuade the European Parliament to introduce a traffic light system also failed.
[200]   Regulation 1169/2011/EU, Article 7.
[201]   Regulation 1924/2006/EC of the European Parliament and of the Council of 20 December 2006 on nutrition and health claims made on foods [2006] OJ L404/9, as amended by: Regulation 107/2008/EC of the European Parliament of the Council of 15 January 2008 amending Regulation (EC) No 1924/2006 on nutrition and health claims made on foods as regards the implementing powers conferred on the Commission [2008] OJ L39/8; Corrigendum to Regulation 1924/2006/EC of the European Parliament and of the Council of 20 December 2006 on nutrition and health claims made on foods [2007] OJ L12/3; Regulation 109/2008/EC of the European Parliament and of the Council of 15 January 2008 amending Regulation (EC) No 1924/2006 on nutrition and health claims made on foods [2008] OJ L39/14; Commission Regulation 116/2010/EU of 9 February 2010 amending Regulation (EC) No 1924/2006 of the European Parliament and of the Council with regard to the list of nutrition claims [2010] OJ L37/16; Commission Regulation 1047/2012/EU of 8 November 2012 amending Regulation (EC) No 1924/2006 with regard to the list of nutrition claims [2012] OJ L310/36.
[202]   Kurzer, 'Non-communicable Diseases: The EU Declares War on 'Fat'' in Greer and Kurzer (eds), (Routledge 2013) above n 29.
[203]   *Commission v Austria*, C-221/00, EU:C:2003:44. On the other hand, the CJEU has held that EU law prohibits promoting wine on the basis of health claims, see: *Deutsches Weintor eG*, C-544/10, EU:C:2012:526, see further below.

Regulation 1924/2006/EC requires 'nutrient profiles' for certain categories of food, and prohibits use of non-compliant nutrition or health claims.[204] The Regulation requires such claims to be supported by scientific evidence, checked by the EFSA. More than 3,000 health and nutrition claims on food had been scientifically evaluated by 2014,[205] about 80 per cent of which had been rejected.[206] A list of 'permitted health claims' was established by Regulation 432/2012/EU.[207]

As the coverage of EU food legislation increases, so both the incidence of litigation based on internal market law decreases, and also the chances of success in such litigation decrease. Taking food additives as an example, we see the CJEU deciding a steady stream of food additives cases in the 1980s and 90s, on the basis that relevant national rules infringed Treaty-based internal market law.[208] But by the mid-2000s, the CJEU was deciding cases by reference only to the EU legislation, and not engaging with possible infringements of the Treaty per se.[209] By the end of that decade, the CJEU turned to the legislation, not the Treaty, as its standard approach. *Darbo*[210] is a good example. The relevant Austrian rule prohibiting the use of the term 'low sugar jam' had the effect of inhibiting the marketing in Austria of jam lawfully produced in Germany. This is a textbook infringement of internal market law, and the CJEU could have approached it as such, applying the Treaty, and balancing national approaches to public health protection, with free trade within the internal market, using the proportionality test. Instead, the CJEU decided the case solely by reference to EU food legislation. EU legislation was increasingly occupying the field, and therefore determining acceptable (and unacceptable) levels of risk to human health. Implicitly, according to the CJEU, EU Treaty rules – which essentially operate to liberalize markets – could not undermine this determination of acceptable risk to human health by the EU legislature.

---

[204] Regulation 1924/2006/EC, Article 3. For further information on nutrient profiles, see: Friant-Perro and Garde, 'From BSE to Obesity: EFSA's Growing Role in the EU's Nutrition Policy' in Alemanno and Gabbi (eds), (Ashgate 2014) above n 141, 141–3.

[205] Geslain-Lanéelle, 'Foreword' in Alemanno and Gabbi (eds), (Ashgate 2014) above n 141.

[206] See the register of all submitted claims: Commission, 'EU Register of nutrition and health claims made on foods' (*Commission*, 12 June 2013). Examples of unauthorised claims are, for instance, "GLA supports weight management GLA reduces re-gaining weight after dieting" and "- supports concentration and mental performance under conditions of mental or physical exertion – helps to maintain working memory and brain performance in aging adults" – the EFSA opinion being that, on the basis of the scientific evidence assessed, these claimed effects for these foods has not been substantiated.

[207] Commission Regulation 432/2012/EU of 16 May 2012 establishing a list of permitted health claims made on foods, other than those referring to the reduction of disease risk and to children's development and health [2012] OJ L136/1, Article 1 and Annex 1.

[208] *Eyssen* EU:C:1981:35; *Denkavit Futtermittel*, C-195/84, EU:C:1985:390; *Motte* EU:C:1985:492; *Commission* v *Greece*, C-176/84, EU:C:1987:125; *Commission* v *Germany (Beer Purity)*, C-178/84, EU:C:1987:126; *Dansk Denkavit*, C-29/87, EU:C:1988:299.

[209] See: *Denkavit Futtermittel*, C-145/02, EU:C:2005:9.

[210] See: *Adolf Darbo*, C-366/08, EU:C:2009:546.

EU obesity law through non-discrimination

During the 2000s and 2010s, EU law has moved beyond a 'food safety' approach, mandated by the BSE crisis, to a concern with food as a major contributor to chronic health problems, particularly those associated with obesity.[211] The European Commission has noted the 'public interest in the relationship between diet and health'.[212] Its White Paper, 'Strategy for Europe on Nutrition, Overweight and Obesity-related Health Issues',[213] along with its 'Consumer Policy Strategy',[214] take the view that the appropriate way to tackle this is through informed consumer choice. The White Paper has been taken forward by the High Level Group on Nutrition and Physical Activity, which provides overviews of EU policies, and facilitates sharing of national policy and practice.[215] The Vienna Declaration of 5 July 2013 on Nutrition and Non-communicable Diseases in the Context of 'Health 2020' provides that European WHO Member States agree to take action on obesity and prioritize work on healthy diet for children. In 2014, Member States agreed an EU Action Plan on Childhood Obesity 2014–2020.[216] This was followed in 2014 by the Council Conclusions on nutrition and physical activity. These focus on fostering health promotion activities and cooperation across Member States. This autonomy-based, non-paternalist approach underpins the more recently adopted EU food legislation, which is very much based on a consumer choice model.

The latest development, not so much in EU food law, but rather in EU law on obesity, has a quite different basis: that of human rights. It falls within EU equality or non-discrimination law. The 'public health and human rights' approach has yet to emerge in EU legislation or policy.[217] But it has arisen before the CJEU. In *Kaltoft*,[218] concerning the dismissal of an obese

---

[211] Hartlev, 'Stigmatisation as a Public Health Tool against Obesity – A Health and Human Rights Perspective' (2014) 21(4) *European Journal of Health Law* 365; Alemanno and Garde, 'The Emergence of an EU Lifestyle Policy: The Case of Alcohol, Tobacco and Unhealthy Diets' (2013) 50(6) *Common Market Law Review* 1745; Friant-Perro and Garde, 'From BSE to Obesity: EFSA's Growing Role in the EU's Nutrition Policy' in Alemanno and Gabbi (eds), (Ashgate 2014) above n 141; Kurzer 'Non-communicable Diseases: The EU Declares War on 'Fat'' in Greer and Kurzer (eds), (Routledge 2013) above n 29. See also: Alemanno and Carreno, 'Fat Taxes in the EU between Fiscal Austerity and the Fight against Obesity' (2011) 2(4) *European Journal of Risk Regulation* 571; Oliver and Ubel, 'Nudging the Obese: A UK-US comparison' (2014) 9(3) *Health Economics, Policy and Law* 329.

[212] Commission, 'Proposal for a Regulation of the European Parliament and of the Council on the provision of food information to consumers' COM (2008) 40 final.

[213] Commission, 'White Paper on a Strategy for Europe on Nutrition, Overweight and Obesity related health issues' (White Paper) COM (2007) 279 final.

[214] Commission, 'EU Consumer Policy strategy 2007–2013 – Empowering consumers, enhancing their welfare, effectively protecting them' (Communication) COM (2007) 99 final.

[215] http://ec.europa.eu/health/nutrition_physical_activity/high_level_group/index_en.htm.

[216] http://ec.europa.eu/health/nutrition_physical_activity/docs/childhoodobesity_actionplan_2014_2020_en.pdf.

[217] Hartlev, 'Stigmatisation as a Public Health Tool against Obesity – A Health and Human Rights Perspective' (2014) 21(4) *European Journal of Health Law* 365.

[218] *Kaltoft*, C-354/13, EU:C:2014:2463.

child-minder employed by the Municipality of Billund, Denmark, the CJEU was asked to consider whether obesity is a disability in EU law. Contrary to much of the media reporting, Karsten Kaltoft was not unable to do his job because of his obesity.[219] It is also not factually established that Kaltoft was dismissed because of his obesity (this will be a matter for the national court); he claims it was given as a reason for his dismissal. The CJEU, agreeing with its Advocate General, held that the EU's Charter of Fundamental Rights does not apply in *Kaltoft*, as the connection to EU law is too remote.[220] On the question of whether obesity is a 'forbidden ground' for discrimination in EU law under the EUCFR or Article 6 TEU, the CJEU held that there is 'nothing to suggest that the situation at issue in the main proceedings, in so far as it relates to a dismissal purportedly based on obesity as such, would fall within the scope of EU law'.[221]

On the question of whether obesity is a disability under Directive 2000/78/EC on non-discrimination in employment, the CJEU held that obesity per se is not a disability.[222] This is consistent with the established principle that illness itself is not a disability under the Directive.[223] However, if the obesity is of such a degree that it 'entails a limitation which results in particular from physical, mental or psychological impairments that . . . may hinder the full and effective participation of that person in professional life on an equal basis with other workers, and the limitation is a long-term one',[224] it is a disability. This would be the case, 'if the obesity of the worker hindered his full and effective participation in professional life on an equal basis with other workers on account of reduced mobility or the onset, in that person, of medical conditions preventing him from carrying out his work or causing discomfort when carrying out his professional activity'.[225] The Advocate General's Opinion is that probably only WHO 'class III obesity', which is 'severe, extreme or morbid', creates limitations such as problems in mobility, endurance and mood, and limitations on effective participation in work or professional life, will meet the test.[226] According to the CJEU, the cause of the obesity (excessive food intake in relation to energy expended; side-effect of medication; metabolic or psychological problem) is irrelevant.[227] This must be correct, otherwise the extent of the protection in Directive 2000/78/EC would not cover disability caused by 'self-inflicted'

---

[219] E.g. it was reported that he could not tie the children's shoelaces, he denied this in a BBC interview (see: Ó Cathaoir, 'Is obesity a disability?' (*EU Law Analysis*, 18 July 2014).

[220] *Kaltoft*, paragraph 39.   [221] *Kaltoft*, paragraph 38.   [222] *Kaltoft*, paragraph 58.

[223] *Chacón Navas*, C-13/05, EU:C:2006:456; *HK Danmark*, C-335/11 and C-337/11, EU:C:2013:222; *Z*, C-363/12, EU:C:2014:159; Opinion of the Advocate General in *Kaltoft* EU:C:2014:2106, paragraph 34.

[224] *Kaltoft*, paragraph 59. See also Opinion of the Advocate General in *Kaltoft* EU:C:2014:2106, paragraph 55.

[225] *Kaltoft*, paragraph 60.

[226] Opinion of the Advocate General in *Kaltoft* EU:C:2014:2106, paragraph 56.

[227] *Kaltoft*, paragraph 56.

risk-taking, for instance, in sports, and this is surely not intended by the legislature. It is consistent with the view that it is not for the EU legislature to reach
moral judgments on individual behaviour that carries the risk of being harmful
to health. The CJEU's approach thus fits well with the consumer-autonomy
approach of the legislature in EU food law.

The overall direction of travel of EU food law is to decrease national autonomy
over food regulation. While much of the EU's food law can be seen through a
standard risk regulation approach, as with the other areas of EU public health
law that we have discussed, such a frame offers an incomplete picture. Questions
of ethics and human rights also arise, and have become increasingly visible in
the legal discussions.

The effectiveness of the EU's approach to food law as a public health measure
is contested. Some point to significant improvements in food safety standards
in the EU over the last ten years.[228] But others note that national politics
continues to impede food-borne disease control.[229] There are also significant
concerns about the permeability of the legislative and administrative structures to the global food industry. It is argued that this prevents an effective
anti-obesity strategy from emerging, at least through hard law.[230] In terms of
administrative capacity, the EFSA has been said to be both 'pro-industry', for
instance, in its scientific assessment of GMOs; and 'anti-industry', in its scientific
assessment of health claims.[231] The EU's institutional structures, especially the
EFSA, may well be stretched 'beyond their comfort zone',[232] particularly with

---

[228] For example, the reduction by half in human cases of salmonella in the EU 2004–2009, see:
Byrne, 'The Genesis of EFSA and the First 10 Years of EU Food Law' in Alemanno and Gabbi
(eds), (Ashgate 2014) above n 141, 22; the tracing of a Legionella outbreak to a resort where
individuals from various Member States were staying, see: McKee, Hervey and Gilmore,
'Public health policies' in Mossialos et al. (eds), (CUP 2010) above n 27.

[229] Greer, 'Catch me if you can: Communicable disease control', in Greer and Kurzer (eds),
(Routledge 2013) above n 29, points to Germany wrongly blaming an e-coli outbreak on
Spanish food in 2011; see also: O'Rourke, 'EFSA's Communication Strategy: A Critical
Appraisal' in Alemanno and Gabbi (eds), (Ashgate 2014) above n 141.

[230] MacMaoláin, *EU Food Law: Protecting Consumers and Health in a Common Market* (Hart
2007) 223–4; Kurzer, 'Non-communicable Diseases: The EU Declares War on "Fat"' in Greer
and Kurzer (eds), (Routledge 2013) above n 29; Greer and Vanhercke, 'The hard politics of
soft law: the case of health', in Mossialos et al. (eds), (CUP 2010) above n 27; Friant-Perrot
and Garde, 'From BSE to Obesity: EFSA's Growing Role in the EU's Nutrition Policy' in
Alemanno and Gabbi (eds), (Ashgate 2014) above n 141.

[231] Alemanno, 'Introduction: Foundation of EU Food Law and Policy' in Alemanno and Gabbi
(eds), (Ashgate 2014) above n 141, 14, Alemanno says the existence of both claims suggest
that they offset each other. See also: Davies, 'The Consumers' Perspective of EFSA'; and Vaqué
and Romero Melchor, 'A Yankee in King Arthur's Court: A Lawyer's perspective of EFSA' both
in Alemanno and Gabbi (eds), (Ashgate 2014) above n 141, which cite evidence to the effect
that the economic impact of the 'permitted list' of health claims in Commission Regulation
432/2012/EU of 16 May 2012 establishing a list of permitted health claims made on foods,
other than those referring to the reduction of disease risk and to children's development and
health [2012] OJ L136/1 will be 'substantial and largely negative'.

[232] Friant-Perro and Garde, 'From BSE to Obesity: EFSA's Growing Role in the EU's Nutrition
Policy' in Alemanno and Gabbi (eds), above n 141.

the EFSA's responsibilities on nutrition. The EFSA encounters significant difficulties in discharging its roles in the scientific substantiation of health claims, the establishment of nutrient profiles, and the setting of dietary 'reference values'.[233] This is unsurprising, given the bifurcation in principle of risk assessment and risk management, in an area as politically charged as food regulation. But, coupled with the under-resourcing and consequent inability of EFSA to cope with requests for approvals of nutrient profiles, it increases the pressure to strip EFSA of these responsibilities altogether. The EFSA committees may be effective for advising on hazards in the food chain. But they are simply not constructed 'to vet and approve thousands of different health claims submitted by the private food sector, which resents the introduction of nutrient profiles in the first place'.[234]

As for the legislature, unlike the tobacco industry, the global food industry was involved in EU anti-obesity lawmaking procedures from the outset in the early 2000s.[235] As Paulette Kurzer and others have observed, despite its professed anti-obesity stance,[236] the European Parliament has proven particularly permeable to the food industry lobby. In the case of both the food labelling Regulation 1169/2011/EU, and Regulation 1924/2006/EC on nutrition claims, the European Parliament was responsible for removing from the Commission proposal some of its more powerful public health features. The final text of the food labelling Regulation offers greater flexibility than originally proposed for producers to shrink font sizes and decide where to place labels. The original proposals on nutrient profiles for Regulation 1924/2006/EC were rejected by the European Parliament,[237] although they were reinstated by Council, in a modified form. The European Parliament's opposition to tough legislation is not a surprise, given the size of the sector and its importance to the European economy and employment, particularly in the context of the Eurozone and global financial crises.

This leaves the pro-health sector to fall back on the 'softer' EU structures, such as the EU 'Platform on Diet, Physical Activity and Health'. Formed in 2005, this is a discussion forum for EU level umbrella organizations representing consumer

---

[233] Dietary Reference Values (DRVs) are 'the complete set of nutrient recommendations and reference values, such as population reference intakes, the average requirement, adequate intake level and the lower threshold intake', see: EFSA, 'Dietary reference values and dietary guidelines' (EFSA, 22 July 2014). On how setting DRVs illustrates the political and cultural nature of 'scientific' evidence, see: Friant-Perro and Garde, 'From BSE to Obesity: EFSA's Growing Role in the EU's Nutrition Policy' in Alemanno and Gabbi above n 141, 147–8.

[234] Kurzer, 'Non-communicable Diseases: The EU Declares War on "Fat"' in Greer and Kurzer (eds), (Routledge 2013) above n 29. See also: Greer, Hervey, McKee and Mackenbach, 'Health Law and Policy of the European Union' (2013) 381(9872) *The Lancet* 1135.

[235] Kurzer above n 232.

[236] European Parliament resolution of 9 October 2008 on 'Together for Health: A Strategic Approach for the EU 2008–2013' (2008/2115(INI))' [2010] OJ CE 9/56.

[237] IMCO (the European Parliament's Internal Market and Consumer Protection Committee) was against them; ENVI (the European Parliament's Environment, Public Health and Food Safety Committee) was split: Kurzer above n 232.

NGOs, public authorities and the private sector. The Platform collaborates to produce voluntary commitments, such as 'not to market to children under 12 years in the internet sphere'. The hope is that this process will lead to beneficial outcomes without using the legislative process.[238] Evidence that this has taken place is inconclusive. According to Holly Jarman, the Platform is now a relatively low-profile forum for information exchange.[239] The process of reaching even modest voluntary commitments keeps the debate open, and avoids legislative stalemate.[240] It should also be recognized that, given the political complexion of the EU legislative institutions at the present time, pushing for hard law may backfire. Reform of EU food law 'would provide as many openings for obesogenic as healthy policy changes'.[241]

Alcohol

Some of the earliest free trade decisions of the CJEU involve alcohol. The seminal *Cassis de Dijon*,[242] in which the CJEU established the principle of mutual recognition of national production and marketing standards, concerned, in part, the protection of public health from alcohol-induced harm. German law provided that a drink marketed as 'cassis' must have an alcohol content of 25 per cent. The German government argued, inter alia, that the fixing of the minimum alcohol content at 25 per cent was justified by the need to avoid the proliferation of alcoholic drinks with a low alcohol content on the German market, since in its view such drinks may more easily induce an unhealthy tolerance towards alcohol than more highly alcoholic drinks. The CJEU was not convinced, pointing out that a very wide range of drinks with a low alcohol content were already permitted on the German market, and, in any case, most high alcohol content drinks are diluted by mixers when consumed. The CJEU concluded 'there is no valid reason why, provided that they have been lawfully produced and marketed in one of the Member States, alcoholic beverages should not be introduced into any other Member State'.[243] Similarly, the CJEU held that the German *Reinheitsgebot* (Beer Purity Law) was not necessary to protect health, as the German government claimed.[244] Although Member States enjoyed

---

[238] Greer and Vanhercke, 'The hard politics of soft law: the case of health' in Mossialos et al. (eds), (CUP 2010) above n 27, 186–230. Director-General Robert Madelin (who left DG-Sanco in 2010) took it seriously, 'it had good attendance and served the interests both of the industry (which could use it to show corporate responsibility and fend off regulation) and of the NGO and scholarly community', see: Greer, et al., above n 233.

[239] Jarman, 'Collaboration and consultation: Functional Representation in EU Stakeholder Dialogues' (2011) 33(4) *Journal of European Integration* 385.

[240] Kurzer above n 232.   [241] Greer et al., above n 233.

[242] *Rewe v Bundesmonopolverwaltung für Branntwein (Cassis de Dijon)*, C-120/78, EU:C:1979:42.

[243] *Rewe v Bundesmonopolverwaltung für Branntwein (Cassis de Dijon)* EU:C:1979:42, paragraph 14.

[244] *Commission v Germany (Beer Purity)* EU:C:1987:126. For a detailed analysis, see: Scott and Vos, 'The Juridification of Uncertainty' in Joerges and Dehousse (eds), *Good Governance in Europe's Integrated Market* (OUP 2002) 262–4.

a margin of discretion in cases where scientific opinion was uncertain as to the potential of health hazards, applying the proportionality principle, consumers could be protected by providing information about ingredients on the label. This autonomy-centred consumer-information approach has reduced national discretion to adopt more paternalistic harm-reduction approaches.

The CJEU continued this approach, even when considering taxation[245] or marketing rules for alcohol, rather than product rules about its content, and even when considering Nordic/Scandinavian Member States, with their distinctive alcohol-related health problems.[246] Even evidence that alcohol-related diseases had risen dramatically in Denmark (which had been a Member State since 1973) was insufficient to convince the CJEU to change its approach to public health arguments justifying restrictions on free movement or competition in the alcohol sector.[247] The position has been used by the alcohol industry to challenge national policies aimed at reducing harm to health from alcohol of specific population groups. For instance, a group of alcohol producers, including the Scotch Whisky Association, the European Spirits Association and the *Comité Européen des Entreprises Vins* sought judicial review of the Alcohol (Minimum Pricing) (Scotland) Act in 2013. The case focused on whether the minimum pricing provisions[248] would be justified by an objective public health interest. The European Commission accepted that Scotland has a significant public health problem caused by alcohol, and that increasing prices would reduce consumption (in general, and particularly by hazardous and harmful

---

[245] *Commission v France (Whisky and cognac)*, C-168/78, EU:C:1980:51; *Commission v Italy (Rum)*, C-169/78, EU:C:1980:52; *COGIS (Compagnia Generale Interscambi) v Amministrazione delle Finanze dello Stato (Wine)*, C-216/81, EU:C:1982:275; *Commission v Italy (Sparkling wine)*, C-319/81, EU:C:1983:71; *Commission v Italy (Sparkling wine)*, C-278/83, EU:C:1985:325; *Commission v Denmark (Johnny Walker)*, C-106/84, EU:C:1986:99; *Commission v Greece (Ouzo)*, C-230/89, EU:C:1991:156; *Joustra*, C-5/05, EU:C:2006:733.

[246] *Franzen*, C-189/95, EU:C:1997:504; *Rosengren*, C-170/04, EU:C:2007:313; *Ahokainen*, C-434/04, EU:C:2006:609. See also the Judgments of the EFTA Court in: *Tore Wilhelmsen AS v Kommune (E-6/96)* [1997] 3 C.M.L.R. 823; *Fridtjof Frank Gundersen v Oslo commune (E-1/97)* [1997] EFTA Ct. Rep 108; *EFTA Surveillance Authority v Norway (E-9/00)* [2002] 2 C.M.L.R. 17. See: Baumberg and Anderson, 'Health, Alcohol and EU Law: Understanding the impact of European single market law on alcohol policies' (2008) 18(4) *European Journal of Public Health* 392; Anderson and Baumberg, 'Alcohol in Europe: A Public Health Perspective' (Institute of Alcohol Studies 2006).

[247] Chenet et al., 'Alcohol policy in the Nordic countries: why competition law must have a public health dimension' (1997) 314(7088) *British Medicial Journal* 1142.

[248] Minimum pricing provisions for tobacco were ruled contrary to Council Directive 95/59/EC of 27 November 1995 on taxes other than turnover taxes which affect the consumption of manufactured tobacco [1995] OJ L291/40 in *Commission v France*, C-197/08, EU:C:2010:111; and *Commission v Ireland*, C-221/08, EU:C:2010:113. The CJEU held that the exemption from excise duties for consumers who buy alchohol in another Member State (relied upon by 'booze cruise' operators) does not apply if the consumer purchases the alcohol on the interet, see: *Joustra* EU:C:2006:733. Directive 2011/64/EU OJ 2011 L 176/24 on tobacco excise duty prohibits different excise duties for cigarettes based on differences in characteristics, or price, effectively prohibiting legislation seeking to set a minimum price for cigarettes, see *Yesmoke Tobacco* EU:C:2014:2263.

drinkers, who tend to buy cheap alcohol, across the socio-economic spectrum). But the Commission took the view that an increase in excise duty would provide equal public health protection, without hindering free movement. The Scottish Court of Session Outer House[249] held that minimum prices could be justified in principle, that a policy seeking to 'get people to build a healthy relationship with alcohol'[250] was within national discretion, that an approach based on excise duties would be insufficiently nuanced to achieve the desired aim without significant negative consequences, and hence the Act was a proportionate protection of an objective public interest, so not contrary to EU law. This is consistent with EU law, as discussed above.[251] But, on appeal,[252] the case was referred to the CJEU on the question of whether the Scottish policy is so justified.[253] In its reasoning, the Court of Session Inner House noted that nine Member States have expressed opposition to the Scottish proposals under the Technical Standards Directive 98/34/EC, and that those Member States may make submissions before the CJEU, whereas they cannot appear before the national court. The ruling thus represents an unusual recognition that the procedures by which national discretion is exercised in EU law do not always ensure that relevant interests are able to be taken into account.[254]

The general food safety and food labelling legislation discussed above also applies in principle to alcohol, as it falls within the definition of 'food'.[255] So, for instance, misleading claims about the properties of alcohol are prohibited in EU law.[256] Specific rules about alcohol labelling, now found in Regulation 1169/2011/EU, have been around since the mid-1980s.[257] These require that alcohol products sold in the EU must indicate their alcoholic strength by volume.[258] But alcohol is exempted from the ingredients and nutrition labelling obligations.[259] The European Commission justified the exemption by 'complexity of production methods', which is unconvincing; and 'political choice', which seems more likely.[260] The question of whether a list of

---

[249] *Scottish Whisky Association v Lord Advocate* [2013] CSOH 70.

[250] [2013] CSOH 70 at [53] (Lord Doherty).

[251] The Court of Session considered it not necessary to refer to the CJEU under Article 267 TFEU.

[252] *Scottish Whisky Association v Lord Advocate* [2014] CSIH 38.

[253] *The Scotch Whisky Association*, C-333/14 (case in progress).

[254] The 'pro-EU' stance may be explained, at least in part, by Scottish politics, and the strong notion of 'Scotland in Europe' which proliferates Scottish society.

[255] Regulation 178/20022002] OJ L31/1 (as amended), Article 1.

[256] The CJEU has held that EU law prohibits promoting wine on the basis of health claims: *Deutsches Weintor eG* EU:C:2012:526.

[257] Commission Directive 87/250/EEC of 15 April 1987 on the indication of alcoholic strength by volume in the labelling of alcoholic beverages for sale to the ultimate consumer [1987] OJ L113/57.

[258] Regulation 1169/2011, Article 9 (1) (k) requires 'beverages containing more than 1.2 % by volume of alcohol' to include on the label 'the actual alcoholic strength by volume', and see Annex XII.

[259] Regulation 1169/2011, Article 9 (1) (l).

[260] Cisneros Örnberg, 'Alcohol policy in the European Union' in Greer and Kurzer (eds), (Routledge 2013) above n 29.

ingredients and the nutrition labelling rules should apply to alcohol has been deferred, and the Commission is obliged to report on the matter by the end of 2014.[261] Until then, national rules requiring ingredients to be listed may continue.[262] No equivalent EU rules to those on tobacco labelling apply to alcohol. National rules are permitted, subject to Commission scrutiny for compliance with free movement law. A handful of Member States have mandatory labelling rules for alcohol.[263]

Otherwise, EU alcohol policy takes the form of soft law only. Following concerns about new products aimed at young people (alcopops), and changes to drinking patterns including an increase in (youth) binge drinking in southern Member States, a Council Recommendation on youth alcohol consumption was adopted in 2001.[264] The Commission's Road Safety Action programme recommends better enforcement of blood alcohol level controls, to reduce drink-driving accidents, and proposes the use of 'alcohol interlock devices' in certain sectors, such as transportation of school children.[265] The European Commission's alcohol strategy communication of 2006,[266] its Action Plan of 2014,[267] and a European Parliament Resolution from 2007[268] envisage classic soft law mechanisms – a committee bringing together national actors for discussion; data-gathering; and the 'European Alcohol and Health Forum, which brings together over 60 stakeholders, from the industry, health professions, and consumer and public health NGOs'. This is a far cry from the approach adopted for tobacco, or even for food.

The observations made above about the EU's tobacco law being based on a 'harm reduction'/ or 'nudging' approach, with a strong focus on young people, and a concomitant assumption that adults are competent to make their own assessments of risk of harm, apply even more strongly to EU alcohol law. There is no *legal* reason for the differences in approach between alcohol and tobacco – the EU is equally competent to act to reduce ill health and disability from alcohol

---

[261] Regulation 1169/2011, Recital 40, Article 16.   [262] Regulation 1169/2011, Article 41.

[263] Cisneros Örnberg above n 259, cites France, which has required warnings on risks of drinking during pregnancy since 2007, and Germany which requires labelling of alcopops.

[264] Council Recommendation 2001/458/EC of 5 June 2001 on the drinking of alcohol by young people, in particular children and adolescents [2001] OJ L 161/38. See: Cisneros Örnberg above n 259; Greer et al., above n 233.

[265] Commission, 'Towards a European road safety area: policy orientations on road safety 2011–2020' (Communication) COM (2010) 389 final. See also: European Parliament Resolution of 5 September 2007 on an European Union strategy to support Member States in reducing alcohol-related harm (2007/2005(INI)) [2008] OJ CE 187/160.

[266] Commission, 'An EU strategy to support member states in reducing alcohol related harm' (Communication) COM (2006) 625 final. The 2006 EU Alcohol Strategy officially came to an end in December 2012 and the European Commission has announced that it will not be updating it. The procedures in place will continue, with an interim action plan.

[267] Commission, 'Action Plan on Youth Drinking and on Heavy Episodic Drinking (Binge Drinking)' (Commission 2014).

[268] European Parliament Resolution of 5 September 2007 on an European Union strategy to support Member States in reducing alcohol-related harm (2007/2005(INI)) [2008] OJ CE 187/160.

as from tobacco, or indeed food. The difference lies in the politics. Indeed, it is possible that the EU's approach in alcohol policy will operate to slow the health agenda in tobacco and food regulation.

The health policy community is highly critical of the EU's (lack of) alcohol law. Jonathan Gornall, writing in 2014 in the *British Medical Journal*,[269] expresses disappointment that the European Commission has failed to push a new alcohol strategy. The aspects of alcohol policy that have been strengthened during 2006 to 2010 are protection of young people, measures against drink-driving, a focus on reducing problem drinking and drinking among certain populations such as pregnant women, and, of course, above all, research and education. These are areas where there is political consensus and, if not actual industry support, at least manageable damage to effects on the industry. More-effective anti-alcohol measures, such as taxation, minimum prices and restrictions on advertising were weakened.[270] Gornall cites industry lobbying as the explanation, giving evidence of close links between the centre-right European Parliament and key industry actors, using similar approaches to those used by the tobacco and food industries. Many of the actors are the same as those involved in the food industry. MEPs from the political centre-left note, for instance, that removal of the original Commission proposal for labelling of calories on the front of alcoholic drinks, and full nutritional labelling on the back, was in response to lobbying from the industry. Health policy advocates are particularly unhappy about the focus on young people and pregnant women. They would prefer a broad population approach.

Some academic commentators are a little less scathing.[271] While the EU could do more in the way of hard law,[272] there is scope for cautious optimism. Alcohol has moved from being framed as a matter for agriculture and free trade to being a social and health concern. Even soft mechanisms keep the relevant stakeholders in dialogue, which can be built on when the political climate is more favourable. The EU provides a place for Member States with shared interests in public health aspects of alcohol to press for their proposals. For instance, a coalition of the UK, Ireland, Baltic and Nordic countries are seeking a new strategy, including minimum pricing rules. The Scottish Health Secretary, Alex Neil, saw the reference to the CJEU of the Scottish minimum alcohol pricing case not as a disappointment, but as an opportunity, to have the

---

[269] Gornall, 'Europe under the influence' (2014) 348 *British Medical Journal* 1.

[270] See also: Bartlett and Garde, 'Time to Seize the (Red) Bull by the Horns: The European Union's Failure to Protect Children from Alcohol and Unhealthy Food Marketing' (2013) 38 *European Law Review* 498.

[271] Greer et al., above n 233; Cisneros Örnberg above n 259; Baumberg and Anderson, 'Health, Alcohol and EU Law: Understanding the impact of European single market law on alcohol policies' (2008) 18(4) *European Journal of Public Health* 392.

[272] For example, minimum excise tax rates on alcohol, set by the EU, last changed in 1993. There insufficient consensus among Member States to change them. Part of the problem is the zero rate on wine, which is particularly politically sensitive.

matter considered at EU level.[273] As we have seen, the CJEU does not always give priority to free trade over public health in free trade cases. However, the lack of a new strategic plan from 2012 may mean that even these potential benefits from an emerging EU alcohol law are receding.

Conclusions (tobacco, food, alcohol)

The examples discussed in this chapter, taken as a whole, tell a story of a gradual replacement of national public health decision-making with EU public health decision-making. The EU takes a particular approach to risk regulation in these contexts. Some aspects of EU tobacco, food and alcohol law are strongly influenced by the precautionary principle, in particular, food safety law, following the BSE/vCJD crisis. But, more often, the EU approach is not particularly precautionary, but is based rather on EU-level scientific advice about known risks to human health. The scope for Member States to justify population-specific regulation at a national level of tobacco, food or alcohol has been increasingly reduced over time. This is so where there is uncertainty about risks to population health. But it also applies where the evidence of risk to health is clear, but the evidence about the relative benefits of different legal or policy options is disputed (as in the case of plain cigarette packaging or minimum alcohol pricing).[274]

Again, as we have seen in previous chapters, the risk of harm to consumers, and to population health, is often seen as balanced against risk of harm to free trade within the internal market. When the demands of the internal market (for a level playing field of fair competition for industry) can be aligned with health objectives, the EU can have a very positive impact on population health.[275] But the converse is also true. Where industry interests pull against health interests, the logic of the single market dominates the political debate, and consequently the legal structures that are politically possible. This is why the health policy community often represents the EU's tobacco, food and alcohol law as a site of missed opportunity.

While the standard risk regulation model is the dominant theme in EU tobacco, food and alcohol law, it is by no means the only theme in play. Not only is the individual freedom to trade and freedom of consumers to choose products in a market at issue, but a human rights/civil liberties agenda forms an

---

[273]   Editorial, 'Alcohol Minimum Pricing Case Referred to European Court of Justice' (*Scottish Legal News*, 30 April 2014).

[274]   The Sheffield Alcohol Research Group offer a 'methodological framework for detailed evaluation of public health strategies for alcohol harm reduction to meet policy-makers needs', see: Brennan, Meier, Purshouse, Rafia, Meng, and Hill-McManus, 'Developing policy analytics for public health strategy and decisions – the Sheffield alcohol policy model framework' (Annals of Operational Research 2013); Booth, Meier et al., 'Independent Review of the Effects of Alcohol Pricing and Promotion' (SchHARR Project Report for the Department of Health 2008).

[275]   Greer et al., above n 233.

important backdrop to EU tobacco, food and alcohol law. Given the 'transversal' nature of this area of EU health law, it is not surprising that free trade remains an important theme. Internal market law is the formal legal basis for virtually all of EU law in these fields. Some commentators see internal market law in opposition to human rights agendas. For instance, Alemanno and Garde[276] argue implicitly that not only is the EU competent to develop lifestyle policy (food, tobacco and alcohol) as part of its internal market competence, but also that it should do so, even if that might be construed as breaching fundamental rights to free trade, autonomy and so on. What we have seen in this chapter is that, increasingly, freedom to trade and freedom to make lifestyle choices about tobacco, food and alcohol consumption are seen as mutually *consistent*. Consumer information is necessary to redress information asymmetries, but more stringent regulation is not justified, because competent adults should be permitted to make autonomous choices. Questions of the costs to health systems of such choices are barely present in EU tobacco, food or alcohol law, or the processes through which the law is developed, be they legislative or judicial. The ways in which such choices are influenced by industry advertising strategies are equally invisible. The strengthening focus on children and young people justifies 'paternalist' interventions, but only for those vulnerable groups, not for the population as a whole. The consequence for EU health law is an approach that is (in general) strong on labelling and information, but weaker on all other kinds of control (whether through taxation, restricted selling arrangements, restricted product requirements or even outright bans).

Conclusions (risk)

We conclude this chapter, and this section of the book, with some observations on the theme of risk in EU health law. How does risk play out in EU health law, and what are the implications, taking a systemic perspective? How do the various strong claims about risk as a theme of EU health law stack up, now that we have immersed ourselves in the legal detail?

The chapters have shown that the EU's law on medical devices, with which we began the book,[277] is an 'outlier' in terms of its relatively light touch approach to risk regulation. Indeed, EU medical devices law may well be moving in the direction of the other areas of law discussed here. EU health law requires a great deal more in terms of pre- and post-market controls of pharmaceuticals, including bio- or nano-technology products that fall within the pharmaceuticals regime. Products involving human blood, tissue and cells or human organs are also subject to significantly greater control at EU level. And EU health law imposes requirements on tobacco and food, and, to a lesser extent, alcohol,

---

[276] Alemanno and Garde, 'The Emergence of an EU Lifestyle Policy: The Case of Alcohol, Tobacco and Unhealthy Diets' (2013) 50(6) *Common Market Law Review* 1745.

[277] See further: chapter 1.

which go further than the rules applicable to ordinary consumer products. There is a discernible 'EU health law' approach to risk, which treats products marketed within health systems, and products that are particularly hazardous to (population) health, differently from other products.

What of the claim that EU health law is more focused on risk assessment (which is said to be 'science based'), than risk management (which is supposed to be democratically legitimated)? The EU's health law considered in these chapters does show that the EU tends to focus on expert calculations of risk, often inspired by a concern to promote a 'safe' internal market. Here the theme of risk to health is mediated through markets, in particular risks to the internal market of protectionist laws, but also risks to industry of the collapse of consumer or patient confidence. The Treaty itself suggests this is the case.[278] We saw it in the context of regulation of pharmaceuticals, for instance the adoption of the ICH standards, and packaging and labelling rules; in EU law on novel technologies; in the EU's human blood safety regime; in the evidence-led changes to EU tobacco law, for instance in changes to emissions statements; and above all in EU food safety law, developed in response to the threat to consumers and the internal market from BSE/vCJD, as well as by mutually reinforcing EU administrative capacity and CJEU decisions. EU food law represents the division between risk assessment and risk management *par excellence*, with its institutionally embedded separation of the EFSA and the European Commission and EU legislature. When the EFSA is asked to expand its role into more politically contentious decision-making, about nutrition profiling, it moves 'out of its comfort zone'. We also see the division in EU pharmaceutical law, with the EMA playing the risk assessment role.

But, equally, many examples in these chapters show that EU has concerned itself with the politics of risk, and not just its technical administration. Technocratically determined assessment of risk to consumers is balanced with the risk to the internal market and European economy more generally, should the EU fail to take political action. We see this strongly in the BSE/vCJD affair, but also, for instance, in the HIV-infected blood scandal, and in Poly Implant Prothèse. Indeed, it may also be suggested that EU risk regulation is driven by the political acceptability of risk, and that the EU uses risk to enhance its political legitimacy. Institutional arrangements, such as the establishment of the European Group on Ethics to advise on ethics of EU law on novel technologies involving human tissues and cells, support that proposition. It cannot be maintained, therefore, that EU health law is concerned only with regulation of risk in the technical, risk assessment sense. But a weaker version of that interpretation of EU health law can be sustained, taking into account the main focus of the EU's activities in the areas discussed in these chapters.

Does risk, in the sense of patient or consumer safety, coupled with risk to the internal market, dominate EU health law, to the exclusion of other important

---

[278] Article 114 TFEU.

themes, principally those of human rights? Again, the detailed analysis in these chapters has shown that this is too strong a claim, though a weaker version of it is defensible. We do see patient safety centre-stage in EU clinical trials law, which seeks above all to prevent harm to trial participants, who are often also patients. Speeding up the clinical trials process, as proposed by the new Clinical Trials Regulation, is justified as being about getting products to market, and new technologies to patients. Lower risk trials are treated differently by EU law in terms of time limits to approval and indemnity rules, as well as simplified procedures for low risk 'big data' trials. EU pharmaceuticals law, with its prior marketing authorization standards of efficacy, quality and safety, and even to some extent product liability law, is justified by the need to prevent another Thalidomide tragedy. EU law on pharmaceuticals marketing authorizations seeks to protect the interests of the pharmaceutical industry, and risks of harm to the European economy should the environment for innovation be insufficiently favourable, as well as being focused on risk of harm to patients. The availability of the centralized procedure removes significant bureaucratic regulatory burdens from pharmaceuticals manufacturers. The desire to support the EU's proprietary pharmaceutical industry, which must compete within global markets, was a significant driver in developing the procedure, which, with its fixed time frames for decision-making, allows speedier marketing approvals and therefore quicker return on investment in new pharmaceuticals.[279] Access to several Member States at once, made possible under the centralized and decentralized procedures, also reduces costs, as the detailed information needed to secure marketing authorization needs to be presented and assessed only once. Quicker procedures are also presented as advantageous to patients who may benefit from new products reaching the market. But EU pharmaceuticals law does not concern itself with relative therapeutic benefit, or (ab)uses of intellectual property rights which result in increased costs to national health (insurance) systems. EU medical devices law is based on a consumer-safety model, but also seeks to protect the internal market. It draws its inspiration from general EU product safety law. The recently proposed changes are driven by the desire to avoid another Poly Implant Prothèse scandal, with its harm to patients/consumers, but also to the competitiveness of the European medical devices industry. EU blood safety law responds to the HIV infected blood crisis of the 1990s, and human tissues and cells law, and organ safety law take their approach from blood safety law. EU food safety law is centrally concerned with risk to consumers and the internal market, from food as a disease vector, following the BSE/vCJD crisis. Recent rules aimed at combating obesity are, at least to some extent, about risks to consumers of over-consumption of unhealthy food. EU alcohol law began with risks to the internal market of protectionism; its (modest) development is justified by the special risks to young people of

---

[279] Abraham and Lewis, *Regulating Medicines in Europe: Competition, Expertise and Public Health* (Routledge 2000) 81.

harmful drinking. The harm-reducing/nudging approach of EU tobacco, food and alcohol law sits more easily within a theme of risk to consumers and/or risk to the internal market than a more protectionist approach, focused on population health and systemic costs to national health (insurance) systems. The failures of the EU to adopt 'traffic lights' food labelling rules, or plain cigarette packaging, provide good examples.

But, while risk is certainly an important, and maybe even a dominant, theme in these aspects of EU health law, this is not to the exclusion of others. We noted many examples where human rights, and biomedical ethical principles such as autonomy and non-paternalism, are also present in EU health law. These include the background to EU clinical trials law in the legacy of Nuremburg, now found in the consent provisions, as well as ethical approval procedures. Ethical considerations and human rights are strongly represented in EU law on human materials, through consent and non-commodification provisions. EU health law includes the elements of choice and patient/consumer autonomy implicit in the packaging and labelling rules for pharmaceuticals, tobacco, food and alcohol. Individual (adult) autonomy over lifestyle choices, and the right to private life, are strongly present in EU alcohol law, present in EU food law, and continue to feature in EU tobacco law. The human rights theme of *Kalkoft* involves a modified interpretation of consumer autonomy, and adds a dimension of the theme of non-discrimination or equality.

What of the claim that the EU is relatively, and increasingly, risk averse, to the detriment of market actors and the economy more generally?[280] Risk may be mediated through markets in EU law, but it is through a particular notion of the EU's internal market, which is constructed as particularly safe for patients/consumers, and particularly ethical.[281] There may well be something in this view. Clinical trials processes are quicker in the USA: the EU time limits rules have inbuilt flexibilities that can be exploited by the authorities where they seek more information; EU rules mean it takes longer to begin a clinical trial; the precautionary principle has stalled technological developments in the EU, such as xenotransplantation or growth hormones in beef; restrictions on pharmaceuticals advertising in the EU are much more stringent than in the USA. However, the precautionary principle is applied differently in different contexts, making generalized conclusions difficult to sustain. Blood safety law, for instance, is no more precautionary in the EU than elsewhere.

---

[280] Wiener, Rogers, Hammitt and Sand, *The Reality of Precaution: Comparing Risk Regulation in the US and Europe* (RFF Press 2010); Jasanoff (Princeton University Press 2007) above n 166; Vogel, *The Politics of Precaution* (Princeton University Press 2012).

[281] Bache et al., 'The Defining Features of the European Union's Approach to Regulating New Health Technologies', and Farrell, 'Legitimacy, and EU Regulation of Health Technologies' both in Flear, Farrell, Hervey and Murphy (eds), *European Law and New Health Technologies* (OUP 2013); Flear et al., call this 'the polar opposite of a "global Vegas", where more or less "anything goes": Flear et al., 'Conclusion: A European Law of New Health Technologies?' in Flear et al. (eds), (OUP 2013) above 405–8.

Another, diametrically opposite, argument in the existing literature is that the EU under-regulates for risks associated with health.[282] Perhaps the better version of this claim is that no state or regulatory order successfully protects against risks of harm to health when industry power is brought to bear on health systems. The power of the pharmaceuticals, medical devices, tobacco, food and alcohol industries is significant, relative to that of health professionals and regulatory authorities, including the EU. We have discussed many examples which support the contention that EU health law on risk is essentially driven by industry preferences. Some of the more obvious examples are in EU tobacco, food and alcohol law, where the focus on young people, rather than the whole population, or the avoidance of evidence-based policy options such as traffic light labelling or minimum tobacco prices, is said to be due to industry preferences and its effective lobbying of the EU legislature. The susceptibility of EU legislative and administrative institutions (such as the EMA or EFSA) to industry influence, described as 'regulatory capture', is well-documented, and we discussed some examples of it in the preceding chapters.

---

[282] The principal source of this set of claims is those who analyse regulation of the pharmaceutical industry. Their analysis is rarely explicitly focused on the EU *per se*, which is understandable given the global nature of the industry. See, for instance: Figert and Bell, 'Big Pharma and Big Medicine in the Global Environment' in Kleinman and Moore (eds), *Routledge Handbook of Science, Technology and Society* (Routledge 2014); Marqusee, *The Price of Experience: Writings on Living with Cancer* (OR Books 2014); advance extract available at: <https://www.opendemocracy.net/ournhs/mike-marqusee/held-hostage-by-big-pharma>; Dukes, Braithwaite, Moloney, *Pharmaceuticals, Corporate Crime and Public Health* (Edward Elgar 2014); Abraham and Davis, 'Science, Law, and the Medico-Industrial Complex in EU Pharmaceutical Regulation: The Deferiprone Controversy' in Flear et al. (eds), (OUP 2013) above n 280; Sahm, 'Of Mugs, Meals and More: the intricate relations between physicians and the medical industry' (2013) 16(2) *Medicine, Health Care and Philosophy* 265; Lemmens, 'Pharmaceutical Knowledge Governance: A Human Rights Perspective' *Perspective'* (2013) 41(1) *Journal of Law, Medicine and Ethics* 163; Womack, 'Ethical and Epistemic Issues in direct-to-consumer drug advertising: where is patient agency?' (2013) 16(2) *Medicine, Health Care and Philosophy* 275; Badcott and Sahm 'The dominance of Big Pharma: unhealthy relationships?' ' (2013) 16(2) *Medicine, Health Care and Philosophy* 245; Bell and Figert, 'Medicalisation and Pharmaceuticalisation at the Intersections: Looking Backward, Sideways and Forward' (2012) 75(5) *Social Science and Medicine* 775; Goldacre, *Bad Pharma: How Drug Companies Mislead Doctors and Harm Patients* (Fourth Estate 2012); Healy, *Pharmageddon* (University of California Press 2012); Jackson, *Law and the Regulation of Medicines* (Hart 2012); Welch, Schwartz, Woloshin, *Overdiagnosed: Making People Sick in Pursuit of Health* (Beacon Press 2011); Fox and Ward, 'Pharma in the Bedroom . . . and the Kitchen . . . The Pharmaceuticalisation of Daily Life' (2008) 30(6) *Sociology of Health and Illness* 856; Fisher, *Medical Research for Hire: The Political Economy of Pharmaceutical Clinical Trials* (Rutgers University Press 2008); Law, *Big Pharma: How the World's Biggest Drug Companies Control Illness* (Constable 2006); Moynihan and Cassels, *Selling Sickness: How the World's Biggest Pharmaceutical Companies are Turning Us All into Patients* (Nation Books 2006); Angell, *The Truth about Drug Companies: How They Deceive Us and What to Do About It* (Random House 2005); Abraham and Lewis (Routledge 2000) above n 278; Payer, *Disease-mongers: How Doctors, Drug Companies, and Insurers are Making You Feel Sick* (Wiley 1992); Braithwaite, *Corporate Crime in the Pharmaceutical Industry* (Routledge 1984).

But, of equal importance are the less obvious ways in which EU health law (and health law in other jurisdictions) is unable to constrain powerful global industries. The critique of industry dominance of pharmaceuticals lawmaking and administrative regulation is only part of the story. A more fundamental point is that the entire structure of the ways in which pharmaceuticals, medical devices, tobacco, food, and alcohol reach patients or consumers is skewed towards an industry-focused, rather than patient- or consumer-focused, perspective. Mike Marqusee describes the global pharmaceuticals industry as 'compromised at its scientific core'.[283] In order to pursue the return on capital investment, in the context of diminishing returns from health problems in the global North,[284] the industry seeks to create new markets to which it can sell its products. So the industry has become focused on selling diseases,[285] rather than serving the needs of health systems and their patients. Research follows the (created) market, and marketing authorization is secured, relying on EU law. But authorization of novel treatments (pharmaceuticals, devices) does not necessarily translate into patient access to those treatments. Those are questions of resource allocation, which are a matter for national health systems. The industry is able lawfully to promote its novel, in-patent products to health professionals, through a range of strategies including education and gift-giving; and to patients' organizations, which are often directly or indirectly industry supported. EU law on advertising of pharmaceuticals is toothless in its control over such practices. These promotional activities, through patient and professional pressure, in turn increase demands on national health systems to make new (and expensive) products available to patients. The 'market pathway' of EU pharmaceuticals regulation reinforces this behaviour. It permits, or even encourages, the 'ever-greening' of patents, and supports a range of other intellectual property rights such as licences, and supplementary protection certificates. Special EU rules for 'orphan medicines' increase pressure on national health systems to pay for highly expensive treatments for relatively rare diseases. Exclusive licensing and other intellectual property rights are justified as a return to investment for research and development. Yet pharmaceutical companies spend more on sales, marketing, lobbying, legal fees, acquisitions, and distribution of profits than on research. And, in any event, technological developments are collective, and cumulative, rather than attributable to any single global pharmaceutical company.[286] They include

---

[283] Marqusee (OR Books 2014) above n 281.
[284] The position is different in the global South, where significant health problems persist for quite different reasons. See the discussion in chapters 17 and 18.
[285] Jackson (Hart 2012) above n 281. The creation of markets for Viagra and statins are examples.
[286] Marqusee cites the oft-mentioned example of Jonas Salk, who refused to take out a patent for the polio vaccine he discovered in the early 1950s. His rhetorical question, "Could you patent the sun?", stands as a byword for this aspect of the critique of the pharmaceutical industry: Marqusee (OR Books 2014) above n 281.

investment from charitable institutions, such as hospitals and universities, as well as small and medium-sized contract research enterprises. In this perspective, EU pharmaceuticals law is about managing industry risks. It misses the opportunity to save or enhance the quality of lives.

The tobacco, food and alcohol industries operate in similar ways. The development of novel products, such as convenience food, or e-cigarettes, is preceded by market creating activities. These are often based on lifestyle or identity, rather than being overtly about consumption. Attempts through (EU) law to control industry's return to capital investment, by reducing consumption, are met with strategies that associate such regulatory moves with culturally unacceptable notions, such as infringement of liberty, autonomy or choice. The entire public debate is reframed, towards the individual consumer, who is barely aware that they are the subject of a carefully orchestrated industry strategy, and away from the costs both in human lives and quality of life; and to national health (insurance) systems.

One of the few potentially effective tools of (EU) law, once we see (EU) health law in this broader context, is that of transparency. The opening of industry activities to public and expert scrutiny offers some hope for increased understanding of the processes at work, and hence increased chance of impetus for change. EU health law has had limited success in promoting transparency. The Poly Implant Prothèse incident demonstrated an almost total lack of transparency over the activities of the 'notified bodies' which certify medical device safety in the EU. The proposed Medical Devices Regulation will require at least some information sharing. Ben Goldacre[287] and others cite the Nordic Cochrane Centre's attempts to gain access to clinical data on two weight-loss drugs. One was authorized by the EMA; the other was not. The EMA maintained that the data were protected by the commercial interests of the companies concerned. It also claimed that it could not remove individual patient data from the files. Eventually, the European Ombudsman intervened,[288] but only some three years and seven months after the original request, and after sustained efforts by the Centre.[289] In June 2014, the EMA announced a new policy, to come into effect from 1 January 2015.[290] EMA is to publish clinical trial data on any drug that receives marketing approval in the EU, for applications received after 1 January 2015, without the need for a formal freedom-of-information request. While this is an improvement in transparency, to begin with at least, the information

---

[287] Goldacre (Fourth Estate 2012) above n 281, 70–79.

[288] European Ombudsman, 'Decision of the European Ombudsman closing his inquiry into complaint 2560/2007/BEH against the European Medicines Agency' (*European Ombudsman*, 24 November 2010).

[289] Gøtzsche and Jørgensen, 'Opening Up Data at the European Medicines Agency' (2011) 342 *British Medical Journal* p. d2686.

[290] EMA (European Medicines Agency), 'European Medicines Agency agrees policy on publication of clinical trial data with more user-friendly amendments' (*EMA*, 12 June 2014); Abbott, 'European Medicines Agency set to publish clinical-trial reports' (*Nature*, 13 June 2014).

(at least the raw data on individual patients) will not be made available in a downloadable form, which limit the practical use to which the information can be put.[291] Furthermore, EU law is still far from making *all* clinical trials data transparent, including the data for unsuccessful trials.

There is undoubtedly something to be said for the argument that (EU) health law is ineffective at promoting patient or consumer interests, and *de facto* supports the continued operation of industries that are more focused on risk to capital investment than patients or consumers. But a more nuanced conclusion recognizes that, perhaps against the odds, EU law has achieved some benefits to health. Transparency rules on marketing authorizations have been tightened, so that details of previous marketing authorization refusals must now be included. Traditional herbal medicines are now within the scope of EU pharmaceuticals law. Tobacco products must have graphic warnings on their packaging, and it is almost impossible to lawfully advertise tobacco in the EU. E-cigarettes are no longer merely 'ordinary' consumer products. Instances of food-borne disease have decreased. All the areas discussed in these chapters could equally be understood as only about internal market law, research and development law, agriculture law and so on. This more nuanced conclusion can only be reached by drawing on the themes of 'EU health law'.

[291] Editiorial, 'European Medicines Agency rejects Ombudsman's concerns on public access to clinical trial data' (*Out-Law*, 20 May 2014).

Part IV
EU external health law

Introduction

In this part of the book, we look outward. We turn from our focus on the EU's internal health law to the global context. Health can be seen as a global opportunity for the EU; it can also be seen as a global challenge. It is implicit in discussions of aspects of the EU's external health law[1] that the EU as a global trade organization is inherently enabled to develop its health law in certain directions, for instance, to pursue trade liberalization and protect property rights. It is also implied that it is inherently impeded from doing so in others, for instance, to pursue equality and justice. We have already touched on some of those enablers and opportunities; limitations and challenges. Much of the law discussed in chapters 9–15 is underpinned by the idea that health contributes to economic growth. Developing the EU's health sector means its potential to compete in global markets is enhanced. The EU seeks to adopt laws which support industrial development. Relevant industries include those that, at least apparently, develop products and services to support national health systems, principally the pharmaceuticals and medical devices sector, but also entities securing human blood, tissue and cells, and organs for European patients. Industries in sectors such as tobacco, food and alcohol, where the products raise particular public health concerns, also contribute to the development of the EU's economy, through global trade. Securing global competitiveness for European industries represents both a challenge and an opportunity for EU health law.

Equally, the law discussed in chapters 4–8 raises issues of global opportunity and challenge for EU health law. Migrant patients do not stop at the borders of the EU. The transnational trade in health services is a significant global business. The EU may attract private consumers of health care services from anywhere in the world, particularly to its centres of medical specialism. There may be consequences for capacities to provide health care for nationals, if health

---

[1] We are not aware of literature that *explicitly* engages with the 'big picture' of EU external health law, although there is, of course, some literature on the EU's contribution to all of the elements of EU health external law that we discuss here. See further chapter 16.

professionals are drawn to lucrative global professional practice and away from serving their home national health (insurance) system.[2] Patients from the EU may seek health care anywhere in the world, as private consumers. If things go wrong, their consumer rights may, or may not, be protected through classical models of private international law, through which liabilities for tortious harm, for instance, involving medical negligence, are determined. But the obligations of solidarity, on which all EU national health (insurance) systems are based, mean that the home state will step in to provide any further aftercare or treatment necessary, once the migrant patient returns home. The ready availability of health products from all over the world via the internet, and the absence of adequate measures for checking quality, safety and efficacy, or for scrutinizing or otherwise regulating advertisement, have raised concerns about harmful, falsified and counterfeit medicines. More fundamentally, internet-based consumption of health technologies has contributed to the consumerization of health care, and to changing relationships between health professionals and their patients. These chapters explore the extent to which some of these strong claims about EU external health law are sustainable.

EU health law is developed, adopted and applied within the broader context of global health law. As Michael Freeman points out,[3] it is unclear when the term 'global health law' first emerged. Its scope remains disputed.[4] But his review of the literature suggests that it may have emerged alongside the general notion of 'globalization'.[5] A more interconnected world, with faster and more frequent physical and virtual[6] communications, raises novel threats from disease.[7] Lawrence Gostin defines global health law as:

---

[2] See: Jarman, 'Healthcare, borders and boundaries: Crossborder health markets and the entrepreneurial state' (2014) 33(1) *Policy and Society* 1; Chen and Flood, 'Medical Tourism's Impact on Health Care Equity and Access in Low-and Middle-Income Countries: Making the Case for Regulation' (2013) 41(1) *Journal of Law, Medicine and Ethics* 286; Cohen, *Patients with Passports: Medical Tourism, Law, and Ethics* (OUP 2015); Eyal and Bärnighausen, 'Conditioning Medical Scholarships On Long, Future Service: A Defense' in Cohen (ed), *The Globalisation of Healthcare: Legal and Ethical Issues* (OUP 2013); Taylor and Dhillon, 'A Global Legal Architecture To Address The Challenges Of International Health Worker Migration' in Cohen (ed), (OUP 2013).

[3] Freeman, 'Global Health: An Introduction' in Freeman, Hawkes, Bennett (eds), *Law and Global Health: Current Legal Issues Volume 16* (OUP 2014); see also: Flood and Lemmens, 'Global Health Challenges and the Role of Law' (2013) 41(1) *Journal of Law, Medicine and Ethics* 9; Cohen (2013) above n 2.

[4] See also: Gostin, *Global Health Law* (Harvard University Press 2014).

[5] See also: Harrington, 'Law, globalisation and the NHS' (2007) 31(2) *Capital and Class* 81; Fidler, 'Global Health Jurisprudence: A Time of Reckoning' (2008) 96(2) *Georgetown Law Journal* 393; Ruger, 'Normative Foundations of Global Health Law' (2008) 96(2) *Georgetown Law Journal* 423; Gostin and Taylor, 'Global Health Law: A Definition and Grand Challenges' (2008) 1(1) *Public Health Ethics* 53.

[6] Although of course disease *per se* cannot be communicated virtually, increased physical movement is supported by virtual communication of information.

[7] Garrett, *The Coming Plague: Newly Emerging Diseases in a World Out of Balance* (Penguin 1995); WHO, 'The world health report 1996 - Fighting disease, fostering development' (WHO 1996).

the study and practice of international law – both hard law (e.g., treaties that bind states) and soft instruments (e.g., codes of practice negotiated by states) – that shapes norms, processes and institutions to attain the highest possible standards of physical and mental health for the world's populations.[8]

It follows that 'global health law' includes responses to communicable diseases, such as SARS, H5N1 and H1N1 influenza, which transcend national and regional borders, and may move around the globe as quickly as aviation technology allows. The increased connectedness of the world and the availability of cheap modes of travel have also contributed to global health tourism. This has a legal dimension, involving protection of the rights of patients in transnational situations.[9]

There is also a long-standing literature on global health rights, seen through the prism of global human rights law.[10] For instance, Gostin sees global health law as encompassing 'the concept of health as a fundamental human rights entitlement'.[11] This entitlement includes international law's right to health:[12] 'the right to the highest attainable standard of physical and mental health'. The minimum core of the 'right to health' covers 'maternal and child care, including family planning; immunization against the major infectious diseases; appropriate treatment of common diseases and injuries; and provision of essential drugs', as well as an 'adequate supply of safe water and basic sanitation; and freedom from serious environmental health threats'.[13] But, equally importantly, 'embedded within a large network of human rights norms, instruments and processes is a growing and expansive field which intersects with health'.[14] Global health law thus involves many legal regimes outside of the health sector. There is a link between the vulnerability of certain individuals or groups to disease, disability and premature death, and the extent to which the general

---

[8] Gostin (2014) above n 4, 59.   [9] See: Cohen (2015) above n 2.

[10] Pogge, 'Human Rights and Global Health: A Research Program' (2005) 36(1-2).
      Metaphilosophy 182; Harrington and Stuttaford (eds), *Global Health and Human Rights: Legal
      and Philosophical Perspectives* (Routledge 2010); Gostin (Harvard University Press 2014) above
      n 4; Eleftheriadis, 'Global Rights and the Sanctity of Life' in Cohen (ed), (OUP 2013);
      Stuttaford, Harrington and Lewando-Hundt, 'Sites for health rights: Local, national, regional
      and global' (2012) 74(1) *Social Science and Medicine* 1; London and Schneider, 'Globalization
      and health inequalities: Can a human rights paradigm create space for civil society action?'
      (2012) 74 (1) *Social Science and Medicine* 6; Mann, Gostin, Gruskin, Brennan, Lazzarini and
      Fineberg, 'Health and Human Rights' (1994) 1(1) *Journal of Health and Human Rights* 6.

[11] Gostin (2014) above n 4, 60.

[12] UN International Covenant on Social, Economic and Cultural Rights, 1966, Article 12.

[13] Toebes, 'The Right to Health', in Eide, Krause and Rosas, (eds), *Economic, Cultural and Social
      Rights* (2nd edn, Martinus Nijhoff Publishers 2001); Toebes, *The Right to Health as a Human
      Right in International Law* (Intersentia 1999. The right to health interacts with other human
      rights, such as the right to life, to physical integrity and privacy, to education and information
      and to housing, food and work. See: Toebes (Intersentia 1999) 243-289, and table at 289.

[14] Gostin (2014) above n 4, 60.

human rights and dignity of those individuals are recognized, respected and protected.[15]

The right to health in international law includes the right to access health services, and essential medicines. Similarly, the literature on access to essential medicines is in part based on human rights, but is also strongly grounded in an ethic of justice. Justice is the basis for many debates on global health.[16] Norman Daniels, for instance, adopting a Rawlsian perspective and drawing on Sen's capability approach, argues that health has a particular moral value, and that global health inequalities are fundamentally unjust.[17] Michael Sandel's work on the moral limits of markets is also concerned with global health questions, such as blood supply and surrogacy.[18] Jennifer Prah Ruger's work on global health institutions and a 'Global Health Constitution' is grounded in theories of justice.[19] John Coggan has suggested the ethical concept of stewardship and the human right to health as bases for global health law.[20] Mark Flear and others have explored the idea of 'super-stewardship' (that is, stewardship in contexts beyond the nation state) in the context of public health.[21] There is a significant literature, largely focused on access to anti-retroviral pharmaceuticals, which are used in the treatment of HIV/AIDS, on how global intellectual property law impedes access to in-patent medicines.[22] More fundamentally, as we already noted in chapters 12, 13 and the conclusions to chapter 15, the global pharmaceutical industry's main focus is on creating novel, or at least patentable, products for the global North. But poor health is more prevalent in the global South.[23] Global health law interfaces here with ethics, and concerns with justice and inequalities

---

[15] Mann, et al., above n 10, 7, cite the example of women in East Africa who are vulnerable to HIV infection: 'women's vulnerability to HIV is now recognised to be integrally connected with discrimination and unequal rights, involving property, marriage, divorce and inheritance'.

[16] See: e.g. Gostin (2014) above n 4, chapter 14: 'Imagining Global Health with Justice'; Baxi, 'The Place of the Human Right to Health and Context Approach to Global Justice' in Harrington and Stuttaford, above n 10.

[17] Daniels, *Just Health: Meeting Health Needs Fairly* (CUP 2008).

[18] Sandel, *What Money Can't Buy: The Moral Limits of Markets* (Allen Lane 2012).

[19] Ruger, *Health and Social Justice* (OUP 2010); see also: Gostin (2014) above n 10, who calls for a global health convention.

[20] Coggon, 'Global Health, Law, and Ethics: Fragmented Sovereignty and the Limits of Universal Theory' in Freeman, Hawkes and Bennett, above n 3.

[21] See: Flear (ed), 'Special Issue: A symposium with Professor Roger Brownsword: super-stewardship in the context of public health' (2011) 62(5) *Northern Ireland Legal Quarterly* 569.

[22] See the discussion in: Aginam, Harrington and Yu (eds), *The Global Governance of AIDS: Intellectual Property and Access to Essential Medicines* (Edward Elgar 2012); Jackson, *Law and the Regulation of Medicines* (Hart 2012) 193-8; Harrington, 'Access to Essential Medicines in Kenya: Intellectual Property, Anti-Counterfeiting, and the Right to Health' in Freeman, Hawkes and Bennett, above n 3.

[23] Commonly known as the '10/90 gap' – 'health problems which affect 90 per cent of the world's population attract only 10 per cent of the global funding for health research', Jackson (Hart 2012) above n 22, 191; see: Global Forum for Health Research, *The 10/90 Gap in Health Research* (GCFR 1999).

on transnational scales.[24] Gostin calls for movement towards an institutional response – a framework global health convention with the message of 'health for all, justice for all' – in order to empower communities to claim the right to health, at both domestic and international levels.[25]

And global health law also includes questions about how, given the massive scale of global inequalities that arise from differences in economic development and the legacies of colonialism, we effectively regulate global markets in human blood, tissues and organs, which we noted in chapter 14. Equally, given the increased transnational 'outsourcing' of clinical trials, the protection of potentially vulnerable participants/patients in trials from which they can gain no conceivable long-term benefit is also a concern of global health law.[26] Finally, we note that the scope of global health law is increasing: it could also include, for instance, tobacco control, obesity,[27] terrorism, global warming and violence against women.[28] In this section of the book, we examine how EU law engages with some of these aspects of health as a global concern.

Health as a global concern

Health tourism has been around in Europe for centuries, with numerous spa towns providing facilities for patients to 'take the waters'.[29] But, in terms of direct medical interventions, health care has long been 'peculiarly and tenaciously local in its character'.[30] For sure, a few patients have always travelled to centres of major medical excellence (in the Western world, such as London's Harley Street[31]) from smaller and less developed countries. Now, with the rise of a global marketplace in health care, and a globalizing health services industry, a new phenomenon is fast replacing this old model of international medical travel: medical tourism.[32] The more common treatments sought

---

[24] Daniels, above n 17; Buse, Gostin, Friedman, 'Pathways towards a Framework Convention on Global Health: Political Mobilization for the Human Right to Health' in Freeman, Hawkes, Bennett, above n 3, 37-39; Goldberg, 'Global Health Care is not Global Health: Populations, Inequities, and Law as a Social Determinant of Health' in Cohen (ed), *The Globalization of Health Care: Legal and Ethical Issues* (OUP 2013).

[25] Gostin (2014) above n 4, 439.

[26] Brownsword, 'The Ancillary-Care Responsibilities of Researchers: Reasonable But Not Great Expectations' in Harrington and Stuttaford, above n 10; Jackson, above n 22.

[27] See: WHO, 'Global Action Plan for the Prevention and Control of Non-Communicable Diseases 2013-2020' (WHO 2013).

[28] Freeman, 'Global Health: An Introduction' in Freeman, Hawkes, Bennett, above n 3, 9.

[29] See: e.g. Bruce, 'Sickness, Health Tourism and the Ever Present Threat of Death: Nineteenth Century Spas and Seasonal Travel' in Botterill, Pennings and Mainil (eds), *Medical Tourism and Transnational Healthcare* (Palgrave Macmillan 2013).

[30] Jost, 'Comparative and International Health Law' (2004) 14(1) *Health Matrix* 141, 141.

[31] Cohen (2015) above n 2.

[32] Cohen (OUP 2015) above n 2; Cohen, 'Medical Tourism and Global Justice' in Cohen (2013) above n 2; Cortez, 'Patients Without Borders: The Emerging Global Market for Patients and the Evolution of Modern Health Care' (2008) 83(1) *Indiana Law Journal* 71; Horowitz,

by such medical tourists include cosmetic surgery, dental treatment, cardiac surgery, orthopaedic surgery, bariatic surgery,[33] human reproduction,[34] gender reassignment, organ and tissue transplantation, including stem cell therapy, and a wide range of diagnostic studies.[35] In general,[36] the destinations of such medical tourists are mainly developing countries,[37] and the main host region globally for medical tourism is Asia.[38] Patients travel for many reasons: to access treatments deemed unsafe, too experimental, immoral or unacceptable by their home state,[39] to access treatments illegal in both home and destination state, where the destination state is more lax in its enforcement of the law,[40] to avoid

Rosensweig and Jones, 'Medical Tourism: Globalization of the Healthcare Marketplace' (2007) 9(4) *Medscape General Medicine* 33.

[33] Such as gastric banding, body contouring subsequent to significant weight loss.

[34] Including commercial surrogacy: in May 2012, the Sunday Telegraph reported a rise in the use of commercial surrogacy by English couples in India. In New Delhi, in the case of one surrogacy clinic run by Dr Gour (an English educated doctor) Indian women carry babies as surrogates for fees of up to 6,000- a sum which is five times the national average salary. The clinic charges individuals and commissioning couples some 25k. Dr Gour was reported as saying "My hospital is an international hub and babies are born through our surrogacy arrangements almost on a daily basis." Over the last year many of the 300 births in the clinic are for children for English commissioning parents, all middle class. In English law commercial surrogacy agreements are criminalized, although the commissioning couple and surrogate are not subject to criminal penalties. Bhatia, 'They queue to donate their eggs and rent out their wombs. One payment can transform their lives' *The Telegraph* (London, 26th May 2012).

[35] Horowitz, Rosensweig and Jones, above n 32, Table 2; Flood and Lemmens, above n 3.

[36] Cohen (2015) above n 2, points to several important exceptions to this rule, including the flow of wealthy patients in developing (low or middle income) countries accessing health care that is not available at home in a developed country.

[37] Cohen (2015) above n 2, discusses Jordan, India, Tunisia, Cuba, Barbados, Panama, Costa Rica, Guatemala, Mexico, Thailand, Singapore, and Malaysia, and notes the strong regional basis of the mobility concerned; Cortez, above n 32, 90-95 states that the most notable destinations are Chile, Cuba, India, Jordan, Malaysia, Singapore, Thailand, the UK, USA. Others include China, South Africa, Mexico and Turkey; Horowitz notes China, India, Israel, Jordan, Malaysia, Singapore, South Korea, Philippines, Taiwan, Turkey, United Arab Emirates, Argentina, Brazil, Canada, Columbia, Costa Rica, Ecuador, Mexico, USA, several European states, including Czech Republic, Hungary, Romania, South Africa, Tunisia, Australia, Barbados, Cuba, Jamaica. Connell, 'Medical tourism: Sea, sun, sand and . . . . Surgery' (2006) 27 *Tourism Management* 1093, 1095 notes India, Singapore, Thailand, Eastern Europe (particularly for dental treatments), Jordan, South Africa, Cuba.

[38] Connell, above n 37, 1099.

[39] See: Mutcherson, 'Open Fertility Borders: Defending Access To Cross Border Fertility Care In The United States' in Cohen (2013) above n 2; Biggs and Jones, 'Tourism: A Matter Of Life And Death In The United Kingdom' in Cohen (2013) above n 2 Levine and Wolf, 'The Roles And Responsibilities Of Physicians In Patients' Decisions About Unproven Stem Cell Therapies' in Cohen (2013) above n 2. For example over many years individuals travelled to Italy to seek IVF treatment unavailable to them in other countries until the regulatory regimes in that jurisdiction tightened, see: Fenton, 'Catholic Doctrine versus reproductive rights: the new Italian law on assisted reproduction' (2006) 14(1) *Medical Law Review* 73. A more recent phenomenon is 'stem cell tourism' – transnational travel of patients seeking highly experimental, and highly expensive, stem cell 'treatments'. See: Master, Zarzeczny, Rachul and Caulfield, 'What's Missing? Discussing Stem Cell Translational Research in Educational Information on Stem Cell "Tourism"' (2013) 41(1) *Journal of Law Medicine and Ethics* 254.

[40] Cohen (2015) above n 2.

domestic infrastructure limitations, to access affordable treatments, or because of long waiting times at home.[41]

Such changes on the demand side for medical tourism are matched by dramatic changes on the supply side. Some developing countries have significantly improved the quality of care they offer.[42] Here it is important to distinguish between 'least developed countries', and countries with 'transitional economies', in particular the BRICS countries.[43] The expansion of the health sector in many transitional economies makes new resources available, as health is seen as an investment opportunity rather than a public good. Health insurance is becoming more portable. New relationships between private providers, including outsourcing, agencies, mergers and other contractual arrangements[44] are springing up in the health sector, with some large global players operating across borders.[45] Specialist medical tourism brokers offer their services to liaise with overseas hospitals and make travel arrangements. Above all, the internet allows providers to market their services (and this marketing is becoming increasingly adept), and would-be patients to access information about those services.

Medical tourism is only one aspect of the increasingly globalized dimension of health law. Globalization of health care can also be seen in responses to cross-border disease transmission. The ineffectiveness of regulation on the basis of a single jurisdiction or even region has long been recognized in the context of communicable diseases.[46] While it seemed that serious communicable diseases had been vanquished (at least for the global North) in the 1950s and 60s, new

---

[41] *Ibid.*

[42] The World Bank found 'significant evidence that the upper end of the quality distribution of both professionals and hospitals in several advanced developing countries lies well above the minimum acceptable standards in industrial countries': Mattoo and Rathindran, 'Does Health Insurance Impede Trade in Health Care Services?' (2005) World Bank Policy Research Working Paper No. 3667, 13.

[43] Brazil, Russia, India, China and South Africa. See: Ruger and Ng, 'Emerging and Transitioning Countries' Role in Global Health: Health Law and Bioethics: Pressing Issues and Changing Times' (2010) 3(2) *Saint Louis University Journal of Health Law & Policy* 253.

[44] Connell, above n 37, 1099 cites the example of the British insurance company BUPA signing an agreement with a hospital in Kolkata (Calcutta).

[45] See examples of international hospital chains, cited in: Cortez, above n 32, 88: 'Two Singapore-based companies, the Parkway Group and the Raffles Medical Group, have acquired hospitals and established joint ventures with local health care providers in Malaysia, India, Sri Lanka, and the United Kingdom. The Parkway Group's international hospital chain, Gleneagles International, is now one of the largest health care organizations in Asia. The Raffles Medical Group has agreed to form fifty-fifty joint ventures with Kaiser Permanente throughout Asia. The Apollo Hospitals Group in India has plans to build hospitals in Sri Lanka, Nepal, and Malaysia. And California-based Adventist Health International runs a network of more than 500 Christian not-for-profit hospitals and clinics, led by Penang Adventist Hospital in Malaysia, a major medical tourist destination.'

[46] See the special issue of: Greer (ed) *Journal of Health Politics, Policy and Law* (2012) 37: Greer, 'Bacteria Without Borders: The European Governance of Infectious Diseases' (2012) 37(6) *Jounral of Health Politics, Policy and Law* 887; and Greer, 'Catch me if you can: Communicable Disease Control', in Greer and Kurzer (eds), *European Union Health Policies* (Routledge 2013). See discussion below.

threats to health from HIV/AIDS, SARS, H5N1 and H1N1 influenza continue into the present day.[47] An increasingly mobile world, with cheaper and more frequent air travel, and a global food industry (as food is an important disease vector[48]), makes communicable disease prevention and control an important aspect of health as a global concern.

Moving beyond communicable disease, public health threats from products that have important health implications, in particular food, alcohol and tobacco, are increasingly the subject of international law. Here, health protection and promotion must take place within the context of powerful and entrenched global trade rules for goods, now governed by the World Trade Organization (WTO), and the economic backdrop of the International Monetary Fund (IMF) and the World Bank.[49] The historical background to these institutions lies in the post-Second World War Bretton Woods agreements, and the General Agreement on Tariffs and Trade (GATT) with its intention to reduce tariffs on trade in goods between participating countries. The WTO seeks to remove barriers to trade, whether these are tariff barriers, legislative barriers or public subsidies. Some limitations are permissible if these concern measures 'necessary to protect human, animal or plant life or health'.[50] Nonetheless, a state may be required to show that such measures are the least restrictive available. The WTO also requires 'harmonization', reducing variations in nations' regulatory standards for goods. While such harmonization may drive up standards in countries where standards were previously poor, there are concerns that this may also operate to drive standards down to the lowest common denominator.

International regulation of particular goods which are used within health care systems is a further important part of the global context of health. The interface with global economic policy is evident in the law on products such as pharmaceuticals or medical devices. International ethical concerns about global trade in such goods, in particular, access to essential medicines, have attracted attention from NGOs and international organizations, and have been framed as both development policies and human rights issues.[51] Practices such as the 'evergreening' of patents (for instance, through changing the delivery mechanism or presentation of a pharmaceutical, though not its underlying pharmacological properties, and securing a new patent in that new product) have been particularly criticized, as they delay the practical access of patients in

---

[47] See: Gostin (2014) above n 4, at chapter 10: 'Getting to Zero: Scientific Innovation, Social Mobalisation and Human Rights in the AIDS Pandemic'; and chapter 12: 'Pandemic Influenza: A Case Study on Global Health Security'.

[48] For example, salmonella in eggs and pork; e-coli in beef; BSE in beef; campylobacter in poultry; foot and mouth disease.

[49] See also: Gostin (2014) above n 4, at chapter 9: 'Global Health, International Trade and Intellectual Property: Towards a Fair Deal for the Global South'.

[50] GATT XX. See: e.g., Scott, The WTO Agreement on Sanitary and Phytosanitary Measures: A Commentary (OUP 2007); Button, The Power to Protect: Trade, Health and Uncertainty in the WTO (Hart 2004).

[51] See further: chapter 17.

the global South to cheaper generic versions of pharmaceuticals, with no clear benefit to public health.[52] These practices are supported by international trade law. Concerns about the safety of new health technologies have led to efforts to agree international rules about clinical trials. There are also important issues about the ethics of such trials. India, for instance, is a prime site for clinical trials,[53] but lacks a comprehensive ethical review system.[54] More fundamentally, the global clinical trials industry is said to adopt morally indefensible exploitative strategies, in terms of the standard of care offered to the control group in a randomized controlled trial; the question of whether 'informed consent' has really been secured;[55] and whether there is any possibility of the community from which trial participants are drawn benefiting from the research.[56] Peter Lurie and Sidney Wolfe drew attention to the phenomenon in their discussion of trials of treatments for mother-to-baby HIV infection. The control group in the trials, which took place in nine developing countries, were not given the best treatment already available, which is standard practice in trials in the global North.[57] Given that the treatments on trial were in-patent, there was no prospect of those in the other group continuing to benefit from the treatments after the trial was over – an infringement of the concept of 'fair benefits'. On the other hand, the participants were not actively disadvantaged by involvement in the trial.[58] International trade law has done little to tackle these ethical concerns. Even where it does attempt to do so, pharmaceutical companies are themselves important actors in global health law, extending their influence through international organizations, such as the International Conference on Harmonisation of Technical Requirements for Registration of Pharmaceuticals for Human Use (ICH).

The WTO also covers trade in services. The World Bank has considered the opportunities and challenges arising from the creation of global health service

---

[52] Jackson, above n 22, 192, 81-82.

[53] This is because of its 'large treatment naïve population, who are increasingly likely to suffer from non-communicable diseases, like diabetes and cancer', Jackson, above n 22, 64.

[54] Jackson, above n 22, 64, citing Cekola, 'Outsourcing Drug Investigations to India: A Comment on US, India and International Regulation of Clinical Trials in Cross-Border Pharmaceutical Research' (2007) 28 *North Western Journal of International Law and Business* 125; and Bhat and Hegde, 'Ethical international research on human subjects research in the absence of local institutional review boards' (2006) 32(9) *Journal of Medical Ethics* 535.

[55] See: Nuffield Council on Bioethics, 'The Ethics of Research Related to Healthcare in Developing Countries' (Nuffield Council on Bioethics 2002).

[56] Jackson, above n 22, 65-71.

[57] Lurie and Wolf, 'Unethical Trials of Interventions to Reduce Perinatal Transmission of the Human Immunodeficiency Virus in Developing Countries' (1997) 337(12) *New England Journal of Medicine* 853. But see: Lie et al., 'The Standard of Care Debate: The Declaration of Helsinki Versus the International Consensus Opinion' (2004) 30(2) *Journal of Medical Ethics* 190.

[58] They were 'no worse off than they would have been if they had not enrolled in the trial', Jackson above n 22, 67.

markets.[59] It is difficult to gain a picture of global trade in health services, as data are simply unavailable.[60] But health care is increasingly conceptualized as a contributor to public finances, and an opportunity for national economies to strengthen their position on global markets. This is in stark contrast to the notion of health care as an exclusively national affair, supported by national mechanisms of solidarity (tax, social insurance) and a major drain on public finance. All four different 'modes of supply' in the WTO's General Agreement on Trade in Services (GATS) are engaged by health services: cross-border service provision where only the service itself moves (telemedicine, outsourced medical transcription); movement of service recipients (medical tourism, discussed above); commercial presence in the host state (foreign companies and foreign direct investment providing health services); and movement of human service providers/professionals (movement of medical professionals across borders to provide services), although not all sectors of the market are covered by GATS.[61] In particular, GATS does not cover 'services supplied in the exercise of governmental authority', defined as 'any service which is supplied neither on a commercial basis, nor in competition with one or more service suppliers'.[62] Thus, health services provided by a public (regional or national) monopoly free at the point of receipt and financed through taxation would not fall within GATS.[63] In terms of the movement of service providers, several international organizations[64] are seeking to set global standards on education of medical professionals.[65] Their

---

[59] Blouin, Drager and Smith, *International Trade in Health Services and the GATS: Current Issues and Debates* (World Bank 2005); Jarman, 'Trade in Services and the Public's Health: A Fortress Europe for Health' in Greer and Kurzer (eds), (Routledge 2013) above n 46.

[60] Krajewski, 'Patient Mobility Beyond Calais: Health Services Under WTO Law' in Van de Gronden et al. (eds), *Health Care and EU Law* (Springer 2011).

[61] Jarman, 'Trade in Services and the Public's Health: A 'Fortress Europe' for Health?' in Greer and Kurzer (eds), (Routledge 2013) above n 46; Krajewski, 'Commodifying and Embedding Services of General Interests in Transnational Contexts: The Example of Healthcare Liberalisation in the EU and the WTO' in C Joerges and J Falke (eds), *Karl Polanyi, Globalisation and the Potential of Law in Transnational Markets* (Hart 2011); Chanda, 'India-EU Relations in Health Services: Prospects and Challenges' (2011) 7 *Globalization and Health* 1.

[62] Article I:3(c), GATS.   [63] Krajewski, (2011) above n 61.

[64] Frenk, Lincoln, Zulfiqar, Cohen, Crisp, Evans, et. al., 'Health Professionals for a New Century: Transforming Education to Strengthen Health Systems in an Interdependent World' (2010) 376(9756) *The Lancet* 1923, mention the WHO, the UN Educational, Scientific and Cultural Organization, the WTO, as well as the International Institute of Medical Education and the World Federation of Medical Education; see also: The Lancet, Education of Health Professionals for the 21st Century: A Global Independent Commission, 'Health Professionals For a New Century: Transforming education to strengthen health systems in an interdependent world' (The Lancet 2010). The Commission on Education of Health Professionals for the 21st Century was launched in January 2010 with the aim of landscaping the field, identifying gaps and opportunities, and offering recommendations for reform a century after the landmark Flexner Report of 1910. This independent initiative was led by co-chairs Julio Frenk and Lincoln Chen working with a diverse group of 20 Commissioners from around the world: Sponsored by the Bill and Melinda Gates Foundation, the Rockefeller Foundation, and the China Medical Board, the co-chairs supervised the research and management teams operating out of the China Medical Board and the Harvard School of Public Health.

[65] See: Cortez, above n 32, 84: 'For example … the International Society for Quality in Health Care created a program to align health care standards and accreditation processes

underlying aims range from promoting 'social accountability' of medical education through to streamlining labour regulation and reducing barriers to trade in medical professional services.

And, beyond these more direct relations between trade and health, health is also an important component of global development. Health and poverty are inter-related, and global health inequalities are related (though not directly and completely) to stages of economic development. Professional mobility also raises ethical questions, as movement is said to be from global South to north.[66] For many reasons, ranging from self-interest to notions of justice,[67] states, third-sector organizations and individuals in the global 'north' seek to support development of states, and alleviation of poverty in the global 'south', particularly, though not exclusively, in 'least-developed countries'. Some of this development policy is carried out through humanitarian aid, responding to natural and human-created disasters, including crop failure and extreme weather conditions. The effects on health of such events are catastrophic, touching both health-related infrastructure (sanitation, nutrition, health services) and individual human health (with famine only the most extreme example). Other areas of development policy are pursued through projects and programmes, and an important area for such programmes is health. From the 1980s onwards, at least in part due to the emergence of HIV/AIDS, health emerged from being a national concern, subject to different national systems, to being a global endeavour. As such, health is now seen as requiring responses from both the global North and South, and the cooperation of a range of governmental and non-governmental agencies (not just medical professionals) to protect and promote health, which is increasingly seen as a 'human right'.[68]

The EU in global health law

To what extent, and how effectively, can the EU respond to the challenges and opportunities presented by global health? Medical tourism may be a positive force, if it ameliorates the global imbalance in supply and demand for health care.[69] Some EU Member States are *receiving* countries of medical tourists,

internationally. A group of countries even created a programme for evaluating the accrediting bodies themselves. Medical education is being standardized by the World Federation for Medical Education and the Institute for International Medical Education, and these standards "are already influencing national and regional systems of recognition and accreditation of medical schools". See also: Cohen (2015) above n 2.

[66] In fact, several global movements of health professionals can be discerned, see: Cohen, (2015) above n 2; Cortez, above n 32; Plotnikova, 'Cross-border mobility of health professionals: contesting patients rights to health' (2012) 74(1) *Social Science and Medicine* 20; Bloom and Cunning, 'Policy Forum: Public Health and the Health and Wealth of Nations' (2000) 287(5456) *Science* 1207.

[67] Daniels, above n 17.

[68] Kickbusch, 'Foreword' in Hein, Bartsch and Kohlmorgen (eds), *Global Health Governance and the Fight against HIV/AIDS* (Palgrave Macmillan 2007) p. x-xi.

[69] See: WHO and WTO, 'WTO Agreements and Public Health: A joint study by the WHO and WTO Secretariat' (WTO Secretariat 2002) 111-124, cited in Cortez, above n 32, 72.

and their economies stand to gain from the encouragement of global medical tourism. Where treatments are available more cheaply elsewhere in the world, the cost savings to public health insurance systems of *sending* Member States could be significant.[70] At the same time there are concerns about patient safety, information asymmetry (or downright misleading information), capacity maintenance in EU Member States, and general questions of equality and equity in access to publicly funded health care. Given its limited competence in health, and the political difficulties entailed in balancing these very different interests, the opportunities for the EU to respond to medical tourism seem seriously constrained. Equally, while it is obvious that communicable diseases do not respect national borders, the EU's technical capacity to combat the threat that they pose, along with other global health threats,[71] is much less than that of several of its Member States.[72] The EU is a member of the WTO. We examine the extent to which it has used that institutional infrastructure to challenge patterns of global trade in goods, such as tobacco, alcohol and food, which negatively affect the health of its populations, or indeed those elsewhere in the world. We are also interested in how the EU's regulation of the pharmaceuticals and medical devices industries, in particular, the development of important new health technologies, plays out in its global contexts. Similarly, we explore the extent to which the EU has become involved in international law on health services. We also consider how, if at all, the EU has influenced the global debates about health and poverty, or responded to global health inequalities.

In the chapters that follow, we develop our discussion of the global dimensions of EU health law. How has the EU's health law embraced the opportunities and responded to the challenges of its global contexts? Has the global context enabled or constrained the EU from pursuing health agendas through what we might call its external health law? What are the implications of broader global debates, for instance, those concerning ethics in bio-medical research and innovation, for EU health law? As implied by the questions we have raised so far, the themes of EU health law (consumerism, rights, competition/equality/solidarity, risk) apply equally to its *external* health law. So we are also interested in the extent to which the claims about EU internal health law, which we have already discussed, are sustainable when applied to EU external health law. Where there are differences, what is their significance for EU health law – its preoccupations, strengths, weaknesses and its trajectories?

---

[70] The World Bank found that the United States could save $1.4 billion if only 10% of patients who needed one of 15 medical procedures travelled abroad. See: Mattoo and Rathindran, 'Does Health Insurance Impede Trade in Health Care Services?' (2005) World Bank Policy Research Working Paper No. 3667, 3 cited in Cortez, above n 32, p 72.

[71] Such as bio-terrorism.

[72] Greer, 'The European Centre for Disease Prevention and Control: Hub or Hollow Core?' 37(6) *Journal of Health Politics, Policy and Law* 1001.

16

The global context: institutions and instruments

Introduction

> The EU's leading role in international trade, global environmental governance and in development aid, as well as its values and experience of universal and equitable quality healthcare give it strong legitimacy to act on global health.

This was the view of the European Commission in 2010, expressed in its communication 'The EU Role in Global Health'.[1] The Commission's optimism is understandable. The Lisbon Treaty changes, which came into effect in 2009, had given the EU greater health competences. The EU Charter of Fundamental Rights, brought within the EU Treaty at Lisbon, recognizes 'the right of access to preventive healthcare and the right to benefit from medical treatment'.[2] Perhaps the new Treaty provisions gave the Commission confidence that the time was ripe to develop a more holistic approach to the explicit competence to 'foster cooperation with third countries and the competent international organisations in the sphere of public health', which had been in the Treaty since the early 1990s. The long-standing 'mainstreaming' obligation, to the effect that 'a high level of human health protection shall be ensured in the definition and implementation of all Union policies and activities', applies to the EU's external relations policies and activities. Greater coherence between its internal and external policies would enhance the EU's reputation as a global actor, or at least its claim to be a global actor. According to the Commission, the EU has a great deal to offer in this regard – its 'social model, strong safety norms and its global trade and development aid position'.[3] At the beginning of this decade, the Commission seemed poised to launch EU external health law, based on a set of guiding principles, and operating across EU law in international trade, global

---

[1] Commission, 'The EU Role in Global Health' (Communication) COM (2010) 128 final; see also: Commission Staff Working Document, 'Contributing to universal coverage of health services through development policy - Accompanying document to the Communication from the Commission to the Council, the European Parliament, the European Economic and Social Committee and the Committee of the Regions - The EU Role in Global Health {COM(2010) 128} {SEC(2010) 380} {SEC(2010) 381}' SEC (2010) 382 final.

[2] Article 35, EU CFR. These rights are enjoyed 'under the conditions established by national laws and practices'.

[3] Commission (2010) above n 1.

environmental law, development aid, and the EU's 'values and experience of universal and equitable quality healthcare'.[4]

But the Commission's communication was not taken up by the other EU institutions.[5] It was 'business as usual' for the EU's external relations law. As we will see, its various strands, to which 'The EU Role in Global Health' referred, continued as before. At the time of writing in 2014, there is no clear commitment from the EU to a holistic EU external health law. Therefore, our concern in this part of the book is rather different from that in Parts II and III. In those chapters, a central part of our research agenda is to provide a critique of existing literature on 'EU health law'. Our analysis is structured around the claims that are made and conclusions that are reached in that literature about EU health law, in terms of its consequences for and resonances with consumerism, rights, competition /solidarity/ equality, and risk. But, so far as we are aware, a holistic (or even relatively holistic) treatment of the EU's external health law has yet to be developed in the literature. This amounts to an implicit assumption that 'EU external health law' is not a meaningful legal category. So we begin our analysis by considering that assumption. In including EU external health law in this book, we are at least open to its existence as a meaningful focus for analysis. If EU external health law is worth exploring, what are its scope and contours? We have outlined emergent understandings of 'global health law'. Much of its substance falls within EU external relations law – particularly EU trade and development law. This chapter outlines the legal and institutional contexts of EU external relations law relevant to health, and, in particular, considers the place of health in EU trade law and in EU development law. In so doing, it considers the extent to which the treatment of health in these contexts can be understood as sufficiently framed by common aims, objectives or values to constitute a meaningful entity. To what extent can 'EU external health law' be understood as distinct from 'EU external relations law'? To what extent can EU external health law be understood as distinct from global health law?

As we said in the Introduction,[6] our focus is on the *law*. This focus becomes more important in this part of the book. International law, with which we are concerned in these chapters, lacks many of the features of EU law that make EU law more like the law of a state – its enforceability by individuals, its density and breadth in terms of substantive coverage, and its legitimation (or at least attempted legitimation) through democratic processes. Generally speaking,[7]

---

[4] Commission (2010) above n 1.

[5] It is mentioned in a single European Parliament resolution: European Parliament, 'Report on healthcare systems in sub-Saharan Africa and global health' (2010/2070(INI), 6 September 2010) and an Opinion of the Committee of the Regions, 'Spring Package: EU action plan for achieving the Millennium Development Goals' (2010/C 267/05, 9-10 June 2010).

[6] See chapter 1.

[7] There are some notable exceptions, principally in the field of human rights. The Council of Europe's Convention on Human Rights, for instance, is enforceable by private individuals in certain, restricted circumstances, and a significant body of jurisprudence has been developed by the European Court of Human Rights.

the techniques of enforcement of international law differ significantly from those of EU (or national) law. They draw on what is commonly called soft law or 'governance' – non-binding processes that nonetheless have, or at least are intended to have, normative effects. Because of that, it is not practical to consider the interactions between the EU and global health law without considering at least some of these processes. But our central concern is the EU's external relations *law* – the legal measures that express the EU's obligations in international law, as well as those of other states and international organizations. In this part of the book, the non-hierarchical nature of the relationships between international, regional, EU and indeed national law is also important. Our focus on the EU should not be mistaken for an implicit claim that the EU is at the pinnacle of a legal hierarchy.

The EU shares many of the capacities of sovereign states in international law: it has international legal personality;[8] and is party to hundreds of international agreements. The EU has competence to conclude an international agreement ('Treaty') 'when its conclusion is provided for in a legislative act of the Union, or is necessary to enable the Union to exercise its internal competence';[9] 'where the Treaties so provide', or 'where the conclusion of an agreement is necessary in order to achieve . . . one of the objectives referred to in the Treaties'.[10] These rules codify the case law of the CJEU on implied external competence.[11] Where the EU does not have exclusive competence to conclude international agreements, or, in practice, where such exclusive competence is in doubt, such agreements are concluded as 'mixed agreements',[12] with both the EU and its Member States as parties to the agreement.

The EU is also a member of numerous international organizations. As, in practice, much of the EU's external health law is pursued through and in collaboration with those international organizations, we begin this chapter by sketching out the main international organizations concerned with global health law, and explaining their relationship with the EU.

Contexts: international organizations

Global health law involves complex and overlapping institutional settings. It includes national interpretations and applications of international law obligations. It also includes international norms (be those adopted as hard or soft law) developed by a range of international and regional organizations.

---

[8] Article 47 TEU.   [9] Article 3 (2) TFEU.   [10] Article 216 (1) TFEU.

[11] Eeckhout, *EU External Relations Law,* (2nd edn, OUP 2011) 70-119; Van Vooren and Wessel, *EU External Relations Law: Text, Cases and Materials* (CUP 2014) 74-94, 99-135.

[12] Eeckhout above n 11, 117; Van Vooren and Wessel above n 11, 55-63. For instance, in Opinion of the Court, *Opinion 1/94 on the WTO,* C-1/94, EU:C:1994:384, the CJEU held that the EU did not have exclusive competence over external trade in services, hence the EU could not join the WTO except through a 'mixed agreement'.

The EU takes its place within those arrangements. In some instances, the EU is also a member of the relevant international organization. In most cases, the relationship is one of cooperation and collaboration. In this section of the chapter, in order to explore the different roles and focus of some relevant international organizations, and how the EU interacts with each in developing aspects of its external health law, we introduce the principal relevant international organizations. In practice, as we will see in the next two chapters, specific areas of global health law may involve several international organizations.

The United Nations: WHO, FAO, CAC, Millennium Development Goals, UNESCR

The 'directing and coordinating authority for health within the United Nations system' is the World Health Organization (WHO).[13] The WHO's Constitution was signed on 22 July 1946, at the International Health Conference in New York, and entered into force on 7 April 1948. The preamble to the WHO Constitution states that its 'principles are basic to the happiness, harmonious relations and security of all peoples'. The Constitution provides that the WHO has the power to seek member state adoption of conventions (Article 19), promulgate regulations (Article 21) and make recommendations (Article 23).

The main decision-making body of the WHO is the World Health Assembly, which meets annually in Geneva and is drawn from delegates from Member States, associate members appointed on the basis of specific expertise, and observers such as the Holy See and the International Federation of the Red Cross.[14] There is also an Executive Board and a Secretariat.[15] The WHO operates through six regional offices: Africa, the Americas, South-East Asia, Europe, Eastern Mediterranean and Western Pacific. Its aims are to provide leadership on global health matters, to shape the global health research agenda, to set norms and standards, to articulate evidence-based policy options, to provide technical support to countries and to monitor and assess health trends. The EU works particularly closely with the WHO Europe office. For instance, since 2008, they have collaborated on disease surveillance, producing joint annual reports on HIV/AIDS and tuberculosis in the WHO Europe region, which covers the EU and its European neighbourhood. The EU also works with WHO Europe on training and capacity building.[16]

The WHO has oversight of the International Health Regulations (IHR), which cover public health risks and public health emergencies of international concern.[17] The EU's trade laws, as well as the work of its European Centre for Disease Prevention and Control, interact with the IHR system.

---

[13] WHO, 'About WHO' (*WHO*, 2014). See: Gostin, *Global Health Law* (Harvard University Press 2014) chapter 4.

[14] See: Gostin above n 13, 93.   [15] See: Gostin above n 13, 94-5.

[16] See: European Centre for Disease Prevention and Control (ECDC), 'Partnerships' (*ECDC*, 2014).

[17] See further: Gostin above n 13, chapter 6; see also the discussion below and in chapter 18.

The WHO's Framework Convention on Tobacco Control, which entered into force in 2005, is the first international treaty agreed under the auspices of the WHO. The Convention marked a new approach for the WHO. It has been described as WHO using its 'global constitutional authority',[18] and hence as a turn to law (alongside 'governance' activity, such as the development and promotion of soft instruments and processes of comparison, and promoting education and policy learning). The EU is a signatory to the Convention. It is therefore under formal obligations to develop its tobacco law consistently with that Convention. The EU also works in partnership with the WHO on global tobacco control, for instance, organizing workshops and events, and preparing and presenting comparative data.[19]

The UN's Food and Agriculture Office (FAO) is mandated to 'raise levels of nutrition, improve agricultural productivity, better the lives of rural populations and contribute to the growth of the world economy'.[20] The European Union is a member organization of its European Commission on Agriculture,[21] which cooperates and makes recommendations on all agricultural problems in Europe. This includes recommendations on food safety, an important aspect of EU health law.

The FAO and the WHO work together in the Codex Alimentarius Commission,[22] of which the EU is also a member. Established by the WHO and UN FAO in 1963, the Codex Alimentarius Commission (CAC) is the key intergovernmental body that sets harmonized standards for internationally traded food.[23] It seeks to ensure consumer protection by enhancing food safety, and to promote fair trade in food.[24] Although the CAC works through guidelines, codes and standards, which are technically voluntary and non-binding, in practice, these are referred to and embedded in binding national (and EU) laws concerning food safety, including the CJEU's case law.[25] The CAC's standards

---

[18] The idea apparently came from the work of Ruth Roemer (Professor Emerita, UCLA School of Public Health) with law Professor Allyn Taylor; see: Roemer, Taylor and Lariviere, 'Origins of the WHO Framework Convention on Tobacco Control' (2005) 95(6) *American Journal of Public Health* 936; Shibuya, Ciecierski, et al., 'WHO Framework Convention on Tobacco Control: Development of an Evidence Based Global Public Health Treaty' (2003) 327(7407) *British Medical Journal* 154.

[19] See: e.g., co-organised information event on 'World No Tobacco Day' 31 May 2012 (see further: WHO, 'Tobacco Free Initiative (TFI): World No Tobacco Day 2014: raise taxes on tobacco' (*WHO*, 2014); Eurobarometer, 'Attitudes of Europeans Towards Tobacco: Report' (Commission 2012).

[20] Food and Agriculture Organization of the United Nations (FAO), 'About FAO' (*FAO*, 2014).

[21] FAO, 'Governing and Statutory Bodies Web site: Agriculture: European Commission on Agriculture' (*FAO*, 2014).

[22] FAO, 'Governing and Statutory Bodies Web site: Food Policy and Nutrition: Codex Alimentarius Commission' (*FAO*, 2014).

[23] MacMaoláin, *EU Food Law: Protecting Consumers and Health in a Common Market* (Hart 2007) 151-173.

[24] See the CAC's Code of Ethics for International Trade in Food 1979, revised 1985 and 2010, a voluntary instrument that seeks to prevent dumping of unsafe or sub-standard food on international markets.

[25] See: in *Smanor*, C-298/87, EU:C:1988:415.

have also been relied on by the WTO Dispute Settlement bodies (see below), as international benchmarks against which national/EU measures are to be assessed, hence there are strong incentives on WTO members to comply with CAC standards.[26] The CAC's capacity to resolve disputes between its different members on questions concerning health (among other matters) is limited, but it operates as an important forum for the sharing and attempted resolution of differences.[27]

Three of the UN's eight Millennium Development Goals[28] directly concern health: child health, maternal health and combating HIV/AIDS. Ending poverty and hunger, and environmental sustainability, also relate to global health. Numerous UN bodies (such as UNICEF, the UN entity for women, the Office of the High Commissioner for Human Rights) work in partnership with other global institutions (such as the WTO, World Bank and International Monetary Fund), and with states, towards the Millennium Development Goals. A 'global action plan'[29] seeks to galvanize development aid and governmental commitments to change law and policy from developed and developing countries. The 'primary aim' of the EU's development cooperation law is to reduce and in the long term eradicate poverty.[30] In pursuing its development cooperation law, the EU is involved in these partnerships. The EU's Development Cooperation Regulation 1905/2006/EC[31] is focused around the Millennium Development Goals.

One aspect of global health law is explicitly human rights-focused.[32] The UN's International Covenant on Economic, Social and Cultural Rights 1966, Article 12 'recognizes' the right to health. This has been interpreted by General Comment 14 of the UN Committee on Economic, Social and Cultural Rights 2000 and by the work of Paul Hunt as UN Special Rapporteur. The UN's right to health is a 'specific, continuing obligation to move ... towards the full realisation of Article 12'.[33] We have already noted the references to the UN's right to health in the context of those aspects of global health law concerned

---

26 See: e.g., *EC-Measures Concerning Meat and Meat Products (Hormones)* [1998] WT/DS26/AB/R, Report of the WTO Appellate Body 1998. For further discussion see: Poli, 'Euro-American Conflicts within the Codex Alimentarius Commission' in Snyder (ed), *International Food Security and Global Legal Pluralism* (Bruylant 2004).

27 Poli, 'Euro-American Conflicts within the Codex Alimentarius Commission' in Snyder above n 26, 229.

28 United Nations, 'Millennium Development Goals and Beyond 2015' (*UN*, 2014).

29 United Nations General Assembly Resolution, 'Keeping the promise: united to achieve the Millennium Development Goals' (A/Res/65/1, UN General Assembly 2010).

30 Article 208 (1) TFEU.

31 Regulation 1905/2006/EC of the European Parliament of the Council of 18 December 2006 establishing a financing instrument for development cooperation [2006] OJ L378/41.

32 See: Harrington and Stuttaford, 'Introduction' in Harrington and Stuttaford (eds), *Global Health and Human Rights: Legal and Philosophical Perspectives* (Routledge 2010).

33 Committee on Economic, Social and Cultural Rights, 'General Comment 14: The right to the highest attainable standard of health' (U.N. Doc. E/C.12/2000/4, UN Economic and Social Council 2000).

with access to essential medicines, as well as with clinical trials in the global South.[34]

The EU does not explicitly recognize Article 12 UNESCR in its own Charter of Fundamental Rights,[35] but Article 12 is a source of the EU's 'right to health care'.[36] Article 35 EUCFR states that 'a high level of human health protection shall be ensured in the definition and implementation of all the Union's policies and activities'. The right to health thus applies as a 'mainstreaming obligation' in relevant EU external relations law. Since 1995, the EU's official policy is to include human rights conditionality clauses in all its external agreements.[37] These clauses are used to promote an environment respectful of human rights. However, the EU has been slow to use such clauses to promote the right to health.[38]

The World Trade Organization

The World Trade Organization (WTO) is the global organization for dealing with trade between nations.[39] Its members are over 150 of the countries of the world, including the EU's main trading partners, such as the USA, China and Japan. The core instruments of the WTO are its trading agreements: the General Agreement on Tariffs and Trade (GATT); the Agreement on Technical Barriers to Trade (TBT); the General Agreement on Trade in Services (GATS); and the Agreement on the Trade-Related Aspects of Intellectual Property Rights (TRIPS). Through these agreements, the WTO seeks to promote free trade, and that is the general principle upon which the agreements are based.

However, in line with the notion of 'embedded liberalism',[40] that is, the idea that governments should be entitled to regulate markets to secure non-economic goals (such as health), the agreements include exceptions for health policy measures.[41] For instance, Article XX (b) of the GATT permits measures 'necessary to protect human . . . life or health', and Article 2.2 of the

---

[34] See further: Introduction to Part IV.

[35] Article 35, EU CFR, Explanatory Note refers only to the European Social Charter, Articles 11 and 13.

[36] See: Hervey and McHale, 'Article 35 – The Right to Health Care' in Peers, Hervey, Kenner and Ward (eds), *The EU Charter of Fundamental Rights: A Commentary* (Hart 2014) 953-4.

[37] Commission, 'Communication on the Inclusion of Respect for Democratic Principles and Human Rights in Agreements between the Community and Third Countries' (Communication) COM (95) 216 final; and, Commission, 'Communication on the European Union and the External Dimension of Human Rights Policy: From Rome to Maastricht and Beyond' (Communication) COM (95) 567. In the event of non-compliance with human rights values and principles, the rights of parties to an international agreement with a human rights conditionality clause are suspended.

[38] Hervey and McHale above n 36, 964.   [39] WTO, 'What is the WTO?' (*WTO*, 2014).

[40] Ruggie, 'International Regimes, Transactions and Change: Embedded Liberalism in the Postwar Economic Order' (1982) 36(2) *International Organization* 379.

[41] See further: Gostin above n 13, chapter 9, 272-289.

TBT provides that states parties must ensure that mandatory requirements concerning product characteristics must not be more restrictive of trade than necessary to meet a legitimate objective, such as human health protection.[42] So, for example, national rules on the ingredients, packaging and labelling for pharmaceuticals, covered by EU pharmaceutical law, fall within Article 2.2 TBT.

The health measures of Article XX(b) GATT have been elaborated in the Agreement on the Application of Sanitary and Phytosanitary Measures (SPS Agreement). If such a measure is in conformity with the SPS Agreement, it is presumed to conform with the GATT.[43] Sanitary measures are defined as including:

> all relevant laws, decrees, regulations, requirements and procedures including, *inter alia*, end product criteria; processes and production methods; testing, inspection, certification and approval procedures; quarantine treatments including relevant requirements associated with the transport of animals or plants, or with the materials necessary for their survival during transport; provisions on relevant statistical methods, sampling procedures and methods of risk assessment; and packaging and labelling requirements directly related to food safety.

aimed at protecting human (or animal) life from pests, diseases, disease-carrying organisms or disease-causing organisms; additives, contaminants, toxins.[44] This is an extremely wide definition. SPS measures must be applied only to the extent necessary, and must be based upon 'scientific principles'.[45] There is an important debate about the extent to which this may be satisfied by 'unscientific' public opinion,[46] and also about how this relates to the 'precautionary principle'.[47] All of the EU's food safety law falls within this provision. Those aspects of its tobacco law aimed at protecting consumers from harmful additives and toxins are also covered. There is a presumption that measures complying with the standards set by the Codex Alimentarius Commission for food (see below)

---

[42] For example, the EC-Tariff Preferences for Developing Countries case concerned the question of whether preferential trade arrangements granted by the (then) EC to countries experiencing drug trafficking problems were consistent with WTO law: *EC – Conditions for the Granting of Tariff Preferences to Developing Countries* [2004] WT/DS246/AB/R, Report of the WTO Appellate Body.

[43] Article 2.4, WTO Agreement on the Application of Sanitary and Phytosanitary Measures (SPS) 1994.

[44] Annex A, SPS.   [45] Article 2.2 SPS.

[46] Scott, *The WTO Agreement on Sanitary and Phytosanitary Measures: A Commentary* (OUP 2007) 77-79; 150-151; Collins, 'Health Protection at the World Trade Organization: The J-Value as a Universal Standard for Reasonableness of Regulatory Precautions' (2009) 43(5) *Journal of World Trade* 1071; Button, *The Power to Protect: Trade, Health, Uncertainty in the WTO* (Hart 2004) 102-113.

[47] Article 5.7 SPS allows provisional measures where scientific information is insufficient, an expression of the precautionary principle, see: *EC-Measures Concerning Meat and Meat Products (Hormones)* [1998] WT/DS26/AB/R, Report of the WTO Appellate Body 1998. For further discussion, see: Scott above n 46; Button (Hart 2004) above n 46, 113-162; Mercurio and Shao, 'A Precautionary Approach to Decision Making: The Evolving Jurisprudence on Article 5.7 of the SPS Agreement' (2010) 2 *Trade, Law and Development* 195.

are SPS compliant,[48] and higher national standards may be set if scientifically justified.[49]

The GATS is relatively less constraining of states parties, as compared to the GATT, as, in general, outside the 'general obligations',[50] the GATS leaves to states which areas of the service economy to open up to transnational trade. These 'specific commitments' vary significantly between countries and service sectors. 'Services supplied in the exercise of governmental authority', which are services supplied outside of commercial or competitive contexts, including health services provided through non-market-based models, are excluded altogether.[51] Even the WTO's own (highly optimistic) website admits that health services are one of the least developed sectors under GATS.[52] The application of WTO law to health services effectively covers only private services.

One of the implications of increasing privatization of health services in (some) Member States is potential application of the GATS.[53] However, as Jarman has argued, the EU's GATS commitments in the health sector suggest that the EU may be creating a 'fortress Europe' for health. While aspects of the EU's *internal* health market are being increasingly liberalized, the EU is contemporaneously setting high *external* barriers to trade in healthcare services.[54] On the other hand, Krajewski argues, in the context of access to services in 'mode 2', where the consumer of the service crosses a border, the EU's position seems to be *more* liberal than that of the USA.[55] This apparently odd legal position

---

[48] Article 3.2 SPS.   [49] Article 3.3 SPS.

[50] These are 'most-favoured-nation treatment' and transparency. The former prohibits preferential arrangements among groups of countries (with exceptions available). The latter requires publication of information on national rules, and establishment of judicial review procedures.

[51] Article 1.3 WTO General Agreement on Trade in Services (GATS) 1994.

[52] WTO, 'Health and Social Services' (*WTO*, 2014).

[53] Krajewski, 'Patient Mobility Beyond Calais: Health Services Under WTO Law' in Van de Gronden et al. (eds), *Health Care and EU Law* (Springer 2011); Jarman, 'Trade in Services and the Public's Health: A 'Fortress Europe' for Health?' in Greer and Kurzer (eds), *European Union Public Health Policy: Regional and Global Trends* (Routledge 2013); Reynolds, Attaran, Hervey and McKee, 'Competition-based reform of the National Health Service in England: A One-Way Street?' (2012) 42(2) *International Journal of Health Services* 213.

[54] Jarman, above n 53.

[55] Krakewski, 'Commodifying and Embedding Services of General Interest in Transnational Contexts: The Example of Healthcare Liberalisation in the EU and the WTO' in Joerges and Falke (eds), *Karl Polanyi, Globalisation and the Potential of Law in Transnational Markets* (Hart 2011): electronic copy available at: <http://ssrn.com/abstract=1732751> at 22: 'One particularly interesting example in the present context is the limitation of the commitments of the United States concerning Mode 2 in hospital services. The US limited the "public re-imbursement of expenses" to facilities in the US. In other words, a US citizen who has received medical treatment in Europe cannot claim the expenses from public health schemes. It should be noted that the EC Schedule of Specific Commitments contains no such limitation. Hence, a EU citizen may travel to the US to receive hospital or non-hospital services and claim the expenses from his or her domestic health system upon the basis of the GATS commitments in conjunction with the ECJ's jurisprudence on patient mobility.' See also Krajewski, above n 53.

may be explicable by the EU's limited competence in the health services field.[56] It thus leaves discretion with the Member States, some of which may choose to be 'receiving' states for migrant patients, and some of which may prefer to protect their health services from influxes of patients.

Thus the main issues in the health field arising from relations between the EU and the WTO concern goods: food, tobacco and alcohol, also pharmaceuticals and medical devices. In some of these areas, in particular food regulation, the EU's regulatory approach is quite distinct from that of other powerful WTO members, such as the USA.[57] This means that many trade disputes between the EU and other WTO members, which are essentially about differences in approaches to health law, have arisen in the context of the WTO.

The WTO resolves trade disputes through its Dispute Settlement Understanding,[58] which establishes the WTO dispute settlement procedure. The procedure involves a structured process, with agreed timetables in each stage. The decisions of the relevant dispute settlement institutions[59] resemble judicial decisions, although the terms of the agreement imply that settlement of disputes by mutual agreement between states is always the preferable outcome.[60] Several such disputes involving the EU concern public health.[61] The approach of the Dispute Settlement Body to the health policy exceptions has been criticized for being unprincipled, inconsistent and unworkable.[62] Other assessments of the WTO 'case law' have suggested, however, that it has been 'fine-tuned' to reflect an increased measure of national regulatory autonomy,[63] in all areas, including health.

---

[56] See discussion below.

[57] See: Snyde above n 26; Young, 'Europe as a global regulator? The limits of EU influence in international food safety standards' (2014) 21(6) *Journal of European Public Policy* 904; Vogel, *The Politics of Precaution: Regulating Health, Safety and Environmental Risks in Europe and the United States* (Princeton University Press 2012).

[58] Uruguay Round of Multilateral Trade Negotiations (1986-1994) - Annex 2 - Understanding on Rules and Procedures Governing the Settlement of Disputes (WTO) [1994] OJ L336/234.

[59] The Dispute Settlement Body, consisting of all WTO members, which may establish 'panels' of experts to consider a dispute, and the Appellate Body, consisting of three members of a permanent seven-member Appellate Body set up by the Dispute Settlement Body and broadly representing the range of WTO membership, not connected to national governments and experts in international trade law. See: WTO, 'Understanding the WTO: Settling Disputes: A unique contribution' (*WTO*, 2014).

[60] The first stage of the procedure is consultation between the states concerned; consultation and mediation are available at all stages of the process. See: WTO, above n 59.

[61] See, for instance, *EC- Measures Affecting Asbestos and Asbestos-Containing Products* [2001] WT/DS135/AB/R, Report of the WTO Appellate Body; *EC - Measures Concerning Meat and Meat Products (Hormones)* [1998] WT/DS26/AB/R, Report of the WTO Appellate Body; *EC-Measure Affecting the Approval and Marketing of Biotechnology Products* [2006] WT/DS291/R, Reports of the Panel.

[62] Scott above n 46; Cheyne, 'Risk and Precaution in World Trade Organization Law' (2006) 40(5) *Journal of World Trade* 837; Collins above n 46.

[63] Du, 'The Rise of National Regulatory Autonomy in the GATT/WTO Regime' (2011) 14(3) *Journal of International Economic Law* 639.

The International Conference on Harmonisation of Technical Requirements for Registration of Pharmaceuticals for Human Use (ICH)

The International Conference on Harmonisation of Technical Requirements for Registration of Pharmaceuticals for Human Use (ICH) was launched in 1990 as a joint regulatory/industry project to make new pharmaceutical development and registration processes more efficient in the interests of patients, public health and cost-effectiveness. Via the ICH, technical requirements for demonstrating the quality, safety and efficacy of new pharmaceuticals have been largely harmonized between the EU, USA and Japan. Work is ongoing with other countries and regions. Although the ICH's guidelines are technically non-binding, in practice they have a 'hard' effect, because, under national or EU law, compliance is necessary for clinical trial authorization or market authorization for products.[64] So, for instance, the European Medicines Agency's 'Guidance Notes' are based on ICH standards.

The International Conference on Harmonisation Global Cooperation Group (GCG), formed in 1999, aims to promote mutual understanding of regional harmonization initiatives in order to facilitate the harmonization process. Its role is to make available information on ICH activities and guidelines to regulatory authorities and pharmaceutical companies which request it. The ICH observers (the WHO, Canada and EFTA) are also part of the GCG. Recognizing the need to engage actively with other harmonization initiatives, representatives from six Regional Harmonisation Initiatives (RHIs) participate in GCG discussions.[65] A further expansion of the GCG was agreed in 2007 and regulators were invited from countries with a history of ICH Guideline implementation and/or where major production and clinical research are done (Australia, Brazil, China, Chinese Taipei, India, Republic of Korea, Russia and Singapore). The GCG serves as a forum for the discussion of harmonization topics and practices.

The Council of Europe

The Council of Europe is the regional human rights organization for Europe. Its forty-seven member countries include all the Member States of the EU. Council of Europe involvement in health includes protection of civil and political rights related to health, as well as social and economic rights through documents such as the Convention on Human Rights and Biomedicine.[66] The EU's Charter of

---

[64] See: European Medicines Agency (EMA), 'ICH Guidelines' (*EMEA*, 2014).

[65] These are Asia-Pacific Economic Cooperation (APEC), Association of South East Asian Nations (ASEAN), the East African Community (EAC) (Kenya, Uganda, Tanzania, Rwanda, Burundi), Cooperation Council for the Arab States of the Gulf (GCC), Pan American Network for Drug Regulatory Harmonisation (PANDRH) and South African Development Community (SADC).

[66] See further: Convention for the Protection of Human Rights and Dignity of the Human Being with Regard to Biology and Medicine: Convention on Human Rights and Biomedicine 1997; Abbing, 'The Convention on human rights and biomedicine: An Application of the Council of Europe Convention' (1998) 5(4) *European Journal of Health Law* 377; and Gevers, Hondius

Fundamental Rights refers to Council of Europe provisions in the 'Explanatory Text' accompanying all of its measures concerned with health rights. These include Article 2 on the right to life;[67] Article 7 on private and family life; Article 8 on protection of personal data;[68] Article 9 on the right to found a family;[69] Article 13 on freedom of the arts and sciences;[70] and Article 35 on the right to health care.[71] Article 3 EU CFR draws on the Council of Europe's Oviedo Convention on Human Rights and Biomedicine, which seeks to protect human rights in the context of medical research. The Council of Europe's Parliamentary Assembly has been active in reporting on potential human rights violations in health care contexts.[72] The Council of Europe, WHO (Europe) and the EU cooperate in pursuing aspects of the health rights agenda, for instance patients' rights.[73]

The EU has a long-standing special relationship with the Council of Europe.[74] Article 6 (2) TEU now obliges the EU to accede to the European Convention on Human Rights and Fundamental Freedoms. Accession negotiations began in 2010, although as Paul Gragl points out, both procedural and substantive obstacles stand in the way of the accession process.[75] For our purposes, what is probably most important is the relationship of mutual respect that has

---

and Hudson (eds), *Health Law, Human Rights and the Biomedicine Convention* (Martinus Nijhoff 2005). See also: chapter 7.

[67] Which refers to Article 2 ECHR.   [68] Both of which refer to Article 8 ECHR.

[69] Which refers to Article 12 ECHR.   [70] Which refers to Article 10 ECHR.

[71] Which refers to Articles 11 and 13 European Social Charter.

[72] E.g. Council of Europe, 'Parliamentary Assembly Recommendation 1611 (2003) on trafficking in organs in Europe' (Council of Europe 2003).

[73] See: WHO (Europe) adopted a Declaration on the Promotion of Patients' Rights in Europe in 1994; Leenen, 'The rights of patients in Europe' (1994) 1(1) *European Journal of Health Law* 5. See further: chapter 8.

[74] There is a significant literature on this question. See: e.g. Gragl, 'Agreement on the Accession of the European Union to the European Convention on Human Rights' in Peers et al. (eds), (Hart 2014) above n 36; Sarmiento, 'Who's Afraid of the Charter? The Court of Justice, National Courts and the New Framework of Fundamental Rights Protection in Europe' (2013) 50 *Common Market Law Review* 1267; Canor, 'My Brother's Keeper? Horizontal *Solange*: An Ever Closer *Distrust* Among the Peoples of Europe' (2013) 50 *Common Market Law Review* 38;3 Rosas, 'The Charter and Universal Human Rights Instruments' in Peers et al. (eds), (Hart 2014) above n 36; Itzcovich, 'Legal Order, Legal Pluralism, Fundamental Principles: European and its Law in Three Concepts' (2012) 18(3) *European Law Journal* 358; Klabbers, 'Völkerrechtsfreundlich? International Law and the Union Legal Order' in Koutrakos (ed), *European Foreign Policy: Legal and Political Perspectives* (Edward Elgar 2011); Walker, 'Beyond boundary disputes and basic grids: Mapping the global disorder of normative orders' (2008) 6(3) & (4) *International Journal of Constitutional Law* 373; Krisch, 'The Open Architecture of European Human Rights Law' (2008) 71(2) *Modern Law Review* 183; Eckes, 'Does the European Court of Human Rights provide protection from the European Community? The Case of Bosphorus Airways' (2007) 13(1) *European Public Law* 47; Douglas-Scott, 'A Tale of Two Courts: Luxembourg, Strasbourg and the Growing European Human Rights *Acquis*' (2006) 43 *Common Market Law Review* 629; Canor, '*Primus Inter Pares*: Who is the Ultimate Guardian of Fundamental Rights in Europe?' (2000) 25 *European Law Review* 3. See further: chapter 7.

[75] Gragl, 'Agreement on the Accession of the European Union to the European Convention on Human Rights' in Peers et al. (eds), (Hart 2014) above n 36, 1737.

developed between the CJEU and the European Court of Human Rights. The CJEU recognized the ECHR as a special source of fundamental rights principles in EU law as long ago as the 1970s.[76] The place of the ECHR in EU law is now also expressed in the Treaty.[77]

The Organisation for Economic Cooperation and Development (OECD)

Established in 1961, the OECD is a forum for governments to share information on common problems and to evaluate policy solutions to questions of growth, or, as its website puts it 'economic, social and environmental change'.[78] As part of its work on development and combating poverty, the OECD collects and compares health indicators. The EU relies on OECD indicators in some of its external relations law with relevance to health. For instance, the EU's development aid programmes refer to OECD definitions to determine 'least developed', other low income, 'lower middle income' and 'upper middle income' countries and territories for the purposes of EU development law.[79]

This brief overview of the main institutions through which the EU is involved in global health law illustrates the key substantive areas of EU external relations law applicable to health.[80] If 'EU external health law' exists, its principal areas of operation are the EU's trade law and its development law. We consider each of these in turn.

Contexts: health in EU trade law

Trade is seen as the 'heart' of EU external relations law.[81] The EU's 'common commercial policy' is the most developed aspect of that body of EU law. The vast majority of international agreements between the EU and other countries concern trade in products ('goods') and services, or cover matters related to trade. The relevance of EU trade law to global health arises from its application to products which either affect population health (food, alcohol, tobacco) or are used within health care systems (pharmaceuticals, medical devices, organs, human tissue and cells, blood), and to health services.

---

[76] In *Rutili*, C-36/75, EU:C:1975:137; in *Kremzow v Austria*, C-299/95, EU:C:1997:254.
[77] Article 6(3) TEU.   [78] OECD, 'About the OECD' (*OECD*, 2014).
[79] Regulation 1905/2006/EC of the European Parliament of the Council of 18 December 2006 establishing a financing instrument for development cooperation [2006] OJ L378/41, Annex II.
[80] There are other important aspects of EU external relations law (or as it is sometimes called 'EU international relations law') which have less direct links to health. These include the external aspects of the EU's 'Area of Freedom, Security and Justice', concerned with global migration, EU environmental law, and the EU's 'common foreign and security policy', concerned with global peace and security.
[81] Eeckhout above n 11, 439; Van Vooren and Wessel above n 11, 276, who also point out that Koutrakos, *EU International Relations Law* (Hart 2006) begins with common commercial policy in its first chapter.

Article 206 TFEU provides that the EU shall contribute to 'development of world trade, the progressive abolition of restrictions on international trade and on foreign direct investment'. To do so, the EU legislature has exclusive competence under Article 207 TFEU[82] to adopt Regulations, which reflect agreements (Treaties in international law) with other states and international organizations. These agreements are negotiated by the Council, on a recommendation by the Commission,[83] and with the consent of the European Parliament in most cases.[84] In general, the Council acts by qualified majority vote.[85] The EU therefore has considerable formal power and indeed autonomy from the governments of its Member States to negotiate trade agreements. The EU has negotiated many such agreements, and adopted many Regulations, to promote free trade. Regulation 260/2009/EU[86] lays down the general rules, and their exceptions. Free trade agreements with specific countries, or groups of countries, operate within the general framework of the World Trade Organization (WTO). They are designed to liberalize trade, by removing customs duties; facilitating transit of goods through customs; setting common technical standards for goods; and opening up opportunities for trade in services. The EU's free trade agreements thus concern various areas concerning health policy, including standards for products used within health systems, and (at least potentially) health services.[87]

There are some important legal constraints on the EU's competence under Article 207 TFEU. Article 218 (8) TFEU provides that, where the field is one where unanimity is needed for an internal EU act, Council must act unanimously in negotiating and concluding agreements with other countries. Article 207 (4) (b) TFEU explicitly provides that actions in the field of trade in health services are subject to unanimous agreement of Council. Most importantly, for our purposes, where the EU Treaties exclude harmonization, Article 207 (6) TFEU applies. The EU's exercise of its competence under Article 207 TFEU, 'shall not affect the delimitation of competences between the EU and the Member States, and shall not lead to harmonization of legislative or regulatory provisions of the Member States in so far as the Treaties exclude such harmonization'.[88]

---

[82] The TFEU extends the EU's common commercial policy to foreign direct investment which, as Piet Eeckhout notes, will develop as an EU policy over time. Eeckhout above n 11, 63-67.

[83] Or the High Representative of the Union for Foreign Affairs, where that agreement relates to common foreign and security policy, Article 218 (3) TFEU.

[84] Article 218 (6) TFEU.

[85] Except where the field is one where unanimity is needed for an internal EU act, for association agreements and for assistance agreements with accession countries, Article 218 (8) TFEU.

[86] Council Regulation 260/2009/EC of 26 February 2009 on the common rules for imports [2009] OJ L84/1.

[87] Jarman, above n 53. But see below.

[88] The idea that the EU external competences are coterminous with its internal competences is known as 'parallelism'. Originally developed through the CJEU's jurisprudence on implied powers, it is now reflected in Article 216 TFEU. See: Eeckhout above n 11, 71-119; Van Vooren and Wessels above n 11, 81-94.

As we have already seen,[89] Article 168 TFEU makes it clear that Member States retain competence for 'the definition of their health policy and for the organization and delivery of health services and medical care'. Similarly, Article 6 TFEU gives EU competence to undertake 'actions to support, coordinate or supplement' national law and policy in areas including 'the protection and improvement of human health' – legislative and regulatory harmonization is excluded. So health is a field to which Article 207 (6) TFEU applies.

If the phrases 'health policy' or 'protection and improvement of human health' were to be defined too widely, the scope of Article 207 TFEU would be significantly constrained. No EU international agreement leading to legal harmonization that touched on anything to do with 'health policy' could be concluded by the EU acting alone. Such Treaties would have to be concluded as 'mixed agreements', and the government of any one Member State would be able to veto such an agreement. In theory, therefore, the extent to which EU competence under Article 207 TFEU reaches into health policy thus has important implications for the scope and nature of EU external health law. In practice, however, the most important agreements have been concluded as mixed agreements.

For instance, the WTO Agreement on Sanitary and Phytosanitary Measures,[90] which falls within EU trade law, has been ratified by both the EU and its Member States. This Agreement forms the basis of EU external health law on the safety of food (and feed). An international convention to which the EU and its Member States are parties[91] concerns harmonization of specifications for pharmaceuticals, through the establishment of a European Pharmacopoeia, administered through a Council of Europe institution responsible for elaborating technical standards for pharmaceuticals in Europe.[92] And long-standing multilateral agreements[93] concern exchange of human blood and its derivatives, and

---

[89] See: chapter 3.

[90] Uruguay Round of Multilateral Trade Negotiations (1986-1994) - Annex 1 - Annex 1A - Agreement on the Application of Sanitary and Phytosanitary Measures (WTO- GATT 1994) [1994] OJ L336/40.

[91] Convention on the elaboration of a European Pharmacopoeia (No 50 Council of Europe) 1974, entered into force for the EU 1994: Convention on the elaboration of a European Pharmacopoeia [1994] OJ L158/19; Protocol to the Convention on the elaboration of a European Pharmacopoeia [1994] OJ L158/22.

[92] Council of Europe, 'Background & Mission of the European Pharmacopoeia (*Council of Europe*, 2014).

[93] European Agreement on the Exchange of Therapeutic Substances of Human Origin (No 26, Council of Europe) 1958, entered into force for the EC 1987: European Agreement on the Exchange of Therapeutic Substances of Human Origin [1987] OJ L37/2; European Agreement of the Exchange of Blood-Grouping Reagents (No 39 Council of Europe) 1962, entered into force for the EU 1987: European Agreement on the Exchange of Blood-grouping Reagents [1987] OJ L37/31; European Agreement on the exchange of tissue-typing reagents (No 84 Council of Europe) 1974, entered into force for the EU 1977: European Agreement on the Exchange of Reagents for Determining Blood Groups - Protocol to the Agreement [1977] OJ L295/8.

sharing of medical, surgical and laboratory equipment,[94] in an effort to pool European resources and meet deficits in one state by sharing excess capacity in another.

However, some agreements within EU trade law concerning free trade in goods are between the EU acting alone, and other countries. So, for instance, specific public health scares, such as the BSE/vCJD crisis, or dioxins in pork, have prompted international agreements with countries such as the USA, Australia and New Zealand,[95] in which the EU agreed very detailed rules on animal slaughter, sterilization, inspection and so on.

When it comes to health services, although the matter has not been definitively determined by the CJEU, the practice of adopted mixed agreements is likely to continue, in spite of the changes made by the Nice and Lisbon Treaties intended to make clear that the EU's trade competences extend beyond trade in goods.[96] Before the Treaty of Lisbon came into force, the boundaries between EU and national competence in external relations law were considered by the Advocate General (Kokott) in a case concerning health services.[97] The question was whether Vietnam's accession to the WTO had to be agreed as a 'mixed agreement' or could be done by the EU acting alone. Under GATS,[98] Articles XVI and XVII, concerning access to the market for services and service providers, some Member States[99] have restricted access to the market for non-national

---

[94] Agreement on the temporary importation, free of duty, of medical, surgical and laboratory equipment for use on free loan in hospitals and other medical institutions for purposes of diagnosis or treatment (No 33, Council of Europe) 1960, entered into force for the EC 1987: Agreement on the temporary importation, free of duty, of medical, surgical and laboratory equipment for use on free loan in hospitals and other medical institutions for purposes of diagnosis or treatment [1986] OJ L131/48.

[95] Council Decision 93/158/EEC of 26 October 1992 concerning the conclusion of an Agreement in the form of an exchange of letters between the European Economic Community and the United States of America concerning the application of the Community third country Directive, Council Directive 72/462/EEC, and the corresponding United States of America regulatory requirements with respect to trade in fresh bovine and porcine meat [1993] OJ L68/1; Agreement between the European Community and the United States of America on sanitary measures to protect public and animal health in trade in live animals and animal products [1998] OJ L118/3; and Agreement in the form of an exchange of letters on the amendments to the Annexes to the Agreement between the European Community and the United States of America on sanitary measures to protect public and animal health in trade in live animals and animal products [2003] OJ L316/21; Agreement in the form of an Exchange of Letters on the amendments to the Annexes to the agreement between the European Community and New Zealand on sanitary measures applicable to trade in live animals and animal products [2003] OJ L214/38.

[96] Article 207 (1) TFEU, which explicitly refers to 'goods *and services, and commercial aspects of intellectual property, foreign direct investment* . . .' (italics added). See: Van Vooren and Wessel above n 11, 279.

[97] Opinion of the Advocate General in *Commission v Council (Vietnam WTO Accession)*, C-13/07, EU:C:2009:190. Withdrawn following entry into force of Lisbon Treaty, paragraphs 142-156.

[98] Uruguay Round of Multilateral Trade Negotiations (1986- 1994) - Annex 1 - Annex 1B - General Agreement on Trade in Services (WTO) [1994] OJ L336/191.

[99] For examples, see Krajewski, above n 53.

companies supplying hospital services through a commercial presence in the host state. They are subject to approval in the framework of national health systems, and in some cases a 'needs' test.[100] Also non-national service providers (health professionals) are subject to many restrictions to market access, including residence or nationality requirements, and economic needs tests. For the Advocate General, these types of restrictions meant that the field of hospital services, at least within the context of national health systems, was one of national competence.[101] A mixed agreement was therefore legally necessary. The case concerned the pre-Lisbon Treaty text, and was settled before being heard by the CJEU, but nevertheless indicates some of the complexities at issue here.[102] Given these, it is not surprising, therefore, that, in the context of health policy, the practical difficulties of regulating global trade in health services have resulted in some 'messy compromises'.[103] This is particularly so in the context of health policy concerning publicly funded services within health care systems. For instance, in its Economic Partnership with the CARIFORUM, the EU undertakes to liberalize trade only in *privately funded* hospital services,[104] even though under the GATS, in principle,[105] the EU's position is one of trade liberalization in both private and public sectors.[106]

The difficulties for the EU in concluding agreements on international trade in health services are illustrated by the proposed bilateral trade agreement with India. The negotiations on this agreement began in 2007.[107] One of a

---

[100] For example, in Belgium the needs test relates to 'the needs in function of the population, age scale, death rate and geographical spread' or in Austria 'due consideration on a case-by-case basis is taken of the density of population, existing facilities, traffic infrastructure, topographical conditions and the distance between hospitals'. See: Opinion of the Advocate General in *Commission v Council (Vietnam WTO Accession)* EU:C:2009:190, paragraph 144, footnote 85.

[101] This might explain why the EU itself has not limited access to hospital services in its schedule of limitations to commitments under GATS; see: Krajewski, n 53.

[102] It is unclear, for instance, whether the AG's reasoning would apply to other types of (non-hospital sector) health services? Does the GATS position really affect the legal position with respect to EU competence? What about other areas of health policy – concerning trade in goods?

[103] Jarman, above n 53.

[104] Economic Partnership Agreement between the CARIFORUM States, of the one part, and the European Community and its Member States, of the other part [2008] OJ L 289/3, Article 69 and Annex IV A; Article 78 and Annex IV B; Article 81 and Annex IV C; Article 83 and Annex IV F.

[105] Subject to national reservations, exceptions for public utilities, restrictions on public investment, or on subsidies provided to foreign firms, and permissible differential treatment for subsidiaries of foreign firms: Jarman, above n 53.

[106] Chanda, 'India-EU Relations in Health Services: Prospects and Challenges' (2011) 7 *Globalization and Health* 1.

[107] On 26 June 2012, in a Joint Statement on the Outcome of the EU-India Trade Ministerial, EU Trade Commissioner Karel De Gucht and Indian Commerce Minister Anand Sharma 'expressed their satisfaction that negotiations towards an ambitious EU-India Free Trade Agreement are making good progress', Commission, 'Joint Statement on the Outcome of the EU-India Trade Ministerial' (*Commission*, 26 June 2012). The negotiations are ongoing, see: Commission, 'Countries and Regions: India' (*Commission*, 14 May 2014).

so-called 'fourth generation'[108] of free trade agreements launched by the EU as part of its *Global Europe* strategy[109] in 2006, the overall ambition of the agreement's proposals for the services sector is one of the difficult issues still to be resolved.[110] It is hoped that the agreement will provide that foreign companies will be permitted to access domestic (EU or Indian) markets, and be treated on the same basis as domestic companies. Health systems in India and in the EU differ significantly, in terms of their resources, priorities, regulatory frameworks and balance between public and private provision. But there are factors that pull towards increased collaboration. These explain the desire for a legal framework within which bilateral arrangements can develop. India has a growing private healthcare sector, emerging world-class hospitals, a young population and significant numbers of medical professionals and other health service providers. The EU has, in general, overburdened public health systems, rising costs and an ageing population. Chanda argues for a 'softly' approach, given the nature of health services as a public good, at least in the EU context, building on successful collaborations selectively and over time.[111] But equally there will be others who argue that, so long as the regulatory frameworks can be guaranteed to provide sufficiently robust human rights protections,[112] global trade in health services, supported by trade agreements, will increase welfare in both the EU and partner countries such as India.

An area of EU external relations law related to its trade law, and with specific relevance to health, is scientific and technological cooperation and research and innovation agreements. These typically aim to encourage exchange of information between researchers in various fields, and fit the EU's

---

[108] See further below. 'First generation' trade agreements covers only trade in goods. 'Second generation' agreements extend to trade in services, public procurement and investment. 'Third generation' agreements, such as the Cotonou Agreement 2000 (revised in 2005 and 2010), include issues such as intellectual property rights, investment, and anti-competitive regulatory measures. There are few 'fourth generation' agreements, which go even further, and seek to achieve a higher degree of economic integration between the parties. Another example of a 'fourth generation' agreement is the Association Agreement between the EU and Chile. See: Scherlin, 'Trade, Association, Aid: Has the Agreement between the EU and Chile Fulfilled its Purposes?' (LLM (unpublished) thesis, Göteborgs Universitat 2009).

[109] Commission, 'Global Europe Competing in the World: A contribution to the EU's growth and jobs strategy' (Communication) COM (2006) 567 final.

[110] Commission, 'Overview of FTA and other Trade Negotiations' (Commission 2014)... Concluding the agreement is likely to prove trickier following the Indian Supreme Court's ruling upholding the Indian Patent Office's decision to reject Novartis' patent application for 'Gleevec', a new form of a known compound. See: t'Hoen 'A Victory for Global Public Health in the Indian Supreme Court' (2013) 34(3) *Journal of Public Health Policy* 370; Chatterjee, 'India's Patent Case Victory Rattles Big Pharma' (2013) 381(9874) *The Lancet* 1263.

[111] Chanda above n 106.

[112] For instance, the data protection arrangements in non-EU countries – see: Directive 95/46/EC of the European Parliament and of the Council of 24 October 1995 on the protection of individuals with regard to the processing of personal data and on the free movement of such data [1995] OJ L281/31.

external relations activities with its 'Framework Programmes' for research and development. Some, such as that with Switzerland, date back to the 1970s.[113] Several, such as those with Brazil[114] and Russia,[115] explicitly mention biomedical and health research. The agreements emphasize that each party must protect intellectual property rights,[116] and for countries that are members of the WTO, fall within the context of the TRIPS, to which the EU is a party. A few, such as the Intelligent Manufacturing Systems Initiative, which includes nanotechnology research,[117] also establish supranational infrastructures. The EU's public health programme, which includes research, also provides for cooperation with non-EU countries.[118]

The fundamental basis of EU trade law is trade liberalization. But this encompasses respect for values other than free trade[119] – in particular for our purposes, protection of consumers and patients from harm, and human rights and ethical values.

Contexts: health in EU development law

The second main area of EU external relations law that is relevant to health is development cooperation. The EU's development cooperation policy affects health in several ways – through the EU's contribution to the 'Millennium Development Goals', which, for instance, include public health concerns and global health inequalities; through infrastructure and capacity building, including human resource development; and through specific project-based work,

---

[113] Framework Agreement for scientific and technical cooperation between the European Communities and the Swiss Confederation [1985] OJ L313/6.

[114] Agreement for scientific and technological cooperation between the European Community and the Federative Republic of Brazil [2005] OJ L295/38.

[115] Agreement 2000/742/EC on Cooperation in science and technology between the European Community and the Government of the Russian Federation [2000] OJ L299/15, renewed 2003, 2009.

[116] See: e.g., Agreement for scientific and technological cooperation between the EC and the Government of the Republic of India [2002] OJ L213/30.

[117] Agreement in the field of intelligent manufacturing systems between the EC and the USA, Japan, Australia, Canada, Norway and Switzerland: Exchange of Letters recording the common understanding on the principles of international cooperation on research and development activities in the domain of intelligent manufacturing systems between the European Community and the United States of America, Japan, Australia, Canada and the EFTA countries of Norway and Switzerland (Switzerland) - Annex: Terms of reference for a programme of international cooperation in advanced manufacturing [1997] OJ L161/41, set up the 'IMS International Steering Committee'. See further: Intelligent Manufacturing Systems (2014) <http://www.ims.org/>.

[118] Regulation 282/2014/EU of the European Parliament and of the Council of 11 March 2014 on the establishment of a third Programme for the Union's action in the field of health (2014-2020) and repealing Decision No 1350/2007/EC [2014] OJ L86/1.

[119] Ruggie's 'embedded liberalism', Ruggie, 'International Regimes, Transactions and Change: Embedded Liberalism in the Postwar Economic Order' (1982) 36(2) *International Organization* 379.

for instance, combating HIV/AIDS, malaria and tuberculosis.[120] Article 208 TFEU provides that the objective of the EU's development cooperation policy is the reduction and eventual eradication of poverty. Its underlying basis thus resonates with ethics of justice and equality, which are part of the global health debate.[121] In this context, 'poverty' must be understood to have an absolute, rather than relative, meaning, as otherwise its eradication could not be a meaningful goal. The correlation between poverty and health is not a perfect or direct one, but many studies show that poverty is a key indicator for poor health. Poverty both causes and is a result of poor health.[122]

The historical context for the EU's involvement in development essentially lies in its colonial and post-colonial history. The shape of EU trade law has also been significantly influenced by the colonial and post-colonial relationships of its powerful Member States, especially those of France, one of its most powerful founding Member States,[123] which viewed its home territory and its colonies as a 'cultural unity'.[124] Development cooperation with other countries was reflected in the original EEC Treaty, and extended the free trade rules of the EEC Treaty to the 'overseas countries and territories'.[125] As these countries acquired independence, the EU entered into a series of multi-lateral framework treaties,[126] reflecting the special relationship between the EU and its former colonies. These treaties are based on both free trade and development aid (called 'financial and technical cooperation'). For instance, the first Lomé Convention 1975 is based on the ideas of the UN Conference on Trade and Development 1964.[127] UNCTAD's broad orientation is towards trade liberalization and market access, in particular for goods.

---

[120] For an early summary, see: Commission, 'Health and Poverty Reduction in Developing Countries' (Communication) COM (2002) 129 final; see also; Commission, 'European Programme for Action to Confront HIV/AIDS, Malaria and Tuberculosis through External Action (2007-2011)' COM (2005) 179 final.

[121] See: Introduction to Part IV; and see: Daniels, *Just Health: Meeting Health Needs Fairly* (CUP 2008); Sandel, *What Money Can't Buy: The Moral Limits of Markets* (Allen Lane 2012).

[122] For some global research see: Dood and Munck, 'Dying For Change: Poor people's experience of health and ill-health' (WHO and World Bank 2000); for European examples see: Koller, 'Poverty, Social Exclusion and Health Systems in the WHO European Region' (WHO Regional Office for Europe 2010) and Koller (ed), 'Poverty and Social Exclusion in the WHO European Region: health systems respond' (WHO Regional Office for Europe 2010) and for recent examples from the USA, see research cited here: Multiple Authors (Spotlight on Poverty and Opportunity, continuous).

[123] See: Bartels, 'The Trade and Development Policy of the European Union' in Cremona (ed), *Developments in EU External Relations Law* (OUP 2008); Broberg, 'The EU's Legal Ties with its Former Colonies – When Old Love Never Dies' (2011) DIIS Working paper 2011:01; Van Vooren and Wessel above n 11, 311-344.

[124] Bartels above n 123,130.   [125] Article 132 (1) EEC Treaty.

[126] Yaoundé I Convention between EAMA (Associated African and Malgache Countries) and EEC 1963; Yaoundé II Convention between EAMA and EEC 1969; Lomé Convention I (1975), II (1979), III (1984) and IV (1990); Cotonou Agreement 2000.

[127] Bartels, above n 123, 146-7. UNCTAD is an institutionalised intergovernmental forum, which meets every four years, and is supported by a permanent secretariat, devoted to considering the place of developing countries in global trade.

Over time, the EU's development cooperation was extended to a wider range of countries, well beyond the Member States' former colonies. The EU began to use a range of different types of trade and development agreements with different 'third countries', depending upon factors such as the stage of development of the partner country or countries, trade patterns with the EU and various political considerations, including post-colonial relations. The EU moved well beyond so-called 'first-generation' trade agreements, which cover only trade in goods, adopting 'second-generation' agreements, which extend to trade in services, public procurement and investment.[128] The EU has also adopted some 'third-generation agreements', such as the Cotonou Agreement 2000, which include issues such as intellectual property rights, investment, and anti-competitive regulatory measures. While remaining intertwined with trade, EU development cooperation has also become more focused on wider concerns, which include human rights, and a range of social matters, including health. The relevant treaties include 'essential elements clauses', which require commitment to human rights (and democracy) as a condition for trade and development cooperation relationships with the EU. These clauses have the potential to change human rights protections in the EU's trading partners. 'Human rights conditionality' is a core element of EU development and trade law.[129]

The EU's approach to development and trade was refocused in 2006, with its *Global Europe* strategy.[130] The strategy made more explicit the links between EU trade and development law, the development of the EU economy and the global competitiveness of EU industry. A new generation of free trade agreements, seeking to go well beyond opening markets in goods, began to be explored. There are few such 'fourth generation' agreements, which seek to achieve a higher degree of economic integration between the parties.[131]

The *Global Europe* strategy ran from 2006 to 2010. In 2010, the European Commission proposed an approach which in many ways is a continuation of the *Global Europe* strategy,[132] focused on trade, and the global competitiveness of the EU, and seeing global development in that context. The European Parliament

---

[128] See further discussion above at n 108.

[129] Commission, 'Communication on the Inclusion of Respect for Democratic Principles and Human Rights in Agreements between the Community and Third Countries' (Communication) COM (95) 216 final; and, Commission, 'Communication on the European Union and the External Dimension of Human Rights Policy: From Rome to Maastricht and Beyond' COM (95) 567; Cremona, 'Human Rights and Democracy Clauses in the EC's Trade Agreements' in O'Keeffe and Emiliou (eds), *The European Union and World Trade Law* (Wiley 1996).

[130] Commission, 'Global Europe Competing in the World: A contribution to the EU's growth and jobs strategy' (Communication) COM (2006) 567 final.

[131] An example of a 'fourth generation' agreement is the Association Agreement between the EU and Chile. See: Scherlin above n 108.

[132] Commission, 'Trade, Growth and World Affairs: Trade Policy as a Core Component of the EU's 2020 strategy' COM (2010) 612 final.

was highly critical.[133] It described the new approach as lacking ambition.[134] The Parliament sought a more holistic approach, which takes account of many other policy areas. Parliament gave a long list of such areas, beginning with human rights but also including 'the fight against poverty within and beyond the EU'; 'development policy'; 'protection of consumer rights and interests'; and 'protection of property rights, including intellectual property rights'.[135] Parliament also wanted a more ambitious approach to international standardization,[136] through which the EU would essentially seek to impose its standards on the global stage. A commitment to free and fair trade should be tempered with flexibility for developing countries, to 'honour the commitment to special and differential treatment' for them as 'engaged in the fight against poverty within and outside the EU'.

Some national governments[137] were also sufficiently dissatisfied with the Commission's proposal to initiate a 'think tank process',[138] designed to inform a broad strategic approach for the EU's external relations, covering all aspects of the EU's external action. The project released its final report in May 2013.[139] It referred to 'ongoing transformations at the global, regional and European levels', which 'demand strategic thinking on an ambitious and assertive external agenda'. It suggested that a proactive, realistic and adaptive approach, that recognizes the limitations of the EU, should be taken forward.[140] The second phase of the process is supposed to be a 'basis and momentum for continued discussion', which the report hopes will be taken forward by the new European Parliament and the new EU Commission appointed in 2014.

According to Article 208 TFEU, the EU's development cooperation policy must complement that of its Member States. The EU and the Member States

---

[133] New trade policy for Europe under the Europe 2020 Strategy: European Parliament Resolution of 27 September 2011 on a New Trade Policy for Europe under the Europe 2020 Strategy (2010/2152(INI)) [2013] OJ CE56/87.

[134] Stating that it 'expected to receive a real future trade strategy, which took account of mid- and long-term developments and did not build on the false assumption of a continuing status quo on the world trade stage'.

[135] According to Parliament, although intellectual property rights should be protected, with effective measures to tackle counterfeiting, 'European IPR policy towards the least developed and poor developing countries, as well as the main producers of generics, notably India and Brazil, should remain within the TRIPS Agreement obligations and must fully respect the 2001 Doha Declaration ... especially in the field of generic medicines and public health'.

[136] International standardization, in Parliament's opinion, 'cannot be carried out at the price of lower technical, health and safety and consumer protection standards'.

[137] Italy, Poland, Spain, and Sweden.

[138] The 'European Global Strategy Process', see: European Global Strategy, 'Towards a European Global Strategy' (*The Swedish Institute of International Affairs*, 2014).

[139] European Global Strategy, 'Towards a European Global Strategy: Securing European Influence in a Changing World' (The Swedish Institute of International Affairs 2013).

[140] "The first-order strategic purpose of the EU is to avoid the conflation of change and conflict and to co-shape the transition of the international system by seeking new deals with other important actors. Such purpose would define Europe as a global power and would also guide the Union's exercise of power. Grevi, 'A progressive European Global Strategy' (Policy Brief No. 140, FRIDE 2012).

are legally obliged to coordinate their policies and aid programmes.[141] Development cooperation must be taken into account in other EU policies 'that are likely to affect developing countries'.[142] The Treaty explicitly requires compliance with commitments made by the EU and its Member States to the UN, or other relevant international organizations.[143]

Coordination of EU and national development cooperation is reflected through the 'European Consensus', adopted by the governments of the Member States, Council, the European Parliament and the Commission in 2006.[144] Its aim is to coordinate funds from national budgets, funds from the EU budget and funds from national budgets which are pooled in the European Development Fund and dispersed under the Cotonou Agreement. Under the multiannual financial framework for the EU 2014–2020, the Commission proposes a European Development Fund of around 34 billion euros.[145] Separating the European Development Fund from the EU budget is a political compromise,[146] which the European Commission hopes will end in 2020.[147]

The EU pursues its development policy through agreements involving 'multiannual cooperation programmes' either with particular countries, or with particular themes.[148] The EU is also competent to enter into agreements with international organizations, in pursuit of its development cooperation policy.[149] The EU's multilateral and bilateral agreements with third countries include both trade and development elements. For instance, the Cooperation Agreement between the European Community and the Republic of India on partnership and development[150] covers access to markets, economic cooperation in various areas, including research in biotechnology, but also development cooperation. The EU provides financial support for projects, including in public health, focused on primary health care, including communicable disease control.[151]

---

[141] Article 210 (1) TFEU. The European Commission is empowered to promote that coordination, Article 210 (2) TFEU.

[142] Article 208 (1) TFEU.   [143] Article 208 (2) TFEU.

[144] Joint statement by the Council and the representatives of the governments of the Member States meeting within the Council, the European Parliament and the Commission on European Union Development Policy: The European Consensus [2006] OJ C46/1.

[145] Commission, 'Preparation of the multiannual financial framework regarding the financing of EU cooperation for African, Caribbean and Pacific States and Overseas Countries and Territories for the 2014-2020 period (11th European Development Fund)' (Communication) COM (2011) 837 final.

[146] Broberg, 'Governing by Consensus – On the Legal Regulation of the EU's Development Cooperation Policy' (2010) DIIS Working Paper 2010:23, 6-7.

[147] Van Vooren and Wessel, (OUP 2014) above n 11, 337-8; Joint Statement on MFF-Related Issues, annexed to Regulation 966/2012/EU (Euratom) of the European Parliament and of the Council of 25 October 2012 on the financial rules applicable to the general budget of the Union and repealing Council Regulation (EC, Euratom) No 1605/2002 [2012] OJ L298/1.

[148] Article 209 (1) TFEU.   [149] Article 209 (2) TFEU.

[150] Cooperation Agreement between the European Community and the Republic of India on partnership and development - Declaration of the Community concerning tariff adjustments - Declarations of the Community and India [1994] OJ L223/24.

[151] Cooperation Agreement between the European Community and the Republic of India on partnership and development - Declaration of the Community concerning tariff adjustments - Declarations of the Community and India [1994] OJ L223/24, Article 16 (3).

Similar 'third-generation agreements' involve other countries which are important in terms of global health law, such as Brazil,[152] Russia[153] or South Africa.[154]
For other 'BRICS' countries, such as China, 'second-generation' agreements
remain the main legal framework for trade and development relations.[155] Many
of the EU's development cooperation agreements with countries such as Bolivia,
Cambodia, Chile, China, Colombia, Laos, Mexico, Pakistan, Peru, Turkey and
Venezuela[156] concern action against international trade in illegal narcotics,
which is, of course, central to the interface between global health and criminal
justice. These agreements concern both the narcotics themselves, and also trade
in 'drug precursors', that is substances that have significant legitimate uses in a

---

[152] Framework Agreement for Cooperation between the European Economic Community and
the Federative Republic of Brazil - Exchange of Letters between the European Economic
Community and the Federative Republic of Brazil on maritime transport [1995] OJ
L262/54.

[153] Agreement on partnership and cooperation establishing a partnership between the European
Communities and their Member States, of one part, and the Russian Federation, of the other
part - Protocol 1 on the establishment of a coal and steel contact group - Protocol 2 on mutual
administrative assistance for the correct application of customs legislation - Final Act -
Exchanges of letters - Minutes of signing [1997] OJ L327/3.

[154] Council Decision 1999/753/EC of 29 July 1999 concerning the provisional application of the
Agreement on Trade, Development and Cooperation between the European Community and
its Member States, of the one part, and the Republic of South Africa, of the other part [1999]
OJ L311/1.

[155] Agreement on Trade and Economic Cooperation between the EEC and the People's Republic
of China [1985] OJ L250/2.

[156] Agreement between the European Community and the Republic of Bolivia on precursors and
chemical substances frequently used in the illicit manufacture of narcotic drugs or
psychotropic substances [1995] OJ L324/3; Cooperation Agreement between the European
Community and the Kingdom of Cambodia - Joint Declarations - Exchange of letters on
maritime transport [1999] OJ L269/18; Agreement between the European Community and
the Republic of Chile on precursors and chemical substances frequently used for the illicit
manufacture of narcotic drugs and psychotropic substances [1998] OJ L336/48; Agreement
between the European Community and the Government of the People's Republic of China on
drug precursors and substances frequently used in the illicit manufacture of narcotic drugs or
psychotropic substances [2009] OJ L56/8; Agreement between the European Community and
the Republic of Colombia on precursors and chemical substances frequently used in the illicit
manufacture of narcotic drugs or psychotropic substances [1995] OJ L324/11; Cooperation
Agreement between the European Community and the Lao People's Democratic Republic
[1997] OJ L334/15; Agreement between the European Community and the United Mexican
States on cooperation regarding the control of precursors and chemical substances frequently
used in the illicit manufacture of narcotic drugs or psychotropic substances [1997] OJ L77/24;
Cooperation Agreement between the European Community and the Islamic Republic of
Pakistan on partnership and development fields, - Final Act - Final Act - Final Act [2004] OJ
L378/23; Agreement between the European Community and the Republic of Peru on
precursors and chemical substances frequently used in the illicit manufacture of narcotic
drugs or psychotropic substances [1995] OJ L324/27; Agreement between the European
Community and the Turkish Republic on precursors and chemical substances frequently used
in the illicit manufacture of narcotic drugs or psychotropic substances [2003] OJ L64/30;
Agreement between the European Community and the Republic of Venezuela on precursors
and chemical substances frequently used in the illicit manufacture of narcotic drugs or
psychotropic substances [1995] OJ L324/35.

range of industries, but are also used in the illicit manufacture of narcotic drugs or psychotropic substances.[157]

An important element of the EU's development policy concerns access to essential medicines and the problem of counterfeit and falsified medicines, and these are explored in detail in chapter 17. The ways in which EU policy on essential medicines interfaces with EU trade law, in particular, the application of TRIPS[158] to pharmaceuticals, stands in contrast to a more justice-based approach to global health.

EU development law has different legal and institutional arrangements from EU trade law. But it is also inextricably entwined with EU trade law. It follows that EU development law is also informed by ideas of modified liberalization. In this respect, EU development law embodies respect for values other than free trade – in particular, protection of consumers and patients from harm, and human rights and ethical values. But others would say that EU and global trade law is in direct competition with global health law.[159] EU development aid, and EU external relations more generally, are being closely linked to the EU's own strategy for growth – 'Europe 2020'.[160] One consequence of this linkage appears to be that the profile of health in EU development law has changed. While in earlier instruments, health is the first substantive or thematic area listed, in more recent documents, climate change, the environment and energy occupy that position, in line with the third 'European 2020' target. Health is largely left implicit. Where it is included, it is as a factor of growth and competitiveness, expressing a capacity-building approach which departs widely from either human rights-based or equality/poverty-based notions of global health law.

Conclusions

Is there enough coherence in the areas of EU law discussed here to suggest that EU external health law has developed sufficiently to be a meaningful analytical category? The evidence is certainly not conclusive. There is undoubtedly something in the claim that it has not done so. The institutional and legal

---

[157] See further, the EU's Drugs Strategies: Council of the European Union, 'EU Drugs Strategy (2005-2012)' (15074/04, Council of the European Union 2004) EU Drugs Strategy (2013-20) [2012] OJ C402/1; and Commission, 'Communication from the Commission to the European Parliament and the Council on an EU Drugs Action Plan for 2009-2012' (Communication) COM (2008) 567 final, and associated legislation.

[158] Uruguay Round of Multilateral Trade Negotiations (1986- 1994) - Annex 1 - Annex 1C - Agreement on Trade-Related Aspects of Intellectual Property Rights (WTO) [1994] OJ L336/214.

[159] Hein, 'Global Health Governance and WTO/TRIPS: Conflicts between 'Global "Market Creation" and "Global Social Rights"' in Hein, Bartsch and Kohlmorgen (eds), *Global Health Governance and the Fight against HIV/AIDS* (Palgrave Macmillan 2007) 38-66.

[160] See: Commission and High Representative of the EU for Foreign Affairs and Security Policy, 'Global Europe: A New Approach to Financing EU external action' COM (2011) 865 final.

arrangements that we have outlined in this chapter can be understood as a barely integrated hotchpotch of different policy areas, which are connected to global health, but share little beyond that. We have some sympathy with that interpretation. Moreover, at least some EU institutions agree. We began this chapter by noting that the European Commission's ambitious 2010 communication 'The EU Role in Global Health'[161] has not been taken further. There is apparently little appetite for a holistic EU global health strategy or policy, much less EU external health *law*.

However, the strongest version of the argument does not quite stack up. Although admittedly at quite a high level of abstraction, there are some discernible common aims, objectives and values in the EU's engagements with global health. EU trade law and EU development law share the values that we have summarized here as modified liberalism. Their trajectory, especially following the global financial crisis and economic downturn, reflects a strong focus on growth. Health is both a contributor to that growth (a productive factor), and an important industry. But growth is not expressed as an objective to be pursued at all costs. Values such as equality and human rights must remain protected. EU trade and development law articulate the EU's values about health – albeit in an imperfect way – but in a recognizably *European* way. Where they meet is, at least arguably, the site for EU external health law. On balance, we suggest that there is sufficient coherence in those of the EU's health-focused external relations activities which rely on international law, to recognize at least an emergent EU external health law.

This tentative conclusion sets the stage for our final set of questions. We consider how the key themes of EU health law, seen through individual and collective or systemic perspectives, play out in the global context. In order to explore this, in the chapters that follow we discuss six case studies, selected to illustrate the themes and perspectives: global organ transplants; access to essential medicines; global health markets and health knowledge in the global economy; communicable diseases law; and global trade law in tobacco and food.

In chapters 4, 5 and 6, we observed that the *very application* of EU law to health products or services perforce requires conceptualizing relationships within a consumerist frame. But the strong version of the claim that EU health law replaces relationships of trust, solidarity or professional ethics with those of consumer relations, with their positive resonances for patient autonomy and choice,[162] cannot be supported in all contexts. How does this conclusion hold up in the global context?

In chapters 7 and 8, we concluded that the strong version of the view that the EU now protects health rights as human rights cannot be supported. On the

---

[161] Commission (2010) above n 1.
[162] Albeit limited to certain patients (in particular, those most able to exercise autonomy and choice).

other hand, neither can it be persuasively asserted that the EU is entirely blind to the idea of health rights as human rights. The EU has articulated a particular version of its internal market law – one in which human rights are protected.[163] Is that also true for the EU's external health law, where it involves itself with global health as a human rights concern?

We have already explored some aspects of the interfaces between competition, solidarity and equality in the discussion above. EU trade law seeks to open up global markets for health services, although it is also attentive to the solidarity-based nature of national health systems within the EU. We extend our discussion of global health markets by considering these themes through the selected case studies. We concluded in chapter 11 that the conclusion that EU health law simplistically promotes free trade and competition, at the expense of solidarity and equality, cannot be sustained. Is this also so if we adopt a global focus?

Finally, what of the view that EU health law is ineffective at promoting patient or consumer interests, and *de facto* supports the continued operation of industries that are more focused on risk to capital investment than patients or consumers? In chapter 15, we concluded that a more nuanced analysis recognizes that, perhaps against the odds, EU law has achieved some benefits to health. To what extent is that conclusion also true for global health law? Has the EU taken its approach onto the global stage?

---

[163] Although the consequences for individual entitlements are minimal.

17

The global context: consumerism, rights, justice and equality; human organs and access to essential medicines

Introduction

Approximately 1.2 billion people (that is around 17 per cent of the world's population) live in extreme poverty, defined by the UN as existing on less than $1.25 a day.[1] The overwhelming majority live in southern Asia and sub-Saharan Africa. Those who have work are often bonded labourers, employed in agriculture, construction, or as domestic servants, living under conditions that are barely distinguishable from outright slavery. They are poorly educated, often illiterate, generally saddled with debt, and have significant numbers of dependants. For these people, access to even the basic conditions for a dignified human existence, as envisaged by international human rights instruments, is a remote possibility. Access to health care is even more remote.

As we saw in the previous chapter, the EU articulates a particular set of rhetorical values pertaining to health. They are shared by the international organizations with which the EU collaborates and cooperates. The EU trades with the countries in which the world's extreme poor live. It has signed development cooperation agreements with those countries. These trade and development agreements include, at least on their face, the idea of human rights conditionality. They also articulate an ethic of justice and equality, on which is based a commitment to end at least the extreme instances of poverty. How does this rhetoric play out in the EU's interactions with global health law? In this chapter, we explore this question through two examples where global health meets consumerism, human rights, justice and equality: the global market in human organs and access to essential medicines.

The global market in human organs

Organ transplantation provides a particularly timely case study as it is affected increasingly by technological developments. The development of immunosuppressant pharmaceuticals, in particular, the increased availability

---

[1] United Nations, 'The Millennium Development Goals Report 2014' (UN 2014) 8–9.

of cyclosporine, has changed the nature of organ donation, because it extends the group of potential organ donors for a particular patient to a much wider group than previously. In this context, wealthy patients (largely in the global North) may seek to source organs from the global South.[2] Indeed, there is some evidence that some patients actively choose to do so.[3] Whether organ transplantation as we currently know it will be needed in the future may depend, for example, on whether developments through stem cell technology or artificial organs provide a viable solution longer term.[4] However, the shortage of organs will remain a matter of concern for at least the next decade or more. The relative costs of artificial or stem-cell based organs, and transplants from living or deceased donors, are likely to mean that a demand for organs continues.

Global commerce in human organs

Only one country in the world currently permits the sale of human organs – Iran.[5] In all other countries, commercial dealing in human organs is a criminal offence. Notwithstanding, in many countries, there is clear documented evidence of a *de facto* black market in organs. For instance, in India, although organ selling has been banned since the Human Organ Transplantation Act of 1994, commentators suggest that there is still a large black market in organ trading. The Voluntary Health Association of India has estimated that about 2,000 Indians sell a kidney every year.[6] There are concerns that UK citizens are travelling to the Indian sub-continent to receive paid organ transplants.[7] In China, the law adopted in 2007 prohibits commercial transplantation, although there remains a trade in providing organs for payment to non-citizens.[8] Particular

---

[2] See the World Health Organisation figures cited in Sperling, 'Human Trafficking and Organ Trade: Does the Law Really Care for the Health of People' in Freeman, Hawkes and Bennett (eds), *Law and Global Health: Current Legal Issues Volume 16* (OUP 2014).

[3] See: Prasad et al. study, cited in Cohen, 'Transplant Tourism: The Ethics and Regulation of International Markets for Organs' (2013) 41(1) *Journal of Law, Medicine and Ethics* 269, 273, ftn 17; Cohen, *Patients with Passports: Medical Tourism, Law, and Ethics* (forthcoming, OUP 2015).

[4] For example, the first synthetic wind pipe transplant was undertaken in Sweden in 2011. Roberts, 'Surgeons carry out the first successful synthetic windpipe transplant' (*BBC News*, 7 July 2011).

[5] Only Iran has a market in organs approved by the state.

[6] Editorial, '"Transplant tourist" defends trip' (*BBC News*, 3 December 2007). Cohen (2013) above n 3, reports a 2001 study of 305 kidney sellers in Chennai, see: Goyal et al., 'Economic and Health Consequences of Selling a Kidney in India' (2002) 288(13) *Journal of the American Medical Association* 1589.

[7] Editorial, '"Transplant tourist" defends trip' (*BBC News*, 3 December 2007).

[8] McNeill and Coonan, 'Japanese flock to China for organ transplants' (*Asia Times online*, 4th April 2006); see also discussion in: Joint Council of Europe and United Nations Study, *Trafficking in organs, tissues and cells and trafficking in human beings for the purpose of the removal of organs* (Directorate General of Human Rights and Legal Affairs, Council of Europe 2009).

concerns relate to this jurisdiction, given the alleged practice of using organs for transplant from executed prisoners.[9] Studies in Pakistan, Bangladesh, Egypt, South Africa, Israel, Singapore and the Philippines also show evidence of illegal sales of human organs.[10] Closer to the EU, a Kosovar court has heard a criminal case against medical doctors involved in kidney donations from Turkey.[11] The WHO in May 2012 estimated that some 10,000 operations concerning organs purchased on the market take place every year.[12]

Paid organ donation and the ethics of commercial dealing in human organs remain the subject of great controversy across global health communities, having been discussed by ethicists, lawyers, policymakers and clinicians over many years.[13] Disapproval of the operation of a market in organs relates to perceptions of the status of the human body, questions of fundamental dignity, of human rights, and, in particular in contexts of extreme poverty, of autonomy. But a ban upon commercial organ selling can also be seen as an interference with personal autonomy, and indeed as such unjustifiable, regardless of whether a market in organs will increase the overall supply.[14] It is also suggested that a utilitarian analysis may justify a market in commercial dealing in human material, and some argue that lifting the statutory prohibitions upon commercial dealing would radically enhance the supply of organs for transplantation.[15] Others, while recognizing some of the challenges of a general market in organs, suggest that a market could operate effectively if it was on a highly regulated basis

---

[9] Branigan, 'Executed prisoners are main source of Chinese organ donations' *The Guardian* (London, 26 August 2009)

[10] See: Naqvi et al., 'A Socioeconomic Survey of Kidney Vendors in Pakistan' (2007) 20(11) *Transplant International* 934; Moniruzzaman, '"Living Cadavers" in Bangladesh: Bioviolence in the Human Organ Bazaar' (2012) 26(1) *Medical Anthropology Quarterly* 69; Yea, 'Trafficking in Parts: The Commercial Kidney Market in a Manila Slum, Philippines' (2010) 10(10) *Global Social Policy* 358; Budiani-Saberi and Delmonico, 'Organ Trafficking and Transplant Tourism: A Commentary on the Global Realities' (2008) 8(5) *American Journal of Transplantation* 925; Francis and Francis, 'Stateless Crimes, Legitimacy, and International Criminal Law: The Case of Organ Trafficking' (2010) 4(3) *Criminal Law & Philosophy* 283; all cited in: Cohen (2013) above n 3 and see further: Cohen (forthcoming, OUP 2015) above n 3; and Sperling, 'Human Trafficking and Organ Trade: Does the Law Really Care for the Health of People' in Freeman, Hawkes and Bennett above n 2.

[11] Peci, 'Kosovo Convicts Five Over Human Organ Trafficking' (*Balkan Transitional* Justice, April 2013); Cohen (2015) above n 3.

[12] Campbell and Davison, 'Illegal Kidney Trade Booms as New Organ is sold every hour' *The Guardian* (Shanghai, 28 May 2012).

[13] Lamb, *Organ Transplants and Ethics* (Routledge 1990) 133–140; Stacey Taylor, *Stakes and Kidneys: Why Markets in Human Body Parts are Morally Imperative* (Ashgate 2005); Price, *Legal and Ethical Aspects of Organ Transplantation* (CUP 2000): Wilkinson, *Bodies for Sale: Ethics and Exploitation in the Human Body Trade* (Routledge 2003); Cohen (2013) above n 3; Cohen (forthcoming, OUP 2015) above n 3.

[14] Savulescu, 'Is the sale of body parts wrong?' (2002) 29(3) *Journal of Medical Ethics* 138.

[15] Radcliffe-Richards, et al., 'The Case for Allowing Kidney Sales' (1998) 351(9120) *The Lancet* 1950.

with individuals, for example, selling their organs directly to the state.[16] While such an approach has the potential to provide a controlled framework enabling health and safety concerns regarding paid donors to be addressed *within* a particular state, it does not address the broader issue as to how to ensure effective regulation in a global market. Glenn Cohen has offered a nuanced analysis in this context, arguing that the outright ban on organ donation is difficult to defend on the grounds of protecting those who sell their organs, if a ban would, on balance, make them worse rather than better off. However, given the conditions under which organs are sold, Cohen argues that prohibition of organ sales is justified on grounds of information deficit, and the conditions of 'bounded rationality' under which organ sellers enter contracts. In some instances, sellers may lack capacity to consent; more seriously, consent cannot be presumed to be informed consent under the conditions of misinformation and downright deceit which are reported in the literature.[17]

While there is some support for commercial dealing in human organs, the prevailing trend in international medical and political communities is one of strong opposition. This opposition is reflected in various legal instruments. In the European context, for instance, the Council of Europe Convention on Human Rights and Biomedicine, Article 21, provides that 'The human body and its parts shall not, as such, give rise to financial gain'. The Parliamentary Assembly of the Council of Europe[18] recommended that states establish criminal responsibility for organ trade in their national criminal codes. Criminal penalties should cover brokers or other intermediaries, hospital-nursing staff and medical laboratory technicians who were involved in illegal transplant procedures. In addition, the Parliamentary Assembly proposed that sanctions should apply to those medical staff who encourage or provide information concerning transplant tourism, or those involved in follow-up care of patients after such transplants, if they fail to inform the enforcement authorities. However, the Parliamentary Assembly recommended that donors should be excluded from criminal liability because they were likely to have been deceived or to have been exploited. A recommendation was made that the Council of Europe should consider drafting an additional protocol to the Council of Europe Anti-Trafficking

---

[16] Errin and Harris, 'A Monopsonistic Market: Or How to Buy and Sell Human Organs, Tissues and Cells Ethically' in Robinson (ed), *Life and Death Under High Technology Medicine* (Manchester University Press 1994).

[17] 'Sellers were misinformed about safety, the quality of the doctor performing their surgery, and falsely assured with the myth of the 'sleeping kidney' [the idea that the remaining kidney will be 'activated' and the patient will suffer no health detriments following the operation], the promises of citizenship or a job, the pleasantness of the conditions … where the transplant will take place, and not informed about the possible physical and stigmatic consequences of the surgery': Cohen (2013) above n 3, 277. See also: Cohen (2015) above n 3.

[18] Council of Europe, 'Parliamentary Assembly Recommendation 1611 (2003) on trafficking in organs in Europe' (Council of Europe 2003).

Convention which was being debated at that time. Donor countries were to be encouraged to include specific provisions on organ trafficking in their criminal code and undertake 'effective measures' to combat trafficking in organs. In demand countries, the recommendation was that national medical insurance should deny reimbursement for illegal transplants abroad and follow-up care of unlawful transplants.[19] In addition, tight control of organ registers and waiting lists was recommended. The Council of Europe's approach was echoed in their subsequent Additional Protocol to the Convention on Human Rights and Biomedicine concerning Transplantation of Organs and Tissues of Human Origin.[20] Subsequently, in July 2014, a Convention prepared by a Committee of Experts on Trafficking in Organs was adopted by the Council of Europe.[21] The declared intention of the Council of Europe Convention against trafficking in human organs is:

(a) to prevent and combat the trafficking in human organs by providing for the criminalisation of certain acts; (b) to protect the rights of victims of the offences established in accordance with this Convention; (c) to facilitate cooperation at national and international levels on action against the trafficking in human organs.[22]

States in the Council of Europe are called upon to create as criminal offences the removal and subsequent use of human organs undertaken without consent or where payment (or 'other comparable advantage') is given to donors, whether in live or cadaver donation.[23] The Council of Europe instruments reflect two aspects of the debate: first, the argument that in itself trading in human material is inherently wrong and an infringement upon the dignity of the individual; and second, the question of autonomous choice in those deciding to sell organs and the risk of exploitation.

The approach of reflecting both aspects of the debate has been replicated in other global contexts.[24] The World Health Organization Assembly has consistently condemned trade in human organs as inconsistent with basic values and

---

[19]   Cohen discusses an equivalent proposal for the USA context, see: Cohen (2015) above n 3.

[20]   Additional Protocol to the Convention on Human Rights and Biomedicine concerning Transplantation of Organs and Tissues of Human Origin 2002, CETS No.: 186; and see also: Council of Europe, 'Parliamentary Assembly Recommendation 1611 (2003) on trafficking in organs in Europe' (Council of Europe 2003); Council of Europe, 'Committee of Ministers Recommendation 2004(7) to member states on organ trafficking' (Council of Europe 2004).

[21]   Council of Europe Convention against Trafficking in Human Organs 2014.

[22]   Council of Europe Convention against Trafficking in Human Organs 2014, Article 1.

[23]   Council of Europe Convention against Trafficking in Human Organs 2014, Articles 4 and 5. For the background to this Convention see: McGuinness and McHale, 'Transnational crimes related to health: How should law respond to illicit organ tourism?' (2014) 34 *Legal Studies* 682.

[24]   See, for instance: Asian Task Force on Organ Trafficking Recommendation on the Prohibition, Prevention and Elimination of Organ Trafficking in Asia, cited in: Joint Council of Europe and United Nations Study, *Trafficking in organs, tissues and cells and trafficking in human beings for the purpose of the removal of organs* (Directorate General of Human Rights and Legal Affairs, Council of Europe 2009).

as being in contravention of the Universal Declaration of Human Rights.[25] In 2004, a resolution of the World Health Assembly, while noting the concern at the shortage of organs for transplantation, went onto urge that governments:

> take measures to protect the poorest and most vulnerable groups from transplant tourism and the same of tissues and organs including attention to the wider problem of international trafficking in human tissues and organs.[26]

A particular concern, highlighted in international reviews of organ commerce,[27] is that those who may be motivated to sell their human material are generally unlikely to be in a position effectively to bargain in the market place and thus they may be at considerable risk of coercion and exploitation.[28] The Declaration of Istanbul on Organ Trafficking and Transplant[29] noted that, while organ brokers charged some £50,000 to £100,000 to facilitate a transplant, the donors could receive sums as little as £500 for donating a kidney, concluding that 'Organ trafficking and transplant tourism violate the principles of equity, justice and respect for human dignity and should be prohibited'. It is also suggested by some commentators that organ selling may result in the vendor being degraded.[30] It can be argued that organ selling is no more exploitative than many other practices which are permitted, such as low-paid work. Moreover, it might be justifiable as a practice if it has the effect of alleviating individuals from extreme poverty,[31] although any such alleviation from poverty is likely to be only temporary.[32]

---

[25] World Health Assembly, 'Resolution WHA 40.13: Development of guiding principles for human organ transplants' (40th World Health Assembly, WHA 1987). See also: WHO, 'WHO Guiding Principles on Human Cell, Tissue and Organ Transplantation' (WHO 2010), endorsed by the sixty-third World Health Assembly in May 2010, in Resolution WHA 63.22.

[26] World Health Assembly, 'Resolution WHA 57.18' (57th World Health Assembly 2004).

[27] In 2003 a report of the Council of Europe Parliamentary Assembly noted that trafficking networks targeted poorer European countries such as Estonia, Bulgaria, Georgia, Russia, Moldavia, Romania and the Ukraine and pressurise people into selling kidneys, see further: Council of Europe, 'Trafficking in Organs in Europe' (Doc. 9822, Council of Europe 2003); see also discussion in: Wilkinson (Routledge 2003) above n 13, 105.

[28] See generally discussion in: Wilkinson (Routledge 2003) above n 13, chapter 6, 126–132; Cohen (2013) above n 3; Cohen (OUP 2015) above n 3.

[29] Steering Committee of the Istanbul Summit, 'Organ Trafficking and transplant tourism and commercialism: the Declaration of Istanbul' (2008) 372(9632) *The Lancet* 5.

[30] See further discussion of this issue and ultimate rejection of this argument in: Duxbury, 'Do Markets Degrade?' (1996) 59(3) *Modern Law Review* 331.

[31] Veatch, 'Why Liberals Should Accept Financial Incentives for Organ Procurement' (2003) 13(1) *Kennedy Institute of Ethics Journal* 19; Cohen (2013) above n 3, 274-6; Cohen (OUP 2015) above n 3.

[32] As research regarding organ trading from India illustrates, see discussion in: Dickenson, *Body Shopping Converting Body Parts to Profit* (Oneworld 2009) 154. See also: Cohen (2013) above n 3; Cohen (OUP 2015) above n 3.

EU law and policy

As we saw in chapter 14, the EU's engagement with organ transplantation is comparatively recent.[33] It reflects the EU's developing public health law and policy flowing initially from what is now Article 168 TFEU, on the use of human material and the Blood Safety and Tissue and Cells Directives.[34] Given the international condemnation of organ trafficking, it is unsurprising that the EU has been consistent in its opposition to commercial dealing in human material in general, and to organ transplantation in particular.[35] The EU Charter on Fundamental Rights, Article 3, on the integrity of the person, echoes the Convention of Human Rights and Biomedicine. It provides that 'in the fields of medicine/biology the following must be respected:... The prohibition on making the human body and its parts as such a source of financial gain'.

EU legislation also reflects opposition to commercial dealing in human blood, tissue and cells, and organs. The Organ Transplant Directive 2010/53/EU[36] mirrors the early Blood Directive and Tissues and Cells Directive.[37] Its core focus is quality and safety of organs within the European Union.[38] The EU does not attempt to harmonize organ donation systems, although the Directive does provide that organ procurement must be consistent with national consent rules.[39] The EU is competent only to set minimum standards on blood, tissues and cells, and organs.[40] Member States may maintain or introduce more stringent national protective measures, for instance, requirements for voluntary and unpaid donations.[41] However, in line with the previous soft law measures

---

[33] Directive 2010/53/EU [2010] OJ L207/14. This is the correct number – see: Corrigendum to Directive 2010/45/EU [2010] OJ L243/68.

[34] Directive 2004/23/EC [2004] OJ L102/48. For a discussion of the background to the Tissue and Cells Directive, see: Hervey and McHale, *Health Law and the European Union* (CUP 2004) 421–426; and see chapter 14.

[35] See: Watson, 'European Parliament tries to stamp out trafficking in human organs' (2003) 327 *British Medical Journal* 1009; Commission, 'Organ Donation and Transplantation: policy action at EU level' (Communication) COM (2007) 275 final; European Parliament Resolution of 22 April 2008 on organ donation and transplantation: Policy actions at EU level (2007/2210 (INI)) [2009] OJ CE 259/1; Commission, 'Action plan on Organ Donation and Transplantation (2009-2015): Strengthened Cooperation between Member States' (Communication) COM (2008) 819 final, page 3.

[36] Directive 2010/53/EU [2010] OJ L207/14. This is the correct number – see: Corrigendum to Directive 2010/45/EU [2010] OJ L243/68.

[37] Directive 2002/98/EC [2003] OJ L33/30; Directive 2004/23/EC [2004] OJ L102/48.

[38] Member States must establish authorized 'competent authorities' responsible for the quality and safety framework required by the Directive: Directive 2010/53/EU of the European Parliament and of the Council of 7 July 2010 on standards of quality and safety of human organs intended for transplantation [2010] OJ L207/14, Article 17.

[39] Directive 2010/53/EU [2010] OJ L207/14, Article 14.

[40] This was necessitated in part by (now) Article 168 (7) TFEU, which states explicitly that provisions adopted under Article 168 (4) may not affect national provisions on organ or blood donation. Directive 2002/98/EC [2003] OJ L33/30, Recital 22; Directive 2010/53/EU, Recital 8.

[41] Directive 2002/98/EC [2003] OJ L33/30, Article 4 (2).

from the Council of Europe and WHO noted above, the Blood Safety Directive provides the strongest possible steer towards voluntary and unpaid blood donations, in Article 20, which states that:

> Member States shall take the necessary measures to encourage voluntary and unpaid blood donations with a view to ensuring that blood and blood components are in so far as possible provided from such donations.

The principle of voluntary and unpaid blood donations has formed a consistent part of EU law on human blood.[42] The relationship between unpaid donation and blood safety is most famously articulated by Richard Titmuss, in his seminal work *The Gift Relationship*.[43] Titmuss argued that the provision of human blood through a classical 'market' mechanism, in which donors are paid for blood, is inappropriate and inefficient. Following the emergence of HIV/AIDS, such arguments are lent even greater weight by the observation that the blood supplied by unpaid donors is also likely to be safer.[44] Most EU Member States do not pay blood donors, and there is no country in Europe with a totally 'for-profit' system of blood collection, but in some Member States, for instance, Germany and Austria, plasma and some whole blood donations to commercial centres are 'remunerated',[45] or rather expenses are reimbursed.[46] International bodies, such as the Council of Europe, the WHO and the Red Cross/Red Crescent, take the view that, ideally, blood and plasma donors should not be remunerated.[47] One of the main reasons for this is the suggestion that clinical paid donors are more likely to conceal potential hazards of the blood they are donating, including the possibility that a donor is seropositive. Unpaid voluntary blood donation has clear resonance with a notion of 'solidarity' between donors and recipients. Solidarity has been seen as part of a set of distinctively

---

[42] See, eg: Farrell, *The Politics of Blood: Ethics, Innovation and the Regulation of Risk* (CUP 2012).

[43] See: Titmuss, *The Gift Relationship: From Human Blood to Social Policy*, Oakley, A. and Ashton, J. (eds), (LSE Books 1997). For a counter-argument in the context of organ donation, see: Fagot-Largeault, 'Does Non-Commercialisation of the Human Body Increase Graft Security?' in Englert (ed), *Organ and Tissue Transplantation in the European Union* (Kluwer 1995).

[44] There is some debate about this among the scientific literature; for a recent overview of various studies, see: Van der Poel, Seifried and Schaasberg, 'Paying for Blood Donations: still a risk?' (2002) 83(4) *Vox Sanguinis* 285; and also the letter responding: Offergeld and Burger, 'Remuneration of blood donors and its impact on transfusion safety" (2003) 85(1) *Vox Sanguinis* 49.

[45] At least this was so in 1993: See: Hagen, *Blood Transfusion in Europe: a "white paper"* (Council of Europe 1993) 50–65.

[46] A reimbursement up to a certain amount is given for direct travel and real time expenses in Germany; see: Von Auer, 'Payment for blood donations in Germany (1995) 310(6976) *British Medical Journal* 399.

[47] Council of Europe, *Guide to the preparation, use and quality assurance of blood components* (17th edn, Council of Europe 2013); International Federation of Red Cross and Red Crescent Societies Blood Programme, *Quality Manual and Development Manual* (International Federation of Red Cross and Red Crescent Societies Blood Programme 1998), cited in: Politis, 'Blood donation systems as an integral part of the health system' (2000) 17(4) *Archives of Hellenic Medicine* 354.

'European' values. It stands in opposition to commercialization of the human body and its parts. The EU institutions may be seen here to be utilizing their legislative competence to express and perhaps shore up this 'European' value of solidarity.

Consistently with the EU's policy on blood donation, and Article 3 EU CFR, the EU Organ Transplant Directive[48] contains a clear statement against commercial dealing in organs, making clear that the practice takes place in a global context. The Preamble to the Directive states that:

> Unacceptable practices in organ donation and transplantation include trafficking in organs, sometimes linked to trafficking in persons for the purposes of the removal or organs which constitute a serious violation of fundamental rights and in particular of human dignity and physical integrity. This Directive although having as its first objective the safety and quality of organs contributes indirectly to combating organ trafficking through the establishment of competent authorities, the authorisation of transplant centres, the establishment of conditions of procurement, and systems of traceability.[49]

The patient safety measures envisaged by the Directive are also to play an indirect role in tackling unlawful global transplant markets. Here, the EU's competence in securing safe and high-quality organs is deployed, in so far as it can be, to tackle the human rights breaches inherent in human trafficking. Quality and safety, in particular traceability, are also brought to bear on the ethical context of global trade in organs. The Preamble also emphasizes that:

> Altruism is an important factor in organ donations. To ensure the quality and safety of organs, organ transplantation programmes should be founded on the principles of voluntary and unpaid donation. This is essential because the violation of these principles might be associated with unacceptable risks. Where donation is not voluntary and/or is undertaken with a view to financial gain, the quality of the process of donation could be jeopardised because improving the quality of life or saving the life of a person is not the main and/or the unique objective. Even if the process is developed in accordance with appropriate quality standards, a clinical history obtained from either a potential living donor or the relatives of a potential deceased donor who are seeking financial gain or are subjected to any kind of coercion might not be sufficiently accurate in terms of conditions and/or diseases potentially transmissible from donor to recipient. This could give rise to a safety problem for potential recipients since the medical team would have a limited capability for performing an appropriate risk assessment.[50]

The Directive mentions the EU Charter of Fundamental Rights, Article 3(2) and the Convention on Human Rights and Biomedicine Article 21, as well as WHO

---

[48] Directive 2010/53/EU [2010] OJ L207/14. This is the correct number – see: Corrigendum to Directive 2010/45/EU [2010] OJ L243/68.
[49] Directive 2010/53/EU, Recital 7.   [50] Directive 2010/53/EU, Recital 19.

principles on transplantation.[51] The Directive requires that donation should be voluntary and unpaid donation.[52]

Thus, the Organ Safety Directive articulates the principle of non-commodification of the human body in what is probably the strongest form consistent with the EU's limited competences. Member States may depart from the measures required by the Directive, to adopt *higher* standards if they wish. Given the ethically controversial dimensions of organ transplants, particularly in transplantation using cadaver organs,[53] it is not surprising that there are widely differing cultural and religious views across the EU's Member States.[54] Any involvement of the EU's institutions must take into account this multiplicity of approaches, in the absence of a 'European' standard. It follows that EU law on organs could not be further from the notion that EU law operates to bring relationships within healthcare settings within a consumerist frame. The provisions of EU legislation are almost (though not totally) blind to the reality of the global market in organs. They certainly do not conceptualize organ 'donation' as a commercial activity. Relations of 'donor' and recipient are constructed within EU law as relationships of solidarity, reflecting a strong ethic of altruism, and human rights related to autonomy, such as respect for the principle of informed consent.

However, in terms of the global realities of vendors and purchasers, with brokers as intermediaries, such legal provisions appear almost naive. Admittedly, it is difficult to envisage effective legal action against unlawful global trade in human organs, with the human suffering that entails. The criminal penalties that apply in virtually every country in the world have not put a stop to the practice. The law seems particularly deficient as a response to the drivers of both demand and, in particular, supply, given the disparities in wealth between the global North and South. EU law is no different from national law in this respect.

Possible additional legal responses that have been mooted include tackling the demand side by restricting access to public health care for those who have purchased organs unlawfully in the state in which the organ was procured. (It will be recalled that this means every state, except Iran.) Cohen reports a provision of the US Medicaid and Medicare system, as part of the consent process, which requires patients to be informed that if their transplant is not from an approved transplant centre they will be ineligible for immunosuppressive pharmaceuticals under the Medicaid or Medicare

---

[51] Directive 2010/53/EU, Recital 19.

[52] Directive 2010/53/EU, Article 13, although note that there are different approaches in different Member States as to the practical interpretation of this provision. See further: chapter 14.

[53] Organs from deceased persons.

[54] See further: Price, *Human Tissue for Transplantation and Research: A Model Legal and Ethical Donation Framework* (CUP 2009); Roels and Rahmel, 'The European Experience' (2011) 24(4) *Transplantation International* 350.

insurance.[55] This could operate as a disincentive to organ recipients seeking organs through the global black market in organs. The EU does not have competence to adopt measures requiring Member States to remove from the protection of the 'basket of care' of national health systems such organ recipients. But it could develop the informed consent provisions within its Organs Directive to steer Member States towards such an interpretation. Notwithstanding, this approach might sail too close to the boundaries of national discretion to be legally justified. But, in particular, should evidence from the USA or elsewhere that this policy is effective in stemming global trade in organs be forthcoming, the EU might justify such an approach from its ethic of non-commodification and on the basis of human rights protection.

Indeed, such an approach might even, with some interpretative imagination, already be envisaged within existing EU law. The EU's Directive 2011/36/EU on preventing and combating trafficking in human beings and protecting its victims requires Member States to ensure that intentional acts of human trafficking, 'for the purpose of exploitation', are 'punishable'.[56] The definition of trafficking adopted in that Directive would cover the act of a broker placing an organ seller in the hands of the medical professional removing an organ. Trafficking need not involve physical force – 'other forms of coercion, . . . fraud, abuse of power or a position of vulnerability or the giving or receiving of benefits' fall within the definition.[57] The definition of 'exploitation' explicitly covers 'the removal of organs'.[58] There is no doubt that the measure covers organ sellers within the criminal jurisdiction of the EU's Member States. Any attempt to purchase organs taking place *within* the EU must be the subject of criminal penalties.[59] These must also be applicable to the brokers of organ sales. Attempts to use national criminal law to prosecute international organ procurement rings have taken place in some countries, including the USA, as well as Brazil, South Africa, Israel, Singapore, Kosovo and Turkey.[60] The Directive could be interpreted to require Member States to do likewise. The problem here is, of course, effective detection, and the priorities of already over-stretched criminal enforcement agencies. But might the Directive also be interpreted to require 'punishment' of those who fuel the 'demand' side of human trafficking? If exclusion from national health system protection were construed as 'punishment', then it could be the basis for the EU to require Member States to go down that route. However, significant legal hurdles pull against that interpretation, not least that the Directive concerns criminal law, rather than access to national

---

[55] Cohen (2015) above n 3.   [56] Directive 2011/36/EU [2011] OJ L101/1, Article 2.
[57] Directive 2011/36/EU, Article 2 (1).   [58] Directive 2011/36/EU, Article 2 (3).
[59] This much is already the case in national law.
[60] Cohen (2013) above n 3, ftn 67; Sperling, 'Human Trafficking and Organ Trade: Does the Law Really Care for the Health of People' in in Freeman, Hawkes and Bennett (eds), above n 2.

health systems. The ethical objections to such an approach are also likely to preclude it being pursued in practice.[61]

There is no *external* EU law directly and explicitly concerned with the global trade in human organs. The EU has not used its external relations competence to seek to regulate organ procurement. The practices of global organ brokers of course fall within the 'human rights conditionality' clauses in EU trade and development cooperation agreements. But, notwithstanding clear evidence that they are being breached, consequences are few. It seems currently unlikely that the EU will use its external relations competence to address the question of illicit commercial organ trafficking with countries outside the EU. Rather, it seems that the EU leaves this to other supranational bodies, in particular the Council of Europe, with its explicitly human-rights and dignitarian focus. Anne-Maree Farrell reports a meeting of national experts which noted that global organ markets are being 'adequately addressed' by the Council of Europe. This was therefore not a priority for the EU.[62] In the global context, therefore, the EU's health law concerning organs – and, by extension, other human materials – is significantly limited. It is true that the EU's competence to act is limited – both legally and practically. But the EU could do more to seek to influence the global debate. It could, as other international organizations have done, articulate and pursue its human-rights and ethics-based position of non-commodification, which is strongly articulated in the policy discourse, through more practical steps, however small or incremental. In its choice not to do so, the EU could be said to be implicitly accepting the fact of the 'consumption' of human organs within a global market.

Access to essential medicines

The concept of 'essential medicines' emerged in the 1970s,[63] when the WHO first produced a list of medicines that satisfy the priority health needs of a population. The lists (for adults and children) are updated every two years, and provide a check for governments, particularly in least developed countries, seeking to optimize their health spending. Equal access to these 'essential medicines', irrespective of class, race, religion, sexuality and other 'forbidden grounds', is

---

[61] Though for discussion on the extension of extra-territorial jurisdiction in the context of the Council of Europe Convention, see: McGuinness and McHale, above n 23.

[62] Farrell, 'Adding Value? EU Governance of Organ Donation and Transplantation' (2010) 17(1) *European Journal of Health Law* 51.

[63] Hein, 'Global Health Governance and WTO/TRIPS: Conflicts between 'Global "Market Creation" and "Global Social Rights"' in Hein, Bartsch and Kohlmorgen (eds), *Global Health Governance and the Fight against HIV/AIDS* (Palgrave Macmillan 2007) 38, 49; Bozik, 'Essential Medicines: The Crisis in Developing Countries' (2011) 7(2) *Yale Journal of Medicine and Law* at 13.

considered to be part of the human right to health.[64] The idea is that these medicines should be made available at a price affordable to individuals and the community.[65] The WHO lists are not mandatory, but may be used by governments in setting their own lists, pricing arrangements and health system priorities. Over time, they have come to embody a powerful statement of global health inequality and injustice, as, in fact, many patients in least developed and developing countries do not have access to essential medicines.[66] Millennium Development Goal (MDG) 8E states that developed countries, in collaboration with the pharmaceutical industry, shall provide access to affordable essential drugs in developing countries.[67] Yet it is reported that there has been no progress overall towards this MDG since 2007.[68]

Putting aside government corruption, which is a serious problem in some countries,[69] there are three main interlocking explanations given for why patients in developing countries, and in particular in least developed countries, do not have access to the medicines that they need.[70] First, it is argued that the cost of in-patent (new) pharmaceuticals is prohibitive for countries in the global South. In order to incentivize development of new pharmaceuticals, global patent protection laws, found in WTO law, desired by the global North and the pharmaceuticals companies based there, in effect prevent the development of cheaper generics. Other intellectual property rights, such as data exclusivity and patent linkage, also affect access to essential medicines.[71] Some adjustments have been made to TRIPS in this respect, but the overall problem remains.

Second is the problem of falsified and counterfeit medicines. Pharmaceuticals are high-value products, and where regulatory enforcement structures

---

[64] Toebes, *The Right to Health as a Human Right in International Law* (Intersentia 1999). Toebes, 'The Right to Health', in Eide, Krause, and Rosas (eds), *Economic, Cultural and Social Rights* (2nd edn, Martinus Nijhoff Publishers 2001) Toebes, 'Right to Health and Health Care', *Encyclopaedia for Human Rights* (2009) vol 1, 365.

[65] WHO, 'Health Topics: Essential Medicines' (*WHO*, 2014)

[66] Approximately one-third of people world wide have access to essential medicines; in developing countries, the cost at public facilities is 270% of the international reference price and at private facilities it is 630%, see: Bozik above n 63.

[67] United Nations, 'Millennium Development Goals and Beyond 2015: Goal 8: Develop a Global Partnership for Development' (UN 2014).

[68] When the UN began tracking this MDG, see: Blue Sky, 'Developing Countries and Intellectual Property Enforcement Measures: Improving Access to Medicines through WTO Dispute Settlement' (2011) 3(2) *Trade, Law and Development* 407.

[69] Emily Jackson cites work of the World Medical Organisation (WMA, 'Resolution on Health and Human Rights Abuses in Zimbabwe' (58th WMA General Assembly 2007) and of Physicians for Human Rights (Physicians for Human Rights, 'Doctors Call Zimbabwe's Ruined Health System a "Man-Made Disaster"' (*Physicians for Human Rights*, 13 January 2009) claiming that Robert Mugabe's government denied access to healthcare to political opponents: Jackson, *Law and the Regulation of Medicines* (Hart 2012) 189–190.

[70] Jackson, above n 69, chapter 7.

[71] See Ho, 'Beyond Patents: Global Challenges to Affordable Medicine' in Cohen (2013) above n 3.

are relatively weak, such as in much of the global South, many of the pharmaceuticals available to patients are actually fakes.[72] Although counterfeit or falsified medicines may be found anywhere in the world,[73] the problem is greater in developing and least developed countries,[74] where the most common counterfeits are for treating life-threatening diseases, such as malaria, tuberculosis and HIV/AIDS.[75] Some of these fakes are benign, though not efficacious. This is a problem for individual patients who need the active ingredient, but can also be harmful to public health as communicable diseases are not effectively treated, and herd immunity can be compromised or drug resistance built up. Other counterfeit pharmaceuticals are positively harmful, either because they have the wrong active ingredient, the wrong dose, or include harmful contaminants.

Third, and more fundamentally, the global pharmaceutical industry is based on private capital. The underlying ('ethical') assumption is that the pursuit of shareholder profits in that context will increase overall welfare, through the operation of markets. But it is argued that a different approach to welfare is needed where access to essential medicines is concerned. Good health affects not only the patient concerned, but also in the case of communicable diseases, others around them. Good health is also crucial to development and well-being in general, for instance, in terms of a healthy workforce or of ability to exercise civil and political rights in a democracy. Moreover, health is a human right. For all these reasons, it is argued that good health should be treated as a public good. From this point of view, there are insufficient incentives for the development of treatments (and especially vaccines) for the kinds of health problems that are prevalent in the global South, as compared to treatments for the non-communicable diseases that concern the majority of patients in the global North, not to mention the increasingly lucrative market in 'lifestyle medicines'.

In order to understand how the EU has responded to these aspects of global health, we need to explore each a little further.

---

[72] There is also an emerging problem with counterfeit medical devices, see: MHRA, 'Counterfeit Medical Devices' (*MHRA*, 2 May 2012) and Council of Europe, 'The Medicrime Convention: Combating counterfeiting of medicial products and similar crimes' (Council of Europe 2011).

[73] The World Health Organisation reports that 50% of internet purchases of pharmaceuticals where the physical address of the supplier was not on the website were of counterfeit medicines: WHO, 'Medicines: spurious/falsely-labelled/ falsified/counterfeit (SFFC) medicines' (*WHO*, May 2012).

[74] WHO above n 73.

[75] According to the World Trade Organization, counterfeit anti-malaria pharmaceuticals are responsible for the deaths of 100,000 Africans a year. The black market in counterfeit pharmaceuticals deprives governments of between 2.5% and 5% of revenue. See: Kannan, 'Counterfeit drugs targeted by technology in India' (*BBC News*, 11 October 2011). In the global North, counterfeit medicines tend to be for treating so-called 'lifestyle' diseases, for example, counterfeit Viagra, hormones or steroids.

In-patent medicines and generics

The WTO's TRIPS agreement aims to harmonize intellectual property law across the globe, by setting agreed minimum standards for national intellectual property regimes.[76] All WTO member countries, and the EU, which is also a member of the WTO, are obliged by TRIPS to bring into force intellectual property laws, including patent protections for inventions. These include recognizing a twenty-year global patent protection for new pharmaceuticals. During that time, generic equivalents may not enter the marketplace. Because these generics are 'reverse engineered' from the on-patent product, they are much cheaper to produce. Before TRIPS entered into force in 1995, many developing countries provided a place where generics could be made, both for home markets, and for markets in other developing and least developed countries.[77] The key example is India, which had only a partial patent protection system in place, and had no patent protection at all for the active ingredients of pharmaceuticals. Signing up to TRIPS could be interpreted to mean that India could no longer be 'the developing world's pharmacy'.[78]

Although obviously the TRIPS agreement is first and foremost a trade agreement, it does include a number of provisions that potentially mitigate any negative effects it may have on health, particularly in the context of developing and least developed nations. The agreement contains several provisions for transitional implementation. In 2002, for least developed countries, the original transitional period for pharmaceutical products was extended to 2016. Developing countries, such as India, were given ten years until implementation was required.[79] The preamble to TRIPS recognizes 'developmental objectives' of national intellectual property law, and 'special needs of least developed country Members in respect of maximum flexibility in the domestic implementation of law and regulations in order to enable them to create a sound and viable technological base'. TRIPS, Article 7 states that intellectual property rights 'should contribute to the promotion of technological innovation . . . in a manner conducive to social and economic welfare' and Article 8 gives states parties power to 'adopt measures necessary to protect public health and nutrition, and to promote the public interest in sectors of vital importance to their . . . development'. This clause can be interpreted to include the health sector, and indeed essential medicines. There are also clauses allowing derogation in times of national emergency,[80] which would include major communicable disease outbreaks, such as influenza or SARS.

During the 'Doha Development round' of WTO negotiations, a group of eighty developing and least developed countries successfully proposed a

---

[76] See further: Gostin, *Global Health Law* (Harvard University Press 2014) 285–295.
[77] Jackson, above n 69, 193.
[78] Oxfam India, 'Oxfam calls on EU not to shut down 'pharmacy of the developing world'' (*Oxfam*, 9 February 2012).
[79] TRIPS, Article 65 (4).   [80] TRIPS, Article 31.

Declaration (the 'Doha Declaration' 2001) interpreting TRIPS in the context of public health issues, including access to essential medicines.[81] The Doha Declaration 'reaffirms the right of WTO members to use, to the full, the provisions in the TRIPS Agreement which provide flexibility... to protect public health and, in particular, to promote access to medicines for all'. In principle, WTO member countries may issue compulsory licences to manufacture in-patent medicines in cases of national emergency, such as 'HIV/AIDS, tuberculosis, malaria and other epidemics'. In practice, the procedures for doing so are cumbersome,[82] and the perceived threat of US economic sanctions (or perhaps the fear of the drain on national resources were currently unafford-able on-patent drugs to be locally produced) in effect dissuaded countries such as South Africa from using the compulsory licence provisions for HIV/AIDS treatments.[83]

One possibility for increasing global equality to access to essential medicines is to encourage developing and least developed countries to take advantage of these TRIPS flexibilities. Some of the literature suggests that the EU has done quite the opposite.[84] Although its policy statements suggest that the EU is concerned about access to essential medicines,[85] the EU's trade law has been used to move global intellectual property law in the opposite direction. TRIPS is a minimum agreement. Countries may freely enter into agreements

---

[81] Correa and Matthews, 'The Doha Declaration Ten Years on and its Impact on Access to Medicines and the Right to Health' (United Nations 2011); Aginam and Harrington, 'Introduction' in Harrington, Aginam and Yu (eds), *The Global Governance of HIV/AIDS: Intellectual Property and Access to Essential Medicines* (Edward Elgar 2012).

[82] They have been used, for instance, for supplying combination HIV/AIDS drugs from Canada to Rwanda, see: Jackson above n 69, 195–196; Blue Sky, above n 68; Tsai, 'Canada's Access to Medicines Regime: Lessons for Compulsory Licensing Schemes under the WTO Doha Declaration' (2009) 50(1) *Virginia Journal of International Law* 1063; for HIV/AIDS drugs in Brazil, and anti-platelet drug clopidogrel, used to treat heart disease, in Thailand, see: Sunder, 'An Issue of Life or Death' (2012) Yale University Press UC Davis Legal Studies Research Paper No 297; and for antiretroviral drugs in India, see: Jain and Darrow, 'Exploration of Compulsory Licensing as an Effective Policy Tool for Antiretroviral Drugs in India' (2013) 23(2) *Health Matrix* 425; Taylor, 'India's First Ever Compulsory Licence: a "game changing move"' (*PharmaTimes Online*, 12 March 2012). For a summary, see: Löfgren and Williams (eds), *The New Political Economy of Pharmaceuticals: Production, Innovation and TRIPS in the Global South* (Palgrave Macmillan 2013) 19–21.

[83] The reasons for the lack of use of compulsory licences are not simple, see: Schüklenk and Ashcroft, 'Affordable Access to Essential Medicines in Developing Countries: Conflicts between Ethical and Economic Imperatives' (2002) 27(2) *Journal of Medicine and Philosophy* 179; Jackson (Hart 2012) above n 69, 196; Sunder, above n 82.

[84] For instance, Arkinstall, et al., 'The reality behind the rhetoric: How European policies risk harming access to generic medicines in developing countries' (2011) 8(1) *Journal of Generic Medicines* 14; Shabalala and Bernasconi, 'The European Approach to Intellectual Property in European Partnership Agreements with the African, Caribbean and Pacific Group of Countries' (2007) CIEL Discussion Paper; Oxfam India, above n 78; Löfgren and Williams (eds), (Palgrave Macmillan 2013) above n 82.

[85] See, for instance, the statements made on the European Commission's website: Commission, 'Access to Medicines' (*Commission*, 28 February 2013).

that go further in protecting intellectual property rights. Since its 2006 *Global Europe* Communication,[86] signalling a new approach, the EU has been actively negotiating many 'third-generation', 'TRIPS-plus' agreements, including free trade agreements, and 'Economic Partnership Agreements',[87] with developing countries across the globe. Although these agreements typically state that the parties recognize and respect the Doha Declaration, they do so in the context of detailed provisions on patent law and enforcement of intellectual property law more generally. For example, the CARIFORUM agreement[88] provides that Article 8 TRIPS applies, and that:

> The Parties also agree that an adequate and effective enforcement of intellectual property rights should take account of the development needs of the CARIFO-RUM States, provide a balance of rights and obligations between right holders and users and allow the EC Party and the Signatory CARIFORUM States to protect public health and nutrition. Nothing in this Agreement shall be construed as to impair the capacity of the Parties and the Signatory CARIFORUM States to promote access to medicines.[89]

But the agreement also includes a section on effective enforcement of intellectual property rights, requiring that they be 'effective, proportionate and dissuasive', providing details on remedies and on enforcement procedures, including border controls. The agreement further provides that the CARIFORUM countries must cooperate with EU-provided support in developing national intellectual property laws, enforcement agencies and human resource training in enforcement.[90] Similarly, in the 2010 'new-generation' free trade agreement with Korea,[91] the parties 'shall commit to (g) promoting strong and efficient intellectual property rights enforcement by customs authorities, regarding imports, exports, re-exports, transit, transhipments and other customs procedures, and in

---

[86] Commission, 'Global Europe: Competing in the world: A contribution to the EU's Growth and Jobs Strategy' (Communication) COM (2006) 567 final.

[87] Commission, 'Overview of EPA Negotiations: Economic Partnership Agreement Negotiations' (Updated July 2014, Commission 2014).

[88] Economic Partnership Agreement between the CARIFORUM States, of the one part, and the European Community and its Member States, of the other part – Protocol I concerning the definition of the concept of 'originating products' and methods of administrative cooperation – Protocol II on mutual administrative assistance in customs matters – Protocol III on cultural cooperation – Final Act – Joint Declarations [2008] OJ L289/3.

[89] Economic Partnership Agreement between the CARIFORUM States, of the one part, and the European Community and its Member States, of the other part – Protocol I concerning the definition of the concept of 'originating products' and methods of administrative cooperation – Protocol II on mutual administrative assistance in customs matters – Protocol III on cultural cooperation – Final Act – Joint Declarations [2008] OJ L289/3, Article 139 (2).

[90] Economic Partnership Agreement between the CARIFORUM States, of the one part, and the European Community and its Member States, of the other part – Protocol I concerning the definition of the concept of 'originating products' and methods of administrative cooperation – Protocol II on mutual administrative assistance in customs matters – Protocol III on cultural cooperation – Final Act – Joint Declarations [2008] OJ L289/3, Article 164 (2) (b).

[91] Council Decision 2011/265/EU [2011] OJ L127/1.

particular as regards counterfeit goods',[92] and a whole Chapter covers intellectual property, specifying rights under TRIPS. The parties recognize the Doha
Declaration, and that they are entitled to rely on it in interpreting the rights
and obligations in the agreement.[93] However, the agreement goes on to specify
the application of these rules in the context of pharmaceuticals authorization.
Data confidentiality and non-reliance on data submitted for the purpose of
gaining marketing authorization for a pharmaceutical product must be guaranteed. National law must ensure that data on safety and efficacy of a new
pharmaceutical is not used to obtain another marketing authorization for a
pharmaceutical product, thereby prohibiting the use of reverse engineering and
bringing of products to authorization authorities without having undergone
fresh clinical trials.[94] This provision is followed by very detailed provisions on
effective enforcement of intellectual property rights.[95] Where bilateral agreements include provisions on private enforcement of intellectual property rights,
they are particularly concerning to those who seek to enhance access to essential
medicines through patent flexibilities.[96] The emergence of new bilateral investment treaties (BITS),[97] which include intellectual property within the definition
of investment, is another example of strengthening patent protection through
the possibility of private litigation.

On the other hand, some aspects of EU law and policy are less disruptive of
the access to essential medicines agenda than the approaches of other developed
countries, such as the USA and Japan. For instance, EU provision of technical assistance to developing countries in intellectual property matters, under
Article 61 TRIPS, puts more emphasis on incorporating TRIPS flexibilities
in national law, including those flexibilities concerning public health, than
technical assistance from other developed countries.[98] And, although the EU's

---

[92] Council Decision 2011/265/EU, Article 6.13 on Customs Cooperation.
[93] Council Decision 2011/265/EU, Article 10.34.
[94] Council Decision 2011/265/EU, Article 10.36.
[95] Council Decision 2011/265/EU, Articles 10.41-10.69.
[96] Oxfam International, 'Novartis launch renewed attack on India's right to produce affordable
    medicines' (Oxfam 2012).
[97] The aim of these international agreements is to limit the ability of states to interfere with
    investments made by foreign investors. In particular, they protect the property and intellectual
    property rights of foreign investors, relying on the principle of non-discrimination, providing
    for compensation in the event of expropriation of property, and protection against unfair
    treatment. International Investment Agreements usually allow foreign investors (in practice,
    multi-national firms) to bring claims directly against governments of states parties, and
    recover damages. International Investment Agreements are found within free trade
    agreements, see: Uruguay Round of Multilateral Trade Negotiations (1986- 1994) – Annex 1 –
    Annex 1A – Agreement on Trade-Related Investment Measures (WTO-GATT 1994) [1994] OJ
    L336/100, (indeed the provisions on freedom of establishment in the TFEU might be counted
    as a form of an international investment agreement) or as separate bilateral investment treaties
    (BITS). The application of BITS in health contexts is just beginning to emerge, for instance in
    the context of emergent multinational healthcare providers, or the tobacco industry. See:
    WHO, 'Workshop on trade-related issues relevant to implementation of the WHO FCTC
    [Framework Convention on Tobacco Control]' (WHO 2012) 9–12.
[98] Matthews and Munoz-Tellez, 'Bilateral Technical Assistance and TRIPS: The US, Japan and the
    EC in Comparative Perspective' (2006) 9(6) *Journal of World Intellectual Property* 629.

'TRIPS-plus' agreements do seek to promote enforcement of intellectual property rights, they tend to be less extensive and less specific than agreements to
which the USA is a party.[99]

The EU has also sought to enable differential pricing schemes for essential medicines being supplied to some of the poorest countries, without the
medicines being diverted back to the global North. Regulation 953/2003/EC to
avoid trade diversion into the EU of certain key medicines[100] sets up a scheme
whereby manufacturers or exporters of medicines used to treat HIV/AIDS,
tuberculosis or malaria may apply for 'tiered pricing' for sales into one of
seventy-six named countries.[101] The Regulation makes it illegal to import tiered
priced products into the EU, or to release them for free circulation, place them in
a free trade zone or a free warehouse.[102] The system has been used to authorize
some nine products.[103] However, the numbers of products sold are declin-
ing, suggesting that this approach is not particularly effective, compared, for
instance, to encouraging generics production, in securing access to essential
medicines.[104]

An alternative possibility to pursuing flexibility in TRIPS, encouraging differential pricing, bypassing patent protection by issuing compulsory licences,
or using patent pools,[105] is to more or less accept the global market conditions, but to use development aid to increase availability of medicines in least
developed and developing countries. This approach has been adopted by the
global pharmaceutical industry, sometimes working in partnership with international aid agencies, and referring to their 'corporate social responsibilities'.
Pharmaceutical companies have offered patented drugs at reduced prices, or
even made private donations of medicines free of charge to developing countries, such as Boehringer-Ingelheim's time-limited donation of Nevirapene to

[99]   Matthews, 'The Lisbon Treaty, trade agreements and the enforcement of intellectual property
       rights' (2010) 32(3) *European Intellectual Property Review* 104.
[100] Council Regulation 953/2003/EC [2003] OJ L135/1 (as amended). See further the proposed
       consolidating legislation: Commission, 'Proposal for a Regulation of the European Parliament
       and of the Council to avoid trade diversion into the European Union of certain key medicines'
       COM (2014) 319 final.
[101] Council Regulation 953/2003/EC, Annex II
[102] Council Regulation 953/2003/EC, Article 2.
[103] Council Regulation 953/2003/EC, Annex I, see also: Commission, 'Annual Report (2009) on
       the application of Council Regulation (EC) No 953/2003 of 26 May 2003 to avoid trade
       diversion into the European Union of certain key medicines' COM (2010) 652. All of the
       authorisations are held by Glaxo Smith Klein.
[104] Commission, 'Annual Report (2009) on the application of Council Regulation (EC) No
       953/2003 of 26 May 2003 to avoid trade diversion into the European Union of certain key
       medicines' COM (2010) 652, page 9.
[105] Discussed in Jackson, above n 69, 196–198. The idea of a patent pool in this context is that
       pharmaceutical companies would voluntarily make their patents available to generics
       producers in developing countries. A patent pool for HIV/AIDS medicines was set up by
       UNITAID. Although it has reduced the annual cost for antiretroviral therapies significantly
       in some developing countries, it is far from a 'cure-all' solution to the problem of access to
       essential medicines. The EU does not appear to have been involved in the patent pooling of
       essential medicines.

South Africa.[106] Likewise, the EU's development aid policy, organized into geographic and thematic strands, has been used to increase access to essential medicines, in particular, anti-retrovirals for the treatment of HIV/AIDS.[107] The thematic strand on 'Investing in People' explicitly refers to activity to 'increase the affordability of key pharmaceuticals and diagnostics' for the major communicable diseases, expressly mentioning HIV/AIDS, malaria and tuberculosis. The EU may use its development funding to 'encourage public and private investment in research and development for new treatments, new medicines, particularly vaccines, microbicides and innovative treatments' for major communicable diseases.[108] The Regulation also explicitly mentions the Doha Declaration's 'clarification' of the TRIPS provisions on public health. The geographic strand mentions health-related development in respect of some regions or countries, for instance, HIV/AIDS is mentioned explicitly for Asia, and South Africa.[109] In the EU's development policy, the financial reference amounts granted to each strand[110] are indicative of the relative importance of particular development concerns for the EU. Although health is not at the bottom of the table, there was greater EU investment in, for instance, food security, or in the ACP Sugar Protocol countries,[111] through the programme for the period 2007–13.[112]

One of the key ways in which the EU carries out its development policy in this area is through the Global Fund to fight HIV/AIDS, Tuberculosis and Malaria (ATM).[113] This is a multi-agency cooperative institution, which works with the 'Global Alliance for Vaccines and Immunisation', a public–private cooperation,[114] the World Bank and the WHO. The EU's 2010 evaluation of the Global Fund ATM, working alongside specific support programmes in individual countries, was extremely positive.[115] The EU thus increased its budgetary

---

[106] Schüklenk and Ashcroft, above n 83; Wogart, 'From Conflict over Compromise to Cooperation? Big Pharma, the HIV/AIDS crisis and the Rise of Countervailing Power in the South' in Hein, Bartsch and Kohlmorgen (eds), (Palgrave Macmillan 2007) above n 63.

[107] Regulation 1905/2006/EC [2005] OJ L304/1, repeals Regulation 1568/2003/EC [2003] OJ L224/7; and amends Regulation 2110/2005/EC [2005] OJ L344/1; and was also amended by: Regulation 1339/2011/EU [2011] OJ 347/30; Regulation 1341/2011/EU [2011] OJ L347/34; and Regulation 127/2013/EU [2013] OJ L43/28.

[108] Regulation 1905/2006/EC Article 12 (2) (a).

[109] Regulation 1905/2006/EC Articles 8 and 10.   [110] Regulation 1905/2006/EC Article 38.

[111] See: Regulation 1905/2006 Annex III: Barbados, Belize, Guyana, Jamaica, Saint Kitts and Nevis, Trinidad and Tobago, Fiji, Republic of the Congo, Côte d'Ivoire, Kenya, Madagascar, Malawi, Mauritius, Mozambique, Swaziland, Tanzania, Zambia, Zimbabwe.

[112] Regulation 1905/2006 Annex IV: Investing in people gets 1 060 EUR million. Food security gets 1 709 EUR million; ACP Sugar Protocol countries get 1 244 EUR million. Geographic programmes (which of course include health interventions) get the lion's share at 10 057 EUR million.

[113] For further discussion, see: Bartsch, 'The Global Fund to Fight AIDS, Tuberculosis and Malaria' in Hein, Bartsch and Kohlmorgen (eds), (Palgrave Macmillan 2007) above n 63, 146–171.

[114] <http://www.gavialliance.org/>.

[115] Commission, 'Investing in People: Mid Term Review of Strategy Paper for Thematic Programme (2007–2013)' (Commission 2010).

contribution to the Global Fund ATM in 2011, and pledged 1,252,500 euros to the Global Fund up to 2013.[116] This is an example of a more general phenomenon in terms of how the EU has become involved in global health. The EU embeds itself in, and contributes (human and financial resources) to, global governance institutions and activities that have a reputation for success. At least, arguably, the possibility of reputational gain, and the pursuit of an efficiency agenda, related to the idea of value for public money, rather than, for instance, a desire to improve global health equality, is a primary driver of the EU's policy choices.

To some extent this might explain why the EU has used the development aid approach, even though it has been criticized on moral grounds as being less effective than the alternatives, especially compulsory licensing.[117] As for the argument that patent enforcement is essential to protect the pharmaceutical industry, and to ensure that new treatments are continually developed, it seems it does not bear scrutiny when the main source of industry profits (the global North) is considered. Even if developing and least developed countries all granted compulsory licences, or simply breached TRIPS rules, it would not significantly affect the pharmaceutical industry's 'bottom line'.[118]

Counterfeit or falsified medicines

The European Medicines Agency defines falsified medicines as 'fake medicines that are designed to mimic real medicines' and counterfeit medicines as 'medicines that do not comply with intellectual property rights or that infringe trademark law'.[119] The two are not identical, but are treated together here as part of the problem of unethical trade in pharmaceuticals in global contexts, contributing to the lack of access to essential medicines experienced by the world's poorest people. The WHO notes that it is virtually impossible to gauge the extent of the problem, but one estimate is that 10 per cent of all pharmaceuticals sold globally are counterfeit or falsified, and in some developing countries it may be as much as one-third.[120] BRICS countries, in particular China, are claimed by the global North to be an important source, due to inadequate regulatory oversight of pharmaceuticals production and marketing.[121]

---

[116] See: The Global Fund, 'Annual Report 2011' (The Global Fund 2011).

[117] Schüklenk and Ashcroft above n 83.

[118] Schüklenk and Ashcroft above n 83, citing Brock, 'Some questions about the moral responsibilities of drug companies' (2001) 1(1) *Developing World Bioethics* 33; Daniels, 'Social responsibility and global pharmaceutical companies' (2001) 1(1) *Developing World Bioethics* 38.

[119] European Medicines Agency (EMA), 'Falsified Medicines' (*EMA*, 2014).

[120] See: MHRA, 'Counterfeit Medical Devices' (*MHRA*, 2 May 2012).

[121] The New York Times reported in 2007 that "China's health officials have known of this regulatory gap since at least the mid-1990s, when a chemical company sold a tainted ingredient that killed nearly 100 children in Haiti. But Chinese regulatory agencies have failed to cooperate to stop chemical companies from exporting drug products. In 2006, at least 138

The problem is compounded by the cost and logistics of testing suspected falsified medicines, although there is now some research into new cheap and effective mechanisms,[122] including through partnership arrangements between industry and international organizations.[123]

The problem of falsified and counterfeit medicines relates to access to essential medicines in two ways. Obviously, access to essential medicines is not achieved where the 'medicines' being made available are fake. Effective regulation is needed to prevent such forgeries reaching the market. The European Medicines Agency cooperates with the European Directorate for the Quality of Medicines and Healthcare,[124] and the WHO's International Medical Products Anti-Counterfeiting Taskforce (IMPACT),[125] as well as with the Council of Europe's 'Medicrime' Convention[126] and the OECD,[127] to seek to enforce the EU's Directive 2011/62/EU on falsified medicines for human use.[128] The Directive requires packaging elements to demonstrate authenticity,[129] increased requirements for supply-chain tracing, inspection obligations,[130] obligations on manufacturers and distributors to report suspect falsified medicines[131] and controls of on-line pharmacies.[132]

But counterfeit medicines also breach intellectual property law, for instance, copyright law, where packaging is also falsified. Intellectual property law is thus a possible regulatory tool to be deployed here. Nevertheless, overenthusiastic

---

Panamanians died or were disabled after another Chinese chemical company sold the same poisonous ingredient, diethylene glycol, which was mixed into cold medicine.", see: Bogdanich, 'Chinese Chemicals Flow Unchecked Onto World Drug Market' *The New York Times* (New York, 31 October 2007); and, Rappeport, 'US Regulator Calls for action on fake drugs' *Financial Times* (New York, 6 June 2012).

[122] E.g., American Chemical Society, 'Simple new test to combat counterfeit drug problem in developing countries' (*Science Daily*, 19 August 2012), involving a test for Panadol/Tylenol, the pain-and-fever-reliever acetaminophen.

[123] "In order to bridge the capacity gap in regular drug quality monitoring on national level in low-income countries and in order to overcome limited access to regular drug quality testing of public, private and faith-based drug supplies, the Global Pharma Health Fund (GPHF) set out to develop and supply inexpensive field test kits with simple test methods for rapid drug quality verification and counterfeit medicines detection." The 'Global Pharma MiniLabs' are marketed by GPHF to developing and least developed countries such as 34 African states. "The Global Pharma Health Fund (GPHF) is a charitable organization initiated and funded exclusively by donations from Merck, Darmstadt Germany." GPHF, 'The Global Pharma Health Fund (GPHF)' (*GPHF*, 2014). It works in partnership with WHO.

[124] Responsible for the European Pharmacopoeia, see: Council of Europe, 'EDQM' (*Council of Europe*, 2014).

[125] Launched in 2006, see: WHO, 'International Medical Products Anti-Counterfeiting Taskforce (IMPACT)' (*WHO*, 2014).

[126] Council of Europe, 'The Medicrime Convention: Combating counterfeiting of medical products and similar crimes' (Council of Europe 2011).

[127] Now on 'indefinite hold', see: OECD, 'OECD project on counterfeiting and piracy' (*OECD*, 2014).

[128] Directive 2011/62/EU.   [129] Directive 2011/62/EU, Article 1 (3).

[130] Directive 2011/62/EU, Article 1 (21) and (22), including a procedure for verifying whether non-EU countries' inspection systems are reliable.

[131] Directive 2011/62/EU Article 1 (24).   [132] Directive 2011/62/EU, Article 1 (20).

application of measures essentially designed to protect the pharmaceuticals industry's intellectual property interests, carried out in the name of protecting patients from falsified or counterfeit medicines, has been criticized as unnecessarily impeding trade flows of (genuine) generic medicines.[133] Regulation 608/2013/EU sets procedures for customs authorities where products, either being released for free circulation, or being found during checks on goods being imported into or exported from the EU, are suspected of breaching intellectual property rights, and where goods are found to have breached intellectual property rights.[134] The Regulation allows holders of intellectual property rights, including patents, to apply to the customs authorities to take action.[135] Customs authorities, in accordance with national law, have significant powers to seize and retain goods, while investigations take place, and even to destroy them, in some cases without a finding of infringement.[136] Goods to be destroyed under the Regulation may not be released for free circulation, brought out of the EU's customs territory, exported, re-exported, or placed in a free zone or warehouse.[137]

In 2008, following careful planning by the European Council and Commission,[138] the Dutch customs authorities seized a shipment of a pharmaceutical (losartan potassium) in transit between India and Brazil, on the basis of the Regulation. Similar seizures took place subsequently, again mainly involving exports from India, destined for several other developing countries, including Venezuela, Columbia, Peru and Nigeria. At least one incident involved a shipment of medicines funded by UNITAID,[139] an international drug purchase organization, supported by twenty-nine (developed and developing) countries and the Gates Foundation, which works with the WHO and the Global Fund ATM.[140] Many of these consignments involved generic drugs, and most were destroyed, or returned to the country of origin. The consequences for access to essential medicines in the developing world of this use by the EU of intellectual property law by customs authorities has been condemned both by governments

---

[133] The right to health has also been deployed as a tool to tackle such legislation, for instance by the Kenyan constitutional court, see Harrington, 'Access to Essential Medicines in Kenya: IP, Anti-Counterfeiting, and the Right to Health' in Freeman, Hawkes and Bennett (eds), (OUP 2014) above n 2.

[134] Regulation 608/2013/EU, Article 1. This Regulation repeals the earlier Regulation 1383/2003/EC.

[135] Regulation 608/2013/EU, Articles 3–6.

[136] Regulation 608/2013/EU, Article 23. This power has been criticized as excessively punitive, see: Arkinstall, et al., 'The reality behind the rhetoric: How European policies risk harming access to generic medicines in developing countries' (2011) 8(1) *Journal of Generic Medicines* 14.

[137] Regulation 608/2013/EU, Article 25.

[138] Abbott, 'Worst Fears Realised: The Dutch Confiscation of Medicines Bound from India to Brazil' (2009) 1 *Bridges, International Centre for Trade and Sustainable Development* 13.

[139] Ruse-Khan, H.G., 'A Trade Agreement Creating Barriers to International Trade?: ACTA Border Measures and Goods in Transit' (2011) 26(3) *American University International Law Review* 645.

[140] Unitaid (*WHO*, 2014).

at the TRIPS Council[141] and by a range of NGOs[142] and other commentators.[143] Their view is that the EU Regulation undermines the TRIPS flexibilities, especially as interpreted in the Doha Declaration. They are critical of the effect of the Regulation on national intellectual property law in both the exporting and receiving states, pointing out that the medicines were lawfully produced in the former, and would be lawfully imported marketed and consumed in the latter.[144] In particular, in effect, they would render compulsory licensing arrangements pointless, as any compulsory licence granted would make no difference to the infringement of a patent right under the Regulation.[145] WTO Dispute Settlement Proceedings were taken by Brazil and India against the EU.[146] India settled in 2011, when the EU agreed to cease its practice unless there was evidence of a substantial likelihood of the generics being diverted to the EU market and to review Regulation 1383/2003/EC,[147] which it has now done. Brazil's is still 'in consultations'.[148]

Following the Lisbon Treaty, the common commercial policy is now an area of EU exclusive competence. Common commercial policy includes the commercial aspects of intellectual property. Regulation 608/2013/EU is therefore based on Article 207 TFEU.[149] This Treaty amendment increases the role of the European Parliament which now has a veto over such agreements.[150] However,

---

[141] Statement by Brazil, Intervention by India (both available here: Mara and New, 'Concerns Continue Over Generic Drug Seizures As Legality Debates Begin' (*Intellectual Property Watch*, 5 March 2009) WTO, 'TRIPS General Council: Meeting of 3–4 February 2009' (*WTO*, 2014).

[142] See: e.g., Unitaid, 'Unitaid Statement on Dutch Confiscation of Medicines Shipment' (*WHO*, 2014) Oxfam International, 'Trading Away Access to Medicines' (*Oxfam International*, 2009).

[143] Arkinstall, et al., above n 84.

[144] Baker, 'Settlement of the India/EU WTO Dispute re Seizures of In-Transit Medicines: Why the proposed EU Border Regulation isn't Good Enough' (2012) Program on Information Justice and Intellectual Property Research Paper No 2012/02.

[145] Abbott, 'Worst Fears Realised: The Dutch Confiscation of Medicines Bound from India to Brazil' (2009) 1 *Bridges, International Centre for Trade and Sustainable Development* 13, Ruse-Khan 'A Trade Agreement Creating Barriers to International Trade?: ACTA Border Measures and Goods in Transit' (2011) 26(3) *American University International Law Review* 645.

[146] *European Union and a Member State – Seizure of Generic Drugs in Transit (India)* [2010] DS408, WTO Appellate Body (Consultation stage). *European Union and a Member State – Seizure of Generic Drugs in Transit (Brazil)* [2010] DS409, WTO Appellate Body (Consultation stage). The consultations were joined by Canada, China, Ecuador, India, Japan and Turkey.

[147] Brazil's dispute has been suspended pending the new EU Regulation. Baker, above n 44.

[148] See: WTO, 'Current status of disputes' (*WTO*, 26 August 2014).

[149] Commission, 'Proposal for a Regulation of the European Parliament and of the Council concerning customs enforcement of intellectual property rights' COM (2011) 285 final.

[150] Under Article 207 (2) TFEU, the 'ordinary legislative' procedure applies. In that procedure both Council and the European Parliament must agree on the Commission's proposal, see: Articles 289 and 294 TFEU. See further on the implications: Matthews, 'The Lisbon Treaty, trade agreements and the enforcement of intellectual property rights' (2010) 32(3) *European Intellectual Property Review* 104.

those who hoped that the European Parliament would exercise its new powers in the proposed amendment to the EU's Regulation on customs enforcement of intellectual property rights, so as better to protect access to essential medicines in developing countries,[151] must be somewhat disappointed. If Regulation 608/2013/EU had responded to such concerns, it would, for instance, be limited in scope to counterfeit trade-mark goods (so as to remove these goods from circulation); apply only to goods destined for the EU market, not goods in transit. The European Parliament's report and proposed amendments keep intact the basic idea of the Regulation, its application to a wide range of intellectual property rights, including patents and supplementary protection certificates for medicinal products, and to goods in transit. However, the new Regulation confirms the implied derogation for parallel trade in Regulation 1383/2003/EC, and explicitly excludes parallel trade.[152] As parallel trade is a practice that *de facto* reduces the price of medicines worldwide, the clarification may be seen as a small step towards increased access to essential medicines.

With respect to the question of goods in transit, the CJEU has ruled that a mere abstract consideration that the goods are to be fraudulently diverted to the EU market is insufficient to trigger the application of the Regulation. However, 'where it is proven that they are intended to be put on sale in the EU', they may be classified as 'counterfeit goods' under the Regulation.[153] Evidence includes where the products have been sold, offered for sale or advertised to customers in the EU, or where other documentary evidence suggests the products are to be diverted to the EU. The 2013 Regulation deals explicitly with access to essential medicines, in the context of the Doha Declaration, and states in recital 11 that customs authorities must take into account 'any substantial likelihood' of the products reaching the EU market. The European Parliament proposed adding a recital 17b, reflecting the CJEU's jurisprudence.[154] However, nothing to this effect was adopted in the final text.

The European Parliament has exercised its veto in the context of the proposed and highly controversial Anti-Counterfeiting Trade Agreement (ACTA). ACTA, which would fall outside the WTO, WIPO (the World Intellectual Property Organization) and the UN, is a proposed multilateral treaty aiming to

---

[151] E.g. Oxfam, see: Oxfam International, 'Public Consultation on the review of Council Regulation 1383/2003' (available: Commission, 'Consultation on the Commission Report on the enforcement of intellectual property rights' (*Commission*, 11 July 2011) ; Oxfam, 'Oxfam Reaction to the May 2011 Proposal for a Regulation of the European Parliament and of the Council Concerning Customs Enforcement of Intellectual Property Rights (replacing Council Regulation 1383/2003)' (Oxfam 2011). See also Baker, above n 144.

[152] Regulation 608/2013/EU, Recital 6.

[153] *Koninklijke Philips Electronics*, C-446/09 and C-495/09, EU:C:2011:796, paragraph 62 and 71.

[154] Committee on the Internal Market and Consumer Protection and Committee on International Trade, 'Committee Report on the proposal for a regulation of the European Parliament and of the Council concerning customs enforcement of intellectual property rights (COM(2011)0285)' (A7-0046/2012, European Parliament 2012).

enhance international enforcement of intellectual property rights. The countries involved are largely from the global North, including the USA, Japan and the EU.[155] ACTA is controversial for several reasons, including the secrecy surrounding its negotiations, which has been criticized by civil society organizations and governments of countries in the global South.[156] Various NGOs, including Oxfam and Médecins Sans Frontières,[157] and others,[158] have criticized ACTA, on the basis that it would limit lawful trade in generic medicines, essential to providing access to essential medicines in the global South. ACTA was open for signature until May 2013, and the EU, along with twenty-two of its Member States, has signed it. ACTA will not come into force unless six countries ratify it. So far only Japan has done so. In July 2012, the European Parliament voted decisively against the measure.[159] The Commission suspended its ratification processes, and referred to the CJEU on the question of competence, though the case was subsequently withdrawn.[160] The Parliamentary opposition in effect means that, for political reasons, the EU will not ratify ACTA, and it seems unlikely that any of its Member States will do so either.[161]

Those who oppose use of intellectual property law in the context of securing access to essential medicines, and reducing the threat from counterfeit and falsified medicines, argue that other regulatory means, for instance, inspection for fake packaging, and cooperative use of the criminal law,[162] would be more effective. In reality, they argue, the kinds of measures like ACTA against

---

[155] For more information on ACTA, see: Commission, 'What ACTA is about' (Commission 2012). Signatories to date are Australia, Canada, the EU (and its Member States), Japan, Mexico, Morocco, New Zealand, Singapore, and the USA, see: Commission, 'Trade: Intellectual Property' (*Commission*, 4 July 2014).

[156] Dutch MEP Sophie in 't Veld has had some success in obtaining access to ACTA negotiation documents, using the EU's transparency rules, see: *in't Veld*, C-350/12 P, EU:C:2014:2039.

[157] Dransfield, 'Oxfam reaction to European parliament vote on ACTA' (*Oxfam*, 4 July 2012); Médicins Sans Frontières (MSF), 'MSF Briefing Document: A Blank Cheque for Abuse' (Médicins Sans Frontières 2012).

[158] Baker, 'ACTA – risks of Third Party Enforcement for Access to Medicines' (2011) 26(3) *American University International Law Review* 579.

[159] 478 votes against, 39 in favour, 165 abstentions.

[160] The referral was under the rarely used procedure in Article 218 TFEU. See: Meyer, 'ACTA gets final stake through heart as EC drops court referral' (*ZDNet*, 20 December 2012); Palmedo, 'Final Blow to ACTA in the EU: European Court of Justice No Longer to Rule on Its Legality' (*Infojustice.org*, 20 December 2012). In a different context, the CJEU has held that only those EU intellectual property laws 'with a specific link to international trade are capable of falling within the concept of 'commercial aspects of intellectual property' in Article 207 (1) TFEU and hence the field of the common commercial policy' over which the EU has exclusive competence: *Daiichi Sankyo*, C-414/11, EU:C:2013:520, paragraph 52. TRIPS, Article 27, on patent protection, falls within Article 207 (1) TFEU, see: *Daiichi Sankyo*, EU:2013:520, paragraph 61.

[161] This means that at least 6 of the 8 non-EU signatories would have to ratify ACTA. They are Australia, Canada, Japan (which has done so), Morocco, New Zealand, Singapore, South Korea, and the USA. The US has expressed renewed commitment to doing so, in its 2013 Trade Policy Agenda, and Canada introduced a Bill to secure legislative compliance in March 2013.

[162] Such as envisaged by the Council of Europe's Medicrime Convention, see: Council of Europe, 'The Medicrime Convention' (*Council of Europe*, 2014).

counterfeit pharmaceuticals have little to do with concerns about the quality or safety of medicines.[163] In using patent law, the EU has essentially supported the interests of the global pharmaceutical industry disproportionately over those of patients in the global South, and pharmaceuticals companies in developing countries. The EU has coincidentally extended the practical reach of the national interpretations of TRIPS in its own Member States to outside the EU's territory, undermining the flexibilities inherent in TRIPS. However, in rejecting ACTA, the EU has not gone as far as other jurisdictions in this respect.

Incentives for developing medicines for the global South

In 1999, the NGO Médecins Sans Frontières won the Nobel Peace Prize. So serious is the deficiency in the current global system for research into, development and marketing of new pharmaceuticals and vaccines for the diseases that affect the poorest patients in the world (so-called 'neglected tropical diseases')[164] that MSF invested its prize winnings in what it describes as a new model for researching and developing these products.[165] Several other similar public–private partnerships, including the Global Alliance for Vaccines and Immunisation (GAVI) mentioned above,[166] pursue similar aims.[167] More than 1 billion people across the world are affected with one or more neglected tropical diseases. Yet, according to the WHO, 'less than 1% of the 1393 new drugs registered during 1975–1999 were for tropical diseases, and less than 0.001% of the US$ 60–70 billion spent on new drugs went towards developing new and urgently needed treatments for tropical diseases'.[168] The disparity is said to be because neglected tropical diseases:

> persist under conditions of poverty and are concentrated almost exclusively in impoverished populations in the developing world . . . tend to be hidden below the radar screens of health services and politicians because they afflict populations that are marginalized, with little political voice . . . and do not pose an immediate threat to Western society.[169]

[163] Arkinstall, et al., above n 84; Menghaney, '"Counterfeit" confusion diverts action from drug quality' (*MSF*, 4 April 2011).

[164] WHO, 'Neglected Tropical Diseases' (WHO 2009). They are diseases such as dengue, rabies, leprosy, sleeping sickness. For a list, see: WHO, 'Neglected Tropical Diseases: The 17 neglected tropical diseases' (*WHO*, 2014).

[165] This is the 'Drugs for Neglected Diseases Initiative (DNDi): at <http://www.dndi.org/>. The EU is not involved in this initiative.

[166] <http://www.gavialliance.org/>, Jackson, above n 69, 199–201.

[167] See: Clemens, et al., 'Ten years of the Global Alliance for Vaccines and Immunization: challenges and progress' (2010) 11(12) *Nature Immunology* 1069; Nwaka and Ridley, 'Virtual drug discovery and development for neglected diseases through public-private partnerships' (2003) 2 *Nature Reviews Drug Discovery* 919.

[168] WHO, 'Neglected Tropical Diseases' (WHO 2009) 13.   [169] *Ibid.*

As Emily Jackson explains, none of the current incentives for developing medicines for the global South ('advance market commitments'; 'priority review vouchers'; 'soft' incentives) is a clear success.[170]

The idea of advance market commitments (AMCs) responds to the fact that market incentives do not work particularly effectively for the production of vaccines, from the point of view of public health. To remove some of the risks inherent in entering the market for vaccines, governments, international organizations or public–private partnerships formally undertake to purchase vaccines in accordance with terms and conditions set out in advance. Manufacturers who might be interested tender for a share in the AMC funding, which funds an agreement to supply a fixed number of doses at a fixed price. The idea is that manufacturers are able to recover investment costs more quickly than under normal market conditions. The donor of the AMC funding only pays if the vaccine is authorized as suitable by the relevant countries, and they are willing to purchase it, albeit at heavily subsidized rates. Early assessments of AMC for pneumococcal vaccines suggested some qualified success,[171] although others have been more critical of the idea.[172] Priority review vouchers allow a company that has developed and brought to market a medicine or vaccine for a neglected tropical disease to have a quicker authorization process for a future product. The system has been used in the USA, and is viewed by some as a success[173] that should be emulated in the EU.[174] However, as with AMCs, there are a number of potential problems with priority review vouchers.[175]

The EU's involvement in this particular aspect of global health is minimal. The principal policy tool used by the EU to encourage development of medicines and vaccines for the global South is through its development cooperation policy. Here, it seems that there is little EU interest. Although the EU stated in 2011 on its website[176] that it supports 'innovative sources of finance for development' including 'advanced market commitments',[177] the website's hyperlink went to GAVI's pneumococcal vaccines AMC,[178] and the EU is not listed as a donor (though Italy and the UK are). The European Commission's EU Accountability

---

[170] See also: Moran, 'Global Health Policy Responses to the World's Neglected Diseases' in Brown, et al. (eds), *The Handbook of Global Health Policy* (Wiley 2014).

[171] Cernuschi, Furrer, Schwalbe, Jones, Berndt and McAdams, 'Advance Market Commitment for pneumococcal vaccines: putting theory into practice' (2011) 89(12) *Bulletin of the WHO* 913.

[172] See: Jackson above n 69, 199–201, and the sources cited therein.

[173] Sonderholm, 'In Defence of Priority Review Vouchers' (2009) 23(7) *Bioethics* 413.

[174] Ridley and Sanchez, 'Introduction of European priority review vouchers to encourage development of new medicines for neglected diseases' (2010) 376(9744) *The Lancet* 922.

[175] See: Jackson above n 69, 201–204.

[176] See also the EU Presidency Statement of Mr. Jarl-Håkan Rosengren (Minister Counsellor, Permanent Mission of Finland to the United Nations, on behalf of the European Union), 'EU Presidency Statement – Macroeconomic policy questions and follow-up to Financing for Development' (*Delegation of the EU before the UN*, 9 October 2006).

[177] In December 2011 <http://ec.europa.eu/europeaid/how/delivering-aid/monterrey_en.htm> (hyperlink no longer works).

[178] GAVI, 'Pneumococcal AMC' (*GAVI*, 2014).

Report, 2012, on financing for development, notes that twelve Member States use, or are planning to use, AMCs to leverage development aid[179] – the EU is not listed as having such plans.[180] The AMC mechanism does not appear to be used or even under consideration by the European Centre for Disease Control. If the EU were serious about this mechanism for developing medicines for the global South, one would expect its principal communicable disease control institution to be at least exploring its potential. As far as we have been able to ascertain, this is not the case, although there is a modicum of interest from some other institutions.[181]

In terms of 'soft' incentives, such as reputation, the notion of 'corporate social responsibility' seems to be having some effect in the area of developing vaccines and medicines for neglected tropical diseases.[182] But, again, there does not appear to be a great deal of EU activity in this respect. The European Commission's Commission 'A Renewed EU Strategy 2011–2014 for Corporate Social Responsibility'[183] does not mention access to essential medicines at all. There was a 'platform' on access to medicines in developing countries with a focus on Africa[184] within the context of DG Enterprise and Industry's Process on CSR in the field of pharmaceuticals. This platform, bringing together industry and other stakeholders, 'facilitated discussion' on 'non-regulatory' aspects of access to essential medicines. The reported activity in the Africa platform is significantly less than the activity reported in the platform on access to medicines in Europe.[185] The work of the platform finished in 2013. Its final report called for continued dialogue and partnerships.[186]

---

[179] France is one of the leading states in this regard, see: France Diplomatie, 'Innovative financing for development' (*France Diplomatie*, 26 December 2013).

[180] Commission, 'EU Accountability Report 2012 on Review of progress of the EU and its Member States: Financing for Development' (Commission 2012).

[181] Searching for 'priority review voucher' in 2011 found nothing on either the Europa website or Eur-lex, suggesting that the EU was not interested in developing or contributing to the development of this mechanism. In 2014, the phrase results in three hits on Europa: A DG Enterprise and WHO sponsored project: Kaplan, et al., 'Priority Medicines for Europe and the World' (WHO 2013) ; a presentation on rare diseases within a DG Research health research project: Pfizer, 'Orphan and Genetic Diseases at Pfizer' (Pfizer 2010) and, Aymé, S. and Rodwell, C. (eds), '2014 Report on the State of the Art of Rare Disease Activities in Europe: Part I: Overview of Rare Disease Activities in Europe' (EUCERD 2014), all of which describe the US system. Eur-lex reveals a Parliamentary question from Mario Mauro: Mauro, 'Parliamentary Questions: Subject: Developing medicines for neglected diseases: the priority review voucher' (European Parliament 2011) and a European Commission staff working document which says that the policy option of priority review vouchers 'needs to be continuously evaluated': Commission, 'European research and knowledge for global health: The EU Role in Global Health' SEC (2010) 381 final.

[182] See: Jackson, above n 69, 203–204.

[183] Commission, 'A renewed EU strategy 2011–14 for Corporate Social Responsibility' COM (2011) 681 final.

[184] Commission, 'Platform on Access to medicines in developing countries with a focus on Africa' (*Commission*, 24 February 2014).

[185] Commission, 'Platform on access to medicines in Europe' (*Commission*, 20 August 2014).

[186] Commission, 'EU-Africa Pharma Business to Business Forum: Final Recommendations (Commission 2013).

If we look at the access to essential medicines debate, overall, there is criticism that the world trading system, in particular TRIPS, as interpreted and applied in practice, is not based on laws that are fair, humane, transparent and even-handed, in the context of imbalances of (economic and political) power between the global North and South.[187] Mary Moran writes of a 'disturbing tendency in policy debates to link or conflate neglected disease R&D with IPRs and access issues'.[188] Vincanne Adams explains how the move to 'global health' policy has privileged 'scientific' interventions which can be measured through randomized, double-blind controlled clinical trials, rather than those which are 'common sense', such as supplying clean water, nutritional supplements or cash transfers to those living in poverty.[189] Overall, and on balance, the discussion above suggests that the EU does little in practice to redress this inequality, and, to the extent that it participates at all, it also conflates access, research and intellectual property protection. The EU's rhetoric of justice and human rights protection does not translate into legal action.

Conclusions

To restate simply our conclusions from Part II of the book, the EU's health law, as applicable within the EU, protects human rights, and relationships of solidarity and equality. But when we consider such protections at the global level, the 'European values' embodied in the EU's internal health law, although still present in the rhetoric, largely disappear from legal texts. For instance, work on patients' rights, under the auspices of the WHO, Council of Europe and the EU, which has translated into national law in several Member States, does not reflect the collectively enjoyed right to adequate health care, implied by access to essential medicines.[190] EU law on counterfeit and falsified medicines is more about protecting intellectual property rights, held by legal persons, than it is about protecting rights held by human beings, or their safety. In part, this is a matter of politics. But there are also important legal considerations – in particular, the EU's external relations competence, which is mainly focused on trade and development law. The global context constrains the ways in which the EU pursues health agendas, which has important implications for EU health law.

---

[187] See: e.g. in the context of food: Aginam, 'Food Safety, South-North Asymmetries, and the Clash of Regulatory Regimes' (2007) 40(4) *Vanderbilt Journal of Transnational Law* 1099.

[188] Moran, 'Global Health Policy Responses to the World's Neglected Diseases' in Brown, et al., above n 170, 242.

[189] Adams, 'Against Global Health? Arbitrating Science, Non-Science, and Nonsense through Health' in Metzl and Kirkland (eds), *Against Health: How Health Became the New Morality* (New York University Press 2010).

[190] See: chapter 8. The European patients' rights agenda converges around rights to privacy and confidentiality; to dignity, especially to consent to or refuse treatment; and to be informed (or choose not to be informed) about risk. All are expressions of individual rights, to be enjoyed and enforced by individual patients.

The consequence is that the EU has little impact on the practical realities of global health inequalities, reflected, for instance, through global trade in human organs, and in lack of access to even the most basic medicines for some of the people in the world who need them most. Of course, tackling global health inequalities is far from easy, and there are obvious limits on the EU capacity to do so successfully. But compared to what we have shown the EU might potentially achieve in this regard, the overall conclusion must be that this represents a missed opportunity.

18

The global context: opportunities and threats; health knowledge; communicable diseases, global food and tobacco law

Introduction

Global health markets involve emergent opportunities – to exploit economies of scale, access new consumers/patients and develop new health technologies. Firms operating within the EU could benefit, and thereby contribute to EU employment and growth. The global pharmaceutical market alone is currently worth $300 billion a year, and the WHO expects this figure to rise to $400 billion by 2017.[1] Health is a growing industry.[2] It is also increasingly an international industry – health 'knowledge production', in the sense of the scientific research that supports health innovations, is fundamentally international, and is increasingly taking place in places beyond the 'global North'.[3] When it comes to novel health technologies, EU law supports and enables their development, and bringing to market, in many ways. As Mark Flear et al. put it:

---

[1] Four of the world's ten largest pharmaceuticals companies are based in Europe, see: WHO, 'Pharmaceutical Industry' (*WHO*, 2014). See also DG Enterprise's analysis at: Commission, 'Pharmaceuticals in Europe: Facts and Figures' (*Commission*, 5 February 2013).

[2] E.g. the UK health and fitness industry has grown its total market value by 1.5% to £3.92 billion, over the twelve month period to end of March 2013, according to the 2013 State of the UK Fitness Industry Report. European Health & Fitness Association, 'The 2013 State of the UK Fitness Industry Report' (European Health & Fitness Association, 17 June 2013).

[3] See: Flear, 'Clinical Trials Abroad: The Marketable Ethics, Weak Protections and Vulnerable Subjects of EU Law' in Albors-Llorens, Armstrong and Gehring (eds), *Cambridge Yearbook of European Legal Studies, Vol 16 2013-2014* (Hart 2014); Figert and Bell, 'Big Pharma and Big Medicine in the Global Environment' in Kleinman and Moore (eds), *Routledge Handbook of Science, Technology and Society* (Routledge 2014); Lemmens, 'Pharmaceutical Knowledge Governance: A Human Rights Perspective' (2013) 41(1) *Global Health and Law* 163; Spielman, 'Offshoring Experiments, Outsourcing Public Health: Corporate Accountability and State Responsibility for Violating the International Prohibition on Nonconsensual Human Experimentation' in Cohen (ed), *The Globalization of Health Care: Legal and Ethical Issues* (OUP 2013); Cortez, 'Patients Without Borders: The Emerging Global Market for Patients and the Evolution of Modern Health Care' (2008) 83(1) *Indiana Law Journal* 71; Fisher, *Medical Research for Hire: The Political Economy of Pharmaceutical Clinical Trials* (Rutgers University Press 2008); Glickman et al., 'Ethical and Scientific Implications of the Globalization of Clinical Research' 360(8) *New England Journal of Medicine* 816.

The entire structure of EU regulation of new health technologies, the way the regulatory measures fit together, cross-refer to each other, and are justified, all concern the marketing of new health technologies.[4]

Health innovation fits with the EU's 'knowledge society', central to its 'Europe 2020' plan for growth and development.[5] The EU has identified the health sector, in particular new health technologies, as an important area for growth. Its activities on the global stage seek to enhance opportunities for EU businesses within that sector. In that sense, EU external health law on global health markets and health knowledge in the global economy fits with the commonly expressed view that we investigated in chapters 9–11, to the effect that EU health law pursues free trade and competition, at the expense of solidarity and equality. Our analysis of the detail of EU internal health law shows a more complex picture. This chapter investigates the extent to which this also the case from a global perspective.

Taking a global focus, health represents a threat as well as an opportunity. This chapter therefore also considers the EU's response to global health threats, focusing first on the challenge of communicable disease control, including through food safety regulation. It then turns to non-communicable diseases, focusing on the role of tobacco and food law in reducing such diseases. These examples have been selected as they represent areas where the EU's law is relatively dense. In chapters 12–15, we considered the claims that the EU is relatively ineffective at protecting those members of its populations at risk of harm to their health, particularly from non-communicable diseases; and that, correspondingly, the ways in which EU health law operates in fact are more focused on risk of harm to industry interests. To what extent does our conclusion to the effect that the EU has developed some aspects of its health law to protect populations and promote public health still hold true when we adopt a global focus? How effectively does the EU succeed in embedding its approaches in the international organizations with which it cooperates to develop global health law?

Opportunities: global health markets and health knowledge in the global economy

Over the last few decades, the global 'bio-pharma' sector has become increasingly prominent in global health discussions. New health technologies (including, but not limited to,[6] those arising from biotechnology) are 'big business' in

---

[4] Flear, Farrell, Hervey and Murphy, 'Conclusion: A European Law of New Health Technologies?' in Flear, Farrell, Hervey and Murphy (eds), *European Law and New Health Technologies* (OUP 2013).

[5] Commission, 'Europe 2020: A Strategy for Smart, Sustainable and Inclusive Growth' (Communication) COM (2010) 2020 final.

[6] Nanotechnology offers another important site for global developments in the health field.

twenty-first-century economies. They offer potential for growth and development. They promise more-efficient, cheaper and clinically improved treatments for ill health and disability, as well as managing and improving quality of life in ageing societies. The new contract research industry, which manages clinical trials for pharmaceuticals, medical devices and biotechnology products (which could be either pharmaceuticals or devices), is a global industry.[7] Both clinical trials and manufacturing of new health products increasingly take place across national borders. Multinational pharmaceuticals and medical devices companies enjoy considerable economic power, leading to the prospect of equivalent political leverage. The global industry is subject to various global governance systems, but also seeks to influence legal and policy developments in its favour.[8]

The EU's global economic strategy includes the idea of the EU as a 'knowledge economy'.[9] The EU's 'European Research Area' involves a commitment to increase investment in research and development[10] in a range of areas, including health and ageing.[11] The health technology sector, includes, for instance, biotechnology, nanotechnology, synthetic biology, or, as Regulation 1291/2013/EU puts it:

> understanding the molecular basis of disease, the identification of innovative therapeutic strategies and novel model systems, the multidisciplinary application of knowledge in physics, chemistry and systems biology, the development of long-term cohorts and the conduct of clinical trials (including focus on the development and effects of medicines in all age groups), the clinical use of '-omics', systems biomedicine and the development of ICT and their applications in healthcare practice, notably e-health.[12]

Development of the EU's health technology sector, so that it can effectively compete in global markets, is a central part of this policy. Both individual EU

---

[7] Fisher above n 3; Figert and Bell, above n 3; Flear, above n 3; Lemmens, above n 3; Spielman, above n 3; Cortez, above n 3; Glickman et al., above n 3; Altavilla, 'Ethical Standards for Clinical Trials Conducted in Third Countries: The New Strategy of the European Medicines Agency' (2011) 18 *European Journal of Health Law* 65.

[8] Jackson, *Law and the Regulation of Medicine* (Hart 2012); Figert and Bell, above n 3.

[9] Commission, 'Europe 2020: A Strategy for Smart, Sustainable and Inclusive Growth' (Communication) COM (2010) 2020 final.

[10] Europe 2020's 'headline target' in this respect is to increase R&D investment to 3% of GDP. The latest headline figure reported (2012) is 2.07% (see: Eurostat, 'Gross domestic expenditure on R&D (GERD)' (*Eurostat*, 28 May 2014)) with a range from 2.98% in some Member States and 0.46% (Cyprus) and 0.49% (Bulgaria). The European Commission's (optimistic) estimate for the EU in May 2012 was 2.65-2.72%, but this ranges from 0.5% in some Member States to 4% in others. Comparator states include South Korea (3.74%), Japan (3.36%) and USA (2.88%), see: Commission, 'Action for Stability, Growth and Jobs' COM (2012) 299 final.

[11] Regulation 1291/2013/EU [2013] OJ L347/104, Annex I, Part III, lists 'Health, demographic change and well-being' as the first of its six funding foci.

[12] Regulation 1291/2013/EU, Annex I, Part III, 1.2.

Member States and the EU itself perceive themselves as part of this technological innovation 'race'.[13]

The globalization of medical research and development and manufacturing presents potential problems for the EU (and the rest of the 'global North'). Where clinical research activities are moved to the developing world,[14] challenges include how to safeguard data integrity; ensure appropriate ethical[15] and human rights protections are in place; and secure sufficient post-market safety information; all in the context of (lack of) confidence in local regulatory arrangements, including poor quality monitoring, supervision and enforcement of standards. The EU's marketing authorization law has an indirect effect here, as products to be marketed in the EU must have clinical trial data which complies with EU ethical standards.[16] Where active pharmaceutical ingredients are manufactured outside of the EU, there is potential for substandard material to enter the supply chain.[17] All of the EU's elaborate risk management processes that seek to ensure that pharmaceuticals and medical devices are as safe as possible when reaching patients[18] become irrelevant if the global context is ignored.

As we have already seen, the EU participates in various global risk management structures and arrangements. These include, for instance, European Commission work on eliminating trade in falsified medicines[19] and the EU's contributions to the ICH,[20] which covers the safety of medicines. The European Commission works through the ICH to promote international technical harmonization of pharmaceuticals standards, so as to minimize the risk that substandard pharmaceutical products enter the EU market. But when it comes to global law on the development of medical devices, or of novel products that fall in the boundaries between the concepts of 'medical device', 'human tissue'

---

[13] Flear et al., above n 4. There is some evidence that the EU's investment in its own industry is not particularly effective, see: Galsworthy et al., 'The academic output of nine years of EU investment into health research' (2012) 380(9846) *The Lancet* 971.

[14] Around one quarter of all clinical trials performed in the EU involve at least one other country outside of the EU, see Commission, 'Assessment of the functioning of the Clinical Trials Directive 2001/20/EC – Public Consultation Paper' (Commission 2009).

[15] E.g., some have argued that the Judgment in *Oliver Brüstle v Greenpeace eV*, C-34/10, EU:C:2011:669, will mean research will exit from Europe. See: e.g., Bache et al., 'The Defining Features of the European Union's Approach to Regulating New Health Technologies' in Flear et al., above n 4, 14, and the literature therein. Probably the most important consequence is that science has moved on and different, less controversial techniques are now being deployed, see Harmon, Laurie and Courtney, 'Dignity, plurality and patentability: the unfinished story of *Brüstle v Greenpeace*' (2013) 38(1) *European Law Review* 92.

[16] Directive 2001/83/EC [2001] OJ L311/67, Article 8 (3) (i) (b). See: Altavilla, above n 7.

[17] European Medicines Agency (EMA), 'Roadmap to 2015: The European Medicines Agency's contribution to science, medicines and health' (EMA 2010) paragraph 4.4.

[18] Discussed in chapter 13.

[19] E.g. through the IMPACT (International Medical Products Anti-Counterfeiting Taskforce) initiative, see: WHO, 'Medicines: IMPACT (Frequently Asked Questions)' (*WHO*, 2014). For further examples, see: Rys, 'Global Health Governance - Multiple Players, Multiple Visions: Challenges and Opportunities' (WHS Working Sessions, 12 October 2010). See further: chapter 17.

[20] See: chapter 16.

and 'pharmaceuticals', the global structures are less developed. New health technologies combine human tissue and non-human materials (both chemical and other materials) in ways that were not foreseen by those who drafted the EU's legislation. EU law distinguishes between 'products', which are the subject of 'ordinary' market trade, although highly regulated to ensure patient safety, and the human body, which is, under EU law, not the subject of ordinary market trade. But, as we saw in chapter 14, in the case, for instance, of advanced tissue engineered products, that use collagen 'scaffolds',[21] or molecular manipulation using nanotechnology,[22] it is not always clear which is the applicable EU law.

The uncertainty here, coupled with the perceived 'lax' EU approach to regulation of medical devices (compared to the USA),[23] has been criticized as being sub-optimal for firms operating within the EU.[24] If regulatory structures are sub-optimal, it is feared that capital will relocate elsewhere. This spectre of a 'regulatory race to the bottom' increases the pressure from global health technology industries both for a different regulatory settlement to apply *within* the EU, but also for the development of *global* regulatory standards. The effect of such standards would be to prevent the exit of capital from the EU, as harmonized global standards would apply everywhere that the global industry might otherwise relocate. Global standardization law would thus be consistent with the EU's economic development strategy. To the extent that the EU pursues standardization, it might also be argued that the EU seeks to position itself as leading global actor in the field of health innovation law[25] – seeking to export its regulatory preferences (for instance, with respect to human rights, such as privacy; or dignity of the human body) to the global stage.[26] As Flear et al. put it:

> European law of new health technologies works to articulate the notion that the European market in new health technologies is safer, more respectful of human rights, and more ethical than other markets. European law of new health technologies is thus constructed as the polar opposite of a 'global Vegas' where more or less 'anything goes'.[27]

This conclusion stands in contrast to our investigation of the EU's missed opportunity to promote its ethical and human rights standards in global organ trade or access to essential medicines.[28]

---

[21] See: Hoppe, 'Innovative Tissue Engineering and Its Regulation: The Search for Flexible Rules for Emerging Health Technologies' in Flear et al., above n 4.

[22] See: Dorbeck-Jung, 'The Governance of Therapeutic Nanoproducts in the European Union: A Model for New Health Technology Regulation?' in Flear et al., above n 4.

[23] See: Greer, Hervey, McKee, and Mackenbach, 'Health Law and Policy of the European Union' (2013) 381(9872) *The Lancet* 1135.

[24] Flear et al., above n 4.

[25] For instance, Commission, 'Europe 2020 Flagship Initiative Innovation Union' (Communication) COM (2010) 546 final, has an entire section entitled 'Leveraging our Policies Externally' (at page 27).

[26] Flear et al., above n 4.   [27] Flear et al., above n 4, 408.   [28] See: chapter 17.

At the same time as pursuing global standardization of health technologies as part of its economic development and growth agenda, at least in its policy aspirations, the EU also pays attention to the global ethics of clinical research. In its Communication on 'The EU Role in Global Health',[29] the European Commission notes that investment should be made in research that 'benefits all', alluding both to 'orphan medicines' (where numbers of patients who will benefit from research are very small) and to the 'access to essential medicines' debate.[30] The Commission suggests that the EU should 'work to ensure more effective use of TRIPS provisions to increase affordability and access to essential medicines.'[31] But, as we saw in the previous chapter, the EU has been very slow to take up the opportunities presented by its growing role in global health. The WHO has now produced a 'Global Strategy and Plan of Action on Public Health, Innovation and Intellectual Property',[32] within which, for instance, a project on health-related technology transfer was funded by the EU.[33] But the EU could do a great deal more. It could also seek to ensure that bilateral and multilateral trade agreements avoid clauses that undermine access to medicines.[34] Furthermore, the EU's 'Framework Programmes' supporting research could prioritize those actions which address global health challenges.[35] Only one of the EU's 'thematic priorities' in its public health programmes does so explicitly.[36] In this regard, the conclusion from the previous chapter to the effect that the EU does not make the most of the opportunity to extend its values of solidarity and equality to the global context, also applies here. That said, the general conclusions about the difficulties inherent in subjecting the global pharmaceutical industry to regulatory control, remain. No jurisdiction (including the EU) has succeeded in responding to the criticisms of the ineffectiveness of laws governing that industry that are found in the literature discussed in chapters 12 and 13.

Threats: communicable diseases law

Disease does not respect international boundaries. This has long been recognized in international law. The current International Health Regulations (IHR) form the global legal framework on infectious diseases.[37] The IHRs originate in the first International Sanitary Conference in Paris in 1851, following the major

---

[29] Commission, 'The EU Role in Global Health' (Communication) COM (2010) 128 final, paragraphs 3.3 and 3.4.

[30] For further discussion, see: chapter 17.

[31] Commission, COM (2010) 128 final, paragraph 4.3.

[32] World Health Assembly, 'Resolution WHA 61.21: Global strategy and plan of action on public health, innovation and intellectual property' (61st World Health Assembly, WHA 2008).

[33] WHO, 'WHO project on improving access to medicines in developing countries through local production and related technology transfer' (WHO, 2014).

[34] Rys, above n 19.   [35] Commission, COM (2010) 128 final, paragraph 4.4.

[36] Regulation 282/2014/EU [2014] OJ L86/1, see below.

[37] See further: Gostin, Global Health Law (Harvard University Press 2014), chapter 6.

cholera epidemics across Europe in the early 1800s.[38] The first International Sanitary Convention was adopted in 1892, and was followed by conventions (international agreements/treaties) in 1897 and 1903. Even at that early stage, the relevant European delegates were concerned to protect European (as opposed to simply national) territory.[39] A European multilateral institution in this area (*L'Office international d'hygiène publique*) (OIHP) was established in 1907, and the Health Organization of the League of Nations (HOLN) was established in 1923. Article XXIII of the League of Nations Covenant provided that members would 'endeavour to take steps in matters of international concern for the prevention and control of disease'.[40] The United Nations Charter, Article 55 provides that a primary objective of the UN is to promote 'higher standards of living' and 'solutions of international . . . health'. The WHO, established in the late 1940s, subsumed pre-existing international health institutions, such as OIHP and HOLN. It is organized into six wide geographical regions, one of which is Europe.[41] Like the EEC, which was set up in the 1950s, WHO Europe included in its vision the reconstruction of Europe in a 'spirit of mutual cooperation'.[42]

The first International Sanitary Regulations, overseen by the WHO, were adopted on 25 July 1951. They were renamed the International Health Regulations in 1969.[43] The current (2005) version of this binding international law instrument entered into force on 15 June 2007, following a revision prompted by major international disease epidemics in the 1990s of cholera, plague and Ebola haemorrhagic fever.[44] The purpose of the IHR is 'to prevent, protect against, control and provide a public health response to the international spread of disease in ways that are commensurate with and restricted to public health risks, and which avoid unnecessary interference with international traffic and trade'.[45] Whether the IHR is effective in this respect is a matter of some concern. Laurence Gostin has noted problems with effective enforcement, and in

---

[38] See further: Gostin, above n 37, 177-181; Gostin, 'The International Health Regulations: A New Paradigm for Global Health Governance' in McLean (ed), *First Do No Harm: Law, Ethics and Healthcare* (Ashgate 2006); and Gostin, 'International Infectious Disease Law: Revision of the World Health Organisations International Health Regulations' (2004) 291(21) *Journal of the American Medical Association* 2623; Livrani and Coker, 'Protecting Europe from Diseases: From the International Sanitary Conferences to the ECDC' (2012) 37(6) *Journal of Health Politics, Policy and Law* 915.

[39] 'European' being defined essentially as 'non-Eastern', and culturally, not only geographically, see: Livrani and Coker, above n 38, 916-7.

[40] Gostin, (2004) above n 38.   [41] See: chapter 16.

[42] WHO, 'Sixty Years of WHO in Europe' (WHO 2010) 10.

[43] The IHR were slightly modified in 1973 (particularly for cholera) and in 1981 (to exclude smallpox, in view of its global eradication).

[44] Gostin, (2006) above n 38, 64; Von Tigerstrom, 'The Revised International Health Regulations and Restraint of National Health Measures' (2005) 13 *Health Law Journal* 35. See also: WHO, '*Global Crisis—Global Solutions: Managing Public Health Emergencies of International Concern Through the Revised International Health Regulations*' (WHO 2002).

[45] WHO, 'International Health Regulations' (WHO 2005) Article 2.

particular with national acceptance for globally determined standards for prevention and control of infectious diseases, in a system which is 'only as strong as its weakest link'. This implies a need to address the significant disparities in health resources between developed and developing countries.[46] Furthermore, the promise of sufficient flexibility to deal with novel health threats has not been fulfilled.[47] Thirdly:

> [i]n many ways, it is in a country's self-interest to overlook WHO recommendations and regulations. Rule compliance may risk national prestige, travel, trade, and tourism. For example, reporting a disease outbreak and offering the WHO full cooperation may incur serious economic harm by impeding the flow of people and goods. This dynamic was illustrated during the SARS outbreaks when China delayed notification to the WHO, and Ontario, Canada, resisted WHO travel advice.[48]

The initial International Sanitary Regulations covered cholera, plague and yellow fever. The latest version has expanded significantly.[49] Other events of potential international public health concern must be considered, in terms of their unexpectedness, seriousness and effects on international spread, travel or trade. Some 194 countries are States Parties to the IHR, including all members of the WHO, and all hence EU Member States. The EU itself is not a signatory to the IHR, although the Presidency of the Council (Portugal at the relevant time) issued several Declarations annexed to the IHR.

The International Health Regulations place formal legal obligations on States Parties. States are required, with the WHO's assistance, to develop sufficient capacity[50] to notify the WHO where these diseases occur[51] and when areas within states are disease free. However, State Parties have failed to give such notifications and have restricted trade and travel unnecessarily.[52] Moreover, limited or no powers are provided to monitor performance of states, or to implement sanctions or incentives.[53] States Parties must develop the capacity to respond to public health emergencies covered by the Regulations.[54] Hygiene measures must be implemented at borders (including ports and airports),[55] to

---

[46] Gostin, (2004) above n 38. See also: Wilson, Brownstein and Fidler, 'Strengthening the International Health Regulations: Lessons from the H1N1 pandemic' (2010) 25(6) *Health Policy and Planning* 505.

[47] Gostin, (2004) above n 38.   [48] *Ibid.*

[49] It includes smallpox; poliomyelitis due to wild-type poliovirus; human influenza caused by a new subtype; severe acute respiratory syndrome (SARS) (must always be notified); cholera; pneumonic plague; yellow fever; viral haemorrhagic fevers (Ebola, Lassa, Marburg); West Nile fever; and other diseases that are of special national or regional concern, e.g. dengue fever, Rift Valley fever, and meningococcal disease'(must be notified where there is a significant risk of international spread and of international travel or trade restrictions). See: WHO, 'International Health Regulations', Annex II.

[50] WHO, 'International Health Regulations', Article 5.

[51] WHO, 'International Health Regulations', Articles 6, 7 and 9 (2).

[52] Gostin (2014) above n 37, 197.   [53] *Ibid.*

[54] WHO, 'International Health Regulations', Article 13.

[55] WHO, 'International Health Regulations', Articles 19-22, Annex I.

ensure that 'baggage, cargo, containers, conveyances, goods, postal parcels and human remains departing and arriving from affected areas... are maintained in such a condition that they are free of sources of infection or contamination, including vectors and reservoirs'.[56] States Parties must require health and vaccination certificates for travellers from countries where there is disease infection.[57] An array of model forms, and procedures for investigations and assessments, are provided in the Annexes. Although there is no obligation to use these, for States with reduced capacity, or which are concerned to be seen to be complying, the effect of the existence of the model is likely to induce compliance. The IHR impose obligations on the WHO, to share information with all the States Parties.[58] The WHO is also obliged to cooperate with other international agencies and institutions.[59] Since the 1990s, WHO Europe has been developing its engagement with communicable disease threats (such as diphtheria and drug-resistant tuberculosis), particularly in central and eastern Europe, following the collapse of the USSR. Its 'Eurohealth' plan involves human resources, HIV/AIDS prevention and environmental health; it has improved information sharing through its computerized Information System for Infectious Diseases.[60] However, for instance, during the H1N1 outbreak, there was variable compliance with the IHR.[61]

The IHR measures were conceived as 'the *maximum measures* applicable to international traffic, which a state may require for the protection of its territory.'[62] The general principle, for instance, is that no further health documentation may be required other than that provided for under the IHR or WHO recommendations.[63] The underlying principle of the IHR, for all that they are about control and prevention, is thus free movement and free trade. In this respect, the IHR fit well with EU free movement/trade law (and indeed with WTO law).[64] The IHR explicitly state that they should be interpreted consistently with other international obligations of the States Parties[65] (which includes obligations in EU (and WTO) law), and that nothing in the IHR prevents closer collaboration between States, for instance, of geographical contiguity.[66] Article 57 (3) explicitly provides that 'States Parties that are members of a regional economic integration organization shall apply in their mutual relations the common rules in force in that regional economic integration organization'.

[56] WHO, 'International Health Regulations', Article 22 (1) (a).
[57] WHO, 'International Health Regulations', Article 23.
[58] WHO, 'International Health Regulations', Article 11.
[59] WHO, 'International Health Regulations', Article 14.
[60] Livrani and Coker, above n 38, 919; MacLehose, McKee and Weinberg, 'Responding to the Challenge of Communicable Disease in Europe' (2002) 295(5562) *Science* 2047.
[61] Gostin (2014) above 37, 197.
[62] WHO, 'International Health Regulations' (WHO 1969), Article 23.
[63] WHO, 'International Health Regulations' (WHO 2005), Article 35.
[64] For discussion of these synergies, see: Von Tigerstrom, above n 44.
[65] WHO, 'International Health Regulations', Article 57 (1).
[66] WHO, 'International Health Regulations', Article 57 (2) and (3).

Overall, the IHR may be an improvement in public health protection. But lessons can be learned from the H1N1 pandemic when strong science-based recommendations issued by the WHO were ignored by a number of States Parties.[67]

EU communicable diseases law

The WHO and IHR at least appear to provide a complete institutional and legal response to the understanding that communicable disease is a problem that requires a global response. All the EU Member States are part of this system. What, then, could the EU contribute, and how does this contribution square with the ways in which the EU manages health risks? What are the consequences for its effectiveness in this respect? Common European communicable disease control law is necessary for the EU's single market: if people, animals and food are to cross borders, then so will bacteria. It would seem wise for the EU to develop the necessary epidemiological and scientific capacity to assess and communicate risks, and perhaps build up the surveillance and treatment capacities of its Member States to reduce the risk of them becoming sources of infection. The significant diversity of European communicable disease control infrastructure, which does not always instil confidence, engendered demands for more consistency. Indeed, from the 1980s, the EU began to fund research, training and disease-specific monitoring networks as well as a rudimentary continent-wide surveillance system. A series of failures of cross-border communicable disease surveillance and control provided the stimulus for more robust EU action, above all legislation creating the EU's own agency for communicable diseases: the European Centre for Disease Control and Prevention (ECDC).[68]

The ECDC, based in Stockholm, is a small agency set up in 2005. Under its founding Regulation,[69] its objectives[70] are to 'identify, assess, and communicate current and emerging threats to human health from communicable diseases'.[71] To do so, the ECDC must collect and disseminate relevant data; provide scientific opinions and 'timely information' to the European Commission and the Member States; build capacity through technical assistance and training; coordinate relevant networks; and disseminate best practice.[72]

---

[67] Gostin (2014) above n 37, 202 and see further on the H1N1 virus and influenza epidemics generally: Gostin (2014) above n 37, ch 12.

[68] On the history of the ECDC, see: Greer and Mätze, 'Bacteria without Borders: Communicable Disease Politics in Europe' (2012) 37(6) *Journal of Health Politics, Policy and Law* (2012) 887; Greer, 'The European Centre for Disease Prevention and Control: Hub or Hollow Core?' (2012) 37(6) *Journal of Health Politics, Policy and Law* 1001; Elliott, Jones, and Greer, 'Mapping Communicable Disease Control in the European Union' (2012) 37(6) *Journal of Health Politics, Policy and Law* 935; Livrani and Coker, above n 38.

[69] Regulation 851/2004/EC [2004] OJ L142/1.

[70] Or rather, as the Regulation has it, its 'mission', Regulation 851/2004/EC, *Recital 7*.

[71] Regulation 851/2004/EC, Article 3 (1).   [72] Regulation 851/2004/EC, Article 3 (2).

The ECDC began life as a series of informal advisory group meetings of heads of national communicable disease surveillance bodies, and several networks and interactions between European epidemiologists.[73] These were coordinated and funded through DG SANCO, and the political moment for promoting the (already existing) idea of an ECDC came with the 11 September 2001 and subsequent anthrax attacks, closely followed by SARS in 2002–03.[74] The broader political context of EU enlargement, and hence the need to ensure harmonized surveillance procedures for goods and people moving around the EU is also important; as is increased interest in health and safety on the EU agenda with the development of ideas of EU citizenship following the Treaty of Maastricht.[75] Key policy advocates (including Fernand Sauer,[76] David Byrne,[77] and John Bowis[78]) were able to seize the moment.[79] Thus the ECDC emerged following a gradual process of European Commission-supported networking of national authorities and expert groups (of varying strengths), each in a specific (vertical) communicable disease area,[80] which were eventually brought together in a horizontal institutional arrangement (the ECDC), responding to specific, high-profile communicable disease incidents or problems.[81]

More recently, the notion that health is a key factor in economic growth has been articulated to support the continued development of EU capacity in communicable disease control.[82] Regulation 282/2014/EU[83] establishing the third EU health programme notes in Recital 15 that the EU's public health programme should 'contribute to the creation and maintenance of robust mechanisms and tools to detect, assess and manage major cross-border health threats'. The programme should 'complement' the ECDC's work. Furthermore 'special efforts' are mandated, to 'ensure coherence and synergies' between the public

---

[73] Livrani and Coker, above n 38, 919-20; Greer, (2012) above n 68, 1004-8.
[74] Greer, (2012) above n 68, 1007-8.   [75] Livrani and Coker, above n 38, 921-3.
[76] High level officer in DG SANCO, had just set up the European Medicines Evaluation Authority (now the European Medicines Agency).
[77] European Commissioner for DG SANCO.
[78] Pro-integration UK Conservative MEP, and Rapporteur for the European Parliament's deliberations on Regulation 851/2004/EC [2004] OJ L142/1.
[79] Greer, (2012) above n 68.
[80] Steffen, 'The Europeanization of Public Health: How Does It Work? The Seminal Role of the AIDS Case' (2012) 37(6) *Journal of Health Politics, Policy and Law* 1057.
[81] McKee, Hervey and Gilmore, 'Public Health Policies' in Mossialos, Permanand, Baeten and Hervey (eds), *Health Systems Governance in Europe: The Role of European Union Law and Policy* (CUP 2010); Greer, (2012) above n 68; Elliott, Jones and Greer, above n 68.
[82] Commission, 'Proposal for a Regulation of the European Parliament and of the Council on Establishing a Health for Growth Programme the third multi-annual programme of EU action in the field of health for the period 2014-20' COM (2011) 709 final, called for the EU to develop "common approaches" and demonstrate "their value for better preparedness and coordination in health emergencies in order to protect citizens from cross-border health threats." The proposal has now been adopted, although that specific wording is not reflected in it, see: Regulation 282/2014/EU [2014] OJ L86/1.
[83] Regulation 282/2014/EU [2014] OJ L86/1.

health programme established by the Regulation and 'global health work carried out under other Union programmes and instruments that address, in particular, the areas of influenza, HIV/AIDS, tuberculosis and other cross-border health threats in third countries'. The second of four 'thematic priorities' for the programme is 'protecting Union citizens from serious cross-border health threats'.[84] Under this priority, the programme may be used to support capacity-building against health threats. Such capacity building includes preparedness and response planning, health threats from global population movements, good practice guidelines, voluntary measures on combating the recent resurgence of infectious diseases and communication strategies. The thematic priority explicitly envisages cooperation with the EU's neighbouring countries and global initiatives.

Since its establishment, the ECDC has been engaged with establishing its infrastructure and relationships with the pre-existing disease networks, with developing and disseminating epidemiological reports, and with capacity enhancement and training, particularly in eastern Europe.[85] The ECDC has put significant effort into managing its relationships with national disease control authorities (which vary dramatically across the Member States). Some seventy-seven 'competent organizations' across the EU are recognized by the ECDC.[86] The types of these organizations, and their particular responsibilities and activities, also differ considerably. The question of their practical competence has also been raised.[87] The ECDC has to manage a crowded and complex policy landscape. ECDC has also worked on its relationships with WHO (Europe). Indeed, the first ECDC Director (Zsuzsanna Jakab) subsequently moved to the position of Director of WHO (Europe).[88] Since 2008, the ECDC and WHO (Europe) have produced joint annual surveillance reports on HIV/AIDS and tuberculosis across the EU and the wider European neighbourhood (the WHO European Region covers fifty-three countries). ECDC and WHO (Europe) also work together on influenza surveillance, and have worked as partners on numerous training and capacity-building initiatives. The ECDC signed an agreement with WHO (Europe) in 2011, following the eighth meeting of senior officials from the European Commission and WHO (Europe).[89] The meeting discussed WHO-EU collaboration at both regional and global levels, considering how EU and WHO officers in third countries could work together more effectively. This can be seen as part of the ECDC's network building, and, if achieved, will enhance the ECDC's global capacity and credibility.

---

[84] Regulation 282/2014/EU, Annex I.   [85] Greer, (2012) above n 68, 1022.
[86] Elliott, Jones and Greer, above n 68, Table 1.
[87] Elliott, Jones and Greer, above n 68; Greer and Mätze, above n 68, 903.
[88] Greer, (2012) above n 68, 1019; Livrani and Coker, above n 38, 926-7.
[89] Commission, 'Report on the European Commission – World Health Organisation Senior Officials Meeting 25 March 2011, Brussels' (*Commission*, 2014).

The first major challenges for the ECDC were the H5N1 (bird flu) outbreak of 2005 and the H1N1 (swine flu) pandemic of 2009.[90] The ECDC worked closely with WHO on influenza (in part because the H5N1 outbreak occurred just as the ECDC was setting up). By 2009, the ECDC was issuing its own advice, in the form of an evidence-based policy recommendation advising national authorities to adopt mitigation strategies (such as vaccination programmes, closing of public buildings, restricting of transport) rather than simply containment. Most countries ignored this advice.[91] Approaches to vaccination and public education varied significantly across the EU.[92] Efforts to create a European stockpile of vaccines and antivirals, proposed after the H5N1 outbreak, came to nothing, as health ministers were unable to agree, even though the scientific case for doing so had been widely debated and was the subject of broad agreement.[93]

Assessments of the ECDC's effectiveness have pointed to its weakness and inability to address this first real challenge. Developing a role in the very political world of European communicable disease control is difficult, as we see in the ECDC's public marginalization during some of the most salient outbreaks, e.g., E.coli in Germany (when the German government wrongly accused Spanish farmers) and in the swine flu episode, when at least arguably its data and networks worked well, but it was often overshadowed by Member States' poorly coordinated actions. Like so much of European public health policy, the ECDC relies on networks, but establishing capable, expert and apolitical networks in Europe is a significant challenge when national capacity is so variable. A 2008 evaluation[94] raised concerns about the quality and the comparability of data supplied to the ECDC. Differences in case definitions, medical consultation patterns, and reporting practices across the EU hamper the development of epidemiological analyses at EU level.[95] This is a major concern since the credibility of the ECDC relies on the robustness of the data it is able to provide (and, if it is not credible, Member States are less likely to furnish it with reliable data).[96] In particular, the question of the extent to which reportedly 'non-scientific' factors[97] had played a role was raised. There is also a tension between those who

---

[90] See the discussion of EU action in: Brattberg and Rhinhard, 'Multilevel Governance and Complex Threats: The Case of Pandemic Preparedness in the European Union and the United States' (2011) 5(1) *Global Health Governance* 1.

[91] Livrani and Coker, above n 38, 925.   [92] Greer and Mätze, above n 68, 892.

[93] Livrani and Coker, above n 38, 926. The consensus on Tamiflu turns out to be controversial, and may be based on unreliable data syntheses produced by the industry, see Lemmens, above n 3.

[94] Oortwijn et al., 'External Evaluation of the ECDC: Final Report' (ECORYS 2008).

[95] Livrani and Coker, above n 38, 925.   [96] Greer, (2012) above n 68.

[97] Of course, the distinction between 'scientific' and 'non-scientific' knowledge is socially and politically constructed. See Jasanoff, *The Fifth Branch: Science Advisers as Policymakers* (Harvard University Press 1998); Everson and Vos (eds), *Uncertain Risks Regulated* (Routledge-Cavendish 2009) 3; Fisher, *Risk Regulation and Administrative Constitutionalism* (Hart 2007) 16-18; Jasanoff, *Designs on Nature: Science and Democracy in Europe and the United States* (Princeton University Press 2007); and see the discussion in chapter 12.

want the ECDC to receive and disseminate information and those who want the ECDC to give advice. In part, these problems are explained by the significant diversities in national disease control practice and institutional form – there is, in short, no 'EU model' of communicable disease control.[98] These factors have led Margitta Mätze to conclude that the ECDC (a weaker institution, operating in very different policy contexts, with different political and administrative capacity) is unlikely to follow the path of the powerful US CDC.[99]

Scott Greer has argued persuasively that it is too soon to assess the ECDC's effectiveness. It is, as yet, 'a tiny organization with a strong strategic position, trying to make its way in a complex and crowded political environment'.[100] The ECDC's effectiveness will be determined by its ability to build and capitalize on its networks, through providing credible and politically neutral advice, and forging political allies.[101] Against the ECDC is the crowded institutional landscape for communicable disease control in Europe, and the mismatch between those Member States (such as Germany, France or the UK) who want the ECDC to remain a weak network, as their own capacities outpace the ECDC, and those Member States who see in the ECDC an opportunity to rectify their capacity deficits through transfer of resources, in particular technical expertise. On its side is its practical institutional construction: the Management Board (which controls the ECDC)[102] is in fact staffed by officials who are 'more concerned about communicable disease control (at every level) than with sovereignty'.[103]

The EU Commission also operates a Health Security Initiative which requires the notification of health threats including the recent Ebola outbreak. The Health Security Committee has a legal basis to act on such threats under Decision 1082/2013/EU on serious cross-border threats to health. The Commission has been working with the member states involved in the Committee and the ECDC and the WHO since the onset of the outbreak in 2014. Support is also being provided through an online information platform the 'Ebola Commission Platform for Clinicians' which aims to bring together experts, and specialist hospital centres across the EU to facilitate exchange of information and expertise in this area.

If the ECDC turns out to be a success, it will have the opportunity to pursue the EU's approach to risk of global health threats from communicable diseases along the risk-management lines discussed in chapter 15. As well as developing its own communicable disease agency, the EU has sought to engage with global health initiatives in this area. Even the Treaty of Maastricht, in the early 1990s, noted the need for EU external relations law to engage with public

---

[98] Elliott, Jones and Greer, above n 68.
[99] Mätze, 'Institutional Resources for Communicable Disease Control in Europe: Diversity across Time and Place' (2012) 37(6) *Journal of Health Politics, Policy and Law* 965.
[100] Greer, (2012) above n 68, 1003.   [101] Greer, (2012) above n 68, 1001.
[102] Regulation 851/2004/EC [2004] OJ L142/1, Articles 14-17.
[103] Greer, (2012) above n 68, 1017.

health.[104] The European Commission asserts that the global nature of communicable disease (and, indeed, health more generally) makes it futile to separate national/EU policy from global policy[105] and also stresses the global security aspects of health. For instance, the EU is a partner in an informal collaboration with Canada, France, Germany, Italy, Japan, Mexico, the UK and the USA, which seeks to strengthen global capacity to respond to threats of bioterrorism and pandemic influenza.[106] The extent to which the EU will be able to work effectively with institutional arrangements that have a global, as opposed to regional, outlook, is one of the major challenges facing the EU.[107] Overall, therefore, the EU has yet to develop its own communicable disease law, in the sense of a distinctive legal approach to the risks that communicable diseases pose to global health.

EU Food safety law and policy

Globalization of food trade has led to widespread international marketing of food products.[108] Food consumed in the EU has been produced and traded around the globe. Food is increasingly bought 'ready to eat', and many food products are processed foods.[109] Food and animal feed are significant vectors for communicable diseases. Risks to health from food also arise from chemical toxins (such as herbicides or harmful dioxins) or from toxins caused by bacterial growth and a variety of organic substances that may be present in certain foods.[110] For some people, particularly children, the presence of allergens in food is also an important health concern. Genetically modified food may have long-term harmful effects on human health.[111] The cultural place of food, and the fact that it is a high-profile consumer product, leads to significant media

---

[104] Now found in Article 168 (3) TFEU: 'The Union and the Member States shall foster cooperation with third countries and the competent international institutions in the sphere of public health'.

[105] Commission, 'Together for Health: A Strategic Approach for the EU 2008-2013' (White Paper) COM (2007) 630 final; Commission, 'The EU Role in Global Health' (Communication) COM (2010) 128 final, paragraph 4.3, 'EU should contribute to the global and third countries national capacities of early prediction, detection and response to global health threats under the International Health Regulations'.

[106] Livrani and Coker, above n 38, 924.

[107] Livrani and Coker, above n 38, 927, arguing that the EU/WHO relations are strained because of this difference in outlook.

[108] For an excellent overview of the many ways in which international law affects global food safety and food security, see: Snyder, 'Toward an International Law for Adequate Food' in Ahmed and Snyder (eds), *Food Security and Food Safety* (The Hague Academy of International Law, Brill Online 2014).

[109] Havinga, 'Transitions in Food Governance in Europe from national towards EU and global regulation and from public towards hybrid and private forms of governance' (2012) Nijmegen Sociology of Law Working Paper No. 2012/02, 4, 'less than half of the food people in the US, Spain and France eat are unprocessed foods such as vegetables, fruit and meat'.

[110] Such as certain mushrooms, oysters, mussels and other seafood.

[111] WHO, 'Food Safety: Frequently asked questions on genetically modified foods' (*WHO*, 2014).

attention where health is threatened through the food chain. Hence, ensuring the management of risk from 'farm to fork', and everywhere along the supply chain, is of high political salience,[112] and a major difficulty for regulators.[113] This is the case both for national governments and for the EU, in the context of the EU's external trade laws.

As we have already seen in chapter 15, the EU's institutional arrangements for food safety are separate from those of communicable disease control more generally. The European Food Safety Authority (EFSA) was established in 2002,[114] in the wake of the emergence of BSE/vCJD. Although not as powerful as some EU agencies (such as the EMA), the EFSA has established itself as the centre of a reasonably credible system for ensuring food safety within the EU,[115] even though some of its expanded role is more challenging.[116] But what about the EU's position in global food safety? The EU is the largest importer and exporter of food in the world; it has stringent health regulations for food; and has highly developed regulatory capacity. We would therefore expect its influence over global food safety to be significant.[117]

EFSA's approach is summarized in its 'Strategic Plan' for 2009–13[118] and its 'Science Strategy' for 2012–16.[119] One of the key challenges addressed by these strategy documents is global food trade. European and international food security, sustainability and the needs of an ageing European population are highlighted. The EU's food safety law requires that food exported or re-exported from the EU must comply with its food law.[120] EU law seeks to prevent disease being communicated to consumers elsewhere in the world, through unsafe food originating in, or transiting through, the EU. This seems to be a 'genuine concern' for global food safety.[121] But the EU is also concerned to protect its own food industry.[122] In addition, the Science Strategy notes the role of the food industry in developing novel products to enhance EU competitiveness within 'Europe 2020'.[123]

---

[112] Negri, 'Food Safety and Global Health: An International Law Perspective' (*Global Health Governance*, 1 September 2009).

[113] Havinga, above n 109.   [114] Regulation 178/2002/EC [2002] OJ L31/1 (as amended).

[115] MacMaoláin, *EU Food Law: Protecting Consumers and Health in a Common Market* (Hart 2007); Alemanno and Gabbi (eds), *The Foundations of EU Food Law and Policy* (Ashgate, 2014).

[116] See: e.g. chapter 15, discussion on nutrient profiling.

[117] Young, 'Europe as a global regulator? The limits of EU influence in international food safety standards' 21(6) *Journal of European Public Policy* (2014) 904.

[118] European Food Safety Authority (EFSA), 'Strategic Plan of the European Food Safety Authority for 2009-2013' (*EFSA* 2008), adopted following a regular evaluation of its activities required by Regulation 178/2002/EC [2002] OJ L31/1.

[119] European Food Safety Authority (EFSA), 'Science Strategy 2012-2016' (EFSA 2012).

[120] Regulation 178/2002/EC [2002] OJ L31/1, Recital 24.

[121] Vos and Weimer, 'The Role of the EU in Transnational Regulation of Food Safety: Extending Experimentalist Governance?' (2013) GR:EEN Working Paper No. 35, 3.

[122] Vos and Weimer, above n 121, 3, describe the EU's external food policy as 'promoting the safety of foods traded on the internal market on the one hand and defending the interests of EU economic actors on the other'.

[123] European Food Safety Authority (EFSA), 'Science Strategy 2012-2016' (EFSA 2012) 10.

Of course, the EU also seeks to protect its own consumers from risks to health from global food trade. Food sold in the EU must comply with the EU's food safety rules, or requirements recognized by the EU as equivalent, or requirements agreed between the EU and another country in a bilateral agreement.[124] Thus, in practice, the EU 'exports' its food safety standards to thousands of food producers across the globe. The requirement to meet stringent EU food safety standards increases pressure on governments in other countries, as the food industry seeks to persuade them to adopt EU-compliant standards, so that they can market food in the EU, but not be subject to a competitive disadvantage in their home country.[125]

The Official Food and Feeds Control Regulation 882/2004/EC[126] establishes the operating framework for official controls on food imported into the EU. Due to sheer volume, the vast majority of goods imported into the EU are not subject to systematic border controls.[127] Rather, Regulation 882/2004/EC and Regulation 178/2002/EC envisage that the EFSA will work within a global network of food safety authorities. The EU establishes import conditions; sets processes for recognizing standards of other countries as equivalent to EU standards, and checks carried out by food safety authorities in other countries; approves pre-import controls;[128] and collects information. According to Ellen Vos and Maria Weimer, the EU's approach to import controls on food is a 'risk-based approach'. Rather than a 'one size fits all' rule, the risks that a specific food import poses to human health (or animal health, or the environment) determine the conditions under which that product may enter the EU. The consequence is a significant need for effective information flow about emergent risks. EFSA is required to work with candidate and applicant countries, third countries and international bodies, in order to fulfil its technical mission – to locate, collect, synthesize, and analyse scientific and technical data on food safety.[129] The ESFA's alert system picks up thousands of notifications for food and feed being imported into the EU every year. High-profile food scares, such as concerning Chinese infant milk in 2008,[130] represent only the visible tip of the iceberg. The European Commission is also obliged to build capacity of food safety authorities,[131] especially in developing countries where costs of compliance with EU standards are high, through providing information about hazard control and assessment procedures, and risk assessment. Opinions differ

---

[124] Regulation 178/2002/EC [2002] OJ L31/1 (as amended), Article 11.
[125] Vos and Weimer, above n 121.   [126] Regulation 882/2004/EC [2004] OJ L165/1.
[127] Vos and Weimer, above n 121.
[128] An approval of pre-import checks means that import controls at the border are less frequent, Regulation 882/2004/EC, Article 23.
[129] Regulation 178/2002/EC, Article 33.
[130] WHO, 'International Food Safety Authorities Network (INFOSAN)' (WHO, 2014); International Food Safety Authorities Network (INFOSAN), 'Enhancing INFOSAN in Asia and Implementation of Regional Food Safety Strategies: Meeting Report' (WHO 2013); see: Havinga, above n 109.
[131] Regulation 882/2004/EC, Article 50 (2).

on whether this constitutes protectionism of the EU food industry, or enhances learning in developing countries.[132]

Where the EU has competence (either exclusive, or shared with its Member States), the European Commission represents the EU in international institutional fora such as the UN's Food and Agriculture Office (FAO), WHO, and the Codex Alimentarius Commission. EFSA has 'built dialogue'[133] with these international organizations. It holds meetings with national food safety agencies in the EU's major food trading partners, particularly the USA, Canada, Australia, New Zealand and Japan. China, Korea and Afghanistan are also highlighted. Some of this work has resulted in formal bilateral agreements,[134] which are said (by the EFSA) to secure 'more appropriate' protection of confidential information under national law in each country. As part of its 'pre-Accession programmes', and 'neighbourhood policy', EFSA has established contacts with authorities in several countries.[135]

The EFSA's 2009 document, 'International Activities: A Strategic Approach',[136] describes EFSA as a 'mature organization'.[137] Yet its own commissioned report on its 'image' (2010) admits that its position in global health networks is not particularly strong.[138] Relations with Codex Alimentarius Commission (CAC), and with national food safety authorities, especially the US Food and Drug Administration, suggest that, in general, the EFSA is still a relatively 'young' institution, and has yet really to become a seriously heavyweight player globally. For instance, the EU (selectively) 'receives' policy from the CAC,[139] as

---

[132] See literature cited in: Vos and Weimer, above n 121.

[133] According to the EFSA website: EFSA, 'International scientific cooperation' (*EFSA*, 2014).

[134] See: e.g., U.S. - EFSA and the U.S. Food and Drug Administration, European Agreement in the Area of Assessing Food Safety Risk (2 July 2007); Memorandum of Cooperation for the promotion of scientific cooperation on data collection and data sharing related to risk assessment, 7 December 2009, signed with the Food Safety Commission of Japan. Regulation 178/2002/EC of the European Parliament and of the Council laying down the general principles and requirements of food law, establishing the European Food Safety Authority and laying down procedures in matters of food safety [2002] OJ L31/1 (as amended), Articles 11 and 12, explicitly envisage such agreements. A full list, of over 50 legal instruments, is here: Commission, 'International Affairs – Sanitary and Phytosanitary Agreements' (*Commission*, 23 September 2013).

[135] 'Albania, Former Yugoslav Republic of Macedonia, Montenegro, Serbia and Turkey'; 'Bosnia & Herzegovina and Kosovo∗ (∗This designation is without prejudice to positions on status, and is in line with UNSCR 1244 and the ICJ Opinion on the Kosovo Declaration of Independence: *Accordance with International Law of the Unilateral Declaration of Independence in Respect of Kosovo, Advisory Opinion, I.C.J. Reports 2010*, p. 403.)'; 'Algeria, Armenia, Azerbaijan, Belarus, Egypt, Georgia, Israel, Jordan, Lebanon, Libya, Moldova, Morocco, the State of Palestine, Tunisia and Ukraine'; see: EFSA, 'International scientific cooperation' (*EFSA*, 2014).

[136] EFSA, 'International Activities – Strategic Approach: Document Describing EFSA's strategic approach to its international activities' (EFSA 2009).

[137] EFSA, (2009) above n 136, 3.

[138] EFSA, 'Image of the European Food Safety Authority (EFSA): Qualitative Research Report' (EFSA 2010).

[139] See: Poli, 'Euro-American Conflicts within the Codex Alimentarius Commission' in Snyder (ed), *International Food Security and Global Legal Pluralism* (Bruylant 2004). AG Fennelly has

in practice the CAC's standards have a normative effect through recognition in the WTO system. But the EU could also seek to *make* CAC policy, in particular since 2003, when the EU Member States were able to speak with 'one voice' in the CAC, as the EU itself acceded to the CAC. This means that the EU effectively has multiple votes in CAC processes.[140] There is some scepticism over whether it has been successful, either in terms of 'uploading' elements of EU food safety law at the level of principle (e.g., the precautionary principle)[141] or in terms of adoption of specific standards. Alastair Young shows conclusively that studies that reach positive conclusions on the EU's influence in the CAC are focused on a few high profile but atypical examples. The EU does not seek to export its food safety standards, nor to block competing standards, through the CAC.[142] The EFSA also seeks to strengthen its dialogue and cooperation with international organizations and food agencies in different parts of the world[143] through a multiannual programme on International Scientific Cooperation.[144] It envisages establishment of an international 'platform' for the development and implementation of harmonized risk communication practices.

Moreover, the EU's contributions to global food safety law must be seen in their specific legal context. Regulation 178/2002/EC is based on the idea that 'it is . . . necessary to establish general requirements for only safe food and feed to be placed on the market'.[145] To that end, it requires that 'food law shall aim to achieve the free movement in the [EU] of food and feed manufactured or marketed according to the general principles and requirements'[146] of the Regulation. The underlying aim of the Regulation is thus free trade – the risk assessment provisions, and exercise of the precautionary principle envisaged by the Regulation[147] operate as exceptions to the rule of free trade in food across the EU, and globally.

Several commentators have pointed out the disparity between the relatively 'hard' provisions of global trade law,[148] especially WTO law, and the 'softer'

---

argued that the Codex's standards should be relied on by the CJEU, see: Opinion in *Fábrica de Queijo Eru Portuguesa*, C-42/99, EU:C:2000:306.

[140] In practice, as many votes as Member States that are represented in a particular meeting, plus the EU's own vote, see: Young, (2014), above n 117, 910.

[141] See: Poli, above n 139, discussing the CAC's approach to the precautionary principle, where the EU is out of line with other members of the CAC; although she contrasts the EU's relative success in gaining CAC recognition for factors other than science-based risk assessment (such as consumer concerns, or economic sustainability); Young, above n 117.

[142] Young, above n 117.

[143] The ECDC will continue to work with agencies in Australia, Canada, Japan, New Zealand and the US. It will develop case by case relations with agencies in countries where the EU is developing or has developed bilateral agreements, such as countries in Asia, South America and Africa.

[144] EFSA, 'Multi-annual programme on International Scientific Cooperation 2014-2016' (*EFSA*, 7 July 2014).

[145] Regulation 178/2002/EC, Recital 27.   [146] Regulation 178/2002/EC, Article 5 (2).

[147] Regulation 178/2002/EC, Article 7.

[148] Button, *The Power to Protect: Trade, Health and Uncertainty in the WTO* (Hart 2004); Negri, above n 112; Snyder, 'Introduction: International Food Security and Global Legal Pluralism'

provisions of international public health organizations, such as WHO, UN FAO or Codex Alimentarius Commission. These different aspects of EU global food law are thus in a non-equal relationship. However, the relationship is not entirely hierarchical: standards such as those developed by the Codex Alimentarius Commission have been recognized by the WTO as international benchmarks of acceptable food regulation.[149] However, the norms of global trade law, like those of EU trade law, enjoy a privileged legal status – they are the standard, the 'rule', against which health protection must be accepted as a permissible exception. The implications for EU health law include that public health protection aims must be pursued within a global context that privileges enforceable rules of trade law. However, as we concluded in chapter 15, this does not mean that the EU is entirely ineffective at protecting the health interests of the consumers of food. The health aspects of the EU's global food law discussed so far are focused on communicable diseases, rather than the significant and growing threats to health through non-communicable diseases associated with obesity. To some extent, the EU's global food law constrains the significant powers of the global food industry – although perhaps in the final analysis not as effectively as might be hoped for, if a health protection agenda were to be pursued. We say a little more about this below.

Threats: global food and tobacco law

According to the UN General Assembly, nearly two-thirds of deaths globally are attributable to largely preventable non-communicable diseases, including cardiovascular diseases, chronic respiratory diseases and diabetes.[150] This final substantive section of the book discusses non-communicable diseases. We consider the extent to which the EU has developed global food law applicable not to the control of spread of communicable diseases through food, but to other aspects of food which are, or may be, harmful to human health. We do not consider in detail the most obvious connection between food and health: that of famine, although our conclusions about the limitations of EU external health law in tackling global health inequalities also apply in this context.[151] As we saw

---

in Snyder, above n 108; Gostin, 'Global Health Law Governance' (2008) 22(1) *Emory International Law Review* 35.

[149] See: e.g., *EC – Trade Description of Sardines (Peru)* [2002] WT/DS231/AB/R, Report of the WTO Appellate Body; *EC – Measures Concerning Meat and Meat Products (Hormones)* [1998] WT/DS26/AB/R - WT/DS48/AB/R, Report of the WTO Appellate Body. See further: chapter 15.

[150] United Nations, 'Political declaration of the High-level Meeting of the General Assembly on the Prevention and Control of Non-communicable Diseases' (Doc A/66/L 1, UN General Assembly 2011); WHO, 'Global Status Report on Non-Communicable Diseases 2010' (*WHO* 2011).

[151] See: Gruni, 'Going from One Extreme to the Other: Food Security and Export Restrictions in the EU-CARIFORUM Partnership Agreement' (2013) 19(6) *European Law Journal* 864; Snyder (2004) above n 108. Another area of EU law which could be considered here is EU water law. As we noted in chapter 3, a 'citizens initiative' on access to water and sanitation was

in chapter 15, food law is a potential way of tackling the diseases associated with obesity. Finally, we consider the EU's contributions to global tobacco regulation as a key component in reducing cancer and cardiovascular diseases.

EU food law and policy

It is still unclear what, if any, the long-term effects on human health of genetically modified food[152] might be, although possible risks include increased antibiotic resistance, increased allergic reactions and poor nutrition. In terms of global food trade, the EU's approach to the regulation of genetically modified organisms within the food chain has been a major issue. European distaste for genetically modified crops and the like relates not only to health concerns – it is also driven by questions of environmental protection,[153] land use and organization,[154] as well as of culturally embedded notions of food.[155] But from our point of view, the relevance of this topic is the extent to which the EU is able to pursue its health policy, by determining its own regulatory approach to genetically modified food, while complying with its WTO obligations. The

---

not taken up by the European Commission, see: Commission, 'Communication on the European Citizens' Initiative "Water and sanitation are a human right! Water is a public good, not a commodity!"' (Communication) COM (2014) 177 final. The Commission refers to its development policy, stating that the human rights dimension of access to clean water is 'at the heart of its development policy' (page 10).

[152] 'Genetically modified food' is defined by the WHO as follows: 'Genetically modified organisms (GMOs) can be defined as organisms in which the genetic material (DNA) has been altered in a way that does not occur naturally. The technology is often called "modern biotechnology" or "gene technology", sometimes also "recombinant DNA technology" or "genetic engineering". It allows selected individual genes to be transferred from one organism into another, also between non-related species. Such methods are used to create GM plants – which are then used to grow GM food crops.' See: WHO, 'Food Safety: Frequently asked questions on genetically modified foods' (*WHO*, 2014).

[153] See: Strauss, 'Feast or Famine: The Impact of the WTO Decision Favoring the US Biotechnology Industry in the EU Ban of Genetically Modified Foods' (2008) 45(4) *American Business Law Journal* 775; Scott, 'European Regulation of GMOs and the WTO' (2003) 9 *Columbia Journal of European Law* 213; Howse and Mavroidis, 'European Evolving Regulatory Strategy for GMOs and the issue of Consistency with WTO Law: of Kine and Brine' (2000) 24 *Fordham International Law Journal* 317; Tiberghien, 'Competitive Governance and the Quest for Legitimacy in the EU: the Battle over the Regulation of GMOs since the mid-1990s' (2009) 31(3) *European Integration* 389; Winham, 'The GMO Panel: WTO and Agricultural Biotech Products' (2009) 31(3) *European Integration* 409. A good example of a European approach is the case brought by Karl Heinz Bablok, a German amateur beekeeper, to seek to prevent Monsanto's MO810 maize from being grown near his beehives, see: Judgment in *Bablok*, C-442/09, EU:C:2011:541.

[154] Anderson and Jackson, 'Why are US and EU Policies Toward GMOs so Different?' (2003) 6(3) *AgBioForum* 95.

[155] Snyder (2004) above n 108. On the cultural resonances of food in the EU see Roth-Behrendt, 'A View of EFSA from the European Parliament' in Alemanno and Gabbi above n 115; Laudan, 'Slow Food: The French Terroir Strategy, and Culinary Modernism. An Essay Review of Carlos Petrini, trans. William McCuaig. *Slow Food: The Case for Taste* (New York: Columbia University Press, 2011)' (2004) 7(2) *Food Culture and Society: An International Journal of Multidisciplinary Research* 133, and see: chapter 15.

essence of the question is whether the EU's approach to genetically modified food, which is more precautionary than that in other northern/western states, in particular the USA,[156] is compatible with WTO law.

There is a significant literature on this question, and here we are able only to touch on the points that are most salient to EU health law. We have already outlined the key elements of WTO law in chapter 16: the WTO system recognizes the interests of States Parties to protect, inter alia, human health. It also establishes a complaints system, whereby national measures purporting to protect health can be assessed to determine whether they constitute disguised protectionism. The EU has been the subject of complaints before the WTO dispute resolution system about various aspects of its food law. The disparities between the EU and USA approaches to food regulation, and the fact that the EU is an attractive market for USA food producers, mean that the WTO challenges to EU food law tend to come from the USA.[157]

During the 1990s, the EU had approved some eighteen genetically modified products under its legislation on genetically modified organisms. But, in 1999, the Council of Ministers agreed to impose a *de facto* moratorium on the approval of such genetically modified products, pending revision of the EU authorization procedures. The context for this decision includes European suspicion of technologically enhanced food,[158] and the BSE/vCJD crisis,[159] during which European publics felt a deep distrust of both their governments and the European Union. Thus, genetically modified food became more associated with health threats than it might otherwise have been. The moratorium remained in place until around 2004, when new EU legislation came into effect.[160] Thereafter, new genetically modified products were authorized, but with much stricter labelling and traceability requirements. In the meantime, aspects of the EU's policy (in particular, the moratorium, but not the labelling and traceability rules) were challenged by the USA, Canada and Argentina using the WTO procedures. Over three years later, in 2006, the WTO Panel reported, finding that, procedurally speaking, the operation of the moratorium between 1999 and 2003 was incompatible with WTO requirements. The EU (probably for pragmatic reasons)[161] declined to appeal this Panel report, ending the formal legal phase of the dispute settlement mechanism.[162]

---

[156] For a detailed summary of the differences, see: Vogel, *The Politics of Precaution: Regulating Health, Safety, and Environmental Risks in Europe and the United States* (Princeton University Press 2012); Strauss, above n 153. Japan and South Korea also follow a precautionary approach, as does China.

[157] MacMaoláin, above n 115.

[158] See the Hormones in Beef WTO dispute: *EC – Measures Concerning Meat and Meat Products (Hormones)* [1998] WT/DS26/AB/R - WT/DS48/AB/R, Report of the WTO Appellate Body.

[159] Winham, above n 153.

[160] Directive 2001/18/EC [2001] OJ L106/1; Regulation 1829/2003/EC [2003] OJ L268/1; Regulation 1830/2003/EC [2003] OJ 268/24.

[161] Winham, above n 153, 414.

[162] The US subsequently began proceedings under Article 22.2 of the DSU, for the EU's failure to comply with the panel report in due time. These proceedings were suspended in 2008: *EC — Measures Affecting the Approval and Marketing of Biotech Products* [2006] WT/DS291/R,

One of the interesting things about the WTO Panel report, for our purposes, is the way in which it interpreted the relationship between genetically modified foods and human health. The Panel found that, of the possible relevant WTO instruments (the Sanitary and Phytosanitary (SPS) Agreement and the Agreement on Technical Barriers to Trade (TBT)), the applicable provision was the SPS. Hence the WTO Panel relied upon an interpretation of the EU's genetically modified food law that focused on its aims of protecting human (and animal) health, rather than protecting the environment more generally (e.g., in terms of biodiversity). This aspect of the Panel decision has been criticized.[163] The Panel report has been heralded as determining the future direction for WTO law on the place of food safety, health and environmental measures within international trade law.[164] However, given the relatively narrow nature of the report, technically speaking, it may be that this is to overstate matters. Certainly both sides were able to claim a political 'win'.[165] Perhaps the most important aspect of the WTO Panel report may be that it *de facto* undermines the WTO's authority to take decisions on sensitive policy areas, such as the protection of human health in the context of global trade.[166] If that is so, then its significance is that, despite its WTO obligations, the EU retains a significant discretion to determine the scope and approach of food law, in the name of human health protection, and adopting a precautionary approach. This discretion has implications for our conclusions below, about a wider range of food law than the genetically modified food example.

Finally, we should note that in some ways the most important aspect of EU food law is its Common Agricultural Policy (CAP). The historical context of the CAP is the major health threat of starvation and malnutrition facing much of Western continental Europe in the late 1940s and into the 1950s.[167] Seen in this context, the CAP, and the EU's external trade policies on food, have been enormously successful. Starvation is not a widespread or even common problem in the EU. But there are significant concerns among health policy communities about the effects of EU food law on eating patterns in the EU. Coupled with increasingly sedentary lifestyles, as patterns of labour are moving away from heavy manual labour, obesity in Europe is on the increase. There is very little evidence that the EU has attempted to use its lawmaking powers to tackle this health threat, for instance, by attempting to influence the global regulation of food labelling and consumer information. The consumer information rules discussed in chapter 15 apply to all food sold in the EU, so will have indirect

---

WTO Panel Report; see further: WTO, 'Dispute Settlement: Dispute DS291: European Communities — Measures Affecting the Approval and Marketing of Biotech Products' (*WTO*, 17 January 2008). Assessments of the EU approach suggest that it does indeed have a negative impact on trade, see: Disdier and Fontagné, 'Trade impact of European measures on GMOs condemned by the WTO panel' (2010) 146(3) *Review of World Economics* 495.

[163] Winham, above n 153, citing Palmer, 'The WTO GMO Dispute: implications for developing countries and the need for an appeal' (GeneWatch UK, RSPB, Forum for Biotechnology and Food Security, and the GM Freeze 2006).

[164] Strauss, above n 153.   [165] Tiberghien, above n 153.   [166] Strauss, above n 153.

[167] See: Judt, *Postwar: A History of Europe since 1945* (Vintage 2010).

effects on food producers elsewhere in the world. But, as we saw in that chapter, their effects are not as far-reaching as they could be.

Given the discretion implied by the WTO procedures on the EU's approach to genetically modified food, global trade *law* is not *per se* an impediment to the EU taking a different approach to other jurisdictions, and seeking to protect human health through stringent food regulation. The EU's failure to do so is not because it is *legally* constrained from so doing. Rather, the power of the global food industry, already noted in chapter 15, and the relative ineffectiveness of the EU political processes to tackle that power, apply equally in the context of the EU's external health law. Whereas in terms of its internal health law, the EU has made some (very) small steps to use food law to tackle obesity, in terms of external health law, the conclusion is that the effects of EU law are indirect at best.

EU tobacco law and policy

At least food, if consumed appropriately, can be good for human health. In these final paragraphs before we turn to our conclusions, we examine a product which is *never* good for human health: tobacco. Given its beginnings, in supporting tobacco producers in the EU through the Common Agricultural Policy, the EU's tobacco law and policy have come a long way in terms of their contributions to health. But to what extent is this internal policy reflected in the EU's engagement with global health? Looking first at global trade law, WTO law, which prohibits discriminatory treatment of the same products,[168] has been used to challenge national tobacco policies. One issue which has arisen is what counts as 'the same products' for these purposes. For instance, Indonesia has challenged the USA's prohibition of clove-flavoured cigarettes, arguing that it is in effect a disguised protection for domestic producers, whose products taste either of tobacco or of menthol.[169] The administration of tobacco tax systems[170] and licensing arrangements[171] have also been challenged. The human

---

[168] Articles III (2) and III (4), GATT: governing 'national treatment', and also the Agreement on Technical Barriers to Trade (TBT).

[169] Compliance proceedings ongoing: *US- Measures Affecting the Production and Sale of Clove Cigarettes* [2012] WT/DS406/R, Report of the WTO Appellate Body. The EU has commenced a separate dispute against Indonesia, challenging the procedure whereby Indonesia has sought to enforce the decision in this dispute against the USA. The EU was a third party in the original dispute, but was not granted third party rights in the enforcement arbitration procedure. The EU requested consultations on its dispute (the first formal step in a WTO dispute procedure) on 13 June 2014. See further: Zagger, 'US, Indonesia Stall WTO Clove Cigarette Arbitration (*Law 360*, 2014); and Strawbridge, 'U.S. Implementation of Adverse WTO Rulings: A Closer Look at the Tuna-Dolphin, COOL, and Clove Cigarettes Cases' (2013) 17(23) *American Society of International Law*. Thanks to Oisin Suttle for explaining this to us.

[170] *Thailand- Customs and Fiscal Measures on Cigarettes from the Philippines* [2011] WT/DS/371/AR/R 17, Report of the WTO Appellate Body.

[171] *Thailand- Restrictions on Importation of and Internal Taxes on Cigarettes* [1990] DS10/R, WTO Panel Report.

health protection provision in Article XX(b) GATT is at issue in such cases. Allyn Taylor et al. have argued that the effect of international trade law was to increase global trade in tobacco and tobacco products through the 1980s and 90s.[172] This is obviously at odds with the EU's tobacco control policies, which focus on improving public health within the EU. But until the EU's involvement with the WHO in developing the Framework Convention on Tobacco Control[173] there is little evidence that the EU seeks to restrict tobacco consumption elsewhere in the world,[174] and certainly no evidence that it seeks to use the WTO as a forum in which to do so.

The differential approach to tobacco regulation between the EU's internal policies and its external policies is illustrated in Case C-491/01 *R. v. Secretary of State for Health, ex parte British American Tobacco and Imperial Tobacco Ltd.*[175] The case concerned the validity[176] and interpretation of various aspects of the Tobacco Products Directive 2001/37/EC,[177] including the labelling provisions. Article 7 of the Directive provides that 'texts, names, trade marks and figurative or other signs suggesting that a particular tobacco product is less harmful than others shall not be used on the packaging of tobacco products'. The question was whether this provision, which in effect bans descriptors such as 'low tar', 'light', 'ultra-light' or 'mild',[178] applies only to tobacco products marketed within the EU, or also to those packaged within the EU for export to third countries.

The CJEU drew a distinction between rules such as those covered by Article 3, covering the composition of tobacco products (where the Directive explicitly covers external trade), and rules such as those covered by Articles 7, concerning the presentation and labelling of tobacco products.[179] The consequences of the latter type of product unlawfully circulating in the internal market were deemed

---

[172] Taylor et al., 'The impact of trade liberalization on tobacco consumption' in Jha and Chaloupka (eds), *Tobacco in Developing Countries* (OUP 2000).

[173] Council Decision 2004/513/EC [2004] OJ L213/8.

[174] The EU's internal tobacco regulations do extend to other European countries, under the European Economic Area Agreement, see further below.

[175] *BAT/Imperial Tobacco*, C-491/01, EU:C:2002:741.

[176] Legal basis for the Directive is Article 95 EC (now Article 114 TFEU) for its internal trade aspects, and Article 133 EC (now replaced by Article 207 TFEU) for its external trade aspects. ECJ held that Article 95 was the only appropriate legal basis for the Directive, and that it was incorrect for the EU legislature to rely also on Article 133 EC: *BAT/Imperial Tobacco*, EU:C:2002:741, paragraph 97. This did not, however, render the Directive invalid as a whole. Although, at the time, the legislative procedures under Articles 95 and 133 EC were different from each other, both procedures provided for QMV in Council. The CJEU also held that the Directive is proportionality and subsidiarity compliant, and compliant with the duty to give reasons, and there was no misuse of powers.

[177] Directive 2001/37/EC of the European Parliament and of the Council of 5 June 2001 on the approximation of the laws, regulations and administrative provisions of the Member States concerning the manufacture, presentation and sale of tobacco products [2001] OJ L194/26 (as amended).

[178] Directive 2001/37/EC [2001] OJ L194/26 (as amended), Recital 27.

[179] *BAT/Imperial Tobacco*, EU:C:2002:741, paragraph 205.

not 'of the same severity',[180] and so did not necessitate the adoption of the same sorts of measures. Hence Article 7 applies only to products marketed within the EU, and does not extend to those intended to be marketed in third countries:[181] 'The provisions of the Directive must be considered in principle to concern only tobacco products which are to be placed on the internal market'.[182]

Notwithstanding the EU's work on global tobacco regulation, in particular the WHO's Framework Convention on Tobacco Control,[183] this did not affect the CJEU's interpretation of the legislative text, in the absence of explicit application to external trade. On the one hand, the CJEU's decision supports global anti-tobacco efforts, in that the CJEU upholds the validity of the Directive, which applies its composition rules not only to tobacco products to be marketed within the EU, but also to those to be marketed elsewhere. These composition rules have similar indirect effects on global industry behaviour to those of the EU's food law, discussed above. But. on the other hand, given the highly addictive nature of tobacco products, and the industry's practice of targeting new smokers – young people, to whom the descriptors such as 'light', 'mild' and so on are aimed – the differentiation between composition rules and labelling rules could be seen as misplaced deference to national regulatory preferences elsewhere. In that respect, it is at odds with the EU's attempts to develop global tobacco law. It is more consistent with the EU's Common Agricultural Policy, through which the EU has subsidized tobacco products aimed at North African and Eastern European markets.[184] A different approach, available to the CJEU, would have been to rely on Article 168 (1) TFEU, which requires that 'a high level of human health protection' is to form a constituent part of all EU policies, and to reason that the correct interpretation of Article 7 of the Directive is to ensure a high level of health protection, hence tobacco regulation, within the EU's external trade law.

Negotiations on the Framework Convention on Tobacco Control began in the mid-1990s. The EU, and especially DG SANCO of the European Commission, made much of the EU's involvement in this instrument. The EU was a full participant in the intergovernmental negotiating body, alongside its Member States.[185] The Convention marks a move on the part of the WHO from a 'charity-based' to a 'norm-based' model. Modelling itself on international environmental law, the underlying idea of the Convention is that an interdependent regulatory

---

[180] *BAT/Imperial Tobacco*, EU:C:2002:741, paragraph 215.

[181] *BAT/Imperial Tobacco*, EU:C:2002:741, paragraphs 214-7.

[182] *BAT/Imperial Tobacco*, EU:C:2002:741, paragraph 212, referring to Article 5 (which covers rules about labelling information concerning harmful substances), and to the main objectives of the Directive.

[183] Opinion in *BAT/Imperial Tobacco*, C-491/01, EU:C:2002:476, paragraphs 72-73.

[184] Taylor et al., above n 172, 354; Roemer, *Legislative Action to Combat the World Tobacco Epidemic* (WHO 1993).

[185] Information on the FCTC is available from WHO, 'Framework Convention on Tobacco Control' (*WHO*, 2014).

environment, such as that for tobacco, needs global regulatory arrangements.[186] In terms of how the EU assists with implementation of the Convention outside its borders, tobacco control has arisen as a global public health concern on which the EU should act, in partnership with other global health actors, in particular the WHO. The EU's mid-term review of its 2007–13 development policy notes that the EU's work in global non-communicable disease control should be in line with WHO objectives.[187] The 'Investing in People' strands of the EU's development policy should, according to the European Commission, be used to provide technical and financial support in developing and least developed countries for the implementation of the WHO's Framework Convention on Tobacco Control.[188]

Other implementation work includes the possibility of using bilateral and multilateral treaties to secure compliance with the Framework Convention.[189] The EU does extend the scope of its tobacco regulation to countries in the European Economic Area, through its free trade agreement with those countries,[190] by extending its free movement law (of which its tobacco regulation is a part) to the European Economic Area. A claim brought in a Norwegian court challenged Norwegian tobacco law, which is more restrictive than EU law, in that it bans displays of tobacco products at the point of sale.[191] The EFTA Court[192] held that the ban would breach the EEA if it had a disproportionate effect on marketing tobacco products imported from other EEA states than on that of imported products which were, until recently,[193] produced in Norway. The question of whether the ban was suitable and necessary for public health protection is a matter for the national court,[194] although the EFTA Court took

---

[186] Kickbusch, 'Foreword' in Hein, Bartsch and Kohlmorgen (eds), *Global Health Governance and the Fight against HIV/AIDS* (Palgrave Macmillan 2007) xiii. See also: Shibuya et al., 'WHO Framework Convention on Tobacco Control: development of an evidence based global public health treaty' (2003) 327(7407) *British Medical Journal* 154; Taylor and Bettcher, 'WHO Framework Convention on Tobacco Control: a global 'good' for public health' (2000) 78(7) *Bulletin of the WHO* 920; Roemer, Taylor and Lariviere, 'Origins of the WHO Framework Convention on Tobacco Control' (2005) 95(6) *American Journal of Public Health* 936.

[187] Set out in the WHO, '2008-2013 Action Plan for the Global Strategy for the Prevention and Control of Non-communicable Diseases' (WHO 2009).

[188] Commission, 'Investing in People: Mid Term Review of Strategy Paper for Thematic Programme (2007-2013)' (Commission 2010).

[189] See: WHO, 'Workshop on trade-related issues relevant to implementation of the WHO FCTC' (WHO FCTC 2012).

[190] Iceland, Lichtenstein, Norway.

[191] 'A total prohibition on the advertising of tobacco products has been in force in Norway since the introduction of such a ban in 1973. That ban, which is based on the Act of 9 March 1973 No 14 relating to the Prevention of the Harmful Effects of Tobacco (Lov om vern mot tobakksskader 9. mars 1973 nr. 14), is wide in scope as it covers all forms of marketing of tobacco products in all kinds of media', *Philip Morris Norway AS v Norway* (E-16/10) [2012] 1 CMLR 24, paragraph 2.

[192] The EFTA Court has jurisdiction over states which are parties to the EEA agreement, see: EFTA Court, 'Introduction to the EFTA Court' (*EFTA Court*, 2014).

[193] Tobacco products were produced in Norway until 2008.

[194] *Philip Morris Norway* (E-16/10) [2012] 1 CMLR 24.

the view that 'in the absence of convincing proof to the contrary, a measure of this kind may be considered suitable for the protection of public health'.[195] The EEA case shows that countries with which the EU has agreed free trade agreements may lawfully impose public health protection measures which are proportionate and justified, including tobacco regulation. But it also implies that the EU could use its free trade agreements indirectly to extend its tobacco control measures to elsewhere in the world. The same is also true of the EU's bilateral or multilateral investment agreements,[196] although these agreements have been used elsewhere as a basis for *challenges* to tobacco regulations.[197] Certainly the underlying rationales of such agreements – which seek to limit the powers of states to interfere with private foreign investments – pull against tobacco regulation, which in essence seeks to constrain the power of the global tobacco industry.

The Framework Convention on Tobacco Control embodies the rhetoric of global health law, and this instrument is quite detailed, and hence potentially powerful. It may be that the EU's capacity developing competences, under its development policy, will enhance compliance with the Convention in countries outside the EU. However the EU's tobacco legislation, as interpreted by the CJEU, means in practice that equivalent protections for tobacco consumers, and potential future consumers, elsewhere in the world, to those within the EU, are not provided by EU health law. The EU's external trade law has yet to be used as a basis to secure the implementation of the Convention.

Conclusions

Health cannot remain solely the preserve of nation states. The global nature of health requires responses beyond national borders. But, given the EU's limited competences in health care, and the political difficulties entailed in balancing the very different interests at stake, the opportunities for the EU to contribute positively or negatively to global health law are seriously constrained. The EU's capacity to engage in the creation of global health law is more restricted than

---

[195] *Philip Morris Norway* (E-16/10), paragraph 84.
[196] The EU's Member States between them have almost 1200 bilateral investment treaties (BITS) (Ireland is the only Member State without at least one such treaty). The EU's Regulation 1219/2012/EU [2012] OJ L351/40, 'grants legal security to the existing Bilateral Investment Agreements between Member States and Third Countries until they are replaced by EU-wide investment deals' (see: Commission, 'Trade: Investment' (*Commission*, 11 June 2014)). The EU is currently negotiating various agreements which include investment, e.g. the FTAs with Canada, India and Singapore. See: Commission, 'Towards a comprehensive European international investment policy' (Communication) COM (2010) 343 final. See chapter 16.
[197] See the claims brought under arbitration under the Rules of the International Centre for Settlement of Investment Disputes, concerning Uruguauy and Australia, discussed in: WHO, 'Workshop on trade-related issues relevant to implementation of the WHO FCTC' (WHO FCTC 2012).

that of specialist international organizations (in particular, the WHO, but also the UN and WTO) or indeed that of several of its larger Member States.

This conclusion is supported in the general literature on EU external relations law and policy. For instance, Young's review of the literature supporting the idea that the EU is a powerful and significant global actor[198] does not include a single example related to health. None of the 'standard examples' of EU global influence (trade, development, security and defence, energy and environment) directly concerns health, or health-related, topics. Although it is claimed that the EU exercises global influence through international organizations concerned with health, particularly those which set regulatory standards, such a conclusion is not supported by the evidence in every policy domain.[199]

But neither is it the case that the EU is completely incapacitated. The literature on the EU's global influences points to the unilateral and extraterritorial impact of the EU's internal market rules – access to that market (the largest single market in the world) requires conformity with EU trade law. Trade law is a significant site for global health law.[200] The EU's role in this regard is highly influential, but ultimately indirect and passive – companies in other countries are not obliged to trade within the EU, but, if they do, they must comply with EU law. The EU plays an active role in 'regulatory diplomacy', in its interactions with states across the world, in a range of fields. It has been described as a 'global producer of risk regulation'.[201] Although the EU, along with all states, is challenged by the mobility of global capital, it is not entirely powerless in the face of that mobility. We agree with Holly Jarman[202] that it should thus be held to account for its actions and lack thereof.

Like Young, we are suspicious of conclusions about the EU's role in global health that purport to be generally applicable. Aspects of EU global health law, defined broadly as we have done here, suggest that EU law may have some positive influences on global health. This is particularly the case where developing the EU's health economy through global free trade and fair competition can be aligned with delivering health innovations that enhance quality of life or health care for patients elsewhere in the world. Another example is where EU health innovation law requires ethical or human rights protections. The EU may 'export' those values, for instance, in securing indirect influence over health research that takes place elsewhere in the world, through requirements

---

[198] Young, above n 117, 905-7.

[199] In the context of food safety, the reason, according to Young, above n 117, is that the EU is a 'preference outlier'. It is unable to impose its food safety standards on the *Codex Alimentarius Commission*, because it is unable to secure sufficient support from other actors within that international institution.

[200] See Agninam, 'Health or Trade? A Critique of Contemporary Approaches to Global Health Diplomacy' 5 *Asian Journal of WTO & International Health Law and Policy* (2010) 355.

[201] Young, above n 117, 905-7.

[202] Jarman, 'Trade in Services and the Public's Health: A Fortress Europe for Health' in Greer and Kurzer, eds, European Union Public Health Policy: Regional and Global Trends (Routledge 2013).

for clinical trials that lead to new products intended for the European market. Another example is reducing spread of communicable diseases through the indirect application of the EU's food safety rules to food producers elsewhere in the world.

But global free movement of the 'factors of production' also has negative effects on health. For instance, the abilities of least developed or developing countries to provide high-quality health care for their populations may be reduced where health professional migration to developed countries is facilitated by global health law.[203] Counterfeit or falsified medicines may circulate more easily, and where attempts to control this phenomenon are focused on intellectual property rights, the safety of patients in the global South may be more compromised than that of patients in the global North. More seriously, equality of access to essential medicines between South and North may be significantly compromised. The 'thematic priorities' of the EU's public health programme 2014–20 pick up several of these topics, including professional mobility and workforce sustainability, access to high-quality, safe medical treatment, protection from communicable and non-communicable diseases. Yet only one of the thematic priorities has any 'outward facing' element – the vast majority focus solely on the health of those *within* the EU, not on global health.

Moreover, where the EU seeks to protect its industries producing products that are, or may be, harmful for health, the effects of free trade may be detrimental. The EU's differential application of its tobacco labelling rules is a case in point. In many instances, the EU has not exported the values of its internal health law, for example, concerning solidarity, equality, ethics or human rights, to the rest of the world.

---

[203] See Agninam, 'Health or Trade? A Critique of Contemporary Approaches to Global Health Diplomacy' 5 *Asian Journal of WTO & International Health Law and Policy* (2010) 355.

Part V
Conclusions

19

Conclusions

The cartography of EU health law

We have been 'mapping' the field of EU health law for over fifteen years. As we have done so, it has expanded, both in breadth and depth of substantive legal coverage. Initially, the field was 'policy-heavy', and correspondingly 'law-light'.[1] 'Governance' became an important feature from the mid-1990s.[2] Ten years ago, we felt that the best way to understand EU health law was as an intersection between 'health law' *and* 'the EU'.[3] But, over time, the contours of EU health law have come to encompass new provisions that fall within an emergent category of 'EU health law', with its own special characteristics and specific legitimacy. The 'holistic' understanding of EU health law is visible, for instance, in the EU Commission's White Paper, 'Together for Health',[4] and in the 'mainstreaming' obligation found in Articles 9 and 168 (1) TFEU. It emanates from the increasing use of the independent 'health' legal basis for EU legislation in Article 168 (4) TFEU.[5] The time has come for *European Union Health Law*.

As we have shown,[6] EU health law will never have the same substantive scope or dominant focus as national medical law, health law or health care law. EU health law has a *presence* in all, or virtually all, of the 'traditional categories' of those areas of law. In some of those categories (for example, pharmaceuticals regulation), EU law more or less occupies the field. But, in others (for example,

---

[1] Hence Hervey, 'Mapping the Contours of European Union Health Law and Policy' 2002 *European Public Law* 69; Hervey, 'Up in Smoke: Community (anti) tobacco law and policy' 26 *European Law Review* (2001) 101.

[2] Hence, e.g., Hervey, 'The European Union and the governance of health care' in de Búrca and Scott (eds), *Law and New Governance in the EU and the US* (Hart 2006) 179.

[3] Hence Hervey and McHale, *Health Law and the European Union* (CUP 2004); Hervey and McHale 'Law, Health and the European Union' (2005) 25(2) *Legal Studies* 200.

[4] Commission, 'White Paper: Together for Health: A Strategic Approach for the EU 2008–2013' (White Paper) COM (2007) 630 final. See further: chapter 3.

[5] We might also point to the arrangement of the European Commission's website on health matters. A decade or so ago, legal scholars would need to plough through diverse material located in different areas on the website. Now much of the relevant material is located in a single portal.

[6] See further: chapters 2 and 3.

end-of-life care), it barely has any effects at all. Equally, we have shown that EU health law is not simply a regional variant of global health law. Global health law differs in its scope and also, importantly, in its normative effects from EU health law.[7] We perceive a distinctively 'European' approach to the modification of liberal global trade, which involves conceptualizing health as a productive factor in economic growth (a capability approach), but also human rights conditionality, elements of an ethic of equality or justice, and risk-based consumer protection.

EU health law interacts with, and therefore has important implications for, both national health law and global health law. For instance, the EU law angle on human rights in health contexts may illuminate questions of consent or autonomy.[8] EU law on privacy may require changes to patient confidentiality rules.[9] EU law on clinical trials may influence and affect the pursuit of medical research.[10] Equally, we have shown that EU health law is a distinct area of EU law, which has implications for other, related, areas of EU law.[11] For instance, EU health law affects social or welfare services and institutions of national importance, such as hospitals or national health insurance entities, as they interact with the internal market and the EU's international relations. EU health law therefore has implications for how EU lawyers understand internal market law, competition law[12] and external relations law.[13] We offer our map of EU health law to health lawyers and EU lawyers alike, as much as to the emergent, and still small, community of EU health lawyers.

The free-standing legal category of EU health law (legislation based on Article 168 (4) TFEU and its interpretation and application) captures only a few features that we seek to include in our map. EU health law includes many more. As we already observed in 2004, these can be read through the internal logic and structures of health law, or those of EU law. These categories are the 'primary colours' (to change metaphor) of our initial cartographic forays. But we have become increasingly dissatisfied with the 'and' approach to EU health law. We need some 'secondary colours', which do more than merely juxtapose the logics of health law and of EU law. This is where the themes of *European Union Health Law* come in.

Themes and perspectives

Our four themes (consumerism; (human) rights; competition/solidarity/equality; risk) provide a way of conceptualizing EU health law through its own internal logic. For the reasons set out in the foregoing, we find this a much

---

[7] See further: chapters 16–18, and see chapters 4–15 by way of contrast.
[8] See further, for instance: chapter 12.   [9] See further: chapter 7.
[10] See further: chapter 12.
[11] Catherine Barnard and Steve Peers were among the first EU lawyers to explicitly recognise this in the context of an academic textbook, by including EU health law as a chapter in Barnard and Peers, *European Union Law* (OUP 2014).
[12] See further: chapters 4–6; 9–14.   [13] See further: chapter 16.

more satisfactory approach to the mapping of EU health law. In this book, the themes are organized and discussed by reference to two perspectives: individual, and collective or systemic. The individual perspective seeks to consider the implications of a particular body of law for an individual person; likewise, the collective/systemic perspective investigates its implications for (health) systems or groups of people. Thus, the principal contribution of the thematic arrangement of *European Union Health Law* is both analytical and contextual.

In each thematically arranged chapter, our discussion is dominated by one theme and one perspective (individual or systemic/collective). Inevitably, of course, the themes and perspectives cut across several chapters, and there are exceptions and qualifications to the overall conclusions we draw. We have discussed these in each substantive chapter, and we draw out this analysis a little further below.

Our approach has six principal benefits. It illuminates EU health law in its own terms, rather than those of EU law or health law. It sheds light on what otherwise present as legal 'puzzles' from the viewpoint of pre-existing legal categories. It supports investigation of the law in context, taking us beyond analysis of legal texts without reference to their effects on practices, policies, institutions or individuals. It allows us to draw out the implications of each theme from more than one perspective. It enhances our ability to develop an informed view of the persuasiveness of claims made in the existing literature. It supports an assessment of the potential for EU health law to tackle some of the problems associated with, or deficiencies of, health law more generally.

Analysing EU health law in its own terms

More than allowing us to answer the question 'what is EU health law?' (an important question in its own right), our approach allows us to consider the field of EU health law in its own terms. We are able to single out for analysis the significance of EU health law in a range of substantive areas organized through a novel taxonomy, rather than through the 'traditional categories' of either EU law or health law. For instance, clinical trials regulation could belong in the category of 'internal market law' or of 'consent to treatment'. Tobacco regulation could belong in 'autonomy', 'public health' or 'consumer protection'. Pharmaceuticals pricing could belong in 'competition law', 'internal market law', 'health systems regulation' or 'consumer law'. Organ transplantation could belong in 'bio-medical ethics', 'consent', 'autonomy', 'regulation of human materials' or 'external trade law'. We could go on. If we discuss the topics in the traditional categories, we may miss the implications or significance of EU health law.

Shedding light on 'legal puzzles'

Areas of law that present as puzzling from the point of view of EU law (or indeed of health law) are susceptible to more satisfactory explanation once the themes are brought into play. A good example is the way in which EU internal market law treats health institutions as compared to patients. In EU internal market law, both institutions and patients are understood as 'factors of production/consumption'. The principles of free movement apply in the same way to legal entities and human beings. Therefore, according to the logic of EU internal market law, there should be no difference in the legal position of an entity seeking to rely on rights of free movement, be they patient or health institution. Nevertheless, when we examine the legal detail, there is such a difference.[14]

The interpretation that leads to the conclusion that patients and institutions should have the same legal entitlements in free movement law is based on assumptions that rely on the themes of consumerism and competition in a market. Our approach to EU health law reveals that those assumptions are not the only themes of EU health law in play. The solidarity basis of health systems in Europe, and the European commitment to the value of equality of treatment according to medical need, are also relevant. The CJEU's jurisprudence on free movement of services and freedom of establishment of health institutions demonstrates this well.[15] There is a temporal element in that, over time, the CJEU is increasingly willing to interfere with or disrupt national health systems by allowing access to institutions or actors from outside of the system. But, more importantly, the jurisprudence is different as between types of institutions and also types of health care or service. The closer that the CJEU perceives a particular institution to be to the 'heart' of the national health (insurance) system, the less likely the CJEU is to follow the consumer and competition-led logic of internal market law. Health insurance itself is the canonical example;[16] hospitals, laboratories and blood centres are others.[17]

Another example is the position of ethically controversial medical treatments in EU law. Again, the logic of EU internal market law implies that we should expect a movement towards convergence on a European market-led norm, for access to, for instance, abortion or euthanasia. But, although the *explicit* discussion of ethical differences in the CJEU (and national courts applying EU law) might be suppressed by the ways in which EU law conceptualizes such health services, the outcomes of the relevant litigation, and the overall lack of such litigation, demonstrate that the consumerizing effects of EU internal market law are not in a hierarchical relationship to ethical settlements expressed in national law.[18] EU legislation, even internal market legislation, often embodies ethical principles.

Investigating the 'law in context'

This book investigates EU health law in its various contexts. We have drawn on, and in some cases reinterpreted, existing analyses of data, from the health

---

[14] Contrast the discussion in chapters 4, 7 and 8, with that in chapters 10 and 11.
[15] See chapter 10; see also chapters 9 and 11.   [16] See further: chapter 9.
[17] See further: chapter 10.   [18] See further: chapter 4.

policy and EU studies literature, across a range of disciplines, such as socio-legal studies, political science and sociology. We go beyond a discussion of substantive topics (clinical trials, anti-obesity law, pharmaceuticals pricing, organ donation and so on), which describes 'what is the law?' – what is the meaning of the legal texts within the scope of our inquiry? Of course, we have sought to answer this question, and have shown that, in many instances, the answer reveals that the question may not be as simple as it sounds.[19]

But we have gone further. We are not only concerned with the meaning of the texts of the law, but also with their effects, or possible effects, in practice. The themes assist in unravelling the modes of legal reasoning and the assumptions and conceptualizations that underpin the texts of the law. In so doing, the themes help to sharpen illustration of how EU health law has shaped or may shape the behaviour of relevant actors, such as national governments, those bodies which finance or otherwise regulate the provision of health care, patients, health care professionals, the pharmaceutical or medical devices industry, health researchers and so on. This inquiry goes to the question of 'law in context'.

The governments of the EU Member States must comply with their obligations in EU law. They must, for instance, ensure that no unjustified restrictions remain in place on patient mobility.[20] In so doing, they may respond to EU health law so as to reassert control on such migration, for instance, by defining the 'basket of care' covered by their health systems with greater precision. While Member States may no longer prevent health professional mobility through, for instance, single registration rules, they may seek to secure sufficient professional capacity through controlling access to professional education.[21] Changes to health professionals' working time have been made in several Member States, improving working conditions and, presumably therefore, the quality of the care professionals are able to provide.[22] Ownership rules of health institutions have had to change in several Member States,[23] opening up possibilities for new business structures for opticians, dental clinics and so on. Some Member States have sought to take advantage of EU law by encouraging the development of specialist capacities in particular medical treatments and also competing in the global market for health services.[24] Private companies have also sought to do so.

Some patients may be able to take advantage of the greater choice and autonomy promoted by EU law. But this ability depends on a range of factors,

---

[19] For example, see the discussion of when health institutions are 'undertakings' within EU competition or state aids law in chapter 9, and consequently whether particular types of health insurance arrangement (chapter 9); particular legal structures of hospitals, pharmacies, laboratories, blood and tissue centres, dental clinics, (chapter 10) involve 'undertakings'. Another example is the meaning of the term 'human embryo' in Directive 98/44/EC [1998] OJ L213/13, see further: chapters 7 and 14.

[20] See further: chapter 4.   [21] Though this is disputed. See further: chapter 6.

[22] See further: chapter 6.   [23] See further: chapters 10 and 11.

[24] See further: Introduction to Part IV, chapter 18.

including their relative wealth (in most instances, patients relying on EU law would have to be sufficiently wealthy to pay for at least travel and accommodation, if not the actual treatment, even if they were to be reimbursed thereafter); their health (cross-border care being particularly suitable for acute, rather than chronic, conditions); their access to and ability to understand information about available health care in other Member States; their linguistic competences and confidence; their ease or comfort in other cultural contexts; their geographical location and proximity to national borders. The available data show some effects of EU law on patient migration patterns, but overall very little evidence of significant changes in patient behaviour.[25]

EU rules on marketing authorizations for pharmaceuticals have secured some changes in behaviour in the pharmaceutical industry, for instance, compliance with rules on clinical trials.[26] The biomedical research industry has focused its efforts in particular directions, following rulings from the CJEU about the lawfulness of particular research practices, and the patentability or otherwise of inventions involving particular processes or human tissue or cells.[27] Overall, though, the evidence suggests significant industry resilience to attempts to address its power. The same is true of industries creating products that are, or may be, harmful to human health, such as the tobacco, food and alcohol industries. It may be that the work of the tobacco industry in developing new products is in part a response to the increasing EU regulation of traditional tobacco products, in particular, the near ban on advertising of cigarettes in the EU.[28]

We should also note that we found some instances where the existence of EU law, particularly 'softer' law, has either been very slow to secure change to practice or, at least so far, made no discernible change. For instance, the swine flu episode did not result in common national policies or procedures of disease containment across the Member States, in spite of the work of the European Centre on Disease Control.[29] Many Member States were very slow to implement changes to working time rules in health contexts.[30]

Revisiting the conclusions on each theme from alternative perspectives

As we noted above, each of our themes can be viewed from either of our two perspectives. In chapters 4–6, we considered the theme of consumerism mainly through an individual perspective. But, of course, the notion of 'consumer' can equally be understood as a collective concept. A group of consumers could be, for instance, a particular group of patients waiting for a hip transplant, or could be the group of all patients covered by a national health (insurance) system. Opening up patient choice may potentially enhance autonomy for both

---

[25] See further: chapter 4. [26] See further: chapters 12 and 13.
[27] See further: chapter 14. [28] See further: chapter 15.
[29] See further: chapter 18. [30] See further: chapter 6.

groups, either through immediate access to services elsewhere in the EU or through longer-term improvements to services through raising awareness of practices elsewhere and improved knowledge about the different treatments that are available. But, from a collective perspective, enhanced patient mobility may be seen as something to be limited rather than welcomed. Some of the negative consequences of enhanced patient autonomy and choice have already been highlighted – there is the potential for individual litigation to disrupt carefully calibrated and democratically legitimated resource allocation models and to force systems to prioritize patients who are 'impatient' and are able to circumvent the rules put in place to secure allocation of resources according to medical need. The greater nuances to patient mobility discussed in chapters 4, 7 and 8, for instance, in the Patients' Rights Directive, already operate as a significant brake on such (perceived) negative consequences. The Patients' Rights Directive enacts in legislation pre-existing principles in the CJEU's jurisprudence which express respect for such concerns, which come into view when one adopts a systemic perspective.

'Consumer rights', a concept that appears in many places in our analysis,[31] involves a collective perspective on consumerism. Where EU law opens up markets in health products or services, and at the same time gives consumers rights to information, or to be heard, so as to protect consumer safety, it involves increased respect for collectively enjoyed public health imperatives.[32] The recognition in EU law of the power of Member States to make such determinations, including by reference to their own populations in some circumstances, facilitates protection of patients/consumers at a collective (state) level. Consumer rights are by no means necessarily aligned with human rights. Consumer markets may enhance individual choice, but may infringe human rights principles in other respects, as, for instance, the debates surrounding organ selling illustrate.[33]

Another example of the collective perspective on consumerism lies in the idea of 'consumer welfare' which underpins competition law (discussed in chapters 9–11, where the focus is systemic). Competition law relies on the idea of consumer choice within markets. Our conclusion in chapters 4–6 to the effect that the very application of EU internal market law to health care involves a *de facto* reconceptualization of relationships between patients, health professionals and health systems, is revisited and disrupted in subsequent chapters, where we discuss competition within (quasi)markets as a way of organizing health systems within the EU. There we show that the individual focused conclusions of the earlier chapters should be understood with greater nuance, given the multiple ways in which EU internal market law respects the 'special place' of health systems, rather than as simply an expression of actors engaging within a market.

---

[31] See, principally: chapter 8, see also chapters 5, 13–15, 18.
[32] See: chapter 5, also chapters 13–15, 18.   [33] See: chapter 17.

Our thematic analysis relies largely on the notion of a 'good' consumer. But what of the consumer who flits between lawful and unlawful markets? We touch on EU law's implications for such consumption in chapter 17 where we discuss organ donation. Where the consumer becomes a cost to the state, the consumer/competition theme is challenged. Questions of equitable treatment of such consumer/patients within national health systems in situations where treatment overseas goes wrong bring attempts to control medical tourism within the themes of equality and solidarity. What is the obligation of the home state, in terms of solidarity, to such a patient, and how should that be embodied in the law? EU health law has done little if anything to answer this question. And organ donation is only one example of the phenomenon – we could also have considered, for instance, global surrogacy markets. Of course, there is a significant body of EU family law which covers families in cross-border situations, including the rights of children.[34] But there is no explicit EU health law on surrogacy.

Turning to rights, most of the (human) rights discussed in chapters 7 and 8 are discussed from the perspective of the rights of an individual human being. The analysis in chapter 8 demonstrates the benefits of bringing together the themes of consumerism and rights, allowing a deeper and more integrated understanding of the different 'strands' of EU health law that are embodied in the Patients' Rights Directive than available in previous analyses. We also bring in the systemic perspective through discussion of 'strand 2', coordination of social security entitlements of migrant patients through cooperation between national health and social security systems. EU law on health rights as human rights that draws on the notion of EU citizenship ('strand 4') could be read as adopting a more collective perspective, focusing on the legal position of EU citizens as a group. But, given that strand 4 is being pursued through litigation, the individual is still very much in the centre of this chapter.

Health rights – particularly the 'right to health care' – may also be conceptualized as a collective concept. Should a Member State seek to adopt a collective rights approach to health care, nothing in EU law would prevent such a project. But, equally, no European state is strongly associated with a collectively enjoyed 'right to health care', for instance, enforceable through class actions.[35] We saw in chapter 17 that the collectively enjoyed 'right to access essential medicines', which has been defined as part of a 'human right to health care', may also be

[34] See, e.g. McGlynn, *Families and the European Union* (CUP 2006); Costello, 'Article 33 – Family and Professional Life' and R Lamont, 'Article 24 – The Rights of the Child' both in Peers, Hervey, Kenner, and Ward (eds), *The EU Charter of Fundamental Rights: A Commentary* (Hart 2014).

[35] Those states which are so associated include South Africa, Columbia and India. See further: Yamin and Parra-Vera, 'Judicial Protection of the Right to Health in Colombia: From Social Demands to Individual Claims to Public Debates' (2010) 33 *Hastings International and Comparative Law Review* 431; O'Connell, *Vindicating Socio-Economic Rights: International Standards and Comparative Experiences* (OUP 2012).

understood in terms of risks of harm to patients who unwittingly consume falsified or counterfeit medicines.

Our discussion of the themes of solidarity, equality and competition, focusing on (national) health insurance providers; health institutions and professions; and key industries, concentrates mainly on the systemic perspective, and draws out the implications of EU health law for national health systems.[36] We also consider overlaps and interactions between solidarity, equality, competition and (patients') rights. Taking an individual perspective, the analysis can be extended to demonstrate the opportunities offered by EU law to individual private actors (legal persons) to capitalize on EU free movement and competition law, so as to strengthen their market positions, or enter new markets. The claim discussed in chapters 9, 10 and 11 to the effect that EU health law moves health systems towards the 'neoliberal' end of a spectrum of types of health system, suggests that there are significant opportunities for such individuals here, and our discussion shows that such opportunities do exist. However, our overall conclusions are that detailed legal analysis more persuasively supports a modified claim. These conclusions show that the individual perspective may be taken too far. Bringing in the systemic perspective reveals the ways in which EU law recognizes the solidarity on which health systems are based.

When we consider individual human beings, the systemic perspective may hide an important dimension of the ways EU health law affects health institutions. The application of free movement or competition law provides opportunities for actions of individual human beings – choosing a pharmacy from which to receive pharmaceuticals paid for by the system or whistle-blowing on collusive actions of hospitals or other providers are two examples. We already noted that separating out the individual and systemic perspective for analysis, and subsequently contrasting them, allows us to draw out a distinction between how competition, solidarity and equality *and* individual and collective interests are resolved in EU health law, especially, but not only, in CJEU jurisprudence. The claims or rights of individual human beings enjoy greater *de facto* protection in these aspects of EU health law than claims brought by legal persons or institutions.

Similarly, the discussion of the theme of risk, within both the EU's internal health law[37] and its external health law,[38] involves both collective or systemic and individual perspectives, and brings in the other themes, particularly consumerism and (human) rights. The risks to individual patient safety arising from development of novel health technologies and treatments are a central concern of EU health law on clinical trials, and pre- and post-market controls on pharmaceuticals, medical devices and products involving human blood, tissues or cells. These could even be understood as constraining consumer choice. Much of the EU law here is also about individual human rights, in particular, the consent provisions of EU clinical trials law. We also draw out the ways in

---

[36] See: chapters 9–11.   [37] See: chapters 12–15.   [38] See: chapter 18.

which risks to the various European industries operating in the health field are managed in the legislation, including the reputational harms from irresponsible industry behaviour.

In chapter 15, the discussion is focused on public health protection, and therefore a collective perspective. But individual consumers, and the providers who seek to promote such consumption, are also very much present. Rather than facilitating individual choice, EU law on tobacco, food and alcohol constrains individual autonomy. The rationale here is the cost to the collective – the interests of national health systems (and, even more broadly, governments in having, for instance, a healthy workforce). This aspect of EU health law focuses on minimizing the costs to the collective consequential upon individual consumer behaviours that are harmful to health. It confronts libertarian notions of autonomy, which run strongly in European legal and cultural contexts. In part, this explains EU health law's focus on the vulnerable (for instance, children who are passive smokers or are targeted by bespoke alcohol products) and on the damages to the economy (for instance, unemployment through ill health) in these contexts. These vulnerable individuals are presented as justifying legal interventions that, if applied to all of the population, would offend against individual freedom of action.

Assessing claims about EU health law in existing literature

A major benefit of our thematic approach is the strengthening of analytical purchase it brings. Through our detailed analysis, we have been able to assess several claims that have been made about EU health law in the existing literature.[39] Some of these are very strong claims, with perhaps shocking implications for health law and health systems in European contexts. Our overall conclusion is that, while each of these claims has some merit, none of them stands up in its strongest form. All need more nuance. All are significantly more context-dependent than their proponents imply.

We investigated in detail, and across several chapters, the idea that EU health law undermines national health systems based on territorial solidarity, social citizenship and equitable treatment on the basis of medical need, by treating health care as a consumer service.[40] In particular, the CJEU has been criticized for paying insufficient attention to the role of national health (insurance) systems in securing equitable access to health care and promoting solidarity between healthy and less healthy people, and across generations, within a particular Member State. The fear is that EU health law moves EU health systems towards neoliberal models of health care provision.[41]

Bringing health services provided within national health (insurance) systems within the scope of EU health law does involve conceptualizing health care as a

---

[39] See: further chapter 1 and Appendix.   [40] See further: chapters 4–6.
[41] See further: Introduction to Part III; chapter 9.

consumer service. Further, the very structure of EU law sets the preferences of an individual consumer of services (patient) against the priorities of a national health (insurance) system, with the former as the rule, and the latter as the exception. But EU health law does not go so far as to treat health services as essentially identical to other consumer services. Health care rarely operates totally as such a 'one-off' transaction. Even in the case of elective surgery, there are periods of aftercare and social/health care support, and in some cases these are necessary for the remainder of a patient's life.[42] Patients frequently do not directly contract with health institutions or professionals at all – provision is mediated through insurers who may direct individuals to specific providers, or through a nationalized health service, where the choice of provider may be very limited indeed. EU health law does not entirely replace relationships of solidarity, trust and a professional ethic of care with those of consumer relations. EU health law recognizes the need to secure financial sustainability of national health (insurance) systems, especially in the context of fiscal austerity. EU health law does have a consumerizing effect, but it is not as strong as some of the existing literature claims.[43]

Nothing in EU health law *requires* Member States to organize their health systems in a particular (neoliberal or other) way. Rather, the EU's legislature, its administrative authorities and also the CJEU find ways to respect national settlements and structures of health (insurance) systems. This is achieved either by drawing the scope of EU competition or free movement law so that aspects of national health systems fall outside of scrutiny for compliance with EU law, or by allowing national institutional arrangements to be readily justified by a 'light touch' proportionality test.[44] Nonetheless, should Member States *choose* to adopt market-like models for aspects of their national health (insurance) systems, EU health law has a 'sticky' quality which impedes subsequent retreat from that position.[45] Furthermore, EU competition and free movement law are used not only to achieve economic efficiency and free trade in a narrow sense. They also support a range of other objectives, including promoting social and ethical goals.[46]

Our analysis suggests that neither the claim that the EU now protects health rights as human rights, nor the opposite claim that EU is blind to or ignores that idea, can be supported in its strong form. EU health law does recognize health rights as human rights; health rights constitute a rhetorical underpinning for much of EU health legislation and provide an important reference point for interpretation in the CJEU's jurisprudence.[47] Nonetheless, the most important practical implications of patients' rights in EU law are procedural and

---

[42] For example organ transplant patients necessarily need to continue taking immune suppressants to prevent organ rejection.
[43] See further: chapters 4–6; 9–11.   [44] See further: chapter 9.
[45] See further: chapters 9–11.
[46] This point is illustrated in all the substantive chapters of the book.
[47] See further: chapter 7.

informational. The indirect influences flowing from transparency of information required by EU legislation may be more significant than individual patients' rights claims pursued through litigation.[48]

Various, and sometimes contradictory, claims have been made about how EU health law treats risk. The EU is said to be focused on risk to the detriment of other considerations, such as human rights or ethical matters. It is said to be more risk-averse in its legal approach than, for instance, the USA, but it is also said to be insufficiently attentive to risks inherent in the circulation of products that are, or may be, harmful to human health. The power of global industries, such as the pharmaceuticals or tobacco industries, is said to be largely unaffected by attempts to regulate such risks, by the EU and by States alike. But the EU is also said to be 'over-regulating' and thus inhibiting innovation. Our wide-ranging discussion of many areas of EU health law suggests that generalized statements about the EU's approach to risk (even within one area, such as clinical trials, or pharmaceuticals regulation) should be treated with caution. There are important distinctions between areas of law where the EU's regulatory oversight increases over time; areas where significant national discretion remains within broad principles set by EU health law; and areas where there is no applicable EU law at all.[49]

Our conclusions about the various claims made about EU health law in the existing literature are not shocking, surprising or revolutionary. They are to be expected. Many of the claims which we discuss are made on the basis of analysis of only part of EU health law – our more holistic approach allows us to show that they are not as universally applicable as it would initially appear. We understand the temptations to make such 'headline grabbing' claims, given professional pressures to be 'original', 'discipline-changing' or 'revolutionary'. We are particularly sympathetic to those who do so when protections for vulnerable people, or values held dear, appear to be under threat from the logics of an 'outsider' legal system. But, in our view, legal scholarship that draws out cautious and measured conclusions, based on careful attention to as wide a range as possible of specific legal details, within specific contexts and during particular time frames, will do more to help to protect such values, and such people.

Assessing EU health law's potential

Finally, although this was not our agenda,[50] we suggest that our approach assists in assessing the potential of EU health law in tackling some of the problems associated with, or deficiencies of, health law more generally (both nationally and globally). Here, of course, we must be first and foremost mindful of the limits of law in securing change. Law can only ever be one factor in altering social,

---

[48] See further: chapter 8.   [49] See further: chapters 12–15, 18.

political, commercial or industrial practice – others must also be deployed. And EU law is more limited than national law in that the EU is constrained by its attributed competences, as well as by the politics of European integration. There are significant disparities in development, and hence investment in national health systems, across the EU as a whole.[51] Hence, even if the EU has formal legal competence, there are limits to the extent to which the EU can effectively mandate common standards, for instance, by setting minimum standards of entitlement to state of the art medical treatment. Ethically controversial areas, such as surrogacy, abortion, euthanasia, are another example where, as a matter of practical politics, EU law will never have more than a tangential effect.

That said, we identified several instances where the EU's health law has, almost against the odds, contributed to improving human health. The EU's tobacco legislation, and the relatively robust approach of the CJEU to the many legal challenges to that legislation, is a prime example;[52] although we note that *externally* applicable EU tobacco law could do more to promote the approach of its internally applicable law to the rest of the world.[53] EU pharmaceuticals and medical devices regulation and non-contractual liability law have secured some protections for some patients.[54] Another example is the ways in which EU health law has promoted respect for the dignity, privacy and autonomy of clinical trial participants/patients. Here the reach of EU law in practice includes trials undertaken outside the EU.[55]

However, our analysis also revealed several missed opportunities for EU health law. For instance, the EU's law on health professionals is replete with such missed opportunities. There is little attempt to develop EU level rules on professional ethics; standards of safety, or of care; on sufficient competency of health professionals; or ability of patients and those who employ the services of health professionals to gain information about such matters. These are matters that fall within a broader agenda, focused on securing state provision of respectful and safe health care, by autonomous (and sometimes powerful) professional groups, in the context of fiscal austerity mandated by the Eurozone crisis. The Patients' Rights Directive enacts such systemic concerns, while at the same time being focused on the mobility of patients within the EU's internal market. Health professional mobility creates some of the same sorts of problems as patient mobility – the potential for direct physical harm to patients, as well as threats to systemic stability – so an intervention through EU legislation would be justified. But there is, as yet, no equivalent EU legislation that focuses sufficiently on those concerns arising from mobile professionals within the EU. An insufficiently regulated 'market' in health professionals

---

[50] See: chapter 1.   [51] See table (Figure 8.1) at the end of chapter 8.
[52] See further: chapter 15.   [53] See further: chapter 18.
[54] See further: chapters 13, 14.   [55] See further: chapters 12, 13, 18.

across the EU may place at risk patients who choose a health professional provider on the basis of assumptions of professional competence and ethical approach.

Another example is EU law on global organ trade or donation.[56] Internally applicable EU law on organs is based on human rights protection, solidarity and equality, and sets itself apart from a consumerist approach. It embodies a legal commitment to non-commodification of the human body in virtually as strong a form as the EU's competence permits, and leaves significant discretion to Member States to set higher human rights standards.[57] By contrast, there is almost no externally applicable EU law on organ donation (only the human rights conditionality clauses of the EU's trade agreements could conceivably fit the bill). The EU has left such global health matters to the Council of Europe, which, given the EU's now-developed human rights law,[58] reveals the serious limitations of EU health law in this context. Access to essential medicines provides another, similar, example.[59]

A thematic analysis supports our conclusions on some of the deficits and missed opportunities of EU health law. Our 'could do better' assessment relies on considering EU health law as distinct from EU trade law or EU development law, and on focusing on the thematic effects of the relevant law. In the EU Member States, health is fundamentally associated with the values of solidarity and equality of access according to medical need. Countervailing values, such as consumer choice or competition, or risk within a market, sit ill with health policy communities. Human rights belong somewhere in the middle, encompassing everything from autonomy (related to choice) to non-discrimination (related to equality). The deficits, the missed opportunities, and hence the potential for EU health law, emerge from a careful, context-specific and detailed exploration of the extent to which EU health law increases or enhances consumerist relationships in health settings; improves equality of access to health care; secures protection against harm from health risks; or respects health rights as human rights.

The story so far, and the future

What has become of the women whose health was affected by the actions of Poly Implant Prothèse, whose stories began this book? Poly Implant Prothèse went into liquidation in 2009. However, a class action is underway against TÜV-Rheinland, the body which certified the safety of the implants.[60] TÜV-Rheinland is a global safety standards provider, operating in over sixty countries,

---

[56] See further: chapter 17.   [57] See further: chapter 14.
[58] See further: chapter 7.   [59] See further: chapters 12, 13, 17.
[60] A separate claim has also been brought by distributors of the implants in Bulgaria, Brazil, Italy, Syria, Mexico and Romania, involving a claim of €28m.

and employing over 17,200 people.[61] The action involves women from several Member States, and other countries. An initial ruling of a Toulon court on 13 November 2013 gave interim damages to over 1,600 women, and ordered that medical assessments of the damage should take place to determine final compensation.[62] The lawyer leading the litigation, Oliver Aumaitre, is reported as expecting damages pay-outs for each woman of between 10,000 and 15,000 euros.[63] Many more women are expected to join the claim by the court's deadline of December 2014, shortly before the date at which we complete this manuscript.

As we saw in chapter 14, the EU's legislative response is reform of its medical devices legislation. As we write, the European Commission's proposals have been adopted with amendments by the European Parliament, and have been discussed in Council.[64] Legal developments continue in a range of other areas. Other legislation in the pipeline includes the proposed new general Data Protection Regulation.[65] Pending cases before the CJEU cover, for instance, minimum alcohol pricing;[66] liability for defective medical devices and pharmaceuticals;[67] pharmacies;[68] and hospitals.[69] The implications of new legislation, such as the Clinical Trials Regulation's effects on existing ethics committee structures,[70] and of CJEU decisions in other fields, such as the effects on data in medical research of the CJEU's 2014 *Google Spain* case on the right to become anonymous online,[71] are yet to unfold. Above all, the implications of the Eurozone austerity rules for health systems, and their legality, are yet to be fully understood. Policy developments, for instance, in EU involvement in the ageing society, with implications for the human rights of older patients, and mental health, may eventually harden into law.

Given the dynamic potential of law, the exercise we have set ourselves of 'mapping' EU health law, and understanding its implications in practice, will of course never be complete. The EU health law is an unfolding process, not a

---

[61] TÜV Rheinland, 'Facts and Figures' (*TÜV Rheinland*, 2014).

[62] Samuel, 'Victims of faulty PIP breast implants win compensation from German firm' *The Telegraph* (London, 14 November 2013); Lichfield, 'Breast implants ruling in PIP scandal could lead to compensation for 400,000 women' *The Independent* (Paris, 14 November 2013).

[63] Ring, 'Women could get €15,000 for faulty implants' *Irish Examiner* (Blackpool, 9 September 2014).

[64] See further: chapter 14.

[65] Proposal for a Regulation of the European Parliament and the Council on the protection of individuals with regard to the processing of personal data and on the free movement of such data (General Data Protection Regulation) COM (2012) 11 final.

[66] *The Scotch Whisky Association v Lord Advocate*, C-333/14 (case in progress).

[67] *Boston Scientific* (Pending), C-503/13 and C-504/13, concerning an implantable cardioverter defibrillator where a malfunction in the device had already occurred in several devices in the same series, but no defect had been detected in the specific device at issue; *Novo Nordisk* (Pending), C-310/13, concerning a national system of liability under which information on the side-effects of pharmaceutical products may be obtained. See further: Opinion of the Advocate General in *Novo Nordisk* (Pending), C-310/13, EU:C:2014:1825.

[68] *Gullotta* (Pending), C-497/12.   [69] *Data Medical Service* (Pending), C-568/13.

[70] See further: chapter 12.   [71] *Google Spain*, C-131/12, EU:C:2014:317.

final product. The contours of the map will inevitably develop and change over time, through weathering, friction and through responses to sudden unexpected events. What we hope is that, as long-standing observers and creators of EU health law, our approach in this book has provided a new conceptual lens for the ongoing analysis of this process.

Appendix

40 Questions answered

A ready reference guide for those readers who would like brief answers to the questions we posed in the Introduction, with an indication of where more detailed discussion supporting these answers is to be found in the book.

Consumerism

Does European Union law on health products (like the implants in the Poly Implant Prothèse case) treat those products as essentially the same as any consumer product available in the European market?

> EU law on the Poly Implant Prothèse implants ('medical devices') is not typical of EU law on health *products* more generally.[1] The majority of such products are not treated in the same way as other consumer products available in the European market. Prior marketing authorization applies, involving oversight of research, development and manufacturing, as well as post-market surveillance. Moreover, EU legislation on medical devices is changing, to bring it more into line with the rest of EU law on health products.[2]

Is the same true of European Union law on health services?

> EU law treats health *services* quite distinctly from the way it treats general consumer services.[3] Overall, there is little EU-level regulation of health services per se – the organization and delivery of such services within national health systems is a matter for national law.

To the extent that it is, what does that mean for how patients are conceptualized by European Union health law? Are patients essentially consumers, subject to rules such as *caveat emptor*, even if they are protected by law from at least some products and services that would harm their health?

> EU health law does not conceptualize patients entirely within a consumerist perspective.[4]

---

[1] See further chapters 5, 11, 12, 13, 14, 17. [2] See further chapter 14.
[3] See further chapters 4, 6, 7, 8, 9, 10, 17. [4] See further chapters 4, 5, 7 and 8.

If that is so, which products or services does European Union health law decide are harmful to health, and through what processes are those decisions made?

> The ways in which EU health law treats health products or services as requiring special legal regimes are incomplete. Some products that are, or may be, especially harmful to health (such as pharmaceuticals, products derived from human blood, tissue or cells, and tobacco) are the subject of EU-level legislation which aims, at least in part, to mitigate those potential dangers.[5] But the regulation of others (such as food or alcohol) is left more to the discretion of Member States.[6]

What about treatments that are ethically controversial, such as beginning or end-of-life health care?

> Where treatments are ethically controversial, EU health law leaves significant discretion to national regulatory settlements.[7]

What are the implications for health care professionals? What happens to notions of a professional ethic of care, or provision of public service, if European Union health law understands the relationships between doctors and their patients through the lens of consumerism?

> EU law touches upon regulation of health professions, and where it does so, it understands the relationships between health professionals, the national health (insurance) systems within which they operate, and the patients for whom they care, through a service-provider/receiver model, which is grounded in consumerism. But, again, the scope of EU law is limited, and national approaches based on a professional ethic of care, patient protection and safety, or provision of public service, remain in place.[8]

(Human) rights

Both nationally and internationally, health rights are often thought of as human rights. Is this the case in European Union health law?

> To some extent, EU health law conceptualizes health rights as human rights.[9]

What about the rights of patients? Are patients' rights seen as *human* rights in European Union health law, or are they more like *consumer* rights?

> EU law on patients' rights incorporates the human right to health. At present, the implications are more symbolic than real, but emergent interpretations of EU citizenship rights may alter this position over time.[10] EU law also understands patients' rights in at least three other ways: patients' rights as a distinct legal category; the social security entitlements of migrant workers; and rights of patients to consume services in the EU's internal market. Particularly the latter is more related to consumer rights than to fundamental human rights.

---

[5] See further chapters 12, 13, 14, 17, 18.   [6] See further chapters 15 and 18.
[7] See further chapter 4.   [8] See further chapters 6 and 10.
[9] See further chapters 7 and 8.   [10] See further chapter 8.

Which, if any, of such health rights are recognized and upheld by European Union health law?

> EU law recognizes and protects rights such as the right to privacy or human dignity, closely associated with health.[11]

If European Union health law involves consumerization of health care, what does that mean for patient autonomy and patient choice, which are both related to human rights?

> Where it opens access to health care across borders in the EU, EU health law enhances patient choice, and patient autonomy, concepts themselves, of course, related to the human rights to privacy and dignity.

What are the implications of the 'right to health care' in the EU's own Charter of Fundamental Rights, for substantive European Union health law? Is its significance more symbolic than practical?

> Human rights are a source to which the CJEU turns when interpreting provisions of EU legislation and when assessing the implementation of EU law in the Member States.[12] However, to date, no EU health legislation or administrative action has been set aside for breach of such human rights.

How does European Union health law deal with conflicting rights in health contexts?

> Where rights conflict in health contexts, in general, EU law leaves resolution of those conflicts to national law.[13]

Might European Union health law strengthen, or weaken, claims to health care resources as claims of right? What might this mean for health care systems?

> The potential of health rights as human rights in EU law, in particular in combination with non-discrimination, has yet to be realized in practice. Specific legal entitlements are very difficult to enforce as human rights in EU law, not least because of the significant national discretion accorded to the interpretation and implementation of relevant human rights provisions. National health care systems are unlikely to be significantly affected by EU health law on human rights.[14]

If patients in different countries end up with very different entitlements to treatment, what are the implications of European Union health law for equality of access to medical care?

---

[11] See further chapter 7.   [12] See further chapter 7.

[13] See further chapter 4, chapter 7. This is hardly surprising, given the significant margin of appreciation given to states under Council of Europe law, in particular the European Convention on Human Rights.

[14] See further chapter 7; chapters 9-11.

On a macro level, EU health law does not affect inequalities of access to medical care across the EU as a whole.[15] The public provision of health care is a matter of national competence, and varies between the Member States.

Solidarity, equality, competition

National arrangements for health care provision in EU Member States allow monopoly, or near monopoly, providers of health care services. What if those providers abuse that position? Does European Union health law scrutinize such behaviour, or the concentration of market power through mergers of health care providers? Or does European Union health law recognize health care as a 'special case', a type of service that is not subject to the ordinary rules that apply to anti-competitive behaviour of companies?

> Monopolistic or near-monopolistic national arrangements for providing health care may be subject to EU law which controls abuse of such concentrations of market power. But important exceptions apply to the application of EU competition law to health institutions. EU health law recognizes health as a special type of service: although it falls within the ordinary rules of competition, state aids and public procurement law, many important exceptions to those rules apply in health contexts.[16]

If so, does this mean that European Union health law is moving health care systems towards market-based models of regulation? To the extent that it does, what are the implications for the organization and underlying ethos of national health systems?

> Nothing in EU health law moves health care systems towards market-based models of regulation, although if national systems do so through political choice, EU law may have the effect of *de facto* preventing or impeding a return to a less market-based system.[17]

To the extent that European Union health law involves more patient choice, how does that increased choice affect the delivery of health care through health care systems that are predominantly funded either by taxation or through social insurance, rather than through private mechanisms?

> Where individual patients enforce rights to consume health services within the EU's internal market, EU health law supports patient mobility and the right to individual freedom of choice. The arrangements of national health systems are subject to scrutiny where they constrain such freedom. As a minimum, their rules concerning access to medical treatment must comply with principles of individual assessment of patient needs, non-discrimination on grounds of nationality, and judicial reviewability.[18] These aspects of EU health law have the potential to affect the solidarity-based provision of health care within the Member States.

---

[15] See further chapter 8.   [16] See further chapters 9, 10 and 11.
[17] See further chapters 9, 10 and 11.   [18] See further chapter 4, chapter 5.

How does European Union health law balance equality and solidarity with fair and effective competition?

> Increased choice for some patients implies reduced choice for others, because health systems have limited resources. Consumer autonomy in patients implies a reframing of doctor–patient relationships, suggesting changes to the way health professionals relate to the health systems within which they offer service.[19] The reconfiguring of health care relationships has positive implications for patient choice and autonomy, and negative implications for equality and access to health care according to professionally assessed patient need.

> But where *legal persons* seek to rely on the rules of EU internal market to trade across borders in ways which disrupt national health systems, we see a different pattern emerging. In areas most integrated within the operation of national health systems, including social insurance provision, hospitals, laboratories and blood centres, EU law operates under a 'light touch' approach, which allows Member States to justify national institutional arrangements, provisions and practices which on their face breach EU free movement or competition law.[20] Furthermore, matters such as the pricing of pharmaceuticals within health systems, which operates through nationally negotiated settlements, have, by and large, not been disrupted by EU law.[21]

If the European Union is supposed to secure safe medical devices, why did Poly Implant Prothèse patients in different European Union Member States have such different experiences? Why doesn't European Union health law offer equivalent protection to all patients?

> The answers to the questions above begin to explain why the health authorities in different countries came to very different conclusions about how patients involved in the Poly Implant Prothèse case were to be treated. In many areas of EU health law, national authorities enjoy significant discretion to determine the organization of health systems, the entitlements of patients, the expectations of institutions and of health professionals.

The fundamental basis of health care in European contexts is solidarity. Does European Union health law challenge, disrupt or even destroy, those fundamentals?

> At a systemic level, EU health law's increased patient choice has much less of an effect than is often supposed on the delivery of health care through systems that are organized on the basis of solidarity. Solidarity-based systems are predominantly funded either by taxation or through social insurance. They seek to secure equality of access to health care according to need. Any effects of EU law are indirect only, because countervailing aspects of EU law prevent patient choice, or other actions of market participants, from 'unravelling' national health systems.[22]

---

[19] See further chapter 6.   [20] See further chapter 9, chapter 10.
[21] See further chapter 11.   [22] See further chapters 4-6; 9-11.

Risk

Under European Union health law, how much control do national authorities have over determining questions of quality, safety and efficacy of health care products, services and procedures?

> In some areas, Member States no longer entirely control or determine the quality, safety and efficacy of health care products, equipment, services and procedures. The quality, safety and efficacy of pharmaceuticals is subject to detailed EU-level regulation, through a long-standing and evolving body of legislation.[23] Medical devices are subject to increasing control under EU law. The purchase of health care products and medical equipment is subject to some extent to EU public procurement law.[24] EU law regulates some aspects of uses of human blood, tissues and cells, and human organs, in health settings.[25] To some extent, EU law affects national health insurance systems.[26] But the majority of health services, arrangements and procedures within national health systems are not subject to EU *legislation* at all. Even where EU law does apply, EU law may be interpreted quite differently in different national contexts.

What is the extent of national autonomy: if the Swedes decide that alcohol is so harmful to health that it should only be sold through one state-controlled monopoly provider, or the Scots decide to change alcohol pricing rules, or the Greeks decide that infant formula milk should only be sold through pharmacies, is that allowed? Can such national decisions, made with a view to promoting good health of the population, be challenged if they disrupt patterns of trade in products or services across European Union borders?

> National autonomy extends to some measures adopted with a view to promoting the good health of the population, that is, public health law. In general, such national decisions may be challenged for non-compliance with EU law if they disrupt patterns of trade in products or services across EU internal borders. Member States may justify such national approaches *only* if the measures are suitable to protect public health, and proportionate, rather than protecting national industry or provider interests. For instance, Swedish and Scottish alcohol control rules have been challenged on this basis.[27] But, for example, Greek rules requiring infant formula milk to be sold only in pharmacies were held to be outside the scope of EU law.[28]

To what extent does European Union law adopt a light touch approach to regulation of health products or services involving assessment of risk?

> When it comes to assessment of risk in EU health law, medical devices regulation is an outlier, but will almost certainly not remain so.[29] EU health law does not have a light touch approach to regulation of pharmaceuticals, bio- or nano-technology

---

[23] See further chapter 12, chapter 13.   [24] See further chapter 11.
[25] See further chapter 14.   [26] See further chapter 9.   [27] See further chapter 15.
[28] See further chapter 5.   [29] See further chapter 14.

products, products involving human blood, tissue or cells, or of whole human blood or plasma, or human organs.[30]

What does European Union health law require in terms of pre- and post-market controls of health care products such as pharmaceuticals, bio- or nano-technology products and medical devices?

> EU law requires significant and detailed pre- and post-market control of pharmaceuticals, bio- or nano-technology products, products involving human blood, tissue or cells, or of whole human blood or plasma or human organs.[31]

What does European Union health law require of other products that are or may be harmful to health, such as tobacco, food, alcohol?

> Some other products which are or may be harmful to public health are also subject to detailed EU legislation, for instance, on labelling, restrictions on advertising, and composition rules. EU law on tobacco is the example of most complete health-focused legislation; food is subject to some detailed EU law aimed at health protection; EU alcohol law leaves significant national discretion.[32] Nonetheless, EU law has secured at least some improvements in public health.

Where European Union law must balance risks to patients with freedom to run a business, how is such law made? Given that health industries make a major contribution to the European economy, what are the implications for the European economy, which so desperately needs to grow to escape from recession? What should we make of the oft-repeated claim that the European Union is *too strict* in its regulatory approach to risk, is significantly more risk-averse than, say, the USA?

> Many have associated EU law with a precautionary approach to risk regulation, favouring on balance the risks of harm to patients against freedom to run a business. But others take the view that EU law is no more restrictive of industry or capital than any other legal system. This is especially so of the restrictions EU health law imposes (or does not impose) on the global pharmaceutical industry.[33]

Are firms operating in the EU therefore saddled with competitive disadvantage when seeking to compete globally? Does this hamper innovation in European health industries? What does this mean for economic growth?

> It is unclear whether EU law results in competitive disadvantage for European health industries which seek to compete globally, and consequent impediments to innovation in such industries, and to economic growth.

What does it mean for patients who are waiting for a treatment for their currently incurable conditions?

[30] See further chapters 12-14.   [31] See further chapters 12-14.
[32] See further chapters 15 and 18.   [33] See further chapters 12, 13, 17 and 18.

From the point of view of patients who hope for novel medical treatments to become available, it may be good news that EU law on clinical trials and pharmaceuticals is centrally concerned with ensuring that products reach the market.[34]

What does it mean for patients across the world, who are dying because the health industry invests in novel products for the rich global North, not in products that are needed by patients in the poor global South? What, if anything, does EU law do to make health products affordable to the poorest in the world? To what extent does European Union health law affect such questions of global health ethics?

> EU law does very little to affect questions of global health ethics, such as securing access to essential medicines for patients across the world, including in the global South; ensuring dignity and equality are protected in the global organ trade; or preventing migration of health professionals from South to North.[35]

What, if anything, are the implications of European Union health law for global 'medical tourism'? And what about global movement of public health threats, both from products that have important health implications (food, alcohol, tobacco), and from communicable diseases? How does European Union health law interact with global health law?

> EU health law has had little effects on global medical tourism. Where health law priorities can be aligned with the EU's external trade law, however, EU health law has had some small positive influence on global health threats both from products that have important health implications (food, alcohol, tobacco), and from communicable diseases.[36]

---

[34] See further chapters 12, 13 and 14.   [35] See further chapters 16 and 17.
[36] See further chapter 18.

Bibliography

Literature (print)

Abbasi, K., 'The World Bank and World Health' (1999) 318(865–9) *British Medical Journal* 933–7; 1003–7; 1206–8

Abbing, H.R., 'The Convention on Human Rights and Biomedicine: An Application of the Council of Europe Convention' (1998) 5(4) *European Journal of Health Law* 377

 'Patients' Rights in a Technology and Market Driven Europe'(2010) 17(1) *European Journal of Health Law* 11

 'Twenty Year WHO Principles of Patients' Rights in Europe, a Common Framework: Looking Back to the Future' (2014) 21(4) *European Journal of Health Law* 323

Abel, F. and Terribas, N., 'The Dynamics of the Bioethical Dialogue in Spain', in L. Pessini, C. de Paul de Barchifontaine and F. Lolas Stepke (eds.), *Ibero-American Bioethics* (Springer, 2011)

Abraham, J. and Davis, C., 'Science, Law and the Medical-Industrial Complex in EU Pharmaceutical Regulation: The Deferiprone Controversy', in M. Flear, A.-M. Farrell, T.K. Hervey and T. Murphy (eds.), *European Law and New Health Technologies* (Oxford University Press, 2013)

Abraham, J. and Lewis, G., *Regulating Medicines in Europe: Competition, Expertise and Public Health* (Routledge, 2000)

Adamini, S., Versluis, E. and Maarse, H., 'European Policy Making on the Tobacco Advertising Ban: The Imbalance of Escape Routes' (2011) 6(1) *Health Economics Policy and Law* 65

Adams, V., 'Against Global Health? Arbitrating Science, Non-Science, and Nonsense through Health', in J.M. Metzl and A. Kirkland (eds.), *Against Health: How Health Became the New Morality* (New York University Press, 2010)

Aginam, O., 'Food Safety, South–North Asymmetries, and the Clash of Regulatory Regimes' (2007) 40(4) *Vanderbilt Journal of Transnational Law* 1099

 'Health or Trade? A Critique of Contemporary Approaches to Global Health Diplomacy'(2010) 5 *Asian Journal of WTO & International Health Law and Policy* 355

Aginam, O. and Harrington, J., 'Introduction', in O. Aginam, J. Harrington and P.K. Yu (eds.), *The Global Governance of HIV/AIDS: Intellectual Property and Access to Essential Medicines* (Edward Elgar, 2012)

Aginam O., Harrington, J. and Yu, P.K. (eds.), *The Global Governance of HIV/AIDS: Intellectual Property and Access to Essential Medicines* (Edward Elgar, 2012)

Ahmed, M. and Snyder, F. (eds.), *Food Security and Food Safety* (The Hague Academy of International Law, Brill online, 2014)

Albors-Llorens, A., Armstrong, K. and Gehring, M.W. (eds.), *Cambridge Yearbook of European Legal Studies*, vol. 16, *2013–2014* (Hart, 2014)

Alemanno, A., 'Introduction: Foundation of EU Food Law and Policy', in A. Alemanno and S. Gabbi (eds.), *Foundations of EU Food Law and Policy: Ten Years of the European Food Safety Authority* (Ashgate, 2014)

'Out of Sight, Out of Mind: Towards a New EU Tobacco Products Directive' (2012) 18(2) *Columbia Journal of European Law* 197

Alemanno, A. and Carreno, I., 'Fat Taxes in the EU between Fiscal Austerity and the Fight against Obesity' (2011) 2(4) *European Journal of Risk Regulation* 571

Alemanno, A. and Gabbi, S. (eds.), *Foundations of EU Food Law and Policy: Ten Years of the European Food Safety Authority* (Ashgate, 2014)

Alemanno, A. and Garde, A., 'The Emergence of an EU Lifestyle Policy: The Case of Alcohol, Tobacco and Unhealthy Diets' (2013) 50(6) *Common Market Law Review* 1745

Alemanno, A., Den Butter, F., Nijsen, F. and Torriti, J. (eds.), *Better Business Regulation in a Risk Society* (Springer, 2013)

Algrahni, A., Bennett, R. and Ost, S. (eds.), *The Criminal Law and Bioethical Conflict: Walking the Tightrope* (Cambridge University Press, 2012)

Alston, P. (ed.), *The EU and Human Rights* (Oxford University Press, 1999)

Altavilla, A., 'Clinical Research with Children: The European Legal Framework and its Implementation in French and Italian Law' (2008) 15(2) *European Journal of Health Law* 109

'Ethical Standards for Clinical Trials Conducted in Third Countries: The New Strategy of the European Medicines Agency' (2011) 18(1) *European Journal of Health Law* 65

Altenstetter, C., 'EU and Medical Devices Regulation in the Member', paper prepared for delivery at 'European Integration and Health Care Systems: A Challenge for Social Policy', conference, 7–8 December 2001

'EU and Member States Medical Devices Regulation' (2003) 19(1) *International Journal of Technology Assessment in Health Care* 228

Medical Devices, European Union Policy Making and the Implementation of Health and Safety in France (Transaction Publishers, 2008)

'Medical Device Regulation and Nanotechnologies: Determining the Role of Patient Safety Concerns in Policymaking' (2011) 33(2) *Law and Policy* 227

Alter, K.J., 'The European Court's Political Power' (1996) 19 *West European Politics* 458

Ancelin, O., Berghe, P., Simmons, I., et al., 'The Pay-for-Delay Settlements in the Pharmaceutical Sector' (2014) 2(65478) *Concurrences Journal* 12

Anderson K. and Jackson, L.A., 'Why are US and EU Policies Toward GMOs so Different?' (2003) 6(3) *AgBioForum* 95

Andrews, L. and Nelkin, D., 'Whose Body is it Anyway? Disputes Over Body Tissue in a Biotechnology Age' (1998) 351(9095) *The Lancet* 53

Angell, M., *'The Truth about Drug Companies: How They Deceive Us and What to Do about It* (Random House, 2005)

Annas, G.J., 'Health Law at the Turn of the Century: From White Dwarf to Red Giant' (1989) 21 *Connecticut Law Review* 551

Applbaum, K., 'Shadow Science: Zyproxa, Eli Lilly and the Globalization of Pharmaceutical Damage Control' (2010) 5 *Biosocieties* 236

Appleby, G. and Wingfield, J., *Dale and Appleby Pharmacy and Medicines Law*, 10th edn (Pharmaceutical Press, 2013)

Arai-Takahashi, Y., *The Margin of Appreciation Doctrine and the Principle of Proportionality* (Intersentia, 2002)

Areen, J., King, P., Goldberg, S., et al., *Law, Science and Medicine* (Foundation Press, 1996)

Arkinstall, J., Childs, M., Menghaney, L., et al., 'The Reality behind the Rhetoric: How European Policies Risk Harming Access to Generic Medicines in Developing Countries' (2011) 8(1) *Journal of Generic Medicines* 14

Arnull, A., *The European Union and its Court of Justice*, 2nd edn (Oxford University Press, 2006)

Arrow, K.J., 'Uncertainty and the Welfare Economics of Medical Care' (1963) 53(5) *American Economic Review* 941

Arrowsmith, S. (ed.), *EU Public Procurement Law: An Introduction* (EU Asia Inter University Network for Teaching and Research in Public Procurement Regulation, 2011)

Ashcroft, R., 'Could Human Rights Supersede Bioethics?' (2010) 10 *Human Rights Law Review* 639

   'The Troubled Relationship between Bioethics and Human Rights' (2008) 11(22) *Law and Bioethics* 31

Ashcroft, R., Draper, H., Dawson, A. and Macmillan, J. (eds.), *Principles of Health Care Ethics*, 2nd edn (Wiley-Blackwell, 2007)

Augenstein, D. (ed.), *Integration Through Law Revisited* (Ashgate, 2012)

Babić, T. and Roksandić, V., *Uvod u zdravstveno pravo* [Introduction to Health Law] (Tipex, 2006)

Bache, G. and Hervey, T.K., 'Incentivising Innovation or Supporting Other Interests? European Regulation of Orphan Medicinal Products: *CSL Behring GmbH* v. *European Commission and another* (2011) 19(1) *Medical Law Review* 123

Bache, G., Flear, M. and Hervey, T.K., 'The Defining Features of the European Union's Approach to Regulating New Health Technologies', in M. Flear, A.-M. Farrell, T.K. Hervey and T. Murphy (eds.), *European Law and New Health Technologies* (Oxford University Press, 2013)

Bache, I., George, S. and Bulmer, S., *Politics in the European Union*, 3rd edn (Oxford University Press, 2011)

Badcott, D. and Sahm, S., 'The Dominance of Big Pharma: Unhealthy Relationships?' (2013) 16(2) *Medicine, Health Care and Philosophy* 245

Baeten, R., 'European Integration and National Healthcare Systems: A Challenge for Social Policy' (2001) 8 *Infose* 1

Baker, B.K., 'ACTA – Risks of Third Party Enforcement for Access to Medicines' (2011) 26(3) *American University International Law Review* 579

Baldwin, P., *The Politics of Social Solidarity: Class Bases of the European Welfare State, 1875–1975* (Cambridge University Press, 1992)

Baldwin, T., Brownsword, R. and Schmidt, H., 'Stewardship, Paternalism and Public Health: Further Thoughts' (2009) 2(1) *Public Health Ethics* 113

Ballet, J., 'The Belgian Supreme Court Held that Obligatory Opening and Closing Hours for Pharmacists Violate the Competition Act' (2006) 15370 *e-Competitions Law Bulletin*

Barber, B., 'Patient Data and Security: An Overview' (1998) 49(1) *International Journal of Medical Informatics* 19

Barnard, C., *EU Employment Law*, 4th edn (Oxford University Press, 2012)

The Substantive Law of the European Union: The Four Freedoms, 4th edn (Oxford University Press, 2010)

'Unravelling the Services Directive' (2008) 45(2) *Common Market Law Review* 323

Barnard, C. and Odudu, O. (eds.), *The Outer Limits of EU Law* (Hart, 2009)

Barnard, C. and Peers, S., *European Union Law* (Oxford University Press, 2014)

Barnard, C. and Scott, J. (eds.), *The Law of the Single European Market: Unpacking the Premises* (Hart, 2002)

Bartels, L., 'The Trade and Development Policy of the European Union', in M. Cremona (ed.), *Developments in EU External Relations Law* (Oxford University Press, 2008)

Bartlett, A. and Garde, A., 'Time to Seize the (Red) Bull by the Horns: The European Union's Failure to Protect Children from Alcohol and Unhealthy Food Marketing' (2013) 38 *European Law Review* 498

Bartsch, S., 'The Global Fund to Fight AIDS, Tuberculosis and Malaria', in W. Hein, S. Bartsch and L. Kohlmorgen (eds.), *Global Health Governance and the Fight against HIV/AIDS* (Palgrave Macmillan, 2007)

Bassetti, C., Gulino, M., Gazzaniga, V. and Frati, P., 'The Old Roots of the Italian Health Legislation' (2011) 2(2) *Mediterranean Journal of Social Science* 9

Baumberg, B. and Anderson, P., 'Health, Alcohol and EU Law: Understanding the Impact of European Single Market Law on Alcohol Policies' (2008) 18(4) *European Journal of Public Health* 392

Baxi, 'The Place of the Human Right to Health and Context Approach to Global Justice', in J. Harrington and M. Stuttaford (eds.), *Global Health and Human Rights: Legal and Philosophical Perspectives* (Routledge, 2010)

Bayens, A., 'Free Movement of Goods and Services in Health Care: A Comment on the Court Cases *Decker* and *Kohll* from a Belgian Point of View' (1999) 6 *European Journal of Health Law* 373

Bayens, A., 'Implementation of the EU Clinical Trials Directive: Pitfalls and Benefits' (2002) 9 *European Journal of Health Law* 31

Beauchamp, T.L. and Childress, J.F., *Principles of Biomedical Ethics* (Oxford University Press, 2001)

Beck, G., 'The Lisbon Judgment of the German Constitutional Court, the Primacy of EU Law and the Problem of Kompetenz-Kompetenz: A Conflict between Right and Right in Which There is No Praetor' (2011) 17 *European Law Journal* 470

Beck, U., *Risk Society: Towards a New Modernity* (Sage, 1992)

'Politics of Risk Society', in J. Franklin (ed.), *The Politics of Risk Society* (Polity, 1998)

Beddard, R. and Hill, D.M. (eds.), *Economic, Social and Cultural Rights: Progress and Achievement* (Macmillan, 1992)

Bell, M., 'Article 20: Equality before the Law', in S. Peers, T.K. Hervey, J. Kenner and A. Ward (eds.), *The EU Charter of Fundamental Rights: A Commentary* (Hart, 2014)

Bell, S.E. and Figert, A.E., 'Medicalisation and Pharmaceuticalisation at the Intersections: Looking Backward, Sideways and Forward' (2012) 75(5) *Social Science and Medicine* 775

Bentley, J.P. and Thacker, P.G., 'The Influence of Risk and Monetary Payment on the Research Decision Making Process' (2004) 30(3) *Journal of Medical Ethics* 293

Berendt, L., Håkansson, C., Bach, K.F., et al., 'Effect of the European Clinical Trials Directive on Academic Drug Trials in Denmark: Retrospective Study of Applications to the Danish Medicines Agency, 1993–2006' (2008) 336(7634) *British Medical Journal* 33

Berg Brigham, K., Cadier, B. and Chevreul, K., 'The Diversity of Regulation of and Public Financing of IVF in Europe and its Impact on Utilization' (2013) 28(3) *Human Reproduction* 666

Besson, S., 'The EU and Human Rights: Towards a Post-National Human Rights Institution' (2006) 6 *Human Rights Law Review* 323

Beyleveld, D. and Brownsword, R., *Human Dignity in Bioethics and Biolaw* (Oxford University Press, 2001)

Beyleveld, D. and Histed, E., 'Anonymisation is not Exoneration' (1999) 4 *Medical Law International* 69

Beyleveld, D., Townend, D., Rouillé-Mirza, S. and Wright, J., *Implementation of the Data Protection Directive in Relation to Medical Research in Europe* (Ashgate, 2004)

Bhat, S.B. and Hegde, T.T., 'Ethical International Research on Human Subjects Research in the Absence of Local Institutional Review Boards' (2006) 32(9) *Journal of Medical Ethics* 535

Biggs, H. and Jones, C., 'Tourism: A Matter of Life and Death in the United Kingdom', in I.G. Cohen (ed.), *The Globalization of Health Care: Legal and Ethical Issues* (Oxford University Press, 2013)

Blaicher, W., Pokorny, H., Rockenschaub, S., et al., 'Organ Transplantation in Austria' (1996) 1(3) *Annals of Transplantation* 41

Bloom, D.E. and Cunning, D., 'Policy Forum: Public Health and the Health and Wealth of Nations' (2000) 287(5456) *Science* 1207

Blouin, C., Drager, N. and Smith, R., *International Trade in Health Services and the GATS: Current Issues and Debates* (World Bank, 2005)

Blue Sky, M., 'Developing Countries and Intellectual Property Enforcement Measures: Improving Access to Medicines through WTO Dispute Settlement' (2011) 3(2) *Trade, Law and Development* 407

Boeger, N., 'Solidarity and EC Competition Law' (2007) 32 *European Law Review* 319

Boisson de Chazournes, L., 'New Technologies, the Precautionary Principle and Public Participation', in T. Murphy (ed.), *New Technologies and Human Rights* (Oxford University Press, 2009)

Bolkestein, F. (Commissioner), Letter to Hans Hoogervorst, Dutch Minister for Health, regarding Dutch Health Insurance System (25 November 2003)

Bonadio, 'Biotech Patents and Morality after Brüstle' (2012) 34(7) *European Intellectual Property Review* 433

Bongers, L.M.H. and Townend, D.M.R., 'The Implementation of the Directive on the Application of Patients' Rights in Cross-border Healthcare in the Netherlands' (2014) 21(1) *European Journal of Health Law* 65

Borgmeier, I. and Westenhoefer, J., 'Impact of Different Food Label Formats on Healthiness Evaluation and Food Choice of Consumers: A Randomised-Controlled Study' (2009) 9(1) *BMC Public Health* 184

Botterill, D., Pennings, G. and Mainil, T. (eds.), *Medical Tourism and Transnational Health Care* (Palgrave Macmillan, 2013)

Bovis, C., 'Recent Case Law Relating to Public Procurement: A Beacon for the Integration of Public Markets' (2002) 39 *Common Market Law Review* 1025

Braithwaite, J., *Corporate Crime in the Pharmaceutical Industry* (Routledge, 1984)

Brattberg, E. and Rhinhard, M., 'Multilevel Governance and Complex Threats: The Case of Pandemic Preparedness in the European Union and the United States' (2011) 5(1) *Global Health Governance* 1

Brazier, M., 'The Case for a No-Fault Scheme for Medical Accidents', in S. McLean (ed.), *Compensation for Damage: An International Perspective* (Ashgate, 1993)

Brazier, M. and Cave, E., *Medicine, Patients and the Law*, 5th edn (Penguin, 2011)

Brazier, M. and Glover, N., 'Does Medical Law Have a Future?', in D. Hayton (ed.), *Law's Futures* (Hart, 2000)

Brazier, M. and Ost, S., *Bioethics, Medicine and the Criminal Law: Medicine and Bioethics in the Theatre of the Criminal Process* (Cambridge University Press, 2013)

Brock, D.W., 'Some Questions about the Moral Responsibilities of Drug Companies' (2001) 1(1) *Developing World Bioethics* 33

Brown, G.W., Yamey, G. and Wamala, S. (eds.), *The Handbook of Global Health Policy* (Wiley, 2014)

Brownsword, R., 'The Ancillary-Care Responsibilities of Researchers: Reasonable but Not Great Expectations' in J. Harrington and M. Stuttaford (eds.), *Global Health and Human Rights: Legal and Philosophical Perspectives* (Routledge, 2010)

    'Code, Control, and Choice: Why East is East and West is West' (2005) 21 *Legal Studies* 1

    'Human Dignity, Ethical Pluralism and the Regulation of Modern Biotechnologies' in T. Murphy (ed.), *New Technologies and Human Rights* (Oxford University Press, 2009)

    'Regulating Nanomedicine: The Smallest of Our Concerns' (2008) 2(1) *Nanoethics* 73

    Rights, Regulation, and the Technological Revolution (Oxford University Press, 2008)

Brownsword, R. and Somsen, H., 'Law, Innovation and Technology: Before We Fast Forward – A Forum for Debate' (2009) 1(1) *Law, Innovation and Technology* 1

Brownsword, R. and Yeung, Y. (eds.), *Regulating Technologies: Legal Futures, Regulatory Frames and Technological Fixes* (Hart, 2008)

Bruce, D.M., 'Sickness, Health Tourism and the Ever Present Threat of Death: Nineteenth-century Spas and Seasonal Travel' in D. Botterill, G. Pennings and T. Mainil (eds.), *Medical Tourism and Transnational Health Care* (Palgrave Macmillan, 2013)

Brunet-Jailly, J., 'Has the World Bank A Strategy on Health?' (1999) 51(161) *International Social Science Journal* 347

Budiani-Saberi, D.A. and Delmonico, F.L., 'Organ Trafficking and Transplant Tourism: A Commentary on the Global Realities' (2008) 8(5) *American Journal of Transplantation* 925

Buijsen, M.A.J.M., 'The Concept of Health Law', 14th World Health Law Congress, Maastricht, 2002

Burchill, R., Harris, D. and Owers, A. (eds.), *Economic, Social and Cultural Rights: Their Implementation in UK Law* (University of Nottingham Human Rights Centre, 1999)

Busby, H., 'Trust, Nostalgia and Narrative Accounts of Blood Banking in England in the 21st Century' (2010) 14 (4) *Health* 369

Buse, K., Gostin, L. Friedman, E., 'Pathways towards a Framework Convention on Global Health: Political Mobilization for the Human Right to Health', in M. Freeman, S. Hawkes and B. Bennett (eds.), *Law and Global Health: Current Legal Issues*, vol. 16 (Oxford University Press, 2014)

Busse, R., 'Border-crossing Patients in the EU' (2002) 8(4) *eurohealth* 19

'Consumer Choice of Healthcare Services across Borders', in R. Busse, M. Wismar and P. Berman (eds.), *The European Union and Health Services: The Impact of the Single European Market on Member States* (IOS Press, 2002)

Busse, R., Wismar, M. and Berman, P. (eds.), *The European Union and Health Services* (IOS Press, 2002)

Button, C., *The Power to Protect: Trade, Health and Uncertainty in the WTO* (Hart, 2004)

Byrne, D., 'The Genesis of EFSA and the First 10 Years of EU Food Law' in A. Alemanno and S. Gabbi (eds.), *Foundations of EU Food Law and Policy: Ten Years of the European Food Safety Authority* (Ashgate, 2014)

Cabral, P., 'Cross-border Medical Care in the European Union: Bringing Down a First Wall' (1999) 24 *European Law Review* 387

Callens, S., 'Medical Civil Liability in Belgium: Four Selected Cases' (2003) 10(2) *European Journal of Health Law* (2003) 115

Cane, P., *Atiyah's Accidents, Compensation and the Law*, 6th edn (Cambridge University Press, 2004)

Canor, I., 'My Brother's Keeper? Horizontal Solange: An Ever Closer Distrust Among the Peoples of Europe' (2013) 50 *Common Market Law Review* 383

'Primus Inter Pares: Who is the Ultimate Guardian of Fundamental Rights in Europe?' (2000) 25 *European Law Review* 3

Cappelletti, M., Seccombe, M. and Weiler, J.H.H. (eds.), *International Through Law: Europe and the American Federal Experience*, 3 vols (de Gruyter, 1985)

Carmi, A., 'Health Law towards the 21st Century' (1994) 1 *European Journal of Health Law* 225

Cartabia, M., 'Europe and Rights: Taking Dialogue Seriously' (2009) 5(1) *European Constitutional Review* 5

Casparie, A.F., Hermans, H. and Paelinck, J. (eds.), *Health Care In Europe After 1992* (Dartmouth, 1992)

Cekola, J., 'Outsourcing Drug Investigations to India: A Comment on US, India and International Regulation of Clinical Trials in Cross-Border Pharmaceutical Research' (2007) 28 *North Western Journal of International Law and Business* 125

Cernuschi, T., Furrer, E., Schwalbe, N., et al., 'Advance Market Commitment for Pneumococcal Vaccines: Putting Theory into Practice' (2011) 89(12) *Bulletin of the WHO* 913

Chadwick, R., Levitt, M. and Shickle, D. (eds.), *The Right to Know and the Right Not to Know: Genetic Privacy and Responsibility*, 2nd edn (Cambridge University Press, 2007)

Chalmers, D., Davies, G. and Monti, G., *European Union Law*, 3rd edn (Cambridge University Press, 2014)

Chanda, R., 'India-EU Relations in Health Services: Prospects and Challenges' (2011) 7 *Globalization and Health* 1

Chatterjee, P., 'India's Patent Case Victory Rattles Big Pharma' (2013) 381(9874) *The Lancet* 1263

Chen, Y.Y.B. and Flood, C.M., 'Medical Tourism's Impact on Health Care Equity and Access in Low- and Middle-Income Countries: Making the Case for Regulation' (2013) 41(1) *Journal of Law, Medicine and Ethics* 286

Chenet, L., McKee, M., Osler, M. and Krasnik, A., 'Alcohol Policy in the Nordic Countries: Why Competition Law Must Have a Public Health Dimension' (1997) 314(7088) *British Medical Journal* 1142

Cheyne, I., 'Risk and Precaution in World Trade Organization Law' (2006) 40(5) *Journal of World Trade* 837

Chico, V., 'Known Unknowns and Unknown Unknowns: The Potential and the Limits of Autonomy in Non-Disclosure of Genetic Risk' (2012) 28(3) *Journal of Professional Negligence* 162

Chico, V., Hervey, T., Stirton, R. and Warren Jones, A., 'Markets and Vulnerable Patients: Health Law after the 2012 Act' (2014) 22(2) *Medical Law Review* 157

Choudhry, S., 'Article 9: Right to Marry and Right to Found a Family', in S. Peers, T.K. Hervey, J. Kenner and A. Ward (eds.), *The EU Charter of Fundamental Rights: A Commentary* (Hart, 2014)

Choudry, N.K., Fletcher, R.H. and Soumerai, S.B., 'Systematic Review: The Relationship between Clinical Experience and Quality of Health Care' (2005) 142 *Annals of Internal Medicine* 26

Chowdhury, N., *European Regulation of Medical Devices and Pharmaceuticals* (Springer, 2014)

Cisneros Örnberg, J., 'Alcohol Policy in the European Union', in S.L. Greer and P. Kurzer (eds.), *European Union Health Policies: Regional and Global Trends* (Routledge, 2013)

Clapham, A., *Human Rights and the European Community: A Critical Overview* (Nomos, 1991)

Clarfield, A.M., Gordon, M., Markwell, H. and Alibhai, S.M.H., 'Ethical Issues in End-of-Life Geriatric Care: The Approach of Three Monotheistic Religions: Judaism, Catholicism, and Islam' (2003) 51(8) *Journal of the American Geriatrics Society* 1149

Clarke, L., 'Abortion: A Rights Issue?', in R.G. Lee and D. Morgan (eds.), *Birthrights* (Routledge, 1989)

Clemens, J., Holmgren, J., Kaufmann, S.H. and Mantovani, A., 'Ten Years of the Global Alliance for Vaccines and Immunization: Challenges and Progress' (2010) 11(12) *Nature Immunology* 1069

Clemens, T., Michelsen, K. and Brand, H., 'Supporting Health Systems in Europe: Added Value of EU Actions' (2013) 9(1) *Health Economics Policy and Law* 49

Cloatre, E. and Pickersgill, M. (eds.), *Knowledge, Technology and Law* (Routledge, 2014)

Coggon, J., *What Makes Health Public: A Critical Evaluation of Moral, Legal and Political Claims in Public Health* (Cambridge University Press, 2012)

'Global Health, Law, and Ethics: Fragmented Sovereignty and the Limits of Universal Theory' in M. Freeman, S. Hawkes and B. Bennett (eds.), *Law and Global Health: Current Legal Issues*, vol. 16 (Oxford University Press, 2014)

'Would Responsible Medical Lawyers Lose their Patients?' (2012) 20(1) *Medical Law Review* 130

Cohen, D., 'Devices and Desires; Industry Fights Toughening of Medical Device Regulation in Europe' (2013) 347 *British Medical Journal* 1

Cohen, I.G. (ed.), *The Globalization of Health Care: Legal and Ethical Issues* (Oxford University Press, 2013)

'Medical Tourism and Global Justice', in I.G. Cohen (ed.), *The Globalization of Health Care: Legal and Ethical Issues* (Oxford University Press, 2013)

Patients with Passports: Medical Tourism, Law, and Ethics (Oxford University Press, 2015)

'Transplant Tourism: The Ethics and Regulation of International Markets for Organs' (2013) 41(1) *Journal of Law, Medicine and Ethics* 269

Cohen, L. and Peirson, L., 'The UK Research and "Bolar" Exemptions: Broadening the Scope for Innovation?' (2013) 8(11) *Journal of Intellectual Property Law & Practice* 837

Colgan, *Trust Betrayed: How the Organ Retention Scandal Devastated Irish Families* (Poolbeg Press, 2009)

Collins, D., 'Health Protection at the World Trade Organization: The J-Value as a Universal Standard for Reasonableness of Regulatory Precautions' (2009) 43(5) *Journal of World Trade* 1071

Connell, J., 'Medical tourism: Sea, Sun, Sand and . . . Surgery' (2006) 27 *Tourism Management* 1093

Copeland, P. and Papadimitriou, D. (eds.), *The EU's Lisbon Strategy: Evaluating Success, Understanding Failure* (Palgrave Macmillan, 2012)

Coppell, J. and O'Neill, A., 'The European Court of Justice: Taking Rights Seriously?' (1992) 29 *Common Market Law Review* 669

Corkin, J., 'Science, Legitimacy and the Law: Regulating Risk Regulation Judiciously in the European Community' (2008) 33(3) *European Law Review* 359

Cortez, N., 'Patients Without Borders: The Emerging Global Market for Patients and the Evolution of Modern Health Care' (2008) 83(1) *Indiana Law Journal* 71

Costello C., 'Article 33: Family and Professional Life', in S. Peers, T.K. Hervey, J. Kenner and A. Ward (eds.), *The EU Charter of Fundamental Rights: A Commentary* (Hart, 2014)

Council of Europe, *Guide to the Preparation, Use and Quality Assurance of Blood Components*, 17th edn (Council of Europe, 2013)

Cousins, M., 'Health Care and Human Rights after Auton and Chaoulli' (2009) 54 *McGill Law Journal* 717

Coward, H., 'South Asian Approaches to Health Care Ethics', in R. Ashcroft, H. Draper, A. Dawson and J. Macmillan (eds.), *Principles of Health Care Ethics*, 2nd edn (Wiley-Blackwell, 2007)

Craig, P., *The Lisbon Treaty: Law, Politics and Treaty Reform* (Oxford University Press, 2010)

Craig, P. and De Búrca, G. (eds.), *The Evolution of EU Law*, 2nd edn (Oxford University Press, 2011)

Cremona, M., 'Human Rights and Democracy Clauses in the EC's Trade Agreements' in D. O'Keeffe and N. Emiliou (eds.), *The European Union and World Trade Law* (Wiley, 1996)

(ed.), *Market Integration and Public Services in the EU*(Collected Courses of the Academy of European Law)(Oxford University Press, 2011)

Cruz, J.B., 'The Case Law of the ECJ on the Mobility of Patients: An Assessment', in J.W. Van de Gronden, E. Szyszczak, U. Neergaard and M. Krajewski (eds.), *Health Care and EU Law* (Springer, 2011)

Cryer, R., Hervey, T.K., Soki-Bulley, B. and Bohm, A., *Research Methodologies in EU and International Law* (Hart, 2011)

Cullen, H., 'The Collective Complaints System of the European Social Charter: Interpretative Methods of the European Committee of Social Rights' (2009) 9(1) *Human Rights Law Review* 61

Culley, L., Hudson, N., Rapport, F., et al., 'Crossing Borders for Fertility Treatment: Motivations, Destinations and Outcomes of UK Fertility Travellers' (2011) 26 (9) *Human Reproduction* 2373

Daniels, N., *Just Health: Meeting Health Needs Fairly* (Cambridge University Press, 2008)

 'Social Responsibility and Global Pharmaceutical Companies' (2001) 1(1) *Developing World Bioethics* 38

Davies, G., 'Health and Efficiency: Community Law and National Health Systems in the Light of Müller-Fauré' (2004) 67 *Modern Law Review* 94

 'Legislating for Patients' Rights', in J.W. Van de Gronden, E. Szyszczak, U. Neergaard and M. Krajewski (eds.), *Health Care and EU Law* (Springer, 2011)

Davies, S., 'The Consumers' Perspective of EFSA', in A. Alemanno and S. Gabbi (eds.), *Foundations of EU Food Law and Policy: Ten Years of the European Food Safety Authority* (Ashgate, 2014)

Dawson A. and Verweij, M., 'Solidarity: A Moral Concept in Need of Clarification' (2012) 5(1) *Public Health Ethics* 1

Dawson, M., *New Governance and the Transformation of European Law: Coordinating EU Social Law and Policy* (Cambridge University Press, 2011)

Dayrit, M., Taylor, A., Yan, J., et al., 'WHO Code of Practice on the International Recruitment of Health Personnel' (2008) 86(10) *Bulletin of the World Health Organization* 737

De Beyer, J., Preker, A. and Feacham, R., 'The Role of the World Bank in International Health: Renewed Commitment and Partnership' (2000) 50 *Social Science and Medicine* 169

De Búrca, G., 'Fundamental Human Rights and the Reach of EC Law' (1993) 13 *Oxford Journal of Legal Studies* 283

De Búrca, G. (ed.), *EU Law and the Welfare State: In Search of Solidarity* (Oxford University Press, 2005)

De Búrca, G., 'The Road Not Taken: The EU as a Global Human Rights Actor' (2011) 105(4) *American Journal of International Law* 649

De Búrca, G. and De Witte, B. (eds.), *Social Rights in Europe* (Oxford University Press, 2005)

De Búrca, G. and Scott, J., 'Introduction: New Governance, Law and Constitutionalism', in G. de Búrca and J. Scott (eds.), *Law and New Governance in the EU and the US* (Hart, 2006)

De Búrca, G. and Weiler, J.H.H. (eds.), *The European Court of Justice* (Oxford University Press, 2001)

 The Worlds of European Constitutionalism (Cambridge University Press, 2011)

De Klerk, C.M., 'Protection of Incapacitated Elderly in Medical Research' (2012) 19(4) *European Journal of Health Law* 367

De La Mare, T. and Donnelly, C., 'Preliminary Rulings and EU Legal Integration: Evolution and Stats', in P. Craig and G. de Búrca (eds.), *The Evolution of EU Law*, 2nd edn (Oxford University Press, 2011)

De La Rosa, S., 'The Directive on Cross-Border Healthcare or the Art of Codifying Complex Case Law' (2012) 49 *Common Market Law Review* 15

De Morpurgo, M., 'The European Union as a Global Producer of Transnational Law of Risk Regulation: A Case Study on Chemical Regulation' (2013) 19(6) *European Law Journal* 779

De Sadeleer, N.M., 'The Precautionary Principle in EC Environmental and Health Law' (2006) 12(2) *European Law Journal* 139

De Schutter, O. and Lenoble, J., *Reflexive Governance: Redefining Public Interest in a Pluralistic World* (Hart, 2010)

De Wispelaere, J. and Stirton, L., 'Advance Commitment: An Alternative Approach to the Family Veto Problem in Organ Procurement' (2010) 36(3) *Journal of Medical Ethics* 180

De Witte, B., 'Direct Effect, Primacy and the Nature of the Legal Order', in P. Craig and G. de Búrca (eds.), *The Evolution of EU Law*, 2nd edn (Oxford University Press, 2011)

Deacon, B., 'Eastern European Welfare States: The Impact of the Politics of Globalization' (2000) 10(2) *Journal of European Social Policy* 146

Delnoij, D. and Sauter, W., 'Patient Information under the EU Patients' Rights Directive' (2011) 21(3) *European Journal of Public Health* 271

Den Exter, A. and Hermans, H., *The Right to Health Care in Several European Countries* (Kluwer Law International, 1995)

Den Exter, A. and Hervey, T.K., *European Union Health Law: Treaties and Legislation* (Maklu, 2012)

Den Exter, A. and Guy, M.J., 'Market Competition in Health Care Markets in the Netherlands: Some Lessons for England?' (2014) 22(2) *Medical Law Review* 255

Den Heijer, M., 'Article 18: Right to Asylum', in S. Peers, T.K. Hervey, J. Kenner and A. Ward (eds.), *The EU Charter of Fundamental Rights: A Commentary* (Hart, 2014)

Denney, D., *Risk and Society* (Sage, 2005)

'Detaining Patients with AIDS', Editorial, *British Medical Journal* (1985) 291: 1002

Devaney S. and Farrell A.M., 'Making Amends or Making Things Worse: Clinical Negligence Reform and Patient Redress in England' (2007) 27 *Legal Studies* 360

Di Federico, G., 'Access to Healthcare in the Post-Lisbon Era and the Genuine Enjoyment of EU Citizens' Rights', in Rossi, L.S. and Casolari, F. (eds.), *The EU After Lisbon: Amending or Coping with the Existing Treaties* (Springer, 2014)

Dickenson, D., *Bioethics: All that Matters* (Hodder and Stoughton, 2013)

Body Shopping Converting Body Parts to Profit (Oneworld, 2009)

Property in the Body: Feminist Perspectives (Cambridge University Press, 2007)

Disdier A. and Fontagné, L., 'Trade impact of European measures on GMOs condemned by the WTO panel' (2010) 146(3) *Review of World Economics* 495

Dixon A. and Poteliakhoff, E., 'Back to the Future: 10 Years of European Health Reforms' (2012) 7 *Health Economics Policy and Law* 1

Dorbeck-Jung, B., 'The Governance of Therapeutic Nanoproducts in the EU: A Model for New Health Technology Regulation?' Flear, M., Farrell, A.-M., Hervey, T.K. and Murphy, T. (eds.), *European Law and New Health Technologies* (Oxford University Press, 2013)

Dorbeck-Jung, B. and Chowdhury, N., 'Is the European Medical Products Authorisation Regulation Equipped to Cope with the Challenges of Nanomedicines?' (2011) 33(2) *Law & Policy* 276

Dorbeck-Jung, B., Bowman, D.M., and Van Calster, G. (eds.), 'Governing Nanomedicine: Lessons from within, and for, the EU Medical Technology Regulatory Framework' (2011) 33(2) *Law & Policy* 215

Douglas, M., *Risk and Blame: Collected Works* (Routledge, 2002)

Dougan, M. and Spaventa, E. (eds.), *Social Welfare and EU Law* (Hart, 2005)

Douglas, M. and Wildavsky, A., *Risk and Culture: An Essay on the Selection of Technological and Environmental Dangers* (University of California Press, 1983)

Douglas-Scott, S., 'The European Union and Human Rights after the Treaty of Lisbon' (2011) 11(4) *Human Rights Law Review* 645

Douglas-Scott, S., 'A Tale of Two Courts: Luxembourg, Strasbourg and the Growing European Human Rights Acquis' (2006) 43 *Common Market Law Review* 629

Du, M.M., 'The Rise of National Regulatory Autonomy in the GATT/WTO Regime' (2011) 14(3) *Journal of International Economic Law* 639

Dukes, G., Braithwaite, J. Moloney, J.P., *Pharmaceuticals, Corporate Crime and Public Health* (Edward Elgar, 2014)

Dupré, C., 'Article 1: Human Dignity', in Peers, S., Hervey, T.K., Kenner, J. and Ward, A. (eds.), *The EU Charter of Fundamental Rights: A Commentary* (Hart, 2014)

Dute, J., 'Medical Malpractice Liability: No Easy Solutions' (2003) 10(2) *European Journal of Health Law* 85

Duxbury, N., 'Do Markets Degrade?' (1996) 59(3) *Modern Law Review* 331

Dwyer, P., 'Retired EU Migrants, Healthcare Rights and European Social Citizenship' (2001) 23 *Journal of Social Welfare and Family Law* 311

Easterbrook, F., 'Cyberspace and the Law of the Horse' [1996] *University of Chicago Legal Forum* 207

Eckes, C., 'Does the European Court of Human Rights Provide Protection from the European Community? The Case of Bosphorus Airways' (2007) 13(1) *European Public Law* 47

Edward, D., 'Freedom of Movement for the Regulated Professions', in R. White and B. Smythe (eds.), *Current Issues in European and International Law: Essays in Memory of Franck Dowrick* (Sweet & Maxwell, 1990)

Edward, D. and Hoskins, M., 'Article 90: Deregulation and EC Law. Reflections Arising from the XVI FIDE Conference' (1995) 32 *Common Market Law Review* 157

Eeckhout, P., *EU External Relations Law*, 2nd edn (Oxford University Press, 2011)

Eldridge, 'Junior Doctors' Hours' (1993) 308 *British Medical Journal* 417

Eleftheriadis, P., 'Global Rights and the Sanctity of Life', in I.G. Cohen (ed.), *The Globalization of Health Care: Legal and Ethical Issues* (Oxford University Press, 2013)
'A Right to Health Care' (2012) 40 *Journal of Law, Medicine & Ethics* 268

Elliott, H.A., Jones, D.K. and Greer, S.L., 'Mapping Communicable Disease Control in the European Union' (2012) 37(6) *Journal of Health Politics, Policy and Law* 935

Elsmore, V. and Obolevich, M.J., 'Thank You for Not Smoking: The Commission's Proposal for a New Tobacco Products Directive – Legally Sound but Does it Hit the Spot?' (2013) 38(4) *European Law Review* 552

Englert, Y. (ed.), *Organ and Tissue Transplantation in the European Union* (Kluwer, 1995)

Erin, C.A. and Bennett, R. (eds.), *HIV and AIDS: Testing Screening and Confidentiality* (Oxford University Press, 1999)

Erin, C.A. and Harris, J., 'A Monopsonistic Market: Or How to Buy and Sell Human Organs, Tissues and Cells Ethically', in I. Robinson (ed.), *Life and Death Under High Technology Medicine* (Manchester University Press, 1994)

Esping-Andersen, G., *The Three Worlds of Welfare Capitalism* (Princeton University Press, 1990)

European Court of Auditors, *The European Union's Public Health Programme 2003–2007: An Effective Way to Improve Health?* (Court of Auditors, 2009)

European Network for Health Technology Assessment (EUnetHTA) (2009) 25 *International Journal of Technology Assessment in Health Care*

Everson, M. and Vos, E. (eds.), *Uncertain Risks Regulated* (Routledge-Cavendish, 2009)

Eyal, N. and Bärnighausen, T., 'Conditioning Medical Scholarships On Long, Future Service: A Defense', in I.G. Cohen (ed.), *The Globalization of Health Care: Legal and Ethical Issues* (Oxford University Press, 2013)

Eysenbach, G. (ed.), *Medicine and Medical Education in Europe: The Eurodoctor* (Thieme, 1998)

Fabre, J., Murphy, P. and Matesanz, R., 'Presumed Consent: A Distraction in the Quest for Increasing Rates of Organ Donation' (2012) 341 *British Medical Journal* 4973

Faden, R.R., Beauchamp, T.L. and Kass, N.E., 'Informed Consent, Comparative Effectiveness and Learning Health Care' (2014) 370(8) *New England Journal of Medicine* 766

Faeh, A., 'A Just Distribution of Health Care in the Case of Orphan Medicinal Products: Aligning the Interests of European Economic Integration and National Welfare Policy' (2012) 14(1) *European Journal of Social Security* 21

Fagot-Largeault, A., 'Does Non-Commercialisation of the Human Body Increase Graft Security?', in Y. Englert (ed.), *Organ and Tissue Transplantation in the European Union* (Kluwer, 1995)

Fahy, N., 'Who is shaping the future of European health systems?' (2012) 334 *British Medical Journal* (2012) e1712

Fallberg, L., 'Patients' Rights in Europe: Where Do We Stand and Where Do We Go?' (2000) 7 *European Journal of Health Law* (2000) 1

'Patients' Rights in the Nordic Countries' (2000) 7 *European Journal of Health Law* 123–43

Farrell, A.-M., 'Adding Value? EU Governance of Organ Donation and Transplantation' (2010) 17(1) *European Journal of Health Law* 51

'Addressing Organ Shortage in the European Union: Getting the Balance Right', in A.-M. Farrell, D. Price and M. Quigley (eds.), *Organ Shortage: Ethics and Pragmatism* (Cambridge University Press, 2011)

'The Emergence of EU Governance in Public Health: The Case of Blood Policy and Regulation', in M. Steffen (ed.), *Health Governance in Europe: Issues, Challenges and Theories* (Routledge, 2005)

'Governing the Body: Examining EU Regulatory Developments in Relation to Substances of Human Origin' (2005) 27(3) *Journal of Social Welfare and Family Law* 427

'Is the Gift Still Good? Examining the Politics and Regulation of Blood Safety in the EU' (2006) 14(2) *Medical Law Review* 155

The Politics of Blood: Ethics, Innovation and the Regulation of Risk (Cambridge University Press, 2012)

'The Politics of Risk and EU Governance of Human Material' (2009) 16(1) *Maastricht Journal of European and Comparative Law* 41

'Risk, Legitimacy, and EU Regulation of Health Technologies', in M. Flear, A.-M. Farrell, T.K. Hervey and T. Murphy (eds.), *European Law and New Health Technologies* (Oxford University Press, 2013)

Farrell, A.-M., Price, D. and Quigley, M. (eds.), *Organ Shortage: Ethics and Pragmatism* (Cambridge University Press, 2011)

Favale, M., and Plomer, A., 'Fundamental Disjunctures in the EU Legal Order on Human Tissue, Cells and Advanced Regenerative Therapies (2009) 16(1) *Maastricht Journal of European and Comparative Law* 89

Feldman, E.A., and Bayer, R. (eds.), *Unfiltered: Conflicts Over Tobacco Policy and Public Health* (Harvard University Press, 2004)

Fenton, R., 'Catholic Doctrine versus Reproductive Rights: The New Italian Law on Assisted Reproduction' (2006) 14(1) *Medical Law Review* 73

Ferge, Z., 'Welfare and "Ill-fare" Systems in Central and Eastern Europe', in R. Sykes, B. Palier and P. Prior (eds.), *Globalization and European Welfare States: Challenges and Change* (Palgrave Macmillan, 2001)

Ferguson, P., *Drug Injuries and the Pursuit of Compensation* (Sweet & Maxwell, 1996)

Ferrera, M., *The Boundaries of Welfare: European Integration and the New Social Politics of Social Welfare* (Oxford University Press, 2005)

Fidler, A.H., Haslinger, R.R., Hofmarcher, M.M., et al., 'Incorporation of Public Hospitals: A "Silver Bullet" against Overcapacity, Managerial Bottlenecks and Resource Constraints' (2007) 81 *Health Policy* 328

Fidler, D.P., 'Global Health Jurisprudence: A Time of Reckoning' (2008) 96(2) *Georgetown Law Journal* 393

Field, M., 'The Concept of the "Health System" at a Macrosociological Level' (1973) 7 (10) *Social Science & Medicine* 763

Figert, A.E. and Bell, S.E., 'Big Pharma and Big Medicine in the Global Environment', in D.L. Kleinman and K. Moore (eds.), *Routledge Handbook of Science, Technology and Society* (Routledge, 2014)

Figueras, J. and McKee, M. (eds.), *Health Systems, Health, Wealth and Societal Well-being: Assessing the Case for Investing in Health Systems* (Open University Press, 2011)

Finch, J., 'Professional Recognition and Training of Doctors: The 1993 EC Directive' (1995) 2(2) *European Journal of Health Law* 163

Fisher, E., *Risk Regulation and Administrative Constitutionalism* (Hart, 2007)

Fisher, J.A., *Medical Research for Hire: The Political Economy of Pharmaceutical Clinical Trials* (Rutgers University Press, 2008)

Flear, M., 'Annotation of Case C-385/99 Müller-Fauré' (2004) 41 *Common Market Law Review* 209

'Clinical Trials Abroad: The Marketable Ethics, Weak Protections and Vulnerable Subjects of EU Law', in A. Albors-Llorens, K. Armstrong and M.W. Gehring (eds.), *Cambridge Yearbook of European Legal Studies*, vol. 16, 2013–2014 (Hart, 2014)

'Does the Free Movement of Persons Cause Change in Healthcare Systems?', unpublished PhD thesis, University of Nottingham, 2006

'The EU's Biopolitical Governance of Advanced Therapy Medicinal Products' (2009) 16(1) *Maastricht Journal of European and Comparative Law* 113

Governing Public Health (Hart, 2015)

'Introduction to "New Technologies, European Law and Citizens" Symposium: New Technologies, European Law and Citizens – Editorial' (2009) 16(1) *Maastricht Journal of European and Comparative Law* 3

(ed.), 'A Symposium with Professor Roger Brownsword: Super-stewardship in the Context of Public Health', special issue (2011) 62(5) *Northern Ireland Legal Quarterly* 569

Flear, M. and Pfister, T., 'Contingent Participation: Imaginaries of Sustainable Techno-scientific Innovation in the European Union', in E. Cloatre and M. Pickersgill (eds.), *Knowledge, Technology and Law* (Routledge, 2014)

Flear, M. and Pickersgill, M., 'Regulatory or Regulating Publics? The European Union's Regulation of Emerging Health Technologies and Citizen Participation' (2013) 21(1) *Medical Law Review* 39

Flear, M. and Vakulenko, A., 'A Human Rights Perspective on Citizen Participation in the EU's Governance of New Technologies' (2010) 10(4) *Human Rights Law Review* 661

Flear, M., Farrell, A.-M., Hervey, T.K. and Murphy, T. (eds.), *European Law and New Health Technologies* (Oxford University Press, 2013)

Flood, C.M., 'Chaoulli's Legacy for the Future of Canadian health Care Policy' (2006) 44 *Osgoode Hall Law Journal* 273

International Health Care Reform (Routledge, 2003)

Flood, C.M. and Lemmens, T., 'Global Health Challenges and the Role of Law' (2013) 41(1) *Journal of Law, Medicine and Ethics* 9

Flood, C.M. and Xavier, S., 'Health Care Rights in Canada: The Chaoulli Legacy' (2008) 27 *Medicine and Law* 617

Fluss, S., 'The Development of National Health Legislation in Europe: The Contribution of International Organisations' (1995) 2 *European Journal of Health Law* 193

Foster, C. and Herring, J., 'What is Health?', in M. Freeman, S. Hawkes and B. Bennett (eds.), *Law and Global Health: Current Legal Issues* vol. 16 (Oxford University Press, 2014)

Francioni, F. (ed.), *Biotechnologies and International Human Rights* (Hart, 2007)

Francis, L.P. and Francis, J.G., 'Stateless Crimes, Legitimacy, and International Criminal Law: The Case of Organ Trafficking' (2010) 4(3) *Criminal Law & Philosophy* 283

Frankel, S. and Gervais, D., 'Plain Packaging and the Interpretation of the TRIPS Agreement' (2013) 46(5) *Vanderbilt Journal of Transnational Law* 1149

Franklin, J., 'Politics and Risk', in G. Mythen and S. Walklate (eds.), *Beyond the Risk Society: Critical Reflections on Risk and Human Security* (Open University Press, 2006)

(ed.), *The Politics of Risk Society* (Polity, 1998)

Freeman, M., 'Denying Death its Dominion: Thoughts on the Dianne Pretty Case' (2002) 10 *Medical Law Review* 245

'Global Health: An Introduction', in M. Freeman, S. Hawkes and B. Bennett (eds.), *Law and Global Health: Current Legal Issues*, vol. 16 (Oxford University Press, 2014)

Freeman, M., Hawkes, S. and Bennett, B. (eds.), *Law and Global Health: Current Legal Issues*, vol. 16 (Oxford University Press, 2014)

Freeman, R., *The Politics of Health in Europe* (Manchester University Press, 2000)

Frenk, J., Lincoln, C., Zulfiqar, et al., 'Health Professionals for a New Century: Transforming Education to Strengthen Health Systems in an Interdependent World' (2010) 376(9756) *The Lancet* 1923

Friant-Perro, M. and Garde, A., 'From BSE to Obesity: EFSA's Growing Role in the EU's Nutrition Policy', in A. Alemanno and S. Gabbi (eds.), *Foundations of EU Food Law and Policy: Ten Years of the European Food Safety Authority* (Ashgate, 2014)

Friedson, E., *Profession of Medicine: Study of the Sociology of Applied Knowledge* (University of Chicago Press, 1988)

Gabbi, S., 'The Scientific Governance of the European Food Safety Authority', in A. Alemanno and S. Gabbi (eds.), *Foundations of EU Food Law and Policy: Ten Years of the European Food Safety Authority* (Ashgate, 2014)

Galsworthy, M.J., Hristovski, D., Lusa, L., et al., 'The Academic Output of Nine Years of EU Investment into Health Research' (2012) 380(9846) *The Lancet* 971

Garanis Papadatos, T. and Dalla Vorgia, P., 'Ethical Review Procedures for Clinical Trials in Greece' (2000) 7 *European Journal of Health Law* 441

Garben, S., 'Case Note on Bressol' (2010) 47 *Common Market Law Review* 1493

Gardner, J.S., 'The European Agency for the Evaluation of Medicines and European Regulation of Pharmaceuticals' (1996) 2 *European Law Journal* 48

Garrett, L., *The Coming Plague: Newly Emerging Diseases in a World Out of Balance* (Penguin, 1995)

Garwood-Gowers, A., Tingle, J. and Lewis, T. (eds.), *Healthcare Law: The Impact of the Human Rights Act 1998*, (Routledge-Cavendish, 2001)

Gekiere, W., Baeten, R. and Palm, W., 'Free Movement of Health Services in the EU and Health Care', in E. Mossialos, G. Permanand, R. Baeten and T.K. Hervey (eds.), *Health Systems Governance in Europe: The Role of European Union Law and Policy* (Cambridge University Press, 2010)

Geslain-Lanéelle, C., 'Foreword', in A. Alemanno and S. Gabbi (eds.), *Foundations of EU Food Law and Policy: Ten Years of the European Food Safety Authority* (Ashgate, 2014)

Gevers, J., 'Medical Research Involving Children' (2008) 15(2) *European Journal of Health Law* 103

Gevers, J., Hondius, E. and Hudson, J. (eds.), *Health Law, Human Rights and the Biomedicine Convention* (Martinus Nijhoff, 2005)

Gevers, S. and O'Connell, R., 'Fixed Points in a Changing Age? The Council of Europe, Human Rights and the Regulation of New Health Technologies', in M. Flear, A.-M. Farrell, T.K. Hervey and T. Murphy (eds.), *European Law and New Health Technologies* (Oxford University Press, 2013)

Geyer, R., *Exploring European Social Policy* (Polity, 2000)

Geyer, R. and Lightfoot, S., 'The Strengths and Limits of New Forms of EU Governance: The Cases of Mainstreaming and Impact Assessment in EU Public Health and Sustainable Development Policy' (2010) 32(4) *European Integration* 339

Gibson, S.G. and Lemmens, T., 'Niche Markets and Evidence Assessment in Transition' (2014) 22(2) *Medical Law Review* 200

Giddens, A., 'Risk Society: The Context of British Politics', in J. Franklin (ed.), *The Politics of Risk Society* (Polity, 1998)

Giesen, D., *International Medical Malpractice Law* (Martinus Nijhoff, 1988)

'Liability for Transfer of HIV Infected Blood in Comparative Perspective' (1994) 10 *Professional Negligence* 2

Gijzen, M., 'The Charter: A Milestone for Social Protection in Europe?' (2001) 8 *Maastricht Journal of European and Comparative Law* 33

Gilbert Welch, H., Schwartz, L. and Woloshin, S., *Overdiagnosed: Making People Sick in Pursuit of Health* (Beacon Press, 2011)

Gillon, R., *Philosophical Medical Ethics* (John Wiley and Sons, 1986)

Gilmore, A. and McKee, M., 'Tobacco Control Policy: The European Dimension' (2002) 2(4) *Clinical Medicine* 335

'Tobacco Policy in the European Union', in E.A. Feldman and R. Bayer (eds.), *Unfiltered: Conflicts Over Tobacco Policy and Public Health* (Harvard University Press, 2004)

Glass, J. (ed.), *Ethics Committees in Central and Eastern Europe* (Institute of Medical Ethics and Bioethics Foundation, 2001)

Glickman, S.W, McHutchison, J.G., Peterson, E.D., et al., 'Ethical and Scientific Implications of the Globalization of Clinical Research' (2009) 360(8) *New England Journal of Medicine* 816

Global Forum for Health Research, *The 10/90 Gap in Health Research* (GCFR, 1999)

Goldacre, B., *Bad Pharma: How Drug Companies Mislead Doctors and Harm Patients* (Fourth Estate, 2012)

Goldberg, D., 'Global Health Care is Not Global Health: Populations, Inequities, and Law as a Social Determinant of Health', in I.G. Cohen (ed.), *The Globalization of Health Care: Legal and Ethical Issues* (Oxford University Press, 2013)

'In Support of a Broad Model of Public Health: Disparities, Social Epidemiology and Public Health Causation' (2009) 2(1) *Public Health Ethics* 70

Goldberg, R., 'The Development Risk Defence and the European Court of Justice; Increased Injury Costs and the Supplementary Protection Certificate', in R. Goldberg and J. Lonbay (eds.), *Pharmaceutical Medicine, Biotechnology and European Law* (Cambridge University Press, 2001)

Medicinal Product Liability and Regulation (Hart, 2013)

Goldberg, R. and Lonbay, J. (eds.), *Pharmaceutical Medicine, Biotechnology and European Law* (Cambridge University Press, 2001)

Goldsmith, Lord, 'A Charter of Rights, Freedoms and Principles' (2001) 38 *Common Market Law Review* 1201

Gornall, J., 'Europe under the Influence' (2014) 348 *British Medical Journal* 1

Gostin, L., *Global Health Law* (Harvard University Press, 2014)

'Global Health Law Governance' (2008) 22(1) *Emory International Law Review* 35

'The International Health Regulations: A New Paradigm for Global Health Governance', in S.A.M. McLean (ed.), *First Do No Harm: Law, Ethics and Healthcare* (Ashgate, 2006)

'International Infectious Disease Law: Revision of the World Health Organization's International Health Regulations' (2004) 291(21) *Journal of the American Medical Association* 2623

Public Health Law: Power, Duties and Restraints (University of California Press, 2000)

Public Health Law: Power, Duty, Restraint, Revised and Explained (University of California Press, 2008)

'Public Health, Ethics and Human Rights: A Tribute to the Late Jonathan Mann' (2001) 29 *Journal of Law, Medicine and Ethics* 121

Gostin, L. and Friedman, E., '*Ebola: A Crisis in Global Health Leadership*' (2014) 384 *The Lancet* 1323–5

Gostin, L. and Lazzarini, Z., *Human Rights and Public Health in the AIDS Pandemic* (Oxford University Press, 1997)

Gostin, L. and Taylor, A., 'Global Health Law: A Definition and Grand Challenges' (2008) 1(1) *Public Health Ethics* 53

Gøtzsche, P.C. and Jørgensen, A.W., 'Opening Up Data at the European Medicines Agency' (2011) 342 *British Medical Journal* d2686

Gower, J. (ed.), *The European Union Handbook* (Fitzroy Dearborn, 2002)

Goyal, M., Mehta, R.L., Schneiderman, L.J. and Sehgal, A.R., 'Economic and Health Consequences of Selling a Kidney in India' (2002) 288(13) *Journal of the American Medical Association* 1589

Goyder, J. and Albors-Llorens, A., *Goyder's EC Competition Law*, 5th edn (Oxford University Press, 2009)

Gragl, P., 'Agreement on the Accession of the European Union to the European Convention on Human Rights', in S. Peers, T.K. Hervey, J. Kenner and A. Ward (eds.), *The EU Charter of Fundamental Rights: A Commentary* (Hart, 2014)

Grant, W., 'Agricultural Policy, Food Policy and Communicable Disease Policy' (2012) 37 *Journal of Health Politics, Policy and Law* 1029

Gray, P., 'The Scientific Committee for Food', in M. Van Schendelen (ed.), *EU Committees as Influential Policy Makers* (Dartmouth, 1998)

Green, F., 'Further Thoughts on the Recruitment of REC Lay Members' (2007) 3(1) *Research Ethics Review* 8

Greer, S.L., 'Bacteria without Borders: The European Governance of Infectious Diseases' (2012) 37(6) *Journal of Health Politics, Policy and Law* 887

  'Catch Me if You Can: Communicable Disease Control', in S.L. Greer and P. Kurzer (eds.), *European Union Health Policies: Regional and Global Trends* (Routledge, 2013)

  'Choosing Paths in European Union Health Services Policy: A Political Analysis of a Critical Juncture' (2008) 18 *Journal of European Social Policy* 219

  'The European Centre for Disease Prevention and Control: Hub or Hollow Core?' (2012) 37(6) *Journal of Health Politics, Policy and Law* 1001

  'Ever Closer Union: Devolution, the EU and Social Citizenship Rights', in S.L. Greer (ed.), *Devolution and Social Citizenship in the United Kingdom* (Policy Press, 2009)

  The Politics of European Union Health Policies (Open University Press, 2009)

  'The Three Faces of European Union Health Policy: Policy, Markets, Austerity' (2014) 33(1) *Policy and Society* 13

Greer, S.L. and Jarman, H., 'Managing Risks in EU Health Services Policy: Spot Markets, Legal Certainty and Bureaucratic Resistance' (2012) 22(3) *Journal of European Social Policy* 259

Greer, S.L. and Kurzer, P. (eds.), *European Union Public Health Policy: Regional and Global Trends* (Routledge, 2013)

Greer, S.L. and Mätze, M., 'Bacteria without Borders: Communicable Disease Politics in Europe' (2012) 37(6) *Journal of Health Politics, Policy and Law* (2012) 887

Greer, S.L. and Sokol, T., 'Rules for Rights: European Law, Health Care and Social Citizenship' (2014) 20(1) *European Law Journal* 66

Greer, S.L. and Vanhercke, B., 'The Hard Politics of Soft Law: The Case of Health', in E. Mossialos, G. Permanand, R. Baeten and T.K. Hervey (eds.), *Health Systems Governance in Europe: The Role of European Union Law and Policy* (Cambridge University Press, 2010)

Greer, S.L., Hervey, T.K., McKee, M. and Mackenbach, J.P., 'Health Law and Policy of the European Union' (2013) 381(9872) *The Lancet* 1135

Grey, C., 'Accidental Torts' (2001) 54 *Vanderbilt Law Review* 1225

Griffiths, J., Weyers, H. and Adams, M., *Euthanasia and the Law in Europe* (Hart, 2008)

Griffiths, S. and Hunter, D., 'Introduction', in S. Griffiths and D. Hunter (eds.), *New Perspectives in Public Health*, 2nd edn (Radcliffe, 2006)

  (eds.), *New Perspectives in Public Health*, 2nd edn (Radcliffe, 2006)

Griller, S. and Ziller, J. (eds.), *The Lisbon Treaty: EU Constitutionalism without a Constitutional Treaty* (Springer, 2008)

Grubb, A., 'Comparative European Health Law' (1999) 2 *European Journal of Health Law* 291

Grubb, A., Laing, J. and McHale, J.V. (eds.), *Principles of Medical Law*, 3rd edn (Oxford University Press, 2010)

Gruni, G., 'Going from One Extreme to the Other: Food Security and Export Restrictions in the EU–CARIFORUM Partnership Agreement' (2013) 19(6) *European Law Journal* 864

Guéguen, D., *'Comitology: Hijacking European Power?'* (European Training Institute, 2010)

Guerra, G., 'European Regulatory Issues in Nanomedicine' (2008) 2(1) *Nanoethics* 87

Guibboni, S., 'Free Movement of Persons and European Solidarity' (2007) 13 *European Law Journal* 360

Gunningham, N., 'The New Collaborative Environmental Governance: The Localization of Regulation' (2009) 36 *Journal of Law and Society* 145

Hagen, P., *Blood Transfusion in Europe: A 'White Paper'* (Council of Europe, 1993)

Haigh, R. and Harris, D., *AIDS and the Law* (Routledge, 1995)

Hajer, M. and Laws, D., 'Ordering Through Discourse', in M. Moran, M. Rein and R. Goodin (eds.), *Oxford Handbook of Public Policy* (Oxford University Press, 2006)

Hall P. and Soskice D., 'An Introduction to Varieties of Capitalism', in P. Hall and D. Soskice (eds.), *Varieties of Capitalism: The Institutional Foundations of Comparative Advantage* (Oxford University Press, 2001)

  (eds.), *Varieties of Capitalism: The Institutional Foundations of Comparative Advantage* (Oxford University Press, 2001)

Hanafin, P., 'Law Biopolitical and Reproductive Citizenship: The Case of Assisted Reproduction in Italy' (2013) 4(1) *Italian Journal of Science and Technology Studies* 45

Hancher, L., 'EC Competition Law, Drugs and Intellectual Property: Recent Developments', in R. Goldberg and J. Lonbay (eds.), *Pharmaceutical Medicine, Biotechnology and European Law* (Cambridge University Press, 2001)

  'The EU Pharmaceuticals Market: Parameters and Pathways', in E. Mossialos, G. Permanand, R. Baeten and T.K. Hervey (eds.), *Health Systems Governance in Europe: The Role of European Union Law and Policy* (Cambridge University Press, 2010)

Hancher, L. and Sauter, W., *EU Competition and Internal Market Law in the Health Care Sector* (Oxford University Press, 2012)

Hall, M., 'The Legal and Historical Foundations of Patients as Medical Consumers' (2008) 96 *Georgetown Law Journal* 583

Hammitt, J.K., Weiner, J.B., Swedlow, B., et al., 'Precautionary Regulation in Europe and the US: A Quantitative Comparison' (2005) 25(5) *Risk Analysis* 1215

Hardcastle, R., *Law and the Human Body: Property Rights, Ownership and Control* (Hart, 2009)

Harmon, S.H.E., Laurie, G. and Courtney, A., 'Dignity, Plurality and Patentability: The Unfinished Story of Brüstle v. Greenpeace' (2013) 38(1) *European Law Review* 92

Harrington, J. 'Access to Essential Medicines in Kenya: IP, Anti-Counterfeiting, and the Right to Health', in M. Freeman, S. Hawkes and B. Bennett (eds.), *Law and Global Health: Current Legal Issues*, vol. 16 (Oxford University Press, 2014)

'Law, globalisation and the NHS' (2007) 31(2) *Capital and Class* 81

Harrington, J. and Stuttaford, M. (eds.), *Global Health and Human Rights: Legal and Philosophical Perspectives* (Routledge, 2010)

'Introduction', in J. Harrington and M. Stuttaford (eds.), *Global Health and Human Rights: Legal and Philosophical Perspectives* (Routledge, 2010)

Harris, J., *The Value of Life: An Introduction to Medical Ethics* (Routledge, 1985)

Harris, J. and Keywood, K., 'Ignorance, Information and Autonomy' (2001) 22(5) *Theoretical Medicine and Bioethics* 415

Hartlev, M., 'Diversity and Harmonization: Trends and Challenges in European Health Law' (2010) 17(1) *European Journal of Health Law* 37

'Stigmatisation as a Public Health Tool against Obesity: A Health and Human Rights Perspective' (2014) 21(4) *European Journal of Health Law* 365

Hatzopoulos, V.G., 'Health Law and Policy: The Impact of the EU', in G. de Búrca (ed.), *EU Law and the Welfare State: In Search of Solidarity* (Oxford University Press, 2005)

'Killing National Health and Insurance Systems but Healing Patients?' (2002) 39 *Common Market Law Review* 683

'Public Procurement and State Aid in National Health Care Systems', in E. Mossialos, G. Permanand, R. Baeten and T.K. Hervey (eds.), *Health Systems Governance in Europe: The Role of European Union Law and Policy* (Cambridge University Press, 2010)

Hatzopoulos, V.G. and Hervey, T.K., 'Coming into Line: The EU's Court Softens on Cross Border Healthcare' (2013) 8 *Health Economics Policy and Law* 1

Havighurst, C., 'American Federalism and American Health Care: Lessons for the European Community', in H.E.G.M. Hermans, A.F. Casparie and J.H.P. Paelinck (eds.), *Health Care in Europe after 1992* (Dartmouth, 1992)

Hayton, D., (ed.), *Law's Futures* (Hart, 2000)

Healy, D., *Pharmageddon* (University of California Press, 2012)

Hearn, J. and Sullivan, R., 'The Impact of the Clinical Trials Directive on the Cost and Conduct of Non-commercial Cancer Trials in the UK', 43 *European Journal of Cancer* (2007) 8–13

Hein, 'Global Health Governance and WTO/TRIPS: Conflicts between Global "Market Creation" and "Global Social Rights"', in W. Hein, S. Bartsch and L. Kohlmorgen (eds.), *Global Health Governance and the Fight against HIV/AIDS* (Palgrave Macmillan, 2007)

Hendriks, A., 'The Right to Health' (1998) 5 *European Journal of Health Law* 389

Henley, J., 'What's the New Buzz?' *Guardian* (6 May 2014)

Hennette-Vauchez, S., 'Biomedicine and EU Law: Unlikely Encounters?' (2011) 38(1) *Legal Issues of Economic Integration* 5

Heringa, J. and Dute, J., 'The Proposed EU Regulation on Clinical Trials on Medicinal Products: An Unethical Proposal?' (2013) 20(4) *European Journal of Health Law* 347

Hermans, H.E.G.M., Casparie, A.F. and Paelinck, J.H.P. (eds.), *Health Care in Europe after 1992* (Dartmouth, 1992)

Herméren, G., 'Accountability, Democracy and Ethics Committees' (2009) 2 *Law, Innovation and Technology* 153

Herring, J., *Medical Law and Ethics*, 5th edn (Oxford University Press, 2014)

Herring, J., Gould, I., Greasley K., and Skene, L. (eds.), *Persons, Parts and Property: How Should we Regulate Human Tissue in the 21st Century* (Hart, 2014)

Herrmann, J.R. and Toebes, B., 'The EU and Human Rights', in B. Toebes, M. Hartlev, A. Hendriks and J.R. Herrmann (eds.), *Health and Human Rights in Europe* (Intersentia, 2012)

Hernandez, R., Cooney, M., Dualé, C., et al., 'Harmonisation of Ethics Committees Practice in 10 European Countries' (2009) 35(11) *Journal of Medical Ethics* 696

Hervey, T.K., 'Buy Baby: The European Union and Regulation of Human Reproduction' (1998) 18 *Oxford Journal of Legal Studies* 207

'EU Health Law', in C. Barnard and S. Peers, *EU Law* (Oxford University Press, 2014)

'The European Union and the Governance of Health Care', in G. de Búrca and J. Scott (eds.), *Law and New Governance in the EU and the US* (Hart, 2006)

'The European Union, its Court of Justice, and "Super-Stewardship" in Public Health' (2011) 62(5) *Northern Ireland Legal Quarterly* 633

'The European Union's Governance of Health Care and the Welfare Modernization Agenda' (2008) 2 *Regulation and Governance* 103

'Health Equality, Solidarity and Human Rights in European Union Law', in A. Silveira, M. Canotilho and P. Madeira Froufe (eds.), *Citizenship and Solidarity in the EU: From the Charter of Fundamental Rights to the Crisis, The State of the Art* (Peter Lang, 2013)

'If Only it Were so Simple: Public Health Services and EU Law', in M. Cremona (ed.), *Market Integration and Public Services in the EU* (Collected Courses of the Academy of European Law) (Oxford University Press, 2011)

'Mapping the Contours of EU Health Law and Policy' (2002) 8 *European Public Law* 69

'The Right to Health in EU Law', in T.K. Hervey and J. Kenner (eds.), *Economic and Social Rights Under the EU Charter of Fundamental Rights* (Hart, 2003)

'The Role of the European Court of Justice in the Europeanization of Communicable Disease Control: Driver or Irrelevance?' (2012) 37(6) *Journal of Health Politics, Policy and Law* 975

'Social Solidarity: A Buttress against Internal Market Law', in J. Shaw (ed.), *Social Law and Policy in an Evolving European Union* (Hart, 2000)

'Up in Smoke: Community (Anti) Tobacco Law and Policy' 26 *European Law Review* (2001) 101

'We Don't See a Connection: The "Right to Health" in the EU Charter and European Social Charter', in G. de Búrca and B. De Witte (eds.), *Social Rights in Europe* (Oxford University Press, 2005)

Hervey, T.K. and Black, H., 'The European Union and the Governance of Stem Cell Research' (2005) 12(1) *Maastricht Journal of European and Comparative Law* 3

Hervey, T.K. and De Ruijter, A., 'Healthcare and the Lisbon Agenda', in P. Copeland and D. Papadimitriou (eds.), *The EU's Lisbon Strategy: Evaluating Success, Understanding Failure* (Palgrave, 2012)

Hervey, T.K. and Kenner, J. (eds.), *Economic and Social Rights under the EU Charter of Fundamental Rights* (Hart, 2003)

Hervey, T.K. and McHale, J.V., *Health Law and the European Union* (Cambridge University Press, 2004)

'Law, Health and the European Union' (2005) 25(2) *Legal Studies* 200

'Article 35: The Right to Health Care', in S. Peers, T.K. Hervey, J. Kenner and A. Ward (eds.), *The EU Charter of Fundamental Rights: A Commentary* (Hart, 2014)

Hervey, T.K. and Trubek, L.G., 'Freedom to Provide Health Care Services within the EU: An Opportunity for Hybrid Governance' (2007) 13(3) *Columbia Journal of European Law* 623

Hervey, T.K. and Vanhercke, B., 'Health Care and the EU: The Law and Policy Patchwork', in E. Mossialos, G. Permanand, R. Baeten and T.K. Hervey (eds.), *Health Systems Governance in Europe: The Role of European Union Law and Policy* (Cambridge University Press, 2010)

Hervey, T.K., Busby, H. and Mohr, A., 'Ethical EU Law: The Influence of the European Group on Ethics in Science and New Technologies' (2008) 33 *European Law Review* 803

Hewson, B., 'Dancing on the Head of a Pin: Foetal Life and the European Convention' (2005) 13 *Feminist Legal Studies* 363

Higson, G.R., *Medical Device Safety: The Regulation of Medical Devices for Public Health* (Institute of Physics Publishing, 2002)

Hirst, M., 'Assisted Suicide after Purdy: The Unresolved Issue' (2009) 12 *Criminal Law Review* 870

Ho, C.M., 'Beyond Patents: Global Challenges to Affordable Medicine', in I.G. Cohen (ed.), *The Globalization of Health Care: Legal and Ethical Issues* (Oxford University Press, 2013)

Hodges, C., 'Developmental Risks: Unanswered Questions' (1998) 61(4) *Modern Law Review* 560

'Do We Need a European Medical Devices Agency?' (2004) 12(3) *Medical Law Review* 268

'The Regulation of Medicinal Products and Devices', in A. Grubb, J. Laing and J.V. McHale (eds.), *Principles of Medical Law*, 3rd edn (Oxford University Press, 2010)

Hoey, R., 'The EU Clinical Trials Directive: 3 Years On' (2007) 369(9575) *The Lancet* 1777

Hofstede, G., *Culture's Consequences: International Differences in Work-related Values* (Sage Publications, 1980)

Holland, D. and Pope, H., *EU Food Law and Policy* (Kluwer, 2004)

Hoppe, N., 'Innovative Tissue Engineering and its Regulation: The Search for Flexible Rules for Emerging Health Technologies', in M. Flear, A.-M. Farrell, T.K. Hervey and

T. Murphy (eds.), *European Law and New Health Technologies* (Oxford University Press, 2013)

Horowitz, M.D., Rosensweig, J.A. and Jones, C.A., 'Medical Tourism: Globalization of the Healthcare Marketplace' (2007) 9(4) *Medscape General Medicine* 33

House of Lords, *Behaviour Change*, Second Report of the Science and Technology Select Committee, Session 2010–2012, HL Paper 179

Howells, G., *Comparative Product Liability* (Dartmouth Publishing, 1993)

Howells, G. and Weatherill, S., *Consumer Protection Law*, 2nd edn (Ashgate, 2005)

Howells, G. and Wilhelmsson, T., *EC Consumer Law* (Ashgate, 1997)

Howse R. and Mavroidis, P., 'European Evolving Regulatory Strategy for GMOs and the Issue of Consistency with WTO Law: of Kine and Brine' (2000) 24 *Fordham International Law Journal* 317

Hughes, J., 'Buddhist Bioethics', in R. Ashcroft, H. Draper, A. Dawson and J. Macmillan (eds.), *Principles of Health Care Ethics*, 2nd edn (Wiley-Blackwell, 2007)

Hunt, P., 'The Human Right to the Highest Attainable Standard of Health: New Opportunities and Challenges' (2006) 100(7) *Transactions of the Royal Society of Tropical Medicine and Hygiene* 603

Huxtable, R., *Euthanasia, Ethics and Law from Conflict to Compromise* (Routledge, 2007)

International Federation of Red Cross and Red Crescent Societies Blood Programme, *Quality Manual and Development Manual* (International Federation of Red Cross and Red Crescent Societies Blood Programme, 1998)

Itzcovich, G., 'Legal Order, Legal Pluralism, Fundamental Principles: European and its Law in Three Concepts' (2012) 18(3) *European Law Journal* 358

Jääskinen, N., 'Fundamental Social Rights in the Charter – Are They Rights? Are They Fundamental?', in S. Peers, T.K. Hervey, J. Kenner and A. Ward (eds.), *The EU Charter of Fundamental Rights: A Commentary* (Hart, 2014)

Jackson, E., *Law and the Regulation of Medicines* (Hart, 2012)

Medical Law: Text, Cases, and Materials, 3rd edn (Oxford University Press, 2014)

Jacobs, J.M., *Doctors and Rules: A Sociology of Professional Values*, 2nd edn (Transaction Publishing, 1999)

Jain, D. and Darrow, J.J., 'Exploration of Compulsory Licensing as an Effective Policy Tool for Antiretroviral Drugs in India' (2013) 23(2) *Health Matrix* 425

Jarman, H., 'Collaboration and Consultation: Functional Representation in EU Stakeholder Dialogues' (2011) 33(4) *Journal of European Integration* 385

'Healthcare, Borders and Boundaries: Crossborder Health Markets and the Entrepreneurial State' (2014) 33(1) *Policy and Society* 1

'Trade in Services and the Public's Health: A Fortress Europe for Health', in S.L. Greer and P. Kurzer (eds.), *European Union Public Health Policy: Regional and Global Trends* (Routledge, 2013)

Jasanoff, S., 'Citizens at Risk: Cultures of Modernity in the US and the EU' (2002) 11(2) *Science As Culture* 363

Designs on Nature: Science and Democracy in Europe and the United States (Princeton University Press, 2007)

The Fifth Branch: Science Advisers as Policymakers (Harvard University Press, 1998)

Jha, P. and Chaloupka, F. (eds.), *Tobacco in Developing Countries* (Oxford University Press, 2000)

Jing-Bao, N., 'The Specious Idea of an Asian Bioethics: Beyond Dichotomizing East and West', in R. Ashcroft, H. Draper, A. Dawson and J. Macmillan (eds.), *Principles of Health Care Ethics*, 2nd edn (Wiley-Blackwell, 2007)

Joerges, C. and Dehousse, R. (eds.), *Good Governance in Europe's Integrated Market* (Oxford University Press, 2002)

Joerges, C. and Falke, J. (eds.), *Karl Polanyi, Globalisation and the Potential of Law in Transnational Markets* (Hart, 2011)

Johnson, T., Larkin, G. and Sachs, M. (eds.), *Health Professions and the State in Europe* (Routledge, 1995)

Joint Council of Europe and United Nations Study, *Trafficking in Organs, Tissues and Cells and Trafficking in Human Beings for the Purpose of the Removal of Organs* (Directorate General of Human Rights and Legal Affairs, Council of Europe, 2009)

Jones, A. and Sufrin, B., *EU Competition Law: Text, Cases, and Materials*, 5th edn (Oxford University Press, 2014)

Jones, J., 'Common Constitutional "Traditions": Can the Meaning of Dignity under German Law Guide the European Court of Justice?' [2004] *Public Law* 167

Jones, M., 'Informed Consent and other Fairy Stories' (1999) 7(2) *Medical Law Review* 104

Medical Negligence, 4th edn (Sweet & Maxwell, 2008)

Jorens, Y., 'The Right to Health Care Across Borders', in M. McKee, E. Mossialos and R. Baeten (eds.), *The Impact of EU Law on Health Care Systems* (PIE/Peter Lang, 2003)

Jost, T.S., 'Comparative and International Health Law' (2004) 14(1) *Health Matrix* 141

(ed.), *Health Care Coverage Determinations: An International Comparative Study* (Open University Press, 2004)

Readings in Comparative Health Law and Bioethics, 2nd edn (Carolina Academic Press, 2007)

Judt, T., *Postwar: A History of Europe since 1945* (Vintage, 2010)

Kattelus, M., 'Implementation of the Directive on the Application of Patients' Rights in Cross-border Healthcare (2011/24 EU) in Finland' (2014) 21(1) *European Journal of Health Law* 23

Keighley, T., 'Nursing and the EU Accession Process' (2006) 53(2) *International Nursing Review* 81

Kelemen, R.D., *Eurolegalism: The Transformation of Law and Regulation in the European Union* (Harvard University Press, 2011)

Kennedy, I., *The Unmasking of Medicine* (Allen & Unwin, 1981)

Kennedy, I. and Grubb, A., *Medical Law: Text with Materials*, 3rd edn (Butterworths, 2000)

Kenner, J., 'The EU Employment Title and the "Third Way": Making Soft Law Work?' (1999) 15 *International Journal of Comparative Labour Law and Industrial Relations* 33

Kentikelenis, A. and Papanicolas, I., 'Economic Crisis, Austerity and the Greek Public Health System' (2012) 22 *European Journal of Public Health* 4

Keown, J., *Euthanasia, Ethics and Public Policy: An Argument against Legalisation* (Cambridge University Press, 2002)

Khosla, M.,'Making Social Rights Conditional: Lessons from India' (2010) 8 *International Journal of Constitutional Law* 739

Kickbusch, I., 'Foreword', in W. Hein, S. Bartsch and L. Kohlmorgen (eds.), *Global Health Governance and the Fight against HIV/AIDS* (Palgrave Macmillan, 2007)

Kilpatrick, C., 'Article 21: Non-Discrimination', in S. Peers, T.K. Hervey, J. Kenner and A. Ward (eds.), *The EU Charter of Fundamental Rights: A Commentary* (Hart, 2014)

'Internal Market Architecture and the Accommodation of Labour Rights: As Good as it Gets?', in P. Syrpis (ed.), *The Judiciary, the Legislature and the Internal Market* (Cambridge University Press, 2012)

King, J.A., 'Constitutional Rights and Social Welfare: A Comment on the Canadian Chaoulli Health Care Decision' (2006) 69 *Modern Law Review* 631

Klabbers, P., 'Völkerrechtsfreundlich? International Law and the Union Legal Order', in P. Koutrakos (ed.), *European Foreign Policy: Legal and Political Perspectives* (Edward Elgar, 2011)

Klein, R., 'Learning from Others and Learning from Mistakes: Reflections on Health Policy Making', in T.M. Marmor, R. Freeman and K. Okma (eds.), *Comparative Studies and the Politics of Modern Medical Care* (Yale University Press, 2009)

The New Politics of the NHS: From Creation to Reinvention, 8th edn (Radcliffe, 2013)

Kleinman, D.L. and Moore, K. (eds.), *Routledge Handbook of Science, Technology and Society* (Routledge, 2014)

Klemperer, F., 'Working Abroad as a Doctor', in G. Eysenbach (ed.), *Medicine and Medical Education in Europe: The Eurodoctor* (Thieme, 1998)

Koch, B.A., 'Austrian Cases on Medical Liability' (2003) 10(2) *European Journal of Health Law* 91

Koch, T., 'Bioethics? A Grand Idea' (2008) 178(1) *Canadian Medical Association Journal* 116

Kotzeva, D., 'International Influence on Bulgarian Health Law and Policy', unpublished PhD thesis, University of Wisconsin-Madison, 2006

Koutrakos, P., *EU International Relations Law* (Hart, 2006)

(ed.), *European Foreign Policy: Legal and Political Perspectives* (Edward Elgar, 2011)

Kovar, J-P., 'Jurisdiction of the French NCA: The French Commercial Supreme Court Rejects an Appeal against a Decision of the Court of Appeal of Paris (CNOCD, Santéclair)' (2011) 3(38200) *Concurrences* 212

Krajewski, M., 'Commodifying and Embedding Services of General Interests in Transnational Contexts: The Example of Healthcare Liberalisation in the EU and the WTO', in C. Joerges and J. Falke (eds.), *Karl Polanyi, Globalisation and the Potential of Law in Transnational Markets* (Hart, 2011)

'Patient Mobility Beyond Calais: Health Services Under WTO Law', in J.W. Van de Gronden, E. Szyszczak, U. Neergaard and M. Krajewski (eds.), *Health Care and EU Law* (Springer, 2011)

Krajewski, M., Neergaard, U. and Van de Gronden, J.W. (eds.), *The Changing Legal Framework for Services of General Interest in Europe: Between Competition and Solidarity* (TMC Asser Press, 2009)

Kramer, D.B., Shuai Xu. and Kesselheim, A.S., 'Regulation of Medical Devices in the USA and the EU' (2012) 366(9) *New England Journal of Medicine* 848

Kranenborg, H., 'Article 8: Protection of Personal Data', in S. Peers, T.K. Hervey, J. Kenner and A. Ward (eds.), *The EU Charter of Fundamental Rights: A Commentary* (Hart, 2014)

Krapohl, 'Risk Regulation in the EU between Interests and Expertise: The Case of BSE' (2003) 10(2) *Journal of European Public Policy* 189

Kreeftmeijer-Vegter, A.R., De Boer, A., Van Der Vlugt-Meijer, R. and De Vries, P.J., 'The Influence of the European Paediatric Regulation on Marketing Authorization of Orphan Drugs for Children' (2014) 9 *Orphanet Journal of Rare Diseases* 120

Kretzschmar, M.D., 'Drug Safe Harbour Provisions in the USA and Europe: Implications for the Emerging Biosimilars Industry' (2014) 9(4) *Journal of Intellectual Property Law & Practice* 298

Krisch, N., 'The Open Architecture of European Human Rights Law' (2008) 71(2) *Modern Law Review* 183

Krishnan, S., 'What's the Consensus: The Grand Chamber's Decision on Abortion in A, B and C v. Ireland' (2011) 2 *European Human Rights Review* 200

Kritikos, M., 'Traditional Risk Analysis and Releases of GMOs into the European Union: Space for Non-scientific Factors?' (2009) 34(3) *European Law Review* 405

Kurzer, P., 'Non-Communicable Diseases: The EU Declares War on Fat', in S.L. Greer and P. Kurzer (eds.), *European Union Public Health Policy: Regional and Global Trends* (Routledge, 2013)

Kulik, M.C., Menvielle, G., Eikemo, T.A., et al., 'Educational Inequalities in Three Smoking-Related Causes of Death in 18 European Populations' (2014) 16(5) *Nicotine and Tobacco Research* 507

Lamb, D., *Organ Transplants and Ethics* (Routledge, 1990)

Lambers Heerspink, H.J., Dobre, D., Hillege, et al., 'Does the Clinical Trials Directive Really Improve Clinical Trial Approval Time' (2008) 66(4) *British Journal of Clinical Pharmacology* 546

Lamont, R., 'Article 24: The Rights of the Child', in S. Peers, T.K. Hervey, J. Kenner and A. Ward (eds.), *The EU Charter of Fundamental Rights: A Commentary* (Hart, 2014)

Latham, M., '"If it ain't broke don't fix it": Scandals, "Risk" and Cosmetic Surgery Regulation in the UK and France' (2014) 22(3) *Medical Law Review* 384
    Regulating Reproduction: A Century of Conflict in Britain and France (Manchester University Press, 2002)

Laudan, R., 'Slow Food: The French Terroir Strategy, and Culinary Modernism', essay review of Carlos Petrini (trans. W. McCuaig), Slow Food: The Case for Taste (New York: Columbia University Press, 2011) (2004) 7(2) *Food Culture and Society: An International Journal of Multidisciplinary Research* 133

Láufs, A., Uhlenbruch, W. and Genzel, H., *Handbuch des Artzrechts* (CH Beck, 2002)

Laurie, G., *Genetic Privacy: A Challenge to Medico-Legal Norms* (Cambridge University Press, 2007)
    'In Defence of Ignorance: Genetic Information and the Right Not to Know' (1999) 6(2) *European Journal of Health Law* 119
    'Protecting and Promoting Privacy in an Uncertain World: Further Defences of Ignorance and the Right Not to Know' (2000) 7(2) *European Journal of Health Law* 185

Laurie, G. and Postan, E., 'Rhetoric or Reality: What is the Legal Status of the Consent Form in Health-related Research?' (2013) 21(3) *Medical Law Review* 371

Law, J., *Big Pharma: How the World's Biggest Drug Companies Control Illness* (Constable, 2006)

Lawless, J., 'EFSA Under Pressure: Emerging Risks, Emergencies and Crises', in A. Alemanno and S. Gabbi (eds.), *Foundations of EU Food Law and Policy: Ten Years of the European Food Safety Authority* (Ashgate, 2014)

Le Grand, J., *The Other Invisible Hand: Delivering Public Services through Choice and Competition* (Princeton University Press, 2007)

Lear, J., Mossialos, E. and Karl, B., 'EU Competition Law and Health Policy', in E. Mossialos, G. Permanand, R. Baeten and T.K. Hervey (eds.), *Health Systems Governance in Europe: The Role of European Union Law and Policy* (Cambridge University Press, 2010)

Lee, M., 'Beyond Safety: The Broadening Scope of Risk Regulation' (2009) 62(1) *Current Legal Problems* 242

   'The Precautionary Principle in the Court of First Instance' (2003) 14(1) *King's College Law Journal* 86

   'Risk and Beyond: EU Regulation of Nanotechnology' (2010) 35(6) *European Law Review* 799

Lee, R.G. and Morgan, D. (eds.), *Birthrights* (Routledge, 1989)

   Human Fertilisation and Embryology: Regulating the Reproductive Revolution (Blackstones Press, 2001)

Leenen, H.J.J., 'Development of Patients' Rights and Instruments for the Promotion of Patients' Rights' (1996) 3 *European Journal of Health Law* 105

   'The European Journal of Health Law: A New Publication' (1994) 1 *European Journal of Health Law* 1

   'The Rights of Patients in Europe' (1994) 1 *European Journal of Health Law* 5

Legido-Quigley, H., Glinos, I., Baeten, R. and McKee, M., 'Patient Mobility in the European Union' (2007) 334 *British Medical Journal* 188

Legido-Quigley, H., Otero,L., la Parra, D., et al., 'Will Austerity Cuts Dismantle the Spanish Health Care System?' [2013] *British Medical Journal* 346:f2363

Leibfried, S. and Pierson, P. (eds.), *European Social Policy: Between Fragmentation and Integration* (The Brookings Institution, 1995)

Lenaerts, K., 'Interlocking Legal Orders in the EU and Comparative Law' (2003) 52 *International and Comparative Law Quarterly* 873

Lenaerts, K. and Foubert, P., 'Social Rights in the Case-Law of the European Court of Justice' (2001) 28 *Legal Issues of Economic Integration* 267

Lemmens, T., 'Pharmaceutical Knowledge Governance: A Human Rights Perspective' (2013) 41(1) *Journal of Law, Medicine and Ethics* 163

Lethbridge, J., 'The Promotion of Investment Alliances by the World Bank: Implications for National Health Policy' (2005) 5 *Global Social Policy* 203

Levine, A.D. and Wolf, L.E., 'The Roles and Responsibilities of Physicians in Patients' Decisions about Unproven Stem Cell Therapies', in I.G. Cohen (ed.), *The Globalization of Health Care: Legal and Ethical Issues* (Oxford University Press, 2013)

Lewis, P., *Assisted Dying and Legal Change* (Oxford University Press, 2007)

Lewis, P. and Black, I., 'Reporting and Scrutiny of Reported Cases in Four Jurisdictions where Assisted Dying is Lawful: A Review of the Cases in Belgium, Oregon, the Netherlands and Switzerland' (2013) 13(4) *Medical Law International* 221

Lewis, R., Harrison, A. and Smith J., *From Quasi Markets to Markets in the NHS: What Does This Mean for the Purchasing of Health Services?* (King's Fund, 2009)

Liddel, K., Bion, J., Chamberlain, D., et al., 'Medical Research Involving Incapacitated Adults, Implications of the EU Clinical Trials Directive' (2006) 14 *Medical Law Review* 367

Lie, R.K., Emanuel, E., Grady, C. and Wendler, D., 'The Standard of Care Debate: The Declaration of Helsinki Versus the International Consensus Opinion' (2004) 30(2) *Journal of Medical Ethics* 190

Littoz-Monnet, A., 'The Role of Independent Regulators in Policy Making: Venue Shopping and Framing Strategies in the EU Regulation of Old Wives' Cures' (2014) 53(1) *European Journal of Political Research* (2014) 1

Livrani, M. and Coker, R., 'Protecting Europe from Diseases: From the International Sanitary Conferences to the ECDC' (2012) 37(6) *Journal of Health Politics, Policy and Law* 915

Loebel, O., 'The Renew Deal: The Fall of Regulation and the Rise of Governance in Contemporary Legal Thought'(2004) 89 *Minnesota Law Review* 262

Löfgren, H. and Williams, O.D. (eds.), *The New Political Economy of Pharmaceuticals: Production, Innovation and TRIPS in the Global South* (Palgrave Macmillan, 2013)

London, L. and Schneider, H., 'Globalization and Health Inequalities: Can a Human Rights Paradigm Create Space for Civil Society Action?' (2012) 74 (1) *Social Science and Medicine* 6

Longley, D., *Health Care Constitutions* (Routledge, 1996)

Lord, C. and Magnette, P., 'E Pluribus Unum? Creative Disagreement about Legitimacy in the European Union' (2004) 42(1) *Journal of Common Market Studies* 183

Luce, B.R., Kramer, J.M., Goodman, S.N., et al., 'Rethinking Randomized Clinical Trials for Comparative Effectiveness Research: The Need for Transformational Change' (2009) 151(3) *Annals of Internal Medicine* 206

Luckhaus, L., 'EU Social Security Law', in A.I. Ogus and N.J. Wikeley (eds.), *The Law of Social Security*, 5th edn (Oxford University Press, 2002)

Lurie, P. and Wolf, S.M., 'Unethical Trials of Interventions to Reduce Perinatal Transmission of the Human Immunodeficiency Virus in Developing Countries' (1997) 337(12) *New England Journal of Medicine* 853

McCarthy, M. and Rees, S., *Health Systems and Public Health Medicine in the EC* (Royal College of Physicians, 1992)

MacCormick, N., *Questioning Sovereignty: Law, State, and Nation in the European Commonwealth* (Oxford University Press, 1999)

McCrudden, C., 'Human Dignity and Judicial Interpretation of Human Rights' (2008) 19(4) *European Journal of International Law* 655

McGlynn, C., *Families and the European Union* (Cambridge University Press, 2006)

McGuinness, S., 'A, B and C leads to D for Delegation!' 19(3) *Medical Law Review* (2011) 476

McGuinness, S. and McHale, J.V., 'Transnational Crimes Related to Health: How Should Law Respond to Illicit Organ Tourism?' (2014) 34(4) *Legal Studies* 682

McHale, J.V., 'Enforcing Health Care Rights in the English Courts', in R. Burchill, D. Harris and A. Owers (eds.), *Economic, Social and Cultural Rights: Their Implementation in UK Law (University of Nottingham Human Rights Centre, 1999)*

'Fundamental Rights and Health Care', in E. Mossialos, G. Permanand, R. Baeten and T.K. Hervey (eds.), *Health Systems Governance in Europe: The Role of European Union Law and Policy* (Cambridge University Press, 2010)

'Law, Regulation and Public Health Research: A Case for Fundamental Reform?' (2010) 63(1) *Current Legal Problems* 475

'Medical Malpractice in England: Current Trends' 10(2) *European Journal of Health Law* (2003) 135

'Nanomedicine and the EU: Some Legal, Ethical and Regulatory Challenges' (2009) 16(1) *Maastricht Journal of European and Comparative Law* 65

McHale, J.V. and Fox, M., *Health Care Law: Text and Materials*, 2nd edn (Sweet & Maxwell, 2007)

McKee, M., Hervey, T.K. and Gilmore, A. 'Public Health Policies', in E. Mossialos, G. Permanand, R. Baeten and T.K. Hervey (eds.), *Health Systems Governance in Europe: The Role of European Union Law and Policy* (Cambridge University Press, 2010)

McKee, M., Mossialos, E. and Baeten, R. (eds.), *The Impact of EU Law on Health Care Systems* (PIE/Peter Lang, 2003)

McLean, A., "From Sidaway to Pearce and Beyond: Is the Legal Regulation of Consent any Better Following a Quarter of a Century of Judicial Scrutiny?' (2012) 20(1) *Medical Law Review* 108

McLean, S., 'Can No-Fault Analysis Ease the Problems of Medical Injury Litigation?', in S. McLean (ed.), *Compensation for Damage: An International Perspective* (Ashgate, 1993)

(ed.), *Compensation for Damage: An International Perspective* (Ashgate, 1993)

MacLehose, L., McKee, M. and Weinberg, J., 'Responding to the Challenge of Communicable Disease in Europe' (2002) 295(5562) *Science* 2047

MacMaoláin, C., *EU Food Law: Protecting Consumers and Health in a Common Market* (Hart, 2007)

'Free Movement of Foodstuffs, Quality Requirements and Consumer Protection: Have the Court and the Commission Both Got it Wrong?' (2001) 26(5) *European Law Review* 413

'Waiter! There's a Beetle in my Soup. Yes Sir, That's E120: Disparities between Actual Individual Behaviour and Regulating Food Labelling for the Average Consumer in EU Law' (2008) 45(4) *Common Market Law Review* 1147

McNeill, P., 'Paying People to Participate in Research: Why Not?' (1997) 11(5) *Bioethics* 390

Madden, D., *Medical Law in Ireland*, 2nd edn (Kluwer Law International, 2014)

Medicine, Ethics and the Law in Ireland, 2nd edn (Bloomsbury Professional, 2011)

Maduro, M. and Azoulai, L. (eds.), *The Past and Future of EU Law: The Classics of EU Law Revisited on the 50th Anniversary of the Rome Treaty* (Hart, 2010)

Magnusson, J., Vanbræk, K. and Saltman, R. (eds.), *Nordic Healthcare Systems: Recent Reforms and Current Policy Challenges* (Open University Press, 2009)

Mahalatchimy, A., 'Access to Advanced Therapy Medicinal Products in the EU: Where Do We Stand?' (2011) 18(3) *European Journal of Health Law* 305

Maher, I., 'Introduction: Regulating Markets and Social Europe. New Governance in the EU' (2009) 15 *European Law Journal* 155

Majone, G., *Regulating Europe* (Routledge, 1996)

'What Price Safety? The Precautionary Principle and its Policy Implications (2002) 40(1) *Journal of Common Market Studies* 89

'Malta, Abuse of Dominant Position, Blood', Case Comment (2007) 28 *European Competition Law Review* 120

Mann, J.M., Gostin, L., Gruskin, S., Brennan, T., et al., 'Health and Human Rights' (1994) 1(1) *Health and Human Rights* 6

Mann, J.M., Gruskin, S., Grodin, M.A. and Annas, G.J. (eds.), *Health and Human Rights: A Reader* (Routledge, 1999)

Marlier, E. and Natali, D. (eds.), with Van Dam, R., *Europe 2020: Towards a More Social EU?* (PIE/Peter Lang, 2010)

Marmor, T.M., 'Canada's Supreme Court and its National Health Insurance Program: Evaluating the Landmark Chaoulli Decision from a Comparative Perspective' (2006) 44 *Osgoode Hall Law Journal* 311

Marmor, T.M. and Klein, R., *Politics, Health and Health Care: Selected Essays* (Yale University Press, 2012)

Marmor, T.M., Freeman R. and Okma, K., 'Comparative Perspectives and Policy Learning in the World of Health Care' (2005) 7(4) *Journal of Comparative Policy Analysis* 331

Marqusee, M., *The Price of Experience: Writings on Living with Cancer* (OR Books, 2014)

Marreé J. and Groenewegen, P., *Back to Bismarck: Eastern European Health Care Systems in Transition* (Ashgate, 1997)

Marshall, J., 'A Right to Personal Autonomy at the European Court of Human Rights' (2008) 13(3) *European Human Rights Law Review* 337

Marteau, T.M., Oliver, O. and Ashcroft, R., 'Changing Behaviour through State Intervention: When Does an Acceptable Nudge Become an Unacceptable Shove?' (2009) 338(7687) *British Medical Journal* 121

Martin-Casals, M., Igualada, J.R. and Feliu, J.S., 'Medical Malpractice Liability in Spain: Cases, Trends and Developments' (2003) 10(2) *European Journal of Health Law* 153

Mason, J.K., 'What's in a Name? The Vagaries of Vo v. France (2005) 17(5) *Child and Family Law Quarterly* 97

Mason, K. and Laurie, G., *Mason & McCall Smith's Law and Medical Ethics*, 9th edn (Oxford University Press, 2013)

Mason, S. and Megone, C. (eds.), *European Neonatal Research: Consent, Ethics Committees and Law* (Ashgate, 2001)

Master, Z., Zarzeczny, A., Rachul, C. and Caulfield, T., 'What's Missing? Discussing Stem Cell Translational Research in Educational Information on Stem Cell "Tourism"' (2013) 41(1) *Journal of Law Medicine and Ethics* 254

Matthews, D., 'The Lisbon Treaty, Trade Agreements and the Enforcement of Intellectual Property Rights' (2010) 32(3) *European Intellectual Property Review* 104

Matthews, D. and Munoz-Tellez, V., 'Bilateral Technical Assistance and TRIPS: The US, Japan and the EC in Comparative Perspective' (2006) 9(6) *Journal of World Intellectual Property* 629

Mätze, M., 'Institutional Resources for Communicable Disease Control in Europe: Diversity across Time and Place' (2012) 37(6) *Journal of Health Politics, Policy and Law* 965

Maurice, 'The European Union Adds Teeth to its Anti-Tobacco Legislation' (2014) 383(9920) *The Lancet* 857

Megone, C., et al., 'The Structure, Composition and Operation of European Research Ethics Committees', in S. Mason and C. Megone (eds.), *European Neonatal Research: Consent, Ethics Committees and Law* (Ashgate, 2001)

Mercurio, B. and Shao, D., 'A Precautionary Approach to Decision Making: The Evolving Jurisprudence on Article 5.7 of the SPS Agreement' (2010) 2 *Trade, Law and Development* 195

Merkur, S., Mossialos, E., Long, M. and McKee, M., 'Physician Revalidation in Europe' (2008) 8 *Clinical Medicine* 371

Metx, C. and Hoppe, N., 'Organ Transplantation in Germany: Regulating Scandals and Scandalous Regulation' (2013) 20(2) *European Journal of Health Law* 113

Metzl, J.M. and Kirkland, A. (eds.), *Against Health: How Health Became the New Morality* (New York University Press, 2010)

Michalowski, S., 'Article 3: Right to the Integrity of the Person', in S. Peers, T.K. Hervey, J. Kenner and A. Ward (eds.), *The EU Charter of Fundamental Rights: A Commentary* (Hart, 2014)

　'Health Care Law', in S. Peers and A. Ward (eds.), *The European Union Charter of Fundamental Rights* (Hart, 2004)

Michielsen, P., 'Presumed Consent to Organ Donation: 10 Years' Experience in Belgium' (1996) 89(12) *Jounal of the Royal Society of Medicine* 663

Millns, S., 'Consolidating Bio-rights in Europe', in F. Francioni (ed.), *Biotechnologies and International Human Rights* (Hart, 2007)

　'Reproducing Inequalities: Assisted Conception and the Challenge of Legal Pluralism' (2002) 24 *Journal of Social Welfare and Family Law* 19

Milward, A., *The European Rescue of the Nation State*, 2nd edn (Routledge, 2000)

Miola, J., 'The Impact of Less Deference to the Medical Profession', in A. Algrahni, R. Bennett and S. Ost (eds.), *The Criminal Law and Bioethical Conflict: Walking the Tightrope* (Cambridge University Press, 2012)

　Medical Law and Medical Ethics: A Symbiotic Relationship (Hart, 2007)

Moniruzzaman, M., '"Living Cadavers" in Bangladesh: Bioviolence in the Human Organ Bazaar' (2012) 26(1) *Medical Anthropology Quarterly* 69

Montgomery, J., *Health Care Law*, 2nd edn (Oxford University Press, 2002)

　'The Impact of EU Law on English Health Care Law', in M. Dougan and E. Spaventa (eds.), *Social Welfare and EU Law* (Hart, 2005)

　'Medical Law in the Shadow of Hippocrates' (1989) 52 *Modern Law Review* 566

　'Medicalizing Crime: Criminalizing Health? The Role of Law', in C.A. Erin and E. Ost (eds.), *The Criminal Justice System and Health Care Law* (Oxford University Press, 2007)

　'Recognising a Right to Health', in R. Beddard and D.M. Hill (eds.), *Economic, Social and Cultural Rights: Progress and Achievement* (Macmillan, 1992)

　'Time for a Paradigm Shift? Medical Law in Transition' (2000) 53 *Current Legal Problems* 363

Monti, G., *EC Competition Law* (Cambridge University Press, 2007)

Moran, M., 'Global Health Policy Responses to the World's Neglected Diseases', in G.W. Brown, G. Yamey and S. Wamala (eds.), *The Handbook of Global Health Policy* (Wiley, 2014)

Moran, M. and Wood, B., *States, Regulation and the Medical Profession* (Open University Press, 1993)

Moran, M., Rein, M. and Goodin, R. (eds.), *Oxford Handbook of Public Policy* (Oxford University Press, 2006)

Moravcsik, A., 'In Defence of the Democratic Deficit: Reassessing Legitimacy in the EU' (2002) 40(4) *Journal of Common Market Studies* 603

Moreno, L. and Palier, B., 'The Europeanisation of Welfare: Paradigm Shifts and Social Policy Reforms', in P. Taylor-Gooby, *Ideas and Welfare State Reform in Western Europe* (Palgrave Macmillan, 2005)

Morgan, D., *Issues in Medical Law and Ethics* (Cavendish, 2001)

Morgan, D. and Lee, R.G., 'In the Name of the Father? Ex parte Blood: Dealing with Novelty and Anomaly' (1997) 60 *Modern Law Review* 840

Mossialos, E. and Abel-Smith, B., 'The Regulation of the European Pharmaceutical Industry', in S. Stavridis, E. Mossialos, R. Morgan and H. Machlin (eds.), *New Challenges to the EU: Policies and Policy-Making* (Dartmouth, 1997)

Mossialos, E., and McKee, M. (eds.), *EU Law and the Social Character of Health Care* (PIE/Peter Lang, 2004)

Mossialos, E., Dixon, A., Figueras, J. and Kutzin, J. (eds.), *Funding Health Care: Options for Europe* (Open University Press, 2002)

Mossialos, E., Permanand, G., Baeten, R. and Hervey, T.K., 'Health Systems Governance in Europe: The Role of EU Law and Policy', in E. Mossialos, G. Permanand, R. Baeten and T.K. Hervey (eds.), *Health Systems Governance in Europe: The Role of European Union Law and Policy* (Cambridge University Press, 2010)

(eds.), *Health Systems Governance in Europe: The Role of European Union Law and Policy* (Cambridge University Press, 2010)

Moynihan, R. and Cassels, A., *Selling Sickness: How the World's Biggest Pharmaceutical Companies are Turning Us All into Patients* (Nation Books, 2006)

Murphy, T., *Health and Human Rights* (Hart, 2013)

(ed.), *New Technologies and Human Rights* (Oxford University Press, 2009)

'Repetition, Revolution, and Resonance', in T. Murphy (ed.), *New Technologies and Human Rights* (Oxford University Press, 2009)

Muscat, N.A., Grech, K., Cachia, J.M. and Xuereb, D., 'Sharing Capacities: Malta and the United Kingdom', in M. Rosenmöller, M. McKee and R. Baeten (eds.), *Patient Mobility in the European Union: Learning from Experience* (European Observatory on Health Systems and Policies, 2006)

Mutcherson, K.M., 'Open Fertility Borders: Defending Access to Cross Border Fertility Care in the United States', in I.G. Cohen (ed.), *The Globalization of Health Care: Legal and Ethical Issues* (Oxford University Press, 2013)

Mythen, G. and Walklate, S. (eds.), *Beyond the Risk Society: Critical Reflections on Risk and Human Security* (Open University Press, 2006)

Naci, H., Spackman, E. and Fleurence, F., 'National Approaches to Comparative Effectiveness Research', in B. Sobolev (ed.), *Handbook of Health Services Research* (forthcoming)

Naqvi, S.A.A., Ali, B., Mazhar, F., et al., 'A Socioeconomic Survey of Kidney Vendors in Pakistan' (2007) 20(11) *Transplant International* 934

National Research Council, *Risk Assessment in the Federal Government: Managing the Process* (National Academy, 1993)

Navarro-Michel, M., 'New Health Technologies and their Impact on EU Product Liability Regulations', in M. Flear, A.-M. Farrell, T.K. Hervey and T. Murphy (eds.), *European Law and New Health Technologies* (Oxford University Press, 2013)

Neergaard, U., 'Services of General Economic Interest: The Nature of the Beast', in M. Krajewski, U. Neergaard and J.W. Van de Gronden (eds.), *The Changing Legal Framework for Services of General Interest in Europe: Between Competition and Solidarity* (TMC Asser Press, 2009)

NeJaime, D., 'When New Governance Fails' (2009) 70 *Ohio State Law Journal* 323

Nelkin, D., *Technological Decisions and Democracy: European Experiments in Public Participation* (Sage, 1977)

Nelkin, D., (ed.), *Controversy: Politics of Technical Decisions* (Sage, 1992)

New, B., Solomon, M., Dingwall R. and McHale J.V, *King's Fund Research Report no. 18: A Question of Give and Take* (King's Fund, 1994)

Newdick, C., 'Citizenship, Free Movement and Health Care: Cementing individual Rights by Corroding Social Solidarity' (2006) 43(6) *Common Market Law Review* 1645

'The Development Risk Defence of the Consumer Protection Act 1987' (1988) 47 *Cambridge Law Journal* 455

'Disrupting the Community: Saving Public Health Ethics from the EU Internal Market', in J.W. Van de Gronden, E. Szyszczak, U. Neergaard and M. Krajewski (eds.), *Health Care and EU Law* (Springer, 2011)

'The European Court of Justice, Transnational Health Care, and Social Citizenship: Accidental Death of a Concept?' (2009) 26 *Wisconsin International Law Journal* 845

'Preserving Social Citizenship in Health Care Markets: There May be Trouble Ahead' (2008) 2 *McGill Journal of Law and Health* 93

Who Should We Treat? Rights, Rationing and Resources in the NHS, 2nd edn (Oxford University Press, 2005)

Nickless, J., 'The Internal Market and the Social Nature of Health Care', in M. McKee, E. Mossialos and R. Baeten (eds.), *The Impact of EU Law on Health Care Systems* (PIE/Peter Lang, 2003)

'Were the ECJ Decisions in *Kohll* and *Decker* Right?' 7(1) *Eurohealth* (2001) 16

Nihoul, P. and Simon, A.C. (eds.), *L'Europe et les soins de santé: Marché intérieur, sécurité sociale, concurrence* (Larcier, 2005)

Normand, E.M. and Vaughan, P. (eds.), *Europe without Frontiers: The Implications for Health* (Wiley, 1993)

Nugent, N. (ed.), *European Union 1996: the Annual Review*, published in association with *Journal of Common Market Studies* (1997)

Nwaka, S. and Ridley, R.G., 'Virtual Drug Discovery and Development for Neglected Diseases through Public–Private Partnerships' (2003) 2 *Nature Reviews Drug Discovery* 919

Nys, H., 'Comparative Health Law and the Harmonisation of Patients' Rights in Europe' (2001) 8(4) *European Journal of Health Law* 317

'Ethical Committees in Belgium' (1995) 2 *European Journal of Health Law* 175

(ed.), *International Encyclopedia of Laws: Medical Law*, 63rd supplement (Kluwer Law International, 1994)

Medical Law in Belgium, 2nd edn (Kluwer Law International, 2012)

La Médicine et Le Droit (Kluwer Édit Juridiques, 1995)

'New European Rules Regarding the Approval of Clinical Trials, the Role of Research Ethics Committees and the Protection of Subjects' (2012) 60(6) *Archivum Immunologiae et Therapiae Experimentalis* 405

'Organ Transplantation and the Proposed Directive on Cross-Border Care' (2010) 17(5) *European Journal of Health Law* 427

'The Transposition of the Directive on Patients' Rights in Cross-Border Healthcare in National Law by the Member States: Still a Lot of Effort to be Made and Questions to Be Answered', Editorial (2014) 21(1) *European Journal of Health Law* 1

O'Cinneide, C., 'Article 25: The Rights of the Elderly', in S. Peers, T.K. Hervey, J. Kenner and A. Ward (eds.), *The EU Charter of Fundamental Rights: A Commentary* (Hart, 2014)

O'Connell, P., *Vindicating Socio-Economic Rights: International Standards and Comparative Experiences* (Oxford University Press, 2012)

O'Donovan, K., 'Taking a Neutral Stance on the Legal Protection of the Fetus' (2006) 14 *Medical Law Review* 115

O'Keeffe, D. and Emiliou, N. (eds.), *The European Union and World Trade Law* (Wiley, 1996)

O'Leary, S., 'Free Movement of Persons and Services', in P. Craig and G. de Búrca (eds.), *The Evolution of EU Law*, 2nd edn (Oxford University Press, 2011)

O'Neill, O., *A Question of Trust* (Cambridge University Press, 2002)

O'Reilly, J., Busse R., Häkkinen, U., et al., 'Paying for Hospital Care: The Experience with Implementing Activity-Based Funding in Five European Countries' (2012) 7 *Health Economics, Policy and Law* 73

O'Rourke, R., 'EFSA's Communication Strategy: A Critical Appraisal', in A. Alemanno and S. Gabbi (eds.), *Foundations of EU Food Law and Policy: Ten Years of the European Food Safety Authority* (Ashgate, 2014)

European Food Law (Palladian Law Publishing, 1999)

European Food Law, 3rd edn (Sweet & Maxwell, 2005)

O'Sullivan, D., 'The Allocation of Scarce Resources and the Right to Life under the European Convention on Human Rights' [1998] *Public Law* 389

Obermeier, A., *The End of Territoriality? The Impact of ECJ rulings on British, German and French Social Policy* (Ashgate, 2009)

Odudu, O., *The Boundaries of EC Competition Law* (Oxford University Press, 2006)

Offe, C., 'The European Model of "Social" Capitalism: Can it Survive European Integration?' (2003) 11(4) *Journal of Political Philosophy* 437

Offergeld, R. and Burger, R., 'Remuneration of Blood Donors and its Impact on Transfusion Safety" (2003) 85(1) *Vox Sanguinis* 49

Ognyanova, D. and Busse, R., 'A Destination and a Source: Germany Manages Regional Health Workforce Disparities with Foreign Medical Doctors', in M. Wismar, C.B. Maier, I.A. Glinos, et al. (eds.), 'Health Professional Mobility and Health Systems: Evidence from 17 European Countries' (WHO, 2011) www.euro.who.int/__data/assets/pdf_file/0017/152324/e95812.pdf?ua=1

Oliver, A. and Ubel, P., 'Nudging the Obese: A UK–US Comparison' (2014) 9(3) *Health Economics, Policy and Law* 329

Olsena, S., 'Implementation of the Patients' Rights in Cross-border Healthcare Directive in Latvia' (2014) 21(1) *European Journal of Health Law* 46

Ost, D.E., 'The "Right" Not to Know' (1984) 9(3) *Journal of Medicine and Philosophy* 301

Palm, W. and Glinos, I.A., 'Enabling Patient Mobility in the EU: Between Free Movement and Coordination', in E. Mossialos, G. Permanand, R. Baeten and T.K. Hervey (eds.), *Health Systems Governance in Europe: The Role of European Union Law and Policy* (Cambridge University Press, 2010)

Pattinson, S., *Medical Law and Ethics*, 4th edn (Sweet & Maxwell, 2014)

Payer, L., *Disease-mongers: How Doctors, Drug Companies, and Insurers are Making You Feel Sick* (Wiley, 1992)

Pearson Commission, *Report of the Royal Commission on the Civil Liability and Compensation for Personal Injury*, Cmnd 7054-1 (1978)

Peers, S. and Prechal, S., 'Article 52: Scope and Interpretation of Rights and Principles', in S. Peers, T.K. Hervey, J. Kenner and A. Ward (eds.), *The EU Charter of Fundamental Rights: A Commentary* (Hart, 2014)

Peers, S. and Ward, A. (eds.), *The European Union Charter of Fundamental Rights* (Hart, 2004)

Peers, S., Hervey, T.K., Kenner, J. and Ward, A. (eds.), *The EU Charter of Fundamental Rights: A Commentary* (Hart, 2014)

Peeters, M., 'Free Movement of Patients: Directive 2011/24 on the Application of Patients' Rights in Cross-Border Healthcare' (2012) 19(1) *European Journal of Health Law* 29

Peeters, M., McKee, M. and Merkur, S., 'EU Law and Health Professionals', in E. Mossialos, G. Permanand, R. Baeten and T.K. Hervey (eds.), *Health Systems Governance in Europe: The Role of European Union Law and Policy* (Cambridge University Press, 2010)

Pennings, G., 'The Draft Patient Mobility Directive and the Coordination Regulations of Social Security', in J.W. Van de Gronden, E. Szyszczak, U. Neergaard and M. Krajewski (eds.), *Health Care and EU Law* (Springer, 2011)

Pennings, G., Autin, C., Decleer, W., et al., 'Cross Border Reproductive Care in Belgium' (2009) 24(12) *Human Reproduction* 3108

Pennings, G., De Wert, G., Shenfield, F., et al., 'ESHRE Task Force on Ethics and Law 15: Cross-border Reproductive Care' (2008) 23(10) *Human Reproduction* 2182

Pereira, A., 'Transplantation of Organs and Tissues and Some Reflections on the "Solidarity" of the Human Cadaver in Portugal' 18(1) *European Journal of Health Law* 55

Permanand, G. and Vos, E., 'EU Regulatory Agencies and Health Protection', in E. Mossialos, G. Permanand, R. Baeten and T.K. Hervey (eds.), *Health Systems Governance in Europe: The Role of European Union Law and Policy* (Cambridge University Press, 2010)

Perrett, R.W., 'Buddhism, Euthanasia and the Sanctity of Life' (1996) 22 *Journal of Medical Ethics* 309

Pessini, L., de Paul de Barchifontaine, C. and Lolas Stepke, F. (eds.), *Ibero-American Bioethics* (Springer, 2011)

Pestieau, P., *The Welfare State in the European Union: Economic and Social Perspectives* (Oxford University Press, 2005)

Petersmann E-U. and Pollack, M.A. (eds.), *Transatlantic Economic Disputes: The EU, the US, and the WTO* (Oxford University Press, 2003)

Phelan, D.R., 'The Right to Life of the Unborn v. Promotion of Trade in Services: The European Court of Justice and the Normative Shaping of the European Union' (1992) 55 *Modern Law Review* 670

Pierson, P., 'Coping with Permanent Austerity: Welfare State Restructuring in Affluent Democracies', in P. Pierson (ed.), *The New Politics of the Welfare State* (Oxford University Press, 2001)

'Increasing Returns, Path Dependence, and the Study of Politics' (2000) 94(2) *American Political Science Review* 251

(ed.), *The New Politics of the Welfare State* (Oxford University Press, 2001)

'The Path to European Integration: A Historical Institutionalist Analysis' (1996) 29 *Comparative Political Studies* 123

Pixton, W., Direick, K. and Nys, H., 'The Implementation of Directive 2001/201 EC into Belgian Law and Specific Provisions on Paediatric Practice' (2008) 15 *European Journal of Health Law* 153

Plomer, A., 'The European Group on Ethics: Law, Politics and the Limits of Moral Integration in Europe' (2008) 14 *European Law Journal* 839

'A Foetal Right to Life? The Case of Vo v. France' (2005) 5(2) *Human Rights Law Review* 311

Plotnikova, E.V., 'Cross-border Mobility of Health Professionals: Contesting Patients' Rights to Health' (2012) 74(1) *Social Science and Medicine* 20

Pogge, T.W., 'Human Rights and Global Health: A Research Program' (2005) 36(1–2) *Metaphilosophy* 182

Polanyi, K., *The Great Transformation: The Political and Economic Origins of our Time*, 2nd edn (Beacon Press, 2002)

Poli, S., 'Euro-American Conflicts within the Codex Alimentarius Commission', in F. Snyder (ed.), *International Food Security and Global Legal Pluralism* (Bruylant, 2004)

Politis, C., 'Blood Donation Systems as an Integral Part of the Health System' (2000) 17(4) *Archives of Hellenic Medicine* 354

Prah Ruger, J., 'The Changing Role of the World Bank in Global Health' (2005) 95 *American Journal of Public Health* 60

Prainsack, B. and Buys, A., *Solidarity, Reflections on an Emerging Concept in Bioethics* (Nuffield Council on Bioethics, 2012)

Price, D., *Human Tissue for Transplantation and Research: A Model Legal and Ethical Donation Framework* (Cambridge University Press, 2009)

Legal and Ethical Issues of Organ Transplantation (Cambridge University Press, 2000)

Prosser, T., 'EU Competition Law and Public Services', in E. Mossialos, G. Permanand, R. Baeten and T.K. Hervey (eds.), *Health Systems Governance in Europe: The Role of European Union Law and Policy* (Cambridge University Press, 2010)

The Limits of Competition Law: Markets and Public Services (Oxford University Press, 2005)

'Regulation and Social Solidarity' (2006) 33 *Journal of Law and Society* 364

Prudil, L., 'Implementation of the Directive 2011/24/EU in the Czech Republic' (2014) 21(1) *European Journal of Health Law* 15

'Public Health Insurance and Freedom of Movement within the European Union', Editorial (1999) 6 *European Journal of Health Law* 1

Quinn, P. and De Hert, P., 'The European Patients' Rights Directive: A Clarification and Codification of Individual Rights Relating to Cross-border Healthcare and Novel Initiatives Aimed at Improving Pan-European Healthcare Cooperation' (2012) 12(1) *Medical Law International* 28

Radcliffe-Richards, J., Daar, A.S., Guttmann, R.D., et al., 'The Case for Allowing Kidney Sales' (1998) 351(9120) *The Lancet* 1950

Randall, E.D., *The European Union and Health Policy* (Palgrave, 2001)

Requejo, T.M., 'Cross-border Healthcare in Spain and the Implementation of the Directive 2011/24/EU on the Application of Patients' Rights in Cross-border Healthcare' (2014) 21(1) *European Journal of Health Law* 79

Reynolds, L., Attaran, A., Hervey, T.K. and McKee, M., 'Competition-based Reform of the National Health Service in England: A One-Way Street?' (2012) 42(2) *International Journal of Health Services* 213

Richardson, R., *Death, Dissection and the Destitute*, 2nd edn (Phoenix Press, 2001)

Ridley, D.B. and Sanchez, A.C., 'Introduction of European Priority Review Vouchers to Encourage Development of New Medicines for Neglected Diseases' (2010) 376(9744) *The Lancet* 922

Rippe, K.P., 'Novel Foods and Consumer Rights: Concerning Food Policy in a Liberal State' (2000) 12(1) *Journal of Agricultural and Environmental Ethics* 71

Rithalia, A., McDaid, C., Suekarran, S., et al., 'Impact of Presumed Consent for Organ Donation on Donation Rates: A Systematic Review' (2009) 338 *British Medicial Journal* 3162

Robinson, E.A.E. and Hampson, H., 'The EU Blood Safety Directive and its Implications for Blood Services' (2007) 93(2) *Vox Sanguinis* 122

Robinson, K. and Andrews, P., '"(More) trials And Tribulations"; The Effect of the EU Directive on Clinical Trials in Intensive Care and Emergency Medicine, Five Years after its Implementation' (2010) 36(8) *Journal of Medical Ethics* 322

Roche, J., 'Advanced Technologies and the Outer Limits of DNA Legislation: New Horizons for Patients or a Scaffold Too Far?' (2008) 3(4) *Journal of Intellectual Property Law and Practice* 210

Roels, L. and Rahmel, A., 'The European Experience' (2011) 24(4) *Transplantation International* 350

Roemer, R., Taylor, A. and Lariviere, J., 'Origins of the WHO Framework Convention on Tobacco Control' (2005) 95(6) *American Journal of Public Health* 936

Rosas, A., 'The Charter and Universal Human Rights Instruments', in S. Peers, T.K. Hervey, J. Kenner and A. Ward (eds.), *The EU Charter of Fundamental Rights: A Commentary* (Hart, 2014)

Rosenkötter, N., Clemens, T. and Sørensen, K., 'Twentieth Anniversary of the European Union Health Mandate: Taking Stock of Perceived Achievements, Failures and Missed Opportunities: A Qualitative Study' (2013) 13 *BMC Public Health* 1074

Rosenmöller, M., McKee, M. and Baeten, R. (eds.), *Patient Mobility in the European Union: Learning from Experience* (European Observatory on Health Systems and Policies, 2006)

Rosner, F., 'Judaism and Medicine: Jewish Medical Ethics', in R. Ashcroft, H. Draper, A. Dawson and J. Macmillan (eds.), *Principles of Health Care Ethics*, 2nd edn (Wiley-Blackwell, 2007)

Ross, A., *On Law and Justice* (University of California Press, 1959)

'Promoting Solidarity: From Public Services to a European Model of Competition' (2007) 44 *Common Market Law Review* 1057

'The Value of Solidarity in European Public Services Law', in M. Krajewski, U. Neergaard and J.W. Van de Gronden (eds.), *The Changing Legal Framework for Services of General Interest in Europe: Between Competition and Solidarity* (TMC Asser Press, 2009)

Rossi, L.S. and Casolari, F. (eds.), *The EU After Lisbon: Amending or Coping with the Existing Treaties* (Springer, 2014)

Rosso-Gill, I., Legido-Quigley, H., Panteli, D. and McKee, M., 'Assessing the Role of Regulatory Bodies in Managing Health Professional Issues and Errors in Europe' (2014) 26(4) *International Journal for Quality in Health Care* 348

Roth-Behrendt, D., 'A View of EFSA from the European Parliament', in A. Alemanno and S. Gabbi (eds.), *Foundations of EU Food Law and Policy: Ten Years of the European Food Safety Authority* (Ashgate, 2014)

Rothstein, M.A., 'The Limits of Public Health: A Response' (2009) 2(1) *Public Health Ethics* 84

'Rethinking the Meaning of Public Health' (2002) 30 *Journal of Law, Medicine and Health* 144

Ruger, J., *Health and Social Justice* (Oxford University Press, 2010)

'Normative Foundations of Global Health Law' (2008) 96(2) *Georgetown Law Journal* 423

Ruger, J. and Ng, N., 'Emerging and Transitioning Countries' Role in Global Health: Health Law and Bioethics: Pressing Issues and Changing Times' (2010) 3(2) *Saint Louis University Journal of Health Law & Policy* 253

Ruger, T., 'Health Law's Coherence Anxiety' (2008) 96 *Georgetown Law Review* 625

Ruggie, J.G., 'International Regimes, Transactions and Change: Embedded Liberalism in the Postwar Economic Order' (1982) 36(2) *International Organization* 379

Runnels, V., Packer C. and Labonté, R., 'Global Policies and Local Practice in the Ethical Recruitment of Internationally Trained Health Human Resources', in I.G. Cohen (ed.), *The Globalization of Health Care* (Oxford University Press, 2013)

Ruse-Khan, H.G., 'A Trade Agreement Creating Barriers to International Trade?: ACTA Border Measures and Goods in Transit' (2011) 26(3) *American University International Law Review* 645

Rynning, E. and Hartlev, M. (eds.), *Nordic Health Law in a European Context: Welfare State Perspectives on Patients' Rights and Biomedicine* (Martinus Nijhoff, 2011)

Sabel, C.F. and Zeitlin, J. (eds.), *Experimentalist Governance in the European Union* (Oxford University Press, 2010)

Sachedina, A., 'The Search for Islamic Bioethics Principles', in R. Ashcroft, H. Draper, A. Dawson and J. Macmillan (eds.), *Principles of Health Care Ethics*, 2nd edn (Wiley-Blackwell, 2007)

Sachs, J., *The End of Poverty: How We Can Make it Happen in Our Lifetime* (Penguin, 2005)

Sahm, S., 'Of Mugs, Meals and More: The Intricate Relations between Physicians and the Medical Industry' (2013) 16(2) *Medicine, Health Care and Philosophy* 265

Saks, M., 'Professionalization, Regulation and Alternative Medicine', in M. Saks and J. Allsop (eds.), *Regulating the Health Professions* (Sage, 2002)

Saks, M. and Allsop, J. (eds.), *Regulating the Health Professions* (Sage, 2002)

Salmon, T., 'The Structures, Institutions and Powers of the EU', in J. Gower (ed.), *The European Union Handbook* (Fitzroy Dearborn, 2002)

Saltman, R., 'The Role of Comparative Health Studies for Policy Learning' (2012) 7 *Health Economics, Policy and Law* 11

Sandel, M., *What Money Can't Buy: The Moral Limits of Markets* (Allen Lane, 2012)

Sanders, A. and Griffiths, D. (eds.), *Medicine, Crime and Society* (Cambridge University Press, 2013)

Sarmiento, D., 'Who's Afraid of the Charter? The Court of Justice, National Courts and the New Framework of Fundamental Rights Protection in Europe' (2013) 50 *Common Market Law Review* 1267

Satz D., *Why Some Things Should Not Be for Sale: The Moral Limits of Markets* (Oxford University Press, 2010)

Sauter, W., 'The Altmark Package Mark II: New Rules for State Aid and the Compensation of Services of General Economic Interest' (2012) 33(7) *European Competition Law Review* 307

  'The European Community's Pharmaceutical Policy', in A.F. Casparie, H. Hermans and J. Paelinck (eds.), *Health Care in Europe After 1992* (Dartmouth, 1992)

  'The Impact of EU Competition Law on National Healthcare Systems' (2013) 38(4) *European Law Review* 457

  'Proportionality in EU Law: A Balancing Act?' (2013) 15 *Cambridge Yearbook of European Legal Studies* 439

Savulescu, J., 'Is the Sale of Body Parts Wrong?' (2002) 29(3) *Journal of Medical Ethics* 138

Sayers, D., 'Article 13: Freedom of the Arts and Sciences', in S. Peers, T.K. Hervey, J. Kenner and A. Ward (eds.), *The EU Charter of Fundamental Rights: A Commentary* (Hart, 2014)

Scharpf, F.W., 'The Asymmetry of European Integration, or Why the EU Cannot Be a "Social Market Economy"' (2010) 8(2) *Socio-Economic Review* 211

  'Economic Integration, Democracy and the Welfare State' (1997) 4(1) *Journal of European Public Policy* 18

  'The European Social Model: Coping with the Challenges of Diversity' (2002) 40(4) *Journal of Common Market Studies* 645

  'The Joint-Decision Trap: Lessons from German Federalism and European Integration' (1988) 66(3) *Public Administration* 239

  'The Joint-Decision Trap Revisited' (2006) 44(4) *Journal of Common Market Studies* 845

Schieber, G.J., Poullier, J.P. and Greenwald, L.M., 'Health Care Systems in Twenty-four Countries' (1991) 10(3) *Health Affairs* 22

Schiek, D. and Lawson, A. (eds.), *European Union Non-Discrimination Law and Intersectionality: Investigating the Triangle of Racial, Gender and Disability Discrimination* (Ashgate, 2011)

Schmidt, V.A., 'Democracy and Legitimacy in the European Union Revisited: Input, Output and "Throughput"' (2013) 61(1) *Political Studies* 2

Schüklenk, U. and Ashcroft, R., 'Affordable Access to Essential Medicines in Developing Countries: Conflicts between Ethical and Economic Imperatives' (2002) 27(2) *Journal of Medicine and Philosophy* 179

Schütze, R., *European Constitutional Law* (Cambridge University Press, 2012)

Schwebag, M., 'Implementation of the Cross-border Care Directive in EU Member States: Luxembourg' (2014) 21(1) *European Journal of Health Law* 56

Sclove, R.E., *Democracy and Technology* (Guilford Press, 1995)

Scott, J., 'European Regulation of GMOs and the WTO' (2003) 9 *Columbia Journal of European Law* 213

'Mandatory or Imperative Requirements in the EU and the WTO', in C. Barnard and J. Scott (eds.), *The Law of the Single European Market: Unpacking the Premises* (Hart, 2002)

The WTO Agreement on Sanitary and Phytosanitary Measures: A Commentary (Oxford University Press, 2007)

Scott, J. and Trubek, D.M., 'Mind the Gap: Law and New Approaches to Governance in the European Union' (2002) 8 *European Law Journal* 1

Scott, J. and Vos, E., 'The Juridification of Uncertainty', in C. Joerges and R. Dehousse (eds.), *Good Governance in Europe's Integrated Market* (Oxford University Press, 2002)

Selgelid, M.J. and Pogge, T. (eds.), *Health Rights* (Ashgate, 2010)

Senden, L., 'Soft Law, Self-regulation and Co-regulation in European Law: Where Do They Meet?' (2005) 9 *Electronic Journal of Comparative Law* 1

Soft Law in European Community Law (Hart, 2004)

Shaw, J. (ed.), *Social Law and Policy in an Evolving European Union* (Hart, 2000)

Sheldon, S. and Thompson, M. (eds.), *Feminist Perspectives on Health Care Law* (Cavendish, 1998)

Shibuya, K., Ciecierski, C., Guindon, E., et al., 'WHO Framework Convention on Tobacco Control: Development of an Evidence Based Global Public Health Treaty' (2003) 327(7407) *British Medical Journal* 154

Sieveking, K., 'ECJ Rulings on Health Care Services and Their Effects on the Freedom of Crossborder Patient Mobility in the EU' (2007) 9(1) *European Journal of Migration and Law* 25

'The Significance of the Transborder Utilisation of Health Care Benefits for Migrants' (2000) 2 *European Journal of Migration and Law* 143

Silano, V., 'EFSA's Science Strategy: Taking Stock and Looking Ahead', in A. Alemanno and S. Gabbi (eds.), *Foundations of EU Food Law and Policy: Ten Years of the European Food Safety Authority* (Ashgate, 2014)

Silveira, A., Canotilho, M. and Madeira Froufe, P. (eds.), *Citizenship and Solidarity in the EU: From the Charter of Fundamental Rights to the Crisis, The State of the Art* (Peter Lang, 2013)

Sindbjerg Martinsen, D., 'Conflict and Conflict Management in the Cross-border Provision of Healthcare Services' (2009) 32 *West European Politics* 792

EU for the Patients: Developments, Impacts, Challenges, Report no. 6 (Swedish Institute for European Policy Studies, 2007)

'The Europeanisation of Welfare: The Domestic Impact of Intra European Social Security' (2005) 43 *Journal of Common Market Studies* 1027

'Social Security Regulation in the EU: The De-territorialisation of Welfare', in G. de Búrca (ed.), *EU Law and the Welfare State: In Search of Solidarity* (Oxford University Press, 2005)

Sindbjerg Martinsen, D. and Blomqvist, P., 'The European Union: Single Market Pressures', in J. Magnusson, K. Vanbræk and R. Saltman (eds.), *Nordic Healthcare Systems: Recent Reforms and Current Policy Challenges* (Open University Press, 2009)

Sindbjerg Martinsen, D. and Vollaard, H., 'Bounded Rationality in Transition Processes: The Case of the European Patients' Rights Directive' (2014) 37(4) *West European Politics* 711

'Implementing Social Europe in Times of Crises: Re-established Boundaries of Welfare' (2014) 37(4) *West European Politics* 677

Sindbjerg Martinsen, D. and Vrangbæk, K., 'The Europeanisation of Healthcare Governance: Implementing the Market Imperatives of Europe' (2008) 86 *Public Administration* 169

Singer, E.A. and Mullner, M., 'Implications of the EU Directive on Clinical Trials for Emergency Medicine: Many Trials in Emergency Medicine Will Not Be Possible' (2002) 324(7347) *British Medical Journal* 1169

Skogstad, G., 'The WTO and Food Safety Regulatory Policy Innovation in the European Union' (2001) 39(3) *Journal of Common Market Studies* 485

Smith, K.E., Fooks, G., Collin, J., et al., 'Working the System: British American Tobacco's Influence on the European Union Treaty and its Implications for Policy: An Analysis of Internal Tobacco Industry Documents' (2010) 7(1) *PLoS Medicine* e1000202

Snyder, F. (ed.), *International Food Security and Global Legal Pluralism* (Bruylant, 2004)

'Introduction: International Food Security and Global Legal Pluralism', in F. Snyder (ed.), *International Food Security and Global Legal Pluralism* (Bruylant, 2004)

'Toward an International Law for Adequate Food', in M. Ahmed and F. Snyder (eds.), *Food Security and Food Safety* (The Hague Academy of International Law, Brill online, 2014)

Sobolev, B. (ed.), *Handbook of Health Services Research* (forthcoming)

Sokhi-Bulley, B., 'Governing (Through) Rights: Statistics as Technologies of Governmentality' (2011) 20 *Social and Legal Studies* 139

Sokol, T., 'Rindal and Elchinov: A(n) (Impending) Revolution in EU Law on Patient Mobility' (2010) 6(6) *Croatian Yearbook for European Law and Policy* 167

Sonderholm, J., 'In Defence of Priority Review Vouchers' (2009) 23(7) *Bioethics* 413

Sorenson, C. and Chalkidou, K., 'Reflections on the Evolution of Health Technology Assessment in Europe' (2012) 7 *Health Economics, Policy and Law* 25

Sox, H.C. and Greenfield, S., 'Comparative Effectiveness Research: A Report from the Institute of Medicine' (2009) 151(3) *Annals of Internal Medicine* 203

Sperling, D., 'Human Trafficking and Organ Trade: Does the Law Really Care for the Health of People', in M. Freeman, S. Hawkes and B. Bennett (eds.), *Law and Global Health: Current Legal Issues Volume 16* (Oxford University Press, 2014)

Spielman, B., 'Offshoring Experiments, Outsourcing Public Health: Corporate Accountability and State Responsibility for Violating the International Prohibition on Nonconsensual Human Experimentation', in I.G. Cohen (ed.), *The Globalization of Health Care: Legal and Ethical Issues* (Oxford University Press, 2013)

Spranger, T.M., *Medical Law in Germany*, 2nd edn (Kluwer Law International, 2012)

Sprumont, D., 'Legal Protection of Human Research Subjects in Europe' (1999) 6(1) *European Journal of Health Law* 25

Stacey Taylor, J., *Stakes and Kidneys: Why Markets in Human Body Parts are Morally Imperative* (Ashgate, 2005)

Stapelton, J., 'Products Liability in the UK: The Myths of Reform' (1999) 34(1) *Texas International Law Journal* 45

Starr, D., *Blood: An Epic Story of Medicine and Commerce* (Alfred A. Knopf, 1998)

Stavridis, S., Mossialos, E., Morgan, R. and Machlin, H. (eds.), *New Challenges to the EU: Policies and Policy-Making* (Dartmouth, 1997)

Steele, J., *Risks and Legal Theory* (Hart, 2004)

Steering Committee of the Istanbul Summit, 'Organ Trafficking and Transplant Tourism and Commercialism: The Declaration of Istanbul' (2008) 372(9632) *The Lancet* 5

Steffen, M., 'The Europeanization of Public Health: How Does it Work? The Seminal Role of the AIDS Case' (2012) 37(6) *Journal of Health Politics, Policy and Law* 1057

(ed.), *Health Governance in Europe: Issues, Challenges and Theories* (Routledge, 2005)

Stein, 'Lawyers, Judges and the Making of a Transnational Constitution' (1971) 75 *American Journal of International Law* 1

Sterckx, S. and Cockbain, J., 'The UK National Health Service's "Innovation Agenda": Lessons on Commercialisation and Trust' (2014) 22(2) *Medical Law Review* 221

Stirton, L., 'Back to the Future? Lessons on the Pro-Competitive Regulation of Health Services' (2014) 22(2) *Medical Law Review* 180

Stjernø, S., *Solidarity in Europe: The History of an Idea* (Cambridge University Press, 2009)

Stokes, E., 'Demand for Command: Responding to Technological Risks and Scientific Uncertainties' (2013) 21(1) *Medical Law Review* 11

'Nanotechnology and the Products of Inherited Regulation' (2012) 39(1) *Journal of Law and Society* 93

'Something Old, Something New, Something Borrowed: Emerging Health Technologies and the Continuing Role of Existing Regulations', in M. Flear, A.-M. Farrell, T.K. Hervey and T. Murphy (eds.), *European Law and New Health Technologies* (Oxford University Press, 2013)

Stone, J. and Matthews, J., *Complementary Medicine and the Law* (Oxford University Press, 1996)

Strauss, D.M., 'Feast or Famine: The Impact of the WTO Decision Favoring the US Biotechnology Industry in the EU Ban of Genetically Modified Foods' (2008) 45(4) *American Business Law Journal* 775

Streinz, R., 'Risk Decisions in Cases of Persisting Scientific Uncertainty: The Precautionary Principle in European Food Law', in G. Woodman and D. Klippel (eds.), *Risk and the Law* (Routledge, 2009)

Stuart Mill, J., *On Liberty* (Penguin, 1985)

Studlar, D.T., 'Tobacco Control: The End of Europe's Love Affair with Smoking?', in S.L. Greer and P. Kurzer (eds.), *European Union Health Policies: Regional and Global Trends* (Routledge, 2013)

Stuttaford, M., Harrington, J. and Lewando-Hundt, G., 'Sites for Health Rights: Local, National, Regional and Global' (2012) 74(1) *Social Science and Medicine* 1

Sunstein, C., *Risk and Reason: Safety, Law and the Environment* (Cambridge University Press, 2002)

Sykes, R., Palier, B. and Prior P., (eds.), *Globalization and European Welfare States: Challenges and Change* (Palgrave Macmillan, 2001)

Syrett, K., 'Health Technology Appraisal and the Courts: Accountability for Reasonableness and the Judicial Model of Procedural Justice' (2001) 6(4) *Health Economics, Policy and Law* 469

Law, Legitimacy and the Rationing of Health Care (Cambridge University Press, 2007)

'Looking After the Orphans? Treatments for Rare Diseases, EU Law, and the Ethics of Costly Health Care', in M. Flear, A.-M. Farrell, T.K. Hervey and T. Murphy (eds.), *European Law and New Health Technologies* (Oxford University Press, 2013)

Syrpis, P. (ed.), *The Judiciary, the Legislature and the Internal Market* (Cambridge University Press, 2012)

Syx, E., 'The Case of the Electronic Cigarette in the EU' (2014) 21(2) *European Journal of Health Law* 161

Szyszczak, E., 'Modernising Healthcare: The Quest for the Holy Grail', in M. Krajewski, U. Neergaard and J. Van de Gronden (eds.), *The Changing Legal Framework for Services of General Interest in Europe* (TMC Asser Press, 2009)

t'Hoen, E., 'A Victory for Global Public Health in the Indian Supreme Court' (2013) 34(3) *Journal of Public Health Policy* 370

Tallacchini, M., 'Governing by Values. EU Ethics: Soft Tool, Hard Effects' (2009) 47(3) *Minerva* 281

Taylor, A., Chaloupka, F., Gundon, E. and Corbett, M., 'The Impact of Trade Liberalization on Tobacco Consumption', in P. Jha and F. Chaloupka (eds.), *Tobacco in Developing Countries* (Oxford University Press, 2000)

Taylor A.L. and Bettcher, D.W., 'WHO Framework Convention on Tobacco Control: A Global 'Good' for Public Health' (2000) 78(7) *Bulletin of the WHO* 920

Taylor, A.L. and Dhillon, I.S., 'A Global Legal Architecture to Address the Challenges of International Health Worker Migration', in I.G. Cohen (ed.), *The Globalization of Health Care: Legal and Ethical Issues* (Oxford University Press, 2013)

Taylor, M., *Genetic Data and the Law: A Critical Perspective on Privacy Protection* (Cambridge University Press, 2012)
  'Health Research, Data Protection, and the Public Interest in Notification' (2011) 19(2) *Medical Law Review* 267

Taylor, M. and Grace, J., 'Disclosure of Confidential Patient Information and the Duty to Consult: The Role of the Health and Social Care Information Centre' (2013) 21(3) *Medical Law Review* 415

Taylor-Gooby, P., *Ideas and Welfare State Reform in Western Europe* (Palgrave Macmillan, 2005)
  (ed.), *New Risks, New Welfare* (Oxford University Press, 2004)

Taylor-Gooby, P. and Zinn, J. (eds.), *Risk in Social Science* (Oxford University Press, 2006)

Teff, H. and Munro, C., *Thalidomide: The Legal Aftermath* (Saxon House, 1976)

Thaler, R. and Sunstein, C., *Nudge: Improving Decisions about Health, Wealth, and Happiness* (Yale University Press, 2008)

Thompson, I.E., 'Fundamental Ethical Principles in Health Care' (1987) 295 *British Medical Journal* 1461

Thompson, R., *The Single Market for Pharmaceuticals* (Butterworths, 1994)

Thomson, S. and Mossialos, E., 'Private Health Insurance and the Internal Market', in E. Mossialos, G. Permanand, R. Baeten and T.K. Hervey (eds.), *Health Systems Governance in Europe: The Role of European Union Law and Policy* (Cambridge University Press, 2010)

Tiberghien, Y., 'Competitive Governance and the Quest for Legitimacy in the EU: The Battle over the Regulation of GMOs since the mid-1990s' (2009) 31(3) *European Integration* 389

Titmuss, R.M., Oakley, A. and Ashton, J. (eds.), *The Gift Relationship: From Human Blood to Social Policy* (LSE Books, 1997)

Tobey, J.A., *Public Health Law: A Manual of Law for Sanitarians* (Williams and Wilkins Co., 1926)

Toebes, B., 'Right to Health and Health Care', in D.P. Forsythe (ed.), *Encyclopaedia for Human Rights* (Oxford University Press, 2009) vol. 1, 365

The Right to Health as a Human Right in International Law (Intersentia, 1999)

'The Right to Health', in A. Eide, C. Krause and A. Rosas (eds.), *Economic, Cultural and Social Rights*, 2nd edn (Martinus Nijhoff Publishers, 2001)

Toebes, B., Hartlev, M., Hendriks, A. and Herrmann, J.R. (eds.), *Health and Human Rights in Europe* (Intersentia, 2012)

Toggenburg, G.N., 'The Role of the New EU Fundamental Rights Agency: Debating the "Sex of Angels" or Improving Europe's Human Rights Performance? (2008) 33 *European Law Review* 385

Trubek, A., *The Taste of Place: A Cultural Journey into Terrior* (University of California Press, 2009)

Trubek, D.M. and Trubek, L.G., 'New Governance and Legal Regulation: Complementarity, Rivalry and Transformation' (2007) 13 *Columbia Journal of European Law* 539

Trubek, L.G., Nance, M. and Hervey, T.K., 'The Construction of a Healthier Europe: Lessons from the Fight Against Cancer' (2008) 26 *Wisconsin International Law Journal* 804

Trubek, L.G., Oliver, T.R., Liang, C.-M. and Mokrohisky, M., 'Improving Cancer Outcomes through Strong Networks and Regulatory Frameworks: Lessons from the US and EU' (2011) 14(1) *Journal of Health Care Law and Policy* 119

Tsadiras, A., 'The European Ombudsman's Remedial Powers: An Empirical Analysis in Context' (2013) 38(1) *European Law Review* 52

Tsai, G., 'Canada's Access to Medicines Regime: Lessons for Compulsory Licensing Schemes under the WTO Doha Declaration' (2009) 50(1) *Virginia Journal of International Law* 1063

Tuohimäki, C., Kaltiala-Heino, R., Korkeila, J. and Tuori, T., 'The Use of Harmful to Others-Criterion for Involuntary Treatment in Finland' (2003) 10(2) *European Journal of Health Law* 183

Tuohy, C.H., *Accidental Logics: The Dynamics of Change in the Health Care Arena in the United States, Britain and Canada* (Oxford University Press, 1999)

'Agency, Contract and Governance: Shifting Shapes of Accountability in the Health Care Arena' (2003) 28 *Journal of Health Politics, Policy and Law* 19

Tur, R.H., 'Legislative Techniques and Human Rights: The Sad Case of Assisted Suicide' (2003) *Criminal Law Review* 3

Turkmendag, I., 'When Sperm Cannot Travel: Experiences of UK Fertility Patients Seeking Treatment Abroad', in M. Flear, A.-M. Farrell, T.K. Hervey and T. Murphy (eds.), *European Law and New Health Technologies* (Oxford University Press, 2013)

Tushnet, M., 'Social Welfare Rights and the Forms of Judicial Review' (2003) 82 *Texas Law Review* 1895

'Two-Speed European Citizenship? Can the Lisbon Treaty Help Close the Gap?', Editorial (2008) 45(1) *Common Market Law Review* 1

UK Human Genetics Commission, *Common Framework of Principles of Direct to Consumer Genetic Testing Services* (UK HHC, 2009)

Inside Information: Balancing Interests in the Use of Personal Genetic Data (UK HGC, 2002)

Urwin, D., *The Community of Europe: A History of European Integration since 1945*, 2nd edn (Longman, 1995)

US National Research Council, *Risk Assessment in the Federal Government: Managing the Process* (National Academy Press, 1983)

Valongo, A., 'Human Rights and Reproductive Choices in the Case Law of the Italian and European Courts' (2014) 24(2) *European Journal of Health Law* 123

Van de Gronden, J.W., 'Cross-Border Health Care in the EU and the Organization of the National Health Care Systems of the Member States: The Dynamics Resulting from the European Court of Justice's Decisions on Free Movement and Competition Law' (2009) 26 *Wisconsin International Law Journal* 705

  'Financing Health Care in EU Law: Do the European State Aids Rules Write Out an Effective Prescription for Integrating Competition Law with Health Care?' (2009) 6(1) *Competition Law Review* 5

  'Purchasing Care: Economic Activity or Service of General (Economic) Interest?' (2004) 25(2) *European Competition Law Review* 87

  'The Treaty Provisions on Competition and Health Care', in J.W. Van de Gronden, E. Szyszczak, U. Neergaard and M. Krajewski (eds.), *Health Care and EU Law* (Springer, 2011)

Van de Gronden, J.W. and Sauter, W., 'Taking the Temperature: EU Competition Law and Health Care' (2011) 38(3) *Legal Issues of Economic Integration* 213

Van de Gronden, J.W., Szyszczak, E., Neergaard, U. and Krajewski, M. (eds.), *Health Care and EU Law* (Springer, 2011)

Van der Mei, A.P., 'Cross-Border Access to Medical Care within the European Union: Some Reflections on the Judgments in *Decker* and *Kohll*' (1998) 5 *Maastricht Journal of European and Comparative Law* 277

  Free Movement of Persons within the European Community: Cross-Border Access to Public Benefits (Hart, 2003) 256

Van der Mei, A.P. and Waddington, L., 'Public Health and the Treaty of Amsterdam' (1998) 5 *European Journal of Health Law* 129

Van der Meulen, B. and Vaskoka, R.S., 'Rule of Science: A Food Law Professor's Perspective', in A. Alemanno and S. Gabbi (eds.), *Foundations of EU Food Law and Policy: Ten Years of the European Food Safety Authority* (Ashgate, 2014)

Van der Poel, C.L., Seifried, E. and Schaasberg, W.P., 'Paying for Blood Donations: Still a Risk?' (2002) 83(4) *Vox Sanguinis* 285

Van Schendelen, M., (ed.), *EU Committees as Influential Policy Makers* (Dartmouth, 1998)

Van Vooren, B. and Wessel, R.A., *EU External Relations Law: Text, Cases and Materials* (Cambridge University Press, 2014)

Van Vooren, B., Blockmans, S. and Wouters, J. (eds.), *The EU's Role in Global Governance: The Legal Dimension* (Oxford University Press, 2013)

  'The Legal Dimension of Global Governance: What Role for the European Union? An Introduction', in B. Van Vooren, S. Blockmans and J Wouters (eds.), *The EU's Role in Global Governance: The Legal Dimension* (Oxford University Press, 2013)

Vaqué, G. and Romero Melchor, S., 'A Yankee in King Arthur's Court: A Lawyer's Perspective of EFSA', in A. Alemanno and S. Gabbi (eds.), *Foundations of EU Food Law and Policy: Ten Years of the European Food Safety Authority* (Ashgate, 2014)

Varju, M. and Sandor, J., 'Patenting Stem Cells in Europe: The Challenge of Multiplicity in EU Law' (2012) 49(3) *Common Market Law Review* 1007

Veatch, R.M., 'Why Liberals Should Accept Financial Incentives for Organ Procurement' (2003) 13(1) *Kennedy Institute of Ethics Journal* 19

Ventola, C.L., 'Direct-to-Consumer Pharmaceutical Advertising: Therapeutic or Toxic?' (2011) 36(10) *Pharmacy and Therapeutics* 669

Vidalis, T. and Kyriakaki, I., 'Cross-border Healthcare: Directive 2011/24 and the Greek Law' (2014) 21(1) *European Journal of Health Law* 33

Vincent-Jones, P. and Mullen, C., 'From Collaborative to Genetic Governance: The Example of Healthcare Services in England', in O. De Schutter and J. Lenoble, *Reflexive Governance: Redefining Public Interest in a Pluralistic World* (Hart, 2010)

Vogel, D., *The Politics of Precaution: Regulating Health, Safety and Environmental Risks in Europe and the United States* (Princeton University Press, 2012)

Von Auer, F., 'Payment for Blood Donations in Germany (1995) 310(6976) *British Medical Journal* 399

Von Bogdandy, A., 'The EU as a Human Rights Organisation: Human Rights and the Core of the EU' (2000) 37 *Common Market Law Review* 1307

'Pluralism, Direct Effect, and the Ultimate Say' (2008) 6 *International Journal of Constitutional Law* 397

Von Bogdandy, A. and Von Bernstoff, J., 'The EU Fundamental Rights Agency within the European and International Human Rights Architecture: The Legal Framework and Some Unsettled Issues in a New Field of Administrative Law' (2009) 46 *Common Market Law Review* 1035

Van Hoof, W. and Pennings, G., 'Cross-Border Reproductive Care around the World: Recent Controversies', in D. Botterill, G. Pennings and T. Mainil (eds.), *Medical Tourism and Transnational Health Care* (Palgrave Macmillan, 2013)

Varkevisser, M., Capps, C.S. and Schut, F.T., 'Defining Hospital Markets for Antitrust Enforcement: New Approaches and their Applicability to The Netherlands' (2008) 3(1) *Health Economics Policy and Law* 7

Veitch, K., *The Jurisdiction of Medical Law* (Ashgate, 2013)

Vinck, I., Hulstaert, F., Van Brabandt, H., et al., 'Market Introduction of Innovative High Risk Medical Devices: Towards a Recast of the Directive concerning Medical Devices' (2011) 18(5) *European Journal of Health Law* 477

von Heydebrand u.d. Lasa, H.-C., 'Free Movement of Foodstuffs, Consumer Protection and Food Standards in the EU: Has the Court of Justice Got it Wrong?' (1991) 16(5) *European Law Review* 391

Von Tigerstrom, B., 'The Revised International Health Regulations and Restraint of National Health Measures' (2005) 13 *Health Law Journal* 35

Vos, E., 'EU Food Safety Legislation in the Aftermath of the BSE Crisis' (2000) 23(3) *Journal of Consumer Policy* 227

Vos, E. and Wendler, F., *Food Safety Regulation in Europe* (Intersentia, 2006)

Vrangbaek, K., Robertson, R., Winblad, U., et al., 'Choice Policies in Northern European Health Systems' (2012) 7 *Health Economics Policy and Law* 47

Wagstaff A., 'Economics, Health and Development: Some Ethical Dilemmas Facing the World Bank and the International Community' (2001) 27 *Journal of Medical Ethics* 262

Walker, N., 'Beyond Boundary Disputes and Basic Grids: Mapping the Global Disorder of Normative Orders' (2008) 6(3–4) *International Journal of Constitutional Law* 373

'The Idea of Constitutional Pluralism' *Modern Law Review* (2002) 65(3) 317

Walker, N., Shaw, J. and Tierney, T. (eds.), *Europe's Constitutional Mosaic* (Hart, 2011)

Walsh, K., *Public Services and Market Mechanisms: Competition, Contracting and the New Public Management*, Public Policy and Politics (Palgrave Macmillan, 1995)

Ward, A., 'Article 51: Field of Application', in S. Peers, T.K. Hervey, J. Kenner and A. Ward (eds.), *The EU Charter of Fundamental Rights: A Commentary* (Hart, 2014)

Warren-Jones, A., 'Mapping Science and New Health Technologies: In Search of a Definition', in M. Flear, A.-M. Farrell, T.K. Hervey and T. Murphy (eds.), *European Law and New Health Technologies* (Oxford University Press, 2013)

Watson, P., *Social Security Law of the European Communities* (Mansell, 1980)

Watson, R., 'EU Legislation Threatens Clinical Trials' (2003) 326(7403) *British Medical Journal* 1348

'European Parliament Tries to Stamp Out Trafficking in Human Organs' (2003) 327 *British Medical Journal* 1009

Weatherill, S., 'Competence and Legitimacy', in C. Barnard and O. Odudu (eds.), *The Outer Limits of EU Law* (Hart, 2009)

'Competence Creep and Competence Control' (2004) 23 *Yearbook of European Law* 1 *Law and Integration in the European Union* (Clarendon Press, 1995)

Weedle, P.B. and Clarke, L., *Pharmacy and Medicines Law in Ireland* (Pharmaceutical Press, 2011)

Weiler, J.H.H., *The Constitution of Europe* (Cambridge University Press, 1999)

'The Transformation of Europe' (1991) 100(8) *Yale Law Journal* 2403

Weiler, J.H.H. and Lockhart, J.S., '"Taking Rights Seriously" Seriously: The European Court and its Fundamental Rights Jurisprudence Part I' (1995) 32(1) *Common Market Law Review* 51

'"Taking Rights Seriously" Seriously: The European Court and its Fundamental Rights Jurisprudence Part II' (1995) 32(2) *Common Market Law Review* 579

Weiler, J.H.H. and Wind, M. (eds.), *European Constitutionalism Beyond the State* (Cambridge University Press, 2003)

Weishaar, H., Collin, J. and Amos, A., 'Tobacco Control and Health Advocacy in the European Union: Understanding Effective Coalition Building'. *Nicotine & Tobacco Research* (2015)

Wiener, J.B., Rogers, M.D., Hammitt, J.K. and Sand, P.H. (eds.), *The Reality of Precaution: Comparing Risk Regulation in the US and Europe* (RFF Press, 2010)

Wellens, K.C. and Borchardt, G.M., 'Soft Law in European Community Law' 14 (1989) *European Law Review* 267

Wells, D.J., 'Animal Welfare and the 3Rs in European Biomedical Research' (2011) 12451(1) *Annals of the New York Academy of Sciences* 14

Wendell, M., 'Lisbon before the Courts: Comparative Perspectives' (2011) 7 *European Constitutional Law Review* 96

Wendt, C., 'Mapping European Healthcare Systems: A Comparative Analysis of Financing, Service Provision and Access to Healthcare' (2009) 19(5) *Journal of European Social Policy* 432

Westerhäll, L., *Medical Law: An Introduction* (Fritzes, 1994)

Westlake, M., '"Mad Cows and Englishmen": The Institutional Consequences of the BSE Crisis', in N. Nugent (ed.), *European Union 1996: The Annual Review*, published in association with *Journal of Common Market Studies* (1997)

Whish, R. and Bailey, D., *Competition Law*, 7th edn (Oxford University Press, 2012)

White, R., 'Article 34: Social Security and Social Assistance', in S. Peers, T.K. Hervey, J. Kenner and A. Ward (eds.), *The EU Charter of Fundamental Rights: A Commentary* (Hart, 2014)

White, R. and Overy, C., *Jacobs, White & Overy: The European Convention on Human Rights*, 5th edn (Oxford University Press, 2010)

White, R. and Smythe, B. (eds.), *Current Issues in European and International Law: Essays in Memory of Franck Dowrick* (Sweet & Maxwell, 1990)

WHO, '*Global Burden of Disease study*' (WHO, 2004)

   Promotion of the Rights of Patients in Europe (Kluwer Law International, 1995)

Wicks, E., 'A, B, C v. Ireland: Abortion Law under the European Convention on Human Rights' (2011) 11 *Human Rights Law Review* 556

   'Article 2: Right to Life', in S. Peers, T.K. Hervey, J. Kenner and A. Ward (eds.), *The EU Charter of Fundamental Rights: A Commentary* (Hart, 2014)

   Human Rights and Health Care (Hart, 2007)

Widdows, H., 'Christian Approaches to Bioethics', in R. Ashcroft, H. Draper, A. Dawson and J. Macmillan (eds.), *Principles of Health Care Ethics*, 2nd edn (Wiley-Blackwell, 2007)

Wilkinson, M. and Moore, A., 'Inducements in Research' (1997) 11(5) *Bioethics* 373

Wilkinson, S., *Bodies for Sale: Ethics and Exploitation in the Human Body Trade* (Routledge, 2003)

Williams, A., *The Irony of Human Rights in the European Union* (Oxford University Press, 2004)

Wilsford, D., Oliver, A. and Mossialos, E. (eds.), 'Special Issue on Legacies and Latitude in European Health Policy' (2005) 30(1–2) *Journal of Health Politics, Policy and Law* 1

Wilson, K, Brownstein, J.S. and Fidler, D.P, 'Strengthening the International Health Regulations: Lessons from the H1N1 Pandemic' (2010) 25(6) *Health Policy and Planning* 505

Winham, G.R., 'The GMO Panel: WTO and Agricultural Biotech Products' (2009) 31(3) *European Integration* 409

Winslow, C.E.A., 'The Untilled Fields of Public Health' (1920) 51 *Science* 23

Wogart, J.P., 'From Conflict over Compromise to Cooperation? Big Pharma, the HIV/AIDS Crisis and the Rise of Countervailing Power in the South', in W. Hein, S. Bartsch and L. Kohlmorgen (eds.), *Global Health Governance and the Fight against HIV/AIDS* (Palgrave Macmillan, 2007)

Womack, C.A., 'Ethical and Epistemic Issues in Direct-to-Consumer Drug Advertising: Where is Patient Agency?' (2013) 16(2) *Medicine, Health Care and Philosophy* 275

Woodman, G. and Klippel, D. (eds.), *Risk and the Law* (Routledge, 2009)

   'Who's Afraid of the European Clinical Trials Directive?', Editorial (2003) 361(9376) *The Lancet* 2167

Yamin, A.E. and Parra-Vera, O., 'How Do Courts Set Health Policy? The Case of the Colombian Constitutional Court' (2009) 6(2) *PLOS Medicine* 147

   'Judicial Protection of the Right to Health in Colombia: From Social Demands to Individual Claims to Public Debates' (2010) 33 *Hastings International & Comparative Law Review* 431

Yea, S., 'Trafficking in Parts: The Commercial Kidney Market in a Manila Slum, Philippines' (2010) 10(10) *Global Social Policy* 358

Young, A.R., 'Europe as a Global Regulator? The Limits of EU Influence in International Food Safety Standards' (2014) 21(6) *Journal of European Public Policy* 904

Young, K., 'The Minimum Core of Economic and Social Rights: A Concept in Search of Content' (2008) 33 *Yale Journal of International Law* 1

Zajac, M., 'EU Accession: Implications for Poland's Healthcare Personnel' (2002) 8 *Eurohealth* 13

Zanon, E., 'Healthcare Across Borders: Implications of the Directive on Crossborder Health Care for the English NHS' (2011) 17(2–3) *Eurohealth* 34

Zilgavis, P., 'The European Convention on Biomedicine: Its Past, Present and Future', in A. Garwood-Gowers, J. Tingle and T. Lewis (eds.), *Healthcare Law: The Impact of the Human Rights Act 1998*, (Routledge-Cavendish, 2001)

Literature (online)

Abbott, A., 'European Medicines Agency Set to Publish Clinical-trial Reports', *Nature* (13 June 2014) www.nature.com/news/european-medicines-agency-set-to-publish-clinical-trial-reports-1.15410

Abbott, F.M., 'Worst Fears Realised: The Dutch Confiscation of Medicines Bound from India to Brazil' (2009) 1 *Bridges, International Centre for Trade and Sustainable Development* 13, available at: www.ictsd.org/i/news/bridges/44192/

Active Citizenship Network, 'European Charter of Patients' Rights' (2002) www.activecitizenship.net/images/patientsrights/ec_english.pdf

'Aids Scandals around the World', BBC News (9 August 2001) http://news.bbc.co.uk/1/hi/world/europe/1482021.stm

Alaimo, A., Alessi, L., Amuso, D., et al., 'An Analysis of the Economic Impact of the Development Risk Clause as Provided by Directive 85/374/EEC on Liability for Defective Products: Final Report' (Foundazione Rosselli, 2004) http://ec.europa.eu/enterprise/policies/single-market-goods/files/goods/docs/liability/2004-06-dev-risk-clause-study_en.pdf

'Alcohol Minimum Pricing Case Referred to European Court of Justice', *Scottish Legal News* (30 April 2014) www.scottishlegal.com/index.asp?cat=NEWS&Type=Commercial&newsID=61631

'Alcohol Use Around the Globe: New Data Trends', EpiAnalysis (28 February 2012) http://epianalysis.wordpress.com/2012/02/28/alcohol/

Alemanno, A., 'The Revised EU's Tobacco Products Directive Seeks to "nudge" Citizens whilst Preserving Individual Choice about Smoking', *London School of Economics* (27 March 2012) http://blogs.lse.ac.uk/europpblog/2012/03/27/the-revised-eus-tobacco-products-directive-seeks-to-nudge-citizens-towards-making-better-decisions-about-smoking-whilst-preserving-individual-choice/

Allekotte, B., 'The Bolar Exemption: The Question of Third Parties', *Life Sciences Intellectual Property Review* (28 February 2014) www.lifesciencesipreview.com/article/the-bolar-exemption-the-question-of-third-parties

Almunia, J., 'Commission Fines Lundbeck and other Pharma Companies for Delaying Market Entry of Generic Medicines: Statement by Vice-President Almunia', Commission (19 June 2013) http://europa.eu/rapid/press-release_SPEECH-13-553_en.htm

American Chemical Society, 'Simple New Test to Combat Counterfeit Drug Problem in Developing Countries', *Science Daily* (19 August 2012) www.sciencedaily.com/releases/2012/08/120819153450.htm

Amnesty International, 'Human Rights and the European Union' (2009) www.end fgm.eu/en/resources/amnesty-international-publications-and-materials/human-rights-and-the-european-union/

Anderson, P. and Baumberg, B., 'Alcohol in Europe: A Public Health Perspective', Institute of Alcohol Studies (2006) http://ec.europa.eu/health-eu/doc/alcoholineu_content_en.pdf

ASPECT Consortium, 'Tobacco or Health in the European Union: Past, Present and Future, Commission' (2004) http://ec.europa.eu/health/archive/ph_determinants/life_style/tobacco/documents/tobacco_fr_en.pdf

Autorità Garante della Concorrenza e del Mercato (AGCM), 'Drugs: Pfizer Sanctioned with 10.6 Million Euro Fine for Abuse of Dominant Position', AGCM (17 January 2012) www.agcm.it/en/newsroom/press-releases/1986-pfizer-sanctioned-with-106-million-euro-fine-for-abuse-of-dominant-position.html

'Flu Vaccines: Antitrust Launches Investigation into Possible Competition-Restricting Agreement between Solvay Pharma and Sanofi Pasteur MSD', AGCM (22 December 2009) www.agcm.it/en/newsroom/press-releases/1433-i726–flu-vaccine.html

'Healthcare: Antitrust, over 5.5 Million in Fines for Competition-Distorting Agreement among 4 Suppliers of Magnetic Resonance Equipment', AGCM (5 August 2011) http://www.agcm.it/en/newsroom/press-releases/1963-i729-healthcare-antitrust-over-55-million-in-fines-for-competition-distorting-agreement-among-4-suppliers-of-magnetic-resonance-equipment.html

'Milleproroghe Decree: Antitrust Authority – No To Amendments Blocking New Parapharmacies', *AGCM* (3 February 2011) www.agcm.it/en/newsroom/press-releases/1931-antitrust-no-to-amendments-blocking-new-parapharmacies.html

'Umbilical Cord Preservation: Antitrust Intervenes to Change the Advertising Messages of Six Companies', *AGCM* (24 October 2011) www.agcm.it/en/newsroom/press-releases/1968-umbilical-cord-preservation-antitrust-intervenes-to-change-the-advertising-messages-of-six-companies.html

Autorité de la concurrence, 'The Autorité de la concurrence Does Not Declare Emergency Measures against Sanofi-Aventis but Continues its Investigation on the Merits Regarding the Complaint by Teva Santé' (18 May 2010) www.autorite delaconcurrence.fr/user/standard.php?id_rub=368&id_article=1404

'The Conseil de la concurrence Fines the National Board of the French Dental Surgeons Association (Conseil national de l'Ordre des chirurgiens-dentistes) and Several of its Regional Boards for Encouraging Dental Surgeons to Rule out a Partnership with the Company Santéclair' (12 February 2009) www.autoritedelaconcurrence.fr/user/standard.php?id_rub=316&id_article=1085

'Conseil de la concurrence Imposes €10 Millions Fine on GlaxoSmithKline for Having Abusively Hindered the Entry of Certain Generic Drugs to Hospitals' (14 March 2007) www.autoritedelaconcurrence.fr/user/standard.php?id_rub=211&id_article=695

'Medical Gases for Use in Hospitals: The Conseil de la concurrence Sanctions Practices by Two Subsidiaries of the Air Liquide Group' (20 January 2003) www.autoritedelaconcurrence.fr/user/standard.php?id_rub=127&id_article=243

Aymé, S. and Rodwell, C. (eds.), '2013 Report on the State of the Art of Rare Disease Activities in Europe', EUCERD (2013) www.eucerd.eu/upload/file/Reports/2013ReportStateofArtRDActivities.pdf

(eds.), '2014 Report on the State of the Art of Rare Disease Activities in Europe: Part I: Overview of Rare Disease Activities in Europe', EUCERD (2014) www.eucerd.eu/upload/file/Reports/2014ReportStateofArtRDActivities.pdf

Baker, B.K., 'Settlement of the India/EU WTO Dispute re Seizures of In-Transit Medicines: Why the Proposed EU Border Regulation isn't Good Enough' (2012), Program on Information Justice and Intellectual Property Research Paper no. 2012/02 http://digitalcommons.wcl.american.edu/research/24/

Bhatia, S., 'They Queue to Donate their Eggs and Rent out their Wombs. One Payment Can Transform their Lives' *Daily Telegraph* (26 May 2012) www.telegraph.co.uk/health/healthnews/9291913/They-queue-to-donate-their-eggs-and-rent-out-their-wombs.-One-payment-can-transform-their-lives.html

Bogdanich, W., 'Chinese Chemicals Flow Unchecked onto World Drug Market' *New York Times* (31 October 2007) www.nytimes.com/2007/10/31/world/asia/31chemical.html

Booth, B., Meier, P., Stockwell, T., et al., 'Independent Review of the Effects of Alcohol Pricing and Promotion', SchHARR Project Report for the Department of Health (2008) www.sheffield.ac.uk/polopoly_fs/1.95617!/file/PartA.pdf

Bozik, A., 'Essential Medicines: The Crisis in Developing Countries' (2011) 7(2) *Yale Journal of Medicine and Law* 13, available at: www.yalemedlaw.com/issues/vol7-issue 2.pdf

Branigan, T., 'Executed Prisoners are Main Source of Chinese Organ Donations' *Guardian* (26 August 2009) www.theguardian.com/world/2009/aug/26/china-organ-donation-prisoners

'Breast Implants: PIP's Jean Claude Mas Gets Jail Sentence', BBC News (10 December 2013) www.bbc.co.uk/news/world-europe-25315627

Brennan, A., Meier, P., Purshouse, R., et al., 'Developing Policy Analytics for Public Health Strategy and Decisions: The Sheffield Alcohol Policy Model Framework', Annals of Operational Research (2013) http://link.springer.com/article/10.1007%2Fs10479-013-1451-z

Briggs, H., 'Full Face Transplant a Success' , BBC News (23 April 2010) http://news.bbc.co.uk/1/hi/health/8639437.stm

Bristol Inquiry Interim Report, 'Removal and Retention of Human Material' (2000) www.bristol-inquiry.org.uk (no longer available)

British Medical Association (BMA), 'Standardised Packaging' (2014) http://bma.org.uk/working-for-change/improving-and-protecting-health/tobacco/standardised-packaging

British Medical Association Ethics Committee, 'Building on Progress: Where Next for Organ Donation Policy in UK?', British Medical Association (2012) www.odt.nhs.uk/pdf/bma_organdonation_buildingonprogressfebruary2012%5B1%5D.pdf

British Medical Council, 'EU Maintains Minimum Length of Medical Training', *British Medical Association* (21 November 2013) http://bma.org.uk/news-views-analysis/news/2013/november/eu-maintains-minimum-length-of-medical-training

Broberg, M., 'The EU's Legal Ties with its Former Colonies: When Old Love Never Dies' (2011) DIIS working paper 2011:01 http://subweb.diis.dk/graphics/Publications/WP2011/WP2011-02%20til%20tryk.pdf

'Governing by Consensus: On the Legal Regulation of the EU's Development Cooperation Policy' (2010) DIIS working paper 2010:23 http://subweb.diis.dk/graphics/Publications/WP2010/WP2010-23-Governing-by-Consensus-web.pdf

Buchan, J., Wismar, M., Glinos, I.A. and Bremner, J. (eds.), 'Health Professional Mobility in a Changing Europe: New Dynamics, Mobile Individuals and Diverse Responses' (WHO, 2014) www.euro.who.int/__data/assets/pdf_file/0006/248343/Health-Professional-Mobility-in-a-Changing-Europe.pdf

Bundeskartellamt, 'Agreement on Price Increase for Pharmaceuticals Retracted after Application for Leniency', *Bundeskartllamt* (7 May 2009) www.bundeskartellamt.de/SharedDocs/Meldung/EN/Pressemitteilungen/2009/07_05_2009_Gr%C3%BCnenthal-Infectopharm.html

'Bundeskartellamt Imposes Fines against Pharmacist Associations and Manufacturers of Pharmaceuticals for Asking Pharmacists to Observe Nonbinding Price Recommendations of Manufacturers', *Bundeskartellamt* (8 January 2008) www.bundeskartellamt.de/SharedDocs/Meldung/EN/Pressemitteilungen/2008/08_01_2008_OTC.html

'Bundeskartellamt Obtains Reversal of Merger between the University Hospital of Tübingen and Zollernalb District', *Bundeskartellamt* (14 May 2009) www.bundeskartellamt.de/SharedDocs/Meldung/EN/Pressemitteilungen/2009/14_05_2009_Uniklinik-T%C3%BCbingen_Zollernalbkreis.html

'Clearance of Two Laboratory Acquisitions: Sonic Healthcare/Lademannbogen and BC Partners/ Futurelab', Bundeskartellamt (5 January 2010) http://www.bundeskartellamt.de/SharedDocs/Entscheidung/EN/Fallberichte/Fusionskontrolle/2009/B3-88-09.pdf?__blob=publicationFile&v=4

'Federal Court of Justice Confirms Merger Control Practice in the Hospital Sector', *Bundeskartellamt* (17 January 2008) www.bundeskartellamt.de/SharedDocs/Meldung/EN/Pressemitteilungen/2008/17_01_2008_Rh%C3%B6n-BGH.html

'Fine Proceedings against Manufacturers of Ophthalmic Lenses', Bundeskartellamt (10 June 2010) www.bundeskartellamt.de/SharedDocs/Entscheidung/EN/Fallberichte/Kartellverbot/2010/B12-11-08.pdf?__blob=publicationFile&v=4

'Fines Against Pharmaceutical Wholesalers are Final', *Bundeskartellamt* (19 April 2007) www.bundeskartellamt.de/SharedDocs/Meldung/EN/Pressemitteilungen/2007/19_04_2007_Rechtskraft-Bußgelder-Pharmagroßhändler.html

'Non-binding Price Recommendations for Ophthalmic Lenses to be Discontinued', *Bundeskartellamt* (25 March 2009) www.bundeskartellamt.de/SharedDocs/Meldung/EN/Pressemitteilungen/2009/25_03_2009_Brillengl%C3%A4ser.html

'Statutory Health Insurance Funds to be Seen as Public Contracting Entities', *Bundeskartellamt* (11 May 2007) www.bundeskartellamt.de/SharedDocs/Meldung/EN/Pressemitteilungen/2007/11_05_2007_Gesetzliche-Krankenkassen.html

Bureau of European Policy Advisors (BEPA), 'Second Dialogue EU–US on Precaution in Risk Management Science and Society Projects (Michael D. Rogers), Project 1: "The Reality of Precaution: Comparing Transatlantic Approaches to Risks and Regulation"', *BEPA* (22 February 2010) http://ec.europa.eu/dgs/policy_advisers/archives/publications/second_dialogue_en.htm

Camilleri, I., 'EU Citizens' Initiative to Force Abortion', *Times of Malta* (19 July 2009) www.timesofmalta.com/articles/view/20090719/local/eu-citizens-initiative-to-force-abortion.265670

Campbell, D., 'Destination Spain: The Rise and Rise of Fertility Tourism' *Guardian* (22 August 2010) www.theguardian.com/lifeandstyle/2010/aug/22/spain-fertility-tourism

Campbell, D. and Davison, N., 'Illegal Kidney Trade Booms as New Organ is Sold Every Hour' *Guardian* (28 May 2012) www.guardian.co.uk/world/2012/may/27/kidney-trade-illegal-operations-who

Chantler, C., 'Standardised Packaging of Tobacco: Report of the Independent Review Undertaken by Sir Cyril Chantler' (Williams Lea, 2014) www.kcl.ac.uk/health/10035-TSO-2901853-Chantler-Review-ACCESSIBLE.PDF

Chief Medical Officer, 'Making Amends: A Consultation Paper Setting out the Proposals for Reforming the Approach to Clinical Negligence in the NHS', Department of Health (2003) http://webarchive.nationalarchives.gov.uk/20130107105354/ http://www.dh.gov.uk/prod_consum_dh/groups/dh_digitalassets/@dh/@en/documents/digitalasset/dh_4060945.pdf

Chrisafis, A.,'PIP Breast Implant Bosses' Trial for Aggravated Fraud Begins in France', *Guardian* (16 April 2013) www.theguardian.com/world/2013/apr/16/pip-breast-implant-bosses-trial

Clarke, T., 'E-cigarettes May Not Be as Safe as You Think' *Huffington Post* (17 April 2014) www.huffingtonpost.com/2014/04/17/more-ecigarette-injuries_n_5165480.html

Commission for the Protection of Competition (Cyprus), 'Annual Report 2009' (2009) 22 www.competition.gov.cy/competition/competition.nsf/All/70DF59AB914E07EAC22577CF003A2A0F/$file/Annual%20Report%202009.pdf?OpenElement

Committee on Economic, Social and Cultural Rights, 'General Comment 14: The Right to the Highest Attainable Standard of Health', UN Doc. E/C.12/2000/4, UN Economic and Social Council (2000) http://docstore.ohchr.org/SelfServices/FilesHandler.ashx?enc=4slQ6QSmlBEDzFEovLCuW1AVC1NkPsgUedPlF1vfPMJ2c7ey6PAz2qaojTzDJmC0y%2b9t%2bsAtGDNzdEqA6SuP2r0w%2f6sVBGTpvTSCbiOr4XVFTqhQY65auTFbQRPWNDxL

Committee on the Internal Market and Consumer Protection and Committee on International Trade, 'Committee Report on the Proposal for a Regulation of the European Parliament and of the Council concerning Customs Enforcement of Intellectual Property Rights (COM(2011)0285)', A7–0046/2012, European Parliament (2012) www.europarl.europa.eu/sides/getDoc.do?pubRef=-//EP//NONSGML+REPORT+A7-2012-0046+0+DOC+PDF+V0//EN

Cook, J., 'Minimum Alcohol Pricing: Five Countries Oppose Scottish Drink Plan', BBC News (25 July 2013) www.bbc.co.uk/news/uk-scotland-scotland-politics-22182607

Correa, C. and Matthews, D., 'The Doha Declaration Ten Years on and its Impact on Access to Medicines and the Right to Health', United Nations (2011) www.undp.org/content/dam/undp/library/hivaids/Discussion_Paper_Doha_Declaration_Public_Health.pdf

'The Cost of Fertility Treatment Tourism' , BBC News (24 April 2011) www.bbc.co.uk/news/uk-scotland-13181119

Council of Europe, 'Background & Mission of the European Pharmacopoeia, Council of Europe (2014) www.edqm.eu/en/background-50.html

'Committee of Experts on Trafficking in Human Organs, Tissues and Cells (PC-TO)', *European Committee on Crime Problems (CDPC)*, Council of Europe (2014) www.coe.int/t/DGHL/STANDARDSETTING/CDPC/PC_TO_en.asp

'Committee of Ministers Recommendation 2004(7) to Member States on Organ Trafficking', Council of Europe (2004) https://wcd.coe.int/ViewDoc.jsp?id=744621

'EDQM', Council of Europe (2014) www.edqm.eu/en/Homepage-628.html

'The European Social Charter', Council of Europe (2014) www.coe.int/t/dghl/monitoring/socialcharter/presentation/aboutcharter_EN.asp

'The Medicrime Convention: Combating Counterfeiting of Medicial Products and Similar Crimes', Council of Europe (2011) www.coe.int/t/dghl/standardsetting/medicrime/medicrime_ENG_BAT_web_v2.pdf

'The Medicrime Convention', Council of Europe (2014) www.edqm.eu/en/the-medicrime-convention-1470.html

'Parliamentary Assembly Recommendation 1611 (2003) on Trafficking in Organs in Europe', Council of Europe (2003) http://assembly.coe.int/Main.asp?link=/Documents/AdoptedText/ta03/EREC1611.htm

'Recommendation Rec(2003)10 of the Committee of Ministers to Member States on Xenotransplantation (Adopted by the Committee of Ministers on 19 June 2003 at the 844th Meeting of the Ministers' Deputies)', Council of Europe (2014) https://wcd.coe.int/ViewDoc.jsp?id=45827

'Towards a Council of Europe Convention to Combat Trafficking in Organs, Tissues and Cells of Human Origin' (Committee on Social Affairs, Health and Sustainable Development), Council of Europe (20 December 2012) http://assembly.coe.int/ASP/XRef/X2H-DW-XSL.asp?fileid=19236&lang=EN

'Trafficking in Organs in Europe', Doc. 9822, Council of Europe (2003) http://assembly.coe.int/ASP/Doc/XrefViewHTML.asp?FileID=10176&Language=en

Council of the European Union, 'Agreement and Ratification Database', Council of Europe (2014) www.consilium.europa.eu/policies/agreements/search-the-agreements-database

'Couple Abandon Battle for Baby of their Choice', *Sunday Times* (Scotland) (23 January 2005), available at: http://www.bionews.org.uk/page_12230.asp

Croatian Competition Agency (AZTN), 'Exclusively Croatian Institute for Health Insurance decides on prescription drug benefit programmes', AZTN (6 February 2012) www.aztn.hr/article/623/exclusively-croatian-institute-for-health-insurance-decides-on-prescription-drug-benefit-programmes

Danish Competition and Consumer Authority, 'Decision by the Danish Competition Appeals Tribunal: The Insolvency Scheme of the Pharmaceutical Sector', Danish Competition and Consumer Authority (8 June 2007) http://en.kfst.dk/Indhold-KFST/English/Judgements/20070608-Decision-by-the-Danish-Competition-Appeals-Tribunal?tc=D5B236A4F02D4495866A6C4A6BE0EEB8

'Regulation of Pharmacies', Danish Competition and Consumer Authority (23 February 2010) http://en.kfst.dk/Indhold-KFST/English/News/20100223-Regulation-of-Pharmacies?tc=51FB8908FD98420B832C134E5E0A6A1D

Davies, G., 'The Process and Side-effects of Harmonisation of European Welfare States', Jean Monnet working paper 2/06 (2006) www.jeanmonnetprogram.org/papers/06/060201.pdf

De Souza, N., 'Competition in Pharmaceuticals: The Challenges Ahead Post *AstraZeneca*', Competition Policy Newsletter (2007) http://ec.europa.eu/competition/sectors/pharmaceuticals/2007_1_39.pdf

De Witte, B., 'Setting the Scene: How Did Services Get to Bolkestein and Why?', Edinburgh Europa Institute Mitchell working paper series 3/2007 (2007)

www.europa.ed.ac.uk/_data/assets/pdf_file/0009/110979/28_settingthescenehow didservicesgettobolkesteinandwhy.pdf

Defossez, A., 'The Danish Competition Council Found an Insolvency Agreement between Three Medical Wholesale Dealers and the Danish Pharmaceutical Association to be Incompatible with Art. 81 EC and Relevant National Competition Law Provision', *Bulletin e-Competitions Healthcare*, Art. N° 24451 (2005) www.concurrences.com/article.php3?id_article=24451&lang=fr

Department for Business Innovation & Skills, 'UK Government Response: European Commission Public Consultation on the Mutual Recognition of Professional Qualifications Directive', Department for Business Innovation & Skills (2011) https://www.gov.uk/government/uploads/system/uploads/attachment_data/file/32276/11-794-uk-government-response-mutual-recognition-professional-qualifications.pdf

Devlin, K., 'Hundreds of Women Risk Health by Fertility Tourism' *Daily Telegraph* (29 June 2009) www.telegraph.co.uk/health/healthnews/5685785/Hundreds-of-women-risk-health-by-fertility-tourism.html

Dood, R. and Munck, L., 'Dying For Change: Poor People's Experience of Health and Ill-health', WHO and World Bank (2000) www.who.int/hdp/publications/dying_change.pdf

Dransfield, S., 'Oxfam Reaction to European Parliament Vote on ACTA', Oxfam (4 July 2012) www.oxfam.org.uk/media-centre/press-releases/2012/07/acta-reaction

Dussault, G. and Buchan, J., 'The Economic Crisis in the EU: Impact on Health Workforce Mobility', in J. Buchan, M. Wismar, I.A. Glinos and J. Bremner (eds.), 'Health Professional Mobility in a Changing Europe: New Dynamics, Mobile Individuals and Diverse Responses', WHO (2014) www.euro.who.int/_data/assets/pdf_file/0006/248343/Health-Professional-Mobility-in-a-Changing-Europe.pdf

EFTA Court, 'Introduction to the EFTA Court' (2014) www.eftacourt.int/the-court/jurisdiction-organisation/introduction/

Estonian Competition Authority, 'Annual Report 2009' (2009) www.konkurentsiamet.ee/public/AnnualReports_/Annual_Report_2009.pdf

'EU's Top Court Hears Dispute over EU Commissioner Dalli', BBC News (8 July 2014) www.bbc.co.uk/news/world-europe-28209161

Eurobarometer, 'Attitudes of Europeans Towards Tobacco: Report', Commission (2012) http://ec.europa.eu/health/tobacco/docs/eurobaro_attitudes_towards_tobacco_2012_en.pdf

European Accreditation Council for Continuing Medical Education (2013) www.uems.eu

European Anti-Fraud Office, 'OLAF press statement, Commission (19 October 2012) http://ec.europa.eu/anti_fraud/media-corner/press-releases/press-releases/2012/20121019_01_en.htm

OLAF Statement in Light of Recent Comments Made by the Maltese Police Commissioner', Commission (2 June 2014) http://ec.europa.eu/anti_fraud/mobile/media-corner/press-releases/2013/20130611_01_en.htm

European Centre for Disease Prevention and Control (ECDC), 'Partnerships', ECDC (2014) www.ecdc.europa.eu/en/aboutus/Partnerships/Pages/partnerships.aspx

European Environment Agency (EEA), 'Impact of Selected Policy Measures on Europe's Air Quality', EEA Technical Report no. 8/2010, EEA (2010) www.eea.europa.eu/publications/impact-of-selected-policy-measures

European Food Safety Authority (EFSA), 'Dietary Reference Values and Dietary Guidelines', EFSA (22 July 2014) www.efsa.europa.eu/en/topics/topic/drv.htm

'Food-borne Zoonotic Diseases', EFSA (19 February 2014) www.efsa.europa.eu/en/topics/topic/foodbornezoonoticdiseases.htm

'Image of the European Food Safety Authority (EFSA): Qualitative Research Report', EFSA (2010) www.efsa.europa.eu/en/mb100318/docs/mb100318-ax8a.pdf

'International Activities: A Strategic Approach – Document Describing EFSA's Strategic Approach to its International Activities', EFSA (2009) www.efsa.europa.eu/en/corporate/doc/intstrategicen.pdf

'International Scientific Cooperation', EFSA (2014) www.efsa.europa.eu/en/networks/international.htm

'Multi-annual Programme on International Scientific Cooperation 2014–2016', EFSA (7 July 2014) www.efsa.europa.eu/en/corporate/pub/iscmap1416.htm

'Science Strategy 2012–2016', EFSA (2012) www.efsa.europa.eu/en/corporate/doc/sciencestrategy12.pdf

'Strategic Plan of the European Food Safety Authority for 2009–2013', EFSA (2008) www.efsa.europa.eu/en/corporate/doc/stratplan09en.pdf

European Global Strategy, 'Towards a European Global Strategy', Swedish Institute of International Affairs (2014) www.europeanglobalstrategy.eu/

European Group on Ethics in Science and New Technologies, Opinion no. 21, *Ethical Aspects of Nanomedicine*, European Group on Ethics in Science and New Technologies (2007) http://ec.europa.eu/bepa/european-group-ethics/publications/opinions/index_en.htm

Opinion no. 25, *The Ethics of Synthetic Biology*, European Group on Ethics in Science and New Technologies (2009) http://ec.europa.eu/bepa/european-group-ethics/publications/opinions/index_en.htm

'Statement of the European Group on Ethics in Science and New Technologies on the Proposal for a Regulation of the European Parliament and the Council on Clinical Trials on Medicinal Products for Human Use and Repealing Directive 2001/20/EC (COM 2012), 369 final', European Group on Ethics in Science and New Technologies (2013) www.eurecnet.org/documents/proposal_for_a_regulation_of_the_european_parliament_and_the_council_on_....pdf

European Health & Fitness Association, 'The 2013 State of the UK Fitness Industry Report', European Health & Fitness Association (17 June 2013) www.ehfa.eu.com/node/324

European Medicines Agency (EMA), 'Common Technical Document for the Registration of Pharmaceuticals for Human Use', CPMP/ICH/2887/99, EMA (2004) www.ema.europa.eu/docs/en_GB/document_library/Scientific_guideline/2009/09/WC500002721.pdf

'European Medicines Agency Agrees Policy on Publication of Clinical Trial Data with More User-friendly Amendments', EMA (12 June 2014) www.ema.europa.eu/ema/index.jsp?curl=pages/news_and_events/news/2014/06/news_detail_002124.jsp&mid=WC0b01ac058004d5c1

'Falsified Medicines', EMA (2014) www.ema.europa.eu/ema/index.jsp?curl=pages/special_topics/general/general_content_000186.jsp&mid=WC0b01ac058002d4e8

'Guideline on Similar Biological Medicinal Products' (CHMP/437/04), EMA (2005) www.ema.europa.eu/docs/en_GB/document_library/Scientific_guideline/2009/09/WC500003517.pdf

'ICH Guideline E11: Note for Guidance on Clinical Investigation of Medicinal Products in the Paediatric Population' (CPMP/ICH/2711/99), EMA (2001) www.ema.europa.eu/docs/en_GB/document_library/Scientific_guideline/2009/09/WC500002926.pdf

'ICH Guideline S6 (R1): Preclinical Safety Evaluation of Biotechnology-Derived Pharmaceuticals' (CHMP/ICH/302/95), EMA (2009) www.ema.europa.eu/docs/en_GB/document_library/Scientific_guideline/2009/09/WC500002828.pdf

'ICH Guidelines', EMA (2014) www.ema.europa.eu/ema/index.jsp?curl=pages/regulation/general/general_content_000035.jsp&mid=WC0b01ac0580027645

'Reflection Paper on Nanotechnology-based Medicinal Products for Human Use' (EMEA/CHMP/79769/2006), EMA (2006) www.ema.europa.eu/docs/en_GB/document_library/Regulatory_and_procedural_guideline/2010/01/WC500069728.pdf

'Roadmap to 2015: The European Medicines Agency's Contribution to Science, Medicines and Health', EMA (2010) www.ema.europa.eu/docs/en_GB/document_library/Report/2011/01/WC500101373.pdf

'European Medicines Agency Rejects Ombudsman's Concerns on Public Access to Clinical Trial Data', Out-Law (20 May 2014) http://www.out-law.com/en/articles/2014/may/european-medicines-agency-rejects-ombudsmans-concerns-on-clinical-data-trial-public-acccess/

European Monitoring Centre on Racism and Xenophobia (EUMC), 'Breaking the Barriers: Romani Women and Access to Public Health Care', EUMC (2003) http://fra.europa.eu/sites/default/files/fra_uploads/180-ROMA-HC-EN.pdf

European Observatory on Health Care Systems, 'Health Care Systems in Transition Studies', WHO (various dates) www.euro.who.int/en/who-we-are/partners/observatory/health-systems-in-transition-hit-series

European Ombudsman, 'Decision of the European Ombudsman Closing his Inquiry into Complaint 2560/2007/BEH against the European Medicines Agency', European Ombudsman (24 November 2010) www.ombudsman.europa.eu/en/cases/decision.faces/en/5459/html.bookmark

'European Ombudsman Reaction to EMA's 12 June 2014 statement Issued after its Management Board Meeting', European Ombudsman (13 June 2014) www.ombudsman.europa.eu/en/resources/otherdocument.faces/en/54540/html.bookmark

European Parliament Committee on Environment, Public Health and Food Safety, 'Draft Report on the Proposal for a Directive of the European Parliament and of the Council on the Approximation of the Laws, Regulations and Administrative Provisions of the Member States concerning the Manufacture, Presentation and Sale of Tobacco and Related Products (COM(2012)0788 – 2012/0366(COD)), European Parliament (2013) www.europarl.europa.eu/sides/getDoc.do?pubRef=-%2f%2fEP%2f%2fNONSGML%2bCOMPARL%2bPE-508.085%2b03%2bDOC%2bPDF%2bV0%2f%2fEN

European Patent Office, 'Guidelines for Examination of Patent Applications: Part G: Patentability', European Patent Office (2013) http://documents.epo.org/projects/babylon/eponet.nsf/0/6c9c0ec38c2d48dfc1257a21004930f4/$FILE/guidelines_for_examination_2013_part_g_en.pdf

'Substantive Patient Law Harmonisation: The Tegernsee Process', European Patent Office (14 May 2014) www.epo.org/news-issues/issues/harmonisation.html

European Traffic Safety Council (ETSC), '2010 Road Safety Target Outcome: 100,000 Fewer Deaths since 2001', 5th Road Safety PIN Report (ETSC 2011) http://archive.etsc.eu/documents/ETSC_2011_PIN_Report.PDF

European Union Agency for Fundamental Rights (FRA), 'Annual Report. Fundamental Rights: Challenges and Achievements in 2010', FRA (2011) http://fra.europa.eu/sites/default/files/fra_uploads/1633-annual-report-2011_EN.pdf

'Assisting Member States to Measure the Progress of Roma Integration', *FRA* (ongoing) http://fra.europa.eu/en/project/2013/multi-annual-roma-programme?tab=member-states

'Choice and Control: The Right to Independent Living', FRA (2012) http://fra.europa.eu/sites/default/files/choice_and_control_en_13.pdf

'Collecting Secondary Data and Mapping Official Data Sources', FRA (ongoing) http://fra.europa.eu/en/project/2013/multi-annual-roma-programme?tab=secondary-data

'Coping with a Fundamental Rights Emergency: The Situation of Persons Crossing the Greek Land Border in an Irregular Manner', FRA (2011) fra.europa.eu/fraWebsite/attachments/Greek- http://border-situation-report2011_EN.pdf

'Inequalities and Multiple Discrimination in Healthcare', FRA (2012) http://fra.europa.eu/fraWebsite/attachments/FRA-Factsheet_InequMultDiscrimination_EN.pdf

'Inequalities in Multiple Discrimination in Access to and Quality of Healthcare', FRA (2013) http://fra.europa.eu/sites/default/files/inequalities-discrimination-healthcare_en.pdf

'Involuntary Placement and Involuntary Treatment of Persons with Mental Health Problems', FRA (2012) http://fra.europa.eu/sites/default/files/involuntary-placement-and-involuntary-treatment-of-persons-with-mental-health-problems_en.pdf

'Legal Capacity of Persons with Intellectual Disabilities and Persons with Mental Health Problems', FRA (2013) http://fra.europa.eu/sites/default/files/legal-capacity-intellectual-disabilities-mental-health-problems.pdf

'Migrants in an Irregular Situation: Access to Health Care in 10 EU Member States', FRA (2011) http://fra.europa.eu/sites/default/files/fra_uploads/1771-FRA-2011-fundamental-rights-for-irregular-migrants-healthcare_EN.pdf

'Multi-Annual Programme', FRA (2013) http://fra.europa.eu/en/project/2013/multi-annual-roma-programme?tab=pilot-survey

'The Race Equality Directive: Application and Challenges', FRA (2011) http://fra.europa.eu/sites/default/files/fra_uploads/1916-FRA-RED-synthesis-report_EN.pdf

'Separated Asylum-seeking Children in EU Member States: A Comparative Report', FRA (2011) http://fra.europa.eu/fraWebsite/attachments/SEPAC-comparative-report_EN.pdf

'The Situation of Roma in 11 Member States', FRA (2012) http://fra.europa.eu/sites/default/files/fra_uploads/2099-FRA-2012-Roma-at-a-glance_EN.pdf

European Union Platform on Diet, Physical Activity and Health, '2010 Annual Report', European Union Platform on Diet, Physical Activity and Health (2010) http://ec.europa.eu/health/nutrition_physical_activity/docs/eu_platform_2010frep_en.pdf

Eurostat, 'Gross Domestic Expenditure on R&D (GERD)', Eurostat (28 May 2014) http://epp.eurostat.ec.europa.eu/tgm/table.do?tab=table&init=1&plugin=0&language=en&pcode=t2020_20&tableSelection=1

The Expert Group on Phase One Clinical Trials, 'Final Report', Department of Health (2006) http://webarchive.nationalarchives.gov.uk/+/dh.gov.uk/en/publicationsandstatistics/publications/publicationspolicyandguidance/dh_063117

Federation of the European Academies of Medicine (FEAM), 'Opportunities and Challenges for Reforming the EU Clinical Trials Directive: Statement', FEAM (2010) https://www.acmedsci.ac.uk/viewFile/51f9051c3b08d.pdf

Finnish Competition Authority, 'Competition: Key to Efficiency: Finnish Competition Authority Yearbook 2009', Finnish Competition Authority (2010) www.kilpailuvirasto.fi/tiedostot/vuosikirja-2010-englanti.pdf

'Finish Competition Authority Yearbook 2003', Finish Competition Authority Yearbook (2003) www.kilpailuvirasto.fi/tiedostot/vuosikirja-2003-englanti.pdf

'Finnish Competition Authority Yearbook 2006', Finnish Competition Authority (2006) www.kilpailuvirasto.fi/tiedostot/vuosikirja-2006-englanti.pdf

'Finnish Competition Authority Yearbook 2009', Finnish Competition Authority (2009) www.kilpailuvirasto.fi/tiedostot/vuosikirja-2009-englanti.pdf

Flear, M. 'Offshoring Clinical Trials: The Mutable Ethics, Weak Protections and Vulnerable Subjects of EU Law', Centre for European Legal Studies Seminar Paper (2013) www.cels.law.cam.ac.uk/Mark_Flear_paper.pdf

Food and Agriculture Organization of the United Nations (FAO), 'About FAO', FAO (2014) www.fao.org/about/en/

'Governing and Statutory Bodies Website: Agriculture: European Commission on Agriculture', FAO (2014) www.fao.org/unfao/govbodies/gsb-subject-matter/gsb-agriculture/detail/en/?dyna_fef%5Buid%5D=76

'Governing and Statutory Bodies Website: Food Policy and Nutrition – Codex Alimentarius Commission', FAO (2014) www.fao.org/unfao/govbodies/gsb-subject-matter/gsb-foodpolicy/detail/en/?dyna_fef%5Buid%5D=211

Fox, B., 'Drugs Supplies to Euro Crisis Countries at Risk, Warn Health Analysts', eu observer, 23 August 2012) http://euobserver.com/social/117316

Fox, N.J. and Ward, K.J., 'Pharma in the Bedroom . . . and the Kitchen . . . The Pharmaceuticalisation of Daily Life' (2008) 30(6) Sociology of Health and Illness 856

France Diplomatie, 'Innovative Financing for Development', France Diplomatie (26 December 2013) www.diplomatie.gouv.fr/en/french-foreign-policy-1/development-assistance/innovative-financing-for/

Galan, A., Olsavszky, V. and Vladescu, C., 'Emergent Challenge of Health Professional Emigration: Romania's Accession to the EU', in M. Wismar, C.B. Maier, I.A. Glinos et al. (eds.), 'Health Professional Mobility and Health Systems: Evidence from 17 European Countries', WHO (2011) www.euro.who.int/__data/assets/pdf_file/0017/152324/e95812.pdf?ua=1

Gallagher, J., 'Tough EU Smoking Rules Approved', BBC News (24 February 2014) www.bbc.co.uk/news/health-26355419

GAVI, 'Pneumococcal AMC', GAVI (2014) www.gavialliance.org/funding/pneumococcal-amc/

General Medical Council (GMC), 'Consent Guidance: Patients and Doctors Making Decision Together', GMC (2008) www.gmc-uk.org/static/documents/content/Consent_-_English_0414.pdf

Geradin, D. and Petit, N., 'The Development of Agencies at EU and National Levels: Conceptual Analysis and Proposals for Reform' Jean Monnet working paper no. 01/04 (2004) www.jeanmonnetprogram.org/archive/papers/04/040101.pdf

'German Medics Challenge New EU Clinical Drugs Trials', BBC News (25 September 2012) http://www.bbc.co.uk/news/world-europe-19711026

'"Get Tough" on Unhealthy: Survey', BBC News (22 November 2005) http://news.bbc.co.uk/1/hi/health/4457330.stm

Glinos, I.A., 'Going Beyond Numbers: A Typology of Professional Mobility Inside and Outside the European Union' (2014) 33(1) *Policy and Society* 25

Glinos, I.A. and Baeten, R., 'A Literature Review of Cross-Border Patient Mobility in the European Union', Observatoire social européen (2006) www.ose.be/files/publication/health/WP12_lit_review_final.pdf

The Global Fund, 'Annual Report 2011' (2011) available at: https://web.archive.org/web/20130409015756/http://www.theglobalfund.org/en/library/publications/annualreports

Global Pharma Health Fund (GPHF), 'The Global Pharma Health Fund (GPHF)', (2014) www.gphf.org/web/en/start/index.htm

Greer, S.L, 'Power Struggle: The Politics and Policy Consequences of Patient Mobility in Europe', policy paper no. 2, Observatoire social européen (2008) www.ose.be/files/publication/policy_papers/OSEPolicypaper2_Greer_EN.pdf

Ham, C. and Walsh, N., 'Making Integrated Care Happen at Scale and Pace', The King's Fund (2013) www.kingsfund.org.uk/sites/files/kf/field/field_publication_file/making-integrated-care-happen-kingsfund-mar13.pdf

Hammarberg, T. (Commissioner for Human Rights of the Council of Europe), 'Human Rights of Asylum Seekers and Refugees', CommDH(2009)31, Council of Europe (2009) https://wcd.coe.int/com.instranet.InstraServlet?Index=no&command=com.instranet.CmdBlobGet&InstranetImage=1521616&SecMode=1&DocId=1501516&Usage=2

Havinga, T., 'Transitions in Food Governance in Europe from National towards EU and Global Regulation and from Public Towards Hybrid and Private Forms of Governance', Nijmegen Sociology of Law, working paper no. 2012/02 (2012) http://papers.ssrn.com/sol3/papers.cfm?abstract_id=2189478

Henley, J., 'E-cigarettes: miracle or health risk?', Guardian (5 May 2104) www.theguardian.com/society/2014/may/05/rise-of-e-cigarettes-miracle-or-health-risk

Heyvaert, V., 'Europe in a Climate of Risk: Three Paradigms at Play' London School of Economics Law, Society and Economy working papers 06/2010 (2010) http://eprints.lse.ac.uk/32904/1/WPS2010-06_Heyvaert.pdf

High Level Group on Nutrition and Physical Activity, 'EU Action Plan on Childhood Obesity', High Level Group (2014) http://ec.europa.eu/health/nutrition_physical_activity/docs/childhoodobesity_actionplan_2014_2020_en.pdf

Hildebrand, M., 'Open Government in the EU: Dalligate Tests the European Parliament's Oversight over the European Commission', ACELG (20 November 2012) http://acelg.blogactiv.eu/2012/11/20/what-does-dalligate-tell-us-about-european-transparency/#more-56

HOSPEEM and EPSU, 'EPSU- HOSPEEM Code of Conduct and Follow up on Ethical Cross-Border Recruitment and Retention in the Hospital Sector', HOSPEEM and EPSU (2008) http://ec.europa.eu/social/BlobServlet?docId=203&langId=en

Howat, C., Ulicna, D. and Harris, P., 'Study Evaluating the Professional Qualifications Directive against Recent Educational Reforms in EU Member States', Danish

Technological Institute (2011) http://ec.europa.eu/internal_market/qualifications/docs/policy_developments/final_report_en.pdf

Human Rights Watch, 'Left to Survive: Systematic Failure to Protect Unaccompanied Migrant Children in Greece', Human Rights Watch (2008) www.hrw.org/sites/default/files/reports/greece1208webwcover_0.pdf

Hungarian Competition Authority, 'Bidders Cooperated in University Hospitals Public Procurement, Municipial Court of Budapest Upheld', Hungarian Competition Authority (21 February 2007) www.gvh.hu/en/press_room/press_releases/press_releases_2007/4438_en_bidders_cooperated_in_university_hospitals_public_procurement_municipial_court_of_budapest_upheld.html

'Implants: France Recommends Removal but UK Does Not', BBC News (23 December 2011) http://www.bbc.co.uk/news/health-16311763

International Food Safety Authorities Network (INFOSAN), 'Enhancing INFOSAN in Asia and Implementation of Regional Food Safety Strategies: Meeting Report' (WHO 2013) www.fao.org/fileadmin/user_upload/agns/pdf/Infosan/Enhancing_INFOSAN_in_Asia_meeting_report.pdf

Irish Competition Authority, 'The Competition Authority and the Irish Medical Organisation: Heads of Agreement', Irish Competition Authority (2014) www.tca.ie/images/uploaded/documents/2014-05-28%20CA%20v%20IMO%20Signed%20Settlement%20Agreement.pdf

'Competition Authority Secures High Court Undertakings from the Irish Medical Organisation', Irish Competition Authority (28 May 2014) www.tca.ie/EN/News–Publications/Press-Releases/Competition-Authority-secures-High-Court-undertakings-from-the-Irish-Medical-Organisation.aspx

'Competition in Professional Services: General Medical Practitioners', Irish Competition Authority (2010) www.tca.ie/images/uploaded/documents/General%20Medical%20Practitioners%20Report.pdf

'General Medical Practitioners (GPs)', Irish Competition Authority (June 2013) www.tca.ie/EN/Promoting-Competition/Market-Studies/Professions/General-Medical-Practitioners.aspx

'Notice in Respect of Collective Action in the Community Pharmacy Sector', Decision no. N/09/001, Irish Competition Authority (2009) www.tca.ie/images/uploaded/documents/Guidance%20Notice%20on%20Community%20Pharmacy%20%2823.09.09%29.pdf

'Notice in Respect of Collective Action in the Community Pharmacy Sector' (23 September 2009) www.tca.ie/EN/News–Publications/News-Releases/Competition-Authority-Publishes-Guidance-on-Collective-Action-in-the-Pharmacy-Sector.aspx?page=5&year=0

'Patients will Benefit from Changes to GP System', Irish Competition Authority (15 September 2011) www.tca.ie/EN/News–Publications/News-Releases/Patients-will-benefit-from-changes-to-GP-system.aspx?page=1&year=0

'What's the story . . . with the IMO representing their members?', Irish Competition Authority (3 July 2014) http://tca.ie/EN/Whats-The-Story/IMO.aspx?page=0

Irish Medical Organisation www.imo.ie/

ITV News, 'Lancashire Firms Legal Challenge Over e-Cigarettes', ITV News (20 August 2014) www.itv.com/news/granada/story/2014-08-19/lancashire-e-cigarette-firm-legal-challenge/

Kannan, S., 'Counterfeit Drugs Targeted by Technology in India', BBC News (11 October 2011) www.bbc.co.uk/news/business-15208595

Kaplan, W., Wirtz, V.J., Mantel-Teeuwisse, et al., 'Priority Medicines for Europe and the World', WHO (2013) http://ec.europa.eu/enterprise/sectors/healthcare/files/docs/prioritymedicines_report_en.pdf

Kautsch, M. and Czabanowsk, K., 'When the Grass Gets Greener at Home: Poland's Changing Incentives for Health Professional Mobility', in M. Wismar, C.B. Maier, I.A. Glinos et al. (eds.), 'Health Professional Mobility and Health Systems: Evidence from 17 European Countries' (WHO 2011) www.euro.who.int/__data/assets/pdf_file/0017/152324/e95812.pdf?ua=1

Kennedy, I., 'The Report of the Public Inquiry into Children's Heart Surgery at the Bristol Royal Infirmary 1984–1995: Learning from Bristol', Bristol Royal Infirmary Inquiry (2001) http://webarchive.nationalarchives.gov.uk/+/www.dh.gov.uk/en/Publicationsandstatistics/Publications/PublicationsPolicyAndGuidance/DH_4005620

Keogh, B., 'Review of the Regulation of Cosmetic Interventions', Department of Health (2013) www.nhs.uk/NHSEngland/bruce-keogh-review/Documents/outcomes/keogh-review-final-report.pdf

Kogustowska, M., 'France Allows Taurine in *Red Bull*', FoodBev (2 June 2008) www.foodbev.com/news/france-allows-taurine-in-red-bull#.VBslV6zwpmo

Koller, T. (ed.), 'Poverty and Social Exclusion in the WHO European Region: Health Systems Respond', WHO Regional Office for Europe (2010) www.euro.who.int/__data/assets/pdf_file/0006/115485/E94018.pdf

Koller, T., 'Poverty, Social Exclusion and Health Systems in the WHO European Region', WHO Regional Office for Europe (2010) www.euro.who.int/__data/assets/pdf_file/0004/127525/e94499.pdf

Koncurences Padome (Latvian Competition Council), 'Existing Regulation Impedes Price Competition in Medicine Market', Latvian Competition Council (13 May 2011) www.kp.gov.lv/en/aktualitates-pagaidam-lv/25-tests-eng

The Lancet Commisions, Education of Health Professionals for the 21st Century, 'Health Professionals For a New Century: Transforming Education to Strengthen Health Systems in an Interdependent World', (29 November 2010) www.thelancet.com/journals/lancet/article/PIIS0140-6736(10)61854-5/abstract

Lawrence, F., 'Horsemeat Scandal: Where Did the 29% Horsemeat in Your Tesco Burger Come From?' *Guardian* (22 October 2013) www.theguardian.com/uk-news/2013/oct/22/horsemeat-scandal-guardian-investigation-public-secrecy

Letter from Emily O'Reilly (European Ombudsman) to José Manuel Barroso (European Commission President) (3 June 2014) www.ombudsman.europa.eu/en/resources/otherdocument.faces/en/54531/html.bookmark

Lichfield, J., 'Breast Implants Ruling in PIP Scandal Could Lead to Compensation for 400,000 women' *Independent* (14 November 2013) www.independent.co.uk/news/world/europe/court-finds-german-firm-liable-over-pip-implants-8940208.html

McNeill, D. and Coonan, C., 'Japanese Flock to China for Organ Transplants', *Asia Times online* (4 April 2006) www.atimes.com/atimes/China/HD04Ad01.html

Maduro, M., 'How Constitutional Can the European Union Be? The Tension between Intergovernmentalism and Constitutionalism in the European Union', Jean Monnet working paper 5/04 (2004) www.jeanmonnetprogram.org/archive/papers/04/040501-18.pdf

Maier-Rigaud, F., 'The Commission Proposal for a European Tobacco Products Directive: A Critical Evaluation of the Roland Berger Studies' IESEG working paper series no. 2013- ECO-06 (2013) www.ieseg.fr/wp-content/uploads/2013-ECO-06_Maier-Rigaud.pdf

Mandal, S., Gilmore, A., Collin, J., et al., 'Block, Amend, Delay: Tobacco Industry Efforts to Influence the EU's Tobacco Products Directive (2001/37/EC)', SmokeFree Partnership (2009) http://esi.praguesummerschools.org/files/esi/12esi.pdf

Mara, K. and New, W., 'Concerns Continue Over Generic Drug Seizures As Legality Debates Begin', Intellectual Property Watch (5 March 2009) www.ip-watch.org/2009/03/05/concerns-continue-over-generics-drug-seizures-as-legality-debates-begin/

Mattoo, A. and Rathindran, R., 'Does Health Insurance Impede Trade in Health Care Services?' World Bank Policy Research working paper no. 3667 (2005) www-wds.worldbank.org/servlet/WDSContentServer/WDSP/IB/2005/07/19/000016406_20050719140725/Rendered/PDF/wps3667.pdf

Mauro, M., 'Parliamentary Questions: Subject: Developing Medicines for Neglected Diseases: The Priority Review Voucher', European Parliament (24 January 2011) www.europarl.europa.eu/sides/getDoc.do?pubRef=-//EP//TEXT+WQ+E-2011-000293+0+DOC+XML+V0//EN&language=LT

Médecins Sans Frontières (MSF), 'MSF Briefing Document: A Blank Cheque for Abuse' (Médicins Sans Frontières 2012) www.msfaccess.org/sites/default/files/MSF_assets/Access/Docs/Access_Briefing_ACTABlankCheque_ENG_2012.pdf

'Not Criminals', Médecins Sans Frontières (2009) www.aerzte-ohne- http://grenzen.at/fileadmin/data/pdf/reports/2009/MSF_Report_Malta_2009.pdf

Menghaney, L., '"Counterfeit" Confusion Diverts Action from Drug Quality', Médecins Sans Frontières (4 April 2011) www.msfaccess.org/our-work/overcoming-barriers-access/article/1312

Merkur, S., Sassi, F. and McDaid, D., 'Promoting Health, Preventing Disease: Is There an Economic Case?', European Observatory on Health Systems and Policies, WHO Europe (2013) www.euro.who.int/__data/assets/pdf_file/0004/235966/e96956.pdf

Meyer, D., 'ACTA Gets Final Stake Through Heart as EC Drops Court Referral', ZDNet (20 December 2012) www.zdnet.com/acta-gets-final-stake-through-heart-as-ec-drops-court-referral-7000009070/

MHRA, 'Counterfeit Medical Devices' (2 May 2012) www.mhra.gov.uk/Safety information/Generalsafetyinformationandadvice/Adviceandinformationfor consumers/counterfeitmedicinesanddevices/Falsifiedmedicaldevices/index.htm

'UK Moves Towards Safe and Effective Electronic Cigarettes and Other Nicotine-containing Products' (12 June 2013) www.mhra.gov.uk/NewsCentre/Pressreleases/CON286855

Mladovsky, P., Allin, S., Masseria, C., et al., 'Health in the European Union: Trends and Analysis', European Observatory on Health Systems and Policies (2009) www.euro.who.int/__data/assets/pdf_file/0003/98391/E93348.pdf?ua=1

Morée, I., Kuipers, G., Hustinx, J.P. and Kokke, M., 'It Might Take Three to Bolar', Lexology (10 February 2014) www.lexology.com/library/detail.aspx?g=138ee0b2-2348-4f12-b40b-3cb326b3c4e0

Mossialos, E., Costa-Font, J. and Rudisill, C., 'Does Organ Donation Legislation Affect Individuals' Willingness to Donate their Own or their Relative's Organs? Evidence

from European Union Survey Data', BMC Health Services Research (2008) www
.biomedcentral.com/content/pdf/1472-6963-8-48.pdf

National Prescribing Centre, 'Non-Medical Prescribing Competency Frameworks' (20
May 2011) www.npc.nhs.uk/guidance_nmp.php

Negri, S., 'Food Safety and Global Health: An International Law Perspective', Global
Health Governance (1 September 2009) http://blogs.shu.edu/ghg/2009/09/01/
food-safety-and-global-health-an-international-law-perspective/

Netherlands Competition Authority (NMa), 'Amsterdam-based Hospitals to Adjust
Their Information Exchange Processes after NMa Investigation', *NMa* (4 January 2011) https://www.acm.nl/en/publications/publication/6523/Amsterdam-
based-hospitals-to-adjust-their-information-exchange-processes-after-NMa-
investigation

'NMa: An Efficient Purchasing Process Helps Control Costs of Medical Equipment',
NMa (15 February 2012) www.nma.nl/en/documents_and_publications/press_
releases/news/2012/04_12_nma__an_efficient_purchasing_process_helps_control_
costs_of_medical_equipment.aspx

'NMa Blocks Merger of Health Care Providers in Central Netherlands',
NMa (20 December 2011) https://www.acm.nl/en/publications/publication/6714/
NMa-blocks-merger-of-health-care-providers-in-central-Netherlands/

'NMa Confirms Investigation into Two Amsterdam-based Hospitals', NMa
(11 February 2010) https://www.acm.nl/en/publications/publication/6257/NMa-
confirms-investigation-into-two-Amsterdam-based-hospitals/

'NMa Fines Dutch National Association of General Practitioners for Illegal
Establishment Recommendations', NMa (9 January 2012) www.acm.nl/en/
publications/publication/6719/NMa-fines-Dutch-National-Association-of-
General-Practitioners-for-illegal-establishment-recommendations/

'NMa Says Proposed Hospital Merger in Western Netherlands Requires a License',
NMa (14 February 2012) https://www.acm.nl/en/publications/publication/6731/
NMa-says-proposed-hospital-merger-in-western-Netherlands-requires-a-license/

NHS, 'Statins', NHS Choices (25 March 2014) www.nhs.uk/conditions/
Cholesterol-lowering-medicines-statins/pages/introduction.aspx

NHS Employers, 'Working Time Directive', NHS Employers (2014) www.nhsemployers
.org/EmploymentPolicyAndPractice/European_employment_policy/Pages/
Working-Time-Directive.aspx

NHS Health Research Authority, 'NIHR Call for Simple and Efficient Trials
(Closed)', NHS Health Research Authority (2014) www.hra.nhs.uk/about-the-hra/
consultations-calls/closed-consultations/nihr-call-simple-efficient-trials-active/

NHS Scotland, 'Patient Rights and Responsibilities: A Draft for Consultation', The
Scottish Executive (2003) www.scotland.gov.uk/Resource/Doc/47034/0030150.pdf

Nicotine Science & Policy, 'Legal Challenge against EU Tobacco Directive' (20
August 2014) http://nicotinepolicy.net/n-s-p/2364-first-legal-challenge-against-
eu-tobacco-products-directive

Nielson, N., 'Barrosso Faces Dalli at EU Court in Tobacco Lobby Case', eu*observer* (8
July 2014) http://euobserver.com/institutional/124890

'Judges to Cross-examine Barroso in Tobacco Lobby Case', *euobserver* (3 July 2014)
http://euobserver.com/institutional/124864

'Tobacco Giant Spent up to €1.25mn on EU Lobbying in 2012', *euobserver* (3 October
2013) http://euobserver.com/institutional/121657

Nuffield Council on Bioethics, 'The Ethics of Research Related to Healthcare in Developing Countries', Nuffield Council on Bioethics (2002) http://nuffield bioethics.org/wp-content/uploads/2014/07/Ethics-of-research-related-to-healthcare-in-developing-countries-I.pdf

Public Health: Ethical Issues (Cambridge Publishers, 2007) http://nuffieldbioethics.org/wp-content/uploads/2014/07/Public-health-ethical-issues.pdf

Ó Cathaoir, K., 'Is Obesity a Disability?', *EU Law Analysis* (18 July 2014) http://eulawanalysis.blogspot.co.uk/2014/07/is-obesity-disability.html

Oortwijn, W., Mathijssen, J., Stoicescu, D., et al., 'External Evaluation of the ECDC: Final Report', Ecorys 2008) www.ecdc.europa.eu/en/aboutus/key%20documents/0808_kd_external_evaluation.pdf

Organisation for Economic Co-Operation and Development (OECD), 'List of Variables in OECD Health Data', OECD (2011) www.oecd.org/dataoecd/62/8/38984666.pdf

'OECD Project on Counterfeiting and Piracy', OECD (2014) www.oecd.org/industry/industryandglobalisation/oecdprojectoncounterfeitingandpiracy.htm

Oxfam, 'Oxfam Reaction to the May 2011 Proposal for a Regulation of the European Parliament and of the Council concerning Customs Enforcement of Intellectual Property Rights (replacing Council Regulation 1383/2003)', Oxfam (2011) www.oxfamsol.be/fr/IMG/pdf/Oxfam_Reaction_to_EC_proposal_for_new_regulation_on_customs_enforcement_of_IPR.pdf

Oxfam India, 'Oxfam Calls on EU Not to Shut Down "Pharmacy of the Developing World"', Oxfam (9 February 2012) www.oxfam.org.uk/media-centre/press-releases/2012/02/oxfam-calls-on-eu-not-to-shut-down-pharmacy-of-the-developing-world

Oxfam International, 'Novartis Launch Renewed Attack on India's Right to Produce Affordable Medicines' (Oxfam, 2012) www.oxfam.org/en/pressroom/pressreleases/2012-08-20/novartis-launch-renewed-attack-indias-right-produce-affordable

'Trading Away Access to Medicines', Oxfam International (2009) www.oxfam.org/en/policy/trading-away-access-medicines

Pallot, P., 'Sympathy Wanes for Sufferers of the "Self-Inflicted Illnesses"', *Daily Telegraph* (24 January 2006) www.telegraph.co.uk/health/expathealth/4198880/Sympathy-wanes-for-sufferers-of-the-self-inflicted-illnesses.html

Palm, W., Nickless, J., Lewalle, H. and Coheur, A., 'Implications of Recent Jurisprudence on the Coordination of Health Care Protection Systems: Summary Report Produced for DG Employment and Social Affairs' (AIM, 2000) http://ec.europa.eu/employment_social/soc-prot/disable/synt_en.pdf

Palmedo, M., 'Final Blow to ACTA in the EU: European Court of Justice No Longer to Rule on its Legality', infojustice.org (20 December 2012) http://infojustice.org/archives/28196

Palmer, A., 'The WTO GMO Dispute: Implications for Developing Countries and the Need for an Appeal', GeneWatch UK, RSPB, Forum for Biotechnology and Food Security, and the GM Freeze (2006) www.genewatch.org/uploads/f03c6d66a9b354535738483c1c3d49e4/WTO_Biotech_case_dcsummaryfinal_1.pdf

Peci, E., 'Kosovo Convicts Five Over Human Organ Trafficking', Balkan Transitional Justice (April 2013) www.balkaninsight.com/en/article/kosovo-convicts-five-over-human-organ-trafficking

Pfizer, 'Orphan and Genetic Diseases at Pfizer', Pfizer (2010) http://ec.europa.eu/research/health/medical-research/pdf/rare-diseases/event03/14-mascioli_en.pdf

Physicians for Human Rights, 'Doctors Call Zimbabwe's Ruined Health System a "Man-Made Disaster"', Physicians for Human Rights (13 January 2009) http://physiciansforhumanrights.org/press/press-releases/news-2009-01-13-zimbabwe.html

'PIP Breast Implant Scandal: Compensation Ruling Upheld' , BBC News (21 January 2014) www.bbc.co.uk/news/world-europe-25831237

'PIP Implant Scandal: German Firm Ordered to Pay Damages' , BBC News (14 November 2013) www.bbc.co.uk/news/world-europe-24936958

The Poison Garden, 'Aristolochia Clematitis, Birthwort' (2014) www.thepoisongarden.co.uk/atoz/aristolochia_clematitis.htm

Polish Office of Competition and Consumer Protection, 'Consent to Concentration: Valeant Pharmaceuticals', Polish Office of Competition and Consumer Protection (17 August 2011) www.uokik.gov.pl/news.php?news_id=2917&news_page=4

'Professional Association of Medical Doctors Violated the Law', Polish Office of Competition and Consumer Protection (8 August 2011) www.uokik.gov.pl/news.php?news_id=2828&news_page=5

President's Council on Bioethics, 'Beyond Therapy', President's Council on Bioethics (2003)   https://repository.library.georgetown.edu/bitstream/handle/10822/559341/beyond_therapy_final_webcorrected.pdf?sequence=1

Private HealthCare UK, 'OFT launches Dentistry Market Study', Private Health-Care UK (16 September 2011) www.privatehealth.co.uk/news/september-2011/oft-dentistry-market-study-35891/

Rappeport, A., 'US Regulator Calls for Action on Fake Drugs' *Financial Times* (New York) (6 June 2012) www.ft.com/cms/s/0/fac4f8fc-b020-11e1-b737-00144feabdc0.html#axzz289Ru8uOV

Redfearn, M., 'The Royal Liverpool Children's Inquiry Report' (HC12-II), The Stationery Office (2001) https://www.gov.uk/government/uploads/system/uploads/attachment_data/file/250934/0012_ii.pdf

Ring, E., 'Women Could Get €15,000 for Faulty Implants' *Irish Examiner* (9 September 2014) www.irishexaminer.com/ireland/women-could-get-euro15000-for-faulty-implants-285481.html

'Rise of the Fertility Tourist' , BBC News (6 March 2001) http://news.bbc.co.uk/1/hi/health/1205247.stm

Roberts, M., 'Surgeons Carry Out the First Successful Synthetic Windpipe Transplant' , BBC News (7 July 2011) www.bbc.co.uk/news/health-14047670

Roemer, R., *Legislative Action to Combat the World Tobacco Epidemic*, WHO (1993) http://apps.who.int/iris/handle/10665/37823

Romanian Competition Council, 'The Competition Council Sanctioned the Companies Baxter, Belupo and their Distributors with Fine of RO 7,8 million', Romanian Competition Council (October 2011) www.consiliulconcurentei.ro/uploads/docs/items/id7151/traducere_comunicat_baxter_si_belupo.pdf

Rosengren, J-H., 'EU Presidency Statement: Macroeconomic Policy Questions and Follow-up to Financing for Development', Delegation of the EU before the UN (9 October 2006) www.eu-un.europa.eu/articles/es/article_6359_es.htm

Ross, G., 'Smoking Kills, So Why Ban Smokeless Tobacco', *European Voice* (9 January 2013) www.europeanvoice.com/article/imported/smoking-kills-so-why-ban-smokeless-tobacco-/76128.aspx

Runner's World, 'Should the NHS Treat "Self-Inflicted" Illness?', Clubhouse, Runner's World (11 February 2014) www.runnersworld.co.uk/forum/clubhouse/should-the-nhs-treat-self-inflicted-illness/30561.html

Rys, A., 'Global Health Governance – Multiple Players, Multiple Visions: Challenges and Opportunities', WHS Working Session (12 October 2010) http://ec.europa.eu/health/eu_world/docs/speech_ar_whs_en.pdf

Saar, P. and Habicht, J., 'Migration and Attrition: Estonia's Health Care Sector and Cross-border Mobility to its Northern Neighbour', in M. Wismar, C.B. Maier, I.A. Glinos et al. (eds.), 'Health Professional Mobility and Health Systems: Evidence from 17 European Countries' (WHO 2011) www.euro.who.int/__data/assets/pdf_file/0017/152324/e95812.pdf?ua=1

Samuel, H., 'Victims of Faulty PIP Breast Implants Win Compensation from German Firm' *Daily Telegraph* (14 November 2013) www.telegraph.co.uk/news/worldnews/europe/france/10449738/Victims-of-faulty-PIP-breast-implants-win-compensation-from-German-firm.html

Savage, M., 'Tobacco Giant Could Sue for £11bn over Plain Pack "Injustice"' *The Times* (12 August 2014) www.thetimes.co.uk/tto/news/politics/article4173198.ece

Scharpf, F.W., 'Legitimate Diversity: The New Challenge of European Integration', *Les Cahiers européens de Sciences Po.*, 01/2002 (Paris: Centre d'études européennes at Sciences Po., 2002) www.cee.sciences-po.fr/erpa/docs/wp_2002_1.pdf

'A New Social Contract? Negative and Positive Integration on the Political Economy of European Welfare States' (1996) European University Institute working paper, RSC 94/44 http://cadmus.eui.eu/handle/1814/1459?show=full

Scherlin, A., 'Trade, Association, Aid: Has the Agreement between the European Union and the Republic of Chile Fulfilled its Purposes?', unpublished LLM thesis, Göteborgs Universitat, 2009 https://gupea.ub.gu.se/bitstream/2077/21095/1/gupea_2077_21095_1.pdf

Shabalala, D. and Bernasconi, N., 'The European Approach to Intellectual Property in European Partnership Agreements with the African, Caribbean and Pacific Group of Countries' (2007) CIEL discussion paper www.ciel.org/Publications/EU_EPAs_Draft_18Apr07.pdf

Smith, J., 'Sixth Report – Shipman: The Final Report', Shipman Inquiry (2005) http://webarchive.nationalarchives.gov.uk/20090808154959/http://www.the-shipman-inquiry.org.uk/finalreport.asp

Spotlight on Poverty and Opportunity (ongoing) www.spotlightonpoverty.org/HealthAndPovertyResearch.aspx

Stotesbury, S., 'Smokeless Tobacco: EU Dogma or Dialogue', *EurActiv* (16 October 2012) http://euractiv.com/health/smokeless-tobacco-eu-dogma-dialo-analysis-515441

Strawbridge, J., 'US Implementation of Adverse WTO Rulings: A Closer Look at the Tuna-Dolphin, COOL, and Clove Cigarettes Cases' (2013) 17(23) *American Society of International Law* www.asil.org/insights/volume/17/issue/23/us-implementation-adverse-wto-rulings-closer-look-tuna-dolphin-cool-and

Sunder, M., 'An Issue of Life or Death' (2012), UC Davis Legal Studies Research Paper no. 297 http://ssrn.com/abstract=2061339

Sweet, M., 'Greek Austerity Illegal Says UK Professor', *Neoskosmos* (30 April 2013) http://neoskosmos.com/news/en/greek-austerity-illegal-says-uk-professor

Taylor, L., 'India's First Ever Compulsory Licence: A "Game Changing Move"', *PharmaTimes online* (12 March 2012) www.pharmatimes.com/article/12-03-12/India_s_first-ever_compulsory_license_-_a_game-changing_move.aspx

Temple-Boyer, S., 'No Abuse of Dominant Position Without a Link between the Predatory Practice and the Dominated Market', Soulier Advocats (2009) www.soulier-avocats.com/upload/documents/Soulier_competition_september_2009_FF.pdf

Thomson, S., 'What Role for Voluntary Health Insurance?', in J. Kutzin, C. Cashin and M. Jakab (eds.), 'Implementing Health Financing Reform: Lessons from Countries in Transition', WHO on behalf of the European Observatory on Health Systems and Policies (2010) www.euro.who.int/__data/assets/pdf_file/0014/120164/E94240.pdf

Thomson, S., Foubister, T. and Mossialos, E., 'Financing Health Care in the European Union: Challenges and Policy Responses', WHO (2009) www.euro.who.int/__data/assets/pdf_file/0009/98307/E92469.pdf

'"Transplant Tourist" Defends Trip' , BBC News (3 December 2007) http://news.bbc.co.uk/1/hi/wales/7123747.stm

Treaty Office, 'Convention for the Protection of Human Rights and Dignity of the Human Being with Regard to the Application of Biology and Medicine: Convention on Human Rights and Biomedicine CETS no. 164', Council of Europe (11 July 2014) http://conventions.coe.int/Treaty/Commun/ChercheSig.asp?NT=164&CM=8&DF=11/07/2014&CL=ENG

TÜV Rheinland, 'Facts and Figures' (2014) www.tuv.com/en/corporate/about_us_1/facts_figures_1/facts_figures.html

UK Competition and Markets Authority (CMA), 'CMA Clears Foundation Trust Hospitals Merger', CMA (14 May 2014) https://www.gov.uk/government/news/cma-clears-foundation-trust-hospitals-merger

'New Competition Authority Comes into Existence' (1 October 2013) https://www.gov.uk/government/news/new-competition-authority-comes-into-existence

'Private Healthcare Market Investigation Final Report' (2014) https://assets.digital.cabinet-office.gov.uk/media/533af065e5274a5660000023/Private_healthcare_main_report.pdf

UK Department of Health (DoH), 'Genetics White Paper 'Our Inheritance, Our Future: Realising the Potential of Genetics in the NHS' (2003) www.geneticseducation.nhs.uk/downloads/0001DH_White_paper.pdf

'NHS Dental Contract Pilots: Learning after Two Years of Piloting' (2014) http://www.gov.uk/government/uploads/system/uploads/attachment_data/file/282760/Dental_contract_pilots_evidence_and_learning_report.pdf

'Organs for Transplant', Organ Donation Task Force (2008) www.dh.gov.uk/en/Publicationsandstatistics/Publications/PublicationsPolicyAndGuidance

'Policy Paper: NHS Dental Contract Reform: Feedback Wanted' (15 August 2013) https://www.gov.uk/government/publications/nhs-dental-contract-reform-feedback-wanted

UK Human Genetics Advisory Commission (HGAC), 'Cloning Issues in Reproduction Science and Medicine (Consultation Document)', HGAC 1998) Annex B http://www.webarchive.nationalarchives.gov.uk/20130107105354/http://www.dh.gov.uk/prod_consum_dh/groups/dh_digitalassets/@dh/@ab/documents/digitalasset/dh_104394.pdf

UK Human Genetics Advisory Commission and UK Human Fertilisation and Embryology Authority (HFEA), 'Cloning Issues in Reproduction, Science and Medicine', HGAC and HFEA (1998) www.hfea.gov.uk/docs/Cloning_Issue_Report.pdf

UK Joint Committee on Immunisation and Vaccination, 'Interim Position Statement on Use of Bexsero Meningococcal B Vaccine in the UK' (24 July 2013) https://www.gov.uk/government/publications/jcvi-interim-position-statement-on-the-use-of-bexsero-meningococcal-b-vaccine-in-the-uk

UK Office of Fair Trading (OFT), 'Consumers benefit from pharmacy liberalisation', *OFT*, 22 March 2010) http://webarchive.nationalarchives.gov.uk/20140402142426/http://www.oft.gov.uk/news-and-updates/press/2010/31-10

 'Dentistry: An OFT market study' (2012) http://webarchive.nationalarchives.gov.uk/20140402142426/http://www.oft.gov.uk/shared_oft/market-studies/Dentistry/OFT1414.pdf

 'OFT Evaluation of Napp Case Finds Increased Competition in Morphine Market' (6 June 2011) http://webarchive.nationalarchives.gov.uk/20140402142426/http://www.oft.gov.uk/news-and-updates/press/2011/63-11

 'OFT Provisionally Decides to Refer Private Healthcare Market to Competition Commission' (8 December 2011) http://webarchive.nationalarchives.gov.uk/20140402142426/http://www.oft.gov.uk/news-and-updates/press/2011/132-11

UK Parliament, 'Statement on Standardised Packaging of Tobacco Products: 3 April 2014' (3 April 2014) www.parliament.uk/business/news/2014/april/statement-on-packaging-tobacco-products-3-april-2014/

UK Royal College of Nurses, 'Policy Briefing 9/14: Tobacco Products Directive' (2014) www.rcn.org.uk/__data/assets/pdf_file/0006/578040/09.14_Tobacco_Products_Directive_2014_40_EU.pdf

 'Royal College of Nursing Briefing: Free Movement of Health Professionals in Europe – Proposed Changes to EU Legislation in 2012' (2012) www.rcn.org.uk/__data/assets/pdf_file/0003/434928/RCN_response_to_December_2011_Mutual_Recognition_of_Professional_Qualifications_legislative_proposals.pdf

UK Royal College of Physicians, 'European Parliament Votes on Doctors' Qualifications', (31 January 2013) www.rcplondon.ac.uk/update/european-parliament-votes-doctors-qualifications

UK Science and Technology Committee, 'Report: Human Reproduction and the Law' (HC 2004–05, HC 7-II [Incorporating HC 559 i-ix of session 2003–04]) www.publications.parliament.uk/pa/cm200405/cmselect/cmsctech/7/7we55.htm

Unitaid, 'Unitaid Statement on Dutch Confiscation of Medicines Shipment' (WHO, 2014) www.unitaid.eu/resources/news/156-unitaid-statement-on-dutch-confiscation-of-medicines-shipment

United Nations, 'Integrated Implementation Framework: MDG 8' (2014) http://iif.un.org/?q=node/10

 'Millennium Development Goals and Beyond 2015' (2014) www.un.org/millenniumgoals/

 'Millennium Development Goals and Beyond 2015: Goal 8: Develop a Global Partnership for Development' (2014) www.un.org/millenniumgoals/global.shtml

 'The Millennium Development Goals Report 2014' (2014) www.un.org/millenniumgoals/2014%20MDG%20report/MDG%202014%20English%20web.pdf

'Political Declaration of the High-level Meeting of the General Assembly on the Prevention and Control of Non-communicable Diseases' (Doc A/66/L 1, UN General Assembly 2011) www.un.org/en/ga/ncdmeeting2011/

'World Abortion Policies 2013', Department of Economic and Social Affairs, United Nations (2013) www.un.org/en/development/desa/population/publications/pdf/policy/WorldAbortionPolicies2013/WorldAbortionPolicies2013_WallChart.pdf

United Nations General Assembly Resolution, 'Keeping the Promise: United to Achieve the Millennium Development Goals' (A/Res/65/1, UN General Assembly 2010) www.un.org/en/mdg/summit2010/pdf/outcome_documentN1051260.pdf

US Department of Justice and US Federal Trade Commission, 'Improving Health Care: A Dose of Competition', US DoJ and US FTC (2004) www.justice.gov/atr/public/health_care/204694.htm

Vestlund, N.M., 'Changing Policy Focus through Organisational Reform? The Case of the Pharmaceutical Unit in the European Commission' (2006) Arena working paper 6/2012 www.sv.uio.no/arena/english/research/publications/arena-publications/workingpapers/working-papers2012/wp6–12.pdf

Vos E. and Weimer, M., 'The Role of the EU in Transnational Regulation of Food Safety: Extending Experimentalist Governance?' (2013) GR:EEN working paper no. 35 www2.warwick.ac.uk/fac/soc/csgr/green/papers/workingpapers/no._35_vos_and_weimer.pdf

WHO, '2008–2013 Action Plan for the Global Strategy for the Prevention and Control of Non-communicable Diseases' (2009) http://whqlibdoc.who.int/publications/2009/9789241597418_eng.pdf?ua=1

'About WHO' (2014) www.who.int/about/en/

'Data and statistics' (various dates) www.euro.who.int/en/health-topics/disease-prevention/food-safety/data-and-statistics

'Declaration of Alma-Ata 1978' (1978) www.euro.who.int/__data/assets/pdf_file/0009/113877/E93944.pdf?ua=1

'Facts and Figures about Abortion in the European Region' (2014) www.euro.who.int/en/what-we-do/health-topics/Life-stages/sexual-and-reproductive-health/activities/abortion/facts-and-figures-about-abortion-in-the-european-region

'Food Safety: Frequently Asked Questions on Genetically Modified Foods' (2014) www.who.int/foodsafety/areas_work/food-technology/faq-geneically-modified-food/en

'Framework Convention on Tobacco Control' (2014) www.who.int/fctc/en/

'Global Action Plan for the Prevention and Control of Non-communicable Diseases 2013–2020' (2013) http://apps.who.int/iris/bitstream/10665/94384/1/9789241506236_eng.pdf?ua=1

'Global Crisis – Global Solutions: Managing Public Health Emergencies of International Concern through the Revised International Health Regulations' (2002) www.who.int/csr/resources/publications/ihr/whocdsgar20024.pdf?ua=1

'Global Status Report on Non-Communicable Diseases 2010' (2011) www.who.int/nmh/publications/ncd_report_full_en.pdf

'Health Topics: Essential Medicines' (2014) www.who.int/topics/essential_medicines/en/

'Healthy Ageing' (2014) www.euro.who.int/en/what-we-do/health-topics/Life-stages/healthy-ageing

'Inequalities in Young People's Health: Health Behaviour in School-Aged Children. HBSC International Report from the 2005/2006 Survey' (2008) www.euro.who.int/__data/assets/pdf_file/0005/53852/E91416.pdf

'International Food Safety Authorities Network (INFOSAN)' (2014) www.who.int/foodsafety/areas_work/infosan/en/

'International Health Regulations', 2nd edn (2005) http://whqlibdoc.who.int/publications/2008/9789241580410_eng.pdf?ua=1

'International Health Regulations', 3rd edn (1969) http://whqlibdoc.who.int/publications/1983/9241580070.pdf?ua=1

'International Medical Products Anti-Counterfeiting Taskforce (IMPACT)' (2014) www.who.int/impact/en/

'Medicines: IMPACT (Frequently Asked Questions)' (2014) www.who.int/medicines/services/counterfeit/faqs/count_q-a/en/index.html

'Medicines: Spurious/Falsely labelled/Falsified/Counterfeit (SFFC) Medicines' (May 2012) www.who.int/mediacentre/factsheets/fs275/en/

'Neglected Tropical Diseases: The 17 Neglected Tropical Diseases' (2014) www.who.int/neglected_diseases/diseases/en/

'Neglected Tropical Diseases' (2009) http://whqlibdoc.who.int/publications/2009/9789241598705_eng.pdf

'Obesity: Data and Statistics' (WHO Europe, 2014) www.euro.who.int/en/health-topics/noncommunicable-diseases/obesity/data-and-statistics

'Pharmaceutical Industry' (2014) www.who.int/trade/glossary/story073/en/

'Poverty and Social Exclusion in the WHO European Region: Health Systems Respond' (WHO Europe, 2010) www.euro.who.int/__data/assets/pdf_file/0006/115485/E94018.pdf

'Poverty, Social Exclusion and Health Systems in the WHO European Region' (WHO Europe, 2010) www.euro.who.int/__data/assets/pdf_file/0004/127525/e94499.pdf

'The Rights of Patients in Europe' (1993) www.who.int/genomics/public/eu_declaration1994.pdf

'Sexual and Reproductive Health' (2014) www.euro.who.int/en/what-we-do/health-topics/Life-stages/sexual-and-reproductive-health

'Sixty Years of WHO in Europe' (2010) www.euro.who.int/__data/assets/pdf_file/0004/98437/E93312.pdf

'Tobacco Free Initiative (TFI): World No Tobacco Day 2014: raise taxes on tobacco' (2014) www.who.int/tobacco/wntd/en/

'What We Do' (2014) www.euro.who.int/en/what-we-do

'WHO Global Report: Mortality Attributable to Tobacco' (2012) whqlibdoc.who.int/publications/2012/9789241564434_eng.pdf?ua=1

'WHO Guiding Principles on Human Cell, Tissue and Organ Transplantation' (2010) www.who.int/transplantation/Guiding_PrinciplesTransplantation_WHA63.22en.pdf?ua=1

'WHO Project on Improving Access to Medicines in Developing Countries through Local Production and Related Technology Transfer' (2014) www.who.int/phi/implementation/TotLCProject.pdf

'Workshop on Trade-related Issues Relevant to Implementation of the WHO FCTC [Framework Convention on Tobacco Control]' (2012) www.who.int/fctc/1-1-1-Summary_Workshop_Content_EN.pdf

'The World Health Report 1996: Fighting Disease, Fostering Development' (WHO, 1996) www.who.int/whr/1996/en/whr96_en.pdf?ua=1

WHO and European Commission, 'Health Status Overview for Countries of Central and Eastern Europe that are Candidates for Accession to the European Union' (European Communities and WHO, 2002) http://ec.europa.eu/health/ph_projects/1999/monitoring/health_status_overview_en.pdf

World Bank, 'Dying For Change: Poor People's Experience of Health and Ill-health' (2005) www-wds.worldbank.org/external/default/WDSContentServer/WDSP/IB/2005/07/28/000160016_20050728152217/Rendered/PDF/331250ENGLISH0Dying0for0change.pdf

'World Development Report 1993: Investing in Health' (1993) http://elibrary.worldbank.org/doi/abs/10.1596/0-1952-0890-0

World Health Assembly, 'Resolution WHA 40.13: Development of Guiding Principles for Human Organ Transplants', 40th World Health Assembly (1987) www.who.int/transplantation/en/WHA40.13.pdf

'Resolution WHA 57.18', 57th World Health Assembly (2004) http://apps.who.int/gb/ebwha/pdf_files/WHA57/A57_R18-en.pdf

'Resolution WHA 61.21: Global Strategy and Plan of Action on Public Health, Innovation and Intellectual Property', 61st World Health Assembly (2008) http://apps.who.int/gb/ebwha/pdf_files/A61/A61_R21-en.pdf

WTO, 'Current Status of Disputes' (26 August 2014) www.wto.org/english/tratop_e/dispu_e/dispu_current_status_e.htm

'Dispute Settlement: Dispute DS291: European Communities – Measures Affecting the Approval and Marketing of Biotech Products' (17 January 2008) www.wto.org/english/tratop_e/dispu_e/cases_e/ds291_e.htm

'European Communities: Measures concerning Meat and Meat Products (Hormones)' (2014) www.wto.org/english/tratop_e/dispu_e/cases_e/ds26_e.htm

'Health and Social Services' (2014) www.wto.org/english/tratop_e/serv_e/health_social_e/health_social_e.htm

'TRIPS General Council: Meeting of 3–4 February 2009' (2014) www.wto.org/english/thewto_e/gcounc_e/meet_feb09_e.htm

'Understanding the WTO: Settling Disputes: A Unique Contribution' (2014) www.wto.org/english/thewto_e/whatis_e/tif_e/disp1_e.htm

'What is the WTO?' (2014) www.wto.org/english/thewto_e/whatis_e/whatis_e.htm

Willis, A., 'Something "Rotten" in EU Pharmaceutical Sector, Says Kroes', euobserver (8 July 2009) http://euobserver.com/news/28430

Wismar, M., Maier, C.B., Glinos, I.A., et al. (eds.), 'Health Professional Mobility and Health Systems: Evidence from 17 European Countries' (WHO, 2011) www.euro.who.int/__data/assets/pdf_file/0017/152324/e95812.pdf?ua=1

Zagger, Z. 'US, Indonesia Stall WTO Clove Cigarette Arbitration (Law 360, 2014) www.law360.com/articles/552574/us-indonesia-stall-wto-clove-cigarette-arbitration

Zamboni, M., 'Legal Realisms and the Dilemma of the Relationship of Contemporary Law and Politics', Stockholm Institute for Scandinavian Law (2010) www.scandinavianlaw.se/pdf/48-34.pdf

Commission documents (chronological order)

Commission Practice Note on Import Prohibitions, 'Communication from the Commission concerning the Consequences of the Judgment Given by the Court of Justice on 20 February 1979 in Case 120/78 (*"Cassis de Dijon"*)' [1980]OJ C256/2

Commission, 'Framework Programme for Research 1984–87' COM (83) 260 final

'Completing the Internal Market: White Paper from the Commission to the European Council' (White Paper) COM (85) 0310 final

'Proposal for a Council Directive concerning Medical Devices' COM (1991) 287 final

'Growth, Competitiveness, Employment' (White Paper) COM (93) 700 final

'Communication on the Inclusion of Respect for Democratic Principles and Human Rights in Agreements between the Community and Third Countries' (Communication) COM (95) 216 final

'Communication on the European Union and the External Dimension of Human Rights Policy: From Rome to Maastricht and Beyond' (Communication) COM (95) 567

'Liability for Defective Products' (Green Paper) COM (1999) 396 final

'Communication from the Commission on the Precautionary Principle' (Communication) COM (2000) 1 final

'Towards a European Research Area' COM (2000) 6 final

'Commission Interpretative Communication: Freedom to Provide Services and the General Good in the Insurance Sector' (Communication) [2000]OJ C43/5

Proposal for a Directive of the European Parliament and Council on the Recognition of Professional Qualifications' COM (2002) 119 final

'Health and Poverty Reduction in Developing Countries' (Communication) COM (2002) 129 final

'Food Safety Member States Support Emergency Suspension of the Sale of Jelly Mini-cups Containing "Konjac" (E425) food Additive' (19 March 2002) http://europa.eu/rapid/press-release_IP-02-435_en.htm

'Green Paper on Services of General Interest' (Green Paper) COM (2003) 270 final

'High Level Process of Reflection on Patient Mobility and Healthcare Developments in the EU' since 2003, European Commission, HLPR/2003/16, (9 December 2003) http://ec.europa.eu/health/ph_overview/Documents/key01_mobility_en.pdf

'Follow-up to the High Level Reflection Process on Patient Mobility and Healthcare Developments in the European Union' (Communication) COM (2004) 301 final

'Amended proposal for a Directive of the European Parliament and of the Council on the recognition of professional qualifications (presented by the Commission pursuant to Article 250 (2) of the EC Treaty)' COM (2004) 317 final

'European Programme for Action to Confront HIV/AIDS, Malaria and Tuberculosis through External Action (2007–2011)' COM (2005) 179 final

'Implementing the Community Lisbon Programme: A Strategy for the Simplification of the Regulatory Environment' (Communication) COM (2005) 535 final

'Community Framework for State Aid in the Form of Public Service Compensation' (Communication) [2005]OJ C297/04

'Amended Proposal for a Council Decision concerning the 7th Framework Programme of the European Atomic Energy Community (Euratom) for Nuclear Research and

Training Activities (2007–2011) (Presented by the Commission Pursuant to Article 250 (2) of the EC Treaty)' COM (2006) 364 final

'Global Europe Competing in the World: A Contribution to the EU's Growth and Jobs Strategy' (Communication) COM (2006) 567 final

'An EU Strategy to Support Member States in Reducing Alcohol Related Harm' (Communication) COM (2006) 625 final

'Green Paper on the Review of the Consumer Acquis' (Green Paper) COM (2006) 744 final

'Commission Interpretative Communication on the Community Law Applicable to Contract Awards Not or Not Fully Subject to the Provisions of the Public Procurement Directives' [2006]OJ C179/2

'Work of the High Level Group on Health Services and Medical Care in 2006' (HLG/2006/8, 10 October 2006) http://ec.europa.eu/health/ph_overview/co_operation/healthcare/docs/highlevel_2006_007_en.pdf

'Organ Donation and Transplantation: Policy Actions at EU level: Consultation Document', Commission (2006) http://ec.europa.eu/health/ph_threats/human_substance/oc_organs/consultation_paper.pdf

'Detailed Guidance on the Application Form and Documentation to be Submitted in an Application for an Ethics Committee Opinion on the Clinical Trials of Medicinal Products for Human Use', revised, Commission (2006) http://ec.europa.eu/health/files/eudralex/vol-10/12_ec_guideline_20060216_en.pdf

'Factsheet: Alcohol-related Harm in Europe – Key Data', Commission (2006) http://ec.europa.eu/health/archive/ph_determinants/life_style/alcohol/documents/alcohol_factsheet_en.pdf

'Report on the Open Consultation Policy Options for Organ Donation and Transplantation at EU Level', Commission (2006) http://ec.europa.eu/health/archive/ph_threats/human_substance/oc_organs/docs/oc_organs_frep_en.pdf

'Organ Donation and Transplantation: Policy Action at EU Level' (Communication) COM (2007) 275 final

'EU Consumer Policy Strategy 2007–2013: Empowering Consumers, Enhancing their Welfare, Effectively Protecting Them' (Communication) COM (2007) 99 final

'Together for Health: A Strategic Approach for the EU 2008–2013' (White Paper) COM (2007) 630 final

'Proposal for a Regulation of the European Parliament and of the Council on the Provision of Food Information to Consumers' COM (2008) 40 final

'Damages Actions for Breach of the EU Antitrust Rules' (White Paper) COM (2008) 165 final

'Proposal for a Directive of the European Parliament and of the Council on the Application of Patients' Rights in Cross-border Healthcare' COM (2008) 414 final

'Communication from the Commission to the European Parliament and the Council on an EU Drugs Action Plan for 2009–2012' (Communication) COM (2008) 567 final

'Proposal for a Regulation of the European Parliament and of the Council Amending, as regards Information to the General Public on Medicinal Products for Human Use Subject to Medical Prescription, Regulation (EC) No 726/2004 Laying Down

Community Procedures for the Authorisation and Supervision of Medicinal Products for Human and Veterinary Use and Establishing a European Medicines Agency' COM (2008) 662 final

'Proposal for a Directive of the European Parliament and of the Council Amending, as Regards Information to the General Public on Medicinal Products Subject to Medical Prescription, Directive 2001/83/EC on the Community Code Relating to Medicinal Products for Human Use' COM (2008) 663 final

'Safe, Innovative and Accessible Medicines: A Renewed Vision for the Pharmaceutical Sector' (Communication) COM (2008) 666 final

'Action Plan on Organ Donation and Transplantation (2009–2015): Strengthened Cooperation between Member States' (Communication) COM (2008) 819 final

'Communication on Patient Safety, Including the Prevention and Control of Healthcare-associated Infections' (Communication) COM (2008) 836 final

Commission, 'Guideline on Aspects of the application of Article 8(1) and (3) of Regulation 141/2000/EC: Assessing Similarity of Medicinal Products Versus Authorised Orphan Medicinal Products Benefiting from Market Exclusivity and Applying Derogations from that Market Exclusivity (Communication) COM (2008) 4077 final

'Ethical Cross-border Recruitment and Retention: European Social Partners in the Hospital Sector Signed a Code of Conduct' (7 April 2008) http://ec.europa.eu/social/main.jsp?langId=en&catId=329&newsId=208&furtherNews=yes

'Recast of the Medical Devices Directives Summary of Responses to the Public Consultation' (ENTR/F/3/D(2008) 39582, Commission 2008) http://ec.europa.eu/health/medical-devices/files/recast_docs_2008/responses/responses_public_consultation_recast_en.pdf

'Scientific Committee on Emerging and Newly Identified Health Risks (SCENIHR) Opinion on: Health Effects of Smokeless Tobacco Products, February 2008' (Health and Consumer Protection Directorate-General 2008) http://ec.europa.eu/health/archive/ph_risk/committees/04_scenihr/docs/scenihr_o_013.pdf

'Solidarity in Health: Reducing Health Inequalities in the EU' (Communication) COM (2009) 567 final

'Guidance on the Commission's Enforcement Priorities in Applying Article 82 of the EC Treaty to Abusive Exclusionary Conduct by Dominant Undertakings' [2009] OJ C45/7

'Assessment of the Functioning of the Clinical Trials Directive 2001/20/EC: Public Consultation Paper', Commission (2009) http://ec.europa.eu/health/files/clinicaltrials/docs/2009_10_09_public-consultation-paper.pdf

'Pharmaceutical Sector Inquiry: Final Report', Commission (2009) http://ec.europa.eu/competition/sectors/pharmaceuticals/inquiry/communication_en.pdf

'Communication from the Commission to the Council, the European Parliament, the European Economic and Social Committee and the Committee of the Regions on the Application of Directive 2002/98/EC Setting Standards of Quality and Safety for the Collection, Testing, Processing, Storage and Distribution of Human Blood and Blood Components and Amending Directive 2001/83/EC' (Communication) COM (2010) 0003 final

'The EU Role in Global Health' (Communication) COM (2010) 128 final

'Towards a Comprehensive European International Investment Policy' (Communication) COM (2010) 343 final

'Towards a European Road Safety Area: Policy Orientations on Road Safety 2011–2020' (Communication) COM (2010) 389 final

'Europe 2020 Flagship Initiative Innovation Union' (Communication) COM (2010) 546 final

'Smart Regulation in the EU' (Communication) COM (2010) 543 final

'Trade, Growth and World Affairs: Trade Policy as a Core Component of the EU's 2020 strategy' COM (2010) 612 final

'Annual Report (2009) on the Application of Council Regulation (EC) No 953/2003 of 26 May 2003 to Avoid Trade Diversion into the European Union of Certain Key Medicines' COM (2010) 652

'Report from the Commission to the European Parliament, the Council, the European Economic and Social Committee and the Committee of the Regions on Implementation by Member States of Directive 2003/88/EC ("The Working Time Directive")' COM (2010) 802 final

'Europe 2020: A Strategy for Smart, Sustainable and Inclusive Growth' (Communication) COM (2010) 2020 final

'Assessment of the Functioning of the Clinical Trials Directive, 2001/20/EC: Summary of Responses to the Public Consultation Paper' (2010) http://ec.europa.eu/health/files/clinicaltrials/2010_03_30_summary_responses.pdf

'Communication from the President to the Commission: Framework for Commission Expert Groups: Horizontal Rules and Public Registers, C(2010) 7649 final (2010) http://ec.europa.eu/dgs/internal_market/docs/expert_groups/C2010_7649_en.pdf

'Investing in People: Mid-term Review of Strategy Paper for Thematic Programme (2007–2013)' (2010) http://ec.europa.eu/development/icenter/repository/investing_people_mid-term_review.pdf

'Declaration concerning the Charter of Fundamental Rights of the EU', European Union (2010) http://europa.eu/pol/pdf/qc3209190enc_002.pdf

Commission and the European Economic Policy Committee, 'Joint Report on Health Systems', European Economy Occasional Papers 74 (December 2010) http://ec.europa.eu/economy_finance/publications/occasional_paper/2010/pdf/ocp74_en.pdf

Commission, 'An EU Framework for National Roma Integration Strategies up to 2020' (Communicaion) COM (2011) 173 final

'Single Market Act: Twelve Levers to Boost Growth and Strengthen Confidence, Working Together to Create New Growth' COM (2011) 206 final

'Proposal for a Regulation of the European Parliament and of the Council concerning Customs Enforcement of Intellectual Property Rights' COM (2011) 285 final

'Green Paper on Modernising the Professional Qualifications Directive' (Green Paper) COM (2011) 367 final

'Fourth Report on the Application of Council Directive 85/374/EEC of 25 July 1985 on the Approximation of the Laws, Regulations and Administrative Provisions of the Member States concerning Liability for Defective Products Amended by Directive 1999/34/EC of the European Parliament and of the Council of 10 May 1999' COM (2011) 547 final

'A Renewed EU Strategy 2011–2014 for Corporate Social Responsibility' COM (2011) 681 final

'Proposal for a Regulation of the European Parliament and of the Council on Establishing a Health for Growth Programme, the Third Multi-annual Programme of EU Action in the Field of Health for the Period 2014–2020' COM (2011) 709 final

'Proposal for a Regulation of the European Parliament and Council Establishing Horizon 2020 the Framework Programme for Research and Innovation (2014–2020)' COM (2011) 809 final

'Preparation of the Multiannual Financial Framework Regarding the Financing of EU Cooperation for African, Caribbean and Pacific States and Overseas Countries and Territories for the 2014–2020 period (11th European Development Fund)' (Communication) COM (2011) 837 final

Commission and High Representative of the EU for Foreign Affairs and Security Policy, 'Global Europe: A New Approach to Financing EU External Action' COM (2011) 865 final

Commission, 'Proposal for a Directive of the European Parliament and of the Council Amending Directive 2005/36/EC on the Recognition of Professional Qualifications and Regulation on Administrative Cooperation through the Internal Market Information System' COM (2011) 883 final

'Consultation on the Commission Report on the Enforcement of Intellectual Property Rights' (11 July 2011) http://ec.europa.eu/internal_market/consultations/2011/intellectual_property_rights_en.htm

'Evaluation of the Professional Qualifications Directive', Commission (2011) http://ec.europa.eu/internal_market/qualifications/docs/news/20110706-evaluation-directive-200536ec_en.pdf

'Revision of Directive 98/79/EC of the European Parliament and of the Council of 27 October 1998 on In Vitro Diagnostic Medical Devices: Summary of Responses to Public Consultation', Commission (2011) http://ec.europa.eu/health/medical-devices/files/recast_docs_2008/ivd_pc_outcome_en.pdf

'Safeguarding Privacy in a Connected World A European Data Protection Framework for the 21st Century' COM (2012) 09 final

'Proposal for a Directive of the European Parliament and of the Council on the Protection of Individuals with Regard to the Processing of Personal Data by Competent Authorities for the Purposes of Prevention, Investigation, Detection or Prosecution of Criminal Offences or the Execution of Criminal Penalties, and the Free Movement of Such Data' COM (2012) 10 final

'Proposal for a Regulation of the European Parliament and of the Council on the Protection of Individuals with Regard to the Processing of Personal Data and on the Free Movement of Such Data (General Data Protection Regulation)' COM (2012) 11 final

'Amended Proposal for a Directive of the European Parliament and of Council Amending Directive 2001/83/EC as Regards Information to the General Public on Medicinal Products Subject to Medical Prescription Amending, as Regards Information to the General Public on Medicinal Products Subject to Medical Prescription, Directive 2001/83/EC on the Community Code Relating to Medicinal Products for Human Use' COM (2012) 48 final

'Proposal for a Directive Relating to the Transparency of Measures Regulating the Prices of Medicinal Products for Human Use and Their Inclusion in the Scope of Public Health Insurance Systems' COM (2012) 84 final

'Proposal for a Directive of the European Parliament and of the Council on the Enforcement of Directive 96/71/EC concerning the Posting of Workers in the Framework of the Provision of Services' COM (2012) 131 final

'National Roma Integration Strategies: A First Step in the Implementation of the EU Framework' (Communication) COM (2012) 226 final

'Action for Stability, Growth and Jobs' COM (2012) 299 final

'Proposal for a Regulation of the European Parliament and of the Council on Clinical Trials on Medicinal Products for Human Use and Repealing Directive 2001/20/EU' COM (2012) 369 final

'Safe, Effective and Innovative Medical Devices and In Vitro Diagnostic Medical Devices for the Benefit of Patients, Consumers and Healthcare Professionals' (Communication) COM (2012) 540 final

'Proposal for a Regulation of the European Parliament and of the Council on *in vitro* Diagnostic Medical Devices' COM (2012) 541 final

'Proposal for a Regulation of the European Parliament and of the Council on Medical Devices, and Amending Directive 2001/83/EC, Regulation (EC) no. 178/2002 and Regulation (EC) no. 1223/2009' COM (2012) 542 final

'Annual Growth Survey 2013' (Communication) COM (2012) 750 final

'Proposal for a Directive of the European Parliament and Council on the Approximation of the Laws, Regulations and Administrative Provisions of the Member States concerning the Manufacture, Presentation and Sale of Tobacco and Related Products' COM (2012) 788 final

'Communication from the Commission on the Application of the European Union State Aid Rules to Compensation Granted for the Provision of Services of General Economic Interest' (Communication) [2012]OJ C8/4

'Communication from the Commission: European Union Framework for State Aid in the Form of Public Service Compensation' (Communication) [2012]OJ C8/15

'Communication from the Commission: Approval of the Content of a Draft for a Commission Regulation on de minimis Aid for the Provision of Services of General Economic Interest' (Communication) [2012]OJ C8/23

'Romania: The Competition Council Imposes Fines on Pharmaceutical Companies Baxter, Belupo and Their Distributors', Commission (January 2012) http://ec.europa.eu/competition/ecn/brief/01_2012/ro_pharma.pdf

'Joint Statement on the Outcome of the EU-India Trade Ministerial' (26 June 2012) http://trade.ec.europa.eu/doclib/press/index.cfm?id=812

'Fostering EU's Attractiveness in Clinical Research; Commission Proposes to Revamp Rules on Trials with Medicines' (17 July 2012)

'Antitrust: Commission Sends Statement of Objections to Lundbeck and Others for Preventing Market Entry of Generic Antidepressant Medicine' (25 July 2012) http://europa.eu/rapid/press-release_IP-12-834_en.htm

'Antitrust: Commission Sends Statement of Objections on Perindopril to Servier and Others' (30 July 2012) http://europa.eu/rapid/press-release_IP-12-835_en.htm

'EU Accountability Report 2012 on Review of Progress of the EU and its Member States: Financing for Development', Commission (2012) http://ec.europa.eu/europeaid/what/development-policies/financing_for_development/documents/20120904-summary-highlights_en.pdf

'EU Competition Policy Newsletter 2012-1', various authors (2012) http://ec.europa.eu/competition/publications/cpn/cpn_2012_1_en.html

'Special Eurobarometer 385: Attitudes of Europeans Towards Tobacco: Report', Commission (2012) http://ec.europa.eu/health/tobacco/docs/eurobaro_attitudes_towards_tobacco_2012_en.pdf

'What ACTA is about', Commission (2012) trade.ec.europa.eu/doclib/docs/2012/january/tradoc_149003.pdf

'Towards Social Investment for Growth and Cohesion Including Implementing the European Social Fund 2014–2020' (Communication) COM (2013) 83 final

'Amended Proposal for a Directive of the European Parliament and of the Council on the Transparency of Measures Regulating the Prices of Medicinal Products for Human Use and their Inclusion in the Scope of Public Health Insurance Systems' COM (2013) 168 final

'Antitrust: Commission Sends Statement of Objections to J&J and Novartis on Delayed Entry of Generic Pain-killer' (31 January 2013) http://europa.eu/rapid/press-release_IP-13-81_en.htm

'Enterprise and Industry: Food Industry' (5 February 2013) http://ec.europa.eu/enterprise/sectors/food/index_en.htm

'Access to Medicines' (28 February 2013) http://ec.europa.eu/trade/policy/accessing-markets/intellectual-property/access-to-medicines/

'EU Register of Nutrition and Health Claims Made on Foods' (12 June 2013) http://ec.europa.eu/nuhclaims/?event=register.home

'Antitrust: Commission Fines Lundbeck and Other Pharma Companies for Delaying Market Entry of Generic Medicines' (19 June 2013) http://europa.eu/rapid/press-release_IP-13-563_en.htm

'Financial Programming and Budget: Interinstitutional Agreements' (14 November 2013) http://ec.europa.eu/budget/explained/budg_system/legal_bases/aii/aii_en.cfm

'International Affairs: Sanitary and Phytosanitary Agreements' (23 September 2013) http://ec.europa.eu/food/international/trade/agreements_en.htm

'Pharmaceuticals in Europe: Facts and Figures' (5 February 2013) http://ec.europa.eu/enterprise/sectors/healthcare/competitiveness/importance/facts-figures_en.htm

'Working Time: Commission Refers Greece to Court for Not Respecting EU Rules in Public Health Services' (20 November 2013) europa.eu/rapid/press-release_IP-13-1108_en.htm

'Working time: Commission Refers Ireland to Court for Not Respecting EU Rules in Public Health Services' (20 November 2013) http://europa.eu/rapid/press-release_IP-13-1109_en.htm

'EU-Africa Pharma Business to Business Forum: Final Recommendations (2013) http://ec.europa.eu/DocsRoom/documents/82/attachments/1/translations/en/renditions/native

'Communication on the European Citizens' Initiative "Water and Sanitation are a Human Right! Water is a Public Good, Not a Commodity!"' (Communication) COM (2014) 177 final

'Proposal for a Regulation of the European Parliament and of the Council to Avoid Trade Diversion into the European Union of Certain Key Medicines' COM (2014) 319 final

'A Decent Life for All: From Vision to Collective Action' (Communication) COM (2014) 355 final

'Withdrawal of Obsolete Commission Proposals' [2014]OJ C153/3

'MEMO: Working Time: Commission Requests SPAIN to Respect Forensic Doctors' Rights to Maximum Working Hours and Minimum Rest Periods' (20 February 2014) http://csdle.lex.unict.it/Archive/LW/Press%20releases/RAPID%20press%20releases/20140220-045838_MEMO-14-116_EN_Spainpdf.pdf

'Working Time: Commission Refers Italy to Court for Not Respecting EU Rules in Public Health Services' (20 February 2014) http://europa.eu/rapid/press-release_IP-14-159_en.htm

'Platform on Access to Medicines in Developing Countries with a Focus on Africa' (24 February 2014) http://ec.europa.eu/enterprise/sectors/healthcare/competitiveness/process_on_corporate_responsibility/platform-africa/index_en.htm

'Countries and Regions: India' (14 May 2014) http://ec.europa.eu/trade/policy/countries-and-regions/countries/india/

'Trade: Investment' (11 June 2014) http://ec.europa.eu/trade/policy/accessing-markets/investment/

'Trade: Intellectual Property' (4 July 2014) http://ec.europa.eu/trade/tackling-unfair-trade/acta/transparency/

'Overview of EPA Negotiations: Economic Partnership Agreement Negotiations' updated July 2014 (2014) http://trade.ec.europa.eu/doclib/docs/2009/september/tradoc_144912.pdf

'Public Health: Health' (1 August 2014) http://ec.europa.eu/health/index_en.htm

'Public Health: Tobacco Policy' (6 August 2014) http://ec.europa.eu/health/tobacco/policy/index_en.htm

'Platform on Access to Medicines in Europe' (20 August 2014) http://ec.europa.eu/enterprise/sectors/healthcare/competitiveness/process_on_corporate_responsibility/platform_access/index_en.htm

'NANDO (New Approach Notified and Designated Organizations) Information System' (25 August 2014) http://ec.europa.eu/enterprise/newapproach/nando/

'Guidance MEDDEVs' (18 September 2014) http://ec.europa.eu/health/medical-devices/documents/guidelines/index_en.htm

'Action Plan on Youth Drinking and on Heavy Episodic Drinking (Binge Drinking)', Commission (2014) http://ec.europa.eu/health/alcohol/docs/2014_2016_actionplan_youthdrinking_en.pdf

'Europe 2020 Targets: Poverty and Social Exclusion Active Inclusion Strategies' (2014) http://ec.europa.eu/europe2020/pdf/themes/33_poverty_and_social_inclusion_02.pdf

'Health and Health Systems' (2014) http://ec.europa.eu/europe2020/pdf/themes/05_health_and_health_systems_02.pdf

'Ireland: The Competition Authority Secures High Court Undertakings from Irish Medical Organisation' (2014) http://ec.europa.eu/competition/ecn/brief/03_2014/ie_imo.pdf

'Overview of FTA and other Trade Negotiations' (2014) http://trade.ec.europa.eu/doclib/docs/2006/december/tradoc_118238.pdf

'Report on the European Commission: World Health Organization Senior Officials Meeting 25 March 2011, Brussels' (2014) http://ec.europa.eu/health/eu_world/events/ev_2011325_en.htm

Commission Staff Working Document, 'Investing in Health: Accompanying the Document Commission Communication, Towards Social Investment for Growth and Cohesion Including Implementing the European Social Fund 2014–2020' SWD (2013) 43 final

'Social Investment through the European Social Fund' SWD (2013) 44 final

Secretary-General of the Commission documents

'Lisbon Strategy Evaluation Document' SEC (2010) 114 final

'European Research and Knowledge for Global Health: The EU Role in Global Health' SEC (2010) 381 final

Commission Staff Working Document, 'Contributing to Universal Coverage of Health Services through Development Policy – Accompanying Document to the Communication from the Commission to the Council, the European Parliament, the European Economic and Social Committee and the Committee of the Regions – The EU Role in Global Health {COM(2010) 128} {SEC(2010) 380} {SEC(2010) 381}' SEC (2010) 382 final

Commission Staff Working Paper, 'Detailed Report on the Implementation by Member States of Directive 2003/88/EC concerning Certain Aspects of the Organisation of Working Time ("The Working Time Directive")' SEC (2010) 1611 final

Index

Lightning Source UK Ltd.
Milton Keynes UK
UKOW07n1815141215

264724UK00005B/100/P